THE FACTS ON FILE
COMPANION TO

AMERICAN POETRY

VOLUME II
1900 TO THE PRESENT

BURT KIMMELMAN
AND TEMPLE CONE

Facts On File
An imprint of Infobase Publishing

The Facts On File Companion to American Poetry, Volume II: 1900 to the Present

Facts On File, Inc.
An imprint of Infobase Publishing
132 West 31st Street
New York NY 10001

Library of Congress Cataloging-in-Publication Data

Kimmelman, Burt.
The Facts On File companion to American poetry, 1900 to the present / [edited by] Burt Kimmelman, Temple Cone, Randall Huff.
p. cm.
Includes bibliographical references and index.
ISBN 978-0-8160-6950-7 (alk. paper)
1. American poetry—History and criticism—Handbooks, manuals, etc. I. Kimmelman, Burt. II. Cone, Temple. III. Huff, Randall. IV. Facts On File, Inc.
PS323.5.F33 2007
811'.509—dc22 2006035417

Facts On File books are available at special discounts when purchased in bulk quantities for businesses, associations, institutions, or sales promotions. Please call our Special Sales Department in New York at (212) 967-8800 or (800) 322-8755.

You can find Facts On File on the World Wide Web at http://www.factsonfile.com

Text design adapted by James Scotto-Lavino
Cover design by Salvatore Luongo

Printed in the United States of America

VB Hermitage 10 9 8 7 6 5 4 3 2 1

This book is printed on acid-free paper.

For Diane and Jane, as always
And for Shannon and Isabelle

CONTENTS

Acknowledgments

This volume is the result of the efforts of a good many people who have my deepest gratitude, some of whom I may neglect to mention here, fallible memory being what it is. I am beholden to Mickey Pearlman, who contacted me and urged me to offer my services to Facts On File; to Anne Savarese, former Facts On File editor, who worked with me to conceive this project and set it in motion; to Jeff Soloway, senior editor at Facts On File, whose patience, care, and acuity have been indispensable; and to Jessica Allen, whose perspicacity in copyediting has been more than one could have hoped for. I must also thank my colleagues at New Jersey Institute of Technology for their encouragement and understanding and, in some cases, their participation—especially Robert E. Lynch and Norbert Elliot, who, along with Doris Zames Fleischer, Robert S. Friedman, Christopher Funkhouser, and Nikki Stiller, contributed essays to this book. I am also profoundly thankful for the intelligence and time Norbert Elliot, Tom Fink, and Sherry Kearns (who also contributed essays), as well as Jeff Soloway, donated to the writing of the book's introduction. And I am grateful to Burton Hatlen for his wonderful foreword to the book. I must also thank the many contributors to this volume, whose knowledge, wit, and graceful writing will surely make it a success. Lastly, I am, as always, most thankful for the good natured love and support of my wife, Diane Simmons, and our daughter, Jane Kimmelman, without whom none of this would have been possible.

—Burt Kimmelman

Preface to the New Edition

Under Burt Kimmelman's editorship, the first edition of this volume, entitled *The Facts On File Companion to 20th-Century American Poetry,* offered a panoramic view of the landscape of modern and postmodern American poetry, striking a fine balance between essays on specific poets, poetic schools and movements, modes and genres, and individual poems and books of poems. In their clarity, authority, and accessibility, the entries satisfied the needs of any student beginning a study of 20th-century American poetry, as well as any scholar looking to supplement knowledge of an unfamiliar work, poet, or scholar. A testament to devoted scholarship, *The Facts On File Companion to 20th-Century American Poetry* revealed to novitiate and skilled readers alike the brave new world of American poetry in the modern and postmodern eras.

Yet while the first edition reflects how much the canon of American poetry has expanded, much of the instruction in poetry today, at least in high schools and college-level introductory literature classes, follows the reading practices associated with one movement in literary criticism, the New Criticism, particularly as articulated in Cleanth Brooks's and Robert Penn Warren's influential textbook, *Understanding Poetry* (1938; 1950). Although varied in theory and practice, the movement is generally associated with the prevalent pedagogical practice of "close reading," which regards the poem as a self-contained verbal entity or artifact, whose meanings are derived from the text itself, with little or no need to refer to the historical or social circumstances of the poem's composition. As a dominant mode of literary criticism, New Criticism was eventually superseded by the powerful and explosive influence of European literary theory from the 1970s onward, which liberated voices that had previously been silenced and attended to voices that had been speaking but ignored all along. One need only compare the tables of contents for the first and recent third editions of the *Norton Anthology of Modern and Contemporary Poetry* (1973; 2003) to see how expansive the poetic canon of the 20th century has become since the waning of New Criticism. Even still, New Critical approaches to interpretation, if not to canonization, remain alive and well in high school and introductory-level college curricula.

Keeping in mind this conflict between a widely inclusive canon and traditional New Critical reading practices, the new, expanded edition, now entitled *The Facts On File Companion to American Poetry, 1900 to the Present* attempts to better serve the high school and introductory-level college students who form its primary audience. Because high-school- and college-level classes rely on the discussion of single texts as a means of testing, challenging, and developing students' interpretive skills, the new edition provides 100 new entries on individual poems, as well as six new biographical entries on poets not represented in the first edition. The poems are drawn from every decade of the post-1900 period and represent work by men and women of diverse races, ethnicities, beliefs, poetic schools, and aesthetic sensibilities. Examples of new poems covered include such American classics as Robert Frost's "Birches," William Carlos Williams's "The Red Wheelbarrow," Langston Hughes's "The Weary Blues," and Wallace Stevens's "Thirteen Ways of Looking at a Blackbird" and many others. More contemporary poems covered here for the first time include Rita Dove's *Thomas and Beulah* and Kenneth Koch's "To My Twenties." Yet all these various poems are linked by their recognizable place in the literary canon, for they appear in the most widely used poetry anthologies. Such canonization alone does not justify the poems' inclusion in this new edition of the companion, for as the critic Jed Rasula convincingly argues, anthologies preserve hierarchies of value that often become rigid, forsaking their own aesthetic self-evaluation for decisions of editors past. Yet in deepening the panoply of topics in the first edition, this new edition continues its pedagogical mission, supplying concise, informative analyses of poems that high-school- and college-level students are most likely to encounter in literature courses.

BIBLIOGRAPHY

Brooks, Cleanth, and Robert Penn Warren. *Understanding Poetry: An Anthology for College Students.* New York: Henry Holt and Company, 1938.

Guillory, John. *Cultural Capital: The Problem of Literary Canon Formation.* Chicago: The University of Chicago Press, 1993.

Rasula, Jed. *The American Poetry Wax Museum: Reality Effects, 1940–1990.* Urbana, Ill.: National Council of Teachers of English, 1996.

—Temple Cone

Foreword

20TH-CENTURY AMERICAN POETRY: SOME GUIDEPOSTS

As Burt Kimmelman emphasizes in his eloquent introduction to this volume, all of the poems, poets, and literary movements described in the pages that follow share a common "Americanness." Yet the very essence of "Americanness" is diversity, the many in the one and the one in the many, as Walt Whitman, grandfather of all American bards, insisted: "I hear America singing, / The *varied* carols I hear" (emphasis mine). Thus it may be useful to attempt a chart of the various kinds of "Americanness" at work in the poetry written in this country during the last 100 years. The chartings that I will here propose are chronological as well as regional and ideological, for the sense of what it means to be an American, and specifically an American poet, has shifted over time. At the beginning of the 20th century, the United States made its first tentative forays toward becoming an imperial power, but most Americans still thought of themselves as a people apart, purified by immersion in a New World Eden. With World War I the United States became a significant player on an international stage, but the interwar years saw a renewed sense of American uniqueness, often summed up in the label *isolationism*. Then World War II and the ensuing decades saw a full-blown efflorescence of a distinctively American variety of imperialism, as the nation set out to become the arbiter of the destiny of the planet. Our poets have sometimes enthusiastically participated in the dominant political mood of the moment, but more often, especially in the imperial epoch extending from World War II to the present, the poets have fiercely questioned beliefs and attitudes that most other Americans have apparently accepted as simply "common sense," so that the poetry community has seemed at times the most insistently skeptical and critical of the various American countercultures. (Robert Creeley, at the start of the 21st century one of the last surviving members of a generation of major poets that emerged in the 1950s, was recently heard to ask, "How is it that I don't know *anyone* who supports the policies of George W. Bush?") Yet regional differences have often been no less important than the historical shifts that have occurred over the course of the 20th century, for New York is not California, and New England is not the Southwest. We must also recognize radically different aesthetic commitments that have sometimes united, sometimes separated poets across both historical epochs and cultural regions. And in the late decades of the 20th century, the very notion that we can define a single American identity has been challenged by poets seeking to speak for a range of previously marginalized communities defined by ethnicity, gender, and/or sexual preference.

"On or about December 1910, human nature changed," Virginia Woolf famously declared, and we may date the birth of 20th-century American poetry to the same pivotal moment. Among the tiny group of American poets whose careers carried across from the 19th into the 20th centuries, only three poets survive to find a place in this encyclopedia: Edwin Arlington Robinson, Adelaide Crapsey, and Jeanne Robert Foster. Aging anthologies and histories of American literature preserve a few other names—William Vaughan Moody, Trumbull Stickney, George Santayana. However, in 1905 the young Ezra Pound, H. D., and William Carlos Williams—Pound and Williams were students at the University of Pennsylvania, and H. D. was a friend of both—formed perhaps the first important literary fellowship of the new century. Although Pound and Williams did not come to know and admire Marianne Moore until later, Moore and H. D. were at least aware of one another during the year they spent as fellow students at Bryn Mawr, so we may add Moore to form a unique quartet of "Philadelphia modernists." Around this nexus of personal relationships a new poetic movement would crystallize, although each of the poets in question would arrive at a unique personal voice. In 1905 Pound and Williams were already writing poetry, but in a distinctly 19th-century idiom: They were, in a phrase from Pound's 1921 poem "Hugh Selwyn Mauberley," in search of "the sublime in the old sense." But by 1910 Pound was in London, acutely aware of new poetic possibilities emerging on the continent. In a series of essays published in 1913 under the collective title *The Approach to Paris,* he directed American poets toward a serious reading of poets such as Jules Laforgue, Tristan Corbiere, and, above all, Arthur Rimbaud, whose work of the 1870s pointed the way toward a poetics of radical disjunction and indeterminacy. By 1913 H. D. had also moved to London, and in that year Pound presented her poetry as the model of *imagisme,* a literary movement consciously modeled on the various aesthetic "isms" emanating from Paris: *symbolism, unanisme,* etc., with cubism a first cousin in the visual arts. Then a year or so later, T. S. Eliot, who had already written portions of "Portrait of a Lady" and "The Love Song of J. Alfred Prufrock" while a student at Harvard, arrived in London and quickly became a central figure in the Pound circle. (Williams detested Eliot's poetry, and Eliot was indifferent to Williams's, but they had Pound in common.)

If to my list of the five poets grouped around Pound we add Wallace Stevens and Gertrude Stein, we have a galaxy of major poets who collectively define the most influential poetic movement of the 20th century, international modernism. Pound showed no interest in Stevens's poetry, but Williams came to know Stevens in New York City during the World War I years, when both were members of a group of artists and writers that met regularly at the home of Walter Arensberg, a wealthy art patron. Moore also moved on the fringes of the Arensberg group, and she, too, came to know and admire Stevens's work at this time. In his role as editor of *Others* magazine during the war years, Williams published Stevens's poetry, while in the 1920s Moore solicited some of his poems for publication in *The Dial.* And in the 1930s Stevens contributed a preface to Williams's first *Collected Poems.* Thus we can perhaps create a subgroup of New York–area modernists encompassing Williams, Moore, and Stevens. Stein was never a close friend of any of the poets mentioned thus far and an outspoken critic of some of them, although Williams visited her in Paris and admired her work. But while she was not part of the network of personal relationships that linked our other poets, she is a crucial figure in this story, as the most important mediator between Parisian modernism—cubism, fauvism, etc.—and American writers, artists, and composers. Conrad Aiken, a friend of Eliot's from Harvard, also perhaps belongs in this list of major modernists, but to most observers he has come to seem a lesser figure. Some critics would add to the list Mina Loy, a British expatriate who arrived in New York during the World War I years and there met Williams and possibly Stevens and Moore. Laura Riding (Jackson), E. E. Cummings, and Hart Crane also belong on any list of major American modernist poets, but they were somewhat younger than the poets mentioned thus far and began to write under the shadow of the first generation modernists.

The modernism of Pound, Eliot, H. D., Moore, Williams, Stevens, and Stein is "international" in a basic way: Four of these seven poets chose to live in and write from Europe. Eliot became a British citizen. After World War I, Pound returned to the United States only once willingly, for a short visit, and then for a second time under duress, after his arrest for treason during World War II. Stein is forever linked to Paris in the popular imagination, although she made an extended celebrity tour of the United States in 1934–35, and H. D. made only two brief visits to the United States after she took up residence in Europe, the first shortly after World War I and the second in the late 1950s. But even Williams, Stevens, and Moore, all of whom chose to live in the United States, maintained a distinctly international perspective. All three lived in or near New York City, the main point of communication between America and Europe. Stevens, although he never went to Europe, read widely in French poetry and cultural commentary, while Williams, who spent a year in Europe during the 1920s, was powerfully influenced by such European literary/artistic movements as cubism and surrealism. And most significantly, all seven of my major international modernists shared with European modernist painters (Picasso, Matisse, Braque, et al.), composers (Stravinsky, Schoenberg, Webern, et al.), and writers (Joyce, Proust, Mann, Apollinaire, Valéry, Rilke, et al.) a determination to interrogate the most fundamental principles of their art forms. A range of formal vocabularies that had endured since the Renaissance all came into question during this period: in painting, the illusion of three-dimensional space, constructed through the application of the "laws" of perspective; in music, the diatonic scale with its attendant harmonies; in fiction, the linear narrative and the controlling authorial point of view; and in poetry, the metrical line and the unitary lyric voice. The seven American poets that I have identified as exemplars of international modernism are very different from each other in some important ways: Williams's insistence on the "American ground" contrasts with the condescension toward all things American that we sometimes see in Pound, Eliot, and H. D., while H. D.'s continuing loyalty to the romantic tradition contrasts with the ostensible antiromanticism of Pound and Eliot, et al. But these writers were bound together not only by (in most cases) a network of personal associations to which they were often deeply loyal but also by a desire to construct alternatives to the traditional formal vocabularies that had defined "poetry" for their predecessors, and they "made it new" ("it" here being poetry itself) in ways that continue to inspire poets of the 21st century.

Today the standard classroom anthologies devote more space to the exponents of international modernism than to any other group of 20th-century American poets, and all of them receive maximum space in this encyclopedia. However, the esteem that these poets enjoy today is largely retrospective, as during their lifetimes other poets often had larger audiences and received more respect from critics. The most acclaimed American poet throughout much of the 20th century was Robert Frost, who also lived during the second decade of the century for a time in London, where he brushed up against Pound. But Frost returned to America and with Edwin Arlington Robinson defined a New England alternative to international modernism. Frost borrowed the title of his first book from Longfellow, and neither Frost nor Robinson saw any need to reject the traditional poetic forms or the lyric voice characteristic of the English poetic tradition. Despite the dark undercurrents in their vision of the world, both Frost and Robinson enjoyed during their lifetimes an audience markedly larger than the audiences of the modernists. No less popular was another native New Englander, Edna St. Vincent Millay, who also saw no need to reject either the metrical line or the lyric voice. Meanwhile, in the years during and after World War I, a group of Chicago poets sought to define a populist alternative both to the radical experimentalism of the international modernists and to the formal decorum of the New England poets. Carl Sandburg and Edgar Lee Masters both employed a loose free verse modeled primarily on Whitman's, while Vachel Lindsay sought to revive a tradition of performance poetry. Looking out to the Pacific from his home in Carmel, California, Robinson Jeffers also adapted the long, cadenced Whitman line in his search for a poetic idiom that could do justice to the vast and still largely empty expanses of the western landscape. His poetry has remained an important influence on later West Coast poets such as William Everson, Kenneth Rexroth, and Gary Snyder.

In the late 1920s and 1930s, a group of southern poets, often grouped under the self-chosen labels of *Fugitives* or *Agrarians;* also affirmed a self-consciously regional alternative to international modernism, and their example became an important force in American poetry. John Crowe Ransom, Allen Tate, and Robert Penn Warren all identified with Eliot's social and cultural conservatism and intermittently adopted his ironic, high-Mandarin tone, but they retreated from the radical formal experimentalism of Pound, Williams, and Moore—an experimental impulse also evident in the Eliot of *The Waste Land,* although this impulse fades in his later work. The southern Agrarians all taught in colleges or universities and wrote criticism as well as poetry. (Warren also wrote a series of successful novels.) In alliance with influential critics such as Cleanth Brooks and with other poet/critics, including Kenneth Burke and R. P. Blackmur, the Agrarians became the founders of a movement generally known as the New Criticism, which sought new ways of addressing a public that found poetry more and more opaque. Living in the West but in dialogue with the southern Agrarians, the poet/critics Yvor Winters and J. V. Cunningham also rejected what they saw as a surrender to chaos in the poetry of the high modernists. Tate and Winters were both friends of Hart Crane, whose spectacular but ultimately disastrous career became for them an example of the dangers of modernist excess. As poets, Ransom, Tate, Warren, Blackmur, Winters, and Cunningham no longer command much attention: all six receive only short entries in this encyclopedia. However, they are historically significant insofar as they established a tradition of what has sometimes been called (usually derisively) "academic" poetry: a relatively decorous, often formally traditional poetry written by men and women who have spent significant time in the classroom. Such poetry tends to be relatively "closed" both in its forms and in its cultural attitudes, as it seeks to build in art a refuge from which the poet can contemplate the various disorders of modern life.

The tradition defined by Ransom, Tate, and Warren passes directly to Robert Lowell, who went to Kenyon College to study with Tate and Ransom. While there, Lowell became friends with Randall Jarrell, and together Lowell and Jarrell became the center of another crucial group of young poets who were, like the Pound circle in an earlier generation, bound together by bonds of personal friendship as well as a common aesthetic that they seem to have arrived at through exchanges among themselves. Eventually this new grouping reached out to include Delmore Schwartz, Elizabeth Bishop, and John Berryman, along with Lowell and Jarrell. The members of this circle, in addition to certain other poets who shared many of their aspirations (for example, Theodore Roethke, Richard Wilbur, and W. D. Snodgrass), were, during the 1950s and 1960s, widely regarded as the most significant poets of the period. Many of these poets followed the example of poets such as Frost, Ransom, and the enormously influential British expatriate W. H. Auden in cultivating an expertise in traditional poetic forms and meters; and the metrical subtleties of Bishop, Berryman, Wilbur, Snodgrass, and Lowell (at least in his earlier work) are often dazzling. Lowell, Berryman, and Snodgrass share a self-lacerating irony that is sometimes taken to be characteristic of the whole group, but once again differences are as important as similarities. Neither Jarrell nor Bishop is primarily an ironic poet. Rather, Jarrell's poetry displays a remarkable capacity for empathetic identification with other people, while Bishop's geographic imagination is unique. Most of these poets were, like Ransom and Warren before them, at least intermittently academics, although again Bishop is an exception. As academic appointments carried these poets about the country, regional affiliations here became less significant. However, Lowell and Bishop were distinctly New England poets, while Roethke stood within an identifiable lineage of midwestern poets (his successors have included, for example, James Wright and Robert Bly), and Jarrell and Berryman both had southern roots. Many influential critics (Helen Vendler, for example) continue to regard the lineage defined by these poets as the "mainstream" of American poetry, a judgment also reflected in such widely used anthologies as J. D. McClatchy's *Vintage Book of Contemporary American Poetry.* At the start of the 21st century, furthermore, many still-active poets continue to write within a poetic mode that passes from Eliot (with the qualifications noted above) and Ransom through Lowell, Jarrell, and their associates: for example, Frank Bidart, Alfred Corn, Mark Doty, Stephen Dobyns, Edward Hirsch, and many others.

The southern Fugitive poet/critics and their heirs recognized that universities were becoming positions of power in American society, offering poets the possibility of both a secure livelihood and a new kind of public visibility, based not on the volume of their book sales (in the postwar period, Frost and Ginsberg were probably the only significant American poets to earn enough to live on from the sale of their books) but on a charismatic classroom style and triumphant reading tours. However, the dominance of the academic poets from the 1930s to the 1950s was challenged from the beginning by other writers who rejected the tacit conservatism—whether political or aesthetic or both—of the mainstream academic poets. In the 1930s a group of left-wing poets grouped loosely around the Communist Party, including Tom McGrath, Kenneth Fearing, Muriel Rukeyser, and Walter Lowenfels, offered an alternative to the social conservatism of Eliot and his various followers, southern Agrarian or otherwise, while Trotskyites such as John Wheelwright and anarchists such as Kenneth Rexroth and Kenneth Patchen sought to define the possibility of an anti-Stalinist left. While the specific aura of doctrinaire political commitment becomes rarer after World War II, some later poets—for example, Philip Levine and C. K. Williams—have sought to preserve the engagement with working-class experience represented by poets like McGrath and Fearing. In the 1930s, most of the left-wing poets listed above (Wheelwright was an exception) were content to write within a Whitmanesque poetic mode, a readily accessible and often assertively colloquial free verse idiom. But another group of poets emerged in the 1930s who combined political radicalism with formal experimentation in the tradition of the modernists. These were the so-called objectivist poets: Charles Reznikoff, Louis Zukofsky, Carl Rakosi, George Oppen, Lorine Niedecker, and the British poet Basil Bunting. In much the same way as Pound was at the center of the modernists, Zukofsky was the nodal point of the objectivists: All were linked to him by personal friendship, even though Oppen and Niedecker, for example, apparently never met, and Rakosi and Oppen did not meet until late in their lives. All the objectivists were sympathetic to the political left, and Rakosi and Oppen both joined the Communist Party for a time. But at the same time, the objectivist poets—inspired by the example of the modernists, especially Pound and Williams—also stimulating one another to pursue a rigorous testing of language and its relationship to the perceived world. Reznikoff remained throughout his life loyal to Pound's imagist aesthetic, while Zukofsky became a close friend of both Pound and Williams and initiated a strenuous polemic on behalf of their work as well as the work of Moore and (later in his life) Stevens. Oppen owed a manifest and freely acknowledged debt to both Pound and Williams; Niedecker, too, distilled her aesthetic from the modernists via her close friend Zukofsky; while Stevens and Eliot exercised a palpable influence on Rakosi. The anticommunist hysteria of the postwar years pushed all of the left poets into the shadows, but starting in the 1960s, poets such as Rukeyser, Zukofsky, and Oppen have been increasingly recognized as major American poets.

In the postwar years, the imperial ambitions of the Soviet Union and the manifestly repressive nature of Soviet society made communism an increasingly unattractive alternative, but a large group of American poets continued to question the inherent perfection both of commodity capitalism as a form of social organization and of the lyric ego as a mode of poetic expression. Beginning in 1951, one important such group came together around Cid Corman's *Origin* magazine, which gave an initial airing to the work of Charles Olson, Robert Creeley, William Bronk, Larry Eigner, Theodore Enslin, and others. Olson and Creeley quickly established themselves at the center of an overlapping poetic network, the so-called Black Mountain group, another one of those affinity groups, bound together both by personal friendship and aesthetic commitments, which have so often set the direction of American poetry. The Black Mountain group numbered among its members Paul Blackburn, Denise Levertov, Joel Oppenheimer, Edward Dorn, Jonathan Williams, and Robert Duncan, all of whom either taught or studied at Black Mountain College, where Olson served as rector in the early 1950s, or were linked to the *Black Mountain Review,* edited by Creeley in the mid-1950s. Duncan served as a link between Black Mountain and an already established San Francisco nexus that included Robin Blaser, Jack Spicer, and Helen Adam; and this link was solidified when Creeley moved to San Francisco after Black Mountain College closed in 1957. In the mid-1950s, San Francisco also become the home base of the Beat poets, notably Allen Ginsberg, Jack Kerouac, Gregory Corso,

Diane di Prima, Michael McClure, John Wieners, and Lawrence Ferlinghetti, who published the early work of many of these poets through his City Lights Press. Kenneth Rexroth briefly served as the impresario of this San Francisco poetry scene, which also included some natives of the West Coast, such as Gary Snyder, Philip Whalen, and Joanne Kyger, all of whom looked to the Buddhist traditions of India and Japan for spiritual and aesthetic guidance. Relationships among the various San Francisco groups were not always harmonious, but among them they created an extraordinarily vital poetic world in the 1950s, with reverberations down to the end of the century.

If Duncan and Creeley served as liaisons between Black Mountain and the San Francisco Renaissance, Paul Blackburn played a similar role with an emerging New York School of poets that included Frank O'Hara, John Ashbery, Barbara Guest, James Schuyler, Ted Berrigan, Kenneth Koch, and, for a time, Amiri Baraka (then Leroi Jones). The New York School (and once again most of these poets were personal friends as well as literary allies) shared a distinctive aesthetic, grounded in a witty subversion of all romantic posturing, an empathy with abstract expressionism in the visual arts (O'Hara and Ashbery were both art critics as well as poets), a delight in the vagaries of American pop culture, and a forthright affirmation of alternative sexual identities. In 1960 an intrepid editor, Donald Allen, ventured to link the East and West Coasts into a movement that he saw as dedicated to the creation of a "New American Poetry," and the publication of his anthology under that title represents a decisive moment in our literary history. The 1960s challenged all the certainties of American life: The Civil Rights movement called into question the degree to which America offered equal justice to its own citizens; the movement against the Vietnam War challenged the assumption that our nation self-evidently embodied "freedom" to all the peoples of the world; and the women's movement questioned power relationships within not only the workplace but even the home. At the threshold of the decade of what has sometimes been called the Third American Revolution (the Second was the Civil War), the Allen anthology defined a clear alternative to the social and aesthetic conservatism of the academic poets: a free-wheeling, process-based poetics that saw the poem not as articulation of already-established truths but as an exploration into untracked territories. ("I write poetry," Duncan said memorably, "to find out what I am going to say,") During the 1960s other new movements sympathetic to the aesthetic of the New American poetry also emerged, including the ethnopoetics of Jerome Rothenberg and Armand Schwerner and the talk-poetry of David Antin; all these poets were initially based in the New York area.

Then the last years of the 1960s saw the emergence of a younger group of poets who continued to identify with the Pound/Williams/Olson/Creeley lineage (or sometimes with a Stein/Pound/Williams/Creeley/Ashbery lineage), but who contended that their predecessors had not gone far enough in the interrogation of language as a self-perpetuating ideological system. Thus the self-labeled "Language poets" set about a deconstruction of "meaning" itself. Once again San Francisco and New York served as the twin centers of this new avant-garde: Ron Silliman, Lyn Hejinian, Bob Perelman, Barrett Watten, Carla Harryman, Kathleen Fraser, Rae Armantrout, and others were all, at least initially, based on the West Coast, while Charles Bernstein, Fanny and Susan Howe, Bruce Andrews, Bernadette Mayer, Joan Retallack, and others have represented the East Coast wing of the Language poetry movement. Silliman's 1986 anthology *In the American Tree* sought to bring together the East and West Coasts of the Language poetry movement, in much the same way that Allen's *The New American Poetry* brought together the two coasts a generation earlier. The latest bicoastal vision of American poetry, like Allen's, might be faulted for leaving out everything between the coasts. Further, the poets that anthologists have sought to constrain within such categories as "the New American poetry" or "Language poetry" repeatedly insist on going their own ways. That John Ashbery was once part of the "New York School" seems, for example, less and less germane as a key to the understanding of his work, while classifying Susan Howe as a "Language poet" doesn't tell us much about the vision of American history that her work unfolds. Still, to the end of the century, the poets of a lineage defined by the Allen and Silliman anthologies have continued to offer themselves as an avant-garde, united by an adversarial cultural stance and questioning all *a priori* assumptions about what a poem should be and do. Meanwhile, and perhaps partly in response to the increasingly uncompromising tone of the manifestos issued by the Language poets, a counter-avant-garde often labeled New Formalism has produced a body of poetry and theory that returns to traditional forms and strives to rebalance poetry in favor of meter and rhyme. Representative New Formalists include Dana Gioia, Mark Jarman, and Robert McDowell.

Much academic discussion of 20th-century American poetry has centered on the clash between, on the one hand, the "mainstream" poets, who have tended to receive most of the prestigious literary prizes and, until recently at least, to dominate the anthologies and, on the other hand, the insurgent poets of what we might now think of, with a full recognition that the specific names here are a bit arbitrary, as the Pound/Zukofsky/Olson/Hejinian/Bernstein lineage. Each of these lineages has also found forceful critical spokespersons, notably Helen Vendler for the "mainstream" poets and Marjorie Perloff for the tradition that extends from Pound to the Language poets. However, the years since World War II have also seen a broad challenge to both of these lineages. Both the mainstream and the avant-garde traditions have defined themselves primarily through their contrasting approaches to poetic form, but a third group of poets has placed primary emphasis on content rather than form, as they have sought to give poetic expression to the experiences of social groups that had previously been effectively silenced. As so often in American life, African Americans, the nation's largest and most brutally dispossessed minority, have been in the forefront of this effort to give voice to the voiceless. African-American poetry has often borrowed forms and modes from the poetic possibilities afloat in the culture as a whole. Thus the early 20th-century African-American poets Claude McKay, James Weldon Johnson, and Countee Cullen generally worked within traditional poetic forms. But with Melvin Tolson and Langston Hughes, African-American poetry also began to explore the new poetic possibilities opened up by the modernists, and in the last half of the century, African-American writing opened into a broad range of poetic modes, from Baraka's "projectivist" early verse, written in dialogue with Olson and O'Hara, through the Beat idiom of Bob Kaufman and the beautifully modulated lyric voices of Robert Hayden and Rita Dove, to the epic aspirations of Derek Walcott, Gwendolyn Brooks, and Jay Wright. The names listed here represent but a small sample of the rich heritage of African-American poetry. This body of poetry has made an active contribution to the ongoing project of African-American self-definition, while at the same time the imaginative scope of this poetry has demanded a fundamental reconception of the American poetic heritage itself.

The corpus of African-American poetry had become, by the end of the century, sufficiently large and various to qualify as a distinct poetic tradition, within an American literature increasingly defined not by its presumed unity but by its diversity. In this respect, African-American poetry has become the prototype of other ethnically defined poetries. Perhaps African-American literature moved ahead of other ethnic literatures in part because English early became the common language of black Americans. Slave owners deliberately broke up African-language communities because they feared the slaves would use their African languages to plot rebellion. Remnants of African languages did, however, linger on in Black English and have thence found their way into much African-American poetry. In contrast, many Native American languages survived as active means of communication into the 20th century, and only relatively late in the century did a body of Native American poetry in English crystallize to define an alternative poetic tradition. By the end of the century, however, such writers as Simon Ortiz, Leslie Marmon Silko, Linda Hogan, Joy Harjo, and Sherman Alexie had begun to chart the lineaments of a Native American poetic tradition. This tradition overlaps at times with a Hispanic-American poetic lineage. The situation of the Hispanic-American poet, who may choose to reject English itself in favor of the rich heritage of Spanish and Latin American literature, is perhaps even more ambiguous than that of the Native American poet. However, a significant group of poets has written out of this position as members of an Hispanic linguistic community (and there are in fact several different such communities in the United States, from the Chicano/Chicana world of the Southwest to the "Nuyorican" world of New York City) surrounded and often overwhelmed by an

English-speaking world: for example, Rafael Campo, Alberto Rios, Martin Espada, Lorna Dee Cervantes, Judith Ortiz Cofer, and Jimmy Santiago Baca.

The emergence of an explicit ethnic consciousness among African-American, Native American, and Hispanic-American writers has also encouraged a renewed ethnic self-consciousness among other groups. In particular, the last decades of the century saw a widespread recognition of a distinctively Jewish-American tradition within our literature. It has come to seem no accident, for example, that almost all of the objectivist poets of the 1930s generation shared a Jewish heritage. The political radicalism of these poets was in part a function of their ethnicity, as immigrant Jews brought a tradition of socialist and communist theory and practice to the United States. And when George Oppen passionately insists that "The self is no mystery, the mystery is / That there is something for us to stand on," his vision of the relationship between the perceiving subject and a larger mystery may owe something to the Jewish heritage. Furthermore, the objectivists' combination of a deep skepticism about language and an impassioned commitment to Truth has been carried forward by a group of younger poets who are also largely Jewish: This Neo-objectivist group might include, for example, Hugh Seidman, Michael Heller, Armand Schwerner, Rachel Blau DuPlessis, and even the editor of this encyclopedia, Burt Kimmelman, who has modestly omitted any entry on his own poetry. A recognition of the role that ethnicity played in the work of the objectivist and neo-objectivist poets also allows us to bring these poets into dialogue with Jewish American poets writing in more rhetorical and incantatory poetic idioms, such as Muriel Rukeyser, Allen Ginsberg, Allen Grossman, or even Adrienne Rich.

However, in many ways the most dynamic literary movement of the late 20th century—a movement that has now carried forward into the 21st century—has been a newly self-conscious and self-assertive tradition of women's writing. Throughout the 20th century, women made up the primary audience for poetry and beginning in the 1960s women readers increasingly demanded a poetry that would speak out of and to their own distinctive experiences as women. By century's end, the women's movement that erupted in the 1960s had permanently transformed the politics not only of the workplace and of the household but also of the poetry community. The voices of Sylvia Plath and Anne Sexton (both too early silenced by suicide) became models (in part cautionary) for a generation of young women writers, while Adrienne Rich offered a more positive, even heroic model: The voices of women, she and her followers and admirers insisted, *were* different, and they *would* be heard. The new women's writing that found its way into print beginning in the 1960s covers an immense formal range, from the Language poetries of Lyn Hejinian, Leslie Scalapino, Beverly Dahlen, Kathleen Fraser, or Joan Retallack, through the neo-objectivism of Rachel Blau DuPlessis, to the more traditional poetic modes of Sandra Gilbert, Marilyn Hacker, or Carolyn Kizer. At the same time as these new poetic voices found their way into print, scholars and poet/critics began to recover a whole galaxy of women poets who had been more or less buried by a male-dominated literary establishment: If writers like H. D., Mina Loy, and Lorine Niedecker have finally assumed their rightful places within the literary canon, we must thank primarily the work of a remarkable generation of women scholars. Further, poets such as Gwendolyn Brooks, Lucille Clifton, Nikki Giovanni, June Jordan, Rita Dove, and Audre Lorde have been increasingly recognized not only as black poets but also as women poets, sharing a broad range of experiences and concerns with all women poets among their contemporaries. At the same time, the work of feminist critics has allowed us to read in new ways already canonical writers such as Gertrude Stein, Marianne Moore, and Elizabeth Bishop. This quiet revolution effected by women poets and scholars since the 1960s might remind us that both American poetry itself and the ways we conceptualize our poetic tradition remain, as we enter the 21st century, still dynamic, fluid, in process—open to new possibilities, as our society as a whole must be, too, if we are to survive the new century.

—Burton Hatlen, Director
National Poetry Foundation
University of Maine

Introduction

"Make it new," the poet and sometime evangelist of the literary avant-garde Ezra Pound insisted, as the 20th century was under way. "Literature is news that stays news" was another of his formulations meant to exhort poets to find their own path, to break ground, to put a literary tradition in its proper perspective. Eras do not neatly begin and end on time; the fact of a new century, as told by a calendar, does not necessarily change how people think and feel. Even so, in January 1900 Americans must have felt excitement at the thought of a new kind of life ahead of them (calendars do lend meaning, after all). For Pound, as well as for other artists and intellectuals, it was easy to imagine that their new century was to be one of great promise. The object of Pound's imperatives was poetry but, whether he meant it or not, he was also putting a broader national impulse into words.

In the early 19th century Alexis de Tocqueville had remarked upon American individualism, noting how central it was to the growth of the new nation he was visiting. That element in the American character comes to the fore in the poetry of the United States during what came to be thought of as "modern" times. Richard Gray describes 20th-century American poetry as one "of radical experiment, the personal address and frequently eccentric innovation" (15). Of course, in the last century there were poets whom readers would not consider to have been experimental—Robert Frost and Edwin Arlington Robinson, for instance—yet even they "seem to speak to us from out of the depths of their solitude; even the distanced, hieratic tone of a John Crowe Ransom or the elaborate patternings of a Marianne Moore cannot disguise the fact that they too are engaged in a lonely confrontation with the real," Gray continues (15). American poetry of the last century embodied the sense of the particular, of the here and now, of what are markedly American—as opposed to British—concerns and language. "For the first time," Louis Untermeyer announced in his 1919 anthology *The New Era in American Poetry*, "a great part of American letters is actually American. We have had, of course, music, art and literature in this country before. But it has not been, as a rule, a native growth; it has merely been transplanted and produced here" (3). When considered as a body of work, the new American poetry was idiosyncratic, not afraid of innovation. Moreover, especially as the century progressed and more voices other than those of principally white Anglo-Saxon males became audible, American poetry evolved and reflected America's diversity. "I contain multitudes," Walt Whitman sang in the 19th century, many years ahead of his time.

In 1913 Pound turned to Whitman, saying in his poem "A Pact," "It was you that broke the new wood, / Now it is time for carving." A number of decades later, Charles Olson echoed Pound in "The Kingfishers" (1949) when he maintained, "What does not change / is the will to change." There is such a thing as a "peculiarly American desire to start over," Ed Folsom asserts;

this impulse made "twentieth-century [American] poets reticent about constructing a tradition as a backdrop for their work" (16). Rather, these poets had to invent a new kind of wheel in a process that has continued up to the present. Decades after Olson composed "The Kingfishers," Adrienne Rich wrote of what she called "The Dream of a Common Language" (*Origins and History of Consciousness* [1978]). As Jay Parini points out (quoting Rich), the "dream is deeply feminist, involving 'women's struggle to name the world.'" (x) In "Transcendental Etude" (1978), Rich spoke of the "beginning" of "a whole new poetry." To be sure, ultimately the struggle was not only taken up by women. From the start, Parini continues, poetry in the United States "has been this dream of a common language" (x).

What makes "common" that language Rich and Parini celebrate? Is it that women as well as men have access to it? More elementally, is it a language that molds the foundation for a uniquely American identity? By the end of the 20th century, a common American language had indeed come into being in poetry as well as in the larger American culture, spoken by a panoply of voices and in a seemingly endless variety of poetic forms, which, collectively, make up a uniquely American sensibility. When the century began there was only an inkling of such a language. In 1919 Untermeyer wrote, "[T]here is still an undeniable beauty in the ancient myths, but to most of the living poets it is a frayed and moth-eaten beauty. Their eyes do not fail to catch the glamor of the old tales, but they turn with creative desire to more recent and less shopworn loveliness" (10).

No period in the life of any nation brought forth as many points of view and poetic oddnesses as did the American 20th century. Whatever would lie ahead, it can be said that during this era—an era of both great turmoil and achievement—American poetry collectively stood as a distinctive testament to human aspiration, to human struggle and salutary accomplishment, and to a condition that is especially American in terms of outlook. The American trait of prizing the individual and adventure, the new and the diverse, was a potential fully realized in what came to be known as the "American Century." As Parini has observed, 20th-century American poetry had a love affair with the image, not least of all because of the influence of the imagist and, later, the objectivist poets. Commenting on that, he says, "even when there is an overarching narrative," imagery tends to be central and the poetry exhibits "an overriding concern with concreteness" (xx). The breadth and multiplicity of 20th-century American poetry are evident in its use of images, in the very fact of their proliferation. The American language starts with and is embodied by things.

In the United States to be open to the new is to embrace the particulars of experience. A poem typical of this sensibility is Pound's "In a Station of the Metro" (1913), with its "snapshot suddenness," as Jed Rasula has put it (98). William Carlos Williams intoned, "no ideas but in things." His poem "The Red Wheelbarrow" (1923), Roger Mitchell has argued, shows that Williams not only "trusted the unadorned image to reveal beauty and truth" but also, more fundamentally, to reveal "unadorned reality itself" (30). Perhaps Williams, among all modernist poets, was the most "radical" in his drive to start over; he was "willing to turn his back on all existing ideas of culture and tradition" (31). Still while someone like Williams was first and foremost an originator, he and others, such as Pound, Olson, and Rich, adhered to a basic understanding of what it meant to be American. This understanding, which transcended any particularity of image, prosodic form, or even voice, came to be fully articulated during Williams's lifetime. Together, these and many other poets forged an American identity at the heart of which lies the fresh and the various.

Beyond the insular world of poetry, the United States in the early 20th century found itself in the throes of invention. Twentieth-century America is normally thought of as a time and place of modernity, and, in fact, the literary movement of modernism began with American formulations and endured, increasingly attenuated, as the century evolved. It is interesting to note, however, looking back from the vantage point of the 21st century, how much of the material and intellectual world normally associated with modern living was already in place by 1900. At the start of the 20th century, the ratio in the United States between agricultural workers and factory workers was shifting dramatically. At the same time there was a flood of immigrants. Cities, the incubators of high culture, were growing quickly. Skyscrapers, which actualized the metaphor of reaching upward to the heavens or, alternately, to the stars, were already being constructed. Over distances, people could communicate by telephone. In 1900 the U.S. per capita income (about $570) was the highest in the world; there were nearly a thousand colleges and universities and more than 2,000 American daily newspapers, which constituted half of all the newspapers being published anywhere. In that year work began on New York City's rapid transit subway system, the photostatic copying machine was invented, the "Brownie" camera was being marketed, and the paper clip was patented. Change was rampant and startling. In 1901 Guglielmo Marconi sent the first transatlantic wireless message. In 1906 a Stanley Steamer automobile attained a speed of 127 miles per hour. In 1911 the first transcontinental airplane flight took place. An older—and surer—world was quickly fading away; the world of surprise had arrived. Henry Adams wrote in 1900 that his "historical neck [was being] broken by the irruption of forces totally new" (382, cf. Gray 30). Life was becoming more complicated. Adams felt that the "child born in 1900 would . . . be born into a new world which would not be a unity but a multiple" (457, cf. Gray 30).

While discoveries in science, especially in physics and biology, in the later years of the 20th century revealed vast landscapes of possibility that inevitably would become the substance of poetry, these discoveries were also presaged in the century's early years. The idea that the universe is comprised of 12 dimensions, for example, as is held by string theory, represents a departure from classical physics, a science that still holds great sway over everyday language—poems, in contrast, work to reshape language and meaning one by one. This rift in the laws of nature as they were propounded by Sir Isaac Newton, in the late 17th and early 18th centuries, appeared with Albert Einstein's theories of relativity (1905, 1916), then Werner Heisenberg's uncertainty principle (1927). Tangibility, objectivity, and subjectivity were to be understood in new ways; predictability came to be conditional. This transformation lay at the heart of, for instance, William Bronk's conclusion to his poem "How Indeterminacy Determines Us" (1962): "Sight / is inward and sees itself, hearing, touch, / are inward. What do we know of an outer world?" The point of view evoked here is a great leap away from Robert Browning's "God's in His Heaven—/ All's right with the world" ("Pippa Passes" [1841]).

While communication technologies, such as television and the Internet, have transformed society in many ways, their effects—the dramatically social and psychological changes they have provoked—are not fundamentally different from those created by the telephone and the wireless radio early in the century. Yet landing on the Moon and sending exploratory spaceships to the ends of the solar system have ultimately challenged definitions of what it means to be a human being; life beyond Earth can currently be contemplated. Still this way of thinking was ushered in by the first airplane flights. Transformation continues within a world predicated on transformation. The virtual reality created by computing, which causes a rethinking of individual identity and boundaries of the self—leading to the rise of cyberpoetry—calls into question those same limits that were challenged by the transformative nature of viewing motion picture shows in the early part of the 20th century. What is important to see in these developments is that the last century discovered how to understand a radically new world, one not anticipated beforehand and not resembling anything that had come before, and the century produced unique methods of expressing this new awareness.

It was not so much that American poetry evolved in the 20th century in conjunction with a modern society. Rather, it was a task of that poetry to examine and express the meaning of this new way of the world. In terms of the arts (with the possible exception of painting), the 19th century seemed not to possess the sense of what was soon to arrive. Even the poetry of Whitman and other key protomodern literary figures of the prior century—including Emily Dickinson, Ralph Waldo Emerson, Edgar Allan Poe, and Herman Melville—did not comprehend the aesthetic and cerebral concerns that were to arise. The 20th-century

American poet was writing a poetry in a fully realized American language—no longer European in its cast—about a United States that by 1900 was becoming a world power. By the time Pound had told poets, "Make it new," the 20th century was already unfolding its unique character that was, in great measure, due to intellectual realizations then revolutionary, which would fundamentally alter the conception of the world. In 1900 the ancient Minoan palace at Knossos was discovered, as was radon, the gamma ray, and quantum energy, and the third law of thermodynamics was postulated. In this same year Sigmund Freud published his influential opus *The Interpretation of Dreams*—without which the work of Robert Lowell, Sylvia Plath (as readers see her in lines like "At twenty I tried to die / And get back, back, back to you," from her 1962 poem "Daddy") or any confessional poet could not have been written.

This was also the year that Theodore Dreiser's novel *Sister Carrie* was published and that Giacomo Puccini's opera *Tosca* was first performed. And in 1901 Booker T. Washington's autobiography *Up from Slavery* became a best-seller, and Pablo Picasso began painting works that are now famously categorized as belonging to his blue period. In 1902 Joseph Conrad published his novel *Heart of Darkness,* while the opera tenor Enrico Caruso made his first gramophone recordings. In 1903 Wassily Kandinsky inaugurated abstract painting with the showing of his *Blue Rider.* In arts and letters breakthroughs were occurring year after year. The year 1913 was especially noteworthy: Willa Cather published her novel *O Pioneers!,* D. H. Lawrence published his novel *Sons and Lovers,* and Frost published his first collection of verse, *A Boy's Will.* And in that same year Cecil B. DeMille produced the feature-length Hollywood film, *The Squaw Man;* a Parisian opera audience rioted in reaction to a performance of Igor Stravinsky's far-reaching musical work *The Rite of Spring;* and Manhattan hosted the New York Armory Show, a transforming event for a poet like Williams, who was amazed at the modern art he was able to view there, including Marcel Duchamp's painting *Nude Descending a Staircase.* Without these and other artistic innovations, would Williams have otherwise postulated, as he did subsequently, that a poem was a "machine made of words," and would the "machine aesthetic" have gained ground in American poetry?

Well before America was to enter World War I—a global conflict that left society profoundly disillusioned about a human being's capacity for destruction and degradation (as is reflected in Robert Graves's monumental book *Goodbye to All That* [1929])—American society was being transformed materially, intellectually, and aesthetically. Invention of the self and of the world in which the self resided are concepts that have always been central to American culture, beliefs epitomized by the American Revolution. Invention in American poetry was a key to how society was to evolve in the 20th century. Something essential changed in poetry as the new century was progressing. This development was to be spurred by cataclysmic events—the world wars and other military conflicts, the sociopolitical upheavals of the 1930s, and of the 1950s and 1960s, the landing of Americans on the Moon—and yet at bottom the stunning diversity and originality of so much of 20th-century American poetry is the result of the will to carve out a territory all of one's own. The American poet in the 20th century required that style and substance bespeak an individuality—as if the poet made up the rules not only of writing but of life. Hence the work of the 20th century exhibited a dazzling array of metrics and prose poetry and as many explorations of the individual psyche and of world events that mark off this century as qualitatively different from all of its predecessors. If the European Middle Ages can be said to have been a time when poets adhered to tradition and emulated what had come before, the 20th-century United States can be called its direct opposite. In this way Whitman was prescient. He looked ahead to a time when originality would be so widespread as to be taken for granted, and he sought an American tongue and a free verse poetic line. Racial and ethnic diversity are part of the equation that gave rise to this collection of poetries; America is the great social experiment. Nevertheless, it is the drive to stand alone that lies at the heart of what has caused the ingenuity and range of this vast body of verse.

There were many schools and trends over the years between 1900 and 2000—imagism, the New York school, Language poetry, to name but three. Remarkably, not only were there these various coalescences of energy, attention, and vision among American poets, but there were also a great many poets who did not fit easily or at all within these groupings. The 20th-century poet went her or his own way and by so doing reshaped the literary canon and the idea of what is beautiful or compelling. This process occurred daily as poetry burgeoned onto the page and into the cafés, galleries, theaters, and other venues that have served as the bases for other social and aesthetic groupings. The example of Allen Ginsberg in 1955 breaking ground with his reading of his long poem *Howl* at San Francisco's Six Gallery, which signaled the emergence of the San Francisco Renaissance, is one of many instances of this poetic dynamic that is not peculiarly American in its substance but is distinctly American in its spirit. American poetry in the 20th century was a protracted revolution in letters and, more broadly, in society. The poetry has been overwritten by the movies, television, and the Internet. Although the news of this revolt is no longer printed much in newspapers or broadcast electronically, the revolution itself survives—indeed, it flourishes—because of the soul's need for meaningful language that arises out of the human labor to shape language.

A great many poets took Pound's urgings to heart, and others followed his dicta even when they were not conscious of the fact that they had been formalized and enunciated by Pound. This happened despite his repugnant political and social ideas, because, poetically, he spoke for his time. As its poetries attest, American arts and culture broke free decisively from Europe in the 20th century and came into its own. There was the need and urge to institutionalize in poetry a distinctly American idiom, to write, as Williams titled one of his books, *In the American Grain* (1925). That was in the early part of the century. By the late century American language in poetry had reached its fullness and explored the human condition as well as the condition of language itself with an unparalleled depth and variety.

ABOUT THIS BOOK

This volume records important and representative articulations of post-1900 American experience and speech.

I have striven to make this book comprehensive; yet, in its treatment of recent poets and poems, and despite the fact that the volume contains commentary on a disproportionate number of them, it still leaves out certain figures, as is inevitable in a project of this size. Time has helped to determine which poets from, for instance, the period of high modernism should be included in a literary companion such as this is. When it came to deciding who from the 1970s or, say, the 1990s—postmodern poets—should be included, the decision-making process was far more difficult, however. To err on the side of caution, this book tends toward inclusion (although, inevitably, a deserving poet may be left out, the result of imperfect human endeavor or the constraints of space). All the major poetic movements of the 20th century are discussed herein, certainly all the major poets, as well as many of the most pivotal and influential poems of the century. Some poets get more attention than they have received thus far. To cite one of several possible examples of this editorial discretion, the late modernist, African -American poet Melvin Tolson is discussed at length, and his epic poem *Harlem Gallery* is examined, alongside the obviously necessary entries on such African-American poets as Gwendolyn Brooks and Langston Hughes, as well as their respective poems ("The Bean Eaters" and "We Real Cool," *A Montage of a Dream Deferred* and "The Negro Speaks of Rivers," respectively). Similarly while Rich is discussed at length (as are her poems "Diving into the Wreck" and "Snapshots of a Daughter-in-Law"), there is also an entry on lesser-known feminist poet Rachel Blau DuPlessis (and another on her serial poem *Drafts*). Going further, this volume includes an extensive entry entitled "Female Voice, Female Language"—one of nearly 500 entries, among which are such topics as "ars poeticas," "long and serial poetry," "prosody and free verse," and "war and antiwar poetry." The book concludes with a glossary of terms, such as, for example, *iambic pentameter,* to aid the novice reader, and a bibliography for those who would desire further commentary.

The United States is uniquely heterogeneous; so is its poetry. This country has often hosted a social vanguard, and this fact also has been reflected in its poetry (and in its other arts). The country dominated the world economically and militarily in the last century—this, too, has been reflected in the poetry of the era, often as praise and, at times, vituperation. This uniquely social, economic, political, intellectual, and aesthetic experiment in the 20th century took root in a dynamic nation, one that is arguably unprecedented. Its poetry justifies such a claim.

—Burt Kimmelman
Newark, New Jersey

BIBLIOGRAPHY

Adams, Henry. *The Education of Henry Adams*. Boston: Houghton Mifflin, 1946.

Folsom, Ed. "Introduction: Recircuiting the American Past." In *A Profile of Twentieth-Century American Poetry*, edited by Jack Myers and David Wojahn, 1–24. Carbondale: Southern Illinois University Press, 1991.

Gray, Richard. *American Poetry of the Twentieth Century*. New York: Longman, 1990.

Mitchell, Roger. "Modernism Comes to American Poetry: 1908–1920." In *A Profile of Twentieth-Century American Poetry*, edited by Jack Myers and David Wojahn, 25–53. Carbondale: Southern Illinois University Press, 1991.

Parini, Jay, and Brett C. Miller. *The Columbia History of American Poetry*. New York: Columbia University Press, 1993.

Rasula, Jed. *The American Poetry Wax Museum: Reality Effects, 1940–1990*. Urbana, Ill.: National Council of Teachers of English, 1996.

Untermeyer, Louis. Introduction to *The New Era in American Poetry*. New York: Henry Holt and Company, 1919, pp. 3–14.

A

"*A*" Louis Zukofsky (1931–1974, 1978) Among the most ambitious and demanding of American long poems (see LONG AND SERIAL POETRY), the composition of "*A*" represents a major bridge from the high modernist epics of T. S. Eliot, Ezra Pound, and James Joyce to a language-oriented postmodern poetry. The title of Zukofsky's masterwork—the first, shortest, and possibly most ubiquitous word in the English language, tellingly highlighted with quotation marks—indicates an attention to discrete and seemingly insignificant detail that avoids heroic postures or subject matter and focuses on the nuances of linguistic possibilities. As Zukofsky remarked: "a case can be made out for the poet giving some of his life to the use of the words *the* and *a:* both of which are weighted with as much epos and historical destiny as one man can perhaps resolve" (*Prepositions* 10). During the 46 years of its composition and irregular publication in sections, "*A*" received little recognition, but after World War II younger poets, such as Robert Creeley and Ronald Johnson, discovered the poem as a major development of experimental MODERNISM in contrast to the dominant conservative modernism exemplified by the work and influence of Eliot. Subsequently, "*A*" has been an exemplary model and resource for many poets of the Language school.

Zukofsky began "*A*" at a remarkably early stage in his career. By 1928, at age 24, he had composed the first four sections, or movements, and would work intermittently on the poem until 1974. At the outset Zukofsky decided the work would have 24 movements, but instead of subordinating them to overarching formal or thematic patterns, he allowed each movement to develop its own distinct form and content. The formal diversity of the poem is immense, including movements with a variety of complicated predetermined forms as well as looser collage structures assembled out of fragments from diverse textual sources. Zukofsky's interest in rigorous formal models is reflected in his attraction to mathematics and scientific thought, and the major intellectual presences in "*A*" tend to be demandingly formalistic, with such figures as Aristotle, Spinoza, and Bach contributing both philosophical and formal ideas to the poem. The poem's opening, "A / Round of fiddles playing Bach," announces both the structural and thematic centrality of music, adhering to a basic tenet of his OBJECTIVIST poetics: "thinking with the things as they exist, and of directing them along a line of melody" (*Prepositions* 12). "*A*" explores a broad range of intricate musical effects that are distinct from more conventional melodic expectations in poetry. Through sound and cadence, Zukofsky hoped to give abstract ideas a sense of density and substance.

The first six movements bear a striking resemblance to the ideogrammic or collage method of Pound's The Cantos, but their themes and perspective reflect the poet's working-class and leftist sympathies. "*A*"-7 mark's a decisive turn toward an increasingly dense and formally intricate verse that is self-consciously artificial.

The movement consists of seven sonnets in which the poet meditates on and transforms seven sawhorses which each form the letter *A*) into words—the poem itself. The movements written up through the 1930s, "*A*"-1 to -10 (excepting the second half of "*A*"-9), probe the possibilities of how the modernist poet might align herself or himself with the workers' revolution, culminating in "*A*"-10's bitter reaction to the triumph of fascism in Europe. The extraordinary "*A*"-9 is a pivotal double-movement, each half written a decade apart on either side of World War II and mirroring exactly the intricate canzone form of the medieval Italian poet Guido Cavalcanti, down to the complex internal and terminal rhyme scheme. Whereas the first half takes its content from Marx on the degradation of value under capitalism, the latter half adapts material from Spinoza's *Ethics* on the theme of love: The revolutionary hopes of the prewar movements give way in the cold war to a concentration on the domestic concerns that will dominate the rest of the poem. The trinity of the poet, his wife, Celia (married in 1939), and son Paul (born 1943) becomes the microcosm in which Zukofsky realizes his utopia despite public neglect and the social upheavals of the 1950s and 1960s.

The later movements of "*A*" become increasingly diverse and daring in their formal experimentation, as well as demanding on readers. The tumultuous events of the 1960s frequently come into the poem: The assassination of President John F. Kennedy figures prominently in "*A*"-15; the Civil Rights movement, Vietnam War, and other news events appear in "*A*"-14 and -18; and sardonic allusions to the space race occur throughout. However, more often than not conventional meaning is submerged in the sound and play of the language. "*A*"-15 opens with a famous homophonic "translation" from Hebrew of a passage from the Book of Job that translates the sound rather than merely the sense of the original text. Zukofsky also deploys this technique extensively in "*A*"-21, a complete transliteration of Plautus's comedy *Rudens.* "*A*"-22 and -23 are each a thousand lines of virtually impenetrable verbal texture that compresses an enormous amount of reading on natural and literary history, respectively. These sections push to an extreme Zukofsky's effort to create a poetic language that embodies a maximum of sight, sound, and "intellection" (*Prepositions* 171), a language that suggests multiple meanings yet is stubbornly resistant to any definitive sense. Zukofsky countered the charge of obscurity by insisting: "why deny what you've not / tried: read, not into, it" ("*A*" 528).

The massive concluding movement of "*A*" was appropriately composed by Celia, who constructed a compendium of the poet's work in five voices: The first consists of the musical score of Handel's *Harpsichord Pieces,* which is counterpointed with selections from Zukofsky's criticism, drama, fiction, and poetry (from "*A*" itself). As a final curiosity, there is an index, including entries for *a, an,* and *the,* as well as topics and names that suggest alternative readings of the poem.

BIBLIOGRAPHY

Ahearn, Barry. *Zukofsky's "A": An Introduction.* Berkeley: University of California Press, 1983.

Scroggins, Mark. *Louis Zukofsky and the Poetry of Knowledge.* Tuscaloosa: University of Alabama Press, 1998.

Terrell, Carroll F., ed. *Louis Zukofsky: Man and Poet.* Orono, Maine: National Poetry Foundation, 1979.

Zukofsky, Louis. *Prepositions +: The Collected Critical Essays.* Hanover, N.H.: University Press of New England, 2000.

Jeffrey Twitchell-Waas

ABSTRACT EXPRESSIONISM Beginning in New York in the late 1930s and influential until the late 1950s, abstract expressionism was the first major international art movement to originate in the United States. In painting, it combined cubism, fauvism, abstraction, expressionism, and SURREALISM. In poetry, as in painting, the style is marked by spontaneity, gesture, focus on process rather than product, invitation of accident, and collaboration. Its influence on American poetry is not limited to a single group of poets, although the ideas, works, and events that gave rise to abstract expressionism are closely associated with the NEW YORK SCHOOL, a group of overlapping and acquainted poets, critics, and painters. Of the New York school poets, JAMES SCHUYLER and JOHN ASHBERY wrote early art criticism of "action painting," another name for the art movement. FRANK O'HARA worked as a curator at the Museum of Modern Art (MOMA), but he modeled for and collaborated with more figural painters associated with the expressionists, including Fairfield Porter and Larry Rivers. The poetry of Ashbery, KENNETH KOCH, and BARBARA GUEST displays surrealism's influence on expressionism; indeed, Koch and Ashbery translated surrealist works. O'Hara's book *LUNCH POEMS* was part of LAWRENCE FERLINGHETTI's City Lights Pocket Poets series, which is more closely associated with the BEATS. The Beats shared abstract expressionism's interest in spontaneity.

Abstract expressionist painters, including Robert Motherwell, taught at BLACK MOUNTAIN College. Painters, such as Franz Kline, Willem de Kooning, and painter and critic Elaine de Kooning, studied there. The poet ROBERT CREELEY, also on the Black Mountain faculty, continued to collaborate with visual artists; CHARLES OLSON's theories of breath and gesture in his essay "Projective Verse" draw on abstract expressionist ideas.

SAN FRANCISCO RENAISSANCE poets also share a relationship to abstract expressionism: ROBERT DUNCAN through Black Mountain, and JACK SPICER through teaching at the California School of Fine Arts (now the San Francisco Art Institute), where abstract expressionist painters, including Mark Rothko, also taught.

Various abstract expressionist purposes and styles continue to cross-pollinate: Some POETRY ANTHOLOGIES combine abstract expressionism–influenced poetics under the term *postmodernism.* Critics generally consider there to be three generations of New York school poets. The second generation of New York school poets includes such varied poets as ANN LAUTERBACH, DAVID LEHMAN, and ALICE NOTLEY, as well as others associated with New York's Poetry Project (see POETRY INSTITUTIONS), which, while unique, nevertheless represents a variety of Black Mountain, Beat, and New York school aesthetics. The third generation consists of poets who have studied at the Poetry Project.

Abstract expressionism in poetry is marked by extreme abstraction of form. Lines, even when the work is written in verse form, are broken by gesture, syntax, or musical "movement." A colloquial tone reflecting an American idiom builds toward forming thematic unity, completing a rhythm, or developing or creating a "return," a minimal version of the LYRIC epiphany. Koch and Ashbery's delirious sestina collaborations retain the envoy, the concluding stanza, albeit a ridiculous one; O'Hara's "WHY I AM NOT A PAINTER" and "THE DAY LADY DIED" build toward the last sentence; and Schuyler's "Morning of the Poem" establishes its unity through an extremely natural repetition and variation. The origins of the poetry are markedly conceptual, based on an idea for a poem; phenomenological, based on an attempt to capture experience; or collaborative, either with an artist working in another medium or with another poet. Poems are identified with experience rather than description. Invitation of "occasion" and tolerance of experiment set the stage for Language poetry's application of the experience of language and reflection of process to critique "art for art's sake." In poetry, abstract expressionism's extended consideration of the pictorial plane and the artistic process—where gesture and field replace the use of arrangement of objects or images to create depth—becomes an open, minimal, or discovered form, uses the page as a canvas, considers the way language handling changes content, and queries the unitary "I."

BIBLIOGRAPHY

Hoover, Paul. Introduction to *Postmodern American Poetry: A Norton Anthology*. New York: Norton, 1994, pp. xxv–xxxix.

Landauer, Susan. *The San Francisco School of Abstract Expressionism.* Berkeley: University of California Press, 1996.

Leja, Michael. *Reframing Abstract Expressionism: Subjectivity and Painting in the 1940s.* New Haven, Conn.: Yale University Press, 1993.

Catherine Daly

ACKERMAN, DIANE (1948–) Author of 16 books, Diane Ackerman is perhaps best known for her natural histories and creative nonfiction, most famously, *A Natural History of the Senses* (1990). Nevertheless she considers herself a poet first and continues to write dazzling collections of verse, six in all. Perhaps following Henry David Thoreau's dictum that before one can write one must live, she has filled her life with rich experience and far-flung adventures, each one culminating in a book. Consequently, her poetry displays a striking breadth of subject matter (scientific study of planets, deep-sea diving, piloting airplanes, gaucho wrangling, Arctic and jungle explorations, and so on).

Hers is an accessible, usually free-verse poetry, written in the first person with NARRATIVE elements, imaginatively realized in brilliant, often exotic imagery, and demonstrating a careful attention to rhythm and the sounds of words.

Born in Waukegan, Illinois, Ackerman received a B.A. from Pennsylvania State University and an M.F.A., M.A., and Ph.D. from Cornell University, where she studied with A. R. AMMONS and the physicist Carl Sagan. She has won the Academy of American Poets' Lavan Award (1985) and grants from the National Endowment for the Arts (1986 and 1976) and the Rockefeller Foundation (1974), as well as a 2003 Guggenheim Fellowship.

In her first collection, *The Planets: A Cosmic Pastoral* (1976), Ackerman began her lifelong mixing of science and art; with Sagan as "technical advisor," she created "scientifically accurate" poems about the planets (Richards 5). Her second collection, *Wife of Light* (1978), continued this interest in science and began her poetry of geographic adventure. *Lady Faustus* (1983) broadened her search for experience as a "sensuist"—her term for one who rejoices in sensory experience—recreating adventures in undersea diving, night flying, and sexuality. In "Christmas on the Reef," when her guide indicates with a sweep of his hand that we have the tide within our bodies, she writes, "My eyes watered . . . and for a moment, the womb's dark tropic . . . lit my thought." Most recently, in *I Praise My Destroyer* (1998), Ackerman's poetry unflinchingly confronts death and suffering while still holding to an edge from which it can praise. From the haunting elegy for Sagan, "We Die," to the final sequence "Canto Vaqueros," the voice ranges far and affirms "this life where wonder / was my job." Perhaps responding to the dissolution of death with a rage for order, the poetry explores these subjects with form, as in the villanelle "Elegy": "My own sorrow starts / small as China, then bulges to an Orient." In a century of poetry whose dominant tone was irony, Ackerman has held fast to a genuine poetry of wonder.

BIBLIOGRAPHY

Richards, Linda. Interview. "At Play with Diane Ackerman." *January Magazine*. Available online. URL: http://www.januarymagazine.com/profiles/ackerman.html. (August 1999), pp. 1–11.

Veslany, Kathleen. "A Conversation with Diane Ackerman." *Creative Nonfiction* 6 (July/August 1996): 41–52.

Michael Sowder

ADAM, HELEN (1909–1993) Helen Adam was a central figure in the SAN FRANCISCO RENAISSANCE, best known for her ballads of the supernatural. ROBERT DUNCAN described her ballads as the "missing link [that] opened the door to the full heritage of the forbidden romantics" (435). Seemingly anachronistic, the eerie power of Adam's ballads stands in sharp contrast to the cerebral sophistication of the late MODERNISM dominant at the midcentury, and her work greatly appealed to younger poets seeking a sense of poetry's primordial power.

Growing up in Scotland, Adam published her first book of ballads, *The Elfin Pedlar,* at age 14. She came to the United States in 1939 with her sister and lifelong companion, Pat, initially living in New York City, but eventually moving to San Francisco in 1953. There she became associated with the BEATS, and especially with the poets who gathered around Duncan and JACK SPICER. Adam was renowned for her readings, which she sang. Her published volumes included illustrations, frequently her own surrealistically inspired collages (see SURREALISM). A major event in the poetry scene of the period was the 1961 premiere of her ballad opera, *San Francisco's Burning,* which was later revived in New York, where Helen and Pat settled in 1964.

While Adam experimented with a range of forms, her central preoccupation remained the narrative ballad; she expertly developed many formal variations without straying far from the essentials of her romantic models. Although she most often reworked 19th-century folk and gothic material, Adam also wrote updated ballads depicting the darker side of contemporary urban life. She had an intimate knowledge of the occult, which particularly manifests itself by showing women as agents of forbidden power. Her ballads depict desire as an insatiable force that lies largely hidden in conventional life due to repression and fear, but which impinges on the everyday and can burst forth as an overwhelming passion or seduction. As with William Blake's *Songs* (1789–94), which are an important precursor, the combination of frightening fables presented in a fairy-tale or childlike manner give her work a sinister charm.

Adam's best-known poem is probably "I Love My Love" (1958). A newly wed husband finds himself increasingly entangled by his wife's diabolical hair, driving him to murder her; the hair springs up from her grave, singing, "I love my love with a capital T. My love is Tender and True. / Ha! Ha!," hunts down the husband, and strangles him. This poem demonstrates Adam's characteristic strengths: the combination of horror and humor with the trancelike repetitions of the ballad form, the unselfconscious directness of the NARRATIVE presentation, the witch-wife manifesting the husband's fear of passion and the irrational, and the vengeful return of the repressed.

BIBLIOGRAPHY

Davidson, Michael. *The San Francisco Renaissance: Poetics and Community at Mid-Century*. Cambridge: Cambridge University Press, 1989, pp. 179–187.

Duncan, Robert. "Biographical Notes." In *The New American Poetry*, edited by Donald M. Allen. New York: Grove Press, 1960.

Finkelstein, Norman M. *The Utopian Moment in Contemporary American Poetry*. 2d ed. Lewisburg, Penn.: Bucknell University Press, 1993, pp. 82–90.

Prevallet, Kristin. "The Reluctant Pixie Poole (A Recovery of Helen Adam's San Francisco Years)," Electronic Poetry Center. Available online. URL: http://wings.buffalo.edu/epc/authors/prevallet/adam.html. Downloaded March 26, 2007.

Jeffrey Twitchell-Waas

"ADVICE TO A PROPHET" RICHARD WILBUR (1961) RICHARD WILBUR's "Advice to a Prophet" is concerned with one of the most ancient of issues—the nature of prophecy—and one of the most contemporary—the threat of nuclear war. Addressed to an anonymous prophet whose imminent arrival parallels the nuclear conflict that seemed inevitable during the early 1960s, the poem suggests that persons in the modern era have become indifferent to nuclear holocaust precisely because the scale of such destruction eclipses the human imagination. Wilbur suggests that to speak against such weapons as a lone voice or with the same unfeelingly scientific and statistical language that governs their construction and deployment will prove futile, because a prophet needs to transform the very terms of the argument. "Spare us all word of the weapons, their force and range," the speaker warns, "Our slow, unreckoning hearts will be left behind / Unable to fear what is too strange." Instead, the speaker advises the prophet not to depict a world emptied of human presence, an idea beyond the scope of the egoistic mind, but a world rid of its individual beauties.

Writing about links between recent poetry and nuclear armament, scholar John Gery argues that nuclear weapons have more of a symbolic than a material presence or effect upon human life; used only twice in the history of human aggression (though tested frequently), they reside almost entirely in the space of the imagination (3–4). Because it works in the realm of the imagination, poetry can confront the dangers of nuclear escalation by "expressing the uncertainty of a world that itself hangs suspended between mutable truths and insufficient lies" (32). "Speak of the world's own change," Wilbur urges the prophet, and his injunction is ultimately for the prophet to act as poet. Two types are suggested here. The prophet must speak in terms of the natural changes to which humans are accustomed, the positive metamorphoses of nature which contrast powerfully against the unnatural changes wrought by nuclear weapons. But the prophet as poet must also depict and intensify the material world that will be lost as a result of nuclear apocalypse, must show the disintegration that will result from such a conflict. Moreover, the speaker seems to be praising the capacity to change that is the mark of a world unharmed by nuclear war; nuclear apocalypse will, ironically, perfect the world, because no change will ensue when everything has been destroyed absolutely; thus, "the white-tailed deer will slip / Into the perfect shade, grown perfectly shy." Punning on the title of his first collection of poems, Wilbur suggests that "the beautiful changes," and that the prophet must ask the people what their lives will be like without the beautiful, ever-changing natural world.

The speaker advises the prophet not to take up the rhetoric of the prophet, which will eventually make him "Mad-eyed from stating the obvious," but to speak, as Peter Sacks explains, as a member of the civic community. Sacks writes, "The need for this kind of mediating (rather than "mad-eyed") speaker is urgently historical—as is the content of his speech, which is also personal, since it focuses on how we may affectively (hence effectively) be made to experience the abstract threat of nuclear war" (555). In short, Wilbur seems to be urging the prophet to behave as a poet would, by suggesting through metaphorical images the extent of the destruction that is approaching, and by striving to "Ask us, ask us whether with the worldless rose / Our hearts shall fail us." The alternative is to go unheard.

The task Wilbur sets before his prophet is by no means easy, because he will not be able to rely on declamations and rage, but must instead draw on the images of peace. He must intensify images of the world that is threatened, not images of the threats, and with such images he must bring the public to feel how the loss of the natural world, which so often provides a mirror for human reflection, will bring about the loss of all meaning in human life: "What should we be without / The dolphin's arc, the dove's return, // These things in which we have seen ourselves and spoken?" And if the prophet cannot find a way to achieve this task, Wilbur's poem clearly presents itself as a model.

BIBLIOGRAPHY

Gery, John. *Nuclear Annihilation and Contemporary American Poetry: Ways of Nothingness.* Gainesville: University Press of Florida, 1996.

Sacks, Peter. "Richard Wilbur." *American Writers.* Supp. 3, Vol. 2. New York: Scribner, 1991: 541–565.

Temple Cone

"AFTER APPLE-PICKING" ROBERT FROST (1914)

One of his most celebrated poems, "After Apple-Picking" draws upon a familiar image from ROBERT FROST's New England landscape—the harvesting of an apple orchard—to consider how life is conducted after "the Fall" of man into sin. The poem's images of rural labor and its deceptively simple language suggest a world of pastoral harmony, but its recurrent figures of sleep and falling resonate with darker, transcendent significance. "Essence of winter sleep is on the night," the speaker remarks, and the poem is haunted by thoughts of the weariness caused by labor, of mortality, and of what follows after death.

A key to reading the poem is to understand its formal qualities. Like many of the other poems published in the collection *North of Boston* (1914), "After Apple Picking" is written in iambic meter, meaning that the cadence of each line is ascending. But the number of iambic feet in each line varies, and the rhymes are irregularly organized, a form poet-critic Timothy Steele calls astrophic iambs (142). As a result, the poem follows no set pattern, though its formal devices give the appearance of order. These variations underscore aurally what the poem addresses thematically: uncertainty about how, or even if, the universe is ordered.

The poem opens with the speaker reflecting upon the apple harvest that has just concluded. He is resigned to disappointment with his labors, uncertain if he completed his work and troubled by the consequences of his failures, for every apple he dropped "Went surely to the cider-apple heap / As of no worth." This unease seems the result of a strange vision experienced while looking through a pane of ice skimmed from a water trough, a trompe l'oeil that disturbed his dreams, making "Magnified apples appear and disappear." At last, weary both from labor and from meditating upon it, the speaker considers his approaching sleep, but in a turn that recalls Hamlet's analogy of the afterlife and sleep, he cannot tell if his sleep will be like the woodchuck's hibernation (cyclical and therefore restorative) or "just some human sleep."

Frost uses biblical allusions throughout the poem to suggest the struggle of mortal life and the uncertain nature of the afterlife. The speaker's work of picking apples is never decisively concluded, reminding us that one consequence of humankind's Fall (for picking an apple) is a life of unending labor, while the distorted vision the ice grants recalls St. Paul's claim that one sees God "as through a glass darkly." But "After Apple-Picking" resists simple symbolic correspondence, and indeed, one of its major themes is that human understanding of the transcendent is limited. Thus, as Robert Faggen notes, the apple-tree can represent both the tree of Paradise, whose fruit caused humankind's Fall, and the Darwinian "Tree of Life," whose fruits endure the process of natural selection. Ultimately, as Richard

Poirier explains, "After Apple-Picking" depends upon a language that evokes metaphysical truths without abandoning the material world from which that language derives. Less important than the symbolic meanings of the poem's various images is the idea that the physical world has a significance beyond itself whose meaning can never be fully determined, and this state of uncertainty, which defines and disturbs the speaker, is for Frost the fullest expression of the human condition.

BIBLIOGRAPHY

Faggen, Robert. "Frost and the Questions of Pastoral." In *The Cambridge Companion to Robert Frost,* edited by Robert Faggen, 49–74. New York: Cambridge University Press, 2001.

Poirier, Richard. *Robert Frost: The Work of Knowing,* 290–301. New York: Oxford University Press, 1977.

Steele, Timothy. "'Across Spaces of the Footed Line': The Meter and Versification of Robert Frost." In *The Cambridge Companion to Robert Frost,* edited by Robert Faggen, 125–153. New York: Cambridge University Press, 2001.

Temple Cone

AFTER LORCA **JACK SPICER (1957)** *After Lorca,* according to Peter Gizzi, "offers a template for reading [JACK] SPICER's other books" (183); it works as an ARS POETICA that introduces serial composition and what is usually called "dictation" as theme and method in the poet's career (see LONG AND SERIAL POETRY). Its attention to language, community, and poetic tradition were significant to both Spicer's contemporaries in the SAN FRANCISCO RENAISSANCE (particularly ROBIN BLASER and ROBERT DUNCAN) and to the later LANGUAGE SCHOOL. The book also demonstrates a paradoxically solemn and irreverent attention to tradition. While Spicer's poetry exists within elevated traditions (the text names a number of poets as influences, including William Blake, HELEN ADAM, MARIANNE MOORE, and William Butler Yeats), it simultaneously critiques the very notion of tradition. *After Lorca* purports to be a translation of the poetry of Federico García Lorca (1899–1936), but, in actuality, it takes Lorca's poetry, particularly his interest in spiritual mediums, as an often radical jumping-off point. Furthermore Spicer's use of source materials (in the form of poetries quoted or alluded to within *After Lorca*) situates him alongside 20th-century writers ranging from EZRA POUND and WILLIAM CARLOS WILLIAMS to SUSAN HOWE.

The poem's description of tradition as "generations of different poets in different countries patiently telling the same story, writing the same poem" indirectly addresses Spicer's idea of poetic dictation. For Spicer dictation is a quasi-mystical writing practice in which the poet, like a radio, receives the poem from an "outside" source (in Spicer's case, purportedly from Martians). "At the base of the throat is a little machine / Which makes us able to say anything," he explains in *After Lorca*'s "Friday the 13th" section. Here the poet's "voice" is dissolved into a poem that exceeds the poet's own subjective control.

After Lorca contains perhaps Spicer's most famous commentary on language in poetry, articulated as a desire to "make poems out of real objects," to make of the poem a "collage of the real." Spicer wants "to transfer the immediate object, the immediate emotion to the poem." The poems themselves are essentially lyrical, though this lyricism is marked by line breaks that frequently respond not to sound or to breath (as described in CHARLES OLSON's essay "Projective Verse") but to meaning; Spicer's line break often works to heighten a word's ambiguity, particularly when combined with an often erratic use of punctuation: "I crawled into bed with sorrow that night / Couldn't touch his fingers." The word *sorrow* fluctuates between being the emotion that informs the speaker's action and the lover with whom the speaker is in bed; it is similarly unclear whether "I" or "night" itself fails in the caress. Meaning's ambiguity heightens the effect here, producing the emotion described. According to Blaser, it is in *After Lorca* that "the reader first notices the presence of this disturbance" characteristic of Spicer's work, in which "all elements of order and resolution draw to themselves a fragmentation of meaning" (308).

BIBLIOGRAPHY

Blaser, Robin. "The Practice of Outside." In *The Collected Books of Jack Spicer.* Santa Rosa, Calif. Black Sparrow Press, 1996, pp. 270–329.

Gizzi, Peter. "Jack Spicer and the Practice of Reading." In *The House That Jack Built: The Collected Lectures of Jack Spicer.* Hanover, N.H.: University Press of New England, 1998, pp. 173–225.

Nathan Austin

AI (FLORENCE OGAWA ANTHONY) (1947–) Ai's work has been important for its explorations of the dramatic monologue, as well as for testing the limits and possibilities of poetic NARRATIVE. Her most significant influence is GALWAY KINNELL, though her work has been frequently compared with that of the poet Norman Dubie. Her fidelity to narrative has produced a widely accessible and popular poetry. Her writing, however, offers a sustained critique of narrative representation, giving voice dispassionately to both the silenced and the iconographic.

Ai was born in 1947 to a Japanese father and a "black Choctaw, Irish and German mother" (Ai 1). She received a B.A. in Japanese from the University of Arizona and an M.F.A. in creative writing from the University of California, Irvine. Her first book, *Cruelty,* was published 1973, and six other books have followed: *Killing Floor* (1979), *Sin* (1986), *Fate* (1991), *Vice* (1999), which won the National Book Award (1999), and *Dread* (2003). She has been the recipient of numerous grants, including those from the National Endowment for the Arts and the Ingram Merrill Foundation.

Ai has spoken against "the tyranny of CONFESSIONAL POETRY—the notion that every thing every one writes has to be taken from the self" and has suggested, instead, that she wants to "take the narrative 'persona' poem as far as [she] can, and [she has] never been one to do things by halves" (Ai 3). Her writing seeks to make apparent the erotic and disturbing desires that sustain American culture's fascination with the cult of personality: She writes with the voice of John F. Kennedy, an abused daughter, James Dean, J. Edgar Hoover, a pedophilic priest, J. Robert Oppenheimer, and others. Of the latter she writes: "To me the ideological high wire / is for fools to balance on with their illusions." A more suitable alternative is "to leap into the void." These lines suggest something of the mocking ambivalence that characterizes Ai's work as it aims both to transcend and critique the political. Her attention to the violence of the everyday and of the monumental also produces a poetry that challenges the distinctions to be made between the two. Although this writing's ability to give voice to the voiceless has implications for both identity politics and cultural revisionism, it actually questions the assumptions of each. Ai's tracing of the limitations of self, her marking of the boundary between the transcendent and the abject, places notions of identity, articulation, and self-knowledge under pressure.

BIBLIOGRAPHY

Ai. "Interview with Lawrence Kearney and Michael Cuddihy." In *American Poetry Observed,* edited by Joe David Bellamy, 1–6. Urbana: University of Illinois Press, 1984.

Ingram, Claudia. "Writing the Crises: The Deployment of Abjection in Ai's Dramatic Monologues." *Lit: Literature, Interpretation, Theory* 8, no. 2 (1997): 173–191.

Wilson, Rob. "The Will to Transcendence in Contemporary American Poet Ai." *Canadian Review of American Studies* 17, no. 4 (1986): 437–448.

Nicky Marsh

AIKEN, CONRAD (1889–1973) Conrad Aiken was a central figure in the 20th-century exploration of human consciousness through poetry. Working within a modernist context and influenced by a modernist preoccupation with the subjective mind (see MODERNISM), he developed a reputation as a poet, critic, novelist, and writer of fine short fiction. In his emphasis on natural imagery, he is influenced by 19th-century romantics, such as William Wordsworth and Ralph Waldo Emerson. In his exploration of the mind, he shares affinities with his contemporaries, such as T. S. ELIOT and EZRA POUND, to whom Aiken introduced Eliot in 1913.

Aiken was born in Savannah, Georgia. After his parents' death—his father killed his mother, then committed suicide—he moved to Cambridge, Massachusetts, to live with an uncle; he was educated at Middlesex School, in Concord, and later at Harvard University. In college, he associated with contemporaries, such as Stuart Chase, E. E. CUMMINGS, Walter Lippman, and, most notably, Eliot. Throughout his career he won the Pulitzer Prize (1930), the National Book Award (1954), and the Bollingen Prize in poetry (1956), among other accomplishments.

Aiken published more than 30 volumes of poetry, short stories, novels, and criticism, all of which involve a strong introspective and autobiographical element. His poetry experiments with musical variation as a poetic device; as a structural principle, this comes into fruition in the six "symphonies" published between 1916 and 1925 (including *The Jig of Forslin, House of Dust, The Charnel Rose, Senlin, The Pilgrimage of Festus, The Divine Pilgrim,* and *Changing Mind*). In these symphonies, his interest in the long poem (see LONG AND SERIAL POETRY) emerged in a highly developed manner. Lines from *The Pilgrimage of Festus* (1923), such as "Beautiful darkener of hearts, weaver of silence" and "Beautiful Woman! Golden woman whose heart is silence!," involve a rhythmic echoing, variation, and repetition that is musical in nature and contemporary in influence, drawing from composers, such as Gustav Mahler, Arnold Schoenberg, and Igor Stravinsky. In all of the verse symphonies, Aiken places his thematic emphasis on the human mind, its identity, and the flux and dynamism of its interaction with physical reality.

During the 1930s, Aiken composed the "Preludes," the works for which he is most remembered. In *Preludes for Memnon: or Preludes to Attitude* (1931), he records the movement of human awareness and mental perception. The focus is on finite memory and the central locale is the individual human consciousness: "Winter for a moment takes the mind; the snow / Falls past the arclight. . . . Winter is there, outside, is here in me." Aiken pursued these themes in later books, such as *Landscape West of Eden* (1934), *The Soldier: A Poem* (1944), *Skylight One: Fifteen Poems* (1949), and *Sheepfold Hill: Fifteen Poems* (1958). Increasingly Aiken has come to be considered as one of the most perceptive poets of the modern experience.

BIBLIOGRAPHY

Martin, Jay. *Conrad Aiken: A Life of His Art.* Princeton, N.J.: Princeton University Press, 1962.

Peterson, Houston. *The Melody of Chaos.* New York: Longmans, Green, 1931.

Stallman, R. W. "Annotated Checklist on Conrad Aiken: A Critical Study." In *Wake II,* edited by Seymour Lawrence, 114–121. New York: Wake Editions, 1952.

Steven Frye

ALEXIE, SHERMAN (1966–) Literary critics and poets alike consider Sherman Alexie one of the most important American Indian poets. In evocations of contemporary American Indian life, Alexie's poems brilliantly render the complex cultural position of American Indians and the feelings that position entails. As Alexie's character Lester FallsApart claims, "Poetry = Anger × Imagination." These poems often fall into one of two thematic categories: investigations of the relationships between the speaker and others, as complicated by centuries of divisive race relations, and new or revised histories that mourn or celebrate American Indian life.

Alexie was born on the Spokane Indian Reservation in Wellpinit, Washington, and began writing in college. His first collection, *The Business of Fancydancing,* appeared in 1992 to critical acclaim. He has since published four more full-length collections as well as several chapbooks, and he has achieved repute as a performer of his poetry by winning the World Heavyweight Championship Poetry Bout for four years in a row (1998–2001) as well as for winning the PEN/Malamud Award (2001) and a Pushcart Prize for poetry (2005). Yet to the general public Alexie may be better known as a fiction writer, having published two short-story collections and two novels, and as the screenwriter of *Smoke Signals,* the first commercial feature film written, directed, and acted solely by American Indians, and *The Business of Fancydancing.*

In his poetry, Alexie writes in free verse and adaptations of traditional forms (see PROSODY AND FREE VERSE). Not only is writing in English a problematic issue for those who regard its use as signaling the loss of indigenous language, as Robin Riley Fast explains (214–215), but the native poet may also feel that he or she can employ the dominant culture's established poetic forms only "at a slant." It thus seems fitting that Alexie's formal adaptations evince both a playful irreverence and a respect for such forms' power. In "Totem Sonnets" (1996), for example, Alexie presents seven varied lists of 14 items grouped into Italian or English stanza patterns. The first sonnet lists 14 people, from Meryl Streep to Muhammad Ali, whom Alexie has elsewhere professed to admire. The opening octave lists white Americans, while the sestet presents six nonwhite people of various international origins. The traditional turn of the sestet takes us from Alexie's heroes in the dominant culture to his heroes among marginalized cultures, whose status renders these individuals' achievements greater while simultaneously indicating why these figures may be fewer in number. "Totem Sonnets" thus provides just one example of how Alexie "makes junkyard poetry out of broke-down reality, vision out of delirium tremens, prayer out of laughter" (Lincoln 270).

BIBLIOGRAPHY

Alexie, Sherman. *The Business of Fancydancing.* Brooklyn, N.Y.: Hanging Loose Press, 1992.

Fast, Robin Riley. *The Heart As a Drum: Continuance and Resistance in American Indian Poetry.* Ann Arbor: University of Michigan Press, 1999.

Lincoln, Kenneth. *Sing with the Heart of a Bear: Fusions of Native and American Poetry, 1890–1999.* Berkeley: University of California Press, 2000.

Carrie Etter

ALGARÍN, MIGUEL (1941–) Miguel Algarín's most important contributions to 20th-century American poetry are his role in the development of the Nuyorican poetry movement, a group of writers and artists working in the 1960s and 1970s to establish a voice for New York Puerto Ricans, his spoken-word poetry (See POETRY IN PERFORMANCE), and his commitment to an alternative arts space that has opened the artistic community—particularly theater, poetry, and music—within the United States to artists of color. Algarín's 14 books and plays engage the mixture of his United States, Puerto Rican, and New York identities. In 1974, seeking to support fellow Nuyorican writers, along with the playwright Miguel Piñero, Algarín played host to the first Nuyorican Poets Café, originally held in his living room. The second, and current, Nuyorican Poets Café, an important site for poetry slams, opened in 1989, after an eight-year hiatus, on the Lower East Side of Manhattan.

Born in Santurce, Puerto Rico, Algarín immigrated to New York City with his family in 1951. They learned to negotiate the difficulties of adjusting to the United States while maintaining strong cultural and ethnic ties to Puerto Rico; this experience forms the basis for much of his work and the work of others he fosters. Algarín received a B.A. from the University of Wisconsin (1963) and an M.A. from Pennsylvania State University (1965). Although Algarín completed all of the work for a Ph.D., he refused to accept the degree because of the turbulent political climate of 1967 and the struggle for civil rights. He joined the English faculty at Rutgers University in 1971. Among many honors, Algarín has received a Bessie Award, for outstanding creative work by independent artists in dance and performance arts in New York City, and American Book Awards, an honor awarded annually by the Before Columbus Foundation, in 1981, 1986, and 1994.

In "Sunday, August 11, 1974," he writes of Latino families who, upon leaving church, "have crossed themselves and are now going home to share in the peace of / the day, *pan y mantequilla, una taza de café* and many sweet recollections." His infusion of Nuyorican language and experience, here demonstrated in the easy mixture of Spanish and English, and his challenge to format poetry in his long, proselike lines, typify his work and that of many young Nuyorican poets. The gritty, urban edge of the Nuyorican Café poets relies on an audience willing to hear new voices, as Algarín explains in the introduction to *Aloud: Voices from the Nuyorican Poets Café*: "[T]he importance of poetry at the Café, is rooted in its capacity to draw in audiences ranging from our immediate working-class neighbors out for a beer and some fun to serious poetry lovers willing to engage the new poets the Café features" (18). Algarín's legacy lies in his own poetry and his vision to provide a forum for other poets and artists.

BIBLIOGRAPHY

Algarín, Miguel. "The Sidewalk of High Art." In *Aloud: Voices from the Nuyorican Poets Café,* edited by Bob Holman and Miguel Algarín, 3–28. New York: Henry Holt, 1994.

Esterrich, Carmelo. "Home and the Ruins of Language: Victor Hernandez Cruz and Miguel Algarín Nuyorican Poetry." *MELUS* 23 (1998): 43–56.

J. Elizabeth Clark

THE ALPHABET **RON SILLIMAN (1979–)** RON SILLIMAN's *The Alphabet* is a multivolume long poem exhibiting the remarkable agreement of generous scope and attention to minutiae displayed in other experimental works, such as LOUIS ZUKOFSKY's *"A"*, bp Nichol's *The Martyrology,* and PAUL BLACKBURN's *THE JOURNALS.* As is true of these works, included in the minutiae of Silliman's poem are the minor events and materials of language itself, an engine propelled here by the alphabet's 26 letters, which constitute the formal occasion for the poem.

Silliman deploys a number of innovative compositional strategies in this project. The mathematical Fibonacci series (wherein each number of the series equals the sum of the previous two numbers: 1, 1, 2, 3, 5, 8, 13 . . .), for example, determines the length of stanzagraphs in the volume *Lit* (1987). One formal impulse marking all the constituent books of *The Alphabet* is Silliman's signature preference for the sentence over the traditional poetic line. Taken individually, his sentences are conventional enough; the seeming disjunctions between them are what make Silliman's work so dynamic. Apparent non sequiturs yield, in fact, multiple concurrent junctions, as they allow for associative links beyond the NARRATIVE segue; that is, logical gaps between sentences allow for a variety of poetic leaps. *The Alphabet* performs the kind of generative tension, the "play of syllogistic movement" (90), which Silliman celebrates in his critical book on experimental poet's prose, *The New Sentence*. Both works are considered seminal texts in that field of creative investigation referred to as the LANGUAGE SCHOOL.

In avoiding plot that could prove distracting, Silliman's poems invite readers to enjoy a more intimate (engagement with the linguistic materials on the page. The primary logic of "Leopards in leotards," for example, is concrete rather than narrative (See VISUAL POETRY). The way the shift of one letter (*p* to *t*) attends a radical shift in pronunciation begs more attention than cats in tights, although they too are a welcome curiosity. The intimate aura of *The Alphabet* is partly achieved, of course, through the imminence of its compositional moments. We are aware of the writer writing. In *Under* (1993) we read, "Wake, walk, wok, woke, waken versus bake, balk, doesn't exist, doesn't exist, bacon." Here the odd appearances of "doesn't exist" alert the reader to failures in procedure so that the process of writing itself becomes part of the poem. We witness the author happily substituting *b* for *w* in the word pairs *wake/bake* and *walk/balk*, then reaching an impasse at "wok" (although we might want to ask him, what about, say, bok choy?).

Although its refusal of simple referentiality may inspire charges of absurdism, *The Alphabet* is, in fact, profoundly connected to the world. Silliman's process tracks all immediate phenomena with an attention at once visceral, philosophical, and documentary. His radically inclusive poetics results in work that is highly mimetic and highly autobiographical (two characteristics that critics and proponents alike frequently deny Language writing). Such a poetics is also highly ethical, its democratic scope prompting us to consider what and whom we routinely edit out of our field of vision. One of Silliman's achievements in the *The Alphabet* is to offer us an "index of the not seen" (*Jones* 1993).

BIBLIOGRAPHY

Bernstein, Charles. "Narrating Narration: The Shapes of Ron Silliman's Work." In *Contents Dream: Essays 1975–1984*. Los Angeles: Sun & Moon Press, 1986.

Silliman, Ron. *Jones*. Mentor, Ohio: Generator Press, 1993.

Vogler, Thomas, ed. *Quarry West 34: Ron Silliman and* The Alphabet. Santa Cruz: University of California at Santa Cruz, 1998.

Susan Holbrook

AMMONS, A(RCHIE) R(ANDOLPH) (1926–2001) A. R. Ammons, one of the most popular and prolific poets of the latter half of the 20th century, managed to be both a member of the academy and a renegade, the heir to ROBERT FROST in his descriptions of domesticated nature and of WILLIAM CARLOS WILLIAMS in his generosity of spirit and freedom with poetic form. A prolific poet, he wrote numerous collections, including a volume called *The Really Short Poems of A. R. Ammons* (1990) and five book-length poems: *Tape for the Turn of the Year* (1965), *Sphere: The Form of a Motion* (1974), *The Snow Poems* (1977), GARBAGE (1993), and *Glare* (1997).

Ammons was born in Whiteville, North Carolina. While serving in the navy during World War II, he began writing poetry aboard a destroyer escort in the South Pacific. After the war, he attended Wake Forest University. Before he began teaching at Cornell University in 1964, he held a variety of nonacademic jobs. He paid for the publication of his first book, *Ommateum* (1955), the title of which refers to the house fly's compound eye. Ammons's *Collected Poems 1951–1971* (1972) won the National Book Award. *Sphere* (1974) received the Bollingen Prize. *A Coast of Trees* (1981) received the National Book Critics Circle Award. *Garbage* (1993) won the National Book Award and the Library of Congress's Rebekah Johnson Bobbitt National Prize. The American Academy of Arts and Letters made Ammons a fellow in 1978. Ammons's other honors include the Academy of American Poets Wallace Stevens Award (1998), the Poetry Society of America's Robert Frost Medal (1994), and *Poetry* magazine's Ruth Lilly Prize (1995).

His experiments with form include typing a poem, *Tape for the Turn of the Year,* on an adding machine tape. The long, narrow paper determined both the length of the poem's lines and of the whole poem. He used this medium for other poems as well, including *The Snow Poems* and *Garbage*. Ammons's innovative approach to form led Marjorie Perloff to argue that one of Ammons's collections of short poems, *Briefings: Poems Small and Easy,* is actually one long poem in small sections (Schneider 68–82). His long poems are sometimes triggered by a single image, such as a photograph of Earth from outer space in *Sphere* or a mound of trash in *Garbage* (see LONG AND SERIAL POETRY). *A Tape for the Turn of the Year,* on the other hand, proceeds more or less chronologically, something like a diary for the end of one calendar year and the beginning of the next. Whatever the trigger, his long poems often include self-mockery for the ambitiousness implicit in undertaking a long poem in the first place.

Ammons's work is often humorous in a nonchalant way, as when a mountain says to the speaker of "Classic" (1971), "I see you're scribbling again." In addition to his deft handling of the long poem, Ammons is also known for very short, often wittily compressed poems, such as "Small Sang" (1971). In the 12 words of the poem—which begins, "The reeds give," and ends, "the wind away"—Ammons both describes and demonstrates a relationship between form and identity.

One of the central concerns in all of Ammons's work is "the one and the many," the search for a single unifying principle to account for the bewildering array of individual objects of which the world is composed. In some ways, this concern reflects a dualism in which "the many" is the world of the senses and "the one" is some form of, perhaps spiritual, transcendence.

In "One: Many" (1965), he warns that people should "fear a too great consistency, an arbitrary imposition" of abstraction on the concrete details of sensory experience. Drawn back to particular details, he may offer such specifics as "the river is muscled at rapids with trout and a birch limb" ("Visit" 1965), but often his particulars are the particulars of type or species, as "The glow-blue / bodies and gold-skeined wings of flies" ("The City Limits" 1971).

Ammons uses the colon as a multipurpose form of punctuation. This stylistic idiosyncrasy allows him to bring closure to individual clauses while suggesting at the same time the ongoing flow of the poem. Such punctuation also implies his sense that any statement—any answer—is conditional and may be dissolved later in the poem's flow.

In an essay on poetry, Ammons likens a poem to a walk in four ways. First, both walk and poem involve the whole body—that is, the mind and the body. Second, every walk, like every poem, is "unreproducible" (Burr 17). Third, a poem, like a walk, "turns, one or more times, and eventually returns" (Burr 17). Fourth, the motion of the walk, or poem, "occurs only in the body of the walker or in the body of the words. It can't be extracted and contemplated" (Burr 18).

This walking motion is illustrated in Ammons's poem "CORSON'S INLET" (1965), which describes a physical walk as "liberating," releasing the speaker "into the hues, shadings, risings, flowing bends and blends of sight." It is noteworthy that even when he tries to free himself from form, he comes back to the particular forms of nature, and though he says, "Overall is beyond me," he is repeatedly drawn by a desire to understand that "Overall." Perhaps the most characteristic summary statement in the poem, Ammons writes, is "I have reached no conclusions, have erected no boundaries." Harold Bloom, one of Ammons's earliest and most ardent admirers, sees the poet's work as belonging to the important line of poetry influenced by Ralph Waldo Emerson in its attempts to approach an American sublime and pinnacle of human thought and activity. Bloom describes Ammons as "the central poet of my generation" (5), a viewpoint many others share.

BIBLIOGRAPHY
Bloom, Harold, ed. *A. R. Ammons. Modern Critical Views Series.* New York: Chelsea House, 1986.
Burr, Zofia, ed. *A. R. Ammons: Set in Motion: Essays, Interviews, and Dialogues.* Ann Arbor: University of Michigan Press, 1996.
Schneider, Steven P. ed. *Complexities of Motion: New Essays on A. R. Ammons's Long Poems.* Teaneck, N.J.: Fairleigh Dickinson University Press, 1999.

Thomas Lisk

ANDREWS, BRUCE (1948–) Bruce Andrews has been a key player in the LANGUAGE SCHOOL, both as a poet and theorist. Along with CHARLES BERNSTEIN and others, Andrews has, over the past 30 years, explored the limitations of language within artistic expression. Employing such devices as radical fragmentation and juxtaposition, Andrews's poetry represents the pinnacle of the avant-garde. Andrews strains the limits of familiar representation, which makes his poetry often difficult to understand but which also gives it power, as the reader must become an active participant. As Bernstein claims, Andrews's "poetics of 'informalism' advocates the continuing radicalism of constructivist noise" (4). His poetry makes reference to familiar objects; however, his extreme linguistic experimentation serves to make the familiar strange, breaking any neat, mathematical equivalence between signifier and a socially constructed signified. Meaning is no longer passed from poet to reader; the reader must take an assertive role in the construction of the text. Andrews thus represents the culmination of a literary tradition dating back to GERTRUDE STEIN. Along with Virginia Woolf and James Joyce, Stein popularized the practice of foregrounding the mechanical structures of written communication, often at the expense of an easily decipherable narrative. This project was expanded by the poets of the NEW YORK SCHOOL, particularly JOHN ASHBERY. Andrews and the Language school followed in this vein, bringing linguistic signification into an apocalyptic phase.

Andrews was born in Chicago, Illinois. Educated at Johns Hopkins and later at Harvard, where he received a Ph.D. in political science (1975), he has worked as a government official (National Institute of Education), an educator (Fordham University), and an entertainer (musical director for Sally Silvers and Dancers).

As a Language poet, Andrews has experimented with many poetic forms. His desire to explore the limits of language extends beyond his poetry: Andrews is also a theorist and at one point coedited, along with Bernstein, the seminal journal *L=A=N=G=U=A=G=E*. In one of his essays, Andrews makes the following declaration: "Words are mere windows, substitutes, proper names, haloed or subjugated by things to which they seem to point. 'Communication' resembles an exchange of prepackaged commodities. Here, active signifying is subordinated, transitive" (133).

The poem "Stalin's Genius" brings together Andrews's fragmented style and equally fragmented narrative: "[A]djudicate your own spermatozoa. Fallout teaches us money burns, all I / can say is: Jessica Christ!—garbage in, garbage out, rest assured." A wonderfully opaque and challenging piece of writing, "Stalin's Genius" provides images of sexuality, religion, and nuclear war, all brought together under the control that language exerts over everyday life. Andrews does not use language merely as a vehicle for passing along meaning; instead, he destabilizes language, creating a system whereby meaning must be constructed not only by associations between separate links in the linguistic chain but by filling in the missing links. By the early 1970s, well before others, Andrews was actively forcing the reader to become a partial author of the text.

BIBLIOGRAPHY
Andrews, Bruce. "Writing Social Work & Political Practice." In *The L=A=N=G=U=A=G=E Book,* edited by Andrews and Charles Bernstein. Carbondale: Southern Illinois University Press, 1984, pp. 133–136.
Bernstein, Charles, ed. *Close Listening: Poetry and the Performed Word.* New York: Oxford University Press, 1998.
Perelman, Bob. "Building a More Powerful Vocabulary: Bruce Andrews and the World Trade Center." *Arizona Quarterly* 50, no. 4 (winter 1994): 117–131.

Andrew Howe

"ANECDOTE OF THE JAR" WALLACE STEVENS (1923) Like many of his poems, WALLACE STEVENS's "Anecdote of a Jar" engages with the work of the romantic poet John Keats, in this case Keats's "Ode on a Grecian Urn," a poem about a Greek funereal urn whose painted scenes prompt Keats to speculate on the nature of mortality, pleasure, and beauty. Stevens's title seems to eschew the focus on aesthetics and traditional Western culture suggested by Keats's title: while Keats addresses his classical "ode" to a stylized cultural artifact, a "Grecian urn," Stevens writes an "anecdote" about a commonplace product, a "jar." In addition, by setting the poem in Tennessee, Stevens voices the dilemma of the American artist, who cannot draw on the cultural heritage of classical Greece or even of Keats's London, but must settle for "the slovenly wilderness" of Tennessee. Yet while Stevens's poem lacks the lushness of Keats's ode, it is no less philosophically engaged with the ordering and organizing effect that art has upon the chaos of reality; his "Anecdote" also raises important questions about the effect of human creations upon the nonhuman, natural world.

While the first two lines both follow the iambic tetrameter rhythm that the poem strives to follow throughout, their phrasings immediately reveal a conflict. "I placed a jar in Tennessee," begins Stevens, describing an act of almost divine creation with unornamented diction, yet the line that follows troubles this plainspokenness with a syntactic inversion characteristic of British verse: "And round it was, upon a hill." Critic Helen Vendler locates this conflict in the context of Stevens's relation to Keats, noting that "Where Keats had cultural and legendary ornamentation, the American poet has a bare surface. . . . The language of the poem deliberately reflects the absurdity of the American artist's attempt to write a lyric" (45–46). Indeed, this absurdity is central to the poem, and it is manifest in the way Stevens contrasts a common object with the occasionally elevated language and complex syntax used to describe it. One might argue that Stevens is creating a genuinely American lyric voice here with these contrasts, and Vendler seems to support such a finding when she advises reading "Anecdote of the Jar" as "a vow to stop imitating Keats and seek a native American language that will not take the wild out of the wilderness" (46).

But the poem is as much about perception as it is about language. The jar, a man-made product, has the immediate effect of organizing the Tennessee wilderness around it, with the jar itself, as James Baird notes, forming the geometric center (81). In one sense, this centralizing force stands for the organizing power of human perception; Robert Buttel observes that "(T)he speaker would arrange, if he could, the wild landscape into the order of a still life. His success is qualified, but art and the imagination do at least impose an idea of order that creates a bond between the speaker and sprawling reality" (166). In another sense, however, the way the jar "took dominion everywhere" also indicates the ego-centeredness of all human endeavors, which tend to view external reality as valuable only inasmuch as it serves the human ends. Thus, Stevens writes that this plain, even ugly jar "took" from the landscape and "did not give of bird or bush, / Like nothing else in Tennessee." These final lines strike an ambivalent chord: the jar's presence in the wilderness gives that setting an identity that it did not possess before, though the jar fails to "give of" anything else, and Stevens does not conjecture whether the wilderness needed that identity. Yet this ambivalence is why Stevens's "Anecdote of the Jar" proves so psychologically astute: it represents how the human imagination organizes the world into a set of recognizable and understandable patterns, so that it can take "dominion everywhere." For right or wrong, the impulse is primitive and original, an integral component of human perception.

BIBLIOGRAPHY

Baird, James. *The Dome and the Rock: Structure in the Poetry of Wallace Stevens.* Baltimore, Md.: The Johns Hopkins Press, 1968.

Buttel, Robert. *Wallace Stevens: The Making of Harmonium.* Princeton, N.J.: Princeton University Press, 1967.

Vendler, Helen. *Wallace Stevens: Words Chosen out of Desire.* Knoxville: The University of Tennessee Press, 1984.

Voros, Gyorgyi. *Notations of the Wild: Ecology in the Poetry of Wallace Stevens.* Iowa City: University of Iowa Press, 1997.

Temple Cone

ANGELOU, MAYA (1928–) Throughout her career, Maya Angelou has both fit into and broken the mold for African-American poets. She has written autobiography, like many black writers of the earlier HARLEM RENAISSANCE, and she has been associated with the Harlem Writers' Guild since the late 1950s. However, she has also transcended the limits society usually sets for African-American as well as female writers, having worked extensively in the Civil Rights movement, written for English-language newspapers in Africa, and succeeded in stage and film by acting, writing, and producing.

Angelou was born Marguerite Johnson in St. Louis. Raped as a young girl, she was mute for several years. In early adulthood she had a short career in prostitution, but she found her niche in performing arts. Angelou published her first volume of poetry, *Just Give Me a Cool Drink of Water 'fore I Diiie,* in 1971, earning a Pulitzer Prize nomination. *And Still I Rise* (1978), *Now Sheba Sings the Song* (1987), and *I Shall Not Be Moved* (1990) followed. Angelou has also garnered a Tony (1973) nomination and an Emmy (1977) nomination for her acting and a National Book Award nomination (1970) for *I Know Why the Caged Bird Sings* (1969).

Angelou's work is marked by the fusion of poetry and autobiography. In childhood Angelou found inspiration in LYRIC POETRY. In her first autobiographical work, Angelou writes that, at age six, she "met and fell in love with William Shakespeare" (14). Shakespeare's whiteness, however, caused her distress. Racial tension pervades Angelou's early work. "And Still I Rise" (1978) indicates her ongoing struggle: "I'm a black *ocean,* leaping and wide, / Welling and swelling I bear in the tide." Still, Angelou has cited as an influence Emily Dickinson, whose "familiar ballad form," Mary Jane Lupton has written, "can be heard in some of Angelou's poems" (49).

In 1993 Angelou read her poem "On the Pulse of Morning" at William J. Clinton's presidential inauguration. Although lauded by the masses, critics attacked the poem. To compare "Pulse" to "The Gift Outright," the poem ROBERT FROST read at John F. Kennedy's inauguration, A. R. Coulthard writes, is to say "something about what has happened to American verse over the intervening decades" (2). Angelou's poem opens with three symbols repeated often: "A Rock, A River, A Tree / Hosts to species long since departed." Coulthard implies that such stock imagery leads readers "mistakenly [to] believe that symbolism equates with profundity, and such thinking may have produced Angelou's Rock, River, and Tree" (4). Her detractors notwithstanding, Angelou moves readers who might not be schooled in Frost. "On the Pulse of Morning" has been set to music and was recently performed by the Winston-Salem Symphony—a clear sign of popular, if not academic, recognition. Angelou continues to write lyric poetry that addresses questions of race and womanhood in a constantly changing society.

BIBLIOGRAPHY

Angelou, Maya. *I Know Why the Caged Bird Sings.* New York: Random House, 1969.

Coulthard, A. R. "Poetry as Politics: Maya Angelou's Inaugural Poem, 'On the Pulse of Morning.'" *Notes on Contemporary Literature* 28, no. 1 (1998): 2–5.

Lupton, Mary Jane. *Maya Angelou: A Critical Companion.* Westport, Conn.: Greenwood Press, 1998.

Andrew E. Mathis

ANTIN, DAVID (1932–) David Antin is an internationally celebrated poet and art critic best known for the "talk poems" that he began in the early 1970s. Unlike the standard procedure whereby a poet composes a poem first and reads it later, Antin improvises his talk before an audience, then transcribes it on paper. Each talk poem is what Marjorie Perloff calls an "associative monologue" (318–319) made up of loosely connected narratives and driven by his encyclopedic knowledge and endless curiosity about the world.

Antin was born in New York City. His undergraduate studies at the City College of New York (B.A., 1955) were in engineering, and his graduate studies at New York University (M.A., 1966) were in linguistic philosophy and poetry (concentrating on GERTRUDE STEIN). During the 1960s and 1970s, he wrote art criticism for such journals as *Art News* and *Artforum.* He is married to the artist,/filmmaker Eleanor Antin.

Although Antin is seldom aligned with a literary group or movement, he has had a strong interest in the BLACK MOUNTAIN SCHOOL, the NEW YORK SCHOOL, and other poets associated with Donald Allen's 1960 groundbreaking anthology *New American Poetry* (see POETRY ANTHOLOGIES). His talk poems converge with JEROME ROTHENBERG's investigation of oral poetry (see POETRY IN PERFORMANCE) and PAUL BLACKBURN's translation of medieval poetry that was sung by a *joglar,* or court musician. To whatever extent the contours of each talk poem are premeditated, the performance before an audience is beyond his individual control. As he says in an essay critiquing poets associated with New Criticism (see FUGITIVE/AGRARIAN SCHOOL) and their heirs (namely ROBERT LOWELL), "poetry is made by a man up on his feet, talking" ("Modernism and Postmodernism" 131).

The published talk poem is a transcription that uses lowercase and no punctuation and arranges its words in proselike blocks with nonjustified margins. Between phrases are spaces that indicate breaths and pauses during the performance, or what Antin calls the "pulse of the speaking" (*Conversation* 63). He initially described the transcription as "notations or scores of oral performances" (61), but more recently he considers it "a text that was generated by talking, that derived its life and its mode of thinking from talking and carried the traces of its origins into the world of the text" (62).

Stephen Fredman observes that Antin can be thought of in the Emersonian tradition as a "new advocate of the panharmonicon" (138). In a given talk poem, he might combine social commentary, philosophical speculation, art criticism, humor, and autobiography. He is also the most uncharacteristically personal of avant-garde poets. In "what it means to be avant-garde" (1993), for instance, his aunt tells him about the unexpected death of his uncle, and he discovers, "nothing within the horizon of my discourse could have prepared me for that moment." For Antin, who is "mainly concerned with the present," this moment testifies to the continued need for poems that are active and restless and that keep their boundaries open.

BIBLIOGRAPHY

Antin, David. *A Conversation with David Antin: David Antin and Charles Bernstein.* New York: Granary Books, 2002, pp. 61–62.

———. "Modernism and Postmodernism: Approaching the Present in American Poetry." *Boundary* 2 1, no. 1 (1972): 131.

Fredman, Stephen. *Poet's Prose: The Crisis in American Verse.* 2d ed. New York: Cambridge University Press, 1990.

Perloff, Marjorie. *The Poetics of Indeterminacy: Rimbaud to Cage.* 2d. ed. Evanston, Ill.: Northwestern University Press, 1999.

Kaplan Page Harris

"APRIL INVENTORY" W. D. SNODGRASS (1959)

"April Inventory" comes from W. D. SNODGRASS's *Heart's Needle,* a book which, Robert Phillips writes, proves that Snodgrass "must indeed be recognized as a cofounder of the school" of CONFESSIONAL POETRY (6). The poem describes the poet turning 30 while in graduate school at the University of Iowa, as well as offers witty insights into why he is not a successful professor in a tenured job. He has shortcomings; as he tells us, "I haven't read one book about / A book or memorized one plot."

The poem includes the autobiographical element of confessional poetry; as Donald Torchiana states, "Behind [the poem] lies a year of meditating that monstrous examination in literary history for the Ph.D. in English" (104). Snodgrass engages in critical self-appraisal, finding that he falls short in comparison to starched-collared scholars with "the degrees, the jobs, the dollars." Unlike them, he teaches as a graduate student who notices, primarily, how young the women he teaches seem, so young that he has "to nudge" himself "to stare" at their attractiveness.

Though the speaker's inventory of his character and his life yield shortcomings, these shortcomings are balanced by the good things he has done: He has taught a girl one of Gustav Mahler's songs, brought comfort to a dying old man, and showed children such things as the beauty of a moth's colors or, more poignantly, how a person can love another. Having found some positives in his life, the poet asserts that there is value to his person other than the silver and gold used to fill cavities in his teeth. In other words, there is more to his identity than the superficial trappings of wealth, whether it be precious metals turned to dental fillings or the dollars that come with a teaching job.

As Snodgrass presents such an inventory, Paul Gaston asserts, "the poem not only records the memories and feelings of the poet's thirtieth year, but also categorizes them implicitly according to the values he has chosen" (54). While the poem tells us directly what has happened in the poet's life as well as what the poet thinks, it also uses the confessional characteristic of directness. Though the poem does use a strict rhyme scheme as well as a rhythm of iambic tetrameter (see PROSODY AND FREE VERSE), he tells us, for example, about his ability to satisfy his lover sexually. Paul Carroll offers that "it's a pleasure to hear a poet finally admit such things without beating around the bush by using metaphor" (176). Snodgrass describes his life directly, and the values he finds important show that there can be loveliness in life beyond professional success.

BIBLIOGRAPHY

Carroll, Paul. "The Thoreau Complex amid the Solid Scholars." *The Poem in Its Skin.* Chicago: Follett, 1968, pp.174–187.

Gaston, Paul L. *W. D. Snodgrass.* Boston: Twayne, 1978.

Phillips, Robert. *The Confessional Poets.* Carbondale: Southern Illinois University Press, 1973.

Torchiana, Donald T. "Heart's Needle: Snodgrass Strides through the Universe." *Poets in Progress: Critical Prefaces to Thirteen Modern American Poets,* edited by Edward Hungerford. Chicago: Northwestern University Press, 1967, 92–115.

Gary Leising

"ARIEL" SYLVIA PLATH (1965) "Ariel" is the title Poem of SYLVIA PLATH's posthumous volume, and it amply demonstrates many of her greatest strengths: emotional intensity, dazzling, associative imagery, and technical virtuosity. "Ariel" is a poem of death and rebirth, as well as emotional, spiritual, and physical transformation, that operates on several levels at once. The title alludes to Plath's horse, which was named after the "airy spirit" from Shakespeare's play *The Tempest* (1611). Ariel is Prospero's servant, and at the end of the play, when Prospero sets him free, it is clear that Ariel represents creative power and poetry. Thus Plath's "Ariel" literally describes the physical sensation of riding a speeding horse across a landscape, while also pointing to the transformative powers of poetic language. As Christina Britzolakis suggests, "the experience of riding a horse becomes a metaphor for the process of writing a poem" (156). This process is also one of self-transformation and transcendence that is both liberating and destructive.

The poem begins in shadow and stillness—"Stasis in darkness"—just before dawn and quickly picks up speed. As the ride commences, rider and horse merge to form a single being dashing through the landscape. The countryside is a blur of "shadows" and "berries," casting "dark / Hooks," as the speaker hurtles by trying to catch her breath in "black sweet blood mouthfuls." The horse literally carries the speaker forward, but the energy "hauling" the speaker along could also be understood as the power of poetic language and meter. The poem is saturated with assonance, alliteration, and rhyme: "berries" leads to "black sweet blood," and "Hauls me through air" leads to a perfect rhyme with "Thighs, hair" in the next line.

As the intensity and speed of the ride continues, the speaker shifts from the passive position of being "hauled through air" to taking control of the process of self-transformation. The speaker asserts herself as a "White / Godiva," and Susan Van Dyne notes that at this point the poem shifts away from fragments toward "intelligible, complete sentences," suggesting that a new version of the self has begun to emerge (160). By the end of the poem, the speaker leaves behind the self of feminine obligation and responsibility. Rider and horse, speaker and creative force are one. She lays claim to both masculine and feminine elements: She is the phallic "arrow" and also its passive target. The conclusion suggests that the speaker has literally ridden from dusk into the sunrise and has been symbolically transformed from a being in thrall to a powerful agent of the poetic "drive" itself. "Ariel" articulates in poetic form what Plath hoped to accomplish in her work: to transcend the limitations of the prevailing order and transform the self into something completely new.

BIBLIOGRAPHY

Britzolakis, Christina. *Sylvia Plath and the Theater of Mourning.* Oxford, England: Clarendon Press, 1999.

Davis, William V. "Sylvia Plath's 'Ariel.'" *Modern Poetry Studies* 3:4 (1972).

Van Dyne, Susan. *Revisiting Life: Sylvia Plath's Ariel Poems.* Chapel Hill: University of North Carolina Press, 1993.

Lisa Sewell

ARK **RONALD JOHNSON (1996)** An elaborately structured long poem in 99 parts (see LONG AND SERIAL POETRY), RONALD JOHNSON's *ARK* is both an architecture of a romantic imagination and an imaginary architecture. The poem is laid out as if each section of it were part of the structure of an ark. Drawing on such eclectic sources as the myth of Orpheus and Euridice, the movie *The Wizard of Oz,* bird songs, and the Bible, *ARK* is a visionary poem that attempts to reconcile human imagination and the natural laws of the universe in musical phrases. Although Johnson himself variously cited such American epics as EZRA POUND's *The CANTOS*, CHARLES OLSON's *The MAXIMUS POEMS*, WILLIAM CARLOS WILLIAMS's *PATERSON*, and LOUIS ZUKOFSKY's "A" as significant influences, he nevertheless distinguished his work from theirs by his desire to write a poem excluding history, "to start all over again, attempting to know nothing but a will to create, and matter at hand" ("A Note" 274). In its creation of an imaginary world incorporating a wide range of materials pieced together, *ARK* resembles the naïve or unschooled art of James Hampton, Le Facteur Cheval, and Simon Rodia, whose *Watts Towers* appears on the book's cover.

As a textual architecture "fitted together with shards of language, in a kind of cement of music" ("A Note"), *ARK*'s construction is based on the number 3 and is divided into "The Foundations," "The Spires," and "The Ramparts," each containing 33 sections. Covering the span of one day, the first section begins at sunrise and ends at noon, the second continues on until sunset, and the third ends again at sunrise. Combining center-justified line breaks, scientific prose, and the visual wordplay of concrete poetry, "The Foundations" provides an overview of *ARK*'s philosophical underpinnings, focusing on the interrelationship of vision, hearing, and thought. With each "Beam" (or section of the poem), a pun on both a ray of light and an architectural support (perhaps alluding to Noah's Ark), these poems propose a scale of correspondence within and between the human mind and the natural world: "Thinking about thinking moves atoms—however mirrored: and so, as in a rainbow the architecture of light is revealed, mind is a revelation of matter" ("Beam 12"). Examining the material components of perception, Johnson investigates "Linkings, inklings, / around the stem & branches of the nervetree" so that in observing different "sensings" the reader sees how "SENSE sings" ("Beam 8"). Such inversions and double-meanings are likewise performed in the work's concrete poetry. For example, when reading the different semantic possibilities present when the line "eartheart-hearth" is repeated over six lines shaped into a square ("Beam 24"), one fulfills the poem's instruction "TO GO INTO THE WORDS TO EXPAND THEM" ("Beam 28").

In contrast, the coherence of "The Spires" and "The Ramparts" is much looser, with a greater emphasis on sound and rhythm. As Eric Murphy Selinger observes, the "'Spires' have a delicate motion quite different from the expansive claims, illumination, and revelations of the 'Foundations.' More lines are lean and streamlined, composed of one or two words; and there are frequent references to birds, mountains, stairs, and other appropriately rising phenomena" ("Ronald Johnson" 154). While these sections continue to address much of the thematic material introduced earlier, they are more concerned with the sound of words, the "swell round of vowels" ("ARK 52") and play of consonants that "compose sonorities / past sense" ("ARK 54"). Musical elements make up a good deal of Johnson's language. Although it can only be described in the published form of the book, "ARK 38, Ariel's Songs to Prospero" is a sound performance constructed from the recordings of different bird songs. In "The Ramparts," each section of which is composed of 18 tercets, *ARK*'s syntax becomes even more disjunctive as the writing insists on "jolt amazements of being" ("ARK 94"). Here, as throughout, words themselves are "innumerable numinosities" ("ARK 96"), and a steadily increasing tone of prophecy ends in a countdown to a rocket launch, a celebratory finale that sends *ARK*'s architecture into the stars. In its emphasis on the vistas that become available when one attends to the sound and sight of language, *ARK* is a work of spiritual vision. Likening the poem to a Buddhist mandala, Peter O'Leary writes that *ARK* "is not a map of the imaginary cathedral it conceives of so much as it is a map *to* this place," in that the work's completion is ultimately up to the reader (20–21).

Despite its romantic belief in coherence, cosmic patterns of order, and mythic archetypes, *ARK* is at times a difficult poem to read. Pieced together as a "mosaic of Cosmos" ("ARK 99") from various sources, the poem, according to Mark Scroggins, "reconceives the modernist poetics of juxtaposition and the 'luminous detail,' revising it downward, as it were, into the realm of folk culture and bricolage" (148) (see MODERNISM). Quotations range from such sources as the Psalms, "The Battle Hymn of the Republic" (1861), Roger Tory Peterson's *A Field Guide to Western Birds* (1941), Henry David Thoreau's *Journals* (1862), and Vincent van Gogh's *Letters* (1963). Overall *ARK* is characterized by at least two potentially significant tensions: The first is between its transcendental spirituality and its faith in contemporary science, and the second is between its romantic imagination and its innovative structure, which, as described by Selinger, "eschews both the grand, romantic 'I' and the oral, organic forms romanticism sponsors" ("Important Pleasures"). In its attempt to resolve these conflicts, Johnson's *ARK* occupies a unique position in 20th-century American poetry.

BIBLIOGRAPHY

Johnson, Ronald. "A Note." *ARK*. Albuquerque, N. Mex.: Living Batch Press, 1996, pp. 247–275.

O'Leary, Peter. "*ARK* as a Spiritual Phenomenon: An Approach to Reading Ronald Johnson's Poem." *Sagatrieb: A Journal Devoted to Poets in the Imagist/Objectivist Tradition* 14 (winter 1995): 19–44.

Scroggins, Mark. "*'A' to ARK:* Zukofsky, Johnson, and an Alphabet of the Long Poem." *Facture* 1 (2000): 143–152.

Selinger, Eric Murphy. "Important Pleasures and Others: Michael Palmer, Ronald Johnson." *Postmodern Culture* 4, no. 3. Available online. URL: http://muse.jhu.edu/journals/postmodern_culture/v004/4.3selinger.html. Downloaded March 2007.

———. "Ronald Johnson." In *Dictionary of Literary Biography 169: American Poets since World War II, Fifth Series*, edited by Joseph Conte. Detroit: Gale Research Press, 1996, pp.146–156.

James L. Maynard

"THE ARMADILLO" ELIZABETH BISHOP (1965)

Representative of the formal qualities of ELIZABETH BISHOP's poetry, as well as the emotional and moral force that underlies her best work, "The Armadillo" describes "the frail, illegal fire balloons" that are a traditional part of saints' days celebrations in Brazil, where the author lived for many years. The poem contrasts the ethereal beauty of the objects as they rise in the night sky to the destruction they cause when they fall in flames onto the wildlife below. As Penelope Laurens argues, Bishop "shapes the reader's response to this beautiful and cruel event" through her use of metrical variation (77). Until the final stanza, "the habitually shifting rhythms of the poem" keep the reader "from 'taking sides'—from becoming, that is, too caught up either in the beauty of the balloons or the terror of the animals" (77). Until a sudden downdraft directs one of these balloons back to Earth in the sixth quatrain, they falter through the air in an irregular rhythm but seemingly in harmony with the natural phenomena around them, being barely decipherable from Venus or Mars. With characteristic attention to descriptive detail, Bishop slowly develops these ambiguous images before moving on to devote the next three stanzas of her poem to miniportraits of the unwitting victims of the fiery crash: a "pair of owls," "a glistening armadillo," and "a baby rabbit." Not until the ninth stanza, when the speaker utters the expletive "So soft!," seemingly in a spontaneous response to the sight of the rabbit, does Bishop allow the reader to identify fully with the animals. This identification then prepares for the final four italicized lines, which form an outcry of futile anguish and despair at the vulnerability of the animals—and by extension of all of us—to senseless destruction and suffering.

As Bonnie Costello observes, because "The Armadillo" is dedicated to Bishop's friend ROBERT LOWELL, some people read it "as a critique of his way of making art out of suffering" (75). Others, however, connect the poem with Lowell's decision to become a conscientious objector when Allied forces started fire-bombing Germany during World War II. Laurens, for instance, claims that "Bishop's poem points directly to these fire bombings, which wreaked the same kind of horrifying destruction on a part of our universe that fire balloons wreak on the animals" (81). In this reading, the closing image of the armadillo's "weak mailed fist / clenched ignorant against the sky" mirrors a soldier's vulnerability and helplessness in spite of his protective armor. After reading "The Armadillo," Lowell himself was inspired to write "Skunk Hour," which he, in turn, dedicated to Bishop. Both poems, as he once remarked, "start with drifting description and end with a single animal" (109).

BIBLIOGRAPHY

Costello, Bonnie. *Elizabeth Bishop: Questions of Mastery*. Cambridge, Mass.: Harvard University Press, 1992.

Laurens, Penelope. "'Old Correspondences': Prosodic Transformations in Elizabeth Bishop." In *Elizabeth Bishop and Her Art*, edited by Lloyd Schwartz and Sybil P. Estess, 75–95. Ann Arbor: University of Michigan Press, 1983.

Lowell, Robert. "On 'Skunk Hour.'" In *The Contemporary Poet as Artist and Critic,* edited by Anthony Ostroff. Boston: Little, Brown, 1964, pp. 107–110.

Sharon Talley

ARMANTROUT, RAE (1947–) Rae Armantrout's poetry is renowned for its often sparse lyricism and sharp social observation. Although she is a key member of the San Francisco poetry community from which the LANGUAGE SCHOOL emerged, Armantrout is suspicious of the term *language-oriented,* because, as she explains, "it seems to imply division between language and experience, thought and feeling, inner and outer" ("Why" 546). Influenced by GEORGE OPPEN, she agrees with him that "however elusive, sincerity is the measure and goal of the poem" ("Interview" 20). An ethical approach is apparent in her poetic practice, which consistently draws the reader to a heightened awareness of the dominant social structures underlying his or her own perceptions. Armantrout's work is also informed by a feminist poetics that deconstructs the autonomous and unified subject still found in much mainstream verse.

Armantrout was born in Vallejo, California, and grew up in San Diego. In 1989 she received a California Arts Council Fellowship and in 1993 the Fund for Poetry Award. She has coordinated the New Writing series at the University of California at San Diego and coedited the *Archive Newsletter.* Armantrout has published nine collections of poetry and an autobiography, *True* (1998).

Armantrout often explores aspects of the poem commonly overlooked. With six parts connected only through the title, "Tone" (1986) demonstrates how the way in which something is spoken may constitute its meaning. In "Poetic Silence," Armantrout argues that prose poems composed of nonnarrative declarative sentences (typifying much Language writing) leave little room for the experience of silence. Silence, she believes, encourages further questions to arise in a poem and may even enable the unthinkable and conceptually paradoxical. Silence may be accommodated by ending a poem abruptly or unexpectedly. It may be created through "extremely tenuous connections between parts of a poem" or through ellipsis, self-contradiction, and retraction (34). Armantrout further notes that she "may deliberately create the effect of inconsequence" or place "the existent in perceptible relation to the non-existent, the absent or the outside" (34–35).

A number of these strategies can be found in the 1978 poem "View" ("Not the city lights. We want / — the moon—"). Through starting with a negative proposition, Armantrout emphasizes the lack that sparks desire. The Moon itself is elliptic, both in the sky (rendered less clear by the haze of city lights) and on the page (separated from the rest of the poem by the dashes that surround it). The poem reinforces a sense of cliché through the repetition of the phrase *the moon,* while considering philosophically the Moon's existence. The unexpected last line, "none of our doing!," undermines the subject as authorizing an authoritative source of reality.

The poem is also an example of Armantrout's predilection for irony, which she believes "marks the consciousness of dissonance" ("Irony" 674). In other works, she makes use of masquerade to dissemble categorical approaches, or what she calls the "morbid glamor of the singular" (*Necromance* 7).

BIBLIOGRAPHY

Armantrout, Rae. "Poetic Silence." In *Writing/Talks,* edited by Bob Perelman, 31–47. Carbondale: Southern Illinois University Press, 1985.
———. "Tone." In *In the American Tree,* edited by Ron Silliman, 148–149. Orono, Maine: National Poetry Foundation, 1986.
———. "Why Don't Women Do Language-Oriented Writing?" In *In the American Tree,* edited by Ron Silliman, 544–546. Orono, Maine: National Poetry Foundation, 1986.
———. "Interview, conducted by Manuel Brito." In *A Suite of Poetic Voices: Interviews with Contemporary American Poets,* edited by Manuel Brito, 13–22. Santa Brigida, Spain: Kadle Books, 1992.
Beckett, Tom et al. "A Wild Salience": The Writing of Rae Armantrout." Cleveland, Ohio: Burning Press, 2000.
Vickery, Ann. "Rae Armantrout." *Dictionary of Literary Biography.* Vol. 193, *American Poets since World War II,* edited by Joseph Conte. Detroit: Gale Research, 1998, pp. 10–20.

Ann Vickery

ARS POETICAS The long tradition of writing poetic manifestoes that follow the original example of the Roman poet Horace's *Ars Poetica,* has become, since the romantic age, a defense of new verse practices against reigning poetic doctrines. William Wordsworth's 1800 preface to *Lyrical Ballads* calls attention to the need for a more common speech in lyric discourse, a nod to the ideals of the French Revolution and a rejection of the aristocratic tradition that had long demanded elevated, rarefied language in poetry. Ever since, manifestos have indicated the shifting ground of social ideals as they affect the writing of new poetry, with wars, depressions, and other major social upheavals precipitating new styles of poetry.

T. S. ELIOT's essay "Tradition and the Individual Talent," published in 1919, is a classic example of poetic revisionism. Coming on the heels of World War I, a new psychology emerges in the essay, akin to the depth psychology developing in the works of Sigmund Freud and Carl Jung, emphasizing the collective life of society in the form of culture and traditions and the individual's use of this collective experience to express one's own nature. This larger culture resides in a poet's mind as the memory of what one has read, seen, felt, said, or heard, fragments of which are fused together into lyric statements by a strong emotion. As Eliot writes in this essay, "The poet's mind is in fact a receptacle for seizing and storing up numberless feelings, phrases, images, which remain there until all the particles which can unite to form a new compound are present" (8).

Since cultural experience is always changing, emotion will be redefined by each generation of writers drawing on their own times and sense of the world to describe their feelings. In his essay "Hamlet" (1920), Eliot called this process of defining emotion through bits of experience an "objective correlative" and observed that an emotion can be reproduced through the personal associations one has with certain objects. A sequence of objects can provoke a specific emotion in the reader, a principle at the heart of modern advertising, which presents a product or service with an array of provocative and pleasing images to provoke a feeling of need or desire.

"Hamlet" went far toward defining the ways in which English and American poets might graft French symbolist ideas onto their own way of writing. Eliot's argument explains how a poet may use landscape and ordinary life as a screen on which to project personal emotions and moods. Eliot had replaced the objectivity of realistic writing for the more subtle, psychological effects of subjective lyricism, where ordinary objects are suffused with an atmosphere of shadows, far-off sounds, murky lights, and other details that communicate the poet's despair or longing, regret, or feelings of exhaustion. By careful selection of details, even a lamppost or a taxi can provide subtle emotional particularity. Eliot's emotional lyricism was closely related to new styles of painting, in particular, the rendering of landscapes in postimpressionism, as in Vincent van Gogh's fiery depictions of the night sky painted during bouts of mental illness.

EZRA POUND's formulation of imagism, which formed the central tenets of the IMAGIST SCHOOL, scattered about in essays and notes collected in "A Retrospect" (1918), reverses Eliot's emphasis on the subjective imagination by placing the focus of imagination outside the poet, in the landscape itself, where one may find patterns emerging out of the shape of flowers and trees, the recurring shapes of wind and water, and the correspondences between the seasons and the ebb and flow of civilizations. Pound emphasized poetry's need for objectivity, for a language of pure description stripped bare of "emotional slither," his phrase for self-indulgent lyricism. The term *imagism* suggests poetry's affinity with the art of photography, a link enhanced by a later movement influenced by Pound and codified as the OBJECTIVIST SCHOOL, objectivism, with its emphasis on a snapshotlike clarity of vision, control of subject matter, and strict avoidance of discursive writing.

For Pound, poetry is a language of visual perceptions derived from close observation of natural events. Not any image will do for poetry, however. Pound stipulates that the events observed must reveal a relation among things and lead the poet to a larger perception of the presence of form uniting the details into a single, composite entity. The most famous example of this method is in his two-line poem, "In a Station of the Metro" (1913), where he discovers that the faces of a subway commuter crowd resemble the arrangement of petals on a rain-soaked tree branch. In detecting the presence of form in unlikely juxtapositions, the poet is drawn to a larger perception of how certain forms reside in the natural world and are a kind of language. Forms abound and repeat their signatures in any medium or substance, from wind in the trees resembling waves at sea to the overlapping petals of a rose and the patterns of history. His ideas about form and poetry were influenced by Ralph Waldo Emerson's transcendental philosophy, which argued that nature was both a physical and a spiritual system of energy and that human consciousness was mirrored in the natural world.

Both Eliot's and Pound's theories of poetry turn on concepts drawn from modern philosophy and science and from vast overarching theories of the unity of culture; their point of opposition is the locus of order and meaning. Eliot is the more conventional theoretician in locating order in the mind alone, a Christian concept, whereas Pound places order in the natural world, aligning his esthetics with the tradition of Greek pre-Socratic pantheism and pagan literature. From these two theories, American poetry evolved along separate courses, one turning inward toward the poet's subjectivity and emotional complexity, the other turning outward to attentive observations of the natural world. Poets coming after found themselves having to choose between a psychological poetry and a poetry that contemplated the divinity of nature.

LOUIS ZUKOFSKY's "Program: 'Objectivists' 1931," which appeared as a brief preface to his anthology of selected poems under that banner in *Poetry* magazine, uses the word *objectivism* in two ways—the ordinary meaning of detaching one's emotions from observation, and as a pun on the word *objective,* the lens by which photographers view the world in magnification. The relation between film and poetry was very rich at that time, with Alfred Steiglitz, an early master of sharp-focus photography, providing visual studies that resembled imagist lyrics in their simplicity and foregrounding of objects. Zukofsky calls attention to the relations among images, allowing the lyric to expand from its focus on one relation to the possibility of the lyric sustaining a sequence of such relations, so long as "form" is perceived to link all of them. GEORGE OPPEN composed such a sequence in *DISCRETE SERIES* (1934), his experiment with an elongated, more discursive mode of imagist writing.

Zukofsky explores the underlying animist principle behind imagism, wherein matter is treated as if its constituent molecules were possessed of a will to cohere and embrace form. In a later note to his theory, published in a collection of his essays titled *Prepositions* (1967), he writes:

> Good verse is determined by the poet's susceptibility involving a precise awareness of differences, forms, and possibilities of existence—words with their own attractions included. The poet, no less than the scientist, works on the assumption that inert and live things and relations hold enough interest to keep him alive as part of nature. ("Poetry" 7)

While the so-called FUGITIVE or AGRARIAN writers of the same period staked out a position that continued the symbolist mode of lyric begun by Eliot, there are no corresponding statements of a poetic position by any of the members of this circle of southern poets—but a series of textbooks written and coedited by Cleanth Brooks and others argued that poetry's main function was to render the complexities of experience by means of metaphor and to order the relations among events by the conventions of closed rhyming, stanzaic verse. Such writers rejected the notion that form would emerge from the assembled contents alone; form was imposed onto language by the poet's imagination and skill, and it was thus independent of nature. Only by means of human artifice could nature be transformed into art.

In 1950 CHARLES OLSON extended the imagist argument a notch further in his essay "Projective Verse." Here he emphasizes the role of the body in composition, with the line length of the poem determined by the poet's "breath" and with the musicality of the language arising from the poet's aural memory of the sounds of nature. Taking Zukofsky a step further, Olson suggests that the poem is a cascade of perceptions unfolding from the meaning of an initial image. To sustain this sequence of perceptions embracing a widening frame of experience requires that the poet abandon self-consciousness altogether to sharpen attention to the surrounding world. In a state of nearly consuming attention to the outside world, the poet will overhear the "secrets objects share."

A self-effacing disposition toward experience is Olson's way of taking the ego away from the center of the act of writing. Events should be recorded as if they were more important than the observer, a notion that was beginning to reshape the approaches in sociology and anthropology, where Western values were thought to have intervened and judged other cultural systems too much, thus distorting their actual natures. "Projective Verse" was perhaps the first assault upon what might be called an imperialist poetics after World War II, the era in which many native cultures were being revived after centuries of European colonization. Olson's objections to European expansion during the last 400 years centered on the imposition of Western values, languages, and attitudes onto colonized native people; by declaring himself a descendant of New World culture, an heir to Mayan and Incan art, as he did in his great poem, "The Kingfishers" (1953), he renounced his ties to the European tradition.

More recently, a number of people writing under the general heading of the LANGUAGE SCHOOL, named after CHARLES BERNSTEIN's and BRUCE ANDREWS's journal *L=A=N=G=U=A=G=E,* asserted that language should not be "absorptive" but instead resistant to a reader's apprehension in order to rescue poetry from the corruptions of language experienced between the Holocaust and the Vietnam War. By disrupting the predictable flow of syntax and narrative sense, the reader is made to confront words as palpable entities rather than as a medium of persuasive fantasies. A similar argument was made by Bernstein against film as the exploitation of violence and cruelty to attract an audience whose exposure to such illusory experience blunts its sensitivity to reality and moral responsibility. Both in his collection of essays, *Content's Dream* (1986), and in *A Poetics* (1992), Bernstein states his intent to counter illusion and "absorptive" art by derailing syntax, randomizing diction, and using other devices to shock the reader back to his or her senses and the real world.

Others in the movement have explored language as a political construct in which only an official reality is permitted expression through the patterns of normal sentences and paragraphs. By dislocating language from its ordinary logic and syntax, words are liberated from their overused functions and stand out once more as unfamiliar things, as "objects," thrust at the reader in all their complexity and ambiguity of meaning. The language poets wage war against clichés and speech that long ago had been preempted by advertisers and politicians for their own purposes. The restoration of corrupted language is an age-old occupation of poets looking back at the abuse of prior generations; the goal of the Language poets is to liberate language from its entanglement in political and corporate power struggles. These poets equate the freedom of language with the freedom of the individual to think independently and to gain access to the world as it is, not as it is portrayed by those in power. Hence, CLARK COOLIDGE's observation in his talk "Words": "Whole edifices of philosophy rising and falling on the momentary basis of what one has said" (11).

Coolidge, like ROBERT CREELEY before him, has argued that the poet has no foreknowledge of her or his acts as a writer but composes in order to discover the possible meanings underlying her or his attention to surroundings: "I have the sensation that the most honest man in the world is the artist when he is saying I don't know" ("Interview" 37). The predisposition of knowing one's intention means that language will narrowly serve the purpose of proving what one knows; Language poets would rather allow language its own flow in order to discover hidden alternatives to one's habitual perspective. This open-ended process also agrees with LYN HEJINIAN's discourse on method, "The Rejection of Closure," in which she specifically objects to the logic that would presume to isolate a strain of thought from its vital connections to the rest of the activities of the thinking self. Her poems are attempts to recreate the multiple tracks of simultaneous thought and sensation that occur in any given moment of consciousness.

Throughout the 20th century, many American poets have been engaged in an effort to distinguish the American lyric from English poetry. Not only are the conventions of the English lyric viewed as belonging to a different cultural experience, rooted in monarchy and a close relation to Christian sacred literature, but the literature itself is the record of a single race that looks back to Rome and Athens for its legacy. As Walt Whitman argued in his own statement of poetics in the preface to *Leaves of Grass* (1855), the diverse racial makeup of America demands a more varied language embracing the many strains of ethnic consciousness in America's story. Other poets have argued that the American Indian origins of the New World must also be taken into account. Each attempt at restating the goals of American poetry widens the boundaries of what is possible and chafes against the restraints that habit and cultural norms impose upon the freedom of the poet.

BIBLIOGRAPHY

Bernstein, Charles. *Content's Dream: Essays 1975–1984.* Los Angeles, Calif.: Sun & Moon Press, 1986.

Coolidge, Clark. "An Interview with Clark Coolidge [with Jim Cohn and Laurie Price]." *Friction* 7 (1984): 7–44.

———. *A Poetics.* Cambridge, Mass.: Harvard University Press, 1992.

———. "Words." *Friction* 7 (1984): 7–44.

Eliot, T. S. *Christianity and Culture: The Idea of a Christian Society and Notes Towards a Definition of Culture.* New York: Harcourt Brace, 1960.

———. "Tradition and the Individual Talent." In *Selected Essays of T. S. Eliot.* New York: Harcourt Brace, 1964, pp. 3–11.

Hejinian, Lyn. "The Rejection of Closure." *Poetics Journal* 4 (1984): 134–143.

Olson, Charles. "Projective Verse." In *Collected Prose of Charles Olson,* edited by Donald Allen and Benjamin Friedlander, 239–249. Berkeley: University of California Press, 1997.

Pound, Ezra. "A Retrospect." In *Literary Essays of Ezra Pound,* edited by T. S. Eliot, 3–14. New York: New Directions, 1968.

Quartermain, Peter. *Disjunctive Poetics: From Gertrude Stein and Louis Zukofsky to Susan Howe.* New York: Cambridge University Press, 1992.

Zukofsky, Louis. "Program: 'Objectivists' 1931." *Poetry: A Magazine of Verse* 37, no. 5 (February 1931): 268–272.

———. "Poetry." In *Prepositions: The Collected Critical Essays of Louis Zukofsky.* Berkeley: University of California Press, 2000.

Paul Christensen

ARTICULATION OF SOUND FORMS IN TIME SUSAN HOWE (1987) The poetry of SUSAN HOWE has often been viewed as part of the LANGUAGE SCHOOL, though Howe does not consider herself to be a language poet. Nevertheless, in her long poem, *Articulation of Sound Forms in Time,* Howe presents an expansive rendering of early American history, which pays particular attention to lesser-known figures from the past. She accomplishes this, in part, by performing an act commonly used by practitioners of Language poetry, namely, examining the use of language itself. The poem might not have been as much of an accomplishment if Howe had relied solely on this self-referential process, so she pays close attention to language's referents, not just to how words and phrases act, and she plays as much with etymology as with the sonic and visual aspects of words. *Articulation* owes as much to James Joyce as it does to Howe's poetic forebears (Emily Dickinson and HART CRANE) and avant-garde contemporaries (CHARLES BERNSTEIN and LYN HEJINIAN). Howe's poem provides an imaginative means of re-viewing the early American experience and, through its complex wordplay and use of language, shows how present-day America is still tied to and affected by the events and discoveries of an earlier time.

Articulation consists of a short introduction followed by two sections, "Hope Atherton's Wanderings" and "Taking the Forest"; each contains numerous short poems. *Articulation* can seem inscrutable when approached as a reader would normally approach a literary work. And yet, as Rachel Tzvia Back puts it, even though "the text is enigmatic and resistant to interpretation . . the repetition of certain words and the highlighting of others through italics or capital letters signal the presence of language system, which signals the presence of meaning" (43). Indeed, there are multiple meanings to be found in *Articulation.* Despite a seemingly incomprehensible babble, Howe has meticulously constructed a map of a landscape in which each word or word fragment is essential, representing, linguistically, the confusion caused when cultures collide, such as what occurred in colonial America. *Articulation* contains common words with Middle English spellings, words in various American Indian tribal languages or the English appropriation of these words, as well as word fragments that could be any combination of the above. Multiple meanings, along with the sounds of the words themselves, construct an uneasy representation of Howe's vision of the American past.

The first group of poems in *Articulation,* "Hope Atherton's Wanderings," refers to the reverend Hope Atherton, an almost forgotten name in early American history. Howe gives an account of Atherton's strange story in an introduction; she writes that she will "assume Hope Atherton's excursion for an emblem" much as she does with Anne Hutchinson in the second group of poems (*Singularities* 4).

Many critics, in the years following *Articulation*'s publication, have joyfully wrestled with the tight stanzas and strange, somewhat codelike strings of words that make up this work. Marjorie Perloff notes of the two lines that open the first poem in *Articulation*—"Prest try to set after grandmother / revived by and laid down left ly"—that "We cannot be sure whom 'he' (if there is a he here) was 'revived by,' or whose 'grandmother' is involved" (525). What we can understand here, however, is that the text consists of a certain language, at once disordered and full of holes (such as, What is the adjective that "ly" seeks to modify?) and capable of offering multiple interpretations (Is "ly" meant to be a partial adverb, or is it an archaic form of the word "lie." Are we meant to think that someone was "laid down" and "left" to lie or "left" in a particular but undetermined fashion?). In addition, assuming "Prest" should be read as a verb, Perloff states that "the absence of the subject or object of 'Prest' brings other meanings into play: 'oppressed,' 'impressed,' 'presto'" (525). It could also be the noun *prest,* which means "a sheet of parchment."

"Prest" is clearly a very fitting beginning to what is a monumental poetic work—a word that, among its many possible meanings, could refer to a piece of paper, one on which Howe has inscribed a poetic rendering of Hope Atherton's journey and Anne Hutchinson's tragedy (she was banned from her community for religious reasons and subsequently was killed by American Indians). Still, as Perloff reminds us, Howe "is not, after all, a chronicler, telling us some Indian story from the New England past, but a poet trying to come to terms with *her* New England past" (533). Ultimately, Howe is as much a part of the poems as Atherton and Hutchinson, and we are not simply reading a series of poems about the latter, but rather, in sum, a long poem that illustrates one poet's sense of history, her relationship to it, and her understanding of how history is constructed through language.

BIBLIOGRAPHY

Back, Rachel Tzvia. "From the American Wilderness." In *Led by Language: The Poetry and Poetics of Susan Howe.* Tuscaloosa: University of Alabama Press, 2002, pp. 17–59.

Howe, Susan. *Singularities.* Hanover, N.H.: Wesleyan University Press, 1990.

Palatella, John. "An End of Abstraction: An Essay on Susan Howe's Historicism." *Denver Quarterly* 29, no. 3 (1995): 74–97.

Perloff, Marjorie. "'Collision or Collusion with History': The Narrative Lyric of Susan Howe." *Contemporary Literature* 30, no. 4 (1989): 518–533.

Dan Coffey

"THE ARTS AND DEATH: A FUGUE FOR SIDNEY COX" WILLIAM BRONK (1956)

In 1956 WILLIAM BRONK's book *Light and Dark,* published by CID CORMAN's Origin Press, contained an elegy to Bronk's mentor at Dartmouth, who died in 1952. "The Arts and Death: A Fugue for Sidney Cox" presents three thematic ideas that Bronk continued to develop throughout his career. These ideas were that the real world is beyond our knowing, that life is a force that defines us (rather than us defining our lives), and that we make up the stories of our lives and then believe the fictions we have created.

The first idea is stated in the first stanza: "we always miss it. Not / anything is ever entirely true." What we miss is the truth, reality. Bronk was concerned about the nature of reality and what could be said and known of it. "The Arts and Death" explains, "we live in a world we never understand." At the end of his life, Bronk was still writing on this subject. Unlike the 19th-century transcendentalists, whose work he admired, Bronk was unable to experience an innate transcendent order. He believed that the nature of the real world could never be known. Bronk originally saw this transcendental ignorance as a source of despair, but he eventually embraced it.

The second idea Bronk presents is that life lives us, instead of the other way around: "[L]ife has always required / to be stated again, which is not ever stated." Life is the active agent here; the statement of it is ourselves. We are objects acted upon. Years later in the poem "Life Supports" (1981), Bronk writes, "Life keeps me alive." Indeed, the poetic persona is not the decisive actor in much of Bronk's poetry. It is this technique that causes some scholars to see Bronk as an OBJECTIVIST, since his use of the language disturbs an English speaker's basic assumptions about subject and object. It is the poem's subject that becomes objectified by this use of theme.

The third dominant idea in "The Arts and Death" is that what we can say of our lives are self-created fictions. In the third stanza human lives are likened to toy soldiers. By the fifth stanza Bronk says we take consciousness and, with it, "make things and persons . . . make forms," although, "the forms / are never real."

In "The Arts and Death," the reader finds three of Bronk's great themes sounded for the first time together. The persistence of these ideas in Bronk's life work reveals this early poem as a seminal one.

BIBLIOGRAPHY

Clippinger, David, ed. *The Body of This Life: Essays on William Bronk.* Jersey City, N.J.: Talisman House. 2001.

Foster, Edward. *Answerable to None: Berrigan, Bronk, and the American Real.* New York: Spuyten Duyvil, 1999.

Kimmelman, Burt. *The "Winter Mind": William Bronk and American Letters.* Madison, N.J.: Fairleigh Dickinson University Press, 1998.

Sherry Kearns

ASHBERY, JOHN (1927–) John Ashbery is among the most influential poets of late 20th-century America. Associated with the NEW YORK SCHOOL, which includes FRANK O'HARA, KENNETH KOCH, and JAMES SCHUYLER, Ashberry's poetry derives from disparate sources, including W. H. AUDEN, WALLACE STEVENS, ELIZABETH BISHOP, French SURREALISM, and American ABSTRACT EXPRESSIONISM. Ashbery's work has influenced a similarly wide-ranging generation of poets, from those in NEW FORMALISM to Members of the LANGUAGE SCHOOL, as his poetry encompasses experimental and investigative poetry, as well as formal and, at times, nostalgic concerns.

Ashbery was born in Rochester, New York. He graduated from Deerfield Academy in 1945; he went on to receive a B.A. from Harvard in 1949 and an M.A. from Columbia in 1951. In 1955 he went to Paris on a Fulbright Fellowship and remained in France for 10 years, working variously as the art editor of the European edition of the *New York Herald-Tribune,* the Paris correspondent for *Art News,* and the editor of the Paris-based *Art and Literature.* From 1960 to 1962 Ashbery edited and published the journal *Locus Solus.* He has won most major poetry and literary awards, including the Yale Series of Younger Poets (for *Some Trees* in 1956), the Pulitzer Prize, the National Book Award, and National Book Critics Circle Award (for *SELF-PORTRAIT IN A CONVEX MIRROR* in 1976), the Bollingen Prize (which he shared with Fred Chappell in 1985), the ROBERT FROST medal from the Poetry Society of America in 1995, and the 2001 Wallace Stevens Award from the Academy of American Poets.

Ashbery's poetry has been placed within the romantic tradition by critics, such as Harold Bloom, who understand Ashbery's poetry as following and expanding on the poetic traditions of Auden and Stevens. Others, however, place Ashbery within a more exploratory tradition of writers, such as GERTRUDE STEIN and LAURA RIDING, and surrealist writers, such as Raymond Roussel. Ashbery seems to place himself among these other traditions, but his self-assessments (in interviews, for example) often seem merely temporary opinions. Such contingency is appropriate given the nature of Ashbery's poetry.

In 1989–90, Ashbery was named the Charles Eliot Norton Professor at Harvard University. The recipient of this esteemed annual position (past recipients include T. S. ELIOT, Robert Frost, and JOHN CAGE) is required to present a series of public lectures. Ashbery's Charles Eliot Norton lectures were published in 2000 as *Other Traditions,* Ashbery's first book-length commentary on poetry (his art criticism has been collected in *Reported Sightings: Art Chronicles, 1957–1987*). Ashbery takes up poets whose work, although not well known, has influenced his own. Of the six, three are American poets (John Wheelwright, Riding, and David Schubert), two British (John Clare and Thomas Lovell Beddoes), and one French (Roussel).

From these curious forebears (as well as from other more conventional poets, such as Stevens and Bishop), Ashbery has developed a poetic that is challenging and disarming, formal and casual, meaningful and accidental; in his lecture on Riding, Ashbery reveals something of how we might read (and misread) his own poems: "What then are we to do with a body of poetry whose author warns us that we have very little chance of understanding it, and who believes that poetry itself is a lie? Why, misread it of course. . . . All poetry is written with this understanding on the part of the poet and reader; if it can't stand the test of what Harold Bloom names 'misprision,' then we leave it to pass on to something else" (101–102). Ashbery's poetry not only withstands such misprision (Bloom's term for a kind of creative misreading), it also invites such active and participatory readings and misreadings.

In the poem "Self-Portrait in a Convex Mirror," we find that the artist is not really in control of the art anyway, so the reader is invited to create her or his own sense of meaning, an activity not unlike the poet's own. Ashbery compares the relationship between the artist's intention and the reader's interpretation to the party game in which "A whispered phrase passed around the room / Ends up as something completely different." Thus the difficulty faced by the reader of an Ashbery poem is deciding which details—which words—are important. It is possible, however, to enjoy Ashbery's poetry even if one is not sure what is going on. As Ashbery says after interpreting a poem by Riding: "At least, that may be her meaning; to me, it doesn't matter because the overwhelmingly spare and beautiful language has already satisfied me" (*Other Traditions* 113).

The formal concerns and digressions of Ashbery's first major publication *Some Trees* (which Auden chose for the influential Yale Younger Poets series [see POETRY PRIZES]) garnered few reviews, although, in retrospect, the poems introduce themes and techniques Ashbery developed in the later poetry: digressions and attentions ("The Instruction Manual"); playful yet serious references to the self or to the poem ("The Picture of Little J. A. in a Prospect of Flowers"); disjunction ("Grand Abacus"); and formal variety ("Pantoum," "Sonnet," "A Pastoral"). Ashbery was already living in France when the book was published and had begun work on what is still considered his most controversial and problematic book, *The Tennis Court Oath*. Ashbery has noted that the difficult and challenging fragments of *The Tennis Court Oath* were partly a response to his living in France away from other English speakers and partly a result of the lackluster critical response to his first book. On the assumption that he would not get a chance to publish another book, he had been experimenting with language fragments, collage, and narrative disruptions, all of which are present in *The Tennis Court Oath,* since the publication of *Some Trees*.

The few critics, such as Bloom, who admired Ashbery's first book were almost uniformly put off by the apparent nonsense of the second. Yet other, more experimental poets have cited *The Tennis Court Oath* as Ashbery's most interesting and valuable book. The place of *The Tennis Court Oath* within Ashbery's oeuvre is still debated: Critics who place Ashbery in the Auden/Stevens high modernist camp view the book as an aberration (see MODERNISM), while those who see Ashbery as a formal innovator call it his breakthrough book (albeit a breakthrough from which Ashbery himself has retreated in his later works).

With Ashbery's next several books, he developed a continuing readership: *Rivers and Mountains* (1966), *The Double Dream of Spring* (1970), *Three Poems* (which consists of three lengthy prose poems [1972]), and *Self-Portrait in a Convex Mirror* are among his most enduring works. *Self-Portrait,* Ashbery's critical and popular 1975 milestone, established Ashbery's reputation as a major American poet. Following his critical success, Ashbery continued to explore aspects of form and disjunction in books that include a bemused, sometimes nostalgic tone, strange yet simple syntax, odd and surrealist similes, experiments with formal innovation, and playfulness (as in, for example, one of his most commonly anthologized poems, "Paradoxes and Oxymorons," from *Shadow Train* [1981]).

April Galleons (1987) contains no single long poem, unlike many of Ashbery's collections, such as *FLOW CHART* (1991). A single long poem, *Flow Chart* includes, for example, a double sestina within its expansive formal explorations. The sestina itself is a lengthy (13 stanza) meditation on death, but it begins with a concern for language: "We are interested in the language, that you call breath / if breath is what we are to become."

Ashbery's poetry has a reputation for difficulty and obtuseness, but much of the apparent difficulty diminishes if the reader accepts the transitory visions and changing mental landscapes of the poems. His tone often shifts radically within individual poems, from the conversational to the mythic, from self-effacing to grand statements. The poems seem to have no still point, no stable ground from which the speaker speaks; this lack of stability is often itself the theme of the poem. Ashbery's widely anthologized "The Instruction Manual," from *Some Trees,* for example, clearly reveals itself as the mental wanderings of a bored author of an instruction manual. The visions of Guadalajara that the poem presents are mental constructions. Unlike in most of Ashbery's poems, however, the narrative's frame (the author looking out his window dreaming of Guadalajara) is visible at the beginning and end; in much of Ashbery's work, the drifting of the mind is not presented within such a stable frame.

BIBLIOGRAPHY

Ashbery, John. *Other Traditions: The Charles Eliot Norton Lectures.* Cambridge, Mass.: Harvard University Press, 2001.

Bloom, Harold, ed. *John Ashbery.* New York: Chelsea House, 1985.

Schultz, Susan, ed. *The Tribe of John: Ashbery and Contemporary Poetry.* Tuscaloosa: University of Alabama Press, 1995.

Shapiro, David. *John Ashbery: An Introduction to the Poetry.* New York: Columbia University Press, 1979.

Shoptaw, John. *On the Outside Looking Out: John Ashbery's Poetry.* Cambridge, Mass.: Harvard University Press, 1994.

Dean Taciuch

ATKINS, RUSSELL (1926–) Russell Atkins, who has been at the center of African-American avant-garde poetics since the late 1940s, has been among the most active small-press publishers, editors, and critics. Early on Atkins discovered, as he has remarked, that "just as contemporary composers had challenged western diatonicism with chromatic dissonance, I could distort grammar to a similar purpose" (12). Such commitments set Atkins outside the mainstream of popular verse, with its emphasis upon CONFESSIONAL experience and voice, and yet his poetics of conspicuous technique and his aversion to the dominance of "natural language" in so much American verse show his independence even from the main course of experimental poetries.

Atkins was born on February 25, 1926, in the city that was to remain his home, Cleveland, Ohio. He established early correspondences with poets, such as LANGSTON HUGHES and MARIANNE MOORE. In 1949 Hughes wrote to Atkins, advising him not to try to be a "social" poet but to write as he felt compelled. In 1951 Moore recited Atkins's poem "Trainyard by Night" on the radio, later writing to tell Atkins that his poem had been the standout of the program. Atkins published his first of eight books of poetry in 1961. Also a composer, playwright, and critic, he has been invited to the Breadloaf Writers Conference (1956), has been a writer in residence at Cuyahoga Community College (1973), and was awarded an honorary doctorate by Cleveland State University (1976). For two decades, Atkins was an editor of the *Free Lance,* one of the longest-lived journals with a black editorship, a determinedly innovative small magazine that grew out of the Free Lance writers workshop. His poetry has been set to music by the composer Hale Smith and has recently been republished in new poetry journals.

Atkins wrote often of his theories of "psychovisualism" and "deconstruction," writing of the latter as early as 1956, well before the term had become popularized in academic circles. He may have been the first African-American concrete poet, and in poems as early as 1947 his writing departed from the standards of high MODERNISM, pointing the way for much that would follow. A late poem, "Shipwreck" (1976), shows his sense of his own independence: "With today's sympathetics who can dare? / in the old days when sailed struck, / sank, who knew? few, comparatively." Though Atkins has been nearly alone in his aesthetic explorations, his work has attracted an increasing number of sympathizers as it has become more widely known.

BIBLIOGRAPHY

Atkins, Russell. "Russell Atkins." In *Contemporary Authors Autobiography Series,* edited by Joyce Nakamura. Vol. 16. Detroit: Gale Research, 1992, pp. 1–19.

Free Lance 14, no. 2 (1970). [Special Russell Atkins issue with commentary by Casper L. Jordan and L. Stefanski.]
Levy, Andrew, and Bob Harrison, eds. *Crayon* 2 (1999).
Nielsen, Aldon Lynn. "Black Deconstruction: Russell Atkins and the Reconstruction of African-American Criticism." *Diacritics* 26, nos. 3–4 (1996): 86–103.

Aldon L. Nielsen

"AN ATLAS OF THE DIFFICULT WORLD XIII (DEDICATIONS)" ADRIENNE RICH (1991)

Addressing all those who seek meaning and clarity in the act of reading, "(Dedications)" is the final poem in ADRIENNE RICH's free verse sequence "An Atlas of the Difficult World," which has been described as "an extended inquiry into the nature of patriotism in time of war" (Gwiazda, 165). Built on the parallelism characteristic of Hebrew poetry, "(Dedications)" achieves a uniformly psalmlike rhythm that bespeaks the way poetry can provide a means of solace and supplication. Each sentence begins "I know you are reading this poem," whereupon the narrator describes the conditions under which various readers are turning to the poem. Their circumstances reveal the readers' different backgrounds, needs, desires, and emotions, enabling Rich to map the spectrum of American society. Ultimately, the breadth of readers to whom "(Dedications)" is in fact dedicated reveals Rich's idea of poetry as a civic force, one that can help link disparate members of society by helping them confront the unresolved contradictions of America, past and present.

Rich titles the sequence "The Atlas of the Difficult World" to suggest the way that poetry maps the multiple, varied topographies of life in America. Like MURIEL RUKEYSER, Rich reveals places and experiences in America the reader might never encounter, while also showing how these unlike areas can share common terrain. Like the 19th-century American poet Walt Whitman, Rich uses catalogue, anaphora, and anecdote in "(Dedications)" to speak both to and for her readers. The speaker of the poem is not identified, though as Cheri Colby Langdell observes, many of the people the speaker addresses are experiencing events and emotions in their lives which Rich knows firsthand, from the lover who has given up heterosexuality for homosexuality and is now running up the stairs of a subway tunnel "toward a new kind of love / your life has never allowed," to the parent depleted by caring for an infant. Such empathy is a unifying force that does not erase individual differences, and that sort of union is important of Rich, says Langdell, because "If Americans have sometimes been a violent people, they have also been a lonely people" (188).

Rich's effort to extend herself into the varied lives and experiences of postmodern America is evident in the first lines. Though much of her earlier work demonstrates a strong feminist focus, in "An Atlas of the Difficult World" she opens her critique to encompass the numerous paradoxes of late 20th-century America, from its sexism and racism to its materialism and exploitative capitalism. In broadening her revolutionary stance, the first individual she addresses is an office worker, a member of the business class, "reading this poem / late, before leaving your office . . / long after rush-hour." Rich also invokes a lonely, geographically isolated reader, a victim of marital abuse, a new lover, a political revolutionary, a reader suffering AIDS, an old reader, a fatigued parent, an immigrant, and a reader "torn between bitterness and hope / turning back once again to the task you cannot refuse." She maintains their individuality, but she is equally concerned with how the legacies of American materialism and social oppression have affected all their lives. As Rich remarked in an interview with Bill Moyers, "There is an audience of those unknown to you but whom your words are going to reach. You can't know them in advance, but you can hope for them" (345). Rich does not want her poetry to be simply another consumable item, a pleasant aesthetic experience the reader can enjoy and then forget. Rather, she dedicates the poem to the many Americans who need and seek community in their lives, calling them to dedicate themselves to the multicultural, postmodern society to which they belong and to work within it for justice.

BIBLIOGRAPHY

Gwiazda, Piotr. "'Nothing Else Left to Read': Poetry and Audience in Adrienne Rich's "An Atlas of the Difficult World." *Journal of Modern Literature* 28, no. 2 (2005): 165–188.
Langdell, Cheri Colby. *Adrienne Rich: The Moment of Change.* Westport, Conn.: Praeger Publishers, 2004.

Moyers, Bill. "Adrienne Rich." In *The Language of Life: A Festival of Poets*, 335–353. New York: Doubleday, 1995.

Temple Cone

"AT LUCA SIGNORELLI'S RESURRECTION OF THE BODY" Jorie Graham (1983)

Jorie Graham's "At Luca Signorelli's Resurrection of the Body" is an ekphrastic poem, or poem about a silent work of art, based on the mural paintings of the Last Judgment by the Italian Renaissance painter, Luca Signorelli. The murals, noted for their innovatively realistic treatment of nude figures and their use of foreshortened perspective, anticipated many of the developments in modern painting, and even influenced Michelangelo's murals in the Sistine Chapel. The mural on which Graham focuses depicts the moment the dead souls reclaim their resurrected bodies, and for her the scene raises important questions about mind-body dualism and about visual perception as a means to empirical, as opposed to religious, truth. Graham further dramatizes these questions by concluding the poem with Signorelli's autopsy of his own murdered son, a systematic confrontation of the violence of reality that paradoxically allows Signorelli, as artist and father, to be reborn into the world.

While Graham captures Signorelli's depiction of the joyful reunion of souls with their bodies at the Resurrection, "how they hurry / to enter / their bodies," she also questions the premised good of that reunion, suggesting that the resurrected flesh differs, perhaps negatively, from its previously mortal incarnation. Such an implication clashes with Christian doctrine, but Graham clearly finds that life achieves intensity when mortality is embraced, not transcended. Yet what the resurrected men and women cannot understand, Signorelli clearly does: "that there is no / entrance / only entering." The resurrection of life after death represents a perfection that is not life, because such a state lacks the incompletion and process that distinguish mortal life. Helen Vendler makes a similar point when she argues that "It is because of his patient dissection that Signorelli can leave behind the flat, symbolic, medieval rendering of persons and depict instead, with unprecedented accuracy and intimacy, the actual beauty of the flesh" (*Given*, 100).

Yet for Signorelli himself to achieve the intensity of mortal imperfection that Graham finds lacking in the Resurrection mural, it is not enough for him to observe models from an impartial distance. The transformation of his art occurs through his immersion in the miseries and vicissitudes of reality, from which he must then try to rescue mortal beauty. This immersion is brought to Signorelli directly in the form of his murdered son's body, which Signorelli dissects and analyzes in his studio. The narrative proves harrowing; Graham shows how Signorelli approached the act with all his artistic concentration, "awaiting the best / possible light, the best depth / of day" before cutting "into bone and sinew and every / pocket." Graham maintains a distance from the emotions Signorelli felt, not wanting dramatic emotion to substitute for or conceal the strangeness and utter desperation required to seek the truth of the body this way. Yet in the end, the opening of his son's body allows Signorelli, as artist and as grieving father, to let his mind "climb into / the open flesh and / mend itself."

For Graham, art is the formalized process of perception, and as "At Luca Signorelli's Resurrection of the Body" demonstrates, attention to art as science, as a way of seeking and knowing empirical truth, is more restorative to the psyche wounded by violence and grief than any promise of resurrection made by religion. Vendler claims that this theme is manifest in Graham's short, free verse sestets, which represent "a faith in the power of the patience of the mind . . . its deliberate respect for the resistance of matter" (*Breaking*, 77), an approach in keeping with the way Signorelli "broke into the body / studying arrival." Although Vendler argues that the sestets "advance, advance, advance—without any real promise of final closure" (*Given*, 99), James Longenbach finds that Graham's poem achieves some sort of completion or fruition, if not closure, for "the poem's hushed final lines suggest that the painter himself is 'mended' not by seeking spiritual wholeness but by confronting the physical evidence of the most unbearable kind of human suffering" (164). In a remarkable inversion of the traditional hierarchy, Graham suggests that the artist's rigorous attention to the material world provides more meaning and solace than the believer's devotion to the abstract world of the spirit.

BIBLIOGRAPHY
Gardner, Thomas. *Regions of Unlikeness: Explaining Contemporary Poetry.* Lincoln: University of Nebraska Press, 1999.
Longenbach, James. *Modern Poetry after Modernism.* New York: Oxford University Press, 1997.
Vendler, Helen. *The Breaking of Style: Hopkins, Heaney, Graham.* Cambridge, Mass.: Harvard University Press, 1995.
———. *The Given and the Made: Strategies of Poetic Redefinition.* Cambridge, Mass.: Harvard University Press, 1995.

Temple Cone

"AT MELVILLE'S TOMB" HART CRANE (1926)

HART CRANE's "At Melville's Tomb" is simultaneously an elegy for the American writer Herman Melville and Crane's own meditation on the project of art. As with many of Crane's poems, "At Melville's Tomb" relies on the connotative import of wide-ranging diction and nonlogical metaphor to achieve a unified vision of reality, though in this instance the poem is as much about Melville's struggle to make death comprehensible as about his success. Crane weaves together bibliographical imagery with the imagery of flowers, the deep sea, and navigational equipment to express his wonder at Melville's art; "The dice of drowned men's bones he saw bequeath / An embassy," Crane writes, though their message is slowly obscured. But the artist must not yield, and after this first contact with the universal force of death, Melville pursues a visionary quest to see how "silent answers crept across the stars."

Herman Melville died in 1891 and was buried next to his wife, Elizabeth Shaw, in Woodlawn Cemetery in the Bronx, New York. Although almost forgotten by the end of his life, Herman Melville's writings enjoyed a considerable revival beginning in the 1920s, inspiring many scholarly and literary responses, one of which was Crane's poem. Whether or not Crane ever visited the gravesite is unclear, but he uses the occasion (fictional or otherwise) to praise the author's visionary effort to encompass the conflicting attributes of reality. In another poem, "The Marriage of Helen and Faustus," Crane attempted to face the confusions of the modern world and derive from them something more than despair, writing that "there is the world dimensional for / those untwisted by the love of things / irreconcilable." It is clear that Crane finds in Melville one who attempted to find that "world dimensional," and "At Melville's Tomb" attempts a linguistic collision of contraries that might illuminate such a world.

Melville's great setting was the sea, which came to symbolize the cosmos in which he saw the dead "obscured," though he came to find "(t)he calyx of death's bounty giving back / A scattered chapter, livid hieroglyphs." As Lee Edelman notes, "This 'giving back,' this poetic return, is Crane's willful answer to death, his recuperation of discontinuity in what Nietzsche would recognize as a lie against time" (263). Crane charts the widening focus of Melville's vision, from "the dice of drowned men's bones" to "the circuit calm of one vast coil," an image of the vast, mysterious order governing far beyond the seemingly scattered, terrifying universe. But whatever "silent answers" Crane's predecessor found, his voice has been silenced by death, by the obscurity of fickle literary history, and perhaps by the simple truth that every visionary quest must ultimately be pursued by the individual alone, without the aid of others; "Compass, quadrant, and sextant contrive / No farther tides." Crane struggles with the lonely burden of the artist, fearing that his own efforts to achieve such a vision as Melville's own are doomed to failure, when he writes that "Monody shall not wake the mariner," but one cannot doubt that in the baroque diction, haunting imagery, and counterpoint rhythms of "At Melville's Tomb," Crane has achieved what he praised in Melville: an unflinching and reverent look at the often terrifying, always contrary forces of life and death that undergird reality.

BIBLIOGRAPHY
Edelman, Lee. "'Voyages.'" In *Hart Crane: Modern Critical Views,* edited by Harold Bloom, 255–291. New York: Chelsea House Publishers, 1986.

Temple Cone

"AT THE WELL" PAUL BLACKBURN (1967)

In her introduction to PAUL BLACKBURN's *Selected Poems* (1989), Edith Jarolim refers to his poem "At the Well" as a "mythic piece" (xviii); yet if it is so, it is a myth caught in the act of performing—that is, questioning—its meaning. Martha King notes that a dominant maneuver in Blackburn's later poetry is to comment on the process of making poetry ("Reading"). Such tendencies position this late 1960s poem squarely within a postmodern tradition of self-reflexivity and uncertainty about one's relation to the world as a whole and to others, in particular, prying the gaps between the self and nonself, between the sense of a voice and identity and the forces (in the environment as well as in the unconscious) that challenge them.

The first three lines of the poem present an exotic setting, but they augment, amend, and revise the initial vision as they go along: "Here we are, see? / in this village, maybe a camp / middle of desert." The writing itself demonstrates the imagination's attempt to find its moorings, thereby making the reader aware of the game we play when we read and indulge in fictional worlds that we "make believe" are real. Stanza 2 introduces an antagonistic element, "these riders / on camels or horses," resignedly "sitting / there" waiting for us the readers to make something of them. Since the figures seated ambivalently on animal backs are presented in tableau, resisting (or lacking) the ability to articulate an identity—set pieces in an (as yet) unscripted drama—they may be continuously created or recreated by the mind. The poem, then, though "narrative" in appearance, behaves not as a literal description, but rather as self-generative play. Even though the figures are made to speak in stanza 9, their speech is immediately denied: "They / say nothing." This highlights the closed circuit of the fictional creation of others, especially the utterances of those invented "others." Rather than representing mythic presences, the mounted riders suggest the rhetorical figure of the straw man, emphasizing the inherent hollowness of an image while evoking further questions and tempting us to keep up the game of inventing and reinventing their meaning. The poem dramatizes the imagination as it struggles with its own process of creation, highlighting the phantasmic nature of image making.

In the final turn of the poem's argument (stanza 15), the speaker directly addresses an ambiguous audience of "gentlemen" observers, asking them to turn their backs on this desert of the imagination. The terminal punctuation delays closure by a space, skipping a beat—"There is nothing here. "—a typographical enactment and acknowledgment of the illusionism that is present even (or especially) in the poem's final gesture.

In a foreword to Blackburn's selected poems, M. L. Rosenthal reflects that a hallmark of Blackburn's poetry is tracking "whatever musings have been set ticking right there in middle of things," bounding from the literal to the philosophical and back (vii). In "At the Well," the "literal" itself is teased out, no more a "thing" than the philosophical or psychological; all are at the service of an imagination that holds up a mirror to the nature of the self in which it must confront, ultimately, its self-deceptive tendencies.

BIBLIOGRAPHY

Jarolim, Edith. Introduction to *The Selected Poems of Paul Blackburn*. New York: Persea Books, 1989, pp. xv–xix.

King, Martha. "Reading Paul Blackburn," Jacket Magazine. Available online. URL: www.jacket.zip.com.au/jacket12/blackburn-martha-king.html. Downloaded May 2003.

Rosenthal, M. L. Foreword to *The Selected Poems of Paul Blackburn*. New York: Persea Books, 1989, pp. vii-viii.

Tom Lavazzi

"AUBADE" **AMY LOWELL (1914)** "Amy Lowell wasn't writing about flowers." So runs the title of Diane Ellen Hamer's essay on coded erotic motifs in AMY LOWELL's floral imagery, and Lowell's "Aubade" is an important example of just how the poet wedded IMAGIST technique to her expressions of lesbian identity, erotic desire, and sexual freedom. In the early 1910s, prompted by her readings of H. D.'s imagist poetry, Lowell began stripping her work of the excessively poetic language and sentimentality she inherited from such poets as John Keats (about whom Lowell wrote a two-volume study). This self-revision was mostly a way of cutting closer to her poetic core, but it also enabled Lowell to express emotions and ideas not acceptable during her era.

In a poem as brief as the five-line "Aubade," the reader must scrutinize each word carefully, and the poem invites a deliberate, though by no means slow or heavy, reading. Lillian Faderman notes that the title itself suggests a sexual encounter, since an *aubade* is "a dawn peace in which, traditionally, the poet thanks the beloved with whom he has spent the night for her sexual favors" (68). "As I would free the white almond from the green husk," writes Lowell, "So would I strip your trappings off, / Beloved." The reader may at first be struck by the intimacy of address, emphasized by the isolation of *Beloved* on a line of its own, and by the sexual passion evoked by the act of stripping. Moreover, as Lillian Faderman notes, Lowell used floral imagery throughout her work as "an evocative and descriptive symbol for female genitalia" (73). Yet such intimacy and lesbian desire is moderated by the conventional formality of Lowell's imagery and diction. Her choice of the formal word *trappings,* which signifies both physical clothing and moral sentiments, balances the image of physical undressing with the metaphor of emotional openness, an emotional connotation emphasized by the choice of the word *husk,* which describes both the almond's shell and an outward emotional toughness protecting the heart's core. Moreover, as Paul Lauter notes, Lowell followed a "calculated strategy of fusing the conventions of amorous male poetry, to encode lesbian desire" (7). Thus, when Lowell uses a simile to compare the lover's body with an almond, she rejects the more feminine floral image for a conventional heterosexual association of fruit and sexuality, and in this way avoids identifying her beloved's gender.

The coding that critics such as Faderman and Lauter identify in Lowell's work, at once communicative and concealing, reflects the conflicted nature of Lowell's lesbianism. Lauter argues that many of Lowell's poems show "painfully contradictory impulses toward revelation, display, or even a certain form of 'flaunting,' and hiding, a poetics of the closet" (5–6), and such contradictions are apparent in the first two lines of "Aubade." It would seem that the isolation of "Beloved" on the third and central line ought to signal a change in the speaker's tone, a resolution of these conflicts, but Lowell continues to encode her sexual desire in conventionally heterosexual figures, with the beloved described as a "smooth and polished kernel" and as "a gem beyond counting." Even following Faderman's suggestion that the image evokes female genitalia, one cannot help but acknowledge the speaker's own seeming lack of gender, an ambiguity that opens the possibility of a heterosexual relation. Yet careful attention to Lowell's use of auxiliary verbs in the poem, the "would . . . would . . should" sequence, suggests the poem follows an arc from desire to fulfillment that is inherently transgressive, an overcoming of boundaries that would not hinder an ordinary (i.e., heterosexual) lover. In "Aubade," Lowell uses imagism as a strategy for negotiating the complexities of gender and sexual politics in the early 20th century, an evocative restraint rejected by the more overt expressions of sexual identity in the 1960s and 1970s, but partly reclaimed toward the end of the 20th century by such poets as May Swenson and Olga Broumas.

BIBLIOGRAPHY

Faderman, Lillian. "'Which, Being Interpreted, Is as May Be, or Otherwise': Ada Dwyer Russell in Amy Lowell's Life and Work." *Amy Lowell, American Modern,* edited by Adrienne Munich and Melissa Bradshaw, 59–76. New Brunswick, N.J.: Rutgers University Press, 2004.
Hamer, Diane Ellen. "Amy Lowell wasn't writing about flowers." *The Gay and Lesbian Review* 10, no. 4 (2004): 13–14.
Lauter, Paul. "Amy Lowell and Cultural Borders." *Amy Lowell, American Modern,* edited by Adrienne Munich and Melissa Bradshaw, 1–8. New Brunswick, N.J.: Rutgers University Press, 2004.

Temple Cone

AUDEN, W(YSTAN) H(UGH) (1907–1973)

W. H. Auden was one of the leading poets of the 20th century. No other poet exhibited his range of genre, style, or subject matter. His poetry drew on such varied resources as fairy tales, Anglo-Saxon myth and meter, Icelandic sagas, songs (ancient, medieval, modern), ballads, lyric poetry, odes, epics, satires, parodies, epigrams, elegies, meditations, arguments, and urbane, witty conversations. Unlike poets of a single voice, Auden mastered, then abandoned voices and styles, not as a dabbler but as a talented virtuoso, with encyclopedic interests and a conviction that no single perspective can reveal the truth. From an early modernist beginning, influenced by T. S. Eliot, his poetry progressed into a middle period of Freudian and Marxist social critique and gradually into a more accessible, conversational style with a broadly Christian perspective. During the 1950s and 1960s, he was a model for American poets writing formal verse, such as John Hollander, Richard Wilbur, and, later, James Merrill; during the later decades of the century, a period dominated by free verse in confessional, imagistic, and more romantic modes, he remained a sophisticated, urbane alternative model (see IMAGIST SCHOOL). The fin de siècle resurgence of interest in formal poetry owes something to his long-standing example.

Auden was born in York, England, into a well-to-do family, the son of a doctor and a nurse, becoming what he later called "a typical little highbrow and difficult child" (322). He was educated at Oxford (1925–28), and when he was 21, Stephen Spender privately printed his first volume, *Poems* (1928). After graduation, he lived for a year and a half in Berlin, exploring his homosexuality in the bar and café life of the city. On T. S. Eliot's recommendation, Faber and Faber published an expanded edition of his *Poems* (1930). His second volume, *The Orators* (1932), established him as the spokesperson for his generation. From 1932 to 1937, he wrote three plays with Christopher Isherwood, *The Dog beneath the Skin, The Ascent of F 6,* and *On the Frontier.* In 1936 a new collection of his poetry appeared, *Look, Stranger* (The U.S. edition, titled *On This Island,* appeared in 1937). After traveling to Iceland with Louis MacNeice and publishing *Letters from Iceland* (1937) and traveling to Spain during the civil war there and publishing *Spain* (1937), Auden returned to England to receive the King's Gold medal for Poetry. In 1938 he went to China with Isherwood, and the two wrote *Journey to a War* (1939).

The year 1939 began a culmination of controversial changes in Auden's life. He immigrated to the United States just before the outbreak of war in Europe, and a year later he became a Christian. Once in the United States, he became romantically involved with Chester Kallmann, a young American poet, and the two lived together, off and on, for the rest of Auden's life. In 1946 Auden became a U.S. citizen. For three decades he made New York City his home, spending his summers in Italy and later outside Vienna. He taught at the New School for Social Research, the University of Michigan, Swarthmore, Bryn Mawr, and Bennington. Of the many awards he received were two Guggenheim awards in 1942 and 1945, a Pulitzer Prize for *The Age of Anxiety* (1947), and a National Book Award for *The Shield of Achilles* (1955). In addition to poetry, he wrote libretti for operas, including (with Kallmann) the libretto for Igor Stravinski's *The Rake's Progress,* and wrote many essays, including those in *The Dyer's Hand and Other Essays* (1962). In 1972 he returned to England to teach at Oxford and died the following year in Vienna.

Critical discussion often divides Auden's work into an early and a late period, his move to the United States standing as the watershed, though such a division oversimplifies his lifelong development. His first volume is *Poems,* influenced by Eliot's *The* WASTE LAND, and is characterized by fragmentation, disjunction, ellipsis, irony, a haunted voice, and a visionary tone. *Poems* creates a landscape of abandoned mines, power stations, and industrial machines set in an unspecified time of war or exile. After taking the reader to such a landscape, the first poem ends, "Go home, now, stranger . . . / This land, cut off, will not communicate," lines that suggest the alienation and sterility of modern life. As Auden inherited from his father an interest in medicine, illness, and diagnosis, he sought to diagnose the modern condition by exploring both psychological and social causes and finding potential remedies in Sigmund Freud's and D. H. Lawrence's valuing of the instinctual over the rational. These concerns appear again in *The Orators,* a booklength poem and Auden's most difficult work. After part one, "The Initiates," parodies the official, public rhetoric, clichés, and false rationalizations supporting modern life, part two, "The Journal of an Airman," offers an intimate account of a failed attempt to heal crisis by looking toward a revolutionary hero. Part three, consisting of "Six Odes" and an epilogue, then seems to offer hope through some unspecified spiritual healing.

As the 1930s progressed, Auden moved toward a more casual style of plain speech and more explicit subjects drawn from everyday experience. This change may have resulted from a desire to reach a broader audience than MODERNISM could reach, a desire born of his deepening commitment to Marxism, his writing of plays, and a religious experience of agape, or universal love, he claimed to have undergone in 1933. Characteristic is the 1936 *Look, Stranger.* Along with a dozen songs, there appear many poems in this new style, in which the poet speaks publicly about contemporary events. In 1939 *Journey to a War* included his famous sonnet sequence, "In Time of War," also in the new style.

By the close of the decade, Auden was reexamining his largest ideas about human being, reading Søren

Kierkegaard, and finding personal echoes in the philosopher's account of an intellectual's journey toward Christianity. His ultimate conversion to Christianity resolved for him the conflict between eros (the instinctual) and logos (the rational) through agape (love transformed by grace). *Another Time* (1940) conveys a new warmth, confidence, and directness, and it includes many of his most famous poems, "Musée des Beaux Arts," the elegies for Freud and William Butler Yeats, and "September 1, 1939." "Musée des Beaux Arts" displays Auden's ability to speak profoundly about serious subjects with ordinary, even comic detail. Commenting on the stark psychological isolation suffering engenders, this poem observes that even martyrdom must always take place in "some untidy corner . . / Where the dogs go on with their doggy life and the torturer's horse / Scratches its innocent behind on a tree." Four important poems in this volume trace his journey from humanism to Christianity: "Voltaire at Ferney," "Matthew Arnold," "Herman Melville," and "Pascal."

Also during the 1940s, four important long poems appeared. "New Year Letter" in *The Double Man* (1941) is an epistle contemplating the state of Western civilization and offering Kierkegaardian solutions. "For The Time Being, A Christmas Oratorio" and "The Sea and the Mirror: A Commentary on Shakespeare's *The Tempest*" appeared in *For the Time Being* (1944); the former was Auden's most openly religious piece, and the latter includes a speech by Caliban that Auden felt to be among his best work. *The Age of Anxiety*, written in Anglo-Saxon meter, presents a theological barroom conversation probing the inner life in accentual verse. *Nones* (1951) uses syllabic meter extensively. *The Shield of Achilles* continued Auden's movement toward an intimate, Horatian style—sober, often witty contemplations about ordinary life, deeply felt, carefully reasoned musings, never overcome with emotion, seeking a balance of ironies and multiplicities rather than solutions from a single perspective. *Homage to Clio* (1960) explores conflicts between nature and history, and *About the House* (1965) canvasses domestic life.

Many criticized Auden's later style as impoverished—too bookish, verbose, and intellectual; offering ironic, often comical chat; a product of thinking rather than feeling. But having rejected the role of spokesperson of his generation and wary of the pretenses of an easy, prophetic, bardic romanticism, he offered himself as a flawed, contemporary subject whose urbanity and chattiness veil a carefully controlled rhetorical power. After his rebellious beginnings in modernism, his last poems seem to find reconciliation with the world. Auden's influence on American poetry cannot be overemphasized. As judge of the Yale Series of Younger Poets (see POETRY PRIZES) from 1947 to 1958, he helped the careers of many now-eminent poets including JOHN ASHBERY and ADRIENNE RICH, and his explorations and discoveries in form, style, and subject matter opened new landscapes for poets to follow.

BIBLIOGRAPHY

Auden, W. H. *The English Auden*, edited by Edward Mendelson. New York: Random House, 1978.

Carpenter, Humphrey. *W. H. Auden*. Boston: Houghton Mifflin, 1981.

Fuller, John. *W. H. Auden: A Commentary*. Princeton, N.J.: Princeton University Press, 1998.

Mendelson, Edward. *Early Auden*. New York: Viking, 1981.

———. *Later Auden*. New York: Farrar Straus & Giroux, 1999.

Wright, George. *T. W. H. Auden*. Boston: Twayne, 1981.

Michael Sowder

"AXE HANDLES" GARY SNYDER (1983) Gary Snyder's "Axe Handles" weaves together themes of fatherhood, literary influence, the value of physical labor, the nature of teaching and learning, the growth of the self, and the relations between generations, achieving a final insight that is breathtaking not only for its profundity, but also for its naturalness. Making allusions to various translations of an ancient Chinese, Snyder recalls teaching his young son Kai how to fashion a new hatchet handle by using the carving hatchet for a model. This simple exchange calls to mind a range of associations for Snyder, enriching and intensifying the moment.

"Axe Handles" is more narrative than much of Snyder's work. The opening lines set the scene, their informal tone not conventionally poetic but demonstrating precision and economy: "One afternoon the last week in April / Showing Kai how to throw a hatchet." The absence of the first person pronoun "I" here is crucial.

Rhythmically, it startles the reader; thematically, it suggests that through Snyder, teachers from many generations are instructing young Kai. When father and son begin making a new handle for a loose hatchet-head, Snyder recalls the Chinese maxim, variously translated, about how the pattern for shaping an axe is always close at hand. Each version Snyder recalls differs slightly according to its translators, who include Snyder's Zen Buddhist teacher, Shih-hsiang Chen; the poet EZRA POUND; Lu Ji, the 4th-century A.D. author of the *Wen Fu* or "Essay on Literature"; and even the 5th-century B.C. folk song from which the maxim originated and which Snyder uses as the epigraph to his collection *Axe Handles.* These differences, however, do not alter the gist of the saying, and this consistency supplies Snyder a metaphor for the transmission of cultural knowledge, wherein knowledge is altered slightly by each individual teacher (and student) but retains its essential qualities.

The synthesis of family bonds, generational instruction, literary connections, spiritual poise, and physical activity that Snyder achieves in "Axe Handles" represents a cultural ideal of continuity. In this respect, Snyder's philosophical vision is radically conservative and highly resistant to the breaking of generational ties typical of the 20th century. While critics focus on different aspects of the cultural model Snyder describes, with Patrick D. Murphy attending to the particular cultural knowledge and Tim Dean examining the role the female figure plays in its preservation, they generally represent it as a model that always loops back to its beginnings. This looping is tied to Snyder's ecological focus on "biofeedback loops," wherein ecosystems grow from their own constantly recycled materials. For Snyder, healthy human communities require cultural feedback loops as much as healthy ecosystems require biofeedback loops. In an era where technology threatens the natural environment and humankind alike, "Axe Handles" offers its own model for a sustainable future.

BIBLIOGRAPHY

Dean, Tim. *Gary Snyder and the American Unconscious: Inhabiting the Ground.* New York: St. Martin's Press, 1991.
Moyers, Bill. "Gary Snyder." In *The Language of Life: A Festival of Poets,* 356–374. New York: Doubleday, 1995.
Murphy, Patrick D. *Understanding Gary Snyder.* Columbia: The University of South Carolina Press, 1992.

Temple Cone

B

BACA, JIMMY SANTIAGO (1952–) Jimmy Santiago Baca has been a premier Chicano poet and essayist. While revealing the soul-searing anguish of a life forced into desperation and incarceration, his work is also a testament to the healing power of language. The complex heritage of Chicano culture is evident in Baca's poetry. In his memoir, he acknowledges WILLIAM CARLOS WILLIAMS's common language and Walt Whitman's long adventurous lines. Furthermore, Baca's channeling of intense passion is informed by a Spanish language tradition: "For me," he writes, "there were no schools, no writing workshops. But there were the voices of [Pablo] Neruda and [Federico García] Lorca, [Jaime] Sabines and [Octavio] Paz . . . who in solitude begged on their knees all their lives for one word, one image, to redeem their misery and celebrate their joy" (*Working in the Dark* 59–60).

Baca was born in Santa Fe, New Mexico. The landscape of the Southwest provides a source of regeneration for the poet and the Chicano people he celebrates, as in *Black Mesa Poems* (1986). Baca's own life was marked by early loss. Later the dehumanizing forces of prison life, as well as the sharp edge of a dominant culture's repression of a people, threatened the young man's existence and capacity for being human. It was by recourse to poetry that Baca survived, physically, emotionally, and spiritually. Poems fashioned in the searing crucible of his personal experiences have received high critical acclaim. He has received a number of honors, including the Before Columbus Foundation American Book Award (1988) and the Pushcart Prize (1988).

Baca's poetry is filled with tension between thematic opposites. In his first major collection, *Immigrants in Our Own Land* (1979), prison threatens, but doesn't succeed in canceling, the life of the spirit. Place again becomes an important protagonist in *Martín & Meditations on the South Valley* (1987), wherein the barrio and the culture found there are celebrated as the foundation for a new life. Metaphors of the South Valley and the Chicano experience are warmly contrasted with the world of the comfortably fortunate, expressed through images of the Heights: "Worth is determined in the Valley / by age and durability" ("Meditations on the South Valley" [1987]).

Baca writes in *Martín,* "My mind circles warm ashes of memories, / the dark edged images of my history." His work draws on the twin streams of memory and imagination, allowing the transformative power of language to envision a future, rescuing Baca from the ravages of prison experience and Chicanos everywhere from destructive negation.

BIBLIOGRAPHY

Baca, Jimmy Santiago. *A Place to Stand.* New York: Grove Press, 2001.

———. *Working in the Dark: Reflections of a Poet of the Barrio.* Santa Fe: Red Crane, 1992.

Moore, George. "Beyond Cultural Dialogues: Identities in the Interstices of Culture in Jimmy Santiago Baca's *Martín and Meditations on the South Valley." Western American Literature* 33, no. 2 (summer 1998): 153–177.

Brian A. Spillane

BARAKA, AMIRI (LEROI JONES) (1934–)

Amiri Baraka, also known as Imamu Amiri Baraka and LeRoi Jones, is a unique force in American poetry. His practice as a cultural activist redefined the role of the modern American poet. He is best known for his powerful contribution, as writer and theorist, to the BLACK ARTS MOVEMENT of the 1960s. Mixing the open forms of 1950s BEATS and BLACK MOUNTAIN SCHOOL poetry with the rhetorical and musical traditions of black culture, he explosively developed an urgent and militant African-American poetry and poetics. Literary historian and critic Arnold Rampersad identifies Baraka as the principal modernizing influence on black poetry and names him, along with LANGSTON HUGHES and others, as one of the eight writers "who have significantly affected the course of African-American literary culture" (qtd. in Harris "Introduction" xviii). Hughes's example and influence on Baraka was profound, and the two poets are clearly in sympathy in terms of formal experimentation, commitment to audience, and historical consciousness, even to the extent that Hughes's "Broadcast to the West Indies" (1943) seems to make possible Baraka's "SOS" (1967), and Baraka's "When We'll Worship Jesus" (1975) becomes a later 20th-century treatment of Hughes's "Goodbye Christ" (1932). Other influences include jazz and blues music and musicians and the theory and practice of politicized black writers, including Frederick Douglass, W. E. B. DuBois, Aimé Césaire, and Malcolm X. A prolific poet since the publication of his first collection, *Preface to a Twenty Volume Suicide Note* (1961), Baraka is also a celebrated playwright, essayist, music critic, fiction writer, and editor.

Baraka was born Everett LeRoy Jones to a lower-middle-class family in Newark, New Jersey. His early work was published under the name LeRoi Jones. In 1967 he adopted the name Ameer Barakat (Blessed Prince), later "Bantuizing or Swahilizing" it to Amiri Baraka (*Autobiography* 267). He attended Rutgers and Howard Universities before joining the United States Air Force in 1954. He has taught at several schools, including the State University of New York at Stony Brook. His many awards and honors include an Obie Award for his play *Dutchman* (1964), the American Book Award's Lifetime Achievement Award (1989), and the Langston Hughes Award (1989): in 2001 he was inducted into the American Academy of Arts and Letters. In 2002 Baraka was appointed to a controversial two-year term as poet laureate of New Jersey.

Partly as a result of his capacity for extreme statement and sense of dramatic timing, Baraka's work is often seen as belonging to distinctly defined periods, what William J. Harris names as "Beat" (1957–62), "Transitional" (1963–64), "Black Nationalist" (1965–74), and "Third-World Marxist" (1974–). During the Beat period, Baraka lived in Manhattan's Greenwich Village and Lower East Side, establishing a reputation as a poet and critic, coediting the avant-garde journals *Yugen* and *Floating Bear* with Hettie Cohen and DIANE DI PRIMA, respectively, and associating with avant-garde musicians, visual artists, and poets, including ALLEN GINSBERG, ROBERT CREELEY, and FRANK O'HARA. In his *Autobiography*, Baraka describes himself at this time as being "'open' to all schools within the circle of white poets of all faiths and flags. But what had happened to the blacks? What had happened to me? How is it that [there is] only the one colored guy?" (157).

As a black poet in an America then being transformed by the Civil Rights movement, Baraka felt a growing dissatisfaction with the role of poet as disaffected outsider. A visit to Cuba in 1960 initiated a conscious process of politicization, which eventually resulted in a vehement rejection of white aesthetics and society in favor of the separatist Black Arts movement, which Larry Neal has defined as "the aesthetic and spiritual sister of the Black Power concept" (62), although Baraka has identified black music as being as fundamental to Black Arts as black revolution.

Baraka's black nationalist period was dramatically announced by his rejection of white bohemia, and his first wife, after the assassination of Malcolm X in February 1965, and his subsequent move uptown to Harlem, where he founded the influential Black Arts Repertory Theatre/School. Later that year he moved back to Newark, where he established the publishing company Jihad Productions and the arts space Spirit

House, in addition to participating in black revolutionary politics and politicization. His best-known poem of this period, "Black Art" (1966), announces his uncompromising poetics: "We want 'poems that kill.' / Assassin poems, Poems that shoot / guns." For Baraka, the poem becomes a lethal weapon, and poetry—in rejection of W. H. AUDEN's well-known dictum to the contrary from "In Memory of W. B. Yeats"—can and will make something happen. Baraka aims to replace the silent reader of modernist poetry with a charged, elated, and articulate audience (see MODERNISM). His poem "SOS" (1967), both distress call and call to arms, issues an opening salvo to which black people are asked to respond: "Black people, come in, wherever you are, urgent, calling / you, calling all black people."

In 1974 Baraka rejected cultural nationalism in favor of Marxism-Leninism as a way forward for black revolution. In contrast to black nationalism, which he now saw as racist, Marxism-Leninism offered solidarity not only among oppressed blacks in the United States, Africa, and the West Indies, but also among oppressed classes everywhere. Although his "hate whitey" phase was more or less spent, Baraka's passionate polemic still boiled in his first marxist volume, *Hard Facts* (1975). "When We'll Worship Jesus" exploits black religious rhetoric while simultaneously ripping it apart, saying that we'll worship Jesus, "When jesus blow up / the white house" and "when he get a boat load of ak-47s / and some dynamite." Baraka, who has resoundingly replaced the hesitant "I" of his early poetry with the collective "we," declares: "We can change the world / we ain't gonna worship jesus cause jesus don't exist." The intensely musical "In the Tradition" (1982), dedicated to avant-garde jazz musician Arthur Blythe, shows Baraka at the top of his form, hooking together references to the great artistic and political traditions of black leadership in a loose and exuberant rap: "our fingerprints are everywhere / on you America, our fingerprints are everywhere."

One of the paradoxes of Baraka's poetry is the continued power of his poems, old and new, to stir strong reactions despite their obvious grounding in specific historical contexts. His poems do not grow stale, perhaps because of their outrageous energy and humor. Baraka continues to be a poet of his time, as indicated by the Internet circulation of his poem, "Somebody Blew Up America," written shortly after the September 11, 2001, terrorist attacks. The poem is a blasting indictment of white greed throughout history and became controversial because of its anti-Semitic questions: "Who knew the World Trade Center was gonna get bombed / Who told 4000 Israeli workers at the Twin Towers / To stay home that day," and Baraka's subsequent statement that the Bush administration had advance knowledge of the attacks. Baraka's refusal to resign as poet laureate led the New Jersey State Senate Government Committee to vote for a bill eliminating the position.

BIBLIOGRAPHY

Baraka, Amiri. *The Autobiography of LeRoi Jones / Amiri Baraka.* New York: Freundlich Books, 1984.
Gwynne, James B., ed. *Amiri Baraka: The Kaleidoscopic Torch.* New York: Steppingstones Press, 1985.
Harris, William J. Introduction to *The LeRoi Jones/Amiri Baraka Reader.* New York: Thunder's Mouth Press, 1991, pp. xvii–xxx.
———. *The Poetry and Poetics of Amiri Baraka: The Jazz Aesthetic.* Columbia: University of Missouri Press, 1985.
Neal, Larry. "The Black Arts Movement." In *Visions of a Liberated Future: Black Arts Movement Writings.* New York: Thunder's Mouth Press, 1989, pp. 62–78.

Mairéad Byrne

"THE BEAN EATERS" GWENDOLYN BROOKS **(1960)** "The Bean Eaters," the title poem of one of GWENDOLYN BROOKS's most widely known collections, fits into what Brooks herself called her "pre-1967" category of poetry. However, the poem bridges Brooks's pre- and post-1967 poetry, with its commentary on an elderly couple's meager existence and the suggestion that these people have no opportunity for economic improvement. The focus on blacks as both subject and audience prefigures the work of poets of the BLACK ARTS MOVEMENT—many of whom influenced her more direct poetic expression after 1967.

Brooks labels much of her work written during her pre-1967 period as "condition literature," meaning that it "whined" about the "lot" of black people in an effort to get whites to help alleviate certain adverse societal conditions (5). Although her post-1967 poetry was more consciously directed to blacks as she became more involved in the community, Brooks insists, "Many of the poems, in my new and old books, are politically aware . . . even [in 1945] I could sense, although not brilliantly, not in great detail, that what was happening to [blacks] was going to erupt at some later time" (42). "The Bean Eaters" certainly fits into this sense of her early work as she describes it. Its politics lie in the resilience of the black poor, and nowhere in the poem does she appear to "whine" to white America. As Jacquelyn Y. McLendon points out, the poem "continues themes found in Brooks's earlier poetry, especially the notion of the tiny, cramped physical and emotional space of the poor, which can be redeemed by the power of memory" (35).

The first two stanzas intertwine form with content, ordinary language, and conventional line lengths and rhyme scheme to convey the humdrum nature of an aging couple's everyday life. Their dinner—"a casual affair"—is defined by the recurrence of a meal of beans, eaten on "Plain chipware," dinner plates cracked by years of use, and "tin flatware" that certainly will not become the stuff of heirlooms. The "old yellow pair" has passed the height of their lives, moved far beyond their youth, and resides in a "rented back room."

Yet, in the third stanza, Brooks switches to free verse to describe the "twinklings" of their memories. The leftovers of their lives suggest the presence once of flowers, children, and days of dressing up and having fun. With little money and no luxuries, the couple are content to find joy in "remembering" how they "have lived their day." An unwavering devotion to well-crafted poetry attentive to the music and clarity of language is evident in this poem, as is true of other poems by Brooks. *The Bean Eaters* has achieved an iconic status within her entire body of work.

BIBLIOGRAPHY

Brooks, Gwendolyn. "Gwendolyn Brooks." In *Black Women Writers at Work*, edited by Claudia Tate. New York: Continuum, 1984.

McLendon, Jacquelyn Y. "Gwendolyn Brooks." In *African American Writers*, edited by Valerie Smith et al. New York: Collier Books, 1991.

Judy Massey Dozier

"THE BEAR" GALWAY KINNELL (1965) GALWAY KINNELL's seven-part free verse narrative "The Bear" transforms a harrowing bear-hunt into an archetypal metaphor for the rebirth of the psyche through poetry. It is one of Kinnell's most celebrated poems, and is also one of the great animal poems of the 20th century. Richly woven with nonvisual images and highly rhythmic anaphora, "The Bear" links the seasonal renewal of nature with psychological rebirth and poetic inspiration.

Set in a desolate, winter landscape, the poem is narrated by an Inuit huntsman who is pursuing a bear. His hunting method is simple: he freezes a sharpened wolf's rib in a ball of fat and leaves it for a bear to find and eat. Later, following the blood trail, he pursues the wounded bear for seven days, becoming more and more bearlike in the process, a change emphasized by the famished hunter's eventual consumption of "a turd sopped in blood" "as I knew I would." Finally, the hunter comes upon the bear the moment it dies, feeding on it and then sheltering inside the still-warm corpse, a sign of the completed unification of the human self with the animal. Sleeping inside the body, the speaker experiences a dream vision in which he relives the bear's life; when he wakes, he rises with a new knowledge of how nature is reborn from winter in an eternal cycle: "Marshlights / reappear, geese / come trailing again up the flyway." Spiritually transformed, the speaker finds himself for the rest of his life "wandering: wondering / what, anyway, / was that sticky infusion, that rank flavor of blood, that poetry, by which I lived?"

Kinnell's free verse is significantly patterned in "The Bear." The seven sections of the poem correspond to the seven days of creation, suggesting that the process of the hunt, with the parallel exhaustion of the bear and the hunter, is creating a new psyche, and that this creation is as significant as the creation of an entire world. Richard J. Calhoun argues that "The poem develops into an account of the death of the ego in the poet. His exclusively human identity is transformed. . . . Through the act of regression he has experienced renewal of life" (69–70). The primitive "regression" Calhoun identifies is enhanced by Kinnell's frequent use of anaphora in the poem, resulting in chantlike rhythms suggestive of the shamanlike vision-quest the hunt seems to become.

Kinnell's choice of imagery is also significant. Noting the traditional association of vision with abstraction, Susan Weston writes that "If Kinnell is a seer, he sees not with his mind's abstracting eye, but with his body" (206). Complete vision is withheld in the poem; the speaker will "sometimes glimpse bits of steam / coming up from / some fault in the old snow," but if he is to confirm that a bear has passed, he must "put down my nose / and know / the chilly, enduring odor of bear." The numerous tactile, olfactory, and gustatory images of "The Bear" return the reader to the experience of the body, the place where life and death maintain a constant dialogue and where, for Kinnell, any glimpse of the truth of reality must begin. Weston acknowledges Kinnell's emphasis on the body as a visionary instrument when she writes that the speaker's experience of the breeze blowing "across / my sore, lolled tongue a song / or screech" is a distortion of "the Romantic metaphor of inspiration—the Aeolian harp" (207).

The poem's origins are not only anthropological but literary as well. John Hobbs notes that Kinnell's sources for "The Bear" included E. E. Cummings's poem "I SING OF OLAF GLAD AND BIG," which concludes "there is some shit I will not eat," and a scene from Hans Ruesch's adventure novel set among the Eskimos, *Top of the World.* Of the former source, Hobbs writes that "For Kinnell to link Olaf's defiant phrase with actual human diets suggests a preoccupation with the interdependence of the lowest and highest forms of life" of the latter, he concludes that Kinnell's occasional breaks from realistic detail (e.g., the hunter's surprising endurance, the pursuit of the blood trail) "emphasize Kinnell's attempts to go beyond the realistic limits of his persona, the primitive Eskimo hunter." Cary Nelson praises Kinnell's mysterious revelation "that in America blood is the spirit's true poetry . . . the blood of a land shared by American creatures and the American people," though he also warns that "this violent commingling has a history more immediate and intransigent than any archetype" (76). While the natural wilderness Kinnell describes may indeed exist beyond the limits of ordinary human existence, the spiritual and psychological wilderness of mortal life that his hunter traverses is common to all.

BIBLIOGRAPHY

Calhoun, Richard J. *Galway Kinnell.* Boston: Twayne Publishers, 1992.

Hobbs, John. "Galway Kinnell's 'The Bear': Dream and Technique." Modern American Poetry. Available online. URL: www.english.uiuc.edu/maps/poets/g-l/kinnell/bear.htm.

Nelson, Cary. *Our Last First Poets: Vision and History in Contemporary American Poetry.* Urbana: University of Illinois Press, 1981.

Weston, Susan. "To Take Hold of the Song: The Poetics of Galway Kinnell." *Critical Essays on Galway Kinnell,* edited by Nancy Lewis Tutten, 205–217. New York: G. K. Hall, 1996.

"BEARDED OAKS" ROBERT PENN WARREN **(1942)** A central early poem of ROBERT PENN WARREN (he included it in each edition of his collected poems), "Bearded Oaks" is a haunting meditation on time, history, mortality, and love. Often compared to the lyrics of the 17th-century Metaphysical poets, the poem nevertheless has an important underlying narrative. It depicts the stillness of two lovers resting beneath bearded oaks, or live oak trees draped with Spanish moss, and from this dramatic situation Warren raises questions about the nature of the human relationship to time. Warren metaphorically transforms the familiar southern setting into an underwater landscape, one that foretells the decay and ruin of all creation, even of love itself, for the lovers will remain only as "Twin atolls on a shelf of shade." Yet this awareness of mortality, of how "(t)he caged heart makes iron stroke," does not diminish the narrator's love; rather, it alters his perspective, so that he comes to see how the stillness of an hour can signify the stillness of eternity.

"Bearded Oaks" demonstrates the mastery of poetic form that made Warren one of the major figures of the FUGITIVE/AGRARIAN SCHOOL, which proclaimed the importance of traditional forms and of imagery for modern poetry. Warren's language is sonorous, made up of elevated diction, a subtle layering of consonance and assonance, and occasional inversions of syntax, yet for all these poetic qualities, the voice is recognizably modern in its preoccupation with history as well as time. "Ages to our construction went," writes Warren, "And violence, forgot now, lent / The present stillness all its power." Composed in rhymed quatrains of iambic tetrameter, the poem recalls the Metaphysical poet Andrew Marvell's "To His Coy Mistress," in which the speaker petitions his lover by telling her how "at my back I always hear / Time's winged chariot hurrying near." Yet Warren's poem negates the urgency of Marvell's impassioned lover; indeed, as Warren's biographer Joseph Blotner observes, the poem seems almost to take place after the occasion of sexual union, when the lovers find themselves becoming part of "the positive night" that follows "the storm of noon," an image of the way time undoes all creation and lays "Foundation for our voicelessness."

For Warren, such nihilism is the problematic and regrettable outcome of naturalism, the belief that human life is identical with material reality and can be explained entirely in physical terms, a belief that characterizes the modern world. Many critics therefore read the final stanza ironically, with the narrator's claim that he and his lover "may spare this hour's term / To practice for eternity" signaling a sort of paralysis that Warren critiques. James Justus argues that the two lovers fall into a condition of total complacency in the face of eternity, while Lesa Carnes Corrigan argues that the conclusion must be read ironically because history can never be undone for Warren, who was so conscious of the South's past. Yet these ironic readings neglect the Christian overtones of the poem, in which mortality and eternity are accepted as part of a religious vision. Warren's own gloss of the poem seems to support such a religious reading; he explained that "Though all of us are trapped in time, and live in time, so little time, there are moments, say in love, that seem outside of time—moments in which 'we practice for eternity'" (Blotner, 162). Ultimately, whether motivated by a sense of history's permanence or by religious impulse, Warren calls for a vision that goes beyond naturalism in "Bearded Oaks," a vision that frees us from the modern fear "that all that light once gave / The graduate dark should now revoke."

BIBLIOGRAPHY

Blotner, Joseph. *Robert Penn Warren: A Biography*. New York: Random House, 1997.

Corrigan, Lesa Carnes. *Poems of Pure Imagination: Robert Penn Warren and the Poetic Imagination*. Baton Rouge: Louisiana State University Press, 1999.

Strandberg, Victor. *A Colder Fire: The Poetry of Robert Penn Warren*. Lexington: The University of Kentucky Press, 1965.

Temple Cone

BEAT POETRY The Beat poets were a group of friends living in New York City in the decade following World War II who, through their collaborations, experiments with poetry rhythms, and questioning of the status quo, forever altered the relationship of poetry to popular culture. The peak of their influence was during the late 1940s through the early 1960s, when their thematic explorations of sexuality and social class ushered in the hippie movement. Building on the free verse, stream-of-consciousness, and collage styles explored by many modernist poets (see MODERNISM), the Beats integrated rhythms found in jazz clubs with invocations of Eastern religions and Buddhist chants. They differed from the poets of the IMAGIST SCHOOL by focusing on the immediacy of experience, as opposed to the precision of images. By representing and embracing the contradictions of contemporary lives on the fringe, they created an especially active and accessible poetry. Today the influence of the Beats is still felt in popular culture, through the popularity of coffee houses, poetry slams, and spoken word poetry.

The term *beat* was coined during a 1948 discussion between writers JACK KEROUAC and John Clellon Holmes about the weariness and alienation or, as Kerouac was to put it, the "beatness" of their generation. Holmes used the term twice in 1952: in a fictionalized biography called *Go* and in a *New York Times Magazine* article, "The Beat Generation" (Watson 3). The name caught on, making the term *beatnik* synonymous with an intellectual form of youth rebellion. Before long, the concept of "beat" was commodified by popular culture, inspiring Beatlike characters on film and television shows, such as on the sitcom *Dobie Gillis*. Media of the 1950s and 1960s were filled with images of the finger-snapping, turtleneck-wearing, goateed archetypal Beat, bearing little resemblance to the actual poets most closely associated with the movement.

A decade before the Beatnik fad began, a small network of outcast students, graduates, and dropouts from Columbia University's English department hunkered down in New York cafés, challenging and encouraging each other to take their own writing in new and surprising directions. Inspired by such poets as Walt Whitman and WILLIAM CARLOS WILLIAMS, the Beats emphasized freethinking and spontaneous writing. Like their BLACK MOUNTAIN SCHOOL counterparts, they celebrated the theme of individual experience and perception, and they saw their very lives as the active impetus by which poems were made.

The writers most central to the movement were ALLEN GINSBERG, Kerouac, and William Burroughs. Their cohorts and muses came to include, over the years, Herbert Huncke, Neal Cassady, GREGORY CORSO, GARY SNYDER, LeRoi Jones (later to be known as AMIRI BARAKA), DIANE DI PRIMA, Carl Solomon, Peter Orlovsky, Carolyn Cassady, MICHAEL MCCLURE, and Lucien Carr. Many other writers were part of the larger Beat constellation, embracing the political and subversive possibilities of poetry and helping shape the rebel-youth culture that still resonates powerfully today.

The friendships among the Beat writers are as famous and enthusiastically chronicled as their actual creative output. During the late 1940s, the Beats often lived together in crowded New York apartments, worked together, and hit the road together to reveal in their writing the "real" America and Mexico. Through their associations, they tested their own spiritual, physical, and sexual boundaries, challenging the limits of their experience. There was a complex web of brotherhood, sexual desire, and emotional tumult.

Their transformative relationships were openly represented in poems and novels, usually with clever yet transparent aliases. And with their shared adventures as both content and context for their writing, they encouraged and critiqued each other. As Kerouac writes of Ginsberg and Cassady in *On the Road,* a novel that openly chronicles and fictionalizes their relationships: "the only people for me are the mad ones, the ones who are mad to live, mad to talk, mad to be saved, desirous of everything at the same time, the ones who never yawn or say a commonplace thing, but burn, burn, burn like fabulous yellow roman candles exploding like spiders across the stars . . . !" (8). Cassady, whom Ginsberg refers to in *HOWL* as the "Adonis of Denver," was of particular personal and metaphoric interest for both him and Kerouac. Cassady's swagger, restlessness, and insatiable sexual drive personified the energy of the archetypal West, and he became muse as much as friend.

Drug use abounded, since the Beats saw it as a tool for mind-expansion and the heightening of the senses, perceptions that could then be applied to creative work. Another venue of inspiration was the be-bop jazz scene in Harlem, the echoes of which can be heard in the twists and turns of their verse and prose rhythms. For a time Kerouac called his spontaneous style "blowing," referring to a be-bop jazz player riffing off a melody with a horn.

The Beats increasingly took a holistic view of writing, questioning the validity of "high" art and rejecting the literary New Critical notion of "art for art's sake" (see FUGITIVE/AGRARIAN SCHOOL). Familiar with the literary canon through their studies at Columbia University, the group aimed to reclaim poetry from the ivory tower and place it squarely in jazz clubs, alleyways, and bedrooms. In this vein, their themes challenged the false sheen of American patriotism, a holdover from World War II's war effort. The resulting proliferation of nuclear weapons, the onset of the cold war, and increasing racial tensions further contradicted America's wholesome image. By exposing the disingenuous use of propaganda, they offered one of the strongest modern-day critiques of America as spiritually bereft and bloated by consumerism. The Beats lived their beliefs by existing hand-to-mouth and befriending criminals, prostitutes, and others who lived on the margins of society. Interestingly, through their immersion into the sordid parts of American life, Beat poetry emerged as largely affirmative of human nature. Throughout their work, the creative process is celebrated, as is the integrity of those who push societal boundaries, foster a spiritual vision, or choose to be different.

Characteristics of Beat poetry include what Cassady called "a continuous flow of undisciplined thought" (Watson 139). Spontaneity as a technique was valued, as was a probing and honest inventory of all of the senses. As Steven Watson writes of Kerouac, the Beats "tried to convey, uncensored, [their] field of perception at the moment of composition," closing the gap between lived experience and the written word (138). Ginsberg, a master of spontaneity, took on the Beat approach later than his comrades, reflecting his ongoing formal studies at Columbia. Both Kerouac and Williams encouraged Ginsberg to let go of verse forms and develop a style of "word sketching." Sharing characteristics with imagist poetry and his idol Whitman, Ginsberg began to pull details from his journals, arranging them in a catalogue style, as is most vividly experienced in *Howl*. Opening it with the line, "I saw the best minds of my generation destroyed by madness, starving, hysterical, naked," Ginsberg creates a mosaic of sharpened images from his experiences with the Beat circle and of his brilliant but troubled mother, Naomi.

In Corso's "Bomb" (1958), published by LAWRENCE FERLINGHETTI's influential City Lights Books as a pull-out centerfold in the shape of a mushroom cloud, the mosaic style is used to create a poem on the threat of nuclear war that is not polemic, but aesthetically spectacular. Through this technique, Corso's poem aims to render the bomb insignificant by its own richness. Another technique of Corso's is the interplay of voices within the poem. In "Marriage" (1959), Corso asks: "Should I get married? Should I be good?" He answers himself rhetorically by proposing to "astound the girl next door with my velvet suit and faustus hood." He proceeds to propose both conventional and unconventional means of courtship, generally leading toward the unconventional. Similarly, his prose poem, "Variations on a Generation" (1959), is a mock interview between the press and the Beat poets. By structuring his poems as an internal or external dialogue, Corso creates a tension between monolithic societal norms and the creativity of the individual mind.

In contrast to Ginsberg and Corso is the comparatively spare writing of Snyder, who is seen as the Beatnik Henry David Thoreau, just as Ginsberg is seen as the Beatnik Whitman. Feeling that symbol and metaphor serve as a distancing device, Synder crafts poems that offer a clear vision of the poet in nature. As the Beatnik most versed in Buddhism and environmentalism, he was the inspiration for Kerouac's novel *Dharma Bums* (1958). And like Ginsberg, Snyder became an icon and activist in the 1960s and eventually a respected college professor.

Despite a largely progressive view on society, the Beat writers were largely antifeminist. With the exception of di Prima, very few women involved in the circle were not girlfriends or wives, and even girlfriends and wives were on the periphery of a sphere devoted to male bonding. Moreover, much of the writing conveyed an underlying misogyny that di Prima challenges in poems such as "The Practice of Magical Evolution" (1958), an ironic response to Snyder's "Praise for Sick Women" (1957). In addition to being male, most members of the group were white, proving to be a limiting landscape for poet, playwright, and black activist Jones (Baraka). Although they had friendships with the core Beat group, di Prima and Jones evolved in directions that the other Beats did not, compelled by their own life experiences and political views. It is noteworthy that Jones and his former wife Hettie Cohen's Totem Press published di Prima's first poetry collection, *This Kind of Bird Flies Backward* (1958). Through 1961–63, both di Prima and Jones edited the poetry newsletter, the *Floating Bear*. Other journals that were important for the Beats and helped them reach an audience were *City Lights Books, Neurotica, Origin Press, Poets Press, Capra Press,* and the *Harvard Advocate*.

A pivotal moment in Beat history was the meeting of East Coast and West Coast Beats during Ginsberg's time in San Francisco. On October 13, 1955, Ginsberg, along with Snyder, McClure, PHILIP WHALEN, and Philip Lamantia, organized a reading at Six Gallery. It is here that Ginsberg introduced the world to *Howl* and secured the opportunity to publish with Lawrence Ferlinghetti of City Lights Books. Thus began the SAN FRANCISCO RENAISSANCE, an important movement in modern American poetry.

Although the Beats began their association in 1943, it was not until after the Six Gallery reading that the group gained national prominence. *Howl* became inadvertently infamous due to a lawsuit over its 1956 publication. Publisher Ferlinghetti and bookstore manager Shigeyoshi Murao were charged with obscenity but were defended broadly by the literary community. National attention was given to the trial, which eventually proved a victory for First Amendment rights, as Ferlinghetti and Murao were acquitted. During the year of the trial, Kerouac's novel *On the Road* (1957) hit the bookstores, prompting both controversy and acclaim. Through these events, the Beats rapidly gained national recognition.

Ironically, as the idea of the "Beat generation" took root in the public imagination, spawning various fashion and music fads, the small circle to whom the term referred began to disperse. Ginsberg and Snyder became involved with the hippie movement; Kerouac became increasingly reclusive; Baraka became a lead artist within the Black Nationalist movement; di Prima focused on holistic medicines and cofounded The New Poets Theater; and Burroughs traveled to Tangiers after accidentally killing his wife and soon underwent his own censorship trial involving his novel *Naked Lunch* (1959).

Some of the Beats burned so brightly and so intensely that they burned themselves out by middle age. Cassady died in Mexico from sun exposure and congestion shortly before his 42nd birthday. On October 1, 1969, less than a year after Cassady's death, Kerouac died of an alcohol-related illness at the age of 46. In contrast, both Burroughs and Ginsberg died in 1997. Burroughs had delved ever deeper into his reclusive persona and paranoia, an active drug user until the end. Ginsberg, however, partook not only of the hippie movement of the 1960s, but he was celebrated by the punk movement in the 1970s and remained an active poet, Buddhist, and gay rights activist until the end, ultimately, as a world-renowned figure. The Beats endure, much as Ginsberg predicted in *Howl,* "with the absolute heart of the poem of life butchered out of their bodies good to eat a thousand years."

BIBLIOGRAPHY

Charters, Ann, *The Portable Beat Reader*. New York: Penguin Books,1992.

Foster, Edward Halsey. *Understanding the Beats.* Columbia: University of South Carolina Press, 1992.

Kerouac, Jack. *On the Road.* Reprint, New York: Penguin, 1991.

Watson, Steven. *The Birth of the Beat Generation: Visionaries, Rebels, and Hipsters, 1944–1960.* New York: Pantheon Books, 1995.

Julie Bolt

BELL, MARVIN (1937–) An interviewer once dubbed Marvin Bell the "tree poet," and Bell's body of work lives up to the nickname. Bell says that his "poems have often made a distinction between what nature is and the uses we make of it" (21). "The Self and the Mulberry" (1977) opens with praises for nature's simplicity, which the speaker determines to emulate: "Like the willow, I tried to weep without tears." The speaker finds that his imitations result in not being able to "cry right," and the poem suggests that contemplating nature will not yield "a natural self." Not all of Bell's verse concerns trees, but all of it possesses a philosophical and contemplative tone. Bell states that he, like WILLIAM CARLOS WILLIAMS, is "a poet of ideas," and he shares with his mentors, JOHN LOGAN and DONALD JUSTICE, a concern for the psychology of loss and interest in conceptualizing self-identity (78).

Bell was born on August 3, 1937, in New York City and grew up in rural Long Island. He studied with Logan at the University of Chicago before working with Justice at the University of Iowa. He published *Things We Dreamt We Died For,* his first book, in 1966 and has published 17 volumes of poetry to date. Bell has received awards and fellowships from the Academy of American Poets, the American Academy of Arts and Letters, the Guggenheim Foundation, and the National Endowment for the Humanities. Iowa named him as the state's first poet laureate in 2000. Bell's former students include RITA DOVE, JOY HARJO, and JAMES TATE.

Tending toward the experimental, Bell's early poems are noted for a nontraditional structure and style, wordplay, and complicated syntax. While Bell's writing developed, his innovations became more subtle; as Richard Jackson observes of Bell's later work, his "poems . . . make stunning leaps and turns with the seeming ease of someone out for a walk" (45).

In his most recent and longest poem cycle, Bell develops his thinking through counterpoint, as he often does. Based upon the contradictions and dialectics of death and life, the Dead Man is an everyman character, who "is dead like a useless gift in its box waiting." ("About the Dead Man"). As Bell writes in "About the Dead Man's Not Telling," the protagonist "encounters horrific conditions infused with beauty," a phrase that embodies the entire cycle. The Dead Man appears in *The Book of the Dead Man* (1994), *Ardor: The*

Book of the Dead Man, Vol. 2 (1997), and "Sounds of the Resurrected Dead Man's Footsteps," included in *Night Works* (2000).

The convoluted becomes clear in Bell's writing, but the mundane and simple turn into the complex. All of it intertwines, producing an aesthetic of paradox and possibility.

BIBLIOGRAPHY

Bell, Marvin. *Old Snow Just Melting: Essays and Interviews.* Ann Arbor: University of Michigan Press, 1983.

Jackson, Richard. "Containing the Other: Marvin Bell's Recent Poetry." *North American Review* 280, no. 1 (Jan.–Feb. 1995): 45–48.

McGuiness, Daniel. "Exile and Cunning: The Recent Poetry Of Marvin Bell." *The Antioch Review* 48, no. 3 (summer 1990): 353–361.

Dallas Hulsey

"BELLS FOR JOHN WHITESIDE'S DAUGHTER" **JOHN CROWE RANSOM (1924)** In "Bells for John Whiteside's Daughter," JOHN CROWE RANSOM uses the death of a child to explore metaphysical questions about human life. Although highly traditional in form, this brief elegy is often anthologized for its achievement in accurately reflecting the conflicts within the modern consciousness. The poem is often compared to Ransom's "The Dead Boy," since each depicts a dead child in a coffin as family and friends struggle to comprehend not only the individual loss of the child but also the resulting loss of innocence for themselves. In both poems Ransom uses seemingly sentimental situations to probe the unsentimental realities of life.

As Alan Shucard, Fred Moramarco, and William Sullivan observe, "Bells for John Whiteside's Daughter" "reverberates with a number of striking contrasts that capture the paradoxical nature of human existence: life-death, past-present, memory-reality, astonishment-vexation, starkness-artifice" (217). The overarching contrast between the poem's somber theme and its playful tone and imagery enables Ransom to develop what ROBERT PENN WARREN calls the "savage irony" behind two central clichés: "'Heaven, won't that child ever be still, she is driving me distracted'; and second, 'She was such an active healthy-looking child, would you've ever thought she would just up and die!'" (238). Ransom intensifies the horrific irony of the wish fulfilled by presenting images of the naturally vital child in life, chasing "lazy geese" and taking "arms against her shadow," which he then juxtaposes against a final picture of the unnaturally still child in death, "lying so primly propped." Warren claims that the poem's ironies attenuate the speaker's grief by allowing him or her to come to terms with the situation through an "exercise of will and self-control" (240). Yet Elias Schwartz argues that the ironic understatement in the line, "But now go the bells, and we are ready," instead "expresses more powerfully than before the speaker's grief" (285). Still, as M. E. Bradford reminds us, regardless of how the word *ready* is taken, "the experience implicit in this poem's order is only minimally reassuring" (47).

Even Warren acknowledges that "the transcendence is not absolute," that the speaker's divergent emotions are not completely resolved (240). In his analysis of Ransom's "effort to dominate the entire range of elegiac possibilities" by mixing heroic and mock-heroic elements, William Vesterman observes a similar "partial transcendence of divergent metrical association"—the poem's prosody in agreement with its themes and diction (see PROSODY AND FREE VERSE)—which also contributes to the poem's "special flavor and makes it [a] unique compound of moral and aesthetic elements" (45, 51). In the end, perhaps the poem is worth reading largely *because* of the inability of the speaker, the poet, and, finally, the reader to fully resolve the conundrums with which they wrestle.

BIBLIOGRAPHY

Bradford, M. E. "A Modern Elegy: Ransom's 'Bells for John Whiteside's Daughter.'" *Mississippi Quarterly* 21, no. 1 (1967–1968): 43–47.

Schwartz, Elias. "Ransom's 'Bells for John Whiteside's Daughter.'" *English Language Notes* 1 (1964): 284–285.

Shucard, Alan, Fred Moramarco, and William Sullivan, eds. *Modern American Poetry, 1865–1950.* Boston: Twayne-Hall, 1989.

Vesterman, William. "The Motives of Meter in 'Bells for John Whiteside's Daughter.'" *Southern Quarterly* 22, no. 4 (1984): 42–53.

Warren, Robert Penn. "Pure and Impure Poetry." *Kenyon Review* 5, no. 2 (1943): 228–254.

Sharon Talley

BENÉT, STEPHEN VINCENT (1898–1943)

Stephen Vincent Benét was an acclaimed poet of American democracy. Though he also wrote novels and short stories (including *The Devil and Daniel Webster* [1936]), he remains best known for *John Brown's Body* (1928), a long narrative poem on the Civil War, whose commercial and literary success brought him to national attention. To open his epic, Benét invoked the "strong and diverse heart" of America as his muse; it became his great lifelong theme. Benét insisted that poetry "is meant for everybody, not only for the scholars" (34), "open to any reader who likes the sound and the swing of rhythm, the color and fire of words" (35). This approachability made him "the most widely read serious poet of his time" (Fenton 80), but his poems have received less subsequent esteem than the more difficult and experimental works of MODERNISM. His influences include Robert Browning and VACHEL LINDSAY.

Born in Bethlehem, Pennsylvania, Benét published his first book, *Five Men and Pompey,* in 1915, during his freshman year at Yale University. In 1921 he married Rosemary Carr, who inspired his love poems and collaborated on *A Book of Americans* (1933). His ballad "King David" (1923) received the *Nation*'s Poetry Prize. On a Guggenheim Fellowship (1926–27) in Paris, he wrote *John Brown's Body,* which won the Pulitzer Prize in 1929. Elected to the National Institute of Arts and Letters in that year, he won its Gold Medal in 1943. In 1933 he became editor of the Yale Series of Younger Poets competition (see POETRY PRIZES). *Western Star* (1943), his unfinished long poem on the settlement of the American West, won Benét a second, posthumous Pulitzer in 1944.

In *John Brown's Body* Benét alternates blank verse with a longer, rougher line, and he continued to use both traditional forms and looser, unrhymed structures throughout his career (see PROSODY AND FREE VERSE). "American Names" (1927), a ballad, joins individual identity to the national identity embodied in place-names with its final demand, "Bury my heart at Wounded Knee." In the 1930s Benét's unrhymed poems increasingly turn from past to future with nightmare visions that are both monitory and elegiac. "Notes to Be Left in a Cornerstone" (1936) commemorates the New York City he lived in and loved, addressing future historians who cannot reconstruct from its ruins "that beauty, rapid and harsh, / That loneliness, that passion or that name."

Benét wrote passionately in democracy's defense from World War II's outbreak until his death. In "Nightmare at Noon" (1940), he acknowledges America's failure to fulfill its ideals, as symbolized by "the lyncher's rope, the bought justice, the wasted land," but he refuses to abandon the promise of democratic freedom that was "bought with the bitter and anonymous blood" of past generations. The radio verse-drama "Listen to the People" (1941) concludes with the commitment to sustain "[t]his peaceless vision, groping for the stars." As the "poet-historian of American democracy," in the words of Parry Stroud (145), Benét brought America's past to life and sought its future.

BIBLIOGRAPHY

Benét, Stephen Vincent. Foreword to *John Brown's Body.* New York: Rinehart, 1941.

Fenton, Charles A. *Stephen Vincent Benét: The Life and Times of an American Man of Letters, 1898–1943.* New Haven, Conn.: Yale University Press, 1958.

Stroud, Parry. *Stephen Vincent Benét.* New York: Twayne, 1962.

Rebecca Melora Corinne Boggs

BERKSON, BILL (1939–)

A precocious member of the NEW YORK SCHOOL, Bill Berkson helped to propel his mentor FRANK O'HARA's poetic project in the years leading up to O'Hara's untimely death. Berkson later encouraged many younger poets who aspired to the New York style and eventually relocated to California, where he continued to pursue a cool, laconic brand of poetry.

Born in New York City, Berkson was trained at Brown and Columbia Universities and also received instruction at the Institute of Fine Arts and the New School, where he studied under KENNETH KOCH. It was in the New York of the early 1960s that Berkson's informal education commenced, enriched by the lively scene of painters and poets he found there. O'Hara was at the center of it all, and he brought Berkson along for the ride. Like O'Hara before him, Berkson is known equally for his art criticism and his poetry. A corresponding editor for *Art in America* and a frequent contributor to *Artforum,* Berkson has also maintained an affiliation as professor and academic director at the San Francisco Art Institute. In the course of a long and varied career, Berkson has received awards from, among others, the National Endowment for the Arts (1980).

Berkson declared a debt to O'Hara in his debut collection of poetry, *Saturday Night* (1961), a volume replete with echoes of O'Hara's nonchalant "I do this, I do that" style, which enumerates the commonplace details of the poet's day. But the debt was equally O'Hara's, for he quickly absorbed the influence of Berkson's unorthodox scattershot spacing, a type of staggered arrangement oriented toward breath and speech patterns.

While the influence between Berkson and O'Hara was mutual, it took Berkson decades to climb out of the late O'Hara's shadow. After a stint as a professor in the same New School workshops where he had first honed his craft, Berkson became the editor and publisher of Big Sky Publications. Through this imprint he produced several new volumes of poetry, including *Enigma Variations* (1975), a collaboration with the painter Philip Guston.

Berkson's poems are most strongly characterized by what EZRA POUND called *phanopoeia,* or "a casting of images upon the visual imagination" (25). His scenes often involve rather mundane subjects, such as a mother and child playing dominos, a trip to the local Italian restaurant, or an unexpected encounter with a movie star in a public restroom. References to everyday existence are everywhere in Berkson's poetry. In "Poem," from *Lush Life* (1984), Berkson describes the experience of suffering a backyard eye injury, along with the ensuing housebound convalescence. Eye bandaged and doped up on codeine, with evening descending, he "watches sundown then 'One Day At A Time.'"

Though afflicted and in pain, Berkson finds repose in both a beautiful sky and a situation comedy. But how do the salves of nature and popular culture differ in their effects on the human psyche? He seems to raise the question for the sake of raising it, rather than answering it, simply calling attention to the strange proximities of the eternal and the transient in everyday life.

BIBLIOGRAPHY

Lehman, David. *The Last Avant-Garde: The Making of the New York School of Poets.* New York: Doubleday, 1998.

Pound, Ezra. "How to Read." In *Literary Essays of Ezra Pound,* edited by T. S. Eliot. London. Faber and Faber, 1954.

Ward, Geoff. *Statues of Liberty.* London: Macmillan, 1993.

Jim Cocola

BERNARD, APRIL (1956–) In the poem "Four Winds" (2002), April Bernard sums up her poetic goal—to produce "untranslatable rainy hootings," a watery word-world between conclusion and impression. JOHN ASHBERY anticipates this project, although Bernard's satirical wit and feminism give her more in common with SYLVIA PLATH.

Born in Williamstown, Massachusetts, Bernard, a poet who is also a novelist, playwright, screenwriter, and essayist, received a B.A. degree at Harvard University, where she studied poetry under ELIZABETH BISHOP. She has worked as an editor for a number of magazines and book publishers and has taught at Barnard, Bennington, Yale, and Columbia. Her *Blackbird Bye Bye* (1989) garnered the Walt Whitman Award from the Academy of American Poets for a first book of poems. She has published three books of poetry.

Bernard's language is typically colorful and demotic but also dreamlike and weird. In "Psalm: It Must Be the Medication" (1993), for instance, Bernard describes a "lion" as having thrown "his head back" to sing "two notes like a veery" (a type of bird); in "I Loved Her, Too" (1989), she muses, "Let's see—you should look / nothing like me, like I used to look." "[B]risk, artfully paced, and wry," in Helen Vendlers words on an early passage (27), Bernard's poems zigzag headily from one such image or remark to another, suggesting narrative without fulfilling it, their breathless brevity recalling Emily Dickinson. Poem sequences and loosely constructed sonnets are forms that Bernard favors. Like her style as a whole, they mix closure and open-endedness, comprehension and doubt.

Bernard's game of "trying to say without saying," as she describes it in "Go Between" (2002), often registers as satire—mockery of a society addicted to its own conventions. The society is patriarchal, and the possibilities it represses are feminine: In "Up Attic" (1989), dulled perception is a sour romantic contract: "I had been struck on the Skull by an oar / And it looked like love to me"; in "Coffee & Dolls" (2002), warped images of femininity—"Yarn-haired, gingham-dressed floppy dolls" in a window—help the "old guys" within to conceal crimes. Comic as well as acerbic, aimed at herself as well as her contemporaries, Bernard's mockery passes easily into gentler modes of speech. Adapting traditional Christian forms of worship, she summons herself, as David Baker writes, "to embrace and even adore the evasive nature of things" (226), praying in "Psalm of the One Who Has No Dwelling-Place" (1993), for example: "May / I rest my head in you, that is, in the uttermost parts of the sea." She also celebrates breaks from convention. This celebratory note has strengthened over the course of Bernard's career and makes for some of her loveliest recent poems: for instance, "Sonnet in E" (2002), where she decides "To fling the particles of person wide, awash on the blue," realizing that she is "no longer obliged to sit like a china dog / on a table in the corner of the room."

BIBLIOGRAPHY

Baker, David. "Plainness and Sufficiency." *Poetry* 164, no. 4 (July 1994): 223–240.

Vendler, Helen. "Four Prized Poets." *New York Review of Books* (17 August 1989): 26–30.

Shaileen Beyer

BERNSTEIN, CHARLES (1950–) From the late 1970s to the present, Charles Bernstein has helped develop the poetry and poetics of the LANGUAGE SCHOOL. He is the key figure behind this literary movement, which includes a diverse range of poets who challenge the customary use of language. Language poetry questions conventional "vocabulary, grammar, process, shape, syntax, program, or subject matter" (Andrews ix). It answers to the earlier modernists, such as EZRA POUND and GERTRUDE STEIN, who were known for their unconventional use of language. It is also influenced by postructuralist theories about the rupture between language and meaning and by Marxist notions about the class inequality embedded in language. By using language differently, Language poetry changes standard poetic forms, encourages multiple interpretations, and contests social and economic disparities. Bernstein continues to develop this poetry of innovation by reinventing it in different media: textual, acoustic, operatic, and electronic. By continually reinventing Language poetry, he sustains its aesthetic and political cantankerousness. He revels in its popular failure as a sign of its disruption of the status quo. He views Language poetry as an intimate "conversation" about the process of generating meaning rather than as a "particular style" (qtd. in Wood 3) driven by "generational and marketing products" (4). Continuing this conversation with other poet-scholars like himself, such as Steve McCaffrey, he participates in creating "a poetry of and for the present" that opposes the commercialization and simplification of poetry and culture in late 20th-century America (3).

Bernstein was born on April 4th, 1950, in New York City. The author of 30 collections of books, essays, and libretti, he is best known for *L=A=N=G=U=A=G=E*, a magazine on experimental poetics that he edited with BRUCE ANDREWS from 1978 to 1981. He has taught at the State University of New York (Buffalo) and the University of Pennsylvania. He was awarded the Roy Harvey Pearce/Archive for New Poetry Prize of the University of California at San Diego in 1999 for a lifetime contribution to poetry and scholarship. In 2006, he was elected a Fellow of the Academy of American Poets.

Bernstein's poetry is characteristic for its intellectual rigor belied by its pedestrian language. His poetry, repudiates narrative, logic, image, and tradition so that it is at once nonsensical and evocative. His 1999 poem, "Don't Be So Sure (Don't Be Saussure)," for example, is lyrical nonsense, but it suggests an alternative stream-of-consciousness coherence. Contesting Saussure's notion that the word is not the thing, he shows that the word may not be a reliable conduit for meaning but is nonetheless an expressive one. Beginning with a cup, the poem progresses through rhyme and association (from "cap" to "slap" to "pap") to "Get me a drink." This nonsensical exploration of sense is the hallmark of this poet-scholar, who continues to promote his oppositional poetics against linguistic platitudes and social power.

BIBLIOGRAPHY
Andrews, Bruce, and Charles Bernstein, eds. *The L=A=N=G=U=A=G=E Book.* Carbondale: Southern Illinois University Press, 1984.
Perloff, Marjorie. *The Dance of the Intellect: Studies in the Poetry of the Pound Tradition.* New York: Cambridge University Press, 1985.
Wood, Tim. "Charles Bernstein: Politics, Poetics and Laughter against Tears [Interview]." *The Word: The Monthly Guide to the Arts in Dallas* (March 2000): 7.

Colette Colligan

BERRIGAN, TED (1934–1983) One of the central figures in the second generation of the NEW YORK SCHOOL of poetry, Ted Berrigan absorbed influences from his predecessors, such as JOHN ASHBERY and FRANK O'HARA, but transformed what he learned into some of the most delicately modulated poems of his generation. Works from *The Sonnets* (1964) to "Things To Do in Providence" (1970) to the late lyrical poems, such as those collected in *A Certain Slant of Sunlight* (1988), exhibit a subtle and graceful manipulation of tone that few of his contemporaries could approach. Berrigan was an important teacher of poets as well, and his collected talks about poetry, *On the Level Everyday* (1997), remains an important text for younger writers.

Born into a working-class family, Berrigan grew up in Providence, Rhode Island. He enlisted in the army, served in Korea, and was stationed in Tulsa, Oklahoma, where he met the poet RON PADGETT, then a high-school student, who would later be closely associated with him in the New York school. Married to the poet ALICE NOTLEY, he was the father of Anselm and Edmund Berrigan, both recognized as important younger poets today. In 1963 Berrigan founded "C" Press, which published both the journal *"C"* and a series of mimeographed books by Padgett and other New York poets of their generation. Berrigan taught at numerous colleges and universities, including Yale, the University of Michigan, and the City University of New York.

Berrigan's *Sonnets* are a collage of lines, some borrowed from his readings. The same set of words—even something as plain and straightforward as "Dear Chris, hello"—appear in various contexts, each time given a different intonation and emphasis. The perfect control of cadence and tone exemplified in these early poems became Berrigan's trademark in a wide range of writing, from his minimalist works in the late 1960s to the more traditional lyric poems written toward the end of his life (see LYRIC POETRY). Among these, "Red Shift" (1980) is generally considered to be his major achievement. A defense of poetry as the prime speech of civilization, it ends famously with the line, "The world's furious song flows through my costume."

"The world's furious song" as it passed through Berrigan's voice has become the measure against which younger poets, especially those associated with the New York school, continue to calibrate their own work. With the possible exception of JACK SPICER, no avant-garde American writer of Berrigan's generation achieved so much both as a poet and as a teacher, and as a defender of his art.

BIBLIOGRAPHY
Foster, Edward. *Berrigan, Bronk, and the American Real.* New York: Spuyten Duyvil, 1999.
Waldman, Anne, ed. *Nice to See You: Homage to Ted Berrigan.* Minneapolis, Minn.: Coffee House, 1991.

Edward Foster

BERRY, WENDELL (1934–) The poetry of Wendell Berry offers a persistent and deliberate response to the environmental and moral crises of 20th-century America. Focused on a sense of place defined by community, work, and respect for the land, Berry relies on pastoral and elegiac poetic forms while avoiding the stylistic experimentation of many of his postmodern literary peers. His themes echo such poets as Walt Whitman, ROBERT FROST, and GARY SNYDER. As a poet, essayist, and novelist, Berry is an active spokesman for the virtues of sustainable farming and bioregionalism, or commitment to place, as a means of living a sincere and ethical life.

Berry grew up in Kentucky and received undergraduate and graduate degrees at the University of Kentucky in 1956 and 1957. After completing a Wallace Stegner Fellowship at Stanford in 1959 and a Guggenheim Fellowship in Italy in 1962, Berry taught briefly in New York before returning to the University of Kentucky in 1964. A year later he bought a 12-acre farm on the Kentucky River, in the same county in which he was born. After a dozen volumes of poetry and more than 20 other books, Berry still inhabits his native ground, a decision that Wallace Stegner has called "as radical as Thoreau's retreat to Walden, and much more permanent" (51). Berry's work has earned him, among other awards, the American Academy of Arts and Letters Jean Stein Award (1987) and a Lannan Foundation Award for nonfiction (1989).

Berry's poetry is a reflection of his decision to return to the rural from the urban. In simple but moving verses, he explores daily and seasonal cycles of life and death, while raising crops, mourning the loss of loved ones, and praising the value of nature. Fidelity is his ideal, and Berry is faithfully "married" not only to his wife but also to his land, his family, and his community. Staying home is Berry's response to the crises of his time, including Vietnam and the cold war in his earlier poems. In "Stay Home" (1980), the fields and woods surrounding his dwelling offer labor "longer than a man's life"; the poem deliberately echoes Frost's "The Pasture." Berry rewrites Frost's refrain, "I sha'n't be gone long.—You come too," with his own: "Don't come with me. / You stay home too." With an ecologist's commitment to place, he hopes that others will stay home as well and protect their own local environments.

Berry's voice shifts throughout his work, from mad farmer to compassionate husbandman to Luddite (with a vehement critique of technology and industrialization), but his implication, as taken from his 1980 poem "Below," is always clear: "What I stand for / is what I stand on."

BIBLIOGRAPHY

Merchant, Paul, ed. *Wendell Berry*. Lewiston, Idaho: Confluence, 1991.

Nibbelink, Herman. "Wendell Berry." In *American Nature Writers*, Vol. 1, edited by John Elder, 89–105. New York: Scribner, 1996.

Stegner, Wallace. "A Letter to Wendell Berry." In *Wendell Berry*, edited by Paul Merchant, 47–52. Lewiston, Idaho: Confluence, 1991.

Michael Lundblad

BERRYMAN, JOHN (1914–1972) Although John Berryman—like his poetic successor ANNE SEXTON—would eventually come to be associated with the CONFESSIONAL movement in American poetry, he first attracted literary acclaim for more traditional poetry published in *Poems* (1942) and *The Dispossessed* (1948). These early books, influenced in part by his reading of William Butler Yeats and W. H. AUDEN, deal with social crises of the times, including the wrenching impact of World War II, in an objective fashion. Berryman's later poetry, however, would turn far more explicitly onto the subject of the poet himself, as with his *Homage to Mistress Bradstreet* (1953), a biographical ode, richly allusive, moving and meaningful to the present day in its inquiry into the personal and spiritual life of the Anglo-American colonial poet Anne Bradstreet. What is most remarkable about the poem is its method of merging the identities of poet and subject, who is imagined to be the poet's mistress across the centuries. Praising *Homage to Mistress Bradstreet,* ROBERT LOWELL called it "the most resourceful historical poem in our language" (107). But Berryman's reputation, that of an agonized poet of the personal, will always be judged in the context of his mental instability, alcoholism, and clinical depression, which led him often to contemplate the idea of ending his own life. As he would write, characteristically, in *Dream Song* 149 (1968), "This world is gradually becoming a place / where I do not care to be any more."

Born John Allyn Smith, Jr., in McAlester, Oklahoma, to John Allyn Smith, a banker, and Martha Little, formerly an elementary schoolteacher, Berryman was raised Roman Catholic, serving for a time as an altar boy and attending Catholic primary schools in both Oklahoma and Florida. But Berryman's boyhood was an unsettled period for his parents, and his writing often reflected the unresolved anguish of familial problems that arose during his youth. The family moved frequently during the early years, finally settling in Tampa, Florida, where his father, who had speculated unsuccessfully in real estate, shot himself to death outside his 11-year-old son's bedroom window in 1926. Several months later his mother married John McAlpin Berryman, whose name was given to the son. Berryman was educated at Columbia University (B.A., 1936) and later in England, where he attended Clare College at Cambridge University on a fellowship and met Yeats,

T. S. ELIOT, Auden, and Dylan Thomas. While at Columbia, he came under the influence of the professor Mark van Doren and began to publish poetry in the *Nation* and taught at Wayne University (later Wayne State University) in Detroit, Michigan.

During his years at Columbia, Berryman won the Van Renssalaer Prize for LYRIC POETRY (1935). The many subsequent honors earned by Berryman included *Poetry* magazine's Guarantors Prize (1948), the Russell Loines Award from the National Institute of Arts and Letters (1964), the Pulitzer Prize in poetry (1965), the Bollingen Prize (1969), and the National Book Award in Poetry (1969).

While he was writing *Homage to Mistress Bradstreet* during the early 1950s, Berryman was also finishing work on 115 deeply personal Petrarchan sonnets that recounted an adulterous love affair, a poetry sequence that would eventually be published as *Berryman's Sonnets* (written in 1947, published in 1967). The love affair, combined with the pressure of writing the sonnets, pressed Berryman to consider suicide and to begin his many years of psychiatric treatment. The volume also established Berryman as one of the modern masters of that difficult poetic form, even as his sudden shifts in thought and feeling and his disruptions of syntax and strict form show his ongoing radical experimentation with the genre, as in sonnet 44: "Bell to sore knees vestigial crowds, let crush / One another nations sottish and a-prowl."

During World War II, he took on teaching assignments at Harvard University before serving for 10 years at Princeton University at the invitation of literary critic and poet R. P. BLACKMUR. While at Princeton, Berryman wrote a psychobiographical study of Stephen Crane (1950) for the American Men of Letters Series. Later he became professor of humanities at the University of Minnesota (1955–72). With *77 Dream Songs* (published in 1964, winner of the 1965 Pulitzer Prize for poetry), part of a long semiautobiographical project begun in 1955, Berryman achieved his highest acclaim as a poet and confirmed his status as the preeminent voice in the confessional movement in poetry, a modern version of the romantic impulse that places the poet and her or his emotional experience at the center of the poem's concerns. In this most important sequence of poems, Berryman unveiled the memorable alter egos "Henry" and "Mr. Bones," the latter of which is written as a character out of blackface minstrelsy. In this long sequence of 18-line, sonnetlike poems, with their complicated syntax, strange diction, and unexpected shifts in language and tone, Berryman investigates the furthest reaches of human psychology and spirituality while probing the most deeply personal aspects of the poet's own inner life.

In succeeding years Berryman added to the sequence of poems, burnishing his reputation as a modern master of the colloquial American language, until there were nearly 400 collected Dream Songs, many of which were included in his important late volume, *His Toy, His Dream, His Rest: 308 Dream Songs* (1968). This final collection of Dream Songs earned Berryman the National Book Award. In his acceptance speech for the award, Berryman explained his iconoclasm and experimental style in this way: "I set up the Dream Songs as hostile to every visible tendency in both American and English poetry" (Mariani 443).

After checking into alcohol rehabilitation once in 1969 and three times in 1970, Berryman experienced "a sort of religious conversion" in 1970 (Mariani 457). He first considered Judaism, then professed Catholicism, and eventually wrote *Recovery* (1971), a vague autobiography about alcoholic rehabilitation. Finally, the 57-year-old Berryman committed suicide in 1972 by leaping from the Washington Avenue bridge in Minneapolis, 30 miles from his father's birthplace.

BIBLIOGRAPHY

Bloom, Harold, ed. *John Berryman.* New York: Chelsea House Publishing, 1989.

Conarroe, Joel. *John Berryman: An Introduction to the Poetry.* New York: Columbia University Press, 1977.

Lowell, Robert. "John Berryman." In *Collected Prose,* edited by Robert Giroux. New York: Farrar, Straus & Giroux, 1990.

Mariani, Paul. *Dream Song: The Life of John Berryman.* New York: William Morrow, 1990.

James Emmett Ryan

BERSSENBRUGGE, MEI-MEI (1947–)

Mei-mei Berssenbrugge's intricate collagist poetry expands the traditions of innovative American lyric and feminist experimentation. Dense abstraction and concrete imagery borrowed from the realms of continental and Eastern philosophy, psychology, religion, architecture, art theory, conventional and alternative medicine, physics, and other sources commingle in her work with a painstaking account of visual experience, emotional states, and surreal drifts. Berssenbrugge makes statements that seem absolutely authoritative, but these are only to be dissolved and displaced by fresh new possibilities and rich uncertainties in the flux of long lines of verse.

The daughter of Chinese and Dutch-American parents, Berssenbrugge was born in Beijing and grew up in Massachusetts. The author of 12 books of poetry, beginning with *Fish Souls* (1974), Berssenbrugge won an American Book Award for *Random Possession* (1979) and *The Heat Bird* (1983), among other awards and fellowships.

Berssenbrugge frequently exerts, as she puts it in "Naturalism" (1989), "an erotic concentration on a vicissitude of light." The preoccupation with ever-shifting perspectives on constantly changing visual impressions is erotic in its intensity, prolonged focus, aesthetic pleasures, and inextricability from meditation on female/male and mother/daughter intimacies. Even as she marks how individuals cannot master each other's subjective truths, the poet suggests that separations between a self's inside and outside are arbitrary; in the long poem *Endocrinology* (1997), a speaker declares: "She can't see where her sadness ends and someone else's is." Furthermore, the "erotic" exploration is fraught with many disruptions and erasures of memory. An apostrophe in "Fog" (1989) plaintively questions: "If you do remember correctly, how can we compare the feeling without being influenced by what has happened since?"

Frequently Berssenbrugge perceives "the body as a space of culture" while also perceiving it "as nature," especially when it is threatened or "taken away by disease," as in *Endocrinology*. In "The Four Year Old Girl" (1998), which alludes to a struggle against a rare "genetic disease," the juxtaposition of sentences about genotypes, phenotypes, and selves with sentences that include water images foregrounds the disjunction between confidence in one's stable identity and movements toward disintegration.

The unpredictable, often disjunctive journey of sensuous, sensory thinking that Berssenbrugge's poetry embodies provides a trenchant criticism of the distortions of efforts at representation, as well as an affirmation of desires for lucid perceptions, intimate interchanges and, as "Value" (1993) has it, "a moving frame" that "reframes the space for utopian content."

BIBLIOGRAPHY

Newman, Denise. "The Concretion of Emotion: An Analytic Lyric of Mei-mei Berssenbrugge's *Empathy*." *Talisman: A Journal of Contemporary Poetry and Poetics* 9 (fall 1992): 119–124.

Simpson, Megan. *Poetic Epistemologies: Gender and Knowing in Women's Language-Oriented Writing*. Albany: State University of New York Press, 2000, pp. 134–144.

Tabios, Eileen R. "Mei-mei Berssenbrugge Bleeds a Poem That Transcends Heartbreak." In *Black Lightning: Poetry-in-Progress*, edited by Tabios. New York: Asian American Writers Workshop, 1998, pp. 133–177.

Thomas Fink

"BIALYSTOK STANZAS" MICHAEL HELLER **(1979)** This poem, collected in MICHAEL HELLER's volume *Knowledge* (1979) and reprinted in his memoir, *Living Root* (2000), was originally conceived by Heller in the late 1960s as a historical novel on the life of Jews in the Polish city of Bialystok, from which his father's family had emigrated. In pursuing this subject, Heller joins the ranks of American Jewish poets writing after the Holocaust, who can neither totally ignore nor totally submerge themselves in the great Jewish tragedy of the 20th century.

The poem's parenthetical subtitle, "from a book of old photos," refers to David Sohn's book *Bialystok: Photo Album of a Renowned City and Its Jews the World Over* (1951), which Heller procured on his father's advice in 1963. Most sections of the poem, then, address photos from Sohn's book. On the series of poems, Heller has said, "I am remembering then, not for the sake of *what was*, but in a sense, in order *to be*" (15). Heller also cites Walter Benjamin on the subject of photography, quoting the German-Jewish philosopher's notion that a photograph is a "posthumous moment" (33).

In his commentary on the poem, Norman Finkelstein sees photography in "Bialystok Stanzas," beyond either Heller's or Benjamin's explicit statements, as "the inevitable violation of a historical space, a psychic zone which can maintain its dignity only in the medium of mute memory" (77–78). Burt Kimmelman expands the implications of the poem to those of Heller's entire theory of poetics having to do with how words and lived experience intersect, writing that a Jew's "first condition" is her or his "relationship to the idea of a text" (70). Here Heller is dealing with photographs as "texts." Part 7 of the poem, subtitled "Terrible Pictures," specifically its lines describing Jews being photographed just before their execution, underscores this point. Heller is making it clear that the extermination of European Jews is both a real experience and a textual one, part of the literary tradition of the Jews that has bound them together throughout the diaspora.

The final section of the poem, the "Coda" entitled "Senile Jew," is the only section not dealing with texts in general or photography specifically. Describing an interaction with his elderly grandfather, Heller asks about a missing boot: "Do you wear the boot? / Or does he who wears the boot / Wear you?" (32). Soon the voice of the grandfather and the grandson become intermingled. However, in ending the poem with the line, "I am the Jew," Heller acknowledges his role in Jewish history as a member of a persecuted people who is, himself, not persecuted. With this line, Finkelstein is able to tie the poem to the OBJECTIVIST school, noting that objectivism "remains an important mode of Jewish-American poetry because Objectivists must acknowledge their responsibility to the circumstances from which their poems arise" (78).

BIBLIOGRAPHY

Finkelstein, Norman. "*Dy-Yanu:* Michael Heller's 'Bialystok Stanzas.'" *Talisman: A Journal of Contemporary Poetry and Poetics* 10 (fall 1993): 77–80.

Heller, Michael. *Living Root.* Albany: State University of New York Press, 2000.

Kimmelman, Burt. "The Autobiography of Poetics: Michael Heller's *Living Root.*" *Talisman: A Journal of Contemporary Poetry and Poetics* 10 (fall 1993): 67–76.

Andrew E. Mathis

BIDART, FRANK (1939–) Frank Bidart writes poems of great philosophical and emotional depth. They show us interior landscapes of desire and loss, crime and self-punishment, righteousness and forgiveness. More recently they have been concerned with love and artistic creation. Although he belongs to no poetic school, Bidart's affinities include ROBERT LOWELL, ELIZABETH BISHOP, and ROBERT PINSKY. LOUIS GLÜCK has called Bidart "one of the great poets of our time" in a blurb for his 2002 volume *Music Like Dirt.*

Of Basque-American heritage, Bidart was born in the Central Valley town of Bakersfield, California. He received a B.A. degree in English from the University of California, Riverside, and an M.A. in English from Harvard, where he studied with Lowell. He has taught at Wellesley College. Bidart's books have won many prizes including the Shelley Memorial Award (1997), the Lannan Foundation Award for poetry (1998), and the WALLACE STEVENS Award (2001). In 2003 he was elected a chancellor of the Academy of American Poets, and in 2006 he was elected to the American Academy of Arts and Letters, and in 2007 he received the Bollingen Prize in Poetry.

Bidart's first volume, *Golden State* (1973), includes a series of indelible characters—some hateful, some beloved, all struggling for meaning. The speaker of the title poem, based on Bidart himself, attempts to reconnect through memory with his deceased father, a difficult and unloving man. Yet the father escapes the son's control, as he did in real life. He remains "unknowable; unpossessable." ("Golden State"). The poem exposes both the tensions and the intensity of the father-child relationship, and it reveals the tarnish on the "Golden State" of California.

"Ellen West" (1977) and "The War of Vaslav Nijinsky" (1983)—published in subsequent volumes and collected in *In the Western Night* (1990)—bring historical personages to life. Both poems vividly reproduce the voices of the title characters and of those who interacted with them. Like "Golden State" these poems reflect on the tragic circumstances of individuals and on their historical situations. "The Second Hour of the Night," published in *Desire* (1997), meditates on longing, pleasure, pain, and death. It begins by reanimating the voices of French composer Hector Berlioz and his wife, actress Henriette-Constance Berlioz-Smithson. It then explores compulsive desire through the Ovidian myth of Myrrha and Cinyras and concludes by evoking an intense encounter with the ghost of a dead lover. In Bidart's most recent sequence, *Music Like Dirt,* he focuses on the central activity of creative "making."

Throughout his career Bidart has given readers a series of greatly original poems. They stretch the limits of language and genre. They examine a darkened world and even darker human natures. They pray for insight that often does not come. And, as in "Lament for the Makers," they explore the power of art to remake life: "Teach me, masters who by making were / remade, your art."

BIBLIOGRAPHY

Glück, Louise. "The Forbidden." *Proofs & Theories: Essays on Poetry.* Hopewell, N.J.: Ecco Press, 1994, pp. 53–63.
Gray, Jeffrey. "'Necessary Thought': Frank Bidart and the Postconfessional." *Contemporary Literature* 34, no. 4 (1993): 714–739.

Steven Gould Axelrod

"BIRCHES" **ROBERT FROST (1916)** Few poems in American literature hold as esteemed a place in the public mind as Robert Frost's blank verse meditation "Birches"; fewer still are as commonly misunderstood. The titular birch trees evoke a pastoral New England setting, one so quaint that even as admiring a reader of Frost's poetry as RANDALL JARRELL laments that the poem leaves a taste "a little brassy, a little sugary" (41). Yet such a response overlooks Frost's careful manipulation of pastoral nostalgia in order to address spiritual longing and the isolating effects of the poetic imagination. Musing about what caused the birches to bend, Frost "like[s] to think some boy's been swinging them," and thereby calls up images of lonely frontier life, adolescent independence, and communion with nature, images of a mythic American past that connect to intensely held American ideals. But this evocation of the solitary country boy proves a metaphor through which Frost masks the actual cause of the birches' misshapenness: the heavy burden of winter ice, which Frost associates with Truth. This Truth shatters faith and denies spiritual aspiration, for when Frost imagines the ice, he writes that "You'd think the dome of heaven had fallen." The speaker's persistent replacement of the imagined with the real, of the boy with the ice storm, is mirrored by the boy's own dropping back to earth after his upward (and thus heavenward) climbs, reflecting the poem's movement toward an imaginative balance between realism and transcendence.

Historically speaking, Frost's evocation of a disappearing rural America is timely, though perhaps already past; this imagined boy's life, "too far from town to learn baseball," is already fading before the rapid urbanization of modern America. But the poem is less about antiurbanization (or antimodernism, despite that frequent charge against Frost) than the way nostalgia for either the real or imagined past reflects an aspiration for purity and transcendence. The structure of the poem reflects this conflict: Frost's initial musing about the boy is broken up by a long, imagistic passage evoking the ice storm that grounded the trees, a passage alive with the sounds of the ice storm: "click," "cracks," "crazes." But Frost returns to his imagined boy in the second half of the poem, writing, "But I was going to say when Truth broke in / With all her matter-of-fact about the storm, / I should prefer to have some boy bend them." This insistence on what the poet prefers to what he must acknowledge as Truth introduces an important conflict in the poem, between imagination and reality, spontaneity and structure, visionary ambition and unrelenting reality. The poem will not resolve the conflict, even though the speaker may be "weary of considerations, / And life is too much like a pathless wood"; indeed, for Frost, the conflict itself is at the heart of human experience. Richard Poirier notes how easy it is to forget that the birches were shaped by ice, not by a boy's swinging. The latter represents the poet's preference, and the plausibility of such a boy demonstrates the power of the poetic imagination in shaping the perception of reality (275). But Poirier also writes that while the speaker of "Birches" would sometimes "'like to get away from earth awhile,' his aspiration for escape to something 'larger' is safely controlled by the recognition that birch trees will only bear so much climbing before returning you, under the pressure of human weight, back home" (172).

Frost slyly transforms the poem into an ARS POETICA with the opening image of the poem and its subtle pun on the lines of a poem: "When I see birches bend to left and right / Across the lines of straighter darker trees" is at one remove Frost's comment on his own poem, on its movement against the straighter and surer background of darker trees (the birch's bark is white), on his restless effort to see the truth but not to deny the visionary experience in the process.

BIBLIOGRAPHY

Jarrell, Randall. *Poetry and the Age.* New York: Vintage, 1955.

Poirier, Richard. *Robert Frost: The Work of Knowing.* New York: Oxford University Press, 1977.

Temple Cone

BISHOP, ELIZABETH (1911–1979) From the beginning of her life as a poet, Elizabeth Bishop was interested in the way that our perceptions can be refined through our encounters with the natural world. Written when she was 16 years old, "To a Tree" (1927) gives us an early glimpse into her way of viewing the world. The tree outside her window, her "kin," asks nothing but "To lean against the window and peer in / And watch [her] move about!" Personified nature is interested in her, but what of her own interest in nature? What does she make of her life, an existence "Full of tiny tragedies and grotesque grieves," as she looks back at nature? Central to our understanding of Bishop's work is our understanding of the tense moment when the poet turns her gaze from herself to the world. As she incorporated the natural world into her poetry, Bishop developed a voice that remains one of the most unique in American poetry. She captures subtle moments that are deeply felt and elegantly rendered, and in this tradition she was influenced by MARIANNE MOORE with whom, beginning in 1934, she maintained a lifelong friendship. In 1947 RANDALL JARRELL introduced her to ROBERT LOWELL, thus beginning a second lifelong friendship and mutual artistic influence. Bishop's impact is felt in the poetry of ANNE SEXTON, SYLVIA PLATH, and RITA DOVE—although Bishop never adopted the tradition of CONFESSIONAL POETRY, as did these poets. Her poems are absorbed with precisely capturing the world through language, and in this emphasis she is more closely aligned with the Metaphysical poet George Herbert, the romantic poet William Wordsworth, and the Victorian poet Gerard Manley Hopkins.

Bishop was born in Worcester, Massachusetts. Her father, William Thomas Bishop, died eight months after her birth. Her mother entered a mental institution in 1916, and Bishop lived in Great Village, Nova Scotia, with her mother's family. Bishop was never again to see her mother. In 1918 her paternal grandparents expressed concern about the rural education Bishop would receive in Nova Scotia, so she was moved to her aunt's house in Massachusetts. She graduated at Walnut Hill, a boarding school, in 1930 and enrolled at Vassar College, where she was a classmate of the poet MURIEL RUKEYSER. But it was travel, not the influence of other contemporary poets, that was the hallmark of her life. In Mexico during 1942–43, she met the Chilean poet Pablo Neruda. She traveled down the Amazon in 1961 with the novelist Aldous Huxley. Even in the final years of her life, while teaching at Harvard University, she continued her travels to Ecuador and Peru. For her work, Bishop was awarded the Pulitzer Prize for poetry in 1956 and the National Book Award in 1976. An important selection of her uncollected work and drafts was published as *Edgar Allan Poe & The Juke-Box* in 2006.

Journey is a central theme in Bishop's poetry; "These peninsulas take water between thumb and finger," Bishop writes in "The Map" (1946), "like women feeling for the smoothness of yard-goods." The landscape is rendered, by simile, into a domestic world: Topographical features become human, embracing the texture of nature. "More delicate than the historians' are the map-makers' colors," she claims. Through a different kind of perception—subtler, more intuitive than those who work with words—the mapmaker becomes the ultimate interpreter of the external world.

And so it is that artistic vision, expressed by the mapmaker, is understood to be a valid guide to our travels both to the external world of nature and to the internal world of individual consciousness. The depth of this vision is examined in "The Man-Moth" (1946) in which Bishop, working in the tradition of SURREALISM, imagines a creature who lives under the surface of the city, emerging, "trembling," to "investigate as high as he can climb." If we catch him, we are told to hold his tear, "cool as from underground springs and pure enough to drink." As a visionary in his own right, the

Man-Moth is the embodiment of the poet. His visionary tear is refreshing only because he holds himself apart from the world, living by night and perception alone. As Bishop makes clear in "The FISH" (1946), elusiveness yields perception; she ends that poem, "And I let the fish go."

"Questions of Travel" (1965) examines the tension that arises in the development of artistic vision itself. Should vision be developed in isolation, the poet asks, or should vision be broadened by experience? Recalling Blaise Pascal, Bishop wonders if we should just sit quietly in our room. The poem begins with an image of too many waterfalls, and the reader realizes that there is too much in the external world to be understood, much less analyzed in the brief time for observation. Yet, the poet concedes, it would have been a pity not to have seen Brazil, not to have had the moment in which, stopping for gasoline, she heard "the sad, two-noted wooden tune / of disparate wooden clogs" moving across the floor. In any other country, she concedes, the clogs would have been tested to have identical sound. The choice to open ourselves to experience is never free. The dilemma—to gain new experiences by travel or stay in one place and write—is made even more complex by the flawed nature of writing itself: There is cost both in the distracting nature of travel (which, paradoxically, yields experience) and in the troublesome, flawed act of writing (which, paradoxically, yields insight).

Bishop often built poems out of moments experienced in her journeys. In 1946 and 1947 she visited Nova Scotia. In a letter dated August 29, 1946, she wrote to Moore of her trip by bus back to the United States: "Early the next morning, just as it was getting light, the driver had to stop suddenly for a big cow moose who was wandering down the road. She walked away very slowly into the woods, looking at us over her shoulder." The bus driver had commented that these were "very curious beasts" (141). It was nearly 30 years before she published the memory of that bus trip in "The Moose" (1976). The 30-year-old memory of a bus ride as rendered in the poem lets us see the way the natural world provides a moment of grace, of easement from our troubling histories. If humans have an eternal tendency to recollect, then the presence of the moose gives us a moment away from our thoughts. As the moose looks the bus over, the poet asks, "Why, why do we feel (we all feel) this sweet / sensation of joy?" For Bishop, as David Kalstone proposes, "the actual existences that lie outside the self—geography, other minds, the world as prior creation—are like rafts, respite and rescue from guilt" (246). Through what Kalstone called her "creaturely" depiction of animals in the natural world, a technique evident also in the appearance of the little mammal in "The ARMADILLO" (1965), Bishop provides solace from thought and attendant regret.

In Bishop's poetry there is a need for respite. In the villanelle "One Art" (1976), the subject is loss. We are told to practice losing something every day, then practice "losing farther, losing faster." The "fluster of lost door keys" or an "hour badly spent" is loss of one kind; the loss of one we love is quite another. In the final quatrain of the poem, however, the poet's voice breaks as certainty dissolves. If the act of writing is taken to be a vehicle to help us cope with loss, then the vehicle is frail. The poet's voice falters in the wake of too great a loss.

"Sonnet" was published in the *New Yorker* after Bishop's death in 1979. At the end of her life, what did the poet think about when she turned her gaze to nature? She begins the poem with a single word: "Caught." The bubble in a carpenter's level is caught—"a creature divided," as too the compass needle is caught, "wobbling and wavering." The second movement in the poem begins with the single word *freed.* The mercury from a broken thermometer is free, as is the rainbow-bird who becomes free, "flying wherever / it feels like, gay!" But the tension remains for Bishop. The poem is, after all, a sonnet—one of the most challenging and potentially restraining of all poetic forms (see PROSODY AND FREE VERSE). A longing for freedom, juxtaposed with the presence of restraint, rests at the center of the poet's vision. The more we examine the description of contrast, the more we understand the poetry of Elizabeth Bishop.

BIBLIOGRAPHY

Bishop, Elizabeth. "Letter to Marianne Moore, 29 August 1946." In *One Art: Letters,* edited by Robert Giroux, 139–141. New York: Farrar, Straus & Giroux, 1994.

Kalstone, David. *Becoming a Poet: Elizabeth Bishop with Marianne Moore and Robert Lowell,* edited by Robert Hemenway, New York: Farrar, Straus & Giroux, 1989.

MacMahon, Candace W. *Elizabeth Bishop: A Bibliography.* Charlottesville: University Press of Virginia, 1980.

Spires, Elizabeth. "Elizabeth Bishop." In *Writers at Work: The Paris Review Interviews,* Sixth Series, edited by George Plimpton. New York: Penguin, 1985.

Norbert Elliot

BLACK ARTS MOVEMENT The Black Arts movement (or Movement) was a controversial literary faction that emerged in the mid-1960s as the artistic and aesthetic arm of the Black Power movement, a militant political operation that rejected the integrationist purposes and practices of the Civil Rights movement that preceded it. The Black Arts movement was one of the only American literary movements to merge art with a political agenda. Because poems were short and could be recited at rallies and other political activities to incite and move a crowd, poetry was the most popular literary genre of the Black Arts movement, followed closely by drama. Poet, playwright, activist, and major figure of the Black Arts movement, AMIRI BARAKA (formerly LeRoi Jones) coined the term *Black Arts* when he established his Black Arts Repertory Theatre/School in New York City's Harlem. Although the Black Arts movement began its decline during the mid-1970s, at the same time as the Black Power movement began its descent, it introduced a new breed of black poets and a new brand of black poetry. It also inspired and energized already established poets like GWENDOLYN BROOKS, and ROBERT HAYDEN. The Black Arts movement created many poetic innovations in form, language, and style that have influenced the work of many of today's spoken word artists and socially conscious rap lyricists.

The poets most often associated with the Black Arts movement include Baraka, SONIA SANCHEZ, ETHERIDGE KNIGHT, NIKKI GIOVANNI, Larry Neal, Mari Evans, Don L. Lee (now known as HAKI MADHUBUTI), Carolyn Rodgers, Marvin X, JAYNE CORTEZ, Askia Toure, and JUNE JORDAN.. A number of important African-American playwrights, fiction writers, and scholars also made significant contributions to the Black Arts movement, creatively as well as philosophically and theoretically, by defining and outlining the objectives and criteria of the movement and its "black aesthetic."

Several publishing houses and workshops were founded during the period of the movement, and several magazines and journals emerged, all of which provided a vehicle for the literary work of Black Arts poets. Literary publications, such as *Freedomways, Negro Digest* (later renamed *Black World*), the *Black Scholar,* the *Journal of Black Poetry,* and *Liberator,* brought Black Arts movement poets to a larger audience when more established publications rejected their work. Two important publishing houses—Dudley Randall's Broadside Press in Detroit and Madhubuti's Third World Press in Chicago—were also instrumental in helping to introduce new poets and to disseminate their work. Umbra Workshop (1962–65), composed of a group of black writers, produced *Umbra Magazine* and gained significance as a literary group that created a distinct voice and often challenged mainstream standards concerning literature. Lastly, Baraka's Black Arts Repertory Theatre/School, founded in 1965, brought free plays, poetry readings, and musical performances to the people of Harlem, thereby carrying out the idea of art as a communal experience.

The Black Power movement, from which the Black Arts movement derived, sought to empower African-American communities economically and politically by relying solely on resources within the black community. It also sought to celebrate blackness and restore positive images of black people from the negative stereotyping that took place in the larger society. Thus slogans, such as "Black Is Beautiful," were prominent during the time. Members of organizations, such as the Student Non-Violent Coordinating Committee (SNCC, under the leadership of Stokely Carmichael, and the Black Panther Party, founded by Huey Newton and Bobby Seale, demanded racial equality, not through the methods of passive resistance associated with Dr. Martin Luther King, Jr., but "by any means necessary" (a slogan of the party), including "violent revolution," as stated by Malcolm X. Moreover, "black cultural nationalism," the belief that blacks and whites had two separate worldviews and outlooks on life, was a prominent idea in both the Black Power and the Black Arts movements. As a result, Black Arts movement writers experimented with methods of artistic expression that were characteristic of African-American culture and experience. First all of the poetry was infused with a certain level of black consciousness, meaning that its subjects and themes reflected the quality and character of black experience. In form, Black Arts movement poets often rejected standard English in favor of Black English, a more colloquial and vernacular language and syntax. They peppered it with street slang and idiomatic phrases that were simple, direct, explicit, and often irreverent. In addition the poetry borrowed greatly from black music, using rhythmical effects from jazz and blues, as well as from other forms of black oral speech, such as sermons, folktales, signifying (an intricate, humorous language style that uses indirection, innuendo, puns, metaphors, and other wordplay to persuade, argue, send a message, or insult), and the dozens (a form of signifying that involves trading insults, primarily about a person's relatives). Other common features of the poetry include free verse, short line lengths, call-and-response patterns, chanting, and free rhyming.

The Black Arts movement had much in common with another period of increased artistic production among African-American writers—the HARLEM RENAISSANCE of the 1920s. During both periods, there was an increased interest in establishing a more assertive black collective identity than had previously existed (during the Harlem Renaissance, it was called "the New Negro") and in searching for ethnic identity and heritage in folk and African culture. Thus poets from both periods experimented with folk elements, such as blues, spirituals, and vernacular idioms in their poetry, and venerated Africa. However, despite these similarities, many Black Arts movement writers were critical of the objectives of the Harlem Renaissance, believing it had failed to link itself concretely to the struggle of the black masses. Adherents of the Black Arts movement were also critical of Harlem Renaissance writers' reliance on white patronage, as well as their tendency to esteem Western art, to desire mainstream recognition, and to write with a white audience in mind. They felt that this compromised black writers' ability to be completely honest in their depiction and expression of black life and struggle.

The Black Arts movement established a number of objectives and criteria for its creative artists to follow. Primary among them was to persuade African Americans to reject the mainstream culture and the process of Americanization and assimilation, instead encouraging them to embrace a "black aesthetic," whereby black people would look to their own culture and aesthetic values to create and evaluate African-American literature. The three major criteria of the Black Arts movement, established by Ron Karenga, were that all black art must be "functional, collective, and committed" (33). The functional nature of black art meant that the literary work must serve a purpose larger than merely the creation of art. It had to be connected to the social and political struggles in which African-American people were engaged. The second criterion, that black art must be "collective," meant that it must serve the people; it must educate, inspire, and uplift them. Reciprocally, the artist must learn from and be inspired and uplifted by the people. The artist must be prepared to sacrifice her or his own individuality and, instead, always write with the good of the people in mind. Third and lastly, black art must be committed to political and social reform and supportive of the revolution that will bring this about. In essence the Black Arts movement's objectives were to reach the masses of black people, to make them understand their message of self-sufficiency and dignity, and to inspire them to act upon it.

Many of the criteria and objectives of the Black Arts movement are discernible within the poetry itself. For example, in "From the Egyptian" in his 1966 collection *Black Art,* Baraka makes clear that violent confrontation with the oppressors of black people is an imminent reality as he asserts that he is prepared to murder "the enemies / of my father." Likewise, in "The True Import of Present Dialogue, Black vs. Negro" in *Black Feeling, Black Talk* (1968), Giovanni tells black people: "We ain't got to prove we can die / We got to prove we can kill." Giovanni also demonstrates the criterion of commitment with "My Poem" (1968), when she writes in support of the revolution and its enduring nature, stating that "if i never do anything / it will go on." The didacticism of much Black Arts poetry is visible in Baraka's "A School of Prayer" (1966). In this poem,

Baraka tells his black audience: "Do not obey their laws." "Their," of course, refers to white society. Essentially Baraka urges black people to rebel against white authority and be wary of the words spoken by those who seek to oppress them because their purpose is to deceive black people and curtail their advancement. The celebration of blackness is also noticeable in Black Arts poetry. Sanchez, perhaps the female poet most closely identified with the Black Arts movement, reclaims the dignity of black womanhood in an unnamed poem in her volume *We a BaddDDD People* (1970), when she links herself as a black woman to a regal African queen who will, "Walk / move in / blk queenly ways." Similarly, in "Ka Ba" (1969), Baraka affirms the uniqueness of black expressive culture and of black people, whom he describes as "full of masks and dances and swelling chants / with African eyes and noses and arms," despite the present condition of oppression and degradation under which many African Americans live. In both of these poems, Sanchez and Baraka seek to restore to black people a positive representation of blackness and raise their collective sense of identity.

Many of the poems in Sanchez's collection *We a BaddDDD People* exemplify experimentation with language. In "indianapolis/summer/1969/poem," Sanchez provides a new spelling of the words *mothers* ("mothas"), *fathers* ("fathas"), and *sisters* ("sistuhs"); the word *about* becomes "bout," the word *black* becomes "blk," and the word I becomes "i." The changes in spelling, as well as the use of nonstandard English in Sanchez's poems, are meant to capture the syntax and vernacular speech of many within the black community, while the abbreviated spelling of "blk" and the lower case "i" are part of Sanchez's refusal to adhere to the rules of standard English. Many Black Arts poets perceived language to be a tool of the oppressor and therefore sought ways to make it their own. Lastly, the use of pejorative terminology and irreverent language was also common among Black Arts poets. The police were often referred to as "pigs," and white people were termed "honkies" or "crackers."

Several criticisms have been leveled against the Black Arts movement. One was that it tended only to address issues of race and to promote racial hatred. Also the functional aspect of the Black Arts movement came to be denounced by newly emerging black literary critics who claimed that the literature itself was often subordinate to the political or social message of the movement. These critics saw this as detrimental to black literature, creating a narrowness of focus that creatively limited the artist and the kinds of literature he or she could compose. In addition there was a tendency in the Black Arts movement to devise theories prior to the creation of an actual body of literature that would prove the theory. Therefore the literature was driven by the theory rather than the other way around. Lastly, some Black Arts movement writers were known to judge harshly any black writer who did not conform to the criteria and objectives of the movement. Even black writers of the past were not exempt from being maligned, and Black Arts movement writers often did criticize them without always taking into consideration the historical period and context in which these past writers were composing their literature.

Still the Black Arts movement's influence and contributions to American poetry were far reaching. It made literary artists rethink the function and purpose of their work and their responsibility to their communities and to society. It also influenced and continues to inspire new generations of poets to experiment with a variety of artistic forms to refuse the pressure to conform to Western standards of art and to write, embrace, and derive their art from within their own expressive culture.

BIBLIOGRAPHY

Baraka, Amiri, and Larry Neal, eds. *Black Fire: An Anthology of Afro-American Writing.* New York: William Morrow, 1968.

Gayle, Addison. *The Black Aesthetic.* Garden City, N.Y.: Doubleday, 1971.

Henderson, Stephen. *Understanding the New Black Poetry: Black Speech and Black Music as Poetic Reference.* New York: William Morrow, 1973.

Karenga, Ron. "Black Cultural Nationalism." In *The Black Aesthetic,* edited by Addison Gayle, 32–38. Garden City, N.Y.: Doubleday, 1971.

Ama S. Wattley

BLACKBURN, PAUL (1926–1971) Paul Blackburn is an indispensable figure in American poetry, not only for his innovations in poetic form but for his other contributions to the contemporary American poetic community. His influences—which include Provençal troubadour poetry of the Middle Ages, EZRA POUND, WILLIAM CARLOS WILLIAMS, CHARLES OLSON, and other figures of the BLACK MOUNTAIN SCHOOL—were many, but, in turn, his influence on late 20th-century American poetry is an essential one. He was an important innovator in the contemporary sound and form of free verse, both on the page and in performance. He also shaped the public poetry reading as we know it today and helped make New York City a vital locale for poetry.

Blackburn was born in St. Albans, Vermont, where his mother, writer Frances Frost, left him to the repressive and sometimes violent care of his grandmother. At the age of 14, Frost took him to live with her in Greenwich Village in New York City. Blackburn went to New York University in 1947, where he studied with M. L. Rosenthal and discovered the work of Pound. In 1949 he transferred to the University of Wisconsin, Madison, from where he would hitchhike to Washington, D.C., to visit Pound, who introduced him to poets, such as ROBERT CREELEY. Blackburn's first book of translations of the medieval Provençal poetry, *Proensa,* was published in 1953, and his first collection of poetry, *The Dissolving Fabric,* was published in 1955, both by Creeley's Divers Press (see POETRY PRESSES). In 1954 Blackburn received a Fulbright Fellowship to study at the University of Toulouse in France. In 1956 he moved to Spain, where he began his lifelong translations of Federico García Lorca, published posthumously as *Lorca/Blackburn.* His other translations include Julio Cortazar's *Blow-Up and Other Stories* and Pablo Picasso's *Hunk of Skin.* While Blackburn neither attended nor taught at Black Mountain College, he briefly worked for *Black Mountain Review* and was grouped with the Black Mountain poets in Donald Allen's influential 1960 anthology, *The New American Poetry 1945–1960* (see POETRY ANTHOLOGIES). In 1967 he received a Guggenheim Fellowship. He taught at the State University of New York at Cortland and elsewhere.

Called by Daniel Kane "the man perhaps most responsible for developing a vibrant poetic community on the Lower East Side" (160), Blackburn organized a Wednesday Night reading series at Le Metro Café, which he suggested moving to St. Mark's Church in 1966, helping to create the still-extant Poetry Project. From 1964 to 1965, he ran a poetry radio show at WBAI. "He was an indefatigable attender of all types of poetry readings, and he carried his large double-reel tape recorder with him wherever he went; his tape collection, now at the University of California, San Diego, is probably the best oral history of the New York poetry scene from the 1950s up until 1970," says Edith Jarolim (xxix).

Creeley, in his preface to *Against the Silences* (1980), says, "Paul was without question a far more accomplished craftsman than I" (11). Blackburn's ear for the poetic "breath" and his eye for how words should be spaced on a page were indeed remarkably acute. His ability, honed by his prodigious reading and translating, allowed him to revolutionize poetic form, integrating natural speech and everyday observations into a vibrant poetic space. "Brooklyn Narcissus" (1958), "Clickety-Clack" (1958/1960)—also an example of Blackburn's sometimes controversial attitude toward women—and "Meditation on the BMT" (1959) are examples of the "subway poem," a form Blackburn is credited with inventing. While these poems may at first appear to be loose, almost journalistic observations (see *The* JOURNALS), the intricate sound and placement of words on the page reveal the poems' craft. In "Brooklyn Narcissus," Blackburn cleverly echoes ROBERT FROST's poem "Stopping by Woods on a Snowy Evening" (1923): "But I have premises to keep / & local stops before I sleep."

"The Watchers" (1963) shows Blackburn's ability to discover significance within the small details of life. Ostensibly about construction workers operating a "CIVETTA LINK-BELT" crane, Blackburn sees poetry in the crane's "graceless geometry" and a reference to the avian crane's meaning to the ancient Greeks: "The crane moves slowly, that / much it is graceful." A sense of eternal, mythological time in human history is also expressed in "AT THE WELL" (1963), a poem of mysterious yet familiar desert figures who seem to indicate, somehow, the origin of human speech: "Can I offer them some sound / my mouth makes in the night?" This poem is one of the most striking examples of

Blackburn's "ear," with complex off rhymes, typographical "pauses" in the form of spaces between periods and words, and unexpected line breaks.

Toward the end of his life, Blackburn wrote in a new poetic form that he titled "journals," which Jarolim calls "Final evidence of Blackburn's continual struggle, often with himself, to extend the boundaries of what could be considered poetry's fit subject and form" (xxxii). While in many ways the logical extension of Blackburn's interest in chronicling everyday details, the journals did indeed extend the boundaries of poetry and what was seen as acceptable poetic vocabulary and content, presenting acute and not always comfortable observations on the nature of his own illness, love, and mortality. In many ways, *The Journals* (1975) were the final push toward achieving a true equality of subject: Nothing should be beneath the interest of the poet, as all is equally compelling.

BIBLIOGRAPHY

Creeley, Robert. Preface to *Against the Silences,* by Paul Blackburn. New York: Permanent Press, 1980, pp. 11–13.

Jarolim, Edith. Introduction to *The Collected Poems of Paul Blackburn*. New York: Persea Editions, 1985, pp. xxix–xxxii.

Kane, Daniel. *All Poets Welcome: The Lower East Side Poetry Scene in the 1960s.* Berkeley: University of California Press, 2003.

Marcella Durand

BLACK MOUNTAIN SCHOOL What came to be known as the Black Mountain school of poetry represented, in mid-20th-century America, the crossroads of poetic innovation. The name of this poetic movement derives from Black Mountain College in North Carolina, an experimental college founded in 1933. By the time the poet and essayist CHARLES OLSON became its rector in 1950, it had become a mecca for a larger artistic and intellectual avant-garde. Until it closed in 1957, the college was the seedbed for virtually all of America's later artistic innovations. A vast array of writers, painters, sculptors, dancers, composers, and many other people involved in the creative arts passed through the college's doors as teachers or students.

The poets most often associated with the name Black Mountain are, primarily, Olson, ROBERT CREELEY, and ROBERT DUNCAN, along with DENISE LEVERTOV, PAUL BLACKBURN, PAUL CARROLL, WILLIAM BRONK, LARRY EIGNER, EDWARD DORN, JONATHAN WILLIAMS, JOEL OPPENHEIMER, JOHN WIENERS, THEODORE ENSLIN, Ebbe Borregard, RUSSELL EDSON, M. C. Richards, and Michael Rumaker (a few of these never attended the college but are nevertheless associated with the college group, because of their poetic styles or their representation in certain literary magazines discussed below). Many other important intellectuals and artists were also involved in what amounted to an artistic revolution.

Today Black Mountain poetry may seem to contain a great variety of styles and themes. Regardless, there are some common characteristics to be noticed in this poetry: the use of precise language, direct statement, often plain (even blunt) diction, and metonymy (a figure of speech whereby a phrase or word stands in for something with which it is closely associated) rather than metaphor or simile. These writerly tendencies evolved in reaction to earlier poetry that was strictly metered, end-rhymed, and filled with grand diction and monumental subject matter. The reaction by the Black Mountain poets was a continuation of a poetic revolution begun by those in the IMAGIST SCHOOL and later the OBJECTIVIST school. In general Black Mountain poets typically refrain from commenting on their personal appraisal of a scene evoked in a poem, and this strategy can even mean the avoidance of adjectives and adverbs. As Ezra Pound had pronounced early in the century (in describing the poetry of H. D.), poetry should be "laconic speech," "Objective," without "slither—direct," and containing "No metaphors that won't permit examination.—It's straight talk" (11). Besides its alignment with imagism and, later, objectivism, Black Mountain poetry can be said to descend, especially in its embrace of individualism, from such 19th-century New England writers as Henry David Thoreau and, particularly, Ralph Waldo Emerson. As EDWARD FOSTER has written, Emerson's essay "Self-Reliance" gave the many Black Mountain poets, "despite their radical differences in personality, sensibility, and general ambitions, a common apprehension about what a poem might achieve" (xiii). The poem could be an extension of themselves as persons, as individuals standing apart from the ideals of an orthodox past.

Philosophically Black Mountain poetry also shares a view of reality—of the physical world and humanity's relationship to it—derived from scientific movements of its time, movements that contradicted the view of a stable and predictable universe set forth in earlier times by thinkers such as Sir Isaac Newton (1643–1727) and, later, Immanuel Kant (1724–1804). Olson, Creeley, Duncan, and others were interested in the modern ideas of Albert Einstein, who formulated the theory of relativity, and Werner Heisenberg, who postulated his theory of uncertainty relations. Physical reality was relative to time, according to Einstein; according to Heisenberg, it was simply indeterminate and incomplete. Creeley has therefore argued:

> The world cannot be "known" entirely. . . . In all disciplines of human attention and act, the possibilities inherent in the previous conception of a Newtonian universe—with its containment and thus the possibility of being known—have been yielded. We do not know the world in that way, nor will we. Reality is continuous, not separable, and cannot be objectified. We cannot stand aside to see it. (115–16)

The reliance in Black Mountain poetry, and its "objectivist" forebears, on direct statement and metonymy is a symptom of this basic outlook on the world. What is unknowable finally can nevertheless be beautiful. This poetry, then, poses a fundamental problem of perception. In "Love," an early poem by Creeley, there are the sure "particulars," such as "oak, the grain of, oak," and there are also, by contrast, "what supple shadows may come / to be here." These details hold within themselves a tension between the stable and the radical, the known and the continually evolving.

The literary magazines associated with the Black Mountain school, the *Black Mountain Review, Origin* and, to a lesser extent, the *San Francisco Review,* were a haven for writers whose aesthetics and point of view were found to be unacceptable by the mainstream POETRY JOURNALS of the time. Indeed it is within the issues of these magazines that the Black Mountain sensibility truly coalesces. Edited by Creeley and CID CORMAN, respectively, the *Black Mountain Review* and *Origin* published now well-known figures such as (besides the poets named above) Jorge Luis Borges, William Burroughs (under the name of William Lee), Paul Celan, Judson Crews, René Daumal, Fielding Dawson, André du Bouchet, Katue Kitasono, Irving Layton, JAMES MERRILL, Eugenio Montale, Samuel French Morse, James Purdy, KENNETH REXROTH, Hubert Selby, Jr., Kusano Shimpei, GARY SNYDER, JOHN TAGGART, Gael Turnbull, César Vallejo, PHILIP WHALEN, RICHARD WILBUR, and WILLIAM CARLOS WILLIAMS. Later issues of *Origin,* in the 1960s, featured work by LOUIS ZUKOFSKY, Snyder, Zeami Motokiyo, Margaret Avison, ROBERT KELLY, Ian Hamilton Finlay, Turnbull, Corman, Duncan, Francis Ponge, Frank Samperi, LORINE NIEDECKER, du Bouchet, Shimpei, Bronk, Josef Albers, and others.

The ARS POETICA, or manifesto, of the Black Mountain movement is usually identified with Olson's 1950 essay "Projective Verse," published in *Poetry New York,* a magazine that preceded these others, Olson's fully defined formula for poetry being projective or open field verse. In this essay, Olson discusses the importance of composing poetry according to the breathing of the individual poet or speaker of a poem and not according to a predetermined set form of speech or verse. There are two aspects of a poem, he maintains: "the HEAD, by way of the EAR, to the SYLLABLE [and] the HEART, by way of the BREATH, to the LINE" (55). The breath of the poet "allows all the speech-force of language." Moreover, a poem should never have any slack, or, as Olson puts it, "ONE PERCEPTION MUST IMMEDIATELY AND DIRECTLY LEAD TO A FURTHER PERCEPTION" (52). Hence the poet must "USE USE USE the process at all points" so that a perception can "MOVE, INSTANTER, ON ANOTHER" (53). Perhaps the essence of what Olson is saying comes from Creeley's belief, as quoted by Olson in this essay, that "FORM IS NEVER MORE THAN AN EXTENSION OF CONTENT" (52).

The openness of the poetry Olson advocated can be seen in Duncan's poem, "Often I Am Permitted to Return to a Meadow," which begins his volume of poetry entitled, fittingly, *The Opening of the Field* (1960). In this poem Duncan is involved with the personal creative process and the bid for freedom that poetry (implicitly, Black Mountain poetry) makes possible; writing is a "place of first permission," Duncan asserts.

The meadow referred to in the poem's title is possibly real, tangible, yet it exists, more importantly, "as if it were a scene made-up by the mind"; still, it is a place apart from the poem's persona and, in fact, it is "a made place, created by light / wherefrom the shadows that are forms fall." Duncan's vision of poetic reality is akin, it seems, to a classically Platonic view of the world in which ideal forms reside beyond human perception, with the things humanity can know similar to them but not perfectly the same, much as shadows of objects are like the objects themselves. The point here is that readers suppose places they inhabit "*as if* . . . certain bounds [could] hold against chaos" (emphasis added), and therefore the poem stresses how very delicate perception is and underscores the individual's seeing.

Likewise, Olson creates, in his epic work *The MAXIMUS POEMS* (1960–83), a towering persona, Maximus, who looks out upon a vast geography informed by a historical past. The singularity of this figure is meant to compare with the immensity of Olson's subject, the vast terrain beneath Maximus's feet, grounded in Gloucester, Massachusetts, and stretching across North America, and the history beginning in ancient Greece and running up through a present American time. There is tangibility, as when Maximus says that there are "facts, to be dealt with"; on the other hand, he asks, "that which matters, that which insists, that which will last, / that! o my people, where shall you find it, how, where"? In Olson's work readers discover an astonishing sweep of history, a breadth of vision, and the eternal verities laid out—yet these truths are tried by Olson, tested, and, finally, undone. Olson is reconceiving both space (physical geography) and time (the history of his civilization) according to the new paradigms set forth by Emerson and Thoreau, Einstein and Heisenberg. Yet this grasp does not neglect the eternally human condition and accounts for death and suffering as well as triumph and splendor. Hence in "The Kingfishers" (1949), he observes that human beings are capable of precision: "The factors are / in the animal and/or the machine"; they "involve . . . a discrete or continuous sequence of measurable events distributed in time." All the same, Olson says that what endures is change itself, a theme he strikes at the poem's outset and reprises throughout: "What does not change / is the will to change." This concept is perceivable in all things: "hear, where the dry blood talks / where the old appetite walks."

Olson's point of view is echoed in Levertov's work. In her poem "Beyond the End" (1953), human destiny is constrained by natural forces, yet the point of it all is not merely to "go on living' but to quicken, to activate, extend." The "will to respond" is a force unbounded by reason, and so we reside always "further, beyond the end / beyond whatever ends: to begin, to be, to defy." What stands out in both Levertov and Olson is the precise stipulation of limits and the recognition of something outside them, which can best be evoked with exacting language.

This use of language is nicely exemplified by Oppenheimer, who was a student of Olson, Creeley, and others at Black Mountain College. Not only is his work precise, coming out of his student experience, but it is also rhythmic according to the measure of a reader's breathing, as was stipulated in Olson's essay. Moreover, Oppenheimer's signature diction is, for its time, breathtakingly casual and candid, reflecting the social revolution in America that was to reach its height in the late 1960s. Oppenheimer's poetry is located in the moments of a daily life. In his poem "The Bath" (1953), the acts of living are simple, for instance, the act of taking a bath. His lover's bathing, Oppenheimer finds, is a ritual, albeit one unremarked upon but for his verse—and yet, he humorously points out, "she wants him" (the poem's persona thinks) "unbathed"; he is gratified by her desire. The routine of life is celebrated in the poem by this nexus between the two of them; there is "her continuous bathing. / in his tub. in his water. wife."

Black Mountain College was the soil for virtually all later experimental poetry in America and much of America's later art and music. Grounded in the poetry of Pound and Williams—as Creeley writes in his homage to Williams, "For W. C. W." (1963): "and and becomes // just so"—as well as demonstrating great sympathy for the objectivist poetry of Louis Zukofsky and the others of this school, the later Black Mountain writers continued a tradition of exact perception, an avoidance of metaphor, and of a celebration of the individual that would also emerge in BEAT POETRY. The Black Mountain contribution to American poetry was not merely a new version of these other movements, but rather it was original and, arguably, the pivotal moment in modern American poetic history.

BIBLIOGRAPHY

Carter, Steven. *Bearing Across: Studies in Literature and Science.* San Francisco: International Scholars Publications, 1998.

Creeley, Robert. *A Sense of Measure.* London: Calder and Boyars, 1973.

Dawson, Fielding. *The Black Mountain Book, a New Edition.* Rocky Mount: North Carolina Wesleyan College Press, 1991.

Foster, Edward Halsey. *Understanding the Black Mountain Poets.* Columbia: University of South Carolina Press, 1995.

Lane, Melvin, ed. *Black Mountain College: An Anthology of Personal Accounts.* Knoxville: University of Tennessee Press, 1990.

Olson, Charles. "Projective Verse." In *Human Universe and Other Essays,* edited by Donald Allen, 51–62. New York: Grove Press, 1967.

Paul, Sherman. *Olson's Push: Origin, Black Mountain and Recent American Poetry.* Baton Rouge: Louisiana State University Press, 1978.

Pound, Ezra. *Selected Letters,* edited by D. D. Paige. New York: New Directions, 1971.

Burt Kimmelman

BLACKMUR, R(ICHARD) P(ALMER) (1904–1965)

R. P. Blackmur's allusive and psychologically complex poetry of the mid-20th century reflects the influence of earlier poets of MODERNISM, such as EZRA POUND, T. S. ELIOT, and HART CRANE. Blackmur's credo, that "only within order can you give disorder room" (Fraser 86), is reflected in his carefully crafted poems on themes commonly explored in the personal lyric (see LYRIC POETRY), including love, death, loneliness, frustration, and faith, while a number of his later poems reflect more worldly concerns with the upheavals of the mid-20th century. Showing restraint and a distrust of the excessively emotional, they reflect Blackmur's wariness of speaking with finality.

Blackmur was born and raised in Cambridge, Massachusetts. His first book of poetry, *From Jordan's Delight,* appeared in 1937, and from 1940 until his death he taught at Princeton University. Blackmur held Guggenheim Fellowships from 1937 to 1939 and was elected to the National Institute of Arts and Letters (1956) and to the American Academy of Arts and Letters (1964).

Blackmur's poems seem often to give the effect of almost straining to find their most effective expression, using striking and subtle juxtapositions of words with a difficult syntax that requires multiple readings. Consonance, assonance, and alliteration are used to subtle effect, and biblical and other literary allusions as well as sea imagery are common. Blackmur writes in a variety of line, meter, and stanza forms and sometimes creates his own formal arrangements, while also using conventional ones, such as the sonnet.

In "Redwing," the first part of "From Jordan's Delight" (1937), stark sea imagery, alliteration, and assonance are used in an iambic pentameter line set in six-line stanzas to portray a seaman long ago jilted, who while "wilted waits for water still." His loneliness is offset, however, by an "excruciation that redeems," made possible through his work in the harsh marine environment. Blackmur writes in his more public mode in commenting on post-World War II political conditions in "The Communiqués from Yalta" (1947). While the "salvo sounds" of conventional warfare have been stilled, Blackmur describes a more insidious conflict symbolized by the sound of a metaphorical "fire raking" the hopes for an ultimate postwar peace. The final lines of the poem allude to the text of Luke 23:31 and end with a feminine rhyme, implying a resignation that such conflicts are bound to be eternal.

While Blackmur wrote poetry seriously throughout his life, he is today primarily known for his critical writings. With fellow poet-critics ROBERT PENN WARREN, ALLEN TATE, and JOHN CROWE RANSOM, Blackmur came to be associated with New Criticism (see FUGITIVE/AGRARIAN SCHOOL). New Criticism greatly influenced the teaching of literature in American universities by introducing close reading techniques focusing on detailed and subtle linguistic and formal analyses of literature, particularly poetry. Blackmur's critical works include *The Double Agent* (1935) and *Language as Gesture* (1952).

BIBLIOGRAPHY

Donoghue, Denis. Introduction to *Poems of R. P. Blackmur.* Princeton, N.J.: Princeton University Press, 1977, pp. ix–xxix.

Fraser, Russell. "The Poetry of R. P. Blackmur." *Southern Review* 15 (1979): 86–100.

Sue Barker

BLASER, ROBIN (1925–) While Robin Blaser claims that 1955 marks the beginning of his lifelong career as a poet ("The Fire" 242), from as early as the late 1940s, he—along with ROBERT DUNCAN and JACK SPICER—played an integral part in the Berkeley-based SAN FRANCISCO RENAISSANCE. During this period he and Spicer formulated a poetics of what they came to call "seriality"—a formulation that expressed aesthetic, political, social, and ethical concerns. Widely acknowledged as a seminal development in 20th-century American poetry, Blaser's engagement with the serial poem (see LONG AND SERIAL POETRY) has influenced both American poets (such as ROBERT CREELEY, CHARLES BERNSTEIN, SUSAN HOWE, CHARLES OLSON, and LOUIS ZUKOFSKY) and Canadian poets (such as bpNichol, George Bowering, and Daphne Marlatt) (see CANADIAN POETIC INFLUENCES). However, despite such a wide-ranging influence, the combination of Blaser's densely packed, philosophically informed writing with his dual citizenship (Blaser is still viewed as a writer who is "indigenous" to neither the United States nor Canada) is generally acknowledged as the most obvious reason for the lack of critical acclaim for his work.

Born in Denver, Colorado, Blaser spent his childhood with his father and grandmother in small communities throughout Idaho. After briefly attending Northwestern University and the College of Idaho, Blaser began a nine-year-long education at the University of California in 1944. He left Berkeley in 1955 with a M.A. and M.L.S. to take up a position in the Widener Library at Harvard. It was at this point that Blaser began to establish himself as a poet separate from his Berkeley counterparts; as he writes in "The Fire" (1967), "I have worked since 1955 to find a line which will hold what I see and hear, and which will tie a reader to the poems, not to me" (242). In the period between his stay in Boston and his acceptance of a position at Simon Fraser University in British Columbia in 1966, Blaser published his first significant works: *The Moth Poem* (1964) and *Les Chimères: Translations of Nerval for Fran Herndon* (1965). Thereafter his work is marked by the piecemeal publication of the major serial poem *Image-Nation* (1962–93), which eventually appears alongside other individual poems in *Syntax* (1983) and *Pell Mell* (1988). To date, the culmination of Blaser's publication history has been the appearance of *The Holy Forest* (1993), which contains most of his major work from 1956 to 1993. In 2006, Blaser received a special lifetime recognition award from the Griffin Trust for Excellence in Poetry.

Even a cursory glance at *The Holy Forest* reveals the foundational importance of the serial poem; works, such as *Image-Nations* (1962–93), *The Truth Is Laughter* (1979–88), and *Great Companions* (1971 and 1988), appear all throughout and enable Blaser continually to work out the correspondences and contradictions between crucial issues, such as the imaginary and the real, self and other, and public and private. In fact the serial poem is a process-oriented form used to make manifest relationships among the verse segments and to allow these relationships to emerge in such a way that denies lyric control and allows the poem to take on a life of its own.

In the poems of *Image-Nation,* image—the image as a nation and the nation as an image—is one of the dominant tropes through which Blaser explores such relations. As he writes in "Particles" (1969), "Greek and Roman political experience argues that to act intelligently in the public realm requires a vision of things. The words themselves, *vision* and *things,* are telling. Vision, full of that sense of seeing and image, which [is] basic to knowing" (36). Images, as the source of vision, then, are necessary to present knowledge (of public, private, political, social, and linguistic life) and future action—without which we are left homeless, living out less-than-human lives: "as the image wears away / there is a wind in the heart." Drawing from the work of philosophers Hannah Arendt, Alfred North Whitehead, Maurice Merleau-Ponty, and Michel Serres, Blaser is able to bring a constellation of sometimes conflicting poetic concerns to his notion of image to tease out the nature of our single and twin existence. In "Image-Nation 2 (roaming)" a scare-marked "'you'" first sees an image of a burning horse, which then transforms into a flaming eye and a charred log; however, while "'you'" sees, "'you'" refuses to take on the larger task of seeing: visioning the world. Because of the dangers inherent in moving from a superficially named position (a 'you' who merely observes, never to become "you" or "I") to a position that is both named and lived, "'you'" refuses participation in the public world: "turned by that privacy / from such public perils as words / are, we travel in company with the messenger." A powerful influence on Blaser's address of the public and the private is Arendt, who argues in *The Human Condition* (1958) that the loss of the public world means the loss of both our sense of singularity and difference and the world we hold in common. Blaser, however, wants to be clear that—guided by a poetics of "roaming"—the public world and its words are always there to be taken up again, to be read and written once more. As he writes in "Image-Nation 15 (the lacquer house)": "the point is transformation of the theme—/ enjoinment and departure—."

BIBLIOGRAPHY

Blaser, Robin. "The Fire." In *The Poetics of the New American Poetry,* edited by Donald Allen and Warren Tallman, 235–246. New York: Grove Press, 1974.

———. "Particles." *Pacific Nation* 2 (1969): 27–42.

Nichols, Miriam. *Even on Sunday: Essays, Readings, and Archival Materials on the Poetry and Poetics of Robin Blaser.* Orono, Maine: National Poetry Foundation, 2002.

Truitt, Samuel R. "An Interview with Robin Blaser." *Talisman: A Journal of Contemporary Poetry and Poetics* 16 (1996): 5–25.

Watts, Charles, and Edward Byrne, eds. *Recovery of the Public World: Essays on Poetics in Honour of Robin Blaser.* Vancouver, British Columbia: Talonbooks, 1999.

Lori Emerson

"A BLESSING" **JAMES WRIGHT (1963)** Exemplifying the midwestern pastoral imagery and plainspoken voice that he developed in his poetry, JAMES WRIGHT's "A Blessing" is one of Wright's best-known and most moving poems. As one of the concluding poems of his groundbreaking collection *The Branch Will Not Break,* in which Wright shifted from his earlier formal verse to an image-centered, highly intuitive free verse, "A Blessing" suggests that the poet has arrived at the state of inner peace he sought earlier in the volume, having tried to escape the inner turmoil documented by a poem like "Lying in a Hammock at William Duffy's Farm in Pine Island, Minnesota." Set in a horse pasture beside a highway, "A Blessing" uses images of human intimacy with nature to explore themes of loneliness, friendship, and spiritual fulfillment.

"Just off the highway to Rochester, Minnesota," the poem begins, immediately emphasizing the reality and ordinariness of the setting as a way of suggesting that the poetic epiphany can take place anywhere. (In the original draft of the poem, this first line was the title, though Wright later changed it to the current title). The speaker, accompanied by a friend, visits a pasture where two ponies graze, and the companions cross over a barbed-wire fence in order to greet the ponies. The scene is pastoral, but Wright alters the traditional pastoral, in which two shepherds speak to each other about beauty or love, by having the speaker and his friend greet the ponies in silence, with the beauty of the scene rendered entirely through imagery. The paired ponies therefore reflect the relationship between the speaker and his friend, who remains a quiet presence throughout. When the speaker (ostensibly Wright) embraces one of the ponies who approaches him, he experiences a remarkable epiphany—"if I stepped out of my body I would break / Into blossom." This insight is brought about by contact with nature, and the image Wright chooses to express it is a metaphor for the blossoming of a flower or tree. But the image also conveys the jubilation that follows the defeat of the accumulated loneliness Wright suffers throughout *The Branch Will Not Break;* indeed, as Peter Stitt notes, the poem "attempts to achieve a miracle. . . . This is the moment of supreme consecration of man by nature in Wright's poetry, and the key to the happiness in the volume" (22). The encounter with the ponies transforms the loneliness that has afflicted the speaker, so that the ponies' solitude is ultimately an affirmative experience of togetherness: "They bow shyly as wet swans. They love each other. / There is no loneliness like theirs."

At the time that Wright finished *The Branch Will Not Break,* he had been living with his friend, the poet ROBERT BLY, at his farm in western Minnesota, after Wright's dismissal from the University of Minnesota and his struggles with alcoholism. His stay on Bly's farm, as Wright often said, saved his life, and this poem expresses the blessing Wright felt came from his friendship with Bly and from his close contact with the natural world. Commenting on the origins of this poem, Bly (who is the speaker's silent companion) writes that "Those years were a moment of genuine longing for a fresh and subtle poetry, and Jim's lines stand as linguistic expressions of that longing" ("Correspondence," 107). The longing for rebirth cannot be understated either thematically or in the context of Wright's life. Echoing personal comments by the poet RICHARD HUGO, critic David Pink connects the poem's theme of reincarnation with Wright's painful recovery from alcoholism (44–45). Pink also notes that with a highway running right beside this pasture, the poem is a fine example of situational irony: while the poet experiences his reverie, cars are perhaps passing in the background. Thus, for as much as the poem is about beauty, reincarnation, and love, it is also about the power of the will, which can shut out the ugliness of the world in order to embrace its beauty.

BIBLIOGRAPHY

Genoways, Ted, Robert Bly, and James Wright. "Robert Bly and James Wright: A Correspondence." *The Virginia Quarterly Review* 81, no. 1 (2005): 104–131.

Pink, David. "Wright's 'A Blessing.'" *The Explicator* 54, no. 1 (1995): 44–45.

Stitt, Peter. "The Poetry of James Wright." *The Minnesota Review* 2, no. 1 (1972): 13–32.

Temple Cone

BLY, ROBERT (1926–) Robert Bly is a central figure for American poetry in the second half of the 20th century, known as much for his roles as editor, translator, and social critic as for poet. Bly as editor shook up the comfortable literary establishment of the 1950s (in his magazine *The Fifties,* its name changing with each decade) by arguing passionately about poetry and politics and by criticizing other poets and editors. As a translator of Pablo Neruda and César Vallejo, Antonio Machado and Federico García Lorca, Georg Trakl and Rainier Maria Rilke, Tomas Transtromer and Rolf Jacobsen, Maulana Jalal al-Din Rumi and Kabir and Ghalib, he has brought Latin American, Spanish, German, Scandinavian, Persian, and Indian poetry into American consciousness. As a founder of American Writers against the Vietnam War in the 1960s and of the men's movement in the 1980s and 1990s, he brought the increasingly isolated world of poetry into contact with public intellectual life. Bly is most often credited as a founder of DEEP IMAGE POETRY, an effort to bring the unconscious into poetry, despite his dislike of that term, coined by ROBERT KELLY. Reading the Spanish surrealists, Bly found a "profundity of association" beyond French SURREALISM or EZRA POUND'S IMAGIST SCHOOL: "Freud's ocean has deepened, and Jung's work on images has been done. To Pound an image meant 'Petals on a wet black bough.' To us an image is 'death on the deep roads of the guitar' or 'the grave of snow' or 'the cradle-clothes of the sea'" (Peseroff 265). Louis Simpson, another deep image poet, said that the movement Bly led was a "renewal of the aborted MODERNISM of the generation of 1910" (qtd. in Peseroff 269).

Bly was born in Madison, Minnesota, where his family farmed. After graduating from high school, he enlisted in the navy in the last year of World War II. Upon discharge in 1947, he attended St. Olaf's College and Harvard University, where he studied with ARCHIBALD MACLEISH and met DONALD HALL, RICHARD WILBUR, JOHN ASHBERY, KENNETH KOCH, FRANK O'HARA, and ADRIENNE RICH. After Harvard, Bly spent three years living alone as a "homemade monk" (Quinn 46), writing 12 hours a day, six days a week, and working at odd jobs on the seventh. When MacLeish noticed that he looked a little gaunt, he put him up for a grant at the Writer's Workshop at the University of Iowa, where Bly taught freshman English, married, took an M.A., and won a Fulbright to Norway for 1956–57 to translate Norwegian poetry. It was in Oslo that he first read Neruda, Trakl, and other poets outside the English tradition. He returned to Minnesota and began to write a new kind of poem for him, not like NARRATIVE POETRY or formal LYRIC POETRY in the English tradition: "I often walked out somewhere and sat down. Usually a poem didn't begin until something happened . . [and] usually the second stanza didn't begin until something else had happened" (qtd. in Quinn 55). These poems usually begin in a small moment before moving inward, as in "Hunting Pheasants in a Cornfield" (1962) and "Driving to Town Late to Mail a Letter" (1962). Bly wrote a hundred or so of these poems from 1958 to 1961 and chose 44 for his first published book of poetry, *Silence in the Snowy Fields* (1962).

With the storm of the Vietnam War striking in 1965, Bly turned from the personal to the public in such poems as "Johnson's Cabinet Watched by Ants" (1967), "Counting Small-Boned Bodies" (1967), and "Driving through Minnesota during the Hanoi Bombings" (1967) and the book-length poem *The* TEETH MOTHER NAKED AT LAST (1970). The calm of the Minnesota farm could not serve as a private solution when there were threats to the larger community. Bly organized antiwar readings with Simpson, JAMES WRIGHT, GALWAY KINNELL, LAWRENCE FERLINGHETTI, and DENISE LEVERTOV, and when his next book, *The Light around the Body* (1967), won a National Book Award, he famously donated the prize money to the antiwar group Resistance. This new poetry showed his reading of Neruda and Vallejo: "Engines burning a thousand gallons of gasoline a minute sweep over the huts with dirt floors. / Chickens feel the fear deep in the pits of their beaks."

Hall called Bly "a born teacher," who is wild in his "weddings of the unweddable" and "a learned, eclectic priest" (qtd. in Peseroff 272). Bly's concerns, whether he is writing about rural Minnesota or the Vietnam War, are fundamentally religious. And his purpose in readings, famously interrupted and accompanied by song, commentary, and repetition, is to teach. Bly's need to make a living led him in the 1970s to begin giving workshops, based on his deepening interest in fairy tales, first on the Great Mother (beginning in 1975) and, later, after meeting the Jungians Joseph Campbell, James Hillman, and Michael Meade, on stories of initiation for men, which resulted in *A Little Book on the Human Shadow* (1988), his best seller *Iron John* (1990), *The Rag and Bone Shop of the Heart: Poems for Men* (1992), and *The Sibling Society* (1996). This teaching work has been controversial and aggravating to those who find such work antifeminist.

After the death of his friend WILLIAM STAFFORD, Bly spent a year writing in bed, often before rising, as Stafford used to do, producing small elegies, poems in stanzaic form—hence the volume's punning title, *Morning Poems* (1997). These are buoyant elegies, however, as befitting Stafford's personality and Bly's own fundamentally idealistic outlook. *Selected Poems* (1986), structured with short essays as a kind of literary autobiography or growth of the poet's mind, has been followed by *Eating the Honey of Words: New and Selected Poems* (1999) and the two volumes of ghazals, *The Night Abraham Called to the Stars* (2001), and *My Sentence Was a Thousand Years of Joy* (2005).

BIBLIOGRAPHY

Nelson, Howard. *Robert Bly: An Introduction to the Poetry.* New York: Columbia University Press, 1984.

Peseroff, Joyce, ed. *Robert Bly: When Sleepers Awake.* Ann Arbor: University of Michigan Press, 1984.

Quinn, Francis. "Robert Bly: The Art of Poetry LXXIX." *Paris Review* 154 (spring 2000): 36–75.

James Persoon

BOGAN, LOUISE (1897–1970) Recognized as one of the finest lyric poets in the United States—in addition to being a well-respected poetry critic—Louise Bogan produced finely wrought, intellectual, and highly formal verse that places her in the tradition of the 17th-century English Metaphysical poets. Yet even as her form and technique were often traditional, the precise language and concentrated effect of her LYRIC POETRY ranks her alongside her more modernist contemporaries and friends as among the best in 20th-century American verse (see MODERNISM).

Born in Livermore Falls, Maine, Bogan was the second surviving child of Daniel Bogan, a white-collar worker in various paper mills, and Mary Helen Shields. Her childhood was painful. The family moved frequently, and her mother was emotionally unstable. Bogan spent a year at Boston University before marrying Curt Alexander, a German immigrant in the U.S. Army, in 1916. After giving birth to Mathilde (Maidie) in October 1917, Bogan separated from Alexander permanently in 1919, sent Maidie to live with her parents, moved into an apartment in New York City, and determined to make herself into an important woman of letters. By 1921 she was publishing in most of the prestigious journals of the day. She won the first of three Guggenheim Fellowships in 1922 (also in 1933 and 1937), and in 1931 she published her first review for the *New Yorker,* for which she would continue to write regularly until 1969. Bogan won *Poetry* magazine's John Reed Memorial Prize in 1930 and the Helen

Haire Levinson Memorial Prize in 1937. She held a Library of Congress Fellowship in American Letters in 1944, was consultant in poetry (now poet laureate) to the Library of Congress from 1945–47, and won the Harriet Monroe Award in 1948. She was elected to the National Institute of Arts and Letters in 1951, the Academy of American Poets in 1955, and the American Academy of Arts and Letters in 1969, and she shared the Bollingen Prize with Léone Adams in 1955. She published three books of criticism and held several visiting professorships.

Bogan's stylized verses eschew simplistic biographical interpretation. Her first book, *Body of This Death* (1923), abstractly addresses the themes of betrayal and impermanence beneath an objective tone and a precise attention to form and rhyme. She abhorred CONFESSIONAL POETRY. According to biographer Elizabeth Frank, the first poem in *Body of This Death,* "A Tale," exemplifies Bogan's search for "a life lived passionately" and "an understanding" of such a life (56). The male speaker in the poem finds, at its end, that nothing endures except in the frozen confrontation where "something dreadful and another / Look quietly upon each other." A similar confrontation is extended in "Medusa," from the same volume, which her friend THEODORE ROETHKE called a "breakthrough to great poetry" (qtd. in Frank 58), while others saw in it an effort to control her depression. Resolving deep emotional response with intellectual nihilism marks much of Bogan's work. Similarly "The Alchemist" (1923), another of her most popular poems, asserts: "I burned my life, that I might find / A passion wholly of the mind."

The darkness noted in her second volume, *Dark Summer* (1929), appears most often as the unconscious, where passion and emotion lurk behind observation and tightly controlled form. In "If We Take All Gold," psychic peace is apparently won at the cost of burying "treasure" "under dark heaped ground." "Simple Autumnal," considered one the finest American lyric poems, attends to controlling the "forbidden grief" that dominated Bogan's life as an artist and as a human being, while "Summer Wish," assessed by Frank as "her one great poem in a major style and major mode" (125), addresses emotional despair.

After divorcing her second husband and traveling in Europe, Bogan returned to writing about the themes that dominated her earlier work—grief, rage, and impermanence—in what some consider her finest volume, *The Sleeping Fury* (1937). Works like "Italian Morning," "Roman Fountain," "Henceforth from the Mind," and the title poem are cited by critics for their mastery of craftsmanship and maturity of sentiment. "Henceforth from the Mind" reflects Bogan's continued struggle to distance herself intellectually from raging emotions: "Henceforth from the mind, / For your whole joy, must spring." The title poem, "The Sleeping Fury," confronts depression, personified as a sleeping child: "You lie in sleep and forget me. / Alone and strong in my peace, I look upon you in yours."

Bogan's "The Dream," first appearing in *Collected Poems, 1923–1953* (1954), marks an outstanding achievement of intensity of emotional impact presented in timeless, traditional lyric form. By the time *The Blue Estuaries: Poems 1923–1968* (1969)—which added only 12 new poems—was released, Bogan's critics were used to reviewing her entire canon as an expression of her pursuit of lyric control and excellence. The 104 poems that compose her final selected volume are a testament to Bogan's commitment to using traditional metrics to achieve concentrated language and effect.

BIBLIOGRAPHY

Bowles, Gloria. *Louise Bogan's Aesthetic of Limitation.* Bloomington: Indiana University Press, 1987.

Collins, Martha, ed. *Critical Essays on Louise Bogan.* Boston: Hall, 1984.

Frank, Elizabeth. *Louise Bogan: A Portrait.* New York: Knopf, 1983.

Ridgeway, Jacqueline. *Louise Bogan.* Boston: Twayne, 1984.

Upton, Lee. *Obsession and Release: Rereading the Poetry of Louise Bogan.* Lewisburg, Penn.: Bucknell University Press, 1996.

Sharon L. Barnes

BOOTH, PHILIP (1925–2007) A native New Englander, Philip Booth has long been identified with coastal Maine, a region whose elemental landscape and nautical culture provide much of the imagery that frames his spare, meditative poems. Though he began writing in the allusive, formal manner that characterized academic poetry in the 1950s, Booth soon modulated his style to incorporate the directness of ordinary speech. At the same time, he continued to employ subtle prosodic techniques—such as syllabics, consonance, and assonance—that would lend his restrained, selective vocabulary a robust physicality, as if each word were braced to bear as many interpretations as the reader might require of it. The critic Milton R. Stern calls attention to Booth's use of "hard, North names and things" and the "structural unity of style and theme" that reveals the poet's debt to the transcendentalism of Henry David Thoreau and Ralph Waldo Emerson (152). Booth's later poems, in particular, consider the characteristics of work and domestic life, acknowledging the plain-spoken strain of MODERNISM associated with WILLIAM CARLOS WILLIAMS.

Born in Hanover, New Hampshire, Booth served as an air force aviation cadet toward the end of World War II and afterward took degrees at Dartmouth (where he studied with ROBERT FROST) and at Columbia. He was awarded the Lamont Prize for his first collection, *Letter from a Distant Land,* in 1956 and has received honors from the National Endowment for the Arts, the Guggenheim Foundation, and the National Institute of Arts and Letters. His retrospective collection *Lifelines* (1999) won the Nicholas Roerich Museum Poet's Prize. He died in Hanover, New Hampshire, in 2007.

The expanses of sea, sky, and shore that frequently appear in Booth's poems emphasize the durability and magnitude of the natural environment that circumscribes human endeavor. The Earth endures with or without our presence, and rather than searching in nature for answers to eternal questions, the poet, as Booth suggests in "Saying It" (1985), might more productively strive "to find some word for / how we bear our lives." As Guy Rotella has noted, in Booth's work, "It is human response to place, not place . . . that determines meaning and value" (92). Meaning's source is thus located in our own individual reactions to the external world.

Booth's poems seem to be written in the moment, acutely aware of life's transience. His short, strongly accented lines convey a restrained sense of urgency. In "Lives" (1976) he inventories nature's progressive signs of seasonal change, concluding that "We grow / to be old." In an interview, Booth observed that art entails "a searching not so much for absolute certainty as for a way through" (Dunn 139), a path that manifests itself only in the particulars of personal growth and change.

Booth has fashioned a poetry that deftly combines economy of expression with connotative resonance, evincing, in Judith Kitchen's words, "a dependable governing sensibility" (384). Framing the immediacies of daily life within the context of their metaphysical dimensions, his earnest but disciplined poems achieve an uncommon degree of consistency and balance.

BIBLIOGRAPHY

Dunn, Stephen. "An Interview with Philip Booth." *New England Review and Bread Loaf Quarterly* 9, no. 2 (winter 1986): 134–158.

Kitchen, Judith. "The Subjective Correlative." *Georgia Review* 54, no. 2 (summer 2000): 367–387.

Rotella, Guy. "'Facing the Deep': The Poems of Philip Booth." *Three Contemporary Poets of New England: William Meredith, Philip Booth, and Peter Davison.* Boston: Twayne, 1983, pp. 64–127.

Stern, Milton R. "Halfway House: The Poems of Philip Booth." *Twentieth Century Literature* 4, no. 4 (January 1959): 148–153.

Fred Muratori

BOTTOMS, DAVID (1949–) David Bottoms has been one of the most important poets writing in the southern United States, although his work, like that of JAMES DICKEY, a significant influence, transcends regional themes to address fundamental problems of the human condition. Confronting the decline of a metaphysical awareness in the modern world, his poetry seeks moments of grace and renovation achieved through a reconnection to primitive instincts, a kinship with animals, and contact with nature and, in his later work, through regenerative moments of human intimacy.

Bottoms was born in Canton, Georgia. His first book of poems, *Shooting Rats at the Bibb County Dump,* was chosen in 1979 by ROBERT PENN WARREN for the Walt Whitman Award of the Academy of American Poets. In 1985 he received the Levinson Prize from *Poetry* magazine, in 1988 an Ingram Merrill Foundation Award and the Award in Literature from the American Academy and Institute of Arts and Letters, and in 1999 a Guggenheim Fellowship in poetry. In 2000 he served as the poet laureate of Georgia. In addition to two novels, *Any Cold Jordan* (1987) and *Easter Weekend* (1990), he has published six full-length books of poetry. He has taught at Georgia State University.

Writing a highly accessible narrative free verse, Bottoms frequently begins his poems in disarming simplicity, recounting the story of an individual, lived experience—floating in a boat down a river and being startled by a tree filled with vultures ("Under the Vulture Tree" [1987]), breaking into an elementary school at night to steal a desktop carved with his father's name ("The Desk" [1987]), or learning how to bunt ("Sign for My Father Who Stressed the Bunt" [1983]). But through figurative devices—metaphor, simile, wordplay, and symbolic associations—the poems enact sudden moments of recognition and connection, epiphanies that appear upon what seemed a lost, alienated subjectivity. Vultures become "dwarfed, transfiguring angels," the desktop suggests what it means to "own [his] father's name," and a lesson in bunting becomes a lesson in sacrifice. In his recent book, *Vagrant Grace* (1999), Bottoms writes, "I love to imagine being startled / into innocence." Through his five books of poetry, one can trace a growth of the imagination toward a renewed innocence reminiscent of William Blake—the early books informed by an austere, often stoic realism, and the more recent books, perhaps beginning with *Under the Vulture Tree* (1987), revealing a growing faith in moments of transcendence and possibilities of connection. In *Vagrant Grace,* one feels a surer sense of belonging, as if the speaker has found his home in the world, a homecoming often voiced in terms of the regenerative possibilities of family and the grace of ordinary life. Still in midcareer, Bottoms can be expected to continue to be a powerful voice in both southern and American poetry of the 21st century.

BIBLIOGRAPHY

Bottoms, David. "Turn Your Radio On: The Spirits of Influence," *Southern Quarterly* 37, no. 3–4 (spring–summer 1999): 85–92.

Suarez, Ernest. "David Bottoms: An Interview." In *Southbound: Interviews with Southern Poets.* Columbia: University Missouri Press, 1999, pp. 85–103.

Michael Sowder

BOWERS, EDGAR (1924–2000) Edgar Bowers's slight poetic output in no way diminishes his well-deserved status as one of the mid-to-late 20th-century masters of blank verse (unrhymed iambic pentameter). His early poems provide a sketch of a stoic voice skilled in the art of creating rhyming lyrics, while the later poems present a poet capable of strong emotional—albeit controlled—feeling in strictly metered elegies and poetic sequences. In all of his work, however, Bowers demonstrates a talent for meter and for using pastoral imagery to highlight moral and ethical ideas. Upon Bowers's death, his friend THOM GUNN summed up his oeuvre in the *Los Angeles Times:* "Edgar wrote very little but it was always perfect" (Woo A18).

Born in Rome, Georgia, Bowers began studying at the University of North Carolina, Chapel Hill, until the intrusion of World War II. He worked in the counterintelligence corps of the army until his honorable discharge in 1946. War, especially its mindlessness and capacity to ruin once-beautiful places, is a common theme throughout his poetry. After graduating from UNC, he went on to earn a Ph.D. at Stanford University, studying under the New Critic YVOR WINTERS, who encouraged him to write in controlled forms. Bowers then taught briefly at Duke University and Harpur College (New York) before joining the English faculty at the University of California, Santa Barbara, as a professor of modern and Renaissance poetry. He retired in 1991 and moved to San Francisco, where he died in 2000. Despite publishing only five full-length books in his lifetime, including *Collected Poems* in 1997, he was awarded two Guggenheim Fellowships (1959 and 1969) and Yale University's prestigious Bollingen Prize in poetry in 1989. His inclusion in the 1963 *Five American Poets* anthology, edited by Ted Hughes and Gunn, led to a wide British readership.

Some critics speculate that Bowers's smaller reading public in the United States stems from his consistent use of rhyme and meter and the nonconfessional, sometimes impersonal nature of his work; these qualities also separate him from his contemporaries. He laments the pervasive use of free verse in some poems, and he reacts to CONFESSIONAL POETRY in his "To the Contemporary Muse" (1965) by calling "honesty" a "little slut" and asking why the muse wants to hear "every dirty word [he] know[s]."

The poems of Bowers reward intelligent readers interested in formal verse, schooled in Greek mythology and Judeo-Christian traditions, and unafraid of serious, philosophical lessons about the reality of death, memory, and nostalgia. In "Noah" (1990), a poem in which he assumes the voice of the ancient figure, he characterizes the sound of rushing water as "formal, true, exact"—three words that provide an apt description of his own verse.

BIBLIOGRAPHY

Woo, Elaine. "Obituaries: Edgar Bowers; Poet Won Bolllingen Prize." *Los Angeles Times,* 5 February 2000, sec A, 18.

Yezzi, David. "The Order Passion Yields." *New Criterion* 19, no. 3 (November 2000): 77–84.

Jessica Allen

BOYLE, KAY (1902–1992) Instrumental in the development of avant-garde poetry and belonging to various communities of American expatriate artists living in Europe between the world wars, Kay Boyle was one of the longest-lived and most prolific writers of the lost generation (other members of this group included Ernest Hemingway, F. Scott Fitzgerald, and GERTRUDE STEIN). Boyle's work reflects the concept of high MODERNISM that a poem should "exist as an object of art on its own terms" (Spanier 133). Yet Boyle believed too that "[t]he writer must recognize and . . . accept his commitment to his times" (quoted in Madden 218).

Born in St. Paul, Minnesota, Boyle moved to New York at age 20. There she was befriended by such leading poets as WILLIAM CARLOS WILLIAMS and Lola Ridge, with whom she edited the little magazine *Broom.* In 1923 she left for Europe, where she remained for 18 years. During this time Boyle signed Ernest Jolas's "Revolution of the Word," a manifesto proclaiming the artist's right to "disintegrate" and thus remake language, and published her first poetry collection, *A Glad Day* (1938). Later, as an English professor at San Francisco State University, Boyle was known as an activist, writing overtly political poetry and joining in student protests. She published nearly 50 volumes in her lifetime, including 14 novels, 10 short-story collections, and six collections of poetry. She twice won the O. Henry Award for short stories, received two Guggenheim Fellowships (1934 and 1961) and a National Endowment for the Arts Senior Fellowship for literature (1980), and was awarded five honorary doctorates. In 1979 she was named to the American Academy of Arts and Letters.

Densely metaphorical and experimental in style, Boyle's poems from the 1920s and 1930s demonstrate her understanding of the avant-garde as a "shock of fresh experience" (quoted in Madden 218). Boyle mixed genres freely, interrupting lyrical passages with prose paragraphs or quotations from contemporary media. Influenced by SURREALISM and the IMAGIST SCHOOL, she was a master of the startling image fragment, as in "A Christmas Carol for Ernest Carevali" (1928), where the wind becomes a horse "with nostrils like wild black pansies opened on the fog." For subject matter, Boyle drew from her expatriate life or focused on social ills in Europe and at home, constantly exploring cultural and psychological boundaries between individuals.

From the 1960s onward, Boyle's poetry followed the tradition of American intellectual radicalism. Many of her poems, such as "For James Baldwin" (1969), whom she praises as a "witch doctor for the dispossessed," manifest her continued identification with the rebel and outsider. In all her writing, whether documenting the 1937 Scottsboro trials or lauding war protesters in 1969, Boyle lived out the belief that poetry demands both "an acute awareness of words . . . and of life" (Madden 216).

BIBLIOGRAPHY

Madden, Charles. "Kay Boyle." In *Talks with Authors,* edited by Madden. Carbondale: Southern Illinois University Press, 1968, pp. 215–236.

Spanier, Sandra Whipple. *Kay Boyle, Artist and Activist.* Carbondale: Southern Illinois University Press, 1986.

Patricia G. King

BRATHWAITE, EDWARD KAMAU (1930–) "One of the most important poets of the Western Hemisphere," as AMIRI BARAKA noted in a blurb to his 1994 volume, *Middle Passages,* Edward

Kamau Brathwaite belongs to a select group of key and influential epic-making Caribbean poets and scholars who have significantly influenced American letters; others include DEREK WALCOTT and Edouard Glissant. Brathwaite's work addresses the postcolonial conditions of culture and language in the Caribbean; it also comments upon the worldwide African diaspora and what Brathwaite calls the "creolization" of West African, European, and American Indian cultures. Brathwaite's work, in its epic use of collage and myth, can be compared with that of T. S. ELIOT and EZRA POUND, but his relation to American poetry is more as an influence than an heir. Among many others, he has influenced the likes of Baraka, RACHEL BLAU DUPLESSIS, AND NATHANIEL MACKEY, as well as the new generation of digital and video poets.

Lawson Edward Brathwaite was born in Bridgetown, Barbados. He earned a bachelor's degree from Pembroke College, Cambridge, in 1953. After receiving a diploma of education from Pembroke College in 1954, he entered the British colonial service and traveled to the Gold Coast (now Ghana), where he worked as an education officer. In 1962 he moved back to the Caribbean and began teaching at the University of the West Indies. In the mid–1960s he returned to England to complete a doctorate in philosophy at the University of Sussex (1968). In 1976 he began to use the split first name "Edward Kamau" as a means of mirroring the Afro-Anglo strains of his Caribbean culture. He has also taught at New York University. He has written nearly 20 books of poetry and two collections of plays, produced a dozen scholarly books, and has won many awards, including the Cholmondely Award (1970), the Casa de Las Americas Prize for poetry and for literary criticism (1986), and the Neustadt International Award for literature (1994).

Inventive at every level, Brathwaite's work is rife with neologism, pun, collage, dialect (which he terms "nation language"), multilingualism, myth, history, theory, and the manipulation of concrete aspects of text, such as font, size, and layout. He has, in fact, his own distinct font, which he calls his "Sycorax 'video style,'" with which he strives toward "a kind of cinema-painting" (Brathwaite 207), in the manner of medieval Islamic illuminated manuscripts, "when the word could still *hear itself speak*" (167).

His elegy for Jamaican dub poet Mikey Smith, who was stoned to death on Stony Hill in Kingston, shows Brathwaite at his most inventive, biting, dense, epic, and loving: "& every mighty word he trod. the ground fall dark & hole / be. hine him like it as a bloom x. plodding sound" ("Stone" [1994]).

BIBLIOGRAPHY

Baraka, Amiri. Commentary on *Middle Passages*. Brathwaite, Kamua. *Middle Passages*. New York: New Directions, 1994. Back cover.

Brathwaite, Edward Kamau. *ConVERSations with Nathaniel Mackey*. Staten Island, N.Y.: We Press, 1999.

Gabriel Gudding

THE BRIDGE **HART CRANE (1930)** HART CRANE'S epic masterpiece was begun in early 1923 and published seven years later. The poem offers an organic panorama of the history of the United States, beginning with Spanish conquest, exploring American Indian, colonial, and Quaker heritages, and ending with the early 20th-century reality of progress and democracy. The Brooklyn Bridge, the primary emblem of the poem, represents American identity as both myth and prophecy, idea and place, past and present. The epic aims at a mystical synthesis of America, in which fact and history become transfigured into abstract and visionary form. Crane wrote *The Bridge* in the spirit of Walt Whitman, whom he considered his poetic precursor. He also envisioned the poem as a response to T. S. ELIOT'S *The WASTE LAND* (1922), whose modernist technique he admired and to a large extent imitated, yet whose thematic skepticism and pessimism he uniformly rejected (see MODERNISM). By contrast, *The Bridge* is an affirmative and anticipatory work, expressing hope in a future regeneration of America.

The poem consists of eight parts, two of them additionally divided into several subsections. It integrates various personages and locations, some of them real, some mythical, and some altogether invented. Though each part of the epic can be read as a separate piece, each contributes to the text as a whole, which follows a meticulously arranged thematic trajectory. In terms of poetic language, *The Bridge* is vintage Hart Crane, offering an exquisite mixture of Elizabethan rhetoric and French Symbolist imagery, further enhanced by an intense oratorical mode reminiscent of the prophetic books of William Blake. But there is also a strong formal influence of *The Waste Land,* especially in the fragmentary nature of certain passages and sheer multiplicity of voices and perspectives: Early explorers, native inhabitants of the land, railway desperados, vagabond sailors, tenacious settlers, and others speak.

The epic begins with "To Brooklyn Bridge," a high-toned invocation to the bridge, identified as a "speechless caravan," "harp," and "terrific threshold of the prophet's pledge," among other things, which ascends above an irreverent and occasionally ruthless world of modern reality. The fervor of this proem is balanced momentarily by sea-swell tones of "Ave Maria," in which Christopher Columbus reflects on his accidental discovery of America. Next come five sections of "Powhatan's Daughter," which take up the theme of exploration of American soil. Here the legendary Indian princess Pocahontas serves as the symbol of the physical body of the continent. "The Harbor Dawn" is an erotic poem that subtly transports the reader from the 17th century to the 1920s; "Van Winkle" is a homage to memory attained through a poignant childhood recollection. "The River," a jazzy rendition of the cultural confusion of the present day of the poem, takes the reader on a train ride westward toward the Mississippi River. Finally, there comes a visionary portrayal of American Indian heritage in "The Dance" and a moving description of settler experience in "Indiana," both of which illustrate the conflict between American Indians and white settlers in the West and rather idealistically try to make a point about spiritual co-ownership of the land.

The epic proceeds with "Cutty Sark," which combines reminiscences of a weathered sailor and popular songs from a nickel-slot pianola, and "Cape Hatteras," Crane's tribute to his artistic and spiritual forebear, Walt Whitman. This is followed by "Three Songs," describing, respectively, nostalgia after impossible ideals, the power of sexual lust, and the innocence of love. Next comes an exploration of New England heritage in "Quaker Hill," then an infernal vision of "The Tunnel," portraying a subway ride from Columbus Circle in Manhattan to Brooklyn. The subway, because it runs below ground (the bridge runs above it), symbolizes a negative alternative to the affirmative side of American experience heretofore celebrated; it is a route of failure, loss, and despair. The epic ends with "Atlantis," in which the poet bestows no less than 12 epithets on the bridge, starting with the "Tall Vision-of-the-Voyage" and ending with "One Song, one Bridge of Fire." This final enraptured vision of cables, wires, granite, and steel poised high in the air between two banks of the East River is the poet's union with the Absolute. Atlantis remains a matter of potential, a utopian answer to the inferno of the subway tunnel; it is an emblem of hope for a better America to be realized some time in the future.

Throughout his short life, Crane faced the difficulty of working at a time in which conventional moral, social, and religious structures had to a large extent become groundless and needed to be invented anew. *The Bridge* is intended to provide a sense of direction to this temporary state of confusion and uncertainty. This is particularly conspicuous in the way Crane deals with contemporary advances in technology and science. A new landscape filled with skyscrapers, radio antennae, trolleys, and steam whistles fascinated him as much as it frightened poets less given to the technological sublime. Crane believed that poetry and science had an antithetical, but not inimical relationship; thus he aims to produce an independent artistic vision and, at the same time, to give an expression to the greatest achievements of modern civilization.

While he was laboring on the poem in his apartment with a direct view of the bridge, Crane was constantly haunted by fears of poetic failure. Even after he began working on the poem seriously, he became skeptical about his ability to carry out his plans and about the poem's effect on American society. When the poem was finally published in 1930, the reviews were mixed. Certain readers immediately perceived its visionary force and originality; others did not. Crane's friend YVOR WINTERS accused him of having fallen victim to inexact poetic verbiage and ultimately condemned the whole epic as a literary wreckage. In general, however, literary history has been kind to Crane's originality. Today *The Bridge* is considered one of the most important long poems of the 20th century.

BIBLIOGRAPHY

Brunner, Edward. *Splendid Failure: Hart Crane and the Making of The Bridge.* Chicago: University of Illinois Press, 1985.

Gilles, Paul. *Hart Crane: The Contexts of the Bridge*. London: Cambridge University Press, 1986.
Sherman, Paul. *Hart's Bridge*. Urbana: University of Illinois Press, 1972.

Piotr Gwiazda

BRODSKY, JOSEPH (1940–1996) Born in Leningrad/St. Petersburg, Brodsky was a child of the Soviet system until he encountered Fyodor Dostoyevsky's writing and internalized the Kierkegaardian existentialist philosophy he found there and, subsequently, inserted into his own work. A poet, essayist, translator, and playwright, Brodsky saw the use of language for art as the only way to address the future; he found poetry "an extraordinary accelerator of conscience," as he explained in his Nobel lecture. Of the writers he read as a young man, T. S. ELIOT and ROBERT FROST, as well as W. H. AUDEN and John Donne, were the Western poets most significant to his development. He believed that "aesthetics are the mother of ethics, that beauty can save an individual from metaphysical nothingness" (MacFadyen *Muse* 162).

Convicted of "social parasitism" in 1964, Brodsky was sentenced to internal exile and spent 18 months in a labor camp; merely being a poet was not considered productive under the Soviet system. Marginally published in his own country, Brodsky did not find a widespread public audience for his work, especially in the United States, until after his 1972 expulsion from the Soviet Union. Brodsky settled in the United States and served as writer-in-residence and visiting professor at various colleges and universities; he was elected to the American Academy and Institute of Arts and Letters (1979), received a MacArthur Foundation Award (1981), won a National Book Critic's Award (1986), and was poet laureate of the United States (1991–92). Brodsky's most prestigious acknowledgment came when he received the Nobel Prize for literature (1987). He was "someone who . . . preferred his private condition to any role of social significance" but stressed the need for societies to embrace literature, not simply literacy, believing that "had we been choosing our leaders on the basis of their reading experience and not their political programs, there would be much less grief on earth" (Brodsky "Nobel Lecture").

Brodsky's poems are full of people and places, more than things; many pieces have dedicatory notations. He memorializes and reflects, and this is his major concern in "Transatlantic" (1992), in which he gathers time, memory, and philosophy in a meditation on his 20 post-exile years. He proposes that time is incomprehensible unless the transformation of people into (and out of) memory can be explained. His prolonged isolation from Russia reveals the gradual disappearance of familiar figures from his dreams, explaining why "eternal rest / cancels analysis": Sufficient passage of time resolves the persistent existence of the dead who populated memory. A gifted lyric poet, translator, and essayist, Brodsky also cofounded the American Poetry and Literacy Project in the hope that poetry would become a more dominant art form in everyday life. For Brodsky, poetry is not only beautiful but also capable of changing the world.

BIBLIOGRAPHY

Brodsky, Joseph. "Nobel Lecture" (translated by Barry Rubin), Nobel e-Museum. Available online. URL: www.nobel.se/literature/laureates/1987/brodsky-lecture.html. Downloaded March 2007.
Loseff, Lev, and Valentina Polukhina, eds. *Brodsky's Poetics and Aesthetics*. London: Macmillan, 1990.
MacFadyen, David. *Joseph Brodsky and the Baroque*. Montreal: McGill-Queen's University Press, 1999.
———. *Joseph Brodsky and the Soviet Muse*. Montreal: McGill-Queen's University Press, 2000.
Polukhina, Valentina. *Joseph Brodsky: A Poet for Our Time*. New York: Cambridge University Press, 1989.

A. Mary Murphy

"THE BROKEN HOME" JAMES MERRILL (1966) A sonnet sequence that narrates the childhood trauma of his parents' divorce (see NARRATIVE POETRY) and recalls the complex patterns of W. H. AUDEN's poetry, JAMES MERRILL's early poem "The Broken Home" is an important justification of his apolitical aesthetics, his dedication to writing, and his focus on his private past. In an apostrophe to the poetic Muse, Merrill writes, "Tell me, tongue of fire, / That you and I are as real / At least as the people upstairs," and in the sonnets that follow, Merrill defends his exploration of memory and his aestheticism. Yet although his self-exploration, particularly through domestic imagery, resembles that of ROBERT LOWELL, Merrill is not a straightforward CONFESSIONAL poet. Through his wittily inverted clichés, delicately beautiful and haunting, and skillful formal play, he transforms his privileged but lonely childhood and the story of his parents' "marriage on the rocks" into an ironic allegory of the conflict between modern history and nature, between tradition and the individual.

Merrill's cultured irony is evident throughout the poem. Distrustful of myth, he nevertheless paints his parents in the roles of Kronos and Gaia, or Time and Earth, imbuing their lives with significance beyond mere biography while simultaneously preventing their elevation to mythological status. Both enviously and resentfully, Merrill writes, "How intensely people used to feel!" He describes his father, Charles Merrill, a founding partner of the investment firm known today as Merrill Lynch, as the embodiment of modern history's often calamitous "progress," a wealthy financier with "[a] soul eclipsed by twin black pupils, sex / And business," who divorced and remarried "each thirteenth year." Rejecting his father's material ambitions and emotional distance, Merrill chooses the life of an artist, not only making art but making his life an aesthetic product. Grudgingly, however, the aesthetic Merrill must admit his inability to escape the sometimes calamitous progress of history, saying "I am no less time's child than some."

By contrast, Merrill's mother Hellen Ingram Merrill (née Plummer), who came from a socially distinguished family, is described as an intensely physical and emotional individual, a suffragette, and, as many critics have observed, the object of desire in Merrill's childhood Oedipal drama. Yet her intense presence in Merrill's life does not provide him the simple affection to spell his childhood loneliness. Merrill recounts following the family Irish setter to Hellen Merrill's room and finding her asleep in her lingerie, her undone hair "of a blackness found, if ever now, in old / Engravings where the acid bit." Although he realizes "I must have needed to touch it," when she startles awake, Merrill writes that "The dog slumped to the floor. She reached for me. I fled." As an adult, Merrill has rejected his mother's romantic passion and devotion to nature and politics, aligning himself instead with modernism's irony and commitment to art. Yet even though he does not "try to keep a garden," which would suggest a love of nature and thus a romantic commitment, he keeps "An avocado in a glass of water— / Roots pallid, gemmed with air," signifying that "I am earth's no less."

This ambivalence is characteristic of Merrill's thematic analysis of postmodern reality. The critic Mutlu Konak Blasing writes that Merrill's parents come to represent the conflict of technological progress with nature, though Merrill reduces that universal conflict to the simple story of his parents' divorce, making it less obviously "poetic" and more palatable to a skeptical, postmodern audience. Ironically, Merrill claims he cannot resist but must obey his parents, yet his aesthetic life and generally apolitical art belie that claim. It is as if Merrill, reluctant to follow the ideologies of the past, nevertheless honors them in the breach; "I rarely buy a newspaper, or vote," he writes. Blasing argues that "From his postmetaphysical perspective, all truths are rhetorical, and all ideologies, whether mastering or marginal, are textual options" (165); that is, in the postmodern world, belief systems are perceived as choices, not as essential truths, and thus may be followed according to the individual's will. Given that no ideology is central, one's life becomes a matter of choice, and therefore of taste, meaning that Merrill's life of art, more tempered and private than the public ambitions of such modern poets as EZRA POUND, HART CRANE, and W. B. YEATS, is in some ways the most authentic postmodern life. Yet Merrill himself rejects this absolutely private focus; in an interview with J. D. MCCLATCHY, Merrill claims that "That bit in 'The Broken Home'—'Father Time and Mother Earth, / A marriage on the rocks'—isn't meant as a joke. History in our time *has* cut loose, *has* broken faith with Nature" (72).

This ironic ambivalence, a refusal to be trapped in one ideological framework, is manifest most powerfully in Merrill's style, form, and tone. Throughout the poem, Merrill inverts established truths, revitalizing the tired ones and questioning the immovable ones. His use of cliché is at once delightfully witty and poignant: "The party is over" for his rich, socialite parents, whose marriage is at once a cocktail and a catastrophe "on the rocks"; his financier father "made history" but discovers at the end of his life that "money was not time"; and the broken home of the title comes to signify not only the aftermath of the divorce, but also the life that came before. Moreover, Merrill's use of the lyrical sonnet form to narrate his story, as well as his variations in rhyme scheme and stanza pattern for each sonnet, suggest a simultaneous reliance on and reluctance about tradition.

To be consistent and just, such ironic skepticism must be turned on the poet himself, and Merrill does this by questioning the project of remembrance. Haunting the poem is a tone of nostalgia, a wish for the innocence of the past of which the adult Merrill is understanding but also cautious. On the afternoon he encounters his mother "clad in taboos," he follows his Irish setter Michael, who "led / The child I was to a shut door," that "child" signifying both Merrill's youth and the degree of his ignorance about this person. Yet he has not completely rejected them; as an adult, Merrill writes, "I see those two hearts, I'm afraid, / Still," yet he can also hearken back to an evening in the fall of 1931 and remark, "They love each other still." In the end, however, the certainty of memory, good or bad, must be relinquished. The final stanza shows Merrill still trying to hold onto the truth of memory when he writes that "A child, a red dog roam the corridors, / Still, of the broken home." Yet when he imagines how the new inhabitant of his old home might "Watch a red setter stretch and sink in cloud," he signals an abdication of the quest for certainty and an embrace of the richly ambiguous inversions of his present artistic vision.

BIBLIOGRAPHY

Adams, Don. *James Merrill's Poetic Quest.* Westport, Conn.: Greenwood Press, 1997.

Blasing, Mutlu Konuk. *Politics and Form in Postmodern Poetry: O'Hara, Bishop, Ashbery, and Merrill.* New York: Cambridge University Press, 1995.

Keller, Lynn. *Re-making It New: Contemporary American Poetry and the Modernist Tradition.* New York: Cambridge University Press, 1987.

Materer, Timothy. "Confession and Autobiography in James Merrill's Early Poetry." *Twentieth Century Literature: A Scholarly and Critical Journal* 48, no. 2 (2002): 150–173.

Merrill, James. "An Interview with J. D. McClatchy." In *Recitative: Prose by James Merrill,* edited by J. D. McClatchy, 72. San Francisco: North Point Press, 1986.

Temple Cone

BROMIGE, DAVID (1933–) David Bromige is a poet with affinities to the New American writing of the post–World War II period (a group that includes poets such as LARRY EIGNER, RON LOEWINSOHN, and JOHN ASHBERY) as well as to the innovations of the LANGUAGE SCHOOL, and yet his poetry, with its conjoining of lyric and what he has termed "obsessively reflexive narrative and meditation," cannot be reductively assigned to any school or movement. "One does not inherit an audience," he writes in *My Poetry* (1980); "one builds one, a reader at a time." Like the jazz saxophonist Coleman Hawkins, whose sound was unmistakably his even as he, unlike so many other musicians of his generation, joined with the BeBoppers and the avant-garde that came after him, so Bromige's writing aligns itself with significant movements of the time, while always pointing a way beyond those movements.

Born in London on October 22, 1933, Bromige moved to Canada at age 15. He returned to England briefly, went back to Canada, and completed his advanced education in the United States, where he has remained since. Bromige was a student at the University of British Columbia when the works of ROBERT CREELEY and others began to take hold among his circle of acquaintance, and he was at Berkeley when CHARLES OLSON and others read at the poetry conference of 1965. During his years in the San Francisco Bay area, Bromige worked closely with ROBERT DUNCAN and was an early associate of such poets as RON SILLIMAN, BOB PERELMAN, RAE ARMANTROUT, and LYN HEJINIAN. His first book, *The Gathering,* was published in 1965, and since then he has published 10 more major collections. His selected poems, *Desire,* won the Western States Book Award for poetry upon publication in 1988.

In *Desire,* Bromige altered each of his earlier poems. "Affair of the Lemming" (1965), for example, lost a phrase and saw a change in spelling. This seems characteristic of the often-remarked-upon reflexivity of Bromige's verse. It is not so much the constant revision and second thoughts of a W. H. AUDEN or MARIANNE

MOORE, but a constant thinking through of our experience in language in the world, of the multiple ways in which language structures our understanding of the world, even as we use language to change the world. In one interview, Bromige noted that "once a mode becomes a habit . . . attention slackens" (Beckett 30). Hence in the same way that he viewed his early book *The Ends of the Earth* (1968) as a critique of the LYRIC POETRY of the 1960s, the reworked poems of *Desire* enact a lyric critique of his own work. He remains "interested" in song, in how we find ourselves caught in the lyric act. "The Point" (1974) ends by catching us out in just such an act: "Someone is pointing at the flames— / attention has been caught, / desire ignites— we see ourselves / as someone points them out."

BIBLIOGRAPHY

Alpert, Barry et al., eds. "David Bromige: An Interview." *Vort* 3 (1973): 2–23.

Beckett, Tom, ed. *Difficulties* 3, no. 1 (1987). [David Bromige Issue.]

Aldon L. Nielsen

BRONK, WILLIAM (1918–1999) William Bronk is best known for his austere view of the world as well as for his writing style. His language—subtle, balanced in tone and diction, essential—is possibly the most distilled in all of 20th-century American poetry. In addition Bronk is always explicit visually and resonant musically. His work keeps alive a New England poetic tradition, evoking nature and the seasons, winter most of all, and delving into the nature of reality or truth. These concerns were firmly established early in the 19th century by Henry David Thoreau (an especially strong influence on Bronk), Ralph Waldo Emerson, and Emily Dickinson, and in the 20th century by the New England poets ROBERT FROST and WALLACE STEVENS, then later by, along with Bronk, ROBERT CREELEY and GEORGE OPPEN.

Bronk was born in Fort Edward, near Hudson Falls, New York, where he lived his entire life except for his student years at Dartmouth College and Harvard University, a period of military service during World War II, and a brief stint as an instructor at Union College. Even after he gained a wide readership, Bronk shrank from public attention and concentrated on his immediate surroundings. His writing expresses his refusal to compromise his lifestyle and point of view, as in his poem "The Abnegation" (1971): "I will not / be less than I am to be more human." He believes that what he knows of the world is at best only a semblance of the truth. Reality exists, and he is able to intuit its existence, but it is finally beyond his grasp. Despite Bronk's asceticism, he was constantly sought out by readers and many poets who would journey to Hudson Falls to visit; for young poets, this trip was something of a rite of passage. Bronk won some major poetry awards, including the American Book Award in 1982 and the Lannan Prize for his life's work 10 years later. When at Dartmouth, he met Frost, and his fellow student and friend was Samuel French Morse, who became a well-known authority on Stevens. Bronk's first publishing successes were due to the efforts of CID CORMAN, who printed Bronk's work in *Origin*, the POETRY JOURNAL he edited, and who published Bronk's first book *Light and Dark* in 1956. Bronk also enjoyed the support of Creeley in his magazine, the *Black Mountain Review* in the 1950s, and Bronk's second book, *The World, the Worldless,* was published by New Directions in 1964 with the help of Oppen and his sister June Oppen Degnan, who was an editor at that POETRY PRESS.

This network of fellow poets and editors should not suggest, however, that Bronk was in any sense a derivative poet. On the contrary, his work is original, his poetic voice singular and unforgettable. His language, indeed, is perhaps the clearest and most even in tone in all of 20th-century American poetry, devoid of unnecessary wording, yet filled with subtle agreements of sound set out in a basic iambic line. Bronk's poetic statements purport to describe the facts of life, yet, paradoxically, Bronk constantly writes about the elusiveness of any fact. He finds, instead, a compromise he can live with. In his poem "The Rain of Small Occurrences" (1955), he writes, "The world is not quite formless; we lean down / and feel the massive earth beneath our feet." Yet the closest to factuality Bronk can come is the poem itself, ultimately a poem that in its sureness—in its reliability of diction, meter, and outlook—insists on a reality beyond his comprehension. The best strategy for living Bronk can come up with is to embrace the present; the poem "On the Failure of Meaning in the

Absence of Objective Analogs" (1971) suggests: "There is only this whatever this may mean / and this is what there is and nothing will be."

What is knowable, on the other hand, is desire, and Bronk spends a great deal of time examining the force of desire (a title of one of his books, published in 1979) in life. Desire is the "single great constant" in Bronk's work, Norman Finkelstein writes (481). Impossibly, Bronk desires "the world," even though knowing the world, all in all, is beyond his capacity. In any case, knowledge is only a logical realization, yet the human condition is not predicated on reason alone. "Despite the self-limiting fact that consciousness is aware of its inability to experience this totality, it continually struggles for the achievement of its goal. Cut off from any ground of belief, secure only in its desire, consciousness therefore creates a world, which despite its insufficiency in metaphysical terms nevertheless allows for the rendering of form—the poem" (481).

There are "reassurances" in our daily lives, Bronk states in his poem "The Inference" (1972): "the far trips / the mind can make!" Our journeys occur within this world of desire, a world tantalizingly unknowable: "There is a world we know from inference. / It isn't here and yet we go to it." Imbued by desire, then, human existence is never absolutely grounded in certainty, and therefore it exists without a real identity, as Bronk explains in the preface to his book of collected essays, *Vectors and Smoothable Curves* (1983). We attempt to find ourselves as a way of knowing who we are; the problem here is that no matter how "direct and immediate our awareness may be it is also devoid of external reference and its strength and centrality is uncertain" (n.p.). We are like vectors, merely "proposals of location and force whose only referential field is internal—not ultimately oriented. We can be grateful for their stabilities even aware as we are of an arbitrariness with them" (n.p.). To live with these propositions means we must recognize the tenuousness of life. To be sure, "Reality is brought to mind by the inadequacy of any statement of it, the tension of that inadequacy, the direction and force of the statement" (n.p.).

Bronk's poem "Some Musicians Play Chamber Music for Us" (1955), in a phrase reminiscent of Stevens, claims that "all we will know are fragments of a world," even through the arts. In "The Mind's Landscape on an Early Winter Day" (1955), a poem whose evocation of winter rivals winter poems by Frost, Bronk writes, with an unparalleled bleakness that, in turn, evokes a delicate beauty of what he calls the "winter mind, the ne'er do well," his alter ego, a "poor blind" that "is always lost and gropes its way . . . even when the senses seize the world." The best comfort against the sense of being lost are our stories and metaphors we come to inhabit. Thus Bronk's poem "The Wanted Exactitude" (1991) ends in a single-line stanza: "let our metaphor be accurate." Metaphor is as close to reality as he can come. In "The Mind's Limitations Are Its Freedom" (1972), Bronk asks, "What else but the mind / senses the final uselessness of the mind?" The irony in this statement is not, of course, lost on Bronk, and so it might be a surprise to realize that his contemplation of the human mind is joyful, even though "the mind of man" is "frail, deep / in disorder" and "always pushed by the falsenesses / of unreality." It is this unreality that is predicated by desire, and so Bronk has no choice but to embrace that desire. "I want to be that Tantalus," Bronk proclaims in "The Abnegation," "unfed forever." He asks that he be spared all compassion and that his reader notice how humankind "takes handouts, makeshifts, sops for creature comfort." These he refuses.

There is no place to rest in Bronk's view of existence. Even physical love is undermined by restlessness. He accuses his lover, naked beside him in bed in the poem "Wants and Questions" (1985), of taunting him simply by "[wearing] those skins and bones." Who is this person and who is he? As Paul Auster has commented, "Bronk's poetry stands as an eloquent and often beautiful attack on all our assumptions, a provocation, a monument to the questioning mind" (30). This is a poetry of sinuous statement, and yet it is musical, refined, and deeply ruminative, advancing the most troubling, often unanswerable human inquiries.

BIBLIOGRAPHY

Auster, Paul. "The Poetry of William Bronk." *Saturday Review* (8 July 1978): 30–31.

Bronk, William. *Vectors and Smoothable Curves: Collected Essays.* 1983. New edition, Jersey City, N.J.: Talisman House, 1997.

Clippinger, David, ed. *The Body of This Life: Essays on William Bronk.* Jersey City, N.J.: Talisman House, 2001.
Ernest, John. "William Bronk's Religious Desire." *Sagetrieb: A Journal Devoted to Poets in the Imagist/Objectivist Tradition* 7, no. 3 (1988): 145–152.
Finkelstein, Norman. "William Bronk: The World as Desire." *Contemporary Literature* 23, no. 4 (1982): 480–492.
Kimmelman, Burt. *The "Winter Mind": William Bronk and American Letters.* Madison, N.J.: Fairleigh Dickinson University Press, 1998.

Burt Kimmelman

BROOKS, GWENDOLYN (1917–2000) While creating a poetry noted for its NARRATIVE sweep and verbal polish, Gwendolyn Brooks epitomized the ways in which 20th-century African-American poets more fully developed their culture's poetic distinctiveness. Brooks drew on the blues, ballad, and jazz traditions found in the work of LANGSTON HUGHES and other poets of the HARLEM RENAISSANCE for her first collection, *A Street in Bronzeville* (1945). Her early poetry, especially in *Annie Allen* (1949), also makes extensive and innovative use of the Anglo-American canon's forms and diction. Brooks always had been concerned with contemporary African-American culture and, in particular, with the racial struggles of ordinary urban blacks. But with the publication of "The BEAN EATERS" (1960) and the new work in *Selected Poems* (1963), Brooks's poetry became more critical of white American society—a move that became more pronounced through the influence of AMIRI BARAKA and the BLACK ARTS MOVEMENT. She sought to develop an explicitly African-American poetry in *In the Mecca* (1968) and in her later volumes, such as *To Disembark* (1981), by writing specifically to blacks and by drawing on a jazz-inflected free verse. Brooks's poetic development parallels the political development of 20th-century African-American culture as it moved from considering racial integration to black separatism and multiculturalism.

Brooks was born in Topeka, Kansas, but lived in Chicago from infancy. She graduated from Wilson Junior College in 1936, married Henry Blakely in 1939, and raised two children. Brooks wrote poetry from an early age and as a teenager received encouragement from JAMES WELDON JOHNSON and Hughes. In 1943 she won the Midwestern Writers' Conference poetry award. In 1950 *Annie Allen* received the Pulitzer Prize for poetry—the first time the award had been won by an African American. Her attendance at the 1967 Fisk University Black Writers' Conference exposed her to the Black Arts movement. In 1968 Brooks was named poet laureate of Illinois, and in 1985–86 she was the consultant in poetry (now poet laureate) for the Library of Congress. She received a National Medal of Arts in 1995.

Critics often divide Brooks's work into distinct stages, Brooks herself divided her work into pre-1967 and post-1967 categories. Norris B. Clark describes Brooks's work as moving from a concern with craft to a concern with culture, a move that also "can be characterized in political language as traditional, prerevolutionary, and revolutionary; or in the language of sociologists as accommodationists, integrationists, and black nationalists, or in racial language as white, colored, and black" (qtd. in Mootry 85). Brooks's early work draws from the Anglo-American poetic tradition. For her first book, Brooks wrote a sonnet sequence, "Gay Chaps at the Bar," about black soldiers during World War II, and *Annie Allen* tells the story of its title character by drawing on a variety of traditional European conventions. "The Anniad," for instance, alludes to Virgil's epic *The Aeneid* but also to Pope's mock epic *The Dunciad,* as it makes references to "Plato, Aeschylus, / Seneca and Mimnermus, / Pliny, Dionysius." Although *Annie Allen* won the Pulitzer Prize, some later critics saw it as an example of how Brooks did not at first write for African Americans. "*Annie Allen,* important? Yes. Read by blacks? No. *Annie Allen* more so than *A Street in Bronzeville* seems to have been written for whites," complained Don Lee (17). The dispute over Brooks's oeuvre is part of a longstanding controversy among black artists and critics over how African-American writers should preserve the integrity of their particular cultural experience in a society that either exploits or ignores black life.

In a 1950 essay, "Poets Who Are Negroes," Brooks herself argues that for an artist to succeed with the masses she must fully develop her abilities: "You have got to cook that dough, alter it, until it is unrecognizable. Then the mob will not know it is accepting something that will be good for it. . . . [N]o real artist is going, to be content with offering raw materials. The Negro poet's most urgent duty, at present, is to polish his technique, his way of presenting his truths and his beauties, that these may be more insinuating, and, therefore, more overwhelming" (*Phylon* 312). But after attending the 1967 Fisk conference, Brooks explicitly sought to develop an African-American poetic. The effect of listening to Baraka and others call for a poetry about, by, and for African Americans was profound: "*I* had never been, before, in the general presence of such insouciance, such live firmness, such confident vigor, such determination to mold or care something DEFINITE" (Brooks *Part One* 85). Brooks said the experience was an epiphany and that she was then "qualified to enter at least the kindergarten of new consciousness now" (*Part One* 86).

Brooks's later poetry more explicitly addresses politics. *In the Mecca,* for instance, has poems in honor of civil rights martyrs Medgar Evers and Malcolm X ("He opened us— / who was a key" ["Malcolm X"]). The volume also describes "Black / boy-men on roofs fist our 'Black Power!" ("The Wall") and develops a sequence on a black gang—"Sores in the city / that do not want to heal" ("The Blackstone Rangers"). In *Riot* (1969), Brooks develops a sequence about the riots that erupted in Chicago after the assassination of Martin Luther King. Beginning with an epigraph from King, "A riot is the language of the unheard," the poem describes the anger behind the uprising: "Fire. / That is their way of lighting candles in the darkness." In "To Those of My Sisters Who Kept Their Naturals," from *Primer for Blacks* (1980), Brooks celebrates black women who "have not wanted to be white" and have not adopted white hairstyles. Brooks's concerns also focused on Africa in such poems as "The Near-Johannesburg Boy" (1986), in which she finds solidarity in the similar struggles of American and South African blacks: "we shall forge with the Fist-and-the-Fury: / we shall flail in the Hot Time."

Yet it is also possible to read Brooks's poetry as demonstrating continuity rather than development through distinct political stages. From her earliest work, Brooks documented the lives and concerns of urban blacks—especially their struggles against racism. The South Side of Chicago provided the setting for much of Brooks's poetry, in her first volume were transplants from the South, preachers, people living in apartments with only kitchenettes, women who have had abortions, an older couple, single mothers, children, women having affairs, and men on street corners who call women "chicks and broads, / Men hep, can cats, or corny to the jive" ("the soft men" [1945). In "The Ballad of Chocolate Mabbie" and in "The Ballad of Pearl May Lee" (both 1945), Brooks focuses on the violence caused by black prejudices against darker-skinned blacks, and in "Gay Chaps at the Bar" she complains about how the sacrifices of black soldiers during World War II will do nothing to stop their subjugation once the war ends: "Listen, listen. The step / Of iron feet again." In "The Womanhood," a sonnet sequence in *Annie Allen,* Brooks urges blacks to "First fight. Then fiddle" and "civilize a space / Wherein to play your violin with grace." In "The Ballad of Rudolph Reed" from *The Bean Eaters* (1960), Brooks describes how white suburban men attack and kill the first black man to move into the neighborhood. In the same volume, Brooks devotes several poems to Emmett Till, a 15-year-old black boy killed by white southerners in Mississippi. Brooks herself underscored the continuity of her work in 1986 when she republished the earlier anthology *The World of Gwendolyn Brooks* (1971) as *Blacks* (1986) and added her later poetry.

Also consistent throughout Brooks's work is her voice. Whether drawing on blues and ballad rhythms, using rhyme and urban slang, writing a sonnet, or developing a politically explicit free verse, Brooks's style is marked by a jazzlike use of alliteration and irregular rhyme, a penchant for the unusual word, the off-rhythm, and a wide-ranging ironic tone capable of describing, praising, and denouncing. Many of these traits are especially noticeable in what is perhaps her most famous poem, "WE REAL COOL," in which Brooks tells the story of doomed black youths. Described by critics as baroque, elliptical, mandarin, and African, Brooks's voice is one of the most distinctive in American poetry.

BIBLIOGRAPHY

Bolden, B. J. *Urban Rage in Bronzeville.* Chicago: Third World Press, 1999.

Brooks, Gwendolyn. "Poets Who Are Negroes." *Phylon* 2 (December 1950): 312.
———. *Report from Part One.* Detroit: Broadside Press, 1972.
Kent, George E. *A Life of Gwendolyn Brooks.* Lexington: University Press of Kentucky, 1990.
Lee, Don. Preface to *Report from Part One.* Detroit: Broadside Press, 1972, 13–30.
Mootry, Maria K., and Gary Smith. *A Life Distilled.* Urbana: University of Illinois Press, 1987.
Wright, Stephen Caldwell. *On Gwendolyn Brooks.* Ann Arbor: University of Michigan Press, 1996.

George W. Layng

BROUMAS, OLGA (1949–) Olga Broumas's poetry explores feminist and lesbian issues. It can be characterized as an investigation of the varied experiences shared by women, with a particular interest in the way language and discourse are linked to the human body. She writes in a style that is erotic, sensual, and politically charged. Her language combines natural imagery, classic Greek mythology, traditional fairy tales, images of the body, and contemporary feminist scenarios. She writes explicitly about lesbian sexuality and love relationships, as well as the oppression of women throughout history. She has also been part of several significant and successful collaborative projects, including with poets Jane Miller and T. Begley, and painter Sandra McKee. Her major influences include ADRIENNE RICH, W. S. MERWIN, DIANE WAKOSKI, AUDRE LORDE, and Rainier Marie Rilke.

Broumas was born in Syros, Greece, but has lived in the United States since 1967, when she came as a student through a Fulbright exchange program to study architecture and modern dance at the University of Pennsylvania. She received an M.F.A. in creative writing with a minor in dance and printmaking from the University of Oregon (1973). Her first collection of poetry in English, *Beginning with O,* was the 1977 winner of the Yale Series of Younger Poets. She has had a number of fellowships and is the author of seven books of poetry, which are collected in *RAVE: 1975–1999* (1999). She has also translated four books of poetry by the Greek poet, Odysseas Elytis, collected in *Eros, Eros, Eros* (1998).

In selecting *Beginning with O* for the Yale prize, STANLEY KUNITZ describes the book as one of "unabashed eroticism" and "integral imagination" (ix). Broumas's work is erotic, musical, and imagistic with "an intuitive sense of dramatic conflicts and resolutions" (Kunitz ix). She writes with lush language and poetic urgency and, often, with a tone of anger and sadness, as in this passage from "Mosaic" (1983): "Anger fill me with clouds I'll cry." In "If I Yes" (1983), she writes elegiacally: "Let me be carried / Ribbonlike from your tongue / as if by language." These passages demonstrate Broumas's use of figurative language, as well as her poetic range and complexity.

Her poems exhibit a sacred delicacy, whereby they are both evocative and elegant. Broumas relishes the thickness of language, as equally as she luxuriates in the sensuality of the body. Often her poetry explores linguistic experiments that challenge dominant and patriarchal assumptions.

BIBLIOGRAPHY

Hammond, Karla. "An Interview with Olga Broumas." *Northwest Review* 18, no. 3 (1980): 33–44.
Horton, Diane. "'Scarlet Liturgies': The Poetry of Olga Broumas." *North Dakota Quarterly* 55, no. 4 (fall 1987): 322–347.
Kunitz, Stanley. Foreword to *Beginning with O* by Olga Broumas. New Haven, Conn.: Yale University Press, 1977.

Mark Tursi

BROWN, STERLING A. (1901–1989) A contemporary of LANGSTON HUGHES and a protégé of JAMES WELDON JOHNSON, Sterling A. Brown is one of the most important and influential African-American poets of the 20th century. Although Brown's first collection of poetry, *Southern Road* (1932), was published around the time of the HARLEM RENAISSANCE, he resisted being labeled a Harlem Renaissance poet, writing at one point that "[t]he New Negro is not . . . a group of writers centered in Harlem during the second half of the twenties. . . . [M]uch of the best [Negro] writing was not about Harlem" (qtd. in Stuckey 15). For although Brown did write on occasion about urban life and Harlem, in *Southern Road* and later writings, his predominant themes have to do with the folk and folk ways of the black South.

Brown was born in Washington, D.C. His father, a distinguished minister and professor of religion at Howard University, had been a slave in Tennessee. Brown received a scholarship to Williams College, from which he graduated Phi Beta Kappa in 1922, and received his master's degree from Harvard in 1923. A professor, scholar, and literary critic as well as a poet, Brown wrote the first scholarly survey of black poetry, *Negro Poetry and Drama* (1938), and was coeditor of *The Negro Caravan* (1941), an early anthology of African-American literature. He was named poet laureate of the District of Columbia in 1984.

Brown's major contributions to American poetry include his adaptations of the blues, spirituals, and work-song rhythms, innovations in the use of black dialect, and an abiding interest in social realism. In his first published poem, "When de Saints Go Ma'ching Home" (1927), the speaker recollects a sidewalk entertainer who finishes his repertoire with his own variation of the well-known spiritual, enumerating his friends and their troubles as he sees them in "[a] gorgeous procession to 'de Beulah Land.'" Throughout the poem, Brown riffs on the spiritual, expanding its meaning to include particular individuals who have suffered in real-life ways. In the title poem of *Southern Road,* Brown adapts the rhythm of the work song to his line—"Swing dat hammer—hunh— / Steady, bo"—to initiate a poem that details the speaker's daily life on the chain gang even as it gives, through rhythm and lineation, the sound and sense of the speaker's toil.

In these and numerous other poems, Brown layers his portrayals of folk life with memorable characters and penetrating rhythms, leaving a body of work that challenges accepted notions of what it meant to be an African American writing poetry in the midst of the Harlem Renaissance.

BIBLIOGRAPHY

Rowell, Charles H. "Sterling A. Brown and the Afro-American Folk Tradition." In *The Harlem Renaissance Re-examined,* edited by Victor A. Kramer. New York: AMS Press, 1987, pp. 315–337.

Stepto, Robert B. "Sterling A. Brown: Outsider in the Harlem Renaissance?" In *The Harlem Renaissance: Revaluations,* edited by Amritjit Singh, William S. Shriver, and Stanley Brodwin. New York: Garland, 1989, pp. 73–90.

Stuckey, Sterling. Introduction to *The Collected Poems of Sterling A. Brown,* edited by Michael S. Harper. Evanston: Northwestern University Press, 1980, pp. 3–15.

Amy Moorman Robbins

BUKOWSKI, CHARLES (1920–1994) Charles Bukowski came to prominence in the late 1960s. He published antiauthoritarian and sarcastic poems in little literary, underground, and mimeographed magazines and in small-press books. Bukowski's poetry is cynically direct and brutally frank. He wrote contrary to polite ideals, and his poetry fell outside the sanctioned limits of conservative, academic poetry. Shunning literary movements, he became a hero and a model for disenfranchised American poets. The raw vigor of his poetry endeared him to legions of fans. He remains one of America's most widely read poets.

The son of an American soldier and a German mother, Henry Charles Bukowski, Jr., was born in Andernach, Germany, and was brought to Los Angeles in 1922. In 1955 after prolonged alcohol abuse, he was hospitalized with a severe bleeding ulcer. After this near death experience, he began to write poetry. His first book was the slim *Flower, Fist and Bestial Wail* (1960). In 1965 Bukowski met John Martin of Black Sparrow Press. Martin published all of Bukowski's major collections of poetry, including *The Days Run Away Like Wild Horses over the Hills* (1969). He also published Bukowski's short stories and his novels, such as *Post Office* (1971). After publishing more than 60 books in a dozen languages, Bukowski died of leukemia in 1994.

Bukowski's poems are obtuse, insightful, philosophical musings composed as narrative vignettes. He was a master of phrase, cadence, and the use of common speech in poetry. Written in unmeasured lines and in irregular stanzas, his poems read smoothly. Engaging the ordinary, his poems often offer cynical observations: "It Was Just a Little While Ago" (2001) begins with the lines, "almost dawn / blackbirds on the telephone wire." The next line is simply the word, "waiting." The poet enters the banal scene and eats a forgotten sandwich, as his eyes fall upon his carelessly heaped shoes. Bukowski ends the short poem with this ironic insight, "yes, some lives were made to be /

wasted." Writing was Bukowski's salvation. In his poem "Only One Cervantes" (1992), he writes, "writing has been my fountain / of youth." His poetry was always in the midst of both life and death, as well as pleasure and pain, and it was always part of both. In his poem "No More No Less" (1992), he writes, "each day is still a / hammer / a flower."

Much of Bukowski's poetry concerned the raucous exploits of the hardboiled Henry Chinaski, Bukowski's persona, and his greatest literary achievement. Chinaski is a hard-drinking writer, working-class gambler, and womanizer. While Chinaski's exploits seem real, his adventures were embellished by Bukowski to bolster the bravado of his American antihero and underground man. Through Bukowski's—and Chinaski's—adventures the ridiculous in American society is often exposed.

BIBLIOGRAPHY

Cherkovski, Neeli. *Hank: The Life of Charles Bukowski*. New York: Random House, 1991.
Sounes, Howard. *Locked in the Arms of a Crazy Life*. New York: Grove Press, 1998.

Michael Basinski

BURKARD, MICHAEL (1947–) Michael Burkard is a poet whose life experiences—as a professor, psychiatric aide, and alcoholism counselor—inform his heartfelt, dreamlike poetry. Coming out of a lineage which could be said to include WILLIAM CARLOS WILLIAMS and ROBERT CREELEY, Burkard's straightforward address and frequent use of CONFESSIONAL detail are complicated by dislocated syntax and lyrical repetition. A poet who is as interested in the musical and visual arts as he is in literature, Burkard has collaborated with painters and composers and has written artists from Leo Tolstoy to Paul Klee into his poems as familiars. As a teacher of poetry at workshops, universities, and colleges across the country, Burkard has been known for his liberating, inclusive approach to thinking about writing, which emphasizes accessing the uncensored self and a reliance on first drafts and on instinct.

Born in Rome, New York, Burkard attended Hobart College and received an M.F.A. from the University of Iowa in 1973, where his peers included BARRETT WATTEN, Denis Johnson, and TESS GALLAGHER, his second wife. His first book was published in 1977. By 2001 he had published 10 volumes of poetry and received numerous honors, including a Pushcart Prize (2000). His work was included in the annual publication *Best American Poetry* in 1989 and 2001.

Marked by an insistence on truth, Burkard's poems also acknowledge that truth often comes in disguise. His work is heavily populated with ghosts past and present—friends, relatives, lovers, historic figures, versions of the self—and haunted by trains, rain, night, the Moon, and the sea—the shadowy, mysterious side of life. In a typically candid move, he confronts the issue of his recurring themes in the poem "Why Do You Think the Sea Is So Central to Your Writing?" (2001): "what sideways / sea or life am I trying to steer / clear of."

Burkard is similarly introspective when writing about his recovery from alcoholism: "I knew more deeply than before I was in trouble with drinking" ("How I Shaded" [1998]). While this and other poems traffic in melancholy, Burkard's poetry nonetheless often reads as an affirmation of love and joy, both spiritual and physical, manifested through honesty, as in the poem "Wanted" (2001): His desire is to create a poetry that "would talk to you only, / to tell you where I have been."

BIBLIOGRAPHY

Gallagher, Tess. "Inside the Kaleidoscope: The Poetry of Michael Burkard." *American Poetry Review* 11, no. 3 (1982): 34–41.
Gervasio, Michael. "My Secret Boat: The Poetry of Before." *Denver Quarterly* 28, no. 3 (1994): 76–79.
Greenberg, Arielle. "A Place for the Poems to Go: Michael Burkard and Diane Wald." *Rain Taxi* 6, no. 1 (2001): 36–38.

Arielle Greenberg

"BURNING THE SMALL DEAD" GARY SNYDER (1968) GARY SNYDER's "Burning the Small Dead" is collected in his book *The Back Country*, published by New Directions in 1968. As in many of the poems collected in the book, "Burning the Small Dead" explores the character of a particular place, regardless of whether that is Snyder's home on Turtle Island in California, the Pacific Northwest, or Japan. Deeply influenced by Zen Buddhism and Japanese poetry and art, Snyder applies the tenets of mindfulness as he observes small branches burning in a fire, and the result is a poem that charts the connectedness of the human and the natural worlds.

"Burning the Small Dead" is included in the first section of the book, titled "Far West," and the poem suggests poetic affinities with other American styles—namely, the visually laden poetics of the IMAGIST SCHOOL, the sparse linguistic terseness of the OBJECTIVIST SCHOOL, and the poetic dynamics delineated in CHARLES OLSON's 1950 essay "Projective Verse" (see ARS POETICAS). But the poem also invokes a Japanese sensibility in its tone, style, and subject matter and reveals an indebtedness to two of Snyder's largest influences of perceiving and honoring the natural world—American Indian and Zen Buddhist philosophies.

Set on Mt. Ritter in California, the poem focuses upon the natural landscape in order to unveil the ecological interconnectedness of all things. While such discovered connections have ecological implications, the poem seems more explicitly concerned with the spirituality implicit in honoring the natural world and celebrating what Zen Buddhism refers to as "interdependence." In this vein, the poem documents how everything that has sustained and helped a white-bark pine tree over its life of 100 years "hiss[es] in a twisted bough" as the branches burn. After this realization, the gaze of the poem shifts to include Mt. Ritter as part of the webbing that connects the branches to the world as well as to the cosmos, which is represented by the two stars Deneb and Altair and their seemingly separate, yet visually immediate "windy fire."

In this sense, the poem is a celebration of the natural world and the cosmos; like many of Snyder's best poems, it captures and honors the mysterious connectedness of the universe and argues for a more reverent and conscientious attitude toward the natural world that nourishes and sustains human existence.

BIBLIOGRAPHY

Davidson, Michael. *The San Francisco Renaissance: Poetics and Community at Mid-Century.* New York: Cambridge University Press, 1989.

McCord, Howard. *Some Notes to Gary Snyder's Myths & Texts.* Berkeley, Calif.: Sand Dollar, 1971.

Murphy, Patrick D., ed. *Critical Essays on Gary Snyder.* Boston: G. K. Hall, 1991.

David Clippinger

"THE BUS TRIP" JOEL OPPENHEIMER (1960)

Unlike the occasionally baroque lines of CHARLES OLSON, JOEL OPPENHEIMER's teacher at BLACK MOUNTAIN College, or, say, the instant intimacy of many NEW YORK SCHOOL poets, Oppenheimer's poems often read with a kind of rhetorical flatness, atypical for his generation. "The Bus Trip," for example, leaves out the first-person singular and other accoutrements of personality, such as cheerful exclamation marks, an extroverted tone, and any details to contextualize place or time.

While many contemporaneous poets who were thought to be of similar sensibility—such as PAUL BLACKBURN and members of the OBJECTIVIST SCHOOL—eschewed symbolism, Oppenheimer starts his poem by comparing the Moon to a lit clock, but a time piece that does not mean anything to the poem's speaker, who seems to be looking at it from a bus window. The Moon is an icon of the romantic poets, and here Oppenheimer devalues it as something irrelevant to a 20th-century bus rider. "The Bus Trip," then, is not just a mundane perceptual account, the urban anecdote typical of postwar poetry; it is an ideological critique of the received English poetic tradition.

Yet the symbol of the Moon does not quite make sense. The Moon may look like a lit clock, but it is unclear why that clock would not remind or instruct the poem's speaker. Also enigmatic is "J—," an unseen character whose images assail the speaker. By substituting dashes for J—'s full name, Oppenheimer uses a literary convention dating back to Richardson's *Pamela* and its antagonist, Mr. B—. *Pamela,* the first English novel, used this convention to hide the real name of its villain, but in "The Bus Trip," it is unclear if J— is even a person. Foreshadowing the postmodern poetics yet to come, here, a "poetic" symbol like the Moon means nothing to the speaker. He is instead terrified by J—, a signifier that leads to nothing, a mere letter.

The idea of a man being terrified by an initial makes "The Bus Trip" read almost like a precursor to poetry of the LANGUAGE SCHOOL. The poem plays with grammar, but Oppenheimer succeeds at making sense because he always grounds his experiments in a romantic tenderness. When the speaker wonders what would happen if his wife "were not beautiful," Oppenheimer writes, "what could he do and live."

While the poem shifts in syntax, it also shifts in plot. The poem starts with a description of the Moon as useless. The reader then learns that this is only the observation of a man on the bus, who spends the rest of the poem meditating on beauty, his wife and child, and death. And, most mysteriously, the poem begins and ends with the same inexplicable line: "images of J— assail him."

BIBLIOGRAPHY
Thibodaux, David. *Joel Oppenheimer: An Introduction.* Rochester, N.Y.: Camden House, 1986.

Ken Chen

"BY THE ROAD TO THE CONTAGIOUS HOSPITAL" WILLIAM CARLOS WILLIAMS (1923)

"By the road to the contagious hospital," the first lined poem in WILLIAM CARLOS WILLIAMS's collection *Spring in All* (1923), follows immediately after Williams's description of the Greek sculptor Phidias's frieze of the Parthenon, which Williams associates with the coming of spring. Williams depicts the slow arrival of springtime in rural New Jersey, evoking not only the wet but persistent vitality of the land as it pushes off winter but also the struggle of birth that is going on in the hospital where "Dr. Williams' is heading: "They enter the new world naked, / cold, uncertain of all / save that they enter." Williams uses "By the road to the contagious hospital" as a means of enacting one of the central ideas of *Spring and All,* "that progress of life which seems stillness itself in the mass of its movements" (182), and he shows how only close scrutiny of the material world can bring language, and thus human experience, into contact with authentic reality.

Having spent most of his professional life in one region of the country (rural New Jersey), it is not surprising that Williams is fascinated by local settings. The poem opens with a scene of general desolation ("Beyond, the / waste of broad, muddy fields . .") that suggests the heavy industrialization already polluting rural New Jersey at the opening of the 20th century. The first three stanzas depict this stagnation, and the mention of "the contagious hospital" (literally, a sick ward separate from other medical wings, to prevent the spread of contagions like tuberculosis) emphasizes the land's disease and isolation.

Yet out of the waste wrought by human development, the natural world renews itself, as suggested by the birth and germination images of stanzas 5 and 8, respectively. "Lifeless in appearance," Williams writes, "sluggish / dazed spring approaches." As James E. Breslin observes, "[T]he awakened consciousness focused sharply and including everything in the scene, discovers novelty and life" (65). The depiction of vegetative resilience counters the traditional romantic treatment of nature as a pristine environment. The poet neither seeks out an exalted landscape, for the changes he witnesses occur "All along the road," nor does he deploy a decorous language to represent the landscape, as evidenced by the absence of simile or metaphor. Instead, he closely attends to a specific location, as demonstrated by the numerous prepositional phrases and the refusal to choose a more "beautiful" scene, and thus approaches reality itself. Breslin argues that "This poem does not simply describe the physical qualities in a landscape; its center is an *act* of perception" (64). Early in *Spring and All,* Williams wrote that "[t]here is a constant barrier between the reader and his consciousness of immediate contact with the world" (177). But now, it seems that careful observation of life can cross that barrier. "One by one objects are defined," he writes, rendering a world that is not a dead representation, but something vibrant and alive itself: "It quickens: clarity, outline of leaf."

"By the road to the contagious hospital" is in many ways an ecological poem, because it concerns itself with restoration, though more than the environment is being restored. The wreckage caused by industrialization is certainly questioned, though Williams seems to accept the fact of its occurrence. More important, perhaps, language is being returned to a state of exactitude, so that the material world can be apprehended in itself. And this exactitude may also provide the means for human nature to achieve a more organic, less spiritualized state, because for Williams, the material self is itself worthy of wonder and praise. In his subtly ambiguous linking of newborn children and opening blossoms, Williams focuses on the simple reality of new physical existence, a fact imbued with dignity beyond any poetic adornment. Revaluing the human is crucial to the establishment of community. Only when the nonspiritual aspect of human life can be as highly praised as the spiritual can those without a developed "inner life" join with those who possess it. Thus, "By the road to the contagious hospital" functions as the keystone to Williams's project in *Spring and All:* careful observation of reality as a way of restoring language, nature, and the human community.

BIBLIOGRAPHY

Breslin, James E. *William Carlos Williams: An American Artist.* New York: Oxford University Press, 1970.

Williams, William Carlos. *The Collected Poems of William Carlos Williams.* Vol. I: *1909–1939.* 5th ed., edited by A. Walton Litz and Christopher MacGowan. New York: New Directions Books, 1986.

Temple Cone

C

"CACTI" JOEL OPPENHEIMER (1985) JOEL OPPENHEIMER's "Cacti" appeared in *New Spaces: Poems 1978–1983* (1985), with other poems about the changes occurring in his life. Oppenheimer and his second wife, Helen, were divorced in 1976, and by the time this poem was written he was then writing his final newspaper columns for the *Village Voice*. He had refined his poetics so that the discursive voice of his early poems was reduced to focus on specific topics, then to explorations of aspects of the topic. He had learned well the lessons of BLACK MOUNTAIN poetics about open form and projecting the content of the poems through its form. His poetic lines had become shorter and organized with sophisticated rhythms. He was looking around for a new lover, a new place to live, and a new imaginative place for his poetry.

"Cacti" takes place in Oppenheimer's apartment in the West Village of Manhattan and is on one level a meditation about the cacti in the apartment. He looks up information about them in a book and sees their great power for lending meaning to his life. Then he proposes a relationship with the cacti. He finds love once a month; the cacti get water once a month. He, like them, is "planted / in sandy dirt / insecurely," but then in the clear self-consciousness of his discursive mode and avoidance of artifice in language, he explains that "it is all / a conceit / of course." He has survived, as the cacti have survived, but now he is learning that he has lost "all the flowering plants" (women, sexual pleasures) of his life because of his neglect, and he is then reduced to the leafless thick skin of the cacti.

The "puntia rufida" grows even when he is away and not caring for it; it puts out "bright green" shoots in defiance of his neglect. There are other cacti in the group, including "euphorbia," which gives him hope to keep living: Confronting its "terrifying beauty," he feels that they are "equal / as we face each other." He knows the kind of "terrible beauty" of which William Butler Yeats wrote. He is learning how to live in his circumstances, and he is not complaining about his lot in life; even though he is growing "older," he is growing "stronger." Toward the end of the poem, he enlarges the "conceit" to a statement about hurting people who demand too much of him and "eat / too ravenously." He has already learned that New York City "is not nature" but is "grime," and now, in the common experience of man/cacti, he will be friendly only to those who see the beauty in his age as he sees beauty in the cacti. Dylan Thomas created an elaborate metaphor of the "green fuse" that drives flowers and people; Oppenheimer finds a commonality with the cacti in his apartment, which he projects in the short lines and intricate rhythms. The form of the poem enforces the sense of the poem—both plant and poet living forward in a hostile climate.

BIBLIOGRAPHY

Butterick, George F. *Joel Oppenheimer: A Checklist of His Writings*. Storrs: University of Connecticut Library, 1975.

Gilmore, Lyman. *Don't Touch the Poet: The Life and Times of Joel Oppenheimer.* Jersey City, N.J.: Talisman House, 1998.
Thibodaux, David. *Joel Oppenheimer: An Introduction.* Columbia, S.C.: Camden House, 1986.

Robert Bertholf

CAGE, JOHN (1912–1992) Although known primarily as a composer of avant-garde music, John Cage's writing has been significant in postwar American poetry, particularly among his colleagues, such as JACKSON MAC LOW and JOAN RETALLACK. Cage's use of chance-operations and other deterministic compositional procedures—that is, formal and lexical selection made by predetermined systems the author creates, instead of the whims and tastes of the author fitted to preexisting verse norms—extends from a unique set of influences, including the American transcendentalist writer Henry David Thoreau, Japanese Buddhist philosopher D. T. Suzuki, and German composer Arnold Schoenberg.

Cage was born in Los Angeles, California. Leaving after two years study at Pomona College, he spent several years in Europe studying architecture and music and writing poetry and painting in his spare time. By 1933 Cage was in New York studying music composition, and by the following year he was back in Los Angeles studying with Schoenberg. By 1942 Cage had relocated to New York, where he would continue to live and work, often with renowned choreographer Merce Cunningham, until his death. Among Cage's many honors and awards was his position as Charles Eliot Norton Professor of Poetry at Harvard University (1988–89) and his induction into both the American Academy of Arts and Sciences (1978) and the American Academy of Arts and Letters (1989).

Cage's first collection of writings, *Silence* (1961), gathers work from as early as 1937's "The Future of Music: Credo" and compositions as widely cited as "Lecture on Nothing" that state a similar theme: "I have nothing to say and I am saying it and that is poetry as I need it." Cage's interest in *nothing* and *silence* stems from an early observation that human beings can never truly escape sound of some kind and that both poetry and music should make use of the entire range of perceptible material. A related conviction regarding the process of writing is, as he put it in a 1976 interview, that one is as often saying "nothing" as saying something. Cage believes in using the element of chance in composing poetry. For him, chance-operations is a matter of "changing the responsibility of the composer, in making choices to asking questions" (50). Cage's most notable method of asking questions consisted in "reading-through" existing texts to form poems he described as "mesostic," a word meaning "middle-of-the-line." This method involves selecting portions of texts based on keywords, whose letters run down the page, capitalized and vertically, as they appear in the source horizontally, but with this rule: that between any two letters of the keywords those same letters may not appear. The keyword of one such poem is "MARCEL." The poem is about the French artist and writer Marcel Duchamp. It begins with the first three letters of his first name and continues in this vein:

questions i Might
hAve
leaRned

These methods were equally inspired by Cage's practice of Buddhism, and later they incorporated a politically anarchist content drawing on the work of Thoreau. In 1978 Cage began to work as a printmaker while continuing his writing and musical composition. His interest in Japanese Zen Buddhism is reflected in works of this later period, such as *Ryoanji* (1983–85), which takes its name from a Japanese Zen garden, and a 1982 book of mesostic poetry *Themes & Variations,* which he called "a chance-determined *renga*-like mix," referring to the ancient Japanese verse form of half-tankas, the *renga.* In his later years, Cage became a proponent of the political ideas of architect and philosopher R. Buckminster Fuller and the art of macrobiotic eating. His influence survives particularly in the formal and political concerns of the LANGUAGE SCHOOL.

BIBLIOGRAPHY

Cage, John. "Interview." In *Desert Plants: Conversations with 23 American Musicians,* edited by Walter Zimmermann. Vancouver, B.C.: A.R.C. Publications, 1976, pp. 50–61.
Kostelanetz, Richard, ed. *Writings about John Cage.* Ann Arbor: University of Michigan Press, 1993.

Perloff, Marjorie, and Charles Junkerman, eds. *John Cage: Composed in America.* Chicago: University of Chicago Press, 1994.

Patrick Durgin

CAMPO, RAFAEL (1964–) Rafael Campo, a lyric poet who is part of the neoformalist tradition (see NEW FORMALISM), uses form to make sense of the body and its functions as he writes about the AIDS pandemic in both poetry and prose. A physician at Harvard Medical School and the Beth Israel Deaconess Medical Center in Boston, Campo's thematic concern—a doctor who writes about his patients—is reminiscent of WILLIAM CARLOS WILLIAMS's work in the early and mid-20th century. Part of the growing multicultural canon of writers, Campo is concerned with his multiple, sometimes conflicting identities as a physician, HIV-negative gay man, and Latino.

Born in Dover, New Jersey, to Cuban immigrant parents, Campo graduated from Amherst College (1987), where he studied poetry with the poet and critic Eve Sedgwick. He then attended Harvard Medical School, with a year's hiatus in his medical education (1990) to pursue an M.F.A. in poetry with DEREK WALCOTT at Boston University. Torn between poetry and medicine, he jokes that he was afraid to "come out" as a poet, something that inevitably happened when his first book, *The Other Man Was Me: A Voyage to the New World* was selected as the winner of the 1993 National Poetry Series Open Competition (*Healing* 114–115). His early critical success was followed by literary recognitions, such as a Lambda Literary Award, finalist for the National Book Critics Circle Award, finalist for the PEN Center West Literary Award, finalist and a recipient of the National Hispanic Academy of Arts and Sciences Annual Achievement Award, and a Guggenheim Foundation Fellowship.

Campo participates in a larger literary and philosophic tradition of healers. Jeffrey Beame writes, "The music of *What the Body Told,*" one of Campo's books, published in 1996, "its healing generosity, alchemizes a balm for the weary soul, the torn body, this feckless world" (33). In "Night Inexpressible," Campo's tight tercets form the structure of his emotion as he describes his relationship with a patient. David L. Kirp of the *Nation* writes that "Campo's voice carries the traces of a host of healers, poets and prophets, a chorus whose members include Wallace Stevens and Mother Teresa, Richard Rodriguez and AIDS physician Abraham Verghese" (31). Campo separates himself from Williams and others by pursuing the larger meaning of AIDS in the context of his proximity to and distance from his subject matter. Campo is complicit in AIDS as a physician who cares for his patients and as part of two at-risk groups: gay men and Latinos. Simultaneously, however, he struggles to versify his distance as someone who understands AIDS and empathizes with it but is ultimately removed by virtue of his own HIV-negative status.

BIBLIOGRAPHY

Beam, Jeffrey. Review of "What the Body Told." *Lambda Book Report.* (July 1996): 33.
Campo, Rafael. "Does *silencio=muerte?*" *Progressive* 63, no. 10 (1999): 20–23.
———. *The Poetry of Healing.* New York: W. W. Norton, 1993.
Kirp, David L. "Doctor of Desire." *Nation* (24 Feb. 1997): 30–32.

J. Elizabeth Clark

CANADIAN POETIC INFLUENCES To speak of "Canadian influences" on 20th-century American poetry is really only to speak of developments over the latter half of the century. Prior to the 1950s, most poetry written in anglophone Canada was derivative of Victorian and Edwardian British models; the innovations being produced by modernists in the United States and abroad were largely ignored in a country that remained for the most part British and colonial in its cultural outlook (see MODERNISM). In a 1974 issue of *Boundary* 2 devoted to "Canadian Literature," Robert Kroetsch made the famous remark that "Canadian literature evolved directly from Victorian into Postmodern" (1), an evolution that also involves a switch from British/European to North American models and traditions. Due to proximity and a shared language, the enormous cultural influence that the United States holds over the world is felt all the more acutely in anglophone Canada. Couple this with the notorious American ignorance of the country of 30 million to its north, and it is apparent that "Canadian influences" on American poetry cannot be discussed in the same way as, say, French or Russian influences: It would be more accurate to speak of conversations.

The earliest cross-border conversations were nurtured through the context of the little magazine (see POETRY JOURNALS). In the early 1950s, CID CORMAN, the American editor of *Origin,* and Raymond Souster, the Canadian editor of *Contact,* established a correspondence that was to last for some time. According to Frank Davey, "Corman quickly became Souster's most important and prolific correspondent: to date [1980] they have exchanged almost one thousand letters" (*Souster,* 16). *Contact* was unusually internationalist in its editorial focus, an internationalism encouraged by Corman, and it was one of the first Canadian literary magazines to recognize and advance the poetry of the EZRA POUND/WILLIAM CARLOS WILLIAMS line, including work by CHARLES OLSON, ROBERT CREELEY, and DENISE LEVERTOV. *Contact* was to publish 10 issues from 1952 to 1954, but, aside from Corman's interest, the magazine did not receive the attention in the United States for which Souster had hoped.

Montreal poet Irving Layton, who was associated with the *Contact* circle, was the first modern Canadian poet to achieve some recognition in the United States. In his essay "Canadian Poetry 1954," Creeley anoints Layton "the first Great Canadian Poet" (232). In the early 1950s, Creeley and Layton began a correspondence between Montreal and Mallorca, Spain, where Creeley was then residing. Their earliest letters are marked by a discussion of Layton's poem "Vexata Quaestio," which Creeley admired—especially, he wrote Layton, its "Damn fine first verse, and all that hardness" (qtd. in Faas and Reed 6): The speaker fixes his "eyes upon a tree / . . . Listened for ship's sound and birdsong." Creeley's admiration of the verse's "hardness" is in praise of Layton's direct treatment of the thing (to echo Pound [see ARS POETICAS]) and the originality of an imagery that refuses the ease of the simile. Creeley and Layton's correspondence would continue for more than 25 years, and Layton published his book *In the Midst of My Fever* in 1954 with Creeley's Divers Press.

In the early 1960s, the cross-border dialogue shifted west to Vancouver, and once again poets, such as Creeley and Olson, associated with BLACK MOUNTAIN poetry were at the center of things. In 1961 a group of aspiring poets at the University of British Columbia, including Davey, George Bowering, and Fred Wah, started *Tish: A Poetry Newsletter, Vancouver.* These young poets were students of the expatriate American professor Warren Tallman, who had invited ROBERT DUNCAN to Vancouver to give a series of lectures in July 1961. Duncan's lectures were the impetus for the creation of *Tish,* and Tallman would later invite and host other important American writers, such as Creeley, Olson, JACK SPICER, and MICHAEL MCCLURE. *Tish* achieved some notoriety in eastern Canada, partly because of its antagonistic stance to the eastern Canadian "establishment" (the Toronto/Montreal axis), but also because of a perceived American or, more specifically, Black Mountain influence. In 1976 Keith Richardson published his study *Poetry and the Colonized Mind:* Tish, in which he accuses Tallman, Olson, Creeley, and Duncan of being cultural imperialists, and the young Vancouverites their dupes in the importation of a pernicious U.S. influence. But such influence was reciprocal: *Tish* and the Vancouver scene became important sites for American writers: LARRY EIGNER and THEODORE ENSLIN would publish in the pages of *Tish,* for instance, and Creeley taught for a short period in Vancouver.

In 1963 a "Summer Poetry Course" was held at the University of British Columbia, in which Olson, Creeley, Duncan, ALLEN GINSBERG, and PHILIP WHALEN were invited to Vancouver to give lectures, seminars, and readings. The poetry course would eventually come to be known as the 1963 Vancouver Poetry Festival, and it attracted a number of young poets from both Canada and the United States, including MICHAEL PALMER and CLARK COOLIDGE. Such intensity of activity was to cement Vancouver's place in a continental experimental poetics network; Andrew Klobucar and Michael Barnholden have recently argued that after San Francisco, Vancouver in the 1960s "was the primary port of call for experimental writers, especially those associated with the New American Poetry [see POETRY ANTHOLOGIES]" (21).

Of contemporary writers, the poets associated with the so-called LANGUAGE SCHOOL have been most active in continuing and extending this North American community. Toronto poet Steve McCaffery would become a central figure in this movement. In the summer of 1977, a year before the first issue of *L=A=N=G=U=A=G=E*, he edited a section of the Canadian journal *Open Letter* on "The Politics of the Referent." This section included essays by McCaffery, BRUCE ANDREWS, CHARLES BERNSTEIN, Ray DiPalma, and RON SILLIMAN. In 1980 McCaffery would collaborate with the same group of poets in the book *Legend,* during which time he was a somewhat regular contributor to *L=A=N=G=U=A=G=E*. McCaffery's best-known work in the United States is probably *Panopticon* (1984). *Panopticon* features many of McCaffery's signature devices, including a juxtaposition of images with text, as well as a "cinematic" gaze: "The focus moves to a woman writing. She is middle aged. / Her pen plastic. The focus moves to a woman reading." These and other lines recur throughout *Panopticon* in various permutations and recombinations, in a manner somewhat similar to Silliman's *Tjanting* (1981). McCaffery's contemporaries in the United States would also have been interested in *Panopticon*'s self-reflexivity and the extent to which it draws attention to the book as a compositional unit. McCaffery was also a participant, along with bpNichol, Paul Dutton, and Rafael Barreto-Rivera, in the Toronto-based performance poetry group the Four Horsemen, whose improvisatory sound-poetry performances earned them international recognition in the 1970s and 1980s. Around this same time the sound poet Bill Bissett was also performing and reading for audiences outside Canada, including those in the United States (see POETRY IN PERFORMANCE).

The Canadian involvement in the development of the Language school continued in 1982, when the final volume of *L=A=N=G=U=A=G=E* was published as a special issue of *Open Letter* (winter 1982)—one of the first book-length collections of the work of writers associated with the school. In August 1985 the "New Poetics Colloquium" was held in Vancouver, hosted by the newly formed Kootenay School of Writing (KSW), a writer-run collective based in Vancouver and Nelson, British Columbia. This was the first large-scale gathering of poets associated with the Language school, including Andrews, Bernstein, Silliman, BARRETT WATTEN, DIANE WARD, LYN HEJINIAN, and SUSAN HOWE. This colloquium would revitalize the Vancouver scene, and over the following years the poets associated with KSW, such as Jeff Derksen, Nancy Shaw, Deanna Ferguson, Kevin Davies, and Lisa Robertson, would achieve recognition and admiration in the United States. Furthermore, Hejinian, Howe, and Andrews, to name a few, would continue to visit Vancouver as KSW's writers-in-residence, offering readings and seminars and cementing poetic relations between Vancouver and U.S. sites, such as San Francisco and New York.

While the poets associated with the American avant-garde line from the New American poetry to the Language writers have shown the most interest in Canadian poetry, other dialogues have taken place outside these groupings. ADRIENNE RICH, for instance, came to know the work of the Trinidadian-Canadian writer Dionne Brand in the early 1990s. Rich, who appears in dialogue with Brand in a National Film Board of Canada documentary entitled *Listening for Something . . . Adrienne Rich and Dionne Brand in Conversation* (1996), recognized in Brand's poetry a negotiation of passage between oppression and beauty and a demonstration that, as Rich puts it, the love of the medium and the love of freedom "are not in opposition" (249). While Brand had explored anticolonial struggles in earlier works, such as *Chronicles of the Hostile Sun* (1984), a response to the U.S. invasion of Grenada, her 1990 book, *No Language is Neutral,* was groundbreaking in the extent to which it combined a linguistically explorative—and aesthetically gorgeous—poetics with a continued sense of political urgency.

The following generation of Canadian poets has had perhaps the strongest influence on American poetry in the past century, including work by Brand, McCaffery, and poets associated with KSW, but also the Québécoise poet Nicole Brossard and Toronto writers, such as Christian Bök, Karen Mac Cormack, and Darren Wershler-Henry, and expatriate Canadian poets working in the United States, such as Norma Cole and Alan Davies. However, it should also be pointed out that this "North American" community is one based primarily on the foundation of American modernist writers and those poets associated with the New American poetry and that most contemporary American readers remain unaware of some of Canada's most important poets, such as Kroetsch and Phyllis Webb. Thus, despite the cross-border conversation that has developed over the past 50 years, the two literatures continue to develop along differing, if parallel, lines.

BIBLIOGRAPHY

Andrews, Bruce, and Charles Bernstein, eds. *Open Letter* 5, no. 1 (winter 1982). [*L=A=N=G=U=A=G=E*, vol. 4, issue.]

Brand, Dionne. *No Language Is Neutral.* Toronto: Coach House, 1990.

Creeley, Robert. *A Quick Graph: Collected Notes & Essays.* San Francisco: Four Seasons Foundation, 1970.

Davey, Frank. *Louis Dudek & Raymond Souster.* Vancouver: Douglas & McIntyre, 1980.

———, ed. *Tish 1–19.* Vancouver: Talonbooks, 1975.

Faas, Ekbert, and Sabrina Reed, eds. *Irving Layton & Robert Creeley: The Complete Correspondence, 1953–1978.* Montreal/Kingston: McGill-Queen's University Press, 1990.

Klobucar, Andrew, and Michael Barnholden. *Writing Class: The Kootenay School of Writing Anthology.* Vancouver: New Star, 1999.

Kroetsch, Robert. "A Canadian Issue." *Boundary* 2 3, no. 1 (fall 1974): 1–2.

Listening for Something . . . Adrienne Rich and Dionne Brand in Conversation. Directed by Dionne Brand. 56 min. National Film Board of Canada, 1996. Videocassette.

McCaffery, Steve. *Panopticon.* Toronto: blewointmentpress, 1984.

———, ed. "The Politics of the Referent." *Open Letter* 3, no. 7 (summer 1977): 60–107.

Rich, Adrienne. *What Is Found There: Notebooks on Poetry and Politics.* New York: Norton, 1993.

Richardson, Keith. *Poetry and the Colonized Mind:* Tish. Oakville, Ontario: Mosaic, 1976.

Jason Wiens

THE CANTOS EZRA POUND (1930–1970)

EZRA POUND's long, sequential poem, *The Cantos,* not only invented the form and much of the style of the 20th-century long poem (see LONG AND SERIAL POETRY), but seized upon themes that have come to represent the major issues of modern society: the role of spirituality in art and everyday life, the uses of money, the rules of conduct of business and government, and the value of the individual in the age of mass culture. Though long maligned as the work of a traitor to America's cause in World War II, *The Cantos* has endured the test of close scrutiny by the Federal Bureau of Investigation (F.B.I.), the universities, and cultural historians representing a wide spectrum of attitudes and approaches, from hostile to furtively apostolic. While agreement about the poem's achievement is still in the making, few would contest the status of the work as a major poem of an innovative and revolutionary period of literature. (See MODERNISM.)

Conceived originally in 1916 as a poem about history, the first three cantos were published in a form Pound eventually deemed too literal in its historical approach. A second draft of the opening poems, published in 1920, enriched the content by employing what Pound would later call his "ideogrammic method." In essence the ideogram, modeled on the multiple references of meaning embedded in a typical Chinese written character, consists of a pair of concrete particulars whose relation to one another generates in the reader's mind an expanding series of associations. Pound cited the Chinese character for "sincerity," which consists of the figures of "man" and "word," or man standing by his word. That junction of two distinct objects creates a flow of association and meaning without the means of abstraction or generalization. Pound's aim in modernizing poetry was to avoid generalities and to draw language ever closer to the world it seeks to describe.

In rewriting the first three cantos, Pound began with a guiding ideogram of a man setting out to discover his relation to the past, using Homer's Odysseus and his long voyage home after the Trojan War to Ithaca as the controlling metaphor of his exploration of history. Canto I begins with the "ideogram" of men and ships, explorers and their vessels, paraphrased from Book XI of Homer's *Odyssey* in a Latin translation Pound was using at the time while researching the poem in the British Museum. Hence the controlling ideogram of travel to the land of the dead, the Kimmerian Islands of Homer's epic, includes Pound's own act of traveling in the realms of the dead through his reading of ancient literature. While the method is not systematically allegorical, Pound's language moves sinuously between allegorical structures and a more ambitious scheme of conflating whole clusters of related themes and events around a single motif or controlling image.

Canto II continues the journey into the past by shifting the attention from ships to water itself, the waters of consciousness, perhaps, as he indulges in a brilliant display of juggled references from literature pertaining to travelers on the sea, the literal ocean and the figurative one of imagination. The literal ocean exhibits its own magic as he describes myriad patterns of waves, each showing order and structure in this seemingly formless and chaotic medium. The sea also stands for time and memory and the difficulty of fixing exact meanings to any "fact." Instead the lyrical method of approaching something as vast as history itself is one of intuitions and the imagination's unique capacity to discern patterns among the shifting surfaces of his subject.

The test of art, Pound seems to say in this and related cantos, is the power of the artist's attention to discern a design amid the bewildering complexity of life. Pound believed that nature was not a body of random events, but instead an energy system whose processes were cyclical and structured according to the rhythms of growth, decay, and reconstruction. Underlying these rhythms were certain forms that were always present in the ebb and flow of natural things, including the civilizations humans built, then allowed to decay. Such formal laws of nature were the bases, Pound believed, for the arts and for culture. Among his intentions in writing *The Cantos* was to discover how nature provided a model on which the most lasting civilizations had built their moral and ethical visions. *The Cantos* is thus a book of forms, first discovered in nature and then applied to human history as a way of understanding which of them contributed the most to making a balanced, virtuous, and creative form of government for humankind.

Canto III completes the elaboration of Canto I's ideogram of travel by sea by locating the scene in Venice, the great maritime capital of medieval Italy, where "Gods float in the azure air." Here myths and the medium of their occurrence in the imagination, equated with the blue of sea and sky, converge to form a meditation on the decay of mythology in the present age, with its values turned from faith to materialism. The frescoes celebrating such mythic deities have fallen into neglect, where "the pigment flakes from the stone, / Or plaster flakes."

The Cantos may be said to follow from each of these three preambles, with the main emphasis on art as sacred perceptions and time as an erratic progression of periods of enlightenment through close attention to nature's ways and periods of chaos and degradation when such attention fades. The work is divided into the various books marking the progressive publication of the poem. Book I contains the "Draft of XXX Cantos," published in 1930, and develops two of the major themes of the poem: the quest for a leader to rescue the fallen modern age and the complex identity of the poem's persona, who speaks through the voice of Homer's Odysseus, Dante's pilgrim in the *Divine Comedy,* as well as Pound's own persona as a young man first encountering Venice in 1906. Modern Europe has its own dual identity in the poem as the home of the Italian Renaissance and as an industrial civilization that has lost much of its grandeur and importance after World War I.

"Eleven New Cantos XXXI–XLI", which followed in 1934, explores the conflicts of interest underlying the American Revolution and the formation of a strong federal power. "The Fifth Decade of Cantos XLII–LI" is concerned with the powers and influences of European banks in the era just before the outbreak of World War II. Much of the discussion follows from Pound's reading of C. H. Douglas's book, *Social Credit* (1933), which argues that government—not banks—should manage and control the creation of credit for industry and trade.

Pound's involvement in fascist ideology and economic theory drew him to the Italian dictator Benito Mussolini, whose fascist government Pound praised on his twice-weekly radio show on Rome Radio. Among his commentaries were direct addresses to American soldiers to quit fighting and to return to the principles of Thomas Jefferson and the unique agrarian vision he and other founders of the nation once espoused. The Federal Bureau of Investigation (FBI) recorded many of Pound's discussions and considered them efforts to demoralize troops in time of war, grounds for high treason, which led to his indictment as a traitor and to his incarceration by American forces at a detention camp in Pisa, Italy, the subject of his next book of *The Cantos,* "The Pisan Cantos LXXIV–LXXXIV." Considered by many to be the best book of *The Cantos,* it is notable for dropping the all-knowing voice of earlier cantos and sharing with the reader Pound's intimate thoughts as a prisoner housed among war criminals, some of whom were executed in his view. *The Pisan Cantos* was published in 1948 and, controversially, received the Bollingen Prize awarded by the Library of Congress the following year (see POETRY PRIZES).

"Rock Drill De Los Cantares LXXXV–XCV" (1955) borrows widely from various Chinese texts as Pound returns to his chief subject of the poem, good government and the principles of order and justice. Pound makes extensive use of his situation as an inmate of St. Elizabeth's Hospital, in Washington, D.C., established by Congress to confine anyone accused of threatening members of the federal government. Pound's perch near the seat of government of a superpower allows him to comment freely on the politics of the cold war era and to compare American attitudes and policies toward other nations from a larger perspective of politics in world history. His comments on American foreign policy are astute, often ironic assessments of how other nations foundered on some of the same issues—notably how to maintain an empire and how to serve its own citizens when the world demands so much of its attention.

"Thrones de los Cantares XCVI–CIX" (1959), as its name suggests, discusses the elements that make for good leadership, including the right instruction of those who intend to lead and the "solicitude" of good advice by those who make the important decisions. Pound's list of heroes is extensive in *The Cantos* and includes ancient kings of Persia, early rulers of China, the great Renaissance princes of Italy, and the visionary founders of America, most notably Jefferson. Pound attempts to extract from each of their examples a style or single ethical principle, which may offer him the key to right rulership as the ideal philosopher king. The search for a new heroic ruler was, he believed, the responsibility of the artist to imagine, define, and offer to his fellow citizens to improve their own lives and system of government.

The poem's final installment, "Drafts and Fragments of Cantos CX–CXVII" (1969), also regarded as among the best passages of the long poem, contain some of Pound's most moving lyricism, the language of an old man full of regrets about his more impassioned outbursts and accusations and of someone who would most want forgiveness from his readers for having tried too hard to change the world. This book reprises the major motifs of the previous books and rounds out his argument on the necessity of a natural religion as the basis of ethics and good government. Other fragments have been added in subsequent editions of *The Cantos*, but the main lines of the work were established in the 1970 edition, *Cantos 1–117*.

BIBLIOGRAPHY

Cookson, William. *A Guide to* The Cantos *of Ezra Pound*. New York: Persea Books, 2001.

Flory, Wendy. *Ezra Pound and* The Cantos: *A Record of Struggle*. New Haven, Conn.: Yale University Press, 1980.

Kearns, George. *Guide to Ezra Pound's Selected Cantos*. New Brunswick, N.J.: Rutgers University Press, 1980.

Kenner, Hugh. *The Pound Era*. Berkeley: University of California Press, 1971.

Terrell, Carroll F. *A Companion to* The Cantos *of Ezra Pound*. 2 vols. Orono, Maine: National Poetry Foundation, 1980–84.

Paul Christensen

CARIBBEAN POETIC INFLUENCES

The influence of Caribbean literary and oral poetic practices on the culture of poetry in the United States has been important but often subtle. It is—and will be—the result of a number of factors, which include the rising number of people of Caribbean descent living and maintaining their cultural identity in the United States and the fact that poets and poetry scholars of Caribbean nationality have increasingly been invited to teach at U.S. universities, where they come into contact with young American poets and poetry readers and introduce them to poetry they might not have otherwise discovered. The influence of these talented visitors and emigrants to the United States increases to the extent that they achieve literary celebrity.

Many American poetry readers have heard of St. Lucian poet and 1992 Nobel Laureate DEREK WALCOTT. Many have read his books and attended his readings, lectures, and plays. Walcott's high profile, his long tenure as a Boston University professor, and other factors, such as his close association with ROBERT LOWELL, would seem to guarantee at least that less established poets would seek him out for the stamp of his approval.

Two other significant Caribbean poets who have become highly visible and influential in the United

States are Jamaican poet Lorna Goodison and Barbadian poet and scholar EDWARD KAMAU BRATHWAITE. If not quite as well known or widely anthologized as Walcott, both of these poets are, like Walcott, at least part-time U.S. residents, recipients of major international literary prizes, and professors at prestigious American universities. Their employment alone has positioned them to mold the tastes and attitudes of a generation or more of young American poets, readers, and future teachers of poetry.

Brathwaite and Goodison, although more recent arrivals than Walcott, are having a greater impact upon readers and writers with inclinations toward themes and styles outside the confines of Walcott's Eurocentrism and classical British diction and style. Goodison is especially appealing to readers and writers who respond best to a poetry that is more down to earth and socially real, as opposed to Walcott's mythic meditations on history and culture, particularly those with a heightened interest in the experience and status of women. Brathwaite's appeal is strongest among African-American poets and readers who find a source of racial pride in his anticolonialist reconstruction of the history of Africa and the African diaspora, but his immense erudition, technical inventiveness, and mastery of rhythm and sound have won him many admirers among poets and readers of other races, nationalities, and backgrounds.

As different as these influential Caribbean poets are in philosophy and style, they have fundamental things in common, apart from their talent and literary success. First they are all descendents of transported slaves. Second they were all raised and educated under the aegis of the British Empire. Third they all write out of a mixed love for their homelands, one embittered by the hardships their people have suffered for centuries under the racist, imperialist system of the British and now under the scourge of economic and environmental decline, factionalism, violence, and class-based prejudice that has marred their respective nations' periods of self-rule. "And so the drought has dried my tropic," writes Brathwaite of the sad state of affairs in his native Barbados ("Sunsong" [1987]), and of Trinidad, Walcott writes, "Hell is a city much like Port of Spain, / what the rain rots, the sun ripens some more" ("The Spoiler's Return" [1981]). Goodison, in her poem "For My Mother (May I Inherit Half Her Strength)" (1986), offers yet another kind of image of a ruined paradise in a glimpse of her own mother, a superwoman who could "feed twenty people on a stew made from / fallen-from-the-head cabbage leaves."

If Brathwaite, a black nationalist visionary, sees the Caribbean region as a depressing wasteland for the survivors of more than four centuries of slavery and colonial domination, he also sees it as a place with hidden cultural roots that, if nourished, will regrow into nations worthy of their precolonial past. For Walcott, on the other hand, there is no such communal hope; what he sees in his native St. Lucia is a place utterly despoiled of its old beauty and of any trace of nourishing identity. He is neither the cultured Englishman of his education and tastes nor the African of his racial heritage but finds himself, like Robinson Crusoe, a lone survivor in an unrecognizable land who must reinvent himself and build a life from the materials of his imagination. Goodison, a realistic feminist, is neither as hopeful for her homeland's future as Brathwaite nor as hopeless in that regard as Walcott. For her, hope seems to come from the gifts that pass from one hand to another even in the worst of circumstances. In their articulation of feelings of racial pride, tragic identity, and grittiness in the face of social and economic challenges, these Caribbean poets are helping to further the politically potent sense of identity between American citizens of African descent and colonized people around the world that has been one of the principal ideologies in African-American politics of the 20th century.

Decades before Walcott, Brathwaite, and Goodison arrived on the United States shores, there came another Caribbean-born poet whose influence on poetry, literature in general, and race consciousness in the United States is beyond conjecture: CLAUDE MCKAY, whose collection *Harlem Shadows* (1922), is credited with launching the HARLEM RENAISSANCE. Among its most celebrated offerings is the widely anthologized sonnet "The Harlem Dancer," in which McKay reveals his tropical sensibility and breaks new aesthetic ground in celebrating the unappreciated dignity and beauty of a black prostitute who suffers abuse from a crowd of urban lowlifes in the street: "She seemed a proudly-swaying palm / Grown lovelier for passing through a storm." McKay can, in fact, be credited with introducing the idea of the beauty of black people into American culture. It is an idea that continued to show itself in the work of numerous African-American poets who followed him, in the ideas of Malcolm X, and in the slogan, "Black Is beautiful," which was a principal phrase of the civil rights struggle of the late 1960s. Another poem from *Harlem Shadows,* "If We Must Die," remains an anthem of courageous resistance for African Americans and was even quoted in a wartime speech by Winston Churchill.

McKay was an artist, but he was also extremely political. An early black nationalist, he contributed articles to the *Negro World,* a weekly newspaper published in New York by fellow Jamaican Marcus Garvey. Although the extreme anticapitalist, antiimperialist critiques that he expressed in his political writing tended to alienate literary colleagues of his time, the radical content of his poetry and his fervid vision for the progress and independence of his race established him as a precursor of American black nationalist poets, such as AMIRI BARAKA and JAYNE CORTEZ (see BLACK ARTS MOVEMENT), as well as their Barbadian colleague Brathwaite.

McKay influenced American poetry not only through his contributions to the Harlem Renaissance, but also in a delayed, indirect way through the influence of his earliest poems on the literary and popular culture of his native Jamaica. He never returned to his homeland after coming to the United States in 1912, yet he left behind two published volumes of poetry written in creole, the first works of literature ever printed in the everyday language of the Jamaican people. These poems, though unknown elsewhere, were widely read and recited among Jamaicans and became the seeds of a cultural revolution that was to be furthered by the better-known creole poetry of Louise Bennett decades later; they were also given an enormous boost through the continued influence of Garvey, whose ideas inspired the Rastafari religion and more secular versions of black nationalism and black power imported from the United States at the time of the civil rights struggles of the 1960s. Poetry has contributed to this ongoing revolution both through elevating the language of poor blacks to the status of literature and internationally popular song (reggae) and through empowering them with admirable images of their race.

The route by which the outbreak of vernacular poetry in Jamaica came to influence American poetry today is quite circuitous. It begins with the effect vernacular wordplay had, first upon the popular culture of young Jamaicans in both the Caribbean and in England, then upon African-American and Latino youth in urban neighborhoods of the United States. McKay and Bennett invested the language of the Jamaican people with a cultural authority that extended beyond literature and into the oral and musical popular culture of Kingston and London, where the largest numbers of expatriate Jamaicans lived. By the 1970s, Jamaican idioms were expressed prominently in the song lyrics of internationally acclaimed reggae artists, such as Bob Marley and Jimmy Cliff, and in the verbal styles of "toasters," such as U-Roy, who spun records and "skanked" (talked) artfully over the instrumental breaks in songs to incite crowds around mobile sound systems in the streets and neighborhoods of Kingston and London.

If the toaster was an entertainer and not exactly a poet, he or she was a master wordsmith and oral historian of her or his community, and her or his art inspired the often highly political spoken-word creations of dub poets, who recited their rhymes against a simplified and somewhat muted reggae background. Among the first and most famous dub poets were Linton Kwesi Johnson (in London) and Oku Onuora (in Kingston). Although dub poetry never caught on in the United States, it had an American cousin that developed in the streets, playgrounds, and dance clubs of New York's South Bronx. It is what is known as rap or hip-hop, and has extended a powerful influence not only through its highly commercial manifestations in pop music and film, but also through the art of a generation of young black and Latino poets who have been reciting hip-hop-oriented work to packed audiences at poetry slams in American cities since the mid–1990s, and, more recently, at respected literary institutions (see POETRY IN PERFORMANCE).

To trace hip-hop's inception, it is necessary to go back to 1967 when a Jamaican later to be known as Kool DJ Herc packed up his reggae records and moved thousands of miles north to the Bronx. An expert in the music-mixing techniques and crowd-inciting rhetoric pioneered by U-Roy, Herc had put together a powerful Jamaican dancehall sound system to play music at parties and in the street. By 1974 he was a star at disco clubs frequented by young African Americans and Latinos from the neighborhood. Herc had a problem, however: The Bronx crowd was not responding to the island sound at that time and probably was not picking up on the creole lyrics or their revolutionary message. Herc wanted to keep his clients—his listeners—happy. He replaced the unpopular reggae with funk, which the crowd preferred, to dance to and, like U-Roy before him, he maintained continuity and intensity through the use of his verbal skills. He talked to the crowd directly, learned their names, and made up rhymes about them; some from the crowd rhymed back.

By 1980 the content of some of the rapping became serious, aggressively taking on issues of social justice and depicting harsh scenes of life in the ghetto, just as the earlier spoken performance group the LAST POETS had done at the height of the black power movement in the late 1960s. The most politically serious of these first-generation rappers were undoubtedly Afrika Bambaataa and his Zulu Nation, whose vision of ghetto life and political anger were comparable to that of the dub poets in England and Jamaica. Hip-hop took on many forms. Those geared more to music and break dancing evolved to become the cash cow of America's recording industry. The more strictly verbal varieties retained the social conscience of the early political rappers and, in their quest for expanded lyrical possibilities and a larger audience, were destined to become linked to a broader, multiracial performance poetry culture that, though it has a life of its own, is not without links to literary poetry. However far it has come, hip-hop poetry's core connection to the other forms of hip-hop has remained perfectly intact.

If hip-hop poetry has gained a nationwide audience through its impact on live audiences, it has achieved even wider exposure after being featured in two successful films. The first was *SlamNation,* a documentary about the 1996 National Poetry Slam, where rapper and now anthologized hip-hop poet Saul Williams and fellow members of the Nuyorican team stole the show in a coup that established the work of young African-American and Latino poets as a central force in the spoken word movement. The other film is *Slam* (1998), a fictional portrayal of a hip-hop poet that stars and was cowritten by Saul Williams. Winning the Grand Jury Prize at the Sundance Film Festival and the Caméra d'Or at Cannes, *Slam* made hip-hop poetry an international phenomenon.

Still, in spite of all the enthusiasm it has generated and the new poets it has created, hip-hop poetry has hardly enjoyed instant acceptance by the American literary establishment. The mere fact that a new kind of poetry created and enjoyed by young blacks and Latinos in their teens and twenties has had a greater cultural impact than poetries arising from university writing programs, literary journals, and major publishers seems to have spawned snobbish denials that it is poetry at all. If the randomly generated word structures of JOHN CAGE, the manic and onomonapoetic improvisations of JACK KEROUAC's *MEXICO CITY BLUES,* and the explicitly oral and in-your-face chants of ANNE WALDMAN's *Fast Talking Woman* have been accepted and anthologized as poetry, hip-hop poetry can hardly be excluded. In his introduction to the hip-hop section of *The Spoken Word Revolution: Slam, Hip Hop & the Poetry of a New Generation* (2003), an anthology introduced by BILLY COLLINS, a poet laureate of the United States, hip-hop poet Jerry Quickley asserts that hip-hop is simply a form of poetry "like sonnets, villanelles, litanies, *renga,* and other forms" and aptly points out that it incorporates "many of the technical devices of other forms, including slant rhymes, enjambment, [and] A-B rhyme schemes" (Eleveld 38).

In addition to the standard poetic features that Quickley points out, hip-hop has a signature four-beat line which, like the sprung rhythm lines of Gerard Manley Hopkins, can accommodate widely varying numbers of syllables to a common measure, as in these lines from Saul William's "Amethyst Rocks" (2003): "I be exHALin' in RINGS that CIRcle SATurn / leavin' STAINS in my VEINS in astroLOGical PATterns" (capitalization added for emphasis). Imagine the syllables as saxophone notes, and you will hear an agile sort of jazz rhythm not unrelated to what LANGSTON HUGHES and later jazz poets, such as Baraka and Quincy Troupe, try to evoke in their verses. While rhyme and rhythm of this type are common and even expected in all forms of hip-hop, hip-hop poets also employ a broader palette. They will allow themselves the liberties of free verse or use alternative kinds of patterning to achieve effects uniquely suited to their content. These unrhymed 10-syllable lines about the pain of a woman who has just buried her young son, from Jerry Quickley's "Hip Hop Hollas" (2003), provide an apt example: "and she didn't know hearts could break this hard / or what black magic makes her still draw breath." All hip-hop is poetry, Quickley explains: "Not all of it is good poetry. But it's all poetry" (qtd. in Eleveld 38).

If the influx of the literary and oral poetic practice from English-speaking nations of the Caribbean has sown seeds of radical politics and aesthetics in the United States, so have the influx of poetry from the Spanish-speaking Caribbean and the growing number of American-born poets of Hispano-Caribbean ancestry who are also descendents of slaves transported from Africa and survivors of European colonial oppression. Nowhere is the resistance against European and Euro-American political and aesthetic dominance more evident than in the poetry written by members of the community of Puerto Rican poets that sprang up on New York City's Lower East Side, or "Loisaida," as they called it, in the early 1970s and for which the Nuyorican Poets Café has served as creative breeding ground and headquarters (see POETRY INSTITUTIONS). VICTOR HERNANDEZ CRUZ, José Angel Figueroa, Pedro Pietri, MIGUEL ALGARÍN and Miguel Piñero (cofounders of the Nuyorican Poets Café), Sandra Maria Esteves, and JUDITH ORTIZ COFER are among the better-known poets of this group.

The newest generation of poets, slam poets, and hip-hop poets of varying ethnic backgrounds, who hone their skills at open mic sessions and scheduled readings at the Nuyorican Poets Café, learned much from these pioneers of Latino poetry written in English or in artful combinations of standard English, urban black English, and Spanish. Although the younger performers and writers have drawn a great deal from English Language poetry of Nuyorican poets of the 1970s and 1980s and from the highly vernacular, jazz-influenced work of the BEAT poets of the 1950s and 1960s, they have also inherited much from the highly political, yet strongly lyrical work in Spanish of some of Puerto Rico's greatest poets. These include Clemente Soto-Velez and Juan Antonio Corretier, Puerto Rican nationalists who were arrested and imprisoned by the U.S. government in the 1930s, and Julia de Burgos, a pioneering feminist and tireless activist on behalf of Puerto Ricans and other victims of imperialism and prejudice. Other poets who have raised political consciousness and bolstered a sense of Caribbean identity in America's bicultural Puerto Rican community include Nicolas Guillen (1902–78) of Cuba and Ernesto Cardenal (b. 1925) of Nicaragua, antecedents of the popular United States-based poet MARTÍN ESPADA. Committed as these earlier Puerto Rican poets were to anticolonialism and issues of social justice, it would be a mistake to think of their art as mere versification of political clichés, for it is spiritually passionate, sensual in its sounds and images, abstract, and boldly imaginative, as in Burgos's "Poems for a Death That Could Be Mine" (ca. 1953): "What does the ocean care if a river is dammed; / How is the wind tormented if a gust dies?" (*Song of the Simple Truth*, trans. Jack Agueros 1997).

The language of more recent Nuyoricans (both Puerto Rican and non-Puerto Rican) tends to be more "urban" in diction and tone than that of Burgos and her generation, which is made clear in Piñero's depiction of himself as a poet with a head full of precious words "strikin' a new rush for gold / in las bodegas" ("La Bodega Sold Dreams" [1985]). This shift away from the literary discourse of the academy in American poets of Hispanic Afro-Caribbean descent parallels the evolution of creole poetry in the formerly British-ruled Caribbean nations and the adoption of dialect in African-American poetry in general since the Harlem Renaissance. If the decades since Claude McKay arrived here on a boat from Jamaica are any indication, it would seem that growth in and cross-fertilization between multiple ethnic discourses in American poetry will continue, and the influence of poets from the scattered nations and territories of the Caribbean will be a significant part of the process.

BIBLIOGRAPHY

Algarín, Miguel, and Bob Holman. *Aloud: Voices of the Nuyorican Poets Café*. New York: Henry Holt, 1994.

Brown, Stewart et al., eds. *Voice Print: An Anthology of Oral and Related Poetry from the Caribbean.* Kingston, Jamaica: Longman Jamaica Limited, 1989.
Eleveld, Mark, ed. *The Spoken Word Revolution: Slam, Hip Hop & the Poetry of a New Generation.* Naperville, Ill.: Sourcebooks MediaFusion, 2003.
James, Louis. *Caribbean Literature in English.* New York: Addison-Wesley Longman, 1999.
James, Winston. *A Fierce Hatred of Injustice: Claude McKay's Jamaica and His Poetry of Rebellion.* London: Verso, 2000.
Turner, Faythe, ed. *Puerto Rican Writers at Home in the USA.* Seattle: Open Hand, 1991.

Steven J. Peyster

CARRUTH, HAYDEN (1921–) Among 20th-century poets, Hayden Carruth is one of the most iconoclastic and difficult to place. Marshall Rand writes of him: "There is some of Whitman, some of Pound, and a bit of Berryman, among others, but the well-known names (pick your own) don't come to mind after reading his poetry. Where does he fit in?" (272). Because of the enormous span of his career—Carruth's first book, *The Crow and the Heart* (1959), included poetry written as early as 1946—and his penchant for changing style, technique, and tone from poem to poem, trying to pigeonhole Carruth's body of work into a single poetic school or tradition proves not only futile, but largely unproductive. The varied nature of Carruth's work is one of the most vital aspects to consider in understanding his career.

Carruth was born in Waterbury, Connecticut. He earned an A.B. in journalism from the University of North Carolina (1943) and an M.A. in English from the University of Chicago (1948). A noted editor and critic, Carruth has worked for *Poetry* magazine, the University of Chicago Press, and *Harper's,* among other places, and has won numerous awards, including the Lenore Marshall Poetry Prize, a National Book Critics Circle Award, and a National Book Award.

In spite of his panoramic approach to subject and style, Carruth's poetry exhibits some important thematic predilections. His 15-month stay at the Bloomingdale Psychiatric Hospital provided him with material that he has constantly returned to throughout his career: definitions of madness, issues of authenticity, the irresolvable tension between hope and hopelessness. He takes great joy in writing dramatic monologues. By writing in the voices and dialects of others in poems such as "Marvin McCabe," "Marge," and "Septic Tanck [*sic*]," he finds both relief from his own psychological demons and a vehicle through which to express "man's existential situation," which David Perkins cites as the central concern of Carruth's poetry (386). When the character Septic Tanck says in his self-titled poem that his name is the quintessential name "for a poet nowadays, the / ending up place for everything," his humorous, slightly perverse, and ultimately courageous logic is meant to bolster not only Carruth himself, and not only poets, but all people: Through the specificity of the voice, Carruth reaches toward the universal and the timeless. Of his work, Carruth writes, "Beyond passion . . honesty, charity and a radical attitude . . have also been my guides."

BIBLIOGRAPHY

Perkins, David. *A History of Modern Poetry: Modernism and After.* Cambridge, Mass.: Belknap Press of Harvard University Press, 1976–87.
Rand, Marshall. "Carruth against the Grain." *Minnesota Review: A Journal of Creative Writing* 43–44 (1994/1995): 272–275.

Carlos Hernandez

CERAVOLO, JOSEPH (1934–1988) A second-generation member of the NEW YORK SCHOOL, Joseph Ceravolo writes poetry marked by a childlike naiveté, the literary equivalent of the American primitive style in painting. Like his mentor KENNETH KOCH, Ceravolo came to develop a nuanced comic voice: primarily whimsical, but peppered with moments of brooding and foreboding.

Born in Queens, New York, Ceravolo was the eldest son of immigrants from Calabria, Italy. Following a tour of duty in Germany with the U.S. Army, he graduated from the City College of New York (1959). Ceravolo began experimenting with poetry in the army, but it was not until 1959, when he took a workshop with Koch at the New School for Social Research, that his distinctive style began to take shape. Ceravolo's collection *Spring in This World of Poor Mutts* (1968) received the FRANK O'HARA Foundation Award, and his posthumously published collected poems *The Green Lake Is Awake* (1994) earned such widespread praise as to mystify many of those less sympathetic to his project.

A contemporary of other experimental New York school poets, such as TED BERRIGAN and RON PADGETT, Ceravolo's writing is nevertheless more aptly compared, as Koch compared it, to that of earlier vanguards, such as Gerard Manley Hopkins and JOHN WHEELWRIGHT. Ceravolo worked as a civil engineer for a quarter of a century, and, fittingly, his poetry is as practical as it is innovative. With as much earnestness as mirth, Ceravolo proposed to found a school called "Everyday Life," with courses taught on each of the seasons. While often surreal (see SURREALISM), Ceravolo's sense of landscape was deceptively keen; when he describes the "June of winter" ("Drunken Winter" [1994]), those living north of the 40th parallel are likely to feel that strange season's aberration in their bones. Yet Ceravolo was also a city poet and regularly depicted people in urban settings, often taking himself and his family as his subject.

Whether concerned with nature or society, there is an economy of expression in Ceravolo's poetry that is almost Japanese. Though elegant at times, many of his verses are so awkward as to seem the work of a nonnative speaker. Frequently staccato to the point of unintelligibility, his poems often "do" as much as or more than they "say." Sometimes they resonate, and sometimes they frustrate, but they are always on their own terms, and it is this strange integrity that captivates, even when sense begins to shade toward nonsense.

When Ceravolo lacked a word or phrase to express his meaning, he coined one, and his work is rife with neologisms and grammatical acrobatics. When, in his poem "Road of Trials" (1968), Ceravolo runs down to "find you flewing," he brings an immediacy to the past progressive tense that the more traditional construction, "were flying," lacks. Whereas one who "was flying" has flown and is finished, one "flewing" has completed the action and yet, paradoxically, continues it as well. With "flewing," Ceravolo effectively deeds the English language a more perfect form of the imperfect tense. Leaps like these, easily written off as amateurism, have been most highly regarded by Ceravolo's New York school peers.

BIBLIOGRAPHY

Myers, John Bernard, ed. *The Poets of the New York School.* Philadelphia: University of Pennsylvania Press, 1969.

North, Charles. *No Other Way: Selected Prose.* Brooklyn, N.Y.: Hanging Loose Press, 1998.

Jim Cocola

CERVANTES, LORNA DEE (1954–)

A leading member of her generation of Chicana/o poets, Lorna Dee Cervantes writes poems that explore her experiences in complex and strikingly imagistic ways. Writing in Spanish and English, she responds to poetic traditions throughout the Americas. Although she has overcome economic, ethnic, and gender barriers, the memory of those struggles remains in her work.

Born in San Francisco, Cervantes grew up in a poor Mexican-American community near San Jose, California. Educated at San Jose State University and other nearby institutions, she has taught at the University of Colorado, Boulder. Her work has won the American Book Award (1982), the Paterson Poetry Prize (1992), and a Lila Wallace–Reader's Digest Award (1995).

Using memory and social observations, the poems in Cervantes's initial collection, *Emplumada* (1981), focus on friends and family members with notable empathy. Poems like "Uncle's First Rabbit" and "Freeway 280" recall childhood landscapes and conflicted family relationships, even as "Visions of Mexico While at a Writing Symposium in Port Townsend, Washington" and "Emplumada" expose a split identity that can be redeemed through poetry. In the first part of "Visions of Mexico" the speaker identifies with the Mexican people she observes but remains separate from them as well: "I don't want to pretend I know more / and can speak all of the names." In the second part of the poem, set in Washington State, she also finds, "I don't belong." She heals her divided self in the creation of poetry, gathering her "feathers" for "quills." In a similar way, "Emplumada" plays on the Spanish words for "feathered" (*emplumado*) and "pen flourish" (*plumada*) in order to interweave imagery of birds, sexuality, Aztec ceremony, and writing.

The poems of Cervantes's second collection, *From the Cables of Genocide: Poems on Love and Hunger* (1991) are more densely textured, allusive, and wide-ranging than the earlier work. Cervantes dedicates the book, in part, to three women artists who depicted their personal anguish: SYLVIA PLATH (a poet from the United States), Frida Kahlo (a Mexican visual artist), and Violeta Parra (a Chilean poet). Many of the poems in this volume, including "Raisins" and "Ode to a Ranger," ponder the painful aftermath of a failed love affair. In contrast, "Pleiades from the Cables of Genocide" explores a variety of cultural stories, revealing the hybridizations that inevitably follow from social change.

Engaged with the personal life as well as with social realities, history, nature, and myth, Cervantes's poems construct a new identity and a new tradition without being trapped in them. They provide a great journey of discovery for contemporary readers.

BIBLIOGRAPHY

Arteaga, Alfred. *Chicano Poetics: Heterotexts and Hybridities.* New York: Cambridge University Press, 1997, pp. 101–105.

Pérez-Torres, Rafael. *Movements in Chicano Poetry: Against Myths, against Margins.* New York: Cambridge University Press, 1995, pp. 85–95, 200–201.

Steven Gould Axelrod

CHA, THERESA HAK KYUNG (1951–1982) The multimedia works of Theresa Hak Kyung Cha—poet, filmmaker, artist, and writer—portray the experimental quality of language that engages multiple senses. The theme of dislocation is central to the way audiences experience Cha's cross-genre work. Her writings, film, and visual art connect individual and collective memory and history. By offering varying degrees of accessibility to readers and viewers of her work, Cha extends an invitation to revise her words. As she writes in her preface to *Apparatus* (1980), "machinery . . . creates the impression of reality whose function . . . is to conceal from its spectator the relationship of the viewer/subject to the work being viewed" (n.p.). Thus Cha encouraged the active participation of the viewer and reader, thereby "making visible his/her position in the apparatus." Like Sappho and Marguerite Yourcenar, Cha adapts the first-person perspective. Her lyric voice follows and subverts the traditions of Greek poetry, feminist experimental writing, and the American long poem inherited from such poets as EZRA POUND, WILLIAM CARLOS WILLIAMS, and CHARLES OLSON (see LONG AND SERIAL POETRY).

Born in Pusan, Korea, Cha and her family moved to Hawaii and then settled in San Francisco in 1964. After attending the all-girl Convent of the Sacred Heart Catholic School, Cha briefly studied at the University of San Francisco and transferred to the University of California, Berkeley. At Berkeley, she met Jim Melchert, her ceramics instructor, who encouraged her work in performance, and Bertrand Augst, a professor of comparative literature who introduced her to French film theory, while she obtained a bachelor's degree in comparative literature and two master's degrees in comparative literature and fine arts in performance. She became closely involved with other artists, such as Yong Soon Min and Reese Williams, who published Cha's *Apparatus* and *Dictée* (1982). In 1976 Cha spent a year in Paris doing postgraduate work in film and theory. She imbued her works with Catholicism, Korean history, French and English languages and cultures, and the Greco-Roman classics. In 1980 Cha moved to New York to work as a writer and a video/filmmaker. She received a National Endowment for the Arts grant and a postdoctoral fellowship to Korea in 1981. She then worked at the Metropolitan Museum of Art.

Dictée, a work that laces together different genres and crosses cultures, was first published at a time when there was an emphasis on cultural nationalism and the politics of identity. Scholars and critics place *Dictée* in critical interpretations that highlight gender, the nation, and postmodernism. Cha's work reimagines the Korean national history of colonialism and displacement through the bodily representations of women: Korean revolutionary Yu Guan Soon, Joan of Arc, and Cha's mother. In a double movement, the prose both effaces and recalls the multiple voices of such characters: "Dead words. Dead tongue. From disuse. Buried in Time's memory. . . . Restore memory." Believing in culture as the site of exchange, Cha also challenged the conventions of storytelling, particularly the linear form of the epic, by drawing upon many narrative forms: second-language exercises, ideograms, prayers, dreams, and historical documents.

On November 5, 1982, seven days after the publication of *Dictée,* Cha, who made art out of politics, was mysteriously murdered in New York City. Her case remains unsolved.

BIBLIOGRAPHY

Cha, Theresa Hak Kyung. *Apparatus.* New York: Tanam Press, 1980.

Kim, Elaine H., and Norma Alarcón. *Writing Self Writing Nation.* Berkeley, Calif.: Third Woman Press, 1994.

Shih, Shu-Mei. "Nationalism and Korean American Women's Writing: Theresa Hak Kyung Cha's *Dictée.*" In *Speaking the Other Self: American Women Writers,* edited by Jeanne Cambell Reesman. Athens: University of Georgia Press, 1997.

Marie-Therese C. Sulit

THE CHANGING LIGHT AT SANDOVER

JAMES MERRILL (1982) *The Changing Light at Sandover* is an elaborate, engrossing, difficult, and controversial epic trilogy produced by a poet who had been best known before its publication as the author of exquisite lyric poems of "love and loss" written for occasions (see LYRIC POETRY). The poem is variously regarded as either a contemporary poetic triumph or as an extravagant aberration by an otherwise estimable lyric master. Whatever ranking one may give it within Merrill's work as a whole, the trilogy must be regarded as an indispensable addition to that relatively small set of ambitious, book-length, narrative epic poems produced by the major poetic figures of the century, such as *THE CANTOS* of EZRA POUND and WILLIAM CARLOS WILLIAMS's *PATERSON* (see NARRATIVE POETRY and LONG AND SERIAL POETRY). The chief modern poetic influence on the poem, however, was the late group of symbolist poems created by W. B. Yeats (1865–1939) in response to the occult material collected in *A Vision,* the series of meditational sequences, such as "NOTES TOWARD A SUPREME FICTION," that punctuate the poetry of WALLACE STEVENS, and the forms and mannerisms practiced and perfected by W. H. AUDEN throughout his long and varied career. Reaching further back, Merrill's trilogy claims as influence the visionary prophecies of William Blake (1757–1827) and Dante's (1265–1321) *Divine Comedy.*

The Changing Light at Sandover was written with the aid of a Ouija board, at which Merrill and his companion, David Jackson, conversed with ghosts of the dead and various other spirits introduced as the poem evolves. The poem contains a complex cosmological system of death and rebirth, historical evolution, and cultural calamity. By poem's end, however, it becomes clear to the discerning reader that Merrill has produced in this enormous (nearly 600-page) epic yet another tale of love and loss, in which, like Marcel Proust (1871–1922) and Dante, his most evident precursors, he has tried to save time from passing into oblivion and humankind from going astray.

In the trilogy's first book, "The Book of Ephraim," Merrill tells the story of how the spirit Ephraim, whom he and Jackson (referred to in the poem as JM and DJ) first met when taking up the Ouija board as an after-dinner parlor game in the mid 1950s, gradually evolved over a 20-year period into the "household heavyweight" who urges them to bring the inspired "WORD" to humankind in order to save the world from annihilation. The annihilation prophesied in "The Book of Ephraim" is largely a matter of personal psychic self-destruction. Merrill, or JM, is in danger of losing his life, in an aesthetic Proustian sense, by refusing to devote himself fully to the task of writing it down, of translating experience to art, history to myth. The trials that JM must undergo in order to become worthy of the elaborate prophecies he is to receive in the trilogy are figured in terms of the Jungian quest-romance, or the search for psychic wholeness. The poet's chief task is to reign in his inhibiting temperamental skepticism, thereby allowing himself access to the voice of the Jungian unconscious, which is equated in "Ephraim" with God.

First Merrill must integrate the various intransigent elements of his particular psychic makeup into the individual whole of a reinvigorated poet-quester; once that is accomplished, he is prepared in book 2 of the trilogy to begin the daunting task, appointed to him by the spirits, of creating "POEMS OF SCIENCE" (the Ouija board spirits' dialogue is presented throughout the poem, aptly enough, in capital letters). In "Mirabell," Merrill interweaves his extensive knowledge of contemporary science with the Ouija board spirits' ominous tales of past civilizations' downfalls, resulting in an overall admonishment to modern people to direct their awesome scientific achievements to positive humanist ends. In particular this poem warns against the hubris of nuclear power, which is viewed as a collective failure of belief in the value of life itself.

In the trilogy's third poem, "Scripts for the Pageant," and in the "Coda," the poet abandons the trials and warnings of books 1 and 2 in order to offer himself, and his reader, the consolation of a happy ending, in art, if not in life. Although the arguments concerning good and evil, matter and spirit, raised by the earlier books continue in "Scripts," the poet is no longer content in this volume with the theme of the potential for individual and collective destruction. Rather, through his conversations with the spirits (which become "legion" in "Scripts," including archangels, poet precursors, and the ghosts of dead friends), Merrill allows his naturally playful, contrary, and extravagant temperament full sway, responding to all weighty arguments with three equivocal sections, "YES," "&," and "NO." This poem is more mannered than the previous two, and represents this poet's embodiment of a highly unusual paradise that is both high camp and low farce. Read in relation to the earnest psychological self-improvement of "The Book of Ephraim" and the far-ramifying historical-cultural prophecies of "Mirabell," "Scripts" and its "Coda" may be seen to offer the consolation of artifice to a poet destined to have traversed the imaginative heights and depths revealed in the trilogy's complex narrative. In this concluding volume, he finds himself growing weary of the draining task of revelation and is increasingly eager to return to the more mundane pleasures of living. He leaves behind him, as proof of one modern master's unlikely journey into realms seldom visited by contemporary literature, an uncanny poem that will serve as a cultural signpost and a daunting intellectual challenge for generations of readers to come.

BIBLIOGRAPHY

Adams, Don. *James Merrill's Poetic Quest.* Westport, Conn.: Greenwood Press, 1997.

Materer, Timothy. *James Merrill's Apocalypse.* Ithaca, N.Y.: Cornell University Press, 2000.

Polito, Robert. *A Reader's Guide to* The Changing Light at Sandover. Ann Arbor: University of Michigan Press, 1994.

Yenser, Stephen. *The Consuming Myth.* Cambridge, Mass.: Harvard University Press, 1987.

Don Adams

"CHAPLINESQUE" HART CRANE **(1926)** HART CRANE's whimsical yet moving "Chaplinesque" takes as its subject the silent film star Charlie Chaplin, whose iconic role as "The Tramp" Crane elevates to an existential ideal. Chaplin's Tramp, with his tight coat, oversized pants, derby hat, and mustache, represents ordinary humankind, those of us who must "make our meek adjustments / Contented with such random consolations / As the wind deposits." Throughout the poem, Crane skillfully draws on imagery and scenes from Chaplin's films as symbols of the challenges, failures, and minor successes that compose human existence. The language of the poem, though slightly less complex and eccentric than in other Crane works such as *The Bridge* and "AT MELVILLE'S TOMB," nevertheless elevates its subject, suggesting the moral and philosophical importance of Chaplin's Tramp as a model of behavior for all who must accept fate as "that inevitable thumb / That slowly chafes its puckered index towards us."

The curious title, suggesting a focus on people and actions that resemble the style or partake of the characteristics of Chaplin, points immediately to Chaplin's role as an Everyman figure. In the 1920s, Chaplin had already attained status as a world celebrity, having signed the first ever million-dollar acting contract, having founded his own movie studio (which allowed him enormous artistic control), and having filmed the feature-length silent films that are considered among his greatest works. Crane draws his imagery directly from Chaplin's films, depicting the peculiar stroll of the Tramp, his pratfalls, his flexible cane, and his discovery and protection of a defenseless being (the kitten). Indeed, as John Norton-Smith observes, the arrangement of these images narrates a Chaplinesque plot: "stroll, encounter with object in need of protection, discovery and accusation, evasions, unsuccessful comic escape and 'recap'" (61). But Crane does not simply transcribe these images; rather, like his literary forebear, T. S. ELIOT, he gathers these fragmentary images and allusions into a unified structure that may be ironic but is nevertheless elevating, as one can see in Crane's figure of the ash can that becomes a sort of holy grail (of laughter) in the moonlight. Ironically, the poem actually contains one literary allusion: to Eliot. Referring to Eliot's "Preludes," Crane wrote in a letter that "I have made that 'infinitely gentle, infinitely suffering thing' of Eliot's into the symbol of the kitten" (qtd. in Norton-Smith, 61).

Having presented the Chaplinesque figure as an Everyman in the first two stanzas (each one a free verse quatrain), Crane signals a change both in plot and theme in the third stanza, which has an additional line and sets the pattern for the five-line stanzas that follow. Richard Hutson characterizes the shift as the transformation of passivity into grace, noting that "His success lies in his vagabondage, in his ability to transcend any quest or even his own clownishness. . . . [T]his Chaplinesque self is open to the pure gratuity of a vision of liberation" (78). Having been reconciled to life's exigencies, yet also having chosen to shelter a "famished kitten" in our "warm torn elbow coverts," the Chaplinesque figure must ultimately come to terms with fate, facing its "dull squint with what innocence / And what surprise!" The comic pratfalls that follow seem a way of avoiding fate, or at least of appeasing it, but though "The game enforces smirks," Crane admits that in the end "We can evade you, and all else but the heart: / What blame to us if the heart live on." Only a restless wanderer like the Tramp, or like Hart Crane himself, unburdened by possessions, status, or rigid systems of belief, is ever truly free to discover and act upon the goodness latent in all humans, sheltering "a kitten in the wilderness."

BIBLIOGRAPHY

Hutson, Richard. "Exile Guise: Irony and Hart Crane." *Mosaic* 2, no. 4 (1969): 77–78.

Norton-Smith, John. *A Reader's Guide to Hart Crane's "White Buildings."* Lewiston, N.Y.: Edwin Mellen Press, 1993.

Temple Cone

"CHICAGO" CARL SANDBURG (1916) Evoking the expansive free verse (see PROSODY AND FREE VERSE) of the 19th-century American poet Walt Whitman, Carl Sandburg's "Chicago" celebrates the grittiness and gusto of the great midwestern city that became his home. In driving rhythms that recreate the robust energy of Chicago itself, Sandburg's narration rambles from the sordid vices of the gaslight district and the misery of the city's poor to its rail yards and construction sites, praising this city "with lifted head singing so proud to be alive and coarse and strong and cunning." This portrait of Chicago thus stands as a figure for America itself, and in its rousing, early-20th-century optimism, Sandburg's poem exemplifies the way that Americans derive their national identity from their local experience.

Sandburg builds "Chicago" on two different types of free verse lines, short and long. The short lines open the poem and punctuate its middle passages; syntactical fragments, they feature only nouns and adjectives, as if in imitation of tough street talk, and Sandburg praises exactly the qualities one would expect a street tough to admire: "Stormy, husky, brawling, / City of the big shoulders." By contrast, the long lines spread out, overrunning the page's margins in the way the great city threatens to spill over its borders. The longer lines allow Sandburg to write complete sentences that not only describe all aspects of the city, from its vice, crime, and misery to its vibrant growth and bustle, but also comment on these same qualities. Thus, Sandburg can challenge "those who sneer at this my city" with his image of Chicago "Flinging magnetic curses amid the toil of piling job on job, here is a tall bold slugger set vivid against the little soft cities."

"Chicago" evinces a stirring populist sentiment that arises from Sandburg's early engagement with American socialism, though the poem is not overtly critical of capitalism. Indeed, Richard Crowder finds that Sandburg praises the Chicagoans for having "a robustness and a blood-tingling pride that are necessary to the foundations of any healthy society. In return for this vitality, some people must suffer" (51). Mark Van Wienen has written convincingly of various efforts to sanitize the popular socialist impulse behind the collection in which "Chicago" appeared, *Chicago Poems*. Van Wienen charges several forces with blunting the radical politics of Sandburg's poetry: the emphasis of Sandburg's lyricism by such avant-garde poets as AMY

LOWELL; the mollifying influence of his image as a folksy, Walt Whitman–like figure; and most overtly, the effort by Sandburg's publisher, Henry Holt and Company (under the editorship of Alfred Harcourt), to censor some of Sandburg's most committed socialist poems for fear of libel lawsuits from the capitalists Sandburg critiqued.

Yet the uplifting spirit of the poem, its appeal to "the heart of the people," cannot be denied. "Under the terrible burden of destiny," Sandburg writes, the city is "laughing as a young man laughs, / Laughing even as an ignorant fighter laughs who has never lost a battle." By the close of the poem, the most frequently repeated word is "laughing" or "laughter," and this focus on rough joy transforms the potentially oppressive images of modern technology in the opening lines. Indeed, Chicago is no mere industrial entity; for Sandburg, the city is "half-naked, sweating, proud to be Hog Butcher, Tool Maker, Stacker of Wheat, Player with Railroads and Freight Handler to the Nation."

BIBLIOGRAPHY

Arenstein, J. D. "Carl Sandburg's Biblical Roots." *ANQ* 16, no. 2 (2003): 54–60.

Crowder, Richard. *Carl Sandburg.* New York: Twayne Publishers, 1964.

Van Wienen, Mark. "Taming the Socialist: Carl Sandburg's *Chicago Poems* and Its Critics." *American Literature* 63, no. 1 (1991): 89–103.

Temple Cone

CHICAGO POEMS CARL SANDBURG (1916)

Chicago Poems, CARL SANDBURG's first published book of verse, was written in the poet's unique, personal idiom, and it embodies soulfulness, lyric grace, and a love of and compassion for the common person. These poems abandon rare words and classical references of Greek and Roman divinities for everyday vernaculars and subjects. As Louis Untermeyer writes in *Modern American Poetry* (1921), speaking of Sandburg's accomplishment, "This new poetry speaks to us in our own language. Life in its glossary, not literature. It speaks to us of what we had scarcely ever heard expressed; it is not only closer to our soil but nearer to our souls" (xxxi–xxxii). Sandburg's poetry was made for people who had never read verse; turning to it, they found they could not only read it but relish it too.

The poems undulate with a tremendous purring of dynamos, the gossip and laughter of construction gangs, the sounds and images of war, and the tireless energy of a modern city. Indebted to Walt Whitman, Sandburg's poems are less sweeping but more varied than those of the older poet; musically Sandburg's lines, containing few connectives or subordinate clauses and relying instead on the dramatic juxtaposition of simple sentences, mark a great change. His style was met with vast amount of criticism, most notably in *Dial* magazine, whose editorial fumed that the title poem was "blurted out in such an ugly fashion," and "in these 'hog-butcher' pieces there is no discernible evidence that culture has been attained" (Payne 231). In the poem "Style," Sandburg seems to have anticipated the criticisms, stating that if you deny his style by killing it, then "you break [Anna] Pavlova's legs, / and you blind Ty Cobb's batting eye."

Debate of style aside, *Chicago Poems* offers a wide range of sensibilities. And few poems are more intense than "To a Contemporary Bunkshooter," which excoriates contemporary evangelist Billy Sunday with lines such as "the same bunch backing you nailed the nails / into Jesus of Nazareth." And few lyrics are as quiet and tender as "Graves," with its "Petals of red, leaves of yellow, streaks of white," leading the poet to conclude: "I love you and your great way of forgetting."

The 150 poems in the collection are forged with a passion of life, not from the mere aesthetic part of it. Sandburg's acerbic accusations are a result of a robust disgust of shams. Behind the force of his phrases exists the great capacity of his pity. The strength of his, at times, intense dislike is exceeded only by the challenge of his love.

BIBLIOGRAPHY

Payne, William Morton. "New Lamps for Old." *Dial* 56 (1916): 231.

Untermeyer, Louis, ed. *Modern American Poetry.* New York: Harcourt, Brace, 1921.

Woolley Lisa. *American Voices of the Chicago Renaissance.* DeKalb: Northern Illinois University Press, 2000.

Gerald Schwartz

CIARDI, JOHN (1916–1986) John Ciardi was one of several poets who came of age in the mid-20th century and turned away from the free verse of much modern poetry to write in modes that paid closer attention to traditional poetic formal elements, such as meter and rhyme, like his contemporaries KARL SHAPIRO, RICHARD WILBUR, and RANDALL JARRELL (see PROSODY AND FREE VERSE). Ciardi was also a notable public man of letters. As poetry editor at the *Saturday Review* from 1956 to 1972, he generated controversy with attacks on sentimental poetry and was a popular lecturer on poetry to general audiences. He was the author of an influential poetry textbook, *How Does a Poem Mean?* The book stresses the formal analysis of poems while acknowledging the validity of more emotional responses to poetry. He was also the director of the Bread Loaf Writers' Conference between 1955 and 1972 and the translator of an innovative edition of Dante's *Divine Comedy* (1954–70) that used an English vernacular to capture the realism of the original.

Ciardi was born in Boston's Little Italy (North End) neighborhood to Italian immigrant parents. After graduating from Tufts University in 1938, he earned an M.A. in English at the University of Michigan in 1939 and published his first volume of poetry, *Homeward to America,* in 1940. Ciardi then taught at Harvard and Rutgers before leaving academia in 1961. His 20 books of poetry include *Other Skies* (1947), *As If* (1955), and *The Little That Is All* (1974). Ciardi was elected to the American Academy of Arts and Sciences in 1953 and to the National Institute of Arts and Letters in 1957.

Ciardi's often autobiographical poems demonstrate craftsmanship and formal control, usually based on an iambic pentameter line manipulated with a variety of metrical forms and rhyme and typically using precise but contemporary diction that forms unexpected images. Ciardi rarely repeated a form, striving to find for each poem the form that best suited its theme and treatment. His poetry frequently reflects seriously on what Ciardi himself ironically called "unimportant" experiences, such as a child being put to bed or the hearing of a bird's call.

In "On a Photo of Sgt. Ciardi a Year Later" (1947), Ciardi makes a colloquial noun an adjective to create an unexpected but apt metaphor in his description of his "newsreel-jawed" image. Studying the photograph leads to deeper knowledge, however: the realization that in producing the deceptively confident image, "The camera photographs the cameraman" rather than photographing its subject. In "Tenzone" (1964) Ciardi takes up the time-honored literary theme of body versus soul. The soul berates the materialistic, pleasure-seeking body that "leaves in a Cadillac"; the body replies by chastising the soul as "a scratcher of scabs" that are merely illusionary. The poem enacts a dialogue that has been interpreted as relating to Ciardi's own struggle between his worldliness as a public figure and his private creative self. Ciardi's legacy is as a presence in both of those spheres in his roles as critic, public personality, and poet.

BIBLIOGRAPHY

Clemente, Vince, ed. *John Ciardi: Measure of the Man.* Fayetteville: University of Arkansas Press, 1987.

Nims, John Frederick. "John Ciardi: The Many Lives of Poetry" *Poetry* 148 (1986): 283–299.

Sue Barker

CLAMPITT, AMY (1920–1994) Amy Clampitt's poetry, which was influenced by John Keats, Gerard Manley Hopkins, Emily Dickinson, and ELIZABETH BISHOP, possessed what T. S. ELIOT called "the historical sense": "a perception, not only of the pastness of the past, but of its presence" (47). Her work has been classified as being a part of the NEW FORMALISM movement; regardless of her membership in a school, critics, such as Willard Spiegelman, agree that Clampitt has "secured a place for herself in our literary history that is, quite simply, unlike that of any other contemporary" (8).

Clampitt was born in New Providence, Iowa, and her early rural life engendered an encyclopedic knowledge of and empathy with nature. After receiving a bachelor's degree from Grinnell College, she lived primarily in New York and Maine, working at the Oxford University Press, for the Audubon Society, and as a freelance writer and editor at E. P. Dutton. Her first critically acclaimed book of poetry, *The Kingfisher,* appeared in 1983 when she was 63. Five more books and a posthumously published collected poems followed. A member of the American Academy of Arts and Letters, she included among her honors Guggenheim (1982) and Academy of American Poets (1984) Fellowships and a MacArthur Prize (1992).

"Nobody can read Amy Clampitt without a dictionary" (xxii), states MARY JO SALTER regarding Clampitt's *Collected Poems* (1997). Clampitt selected each word so as to heighten a finely crafted sensory experience. Describing the Maine coastline as seen through a veil of low-lying clouds in "Fog" (1983), Clampitt allows us not only to hear but somehow also to see "the ticking, linear / filigree of birdsongs," revealing how the clicking and trilling of various bird voices combine to create a lacy symphony permeating the foggy atmosphere, each one "a blurred flute note" ("Low Tide at Schoodic" [1985].) Her consideration of the smallest details demonstrates one of her major themes: the significance and connectedness of the most seemingly trivial elements of experience. Other important ideas she treats are journeying, loss, death, and transcendence.

In "Beach Glass" (1983), Clampitt claims, "For the ocean, nothing / is beneath consideration," words that are true of the poet herself. As Richard Wakefield notes, Clampitt maintained "an abiding belief that the correspondence between the human heart and the world outside is more than an illusion" (2).

BIBLIOGRAPHY

Eliot, T. S. "Tradition and the Individual Talent." In *The Sacred Wood.* London: Methuen, 1960, pp. 47–52.

Spiegelman, Willard. "What to Make of an Augmented Thing." *Kenyon Review* 21, no. 1 (winter 1999): 173–181.

Wakefield, Richard. "A Clearly Discernible Constellation." *Sewanee Review* 109, no. 1 (winter 2001): xxv–xxviii.

Nan Morelli-White

CLARK, TOM (1941–) With a cavalcade of irreverent lyrics, Tom Clark brought a carnival atmosphere to the poetry scene in the radical 1960s. In addition his discriminating eye as an editor helped shape the tastes of his generation. Clark's offhand but poignant style and his sporadic output link him with predecessors, such as FRANK O'HARA, and contemporaries, such as BILL BERKSON.

Born in Chicago, Clark was trained at the University of Michigan and later at Cambridge University on a Fulbright scholarship. At just 22, he was named poetry editor of the *Paris Review* by his mentor DONALD HALL. During his ensuing decade-long tenure as editor, he promoted the careers of several influential young NEW YORK SCHOOL poets, such as JOHN ASHBERY and TED BERRIGAN. At the same time, Clark published his first volumes of poetry, debuting with *Stones* (1969), which was followed by *Air* (1970). One of his most memorable early efforts was an iconoclastic take-off on the IMAGIST style of WALLACE STEVENS, titled "Eleven Ways of Looking at a Shitbird" (1966).

Though his poems are capable of being caustic, they are also by turns surreal and sentimental (see SURREALISM). Surprising twists abound, as in the frequently anthologized "Going to School in France or America" (1969), wherein Clark declares money to be a means "to certain kinds of killing," only to shift from the critical to the comedic in providing the example of "dropping millions of pennies / on someone from a helicopter." A prolific and versatile author, Clark has produced dozens of chapbooks and larger volumes of poetry. Notable among them are three volumes of collected poems published by Black Sparrow Press, including *When Things Get Tough on Easy Street* (1978). Though irreverent as ever, Clark's later work places a stronger emphasis on history and narrative. Often the poem is used as an occasion for a direct address to a celebrity or historical personality, such as Lenny Bruce or Henry Kissinger.

Clark has also enjoyed an accomplished career as a journalist and an investigative reporter. In *The Great Naropa Poetry Wars,* he examines a confrontation that occurred at the Naropa Institute between W. S. MERWIN and the Buddhist monk Chogyam Trungpa (see POETRY INSTITUTIONS). But in criticizing the Jack Kerouac School of Disembodied Poetics, and, by implication, its founding director ALLEN GINSBERG, Clark found himself ostracized by many in the poetry establishment.

Recent works of nonfiction by Clark include prose biographies of ROBERT CREELEY and CHARLES OLSON as well as poetic narratives on the life of John Keats and on the history of the fur trade in the Pacific Northwest. Clark has also dealt extensively with the subject of baseball in poetry and prose and in a parallel career as a painter.

BIBLIOGRAPHY

Murray, Timothy. "Tom Clark: A Checklist." *Credences: A Journal of Twentieth Century Poetry and Poetics* 1, no. 1 (1981): 121–165.

Perloff, Marjorie. "Poetry Chronicle: 1970–1971." *Contemporary Literature* 14, no. 1 (winter 1973): 97–131.

Warsh, Lewis. "Review of *Stones*." *Poetry* 65, no. 6 (March 1970): 440–446.

Jim Cocola

CLIFTON, LUCILLE (1936–) A prolific writer of poetry and children's books, Lucille Clifton has had a long and distinguished career. She was first published in the 1960s, her early work was influenced by the BLACK ARTS MOVEMENT, especially by poets AMIRI BARAKA (LeRoi Jones), ISHMAEL REED, and GWENDOLYN BROOKS. But the themes of spirituality and self-acceptance that infuse her later work also show the influence of Emily Dickinson, Walt Whitman, and, most important, the culture and stories of African-American women passed down from mother to daughter (see FEMALE VOICE, FEMALE LANGUAGE).

Born in Depew, New York, Thelma Lucille Sayles and her parents moved to Buffalo when she was a child. When she was 16, she received a full scholarship to Howard University in Washington, D.C. In 1955 she returned to Buffalo and studied at Fredonia State Teachers College (now the State University of New York at Fredonia). She married Fred James Clifton in 1958 and had six children within seven years. Clifton juggled writing with the demands of being a wife and mother, and her first poem, "In the Inner City," was published in 1969 in the *Massachusetts Review*. Clifton has taught at a number of schools, including the University of California at Santa Cruz. Returning to Maryland in 1989, she joined the faculty of St. Mary's College of Maryland, where in 1991 she became a distinguished professor of humanities. Clifton received her first National Endowment for the Arts Fellowship in 1970 and a grant from the American Academy of Poets in 1973. She was named poet laureate of Maryland in 1976, a post she held until 1985. Her book *Two-Headed Woman* was nominated for the Pulitzer Prize in 1980. In 1988 she became the only author to have two books of poetry as finalists for the Pulitzer Prize at the same time: *Good Woman: Poems and a Memoir, 1969–1980* and *Next: New Poems*. In 1992 she received the Poetry Society of America's Shelley Memorial Prize. Her book *The Terrible Stories* was nominated for the National Book Award in 1995. In 1996 she received the Lannan Foundation Award for poetry, and in 1999 Clifton was named a chancellor by the American Academy of Poets. In 2000 her book *Blessing the Boats: New and Selected Poems, 1988–2000* received the National Book Award.

A primary strength of Clifton's work is her ability to express themes of great depth—spiritual strength, self-affirmation, sexuality, African-American history—using everyday diction. "I use a simple language," she has said. "I have never believed that for anything to be valid or true or intellectual or 'deep' it had to be first complex" (137). In a voice ranging from African-American idiom to Caribbean dialect, Clifton writes about her family and, especially, about the lives of women. She explores the linkage between generations, within the African-American culture, and in the church, with family, community, and religion as equal sources of spiritual strength and optimism. But it is the women she writes about—whether they are wives, mothers, homeless, saints, or goddesses—who stand out in her poems. Clifton "has written more poems about women's lives than any other African-American poet except Gwendolyn Brooks" (Rushing 218). Among Clifton's ancestors are Caroline Sale, a Dahomey-born woman and former slave who died in 1910, and her great-grandmother and namesake Lucille Sayle, who was hanged after shooting the white man who made her pregnant. Rather than write bitterly about these women's lives, Clifton honors their strength: "and I come from a line / of black and going on women" ("For deLawd" [1969]). The simple phrase *going on women* speaks volumes about the courage and endurance of black women in a culture that has, until recently, little valued them.

Clifton's poems often have a strong narrative thread (see NARRATIVE POETRY), similar to stories told by women around a kitchen table, a quality that makes Clifton's work accessible to readers of all ages and backgrounds. She "gives identity and substance to the everyday people in her poems by giving them names, and therefore a history" (McCluskey 143). She writes of women like Miss Rosie, a "wet brown bag of a woman / who used to be the best looking gal in georgia" ("Miss Rosie" [1969]) or Aunt Nanny, who sat "humming for herself humming / her own sweet human name" ("Slave Cabin, Sotterly Plantation, Maryland, 1989" [1990]). Poems such as these provide a keen insight into the lives of black women, for whom "[r]age and shame and grief must be acknowledged and harnessed for life-saving purposes" (Ansporte-Easton 119). Clifton's themes of healing, self-love, and self-affirmation are also evident in her many children's books.

BIBLIOGRAPHY

Ansporte-Easton, Jean. "'She Made Herself Again': The Maternal Impulse as Poetry." *13th Moon: A Feminist Literary Magazine* 9, nos. 1–2 (1991): 116–135.

Clifton, Lucille. "A Simple Language." In *Black Women Writers (1950–1980): A Critical Evaluation,* edited by Mari Evans. Garden City, N.Y.: Anchor-Doubleday, 1984.

McCluskey, Audrey T. "Tell the Good News: A View of the Works of Lucille Clifton." In *Black Women Writers (1950–1980): A Critical Evaluation,* edited by Mari Evans. Garden City, N.Y.: Anchor-Doubleday, 1984.

Rushing, Andrea Benton. "Lucille Clifton: A Changing Voice for Changing Times." In *Coming to Light: American Women Poets in the Twentieth Century,* edited by Diane Wood Middlebrook and Marilyn Yalom. Ann Arbor: University of Michigan Press, 1985.

Patricia Valdata

"COAL" AUDRE LORDE (1968) AUDRE LORDE's free verse (see PROSODY AND FREE VERSE) poem "Coal" draws upon metaphors of coal, diamonds, darkness, and fire to express an affirmative vision of Lorde's complex identity as an African American, a feminist, a lesbian, a socialist, a mother, and a poet, and to confirm her view of the poet's dual role as activist and cultural spokesperson, a view Lorde shared with her friend, the poet ADRIENNE RICH. Though Lorde begins with the one-word line "I," emphasizing the importance of identity and the power of the lyric voice, the poem ironically shows how "There are many ways of being open." The poem's elemental imagery resonates with Lorde's varied but united identities, and in a more public sense, the "openness" of her imagery, its applicability to a range of subjective experiences, enables Lorde to celebrate all selves, helping their voices find expression so that they will not suffer from neglect or denial.

"Coal" has often been read as an unself-conscious expression of an essential African-American identity, with the recurrent imagery of coal and underground darkness contributing to this view. In this reading, the transformation of coal into diamond and the final excavation of that diamond stand allegorically for the transformation of African-American identity under the pressures of racism and for its public celebration by such cultural movements as the BLACK ARTS MOVEMENT. But Sagri Dhairyam cautions against such a uniformly celebratory and transcendent reading, finding that the images are more ambivalent in their values. Diamonds are luxuries that inversely signify the social poverty and neglect afflicting African Americans, while coal itself remains valuable as a fuel that can bring warmth and energy to homes. Moreover, the mining of diamonds represents a raping of the traditionally feminine earth.

Yet for as much as "Coal" is an affirmative expression of identity, it is also a meditation upon the ways language is used to express and address issues of identity. While early on Lorde emphasizes the capacity of words to "open," a figure for the revelation of identities previously repressed by society, other forms of communication exist. Identity can be articulated by the pure lyric voice "like a diamond / on glass windows," yet it can also be found in choked expressions of rage, like an "ill-pulled tooth with a jagged edge," as well as in the secrecy of cultural isolationism or even in violence, as words "explode through my lips / like young sparrows bursting from a shell." Lorde claims knowledge of all these forms of communication, and she even acknowledges her experience of expressions of identity that fail when she admits that "Some words / Bedevil me."

In the final stanza, Lorde suggests that social harmony is also a way of expressing identity, though she remains ambivalent about this possibility, writing that "Love is a word, another kind of open," but not necessarily the most important kind. Fred Moramarco and William Sullivan note that "For Lorde, anger is a sustaining poetic force, and the articulation of anger gives voice to her deepest self" (175). The expression of identity through poetry is a way of combating the oppressive force of patriarchy; given the widespread racism, sexism, and social oppression Lorde observes throughout America, expressions of anger might well be the transmuted form of love.

BIBLIOGRAPHY

Dhairyam, Sagri. "'Artifacts for Survival': Remapping the Contours of Poetry with Audre Lorde." *Feminist Studies* 18, no. 2 (1992): 229–256.

Lorde, Audre. *The Cancer Journals.* Argyle, N.Y.: Spinsters Ink, 1980.

Moramarco, Fred, and William Sullivan. *Containing Multitudes: Poetry in the United States Since 1950.* New York: Twayne Publishers, 1998.

Temple Cone

CODRESCU, ANDREI (1946–) A wry sense of humor and a talent for shrewdly accurate observations of human culture and society have made Andrei Codrescu a popular poet, novelist, essayist, screenwriter, radio commentator, and editor. His work is characterized by keen satire of the absurd aspects of life in a materialistic society, as seen through the eyes of a person who grew up in a repressive, totalitarian state. His poetry shows the influence of European SURREALISM played against themes of American consumerism, a blend that places his poetry within the postmodern movement. Thus his writing is a mix of European and American sensibility, influenced by poets like Fernando Pessoa, Walt Whitman, the BEATS, and NEW YORK SCHOOL poet TED BERRIGAN, whom Codrescu refers to as a "father" (Hoover 480).

Born in Sibiu, Romania, Codrescu immigrated to the United States when he was 19. His writing career began with the publication of his first book, *License to Carry a Gun* (1970), while Codrescu was still learning to speak English. He became a U.S. citizen in 1981 but went back to Romania after the fall of the Ceausescu government, describing his trip in commentaries on National Public Radio and later on television. In 1983 he founded the literary magazine *Exquisite Corpse: A Journal of Letters and Life* (see POETRY JOURNALS), which was named for a word game invented by French surrealists in the 1920s. He wrote the screenplay for the award-winning film *Road Scholar,* which premiered on public television in 1994. Codrescu has received numerous awards, including three fellowships from the National Endowment for the Arts (1973, 1985, 1989), the Peabody Award for *Road Scholar* (1995), the American Civil Liberties Union Freedom of Speech Award (1995), and the Literature Prize of the Romanian Cultural Foundation in Bucharest (1996).

Codrescu is consistent in his use of humor to point out the ridiculous aspects of modern life, without mincing words: "But through a little hole in the boring report / God watches us faking it" ("Against Meaning" [1996]). He pokes fun at the American idolatry of capitalism by portraying God as a bored executive and underscores the insincerity of life in a country obsessed by the marketplace, where to get by everyone is merely "faking it." In his poetry, prose, and commentaries, Codrescu wants his readers to "acknowledge the paradoxical nature of the postmodern world and to make choices to live meaningfully in that world" (Lehnert 41).

BIBLIOGRAPHY

Hoover, Paul, ed. *Postmodern American Poetry.* New York: W.W. Norton, 1994.

Lehnert, Tim. "Codrescu versus America: A Postmodern Poet Turned Loose." *Xavier Review* 20, no. 2 (2000): 31–42.

Patricia Valdata

COFER, JUDITH ORTIZ (1952–) Judith Ortiz Cofer emerged as an important writer of multicultural and feminist poetry at the end of the 20th century. She is representative of the latest generation of poets who express a new, more inclusive sense of ethnic American identity. Her method of combining poetry with prose also places her at the forefront of a contemporary movement that is in the process of expanding and redefining literary genres and that includes Gloria Anzaldua and THERESA HAK KYUNG CHA. Her literary influences, which include Virginia Woolf, Lillian Hellman, and Emily Dickinson, reflect her interest in a variety of genres as well as her attraction to the power of the female perspective.

Cofer was born in Hormigueros, Puerto Rico. She was raised in Paterson, New Jersey, and became a resident of Georgia as a teenager. Her first collection of poems won the Riverside International Poetry Competition in 1985. In 1994 her collection of poetry and prose, *The Latin Deli,* received the Anisfield-Wolf Book Award, and in 1999 she was honored with a Rockefeller Foundation Residency in Bellagio, Italy. In addition to volumes of poetry, Cofer has published a novel and mixed-genre collections of essays, stories, and poems, as well as a creative nonfiction memoir.

Cofer primarily writes NARRATIVE POETRY, and most of her short, descriptive poems depict the tensions of characters who move between cultures or the complex lives of women in patriarchal societies. Though her poetry is in English, Cofer often incorporates select Spanish words or phrases into her writing. Juan Bruce-Novoa describes this technique as a way to create "the inter space where new meanings are negotiated in a process of synthesis" (96). Most often the themes of family, identity, culture, and spirituality are woven into detailed poems marked by their economy of language and multiple levels of signification.

One of Cofer's most prevalent themes, and the theme that speaks most directly to the condition of living at the turn into the 21st century, is that of multicultural experience. Some of her poems depict the clash of cultures and the fear and division that it can produce. "El Olvido" (1986) begins, "It is a dangerous thing / to forget the climate of your birthplace." The imagery of young Puerto Ricans trying "to choke out the voices of dead relatives" in "bare, cold rooms with no pictures on the wall" reflects the conflict inherent in the desire to assimilate into mainland society. Other poems, such as "To Understand *El Azul*" (2000), represent the fusion of cultures as something positive. The opening line, "We dream in a language that we all understand," expresses unity, and as the poem progresses Cofer fluidly integrates the imagery of Puerto Rico with that of her adopted home in the American South.

Cofer's most memorable poems deal with the places where the intersections of culture create something new, interesting, and even painful out of which to make art.

BIBLIOGRAPHY

Bruce-Novoa, Juan. "Judith Ortiz Cofer's Rituals of Movement." *Americas Review: A Review of Hispanic Literature and Art of the USA* 19, nos. 3–4 (winter 1991): 88–99.

Ocasio, Rafael, and Rita Ganey. "Speaking in Puerto Rican: An Interview with Judith Ortiz Cofer." *Bilingual Review/La Revista Bilingue* 17, no. 2 (May–August 1992): 143–146.

Margaret Crumpton

COLEMAN, WANDA (1946–) Wanda Coleman is a political artist whose vivid, energetic poetry depicts the everyday struggles of poor urban blacks. A poet who prefers the rhythms and language of natural speech to poetic diction, the gritty reality of lived experience to honed imagery, Coleman was instrumental—along with DIANE WAKOSKI, CLAYTON ESHELMAN, and CHARLES BUKOWSKI—in the formation of an alternative literary forum in Los Angeles during the 1970s and 1980s. It was during this time that Coleman earned her reputation as a gifted performance poet (see POETRY IN PERFORMANCE). Coleman draws on diverse and divergent literary traditions, including Euro-American open-form poetics and the African-American vernacular.

Coleman was raised in the Watts district of Los Angeles. She began publishing poems when she was still in her teens and has written many books of poetry, including *Mad Dog Black Lady* (1979), *Imagoes* (1983), and *African Sleeping Sickness* (1990). Her collection *Bathwater Wine* (1998) won the 1999 Lenore Marshall Prize.

Racism is a central concern in Coleman's poetry, and her hard-edged portrayals of life in the Watts ghetto—its prostitutes, alcoholics, welfare mothers, workers, and children—show the damage done to individuals by poverty and racism. "As a writer I feel I best serve my readership when I rehumanize the dehumanized, when I illuminate what is in darkness, when I give blood and bone to statistics that are too easily dismissed," she explains (qtd. in Magistrale and Ferreira 497). Especially interested in the experiences of black women, Coleman writes about sexuality, vulnerability, and resilience, about "being on the bottom where pressures / are greatest" ("Women of My Color" [1979]). The women in Coleman's poems work at jobs in which they are "reduced to rubber-tipped fingers" ("Accounts Payable" [1979]) or to sexual commodities. In "Things No One Knows" (1998), the speaker is a poet who has not reaped much financial reward from her labors: "three months behind in my rent for thirty years," she expects "to die poemless and to be / cremated in state ovens."

Coleman's poems are formally innovative, and her experiments with lineation, spacing, word forms, sound, and integration of blues and jazz cadences achieve varied effects. Her poems tend to resist closure and fixed meaning, eliciting instead immediate psychic and emotional responses. This is a poetry of action and experience, fueled by anger and guided by honest, accurate perception.

BIBLIOGRAPHY

Comer, Krista. "Revising Western Criticism through Wanda Coleman." *Western American Literature* 33, no. 4 (winter 1999): 357–383.

Magistrale, Tony. "Doing Battle with the Wolf: A Critical Introduction to Wanda Coleman's Poetry." *Black American Literature Forum* 23, no. 3 (autumn 1989): 539–554.

———, and Patricia Ferreira. "Sweet Mama Wanda Tells Fortunes: An Interview with Wanda Coleman." *Black American Literature Forum* 24, no. 3, (autumn 1990): 491–507.

Megan Simpson

COLLINS, BILLY (1941–) The critic John Taylor describes Billy Collins's poetry as a "charming mixture of irony, wit, musing, and tenderness for the everyday" (273), qualities that make him one of the most accessible American poets writing in the late 20th century. Unlike many poets of his generation, Collins often uses humorous anecdotes as the basis for his work. This sense of humor, tempered with wise observation and skillful manipulation of image and story, attracts both an academic and a nonacademic audience. Critics praise his craft, which transforms the apparent superficial image or idea into verse that is metaphysically and lyrically surprising.

Born in New York City, Collins received a B.A from the College of the Holy Cross in 1963 and a Ph.D. in 1971 from the University of California, Riverside. He is the author of nine books of poetry and has received many fellowships and awards. In 2001 he was named poet laureate of the United States.

Collins's poems often begin with conversational language and a deceptively simple idea or image. He uses these as the basis for a more complex meaning that emerges near the end of poems. For example, in "Victoria's Secret" (1998), a speaker pores over glossy photos from a Victoria's Secret lingerie catalog; by the end of the poem, these glimpses of flesh symbolize one way for the speaker to forestall death. In "Going Out for Cigarettes" (1999), the speaker contemplates the trajectory of a man who runs away from his life.

Collins's poems sometimes begin lightheartedly, yet his prevalent themes often include death, the effects of aging, disconnectedness, and the ambiguity of language. Though he bases much of his work on life in the real world, his more hopeful poems explore imaginative possibility. As John Updike explains in a blurb to Collins's *The Art of Drowning* (1995), "they describe all the worlds that are and were and some others besides." In "The Blue" (1988), Collins illustrates this characteristic poetic stance as his speaker makes a leap into that "other world": "A jaded traveler with an invisible passport, / I am at home in the heaven of the unforeseen."

Collins's lyrical mastery and his use of the everyday as well as the oft imagined allow him to examine what seems to be the ordinary with extraordinary detail and illumination.

BIBLIOGRAPHY

Taylor, John. *Review of Picnic, Lightning,* by Billy Collins. *Poetry* 17, no. 5 (February 2000): 273.

Weber, Bruce. "On Literary Bridge, Poet Hits a Roadblock," *New York Times.* Available on-line. URL: http://www.nytimes.com/library/books/121999collins-publish-war.html. Downloaded March 2007.

Beckie Flannagan

"THE COLONEL" CAROLYN FORCHÉ (1982) CAROLYN FORCHÉ's chilling prose poem "The Colonel" is based on Forché's own experiences as a human rights worker for Amnesty International in El Salvador in the late 1970s. Written in a documentary style laced with increasingly evident SURREAL images, the poem recounts a dinner Forché attended at the home of a local military colonel noted for his extreme violence towards political opposition. The poem conveys the strangeness, absurdity, and fear that the speaker (ostensibly Forché) feels as the colonel's violent character becomes increasingly apparent, culminating in a shockingly graphic act, the dumping of a sack full of human ears, taken from torture victims. But the poet ironically transforms the colonel's horrifying act into an indictment against him, not by suggesting his own sense of guilt, but by appealing to a higher sense of justice.

Forché has referred to her own work as "poetry of witness," claiming it occupies a "place of resistance and struggle" (10) in between the emotionally expressive, but ultimately private, LYRIC, and the highly public but ultimately partisan expressions of political writing. If political protest addresses verifiable acts of injustice, the poetry of witness exists in "the sphere in which claims against the political order are made in the name of justice" (10). Thus, although Forché has acknowledged that the event she documents actually occurred, its impact upon readers (as evidenced by the poem's inclusion in numerous anthologies) is the truest measure of its power to resist political oppression.

"What you have heard is true," Forché begins, and her dual focus on the truth of her account and on the need to perceive accurately is immediately clear. The speaker details an evening spent in the home of a Latin American military leader, and while the setting appears mundane, some of its details ambiguously suggest violence of a dangerously political sort. A "cop show" is playing on the television, the colonel keeps a pistol on the couch, and the garden walls are topped with broken bottles "to scoop the kneecaps from a man's legs." The rage and violence latent in the atmosphere become manifest when the colonel talks "of how difficult it had become to govern," and when he rises from the table, Forché's friend silently warns her not to speak. The colonel returns with a grocery sack and empties onto the table a great number of human ears, dried and obviously taken from victims of political torture. Forché's description of the scene is poised and unemotional, in keeping with her documentary style and her desire for the poem to be an act of witness, presenting the image without filtering so that the reader herself must come to terms with it. "Something for your poetry, no?" the colonel asks, challenging the poet about the efficacy of poetry in the face of political injustice. At the time it happens, the speaker does not respond, but she fixes her gaze on the ears, and her description of them suggests that while poetry may lack the immediate power of political force, its concern for justice can resonate throughout both the living and the dead, drawing them together in alliance against injustice: "Some of the ears on the floor caught this scrap of his voice. Some of the ears on the floor were pressed to the ground."

BIBLIOGRAPHY

Forché, Carolyn. "Twentieth Century Poetry of Witness." *American Poetry Review* 22, no. 2 (1993): 9–16.

Temple Cone

CONCRETE POETRY See VISUAL POETRY.

A CONEY ISLAND OF THE MIND LAWRENCE FERLINGHETTI (1958)

LAWRENCE FERLINGHETTI's poems in *A Coney Island of the Mind,* a collection of 49 pieces, are typical of much of the avant-garde poetry being composed in the mid–1950s, with an eclectic selection of personal references, as well as allusions to the arts and politics. Their vocabulary, part of a mid-century shift in poetic sensibility, seeks to re-create ordinary speech, a goal articulated and sought earlier by E. E. CUMMINGS and WILLIAM CARLOS WILLIAMS. Ferlinghetti, who published ALLEN GINSBERG's controversial *HOWL,* was a central figure of the SAN FRANCISCO RENAISSANCE, a West Coast parallel to the New York BEATS. He embraced jazz poetry, also found in Beat literature (most notably in JACK KEROUAC's *MEXICO CITY BLUES*).

Ferlinghetti's book received mixed reviews. HAYDEN CARRUTH was especially harsh, judging the book equivalent to the "Sentimentality, fakery, [and] prop cardboard slums on a Hollywood lot" (115). While Ferlinghetti sought to achieve musical verse, Carruth found it "mostly tuneless, mostly arrhythmic" and concluded that the poet's "idea of the new is merely a resuscitation of squabbles that died thirty years ago" (116). D. J. Enright dismissed as "rot" the "description of these poems as 'true mirror-images of our era's tormented face'" (720). Gerald McDonald, however, defended the poems for the way "They mirror [the] time and express an attitude toward it," and he praised them for their "rhythm, lyric strength and immediacy of communication" (1937).

In the first and last sections of *Coney Island,* lines start at various points across the page to stress their musicality. Poem 2 reaches forward and backward in time, with nonsense language and impossible images, such as "elephants in bathtubs / . . . strumming bent mandolins." This hallucinatory quality is consistent in the "Coney Island" and "Gone World" sections that open and close the book, where Ferlinghetti reveals he "fell in love with unreality" (poem 20). In poem 4, Ferlinghetti's World War II military experience, specifically his arrival in Japan soon after the atomic bombing, enters the poem in its depiction of "an inedible mushroom button / and an inaudible Sunday bomb." Even more politically, the absurdist "Dog," which makes the simple substitution of a dog for a man who has the freedom of the streets, makes clear Ferlinghetti's activity as a moral watchdog. The dog sees what anyone might see, including the city's homeless and derelict. Like any anarchist dog, he has no tolerance for uniformed authority figures, but it is what the dog hears while roaming the streets that is particularly distressing, especially "to a sad young dog like himself / to a serious dog like himself." The shared Beat disdain for corrupted politics cannot be silenced or made toothless; the politician is dismissed as nothing more than a suitable scent marker for the dog's territorial perimeter. Central to Ferlinghetti's work is this relentless attention, as Michael Skau observes, to "virtually every issue which has become politically prominent since the mid–1950s" (1).

BIBLIOGRAPHY

Carruth, Hayden. Review of *A Coney Island of the Mind,* by Lawrence Ferlinghetti. *Poetry* 93 (November 1958): 107–116.

Enright, D. J. Review of *A Coney Island of the Mind,* by Lawrence Ferlinghetti. *Spectator* 20 November 1959: 720–721.

McDonald, Gerald D. Review of *A Coney Island of the Mind,* by Lawrence Ferlinghetti. *Library Journal* 83 (15 June 1958): 1937–1938.

Skau, Michael. *'Constantly Risking Absurdity': The Writings of Lawrence Ferlinghetti.* Troy, N.Y.: Whitston, 1989.

A. Mary Murphy

CONFESSIONAL POETRY During the 1950s and 1960s, confessional poetry took shape as a logical progression of one aspect of BEAT POETRY, focusing on the extremely subjective and private experience of the poet. The practice was opposed to, and a reaction against, what had gone immediately before: the erasure of self espoused by such poets as W. H. AUDEN and T. S. ELIOT. These poets had attempted a complete detachment from the speaking subject; the confessional poets immersed themselves (some might say wallowed) in it. In Eliot's MODERNISM, poetry exists as a thing apart from its writer, and the writer is supposedly immaterial to interpretation of the poem; in confessionalism, however, the "I" is central and is an explicit expression of personal experience. Confessional poetry has existed as long as poetry itself, but what marks the mid-20th-century American emergence of an identifiable school is the aesthetic conviction that WILLIAM CARLOS WILLIAMS's claim was right: There is no subject unsuitable for poetry. Whereas other poets in other times were generally too polite or genteel to mention certain matters either directly or even metaphorically, the confessionals sometimes shockingly engaged directly with the most unseemly subjects: mental and physical illness, domestic breakdown, sexual satisfaction or frustration, and functions of the female body—menstruation, pregnancy, childbirth, miscarriage, abortion. This was a movement that had a woman's voice as much as a man's, expanding on EDNA ST. VINCENT MILLAY's unladylike declarations of the 1920s and 1930s (see FEMALE VOICE, FEMALE LANGUAGE).

As with any school, confessional poets knew each other and, in some cases, studied together in workshops. ROBERT LOWELL taught at Boston University, and there encountered the poems of other developing confessionals at the same time as he was beginning work in the mode. SYLVIA PLATH and ANNE SEXTON attended Lowell's poetry workshops in the late 1950s; Sexton and W. D. SNODGRASS had both showed Lowell their poems, and he drew from what was happening in their poems as he worked on his own. Sexton learned from Plath how to articulate hatred in her poems. Snodgrass published *Heart's Needle* in 1959, the same year Lowell's *Life Studies* came out. Sexton followed with *To Bedlam and Part Way Back* in 1960. These three works together claimed the ground first marked out by THEODORE ROETHKE in *The Lost Son* in 1948. These are confessional books, not simply collections that contain a few confessional pieces. Plath "identified with what

Sexton wrote; she also admired her innovative techniques" (Wagner-Martin 159). In an interview near the end of her life, Plath "criticized British poetry for its gentility and praised American poetry for its immediacy. She stated that the subjects of the best poems must be both real, based on genuine emotion, and relevant" (224). Sexton, Snodgrass, Plath, STANLEY KUNITZ, and MAXINE KUMIN all wrote about their surgeries and hospitalizations. The testimonial nature of these confessions includes anything that affected the poet, detailing the impact of other people's behavior as well. In other words, the confessions were not secret in any sense, nor were they confined to the thoughts of the poet. They were sometimes very public declarations of what others had to confess, including "Lowell detailing his father's financial bust, Kunitz confessing his father's suicide, . . . Sexton and Roethke their father's drinking habits, [Allen] Ginsberg his mother's madness" (Phillips 14).

Confessional poetry is not mere prosaic whining. While the subject matter is nontraditional, the traditional literary devices remain available, even indispensable, to any treatment of those subjects. Therefore Sexton can offer up her conclusion that "life is a trick, life is a kitten in a sack" ("Some Foreign Letters" [1960]). There is no more shocking and compelling way than this simile to express the conviction that life is a gigantic fraud, nothing more than drowned innocence and promise. It goes much farther than straightforwardly remarking how disappointed by life one can be. Likewise Ginsberg does not say in passing that he misses and remembers his mother, Naomi; he makes the reader lonely for her when he describes his mother singing with her mandolin. Ginsberg's marvelous poem for his mother, *KADDISH,* openly exhibits his love and tolerance for her and does not shrink from the repulsiveness of his mother's abject body, but instead describes the horrid surgical scars and shows her naked in a way few men or women could. There is a particular courage in the public suffering of confessional poets, a courage that makes it possible to approach the mother's naked body, a courage to show the speaking poet naked before the world too, not narcissistically but dejectedly naked. Confession is an act of ownership, but of sorrows and burdens more than joys. Where joy is present, it is a lost or passing joy, such as Ginsberg's adoring 1956 recollection of Neal Cassady—"So gentle the man, so sweet the moment, so kind the thighs . . . That my body shudders and trembles with happiness, remembering" ("Many Loves" [1996])—a memory of joy, of a body no longer embraced, written with the courage of a midcentury homosexual man.

Losses and sufferings such as these speak directly to the losses and sufferings of the reader. Little wonder, then, that the force required to accomplish such a feat might exact a tremendous cost from the speaker at the same time that it serves a therapeutic purpose. RANDALL JARRELL attempted suicide, and, after more than one attempt each, JOHN BERRYMAN, Plath, and Sexton all succeeded, while Lowell and Roethke both had prolonged struggles with mental illness. In *HOWL* (1956), Ginsberg confesses that he "saw the best minds of [his] generation destroyed by madness, starving hysterical naked." As part of that postwar generation, the confessional poets, in spite of their obvious measure of destruction, practiced a poetry that in some sense hearkened back to the early English Romantics. Their poems are not open wounds on the page. Their work is a crafted response to their overwhelming emotional impulses. They use the sharply defined sensory prompts and the everyday language of the common person learned from the IMAGIST SCHOOL. The profound intimacy of the poetry demands such an accessibility. After all, there is no good in a confession no one comprehends. Crucial to accomplishing the purpose of the poet is the confidence that someone will understand. Otherwise, experience is not validated; for every speaker there must also be a listener. There is some private satisfaction in articulation of the wound, but there is no confession until someone hears.

While confessional poetry as a phenomenon has not generated a great deal of critical interest—perhaps because the period has never really ended—the individual poets most certainly have. Fittingly, biographers have embraced them with a vigorous enthusiasm driven to probe still further behind the confessions. The greater danger is that readers might believe what a confessional poet writes to be true. Use of the "I" and the "you" is a powerful choice because those pronouns carry the weight of eyewitness testimony and speak directly from one person to another or allow a third person (the reader) an eavesdropper's access to private conversation. The strength of eyewitness accounts is that it is very difficult to argue with personal experience, to tell people they did not see what they saw or feel what they felt. However, poets make creative use of experience; perhaps a poem is what it appears to be, perhaps not, but it is always fictionalized to some degree. And each poem has to be questioned on its own merit and contents. Plath's much-discussed poem "DADDY" is a perfect example of the necessity of careful interpretation. Plath understands that sometimes the best way to make a reader understand how a poet feels is to make the reader feel that way too, rather than to describe what is felt. In sum, confessional poetry has all the complexity of any other poetry.

Harry T. Moore complains that confessional poetry is fixed "too exclusively upon the pain, anguish, and ugliness of life at the expense of its pleasure, delight, and beauty" (xiii), but if poets experience more pain than pleasure, then quite naturally that is what will dominate the tone of what they write. Further, Moore concedes that we encounter "more garbage disposals than Grecian urns" (xiii) in 20th-century daily life; surely, it is as much a wonder that a poet finds a way to package the garbage in a beautiful way, as to reflect artistically on classical art. No other group of poets working in the mid-20th century has been so showered with formal recognitions. KARL SHAPIRO (1945), Lowell (1947 and 1974), Roethke (1954), Kunitz (1959), Snodgrass (1960), Berryman (1965), Sexton (1967), Kumin (1973), and Plath (posthumously, 1982) all won the Pulitzer Prize. Certainly, for the confessionals, tangible and public reward of this kind is a fitting part of the process of confession; it verifies a listener, validates the confession, and vindicates the confessor.

BIBLIOGRAPHY

Moore, Harry T. Preface to *The Confessional Poets,* by Robert Phillips. Carbondale: Southern Illinois University Press, 1973.

Phillips, Robert. *The Confessional Poets.* Carbondale: Southern Illinois University Press, 1973.

Sexton, Anne. *The Complete Poems.* Boston: Houghton Mifflin, 1981.

Wagner-Martin, Linda. *Sylvia Plath: A Biography.* New York: St. Martin's Press, 1988.

Yezzi, David. "Confessional Poetry & the Artifice of Honesty." *New Criterion* 16, no. 10 (June 1998): 14–21.

A. Mary Murphy

COOLIDGE, CLARK (1939–) Clark Coolidge is a leading figure in the poetry of language-oriented experimentalism. His early work associated him with both the NEW YORK SCHOOL and BEAT POETRY, and he has since come to be seen as a strong precursor to the LANGUAGE SCHOOL. Coolidge's writing also displays his deep immersion in improvisatory jazz and the visual arts. Writing across a range of forms, from short objectlike poems to seemingly endless longer forms, including poetically charged prose, Coolidge talks of hoping to achieve the "Everything Work," which would use language to record the ever-changing range and expanse of language and consciousness (256).

Coolidge was born in Providence, Rhode Island, where he attended Brown University (1956–58). In the 1960s he lived in New York and San Francisco, where he had a brief career as a jazz drummer. From 1970 to 1997 he lived in the Berkshires on the border between New York and Massachusetts, and since 1997 he has lived in Petaluma, California. He has taught at the Naropa Institute's Jack Kerouac School of Disembodied Poetics since 1977. He was a fellow at the American Academy in Rome in 1984–85.

In 1970 Harper & Row published Coolidge's *Space,* a collection which draws in part on three earlier small-press books. Poems, such as "ounce code orange," which consists of five lines and eight words, show Coolidge's early objectlike language constructs. As Tom Orange writes, the poem "illustrates arrangement and density at work: the placement of words on the page with attention to their sound and semantic values" (54). Coolidge's longer experimental works from the 1970s, including *The Maintains* (1974) and *Polaroid* (1975), extend his improvisatory language investigations in a way that BARRETT WATTEN has compared to the practice in SURREALISM of automatic writing.

Coolidge's poetry of the late 1970s and 1980s takes a turn into more immediately accessible forms of expression. In *The CRYSTAL TEXT* (1986) he writes, "To grasp the relation of words to matter, / mind, process, may be the greatest task." This meditative work also poses the question: "How much of poetry is unprovoked thought?" The work of Coolidge never ceases to expand the boundaries of language art in a writing process that is as inventive as it is prolific.

BIBLIOGRAPHY

Baker, Peter. "Language, Poetry and Marginality." In *Obdurate Brilliance: Exteriority and the Modern Long Poem.* Gainesville: University of Florida Press, 1991, pp. 150–161.

Coolidge, Clark. "Letter to Peter Baker." In *ONWARD: Contemporary and Poetics.* New York: Peter Lang, 1996, pp. 256–258.

Orange, Tom. "Arrangement and Density: A Context for Early Clark Coolidge." *New American Writing* 19 (2001): 50–64.

Watten, Barrett. "Total Syntax: The Work in the World." In *Total Syntax.* Carbondale: Southern Illinois University Press, 1985, pp. 65–114.

Peter Baker

CORMAN, CID (1924–2004) Cid (Sidney) Corman was a prolific writer whose reputation as the author and translator of poems of acute brevity and compression is exceeded only by his importance as an editor and literary facilitator. His poems are steeped in what he calls "the [Ezra] Pound and [William Carlos] Williams, [Wallace] Stevens and [Marianne] Moore mainstream" of American MODERNISM (Charters 137). In their attention to the details and disjunctions of everyday life, his poems can be situated alongside the OBJECTIVIST poetry of LOUIS ZUKOFSKY and GEORGE OPPEN. They are also influenced by his long association and correspondence with CHARLES OLSON, ROBERT CREELEY, and LARRY EIGNER. Corman's poems have been compared to Japanese examples, such as the haiku of Bashō, whose work Corman has published in several volumes of free translations. A tireless cheerleader for poets and poetry alike, Corman was the author of more than 100 books (often from his own small presses), including more than 70 volumes of poetry, several volumes of essays, and translations from many languages, notably Japanese and French.

Corman was born in Boston and studied at Tufts University, graduating in 1945. His first book of poems, *subluna* (1944), was privately printed. Corman pursued graduate studies at the University of Michigan, where he won an Avery Hopwood Prize for poetry (1947) and at the University of North Carolina, Chapel Hill. In 1947 he returned to his parents' Boston home "bursting with a desire to foment a poetic community," soon founding a series of poetry discussion groups based in public libraries (Corman xvi). Corman was among the first to promote radio as a medium for poetry, creating and hosting *This Is Poetry,* a weekly show broadcast on WMEX Boston from 1949–52, featuring live readings by poets, such as JOHN CROWE RANSOM, THEODORE ROETHKE, Stephen Spender, and RICHARD WILBUR. Corman won a 1954 Fulbright grant to study at the Sorbonne, Paris. In 1957 he moved to Kyoto, Japan, where he lived on and off ever since.

In 1951 Corman founded *Origin* magazine (see POETRY JOURNALS), the publication with which he is indelibly associated. Corman claimed that "the story of *Origin* is, in many ways, that of my own development as a poet" (xv). *Origin* ran quarterly until 1957 and soon became a significant venue both for emerging new American poets (recalling the significant anthology by that name edited by Donald Allen and published in 1960 [see POETRY ANTHOLOGIES]) and major works of American and European modernism. *Origin* and, later, Origin Press (founded in 1956) published younger poets as different as WILLIAM BRONK, ROBERT DUNCAN, DENISE LEVERTOV, and JAMES MERRILL (see POETRY PRESSES). Allen, in his seminal anthology, cites *Origin,* along with Creeley's *Black Mountain Review,* as one of "the two important magazines of the period" (Allen xii). Subsequent series of *Origin* were published between April 1961–July 1964 and April 1966–January 1971, Corman financing the rebirths of his magazine through sales from his private collection of letters and manuscripts.

Corman's experience with *Origin* gave him a new confidence in his own poetry. He inscribed a copy of *The Precisions* (1955) to Olson with the request to "be patient that I may learn, having such good teachers." But these poems are more reminiscent of Williams or Stevens than Olson's encyclopedic style, as we see in "The Possessed": "I walk slowly through the closeness / drawing each detail out." In Kyoto Corman began his translations and adaptations of classical Japanese poetry, committing himself, as he wrote in the preface to *Cool Melon* (1959), to the recording of "perception mounted on perception in the joy of language." These qualities are visible in his best-known book of this period, *Sun Rock Man* (1962), written after a stay in Matera, Italy. The poem "the afterthought" seems at first like a parody of Williams, since the poet watches old women "gabbling" out loud, holding onto trussed chickens. But accuracy of perception is not the sole point of the poem: Detail leads instead to whimsical analogy and a bittersweet moral about "doing / what isn't done."

Corman's subsequent collections demonstrate this same mordant humor, often combined with a feeling for the sublime. The 1999 collection *nothing doing* contains examples of both tendencies, as in an untitled three-line poem that describes poetry's potential to be "that conversation we could // not otherwise have." Meanwhile the poem "alighieri" deflates Dante and exalts art in seven lines that point out the irony inherent in the Western tradition's most famous evocation of hell—Dante's *The Inferno*—as being, in the end, "a / comedy."

It would be a mistake, however, to dismiss these disarmingly slight poems as lacking ambition or meditative force. *Of*, a multivolume collection that Corman began publishing in 1990, brings together the many languages and cultures among which he lived and wrote about in five books of 750 poems each. Corman described it as his "new Bible . . . written in a way that even a child could enjoy" (Rowland n.p.). His poems are often overtly concerned with the relation between words and the world, containing profound and disturbing insights. "The Twitch," from book one of *The Despairs* (2001), links eroticism and martyrdom while skewering the Czech poet Miroslav Holub. After citing a Holub aphorism about the possible length of a "moment," Corman compares this abstract idea to the "twitch" of an orgasm, then asks the reader to "tell that to Joan / at the stake." Paraphrasing a Corman poem is very challenging: He describes his work as "direct poetry: if you have to ask somebody to explain the poem then I've failed" (Rowland n.p.). This directness is rooted in the magical banality of words, where the building blocks of writing pay "homage // to themselves / as human" (*For Dear Life* [1975]). Corman was devoted to the complex simplicity of human expression. As he writes in an often-quoted poem from *nothing doing:* "There's only / one poem: / this is it."

BIBLIOGRAPHY

Allen, Donald M. Preface to *The New American Poetry,* edited by Allen. New York: Grove Press, 1960, pp. xi–xiv.

Charters, Ann. "Cid Corman." *Dictionary of Literary Biography*. vol. 5, *American Poets since World War II: Part I: A-K,* edited by Donald J. Greiner. Detroit, Mich.: Gale Research, 1980, pp. 136–142.

Corman, Cid, ed. Introduction to *The Gist of Origin 1951–1971 / an anthology,* edited by Corman. New York: Grossman Publishers, 1975, pp. xv–xxvii.

Rowland, Philip. "Cid Corman in Conversation." *Flashpoint* 4. Available online. URL: http://www.flashpointmag.com/corman1.htm. Downloaded February 2002.

Matthew Hart

CORN, ALFRED (1943–) Alfred Corn is most often associated with such cosmopolitan poets as RICHARD HOWARD, JAMES MERRILL, and J. D. MCCLATCHY, whose sophistication and elegance are among their most distinguishing features. But although Corn's lyrics can contain ornamentation, his finest works often have a directness derived from Walt Whitman and WILLIAM CARLOS WILLIAMS. In his first book, *All Roads at Once* (1976), he writes of his "wanting simple order," and his second volume, *A Call in the Midst of the Crowd* (1978), takes its title from Whitman. Like Williams's *PATERSON, A Call in the Midst of the Crowd* alternates between LYRIC POETRY and prose fragments gleaned from historical sources.

Corn was born in Bainbridge, Georgia, and attended Emory University (B.A., 1965) and Columbia University (M.A., 1970), where he studied French literature and was attracted to the more avant-garde French writers of the time. He has won the Gustaf Davidson Prize (1982) from the Poetry Society of America and the Levinson Prize from *Poetry* magazine (1982), as well as many fellowships from various foundations.

Autobiography is an important element of Corn's work, not just in *Autobiographies* (1992) but also in *Notes from a Child of Paradise* (1984), a three-part poem of 100 sections, obviously modeled on Dante's *Divine Comedy,* which recounts his courtship, marriage, and growing awareness of homosexual feelings. Yet Corn is not a particularly CONFESSIONAL poet. He insists on placing his life within a historical, social, or literary context, which gives it shape. In his long poem "1992," Corn intercuts the story of his life with vignettes of a nurse, an out-of-work house painter, a teenage dishwasher, and other ordinary folk. The interpolated biographies have a particularly documentary style, which although not as severely reduced to evidence as in CHARLES REZNIKOFF's *Testimony,* which is drawn from legal documents, nonetheless holds a special regard for fact. Thus in the account of Dolores Curtis in 1949, he records that her radio is a Zenith, that her boyfriend's car is a Packard, that her boyfriend wears Lucky Tiger hair tonic, and that they eat at the Shangri-La Drive-In, where they order a Schlitz beer.

In addition Corn is interested in writing dramatic monologues. Usually historical figures, the personae vary from Madame de Sévigné to Corn's Revolutionary War ancestor, from Byron to Frances Trollope and Johann Sebastian Bach. An inveterate traveler, Corn has poems set across the United States, Europe, and the Middle East. Corn's work is also informed by his deep religious faith; besides nine volumes of poetry, he has edited *Incarnation* (1990), a collection of essays by contemporary writers on the New Testament.

BIBLIOGRAPHY

Abowitz, Richard. "The Traveler: On the Poetry of Alfred Corn." *Kenyon Review* 15, no. 4 (fall 1993): 204–216.

Martin, Robert K. *The Homosexual Tradition in American Poetry.* Austin: University of Texas Press, 1979.

David Bergman

CORSO, GREGORIO NUNZIO (1930–2001)

Gregory Corso met ALLEN GINSBERG in 1950 in a Greenwich Village bar; with Ginsberg and JACK KEROUAC, he formed the poetic nucleus of the BEAT movement, which would overhaul the form and content of American literature. Frequently living and traveling together internationally over the next few decades, these three and others unavoidably developed similar styles and methods concurrently, demonstrating marked influence on each other. Together they produced unrefined works of such immediacy that the energy and language of experience were, and still are, explicit and shocking in their poetic rejection of boundaries, such as appropriate subject matter, form, and vocabulary.

Corso was born in New York City's Greenwich Village. Abandoned as a small child, he was raised in a series of foster homes until he was 11, when he went to live briefly with his birth father. He was a runaway and a street kid, first arrested in early adolescence for stealing food. Corso's prison career included reform school, New York's infamous jail nicknamed the "Tombs", and a three-year term for armed robbery when he was only 17. Although his formal education ended after elementary school, Corso used his time in Clinton Prison to educate himself; reading voraciously from the prison library, he absorbed an eclectic assortment of writers, which established an idiosyncratic foundation for his own work. He also studied an old dictionary, which might explain an unusually dated language in some of his poems. Although widely hailed in the American intellectual underground, Corso never received any major literary awards.

Because of his poverty, street life, imprisonment, and lack of parenting and education, Corso grew into "a tangled man" (Skau 2), an undisciplined adult, with an unpredictable personality. He "didn't talk—he'd just blurt out or shout some sentence" (Cassady 231), as ill behaved as a recalcitrant child. Corso antagonized everyone, gambled, borrowed money incessantly, developed a 20-plus-year drug addiction, had at least one mental breakdown requiring hospitalization, married three times, and fathered five children. He was also a "poetic wordslinger . . . a poet's, Poet . . Captain Poetry" (Ginsberg xii). For Corso, the duty of the artist was to be a site of resistance to everything negative (Stephenson 13).

One of his best-known poems, "Marriage" (1960), is a light-hearted soliloquy on whether or not to marry, and whether to meet the parents with his disheveled appearance and lack of social graces. He envisions a wedding crowded with the bride's relatives and friends, but with only a token number of his friends because they are social outsiders. The poem makes very clear, though, that becoming an insider, through the respectability of marriage, is not without its appeal.

He imagines a beautiful bride in domestic bliss, but a moment later he also imagines utility bills, crying babies, and television. He even fears that the lovely bride will be transformed into "A fat . . . wife screeching over potatoes Get a job." Bills and responsibility are a frightening specter for a bohemian poet. He embraces the fantasy of family life but is wary of what reality might develop after the wedding.

Corso's poems are widely allusive, often imagistic (see IMAGIST SCHOOL) and surreal (see SURREALISM), and full of common speech alongside archaisms. "Bomb" (1960) is a poem shaped like a mushroom cloud, and it collapses geography and time (so we see the Greek god "Hermes racing [the American track star Jesse] Owens") to create multiple meetings of figures from history and myth. The poem marshals the weapons of history from sticks to knives to guns and proclaims a love of the bomb, which was shocking in the 1950s; it also prophesies an ominous future, considering human nature. The obvious contradictions of humanity are made clear: He lists things that are at stake in nuclear struggle, from Goldilocks to Mozambique, and reminds readers that "earth's grumpy empires" would willingly sacrifice it all.

Nevertheless Corso's poems show a fervent belief in beauty and goodness. Although his poems have a raw, unsophisticated quality, as might be expected from an undisciplined poet, he is consistent—even while treating subjects of brutality—in that "the theme and element of delight are manifest in virtually every poem, every play and prose piece" (Stephenson 8). Living his life outside structured norms, Corso wrote poems that are rigorous in their rejection of formulaic predictability; there are no firm, fast rules or boundaries in his life or art. In Corso, as in the work of other Beat writers, there is the ever-present spontaneous impulse and joy in freedom. Corso wrote three short plays, a variety of short prose pieces, and a single novel (*The American Express* [1961]), but it is as a poet, in eight books of verse, that he is most known.

BIBLIOGRAPHY

Cassady, Carolyn. *Off the Road: My Years with Cassady, Kerouac, and Ginsberg.* New York: Penguin, 1991.

Ginsberg, Allen. "On Corso's Virtues." In *Mindfield,* by Gregory Corso. New York: Thunder's Mouth Press, 1989.

Miles, Barry. *The Beat Hotel: Ginsberg, Burroughs, and Corso in Paris, 1958–1963.* New York: Grove, 2000.

Skau, Michael. *"A Clown in the Grave": Complexities and Tensions in the Works of Gregory Corso.* Carbondale: Southern Illinois University Press, 1999.

Stephenson, Gregory. *Exiled Angel: A Study of the Work of Gregory Corso.* London: Hearing Eye, 1989.

A. Mary Murphy

"CORSON'S INLET" A. R. AMMONS (1965)

In "Corson's Inlet," a vibrant refashioning of the traditional romantic poem about a nature walk, A. R. AMMONS draws on the shifting terrains of coastal New Jersey both to suggest and to delight in the limitations of human knowledge. Evoking both William Wordsworth's meditative lyric "Tintern Abbey" and Ralph Waldo Emerson's essay "Nature," "Corson's Inlet" links the process of thought to a natural landscape. But where Wordsworth sought and Emerson found a sense of universal permanence in nature, Ammons views the ever-changing shoreline as a challenge both to language's attempt to encapsulate reality through description and to reason's effort to encompass the world through abstraction. Thus, the marine 'edge effect' offers Ammons an important epistemological insight: knowledge is always partial, but to be alert and not averse to such limitation may allow for a more expansive sensibility, one which does not hanker for limited and limiting definitions of reality, but which can find "change . . . clear / as any sharpness."

The poem opens with the speaker's description of a morning walk along the dunes, and the poem appears ready to participate in the romantic tradition, until the speaker calls "the walk liberating, I was released from forms," whereupon the conventional treatment of nature as a scene that might reveal a more universal order is challenged. Frederick Buell notes that Ammons's walk is "somewhere between the uniqueness and goal-directedness of a quest and a passive vacancy of receptivity to its surroundings" (201), and this in-between is crucial to Ammons's theory of knowledge. Nature is not necessarily meaningless or chaotic, but its own patterns shift so quickly that the human mind can never grasp them, nor the universe beyond them, in their entirety. Thus, as he watches the sea and the dunes, Ammons finds he can "allow myself eddies of meaning: / yield to a direction of significance," but these directions are intimations at best; ultimately, "Overall is beyond me." Such limitation need not produce anxiety; indeed, it can prevent it. In the romantic tradition, exposure to the grandest scenes of nature produced a sublime experience, which elicits in the viewer both fear and awe, but for Ammons, the scene at Corson's Inlet produces "no arranged terror: no forcing of image, plan, / or thought." Moreover, as the capitalization of "Scope" in the final lines suggests, such limitations imply as-yet-unrealized possibilities, and Ammons can enjoy "the freedom that / Scope eludes my grasp, that there is no finality of vision, / that I have perceived nothing completely." Ultimately, notes poet and critic ROBERT PINSKY, "Ammons' voice conveys the difficulty and tentativeness of its own role in the world, a role within which neither praise nor vision can come with finality or for long" (191).

Ammons's masterful use of free verse, particularly the shifting margins of his lines, provides a visual cue for the shifts of thought and geographic space that occupy the speaker's attentions, indicating the powerful relation between sight and thought, a core romantic tenet. Thus, the poem is very much about how perception is a creative act; poet and critic RICHARD HOWARD writes of "the interrelations of *making* and of a beneficent destruction . . . the actions of sea and land serving as the just emblem of the mind's resources" (45). Reality is never completely ascertainable for Ammons, Howard insists: "Ammons rehearses a marginal, a transitional experience, he is a littoralist of the imagination because the shore, the beach, or the coastal creek is not a *place* but an *event,* a transaction where land and water create and destroy each other, where life and death are exchanged, where shape and chaos are won and lost" (46). One passage in particular evokes this sense of transition by shifting rapidly between images of individuals and collective groups. While watching "thousands of tree swallows / gathering for flight" at the start of the fall migratory season, Ammons describes them as "an order held / in constant change," and just as one may identify individuals amidst a flock, Ammons writes that they are "separable, noticeable / as one event, / not chaos." He evokes their voices both individually and as a mass of voices, which ironically unite in a single sound: "cheet, cheet, cheet, cheet, wings rifling the green clumps . . . / a perception full of wind, flight, curve, / sound." In this and other passages, Ammons challenges the possibility of a complete vision of truth—whether scientific, metaphysical, or sensory—or even of the possibility that reality itself is a unified whole. Yet if reality and our perception of it can be accepted as partial and imperfect, but nevertheless rich and endlessly unfolding, then "there is serenity."

BIBLIOGRAPHY

Buell, Frederick. "'To Be Quiet in the Hands of the Marvelous.'" In *A. R. Ammons: Modern Critical Views,* edited by Harold Bloom, 195–212. New York: Chelsea House Publications, 1986.

Howard, Richard. "'The Spent Seer Consigns Order to the Vehicle of Change.'" In *A. R. Ammons: Modern Critical Views,* edited by Harold Bloom, 33–56. New York: Chelsea House Publications, 1986.

Pinsky, Robert. "Ammons." In *A. R. Ammons: Modern Critical Views,* edited by Harold Bloom, 185–95. New York: Chelsea House Publications, 1986.

Temple Cone

CORTEZ, JAYNE (1936–) A poet who first came to wide notice during the rise of the BLACK ARTS MOVEMENT, Jayne Cortez's work brings forth the diasporic influences of negritude and *negrismo,* jazz-inflected traditions of contemporary black American verse. She has pursued her own course through the most innovative of 20th-century modes of composition, following Léopold Senghor in the movement from SURREALISM to an African-derived poetics they both prefer to call "super realism." She writes at a certain moment in history, like the Aimé Césaire of her poem in tribute to him (1996), a "moment of no compromise" when "his poetry became poetry unique to poetry." In 1969 she published her first volume of poetry, *Pissstained Stairs and the Monkey Man's Wares.*

Cortez was born on May 10, 1936, in Fort Huachuca, Arizona. Like JAY WRIGHT, she is a poet whose career underscores the contributions of the American Southwest to African-American literature. She spent most of her youth in Los Angeles, where she did important early work among musicians and artists in such venues as the Ebony Showcase and the Watts Repertory Theater

Company. During this same period, she traveled to Mississippi to participate in voter registration drives. Her activism has continued throughout her life, as in her work on the 1997 conference "Yari Yari, Black Women Writers and the Future." In 1954 Cortez married composer and musician Ornette Coleman. Their son, Denardo, has taken an active role in his mother's works, combining poetry with music. Cortez has also been one of the most prolific recording jazz poets, releasing a series of recitations to jazz accompaniment. The marriage to Coleman ended, and in 1975 she married visual artist Melvin Edwards. Edwards has contributed artwork to many of Cortez's most significant books. Cortez migrated to New York in 1967. Among her awards are the American Book Award (1980) and the Langston Hughes Medal (2001). To date she has published seven major collections of verse.

Cortez weds intensely physical imagery to progressive politics and a free-verse line built out of the rhythms of blues and jazz. In "Poetry" (1996), she contrasts her aesthetic to poems that "are like flags / flying on liquor store roof." Hers is an "unsubmissive blues," a poetry, like the dance of Josephine Baker described in "So Many Feathers" (1977), that earns a "rosette of resistance."

BIBLIOGRAPHY

Bolden, Tony. "All the Birds Sing Bass: The Revolutionary Blues of Jayne Cortez." *African American Review* 35, no. 1 (2001): 61–71.

Melhem, D. H. *Heroism in the New Black Poetry*. Lexington: University of Kentucky Press, 1990.

Nielsen, Aldon Lynn. "Capillary Currents: Jayne Cortez." In *We Who Love to Be Astonished: Experimental Women's Writing and Performance Poetics,* edited by Laura Hinton and Cynthia Hogue. Tuscaloosa: University of Alabama Press, 2002, 227–236.

Aldon L. Nielsen

CRANE, HART (1899–1932) Hart Crane was literary heir to Walt Whitman, an authentically American male voice expressing his vision of America; thus he became ancestor to the BEAT poets, particularly ALLEN GINSBERG, who traced his own poetic lineage through Whitman and Crane. Crane's poetry was also affected by his contemporaries, such as WALLACE STEVENS, T. S. ELIOT, and EZRA POUND; he admired ROBERT FROST and E. E. CUMMINGS, whom he occasionally copied, as he also did WILLIAM CARLOS WILLIAMS. During the first half of his writing life, Crane's style variously employed, as Edward Brunner has said, an "Eliotic ennui," "sumptuous imagism" (see IMAGIST SCHOOL), "Gusto of a Poundian sort," and characters reminiscent of "a Wallace Stevens seascape" ("Hart Crane"). Among Crane's close friends were ALLEN TATE, who once called Crane "the greatest contemporary American poet" (qtd. in Mariani 113) and later wrote the introduction for Crane's first book, *White Buildings* (1926), JEAN TOOMER, and YVOR WINTERS, who later negatively reviewed Crane's second book, *The BRIDGE* (1930). From Eliot, Crane sought to learn as much technique as possible, and with Pound he shared a desire to protect ancient myth from religious revisionism.

Harold Hart Crane was born in Gainesville, Ohio. He never finished high school, and although he occasionally made plans to pursue a degree, he never did so. His first publication appeared when he was only 17 years old. After he started publishing his poems, he began using his middle name at his mother's suggestion—it was her maiden name; his father called him Harold for the rest of his life. His parents' conflicted relationship was a major element in Crane's unsteady mental development, and the issue of his name is an indication of the extent of their efforts to manipulate him. As an only child, Crane bore the full force of his parents' machinations, especially his mother's, during their marriage and after their divorce. This fact played no small role in the adult Crane's general disparagement of women, which is made especially plain in his lack of respect for the work of female poets—with the single exception of Emily Dickinson. Paul Mariani suggests that Crane grudgingly acknowledged MARIANNE MOORE (243) but dismissed EDNA ST. VINCENT MILLAY as "too derivative" (84); Crane likewise discarded what he categorized as the "scullery permutations of AMY LOWELL" (qtd. in Mariani 243). The only formal, financial recognition he ever received was the conditional patronage of Otto Kahn, a New York banker and arts patron, beginning in late 1925, and a Guggenheim Fellowship in 1931.

Unfortunately Crane was never able to establish a secure and permanent relationship of any kind for himself. He was constantly in motion—emotionally, physically, and mentally. He relocated frequently, from Cleveland, where he had grown up, to New York, a city that had a mythical fascination for him, to Cuba, where his family had a vacation home, to an isolated farm in Connecticut, and back again to all of them repeatedly, all the while hoping and believing that a change of space would enable him to be a more disciplined writer. Likewise he never was able to sustain himself financially by maintaining a regular day job, always complaining that whatever kind of work he had at the time was beneath him and did not pay him enough, whether it was working in his father's Ohio factory or writing ad copy in New York. His emotional relationships waxed and waned as swiftly as his physical ones. Tate explained, as Paul Mariani relates it, that "Crane always saw things in terms of his own insatiable ego" (213).

Crane's early writing was influenced by MODERNISM, but he soon began to develop a clear voice of his own, maintaining all he had absorbed of technique but embracing new ideas as poetry became liberated from its highbrow constraints. He incorporated elements of common speech and believed that jazz had an important role to play in the maturation of American poetry, not only because it was an American musical form, but also because it could accommodate both heights and depths. Crane was convinced that the task of the poet was to confront the historical moment through experience, not detached observation, and to articulate the experience in a neoromantic fashion. As a young poet he emerged from Eliot's influence and in fact disliked *The WASTE LAND*, but he never left Whitman behind. The first movement of Crane's six-part "Voyages" (1926) echoes the second movement of Whitman's "Song of Myself" in its unobserved speaker who watches others frolic on the beach. Written when Crane was 22, this first section nevertheless has a tone of hard-earned worldly wisdom: The speaker warns that "there is a line" of acceptable behavior beyond which these bathers must not go. If they do, they will learn what he already has learned: "The bottom of the sea is cruel." "Voyages" developed as a love sequence to Crane's longest-lasting relationship. Crane was gay, and although he was careful to keep the gender of the poem's beloved unspecified, he speaks in this set of poems to the dearest of his many male sailor lovers when he asks, "Permit me voyage, love, into your hands" at the close of the third movement.

Crane's enduring friend, Waldo Frank, agreed with Tate's early opinion that Crane's significance to American poetry could be based on "For the Marriage of Faustus and Helen" (1923) alone. Certainly the poem is Crane's entrance into his own voice. If the three-part poem is an "uneven, erratic, volatile performance, more defiant than poised, more assertive than assured" (Brunner *Failure* 2), it is so because Crane himself was just such a performance. Like him, the poem exudes energy and might be forgiven for its lack of maturity, because of its promise. In part I, Crane brings Faustus and Helen forward into a very American, very 20th-century world of "baseball scores" and "stock quotations," where the intellect is in danger of stagnation, becoming "Too much the baked and labeled dough." In part II Crane then announces his preference for "New soothings, new amazements" and demonstrates it with a new diction filled with "Glee" and "Brazen hypnotics," where people dance all night "Beneath gyrating awnings." The third and final movement of the poem is even more urgently sensual and erotic; it speaks of "Anchises' navel, dripping of the sea" and "the voltage of blown blood and vine." The poem ends with a gathering momentum emblematic of the newness and vitality Crane felt in his poetry and in his country.

The poem is an important one not only because it represents Crane's break with his own poetic past, but also because it articulates a clear direction for his future. In spite of, or perhaps because of, the poem's somewhat undisciplined images and shape, "For the Marriage of Faustus and Helen" is an announcement made in a clear excited voice. Crane developed a framework for his famous work *The Bridge* in the same year "Faustus and Helen" appeared, but it was a design too conventionally grounded in chronology and history. The breakthrough came when he conceived a new plan that discarded the idea of summing up America's accomplishments. Instead, Crane would write of the past as still in process. The rewritten, 1926 version of the poem was "a breathtaking achievement" (Brunner

Splendid Failure 186), but Crane meddled with his own masterwork, making additions and reorganizing the poem in 1929. Some scholars believe the end result is flawed.

Inextricable from each other, Crane's literary gift and psychological curse developed concurrently. He first attempted suicide when he was 15, approximately when he started writing. From then on his life was a fight to the death. The majority of his work was written in the early 1920s, and as he deteriorated mentally he wrote less and less. By his late twenties he was an alcoholic, vividly so in the effects of drink on his body, and while he unabashedly believed in his own genius, he was incapable of helping himself. He alienated all of his friends through his incessant borrowing and outrageous behavior. Crane arrogantly took the position that the world quite simply owed him a living in return for his brilliance. Well aware that "he was killing the poet within him with his drinking" (Mariani 368), Crane's drive to self-destruction was monumentally strong. Early in his writing life he declared in "Legend," "I am not ready for repentance" (1926), and by the time he was ready the only redemption still available to him was the taking of his own life. In keeping with his fascination with heights, his lust for sailors, and his youthful proverb, "The bottom of the sea is cruel," he leapt from a ship voyaging home from Mexico in 1932.

BIBLIOGRAPHY

Brunner, Edward. "Hart Crane: Biographical Sketch," Modern American Poetry. Available online. URL: www.english.uiuc.edu/maps. Downloaded March 2007.

———. *Splendid Failure: Hart Crane and the Making of the Bridge*. Chicago: University of Illinois Press, 1985.

Mariani, Paul. *The Broken Tower: The Life of Hart Crane*. New York: W. W. Norton, 1999.

A. Mary Murphy

CRAPSEY, ADELAIDE (1878–1914) "We should not let them disappear," YVOR WINTERS said of Adelaide Crapsey's poems in the 1930s, when her name was still known but was already in danger of extinction (331). Indeed the many critics who discovered her slim posthumous volume, *Verses* (1915, 1922, 1934) noted the ephemeral quality of her poetry and the personality behind it. Artists and poets as different as Marsden Hartley, CARL SANDBURG, and Lola Ridge praised Crapsey's work with articles and poems. The reasons for praise, however, were the emotional effect of her works, not initially her innovative form, the cinquain. And her Japanese-influenced imagism, independent of EZRA POUND's work and influence, was eclipsed by more influential poets (see IMAGIST SCHOOL). Nevertheless her poems remain popular and are widely imitated.

Crapsey was born in Brooklyn, raised in Rochester, New York, and educated at Vassar College, where she met Jean Webster, who wrote *Daddy Long-Legs* and other novels about the New Woman, the emancipated, enlightened, and educated woman of the 1890s, with the character of Crapsey in mind. Crapsey's plans for further studies and a career in writing were repeatedly interrupted by recurrent, undiagnosed weakness and the financial setbacks caused by her minister father's conviction for heresy. She taught at various schools, including Smith College, but her career was cut short by a diagnosis of tuberculosis, from which she died more than a year later. A manuscript of verses and other uncollected poems and her incomplete study of English metrics were published in the years following her death.

One of her most popular poems, frequently reprinted and discussed, is "To the Dead in the Grave-Yard under My Window" (1914), an autobiographical work expressing great desire for an active life, despite the enforced rest determined by treatment for tuberculosis and the knowledge of her impending death. But it is for her cinquains that Crapsey is most frequently mentioned. Analogous to the Japanese forms of haiku and tanka, the cinquain is constructed of five lines of different lengths. The first and last lines consist of two syllables or one stress, the second line has four syllables or two stresses, the third line six syllables or three stresses, and the fourth line has eight syllables or four stresses. The result is a visual, rhythmic, and auditory experience that gives the effect of increasing anticipation that ends in completion. Her cinquains often seemed to anticipate some of the principles and structure of WILLIAM CARLOS WILLIAMS in their determination to force the reader to pay attention, attempting to engage the reader in optimistic anticipation and see through the wasteland to hope. "Look Up," she begins her poem "Snow" (1914), and "Listen," she commands in "November Night" (1913), to the way the leaves fall. In these and other poems, the attention to the delicate details of nature point to a gradually expanding spiritual revelation that parallels the cinquain structure.

BIBLIOGRAPHY

Alkalay Gut, Karen. *Alone in the Dawn: The Life of Adelaide Crapsey*. Athens: University of Georgia, 1988.
Butscher, Edward. *Adelaide Crapsey*. Boston: Twayne, 1979.
Winters, Yvor. *In Defense of Reason*. Denver: Swallow, 1947.

Karen Alkalay-Gut

CREELEY, ROBERT (1926–2005) Robert Creeley stands among the company of contemporary American poets who think carefully, in the process of making a poem, about what poetic language can and cannot achieve. Despite affinities with several other modernist precursors (see MODERNISM), Creeley is less concerned with the presentation of sensory observation than WILLIAM CARLOS WILLIAMS and LOUIS ZUKOFSKY, and he turns away from the lush, extravagant imagery and metaphors of WALLACE STEVENS by embracing a more minimalist or pared-down style. Creeley's poetry features a spare, partly colloquial (but never chatty) and partly formal diction, a compression of narrative and lyric gestures, a use of precise quatrains (as well as couplets and tercets), and a preference for metonymy or rather contiguity over metaphor that is based on analogy. His syntax, full of qualifications, sometimes strains traditional grammatical rules. Creeley is a master of surprising, artful enjambment. Like Williams, he breaks lines in unexpected places that emphasize the "hinges" of language—prepositions and transitional terms, as well as underappreciated articles and other words often thought to contain no meaning in themselves. Though his stylistic traits differ considerably from BLACK MOUNTAIN SCHOOL poets like CHARLES OLSON, ROBERT DUNCAN, and DENISE LEVERTOV, with whom he is historically affiliated, he shares their advocacy of a poetry that openly explores all possible experience against one with a unified theme and closed form that might shut out realms of experience evoked by language.

Creeley was born in Arlington, Massachusetts. At age two, he lost his left eye in a car accident, and two years later his father, a physician, died suddenly. After attending Harvard University for a year, he served as an ambulance driver in Burma during the last two years of World War II. He returned to Harvard after the war but soon left without obtaining a degree. In the 1950s Creeley established a strong connection with Olson, CID CORMAN, and other members of the Black Mountain school. He became an instructor of poetry at Black Mountain College and simultaneously earned his B.A. there. He also edited the *Black Mountain Review*. Creeley later earned an M.A. in English at the University of New Mexico, where he also taught.

Creeley's first collection of poetry was *Le Fou* (1952); his first widely distributed book, *For Love: Poems, 1950–1960*, was published 10 years later. Besides his many books of poems, he has published a novel, two books of short stories, and several books of essays. Creeley, who was a professor of English from 1967 until 2000 and held endowed chairs in poetry at the State University of New York at Buffalo and Brown University, is the recipient of two Guggenheim Fellowships, a Rockefeller Grant, the Shelley Memorial Award, the Robert Frost Medal, and numerous other honors. He was also the state poet of New York (1989–91) and was elected a chancellor of The Academy of American Poets in 1999. He died in Odessa, Texas, in 2005.

Several early poems, written shortly before the full flowering of the U.S. women's movement, evince anxiety about the erosion of male confidence in love relationships. In "The Gift" (1962), "the lady" dismisses a man's gift of "precious understanding" with the retort, "is / that all, is / that all." "The Whip" (1962) stages a conflict in the mind of a man who is in bed with one woman but haunted by another and seeks an "exorcism" of the latter by the former. In "Words" (1967), the speaker tries to represent his sense of unity with the beloved, but dislocation in time and space, as underscored by Creeley's characteristic enjambment—"You are always / with me"—ironically undermines the effort, and he goes on to present further obstacles to such unity, as emerging experience replaces what came before.

Well before it became fashionable to do so, Creeley's poetry explored the extent to which the self is shaped by the workings of language. The opening lines of "The Pattern" (1967) articulate the gap between the correct use of the first-person singular and the way in which language creates the self: "As soon as / I speak, I / speaks." The self's freedom is constrained by "the direction / of its words." In Creeley's work there is often an acute consciousness of the division between the I/eye in the midst of experience and the self that tries to stand outside of the experience to perceive and comment on the "I" and its activities. Exploration of language's effects is also extremely evident in *Echoes* (1994), which features various title-poems and other pieces entitled "Echo." Creeley's preoccupation with reverberation as reiteration often traces the breach in space and time between the representing word and the thing, concept, or flux the word is trying to capture, as well as the gap between an experience in process and a stable understanding of it. After imagining that "time" can magically "pass vertically" to enable one to have a full understanding of events, the speaker in one such "Echo" speaks of acoustic after-effects as "shreds of emptying / presence."

Like such OBJECTIVIST predecessors as Zukofsky, GEORGE OPPEN, and Williams, and like the Black Mountain school's Olson, Creeley examines how the clash of an individual's particular, often peculiar, circumstances and her or his desire to shape experience influences the dynamic process of perception. While he begins "The Window" (1967) with the assertion, "Position is where you / put it," the "heaviness" of "the slow / world" seems overwhelming by the poem's end, as evinced by a poignant autobiographical allusion: "I can / feel my eye breaking." A logical extension of Creeley's interest in the unpredictable processes of perception and reflection is his experiment with the serial form in *Pieces* (1969), *A Day Book* (1972), and long sequences in later books (see LONG AND SERIAL POETRY). Joseph Conte argues that such texts are energized by "a conflict . . . between the continuum of experience and the ability of the poet to record only fixed moments, or a series of such moments. . . . Creeley is not interested in what the series says, but in the diverse ways in which one thing finds its place with another" (93, 97).

Much of Creeley's poetry seeks to measure what is common, hence shareable, in human existence. In "I Know a Man" (1962), recognition of how "the darkness sur- / rounds us" breeds a longing to communicate with others about this common ground of uncertainty and "what" to "do against / it." Whereas the speaker would respond by taking aggressive action (purchasing a "goddamn big car"), his friend stresses the importance of self-preservation. The sense of fragmentation that Creeley explores is an important bond with his audience, even as he tries to share a sense of small bits of coherence. In an untitled poem (1969) in *Pieces,* "pieces of cake" are "crumbling / in the hand trying to hold / them together" as an offering to "the seated guests." Tender regard for human struggles for self-actualization is often present; among the 24 discrete quatrains of "Eight Plus" (1988) is the injunction: "Wish happiness / for most of us, / whoever we are, / wherever." Another aspect of the common place is embodied in an arresting maxim in "Credo" (1998): *"I believe in belief."* For Creeley, as for many others, life's tremendous uncertainties, "a void of pattern," and the certainty of death are so powerful that an absence of belief would lead to overwhelming despair.

Indeed, the confrontation of human mortality is a major area in which thinking about the "common place" occurs in Creeley's later work. Various poems written after his mother's death grope, in retrospect, toward a sense that the mother and son shared a deep bond that their reticent, imperfect communication could not destroy. At the beginning of "Histoire de Florida" (1998), the speaker invites his "brother face" that remains "behind the mirror" to make use of whatever is left of life "to come out / . . to play." The poem's "play" involves juxtapositions of passages about death and dying gleaned from the poet's memories of conversations, television narratives, details of Florida history, famous quotations, and news stories alongside images and gestures marking the continuation of life, the "practice" of "survival" through simple routine and ordinary perception.

With its hesitations, qualifications, and provisional clarifications, Creeley's poetry—which has strongly influenced later experimental writers, such as the poets of the LANGUAGE SCHOOL—affords the pleasures, anxieties. and challenges of sensuous thinking about fundamental uncertainties and searching for signs of common ground.

BIBLIOGRAPHY

Altieri, Charles. *Self and Sensibility in Contemporary American Poetry*. Cambridge, England: Cambridge University Press, 1994.

Butterick, George F., ed. *Charles Olson and Robert Creeley: The Complete Correspondence*. Nine volumes. Santa Rosa, Calif.: Black Sparrow Press, 1980–90.

Clark, Tom. *Robert Creeley and the Genius of the American Common Place: Together with the Poet's Own Autobiography*. New York: New Directions, 1993.

Conte, Joseph. *Unending Design: The Forms of Postmodern Poetry*. Ithaca, N.Y.: Cornell University Press, 1991.

Edelberg, Cynthia Dubin. *Robert Creeley's Poetry: A Critical Introduction*. Albuquerque: University of New Mexico Press, 1978.

Paul, Sherman. *The Lost America of Love*. Baton Rouge: Louisiana State University Press, 1981.

Thomas Fink

"CRUSOE IN ENGLAND" ELIZABETH BISHOP **(1976)** ELIZABETH BISHOP's "Crusoe in England" is a dramatic monologue in FREE VERSE that is narrated by Robinson Crusoe, the castaway protagonist of Daniel Defoe's novel by the same name, years after his return to England from the Caribbean island on which he was marooned. Bishop's Crusoe now spends his days reading of geographical and geological discoveries in the New World, musing over his own island experience, and remembering Friday, his native friend who we learn "died of measles / seventeen years ago come March." Friday's place in the poem, though not a narrative focal point, proves to be the emotional core of the poem; Crusoe describes their friendship in such understated terms that he suggests a powerful, perhaps homosexual, bond that words cannot adequately explain. In the figure of Robinson Crusoe, Bishop has found an identity quite like her own: both she and Crusoe attend to the precise, physical details of this world for their survival, both literal and artistic; both suffer from loneliness in the midst of a solitude that brings them independence; and both feel great love toward another individual of the same gender, now dead, about which and about whom they can speak only indirectly.

Many critics view "Crusoe in England" as perhaps Bishop's most ambitious poem, one which explores romantic ideas about nature, the experience of exile, the work of memory, loneliness and the desire for companionship, and even Bishop's own lesbian identity. Bishop's satire on the romantic ideal of nature is rendered with characteristic humor. Steven Hamelman writes that the island is not a romantic paradise of unspoiled nature but "an inverted Eden" (51), and while the poem features many well-realized details, with oceanic waterspouts described as "(g)lass chimneys, flexible, attenuated" and careful attention paid to the island's one variety of "tree snail, a bright violet-blue / with a thin shell," Crusoe ultimately remembers the island, with sardonic humor, as "a sort of cloud-dump." This summary anachronistically alludes to Wordsworth's peaceful meditation on nature, "I Wandered Lonely as a Cloud," which Bishop's Crusoe tries to recite as a pastime: "'They flash upon that inward eye, / which is the bliss. . . ' The bliss of what?" The missing word here is *solitude,* and when Crusoe says that "One of the first things that I did / when I got back was look it up," his failure to complete the line clearly shows that his own experience of solitude belies Wordsworth's rhapsody.

Bonnie Costello notes that Crusoe compensates for his solitude by means of creative pursuits, from fermenting alcohol to playing flute music, which are themselves efforts to construct "orders and values . . . based on memories but created out of and for the present circumstance" (205). Yet these "island industries" reinforce rather than abnegate Crusoe's loneliness, for they become repetitious without the attentive and responsive community that the arts and culture ultimately require. Thus Crusoe, who becomes an artist while in exile, also stands for the artist in social exile, marooned on an island of indifference. His dreams become troubled with images of violence and endless, unrewarding labor, until "Just when I thought I couldn't stand it / another minute longer, Friday came." Having nullified the romantic faith in solitude and nature, Bishop shows that open, authentic human relations offer the possibility for wholeness, passion, and imaginative inspiration. Yet the stanza in which Bishop's Crusoe introduces Friday is curiously plainspoken and unadorned. Following immediately after his nightmare of having to register, for an infinite number of islands, "their flora, / their fauna, their geography," this passage may be an expression of Crusoe's desire for the forthrightness of simple friendship, which would contrast with the lonely effulgence of Crusoe's island, itself a metaphor for the artist's complex, solitary life. Costello offers a keener insight into the passage, noting that Bishop's description of Friday is "conspicuously simple and direct, free of trope, perhaps expressing an emotion too intense, too deviant, or too private for rhetoric to contain" (205–206).

The emotion to which Costello refers is love, which in the case of Bishop's Crusoe and Friday would be a homosexual love. Such a reading finds an immediate link with details from Bishop's own life; Renée R. Curry argues that the subtext of "Crusoe in England" is Bishop's response to the suicide of her lesbian partner, Lota de Macedo Soares, whom Bishop had left but for whom she still felt affection. The difference in genders would have offered the very private Bishop some protective distance from the emotions suggested by the narrative, though like Crusoe's old knife, the story of a lost bond would have "reeked of meaning, like a crucifix." While such a biographical reading risks being constraining, it brings to the surface the loneliness and desolation Crusoe feels back in England at the end of the poem. Home is an abstraction for Crusoe; England proves to be just another island, a place of shipwreck and exile like his old island, which he found "Beautiful, yes, but not much company." The only home for the artist, and here we see that Bishop's "artist" is any individual who does not fit perfectly with society, is in the intimate, reciprocal bond of human love, which can transcend the barriers of gender, race, and language, but which is as fragile as Crusoe's old knife because it is so valuable: "It lived. How many years did I / beg it, implore it, not to break?"

BIBLIOGRAPHY

Colwell, Anne. *Inscrutable Houses: Metaphors of the Body in the Poems of Elizabeth Bishop.* Tuscaloosa: The University of Alabama Press, 1997.

Costello, Bonnie. *Elizabeth Bishop: Questions of Mastery.* Cambridge, Mass.: Harvard University Press, 1993.

Curry, Renée R. "Augury and Autobiography: Bishop's 'Crusoe in England.'" *Arizona Quarterly* 47, no. 3 (1991): 70–91.

Hamelman, Steven. "Bishop's 'Crusoe in England.'" *The Explicator* 51, no. 1 (1992): 50–53.

McCabe, Susan. *Elizabeth Bishop: Her Poetics of Loss.* University Park: Pennsylvania State University Press, 1994.

Temple Cone

CRUZ, VICTOR HERNÁNDEZ (1949–)

A prodigy who first came to wide public attention as a poet while still in his adolescence, Cruz has proved his staying power with a succession of significant publications culminating in his volume of selected poems, *Maraca* (2000). One of the few American poets generally considered important in the evolution of both African-American and Latino verse, his innovative poetry defies easy classification. Equally the progeny of BEAT POETRY and the BLACK ARTS MOVEMENT, Cruz's poems straddle the realms of English and Spanish as readily as they leap generational boundaries.

Born in Aguas Buenas, Puerto Rico, Cruz migrated to New York's Lower East Side when he was six. He began to write seriously while still a teenager, publishing his own first collection, *Papo Got His Gun* (1966), on a mimeograph machine and calling his enterprise Calle Once Publications. A selection of these poems was reprinted in a special section of *Evergreen Review* the following year, and Cruz was soon to publish his first major work with Random House, his collection *Snaps* (1969). Though Cruz had left high school before graduating, he was later to tutor students at Columbia University and taught a poetry workshop at Berkeley. He was a founder of the East Harlem Gut Theater in 1968 and worked closely with the poets of the legendary Umbra group. He has been widely anthologized, and Cruz's subsequent books of poetry and prose include *Tropicalization* (1976), *By Lingual Wholes* (1982), *Red Beans* (1991) and *Panoramas* (1997). He has been the recipient of two Creative Artists Program Service grants, in 1974 and 1978. In both 1979 and 1980, he was invited to appear in the One World Poetry Festival held in Amsterdam, and he is featured in the Bill Moyers PBS television series, *Language of Life*.

In a blurb that appeared on the cover of Cruz's first book, and that has reappeared on *Maraca*, ALLEN GINSBERG saluted the advent of a new talent as "Poesy news from space anxiety police age inner city, spontaneous urban American language as [William Carlos] Williams wished." The excitement attendant upon those early Cruz poems accrues still to his poems of later life, as he continues to build a poetics out of the rhythms of a multilingual American idiom. As he writes in "Nebraska," a poem from his 1973 collection *Mainland:* "In this part of Mexico / Se habla inglish." Steadily resisting the political pressures toward a false monoculturalism, Cruz nonetheless achieves a remarkable singularity. His is, as he writes of Vladimir Nabokov in *Maraca,* "A nationality of language / spread on butterfly wings / Crossing borders."

BIBLIOGRAPHY

Sheppard, Walt. "An Interview with Clarence Major and Victor Hernández Cruz." In *New Black Voices,* edited by Abraham Chapman, 545–552. New York: New American Library, 1972.

Wallenstein, Barry. "The Poet in New York: Victor Hernández Cruz." *Bilingual Review* 1 (1974): 312–319.

Aldon L. Nielsen

THE CRYSTAL TEXT CLARK COOLIDGE (1986)

Though sometimes associated with the LANGUAGE SCHOOL, CLARK COOLIDGE arrived at his poetics in advance of that group and has demonstrated a meditative or reflective tendency in works like *Melencolia* (1978) and *Mine: The One That Enters the Stories* (1981). *The Crystal Text* extends this tendency. A 150-page thought-excursion on the relations between language, perception, and the material world occasioned by a colorless quartz crystal, it was published simultaneously with *Solution Passage: Poems 1978–1981* (1986), a nearly 400-page collection of short lyrics and lyric sequences (see LYRIC POETRY). "Either of these books," Geoffrey O'Brien observed, "by itself would be a peak; to be given both at once seems a natural wonder" (45).

"To grasp the relation of words to matter, / mind, process," we read on the poem's second page, "may be the greatest task" (8). For the OBJECTIVIST poet LOUIS ZUKOFSKY, the test of poetry is "the range of pleasure it affords as sight, sound, and intellection" (xi), three categories that roughly correspond to matter, process, and mind in these lines. But while the perfect objectivist poem, for Zukofsky, is itself a complete object that achieves what he calls a "rested totality" (13), Coolidge's poems are restless and ongoing processes that reflect the improvisational nature of his work (stemming from his time as a jazz drummer and his deep affinity for the spontaneous be-bop prosody of JACK KEROUAC). The meditative qualities of *The Crystal Text* have precedents in his earlier works. In the early 1970s Coolidge began a close friendship with the artist Philip Guston. The two engaged in regular discussions about the nature and function of art and writing; Coolidge recorded some of these observations in notebooks, which provided material that went into not only Coolidge's collaborations with Guston (*Baffling Means*) but also the opening pages of *The Crystal Text.*

Critic Krysztof Ziarek identifies the crystal as a metaphoric link among language, the being of self, and the material world. In an interview, however, Coolidge says the crystal is not a metaphor and that he "was interested in the crystal in the sense of what the crystal might do to things, to me, to the writing, to the day, to the mood, to whatever might come along" (41). In other words, the poem is less *about* the crystal—only a fraction of the text mentions the crystal itself—and more the thoughts, objects, and associations the crystal occasions. Or, as the poem states: "The crystal is but one nexus in the drain / of possibles" (94).

BIBLIOGRAPHY

Coolidge, Clark. "From Notebooks (1976–1982)." In *Code of Signals,* edited by Michael Palmer. Berkeley, Calif.: North Atlantic, 1983.

———. "Interview with Edward Foster." *Talisman* 3 (1989): 16–46.

O'Brien, Geoffrey. "Say What?" *Village Voice* 31, no. 25 (June 1986): 45.

Ziarek, Krysztof. "Word for Sign: Poetic Language and Coolidge's *The Crystal Text.*" *Sagetrieb* 10 (spring & fall 1991): 145–166.

Zukofsky, Louis. *A Test of Poetry.* Hanover, N.H.: Wesleyan University Press, 2001.

Tom Orange

CULLEN, COUNTEE (1903–1946)

Countee Cullen was a central figure in the HARLEM RENAISSANCE in the 1920s and one of this period's finest practitioners of LYRIC POETRY. Publishing his first volume of poetry, *Color,* with Harper & Brothers in 1925, Cullen was one of the most promising and popular young African-American writers to emerge during an era that produced such writers as LANGSTON HUGHES and JEAN TOOMER.

Cullen's poetry is known for its formal lyricism influenced by the romantics, religious concerns, and, notwithstanding the author's declarations otherwise, racial themes. Although he differed with his peers, such as Hughes, over the relationship of racial identity to poetry (a view articulated in *Caroling Dusk,* the 1927 anthology of African-American poetry that he edited), racial matters figure prominently in many of his best-known works.

Cullen was adopted as a child by Reverend Frederick Cullen, an activist Harlem pastor, and Carolyn Belle Cullen. After writing a senior thesis on EDNA ST. VINCENT MILLAY and graduating Phi Beta Kappa from New York University, he continued his studies at Harvard, where he received an M.A. in 1926. During his undergraduate years, the literary prodigy won the Witter Bynner Poetry Award and prestigious contests sponsored by *Crisis, Opportunity, Palms,* and *Poetry* magazines. According to many people who knew Cullen, the Harlem social event of the decade was his 1928 wedding to Yolande DuBois, the only child of the era's leading intellectual and activist, W. E. B. DuBois. A few years after their 1930 divorce, Cullen began teaching French at Frederick Douglass Junior High School, where he worked until his untimely death.

The poet's dilemma concludes his oft-cited sonnet "Yet Do I Marvel" (1925): "Yet do I marvel at this curious thing: / To make a poet black and bid him sing!" "HERITAGE" (1925), one of the longer works in *Color,* emphasizes the challenges posed by its query, "What is Africa to me?" In the widely anthologized "Incident" (1925), Cullen moves from a single to a double to a triple rhyme over the course of the poem's three ballad stanzas. He extends the iambic trimeters of the second and third quatrains by one syllable, using feminine or light endings. This method gives the work a strong, unpretentious rhythm that suits the poem's recollection of a childhood incident when a boy in Baltimore returned the narrator's smile with a racist epithet.

Like "Incident," "The Black Christ" (1929) turns on a racial insult. In rhymed couplets accented by periodic triplets, Cullen explores Christianity and racism, forces that the first line of the poem labels "God's glory and my country's shame," by equating crucifixion with lynching. The skillful application of formal mastery to unique thematic concerns characterizes Cullen's lyric achievements.

BIBLIOGRAPHY

Baker, Houston A., Jr. *Afro-American Poetics.* Madison: University of Wisconsin Press, 1988.

Early, Gerald, ed. *My Soul's High Song: The Collected Writings of Countee Cullen, Voice of the Harlem Renaissance.* New York: Anchor, 1991.

Perry, Margaret. *A Bio-Bibliography of Countee P. Cullen.* Westport, Conn.: Greenwood, 1971.

Shucard, Allen. *Countee Cullen.* Boston: Twayne, 1984.

Ira Dworkin

CUMMINGS, E(DWARD) E(STLIN) (1894–1962)

E. E. Cummings was both a painter and a poet whose art was affected by literary MODERNISM, as well as by postimpressionist and cubist art he encountered during his university days. Particular influences included GERTRUDE STEIN's lively cubist literary experiments, her word portraits of things in *TENDER BUTTONS* (1914), and Pablo Picasso's visual practice of cubism. Likewise he internalized EZRA POUND's IMAGIST criteria after reading Pound's "The Return" (1912), the anthology *Des Imagistes* (1914), and AMY LOWELL's *Sword Blades and Poppy Seeds* (1914). This background becomes hybrid in Cummings's striking verbal images arranged as visual images on the page, not as concrete shapes of things, but as representations of the sense and delivery of the words.

Cummings was born in Cambridge, Massachusetts. His father taught sociology at Harvard College before leaving to become a Unitarian minister and taught his son about the woods and everything in them; Cummings's mother introduced him to poetry and hoped he would become a poet. He received a thorough education at home and at Cambridge Latin School before he entered Harvard College in 1911 at the age of 17. By the time he left five years later, graduating magna cum laude with an A.B. (1915) in literature, especially Greek and English, and an A.M. (1916), "he was one of the best-educated American literary figures of his time, T. S. Eliot, Archibald MacLeish, and Ezra Pound being his only rivals" (Kennedy *Cummings* 15). Cummings had written poetry since he was a child. He and some friends, one of whom was John Dos Passos, prepared a manuscript of their poems, which was published while Cummings was in France during World War I. In a poem that focuses on thoughtless readiness to obey and the illusion of glorious war, Cummings's commentary asks the ironic question, "why talk of beauty what could be more beaut- / iful than these heroic happy dead" ("next to of course god america i" [1926]). Falsely accused of espionage when serving as an ambulance corps volunteer in France, Cummings and a friend were imprisoned on the basis of the friend's letters espousing pacifism and because of Cummings's refusal under interrogation to say he hated the Germans. Subsequent imprisonment led to his novelistic account of the experience in *The Enormous Room* (1922).

After moving to New York, Cummings exhibited his paintings and published his poems in avant-garde magazines during the 1920s. He began to write naturalist and realist poetry, "sonnets and free-verse vignettes that presented nightclubs, crowded tenement districts, ethnic restaurants, prostitutes and their customers, bums, drunks, and gangsters" (Kennedy *Cummings* 34). Formal recognition came to Cummings in the form of a *Dial* Award (1925), the Charles Eliot Norton Professorship at Harvard (1952–53), a National Book Award special citation (1955), the Bollingen Prize (1958), and election as a member of the National Academy of Arts and Letters, among other honors.

Known for his play with language, including the use of lowercase letters, Cummings had been charmed by the correspondence he received from the caretaker on his New Hampshire farm and was inspired by the caretaker's idiosyncratic use of language to experiment with unconventional use of punctuation and capitalization (Kennedy *Cummings* 28). He did not, however, use lowercase letters for his own name, signing his books and paintings with the uppercase "E. E. Cummings" whenever he did inscribe his signature. His poems include shocking moments, such as his discussion of "pubic lice" ("my specialty is living said" [1938]) or a "twot" ("red-flag and pink-flag" [1940]), but his innovations are the most noteworthy. He is a liberating poet to read because he shows by example that language is meant to serve, not to be served; he bent and broke the mechanical conventions of language to meet his literary needs. Cummings's neologisms, or word inventions, include the adjective *smallening* ("a clown's smirk in the skull of a baboon" [1931]), the adverb *smoothloomingly* ("what a proud dreamhorse pulling [smoothloomingly] through" [1935]), and the verbed noun *septembering* ("my father moved through dooms of love" [1940]). He would also incorporate phonetic utterance, such as "jennelman" ("a salesman is an it that stinks Excuse" [1944]), compressed spacing for effect in "Bothatonce" ("she being Brand" [1926]), and odd punctuation for effect as in "slo-wly;bare,ly nudg. ing(my / lev-er" ("she being Brand" [1926]). His whimsy and satire combine to describe a man who was "dressed in fifteen rate ideas / wearing a round jeer for a hat" ("a man who had fallen among thieves" [1926]). Other earmarks of a Cummings poem are the childlike exuberance found in words, such as "mud- / luscious" or "puddle-wonderful" ("IN JUST-" [1923]); in phrases, such as "leaping greenly spirits of trees" ("i thank You God for most this amazing" [1950]); and in the disrupted syntax of such lines as "a pretty girl who naked is" ("my youse needn't be so spry" [1926]).

Cummings's love poems exhibit his most delicate and endearing touch. He says, as a result of one woman's kisses, "the sweet small clumsy feet of April came / into the ragged meadow of my soul" ("if i have made,my lady,intricate" [1926]). Here we see the woman as the breath of spring itself (a favorite subject for Cummings) breezing into the beleaguered life of a man who feels himself in tatters. Physical affection is also important to this poet, who declares, "kisses are a better fate / than wisdom" ("since feeling is first" [1926]). He warns us, "beware of heartless them / (given the scalpel,they dissect a kiss;" ("one's not half two. It's two are halves of one:" [1944]). He says with wonderment that "your slightest look easily will unclose me" ("SOMEWHERE I HAVE NEVER TRAVELLED, GLADLY BEYOND" [1931]), since he is a man who has tightened himself like a closed fist. At the opposite pole from his love lyrics are his biting political remarks. He writes of a man brutally treated for his moral objection to military service, a man "whose warmest heart recoiled at war" ("i sing of Olaf glad and big" [1931]), but who faces violence and dies at the hands of his own side for his resistance.

During his lifetime, Cummings published 10 books of poetry, from *Tulips and Chimneys* (1923) to *95 Poems* (1958), plus two volumes of collected poems. *73 Poems* (1963), *Etcetera: The Unpublished Poems of E. E. Cummings* (1983), and *Complete Poems 1904–1962* (1991) were published posthumously. His nonfiction writings, in addition to the autobiographical novel *The Enormous Room,* are *Eimi* (1933), based on his travels in the Soviet Union, and *i: six nonlectures* (1953), from his tenure as Norton professor at Harvard. Cummings also published three dramatic works, a collection of absurd / Dada pieces (see SURREALISM), and a book of his paintings and drawings. Cummings's style remained fundamentally the same throughout his writing career, but he was by no means stagnant; while his aesthetic convictions did not change, he persistently worked at crafting and perfecting his method. Thus, through his genuine care, his poems have a lasting, delightful freshness about them.

BIBLIOGRAPHY

Fairley, Irene. *E. E. Cummings and Ungrammar: A Study of Syntactic Deviance in His Poems.* New York: Watermill, 1975.

Friedman, Norman. *E. E. Cummings: The Art of His Poetry.* Baltimore: Johns Hopkins University Press, 1960.

———. *(Re)valuing Cummings: Further Essays on the Poet.* Gainesville: University Press of Florida, 1996.

Kennedy, Richard S. *Dreams in the Mirror: A Biography of E. E. Cummings.* New York: Liveright, 1980.

———. *E. E. Cummings Revisited.* New York: Twayne, 1994.

A. Mary Murphy

CUNNINGHAM, J(AMES) V(INCENT)

(1911–1985) J. V. Cunningham, a master of the epigram and the short poem, was closer in style and spirit to the classical and Renaissance poets Horace, Martial, Ben Jonson, and Robert Herrick than to the modernists or the descendents of Walt Whitman (see MODERNISM). His small body of work, characterized by brevity, complexity, and exactitude of statement, was, by his own admission, unfashionable, and his poetry is comparable with that of YVOR WINTERS and EDGAR BOWERS.

Born in Cumberland, Maryland, Cunningham grew up in Billings, Montana, and Denver, Colorado, where he attended a Jesuit high school. During the depression, he traveled the Southwest, writing for trade journals. In 1931 Cunningham entered Stanford, earning a B.A. in classics (1934) and a Ph.D. in English (1945). In 1953 he joined the faculty at Brandeis, where he remained until retirement in 1980. *The Poems of J. V. Cunningham,* edited by TIMOTHY STEELE, was published in 1997.

Cunningham's theory of poetry, developed throughout his *Collected Essays* (1976), influenced the NEW FORMALISM movement. Cunningham claimed romantic definitions of poetry erected pretensions no poem could satisfy and limited the kinds of poetry that could be written. According to him, the situation worsened when the modernists championed free verse, proclaiming meter monotonous and artificial, leaving the poet with only associations, images, and moods. Cunningham considered a good poem a system of propositions and "the definitive statement in meter of something worth saying" because meter, "the ground bass of all poetry," allows a poet to more subtly and accurately convey a wider range of meanings and feelings than can be conveyed by nonmetrical language (431, 250). He preferred "verse" to "poetry" (see PROSODY AND FREE VERSE): "Verse is a professional activity, social and objective, and its methods and standards are those of craftsmanship." The virtues of verse, he wrote, "are civic virtues. If [verse] lacks much, what it does have is ascertainable and can be judged" (406). Cunningham considered poetry "amateurish, religious, and eminently unsociable" because "it dwells in the spiritual life, in the private haunts of theology or voodoo" (406).

In the early poem "For My Contemporaries" (1942), Cunningham details his conversion from poetry to verse in rhymed, dimeter lines: "I now make verses / Who aimed at art." Unlike the mad "ambitious boys" with their "spiritual noise," Cunningham prefers the sanity of verse, which he says cured him of poetry's madness. Like the CONFESSIONAL poets, Cunningham could turn the matter of his life into poetry, but he managed it elegantly and acerbically, as in the late epigram "The Lights of Love" (1942): "The ladies in my life, serially sexed, / Unscrew one lover and screw in the next."

Stoical, abstract, tightly formal, and rhymed, Cunningham's poems spurn the conventions of modern poetry. He nearly single-handedly revived the classical epigram and, with Winters and Bowers, introduced the urbane plain style—the "styleless style" notable for its compression, directness, seeming simplicity, and lack of ornamentation, unusual syntax, conceits, and figurative language—into American poetry.

BIBLIOGRAPHY

Barth, R. L. "The Vacancies of Need: Particularity in J. V. Cunningham's *To What Strangers, What Welcome.*" *Southern Review* 18 (1982): 286–298.

Cunningham, J. V. *The Collected Essays of J. V. Cunningham.* Chicago: Swallow Press, 1976.

Winters, Yvor. *Forms of Discovery.* Denver: Swallow, 1967, pp. 299–311.

Richard E. Joines

CYBERPOETRY Cyberpoetry is one of the many terms used to refer to relationships between poetry and technologies, particularly computer technologies. The prefix *cyber* was derived from the scientist Norbert Weiner's 1947 coinage *cybernetics,* from the Greek for "one who steers." Cyberpoetry is concerned with machine control of the writing process, delivery of poetry in more than one medium, and machine-mediated interactivity between audience and reader or writer and text. Most cyberpoetry is art or institutional poetry and is presented on the Internet or available on storage media such as CD-ROMs. However, most poetry on the Internet is not cyberpoetry. Few poems on the Web embrace new media in ways important to their form, content, or interpretation, as cyberpoetry does.

There are different types of cyberpoetry. These types may be defined by the techniques or processes according to which they are written and by the way they are historically related. One type is procedural poetry. Early procedural writing practices, such as those of SURREALISM, preceded the advent of popular computing but anticipated many of the means of making cyberpoetry. For example, a surrealist poem might have involved choosing words written on pieces of paper drawn from a hat, while a cyberpoem might involve randomizing or sorting words using a computer program. A second type of cyberpoetry is multimedia poetry. Concrete poetry, which uses the graphic possibilities of the page (see VISUAL POETRY), and sound poetry, which uses language as it is pronounced, can be "put in motion" by multimedia poetry. A third type is hypertext poetry, which links objects in a poem in a variety of ways. Early hypertext poems and early computing philosophies define many of the concepts cyberpoetry embodies today. Machine languages and English continue to evolve, and cyberpoetry evolves along with them.

PROCEDURAL POETRY

Throughout the 20th century, some poets have used procedures to produce poems rather than relying on "inspiration." The dada movement employed chance as a method. More recently, a group called the Ouvroir de littérature potentielle (Workshop of potential literature), or OuLiPo, uses processes based on mathematical algorithms to write new literature. The art movement Fluxus has produced mail art, which uses the mail as a medium for a flow of art and which has led to the development of on-line chat, network, e-mail, and FTP exchange of poetry. These movements all use procedures of various sorts to manipulate meaning through art.

For example, composer and poet JOHN CAGE wrote "mesostic" poems, which are procedural poems related to concrete poetry (see VISUAL POETRY). This method involves the use of an array of typefaces and sizes from Letraset letter stickers, which graphic designers used before computers were used for typesetting. Cage created his mesostics by generating numbers using the *I Ching* to help him compose the poem. He later replaced this procedure with computer programs built to his specifications, operating on texts he chose. In this way he reduced human intention in the writings. JACKSON MAC LOW, an artist associated with Fluxus, creates "diastic texts," which, like mesostics, are related to acrostic poems. Diastic texts "read through" and select words from one text (the "text bed") with a piece of that text (the "seed text") chosen by the maker. For example, to make his poem "Words nd Ends from Ez," Mac Low used EZRA POUND's *CANTOS* as a text bed and Pound's name as a seed text: The first word of Mac Low's diastic poem is the first word in *The Cantos* beginning with *e,* the first letter of Ezra Pound's name. The second selection is a fragment consisting of the next *z* in *The Cantos* and the letter in front of it (so that "z" is the second letter of the fragment). The understanding of fragments was important to Pound in the writing of *The Cantos;* thus this diastic comments on its source. Charles O. Hartman created DIASTEXT, a computer program that mimics some of Mac Low's diastic procedures. Hartman and Hugh Kenner used DIASTEXT and other programs to create poems from text beds. Mac Low himself began to use DIASTEXT rather than his manual process.

Electronic availability of literature makes creating procedural poems based on existing texts easy. "Poem generator" programs use text beds, dictionaries, and concordances to generate their "computer written" poems. Other programs manipulate input words into forms of light poetry, such as the limerick. Influenced by procedural poetry, "cyberpoets" closely examine the possibilities of analogy, metaphor, and logic to determine new procedures to generate new poems. Thus procedure in this particular sort of new cyberpoetry replaces traditional form.

MULTIMEDIA POETRY

Multimedia cyberpoetry uses sound, graphics, and text in ways important to the poem's form and content. A cyberpoem audio track is generally not a soundtrack for the poem or a recorded performance of the poem. It adds another level of meaning. For example, the audio portion of "Projects for Mobile Phones" (2000) by Alan Sondheim uses the sounds of mobile phones to divide the poem into "calls" or "exchanges" rather than sections.

The interpretation of multimedia cyberpoetry frequently depends upon decisions the artist makes to define the level of access users have to the work. Some multimedia cyberpoetry is like short film: Audience experience is controlled, and interaction is limited. Other multimedia cyberpoems are like computer games: The audience juxtaposes, rearranges, or "clicks through" words to make more than one poem within a controlled environment. Multimedia cyberpoetry can be more dependent upon poets' and audiences' technical skills, creativity, design skills, and software and hardware purchasing power than procedural poetry or patois poetry.

UBUWEB online is an important archive hosting historical sound poetry, such as the artist Kurt Schwitters's wordless "Ur Sonata" (1922–32), alongside contemporary multimedia cyberpoetry. Other Web sites feature videos of contemporary poets and performance artists, such as Tracie Morris. Some poets who wrote sound, performance, and visual works that challenged relationships of text to language to word to page are now embracing the new challenges of the screen, including Steven McCaffrey, Anne Tardos, and JOAN RETALLACK.

HYPERTEXT AND CYBERTEXT

Hypertext poetry links electronic objects in a variety of ways so that users can navigate through a poem along various textual paths. The reader/operator has a choice of one or more links to follow or actions to perform from within a hypertext. Hyperlinks literally and figuratively connect electronic objects, such as pages of coded text and pages of graphics files, allowing manual or automatic navigation from one object to another. Programmed links can vary the objects linked and the means of linkage. Pop-up links allow the display of more than one set of objects at the same time. Authors may use links to join a set of "written" objects to each other or to join objects within the text to objects outside the hypertext. In this way a simile or metaphor in a poem might be a linked reference in a hypertext. A given poem might be extremely disjunctive or extremely linear, depending on choices the reader makes as she or he clicks links to experience objects in an order the author cannot completely determine and the reader cannot completely anticipate or decide. A company called Eastgate created a computer program for composing electronic literature called Storyspace.

It enables writers of prose and poetry to develop writings containing links and graphics without coding. Early Eastgate poets, such as STEPHANIE STRICKLAND (*True North* [1998]) and Robert Kendall (*A Life Set for Two,* [1996]), continue to write hypertext poetry. Many poets now possess the technical skills, machinery, and software, or they collaborate with programmers and designers, to create hypertext poetry.

While hypertext poetry presents poets and readers with opportunities to consider linear and nonlinear narrative and reader response beyond the limited analogy, metaphor, and logic in procedural poetry, cybertext poetry moves beyond the link and investigates reader response on a deeper level. Interacting with cybertexts involves readers' queries, assumptions, and actions, which change readers' perceptions of the cybertext during the course of the interaction. Critic Espen Aarseth suggests that cybertext is similar to traditional oracles, where the user asks a question and then interprets the results in order to achieve a "reading."

LANGUAGES AND SPECULATIVE LINGUISTICS

Cyberpoetry transcends national boundaries, since it does not rely on a single language or set of letter forms. In this way it is similar to international concrete poetry and visual poetry. However, high-level programming languages are English-based. Computers are operated by predominantly English words. Some poets, such as John Cayley, employ this linguistic interchange and physicality by writing poems that execute as code. Cyberpoems can employ the substance of the Internet or of virtual reality, or they can perform actions in the real world.

Mary Anne Breeze (a.k.a. "mez"), Strickland, and other poets mix English with its computer languages to increase the meanings of words. Breeze's work is characterized by the use of tags and symbols familiar to computer users. Brackets and parentheses indicate multiple words within a single word. For example, dots ordinarily separate a file name from a file extension, which identifies the type of file. In Breeze's main site title, "mo[ve.men]toin," the dots label or categorize movement as a type of talk. Brackets enable her to express multiple words within her coinage. This method is also used to highlight literary-critical concerns, such as the ways that languages convey meaning, the ways that languages exist, and the multiple interpretations offered even within single words.

COMPUTING ENVIRONMENTS, INTERACTIVE POEMS

These languages are frequently used in on-line environments that allow real people or created characters to interact. Electronic environments are also conducive to collaboration and enhance the interactive quality of poetry. Chat rooms allow written conversations in real time online. MOOs (Multiple User Dungeons Object-Oriented), which are similar to early computer game environments called MUDs, or "multiuser dungeons," based on the game "Dungeons and Dragons," allow characters with various sorts of attributes to interact through typed commands. MOOs have been used as on-line classrooms. Bulletin boards, where messages are posted and read, and listservs, where e-mails sent to an address are forwarded to each member of a group, allow electronic communication over time. MOOs, MUDs, chat, and listserv environments allow cyberpoets Miekel And, Alan Sondheim, and others to manipulate the ways that a poet, narrator, speaker, or character may write or be written in a poem and the time reading or writing a poem may occupy. For example, some collaborations are based on historical collaborative forms, such as Japanese *renga,* with progressive stanzas written by different poets, and surrealist "exquisite corpses," with progressive lines written by poets who have not read the preceding lines.

CYBERPOETRY DISSEMINATION

Popular and long-established listservs and other places on the Internet containing cyberpoetry include Sondheim and Laurie Cubbison's WRYTING, for collaborative writing, where Sondheim, Shiela E. Murphy, Peter Ganick, Ivan Arguelles, and others write poems together; CHARLES BERNSTEIN's POETICS, for discussions of poetics and innovative post–LANGUAGE poetry; ANNIE FINCH's WOM-PO, for women's poetry; and John Kinsella's POETRYETC, for international poetry in English. On-line hubs of American cyberpoetry and poetry include Loss Pequeño Glazier's Electronic Poetry Center and Michael Neff's Web del Sol. The Web site Poetry Daily offers a new poem each day. Most of its poems are traditional, and not cyberpoetry, but the dissemination of traditional poetry on-line offers poets an introduction to reading and writing cyberpoetry.

BIBLIOGRAPHY

Aarseth, Espen. *Cybertext: Perspectives on Ergodic Literature.* Baltimore: Johns Hopkins University Press, 1997.

ELO (Electronic Literature Organization). Available online. URL: http://www.eliterature.org. Downloaded March 2007.

Landow, George P. *Hypertext: The Convergence of Contemporary Critical Theory and Technology.* Baltimore: Johns Hopkins University Press, 1992.

North American Centre for Interdisciplinary Poetics. Available online. URL: http://www.nacip.net. Downloaded March 2007.

Perloff, Marjorie. *Radical Artifice: Writing Poetry in the Age of Media.* Chicago: University of Chicago Press, 1992.

Catherine Daly

D

"DADDY" SYLVIA PLATH **(1965)** Written during the final months of her life, "Daddy" is one of SYLVIA PLATH's most famous poems. It may also be one of the best-known examples of CONFESSIONAL POETRY in 20th-century literature, demonstrating both the positive and negative connotations associated with the term. It has been praised by critics, such as George Steiner, for successfully "translating a private, obviously intolerable hurt into a code of plain statement, of instantaneously public images which concern us all" (218). Some scholars, such as Helen Vendler, consider the poem an outstanding example of the possibilities of LYRIC POETRY. Feminist critics have found it to be an effective exploration of feminine rage against male power structures. Other readers, however, protest that "Daddy" indulges in self-aggrandizement because the speaker aligns her suffering with that of Jewish victims of the Holocaust. "Daddy" elicits conflicting responses from readers, for it is a poem that explores and enacts one of the contradictions at the heart of identity: the need for, but impossibility of, self-definition.

Like much of Plath's work from this period, "Daddy" expresses anger and bitterness, blending terse statements with repetitive phrasing and violent imagery. The poem rehearses Plath's unresolved feelings about her father, who died when she was only eight, through a speaker who attempts to exorcise ritualistically the father's malevolent and domineering spirit: "Daddy, I have had to kill you." Presenting herself as his victim, the speaker transforms the father into a range of monstrous figures—Nazi, vampire, devil—and resurrects him in the husband, "A man in black with a Meinkampf look," whom she must kill as well.

In the end, the speaker seems to triumph: "Daddy, daddy, you bastard, I'm through." But it is unclear whether the speaker is through *with* the father or has gotten through *to* him. For along with rage and vitriol, the speaker expresses affection for the father and a desire to connect with him. Nursery rhyme cadence and relentless repetition of "oo" sounds create a sense of helpless entrapment that conflicts with the assertive and aggressive stance of the speaker, underscoring the impossibility of ever genuinely achieving clear disengagement. As Jacqueline Rose notes, it is clear "that such an ending is only a beginning or repetition" (224).

While the conflict "Daddy" expresses has most often been understood as personal rage, as Barbara Hardy has suggested, by turning the father into a Nazi, Plath is able "to promote the private concern to a public status" (222). Certainly Plath makes shocking use of the Holocaust in this poem, but it is clear that she *aims* to disturb and disrupt; the shock is part of her poetic point.

BIBLIOGRAPHY

Hardy, Barbara. "The Poetry of Sylvia Plath." In *Women Reading Women's Writing,* edited by Sue Roe. Brighton, United Kingdom: Harvester Press, 1987, pp. 209–226.

Rose, Jacqueline. *The Haunting of Sylvia Plath.* Cambridge, Mass. Harvard University Press, 1992.

Steiner, George. "Dying Is an Art." In *The Art of Sylvia Plath: A Symposium,* edited by Charles Newman. London: Faber and Faber, 1970, pp. 211–218.

Lisa Sewell

DAHLEN, BEVERLY (1934–) Working in the broadly defined avant-garde tradition, Beverly Dahlen experiments with form in her poetry while drawing from a range of sources for her thematic concerns, including art, philosophy, psychology, and critical theory. ROBERT DUNCAN offered both inspiration and support for Dahlen's early work. Like H. D. and GERTRUDE STEIN before her, Dahlen brings intellectual breadth to her feminist exploration of the relationship between thought and language. Interested in examining the operations of language itself, Dahlen is most often associated with the LANGUAGE SCHOOL of poetry.

Dahlen was born on November 7, 1934, in Portland, Oregon. She earned a B.A. from California State University, Humboldt, and attended San Francisco State University for postgraduate studies. Dahlen's verse and essays have appeared in numerous journals, and she has published six collections of poetry. Her major poetic work, *A Reading,* is published in three volumes: *A Reading (1–7)* (1985), *A Reading (11–17)* (1989), and *A Reading (8–10)* (1992).

Conceived as a lifelong project, *A Reading* suggests that writing is a process of discovery rather than mere description. Dahlen's subject in the work's untitled, numbered sections is, in the broadest sense, herself: a self comprised of lived experience, an unconscious, language, culture, and history. Modeled after Sigmund Freud's (1856–1939) method of free association in psychoanalysis and composed in verse as well as prose, *A Reading* resists any final conclusions. Through this "interminable reading, the infinite analysis" (1985), Dahlen is trying to reveal the contents of the unconscious itself. And because "there is nothing in the unconscious which corresponds to *no*" (1985), *A Reading* is all inclusive as well, roping in memory, dreams, myth, literary theory, psychology, and a range of other poetry.

Dahlen is especially concerned with Western definitions of gender that sharply distinguish between male and female. She resists these, as well as fixed and limited notions of femininity, by conceiving a self always in the process of construction. In *A Reading (1–7),* she writes, "this interminable work is women's work, it is never done, it is there again and again. I live here, an unreconstructed housewife" (1985). The "house" is the "here" where the speaker lives, the writing/reading process itself. Like the poem, her identity is indeterminate, fluid, and multiple; the speaker can write and rewrite herself.

Dahlen's desire to know, the primary impetus of *A Reading,* is tied up with a profound sense of language's limited abilities actually to reveal or represent reality: "language language it is all made of language" (1989). The way to proceed, then, is by direct engagement with language, its play and endless possibilities.

BIBLIOGRAPHY

DuPlessis, Rachel Blau. *The Pink Guitar: Writing as Feminist Practice.* New York: Routledge, 1990.

Perelman, Bob. "Facing the Surface: Representation of Representation." *North Dakota Quarterly* 55, no. 4 (fall 1987): 301–311.

Simpson, Megan. *Poetic Epistemologies: Gender and Knowing in Women's Language-Oriented Writing.* Albany: State University of New York Press, 2000.

Megan Simpson

DAVIDSON, DONALD (1893–1968) Donald Davidson is the third member, with JOHN CROWE RANSOM and ALLEN TATE, of the tripartite leadership of the literary group known as the southern FUGITIVES/AGRARIANS. Although Davidson is perhaps the least known of this group of poet-critics, he was a vital force in the development of a body of poetry and a distinctive critical vision that sought to incorporate Anglo-Saxon and southern traditions within a modern context.

Born in Campbellsville, Tennessee, Davidson entered Vanderbilt University in 1909, eventually earning a master's degree and becoming a literature professor. At Vanderbilt he became part of a coterie that formed the southern Fugitives and, between 1922 and 1925, published an influential literary magazine called the *Fugitive.* His works of poetry include *The Outland Piper* (1924), *The Tall Men* (1927), and *Lee in the Mountains and Other Poems* (1938).

Davidson's conception of poetry embraced the oral tradition as an element essential to the community, necessary both for identity and survival. Poetry, therefore, must always give form to communal experience, thus providing a medium through which traditions are preserved. For the Fugitives-Agrarians, this belief derived from the southern sensibility that included a strong attachment to the traditional values of loyalty to family, place, and God. Contrary to many of the other Fugitives, however, who tended to bemoan the encroaching loss of such traditional attachments in the modern world, Davidson emphasized their enduring presence. His best poem, "Lee in the Mountains, 1865–1870" (1934), depicts Robert E. Lee while president of Washington College—far from Appomattox and the Confederate surrender. Lee contemplates the southern virtues that guided his actions during the "War between the States" and considers how they continue to guide his life. He concludes that although the Civil War may have been lost, the significance of cultural traditions was not. Thus the poem emphasizes the importance of such loyalty, as the narrator observes that God waits "To bring this lost forsaken valor . . Unto all generations of the faithful heart."

Some of Davidson's distinctive traits include his insistence on the necessity of a relationship between high art and folk art, the need for a writer to preserve regional ties, and a preference for the committed lyric and the heroic voice rather than the more obscure, impersonal style of the poets of MODERNISM. Moreover he recognized the difficulty of the southern writer: He was both unable to embrace the modern trends that scorned southern heritage and unwilling to endorse a backward-seeming culture. His figurative compromise was to embrace southern qualities, including what he identified as "exuberance, sensitiveness, liveliness of imagination, warmth and flexibility of temper" (Cowan 52). These traits can be seen particularly in "Randall, My Son" (1955), "Sanctuary" (1938), and "Hermitage" (1943), all of which use narrative within the poetry, commemorating familial and cultural events in the process. One notable poem, "On a Replica of the Parthenon" (1955), refers to contemporary Nashville, Tennessee, and its full-scale replica of the Greek Parthenon, built to commemorate the state's centennial. Davidson's wry depiction of the oblivious passersby suggests the risks faced by ignoring tradition as the speaker criticizes those who would turn tradition into mere convention because they do not understand their cultural foundation.

BIBLIOGRAPHY

Cowan, Louise. *The Southern Critics.* Irving, Texas: University of Dallas Press, 1972.

Davidson, Donald. *Still Rebels Still Yankees and Other Essays.* Baton Rouge: Louisiana State University Press, 1957.

Carol Marion

DAVIDSON, MICHAEL (1944–) ROBERT DUNCAN, in a blurb that appeared on Michael Davidson's first book-length collection, *The Mutabilities* (1976), wrote that Davidson "is the full heir of the New American Poetry (see POETRY ANTHOLOGIES) that has its roots in the late works of WILLIAM CARLOS WILLIAMS and WALLACE STEVENS. He has developed beyond the work of my own generation." Duncan's statement signals Davidson's success in combining the most important midcentury advances in poetics with the new communities that would soon come to be known as poetries of the LANGUAGE SCHOOL.

Born in Oakland, California, Davidson has been a lifelong Californian despite his many visits to other parts of the world. He earned a B.A. at San Francisco State University in 1967 and went on to complete a Ph.D. at the State University of New York, Buffalo, in 1972. He has been the recipient of a National Endowment for the Arts grant (1976) as well as two grants from the California Council for the Humanities (1979, 1980). In 1993 and 1995, he also received awards from the Fund for Poetry. In addition to his work as a poet, Davidson is an internationally recognized critic and scholar. Long associated with the Language poets, he traveled with other associates from that community to the Soviet Union and subsequently published *Leningrad* (1991), jointly authored with LYN HEJINIAN, RON SILLIMAN, and BARRETT WATTEN. His major works of poetry include *The Prose of Fact* (1981), *The Landing of Rochambeau* (1985), *Post Hoc* (1990), and *The Arcades* (1998).

In a special issue of *Occident* devoted to Davidson and MICHAEL PALMER, DAVID BROMIGE remarks that the "satirical, scandalous and life-affirming elements in

Davidson's poetry co-exist in a happy solution" (42); that happy solution is readily evident in *Post Hoc:* "nothing in the desert / is left over / even the sand / is an example." Equal parts philosophy and lyric, Davidson's poems make music of their own self-inspection: "between them / difference forms on a slide / like a chair made out of flesh / in the phrase 'I'll think on it.'" ("The Last Word on the Sign" [1990]). Not since LOUIS ZUKOFSKY has an American poet placed such lyric weight upon such a simple preposition: Is the speaker on the chair, thinking, or is the speaker thinking of the chair? Seldom has a final pronoun been so deliciously ambiguous, and yet *it* shows us how our language supports our every day. Bruce Campbell notes that there is "a fine distinction between poetry (or art) and philosophy, but it is the kind of distinction which can be *used*" (111). From *Discovering Motion* (1980) through *Analogy of the Ion* (1988), Davidson has made a practice of turning such distinctions back upon themselves, demonstrating for readers how that kind of useful practice of poetry might sound.

BIBLIOGRAPHY

Campbell, P. Michael, ed. *Occident: Special Issue on Michael Davidson and Michael Palmer.* CIII, no. 1 (1990).

Aldon L. Nielsen

"THE DAY LADY DIED" FRANK O'HARA **(1964)** This postmodern elegy for Billie Holiday is an example of FRANK O'HARA's tendency to write occasional poems and often to write them on the occasion of death. It is also a prime example of what he called "I do this, I do that" poems, wherein the speaker catalogues events in a running commentary (Gooch 288). O'Hara likened his poems to "unmade telephone calls" (qtd. in Gooch 150), and, indeed, this poem has, at the end of the second line, the implied listener found in a dramatic monologue when the speaker confirms something to the listener (the recipient of the "telephone call") as though the listener has spoken. In fact, the poem's "call" was merely delayed a few hours because O'Hara read it that same evening to the friends he buys gifts for, according to the poem's account. The poem is, on the surface, what its title claims for it; it is about the day itself, and not explicitly about the death of Billie Holiday (or Lady Day) until almost the end.

Implicitly, however, the poem points to its conclusion through the variety of specific references to African and African-American subjects. The first of these occurs when O'Hara has his shoes shined, presumably by a black man because of the poem's explicit situation in place and time, America in 1959. He also mentions Ghanaian poets seemingly in passing and includes Jean Genet's (1910–86) play *Les Nègres* among the books he considers purchasing. It is only from the perspective of the jazz bar, the renowned Five Spot, at the end of the poem that the poem's investment in race becomes clearly visible. O'Hara, yielding to his personal preferences, also salts his account with all manner of things French: brands of cigarettes, names of playwrights and poets, even a national holiday (which again neatly suggests his somewhat-secret subject's identity). The poem is filled with very specific names and places. O'Hara does not go into an unidentified shop to buy an unnamed item for an anonymous friend; rather he states that "in the GOLDEN GRIFFIN I get a little Verlaine / for Patsy" and through these details grants readers intimate entry into the poem's places and events. By the time he arrives in the past—in his memory of Billie Holiday singing—a reader is there with him, "leaning on the john door in the 5 SPOT," just as that reader has already eaten lunch, bought liquor, and sweated in the summer heat.

In this poem O'Hara captures an experience everyone knows, and does so best because he does it through a specific surreal experience. He demonstrates how mundane activities can become significant retrospectively, how things that otherwise would never be remembered are magnified by their proximity to something that makes the world stop breathing. And he gently makes a reader remember a moment when it seemed impossible that the world could go on shopping and shining its shoes because something cataclysmic has happened.

BIBLIOGRAPHY

Ellridge, Jim, ed. *Frank O'Hara: To Be True to a City.* Ann Arbor: University of Michigan Press, 1990.
Gooch, Brad. *City Poet: The Life and Times of Frank O'Hara.* New York: Knopf, 1993.

A. Mary Murphy

"DEAR JOHN, DEAR COLTRANE"

Michael S. Harper (1970) A eulogy for the late jazz saxophonist John Coltrane, "Dear John, Dear Coltrane" is the title poem of Michael Harper's first collection, a National Book Award nominee. Harper's live readings of the poem emphasize its musical qualities, especially with his rhapsodic chanting of the refrain "a love supreme," which was both the title and the refrain chanted by band members on Coltrane's best-known album, a four-part suite expressing Coltrane's love for God transcendent. Mingling song lines with events from Coltrane's own biography, "Dear John, Dear Coltrane" memorializes a life marked by drug abuse and later by spiritual epiphany, while also offering a testament to the healing power of jazz and to the endurance of African-American identity in the face of social iniquity.

Evoking the image of a slave market in the opening lines—"Sex fingers toes / in the marketplace"—Harper takes events from Coltrane's youth in racially segregated Hamlet, North Carolina, to suggest the great influence of Coltrane's personal and racial history on his music. When Coltrane was seven, he lost three members of his close-knit, religious family—his aunt, his grandfather, and his father—and it was at this time that he began practicing and playing music devotedly. Calling the young Coltrane "witness to this love," Harper acknowledges that "there is no substitute for pain," his early loss driving him to "turn back, and move / by river through the swamps, / singing: *a love supreme, a love supreme.*" Here, Harper's swamp imagery suggests the paths to freedom taken both by runaway slaves and by African Americans in the Great Migration to the urban centers of the north (Coltrane himself moved to Philadelphia), with the music Coltrane performs in the city—"your song now crystal and / the blues"—simultaneously preserving and transforming the historical injustices suffered by African Americans.

For Harper, this doubleness in Coltrane's music lies at the heart of jazz, the blues, and the African-American experience, a fullness that can only be spoken of in the religious terms reserved for divine love; thus, during the chanted call-and-response lines of the poem's middle stanza, Harper writes, *"why you so black? / cause I am / a love supreme, a love supreme."* Harper has spoken elsewhere of how jazz artists like Coltrane facilitate connection to broader African-American traditions of improvisation and resilience: "I am connected to Coltrane . . . and to all the master musicians who operate in our tradition, to expand it, carry it on, refine it, enliven it, and make it consistent with the aspirations, the human aspirations, of the people in the particular context in which they live, where the music is a vibrant kind of exponential factor directed toward their desires, toward their dreams, their visions of themselves as irreducible spirits" (469).

Much of the poem is an apostrophe, or address, to Coltrane, interspersed with song lines chanted in Coltrane's own voice, but in the final stanza, Harper reveals that it is not only the poet, but a whole audience, perhaps a people ("we"), that has been addressing the musician. This revelation parallels a shift in attention to the circumstances of Coltrane's death, suggesting the immense impact of his loss. Liver cancer, likely caused by early (but later kicked) addictions to heroin and alcohol, killed Coltrane at the age of 40, and Harper imbues his death with a sense of Christian sacrifice: "we ached / for song you'd concealed / with your own blood." Harper is not the only poet to elevate John Coltrane in such a manner; Gerald Early, in a somewhat critical assessment of John Coltrane's status as a symbolic figure in African-American poetry, notes that Coltrane inspired more poetic homages to him and his music than any other jazz musician, including the charismatic Charlie "Bird" Parker. Early postulates that the attraction lies in Coltrane's particular character—he was a shy, focused performer who epitomized artistic commitment—and in his quest for spiritual purity, which during the years of Coltrane's greatest artistic achievement (1960–67) corresponded with Martin Luther King's preaching of redemptive love as the answer to American racism. Like King, Coltrane died before his time, and Harper finds in Coltrane's music a power similar to King's—"the inflated heart / pumps out, the tenor kiss, / tenor love"—to heal injustice and restore the supreme love of humans for their fellow humankind.

BIBLIOGRAPHY

Chapman, Abraham. "An interview with Michael S. Harper." *Arts in Society: The Arts in the Post-Industrial Society* 11, no. 3 (1974): 463–471.

Early, Gerald. "Ode to John Coltrane: A Jazz Musician's Influence on African American Culture." *Antioch Review* 57, no. 3 (1999): 371–385.

Temple Cone

"THE DEATH OF THE BALL TURRET GUNNER" RANDALL JARRELL (1945) Shocking the reader with its concise, gruesome ending, this is among the most powerful and successful American poems about World War II. The poem briefly tells the story of a young airman who is horrifically killed during a mission. Because he "washed out" of pilot training, RANDALL JARRELL never experienced aerial combat. He did, however, train bomber crews. It was probably through the carrying out of his instructional duties that Jarrell became familiar with the ball turret, a small Plexiglas bubble protruding from the underside of a bomber plane.

Sitting in an upside-down position in the revolving turret, with his knees drawn up to his chin, the gunner, resembling a fetus in the womb, would operate two machine guns. The bubble's exposed location and relatively flimsy construction made the turret and its operator vulnerable to machine-gun and cannon fire from fighter planes. A gunner also faced danger from "flak" (exploding shells fired from ground-based antiaircraft artillery); as the last line of Jarrell's poem makes poignantly clear, a direct hit from "flak" could, quite literally, liquefy an unfortunate gunner: "When I died they washed me out of the turret with a hose."

The poem confronts both its speaker and readers with what Leven Dawson terms "a series of paradoxes or reversals" (238). For example, the gunner emerges from one womb—a natural, life-nourishing space provided by his mother—only to enter another, the turret into which the state, in need of "human resources," summarily deposits him. This second womb, though, does not provide nurturing and sustenance; instead, it offers only combat, fear, and, ultimately, death. Indeed, David K. Cornelius expands the metaphor of turret as womb by asserting that the poem's final line suggests an abortion (240). Jarrell's use of the phrase *washed out* also suggests an aviator's having failed in training. In the gunner's case, however, his very success in completing training speeds him toward the ultimate failure, his own destruction. In addition the poem inverts the traditional significance of the positions *up* and *down*. Whereas the former generally signifies life or spirituality and the latter death, in Jarrell's poem, the gunner ascends only to realize his own demise. Dawson suggests that the six-mile altitude of the gunner's plane stands as a symbolic inversion of a grave's traditional six-foot depth (238). Finally, the transition to wakefulness from sleep is generally characterized as a journey from dream or nightmare to clarity or sanity. The gunner, however, awakens from his "dream of life" only to discover the nightmare of aerial and, ultimately, mortal combat.

BIBLIOGRAPHY

Cornelius, David K. "Jarrell's 'The Death of the Ball Turret Gunner.'" In *Critical Essays on Randall Jarrell,* edited by Suzanne Ferguson. Boston, Mass.: G.K. Hall, 1983, p. 240.
Dawson, Leven. "Jarrell's 'The Death of the Ball Turret Gunner.'" In *Critical Essays on Randall Jarrell,* edited by Suzanne Ferguson, 238–239. Boston, Mass.: G. K. Hall, 1983.

Douglas W. Texter

"THE DEATH OF THE HIRED MAN" ROBERT FROST (1914) Robert Frost's BLANK VERSE narrative "The Death of the Hired Man" is best known for two claims made by its married protagonists, Warren and Mary, about the nature of home. "Home is the place where, when you have to go there, / They have to take you in," says Warren when told that the old farm laborer Silas has returned, not just for work, but for a home or homelike place where he can die. "I should have called it / Something you somehow haven't to deserve," replies Mary. As memorable as folk sayings, these two maxims demonstrate Frost's mastery of the moralizing rhetoric of fireside poetry, but upon closer reading, they reveal Frost's pointedly unnostalgic concern with the problems of modern American life. Rural poverty, alienation, the breakdown of family and community bonds, the failure of communication, and the vulnerability of the indigent are all at issue in Warren and Mary's seemingly quaint musings on home. In its pastoral New England setting, its focus on life lived close to the earth, and its attention to the psychology of ordinary American life, the poem is characteristic of

Frost's work. Yet the conflict between Warren and Mary, and the eventual death of Silas described in the title, demonstrate what the critic Lionel Trilling famously called Frost's "representation of the terrible actualities of life."

Outside of a few short narrative passages, the poem is told largely through the dialogue of Mary and Warren. Their speech demonstrates Frost's commitment to evoking the logic of thought through the patterns of ordinary speech, as well as his thematic focus on communication itself, particularly between the different sexes. While Mary and Warren conflict less than the married couple in Frost's "HOME BURIAL," their conversation nevertheless reveals important differences in character. Warren initially shows skepticism about Silas's motives and commitment to work, sarcastically exhorting Mary to "confess / He said he'd come to ditch the meadow for me," to which Mary replies, with sympathy for Silas and exasperation for her husband's lack of feeling, "Of course he did. What would you have him say? / Surely you wouldn't grudge the old man / Some humble way to save his self-respect." Radcliffe Squires argues that the characters in the poem are "accomplished" and thus "incapable of change" (78), yet this obstinacy seems so typically New England in character that one ought to assume Frost is ironically undermining it. Although they seem fixed in their ways, the characters' attitudes change subtly over the course of the conversation, lending the poem its dramatic force. Mary comes to feel overwhelming pity for Silas's reduced condition, while Warren at last stands up for Silas's strength of character, saying, in response to Mary's claim that "His working days are done," that "I'd not be in a hurry to say that." And Silas himself, who never appears in the poem, changes in the way Mary and Warren characterize him, from being a ne'er-do-well to an object of pity to a tragic figure whose failure to accomplish his life's great work, the ironically minor feat of ditching a meadow, intensifies his humanity.

The contrast between Warren's hardened, masculine attitude toward Silas and Mary's more conventionally feminine and thoughtful nature has an interesting parallel in the conflict between Silas and Harold Wilson. Four years prior, Silas had worked with Harold, a college student whom Warren had hired for the summer. The two men would quarrel about the values and purposes of knowledge, with Harold claiming "He studied Latin like the violin / Because he liked it," while Silas tried to "make the boy believe / He could find water with a hazel prong." Harold's learned but idealistic knowledge and Silas's practical but superstitious lore reflect a central conflict in Frost's work between intellect and experience.

Like the conflict between Mary and Warren and their competing ideals of home, this conflict between intellect and experience cannot be resolved, but it can be peacefully reconciled, as Frost suggests through the poem's setting. Mary and Warren hold their conversation at night under the moon, a traditional symbol of femininity, yet it is Mary who narrates the story of Silas's summer work, which was done "All through July under the blazing sun." Mary thus reconciles the masculine sun and the feminine moon, and by extension, she reconciles Warren to Silas, so that when she touches the moonlit stems of some morning glories, which Frost compares to the strings of a musical instrument, it is "As if she played unheard some tenderness / That wrought on him beside her in the night." For Richard Poirier, the "tenderness" Warren comes to feel "can therefore be said to emanate from her alone but from an environment, both natural and of her own creation. And it is this shared environment which is 'their home'" (107).

The idea of home as an imaginative construction, rather than as a particular place or as a social bond, proves crucial to the story of "The Death of the Hired Man." As Warren reveals, Silas in fact has what would normally stand for a "home": he has a brother in town, "rich, / A somebody—director of a bank," who could and perhaps even ought to take Silas in, according to both Warren's and Mary's earlier definitions of home. Yet neither man will move toward that reconciliation. Mary conjectures that Silas's lack of material success in life makes him an outcast, but also that he refuses to "be made ashamed to please his brother." As in the case of Silas and Harold, the bond between men (and thus between the types of knowledge Frost associates with men) cannot be made a home. Instead, there must be unification of mind and heart, intellect and experience, which is figured in the increasingly tender exchanges between Mary and Warren, who goes off to find Silas and take him back in. Yet even though Frost can acknowledge the impulse to reconcile these warring aspects of human nature, the conclusion of "The Death of the Hired Man" questions the possibility that such reconciliation can occur. When he gets up to find Silas, Mary tells Warren that "I'll sit and see if that small sailing cloud / Will hit or miss the moon," a simple pastime that resonates with the poem's themes of homelessness and tenderness. The cloud hits the moon, Frost writes, but when Warren returns, "'Dead,' was all he answered." For Frost, the actualities of human life are tragic, though the desire to reconcile intellect and experience and thereby find a sort of home in the world will never cease.

BIBLIOGRAPHY

Poirier, Richard. *Robert Frost: The Work of Knowing.* New York: Oxford University Press, 1977.

Squires, Radcliffe. *The Major Themes of Robert Frost.* Ann Arbor: University of Michigan Press, 1963.

Temple Cone

DEEP IMAGE POETRY Deep image poetry was part of the post–World War II, New American poetry inspired by the BEATS and the BLACK MOUNTAIN SCHOOL. The "deep" of deep image refers not to some attempt at political or philosophical "profundity" but to the "direction of seeing" (Rothenberg 31). It refers to the inwardness of the poetry, which plumbs the self in order to express, and perhaps transform, the world. The depth of the image is the measure of how far it can provide a link between the internal and external worlds.

The term *deep image poetry* refers to poems produced by a loose collection of poets spread geographically across the United States and chronologically over a period that included most of the 1960s and the early part of the 1970s. Mainly it refers to three groups surrounding ROBERT KELLY, JEROME ROTHENBERG, and ROBERT BLY. What the three groups shared and what distinguished deep image poetry from other contemporary forms of poetry was, in the words of Dennis Haskell, the "rational manipulation of irrational materials" (142). The deep image poets tried to avoid highly polished philosophical poetry in favor of a poetry that expressed the chaos of the psychological world.

Given the manifold forms of psychological chaos, there is no such thing as a typical deep image poem. However, the description of the eponymous night in Robert Kelly's "Of this night" (the first poem in *Armed Descent* [1961]) as something that comes alive with a "roar of things out of the streets" is typical of the interpenetration of the internal world of the psyche and the external world. In this case the idea or feeling of "night" has just been explicitly "covered with skin"—made into something internal that can exist outside—but it is still a confused and "savage" personification. "This night" takes its life from the internal life of the poet and provides, as a consequence, "an entrance to a living house"—an entrance by way of the night and the poem, to the inner world of the speaker.

Individual poets had been writing poetry that could be called deep image poetry for some years, but they were not identifiable as a coherent group until several of them were included in DONALD HALL's 1964 anthology *Contemporary American Poetry* (see POETRY ANTHOLOGIES). Rothenberg had coined the term in 1960: It is a significant part of a published letter to ROBERT CREELEY in which Rothenberg explains the principles underlying his own poetic practices. Kelly picked up on the term, and deep image poetry is the subject of two theoretical notes in Kelly's *Trobar* journal as well as, arguably, the primary content of the POETRY JOURNAL.

No single event marked the end of deep image poetry, but as the 1970s wore on the term became more open to parody and met with increasing disapproval from both critics and early exponents, who felt that the earlier styles, subjects, and tones of the poetry had become superficial and clichéd. In 1976 ROBERT PINSKY articulated this feeling in his book *The Situation of Poetry,* which critiqued the debased deep image poems that were by that time standard in contemporary books and magazines. Although this critique marked a decisive blow to those who were still identifying themselves as deep image poets in the late 1970s, in 1979 it was still possible for Haskell to refer, in an article in *Southern Review,* to deep image poetry as part of the "current state of American poetry" (137).

No single acknowledged manifesto defined deep image poetry in the way CHARLES OLSON's 1950 "Projective Verse" had declared the intentions of the Black

Mountain School (see ARS POETICAS), or ALLEN GINSBERG'S *HOWL and Other Poems* (1956) had inspired the Beat poets. Since it was founded for neither ideological nor programmatical reasons, deep image poetry could comfortably include a bewildering variety of styles, content, and even personnel. It is evident in the pages of *Trobar* that, with no explicit membership criteria, poets became deep image poets by association. Not many of the larger group of Beats, apart from GARY SNYDER, were in any way affiliated with deep image, but many of the influential poets formerly associated with the Black Mountain school can be found in the pages of *Trobar,* including Olson, Creeley, PAUL BLACKBURN, ROBERT DUNCAN, and EDWARD DORN.

Since the size and orientation of the three interwoven groups gathered around Rothenberg, Kelly, and Bly was continually changing, the membership of the "movement," even at a given point in time, is difficult to delineate. It is important to note, however, that the three groups comprised separate poets and groups of poets whose ideas, writing and thoughts converged—they were not members of a single group that splintered through specific disagreements. Each of the groups had its own journal, but the poets in each group wrote, spoke, and contributed work to each other regularly.

The first of these groups, the neosurrealists, was gathered around Rothenberg and the journal he edited, *Poems from the Floating World.* Although he did not manifest this at the time, he later said that he always thought of the journal as an ongoing anthology of deep image poetry. Including DAVID ANTIN, ARMAND SCHWERNER, and JACKSON MAC LOW, this group was particularly interested in tapping into "a *general* subjective life" (Haskell 142). In their schema, deep image poetry is an attempt to bring the personal (the specific) and the external (the general) into communication by using the image. Their poetry, especially that of Rothenberg, displayed a symbolist belief that the hidden world could be perceived through its external manifestations and that an image unifying the inner and outer could be found inside one's own observations.

Rothenberg was fascinated by the potential of a deeply inward image to link the specific self to the general world. He quotes from French poet Charles Baudelaire to make his point that "the poem 'will contain, at one and the same time, the object and the subject, the external world and the artist himself'" (32). His poem series "Whichever Road I Took, I Somehow Kept Coming Back to the Place Where I Had Started" (1961), published across *Trobar* 2 and 3, narrates the journey of a self in a "strange country" and the difficulty of relating to others in it. The series ends with "A word of greeting [that] passes when we touch," suggesting that, with the word of greeting, the artist has somehow achieved a correspondence between the internal and external world.

The second group formed around Kelly and *Trobar.* Despite more optimistic intentions, *Trobar* was published only five times between 1960 and 1964, but it provided a central forum. It was edited by Robert and Joan Kelly along with GEORGE ECONOMOU and was dedicated to deep image poetry. In addition to poetry by Economou, Kelly, and Rothenberg, the output of this group included work by DIANE WAKOWSKI, ROCHELLE OWENS, CLAYTON ESHLEMAN, LeRoi Jones (AMIRI BARAKA), Margaret Randall, and GERRIT LANSING (all of whom contributed to two or more issues of *Trobar*). This was an even looser grouping than the neosurrealists. *Trobar* published two of the only theoretical notes (written by Kelly and Rothenberg) that discuss what might be meant by deep image poetry and what might be gained by its adoption, and so the journal makes for eclectic reading.

In his 1961 "Notes on the poetry of deep image," Kelly makes clear that context is crucial: "Nothing can be known unless it is known in situ" (14). At the heart of his project is a hope that, by placing images in a poem where the context allows them to resonate through each other, deep image poetry can effect the "transformation of the perceived world." For Kelly deep image poetry comes from an attempt, in language, to link together *percepts,* the basic units of perception—an impression of the senses in the mind. The image is "the clothed percept" (16). Perhaps closer to Olson than either Bly or Rothenberg, Kelly claims that the image is inextricably related to the line: "the image is the measure of the line" (16). It is not a single image that imbues the poem with power but the sequence of images for which the lines have been created: "The line is cut with the image in mind" (16).

Bly and JAMES WRIGHT were the main figures in the third group, which founded and published the *Fifties* (the journal subsequently became the *Sixties* and, briefly, the *Seventies*). According to MICHAEL DAVIDSON and Haskell, this group also included W. S. MERWIN, GALWAY KINNELL, Hall, MARK STRAND, and LOUIS SIMPSON. Bly was only reluctantly a deep image poet. He did not like the term and preferred to call it "leaping poetry" to distinguish it from the work of the IMAGIST SCHOOL, which he thought was misguided. Bly was particularly interested in trying to combine inward reflection with a lightness and an energy that would then have a positive impact on and insight into the external world. He preferred to define the poetry in terms of its energy instead of its chosen image.

Bly thought of the image as a "physical thing"—"a body where psychic energy is free to move around." For Bly "leaping" meant expressing energy in jumps of association that mapped out an image through a poem ("Looking" 4). He felt that contemporary poets were so overwhelmed by rules that they were no longer capable of recognizing the power of a thought: "It's as if a bull woke up one day with so much energy, he ignored the fence posts and barn door of his pasture and created Assyria instead!!" ("Infantilism" 259). Despite the fact that the energy of "the bull" (the image) might let it define "Assyria," his direct predecessors were obsessed with the "fence posts" and were unable to see the "bull." For Bly "the bull" embodied the energy of a poem and defined it far more than the delineating "fence posts" of convention. The poet's mandate was not to dwell within barn doors but to leap with the bull to map new realms symbolized by "Assyria."

Bly claims that this "fantastic freedom of association" was evident in "ancient art" ("Looking" 6), but it was gradually excised from mainstream English poetry after "Chaucer and Langland" (4). All three groups were influenced by the Spanish example of *duende* (Federico Garcáa Lorca's elusive term meaning something between "inspiration" and "energy") and by examples of associative ability that come to us through modern psychologists like Sigmund Freud and Carl Jung, older poets like Friedrich Hölderlin, Novalis, and William Blake, and contemporary poetry in other languages, most notably from Spanish—especially Pablo Neruda, César Vallejo, Antonio Machado, and Lorca, many of whom Bly translated for publication.

As part of its psychologized interest in the mind, deep image poetry was heavily influenced by foreign thinkers, writers, and spiritualists. Rather than trace its genealogy from contemporary English poetry, it saw itself as an inheritor of poetic/prophetic practice that, as has been mentioned, it shared with contemporary surrealist poets in French and Spanish and that stretched back through Martin Buber and Jung to visionaries like Blake and Jacob Boehme. This was a positive decision in favor of writers whose subjects and tone were more appealing, but it was also part of a rebellion against the strictures of New Criticism (see FUGITIVE/AGRARIAN SCHOOL) and its accompanying poetry.

Bly rebelled not only against established ideas of poetry but also against establishment politics. He wrote exuberant poems whose images leapt from personal psychology to the national psyche to global events. Initially these were humorous—such as when he describes how he had behaved when he was president: crushing snails barefoot, sleeping in his underwear, eating Cubans with a straw ("Three Presidents" [1968]). Increasingly, however, as with many deep image poets, his poems became infused with a bitterness about the involvement of the United States in Vietnam.

Among other poems from Bly's *The Light around the Body* (1967), both "At a March Against the Vietnam War" (23) and "Driving through Minnesota during the Hanoi Bombings" (27) trace the movement of the image from the internal world to the domestic political world to global consequences. In "At a March" the speaker's personal vision of feet moving turns into a collective burden—a "cup of darkness" inherited from the Puritans, "As they went out to kill turkeys." Inexorably the same feet carry the reader to the time when, using the "cup of darkness," the same collective makes war, "Like a man anointing himself." "Driving" also traces the connections between a Minnesota summer and the Hanoi bombings. The ramifications of parties in Minnesota are felt as hangovers that end up "In Asia." Self-disgust mixes with self-love in America so that although "We were the ones we intended to bomb!" an inexorable chain of events and images means that it is the "small rice-fed ones" who suffer.

The deep image movement was roughly contemporary with the war in Vietnam and became caught up in many aspects of it. The protests and social changes around the end of the Vietnam War had transformed the practice of the leading deep image writers in ways that varied from one to the other. As these originators moved on to follow their own diverging stylistic and political paths, derivative poets and poetry were left to carry on deep image poetry. With the ending of the war, a new paradigm was needed for American society and its poetry; although Haskell could still write of it in the present tense in 1979, deep image poetry had already ended by then as a viable movement.

BIBLIOGRAPHY

Bly, Robert. "Infantilism and Adult Swiftness: An Interview with Ekbert Faas." In *Talking All Morning.* Ann Arbor: University of Michigan Press, 1981, pp. 251–283.

———. "Looking for Dragon Smoke." In *Leaping Poetry: An Idea with Poems and Translations.* Boston: Beacon Press, 1972.

Davidson, Michael. "American Poetry." In *The New Princeton Encyclopedia of Poetry and Poetics,* edited by Alex Preminger and T. V. F. Brogan. Princeton, N.J.: Princeton University Press, 1993, pp. 47–66.

Haskell, Dennis. "The Modern American Poetry of Deep Image." *Southern Review* 12 (1979): 137–166.

Kelly, Robert. "Notes on the Poetry of Deep Image." *Trobar* 2 (1961): 14–16.

Rothenberg, Jerome. *Pre-faces & Other Writings.* New York: New Directions, 1981.

———. "Why Deep Image?" *Trobar* 3 (1961): 31–32.

Dan Friedman

"DESIGN" ROBERT FROST (1936) "Design" is one of many poems in which ROBERT FROST's speakers express alienation from nature. John Lynen asserts that Frost's conception of nature differs from those of his romantic and Victorian predecessors: "By insisting on the gulf separating man and nature, [Frost] directly opposes the romantic attempt to bring the two together. While the romantics sought a place for sensations, feelings, and values within physical nature, he conceives of the physical world as a distinct level of being" (181). In "Design," Frost sees nature as inscrutable and frightening. This view is related to an alienation from society and even from self that characterizes many American poems of the 20th century.

The poem is an Italian sonnet, consisting of an octave (eight lines describing a scene or situation) and a sestet (six lines of commentary). The octave describes a microcosmic scene, in which a spider on a flower holds up the severed wings of a moth it has caught in the night. Frost employs sardonic similes and metaphors that belie the gruesome character of the scene: One comparison associates the spider's actions with playfulness. Moreover the speaker remarks that such elements of destruction and disease seem quite natural. As Mordecai Marcus observes, "Design" is "[p]erhaps the most often initially misunderstood of Frost's poems . . because of its apparent matter-of-factness and mock cheerfulness" (152).

In the sestet, Frost's speaker asks a series of questions about the scene and its purport. The flower is normally blue: Why is the one on which the spider caught the moth an anomalous albino? Why did the moth alight on this flower? Was it drawn in the dark by its whiteness? Why did the spider choose to climb this flower? Frost's use of verbs suggests a force—divine intervention, fate, natural law—that governs all occurrences. Frost seems to imply that they are not merely happenstances at all. His word for this force is *design.* He implies with his rhetorical questions that the microcosm of the spider, flower, and moth may be extrapolated to the macrocosm of human fate. It is perhaps this recognition that proves most frightening to the speaker and, by extension, to the reader. As the critic Lionel Trilling once observed in a speech in Frost's honor, "I think of Robert Frost as a terrifying poet. . . . The universe that he conceives is a terrifying universe. Read the poem called 'Design' and see if you sleep the better for it" (qtd. in Lynen 189–190).

BIBLIOGRAPHY

Lynen, John. "Frost as Modern Poet." In *Robert Frost: A Collection of Critical Essays,* edited by James M. Cox. Englewood Cliffs, N.J.: Prentice Hall, 1962, pp. 177–197.

Marcus, Mordecai. *The Poems of Robert Frost: An Explication.* Boston: G. K. Hall, 1991.

Edwin J. Barton

DICKEY, JAMES (1923–1997) Emerging from no specific "school" but clearly allied with modern "primitive" poets, such as THEODORE ROETHKE and ROBERT PENN WARREN, James Dickey early on exhibited, in tone and diction, a kinship with the FUGITIVE/AGRARIAN SCHOOL, but his driving rhythms also echoed the popular poetry of Edgar Allan Poe and Robert Service. Visionary and surrealistic, grounded in the southern landscape both geographically and metaphysically, Dickey was ideologically and stylistically at odds with antimilitaristic contemporaries like ROBERT BLY, with whom he publicly feuded, and CONFESSIONAL poets like ROBERT LOWELL, SYLVIA PLATH, and ANNE SEXTON, whom he dubbed the "school of gabby agony" ("Lecture"). The distinctive margin-to-margin lines he developed in his later work, which use space—rather than line breaks or punctuation—to indicate pauses and highlight rhythm, derive from the influence of Walt Whitman and HART CRANE.

Dickey was born in Buckhead, Georgia. His father, Eugene Dickey, was a lawyer who encouraged a love of oratory in his second son through the reading of famous legal trials aloud. His mother, Maibelle Swift Dickey, who frequently quoted Alfred, Lord Tennyson and Henry Wadsworth Longfellow, was an invalid who whistled as she lay in bed, a practice that would inspire one of Dickey's greatest poems, "Buckdancer's Choice" (1965): "Warbling all day to herself / The thousand variations of one song." Dickey attended Clemson A&M (now Clemson University) in South Carolina for one semester before enlisting in the U.S. Army Air Corps in 1943. He served as a bombardier in the 418th Night Fighter Squadron in the South Pacific through 1945, flying in approximately 100 combat missions between 1943 and 1945. During the long idle periods between missions, he began to read poetry seriously; when the war ended, he enrolled at Vanderbilt University, earning a B.A. in 1949 and an M.A. in 1950. It was at Vanderbilt that he began to write poetry. Dickey joined the faculty at Rice Institute in the fall of 1950 but was recalled to active military duty in the Korean War four months later. After serving two years, he returned to Rice, where he taught until 1954, when he received a *Sewanee Review* fellowship, which he used to travel to Europe and concentrate on his writing.

At the age of 34, he sought a new career in New York and entered the advertising field while continuing to write poetry, eventually relocating to Atlanta. Upon being awarded a Guggenheim Fellowship for 1961–62, Dickey abandoned advertising and traveled to Positano, Italy, where he wrote *Drowning with Others* (1962), his first full-length volume of poetry. Upon his return to the United States, he served as poet-in-residence at several colleges and published two more volumes of poetry. The second of these, *Buckdancer's Choice* (1966), won the National Book Award, the Melville Cane Award from the Poetry Society of America, and a National Institute of Arts and Letters Award. Dickey served as consultant in poetry for the Library of Congress from 1966–68. From 1968 until his death, he taught at the University of South Carolina. In 1977 he wrote and read "The Strength of Fields" for Jimmy Carter's inaugural celebration, and in 1988 he was inducted into the American Academy of Arts and Letters. During his career he published three novels, including the extremely successful *Deliverance* (1970), several books of criticism, and two children's books, in addition to his many volumes of poetry, the last of which, *The Eagle's Mile,* was published in 1990.

Dickey was dubbed "the unlikeliest of poets" by *Life* magazine in 1966—a characterization he reinforced through his frequent and electrifying readings (O'Neill 68). He called his tireless attempts to bring poetry to the people—through readings, interviews, teaching, his role as consultant to the Library of Congress, and casual encounters—"barnstorming for poetry" ("Lecture"), and his ideal of the poet was a man of action—both master and student of the natural world—the "energized man" ("The Energized Man" 163). Dickey described the energized man as "the man with vivid senses, the man alert to the nuances and meanings of his own experience, the man able to appreciate and evaluate the relation between words in the right order" ("The Energized Man" 163–164). Although Dickey emphatically stated that he was not this man, he is evoked in Dickey's poetry.

In "Sleeping Out at Easter" (1960), the speaker is transformed into the energized man through his contact with nature as he camps out in his backyard with his child. He is able to see beyond the dark night, his human fear and alienation, and to tap into a larger understanding of the universe: "One eye opens slowly without me. / My sight is the same as the sun's." Through his heightened awareness to his surroundings, the speaker enters a visionary state wherein the physical world reveals the metaphysical. In this state, he grasps "The source of all song at the root." In this poem and in much of Dickey's work, the speaker is actively engaged with the world around him and is frequently in conflict—with nature, family history, military enemies, lovers, his own body—but he is also marvelously attuned, literally transforming himself into the objects, events, animals, and people he observes and envisions. While his work often deals with dark subjects—bestiality, death, rape, adultery, voyeurism, execution, firebombing—it always affirms the life force and the power of the imagination to transform existence. One of his best-known poems, "Falling" (1981), is based on the death of a flight attendant who was sucked from a plane. Dickey transforms this bizarre and tragic event into a mythical visitation, with the flight attendant—from whose point of view the poem is imagined—reimagined as a fertility goddess blessing the earth with her death: As the farmers walk toward her broken body, they move "Toward the flowering of the harvest in their hands."

BIBLIOGRAPHY

Baughman, Ronald. *Understanding James Dickey*. Columbia: University of South Carolina Press, 1985.

Dickey, James. "The Energized Man." In *The Imagination as Glory: The Poetry of James Dickey*, edited by Bruce Weigl and T. R. Hummer, 163–165. Urbana: University of Illinois Press, 1984.

———. "Lecture." Lecture given as part of the American Poetry Course at the University of South Carolina, Columbia, S.C., spring 1994.

O'Neill, Paul. "The Unlikeliest Poet." *Life* 61 (22 July 1966): 68–70.

Melissa Johnson

DIGGES, DEBORAH (1950–) Deborah Digges writes highly wrought and musical LYRIC POETRY that connects personal revelation to historical contexts and social consequences. Her poems combine complex syntax, formal music, and erudition with a deep and startling compassion for all forms of life. At times her poetry evokes the dense ecstatic music of Gerard Manley Hopkins and Dylan Thomas, but she brings a distinctly feminine sensibility to this synthesis of song and intense feeling. Peppered with allusions to the natural sciences, philosophy, astronomy, archaeology, and ancient and contemporary history, her poems are challenging but engaging as she shifts mercurially between celebration and despair, rumination and ecstasy, rebellion and remorse. THEODORE ROETHKE has influenced her work, and her eye for significant detail recalls ELIZABETH BISHOP, though Digges is more direct in her exuberance and less restrained in her sorrows.

Digges was born and raised in Jefferson, Missouri. Her first book, *Vesper Sparrows* (1986), received the Delmore Schwartz Memorial Prize in 1987. Her third book, *Rough Music* (1995), won the Kingsly-Tufts Prize in 1996. Besides her poetry, Digges has translated the work of Cuban poet Maria Elena Cruz Varela and is the author of two memoirs, *Fugitive Spring* (1992) and *The Stardust Lounge* (2001). She has also been awarded a number of fellowships.

Early in her career, Digges was praised for her "effortless music" and "passionate intuition," by JORIE GRAHAM, and she retains these qualities throughout her work (31). In *Vesper Sparrows* and *Late in the Millennium,* Digges demonstrates her ability to merge formal writing with personal concerns, as in "The Rockettes," a modified villanelle about her mother, and "Hall of Souls," a brilliant sestina about cycles of birth and loss (see PROSODY AND FREE VERSE).

Rough Music marks a decisive shift in Digges's work. The volume mourns a broken relationship but, as David Baker writes, "without self-pity or blame, without the rehearsal of confessions or accusations" (201). Digges reveals her considerable erudition with allusions to Ralph Waldo Emerson, Charles Darwin, Sigmund Freud, medical procedures, and medieval rituals, but she also injects the poems with a rougher cadence and harsher, grittier imagery. "Broom" ritualizes loss by focusing on an ordinary household object and imaginatively transforming it into "an oar that parted waters, raft-keel and mast, or twirled / around and around on the back lawn, / a sort of compass." Writing about graffiti-making street gangs in "Tombs of the

Muses," Digges displays her ability to identify with those outside her immediate experience as well as her musical ear and keen eye: "they balance on a car door riding rat-chewed coach seats, / they roller-spread a sky." In *Rough Music,* the formal elements are more diffuse, but they help to contain the ratcheting up of emotion. As Baker suggests, in these poems, technical strategies provide "a series of frames by which to contain grief and to 'atone' for disaster or destruction with discipline" (201).

In her poetry, Digges draws on public rituals and forms to make sense of private, often painful experience. Her willingness to delve intensely into emotional turmoil is balanced by a skillful and inventive use of form.

BIBLIOGRAPHY

Baker, David. "Line by Line." *Kenyon Review* 18, nos. 3–4 (summer–fall 1996): 191–205.

Boruch, Marianne. "Comment: The Feel of a Century." *American Poetry Review* 19, no. 4 (July–August 1990): 17–20.

Graham, Jorie. Review of *Vesper Sparrows,* by Deborah Digges. *New York Times Book Review* (28 September 1986): 32.

Lisa Sewell

DI PRIMA, DIANE (1934–) Diane di Prima is arguably the most well-known female BEAT writer. However, her work extends beyond the affiliation with the Beats to address nature and ecological concerns, family and children, revolutionary politics, American Indian mysticism, and Buddhism. She embraced feminism early (see FEMALE VOICE, FEMALE LANGUAGE), and although she appears at times to depict women in a submissive position to that of men, she, in fact, advocates an active participation for women, a role, as she says in *Memoirs of a Beatnik* (1969), that will "initiate the dance" (5).

Di Prima was born in New York City. In the early 1950s, she left Swarthmore College for Greenwich Village, where she met ALLEN GINSBERG, JACK KEROUAC, and LeRoi Jones (AMIRI BARAKA). With Jones, she founded the newsletter the *Floating Bear;* she also helped to found Poets Press and the New York Poets Theater. She has lived and taught in California since the 1970s and has published more than 30 books of poetry and prose, including *This Kind of Bird Flies Backward* (1958), *Revolutionary Letters* (1968), and the book-length poem LOBA (1978; expanded 1998). In 1993 she received the National Poetry Association Lifetime Service Award and in 1994 the Aniello Lauri Award for creative writing.

Although she experiments with rhyme and standard meter in her early poetry, di Prima generally follows the free verse form that other Beat writers employed (see PROSODY AND FREE VERSE). The subjects of her poetry vary from the role of the artist to issues of motherhood. In the first of "Three Laments" (1961), the speaker criticizes the rigidity she sees in the academic tradition as she considers wistfully that she might have become a well-known writer; unfortunately "the chairs / in the library / were too hard." And, in "Song for Baby-o, Unborn" (1961), the speaker vows that, although the world can be a harsh place, she will guide her child to see "enough to love / to break your heart / forever."

The *Loba* poems blend American Indian myth with characters from Greek, Hebrew, and ancient mythologies, such as Lilith and Persephone. Di Prima invents an archetypal wolf goddess ("Loba") as a model for women united by their cultural marginalization. Each woman is a part of every other; the speaker says, "I am you / and I must become you." The poems also position the Loba as a form of creativity that is both "feminine and maternal" (Friedman 207), one that can "chant / a new / creation myth." Like the Loba, di Prima offers a vision of power for women.

BIBLIOGRAPHY

Butterick, George. "Diane di Prima." *Dictionary of Literary Biography,* Vol. 16. In *The Beats: Literary Bohemians in Postwar America,* edited by Ann Charters. Detroit: Gale Research, 1983.

Friedman, Amy L. "'I saw my new name': Women Writers of the Beat Generation." In *The Beat Generation Writers,* edited by A. Robert Lee. London: Pluto Press, 1996, pp. 200–216.

Libby, Anthony. "Diane di Prima: 'Nothing Is Lost; It Shines in Our Eyes.'" In *Girls Who Wore Black: Women Writing the Beat Generation,* edited by Ronna C. Johnson and Nancy M. Grace, 45–68. Piscataway, N.J.: Rutgers University Press, 2002.

Gordon Beveridge

"DIRECTIVE" ROBERT FROST **(1947)** Critical reception of "Directive" has varied greatly, from Richard Poirier's rejection of it as "a tricky and devious poem not because it has a lot to say but because it is not sure of what it does want to say, or do" (100) to Frank Lentricchia's assessment of it as "Frost's *summa*" that shows "the poet's commitment to his art as a way of saving himself" (112). On its surface, and it is a poem greatly occupied with surfaces and depths, ROBERT FROST's "Directive" is a guidance or set of directions, which literally lead the reader through a pastoral New England landscape towards some figurative truth, but which also prove deceptive, confusing, and designed to keep the reader away from that truth. Such paradoxes have created a range of interpretations that vary almost as widely as its critical reception. To some, it is a Grail narrative, though others claim it parodies such quests. S. P. C. Duvall sees the poem as an important homage to Thoreau's *Walden* and an argument for the restorative powers of American literature, while John F. Lynen claims the poem mirrors the poetic process itself, a claim enhanced by Theodore Morrison's focus on the connection Frost made between understanding parables and understanding poetry. Whatever critical assessment or interpretation one resolves to accept, it is clear that Frost's "Directive" incites readers to powerfully held views, though it may be that the poem, like the Grail itself, is "Under a spell so the wrong ones can't find it."

As with so much of Frost's work, the meaning is subtly and significantly inflected by the play of the formal features. "Directive" is filled with numerous puns, allusions, and syntactical complexities designed to misdirect or snare the unwary reader. As Tyler Hoffman observes, Frost enhances the sense of quest at the opening by deferring the main clause till the fifth line, making the reader undertake a sort of syntactical quest through a maze of prepositional phrases to complete the sentence and "triumph over indirection to secure salvation" (76). Frost's blank verse also provides a subtle test for those seeking the salvation of meaning. The opening two lines offer a metrical challenge, for in several places Frost promotes a stressed syllable where conversational English leaves it unstressed, and vice versa. "Back out of all this now too much for us," Frost begins, and "this" seems to invite the stress that the iambic pentameter pattern reserves for "now." Moreover, it is unclear initially whether the repeated word "Back" should be read as a command or a preposition, resulting not only in metrical ambiguity but in an ambiguity of meaning.

Ambiguity, or confusion, is the greatest threat in "Directive," but ironically it is also the precondition for the salvation Frost hints at. The opening lines describe a house that no longer exists, which can be reached "if you'll let a guide direct you / Who only has at heart your getting lost." This claim is both paradoxical and self-referential, for Frost has already gotten the reader lost, the quest for the house having begun without the speaker revealing why one should bother to seek it. One cannot help but pursue the meaning that the syntax and the progression of images continually defer, and here Frost seems to represent the inexorable quality of the Grail quest accurately. For Frost the promise of the Grail is not spiritual grace, but coherent meaning, which would be an anodyne in an era of fragmentation and skepticism represented by that other modern Grail poem, T. S. ELIOT's The WASTE LAND. Yet meaning cannot be had easily, or it will not be true meaning, so the reader must negotiate a range of ambiguous pronoun references, must learn to exercise the imagination and "Make yourself up a cheering song of how / Someone's road home from work this once was," and finally become so sensitive to the absence of meaning that one craves and can effect its discovery, having become "lost enough to find yourself."

Such a claim links the quest for self-knowledge to the quest for meaning, yet Frost defers even that discovery, for it is neither "the children's house of make believe" nor "the house that is no more a house / . . . a house in earnest" to which the reader is directed; rather, "Your destination and your destiny's / A brook that was the water of the house." This brook may allude to various other waters, including the pre-Socratic philosopher Heraclitus's claim that "One cannot step in the same river twice," an admission that the world is in flux and that knowledge is never absolute, the "still waters" of the Twenty-third Psalm, which offer solace after the valley of the shadow of death, and even to Frost's poem, "West-Running Brook," a poem about the human tendency to contrariness. Ultimately, the brook represents not one meaning, but the totality of possible meanings in which the reader, and perhaps also the poet, must get lost in order to "get saved." When Frost offers his remarkably clear conclusion, "Here are your waters and your watering place. / Drink and be whole again beyond confusion," the effect is that of the wisest parable, which makes itself available to even the poorest reader, but which can only be comprehended fully by those who have suffered to find its meaning.

BIBLIOGRAPHY

Duvall, S. P. C. "Robert Frost's 'Directive' Out of *Walden*." In *Critical Essays on Robert Frost,* edited by Philip L. Garner, 138–143. Boston: G. K. Hall & Co.

Hoffman, Tyler. *Robert Frost and the Politics of Poetry.* Hanover, N.H.: Middlebury College Press and the University Press of New England, 2001.

Lentricchia, Frank. *Robert Frost: Modern Poetics and the Landscapes of Self.* Durham, N.C.: Duke University Press, 1975.

Lynen, John F. *The Pastoral Art of Robert Frost.* New Haven, Conn: Yale University Press, 1960.

Morrison, Theodore. "The Agitated Heart." *Atlantic Monthly* 220, no. 1 (1967): 72–79.

Poirier, Richard. *Robert Frost: The Work of Knowing.* New York: Oxford University Press, 1977.

Temple Cone

DISCRETE SERIES George Oppen (1934)

Prior to publishing his first volume of poetry, GEORGE OPPEN was mainly known for his association with the OBJECTIVIST SCHOOL; *Discrete Series* (1934), however, brought him individual attention. Measured purely by word count, *Discrete Series* is shorter than this entry. In its original form, the white space around the poems gives the words a concrete presence that LOUISE GLÜCK refers to as "restraint, juxtaposition, nuance" (29). Indeed, the first thing that strikes the reader of *Discrete Series* is how the few words of the poetry cling to visibility against the overwhelming white of the page. In the original edition (as opposed to its placement in later collections), where the words are distributed over 30 pages, there are rarely more than four words per line or 10 lines per page, and there are never more than 50 words on a page.

The ostensible subjects of the poems are everyday objects and people in Oppen's New York life. A car, elevator signs, tug boats in the harbor, refrigerators—Oppen finds them all noteworthy. This tangible, empirical world of objects that Oppen describes is mirrored by the sparse, hard words that comprise a poetry joined together more physically than grammatically. Oppen explained that he took the title of his work from mathematics, where the term *discrete series* refers to "a series of terms each of which is empirically derived, each one of which is empirically true" (161). Each page, each poem, indeed, each word is so concrete as to have been "empirically derived" and placed in the series as a constitutive term to be read on its own. This discrete nature makes it difficult to know how many poems there are in the series or whether the poetry is even divided into "poems."

Out of print for many years in its original form, the series is available in both the 1975 *Collected Poems,* where the poems are crammed into 12 pages, and the *New Collected Poems* (2002), where the poetry is paginated more like the original. The series itself is punctuated by numbers and lines in bold type that both *Collected Poems* take to be titles. According to this schema, the contents page (notably absent from the original volume of *Discrete Series*) would list seven poems: an untitled preface; two pairs of poems, each numbered 1 and 2; the longish "Party on Shipboard," which takes up more than half the book; and the short final poem, called "Drawing."

The organization in later collected poems volumes is logical, but it reduces the tension between the terseness of the words and their sparing distribution. Just as depression-era society called for new groupings and new understandings of old groupings, the ambiguity of these pages lies in the problem of deciding how the individual words, pages, and poems constitute themselves as a group (or series) and what the ramifications of those arrangements might be for the silence and space that the words implicate.

Written during the Great Depression, just after Oppen had returned from France to New York, *Discrete Series* addresses the "bad times," in which anonymous "cars pass" and a syntactically and semantically disconnected "man sells post-cards" (32). Oppen's careful minimalism makes the poem's general sense, or specific referents, difficult to pin down. Even a seemingly straightforward "T" has been variously understood as a subway sign, a Pierre Bonnard nude, or a T-shape sign showing the direction of an elevator. Whether "T" refers to one, all, or none of these, it certainly also refers to the poems themselves, as they emerge from the white space under the right arm of the fancy T of the opening word of the book—"THE." This detail exemplifies the type of crafted ambiguity that caused Oppen to be, from the beginning, both obscure and appreciated.

Oppen brings daily life into the poem without subsuming it in his own thoughts: The tug never ceases to be a tug; the car remains a car. The intensity of the poetry lies in the performative assertion of the importance of objects, as well as the poem's corollary that words are objects. Oppen refuses to accede to simple metaphorical, symbolic, or grammatical strategies, which makes the poetry difficult to read. Despite its impenetrability, *Discrete Series* was well received, winning an important review from WILLIAM CARLOS WILLIAMS. The work's reception was also helped by a preface provided by EZRA POUND (whose acquaintance Oppen had made in France), in which he compared Oppen to Williams and referred to him as "a serious craftsman" (vi).

Beginning with a parody of languid conversation typical of the writing of Henry James, Oppen takes readers away from the prudish gentility of a drawing room. He brings them out "past the window-glass" onto the "world, weather-swept, with which / one shares the century." The confusing phrases of genteel conversation and description that continually interject themselves into one another give way first to a sweeping alliteration and then, on the next page, to a whole new start: "1 / White." Oppen alludes to the previous ways of writing but rejects them in favor of a new beginning—a numbering that begins over again and a blank page of "White."

The "White" refers not only to a new page (turning over a new leaf) but also begins a description: "White. From the / Under arm of T // The red globe." The "T" of these lines refers to a type of contemporary elevator signal comprised of one white and one red light bulb under the bars of a T-shaped figure. The indicated direction of the elevator depended on which light was illuminated. By referring to the two bulbs, Oppen begins a movement from the vague rhetoric of "weather-swept" centuries to the cold, hard question of whether we are going up or down. The elevator signal is a symbol for the whole building and for the culture that created it, a figure for the uncertainty and hope of that culture.

Although the opening is striking, it is in the closing movement that Oppen's care and skill with words is at its most evident. Here, in what the older *Collected Poems* calls "Drawing," the relation between the layout of the words and the taut economy of meaning is most closely expressed through the triple wordplay on "the / Paper, turned" (35). The verb *turned* answers the apparently rhetorical question of the previous page, "what will / Bring us back to / Shore," in a threefold manner.

First the paper turns like a winch, providing an alternative winding motion to the "rope" that coils "on the steel deck" as it pulls the barge to shore. The paper, in this case standing metonymically for the poem, *turns* (that is, it skillfully fashions language) around the "tug" and "two barges" and the "shore" and, instead of pulling one to the other, contains the "entire volume," reuniting them once again. Second the paper is "turned" in the same way that wood is turned on a lathe by a craftsperson to produce a beautiful object. Third, moving the onus from the author to the reader (who *turns* the pages), the word is a perfect description of how the discrete series is encompassed by the act of reading—"the / Paper, turned, contains / This entire volume." Oppen impresses, despite the economy of the "entire volume," through his ability to include the mundane and concrete in a minimal, almost elegiac form without betraying the everyday use of everyday words.

BIBLIOGRAPHY

Glück, Louise. "On George Oppen." In *Proofs & Theories.* Hopewell, N.J.: Ecco Press, 1994, pp. 29–33.

Oppen, George. "George Oppen." Interview by L. S. Dembo. *Contemporary Literature* 10, no. 2 (1969): 159–177.

Pound, Ezra. Preface to *Discrete Series,* by George Oppen. New York: The Objectivist Press, 1934, vi.

Williams, William Carlos. "The New Poetical Economy" *Poetry* 44 (July 1934): 220–225.

Dan Friedman

"DIVING INTO THE WRECK" ADRIENNE RICH (1973) ADRIENNE RICH'S collection *Diving into the Wreck* won the National Book Award in 1974, marking one of the first times that a mainstream American institution recognized the achievement of radical feminist poetry. Its title poem presents, through the extended metaphor of a sea diver, an exploration of what it means to be a woman and, specifically, a woman-poet. The sea symbolizes the mind of the creative woman, and the "wreck" is its all-but-destroyed potential, which the explorer must discover and reclaim.

Around the time that Rich wrote "Diving into the Wreck," she began to identify herself explicitly as a feminist and political poet, looking more and more to her art to reinforce bonds between women and to reveal injustices as the first step toward social change. Like many of Rich's poems, "Diving" focuses more on observation and revelation than on recommending specific political action. Nevertheless the poem implies that the new knowledge the diver discovers will be put to use in altering the cultural "scene" to which she returns at the end of the poem. Because the poet seeks a truth that runs contrary to social norms, the quest on which she embarks is a dangerous one: She wears a protective suit, carries a knife, and momentarily finds herself "blacking out" as she enters the unfamiliar world of the sea. Furthermore her status as a woman puts her in an especially risky position: Unlike men—represented by Jacques "Cousteau with his / assiduous team"—this underwater explorer proceeds on her journey alone.

The diver-poet begins her quest only after "First having read the book of myths." These myths, established by custom and reinforced by language and the verbal arts, proclaim that women are inferior to men. In referring to "myth" and a "book," Rich confirms the power of literature to form self-knowledge and to determine cultural values, and the poem as a whole points to the faith she has in her own literary efforts to correct our mistaken perceptions about ourselves and the flaws in our social systems. The poet claims, "The words are purposes. / The words are maps," suggesting that conscientiously used language can guide us to a place of understanding and living that is superior to the current one. Rich again mentions at the poem's end the book of myths, this time naming it as one "in which / our"—that is, women's—"names do not appear." The world and the stories that inform it have not changed, but the poet returns, confident that she is part of a community of women, armed with a new knowledge about the ideal for them, and determined to make it a reality.

BIBLIOGRAPHY

Atwood, Margaret. Review of *Diving into the Wreck,* by Adrienne Rich. In *Reading Adrienne Rich: Reviews and Revisions,* edited by Jane Cooper, 238–241. Ann Arbor: University of Michigan Press, 1984.

Templeton, Alice. *The Dream and the Dialogue: Adrienne Rich's Feminist Poetics.* Knoxville: University of Tennessee Press, 1994.

Jeannine Johnson

DOBYNS, STEPHEN (1941–) Despite his 21 novels, Stephen Dobyns considers himself a poet. In a letter to *Contemporary Authors,* he writes, "Although I sometimes write fiction, I do it only as a diversion. I consider myself entirely a poet, am concerned with it twenty-four hours a day, . . . feel that myself and any poet is always at the beginning of his craft." Dobyns's 10 books of poetry hold 30 years of discerning narrative and are colored by the dissolution, irony, and tenderness that have, at turns, dominated his perspective. Despite his productivity, Dobyns—who in LOUISE GLÜCK'S words is a "cross between Jonathan Edwards and Quentin Tarantino"—has received little critical attention except from "other poets, among whom he has the status of a hero."

Born in West Orange, New Jersey, and raised in Detroit, Dobyns earned degrees at Wayne State University and the University of Iowa before pursuing brief careers as an English teacher and a reporter for the *Detroit News.* Overwhelmed by the violence on which he had to report, both in Detroit and coming out of the Vietnam War, he quit his newspaper job to produce his first book of poetry, *Concurring Beasts,* which was the Lamont Poetry selection for 1971. During his career he has received a number of honors, including the Poetry Society of America's Melville Crane Award for

Cemetery Nights (1987); his volume *Black Dog, Red Dog* was selected for the National Poetry Series in 1984.

The violence of many of Dobyns's poems is sharpened by his unflinching description of snapshot scenes, from one boy forcing another at gunpoint to expose himself ("The Gun" [1984]), to the body of a man in a stream killed for the sport of Santiago police ("Pacos" [1984]). But stunning moments of passion ameliorate Dobyns's disgust with the bleakness around him. In "Leaving Winter" (1984), he writes of the coming of spring in his Santiago back yard, where the blue of the sky leaves him "unable to catch my breath. I ask myself, What new / pain is this? Then I realize I am happy."

Throughout his work, Dobyns has unexpected gleams of hope that vie for supremacy with his dark imagination and self-deprecating sense of humor. In "I'm Muscle, I'm Brawn" (2000), the narrator Heart ironically contemplates "the human condition—how courtesy and compassion go right to the bottom." Dobyns is a somewhat reluctant poet of the human condition, in all of its quirky and unexpected glory.

BIBLIOGRAPHY

Bosselaar, Laurie Ann. "An Interview with Stephen Dobyns." *Ploughshares* 24, no. 4 (winter 1998–99): 64–73.

Dobyns, Stephen. "Stephen Dobyns." Contemporary Authors Online. Available online. URL: www.galenet.com. Downloaded March 2007.

Glück, Louise. "Storytellers." *American Poetry Review* 26, no. 4 (1997): 9–12.

Stitt, Peter. "The Uncertainties of Narrative." In *Uncertainty and Plentitude: Five Contemporary Poets.* Iowa City: University of Iowa Press, 1997.

Aimee Fifarek

"DOG CREEK MAINLINE" CHARLES WRIGHT **(1973)** Set in his native Tennessee, "Dog Creek Mainline" is an early example of CHARLES WRIGHT's noun-rich, highly consonantal FREE VERSE style. While more orderly than the visually expansive, margin-to-margin lines of Wright's middle period, and lacking his late period's numerous direct allusions to literary and religious figures, the poem embodies the lasting preoccupations in Wright's work: a focus on autobiography not as confession but as spiritual exercise (see CONFESSIONAL POETRY) and a devotion to the natural landscape as a surrogate for religious observance and ceremony. For Wright, Dog Creek not only recalls his childhood, but prompts him to meditate on its distance from him. A *memento mori* or reminder of death, the creek evokes "the black throat / You ask redemption of."

Wright has spoken of his first nine books of poetry as a trilogy of trilogies, with every three books reflecting a different style and set of thematic preoccupations. Wright often compares this project to the three parts of Dante Alighieri's epic, *The Divine Comedy,* in which case "Dog Creek Mainline" corresponds to the *Inferno,* a fitting analogy because of the former's rich physical detail, intense link between setting and character, and the experience of spiritual crisis. The structure of the poem itself reflects Wright's preoccupation with trinities, being broken into three sections of three six-line stanzas each. The three sections have different functions: homage to place, elegy, and lyric meditation, and their sequence traces an arc of partial spiritual insight that achieves only a glimpse of visionary truth.

The opening stanza demonstrates a deeply felt tension between the physical and metaphysical qualities of place. The first and last words of the opening stanza are "Dog Creek"; in between are a series of highly sensuous noun phrases describing the place. This bracketing of "cat track and bird splay, / Spindrift and windfall; woodrot; / Odor of muscadine" represents a failed effort to focus only on sensory details, for Wright enjambs this stanza into the next, using a key metaphor to show how the memories and emotions associated with an experience of place are woven into the very fabric of the human subject: "Dog Creek // Starts in the leaf reach and shoal run of the blood."

But for Wright, memories of childhood friends and the love of place are themselves changed in the process of recollection. As David Garrison observes, memory and emotion are "translated first from sensibility into "sense" and then transcribed into sound and image, into melody against rhythm, into a fresh cognitive activity meant to generate, a literacy of emotion and felt thought" (35). Linking the human tongue, a symbol for poetic creation, with the creek itself, Wright extols the baptismal, restorative power of the imagination in the final stanza. In the waters of poetry, the sunlight that illumined Dog Creek "Gathers, and is refracted, and moves / Outward, over the lips, / Over the dry skin of the world." Such reciprocity changes the human self as well, which Wright suggests by echoing the poem's first stanza. While the poem began with a series of noun phrases, suggesting Wright's rootedness in place but also the paralysis resulting from an obsession with memory, the last stanza features several active verbs, all suggestive of motion and metamorphosis. The speaker signals his movement away from the possessive imagination by concluding the last stanza as he did the first, with the words that began it, but now the repeated words are not merely a proper noun, "Dog Creek," but a complete, psalm-like sentence: "The tongue is a white water."

Yet the poem does not offer total absolution. As the title indicates, Wright's focus is not on Dog Creek, but on the railway that runs past it, and its track suggests that spiritual insight is not a destination but an unending, often difficult journey. "Hard freight," he writes, "It's hard freight / From Ducktown to Copper Hill, from Six / To Piled High: Dog Creek is on this line." For Wright, the imagination must transform and return whatever perceptions, memories, or emotions it receives. Yet the method of transformation cannot become fixed and formally stylized but must continue on, without promise of fulfillment. In this way, Wright foreshadows the radical stylistic and thematic revisions his own poetry will undergo during his career, paralleling the creative work of the imagination with those spiritual exercises that encourage, but can never promise, the fruition of the human soul.

BIBLIOGRAPHY

Andrews, Tom, ed. *The Point Where All Things Meet: Essays on Charles Wright.* Oberlin, Ohio: Oberlin College Press, 1995.

Garrison, David. "From Feeling to Form: Image as Translation in the Poetry of Charles Wright." *Midwest Quarterly: A Journal of Contemporary Thought* 41, no. 1 (1999): 33–47.

Hirsch, Edward. "The Visionary Poetics of Philip Levine and Charles Wright." In *The Columbia History of American Poetry,* edited by Jay Parini and Brett C. Miller, 776–806. New York: Columbia University Press, 1993.

Temple Cone

DORN, EDWARD (1929–1999) Edward Dorn is identified with the BLACK MOUNTAIN SCHOOL of poetry and shares this group's use of free verse, which avoids regular metrics and rhyme (see PROSODY AND FREE VERSE), and of precise and blunt language, filtered through his personal and sometimes idiosyncratic poetics and his impassioned politics. As a student at Black Mountain College, Dorn worked closely with CHARLES OLSON, who stimulated his interest in place and geography as themes and in non-Western cultures as alternative and more authentic modes of living. Coming of age as a poet in the 1960s, Dorn's poetic voice was that of a self-exile standing skeptically outside mainstream culture, intensely distrustful of wealth and authority and its abuses and acutely aware of their effects on national and personal life. Dorn wrote disparagingly of the commercialism of American culture and of hypocritical governmental exploitation of foreign cultures, minorities, and the environment while also writing poignantly observant poems on personal and family relationships in a career that produced more than 25 books of poetry, as well as fiction, essays, and translations. His poems of place provide what TOM CLARK has characterized as unique "apprehensions variously geological, geographical, cultural, social, historical, continuously interlaced" of locales in Idaho, England, the American Southwest, and other places (46). Dorn's *GUNSLINGER* (1967–75), an episodic and often humorous tale of a mock heroic quest through the West in search of Howard Hughes, is a major American narrative poem that reflects the tumultuous time of its writing (see NARRATIVE POETRY). Formally it is significant in its movement from earlier poetry that presents itself as the creation of one consciousness to the more multivocal poetics of the late 20th century, which self-consciously draws on and cites many sources.

Dorn was born in Villa Grove, Illinois, and grew up in rural poverty there during the Great Depression. His father, a railroad brakeman, deserted the family when Dorn was an infant, and Dorn's poetry often reflects this early experience of economic and social vulnerability. Dorn attended the University of Illinois from 1949 to 1950, then moved to North Carolina to attend the nontraditional arts-oriented Black Mountain College. Dorn completed a bachelor's degree in 1955.

After leaving school he led a nomadic life, living in Washington's Skagis Valley, New Mexico, and Idaho, at times barely supporting his family through manual labor, but all the while writing poetry. He taught at the University of Idaho from 1961–65, publishing his first book of poetry, *The Newly Fallen,* in 1961. As a Fulbright lecturer, Dorn was in residence at the newly founded University of Essex for most of 1965–70 and, while there, wrote the first book of *Gunslinger,* which expanded to five parts from 1968 to 1975. Dorn then taught at universities from Illinois to California before settling at the University of Colorado in 1977, where he headed the creative writing program until his death. His *Collected Poems: 1956–1974* was published in 1975.

Dorn wrote a loosely structured free verse, the lines shaped to amplify the content of each poem, a style influenced by Olson's "Projective Verse" (see ARS POETICAS). Irregular metrics and frequent enjambment give an asymmetrical rhythm and dissonant quality to the poems and are used to provoke surprise and humor. Lengths of poems range from epigrammic to entire books, with the poetry's tone alternately vulnerable, caustically critical, sensitively attentive, and parodic, sometimes changing abruptly within works. Dorn's creative diction, employing references to popular culture, philosophical theory, historical figures, archaic cultures, nonsense words, and drug and other jargons, produced striking juxtapositions and combinations of words; Dorn himself characterized his writing as coming in "clots of phrase" (5). Puns, internal rhyme, and unusual and ambiguous uses of punctuation also are typical of his poetry.

In "On the Debt My Mother Owed to Sears Roebuck" from *Hands Up!* (1964), a poem of place as well as personal and political implications, Dorn connects domestic economies to those of the Second World War. Arrested opportunity and unwitting complicity are suggested in Dorn's description of his mother as "part of that *stay at home army,*" one who necessarily but unknowingly kept "things going, owing that debt." Internal rhyme, colloquial diction, and the use of italics to emphasize ironically a phrase borrowed from wartime propaganda are used in fashioning a pointed but accessible poem of both personal and social commentary. "An Idle Visitation" from *The North Atlantic Turbine* (1967) first introduced the character of the Gunslinger, later expanded into what became Dorn's best-known poem. Dorn's capsule description of the Gunslinger's "impeccable personal smoothness" implies the satirically heroic, prototypical individualist of the mythical American West. Punning humor is brought about by enjambment in the lines—for instance, "or simply a retinal block / of seats"—and is intertwined with the thematic concern of the difficulty of perceiving reality, creating a tonal and formal instability characteristic of the poem and its later expansion to a book-length work. "Christopher Beach" characterizes Dorn's more playful and difficult style, with its shifting perspectives and evasion of fixed meaning, as a "dissolving of voices" that signals Dorn's movement towards a more postmodern style of writing (215).

In later works Dorn often wrote in a caustic, bitterly humorous, satirical style. In "Homo Sap" from *Abhorrences* (1990), Ronald Reagan is dubbed "the great Teller," and the national obsession with youth is castigated as one of a number of vacuous "life-style frauds" in "Ode of the Facelifting of the 'statue' of Liberty." And in one of his last poems, "Chemo du Jour: The Impeachment on Decadron" (1999), Dorn mixed his experience of treatment for pancreatic cancer with a critique of the Clinton presidency, assuming the role of poet as cultural commentator until his death. It was this role that defined Dorn's life and poetry.

BIBLIOGRAPHY

Beach, Christopher. "Migrating Voices in the Poetry of Edward Dorn." *Contemporary Literature* 32, no. 2 (1991): 211–228.

Clark, Tom. *Edward Dorn: A World of Difference.* Berkeley, Calif.: North Atlantic Books, 2002.

Dorn, Edward. *Interviews,* edited by Donald Allen. Bolinas, Calif.: Four Seasons, 1980.

Wesling, Donald, ed. *Internal Resistances: The Poetry of Edward Dorn.* Berkeley: University of California Press, 1985.

Sue Barker

DOTY, MARK (1953–) Mark Doty has written openly and passionately about being gay and about the personal grief he has felt in the AIDS epidemic, but his concerns and sensibility have never been confined by identity politics or by championing a particular group or movement, although such a poem as "Homo Does Not Inherit" (1995) is an unflinching indictment of religious homophobia. Like MARIANNE MOORE, an important influence, he responds to the natural world with a precision and discrimination that may include allegory or autobiography. In "Difference," from *My Alexandria,* a volume selected for the 1993 National Poetry Series, he writes about a jellyfish that looks like "a plastic purse swallowing itself," a description as odd and accurate as any of Moore's metaphors. Moreover his call at the end of the poem to look "unfettered" at "alien grace" suggests the moral, aesthetic, and personal terms that underlie Moore's poems. Nevertheless Doty's work contains sinuousness, a consolation, even a hedonism, not found in Moore. In his book-length essay, *Still Life with Oysters and Lemon* (2001), he points out that people are not "born knowing how to love the world," but, insofar as they do, it is because they have learned "that pleasure is to be honored" (5).

Born in Maryville, Tennessee, Doty moved frequently through the South, since his father, an army engineer, was repeatedly transferred. His mother was religious, and his poetry is often informed by the austerely grand eloquence of devotional literature. He attended Drake University in Iowa (B.A., 1978) and received an M.F.A. from Goddard College (1980). He has taught at many colleges and universities, including Brandeis University, the University of Utah, and the University of Houston. He has won the National Book Critics Circle Award (1994), the T. S. ELIOT Prize (1996), the Lambda Literary Award (1996), and the Ambassador Book Award (1996); he has also received a number of fellowships from various foundations. In addition to his poetry, Doty has published three works of prose: *Heaven's Gate* (1996), which won the PEN/Martha Albrand Award, and *Firebird* (1999), both autobiographies, as well as *Still Life with Oysters and Lemon.* He has also published, under the pseudonym M. R. Doty, several verse collections written with his former wife.

While living in New York, Doty met Wally Roberts, with whom he lived until Roberts's death from AIDS. This experience of love, loss, and caregiving found voice in *My Alexandria* (1993), Doty's third book, whose touchstone is the poetry of C. F. Cavafy, *Atlantis* (1995), and his memoir *Heaven's Gate* (1996). In these works Doty searches for a means of transcending the mutability or decomposition of the world. In his more recent work, *Sweet Machine* (1998), he has sought ways to ground himself in the material world by enjoying quotidian experiences, such as a sidewalk turtle seller, and in *Source* (2001) he searches for the "generous, cold nothing" from which everything is derived.

BIBLIOGRAPHY

Doty, Mark. *Still Life With Oysters and Lemon,* Boston: Beacon 2001.

Jarraway, David R. "'Creatures of the Rainbow': Wallace Stevens, Mark Doty and the Poetics of Androgyny." *Mosaic* 30, no. 3 (Sept. 1997):169–183.

Wunderlich, Mark. "About Mark Doty." *Ploughshare* 25, no. 1 (spring 1999): 183–189.

David Bergman

DOVE, RITA (1952–) Rita Dove is one of the most prominent figures in contemporary African-American poetry. From 1993 to 1995 she was the first African American to serve as United States poet laureate and the youngest person ever to hold the office. A literary descendant of African-American poets LANGSTON HUGHES, ROBERT HAYDEN, and GWENDOLYN BROOKS, Dove frequently examines in her poetry the particulars of family relationships and American race relations past and present, most often in short narrative poems. Still, overall, the varied subject matter and the range of references in Dove's poetry makes her work difficult to categorize. In addition to her numerous volumes of poetry, Dove has published a book of short stories (*Fifth Sunday* [1985]), a novel (*Through the Ivory Gate* [1992]), a verse drama (*The Darker Face of the Earth* [1994]), and a book of her poet laureate lectures (*The Poet's World* [1995]). She was elected a chancellor of The Academy of American Poets in 2006.

Dove was born and raised in Akron, Ohio. In 1986 ROBERT PENN WARREN (who was then the first U.S. poet laureate) selected Dove for a Lavan Younger Poet Award from the Academy of American Poets. Since then Dove has won many prizes and awards, including, for her most famous book, the poem cycle *Thomas and Beulah* (a collection based on the lives of Dove's grandparents), a Pulitzer Prize in 1987. Dove was only the second African-American poet (after Brooks) to win a Pulitzer. In 1999 Dove was reappointed as special consultant in poetry for the 1999–2000 bicentennial year celebration of the Library of Congress. Since 1989 she has taught at the University of Virginia.

Although the historical particulars of slavery, segregation, and American race relations are frequent concerns of her poetry, Dove's work also demonstrates her wide-ranging interest in world history, culture, and religion. Poems that deal directly with the wrongs of racism may appear alongside poems that forsake visible social concerns in favor of examining individual characters or events separated from modern America by geography or history. This broad range of reference is evident even in Dove's early work. In *The Yellow House on the Corner* (1980), Dove's first book of poems, for example, the poems "The Transport of Slaves from Maryland to Mississippi," "The House Slave," "The Slave's Critique of Practical Reason," and "Kentucky, 1833" appear along with "Robert Schumann, Or: Musical Genius Begins with Affliction" and "The Bird Frau." This dual interest in African-American identity and unrelated issues that are more obviously within the traditional realm of American poetry—a tradition that tended to avoid confronting racial injustice—persists throughout Dove's work.

Dove frequently divides her books into separate sections that cohere more or less thematically, which helps readers make sense of the vast thematic differences between such poems. Most critics consider Dove's willingness to address such widely varying subject matter a great strength. The diversity of subject matter in Dove's poetry reminds readers that an African-American writer need not choose between social engagement and the kind of historical, imaginative, and multicultural awareness often identified with literary MODERNISM. As literary critic Therese Steffen explains, Dove's work "documents and enriches the American European literary and humanist dialogue. Particularly intriguing and fruitful is Dove's fusion of African-American, German, and Greek backgrounds" (163).

It is worth noting that, although in past generations America's literary critics and audiences might have been more likely to praise an African-American poet's willingness to turn away from social issues toward the type of poetry more concerned with art, history, or other aspects of high culture, Dove has garnered great acclaim for books that deal most deeply with race. *Thomas and Beulah* constructs a social background of inequality and racial tension while telling the stories of the title characters' lives. In "Roast Possum," Thomas reads to his grandchildren from an old encyclopedia, omitting racist details, such as the encyclopedia's claim that, although black children were intelligent, this intelligence "clouded over at puberty, bringing / indirection and laziness." In "The Great Palaces of Versailles," reading a library book's account of how French ladies would defecate in the beautiful gardens of Versailles reinforces Beulah's distaste for white people as she irons clothing for white customers: "*Nothing nastier than a white person* // She mutters . . . in the backroom of Charlotte's Dress Shoppe." Dove's acclaimed 1999 collection *On the Bus with Rosa Parks* deals extensively with characters and events related to the Civil Rights movement, particularly the 1955–56 bus boycott in Montgomery, Alabama.

Dove's poetry avoids making grand statements about race and racism; instead, Dove works through individual characters, specific events, and the ways those events shape the lives and minds of the characters. In the introduction to her *Selected Poems*, Dove writes, "The mystery of destiny boils down to the ultimate—and ultimately unanswerable—questions: How does where I come from determine where I've ended up? Why am I what I am and not what I thought I'd be? What did I think I'd be? Where do I reside most completely?" (xxi). Dove's is clearly not protest poetry in the standard sense. It is not didactic, not a poetry that directly proclaims things about the historic injustices of race relations in America. Instead Dove's presentations of individual characters and their experiences provide a more subtle rendering of race and racism along with eloquent reminders that her poetry is inspired by other things as well: Dove says, "I'm very interested in getting inside a person's head, with all of those intricate thoughts; then that person can never be lumped into a stereotype again" (Mullaney 33).

BIBLIOGRAPHY

Dove, Rita. Introduction to *Selected Poems*. New York: Vintage Books, 1993.

Mullaney, Janet P. "Rita Dove." In *Truthtellers of the Times: Interviews with Contemporary Women Poets.* Ann Arbor: University of Michigan Press, 1998.
Therese Steffen. *Crossing Color: Transcultural Space and Place in Rita Dove's Poetry, Fiction, and Drama.* New York: Oxford University Press, 2001.

Sean Heuston

"THE DOVER BITCH" ANTHONY HECHT (1967)

ANTHONY HECHT's often anthologized "The Dover Bitch" is a parody of the Victorian poet Matthew Arnold's "Dover Beach," which was published exactly 100 years earlier. Arnold uses the crashing tides of the seaside at Dover, which marks the closest point between England and France, to symbolize the diminished possibility of happiness in a world bereft of faith. Yet by evoking such a diminished condition, Arnold identifies humankind itself as the prime source of enduring love now that the Sea of Faith has retreated "down the vast edges drear / And naked shingles of the world." By contrast, Hecht's "The Dover Bitch" suffers no such anxieties about modern moral relativity, and rather flippantly endorses the value of short-term, self-satisfying relations. Ironically questioning Arnold's claim that "Art is a criticism of life," Hecht mocks "Dover Beach" not as a call to love, but as a way of turning one's fellow human beings into mere psychological crutches or mirrors for one's own self-aggrandizement.

Hecht narrates the poem in the persona of a rake who knows the "Dover Bitch," a girl whom Arnold invites to Dover and who may, based on her vulgarity and her casual sexual relations with the narrator, be a prostitute. The narrator begins by imagining the scene of "Dover Beach" as an actual exchange between two people: "So there stood Matthew Arnold and this girl / With the cliffs of England behind crumbling away behind them." From the start, the tone is urbane and ironic, and the narrator mocks the philosophical seriousness of Arnold's poem with offhand colloquialisms ("this girl") and a satirically melodramatic setting (the crumbling cliffs symbolize crumbling civilization). Like Arnold, the narrator makes a number of allusions in the poem, but whereas Arnold uses them as ways of explaining and enduring the troubling state of the world, the narrator debunks them as philosophical pretensions that ignore or reject the very people who compose that world. For instance, while the girl understands Arnold's reference to Sophocles, she feels saddened and later angry "To have been brought / All the way down from London," not for the pleasure of her companionship but to provide an audience for Arnold's pessimistic speeches.

Whereas Arnold's relationship with the "Dover Bitch" is philosophically elevated and inclined toward a tragic vision of the world, the narrator's relationship with her is merely social and pleasure-focused. Yet for Hecht such a relationship is more honest because it admits to its own baseness, whereas Arnold remains deceptive (and self-deceptive) about his use of the woman as an audience for his own pontificating. As Harold Bloom observes, Hecht sees "the tragic vision itself, or rather the romantic melancholy which it could lead to . . . [as] a passive state of might that could be otherwise dealt with by the modern intelligence" (121). Joseph Girard notes a sharp epistemological contrast between the constancy embodied in Arnold's message of love and the short-term, self-satisfying relations advocated by Hecht's witty, flippant speaker. Arnold's view is thoroughly Victorian, and it asserts a conservative resistance to the changing tides of modern history, culture, and society. By contrast, Hecht's view reflects such American values of the 1960s as free love, the importance of the individual, and distrust of traditional cultural authority. Such counterarguments are not intended to debunk Arnold's poem nor his humanism, however; as Bloom notes, Hecht often recited the two poems in tandem at public readings. As with the best parodies, Hecht's "The Dover Bitch" strengthens the philosophical position of Arnold's "Dover Beach" even as it criticizes it. As Arnold urges, humankind should indeed "be true / to one another," but as Hecht points out, "all the time he was talking she had in mind / The notion of what his whiskers would feel like / On the back of her neck." Being true to one another, Hecht insists, means accepting the possibility of a coarse but unpretentious truth: that humans may desire physical pleasure and good company more than the consolations of abstract philosophy.

BIBLIOGRAPHY

Bloom, Harold. "The Poetry of Anthony Hecht." In *Contemporary Poets,* edited by Harold Bloom, 113–126. New York: Chelsea House Publishers, 1986.

Gerhard, Joseph. "'The Dover Bitch': Victorian Duck or Modernist Duck/Rabbit?" *Victorian Newsletter* 73 (1988): 8–10.
O'Brien, Timothy D. "Hecht's 'The Dover Bitch.'" *The Explicator* 44, no. 2 (1986): 52–54.

Temple Cone

DRAFTS RACHEL BLAU DUPLESSIS (1991, 1997, 2001)

A feminist revision of the long poems of MODERNISM (see LONG AND SERIAL POETRY), *Drafts* is an open-ended series of poems that RACHEL BLAU DUPLESSIS has been writing and publishing (in journals and in book form) since the mid-1980s. Influenced by various projects, such as *The CANTOS* of EZRA POUND, *"A"* by LOUIS ZUKOFSKY, and H. D.'s *HELEN IN EGYPT,* DuPlessis's poems carry on an avant-garde tradition of formal innovation and linguistic experimentation. Yet *Drafts* strongly emphasizes the ways in which language shapes identity, particularly in terms of gender (see FEMALE VOICE, FEMALE LANGUAGE). In this regard, *Drafts* shows influence from LANGUAGE SCHOOL poets and experimental women writers, such as SUSAN HOWE and KATHLEEN FRASER.

Drafts represents a lifelong project for DuPlessis, who is dedicated to the concept of ongoing revision. DuPlessis's is a poetics of process that resists the finality associated with the epic poem, traditionally viewed as the masterwork of the male poet. In resistance to notions of closure, the form of *Drafts* emphasizes its provisional nature. DuPlessis refers to the project's unfinished quality as a "rhetorical texture one might describe as a flow of interruption across a surface" (123). And, as Lynn Keller points out, DuPlessis conceives of the serial form, in particular, as "speculatively instructive" and "subject to change according to immediate response, in the process of or in the means of investigation," oftentimes one that explores the female as author (276).

Employing visual and irregular typography, as well as the repetition of words and phrases, *Drafts* challenges normal, linear reading practices, which DuPlessis and other experimental women writers associate with a limiting, traditionally masculine poetics. With their collagelike structure and refusal of narrative unity, the poems therefore can be considered an effort to recover previously lost female voices buried beneath patriarchal discourse and recognizable only in fragments. As Linda Kinnahan writes, "the practice of deciphering meaning that resides in and under layers of writing often becomes the subject of [DuPlessis's] poetry." DuPlessis also borrows from diverse feminist philosophies as well as from the Jewish practice of midrash, a tradition of marginal notation and commentary (14).

While *Drafts* takes up a wide range of subjects from the global to the deeply personal—from the Gulf War to the poet's own experiences with motherhood—memory and its exile are recurrent motifs. The poems frequently circle back to a focus on the text and its ability to represent experiences accurately. In "Draft 6: Midrush," DuPlessis makes attempts at first "sighting," then "citing / The writing under the writing"; yet, as far ahead as "Draft 21: Cardinals," the poet still questions "What to ask, of what past or path. / Some texts conjure memory" (135). Challenging on intellectual and personal levels, *Drafts* encourages reassessment of the ways in which texts shape one's perception of the world and of the self.

BIBLIOGRAPHY

DuPlessis, Rachel Blau. "Haibun: 'Draw your / Draft.'" In *H. D. and Poets After,* edited by Donna Krolik Hollenberg, 112–129. Iowa City: University of Iowa Press, 2000.
Keller, Lynn. *Forms of Expansion: Recent Long Poems by Women.* Chicago: Chicago University Press, 1997.
Kinnahan, Linda. "Experiments in Feminism." Review of *Drafts 1–38, Toll,* by Rachel Blau DuPlessis. *Women's Review of Books* 19, no. 8 (2002): 14.

Megan Swihart Jewell

THE DREAM SONGS JOHN BERRYMAN (1969)

In *The Dream Songs,* JOHN BERRYMAN brought together his two previous collections of "dream songs," *77 Dream Songs* (1964), which was awarded the Pulitzer Prize for poetry in 1965, and *His Toy, His Dream, His Rest: 308 Dream Songs* (1968), which won the National Book Award for poetry in 1969. After Berryman's death in 1972, a further collection appeared under the title *Henry's Fate and Other Poems, 1967–1972;* among the previously uncollected poems and fragments in that book are 45 dream songs from among the hundreds of songs Berryman had elected not to include in books published during his life. *The Dream Songs* is difficult to situate among other works in the American 20th century, because the book simply is unlike anything else produced during the period. However, it does take its place alongside noteworthy long poems (see LONG AND SERIAL POETRY), such as HART CRANE's *The BRIDGE,* EZRA POUND's *The CANTOS,* and WILLIAM CARLOS WILLIAMS's *PATERSON.*

Berryman's prefatory note to the single-volume edition explains that the poem concerns itself with "an imaginary character . . . named Henry, a white American in early middle age sometimes in blackface, who has suffered an irreversible loss" (vi). This Henry is not to be confused with Berryman, a distinction made difficult by the fact that Henry's experiences, sorrows, and travels are very similar to Berryman's own. Berryman's disclaimer frees him from whatever constraints he might perceive if he were working in the explicit autobiographical mode of his usual CONFESSIONAL POETRY. The songs are further complicated in terms of the speaker's identity by the fact that Henry slips between pronouns when speaking of himself, using both "I" and "he"; the presence of Henry's unnamed friend, who speaks only occasionally and who calls Henry "Mr. Bones," also distorts questions of self in the poem.

The songs share the same structure; each one is made up of three six-line stanzas occupying no more than a page—a controlling device similar to JACK KEROUAC's *MEXICO CITY BLUES.* The rhythms of Berryman's songs are "like jazz scat and . . . like jazz wailing," notes Frederick Seidel (257), another feature in common with Kerouac's *Blues.* The songs are delivered in widespread experiments with speech, including minstrel-show dialect, baby talk, disrupted syntax, and "comical, boozy private language" (Seidel 257), and they seek an American idiom, as has the work of many American poets, particularly since Pound and Williams in the 1920s. The songs' subject matter, aside from "Henry's" life, is drawn heavily from current events and ranges all over the world. Berryman's name-dropping includes Dwight Eisenhower and Adlai Stevenson in politics, Humphrey Bogart and Hoot Gibson in entertainment, Bodhidharma and St. Simeon in religion, Robert Oppenheimer and Albert Einstein in science, August Strindberg and Raïner Maria Rilke in literary history; he encompasses whole national groups—French, Egyptian, Sudanese, Swedes, and "Paks"—in an overall cataloguing reminiscent of Walt Whitman.

A central concern in many songs is Berryman's address to his fellow poets, both ancestors and contemporaries. Pound, ROBERT FROST, WALLACE STEVENS, Williams, and R. P. BLACKMUR all have a place in these pieces as writers to whom the author expresses a debt, and RANDALL JARRELL, DELMORE SCHWARTZ, SYLVIA PLATH, YVOR WINTERS, T. S. ELIOT, and Crane are grieved and mourned. KARL SHAPIRO calls the poems collectively "elegies (laments, drinking toasts, historical ascriptions, exhortations, curses, dedications, eroticisms, epitaphs, love poems, descriptions, imitations)" (4). ADRIENNE RICH describes *77 Dream Songs* as "a creepy, scorching book" with an "often surrealistic quality" (see SURREALISM), which Berryman's brilliance successfully anchored in Henry (538). *The Times Literary Supplement*'s reviewer vociferously disagreed, declaring that the book "was garbled, and the reviewers who said so and later took it back are foolish" (680); the same writer described *His Toy, His Dream, His Rest* as "a disorderly desperate, and besotted funeral for Berryman's literary heroes" (680), particularly condemning the "thumping exercise in bad taste" of the elegy for Louis MacNeice. Berryman's confessional contemporary, ROBERT LOWELL, admitted that initially the songs are dense with "darkness, disorder and oddness," but with patience "the repeated situations and their racy jabber become more and more enjoyable," eliciting either laughter or tears (3).

Whether Berryman's songs are "a brave original work" (Seidel 259), "dazzling even when they befuddle" (257), or a self-indulgent incoherent jumble, they possess an awe-inspiring scope and vision that they succeed in rising to at least some, and perhaps even most, of the time. Larry Vonalt believes that *The Dream Songs* is "one of the most significant religious poems of the twentieth century," concluding that it "depicts the emptiness and confusion of our world" (467) and is "a complex and meaningful investigation of love and death" (469). Certainly the fact that "There sat down, once, a thing on Henry's heart / só heavy" (#29), a grief that never got up, is the source of these sorrowful songs. Henry is "scared a lonely" (i.e., "scared and lonely") (#40), afraid of himself most of all; he thinks it "easy be not to see anyone" (#40). Admissions such as these deserve a listener, because of their courage and vulnerability, in spite of their confusing inaccessibility. Henry might experience the more conventionally poetic desire for a woman, "Filling her compact and delicious body / with chicken páprika" (#4), a woman whose virtue is saved only by the fact that she and Henry are in the company of five other people, but he still has that thing sitting on his heart, and, as long as it sits, Henry needs to talk out his own therapy: "He stared at ruin. Ruin stared straight back" (#45). It may be that these songs are Berryman addressing his own ruin, trying to stare it down, even though he is "scared a lonely."

BIBLIOGRAPHY

Berryman, John. Note to *The Dream Songs*. New York: Farrar, Straus & Giroux, 1969, v–vi.

"Congested Funeral: Berryman's New Dream Songs." *The Times Literary Supplement* (26 June 1969): 680.

Lowell, Robert. "The Poetry of John Berryman." *New York Times Book Review* (28 May 1964): 3.

Rich, Adrienne. "Mr. Bones, He Lives." *Nation* (25 May 1964): 538–539.

Seidel, Frederick. "Berryman's Dream Songs." *Poetry* 105 (January 1965): 257–259.

Shapiro, Karl. "Major Poets of the Ex-English Language." *Book World* 3 (26 January 1969): 4.

Vonalt, Larry P. "Berryman's *The Dream Songs*." *Sewanee Review* 79 (July 1971): 464–469.

A. Mary Murphy

DUGAN, ALAN (1923–2003) Alan Dugan is a loner in American poetry, avoiding all schools of both poetry and thought, even though he has been associated with the CONFESSIONAL poets for his unflinching use of personal experience. Although his poetry has been dropped from recent academic anthologies, Dugan has influenced many young poets to work for the "hard-earned affirmation," in the words of William Martz (244).

Dugan was born in Brooklyn, New York, and graduated from Mexico City College in 1949. His first book, *Poems* (1961), won the Yale Series of Younger Poets Award. Other prizes followed: the Prix de Rome, the Shelley Memorial Award from the Poetry Society of America (1982), the award in literature from the American Academy and Institute of Arts and Letters (1985), a Pulitzer Prize, and two National Book Awards, most recently for *Poems Seven: New and Complete Poetry* (2001). Married to the artist Judith Shahn, he taught at Sarah Lawrence College (1967–71) and at the Fine Arts Work Center in Provincetown, Massachusetts.

While most of his poems confront the banalities of war and everyday life, Dugan deals with these inconveniences with acid humor and epigrammatic irreverence. Like his British contemporary Philip Larkin, Dugan is determined to "walk out bravely into the daily accident" ("Morning Song" [1961]). Yet the pessimism of poems like "Adultery" (1967) provides the dark background for such lyrical triumphs as "Love Song: I and Thou" (1961), "Lament for Cellist Jacqueline DuPré" (1989), and "Poem for Elliot Carter on his 90th Birthday" (2001), which offer the hard-won consolations of love and art.

His matter-of-fact titles reflect a down-to-earth reticence and a belief that poetry should always be at least as good as good prose. Showing less attention to meter and rhyme than to terse phrasing and exact lineation, Dugan's classical concision is reflected in his martial imagery and frequent allusions to Greek culture. In "Fragment on the British Museum" (1963), Dugan does not mind that "faces are chopped off" because the "reasonable patterns" thus exposed allow us to appreciate the "stone thought of the stone / figures." Dugan's poetry itself shows a higher respect for art's struggle with its medium than for mere personal expression.

While no one would question its honesty, Dugan's poetry can appear self-indulgent and nasty, especially in the poems that seem closest to the poet's own experience. In "Internal Migration: On Being on Tour" (1983), the poet whines about being paid for reading his work at such places as "Asshole State University at Nowheresville"; in the age of creative writing programs, such rants have become a genre, but the complaint is a sin against hospitality that Dugan would never commit in one of his classical moods. In Dugan's homages to the ancients and other artists, especially musicians, however, his poetry reaches the poignancy that comes from facing the most difficult beauties of life.

BIBLIOGRAPHY

Gery, John. "'Pieces of Harmony': The Quiet Politics of Alan Dugan's Poetry." In *Politics and the Muse: Studies in the Politics of Recent American Literature,* edited by Adam Sorkin. Bowling Green, Ky.: Popular Press, 1989, pp. 206–221.

Martz, William J., ed. *The Distinctive Voice: Twentieth-Century American Poetry.* Glenview, Ill.: Scott, Foresman, 1966, 243–244.

Richard Collins

DUHAMEL, DENISE (1961–) To the tradition of American feminist poetry (see FEMALE VOICE, FEMALE LANGUAGE), Denise Duhamel contributes irreverent and playful humor, multifaceted irony, surreal fantasy, startlingly precise social and physical description, and intriguing weaves of compelling narratives. As in *Kinky* (1997), which features dozens of refashionings of the Barbie doll, Duhamel crafts energetic feminist revisions of irksome myths of male dominant culture. Her poetry spotlights the intricate weirdness and mystifications of numerous cultural symbols.

Duhamel was raised in Woonsocket, Rhode Island. In the 1990s, beginning with *Smile!* (1993), she published five collections of poetry, and her *Queen for a Day: Selected and New Poems* appeared in 2001. She has also collaborated with Maureen Seaton on two books of poetry. Duhamel's poems have appeared in the 1993, 1994, 1998, and 2000 editions of the *Best American Poetry.* She earned a National Endowment for the Arts Fellowship in 2001.

Duhamel often portrays the female body as a site of cultural struggle. "Bulimia" (1993) investigates how a woman internalizes male-dominant notions about the body and scrambles to realize conflicting desires for release of energy and self-control. Using bulimia to control her appearance, the speaker obsessively works to make her bulimic routine invisible. "The Limited Edition Platinum Barbie" (1997) critiques fashion industry misogyny: "A model whose legs truly make up / more than half her height," Barbie weighs "less than a quart of milk." However, other poems, such as "Playa Naturista" (1999), describe successful struggles toward women's bodily self-acceptance.

Contemplating feminist community, Duhamel worries about how women's values could be transformed into servitude to male "needs." In "Feminism" (1996), the Girl Scout organization's way of trying to equate "empathy" and "power" is both applauded and questioned. "Assumptions" (1993) catalogues commonalities of experience that foreground race, class, and gender differences and suggest ways to diminish unproductive conflict.

Poems such as "My Grandmother Is My Husband" in *The Woman with Two Vaginas* (1995), which are adaptations of Inuit tales, explore implications of the crossing of gender roles. Suggesting that anatomy does not preordain gender, such poems comically question whether such gender-crossing role reversals can subvert male-dominant arrangements.

Recent Duhamel poems explore class distinctions and social dimensions of attempts to bolster one's ego while playing on the chattiness, name-dropping, and self-referentiality of the NEW YORK SCHOOL of poetry. "Mia and Darger, Ashbery and Gina" (2001) meditates on mortality, on "how artists take the suffering of others / . . . and try to make it art," on their guilt and fascination in doing so, and on how they cannot make actual their most interesting ideas before others do.

Even at its most comic, Duhamel's poetry offers poignant social analysis, and even at its grimmest, it provides humorous touches that prevent difficult truths from having a paralyzing effect.

BIBLIOGRAPHY

Duhamel, Denise. Interview by Sonia Parkes. *Inkshed* 26 (January–June 1994): 16–20.

Fink, Thomas. *"A Different Sense of Power": Problems of Community in Late-Twentieth-Century U.S. Poetry.* Madison, N.J.: Fairleigh Dickinson University Press, 2001, pp. 74–93.

Thomas Fink

DUNCAN, ROBERT (1919–1988) With CHARLES OLSON and ROBERT CREELEY, Robert Duncan defined the BLACK MOUNTAIN SCHOOL of poetry. All three poets discovered their mature styles in the journal pages of the *Black Mountain Review* and *Origin* (see POETRY JOURNALS), and all three originated a poetics based on the generation of poetic forms from within the poem—form was a projection of content. Duncan was also part of the SAN FRANCISCO RENAISSANCE; accordingly he was associated with KENNETH REXROTH—but not with the related BEAT poets ALLEN GINSBERG, LAWRENCE FERLINGHETTI, and GREGORY CORSO, who dominated the public views of the period. Duncan assumed the inherited traditions of high MODERNISM. He took EZRA POUND, H. D., and D. H. Lawrence as his masters, along with James Joyce, WILLIAM CARLOS WILLIAMS, MARIANNE MOORE, Dante, and Walt Whitman. Duncan claimed he was a derivative poet who combined various poetries and traditions into a poetics known as a "grand collage," an assemblage of multiple ideas.

Duncan was born in Oakland, California. His mother died in childbirth, and a family who believed in occult theosophy adopted him. The family soon moved to Bakersfield, where Duncan attended high school in preparation for enrolling at the University of California, Berkeley, in September 1936. After reading *XXX Cantos* (see *The CANTOS*), he became a serious student of Pound's poetry. Between 1938 and 1946, he spent most of his time in the East, living in Philadelphia, New York, Boston, Provincetown, and Woodstock, while returning to Berkeley for short periods. In 1946, when he met ROBIN BLASER and JACK SPICER in Berkeley, he was already a published and experienced poet. His first book of poems was *Heavenly City, Earthly City* (1947). With Blaser and Spicer, he launched the "Berkeley Renaissance" of poetry. In 1951 he began living with Jess Collins, an artist, and also entered a period of high creativity in poetry, art, and poetics. The two men collaborated on a series of books, *Caesar's Gate* (1955), *A Book of Resemblances* (1966), and *Names of People* (1968); *Letters* (1958) transformed Duncan's poetry from rhetorical structures to a poetry that created form based in the musical structures of lines. From 1955 to 1956 Duncan and Collins lived on Mallorca. In 1956 Duncan taught at Black Mountain College, then returned to San Francisco to become assistant director of the Poetry Center at San Francisco State University. He published his first trade book, *The Opening of the Field* (1960); other pamphlets and books followed, including *Roots and Branches* (1964), *Bending the Bow* (1968), *The Truth and Life of Myth* (1968), *Ground Work: Before the War* (1984) and *Ground Work II: In the Dark* (1987). From 1961 to 1963, Duncan wrote an extended study of modernism and H. D.'s poetry, which appeared in chapters as *The H. D. Book.* Duncan received a series of awards, including the Harriet Monroe Memorial Prize (*Poetry* magazine), 1961; the Levinson Prize (*Poetry* magazine), 1964; the National Poetry Award, 1985; and in the same year the American Book Award from the Before Columbus Foundation.

After finishing the book *Letters* (1956), Duncan began writing the poems for *The Opening of the Field* (1960). This volume was conceived and written as a unified book and sequence of poems working variations on themes of the dance, spiritual wonder, the goddess of poetry, and writing poems. These themes appear in the first poem, "Often I Am Permitted to Return to a Meadow." The meadow is an invention that is as real as an actual meadow: "Wherefrom fall all architectures I am." Through a series of appositions, the poem expands the possible meanings of the "field" as a place of inspiration where the Muse, the First Beloved as an avatar of Persephone, or Brigit, "Queen under the Hill," appears. The vision is not unlike a circle of children dancing in a ring, which Duncan explains, refers to an Atlantean dream of his childhood, and finally a "place of first permission, / everlasting omen of what is." The vision in the field gives permission for continuing imaginative invention. The poem contains layers of meaning as carefully placed as an image in a complex collage.

In *The Opening of the Field,* Duncan began a serial poem called "The Structure of Rime," which continues in subsequent books (see LONG AND SERIAL POETRY). The series is a sequence of poems without a defined ending. In *Roots and Branches* (1964), the series combines with other long poems in parts, "A Sequence of Poems for H. D.'s 73rd Birthday," "Apprehensions," and "The Continents," to make a book of poems that challenge and explore the various forms poetry can take. The field, or meadow, as a metaphor for the multiple possibilities of poetry, continues into the poems of the following book, *Bending the Bow* (1968). In this book Duncan began another serial poem, "The Passages Poems," which becomes a place for prophecy and spiritual exercises, where he can talk about the obligations of a spiritualistic poetics. The serial poems are imbedded in the context of the other poems, and here the idea of a large collage poem takes the form of a "grand collage," collecting and modifying ideas and images in shifting relationships with other contexts.

The conflicts raised in the cultural and poetry communities by the war in Vietnam dominate poems such as "Up Rising, Passages 25" and "The Soldiers, Passages 26." That theme continues in the following book, *Ground Work: Before the War* (1984). This volume collects groups of poems published separately: "Tribunals," "Poems from the Margins of THOM GUNN's *Moly*," "A Seventeenth Century Suite," and *Dante Études*. Duncan stands before the war as he would stand before a mirror contemplating the themes of corrupt manipulation of government against the will of the people, the destruction of natural geography and the spiritual landscape, and the grimness of war suppressing human desire. "Passages 35, Before the Judgment" is Duncan's prophecy about the power of war over the human will. Duncan summons the support of ancient gods of wisdom, "The Golden Ones," who "move in invisible realms" to fight against political leaders, in whom "stupidity thickens," and to reveal the laws of eternal goodness "against the works of unworthy men, unfeeling judgments, and cruel deeds." The intensity of this prophecy also shows up in Duncan's everyday life. As shown in "The Torn Cloth," his friendship with DENISE LEVERTOV was shattered under the strain of political and poetic protests. "Years of our rapport," he writes, were wrecked by "War and the Scars upon the land." The *Dante Études,* on the other hand, trace the origins of Duncan's poetics in Dante's ideas of empire and human worth. The volume ends with Duncan's dynamic affirmation of human love in "Circulations of the Song."

The theme of the darker meaning of life in a constant state of war continues into the final volume, *Ground Work II: In the Dark* (1987). Again, poems appear in groups—"Veil, Turbine, Cord & Bird," "Regulators," "Structure of Rime: Of the Five Songs"—as well as separately. In "To Master Baudelaire," the French poet becomes a model for defining the sickened life of the mind, as the theme of entering a "foyer," the entrance to a new language, tries to lift the gloom of the dark to reassert human vision and worth. In the late poem "Passages, the Dignities," Duncan takes stock of his life in poetry; his ties with Olson—"Wisdom as such must wonder"; and his relationship with Blaser, "the moth's / ephemeral existence." Despite the "black Night that hides the elemental germ," he perceives that the persistence of "the extending scale of imagined humanity" has a difficult time surviving in the bleak contemporary world. The elegiac mode of his early poems now reaches points of despair about the possibilities of humankind redeeming itself. The final poem of the volume, "After a Long Illness," recounts the failure of Duncan's kidneys that controlled his life from 1984 onward, even as the darkness of war and spiritual suppression controlled society. Only "the imagination knows" the vision in the meadow, the brilliant "pool of thought" that redeems life itself. Duncan's imagination transforms the elegiac lament of his early poetry into that "grand collage" of poetry powerful enough to gather the persistent wisdom of humanity into a prophecy of fulfillment, surrounded by the darkness of corrupted political systems.

BIBLIOGRAPHY

Bertholf, Robert J. *Robert Duncan: A Descriptive Bibliography.* Santa Rosa, Calif.: Black Sparrow Press, 1986.

Cuddihy, Michael, ed. *Ironwood* no. 22 (1983). [Robert Duncan: Special Issue]

Faas, Ekbert. *Young Robert Duncan: Portrait of the Poet as Homosexual in Society.* Santa Barbara, Calif.: Black Sparrow Press, 1983.

Johnson, Devin. *Precipitations: Contemporary American Poetry as Occult Practice.* Middletown, Conn.: Wesleyan University Press, 2002.

Paul, Sherman. *The Lost America of Love.* Baton Rouge: Louisiana State University Press, 1981.

Terrell, Carroll F., ed. *Sagetrieb* 4, nos. 2/3 (1985). [Robert Duncan Special Issue]

Robert J. Bertholf

DUNN, STEPHEN (1939–) That Stephen Dunn's work is difficult to categorize may account for his slow but steady rise to recognition. After working himself out of his IMAGIST training, he eventually found his mature voice in a discursive, abstract, but highly accessible style. Dunn has forged his own way, writing lyric poems composed of an appealingly intimate voice and a restrained, if pulsating, emotional fabric (see LYRIC POETRY).

Born in New York City, Dunn received a B.A. in history from Hofstra University and an M.A. from the creative writing program at Syracuse University. A prolific writer, he has won many awards and fellowships. His book *Different Hours* earned him the Pulitzer Prize for poetry in 2001.

Dunn has been criticized for flatness of language, and it is true that he avoids rhetorical and linguistic extravagance. A poet of the local and the ordinary, Dunn is suspicious of high passion and purple verbiage. The quiet intimacy of his voice gains power from his use of anecdotal material as a basis for philosophical reflection.

Where Dunn's poetry gauges the nuances of emotional states, he risks courting the maudlin or sentimental. But he successfully avoids this trap in the dialectical movement of his poetry: An idea is proposed, then qualified, with the goal of swerving away from the conclusive and toward the paradoxical.

Dunn's verse is controlled without a reliance on traditional forms, though the line break and the stanza have always held weight as formal elements in his work. One recurring form is a tercet, or three-line stanza, with a truncated second line. Over this unique stanzaic form, Dunn brushes loose-limbed sentences, enjambed and punctuated to bump gently and swerve; the meter then bubbles up from syntactical groupings rather than from variations on a set beat. Note, for example, how this rhythmic effect is created in one such tercet, from "Diminuendo" (1996), which begins: "These were among the unreachables; emblems / of how they felt / once, about each other."

A recurrent theme of Dunn's poetry is how we live together in a fallen world. Hence, the aesthetic dimension is deeply informed by the moral. But that moral dimension is empathic rather than didactic or political in nature. Characteristically, Dunn questions the efficacy of political gesturing in art; yet, a true poet of paradoxes, he does not absolve himself of complicity in the world. In "Loosestrife" (1996), whose background includes the Oklahoma City bombing, a philosopher-speaker is imagined sipping a drink in the ambivalent quiet of afternoon; meanwhile: "Far away, men were pulling bodies from debris, / a moan the sweetest, most hopeful thing."

Although Dunn admits the darkness of human experience, hope usually wins out in his work. Suffering a career crisis, the eponymous character of "The Guardian Angel" knows that his guardianship has been useless. But even though he cannot keep the poor from being thrown in the street or stop insults from hitting their targets, the angel tries to convince himself that "everything he does takes root, hums / beneath the surfaces of the world."

BIBLIOGRAPHY

Elliott, David L. "Precarious Balances." *Mid-American Review* 15, nos. 1–2 (1995): 6–17.

Kitchen, Judith, and Stan Sanvel Rubin. "'Only the Personal Matters': A Conversation with Stephen Dunn." *Literary Review* 30, no. 4 (1987): 559–570.

Vendler, Helen. *The Music of What Happens*. Cambridge, Mass.: Harvard University Press, 1988.

Jayme Stayer

DUPLESSIS, RACHEL BLAU (1941–)

Rachel Blau DuPlessis is a poet-scholar known for feminist experimentation (see FEMALE VOICE, FEMALE LANGUAGE). Her work is associated with the LANGUAGE SCHOOL and the OBJECTIVIST ideals of GEORGE OPPEN and LOUIS ZUKOFSKY, especially in its attention to the relationships between poetics, language, and lived social practices. Additionally DuPlessis's poetry continues the experimentation of modernist writers, including WILLIAM CARLOS WILLIAMS, EZRA POUND, and H. D. (see MODERNISM).

DuPlessis was born in Brooklyn, New York, and remained a New Yorker through her childhood and college years. In 1973 DuPlessis settled in the Philadelphia region, where she has been a professor of English at Temple University. She has published nine books of poetry since 1980, including a long, continuing project, *DRAFTS*. She has received a Pennsylvania Council of the Arts grant for poetry (1990), a Fund for Poetry award (1993), and Temple University's Creative Achievement Award (1999).

Formal innovation in DuPlessis's poetry calls attention to reading and language practices. At times DuPlessis's page resembles a painter's canvas layered with texts. "Writing" in *Tabula Rosa* (1987), for example, includes regular type, bold handwriting, and reproduced collages of text, and it describes this as an "interplay between selection, / imbedding, and loss." DuPlessis regularly disrupts her own writing with the awareness that utterances are always partial, yet she revels in possibilities of language as she plays with words and syntax. "Draft 6: Midrush," for instance, makes a theme of loss and the irrecoverable ("'Where are they now / dead people?' / 'Nowhere'"), but it regularly uses phrases that resonate with multiple meanings, as in "had to be set rite" or "How even is with odd." DuPlessis's poetry acknowledges the limits and possibilities of language while proposing a poetics of process.

This play with form and language is intimately related to the political nuances of DuPlessis's poetry. As Burton Hatlen explains, DuPlessis "writes always as a feminist" (131). Often, then, the poetry recognizes and resists patriarchal traditions that render women voiceless, as in this ironic quote from "Draft 2: She": "'I be good girl with my magic / markers.'" DuPlessis's feminism is expressed more subtly, however, in her refusal of authoritative writing practices that position the poet as the bearer of truth who enlightens worthy readers, often by relying on a single, lyric voice and the objectification of others. Instead DuPlessis favors layered meanings and disruptions to form a theme that encourage a dialogue between poet and reader. This open form, along with a merging of the everyday with the historical, is used to encourage careful attention to social practices and related belief systems.

DuPlessis's poetry is at once unsettling and invigorating, highlighting the problems involved in representation while challenging the reader to participate in meaning-making. In her writing closure is temporary, because more can always be said.

BIBLIOGRAPHY

Hatlen, Burton. "Renewing the Open Engagement: H. D. and Rachel Blau DuPlessis." In *H. D. and Poets After*, edited by Donna Krolik Hollenberg, 130–162. Iowa City: University of Iowa Press, 2000.

Lazer, Hank. "'Travelling many direction'd crossings': The Poetry of Rachel Blau DuPlessis." In *Opposing Poetries*. Vol. 2, *Readings*. Evanston, Ill: Northwestern University Press, 1996, pp. 34–59.

Laurie McMillan

"DURING THE EICHMANN TRIAL"

DENISE LEVERTOV (1961) After a decade of immersing herself in Martin Buber's accounts of 18th century mystical rabbis in *Tales of the Hasidim*, DENISE LEVERTOV published her collection *The Jacob's Ladder* (1961), one of the principal themes of which is Buber's ideal of an authentic relation with all other beings than oneself. Connecting Levertov's desire to Thoreau's notion of "a poetic or divine life," Avis Hewitt writes that "A 'divine' life makes quotidian reality holy, makes it sacred by the infusion of that which quickens the spirit; early on, Levertov named that source 'the authentic'" (67). The term *presence* appears throughout her poetry, indicating the moral and aesthetic importance of keeping the individuality of the other fresh and central in one's relations with the world. At the close of *The Jacob's Ladder*, Levertov portrays the tragedy of the failure to acknowledge presence in "During the Eichmann Trial."

Adolf Otto Eichmann, known as the "Chief Executioner" of the Third Reich, was a high-ranking Nazi official who was directly responsible for the logistics of the extermination of millions of people, particularly Jews, in the Holocaust. Having escaped imprisonment at the end of World War II, he fled to Argentina, where he was eventually captured and taken to stand trial in Israel for crimes against humanity. At the conclusion of his publicly televised trial, he was found guilty and was hanged on June 1, 1962. In her analysis of Eichmann's motivation, the philosopher Hannah Arendt concluded that Eichmann was neither psychopathic nor frankly anti-Semitic, but was simply the embodiment of "the banality of evil," for he appeared at his trial to be an utterly ordinary person. Arendt's analysis was controversial, but influential, and Levertov's poem attempts to make sense of the type of this chillingly normal evil that Arendt identified in Eichmann.

Because all humans are capable of entering an authentic relation with the other, and because all are likewise liable to reject such a relation as being too difficult to enter and sustain, all are complicit in Eichmann's crimes against the Jews. Though the product of

Eichmann's crime far outstrips any crime of omission, the objectifying attitude out of which his crime arose is enacted by many; Levertov describes Eichmann as a pitiful man who "had not looked" and "whom all / must pity if they look // into their own face." Paul Lacey remarks, "(T)here is another kind of meditation, found in the poetry of . . Denise Levertov, where the discovery or creation of the self is unimportant, and only *seeing* matters" (117). For Levertov, the egoistic, ultimately solipsistic mind breeds an indifference to life, the consequences of which can be catastrophic, as emblematized by Eichmann's "banality of evil."

"When We Look Up," the first section of "During the Eichmann Trial," is the thematic key to the series, and it infers that acts of evil originate from individual instances of failure to relate directly with an other. The two sections that follow serve as studies for the consequences of such an attitude: The first depicts Eichmann's murder of a Jewish boy for stealing a peach, and the second depicts *Kristallnacht,* or the Night of Broken Glass, the nationwide pogrom that preceded the Holocaust. While Levertov does not aim at a facile equation of one boy's death with the deaths of several million, the implication that the spiritual attitude required to commit a single murder is little different from that required to commit a million cannot be missed. In each case, Levertov suggests, the crime arises from Eichmann's indifference to the faces of those who confront him and seem to say, "Here is a mystery // a person, an / other, an I."

The first section documents Eichmann's trial, featuring various quotes from the court transcript, but it also presents the poet's reactions to Eichmann himself. During the trial, Eichmann speaks of his always having had "Corpselike // obedience," and he shows nothing but apathy toward his own involvement in the Holocaust, but Levertov's response is passionate, though painful. Having heard Eichmann speak almost poetically of the Holocaust as "A spring of blood / [That] gushed from the earth," Levertov herself sees "a spring of blood gush from the earth," except that her vision is not one of beauty, but of horror, for "Earth cannot swallow / so much at once." This flood washes over all humanity, drowning and condemning all with the sin of his murders: "he, you, I, which shall I say?" The poem represents Levertov's attempt to reassert the eminence of authentic presence in the wake of the Holocaust. To do so, she must not only restate the potential for destruction implicit in any failed relation, but try to understand Eichmann's own rejection of the other and to "(p)ity this man who saw it / whose obedience continued."

The second section, "The Peachtree," allegorizes Eichmann's confessed murder of a Jewish boy for stealing a peach from his orchard by alluding to the expulsion of man from the Garden of Eden, an allegory that equates the failure of presence with original sin. Initially, the poem is narrated in the third person while describing the boy, but it switches to Eichmann's perspective ("mister death") at the moment of the theft. The utter refusal of the poem to return to the boy's position suggests how Eichmann objectifies him, all for the sake of an object (the peach): "mister death who signs papers / then eats / telegraphs simply: Shoot them." Ultimately, of course, such objectification numbs the self and blights the world it turned to for sustenance; Eichmann, who "would have enjoyed / the sweetest of all the peaches on his tree / with sour-cream / with brandy," now finds that "there is more blood than / sweet juice / always more blood." At the moment he was apprehended, the boy stood before Eichmann in utter vulnerability—as a thief, a young boy, and a Jew, he could have no power—his being completely revealed, which for Levertov could be the sort of "meeting" through which the authentic relation of presence might be entered. But Eichmann, out of greed, perhaps, or perversion, cruelty or simple indifference, saw the boy instead as one more entity in a world of unrelated, useful "things," denied him and thereby murdered him.

The third and final section, "Crystal Night," follows almost as a result of this rejection of the intersubjective relation. From a single denial of "love," as Levertov understands it, can arise a "Night of Broken Glass," the historic beginning of the Nazi pogrom against the Jews. The poem evokes the speed and confusion of the night of November 9, 1938, when in alleged retaliation for the murder of a German ambassador, the Nazi party initiated a nationwide pogrom against Jews which resulted in massive destruction of Jewish properties, more than 2,000 deaths, and 30,000 arrests, and portended the mass eradication of the Holocaust. Through a subtle use of key words that link stanza to stanza, Levertov emphasizes the terror of the night and implies that it will be repeated again in the future, "smashing the windows of sleep and dream / smashing the windows of history."

In his remarks on the "lack of a serious treatment of evil" (117) in *The Jacob's Ladder,* Lacey writes that although Levertov does base "During the Eichmann Trial" on a contemporary instance of human evil, she focuses "on the appropriate inner response to the issue rather than arguing a course of action" (118). In fairness to Levertov, the trial preceded the heightened American involvement in Vietnam, which proved the impetus for her later, committed political activism. Later in her career, Levertov did use her poetry to pursue political causes, even reprinting an information sheet for demonstrators in her 1971 collection *To Stay Alive* (*Poems 1968–1972,* 154), though she eventually united the political and spiritual strains of her verse in her final volumes. "As is noticeable in her writing of the last several decades she . . . acknowledges that the poet with a vision believes *and* acts," writes Hallisey ("Unheard," 88). "During the Eichmann Trial" represents an attempt, within Levertov's religious and political sensibilities at the time, to address the issue of evil.

BIBLIOGRAPHY

Buber, Martin. *I and Thou.* Translated by Walter Kaufmann. New York: Scribner, 1970.

———, ed. *Tales of the Hasidim: The Later Masters.* Translated by Olga Marx. New York: Schocken Books, 1948.

Hallisey, Joan F. "Denise Levertov Sings 'The Unheard Music of That Vanished Lyre.'" *Renascence* 50, nos. 1–2 (1997): 83–93.

———. "Denise Levertov's 'Illustrious Ancestors.'" In *Denise Levertov: Selected Criticism,* edited by Albert Gelpi, 260–267. Ann Arbor: University of Michigan Press, 1993.

Hewitt, Avis. "Hasidic Hallowing and Christian Consecration: Awakening to Authenticity in Denise Levertov's 'Matins.'" *Renascence* 50, nos. 1–2 (1997): 97–107.

Lacey, Paul. *The Inner War: Forms and Themes in Recent American Poetry.* Philadelphia: Augsburg Fortress Publishers, 1972.

Levertov, Denise. *Poems 1960–1967.* New York: New Directions, 1966.

———. *Poems 1968–1972.* New York: New Directions, 1987.

Marten, Harry. *Understanding Denise Levertov.* Columbia: University of South Carolina Press, 1988.

Temple Cone

E

EADY, CORNELIUS (1954–) Cornelius Eady's poetry offers a misleadingly casual, even jaunty chronicle of its times that can turn razor sharp in an instant. In poems spoken through many masks, in syncopated rhythms and colloquial sentences studded with striking figurative language, he conveys an exuberant engagement with the world, even when the experiences the world offers are painful ones. In this, he might aptly be called a blues poet—not because he often writes in blues form, as did LANGSTON HUGHES, but because his poems are full of the mordant wit and occasional swagger that, along with grief and struggle, inform the spirit and knowledge of the blues. He shares with the BLACK ARTS poets the conviction that in music especially we find a quintessentially black American culture expressed, but Eady, like MICHAEL S. HARPER, presents his perceptions without the formal and verbal aggressiveness typical of that movement.

Eady was born and raised in Rochester, New York. He published the first of his six books of poems in 1980, and his second, *Victims of the Latest Dance Craze,* won the 1985 Lamont Prize from the Academy of American Poets and he has received several distinguished fellowships. An active teacher throughout his career, Eady has taught at the State University of New York, Stony Brook, and American University.

Eady's African-American identity is central to his work, as it is central to the jazz, blues, and Motown figures and titles that dominate his profuse musical references. "Gratitude" (1991) celebrates the "loose-seed-in-the-air glee . . . this rooster-pull-down-morning glee" of his identity and vocation, his sense that, as a professional black American poet, he has beaten some tall odds. Nevertheless rage is present in his poems, too, not always disguised by the blues perspective. "Anger" (1997) responds bitterly to network coverage of the riots that followed the acquittal of the police officers charged in the beating of Rodney King. *Brutal Imagination* (2001) places Susan Smith's infamous accusation of an imaginary black man after murdering her own children in 1995 in the context of decades of demeaning or demonizing popular images of African-American men.

Eady sees the job of the poet as revelation and discovery—"I am a person / who can't keep a secret" ("Publicity Agent" [1980])—and what he reveals is certainly not limited to African-American concerns. His poems articulate discoveries that all readers can recognize, particularly about the complexities of family life. With a gift for scene and a novelist's interest in contexts and concepts developed gradually and deliberately, Eady creates poems and sequences of poems that tell their secrets less by confession than by dramatization.

Eady's poems are most notable for their energy and flexibility of voice, for their democratic respect toward subjects and readers alike, and for their outward-looking perspective that links private with public concerns.

BIBLIOGRAPHY

Carroll, Rebecca. *Swing Low: Black Men Writing.* New York: Crown Publishers, 1995.

Peters, Erskine. "Cornelius Eady's *You Don't Miss Your Water:* Its Womanist/Feminist Perspective." *Journal of African American Men* 2, no. 1 (summer 1996): 15–31.

William Waddell

EBERHART, RICHARD (1904–2005) Richard Eberhart's poetry includes meditations on landscape and, widely conceived, on spiritual aspects of the human experience. A contemporary of T. S. ELIOT and other poets of MODERNISM who often shunned formal poetry, Eberhart often wrote in form. According to Bernard Engel, Eberhart is "not a follower of William Carlos Williams, Ezra Pound, Robert Frost or any of the other influential figures in the generation immediately preceding his own. Wordsworth, Blake and perhaps Gerard Manley Hopkins are, Eberhart feels, his real poetic ancestors" and he can be considered both a transcendentalist and a visionary poet (24).

Eberhart was born in Austin, Minnesota. He worked a variety of jobs, including deckhand on a steamship, tutor to the son of King Prajadhipok of Siam (1931–32), gunnery instructor in the U.S. naval reserve (1942–46) and various college teaching positions. He lived a great deal of his life in New England, especially New Hampshire, where he was a professor of English at Dartmouth College. Among his many honors are the Bollingen Prize (1963), a Pulitzer Prize (1966), a National Book Award (1977), and the position of consultant in poetry at the Library of Congress from 1959 to 1961, the position which is now known as poet laureate of the United States. His first book, *A Bravery of Earth,* was published in 1930, and his most recent volume of poetry is *New and Selected Poems, 1930–1990.*

Eberhart's poems meditate on the relationship of the cosmos to the lived experience of the individual. In "The Groundhog" (1936), the speaker meditates upon a dead groundhog's decomposition. The death disturbs him deeply for his "senses shook, / And mind outshot our naked frailty," but two years hence the field where the groundhog died is "Massive and burning, full of life." Thus does the poem "bring the theme of death to intense life—a life that involves us who are human beings" (Brooks 3). Another of Eberhart's most famous poems is "The Fury of Aerial Bombardment" (1947), in which he laments the deaths of the young men he taught as a gunnery instructor. As in other poems, he asks metaphysical questions, such as "Was man made stupid to see his own stupidity? / Is God by definition indifferent, beyond us all?"

The critical response to Eberhart largely echoes GALWAY KINNELL, who speaks of Eberhart's "powerful, loving and exuberant wakefulness to the world and its things and creatures," and Daniel Hoffman, who points out Eberhart's "depth of perception" and "spiritual sense of revelation" (qtd. in Lund 13).

BIBLIOGRAPHY

Brooks, Cleanth. "A Tribute to Richard Eberhart." *South Atlantic Review* 50, no. 4 (Nov. 1985): 21–33.
Engel, Bernard F. *Richard Eberhart.* New York: Twayne, 1971.
Lund, Elizabeth. "Poets Offer Tribute to a Life Lived in Verse." *Christian Science Monitor,* 3 December 1996, 13.

Gregory Byrd

ECONOMOU, GEORGE (1934–) George Economou started his career at the forefront of the New York spoken-word scene and, most recently, has translated the medieval poem *Piers Plowman.* Thus, like EZRA POUND, Economou examined the old and the new, the anachronistic and slang—and found that they were often indistinguishable. Also like Pound, Economou was influenced by the Provençal troubadours; he edited PAUL BLACKBURN's translations of them, and the name of *Trobar,* a magazine he founded and edited with ROBERT KELLY, devoted to DEEP IMAGE POETRY, refers to the Old Provençal word for poetry—literally, "to find" or "to invent." The terms are descriptive: Economou used what he found in medieval poetry to invent the new oral poetry of modern New York (see POETRY IN PERFORMANCE). Like many poets of his generation—JEROME ROTHENBERG and Blackburn—Economou saw poetry as "something *said, spoken*" and not something that "merely lands on the page" ("Some Notes" 657).

Born in Great Falls, Montana, Economou taught at Long Island University and the University of Oklahoma. He also cofounded the *Chelsea Review* and received fellowships from the National Endowment for the Arts (1988, 1999). At Columbia University, his "ambitious" dissertation described the Goddess Natura in medieval allegory (Witke 132); it was subsequently published as *The Goddess Natura in Medieval Literature* in 1972 (and reprinted in 2002).

In his poems, Economou declares war against pomposity. He describes his poems as "composition / not eloquence" ("Ameriki: I" [1977]). And what does Economou think of eloquence? There is "no such thing / behind any forehead." Repetition, jittery typesetting, and onomatopoeia make Economou's voice jump off the page. His poems initially sound self-consciously brash, a young man's poems, spoken not in English but in American, as in "Your Sexability Questionnaire" (1977). Yet Economou can also write with an almost innocent tenderness, such as in "Nights of the Half-Eaten Moon" (1969), a poem to his wife (poet ROCHELLE OWENS). The speaker waits all night for his lover, and when she appears from the darkness, Economou writes, he "awoke in your arms / and never let go." The goal of these poems is the same as in much performance poetry—you are supposed to hear Economou sound like himself and no one else. Yet Economou's work, in all his down-to-earth geniality, also shows a more impersonal concern with history—that is, he can sound exactly like others too. In his *Piers Plowman,* he often sounds like Hopkins: "Christ keep you and your kingdom, king."

The translator and the troubadour come together in Economou's most ambitious work, *Century Dead Center* (1997). The poem begins by asking, "Is it half our century," since "the black hole at its center?" He is referring to the Holocaust (our century's center) but also to the "dead center," where our ideas begin to unravel.

BIBLIOGRAPHY

Economou, George. "Some Notes towards Finding a View of the New Oral Poetry." *Boundary* 2 3, no. iii (spring 1975): 653–656.

Nash, Susan Smith. "Century Dead Center." *World Literature Today* 72 (Spring 1998): 377–378.

Witke, Charles. Review of *Goddess Natura in Medieval Literature,* by George Economou. *Speculum* 51, no. 1 (Jan. 1976): 132–134.

Ken Chen

EDSON, RUSSELL (1935–) Russell Edson has proven instrumental in popularizing and legitimizing the prose poetry genre in America. Charles Baudelaire and Arthur Rimbaud, 19th-century French poets, originated the prose poem when they challenged existing literary conventions related to rhyme, rhythm, and line, choosing instead a structure more malleable and natural. Although in 1848 Edgar Allan Poe produced "Eureka—A Prose Poem," it was the length of a novella. American prose poetry truly begins with Russell Edson. As Edson points out, in 1960s America, "the term prose poetry seemed more related to French toast or French fries" (qtd. in Johnson 30). Now a book of prose poetry has won the Pulitzer Prize (CHARLES SIMIC's *The World Doesn't End* [1990]), and many writers embrace the form, including ROBERT BLY and Michael Benedikt. Unquestionably Edson has played an important role in broadening the scope of contemporary American poetry.

Edson was born in 1935. He received a Guggenheim Fellowship in 1974. To date Edson has published 17 books and three pamphlets, all written exclusively in the prose poetry format, along with a novel.

In an Edson poem, all is possible and nothing certain, except perhaps the pervading feelings of isolation and alienation that torment his characters. Often Edson provides his own surreal illustrations, complementing his content with humor and poignancy. We may find a woman replacing her husband with a stone, a suitor whose knees crumble as he proposes marriage, toilets swallowing people. However, Edson shows that no matter how bizarre the scenario, it scarcely competes with the lunacy of reality. In "A Machine" (1961), a poem that now seems especially prophetic, a son pleads, "Father, if you would only stare at the machine for a few hours, you would learn to love it, to perhaps devote your life to it." In comparison the father's fears that the machine will nest on their roof and produce "baby machines" are benign.

A more overt social commentary, "The Philosophers" (1985), shows a mother countering her son's proclamation, "I think therefore I am," by pronouncing instead, "I hit therefore I am," ultimately knocking her son unconscious. In Edson's world, philosophy is worthless: A weakling is bullied by an old woman, powerless against the antiintellectualism of the modern, and still violent, world.

Edson's vision of dominating machines, dysfunctional families, and a rational absurdity rests on a form that allows all manner of literary techniques—poetic, rhetorical, syntactical. In a 1999 interview with Edson, Peter Johnson noted that writers still "treat the prose poem like a one-night stand." Edson's response? "If one cannot accept failure and scorn, how is he to make his art? It's like wanting to go to heaven without dying" (Johnson 30–31).

BIBLIOGRAPHY

Edson, Russell. "An Interview with Russell Edson," by Peter Johnson. *Writer's Chronicle* 31, no. 6 (May/summer 1999): 30–36.

Upton, Lee. "Structural Politics: The Prose Poetry of Russell Edson." *South Atlantic Review* 58, no. 4 (November 1993): 101–115.

Nancy Effinger Wilson

EIGNER, LARRY (1926–1996) Over a career spanning 36 books of poetry, one prose collection, and a volume of essays and letters, Larry Eigner developed a singular poetry, engaged equally with questions of perception and inhabitation in the world, as with explorations and experimentations in language. His poetry is associated with two particular schools, BLACK MOUNTAIN and what is now called the LANGUAGE SCHOOL.

Eigner was born in Lynn, Massachusetts. The classic Eigner phrase, "the self is some head you can't go around" ("Rambling (In) Life" [1989]), retains some literal, biographical weight: A forceps injury sustained at birth developed into cerebral palsy, as well as a spastic condition until the age of 35, when cryosurgery froze the poet's left side. Wheelchair-bound, Eigner spent much of his life at home in Swampscott, Massachusetts, with his parents or with his brother in Berkeley. With the windows open and "only [his] right finger to type with," Eigner composed most of his poems, letter by letter, in the same "sun parlor," in which, "facing the small audience, [his] first one," he made his bar mitzvah (Eigner 127). In 1984 Eigner's *Waters/Places/A Time* received the San Francisco State University Poetry Center Award.

At first sight an Eigner poem seems little more than an elliptical notation of the quiet, weekday business a suburban backyard offers up to perception: "A n i m a t e s // squirrels and phone wires and birds / how many roads distance the hills" (untitled poem [2001]). But typographical features, notably the spacing between lines and even between the letters of "A n i m a t e s ," which may be the poem's title or its first word, lead the eye back through the poem, filling its gaps with multiple syntactic layers. "A n i m a t e s," like "distance" may be noun or verb or, on closer inspection, a collection of letters which animate the "phone wires," communicating the equal weight given hills, animals, roads, wires, words, and letters in what Eigner terms "the discovery and initiation of attention" (6).

In his essays, Eigner expresses a consistent concern with the human need to measure an incommensurate world and a sustained ecological approach. As poet of the suburban environment, Eigner's contribution to nature writing is unique, reflected in the unified quality of his trademark minimalism—a result of exacting attention to the measures of his writing, as well as of the enormous physical effort each poem cost him, but also of an ethical imperative Eigner felt was common to the lot of humans, and the special prerogative of poetry, to do more with less.

BIBLIOGRAPHY

Eigner, Larry. *Areas Lights Heights: Writings 1954–1989,* edited by Benjamin Friedlander. New York: Roof Books, 1989.

Friedlander, Benjamin. "Larry Eigner." In *Dictionary of Literary Biography.* Vol. 193, *American Poets since World War II,* edited by Joseph Conte. Detroit: Gale Research, 1998.

Watten, Barrett. "Missing 'X': Formal Meaning in Crane & Eigner." *Total Syntax.* Carbondale: Southern Illinois University Press, 1985.

Jonathan Skinner

ELIOT, T(HOMAS) S(TEARNS) (1888–1965) T. S. Eliot is one of the 20th century's most important poets, whose work is a part of what is known as the modernist movement in poetry. Critic C. K. Stead has gone so far as to claim that Eliot took part, along with EZRA POUND, in "invent[ing] MODERNISM" (39). Eliot not only influenced the so-called Lost Generation that followed World War I but may be seen as a herald of the "principal tidal movement of poetry in English in the twentieth century" (Stead 4–5). Eliot's early influences were French, including philosopher Henri Bergson, while his poetic maturation came as a result of reading

Arthur Symons's *The Symbolist Tradition in Literature* (1899) and the poetry of the French symbolists Jules Laforgue and Charles Baudelaire. As an American poet, however, it is hard to deny his American poetic predecessors Walt Whitman and Ralph Waldo Emerson as inspiration, as well as novelist Henry James, whose journalistic style, based on objective observation, Eliot adopted and remade into his own, with the help of Pound. Eliot's recreating of these continental and American influences led to a revolutionary new style of writing and reading poetry that, according to Leroy F. Searle, "opened the way to more explicitly speculative and theoretical studies of literature" and provided an early model for New Criticism (see FUGITIVE/AGRARIAN SCHOOL) (529).

Eliot was born in St. Louis, Missouri. He attended Harvard University (1906–10) and studied at the Sorbonne (1910). There he read the symbolists, who believed that language, particularly the use of symbol, is the vehicle for transcendence and allows the reader's imagination, by use of association, allusion, and allegory, an alternate reality. He returned to Harvard to pursue a dissertation on F. H. Bradley, whose book *Appearance and Reality* (1893) made an impression, by Eliot's own account, on Eliot's prose style. Eliot eventually settled in London (without a Ph.D.) in 1914, where he met Pound and T. E. Hulme, whose writings and theories on imagism extended the symbolist influence; the IMAGIST SCHOOL's "dry hard image" became the new vehicle for transcendence (Stead 38), enacting what Bergson called a true understanding of experience that is reflected by an immediate datum of consciousness. In other words, truth is found in the contemplation of whatever is present. Eliot was confirmed in the Church of England and became a naturalized British citizen in 1927. These experiences greatly affected his writing, especially in poems like *The WASTE LAND* (1922) and the *FOUR QUARTETS* (1943). Eliot was presented the *Dial* Award in 1922 for *The Waste Land.* He was also awarded the Nobel Prize in literature, as well as the British Order of Merit, in 1948, and the American Medal of Freedom in 1964.

In his first collection of poems, *Prufrock and Other Observations* (1917), Eliot demonstrates the admiration he held for James who, in Eliot's opinion, was able to control his work yet remain impersonal. To accomplish this invisible control as James did, Eliot turned toward character, revealing the psychological complexity of culture through what amounted to studies and portraits of people. The poems in *Prufrock* largely survey characters of the "decorous" set, such as Miss Nancy Ellicott of "Cousin Nancy" and Miss Helen Slingsby of "Aunt Helen." By focusing on character, Eliot reveals the vacuity of a culture ravaged by world war and unable to be restored by its impotent citizens. In "The *Boston Evening Transcript,*" the speaker "wearily" fetches the paper for his Cousin Harriet and says that the readers of this paper "sway in the wind like a ripe field of corn." Incapable of achievement, like unpicked corn, their only movement is slight and meaningless. The reader imagines that they will rot on the stalks.

Eliot may also be suggesting that the literature of the day is guilty of such meaninglessness, even his own poetry. "The LOVE SONG OF J. ALFRED PRUFROCK" is the study of a man who is aware of the debased state of his culture and wants to change it, yet he is also a product of this culture, living an empty life, which is measured out "with coffee spoons." Prufrock aspires to the heroic, but he cannot enact change; he cannot "disturb the universe" and tell what he knows of the apparent dissolution of civilization. The poem implies that Eliot, like Prufrock, also fails to write of the despair he sees; he is "deferential," perhaps because he is a new poet trying to find both confidence and an effective method to deliver his message. Eliot may be comparing himself to Prufrock, who like his forebear James, is "meticulous," "full of high sentence, but a bit obtuse."

The Waste Land is the seminal example of Eliot's modernist style and theory. The poem is a collage of disparate images that recall both the ancient and contemporary to demonstrate how much civilization has lost and, perhaps, to make a path for redemption. Eliot uses an impersonal, objective technique that defined poetry as an escape from emotion and personality and allowed for the recapture of what he termed the "historical sense" (*Prose* 38) by employing a "dissociation of sensibility" (*Essays* 248) that denies contemporary influence in order to regain the past magnificence of civilization by way of literary history and tradition.

Eliot's fragmented poetry mimics the fragmentation of culture. And yet Eliot's poetry makes sense of the fragments that it collects by involving human thoughts, dialogue, and activity. This modern poem acts as a new version of the *Boston Evening Transcript,* a report of the apathy, ennui, and the "unreal" quality of civilization, as represented by the various voices that speak the poem. Eliot continued to have newspapers in mind as he drew on the dialogue and concrete activities of people for what he called "objective correlatives" that express a particular emotion solely through the use of external facts (*Essays* 124). Eliot gives us, in fragments, his version of the Anytown's *Daily Herald,* and he seemed to be acutely aware of his journalistic method. He originally titled *The Waste Land* "He Do the Police in Different Voices," a reference to a line in Charles Dickens's *Our Mutual Friend* (1865), in which an orphan named Sloppy reads the newspaper aloud to an old woman.

In spite of Eliot's own critical justification for his intellectual and impersonal style, he maintains a personal aspect in his work, embodied in the sometimes narrative quality of his study of people. He replicates the pattern of *The Waste Land* in his last major poetic work, *Four Quartets,* a collection of four poems based loosely on the last quartets of Beethoven which are thematically entwined with each other. The progression of these poems illustrates Eliot's midlife conversion to Anglicanism. They embody a subjective and didactic impulse, ultimately attempting to help readers transcend the despair of the world.

In their musical quality, these poems are spiritual, inspirational, and intended to evoke action. The world is the place, as suggested in the third of the quartets, "The Dry Salvages," where "music [is] heard so deeply / that it is not heard at all, but you are the music." Eliot ultimately believed it was up to him to transcribe that music, the world, for his readers.

He writes in "Little Gidding," the last of the quartets, that "the end of all our exploring / Will be to arrive where we started." Eliot spent his artistic career theorizing and writing in an innovative style, yet borrowing content from history. It is a career representative of modernism—although it projects the individual poet embarking on a lifelong romantic quest for the regeneration of self. In this way Eliot follows Whitman and Emerson in the sustained American tradition of the authentic poetic impulse, to seek, find, and, instead, create anew, in Eliot's case, to reconstitute what has been lost. His steady development of what Stephen Spender describes as "ritual" and the observance of the ritual separates Eliot from the other poets, as ritual becomes for Eliot and his readers the "foremost aim of living" that joins "the living with the dead" as well as "the present with the past" (7).

BIBLIOGRAPHY

Eliot, T. S. *Selected Essays.* 3d ed. New York: Harcourt, 1950.
———. *Selected Prose of T. S. Eliot,* edited by Frank Kermode. New York: Harcourt, 1975.
Searle, Leroy F. "New Criticism." In *Johns Hopkins Guide to Literary Theory and Criticism,* edited by Michael Groden and Martin Krieswirth. Baltimore: Johns Hopkins University Press, 1994.
Spender, Stephen. *T. S. Eliot.* New York: Viking Press, 1975.
Stead, C. K. *Pound, Yeats, Eliot and the Modernist Movement.* New Brunswick, N.J.: Rutgers University Press, 1986.

John R. Woznicki

"THE EMPEROR OF ICE-CREAM" WALLACE STEVENS **(1923)** "Call the roller of big cigars," intones the speaker at the beginning of WALLACE STEVENS's "The Emperor of Ice-Cream," a FREE VERSE lyric ostensibly about the preparations for a funeral and the wake that follows. The poem is narrated as an impersonal address, and while this device adds greatly to the poem's mystery, it also conceals the poem's implicit narrative, as the critic Helen Vendler has noted (Columbia, 382). Stevens uses a baroque diction and gaudy imagery to contrast the sensuous world of the living with the austerities of death, thereby expressing a core theme of his early work that can also be heard in such poems of Stevens's as SUNDAY MORNING: that the myths of institutional religion, particularly its focus on the hereafter, have become hollow and no longer suffice to give existence meaning. In place of a focus on the afterlife, Stevens urges, we must attend to the luscious delicacies of present existence, which are imbued with a spiritual profundity heretofore overlooked.

In the opening stanza, Stevens describes with sensuous detail a number of festivities, though it is not until the introduction of the corpse in the second stanza that he reveals these are funeral festivities. The speaker calls for "concupiscent curds" to be whipped up, describing a tasty dessert in extravagant diction that makes the vivid sensory image sensual (since concupiscence is lust). Such a transformation suggests that for Stevens, language is filled with pleasures akin to desire, and like the desserts served at funerals, language serves as a reminder, in the face of somber death, of the pleasures of living. Sensuousness and language join together in poetry, and poetry, not religion, is all that Stevens can trust in the wake of death, so that the speaker's command, "Let be be finale of seem," argues for material reality not as an intermediary truth before the greater truth of the afterlife, but as truth itself.

Yet Stevens does not render such philosophical musings with a somber tone. The poem delights in all sensory details, be they elaborate or plain. When the speaker orders the serving girls to "dawdle in such dress / As they are used to wear" and for boys to "Bring flowers in last month's newspapers," high ceremony is linked to quotidian detail, suggesting that the ordinary world of housedresses and old newspapers can provide its own elegance. The very title of the poem, "The Emperor of Ice-Cream," embodies just such a paradoxical mixture of the ceremonial and the profane. The pomp and circumstance of empire are incongruous with such a common pleasure as ice cream, but for Stevens, there can be no earthly greatness that does not embrace the senses, nor can those who embrace the senses experience life except as emperors; for Stevens, "the only emperor is the emperor of ice-cream."

The primacy and power of sensory experience is challenged in the second stanza, however, when the speaker must face the corpse, and thus the fact of mortality. At first, the body repels the speaker, who seeks a sheet "to cover her face," but the sheet proves too short to conceal the entire body. Here one should note Stevens's pun on the sheet of paper on which this very poem is printed, which suggests his scorn for language and poetry that try to conceal mortality. Yet for Stevens, who wrote in "SUNDAY MORNING" that "Death is the mother of beauty," mortality has the force of sensory truth, and because ideas of the afterlife lack such power, death paradoxically invigorates and elevates sensory experience. "If her horny feet protrude," Stevens writes, "they come / To show how cold she is, and dumb," yet he balances the somberness of this revelation with attention to such details as the "embroidered fantails" on the sheet and "the dresser of deal, / Lacking the three glass knobs" in which the sheet has been stored. By the poem's close, the speaker's repeated assertion that "The only emperor is the emperor of ice-cream" has been tested, and though it is now more melancholy in tone, it is no less certain of the plenipotentiary power of the sensory world, language, and poetry.

Helen Vendler notes that the poem has a pitiless gaze embodied by the image of the lamp in the penultimate line, which "affix[es] its beam" like the lamp of the ancient Greek Diogenes, who spent his life seeking one honest man. For Stevens, life and death coexist, and any myth of the afterlife essentially evades this truth. Such views are even more poignant when considering the possible biographical origins of the poem. Helen Vendler speculates that "The Emperor of Ice-Cream" is set in Key West, where Stevens sometimes vacationed, and that it resonates with the death of Stevens's mother; Vendler also notes that ELIZABETH BISHOP, who was familiar with the area, likewise believed the poem's setting to be Key West because Cubans in the area worked in cigar factories and customarily ate ice cream at funerals. Yet whether the dead woman is Stevens's mother, a friend, or one of the wenches, the speaker's unflinching attention to sensory detail at the very moment when death is confronted affirms the imagination's responsibility to embrace this world with all the reverence previously reserved for heaven.

BIBLIOGRAPHY

Baird, James. *The Dome and the Rock: Structure in the Poetry of Wallace Stevens.* Baltimore, Md.: The Johns Hopkins Press, 1968.

Bates, Milton J. *Wallace Stevens: A Mythology of Self.* Berkeley: University of California Press, 1985.

Buttel, Robert. *Wallace Stevens: The Making of Harmonium.* Princeton, N.J.: Princeton University Press, 1967.

Vendler, Helen. "Wallace Stevens." In *The Columbia History of American Poetry,* edited by Jay Parini and Brett C. Miller, 369–394. New York: Columbia University Press, 1983.

———. *Wallace Stevens: Words Chosen out of Desire.* Knoxville: The University of Tennessee Press, 1984.

Temple Cone

ENSLIN, THEODORE (1925–) Theodore (Ted) Enslin is one of the most prolific poets of the late 20th century. His work has often been associated with the OBJECTIVIST and BLACK MOUNTAIN SCHOOLS. His lyrical verse, however, although esteemed by writers and critics alike, is not widely known because Enslin is not a self-promoter, has no academic affiliation, and has published almost exclusively with small POETRY PRESSES. Enslin's professional obscurity also underscores his generous spirit, which infuses each poem with uncompromising singularity and intimacy. He writes neither for a partisan audience nor for a literary market trend, but simply for the sheer pleasure of discovery that poetry discloses between writer and reader, which he describes as "the only joy" in writing (Taggart *Truck* 118). Influenced by the works of CID CORMAN, GEORGE OPPEN, WILLIAM CARLOS WILLIAMS, and LOUIS ZUKOFSKY, Enslin's writing has also been compared to that of ROBERT CREELEY, LARRY EIGNER, LORINE NIEDECKER, and CHARLES OLSON.

Enslin was born in Chester, Pennsylvania, to parents who were classical scholars and educators. During the war years, he studied musical composition in Cambridge, Massachusetts, with Nadia Boulanger and Francis Judd Cooke and later attended the New England Conservatory of Music. Enslin moved to Cape Cod in 1946, then to Maine in 1960, where he currently resides, writes, and crafts walking sticks. Enslin won the Niemann Award (1955) for his weekly newspaper column, "Six Miles Square," in the *Cape Codder*. Origin Press published his first book, *The Work Proposed* (1958). Enslin has since produced more than 70 volumes, including *To Come, To Have Become* (1966), which won the Hart Crane Award, *The Weather Within* (1985), and *Re-Sounding: Selected Later Poems* (1999).

Although landscape figures significantly in Enslin's poetry and poetics, he considers himself neither a poet of nature nor a regional writer. Three major, interconnected themes inform this poet's oeuvre: music, observation, and discovery. Enslin recalls that, as early as 1959, he became aware that his musical training "was something that [he] was using in the writing of poetry" (Nowak 396). *Love and Science* (1990), for example, reflects a patient attunement to the poem as lyric, object, and gift by embracing the cadence of things both present and absent, sonorous and silent: "as a movement from itself the sound . . . is discovery" (#49).

BIBLIOGRAPHY

Foster, Edward, ed. *Talisman 12: Theodore Enslin Issue.* Jersey City, N.J.: Talisman House, 1994.

Nowak, Mark. "Interview." In *Theodore Enslin: Then, and Now: Selected Poems*, 389–418. Orono, Maine: National Poetry Foundation, 1999.

Taggart, John. "An Ongoing Conversation." In *Songs of Degrees.* Tuscaloosa: University of Alabama Press, 1994, pp. 179–187.

———, ed. *Truck 20: Theodore Enslin.* Saint Paul, Minn.: Truck Press, 1978.

W. Scott Howard

"EROS TURANNOS," E. A. ROBINSON (1916) "Eros Turannos" is E. A. Robinson's subtly devastating lyric about a woman who continues in a troubled relationship, likely a marriage, despite "her doubts of what he says" and despite the unwanted attentions of small-town gossip. Written in octets that seem "hypertrophied ballad stanzas" (Pinsky, 91), with an ABABCCCA rhyme scheme that repeats the word "him" nine times in the first three stanzas, the poem showcases Robinson's formal control, relying on subtle shifts of voice, an abstract yet precise diction, and well-timed images to evoke the female protagonist's struggle to reconcile failed hopes, personal pride, and social convention with the demands of 'tyrant Love' (the title, translated from Greek). The poem challenges the pieties of society as a whole, contrasting them with the stoic resignation of a secluded, fractured existence, which Robinson does not falsely praise, but upon which he looks with compassion for its integrity and its fidelity to experience.

The first three stanzas concern the woman's husband and her reasons for not leaving him. Robinson conceals the details of their conflict, particularly the husband's misdeeds, thereby suggesting the impossibility of ever truly knowing another person: "As if the story of a house / Were told, or ever could be." In a lecture on Robinson, poet JAMES DICKEY characterizes the woman's husband as "a charming younger man, but who maybe didn't have anything much to him, who's living off her money" (105), yet at heart, Dickey claims, Robinson is "a poet of *contingency*. He realizes . . . that you can't have certainty" (91).

The woman's reasons for continuing the marriage seem clear initially. She fears "the downward years, / Drawn slowly to the foamless weirs / Of age, were she to lose him." But more important, given the poem's title, she still cannot forsake "Love, that will not let him be / The Judas that she found him." In the fourth stanza, the woman stoically accepts contingency and unhappiness along with whatever happiness existed before; for her, "home, where passion lived and died, / Becomes a place where she can hide." Ironically, however, the literal house and metaphorical home (of marriage) in which she hides continue to hinder psychological insight into the woman's experiences, so that by the close of the poem, Robinson suggests that no one can ever know the reasons for human actions, except that one must "Take what the god has given."

In the fifth stanza, Robinson makes a subtle shift of voice, introducing for the first time the first person plural speaker who has, unbeknownst to the reader, been narrating the poem until this point. Poet and critic ROBERT PINSKY identifies this voice as the town community itself, writing that "the first-person plural as 'we' tap our brows and tell the story impersonates the communal, but also heightens the central character's loneliness and lack" (83). Unable to comprehend the woman's decisions, the narrator admits to inventing stories to get at the truth, and thus serves as a proxy for the reader, with one difference: the reader recognizes the irony of the intrusive, gossipy townspeople's professed "need" to invent stories to explain the woman's unconventional life. For all its insistence on transparency—"We'll kindly have no veil between / Her visions and those we have seen"—the narrator cannot see that demanding complete access to the human soul causes seclusion and mystery. No individual, Robinson suggests, can ever be fully known, and to pretend otherwise violates the individual's integrity, and Robinson's own distant, ironic characterizations (in "Eros Turannos" and elsewhere) show this belief in practice. In the final stanza, Robinson can acknowledge that the woman is one of those "That with a god have striven," but regarding the outcome of the woman's struggle, Robinson only offers three images of varying degrees of change, no one of which can assert itself as the truth.

Like much of Robinson's work, "Eros Turannos" seems to be read and celebrated more among poets than among scholars. Pinsky notes that "There is something heroic in Robinson's simultaneous resistant loathing and meticulous love for the provincial settings and figures he imagined" (91), and this ambivalence troubles conclusive interpretations. Dickey suggests that such ambivalence represents a remarkably compassionate resignation when he concludes that "if you've had what love gives, some years of passion and love and mutual esteem, if you've had *that* part, the good part, you also have to take the rest" (106). Throughout his poetry, Robinson dramatizes the terrible challenge individuals face from the loneliness of seclusion and the hypocrisies of community, and "Eros Turannos" stands as one of the greatest examples of Robinson's stoic acceptance of the mystery of Truth.

BIBLIOGRAPHY

Dickey, James. *Classes on Modern Poets and the Art of Poetry*, edited by Donald J. Greiner. Columbia: University of South Carolina Press, 2004.

Pinsky, Robert. *Democracy, Culture, and the Voice of Poetry*. Princeton, N.J.: Princeton University Press, 2002.

Temple Cone

ESHLEMAN, CLAYTON (1935–) Clayton Eshleman is important to the story of American literature not only for his own poetry, which is substantial, but also for his activities as magazine editor and translator. His work is related to movements in poetry, visual art, even psychology. His influences include poet CHARLES OLSON, painter Francis Bacon, and psychologist James Hillman. By turns visionary, gothic, daily, political, grotesque, sexual, and comic, Eshleman's poems provoke on multiple levels simultaneously, demanding that readers reevaluate their lives.

Born in Indianapolis, Eshleman has lived in Mexico, Japan, Peru, and France. In 1967 he founded the influential magazine *Caterpillar* and in 1981 started *Sulfur*, an interdisciplinary magazine of poetry and art (see POETRY JOURNALS). Among many awards, he was a recipient of the National Book Award in 1979 for his cotranslation of César Vallejo's *Complete Posthumous Poetry*. He has taught at Eastern Michigan University. His first book of poetry, *Mexico & North*, was published in 1962.

Eshleman's chief preoccupation is with the caves of southern France, the birthplace of human image-making. The hybrid, primordial pictures inscribed on the cave walls underground serve as metaphors for Eshleman's conception not just of poems but of poem-making. As stated in "Notes on a Visit to Le Tuc D'Audoubert" (1983), "image is crossbreeding," and such operations take place within the mind's most turbulent zones. Eshleman recounts in the introduction to *Fracture* (1983) how he "began to see prehistoric psychic activity as a swamp-like churning, in which construction and destruction were twined forces" (12). An Eshleman poem develops in a similar fashion. Its images or thoughts never follow a linear progression, but grow in an organic, free-associative way, in which origins and ends are indistinguishable from each other. Such free association is enacted at the sentence level, where words are often generated by permutations of previous ones. All this produces a reflection of an endlessly proliferating, interconnected world. "Short Story" (1994) opens, ironically, "Begin with this: the world has no origin."

A translator of, among others, Antonin Artaud, Aimé Césaire, and Vladimir Holan, Eshleman's sympathies lie with the outsider and transgressor—visionaries pitted against the oppression of monolithic culture. While his long-term project has been to unearth subterranean materials, it is also to unmask the way in which atrocities are linked, inexorably, to the prosperities of Western life. It is, as Eshleman describes it in "Short Story" (1994), "A poetry so full of claws / as to tear the reader's face off."

BIBLIOGRAPHY

Christensen, Paul. *Minding the Underworld: Clayton Eshleman and Late Post-Modernism*. Santa Barbara, Calif.: Black Sparrow, 1991.

Eshleman, Clayton. Introduction to *Fracture*. Santa Barbara, Calif.: Black Sparrow, 1983.

Sattler, Martha. *Clayton Eshleman: A Descriptive Bibliography*. Jefferson, N.C.: McFarland, 1988.

David Chirico

ESPADA, MARTÍN (1957–) Martín Espada is recognized for his contributions to political poetry in both English and Spanish. An important part of what has been called the Latino Renaissance, Espada's poetry is a unique intermingling of advocacy, narrative, writings from the margin, and formal innovation, which is clearly influenced by questions of Latino-American identity and the history of colonialism in the Americas. Espada has argued that political convictions and poetry must relate: "The question is not whether poetry and politics can mix. That question is a luxury for those who can afford it. The question is how best to combine poetry and politics" (100). Drawing on Pan-American traditions, Espada has been influenced by the works of Pablo Neruda, Ernesto Cardenal, Eduardo Galeano, and Walt Whitman and their respective traditions of NARRATIVE POETRY of protest.

Espada was born in 1957 to a Puerto Rican father and Jewish mother in Brooklyn. Trained as a lawyer, Espada published his first collection of poetry, *The Immigrant Iceboy's Bolero*, in 1982. His collections of poetry include *Rebellion Is the Circle of a Lover's Hands* (1990), which won the Paterson Poetry Prize and a PEN/Revson Foundation Fellowship (1993), and *Imagine the Angels of Bread* (1996), which won the American Book Award (1997). He has edited several anthologies of poetry, including *El Coro: A Chorus of Latino and Latina Poetry* (1997), which won a Gustavus Myers Center Outstanding Book Award, and he has published a prose collection, *Zapata's Disciple* (1998), which won an Independent Publisher Book Award (1999). He has also received the PEN/Voelker Award for poetry, 1986 and 1992, a Guggenheim Fellowship (2006), two fellowships from the National Endowment for the Arts (1986), and a Massachusetts Artists Foundation Fellowship (1984). Throughout 1994 Espada read several of his poems as part of National Public Radio's *All Things Considered* program. He has taught at the University of Massachusetts, Amherst.

Espada's poetry is marked by an attention to the continuing effects of history on the individual—as migrant, laborer, dispossessed, and disenfranchised—and by an ironic reimagining of fate. In "Imagine the Angels of Bread" (1996), for instance, reversals of fortune abound: "squatters evict landlords," "refugees deport judges," peasants "uproot the deed to the earth that sprouts the vine." "The New Bathroom Policy at English High School" (1990) depicts a principal who bans Spanish in the bathrooms in order to relieve his constipation. Lyrical and bold simultaneously, Espada's poetry in its most populist forms confronts the realities of history's speechless and marginalized masses. His more speculative poetry contemplates metaphysical questions about his family and his past.

BIBLIOGRAPHY

Creeley, Robert. Foreword to *Trumpets from the Islands of Their Eviction,* edited by Martín Espada. Tempe, Ariz.: Bilingual Press, 1994.

Espada, Martín. *Zapata's Disciple: Essays.* Cambridge, Mass.: South End Press, 1998.

Gonzalez, Ray, ed. *Touching the Fire: Fifteen Poets of Today's Latino Renaissance.* New York: Anchor Books, 1998.

Ratiner, Steven. "Martín Espada: Poetry and the Burden of History." *Christian Science Monitor* (6 March 1991): 16.

Shorris, Earl. *Latinos: Biography of a People.* New York: W.W. Norton, 1992.

Snehal Shingavi

ETHNOPOETICS The term *ethnopoetics* signifies an informal movement in poetry and scholarship. Coined by JEROME ROTHENBERG, it refers narrowly to collaborations among poets, anthropologists, linguists, and literary scholars during the late 1960s and 1970s. Ethnopoetics has come to designate writing that reflects a heightened awareness of the artfulness of oral and traditional poetries and the ways in which diverse verbal arts illuminate world cultures; this writing can also reflect innovative theorizing and the practice of transcription or translation.

POETRY ANTHOLOGIES edited by Rothenberg—*Shaking the Pumpkin* (1991) and *Technicians of the Sacred* (1985)—helped bring attention to oral poetry and other ancient literary forms generally neglected within literary and academic circles. The availability of ethnopoetic texts influenced the translation, study, and making of poetry by writers associated with ethnopoetics, as well as some associated with the BLACK MOUNTAIN SCHOOL and BEAT POETRY; more recent trends toward multiculturalism, POETRY IN PERFORMANCE, and cross-cultural poetics reflect the influence of ethnopoetics. During the 1970s the journal *Alcheringa/Ethnopoetics* balanced translations of traditional world poetry and contemporary creative work by poets, including DAVID ANTIN, GEORGE ECONOMOU, ROBERT KELLY, George Quasha, Rothenberg, ARMAND SCHWERNER, and GARY SNYDER, some of whom were earlier associated with the short-lived DEEP IMAGE school. Anthropologists and linguists involved included coeditor Dennis Tedlock, Stanley Diamond, Dell Hymes, and Nathaniel Tarn.

The marginalization of traditional world poetries prior to ethnopoetics can be partially attributed to the poverty of available translations. An ethnopoetic translation requires more than mastery of the language. From the scholarly side, ethnopoetics emphasizes the necessity of acquiring deep knowledge of the cultures and performance context of the poetry; in retranslating the 16th-century Mayan *Popol Vuh,* for example, Tedlock not only learned the Quiché Maya language and collaborated with contemporary Mayans but apprenticed himself to an indigenous spiritual leader. Ethnopoetics scholars developed influential methods of transcription and total translation that aim to carry over the qualities of oral performance to the printed page, thereby improving translations on the formal level as well. By making the artfulness of traditional poetries more apparent on the page, this innovation influenced contemporary poets.

Two classic examples of the innovation inspired by ethnopoetics are *Fast Speaking Woman* (1975) by ANNE WALDMAN and *The TABLETS* (1968, 1989, 1999) by Schwerner. Waldman's book of poems uses techniques of repetition and parallelism learned from the work of an oral poet, Maria Sabina. Ethnopoetics allows Waldman to craft poems that convey an appropriately chant-like power not possible using either traditional English prosody (rhyme and meter) or the looser, speech-oriented patterns of free verse (see PROSODY AND FREE VERSE). Schwerner's *The Tablets* appears, at first glance, to be an English translation of a recovered ancient text; in fact, Schwerner has created a poetic fiction, conjuring up both the original and the "translation," complete with footnotes, indecipherable passages, and an imagined scholar/translator. As ethnopoetics enriches our understanding of traditional poetries in formal, philosophical, and spiritual terms, it alters received ideas about the Western canon and privileged literary forms, thereby enlarging the domain of poetry. Moving beyond a canon centered on the "classics," writers influenced by ethnopoetics study, absorb, and are influenced by a wider range of sources, including Aztec, Mayan, Zuni, Navajo, Egyptian, Yoruban, Ashanti, Indian, Tibetan, and other poetries.

Ethnopoetic scholarship may involve analysis, translation, or transcription of texts gained from living traditional poets, singers, and storytellers, or it may take up previously collected ethnographic texts and retranslate them to expose their aesthetic and culturally informative dimensions. Some of the most valuable ethnopoetic texts have entailed collaboration between formally trained scholars and traditional artists. *Finding the Center* (1978) presents an exemplary collection of poetic narratives performed by Walter Sanchez and Andrew Peynetsa, two traditional Zuni tellers from New Mexico; Tedlock produced the book by making an audio recording, translating, then transcribing the pieces for performance. The result is a book that allows one to read the works and feel nearly present in the performances. Also from the American Southwest, *Yaqui Deer Songs,* Maso Bwikam: *A Native American Poetry* (1987) is a remarkable collaboration between scholar Larry Evers and singer Felipe S. Molina. It presents cycles of traditional songs in bilingual format, which one may read along with an audio cassette of the singing. Most powerful, however, is the way it conveys the sense of how the performers and native audience think of this art by contextualizing the songs with interviews and conversations between Yaqui singers and participants in the deer song performances.

As motto for ethnopoetics in all its facets, the first words of Rothenberg's first anthology—"Primitive means Complex"—serve as a simple measure of its continued influence. Valuing marginalized art—the so-called primitive, preliterate, tribal, or uncivilized—ethnopoetics anticipates multiculturalism. As an exploration of oral poetry and traditions, it resonates with the recent reemergence of performance poetry. The intense, interdisciplinary collaborations of ethnopoetics in its first phase have subsided, but a conversation between poetry and the new interpretive anthropology began with the advent of the journal *XCP: Cross-cultural Poetics* in 1997. In the work of individual poets, ethnopoetic concerns continue to be reflected, as when, for instance, CLAYTON ESHLEMAN delves into the prehistoric imagination in *Hotel Cro-Magnon* (1989), Cecilia Vicuña remembers lost threads of the Quechua in *Unravelling Words and the Weaving of Water* (1992), Snyder imagines his place in North America through Asian art in *Mountains and Rivers without End* (1996), NATHANIEL MACKEY converses with the Dogon in *School of Udhra* (1993), SIMON ORTIZ calls up the trickster in postindustrial America in *Woven Stone* (1992), and EDWARD KAMAU BRATHWAITE forges a poetic Nation Language embodying the African *nommo* in *Middle Passage* (1993). Whether captivated by the oral artfulness or some other feature brought to light by ethnopoetics, 20th-century poets working in this domain continue to share an excitement for the way it expands the vision of the possible for poetry.

BIBLIOGRAPHY

Alcheringa/Ethnopoetics. 9 vols. 1970–80.

Rothenberg, Jerome, and Diane Rothenberg, eds. *Symposium of the Whole: A Range of Discourse toward an Ethnopoetics.* Berkeley: University of California Press, 1983.

Kenneth Sherwood

EUROPEAN POETIC INFLUENCES A signal comment that captures Europe's influence on 20th-century American poetry is FRANK O'HARA's poignant observation: "My heart is in my / pocket, it is Poems by Pierre Reverdy" ("A Step Away from Them" [1956]). While many 19th-century American poets looked across to Europe for culture, the extent to which their 20th-century counterparts were influenced by European poetry and poetics was more than significant. The intellectual and cultural ferment of Europe in the early 20th century sparked a revolution in American poetry that has continued to the present day. Movements such as symbolism (France), imagism and vorticism (England), expressionism (Germany), futurism (Italy), cubo-futurism (Russia), dadaism (Switzerland),

and SURREALISM (France) utterly changed the way American poets wrote and thought (see IMAGIST SCHOOL). And as the work of European poets continues to be translated, so do the ideas of such groundbreaking poets as Charles Baudelaire, Arthur Rimbaud, Stéphane Mallarmé, Guillaume Apollinaire, Rainer Maria Rilke, Filippo Tommaso Marinetti, Vladimir Mayakovksy, Velemir Khlebnikov, Anna Akhmatova, Tristan Tzara, and Federico García Lorca continue freshly to inspire.

"America is my country, and Paris is my home town," wrote GERTRUDE STEIN (61), who moved to Paris in 1903 and who was part of a huge migration of American writers who emigrated to Europe in the 1900s to 1920s. Stein was at the forefront of the burgeoning modernist sensibility and one of the first collectors of work by "new" painters, such as Henri Matisse and Pablo Picasso (see MODERNISM). In her works, such as *TENDER BUTTONS* (1914), she applied to her own writing many of the same cubist techniques that Picasso was using in his art. However, when seeking the conduits through which the European revolution in thought and aesthetics found its way to American shores, American poet and editor EZRA POUND may be the most important. With British poets T. E. Hulme, Richard Aldington, and F. S. Flint and fellow American emigré H. D., inspired by the poetry of French symbolist poets Baudelaire, Mallarmé, Jules Laforgue (called "the father of free verse" [see PROSODY AND FREE VERSE]), and Arthur Rimbaud, Pound introduced imagism in London in 1912. Imagism was the first movement to bring to American poets symbolist ideas about using new language, verse forms, and images to express the rapid changes of the "modern" world.

Symbolism became a major influence on many American poets, including T. S. ELIOT, who incorporated many symbolist ideas into his own poetry, particularly his epic poem, *The WASTE LAND,* as well as HART CRANE, WALLACE STEVENS, ALLEN GINSBERG and other BEAT poets, and JOHN ASHBERY, KENNETH KOCH, and O'Hara, members of the NEW YORK SCHOOL. The poetry critic Marjorie Perloff feels that the "French connection" is the missing link in understanding the two primary strains of contemporary American poetry; she argues that American poetry stemmed from a divergence in thought between Eliot and Pound, influenced respectively by Mallarmé and Rimbaud (4).

"[I]magism all but fizzled out in England where in America it transformed itself to become a complex tradition of free verse that left few poets untouched," says Geoffrey Thurley (110). Because of some inherent problems in imagism, and perhaps because of its overenthusiastic reception by American poets, such as AMY LOWELL, Pound abandoned it to found vorticism with British writer Wyndham Lewis. Vorticism demanded that poetic images be like vortexes—moving, swirling sources of energy. Pound himself was much like a vortex, through whom much European poetry was channelled to the United States and to American poets, such as Stevens, MARIANNE MOORE, and WILLIAM CARLOS WILLIAMS. Pound was the "foreign correspondent" for three of the most important POETRY JOURNALS of the time, *Poetry,* the *Dial,* and the *Little Review,* and he became a primary supporter for European writers, such as William Butler Yeats and James Joyce.

Events such as the 1913 Armory Show in New York City, where Williams was among the crowds viewing avant-garde artwork by Marcel Duchamp, Henri Matisse, and Francis Picabia for the first time, also introduced modernist ideas to the United States. As Williams recalled later, "There had been a break somewhere, we were streaming through, each thinking his own thoughts, driving his own designs toward his self's objectives. Whether the Armory Show in painting did it or whether that also was no more than a facet—the poetic line, the way the image was to lie on the page was our immediate concern" (138).

More radical movements, such as dadaism and futurism, which occurred between the two world wars, were to have a more delayed influence on American poetry. Futurism, an early movement founded by Filippo Iommaco Marinetti in Italy in 1909, inspired many other literary movements in Europe. However, his writings were not translated until recently—this may be due to futurism's disturbing links to war and nationalism. Futurism's indirect contributions to American poetry are nevertheless undeniable, despite Marinetti's seeming eclipse by more lyrical Italian writers widely translated in the 1950s, such as Giuseppe Ungaretti, Salvatore Quasimodo, and Eugenio Montale.

Cubo-futurism in Russia is another movement more recently discovered by American poets. The cubo-futurists abandoned traditional metrical structures in favor of new rhythms and powerful new images, and presented the poet as a revolutionary figure. Mayakovsky, who inspired Ginsberg, is the best known; however, Khlebnikov was the primary innovator of the cubo-futurists, and his ideas were important in the development of postmodern poetry and its nonlinear, dissociative qualities. Perloff maintains that Khlebnikov, because of his many innovations in poetry, is a major influence on "an important thread of twentieth-century poetry from Russian Futurism and Dada to Aimé Césaire and [EDMUND] KAMAU BRATHWAITE, to Mac Wellman and Steve McCaffery, SUSAN HOWE and Maggie O'Sullivan" (126). One of Khlebnikov's important innovations was the idea of *zaum,* "a poetic language beyond (*za*) mind or reason (*um*)," achieved through intense wordplay and multidimensional, nonsequential language (Perloff 123).

Interestingly the irreverent and iconoclastic movement of dadaism, founded in Zurich in 1916 by Tristan Tzara, had a protomanifestation in New York City. Alfred Stieglitz published work by what became the "New York dada" group—Man Ray, Picabia, Djuna Barnes, Marsden Hartley, Marius de Zayas, and others—in a literary journal titled *291.* "*291* was in a sense the prototypical Dada journal, except, of course, that Dada did not yet exist," write Guy Bennett and Béatrice Mousli (31). Picabia started his own journal, titled *391,* whose list of contributors "reads like a who's who of the early 20th century avant-garde," explain Bennett and Mousli (33), including Apollinaire, André Breton, Jean Cocteau, Robert Desnos, Duchamp, Paul Éluard, Max Jacob, Man Ray, René Magritte, Pound, Eric Satie, Tzara, and others. The only American journal officially affiliated with dadaism, titled *New York Dada,* was edited by Ray and Duchamp in 1921. However, it was not until the 1960s that dadaism found a more receptive audience. The Beat poets, JOHN CAGE, and JACKSON MAC LOW used dada's tools of collage, discontinuity, and chance, while poets associated with the New York school created delicious juxtapositions between lowbrow elements of culture, such as comic books, with traditional poetic forms, such as the sestina.

Surrealism reached an even wider audience, and, in fact, it is difficult to find a postwar American poet who does not show at least some awareness of it. Surrealist poets, such as Breton, Desnos, and Éluard, abandoned established rules of poetry and prose to create new images and associations, advancing the primacy of the imagination. The surrealist writer was a spiritual explorer—process was more important than product. "Thus while rejecting, as vehemently as the Dadaists, all fixed categories, dogma (including revolutionary dogma), and rationalizations that threatened to impoverish man and diminish the options open to him, the Surrealist is confident in the capacity of the mind to sustain itself in the midst of chaos," claims Robert Short (302). These ideas proved irresistible to many American poets, particularly the Beats, who adapted the surrealist technique of "automatic writing" into their own "spontaneous prose."

Ashbery, Koch, and O'Hara together revitalized interest in European writing at a time when the United States was experiencing postwar isolation, and Ashbery, who lived in Paris in the 1950s and 1960s, was particularly diligent in reviving neglected European writers, such as Raymond Roussel, Max Jacob, and Reverdy. Their timely reintroductions paved the way for younger American poets to continue translating important works, such as Apollinaire's poem "Zone," which was retranslated by RON PADGETT in the 1970s. Says Ginsberg, who wrote a homage to one of his favorite poets, entitled "At Apollinaire's Grave": "The point of the Apollinaire poem was to show my literary antecedents with the hope that others would go out and read them. . . . Everybody said, 'Oh, Ginsberg is imitating [KENNETH] PATCHEN and CARL SANDBURG.' There was no notion at all of the European tradition. The montage, free association, nonpunctuated *Zone* style that I used in that poem was largely missed" (qtd. in Sawyer-Lauçanno 265). In 1992 Padgett published the complete poems of Swiss poet Blaise Cendrars, whom he had been translating for decades. HARRY MATHEWS, a close friend of Ashbery's, became closely involved with the European group of Oulipo, whose complicated, rigorous, and playful forms inspired many contemporary writers to explore new techniques (see CYBERPOETRY).

There are many poets who were not part of any major literary movement and who were "discovered" by individual American poets. Many poets translated their findings themselves, and some European poets who had emigrated to the United States became translators of their native language (see POETRY TRANSLATION). The German poet Rainer Maria Rilke's gravity and meditative qualities were particularly seductive to American poet-translators of a certain generation, such as ROBERT LOWELL, RANDALL JARRELL, and ROBERT BLY (Heep 4). LANGSTON HUGHES and W. S. MERWIN both translated Lorca, whose tragic death captured many poets' interest. GEORGE ECONOMOU, JAMES MERRILL, ROBERT PINSKY, and W. H. AUDEN all translated the Greek poet C. P. Cavafy, and MURIEL RUYKEYSER translated the Swedish poet Gunnar Ekelof. Some poetic translation relationships include ROSMARIE WALDROP and Edmond Jabès, CLAYTON ESHLEMAN and Antonin Artaud, PAUL BLACKBURN and Lorca, and ROBERT HASS and Czeslaw Milosz. JOSEPH BRODSKY, born in Leningrad in 1940, was exiled in 1972 after serving in a labor camp. Brodsky then emigrated to the United States, where he worked to make poetry more central to American culture, even serving as poet laureate from 1991 to 1992. JEROME ROTHENBERG continues to produce multinational anthologies containing overlooked work by poets such as Kurt Schwitters (see ETHNOPOETICS). CHARLES SIMIC, born in Yugoslavia, has translated Yugoslav poets, such as Vasko Popa, and ANSELM HOLLO, born in Finland, translates Finnish poets Paavo Haavikko and Pentti Saarikoski.

The list of American poets who traveled across the Atlantic to visit or live in Europe—from Stein, Pound, H. D., Eliot, Crane, Cummings, Hughes, COUNTEE CULLEN, CLAUDE MCKAY, Ashbery, Koch, Mathews, Padgett, ALICE NOTLEY, and others—is as impressive as European poets who have traveled the reverse route. American poetry can identify many of its roots in what is not American, just as American identity itself consists of different, but essential "foreign" influences. To explore this hidden debt that American poetry owes to European poets is to continue to revitalize our own language.

BIBLIOGRAPHY

Bennett, Guy, and Béatrice Mousli. *Charting the Here of There: French & American Poetry in Literary Magazines from 1850–2002.* New York: Granary Books, 2002.

Bradbury, Malcolm, and James McFarlane, eds. *Modernism, 1890–1930.* Middlesex, England: Penguin Books, 1978.

Heep, Hartmut. *A Different Poem: Rainer Maria Rilke's American Translators Randall Jarrell, Robert Lowell, and Robert Bly.* New York: Peter Lang, 1996.

Perloff, Marjorie. *The Poetics of Indeterminancy: Rimbaud to Cage.* Evanston, Ill.: Northwestern University Press, 1983.

———. *21st-Century Modernism: The "New Poetics".* Malden, Mass.: Blackwell Publishers, 2002.

Rothenberg, Jerome, and Pierre Joris, eds. *Poems for the Millennium: The University of California Book of Modern and Postmodern Poetry.* Vols. 1 and 2. Berkeley: University of California Press, 1995.

Sawyer-Lauçanno, Christopher. *The Continual Pilgrimage: American Writers in Paris, 1944–1960.* New York: Grove Press, 1992.

Short, Robert. "Dada and Surrealism." In *Modernism, 1890–1930,* edited by Malcolm Bradbury and James McFarlane. Middlesex, England: Penguin Books, 1978.

Stein, Gertrude. *What Are Masterpieces?* New York: Pitman, 1970.

Thurley, Geoffrey. *The American Moment: American Poetry in Mid-Century.* London, England: Edward Arnold, 1977.

Williams, William Carlos. *The Autobiography of William Carlos Williams.* New York: Random House, 1951.

Marcella Durand

EVERSON, WILLIAM (BROTHER ANTONINUS) (1912–1994) By virtue of early literary friendships with ROBERT DUNCAN and KENNETH REXROTH, William Everson is often counted among the poets of the SAN FRANCISCO RENAISSANCE. He saw his life and work proceed in three phases: the first a quest to understand his place in the physical world, the second a rejection of that world in an effort to achieve union with God, and the third a period of synthesis, or reconciliation of the former two. Moving between the polarities of acceptance and renunciation that characterized his personal life, Everson's poems combine a deep knowledge of psychoanalysis and theology with autobiographical candor to investigate what he called, "The divisible selves, / Ill eased with each other." ("The Chronicle of Division" [1946]). Narrative, CONFESSIONAL, keenly descriptive, and presented with, in David A. Carpenter's words, "incantatory intensity and insistence" (173), his poems travel the rugged physical and emotional trails famously broken by ROBINSON JEFFERS, whose expansive evocations of the wave-battered Pacific coast served as models for Everson's own work.

Born in Sacramento and raised in California's San Joaquin Valley, Everson's early life was rural and modest. He began to write poetry in high school, and after graduation he attended Fresno State College, dropping out in 1935 to devote himself to writing, growing grapes, and learning the printer's trade. A conscientious objector, Everson spent World War II in a civilian public-service camp. After the war he moved to Berkeley, where, championed by Rexroth, he gathered increasing recognition for his poetry. In 1948, after experiencing a religious epiphany during a Christmas mass, he converted to Catholicism and three years later was accepted as a lay brother in the Dominican order, receiving the name Brother Antoninus, the name under which he would write until—unable to accept the condition of celibacy—he publicly resigned from the order in late 1969. From 1971 until his retirement in 1981, he was poet in residence at University of California, Santa Cruz. His poems are collected in three volumes: *The Residual Years* (1997), *The Veritable Years* (1998), and *The Integral Years* (2000).

Everson's best-known poem, "Canticle to the Waterbirds" (1950), illustrates his acute sensitivity to the intricate music of language—"Clack your beaks you cormorants and kittiwakes"—as well as his ability to infuse earthly things with divine presence: "Send up the strict articulation of your throats, / And say His name." After Everson left monastic life, he continued to explore the physical manifestations of spirituality, including, as critic Albert Gelpi observes, the erotic aspects of mysticism. While some critics found Everson's work melodramatic, few poets since the romantic era have so fully engaged the paradoxes and conflicts that at once torment and enliven the human psyche.

BIBLIOGRAPHY

Bartlett, Lee. *William Everson: The Life of Brother Antoninus.* New York: New Directions, 1988.

Carpenter, David A. *The Rages of Excess. The Life and Poetry of William Everson.* Bristol, Ind.: Wyndham Hall Press, 1987.

Gelpi, Albert. "'I Am Your Woman': The Erotic Mysticism of William Everson." *Religion and the Arts* 2, no. 2 (1998): 149–181.

Fred Muratori

F

"FACING IT" YUSEF KOMUNYAKAA **(1988)** A LYRIC meditation on the Vietnam Veterans Memorial in Washington, D.C., YUSEF KOMUNYAKAA's "Facing It" confronts the aftermath of the Vietnam War and of racism during the Civil Rights era. Along with numerous PUNS, Komunyakaa uses the IMAGE of the reflective black walls to represent black America's conflicted ambivalence toward the war, which claimed a statistically unbalanced number of African-American soldiers' lives and drained significant financial resources from President Johnson's War on Poverty. In Komunyakaa's poem, whoever faces the granite becomes a part of it, just as anyone who confronts the history of the Vietnam War must become emotionally involved with it. The resulting layers of images reveal that, however traumatic, the experience of Vietnam offers its survivors a common ground that might help resolve the racial differences that haunted the war. Yet to achieve this common ground, one must learn how to hold the multiple, unrelated images together, to read between the lines of the names of the dead, to make sense of the memorial, and thus of America's recent history, as a whole.

"Facing It" is the final poem in Komunyakaa's collection *Dien Cai Dau* (a Vietnamese expression for American G.I.s meaning "crazy"), which explores the conflicted African-American experience of the Vietnam War. The poem is built upon a series of puns and ambiguities, the double meanings serving as a linguistic parallel for the double image created by the memorial's walls, those double images themselves serving as metaphors for Komunyakaa's ambivalent attitude about the Vietnam War and about America itself. "My black face fades, / hiding inside the black granite," Komunyakaa begins, introducing the first of many puns on blackness and whiteness. From the start, the African-American speaker finds his black face simultaneously contained in the wall (suggesting that racial identity cannot be ignored when reflecting upon Vietnam), lightened by contrast with the deep black granite (a figure for the common experience the speaker shares with white veterans), and reduced or weakened (made pale and ghostlike). If the speaker is literally to "face it," he must hold together these opposing values and acknowledge their authenticity and their interconnections; as Vicente F. Gotera observes, "This is what Vietnam poetry . . . *must* do—enlighten, give light, illuminate, the better for all to see and see well" (298).

Looking into the memorial's surface, which is engraved with the names of the dead servicemen and servicewomen from Vietnam, the speaker sees reflected all the individuals wandering through the memorial, including the memories of his fallen comrades and the present image of himself. Gotera notes that this mirror imaging makes the poem "literally a reflection about reflections; it is a 'facing' of the dualities that govern this everyday life: there and here, America and Vietnam, living and dead, night and day, old and young, white and black" (298). Like the reflections, Komunyakaa's puns multiply as the poem progresses, so that when "A white vet's image floats / closer to me, then his pale eyes / look through mine," one cannot determine if the vet is attempting to understand Komunyakaa's racialized perspective or simply attempting to ignore Komunyakaa and avoid his ambivalent judgment of the war and of America.

Ultimately, Komunyakaa suggests, the only way to recover from the Vietnam War and the racial conflicts of the era in which it occurred is to "face it," but such an act is double-sided, just as the poem's title is itself a pun. To face the war is to confront its ugliness and suffering, but also to stand opposite that period of history in which it occurred and so recognize oneself as separate from it (as facing the wall implies). Komunyakaa's artistic achievement is not in resolving the conflict the title implies, but in embracing its paradox as the only legitimate way to authenticate and yet grow beyond the contradictions of the American experience. The final, ambiguous image registers the intellectual and psychological complexity of such a position. The speaker sees in the reflective surface that "a woman's trying to erase names," then corrects himself: "No, she's brushing a boy's hair." As Alvin Aubert argues, "(T)he closure of the poem posits redemption only as a future possibility . . . [ending] on a note of hope in the interaction between the woman, presumably a war widow, and her young son, in gestures that suggest that life must go on" (71). But to earn this hope, Komunyakaa suggests, one cannot relinquish understanding of racial prejudice and its brutal consequences, and thus one must always live in a dual state, never being lured by false hope, never being crushed by despair: "No tears. / I'm stone. I'm flesh."

BIBLIOGRAPHY

Aubert, Alvin. "Rare Instances of Reconciliation." *Epoch* 38, no. 1 (1989): 67–72.

Gotera, Vina F. "Depending on the Light: Yusef Komunyakaa's *Dien Cai Dau*." In *America Rediscovered: Essays on Literature and Film of the Vietnam War,* edited by Owen W. Gilman, Jr. and Lorrie Smith, 282–300. New York: Garland Publishing, 1990.

Temple Cone

"FALLING" JAMES DICKEY (1967) James Dickey wrote his hallucinatory and sublime "Falling" after reading two articles in the *New York Times* about a 29-year-old airline stewardess who fell to her death when the plane's emergency door accidentally opened. The poem dramatizes the woman's experience as she plummets earthward, capturing her thoughts and depicting through a series of metaphors her spiritual transformation as she comes to terms with her quickening death. Featuring the FREE VERSE "split line" that Dickey developed in his National Book Award–winning volume *Buckdancer's Choice* (1967) as a way of breaking from the tight formalism of his early verse, the poem produced more reader mail when it was published in the *New Yorker* than any poem its poetry editor, Howard Moss, had published (Hart, 368). Ultimately, "Falling" confirms Dickey's persistent faith in the human imagination to confront any crisis, even death, and by transforming it, save the individual self.

While the poem's narrative traces the woman's descent, from the moment before the accident to the moment her broken body dies, each stanza describes a stage of spiritual growth running counter to what Robert Kirschten calls "the tragic journalistic narrative" (148) suggested by the epigraph from the *Times* article. Dickey entwines these physical and spiritual narratives, revealing his thematic focus on the individual's rebirth through confrontation with mortality, a theme running through much of his poetry and suggested by the title of his commercially successful novel *Deliverance* (1970). Dickey first describes the boredom of the airline flight, then the accident and the stewardess's terror at the start of her high-atmosphere fall. This terror is replaced by an expansive serenity brought on by her acceptance of death as she finds "more and more breath in what she has been using / For breath." As she descends through the clouds, Dickey describes her metaphorical transformation into a bird of prey, with "the long-range vision of hawks enlarging all human lights of cars / Freight trains looped bridges enlarging the moon racing slowly."

In the middle of the poem, the woman begins imagining ways that she might survive by falling in water, and Dickey, almost comically, supplies her with an image drawn from his past experience as an advertisement writer for Coke: the woman will "insert her feet into water like a needle to come out healthily dripping

/ And be handed a Coca-Cola." When she first sees Kansas, Dickey describes her as a nature goddess who inspires the women below her, but this apotheosis is countered by her realization that there is no water anywhere for her to land. Despite a momentary loss of hope, the woman chooses to embrace the fullness of this moment in her life. In a scene labeled as objectifying by a few feminist critics but praised as mystical and unifying by most other critics and scholars, she strips off all her clothes and experiences a moment of erotic and spiritual self-possession as she caresses her body the moment before she crashes. After the crash, Dickey contemplates the sense of mystery that her death will instill in others, and while her clothes fall to earth, he evokes the spiritual expansiveness of the woman's last sensations as her body dies.

While debate over "Falling" has tended to focus on whether Dickey represents the stewardess as a passive victim or a powerful, visionary goddess, fuller discussions attend to the ways that time is perceived in the poem. Throughout her free fall, Dickey repeats that "There is time" and "There is still time" for the woman to embrace her life even as it ends, an intensification that inverts the fatigue of T. S. ELIOT's "THE LOVE SONG OF J. ALFRED PRUFROCK," where the speaker whispers almost wearily that "There will be time." Dickey himself claims he was interested in the experience of lived, as opposed to chronological, time described by the French philosopher Henri Bergson, whose ideas about the associative imagination profoundly influenced the modernist poets, and to an extent, the associative patterns of word clusters in Dickey's own split lines (see MODERNISM). Thus, although the woman's fall reportedly took less than a minute, the length of "Falling" suggests an intense experience of great duration. Working with these different senses of time, John Vernon concludes that time in "Falling" is a paradoxical union of opposites, in which such experiences as death and growth, falling and rising, helplessness and power, are not reduced but experienced most fully by their proximity to one another. Thus, although Dickey suggests the horror of this accident when he writes that the woman is "falling living beginning to be something / That no one has ever been and lived through," he also calls upon the language of mysticism to evoke an experience of spiritual rebirth.

BIBLIOGRAPHY

Dickey, James. *Self-Interviews.* Recorded and edited by Barbara and James Reiss. Garden City, N.Y.: Dell Publishing Co., 1970.

Ellmann, Mary. *Thinking about Women.* New York: Harcourt, Brace Jovanovich, 1968.

Hart, Henry. *James Dickey: The World as a Lie.* New York: Picador USA, 2000.

Kirschten, Robert. "Form and Genre in James Dickey's 'Falling': The Great Goddess Gives Birth to the Earth." *South Atlantic Review* 58, no. 2 (1993): 127–154.

Vernon, John. *The Garden and the Map: Schizophrenia in Twentieth-Century Literature and Culture.* Urbana: University of Illinois Press, 1973.

Temple Cone

FEARING, KENNETH (1902–1961)

"No other American poet speaks to us more directly and consistently about the era of the Great Depression," the critic Sy Kahn has written about Kenneth Fearing (134). A product of his times, his poetry reflects the circumstantial and emotional history of depression-era culture. Certain adjectives consistently describe Fearing's work: dark, ironic, urbane, and satirical. A prominent rebel poet in the 1930s and 1940s, as well as a novelist, Fearing named Walt Whitman as a major influence (Barnard 47), and many associate his later poems with the conventions of CARL SANDBURG and the high modernist style (see MODERNISM) of T. S. ELIOT (Ryley xxix–xxx).

Fearing was born in Oak Park, Illinois. After almost completing a degree at the University of Wisconsin (he was later awarded an honorary degree), he moved to New York and supported himself through freelance writing, largely using a pseudonym and writing pulp fiction for magazines. Later, however, he garnered acclaim for his seven books of poetry and eight novels, one of which, *The Big Clock* (1946), became a national best seller and a hit movie. He gained critical success for his poetry with his second collection, *Poems* (1935). Awarded Guggenheim Fellowships in 1936 and 1939, he also received an American Academy of Arts and Letters Award in 1940.

Often using 1930s slang and pop-culture images, Fearing centers his poems on city life, deception, capitalism, and the demoralization of modern people. His work has been described as "hard-boiled" (Barnard 43); he was often regarded as a communist poet, but his family has attested that Fearing was not political, and when questioned by the Federal Bureau of Investigation (FBI), Fearing denied being a member of the party (Ryley xx).

Fearing recorded images he saw around him, whether they were of taxis, subways, and billboards or breadlines, money-lenders, and crooked politicians. He, like Whitman, spoke for the common person, using a simple vocabulary and long, all-encompassing lines that display a prosy, distinctly American style. Fearing differs from Whitman, however, in tone. While Whitman's poems are songs of hope, Fearing's are of loss and desperation. For Fearing, the America that Whitman painted with such promise had become a corrupt wasteland.

Ultimately, in poems like "Devil's Dream" (1938), Fearing helps readers deal with the impossible circumstances of their individual and universal tragedies: "Because it is not, will not, never could be true / That the whole bright, green, warm, calm world goes: / CRASH." Despite Fearing's pessimism, during his time, his poetry was popular and far-reaching; he reflected the pain, struggle, and physical and emotional hunger of an entire generation.

BIBLIOGRAPHY

Barnard, Rita. *The Great Depression and the Culture of Abundance: Kenneth Fearing, Nathanael West, and Mass Culture in the 1930s.* New York: Cambridge University Press, 1995.

Kahn, Sy. "Kenneth Fearing and the Twentieth Century Blues." In *The Thirties: Fiction, Poetry, Drama,* edited by Warren French, 133–140. Deland, Fla.: E. Edwards, 1967.

Ryley, Robert M. Introduction to *Kenneth Fearing: Complete Poems.* Orono, Maine: National Poetry Foundation, 1994.

Kelly D. Whiddon

FELDMAN, IRVING (1928–) Irving Feldman remains a poet's poet, although much of his work, while thorny, is not beyond the intelligent reader. Influences on him include William Butler Yeats and Rainer Maria Rilke, their solemnity later tempered by Jules Laforgue and Tristan Corbiere ("Conversation"). But Feldman has remained his own poet. The very idea of a school of poetry is "repugnant" to him, he explains, and as the diversity of his work shows, he finds it difficult even "to join himself" ("Conversation"). His earlier work is delicately lyrical, as exemplified by the metaphysical poem "X" (1972), but the later work has a rugged thoughtfulness. Feldman can write about anything: a quarrel, baseball, smoking cigarettes, Nazi atrocities. All of his work, as he puts it in *Teach Me, Dear Sister* (1983) is "required, requested, rich / in society, in obligations." The poet stands apart to observe, but is still bound—uncomfortably, fretfully—by myriad ties to the rest of life.

Feldman was born in Brooklyn, New York, to a working-class Jewish family. He began teaching at the State University of New York, Buffalo, in 1964. Among his most important works are *New and Selected Poems* (1979), *The Life and Letters* (1994), and *Beautiful Dead Things* (2000). He was twice nominated for a National Book Award.

The titles of Feldman's poems—"Assimilation," "The Nurses," "Family History," "Genealogies," "The Human Circle" and of his books *Teach Me, Dear Sister* (1983) and *All of Us Here* (1986)—point to this poet's insistence on the primary importance of human relations in his work. Many of these poems derive their significant metaphors from our exchanges, inventions, interactions, as well as from our dramas and their consequences. In "The Heir" (1979), for example, a bereaved son is trying to replace his own heart with that of his dead father; he struggles with the corpse that "sits up and shouts at him 'You idiot / do you know how to do anything right?'" The painful conversation continues with the son accepting his "father's dead heart, commonplace, appalling," while the father's "misery and maiming / return in the son's chest to their brutal beating." Many of the poems in *Beautiful Dead Things,* "Bad Brunch," for example, describe the perimeters of male-female relations.

The fine collection *All of Us Here,* as its title indicates, reveals the same insistence on the primary importance of man relating to man, to woman, woman to child, each to each. In "They Say to Us" (1986), a family is looking at a stack of photographs, "the living and the dead who mingle here / as nowhere else." To Feldman, "This ritual is profound, / solemn, religious—

'those who participate feel themselves' weighty" and are "judicious, like gods." In his work Feldman "continually engages the problems of the human condition" (Schweizer 42).

BIBLIOGRAPHY

Feldman, Irving. Conversation with Nikki Stiller. New York City, N.Y., 6 January 2002.

Schweizer, Harold, ed. *The Poetry of Irving Feldman*. Lewisberg, Penn.: Bucknell University Press, 1992.

Nikki Stiller

FEMALE VOICE, FEMALE LANGUAGE

The ascribing of a specific meaning in American poetics to female voice and female language coincided with the emergence of the American second-wave feminist movement. Although this movement had important poetic precursors—poets such as ELIZABETH BISHOP, H. D., AMY LOWELL, MINA LOY, and MARIANNE MOORE had long been concerned with questions surrounding gender and the role of the woman poet—attention to the specifics of a female voice and a female language gained real critical and creative momentum in the postwar period. The second-wave feminist movement, heralded by the publication of such works as Betty Friedan's *The Feminine Mystique* in 1963, brought about profound changes in American society's organization of, and attitude toward, gender difference. Feminist critics and activists resisted the division between public and private and exposed the patriarchal assumptions that supported a broad host of male-dominated cultural practices in the workplace, the family, education, religion, medicine, and sexuality. The discovery of a woman's individual voice and the production of a collective woman's language were both vital to these processes. One of the first woman poets to be identified with this historical and aesthetic moment was MURIEL RUKESYER, whose influential poem "The Poem as Mask" (1968) articulated the divisions—"myself, split open, unable to / speak, in exile from myself"—that the discovery of a woman's voice and language was intended to heal.

This emergence of a female voice in American poetry can be traced to three broader shifts in post–World War II American poetics. First feminist poetry was assisted by the move in American poetics toward open form and free verse. The poet ADRIENNE RICH famously described how her early work was written with the "asbestos gloves" of formal constraints that she eventually had to discard in order to find a voice and a language that could speak "to and of women" in poems written from a "newly released courage to name, to love each other, to share risk, and grief and celebration" (176). The need for this voice is suggested by the angry frustrations of such poems as Rich's 1968 "The Burning of Paper Instead of Children," which ends with an inelegant faltering—"the typewriter is overheated, my mouth is burning, I cannot touch you and this is the oppressor's language." Rich demonstrates the productive possibilities of a female language in the fluid and tender eroticism of "Twenty-One Love Poems" (1977), which frankly articulates lesbian desire. Rich was also an influential figure for combining poetic writing with prose and feminist theory, and her critical work includes seminal essays, such as "Of Woman Born" (1976) and "Compulsory Heterosexuality and Lesbian Existence" (1980).

The second important influence on the development of a feminist poetics in the late early 1950s and early 1960s was the increased attention paid to the role of the poets themselves within their poems. SYLVIA PLATH and ANNE SEXTON worked with the poet ROBERT LOWELL in the mid-1950s and were influenced by his move, in the collection *Life Studies* (1959), toward what has been since labeled CONFESSIONAL POETRY. Sexton and Plath provided intimate and painful insights into the visceral frustrations and contradictions of midcentury femininity in marriage, motherhood, sexuality, and poetic ambition. Plath's posthumously published collection, *ARIEL* (1965), was influential for its rendering of the psychological struggle for a female voice. In poems such as "Ariel," "LADY LAZARUS," and "DADDY," the authorial voice is forged from a fusion of the extremes of femininity. The sexualized climax of the poem "Fever 103," for example, describes the poet as a "pure acetylene / Virgin / attended by roses." The combination of autobiographical honesty and open form that these poets pioneered for a feminist poetics is evident in the work of later poets, such as LOUISE GLÜCK and SHARON OLDS.

The third development in American poetry that contributed to the development of a female voice was the changes in the public circulation of poetry, initiated by movements such as BEAT writing in the 1950s and then by the antiwar and Civil Rights movements in the 1960s. These movements, within which women poets, such as DIANE DI PRIMA and DENISE LEVERTOV, were active, highlighted the public possibilities of contemporary poetry through readings, performances, and the distribution of broadsides and small POETRY JOURNALS. Feminist poetry, in such works as Judy Grahn's *The Common Woman* (1978), sought to use the female voice in poetry as a basis for the collective empowerment of a female audience. Women's poetry was important in these contexts, as Kim Whitehead has recently suggested in *The Feminist Poetry Movement,* for its direct contribution to the public life of the feminist movement as it sought to become a site of cultural production. Whitehead demonstrates the ways in which feminist poetry's sensitivity to the "matrix" of poetic meaning allowed it to serve "as a kind of political clarion call to women to take notice and take action; the consciousness-raising groups and organising cells of radical feminism proved to be especially fertile grounds for preparing women to hear this call" (18).

The development of a female voice and a female language in poetry has received much critical attention from a growing academic community of feminist writers and theorists. In the 1970s and 1980s critics, such as Suzanne Juhasz and Alicia Ostriker, read the possession of a female voice in poetry—defying what Juhasz described as the double-bind of the woman poet: "if she is a 'woman' she must fail as a poet; 'poet' she must fail as 'woman'"—as both deeply subversive of the masculine norms of American poetics and as affirming of the alternative possibilities of women (3). These critics were also important for constructing, along with anthologizers, such as Florence Howe, a genealogy and critical tradition for the female voice that was able to incorporate retrospectively the work of earlier poets such as H. D., Emily Dickinson, and Anne Bradstreet. This largely celebratory critical tradition examined the way in which the voice of women poets was used to breach the cultural silences about female anger, female sexuality, sexuality and body, motherhood, and domesticity. A second generation of academic critics, such as Jan Montefiore, drew upon the emerging field of poststructuralist theory in order to examine the relationship between women's poetry and the disruptive presence of the "feminine" in language. This shift involved moving away from examining the role of women's poetry in the feminist movement to examining, instead, the philosophical nature of the relationship between language and the subject speaking or being spoken of.

By the mid-1980s, however, feminist critics had begun to question the implications of feminist assumptions about what constituted a female voice or language. The models of identity politics that assumed gender to be either an inherent or homogenous characteristic were gradually reproached for their essentialist implications—for assuming, to cite an example, that women possessed inherent biologically determined characteristics. In addition to this, models of poetry based on the text, rather than on the voice, began to receive increased critical attention.

The first of these concerns was most clearly articulated by feminist critics seeking to make apparent the implicit racial exclusions of the feminist movement, which had failed to consider sufficiently the distinct experiences of women of color. The work of such poets as GWENDOLYN BROOKS, LUCILLE CLIFTON, NIKKI GIOVANNI, AUDRE LORDE, JUNE JORDAN, and SONIA SANCHEZ questioned, in a variety of ways, the assumptions about form, self, community, and gender that had been prevalent in the feminist poetry movement. Although many of these poets were committed to this movement, their commitment was often complicated by an identification with the Civil Rights and BLACK ARTS MOVEMENTS that emphasized both an alternative set of political priorities and an alternative deployment of voice and language in literature. Jordan's work was influential for creatively exploiting and reconciling the tensions between her feminist perspective and her fidelity to an African-American oral tradition. Poems such as "Getting Down to Get Over" (1973) disrupt narrative and identification in their emphasis upon the complexities of a woman speaker occupying a variety of culturally specific oral registers. Alternatively Chicana poets, such as Gloria Anzaldua and LORNA DEE CERVANTES, drew attention to the bilingual and interlingual pressures upon an American female voice. Texts, such as

Anzaldua's *Borderlands* (1987), written in English and Spanish, highlight the limitations of the monolingual assumptions upon which much "American" speech-based poetry was predicated.

Feminist experimental writing in the 1980s and 1990s often emphasized the idea that a female voice and language implied an overly simple understanding of language itself. This writing, which emphasized the complicated meanings available in written language rather than the assumed simplicity of its spoken form, claimed an alternative tradition of feminist poets, one that included modernists, such as GERTRUDE STEIN, and OBJECTIVISTS, such as LORINE NIEDECKER. These poets, often associated with the LANGUAGE SCHOOL, included RAE ARMANTROUT, RACHEL BLAU DUPLESSIS, KATHLEEN FRASER, CARLA HARRYMAN, LYN HEJINIAN, SUSAN HOWE, and LESLIE SCALAPINO. These poets share an interest in understanding gender and femininity as things constructed by society rather than as foundations that can be "discovered" through a female voice or language. This writing often relinquished a concern with either the lyrical "I" or the processes of *feminine écriture* in favor of a more fragmented writing style that was intended to explore the multiple meanings available in language. This writing required readers to be engaged actively in the production of meaning, to pay attention to the visual and material aspects of language, and to question the meaning and assumptions supporting narrative and identification. Hejinian's book-length poem *My Life* (1987) became one of the most successful examples of this. This lengthy poem, in which each stanza corresponds to a year of the poet's life, complicates poetic autobiography's reliance on narrative and lyrical self-knowledge by stressing the physicality, the patterning, and the unreliability of memory. At the same time this attention to the sensuality of memory, suggested in repeated phrases, such as "a pause, a rose, something on paper," enriches what this form can be assumed to contain. The scrutiny given in such experimental writing to the politics of representations of women in a variety of social and historical contexts means that, despite its controversial relationship to many of the assumptions about second-wave feminist poetry, it remains committed to many of the aims of the women's movement as they have developed during the past 30 years.

BIBLIOGRAPHY

Juhasz, Suzanne. *Naked and Fiery Forms: Modern American Poetry by Women, a New Tradition.* New York: Harper & Row, 1976.

Montefiore, Jan. *Feminism and Poetry: Language, Experience, Identity in Women's Writing.* London: Pandora, 1987.

Ostriker, Alicia. *Stealing the Language: The Emergence of Women's Poetry in America.* Boston: Beacon Press, 1986.

Rich, Adrienne. *Adrienne Rich's Poetry and Prose,* edited by Albert Gelpi. New York: W. W. Norton, 1993.

Simpson, Megan. *Poetic Epistemologies: Gender and Knowing in Women's Language-Orientated Writing.* Albany: State University of New York Press, 2000.

Whitehead, Kim. *The Feminist Poetry Movement.* Jackson: University Press of Mississippi, 1996.

Nicky Marsh

FERLINGHETTI, LAWRENCE (1919–)

Lawrence Ferlinghetti is significant to the development of 20th-century American poetry as both a poet and publisher. He opened the San Francisco bookstore and publisher City Lights Books in 1953 in partnership with Peter Martin and bought Martin's interest in the business in 1955, the same year he published his own first book; by then, he had developed "a unique style, owing more to E. E. CUMMINGS and KENNETH PATCHEN than either T. S. ELIOT or EZRA POUND, his great influences of the 1940's" (Cherkovski 83). His publisher in the future was to be James Laughlin at New Directions, an avant-garde publishing house on the East Coast as City Lights was on the West (see POETRY PRESSES). Through KENNETH REXROTH, Ferlinghetti met other artists and writers, with whom he became part of the SAN FRANCISCO RENAISSANCE. Among his notable editorial decisions at City Lights were to publish ALLEN GINSBERG'S *HOWL and Other Poems,* which resulted in an infamous and successfully defended obscenity trial, Ginsberg's *KADDISH and Other Poems,* and GREGORY CORSO'S *Gasoline,* each a major work of midcentury American poetry. Ferlinghetti strove to extend the City Lights list beyond BEAT and San Francisco Renaissance works, and therefore he also published translations of new poetry from around the world.

Born in Yonkers, New York, Ferlinghetti had an early childhood fraught with upheaval. His father died before Lawrence, the youngest of five sons, was born.

His birth mother broke down under the difficulties she faced and was institutionalized for a number of years. Separated from his brothers, Ferlinghetti was subsequently abandoned without warning by his foster mother and left in the care of her employers. Thomas Wolfe's literary appeal led Ferlinghetti to choose Wolfe's alma mater, the University of North Carolina, for his postsecondary education, and he graduated with a bachelor's degree in 1941. After naval service in World War II, he earned a master's degree from Columbia in 1947 and a Ph.D. at the Sorbonne in 1949. His dissertation examined "The City as a Symbol in Modern Poetry," and urban geography is a significant figure in Ferlinghetti's creative work.

His poetry consistently considers his personal and public concerns: identity and society. Ferlinghetti, like many poets of the postwar period, discovered the therapeutic value of writing his way through personal experiences as a means to understanding himself and his world, and his background provided him with an abundance of material to be resolved. "A chief subject of Ferlinghetti's poetry is often Ferlinghetti himself" (Skau 52), a statement applicable to the work of virtually every other writer who emerged in the same period. Ferlinghetti's social and political activism, as well as his commitment to and participation in the arts, received numerous acknowledgments. In 1998 he was declared poet laureate of San Francisco, while City Lights Bookstore has been granted historic landmark status. His list of recognitions for lifetime achievement includes the American Book Award (1998), the National Book Critics Circle Ivan Sandrof Award (1999), and the American Civil Liberties Union's (ACLU) Earl Warren Civil Liberties Award (1999).

Urban people, their sounds and issues, populate Ferlinghetti's poetic cityscapes. He explains that "The Long Street" (1959) "passes around the world / filled with all the people of the world." Colloquial speech, set in a consciously constructed musical background occasionally represented by idiosyncratic arrangement of lines across the page, addresses fundamental concerns of the poet's social conscience: the abuse of political and economic power. Ferlinghetti reveals an anarchist ideology and a tireless social and ecological activism. He saw the upheaval of the 1960s as a possible route to a solution of these social ills, particularly the dissolution of the system of nations (Cherkovski 181); one of the appealing features of 1960s radicalism was liberated sex, and "sex is a major process and product in Ferlinghetti's view of a transformed social order" (Skau 12).

These goals are conflated in his 1965 poem "The Situation in the West, Followed by a Holy Proposal," in which he declares "blessed be the fruit of transcopulation" and "blessed be the fucking world with no more nations." In Ferlinghetti's work there is a real hope in the strength of human energy, real "Wild Dreams of a New Beginning" (1988). His literary body of work includes his novel *Her* (1960); a collection of short plays titled *Routines* (1964); travel writings from journeys to Italy, France, and Mexico; translations of French and Italian poetry; and a dozen books of his own "little charleychaplin man" poetry, as he termed it in the poem "Constantly risking absurdity" (1958), starting with *Pictures of the Gone World* (1955) through to *How to Paint Sunlight* (2001).

Ferlinghetti paints, writes, speaks, and works in order to keep corruption from finding a place to hide and to provide beauty and conscience with a voice.

BIBLIOGRAPHY

Cherkovski, Neeli. *Ferlinghetti: A Biography*. Garden City, N.Y.: Doubleday, 1979.
Silesky, Barry. *Ferlinghetti: The Artist and His Time*. New York: Warner, 1990.
Skau, Michael. *'Constantly Risking Absurdity': The Writings of Lawrence Ferlinghetti*. Troy, N.Y.: Whitston, 1989.
Smith, Larry R. *Lawrence Ferlinghetti, Poet-at-Large*. Carbondale: Southern Illinois University Press, 1983.

A. Mary Murphy

FINCH, ANNIE (RIDLEY CRANE) (1956–)

Annie Finch is important to several traditions of writing outside MODERNIST free verse and its descendants (see PROSODY AND FREE VERSE), and she is often associated with NEW FORMALISM and women's poetry (see FEMALE VOICE, FEMALE LANGUAGE). Her formal verse emphasizes direct, unmediated relationships between a poetic self and the world over the complex and ambivalent attitudes toward knowledge, self, and language favored in much contemporary poetry. Poems about seasonal events, life cycles, relationships, and the interpenetration of the natural and the cosmic draw upon the often overlooked tradition of American women poets, including Emily Dickinson, SARA TEASDALE, and CAROLYN KIZER.

Born in New Rochelle, New York, Finch earned a B.A. from Yale University, an M.F.A. from the University of Houston, and a Ph.D. in English from Stanford. She has published two books of poetry, *Eve* (1997) and *Calendars* (2002), as well as critical studies, including *The Ghost of Meter: Culture and Prosody in American Free Verse* (1993), *An Exaltation of Forms* (2002, with Kathrine Varnes), and *New Formal Poets* (2003, with Susan Schultz). The founder and moderator of WOM-PO, a national internet listserv on women's poetry, Finch once remarked that her scholarship is motivated by her need to create a critical context for women's poetry (135). She has taught at Miami University in Ohio.

Finch's poetry combines her interests in the feminine and in form. For example, in *Eve,* poems such as "Running in Church," use an array of poetic forms, from chants to triple meters in order to invoke patterns and traditions of female power. Here the lines, "You made the long corridors ring, tintinnabular / echoes exploring the pounded cold floor," employ dactylic rhythms to emphasize a free feminine presence within the church's patriarchic, constrained space. In *Calendars* this interest in the feminine manifests in an attention to the interpenetration of natural seasons and major life events. From "A Wedding on Earth" to "Belly," a poem to her unborn child, Finch infuses fresh feeling into occasional verse while embracing such poetry's domestic and communal function. "Elegy For My Father" most palpably invokes these themes as it portrays the poet's deceased father merging into the cosmic world: "Night, take his left hand, turning the pages. / Spin with his dry independence, his arms."

Finch's current writing still embraces a female voice but with a new spin. Her poems and essays invoke the sentimental poetry of minor American women writers as a critique of the traditional lyric and its emphasis upon originality and self-expression. Where most critics have dismissed this verse as conventional and artless, Finch tries to reinvent the poetess tradition as an avant-garde postmodern poetry that is as radical and interesting as other contemporary experimental schools.

BIBLIOGRAPHY

Finch, Annie. "Confessions of a Postmodern Poetess." In *By Herself: Women Reclaim Poetry,* edited by Molly McQuade, 213–225. St. Paul, Minn.: Graywolf Press, 2000.

"Finch, A.R.C." *Contemporary Authors New Revision Series* 94, edited by Scot Peacock (2001): 134–137.

Natalie Gerber

FINKEL, DONALD (1929–) Donald Finkel created a voice that combined a New York City street toughness with a classicist's cultural reference and a metaphysician's concern with experience and its implications. His metaphysical bent, along with his early inspiration from jazz and visual art, connect him to the NEW YORK SCHOOL, but he drew away both geographically and thematically. Like ALAN DUGAN, he became a maverick presence on the American poetic landscape, as much defined by his differences from major trends as by his similarities. Finkel himself cites ROBERT FROST as his most important influence ("Conversation").

Born in New York City, Finkel has spent much of his life in the Midwest. After earning a B.S. and M.A. from Columbia University, he attended the University of Iowa Writers Workshop. In 1960 he became poet in residence at Washington University. The author of 14 books of poetry, he has been nominated twice for the National Book Critics Circle Award (1975 and 1981), has been a finalist for the National Book Award (1970), and won the Dictionary of Literary Biography's Yearbook Award in 1994. Finkel's 1991 collection of translations, *A Splintered Mirror: Chinese Poetry from the Democracy Movement,* brought English-speaking readers an important perspective on the Chinese dissident movement of the 1980s.

Finkel's early subject matter included jazz musicians, junkies, and St. Simeon Stylites, the fifth-century saint whose 40 years on top of a pillar provided Finkel with a hero for his second book, *Simeon* (1964), in which he introduced the technique of building a long narrative or character study through series of connected lyric poems. With his fourth book, *Answer Back*

(1968), he would add another element to his lyric-narratives, that of found lines. As with his earlier street tough-classicist melange, Finkel now began the collaging of lines from philosophy, science, popular culture, and, in the case of *Answer Back,* correspondence with a prisoner, with his own tightly crafted, image-rich voice.

The subjects of Finkel's lyric sequences include cave exploration, experiments in communicating with primates, and a bizarre round-the-world sail that never went anywhere. Perhaps the unifying subject of all of these is a meditation on the limits of our humanity. A trip to the South Pole in 1970, as part of a scientific expedition, produced Finkel's most arresting subject, and most powerful extended metaphor, in *Adequate Earth* (1972) and "Endurance" (1978), about the Ernest Shackleton expedition to the pole. Finkel has recently addressed issues of aging in "A Question of Seeing" (1998) and "Burden" (2001), which describes a poet's descent into Alzheimer's "as if words were the burden / he'd been bearing, all his life."

BIBLIOGRAPHY

Cargas, Harry James. "Interview with Constance Urdang and Donald Finkel." *Webster Review* 1, no. 2 (1974): 57–70.

Howard, Richard. *Alone with America: Essays on the Art of Poetry in the United States since 1950.* New York: Atheneum, 1980, pp. 158–175.

Richards, Tad. Telephone Conversation with Donald Finkel, Saugerties, N.Y.: 7 August 2002.

Tad Richards

"THE FISH" ELIZABETH BISHOP (1946) "The Fish," one of ELIZABETH BISHOP's best-known poems, first appeared in her collection *North and South* (1946). With its detailed descriptions of an animal, "The Fish" displays the influence of MARIANNE MOORE, who herself has a poem titled "The FISH," but its strategy of anecdotal first-person narration resembles not Moore's MODERNISM, but instead the lyrics of Bishop's midcentury contemporary ROBERT LOWELL.

Bishop begins with the simple statement, "I caught a tremendous fish"; on its most basic level, the poem recounts catching, observing, and releasing a fish. Like much of Bishop's poetry, however, straightforward tone begs deeper investigation. "The Fish" contains 76 lines of meticulous, inventive description, such as how the fish's "skin hung in strips / like ancient wallpaper" and its eyes resemble "old scratched isinglass." The speaker pores over this battered creature with a painter's sight and helps the reader to see many strange and wonderful details.

The poem is not only about the fish, however; it is also about the speaker who has caught it. In the first half of the poem, she appears to be masterfully in control of her situation. Her actions are denoted by simple verbs, such as "I caught," which suggest a detached perspective on the situation, contrasted by the fish, which "hung a grunting weight" and is infested with parasites. In the second half of the poem, there is a shift in tone. The verbs used for the speaker now suggest her psychology: She "admired" the fish and "stared and stared" at it. Here the speaker looks, just as before, but she looks because something about the fish compels involuntary fascination. The fish has a "weapon-like" lower lip from which hang "five old pieces of fishing line," which tells us that the fish has been hooked five times before but has always survived. The fish is a battle-scarred warrior. The speaker no longer merely observes the fish, but she also admires it.

At the end of the poem, the boat fills with a sense of "victory" as the "rainbow" of oil on the water seems to spread everywhere. The speaker lets the fish go. Her sense of "victory" stems not from catching the fish, which happens at the start of the poem, but from a change that occurred during her meditations on it. As Willard Spiegelman argues, victory does not come from "the elimination, or conquest, of the enemy, but the embracing, subsuming, and internalizing of him" (110). The poem represents an epiphany about beauty, heroism, and the ethics of aesthetic sensitivity.

BIBLIOGRAPHY

Costello, Bonnie. *Elizabeth Bishop: Questions of Mastery.* Cambridge, Mass.: Harvard University Press, 1991.

Spiegelman, Willard. "Elizabeth Bishop's 'Natural Heroism.'" In *Elizabeth Bishop,* edited by Harold Bloom. New York: Chelsea House, 1985.

Ben Johnson

"THE FISH" MARIANNE MOORE (1918) A prominent figure in imagism (see IMAGIST SCHOOL), MARIANNE MOORE relies on carefully constructed images to convey an idea or a feeling. In "The Fish" she develops stunning visual imagery that, on the surface, describes an undersea world while, on a deeper level, also represents ideas as diverse as language's complexities, the poet as observer, and the power and endurance of the sea.

The poem depicts with precision the vitality of the undersea world, examining with detached observation how life and light interact to reveal all that is seemingly invisible beneath the surface of the sea. "The Fish" has been widely celebrated for its aesthetics by such poets as T. S. ELIOT, WALLACE STEVENS, and DONALD HALL, but readers differ widely in their analysis of its meaning. Darlene Williams Erickson observes, "Moore seems to lead her readers to ambiguity. Like the abstract painter, she demands that her audience participate in the lines, turning them slowly until meaning takes shape within the parameters of her images" (136–137). Individual readers themselves must perform the work of wading into the sea of Moore's overwhelmingly visual images.

As with so many of her poems, Moore revised "The Fish" at least three times, experimenting with line length and syllabic meter. First written in 1918, "The Fish" was composed of six lines with syllables distributed according to a 1,3,8,1,6,8 pattern. In her revision of the poem 12 years later, Moore condensed each stanza to five lines with a 1,3,9,6,8 syllabic pattern and an *aabbc* rhyme scheme, thus dramatically reshaping the layout of the poem to enact more visually the swelling waves of the sea. Hugh Kenner describes these as "little intricate grids of visual symmetry" and remarks: "It is a poem to see with the eye, conceived in a typewriter upon an 8 ½ × 11 sheet of paper" (18). A distinctly modernist poem (see MODERNISM), "The Fish" creates an image with both form and content for the eye to track, and as a result it relies as much upon the reader's sight as upon the music of the language.

However, Moore guides the reader into subsurface depths by blurring the boundary between title and poem. The verb *wade,* which opens the poem, literally invites readers to enter into an exploration of the image. Once in the poem, readers, like the fish and like the poet, glide through a catalogue of visual undersea images, the poet's language illuminating the unseen world of the sea like the sunlight that moves "with spotlight swiftness / into the crevices." These images of light and motion are balanced by the rocky "defiant" cliff, whose presence suggests both a terrible power and the will to endure. Yet the images maintain an ambiguity characteristic of Moore's poetry and elude formulaic decoding. "The poem pretends that it works visually," Taffy Martin notes, "whereas it should warn readers that images in poems are not always what they seem to be" (95). Ultimately the paradox of "The Fish" is that it invokes the visible even as it explores, both literally and metaphorically, that which evades sight.

BIBLIOGRAPHY

Erickson, Darlene Williams. *Illusion Is More Precise than Precision: The Poetry of Marianne Moore.* Tuscaloosa: University of Alabama Press, 1992.

Kenner, Hugh. "The Experience of the Eye." In *Modern Critical Views: Marianne Moore,* edited by Harold Bloom, 11–24. New York: Chelsea House, 1987.

Martin, Taffy. *Marianne Moore: Subversive Modernist.* Austin: University of Texas Press, 1986.

Terry Lynn Pettinger

FLETCHER, JOHN GOULD (1886–1950)

John Gould Fletcher was a modernist poet from the American South. Because of his experimentation with different subjects and poetic techniques, and because of his affiliation with different poetic movements, his work has been described as religious, mystical, symbolist, impressionist, IMAGIST, and southern FUGITIVE/AGRARIAN. While these classifications may be applied to particular poems or stages of his work, his poetry as a whole suggests a larger goal. Fletcher's understanding of the artist's duty is clear in the following statement from his book on the painter Paul Gauguin: "to affirm the dignity of life, the value of humanity, despite the morbid prejudices of Puritanism, the timid conventionality of the mob, despite even his own knowledge of the insoluble riddle of suffering, decay and death" (180–181). This visionary focus informs all of Fletcher's work.

Fletcher was born in Little Rock, Arkansas. He attended Harvard from 1903 to 1907 and traveled through the American Southwest and Italy before moving to London in 1909. While abroad, he self-published his first five collections of poetry, met many of the imagist poets, including EZRA POUND and AMY LOWELL, and contributed work to the imagist POETRY ANTHOLOGIES. In the late 1920s, while lecturing in the United States, he encountered the southern Fugitive/Agrarian poets JOHN CROWE RANSOM, DONALD DAVIDSON, and ALLEN TATE. His poetry appeared in the *Fugitive* magazine, and he contributed his essay "Education, Past and Present" to the Agrarian anthology, *I'll Take My Stand* (1930). He returned to Arkansas in 1933. Fletcher published 24 books of poetry and prose during his lifetime, and his *Selected Poems* received the 1938 Pulitzer Prize.

Fletcher's poetry underwent many formal shifts during his career. His symbolist-inspired first books contain traditional forms, such as heroic couplets and sonnets, while his imagist poems are usually in free verse and emphasize direct treatment of the poetic subject and concise description (see PROSODY AND FREE VERSE). His religious and philosophical poetry employs elegies and the religious epic, while his final collections combine free verse and traditional forms to address southern Agrarian concerns. In fact elements of southern MODERNISM run throughout his work, although they are most prevalent in his later poems. Consider how he juxtaposes an image of death with images of the natural world in the title poem of *South Star* (1941): "Over the hill where so many men found the dignity to die," winter "Turns over its burning heap of leaves and brown, dried grasses again." Fletcher uses images of nature to mirror "something of the despair and sadness of the Old South and its lost cause" (Stephen 134).

Fletcher's poetry is grounded in his sense of history and the possibilities for the future. While his poetic explorations take many forms, they are always in service to his visionary goals.

BIBLIOGRAPHY

Carpenter, Lucas. *John Gould Fletcher and Southern Modernism.* Fayetteville: University of Arkansas Press, 1990.

Fletcher, John Gould. *Paul Gauguin, His Life and Art.* New York: Brown, 1921.

Stephens, Edna B. *John Gould Fletcher.* New York: Twayne, 1967.

Ce Rosenow

FLOW CHART **JOHN ASHBERY (1991)** In the book-length poem *Flow Chart,* JOHN ASHBERY synthesizes themes typical of his decades-long career: the instability of meaning and of the objective "I," the poet's struggle with his literary predecessors, and mortality. *Flow Chart* especially laments the end of the poet's role as spokesperson for an organized tribe. The aging poet sets himself adrift on a river of language that streams luxuriously and maddeningly toward no end at all, "the plaited lines that extend / like a bronze chain into eternity."

Flow Chart can be read as a postmodern travel narrative. The poem alludes, for example, to the story of Noah's Ark and refers throughout to the theme of "beginning / and something also in the way of returning," thus placing itself within the context of epic travel narratives, including The *Odyssey, The Iliad,* and Dante's *Divine Comedy.* Unlike its predecessors, however, there is no closure offered in *Flow Chart,* as the "river god" never returns to anything resembling home. Most important, the travel that takes place in *Flow Chart* is not so much in the physical world as it is within the interior world of language, meditation, and narcissistic reverie.

Why is this long poem called *Flow Chart*? A flow chart is a diagram that charts the operations of a sequence of events. Thus one can imagine the poem charting the course of a *consciousness* moving on a continually eddying river of language. The metaphor of the flow chart also reestablishes Ashbery's connection with his community of readers, most of whom "have charted his development as a writer with something of the systematic organization of a flow chart" (Moramarco 40).

The knowledgeable reader of Ashbery's "life work" will recognize that, in *Flow Chart* as in his earlier texts, Ashbery is fascinated by what constitutes authorship. Ashbery as an authorial persona appears only to assert that a conception of Ashbery as a reliable presence is impossible: "I called John but he couldn't come to the phone." The author as the determiner of a poem's "meaning" is unavailable here—the reader, holding a phone with no one on the other end, imposes meaning on the text. Ashbery, aware that he does not have the power to transmit a specific meaning via his poetry, acknowledges the crucial role that an almost arbitrary, highly subjective interpretation plays in determining what a poem is about. There is no privileged meaning, as every potential reading of *Flow Chart* multiplies according to how many times one reads or speaks the poem.

The shaky quality of meaning as it is transmitted through language is directly connected to Ashbery's awareness of writing within a tradition, especially a poetic tradition, in which truth is imagined as a real possibility as opposed to merely another social and linguistic construct. The "anxiety of influence"—critic Harold Bloom's theory that states successful writing is determined by an individual poet's heroic rejection of a literary predecessor, or "father" figure—is in effect throughout *Flow Chart*. Ashbery comically acknowledges Bloom, an early and vocal Ashbery supporter, in the line "Should he have been feeling more anxiety? Nah," and he then proceeds to incorporate and struggle with themes specific to predecessor poets.

Poets, including WILLIAM CARLOS WILLIAMS, Walt Whitman, William Blake, and John Keats, are alluded to throughout *Flow Chart*. Whitman (author of *Leaves of Grass*), in particular, is evoked, yet all of the many references Ashbery makes to Whitman's grass insist on portraying the grass as withered. The elegiac tone, while tempered with humor, is unmistakable.

Referring to Whitman's declaration in *Leaves of Grass* that the poet "contain[s] multitudes," Ashbery asks, "But if all space is contained within me, then / there is no place for me to go, I am not even here, and now." The act of assertion for Ashbery is, at the same time, an act of negation. For the postmodern poet, the capacious Whitmanic acts of tallying and encompassing are transformed into ones of gesturing and redistributing. The democratic impulse in Whitman is, in Ashbery, a failed experiment.

Ultimately, though, *Flow Chart* is as much an elegy for the death of what might be called a "collective spirit" as it is an elegy for the aging body. As James McCorkle recognizes in discussing the role of subjectivity in *Flow Chart*, "The awareness of mortality . . . surfaces throughout the poem. . . . The ambiguity of the 'you' persists in the passage from *Flow Chart*, but what it offers is not a strict dispersal or indeterminacy of identities but an inclusiveness or community that faces suffering and a crisis of hope" (111). *Flow Chart* manifests the universal preoccupation with mortality. The poem thus manages, in the best Whitmanic sense, to contradict itself. Even as it muddies the notion that there is a stable author writing the text, *Flow Chart* nevertheless succeeds in foregrounding itself as a work specific to an aging poet.

BIBLIOGRAPHY

Gardner, Thomas. *Regions of Unlikeness: Explaining Contemporary Poetry*. Lincoln: University of Nebraska Press, 1999.

Kevorkian, Martin. "John Ashbery's *Flow Chart:* John Ashbery and the Theorists on John Ashbery Against the Critics Against John Ashbery." *New Literary History* 25 (1994): 459–476.

McCorkle, James. *"Nimbus of Sensations:* Eros and Reverie in the Poetry of John Ashbery and Ann Lauterbach." In *The Tribe of John: Ashbery and Contemporary Poetry,* edited by Susan M. Schultz, 101–125. Tuscaloosa: University of Alabama Press, 1995.

Moramarco, Fred. "Coming Full Circle: John Ashbery's Later Poetry." In *The Tribe of John: Ashbery and Contemporary Poetry,* edited by Susan M. Schultz. Tuscaloosa: University of Alabama Press, 1995, pp. 38–59.

Daniel Kane

"FOR A COMING EXTINCTION" W. S. MERWIN (1967) W. S. Merwin's haunting meditation on extinction and the sense of global environmental crisis in the 1960s, "For a Coming Extinction" features an apocalyptic vision of the vulnerable natural world, though nature is no less valued for being threatened. The poem is written as an apostrophe to the "Gray Whale," a totemic figure for the entire species (which was first listed on the Endangered Species Act in 1970), and it features the carefully lined and unpunctuated free verse that characterizes Merwin's postmodern work. The speaker is a persona whose arrogant tone represents the selfish indifference of the global community toward environmental issues, even issues as devastating as extinction, and the dramatic bleakness of the poem is due in large part to the distance between the voice of this speaker and that of Merwin himself, who has been a lifelong activist. "For a Coming Extinction" is perhaps the bitterest expression of the bleak vision Merwin develops in *The Lice,* a landmark volume that combined aspects of SURREALISM with political protest (on topics like the environment, nuclear escalation, and the Vietnam War).

In her study of Merwin's environmental poetry, *From Origin to Ecology,* Jane Frazier says of this poem and others like it, "Because Merwin is so personally involved with this issue [of the extinction of animals], many of these poems are bitter or ironic in tone. To Merwin, ecological damage must be dealt with in a polemic manner because it is so serious a subject and so irreversible an action" (101). Rather than enduring or even just surviving, the natural world for Merwin is always on the verge of collapse, either through extinction and species eradication or because of imminent nuclear holocaust. The speaker reflects that the disappearance of the whale may bewilder the Creator, perhaps all Creation, but that "The bewilderment will diminish like an echo . . / Leaving behind it the future / Dead." For Merwin, this disruption in the order of nature both reflects and results from a breakdown in the way humans relate to their natural environments, largely due to the increasingly technological character of human life. Merwin underscores this breakdown with the speaker's devastatingly ironic tone, which reflects the discrepancy between the way humans should relate to nature and the way they actually do.

By the end of the poem, Merwin returns his attention to the contemporary topic of the gray whale's looming extinction. He uses this ecological and political crisis to encapsulate his ironic indictment of humankind for creating these massive environmental losses. In the afterlife, the speaker says, the whale will encounter all the creatures humans have eradicated throughout history, as well as those also on their way to extinction: "The sea cows the Great Auks the gorillas." The speaker's arrogance is beyond hubris, for he tells the departing whale to inform the divine Creator "That we who follow you invented forgiveness / And forgive nothing." Clearly Merwin (though not the speaker) broaches the issue of species extinction in order to play upon his audience's environmental concerns, and to push them to forsake the technologically grounded ideology the speaker exhibits for the morally stable platform of ideas upon which the poet himself stands. Moreover, the speaker's supreme arrogance sets him up for a tragic downfall, and by subtle references to an almost inevitable apocalypse, Merwin warns his readers that the speaker's fate will be their own if their Western, technology-centered ideologies are not grounded in a care and devotion to the environment: "I write as though you could understand," the speaker tells the whale and his audience, "One must always pretend something / Among the dying."

BIBLIOGRAPHY

Frazier, Jane. *From Origin to Ecology: Nature and the Poetry of W. S. Merwin.* Madison, N.J.: Fairleigh Dickinson University Press, 1999.

———. "Writing Outside the Self: The Disembodied Narrators of W. S. Merwin." *Style* 30, no. 2 (1996): 341–350.

Temple Cone

"FORK" CHARLES SIMIC **(1971)** One of his most anthologized poems, Charles Simic's brief surrealist lyric "Fork" makes a commonplace household object terrifyingly unfamiliar, startling the reader's attention and restoring to the quotidian world a measure of wonder often dulled by the veneer of habit and ordinary use. By granting the fork an infernal, nightmarish quality—"This strange thing must have crept / Right out of hell"—Simic signals his interest in the workings of the unconscious, both its capacity to make metaphorical connections and its tendency to evoke foreboding and violence.

Simic's work from the 1960s and 1970s participated in what was at the time a burgeoning interest in surrealist poetry, popularized in large part by the work of such poets as JAMES WRIGHT and ROBERT BLY, whose DEEP IMAGE poems are often called "neosurrealist." Though he occasionally found deep image surrealism "programmatic," Simic was similarly influenced by Spanish, South American, and Eastern European surrealist poetry. These poets offered Simic and other surrealist poets like Bill Knott, JAMES TATE, and MARK STRAND a way to "throw everything out of poetry except what really makes poetry distinct—which is metaphor, one metaphor after another, wild flights of imagination" ("The Toy of Language," 78), and "Fork" demonstrates such imaginative leaps.

The conceit, or extended metaphor, of "Fork" originates from Simic's transformations of the visual image of a fork. In the first stanza, Simic imagines that the fork most closely resembles "(A) bird's foot / Worn around the cannibal's neck," and though this image evokes great physical violence (butchery, cannibalism), the violence is mediated by the suggested religious function of the leg as a totem. Writing about Simic's sacred profanities and profane sanctity, critic Helen Vendler notes that Simic attributes the proliferation of "working-class litter, both rustic and urban" (103), in his poems to the blue-collar background of his hard-drinking, humorous father, with the corresponding ideal and heavenly images in his poems owing to his middle-class, musically oriented mother. Borrowing figures from one of Simic's own poems, Vendler describes this linking of the profane and the divine in Simic's work as the cohabitation of the pig and the angel (103). While Simic's opus demonstrates multiple ways of spiritualizing the litter of this world, or of sullying the furniture of the next, "Fork" reveals Simic's particular delight in evoking the inferno as a place that mingles the metaphysical or divine realm with the physical or secular.

Having identified the hellish qualities of the fork in the first stanza, Simic then implicates the user of the fork in its violence, describing how "you stab with it into a piece of meat." Having made an everyday utensil unfamiliar and discomforting, Simic now raises the possibility that the fork's implicit violence serves to unlock our own, freeing the Freudian id from repression. But Simic's final discomfiture, and his most evocative use of the surrealist imagination, comes when he imagines, not the fork as a bird leg, but the bird to which the fork might once have been joined. This creature "Is large, bald, beakless and blind," a terrifying carrion bird, whose head is "like your fist." Having made the human hand part of the bird itself, Simic suggests not only that objects can contain a violence that precipitates our own, but that objects derive their potential for violence entirely from the dark urges of the human unconscious, which is primitive and mythic. For Simic, the nightmares of the psyche are present everywhere, and take only the most ordinary of objects to be unleashed.

BIBLIOGRAPHY
Ratiner, Steven. "Charles Simic—The Toy of Language." In *Giving Their Word: Conversations with Contemporary Poets*, compiled by Steven Ratiner, 75–93. Amherst: University of Massachusetts Press, 2002.
Vendler, Helen. *Soul Says: On Recent Poetry*. Cambridge, Mass: The Belknap Press of Harvard University, 1995.

Temple Cone

"FOR MY DAUGHTER" WELDON KEES (1943)

Weldon Kees's early sonnet "For My Daughter" is a fierce and bitter attack on the sentimental fictions of poetry and on the reader's willing suspension of disbelief. With the opening line, Kees lures the unwary reader into trusting or even identifying with a prefabricated, conventional sentiment, a father's love for his daughter, without first assessing the speaker's character or even viewing that relationship in action (Kees, in fact, was childless). But the poem undercuts and eventually demolishes these false sentiments through careful turns in the metrical pattern and through an increasingly repulsive range of images.

Kees is praised by such poets as DONALD JUSTICE for his skillful use of form, and in "For My Daughter," Kees's manipulations of form correspond closely with the poem's debunking of sentiment. At first, the poem appears to be a Shakespearean sonnet, for its first four lines follow the rhyme scheme of that form (ABAB), its meter seems reliably iambic, and its initial sentiment is an expression of love (filial, not romantic). Yet these patterns begin to fray quickly. The fifth and sixth lines form a rhyming couplet, which would appear out of place in a Shakespearean sonnet; moreover, the rhyme itself (hands / band) is a slant rhyme, not a full one, signaling a breakdown in the sound patterns. The third line of the poem features an important metrical reversal from a rising to a falling cadence in the word *hintings*. The reversal surprises the listener and suggests that beneath the pleasing sentimentality of the scene, darker forces are at work: "Looking into my daughter's eyes," the speaker begins, "I read / Beneath the innocence of morning flesh / Concealed, hintings of death she does not heed."

From this moment on, notes JONATHAN YAU, the poet "squeezes out any belief we might have about the goodness of the future until nothing but his grotesque imagining is left for us to ponder" (11). The speaker's imagination conjures all the horrors that might conceivably befall his child, from "(t)he night's slow poison" to "certain war" to marriage to "a syphilitic or a fool." Yau claims that these imaginings are themselves extreme to the point of parody, so that Kees may even be undercutting the 'woe-is-me' sentimentality of the absolute pessimist. Certainly the poet's admission that "These speculations sour in the sun" indicates a disgust at his mood which is equivalent to the poem's biting skepticism about the sentiment of fatherly love. Bitter indeed, but resolutely truthful, these lines offer an uncompromising, self-lacerating clarity at odds with the exaggerated and false extremes of love and pessimism that most readers seem ready to admit as the basic character of human experience.

The last line, "I have no daughter. I desire none," offers the poem's most surprising and chilling disclosure. Fred Moramarco and William Sullivan read this as the inevitable outcome of Kees's absolute pessimism, his conclusion that "existence is so meaningless that the desire for children is futile, for we are cut off forever from a world of innocence and peace" (4). Futility certainly motivates this final expression, but its bitterness may also be in response to the reader's willingness to accept the illusion of absolute innocence and peace, a falsehood perpetuated by bourgeois art but here questioned and derided by the avant-gardist Weldon Kees's unwavering commitment to truth, however ugly it may prove.

BIBLIOGRAPHY

Lane, Anthony. "The Disappearing Poet: Whatever Happened to Weldon Kees?" *The New Yorker* 81, no. 19 (2005): 74–80.

Moramarco, Fred, and William Sullivan. *Containing Multitudes: Poetry in the United States since 1950.* New York: Twayne Publishers, 1998.

Yau, John. "At the Movies with Weldon Kees and Frank O'Hara." *American Poetry Review* 34, no. 5 (2005): 11–17.

Temple Cone

"FOR THE UNION DEAD" **ROBERT LOWELL (1959)** "For the Union Dead," the title poem of ROBERT LOWELL's fifth full-length collection of poetry, represents a growing apprehension surrounding the many cultural and social changes in the America of the 1950s. The poem laments the loss of the morally upright and civically conscientious tradition of 19th-century Bostonian (and, by extension, American) culture, while it looks with foreboding at the present age of deteriorating social ethics, impending space travel, and threatening nuclear war. Real fish in the old city aquarium (torn down to create a parking lot) become, by the poem's end, "giant finned cars nosing forward like fish." Colonel Robert Shaw (1837–63), commander of the first African-American Civil War regiment in a free state, however, plays the prominent role, symbolizing traditional values—morality, self-sacrifice, duty, and honor—of the bygone age with which Lowell aligned himself. Shaw was killed in the assault of Fort Wagner, South Carolina. Lowell's respect for Shaw is in opposition to his loathing for the advancing culture of forgetfulness and historical indifference, a sentiment epitomized by a "commercial photograph" on Boylston Street depicting "Hiroshima boiling / over a Mosler Safe." This poignant image of the capitalist exploitation of war atrocities also serves as a demented, contemporary version of a war memorial.

Lowell was commissioned by the city of Boston to write the poem for the annual Boston Festival; the poem was to be recited in the Boston Common, where Augustus St. Gaudens's statue of Shaw stands. Meanwhile Lowell's wife at the time, Elizabeth Hardwick, was at work on an edition of the letters of William James (1842–1910), who had delivered the speech at the original unveiling of the statue. Finally, Shaw himself was linked, by marriage, to ancestors of Lowell and had been celebrated previously in a poem by James Russell Lowell (1819–91), also related to the poet (Hamilton 278). This poem, therefore, brought together many of Lowell's ambitions and obsessions, giving him the opportunity to write his own memorial to a past he saw as glorious.

The poem is among the strongest examples of Lowell's transitional period, when he wavered between the highly gothic and formally wrought elegiacs found in *Lord Weary's Castle* (1946) and the explicit candor and raw autobiography of the later and formally looser *Notebook* (1970). Echoes of EZRA POUND become progressively muted by his ever deepening relationship with free-verse champion WILLIAM CARLOS WILLIAMS, as well as by his rivalry with fellow poets THEODORE ROETHKE and JOHN BERRYMAN. Ultimately it is Lowell's own mental instability, marked by annual, manic emotional swings, that most pervasively informs his best poems, poems capable of entertaining at once gothic highs and CONFESSIONAL lows. The free verse quatrains of "For the Union Dead"—haunted by both his early formal training and his turbulent relationship with Bostonian culture—remain the form most associated with Lowell and helped mark him as the preeminent American poet of his time.

BIBLIOGRAPHY

Hamilton, Ian. *Robert Lowell: A Biography*. New York: Random House, 1982.

Hobsbaum, Philip. *A Reader's Guide to Robert Lowell*. London: Thames and Hudson, 1988.

Chad Davidson

FORCHÉ, CAROLYN (1950–) Carolyn Forché once remarked, "I had been told that a poet should be of his or her time. It is my feeling that the twentieth-century condition demands a poetry of witness" ("El Salvador" 236). Drawing from a variety of poetic forms (see PROSODY AND FREE VERSE), Forché's work revises these forms to suit the 20th-century human condition, mediating the horror of war and its effects on identity and the body. From the elegy and LYRIC POETRY to free verse, Forché's work reflects a profound affinity with poets Anna Akhmaktova, ADRIENNE RICH, and Pablo Neruda, among others.

Born in Detroit, Michigan, Forché comes from a working-class, Eastern European background with a strong Catholic upbringing; she has been greatly influenced by the historical events of the 1960s, such as the Civil Rights movement and the Vietnam War. Throughout her poetry, Forché increasingly identifies with an international audience and embodies an ecumenical spirituality, drawing especially from the Kabbalah and Buddhism. *Gathering the Tribes* (1976) won the Yale Series of Younger Poets Award. Enabled by a Guggenheim Fellowship, she traveled to El Salvador in 1978, where her experiences produced *The Country between Us* (1981), which won the Lamont Award from the Academy of American Poets. Her anthology *Against Forgetting: Twentieth-Century Poetry of Witness* (1993) presents the voices of 145 poets across the globe. *The Angel of History* (1994) won the Los Angeles Times Book Award, and she received other honors as well.

The search for a communal voice highlights all of Forché's work, as she uses the events of the 20th century to forge connections among individuals and experiences. In "A Lesson in Commitment," Forché submits that "no single voice lifts pure from the cacophony of voices." In her lyric poem "Ourselves or Nothing" (1981), the process of memory acts as the vehicle for connection, manifesting a movement between the lyrical "I" and the communal "we": "I have come from our cacophonous / ordinary lives." As a poet, Forché foregrounds the paradox between a socially conscious intellectual and a solitary poet whose experiences stretch her poetic sensibility.

BIBLIOGRAPHY

Forché, Carolyn. "El Salvador: An Aide-Mémoire." *Granta* 8 (1983): 222–237.

———. Interview by Constance Coiner and Stathi Gourgouris. *Jacaranda Review* (winter 1988): 47–68.

———. "A Lesson in Commitment." *Tri-Quarterly* 65 (winter 1986): 30–38.

Marie-Therese C. Sulit

FOSTER, EDWARD (1942–) Edward Foster is a leading contributor to American experimental LYRIC POETRY. His Gnostic poems—poems in which what is known is received through, rather than proposed by, language—are deeply and often darkly rooted in the New England transcendental tradition. They surface, as Foster has written of Ralph Waldo Emerson, "as part of an emerging language . . . offered as the process of meaning rather than as conclusive insight or finality" (*Answerable* 20–21). While Emerson, Manoah Bodman, and WALLACE STEVENS are clear early influences on his work, Foster cites JACK SPICER, WILLIAM BRONK, and Constantine Cavafy as the "'gods' in [his] pantheon" (*Answerable* 126).

Foster was born and raised in rural Williamsburg, Massachusetts, leaving for Columbia University, where he earned a Ph.D. in 1970. As a Fulbright lecturer in

Turkey, he grew to love that country's exotic culture, finding sources there for many poems. Foster's numerous early publications were critical and biographical. His first book of poetry, *The Space between Her Bed and Clock,* was published in 1993. His fifth book, *The Angelus Bell* (2001), won critical acclaim, as has his latest, *MAHREM: Things Men Should Do for Men* (2002). Codirector of the Russian/American Cultural Exchange Program, he has received a number of grants and awards. Additionally, as founding editor in 1987 of the POETRY JOURNAL *Talisman* and in 1993 of Talisman House Publishers, Foster has provided an arena for many extraordinary poets writing outside the mainstream.

Foster's work, while meticulously engineered to revelatory movement through cadence and tonality, simultaneously acknowledges the work's source, one that precedes consciousness and personality, yet uses these as a means through which its intent can be manifest in language. Foster explains this best in his own words: "There is a god in the wind, and a wind in the god, and, as Ted [Berrigan] says, you attend to the gods. It is the wind that shapes our course along the road and, invisible, announces its presence in the act, the curve that is the poem" (*Answerable* 113). In "Family and Friends" (2001), for example, Foster writes of "a film / where ancient looks / educate the eye." Around a complex core of contradictions, Foster layers lean but luminous imagery, allowing the reader access into the experience that informs it through grainy half moments captured in the language, then released.

Termed "inveterately Apollonian" by John Olson (13), Foster can well be compared to Apollo, the masculine god of light, divination, and form: "I met / the young boy once to contradict his stare" ("The Blessed Wall Comes Down" [2001]). Here, as elsewhere, in Foster's work, the dominant cultural distribution of authority and power is confronted by homoerotic imagery. Through unswerving integrity and anarchistic rigor, Foster's lines, like these from "Hadrian's Will" (2001), "have the wings / that lead us back / to angels in the street."

BIBLIOGRAPHY

Foster, Edward. *Answerable to None: Berrigan, Bronk and the American Real.* New York: Spuyten Duyvil, 1999, pp. 20–21, 113.

———. "Edward Foster." In *Contemporary Authors Autobiography Series,* Vol. 26, edited by Shelley Andrews, 109–30. Detroit: Gale Research, 1997.

Olson, John "Revving the Real." *American Book Review* 21, no. 6 (September/October 2000): 13.

Lisa Bourbeau

FOSTER, JEANNE ROBERT (1879–1971)

Jeanne Robert Foster's poetry contrasts the importance of the individual and the natural world against the devaluation of human life and the exploitation of nature inherent in what the 20th century came to define as progress. Her dramatic narratives and monologues recreate the hardships and joys of a people whose birthright was "a low-roofed farmhouse or a log shanty" (n.p.). Seemingly a regionalist poet of the Adirondack area, Foster embodies a modernist trend toward understatement, powerful use of images, and introspection apparent in the work of EZRA POUND, her mentor. Although Foster's publicized connection to the modernist movement has been limited to third-party references in studies of such literati as the William Butler Yeats, Ford Madox Ford, Pound, patron of the arts John Quinn, and painters Gwen and Augustus John (see MODERNISM), Foster was at the movement's center, having worked as an editor for the *Review of Reviews* (1910–33), *transatlantic review* (1923–24), and *This Quarter* (1925). Foster's first publication was a collection of poetry, *Wild Apples* in 1916, followed by four more publications in her lifetime and one posthumous volume, *Adirondack Portraits* (1986).

Foster was born Julia Elizabeth Oliver in Johnsburg, New York, and she learned early to survive in the beautiful, punishing wilderness of the Adirondacks. By 1910 she was working as a model for illustrators Harrison Fisher and Charles Dana Gibson as well as the painter André Derain and developing as a journalist under *Review of Reviews* publisher Albert Shaw. Her encounters with modernity sent her back imaginatively to her mountain heritage for ways to cope with the demands of a new world: "Dig deep, you new men and you new women, / Into the past / . . find the American that was, / Or lose in the World-Game" (*Neighbors of Yesterday,* Epigraph, 1916). Struggling to affirm the value of human life, Foster locates modern tragedy in a disregard for the individual and destruction of the natural resources that nourish us: "But lovely things vanish; / They are going as the feet of destruction / And progress climb the high peaks." ("Neighbors").

While her early poetry depended on end-rhyme and iambic pentameter, Foster settled into the natural cadences of Adirondack speech—laconic, simple in form, broad in its tones, evoking the rhythms of the Psalms—to interpret a modern world in free verse (see PROSODY AND FREE VERSE). Alfred Kazin cited her "matter-of-fact plainness" as reminiscent of ROBERT FROST's in creating "artfully conversational pastorals" (n.p.). Like Frost, Foster rejects nostalgic escape, employing a subtly critical, ironic stance to comment on the purpose of life through its vicissitudes: "The hopelessness is in the tragedy / Of those / Who cannot feel repentance or regret" ("Country Tragedy" [1916]).

BIBLIOGRAPHY

Foster, Jeanne Robert. *Foreword to Neighbors of Yesterday.* Schenectady, N.Y.: Riedinger and Riedinger, 1963.

Kazin, Alfred. Foreword to *Adirondack Portraits: A Piece of Time,* by Jeanne Robert Foster, edited by Noel Riedinger-Johnson. Syracuse, N.Y.: Syracuse University Press, 1986.

Cathy E. Fagan

FOUR QUARTETS T. S. ELIOT (1935–1943)

An extended poetic sequence concerned with the nature of time and place, the *Four Quartets* were published by T. S. ELIOT in the years leading up to and during the Second World War. Recalling the spiritual resolve established by his poem "Ash Wednesday" (1930), they stand in stark contrast to his experimental works, such as "The LOVE SONG OF J. ALFRED PRUFROCK" (1917) and *The WASTE LAND* (1922).

Each of the *Four Quartets* is set in a specific season and locale. Further, each is divided into five carefully crafted movements, with a catalogue of Christian symbolism recurring throughout. For this arrangement they are often hailed as the crowning achievement of a poet who abandoned his modernist roots (see MODERNISM) by assuming a stance that was "classicist in literature, royalist in politics, and Anglo-Catholic in religion" (Eliot vii).

Eliot's original ambitions for the project were quite modest and almost accidental. The first poem of the sequence, "Burnt Norton" (1935), had its genesis in a series of outtakes from his verse drama *Murder in the Cathedral* (1935). Eliot gradually shaped these fragments into a coherent poem which explored "what might have been and what has been," with regard to his own personal maturation.

During the war Eliot's concerns of place and time enlarged and with these changes emerged "East Coker" (1940), a poem as much devoted to family history as to individual history. By tracing his lineage back to a Somerset hamlet in England, his adopted home, Eliot announced that "in my end is my beginning."

Such closure is denied in "The Dry Salvages" (1941), in which simple approaches to meaning melt into a mere muddle of detail. Here Eliot is at his most unfocused, concluding "that the past has another pattern, and ceases to be mere sequence—."

Clarity comes only through the religious lens of "Little Gidding" (1942), a country parish arrived at "to kneel / Where prayer has been valid." This sense of reverence gives Eliot the strength to relate his personal experience to the larger world about him and to comprehend his place anew, more fully than ever before.

Many of Eliot's contemporaries criticized *Four Quartets* as uneven, and some declared them insincere. George Orwell, for instance, dismissed them as an enervated, half-hearted retreat into orthodoxy. Had Eliot fully rejected atheism and nihilism? Even today a debate continues to rage over the true philosophical and religious import of *Four Quartets.*

Despite the controversy, *Four Quartets* has been celebrated widely, then as now, and was instrumental in propelling Eliot to the Nobel Prize for literature in 1948. Sensitive to subtleties of sound and sense, the product of a complex mind imbued with an evolving historical consciousness, *Four Quartets* stands as one of Eliot's finest portraits of 20th-century humanity.

BIBLIOGRAPHY

Eliot, T. S. *For Lancelot Andrewes: Essays on Style and Order.* Garden City, N.Y.: Doubleday, 1929.

Gardner, Helen. *The Composition of Four Quartets.* London: Faber, 1978.

Lobb, Edward, ed. *Words in Time: New Essays on Eliot's Four Quartets.* London: Athlone, 1993.

Jim Cocola

FRASER, KATHLEEN (1935–) Kathleen Fraser has been an important voice in the rich tradition of women writers within the avant-garde. Her own poetry often addresses issues of influence and location. While SYLVIA PLATH was an early role model, Fraser also became attracted to the linguistic attention of BARBARA GUEST's compositions and the precision and silence in the work of LORINE NIEDECKER, JACK SPICER, and GEORGE OPPEN. While Fraser's work first reflected the accessible, self-expressive LYRIC POETRY of the BLACK MOUNTAIN and NEW YORK SCHOOLS, she began investigating how a more complex, specifically female sense of time and interiority might be articulated. She used the word gestate to define a poetic form of "unnumbered discrete phrases, unfolding and proliferating as rapidly or as slowly as one's perceptions do" (*Translating* 44).

Born in Tulsa, Oklahoma, Fraser graduated from Occidental College in California and moved to New York City. There she attended workshops directed by STANLEY KUNITZ, ROBERT LOWELL, and KENNETH KOCH. Fraser herself taught at the Iowa Writers Workshop (1969–71) and Reed College (1971–72) before becoming professor of creative writing at San Francisco State University, where she directed the Poetry Center (1973–76) and founded the American Poetry Archive. She edited *HOW(ever)* (1983–92), a journal focusing on contemporary and modernist women's poetry, and founded its successor, *HOW2*, in 1998. In 1964 Fraser won the FRANK O'HARA Poetry Prize and the American Academy's "Discovery" Award. Other awards include two National Endowment for the Arts poetry grants (1971 and 1978) and a Guggenheim Fellowship (1981).

In "this.notes.new year" (1997), Fraser incorporates a typographical error into her writing, beginning an investigation of "error": "She wanted a 'flow' she thought, but in the translation it was corrected, displacing the *o* and substituting *a*. She could give herself to an accident. She was looking out the window." Here the speaking subject is allowed to be unreliable. At the same time, the poem tracks an alternative perspective known in Italian as *distacco,* an emotional distancing from a situation or exchange. As in painting, the poet momentarily stops to observe how the words, spaces, lines, or phrases have amassed and occur in relation to one another before deciding how to proceed with the poem.

Fraser shifted from traditional lyric form to writing based on the sentence as well as the informal genres of the journal and the letter. Visually inventive, her later work extends CHARLES OLSON's concept of "field poetics" in attempting graphically to represent the dynamics of speech and thought. Fraser also coined the term *devolution* to describe the process of listening through existing written forms, of revisualizing and reassembling them in order to depart from the known to the new or previously uncontainable. Fraser remains an important feminist presence in contemporary poetry.

BIBLIOGRAPHY

Fraser, Kathleen. *Translating the Unspeakable: Poetry and the Innovative Necessity.* Tuscaloosa: University of Alabama Press, 2000.

Kinnahan, Linda. *Poetics of the Feminine: Authority and Literary Tradition in William Carlos Williams, Mina Loy, Denise Levertov, and Kathleen Fraser.* New York: Cambridge University Press, 1994.

Ann Vickery

FREE VERSE See PROSODY AND FREE VERSE.

FROST, ROBERT (1874–1963) Robert Frost occupies a unique position in American poetry. He is more widely known than any other 20th-century American poet, yet his reputation among critics of literary MODERNISM has tended to lag behind the reputations of his contemporaries, such as T. S. ELIOT, WALLACE STEVENS, and WILLIAM CARLOS WILLIAMS, even as his book sales have surpassed theirs and his popular acclaim has grown. In his use of New England settings and weather to explore questions about nature, reality, and human consciousness, Frost situated his work in a line of descent from 19th-century American poets, such as Ralph Waldo Emerson, Henry David Thoreau, and Emily Dickinson. Later 20th-century American writers, such as WILLIAM BRONK, ROBERT CREELEY, GEORGE OPPEN, and GALWAY KINNELL, have continued to explore these issues and extend this tradition.

Although Frost is strongly identified with rural New England, he was born on March 26, 1874, in San Francisco, California, where he lived until shortly after his father's death in 1885. Frost's family then moved to the mill town of Lawrence, Massachusetts, where his paternal grandparents lived. Obviously life in a busy mill town was very different from life on the isolated farms where Frost and his family lived for much of his young adulthood, especially in the years before rural electricity, telephones, automobiles, and paved rural roads. By the time Frost moved to the rural New England of his poems, he was 25 years old and married, with a young daughter. He had worked in mills (11 hours a day, six days a week) and had made two abortive attempts at college (one semester at Dartmouth in 1892 and he was at Harvard from 1897 to 1899). In 1912 Frost and his family moved to England, where they lived until 1915. By the time he returned to America at age 40, Frost had published his first two books of poetry, *A Boy's Will* (1913) and *North of Boston* (1914), to favorable reviews. It is important to note that this success came years before modernist touchstones, such as Eliot's *The WASTE LAND* (1922) or James Joyce's *Ulysses* (1922), drastically changed the literary landscape. Frost went on to win four Pulitzer Prizes (1924, 1931, 1937, and 1943), to receive honorary degrees from dozens of colleges and universities in the United States and England, to visit Nikita Khrushchev in Moscow during the height of the cold war, and, at the age of 87, to read his poetry at the presidential inauguration of John F. Kennedy.

Frank Lentricchia explains the tendency of literary critics to think of Frost as something other than modernist by pointing out the problem with oversimplifying modernism in retrospect: "I understand how odd it must appear to include Robert Frost in modernist company. One of the reasons for the oddity is that we have forgotten the heterogeneous character of modernist literature" (xiii); he continues later, "If the poetry of modernism could include Frost, Stevens, [Ezra] Pound, Marianne Moore, and Langston Hughes, then perhaps the phenomenon of modernism embraced a diversity of intentions too heterogeneous to satisfy the tidy needs of definition" (77).

Frost's disavowals of free verse poetry in favor of meter and rhyme (including his oft-quoted declaration that he would as soon play tennis with the net down as write free verse) set him apart from the vast majority of his modernist poetic contemporaries, as did his deliberate self-presentation as a crusty Yankee farmer who existed beyond the pale of the literary establishment (see PROSODY AND FREE VERSE). Like Lentricchia, Richard Poirier calls for a reconsideration of Frost's status among modernists, asking, "what can we learn from the fact that in the first quarter of the [twentieth] century Frost was considered—and I think still ought to be—an exponent of the new?" (5). Poirier warns readers and critics that Frost "is likely to be most evasive when his idioms are so ordinary as to relax rather than stimulate attention" (xxii). Frost's idiom itself was an important aspect of his innovation. Comparing *A Boy's Will* and *North of Boston* highlights the differences in diction that separate the two books. *A Boy's Will* (with a few notable exceptions, such as the brilliant sonnet "Mowing") sounds somewhat old-fashioned and stilted next to the colloquial speech and dramatic dialogues of *North of Boston*. The latter book abounds with examples of another aspect of Frost's innovation, namely his subject matter. Early in the 20th century, as the United States continued to grow more industrial and urban, rural life had primarily negative connotations, such as poverty, disease, illiteracy, general backwardness, and insanity. In such poems as "The Death of the Hired Man," "A Servant to Servants," "Home Burial," and "The Fear," *North of Boston* challenged the prevailing ideas about the proper subject matter of poetry.

In order to understand why critics have thought of Frost as premodernist, it also helps to know a few things about Frost's *age,* in both senses of the word. Frost was significantly older than the other major American modernist poets. During Frost's formative years as a young poet, the dominant type of verse in America was what has come to be known as "fireside poetry." The era of modernist poetic experimentation had not yet arrived, and widespread small, specialized, experimental literary magazines did not yet exist. Most poetry was published in mass-market magazines and newspapers; this meant that in order to get his or her work published a poet had to appeal on some level to a general audience. Fireside poetry—so-called because it was suitable for the whole family to read together in front of the fireplace or in some other cozy domestic setting—was explicitly instructive and moralistic, and it often contained maxims that readers could detach from the poems and use in everyday life.

Frost's poetry often contains clear, memorable, seemingly detachable tag lines that appear to function according to the conventions of fireside poetry. The famous final lines of "The ROAD NOT TAKEN" (1915), in which the poem's speaker has encountered two diverging roads and takes "the one less traveled by," which "has made all the difference," the final line of "Hyla Brook" (1917)—"We love the things we love for what they are"—and the final lines of "Two Tramps in Mud Time," (1936), which declare that only when love and need are unified "And the work is play for mortal stakes" is an action performed "For Heaven and the future's sakes," exemplify this tendency in Frost's poetry. Although these quotations may appear to be simple and didactic, while Frost is providing the kind of direct reassuring messages that readers of fireside poetry came to expect, he is simultaneously undermining these messages. "The Road Not Taken" contains hints and contradictions that work against the comforting certainty of its final lines. "Hyla Brook" is a poem about loving a brook that is literally no longer a brook; understanding this makes it difficult to accept the simple declaration of loving things for what they are. The final lines of "Two Tramps in Mud Time" appear ready-made to be carried away from the poem and used as portable wisdom; although they sound absolutely convincing, it is not at all clear exactly what they mean on a literal level. Frost enjoyed duplicity and further enjoyed toying with audiences by hinting at the hidden implications beneath his poems' surfaces; he also maintained an adversarial attitude toward literary scholars and critics, who, he thought, too often failed to notice the intellectual complexities of his work. In "On Taking Poetry," his 1955 Bread Loaf English School Address, he said, "I suppose a poem is a kind of fooling," continuing later, "these things are said in parable so the wrong people can't understand them and so get saved. . . . That meant so professors won't understand it" (819). From the beginning, Frost very much wanted to appeal to a mass audience, as is evident in a 1913 letter to John Bartlett. Frost writes that he does not want to be merely "a success with the critical few who are supposed to know. . . . I want to be a poet for all sorts and kinds" (668).

By the autumn years of his life, Frost was a national celebrity. Still he felt that serious literary critics continued to underestimate him despite (and, in part, because of) his popular acclaim. Lentricchia comments that "judging from the reaction to him from high modernist quarters, Frost buried his subtleties right out of sight. For by choosing to fashion a transparent instead of a forbidding surface, he succeeded in telling his highbrow critics that his writing was undergirded by no challenging substance" (71). The penultimate poem from *In the Clearing* (1962), Frost's final book, reminds readers and critics of his concern with being misinterpreted or underinterpreted, and it does so in the memorable, seemingly simple style that brought him great fame and led many critics to overlook the complexities of his work. The poem, an untitled two-line fragment, warns readers that Frost's poetry is deceptively complicated and that conventional education alone will not prepare readers to understand it fully.

In the decades since Frost's death, his poetry has inspired numerous poets who have wanted to explore the potential of formal, metrical verse in a poetic landscape dominated by free verse. Nobel laureates Seamus Heaney, DEREK WALCOTT, and JOSEPH BRODSKY collaborated on a 1997 book called *Homage to Robert Frost;* poets MARK JARMAN and DANA GIOIA, along with other poets who are identified with the movement called NEW FORMALISM, have also been more attentive to Frost's complexities and his astonishing technical virtuosity than most academic critics. At the present, a generation of younger scholars is expanding on the work of the handful of excellent scholars who have long recognized Frost's achievement, and this ongoing reconsideration of his work suggests a coming increase in Frost's appreciation in academic circles.

BIBLIOGRAPHY

Frost, Robert. "On Taking Poetry." In *Robert Frost: Collected Poems, Prose, and Plays,* edited by Richard Poirier and Mark Richardson. New York: The Library of America, 1995.

———. Letter to John H. Bartlett, July 4, 1913. In *Robert Frost: Collected Poems, Prose, and Plays,* edited by Richard Poirier and Mark Richardson. New York: The Library of America, 1995.

Lentricchia, Frank. *Modernist Quartet.* New York: Cambridge University Press, 1994.
Parini, Jay. *Robert Frost: A Life.* New York: Henry Holt and Company, 1999.
Poirier, Richard. *Robert Frost: The Work of Knowing.* Stanford, Calif.: Stanford University Press, 1977.

Sean Heuston

FUGITIVE/AGRARIAN SCHOOL The Fugitives, a group of poets from Nashville, Tennessee, led the vanguard for modernist verse in the South in the 1920s (see MODERNISM). In contrast to the IMAGIST movement centered in England, the Fugitives emphasized traditional poetic forms and techniques, and their poems developed intellectual and moral themes focusing on an individual's relationship to society and to the natural world. The Fugitive group met relatively briefly, from the end of World War I to the late 1920s, and they published a journal of verse, the *Fugitive,* for only three years (1922–25). As poets, fiction writers, social critics, and literary theorists, however, the leading members of the group—JOHN CROWE RANSOM, ALLEN TATE, DONALD DAVIDSON, and ROBERT PENN WARREN—have had an enormous impact on modern literature.

Initially the men who became the Fugitives met regularly for friendly conversations that ranged over history, religion, philosophy, art, and poetry in the home of an eccentric Jewish aesthete, Sidney Mttron Hirsch. Most of the members were professors from Vanderbilt University, and they naturally gravitated toward Ransom, a young English professor, Rhodes scholar, and war veteran who had recently published his first volume of poems. Eventually Ransom and the other members of the group began exchanging poems, and their poems reflected Ransom's artistic influence. His poems, such as "BELLS FOR JOHN WHITESIDE'S DAUGHTER," tended to develop abstract, fantastic images in a detached tone and to explore the relationship between the intellect and the imagination. Later, a precocious undergraduate, Tate, joined the group, and he added a dynamic sense of poetic energy to the group's collective style. The most thoroughly modernist writer, Tate encouraged the Fugitives to experiment with poetic form and to write in free verse, which shifted the Fugitives' traditional foundation (see PROSODY AND FREE VERSE).

In 1922 the Fugitives began publishing a little magazine. In the first issue, they explained that they named their journal the *Fugitive* because they intended to "flee from nothing faster than from the high-caste Brahmins of the Old South," meaning that they rejected the tendency among southern writers to romanticize the antebellum South. At first they considered only contributions from within the group, and they chose to use pseudonyms in the first two published issues, but they took offense to the suggestion that the entire journal had been written by one person, presumably Ransom, under a variety of different names. As the magazine became more established, they printed poems from outside contributors, including HART CRANE, JOHN GOULD FLETCHER, Robert Graves, LAURA RIDING, William Alexander Percy, CARL SANDBURG, and Louis Untermeyer, but the vast majority of poems in each issue came from members of the Fugitive group. At the height of its membership, in 1924, the group listed all of its members on the masthead of the *Fugitive:* Walter Clyde Curry, Davidson, William Yandell Elliott, James M. Frank, William Frierson, Hirsch, Stanley Johnson, Merrill Moore, Ransom, Alec Brock Stevenson, Tate, Warren, Jesse Wills, and Ridley Wills. At age 19, Warren was the youngest member of the group and a literary prodigy who would become one of the 20th century's finest poets.

During the period of the *Fugitive*'s publication, however, Ransom and Tate were the most mature and most dominant poets, and their contrasting styles defined Fugitive verse. Deeply influenced by the metaphysical poets and French symbolism, Ransom's poems frequently describe images of decay and decadence. For example, the poem "Piazza Piece" (1927) juxtaposes the voice of death, personified as a gentleman in a dustcoat, with a beautiful, vital young lady preoccupied with ideas of love; the man tells the woman, "Your ears are soft and small / And listen to an old man not at all." In spite of the evidence of mortality in her presence, specifically roses dying on a trellis, the maiden fatuously refuses to hear the gentleman in a dustcoat. For her, death has less consequence than romance, yet she, like the lovely roses, will inevitably die.

In contrast to Ransom's bleak poems, Tate's intellectually challenging and formally adventurous poems explore the artist's relationship to society. In one of his best early poems, "Mr. Pope" (1928), Tate imagines the crippled 18th-century British poet Alexander Pope enduring the pity of his contemporaries, who feel sorry for his physical deformity but who fail to understand that his poetic art transcends the mortal coil. Tate describes Pope as a snake wrapped around a tree, hissing verses of wit and rage. In the poem's final lines, the image of the coiled snake changes into an emblem: "Around a crooked tree / A moral climbs whose name should be a wreath." The last line of Tate's poem alludes to the ancient practice of crowning the accomplished poet with a wreath of laurel, symbolizing his rhetorical skill and his value to society.

Ransom and Tate engaged in a spirited debate about the nature of modern poetry in the *Fugitive.* In an editorial column, Ransom describes the modernist tendencies to emphasize images over themes and language over form. He claims that stripping poetry of meter reduces it to prose, which undercuts its social value and dissolves its artistic integrity, and he sees the modern poet as forced to choose between the inherent value of traditional formal poetry and the vulgar inanity of free verse. In a rebuttal column, Tate offers a solution to Ransom's dilemma. He suggests that the new mode of versification is an extension, rather than an abandonment, of the established tradition. He explains that writing in free verse requires as much artistry to accomplish effective poetry as formal verse, and he claims that the modern world, in which cultural standards have become more relative, requires a more flexible form of rhetorical expression. In many respects, Tate's argument echoes T. S. ELIOT's essay "Tradition and the Individual Talent" (1919), and, indeed, he found Eliot profoundly influential (see ARS POETICAS).

The Fugitives thought of themselves as peculiarly southern poets. When they began their discussions, however, they felt critical of the southern writers' tendency to mythologize the Old South. Instead they intended to create an artistic vision for the Modern South. Influenced by the South's most outspoken critic, H. L. Mencken, a powerful journalist, they embraced the social, economic, and intellectual changes sweeping the South in the wake of World War I. But in 1925, the same year that they chose to end the *Fugitive,* an event occurred that led them to reconfigure their notions of southern identity. That year John T. Scopes was arrested for teaching evolution in a rural Tennessee school, and the ensuing trial pitted Clarence Darrow, a famous liberal attorney, against William Jennings Bryan, an evangelist and perennial presidential candidate, as they argued science versus scripture. Some of the Fugitives, especially Ransom, Tate, and Davidson, objected to the ridicule heaped upon the South, much of it from Mencken. They reconsidered their earlier position on the idea of progress and its impact on southern culture, and they began to wonder if change, specifically the shift from an agricultural society to an industrial society, would benefit the South.

In 1930 four of the original Fugitives—Davidson, Ransom, Tate, and Warren—and eight other southern intellectuals, including Fletcher, Andrew Lytle, and Stark Young, collected a group of essays that addresses the social and economic changes in the South. *I'll Take My Stand: The South and the Agrarian Tradition* by "Twelve Southerners," who have become known as the Agrarians, reexamines the values of the Old South in the 20th century. The essays maintain that an industrial society commodifies people, regarding them in economic terms as laborers, investors, or consumers, thus destroying individualism and damaging all levels of society—religion, art, education, community, and even family. At the time of its initial publication, soon after the collapse of the stock market, *I'll Take My Stand* received little recognition, and the few critics who did notice it dismissed the Agrarians as a group of conservative reactionaries. But later generations have found the collection to be an especially prophetic analysis of an individual's relationship to an industrial society and an intriguing articulation of the values, good and bad, of the American South.

Three of the original Fugitives also played important roles in the development of contemporary literary theory. In 1941 Ransom published a book titled *The New Criticism* that outlined a revolutionary method of literary criticism. He explained that critics should focus their attention directly on the work, rather than on history or the details of an author's life. Meaning, he contends, emerges from the relationships among the words within the writing or the form of the text, not from the external context of a literary work. New Criticism had an enormous effect on literary scholars in the United States, and numerous critics aligned themselves with the movement, including R. P. BLACKMUR, Kenneth Burke, and YVOR WINTERS. Ransom's technique also influenced the former Fugitives Tate and Warren. Tate wrote numerous elegant essays on literature in the New Critical style that have been collected in *Essays of Four Decades* (1968). Warren and fellow Vanderbilt alumnus Cleanth Brooks, a former student of Ransom, established New Criticism as the dominant mode of literary criticism in America with their series of college textbooks—*Understanding Poetry* (1938), *Understanding Fiction* (1959), and *Modern Rhetoric* (1949). Although Warren divided his attention between creative writing and literary criticism, Brooks devoted his career to the development of literary study, and he became the finest practitioner of New Criticism.

Ransom, Tate, and Warren—the three writers most closely associated with the Fugitive group and the Agrarian movement—had extremely prolific and productive careers as writers, teachers, and editors. Ransom taught at Vanderbilt University and Kenyon College, where he founded the *Kenyon Review*. He published a few collections of poetry, including *Chills and Fever* (1924), *Two Gentlemen in Bonds* (1927), and *Selected Poems* (1969), and, in addition to *The New Criticism,* he wrote two books of intellectual inquiry, *God without Thunder* (1930) and *The World's Body* (1964). Among his most frequently anthologized poems are "Bells for John Whiteside's Daughter," "Janet Waking" (1927), and "Blue Girls" (1927). Tate taught at several universities, including the University of the South and University of Minnesota, and he briefly edited the *Sewannee Review and Hound and Horn.* He wrote a novel, *The Fathers* (1960), biographies of Stonewall Jackson and Robert E. Lee, and several books of poems. His *Collected Poems* appeared in 1977. His most frequently anthologized poems include "ODE TO THE CONFEDERATE DEAD," "The Swimmers" (1953), and "The Mediterranean" (1936). Warren taught at Louisiana State University, University of Minnesota, and Yale University; while at LSU, he and Cleanth Brooks founded and coedited the *Southern Review.* He wrote many novels and short stories, winning a Pulitzer Prize for *All the King's Men* (1946), as well as several books of social and literary criticism. But his reputation rests on his poetry, which won two more Pulitzer Prizes for *Promises* (1957) and *Now and Then* (1978). In 1985 he became the first poet laureate of the United States, and his *Collected Poems* appeared in 1999. The lyrics "Bearded Oaks" (1942), "There's a Grandfather's Clock in the Hall" (1974), and "The Ballad of Billie Potts" (1944) and the long poems *Brother to Dragons* (1953) and *Audubon: A Vision* (1969) are among his most famous works. Together, they taught or influenced numerous poets and writers, including JOHN BERRYMAN, JAMES DICKEY, RANDALL JARRELL, and ROBERT LOWELL.

BIBLIOGRAPHY

Cowan, Louise. *The Fugitive Group: A Literary History*. Baton Rouge: Louisiana State University Press, 1959.
Davidson, Donald, ed. *The Fugitive: April, 1922–December, 1925.* Gloucester, Mass.: Peter Smith, 1967.
Pratt, William, ed. *The Fugitive Poets: Modern Southern Poetry in Perspective.* Nashville: J. S. Sanders & Co., 1991.
Rubin, Louis. *The Wary Fugitives: Four Poets and the South.* Baton Rouge: Louisiana State University Press, 1978.
Twelve Southerners. *I'll Take My Stand: The South and the Agrarian Tradition.* 1930. Reprint, edited by Louis Rubin. Baton Rouge: Louisiana State University Press, 1977.

David A. Davis

FULTON, ALICE (1952–) Alice Fulton's work is deep, complex, and fun. It exploits elements of several types of poetry, particularly LYRIC POETRY and otherwise avant-garde forms, with postmodern feminism at the core (see FEMALE VOICE; FEMALE LANGUAGE). Her engagement with the material aspect of words connects her to the LANGUAGE poets, but emotion and autobiography separate them from her. Often compared to Emily Dickinson, she shares with Dickinson a cryptic and personal use of language.

Fulton was born and raised in Troy, New York, and earned an M.F.A. from Cornell University in 1982. Her many prizes and awards include MacArthur (1991) and Guggenheim (1986) grants. After teaching at the University of Michigan for 18 years, she moved on to Cornell.

The impact of studying with A. R. AMMONS can be seen in Fulton's exploration of science in concentrated language with maximalist verse—that is, typically, long poems made up of fragments, disparate diction, style, and line length, which mix concrete observations with abstract questions or conclusions and are stylistically reminiscent of CHARLES OLSON'S *MAXIMUS POEMS* or Ammons's "CORSON'S INLET." The natural world leads her to questions that seem philosophical rather than poetic. Some readers have called her "difficult," because she expresses abstraction as well as emotion with such expansive compression. Fulton's aesthetic of ambiguity, of probing boundaries, is exemplified by what she calls "fractal poetry" and by her own invention, the "bride sign" (==), which marries but separates what it comes between, like a hinge. *Feeling as a Foreign Language* (1999) elaborates fractal poetry—a poetry of accumulation. Reliant on chaos theory, fractal poetry is Fulton's attempt to apprehend order in apparently disordered free verse.

Fulton's early short lyric poems show her talent for creating ambiguity with puns and enjambment, her humor, and her engagement with the world. Titles of these early poems indicate Fulton's jazzy lightheartedness and rollicking adventures in language: "How to Swing Those Obbligatos Around" (1983) and "My Second Marriage to My First Husband" (1986). Seriousness emerges in "The Gone Years" (1983), about the death of her father, but even in the midst of sorrow there is wry humor. The speaker imagines her father moving "over the snow, leaving / the snow unmoved" and says, "The snow has no imagination." This twist on *unmoved* is characteristic of Fulton's ability at exacting multiple meanings from words.

With *Powers of Congress* (1990), Fulton's tone deepened, and she began to write longer, less semantically ordered works. Humor still abounds in *Sensual Math* (1995) and *Felt* (2001), but it is incorporated into poems of what Fulton calls "cultural incorrectness." Each book is a long interconnected poem. In "The Profit in the Sell" (1995), she uses the evolution of a bee-imitating orchid to question the difference between "real" and "artificial," and, in the process, she upends typical attitudes toward these perceived opposites. This subversion of cultural assumptions drives much of Fulton's writing.

BIBLIOGRAPHY

Keller, Lynn. "The 'Then Some Inbetween': Alice Fulton's Feminist Experimentalism." *American Literature* 71 (June 1999): 311–340.

Marsh, Alec. "A Conversation with Alice Fulton." *Tri-Quarterly* 98 (winter 1996/97): 22–39.

Wilma Weant Dague

"FUNERAL BLUES" W. H. AUDEN (1936)

Popularized by the film *Four Weddings and a Funeral,* W. H. AUDEN'S "Funeral Blues" is a dirge renamed from an untitled poem in a sequence of four songs in "Four Cabaret Songs for Miss Hedli Anderson," dedicated to a cabaret performer who was married to Auden's friend, classmate, and collaborator, Louis MacNeice. Auden included a different version of the poem in *The Ascent of F6,* a play Auden coauthored with Christopher Isherwood, though both versions are brief lyrics spoken (or sung) by a lover for a dead beloved. However, while the play version of the poem specifically refers to members of the cast, the better-known version generalizes the identity of the beloved and draws on the powerful grief and exaggerated imagery of the traditional blues lyric, though it lacks the refrains commonly associated with that form.

"Stop all the clocks, cut off the telephone," commands the speaker in the opening line, granting objects from the mundane world (clocks, telephone) emotional weight more often associated with the lamentations of classical elegy. This mingling of high and low cultures is a powerful MODERNIST move, one which suggests that only by embracing the modern world can art come to terms with the complexities of human experience. In the lyric's four rhymed quatrains, Auden draws upon ordinary, largely urban images to describe a funeral cortege, with "crêpe bows round the white necks of the public doves" and "traffic policemen wear[ing] black cotton gloves." The poem derives its emotional force through a series of imperatives that change in tone from authoritative command to stoic resignation ("Stop," "cut off," "prevent," "Silence," "Bring out," "Let," "Put," "Let"), before arriving at the speaker's description of the beloved in stanza three, where the beloved is variously figured as every point of the compass, as every day of the week, as every hour of the day, and as the different forms of human communication. When the speaker admits, "I thought that love would last for ever: I was wrong," the admission reveals the devastating effect of this loss. The poem rightly concludes with imagery suggesting not only the speaker's emotional annihilation, but the end of the world itself: "Pour away the ocean and sweep up the wood. / For nothing now can ever come to any good."

In *The Ascent of F6,* the last two stanzas of the poem are quite different, making the lyric ironic, almost doggerel, in its supposed lament for the death of the weak, politically ambitious character, James Ransom: "Hold up your umbrellas to keep off the rain / From Doctor Williams while he opens a vein; / Life, he pronounces, it is finally extinct" (92). When Auden rewrote the poem, essentially as a cabaret piece, he removed these particular references and generalized the emotion. In the revised version, the speaker laments a dead lover in a tone of inestimable loss, but the beloved's gender and particular character remain unspecified, making it easy for any listener to assimilate the emotions of the song. Like the best lyrics from the blues tradition that Auden sought to emulate, the particular circumstances of the speaker's loss create the emotion, but the poem universalizes it, so that the sadness the speaker intones can be shared by any and all.

BIBLIOGRAPHY
Auden, W. H. and Christopher Isherwood. *The Ascent of F6 and On the Frontier.* London: Faber & Faber, 1961.
Callan, Edward. *Auden: A Carnival of Intellect.* New York: Oxford University Press, 1983.

Temple Cone

"THE FURY OF AERIAL BOMBARDMENT" RICHARD EBERHART (1945) Like many of RICHARD EBERHART's poems, "The Fury of Aerial Bombardment" depicts the heroic struggle of reason to come to terms with a philosophical problem grounded in human reality. Taking as his subject the heavy use of aerial bombing in World War II (during which time Eberhart himself served in the U.S. Naval Reserve), Eberhart questions the nature of a Supreme Being or God who could allow for the mass deaths of innocents, the "shock-pried faces," that are the inevitable consequences of warfare conducted at a distance from the targeted battleground.

Eberhart opens with a philosophical assertion, "You would think the fury of aerial bombardment / Would rouse God to relent," before presenting evidence to the contrary, noting that "the infinite spaces / Are still silent." This is a customary rhetorical strategy for Eberhart, claims poet PHILIP BOOTH: "Eberhart very often . . begins with a cosmic assertion, and deduces *in the process of writing* whatever evidence may sustain it" (67). The poem portrays God as a distant, indifferent being who not only lacks compassion for human beings, but even seems to lack an understanding of the experience of suffering. For Eberhart, it is as if the humans conducting the bombings are guided by this divine being who has learned nothing over the centuries except how better to cause violence and ruin. Human stupidity thus seems to mirror divine stupidity in this world, and Eberhart is forced to ask "Is the eternal truth man's fighting soul / Wherein the Beast ravens in its own avidity?" After the emotional rage that produces such terrifying questions, Eberhart offers no answers, but can only act as a witness to the misery, naming the names of dead airmen he knew and taught but cannot remember clearly, who went to die in war.

At first, the poem seems, like John Milton's *Paradise Lost,* a theodicy designed to "justify the ways of God to man," but after the hesitant assumption of the first line, the speaker soon finds he can offer no justification at all for God's ways. Asking unsolvable questions about good and evil which hearken back to William Blake's "The Tyger," in which the poet asks the tiger, "Did He who made the Lamb make Thee?" Eberhart comes to see that in the midst of meaninglessness, the poet can exercise reason imaginatively, asking questions that challenge not so much the politics of war but the underlying metaphysical conditions that occasion it. Thus, there is a noticeable shift in tone in the final stanza, which is calm and objective but just as devastating as the earlier stanzas; Eberhart himself claimed that, after having written the first three stanzas, "Sometime later . . . with an analytical mind, quite removed from the passionate one of the three first stanzas, I composed the last four lines" (41). Yet this shift is not an escape from the reality of war or of the poet's participation in it; as scholar Cleanth Brooks notes, "(T)his very same man who, in his indignation, feels that God himself had a hand in bringing these young men to death . . . [now] seems to sense his own complicity" (25). As the instructor who taught these men to fight, Eberhart finds himself ironically entangled in their deaths, and since they went to combat precisely because of their felicity with language, because they "(d)istinguished the belt feed lever from the belt holding pawl," they are likened to him, the poet, and their death is symbolically his own.

If even the most reasoned people can be lured to war and death, Eberhart seems to ask, who shall survive? His reasoned but emotional lines, marked with a regular rhyme scheme and an iambic, occasionally broken meter (as if by spasms of emotion), offer an indirect answer: those who can use their reason and not neglect their compassion for their fellow man may not only survive but may themselves help make "the fury of aerial bombardment . . . relent."

BIBLIOGRAPHY

Booth, Philip. "The Varieties of Poetic Experience." *Shenandoah* (1969): 62–69.

Brooks, Cleanth. "A Tribute to Richard Eberhart." *South Atlantic Review* 50, no. 4 (1985): 21–33.

Eberhart, Richard. *Of Poetry and Poets.* Urbana: University of Illinois Press, 1979.

Temple Cone

G

GALLAGHER, TESS (1943–) Tess Gallagher's poetry continually revisits seemingly unremarkable events to explore issues of identity and relationship. With its focus on details of daily life and its use of personal experience, Gallagher's writing reflects the influence of the CONFESSIONAL POETRY of her immediate predecessors, including ROBERT LOWELL and SYLVIA PLATH; like contemporaries LOUISE GLÜCK, JORIE GRAHAM, and SHARON OLDS, Gallagher uses individual experience consciously to evoke larger patterns of history and humanity.

The oldest of five children, Gallagher was born and raised in Port Angeles, Washington. Having worked for the *Port Angeles Daily News* since the age of 16, she began her studies at the University of Washington in journalism but changed her focus after studying creative writing with mentor THEODORE ROETHKE. She received a B.A. (1968) and an M.A. (1970) from the University of Washington and an M.F.A. from the University of Iowa's Writers Workshop (1974). Writer Raymond Carver, with whom the poet had a longstanding relationship and whom she later married, was perhaps the single most significant collaborator, influence, and inspiration of her literary career. She has published 11 collections of poetry to date, including *Instructions to the Double* (1976), *Willingly* (1984), *Moon Crossing Bridge* (1992), *My Black Horse: New and Selected Poems* (1995) and *Dear Ghosts* (2006). She has received numerous awards and prizes, among them two National Endowment for the Arts grants (1976 and 1981) and a Guggenheim Fellowship (1978–79).

In "Amplitude" (1987), a Christmas visit to Port Angeles prompts a reflection on her ambivalent relationship to childhood memories and the decaying mill town. As she and her brother pass the cemetery where her father is buried, she is surprised to find them in "Ray's Mercedes"–: "in the guise of those we'd learned to / hate as having more than their share." In this poem we see Gallagher's recurrent themes of beginning and persevering, of departure and return, and of the self and its doubles, which are always grounded in common human experience rooted in place and time. As it is here, the time of Gallagher's poetry is often that of memory and of elegy, as she recalls events in her own life and in those of friends and family, who become the poet's doubles. Use of concrete images—here the urban landscape—and of common speech—"'Let's / go Sis,' handing me the Scaggs tape" ["Amplitude" 1987]) reflect not only Gallagher's working-class upbringing and background in journalism, but also the increasing drive, over the course of her career, toward narrative. Throughout her career, Gallagher's poetry has explored issues of the self—and of the relationship between self and other—through the studied investigation of common human experience.

BIBLIOGRAPHY

Bromley, Anne C. "The Home of Uncertainty in the Poetry of Tess Gallagher." *Northwest Review* 26, no. 3 (1988): 96–102.

Gallagher, Tess. "My Father's Love Letters." In *A Concert of Tenses: Essays on Poetry*. Ann Arbor: University of Michigan Press, 1986, pp. 1–23.

Maggie Gordon

GANDER, FORREST (1956—) Forrest Gander is one of the foremost innovators in recent American poetry, blending OBJECTIVIST and LANGUAGE poetics with the cadences of southern dialect and the vocabulary of geology and the biological sciences. His work rejects the romantic vision of transcendent nature for one concentrated on the sheer mass of detail present in the material world. Understanding that the objective world is inseparable from our sensory perceptions and our linguistic accounts of it, Gander seeks not the one reality but varieties of reality, "Because cognition comes only / by contrast" ("The Ceremony of Opening the Mouth and the Eyes").

Gander was raised in western Virginia. He studied at William and Mary College with the poet Peter Klaeppert and became interested in the objectivist poets, including CHARLES OLSON and GEORGE OPPEN. After taking dual degrees in English and geology in 1979, he underwent major surgeries for an undetected skin cancer, during which time he concluded that his knowledge of natural science needed to be incorporated into his poetry. He moved to San Francisco that year, where he associated with many Language poets, including C. D. WRIGHT, whom he married in 1983. In 1997, Gander received a Whiting Writers Award and his second Gertrude Stein Award for North American Experimental Writing (the first came in 1993); in 1999, Gander was chosen as the Briggs-Copeland Poet at Harvard, a position he left in 2001 to become the director of the graduate program in literary arts at Brown, where he continues to work to this day.

A scientific poet resistant to definitive descriptions of objective reality, Gander writes that "We say we are somehow rich enough / for multiple, even inconsistent accounts" ("A Dissonance Leading to a Modulation"). The range of Gander's work reflects this richness: he experiments with SERIAL POEMS, dramatic monologues, narratives, regional poems imitating local speech patterns, and personal lyrics expressed through geology. Layered with geology, biology, and cosmology, his poetry rejects the possibility of absolute knowledge implied by the Cartesian scientific view, returning the reader instead to the dual mysteries of the material world and the human mind, with particular focus on language's struggle to describe nature and human interaction with it. Gander searches over a range of settings—often the rural South of western Virginia, the Ozarks, and the Mississippi delta, which teems with scenes of growth and corruption and a lush, archaic diction to match, but also Russia and a contemporary Japan still characterized by ancient customs—in order to locate the interface between perception, language, and reality. Ultimately, he finds that connection in our bodily experience of nature; his poems are saturated with an almost erotic longing to pass through "a new range of feeling. Torn awake" ("The Hugeness of That Which Is Missing: Contact").

Following the critical success of his book *Science & Steepleflower* (1997), which one critic claims "establishes Gander as part of the great American tradition of Emerson, Thoreau, and . . . Audubon," Gander wrote *Torn Awake* (2001), the most intimate of Gander's books, featuring many poems about fatherhood and family that continue Gander's focus on the links between bodily experience, nature, and language. Many of the poems in *Torn Awake* turn to the natural world not as a mirror for the self but as a source for language needed to achieve self-understanding. The speaker in "Line of Descent" uses the image of sedimentary layers to suggest the lasting psychological impact of grabbing his son in anger, while in "Love's Letter: To the Invisible World," the speaker metonymically compares the surprise of his lover's (and the universe's) conversation to Karl Jansky's accidental discovery of radio galaxies. These poems return to the Emersonian view of the natural world as replete with symbols, though Gander's attention is less concerned with what the natural world symbolizes as with the specific symbols themselves—the scientific particulars of material reality—and how human engagement with them constitutes reality. In a 2001 essay, he remarks: "The objective world is not directly accessible but is constructed on the basis of constraints on our perception and on our language. . . . There is no one real world toward which science proceeds by successive approximations."

BIBLIOGRAPHY

Gander, Forrest. E-mail interview. 31 March 2004.

———. "Nymph Stick Insect: Observations on Poetry, Science, and Creation." In *The Measured Word: On Poetry and Science,* edited by Kurt Brown, 38–46. Athens: University of Georgia Press, 2001.

———. *Science & Steepleflower.* New York: New Directions, 1998.

———. *Torn Awake.* New York: New Directions, 2001.

Irwin, Mark. "'Otherwise Than Being': Imaged Simultaneity and Collapsed Space in Two Contemporary Poems." *Denver Quarterly* 36, nos. 1–2 (2002): 83–93.

Temple Cone

GARBAGE **A. R. AMMONS (1993)** *Garbage* is a book-length poem by A. R. AMMONS, written in late spring of 1989. It is one of a series of long poems Ammons composed during his prolific career and certainly one of the most outrageous. The manner in which the poet interprets the visible world through the prism of his never-resting, larger-than-life speaker-self suggests that his major precursors are Walt Whitman and, in a somewhat different sense, WALLACE STEVENS. *Garbage* is also akin to JOHN ASHBERY's long poems in its tendency to absorb disparate portions of ordinary experience and furnish a transcript of seemingly unrehearsed and uninterrupted mental process.

The central symbol of the poem is a mound of rubbish seen off Highway I-95 in Florida. An enormous landfill induces the poet to examine modern practices of waste disposal and, eventually, to reconsider human relationship with nature. The geometrical shape of the garbage dump appeals to him as a hierarchical image, among other things, with the top corresponding to unity, the base to diversity (as a poet, Ammons is fascinated with tracing connections between the one and the many). *Garbage* is also a poem about old age—at 63, Ammons contemplates his retirement, poor health, and inevitable death. Fittingly enough, the poem is dedicated to "bacteria, tumblebugs, scavengers, / wordsmiths—the transfigurers, restorers." *Garbage* received the National Book Award in 1993.

Garbage is written in an improvisatory mode. In a method similar to that of *Tape for the Turn of the Year* (1965), Ammons writes on a wide roll of adding machine tape and tears off sections of it in lengths of a foot or more. Although aware of the arrogance that goes with trying to get something right the first time, Ammons decides that the poem should attempt to do just that—to be a more or less an immediate transcript of his continuous meditations on the subject of human waste, even if this means that some passages will have to appear as abstract, prosaic, or dull. On a few occasions, Ammons almost apologizes for his lack of brevity, explaining that "what I want to say is saying"; he digresses, takes detours, hits dead ends, but he always manages to return to his primary subject. As a result the poem boasts a music of its own, undergoing a series of rhetorical rises and falls in a kind of continuous verbal stream. The colon remains Ammons's favorite punctuation mark, providing linkages between phrases and sections. There is also a great range of tone and vocabulary in *Garbage*; the poem is both serious and funny, urbane and folksy, profound and witty, filled with technical words, such as *lecithin,* and strikingly imaginative phrases, such as *roseate rearend.* Eventually the poem adds up to 18 sections of unrhymed, heavily enjambed two-line verse units. Each section runs several pages and is written in a language that sometimes sounds like a conversation with hypothetical readers and sometimes like a conversation the poet might be having with himself.

Ammons begins his poem in medias res. An inner voice chides him for wanting to lead a simple and quiet life while the world is waiting for a great poem of the age. The time has come to recover "values thought lost." The poet then asserts that garbage, symbolized by the mound of waste he had seen recently among the flatlands of Florida, must be the poem of our time because it keeps us from dangerous delusions. He intends to write a scientific poem, asserting that nature dictates our values, all values, and that it is a place where we both begin and complete our earthly existence. The grief of failure, loss, and error makes us approach nature with humility and seek spiritual renewal in it. The mound is the "gateway to beginning" because only there does the real change occur.

Throughout the poem Ammons reflects on his own vocation, language, art, and its relationships with human existence. He likens the garbage mound to a poetic mind, in which language and its inexhaustible energies constantly replenish themselves and take a new shape. He says that life, like art, should make shape, order, meaning, and purpose. He offers essential suggestions to humankind: Do not complain too much, count your blessings, take action, and keep the mind "allied with the figurations of ongoing." Overall the whole poem is a celebration of human life and its relationship with nature; among other topics Ammons explores in his multifaceted poetic commentary are food, beauty, ugliness, holiness, fear of death, matter and spirit, and joys of transcendence.

Garbage contains a strong environmental message, as Ammons questions the practices of disposal of organic and inorganic waste and their consequences to the planet at large. He is aware of the dangers of pollution, arguing that it shuts us in "as into a lidded kettle." He anticipates global crises that bring and will continue to bring nations together at international conventions, such as those held in Rio de Janeiro and Kyoto in the 1990s. Above all, he makes us conscious of the reality of garbage, which grows around us, strives for our attention with its appearance and smell, and, ultimately, encompasses us as well.

The poem also shows Ammons as a superb nature poet. The main characteristics of his verse—visionary range, meticulous observation, sensible descriptions of places and people (more of places than of people)—are all present here, emphasizing the poet's conception of nature as a benign, generous, scrupulous, and inexorable force to which we are all subjected. Like his famous shorter poem "The City Limits" (1971), *Garbage* affirms the recuperative radiance that informs all things even in the landscape of waste and death, which is, for Ammons, the very heart (or bowels, perhaps) of the natural world. Notwithstanding its focus on the lowly, dirty, and smelly, *Garbage* is still a poem about praise, celebration, and redemption. Like *Sphere* (1974), one of its book-length predecessors, the poem achieves a truly cosmic vision through a resourceful interlocking of nature and art.

BIBLIOGRAPHY

Kirschten, Robert, ed. *Critical Essays on A. R. Ammons.* New York: G. K. Hall, 1997.

Schneider, Steven P., ed. *Complexities of Motion: New Essays on A. R. Ammons's Long Poems.* Madison, N.J.: Fairleigh Dickinson University Press, 1999.

Piotr Gwiazda

GILBERT, JACK (1925–) Jack Gilbert's reputation comes more from the quality of his work than from the quantity. Although he has only published three volumes of poetry since 1962, he is revered by many contemporary poets. Gilbert once said, "I have no need to publish. My writing doesn't come first. My life comes first" (qtd. in Adamo 157). But for Gilbert, his life is his work. Eschewing careerism, he has established himself as a poet's poet by magnifying the possibilities for elegiac poetry.

Gilbert was born and raised in Pittsburgh. He has spent much of his adult life abroad. In 1962 Gilbert was awarded the Yale Series of Younger Poets Award for *Views of Jeopardy*. In 1975 he became chief lecturer on American literature for the U.S. Department of State. His second book, *Monolithos* (1975), won the *American Poetry Review* Prize and was nominated for a Pulitzer Prize and a National Book Critics Circle Award. *The Great Fires* (1994) also met with great critical acclaim. In 2005, his book *Refusing Heaven* won The National Book Critics Circle Award and the Los Angeles Times Book Prize.

Gilbert's work engages a wide variety of landscapes: Pittsburgh, Italy, Greece, and Japan, among others. His passionate commitment to physical place, in addition to his well-crafted descriptions of his emotional landscape, help Gilbert transcend the easy category of CONFESSIONAL poet that some critics apply. Janet Moore explains this transcendence best when she writes that his "poetry is about the reciprocal relationship between experience and language; it shows how these relationships are parallel" (1). Gilbert extends the elegiac project that began with romanticism into the realm of a less certain, more troubled, world. He does not, however, allow a postmodern cynicism to undermine that project.

In "Michiko Nogami" (1994), he laments the loss of his wife, "a dead woman filling the whole world." In "Tear it Down" (1994), he argues, "We find out the heart only by dismantling what / the heart knows," and insists that poetry should respond to loss with well-earned audacity—an audacity that comes from the power of experience and the power of language. This insistence is the generative force behind his poetry.

Gilbert's work moves beyond cosmetic attention to mechanics—that is, formalism for its own sake—while avoiding an indulgence of the self. His work transforms experience into engaging poetic figures.

BIBLIOGRAPHY

Adamo, Ralph, and John Biguenet. "An Interview with Jack Gilbert." *New Orleans Review* 22, no. 3 (1996): 153–177.

Hoey, Allen. "Between Truth and Meaning." *American Poetry Review* (January–February 1998): 37–45.

Moore, Janet. "Jack Gilbert: Now Getting Overview." *Hollins Critic* 35, no. 1 (1998): 2–14.

Ron Brooks

GILBERT, SANDRA (1936–) Sandra Gilbert's poetry is very much about maintaining emotional balance and integrity in the face of adversity and loss. Gilbert is primarily known for advancing feminist theory; she wrote, with Susan Gubar, *The Madwoman in the Attic* (1979), a seminal study of 19th-century literature that gave feminism a strategy for understanding the conflicts of women writers. Some of her poetry, influenced by SYLVIA PLATH, has an ironic, bitter tone. Many of her poems express personal history in a CONFESSIONAL style derived from ROBERT LOWELL. Gilbert also creates surrealistic portraits and adventures that stretch empirical limits (see SURREALISM).

Gilbert was born and raised in New York City, the only child of Angela Caruso of Sicily, a grammar school teacher, and Alexis Joseph Mortola, a Parisian of Russian descent and a civil engineer. She graduated from Cornell with a B.A. in English (1957), married Eliot Gilbert in 1957, and became the mother of three children. She received an M.A. at New York University in 1961, then a Ph.D. from Columbia in 1968, and she has taught at several prestigious universities. Gilbert has published six scholarly books and six books of poetry. She has received awards from the National Endowment for the Arts (1980–81) and the Guggenheim Foundation (1983), and she was named Woman of the Year by Ms. magazine (1986).

Gilbert's poetry brings balances to a world that can be harsh. *In the Fourth World* (1978) after "[taking] possession of the house" and replacing her collected books with "black paper backs," the speaker receives a letter of dismissal, which gets personified as a "bad-tempered old uncle" with whom the children become familiar ("Getting Fired, or 'Not Being Retained'"). Images gain surreal proportions in "The Giant Rat of Sumatra." When Sherlock Holmes finds no solution to imminent death, he and Watson favor friendship while the Giant Rat devours London. In "The Third Hand" (1984), imagination stirs the mundane "like a new metaphor in every bubble." Gilbert's metaphors transform humdrum experience into inspiration.

Most of Gilbert's poetry takes the reader "on a journey into psychic recesses and through family and personal history," in the words of Bruce Bennett (38). In *Summer Kitchen* (1983), domestic activities produce odes to flowers and vegetables. Exploring perception in *Blood Pressure* (1988) and memory in *Ghost Volcano* (1995), Gilbert discovers the gain of love in the former and, in the latter, explores grief as she mourns the loss of her husband by wrongful death. A confessional mode of poetry restores balance as it asserts the power of metaphor to heal, to reconnect self to world. *Kissing the Bread: New and Selected Poems* (2000) yields a sequence of verses that expresses romance in mathematical terms stretched beyond the limits of ratio. Gilbert's work is an efficient machine for combat in times of personal crisis as well a means to celebrate family values.

BIBLIOGRAPHY

Baker, Wendy. "Sandra M(ortola) Gilbert." In *Dictionary of Literary Biography*. Volume 120, *American Poets since World War II,* edited by R.S. Gwynn. Detroit: Gale Research, 1992, pp. 79–83.

Bennett, Bruce. "Dissatisfactions and Contents." *New York Times Book Review* (12 March 1989): 38.

Bernard Earley

GINSBERG, ALLEN (1926–1997) Allen Ginsberg is the one person in American poetry whose name belongs alongside the prominent and influential writers of almost every mid-20th-century literary movement, including BEAT POETRY, CONFESSIONAL POETRY, the SAN FRANCISCO RENAISSANCE, and even the NEW YORK

SCHOOL. However, he is most well known as the central figure among the Beats, and he lived and worked intimately with JACK KEROUAC, GREGORY CORSO, Peter Orlovsky and William S. Burroughs. Ginsberg's controversial poem *HOWL* (1956) was published by LAWRENCE FERLINGHETTI, who subsequently defended the poem in the infamous obscenity trial that secured its place, and its poet's place, in literary history. At one time or another, Ginsberg knew well or was at least acquainted with almost everyone writing poetry of any consequence, from the first public performance of *Howl* at San Francisco's Six Gallery to the end of his life. When *Howl* was published, it boasted an introduction by WILLIAM CARLOS WILLIAMS, and Ginsberg likewise subsequently championed the work of all his friends. His tireless efforts to publish the work of others as well as his own poems, as EZRA POUND had done among his circle, is responsible for much of the impact of Beat writing on American literature and culture. Without Ginsberg, although the Beat sensibility would have developed, there would be no cohesive Beat Generation as we recognize it today.

Ginsberg was born in Newark, New Jersey, to politically active Marxist parents. Louis Ginsberg was a published and anthologized poet. By the time Allen was four, when the family relocated to Paterson, New Jersey, Naomi Ginsberg had been hospitalized following a nervous breakdown. His formative years laid the foundations for a life of political activism and literary production because his parents modeled these values for him; his childhood also predisposed his development as a man of extraordinary tolerance and exploration because of his mother's mental instability and his parents' openness to new and liberal ideas. Most explicitly, these factors are found in *KADDISH,* Ginsberg's eloquent mourner's cry for his mother. Ginsberg graduated from Columbia University with a B.A. in 1949, and he returned as a visiting professor for 1986–87. He was a distinguished professor at Brooklyn College, the City University of New York, late in life, and cofounded (with ANNE WALDMAN) the Jack Kerouac School of Disembodied Poetics at the Naropa Institute, in Boulder, Colorado. Ginsberg's many awards and honors include being elected King of May by university students in Prague (1965), an American Academy and Institute of Arts and Letters Award for literature (1969), a National Book Award (1974) for *The Fall of America,* election to the American Academy of Arts and Letters (1992), and the French medal of the Chevalier de L'Ordres des Arts et Lettres (1993).

Ginsberg's neoromanticism traces its American lineage from Walt Whitman through HART CRANE, but it reaches back to England's William Blake for the origins of its mystical and visionary impulses. His early poems adhered to the conventions of traditional poetry, including rhyme, as it was practiced by his father. But while he was at Columbia, his life and his work were expanded and transformed more by experiences outside the academy than those inside the classroom. It was during his student days that he met Kerouac and Burroughs, who likewise were students at Columbia; he also met Neal Cassady, with whom he had his first homosexual relationship and who served as muse for both Ginsberg and Kerouac. In 1948 Ginsberg experienced an auditory encounter with William Blake, beginning with a voice external to himself reciting the poem "Ah! Sunflower," from Blake's 1826 *Songs of Experience.* In subsequent days he also experienced visions which he connected with Blake, and thus he began his very long experimentation with hallucinogenic drugs in the attempt to recapture his Blakean vision and to explore the far reaches of eternity. In 1953 he turned his attention to Buddhism. Many writers on both coasts did, but Ginsberg and GARY SNYDER are the most notable of those who made genuine philosophical and ideological commitments for a lifetime. With the addition of this final component part of his equation, Ginsberg was fixed as a gay Marxist Buddhist Jew, visionary political poet, and activist. His writing and his life clearly proclaim and embrace each and all of these aspects of his self.

Ginsberg's one-time friend, Norman Podhoretz, remembers "the amazing virtuosity that enabled [Ginsberg] to turn out polished verses in virtually any style" (26) during his Columbia days; what came after, however, seemed to Podhoretz "hysterical and unmodulated" (27). In spite of this general complaint, the former friend admires the metrical rigor, cleverness, and the imaginative originality of *Howl* and some of the other poems of that period (27) (see PROSODY AND FREE

VERSE). Along with incorporating the pacing and language of common speech advocated by Williams and Pound into contemporary verse, Ginsberg looked to and utilized Whitman in experimentation with line length; as his consciousness expanded thanks to Buddha and Blake, so too did his poetic constructions. In spoken performance, Ginsberg's, long lines demand careful breath control to be delivered in rhythmic fullness, similar to what CHARLES OLSON prescribed in his formative 1950 essay "Projective Verse" (see ARS POETICAS), but in form they owe more to Whitman and Kerouac. For Ginsberg, poetry became a physical undertaking, as well as an emotional, intellectual, and spiritual one; the presentation and reception of the work requires all facets of the human in the same way that production of the work does. Ginsberg's poetry, at every stage of the process and product, is concerned with the whole person—body, mind, and spirit. The result is a poetry that possesses not only a wildness in its all-inclusive scope but also a control in its dependence on conscious attention to rhythm and image.

Ginsberg not only traveled endlessly, giving readings, he also recorded stylistically diverse performances, from Blake to punk, both spoken and sung. Among the recorded treasures is his first performance of "America" (1956) given on the same night in 1956 that he gave the first full reading of *Howl*. Ginsberg said of "America," which neither he nor Kerouac thought "was much of a poem," that it consists of "one-liners in different voices, sardonic schizophrenic, the tone influenced by [Tristan] Tzara's Dada manifestos" (n.p.). Nevertheless those "one-liners" are a kind of Ginsberg manifesto. The voice, however "sardonic schizophrenic" it may be, is a voice madly in love with its country at the same time as it is demonstrably disappointed and angry with it. This voice anachronistically insists that "Sacco & Vanzetti must not die," prophetically declares its "ambition is to be President despite the fact that [it is] a Catholic," and historically catalogues American political impulses and actions, from communism to capitalism to racism. It is a voice that never forgets to whom it is speaking. And then, suddenly, it realizes that America is not some external entity but that each American is America, that each is responsible for what America does inside and outside its borders. Every line is dense with events and ideologies grounded in the collective American consciousness, and the poem is propelled from line to line with the relentless and legendary American energy expressed in Ginsberg's scattergun approach to national documentary.

One of Ginsberg's "Cosmopolitan Greetings" (1994) is the maxim "Candor ends paranoia." Certainly there is no more open and honest poet than Ginsberg, living or dead. Freedom resides in the truth, available to everyone, because "Ordinary mind includes eternal perceptions." Ginsberg's entire adult life was engaged in advocacy, and, as Barry Miles has said, his "greatness as a writer is partly the result of the enlargement of sympathy that he demands for society's victims" (533). To some, Ginsberg's graphic sexual references border on pornography, but no one comes to Ginsberg for discretion and decorum. Readers come to him for the freshness and relief of his daring and for "a big artistic tipsy kiss" ("City Midnight Junk Strains" [1973]).

BIBLIOGRAPHY

Ginsberg, Allen. Liner Notes to *Holy Soul Jelly Roll—Poems and Songs (1949–1993)*. Performed by Allen Ginsberg. CD. Rhino Records, Inc. Compact disc.

Hyde, Lewis, ed. *On the Poetry of Allen Ginsberg*. Ann Arbor: University of Michigan Press, 1984.

Lardas, John. *The Bop Apocalypse: The Religious Visions of Kerouac, Ginsberg, and Burroughs*. Urbana: University of Illinois Press, 2001.

Miles, Barry. *Ginsberg: A Biography*. New York: Simon and Schuster, 1989.

Podhoretz, Norman. *Ex-Friends: Falling out with Allen Ginsberg, Lionel and Diana Trilling, Lillian Hellman, Hannah Arendt, and Norman Mailer*. San Francisco: Encounter Books, 2000.

Schumacher, Michael. *Dharma Lion: A Biography of Allen Ginsberg*. San Francisco: City Lights, 1994.

A. Mary Murphy

GIOIA, DANA (1950–) Perhaps the best-known poet associated with NEW FORMALISM, Dana Gioia is a prominent advocate for the restoration of meter, rhyme, and traditional formal structures to American poetry (see PROSODY AND FREE VERSE). He is a prolific essayist, critic, editor, translator, cultural commentator, and librettist whose own poetry consistently embodies the conservative aesthetic values he champions in his prose. His 1991 essay "Can Poetry Matter?" gained national attention for its claim that poetry had lost touch with the wider American culture and had become the exclusive property of professional enthusiasts. Scholarly in scope but not pedantic in tone, Gioia's poetry encompasses a wide spectrum of subjects, from classical myth in "Juno Plots Her Revenge" (2002) to jazz in "Bix Beiderbecke" (1986) to the natural landscape of "Rough Country" (1991) to personal grief in "Prayer" (1991), yet, in nearly every piece, he attempts to achieve grace and clarity through the fusion of formal design with—as he writes in "The Next Poem" (1991)—the "music . . . of common speech."

Of Sicilian and Mexican parentage, Gioia was born and raised in Hawthorne, California, near Los Angeles. He received a B.A. in English from Stanford University in 1973 and in 1975 earned an M.A. in comparative literature from Harvard, where he studied with ELIZABETH BISHOP. Returning to Stanford for a master's degree in business administration in 1977, he worked as a corporate executive until 1992. His poetry collection *Interrogations at Noon* (2001) won a 2002 American Book Award. In January 2003 he was appointed chairman of the National Endowment for the Arts.

While Gioia's poems showcase his metrical skills, their diction is rarely ornate or lavish. More often they are subtle and muted in their explorations of "the modest places which contain our lives" ("In Cheever Country" [1986]). As Bruce F. Murphy notes, "Gioia's is a public poetry that retains a sense of privacy, and a feeling for the limits of language" (291). Greg Kuzma takes a more negative view of the poet's conservative metrical style when he says that Gioia's iambic pentameter is executed "so much and so loosely that there is a humming monotony to the poetry" (114).

The difficult balance between form and feeling is most explicitly realized in the elegiac lyrics written after the death of Gioia's infant son, which range from the rhymed quatrains of "All Souls'" (1991) to the more expansive, variable lines of "Planting a Sequoia" (1991). Restraint and metaphor are used to channel otherwise overpowering emotions. In a later poem, "Corner Table" (2001), he writes, "What matters most / Most often can't be said." Still Gioia effectively expresses what matters to him through the time-tested methods that poets have relied upon for centuries.

BIBLIOGRAPHY

Kuzma, Greg. "Dana Gioia and the Poetry of Money." *Northwest Review* 26, no. 3 (1988): 111–121.

Murphy, Bruce F. "Music and Lyrics." *Poetry* 179, no. 5 (February 2002): 283–295.

Walzer, Kevin. "Dana Gioia and Expansive Poetry." *Italian Americana* 16, no. 1 (winter 1998): 24–40.

Fred Muratori

GIOVANNI, NIKKI (1943–) The term *popular poet* is often used to describe Nikki Giovanni. Some employ this term to refer to her positive reception by large, diverse audiences; others position her a notch below a first guard of "great" poets. Regardless of the value they attach to Giovanni's popularity, however, critics and reviewers agree that Giovanni is one of the most widely read and appreciated contemporary American poets. One of the first African-American poets of her generation to be published by a large mainstream publisher, Giovanni entered the canon of American poetry early in her career. Her candid voice and her socially conscious persona continue to inspire black female poets as well as upcoming writers in general.

Giovanni was born Yolande Cornelia, Jr., on June 7, 1943, in Knoxville, Tennessee. A 1967 honors graduate of Fisk University, Giovanni also attended the University of Pennsylvania and Columbia University. Before taking a permanent professorial position at Virginia Polytechnic Institute and State University, she held other academic appointments and worked as a full-time writer/publisher. Giovanni is the recipient of more than 30 honors and awards, including Ford Foundation and National Endowment for the Arts grants (1967; 1968), a National Association for the Advancement of Colored People (NAACP) nomination for Woman of the Year (1989), the LANGSTON HUGHES Award (1996), and honorary doctorates from—among others—Smith College (1975) and Indiana University (1991).

Giovanni began her career during the BLACK ARTS MOVEMENT, and while she did not allow her art to be completely absorbed by it, Giovanni's early writing clearly reflects the central issues that characterized the movement. It is her refusal to give up individuality in favor of a streamlined common cause, however, which has remained a more prominent marker of her work over the years. An excellent example of an artist/activist who has honed rather than outgrown the revolutionary voice, Giovanni continues to be an inspiration for those dedicated to using poetry as a means of social change.

From early battle calls, such as "The True Import of the Present Dialogue, Black vs. Negro"—the 1968 poem that sports the often-cited lines "Nigger / Can you kill"—or her signature poem "Nikki-Rosa" (1968) to more recent statements, such as "I couldn't see how I could grow if I thought of myself as anything other than Nikki" (Fowler 136), Giovanni foregrounds the power of self-definition. "[A]nd if this seems / like somewhat of a tentative poem," she remarks in "Categories" (1972), "it's probably / because I just realized that / I'm bored with categories"; in *Cotton Candy* (1978), she adds, "I am tired of being boxed."

Conversational, playful, mischievous, perhaps also careless or in need of fine-tuning, Giovanni's poetry addresses race, gender, love, sex and sexuality, motherhood, childhood, personhood, even popularity and prominence. And "Nikki Giovanni"—whether as poetic personality or engaged artist/activist—continues to draw considerable audiences nationwide.

BIBLIOGRAPHY

Fowler, Virginia C. *Nikki Giovanni.* New York: Twayne, 1992.
Evans, Marie, et al. "Nikki Giovanni." In *Black Women Writers (1950–1980): A Critical Evaluation,* edited by Mari Evans, 205–229. Garden City, N.Y.: Anchor-Doubleday, 1984.

Sabine Meyer

GLÜCK, LOUISE (1943–) Louise Glück's work is best known for its intense lyricism and its brilliant use of persona and myth. While her first book, *Firstborn* (1968), with its painful exploration of family conflict, is reminiscent of CONFESSIONAL POETRY, Glück herself views the confessional mode as alienating to readers. Her later works rely more heavily upon communally held archetypal and mythic themes for insight into the personal. Despite its autobiographical tendencies, the overall voice of the poet easily brings the reader to a mythic and universal space. Glück was influenced by William Butler Yeats, by the modernists T. S. ELIOT and EZRA POUND, and by postmodernist ROBERT LOWELL's *Life Studies* (1959) (see MODERNISM). In respect to her myth-making and her belief in the power of poetry to sustain life, she is perhaps most philosophically aligned with WILLIAM CARLOS WILLIAMS.

Born in New York City and raised on Long Island, Glück's publications include *Firstborn, The House on Marshland* (1975), *The Garden* (1976), *Descending Figure* (1980), *The Triumph of Achilles* (1985), which won the 1985 National Book Critics Circle Award, *Ararat* (1990), which received the 1992 Rebekah Johnson Bobbitt National Prize, *The Wild Iris* (1992), winner of the 1993 Pulitzer Prize, *Proofs and Theories: Essays on Poetry* (1994), *Meadowlands* (1996), *Vita Nova* (1999), and *Averno* (2006). Additional awards include the Lannan Literary Award (1999), the Bollingen Prize (2001), and a wealth of fellowships. In 2003 she was named poet laureate by the Library of Congress.

Glück's lyrical voice is mystical and magical (see LYRIC POETRY). General themes include motherhood, sex, and family. She draws heavily on classical myth, biblical stories, and fairy tales, eliciting a profound sense of the sacred that persuades readers to acknowledge forces beyond their control as they question their own place in the universe. Glück is a master of persona. *Meadowlands,* for example, is a revisioning of Homer's *The Odyssey,* in which Telemachus is perceptive ("I know / what he wants: he wants / *beloved*") and Circe is wise and experienced ("every sorceress is / a pragmatist at heart"). While many of her persona poems are mythological in nature, she demonstrates a wide range of voices. "Gretel in Darkness" (1975) revisits the story of Hansel and Gretel years after the witch has been thrown into "that gleaming kiln" and explores the struggle to keep history alive in a post-Holocaust world growing increasingly forgetful. *The Wild Iris* has three major speakers: the flowers, the gardener, and a god of the garden.

The poems in her earliest two works were, by and large, persona poems and thrilled as many critics as they troubled; however, her brilliant use of rhyme and meter overall overshadows any problems. If anything binds Glück's poetry together it is the simple and elegant specificity of language where archetypal and mythic themes create a new vision of a shared culture and its history.

BIBLIOGRAPHY

Dodd, Elizabeth. *The Veiled Mirror and the Woman Poet: H. D., Louise Bogan, Elizabeth Bishop, and Louise Glück.* Columbia: University of Missouri Press, 1992.

Vendler, Helen. "Flower Power: Louise Glück's *Wild Iris*." *New Republic* (May 24, 1993): 35.

Salita S. Bryant

GOLDBARTH, ALBERT (1948–) Arguably the most prolific poet of the post–World War II, baby-boom generation, Albert Goldbarth has earned acclaim for his encyclopedic range of arcane subject matter, his allusive wit, and his ability to establish meaningful connections among seemingly unrelated events, people, and things. Critic David Baker states that Goldbarth's poems exploit "the points of collision between the comic and the solemn, and between the fabular or mythic and the personal" (173). By linking, for example, the rituals of ancient cultures, the exploits of alchemists and early astronomers, 1950s science fiction movie plots, and memories of his urban Jewish upbringing, Goldbarth assembles unpredictable narratives that lend a sense of cultural integration and continuity to our own personal histories. His exuberant, densely textured monologues have prompted comparisons to the work of Walt Whitman and ALLEN GINSBERG.

Born in Chicago, Goldbarth received his undergraduate degree from the University of Illinois and in 1971 earned an M.F.A. from the University of Iowa. He has taught writing at the University of Utah, Cornell and Syracuse Universities, the University of Texas, and Wichita State University. Among his numerous honors are a National Book Award nomination for *Jan. 31* in 1975, the National Book Critics Circle Award in 1991 for *Heaven and Earth: A Cosmology*, two National Endowment for the Arts Creative Writing Fellowships (1979–80 and 1986–87) and the National Book Critics Circle Award in 2002 for *Saving Lives*. In the past 30 years, he has published more than 20 volumes of poetry and several collections of essays.

Throughout his career, Goldbarth's poems have resembled grand scavenger hunts in which, as he writes in "The Saga of Stupidity and Wonder" (1996), the tiniest facet of knowledge, if "gripped right and studied long, contains the telescoped / story of everything," echoing in microcosm the forces and patterns beneath natural and historical processes. But unlike many academically minded poets, he demonstrates his erudition and ultimate seriousness of purpose with engaging comic brio and irreverence, as in Voices" (1993), which begins, "The dead will speak through anything. / Give them a rock and they'll call it a PA system." Goldbarth's penchant for comedic showmanship and pop culture trivia is tempered, in the words of David Barber, by "a deep and abiding soulfulness, a generosity of spirit that elevates clowning into eloquent feeling and places brashness at the service of spacious passions." (46)

Eschewing prosody and traditional stanzaic forms for wide, randomly enjambed lines and densely packed pages, Goldbarth has been faulted for his lack of attention to poetic niceties, but the reviewer Ben Downing, by regarding the poet as a distant heir to the hyperbolic Walt Whitman—"He too harbors multitudes" (286)—and the linguistically adventuresome James Joyce, suggests that the anarchic propulsion of Goldbarth's poems resists conventional stylistic constraints.

Idiosyncratic and daunting in their breadth, Goldbarth's poems discourage imitation, but they stand as laboratories of thought that evoke a sense of wonder at the world's infinite profusion of coincidences and disparities.

BIBLIOGRAPHY

Baker, David. "Hieroglyphs of Erasure." *Kenyon Review* 19, nos. 3–4 (summer/fall 1997): 173–179.

Barber, David. "Life Studies." *Poetry* 166, no. 1 (April 1995): 46–51.

Cording, Robert. Review of *Original Light: New and Selected Poems 1973–1983*, by Albert Goldbarth. *Carolina Quarterly* 36, no. 2 (winter 1984): 91–95.

Downing, Ben. "The Wizard of Wichita." *Parnassus* 21, nos. 1–2 (1996): 277–296.

Fred Muratori

"THE GOOSE FISH" HOWARD NEMEROV (1955) In many Renaissance and neoclassical still-life paintings, a human skull would be placed in one corner, sometimes with the motto *Et in Arcadia ego* ("I am also in Arcadia"), a memento mori or reminder of human mortality, spoken by Death personified. Howard Nemerov's "The Goose Fish" updates the memento mori by placing the scene in a more familiar contemporary scene than the pastoral setting in which the reminder conventionally appears. In Nemerov's poem, two lovers embrace on a beach (an image ironically recalling the iconic seaside embrace of Montgomery Clift and Donna Reed in the film *From Here to Eternity*), and according to Nemerov, "for a little time they prized / Themselves emparadised." But then the couple is confronted by the rotting remains of a goose fish, a large bottom-dwelling fish with a bony, prehistoric-looking head, washed up in the surf. How the lovers respond to this reminder of the end of all mortal endeavors, even love, testifies to Nemerov's ultimate faith in the human imagination as a moral force, but the way the dead fish seems to grin at some mysterious joke balances this faith with Nemerov's sense of cosmic absurdity.

"The Goose Fish" divests the natural world of the comforts and consolations traditionally associated with the romantic depiction of nature. Poet and scholar PETER MEINKE notes that the image of the dead grinning fish head is a recurrent one in Nemerov's work, appearing also in Nemerov's first novel, *The Melodramatists*. Meinke writes that "Human love, Nemerov realizes, has 'pitched his mansion in / The place of excrement' [lines from the Irish poet W. B. Yeats's "Crazy Jane Talks with the Bishop"]; more than that, there are no lights in this mansion and one needs luck to stumble into someone's arms" (37). Ross Labrie further emphasizes the blighted view of nature Nemerov leaves in "The Goose Fish" when he writes that "one is left without even a view of the gracefulness of nature even if the speaker's fascination remains. . . . The moonlit passion of the lovers had insulated them temporarily from the outside world until they came across the 'hugely grinning head' of the dead fish" (81). As the myth of consoling nature is falsified, so too is the myth of consoling human relations, and Nemerov leaves his lovers standing at the edge not only of the ocean, but of the void itself.

Yet Nemerov is not an abject nihilist. The fish's smile is ambiguous, and as much as it might be mocking the futility of love in the face of mortality, it might also be sanctioning it; as a comment on the possibility of how their love might "make a world their own," Nemerov notes that the goose fish's grin "might mean failure or success." For Nemerov, the threat of mortality to human love does not negate it but should instead prompt a reasonable balance of enthusiasm and stoic resignation. The lovers, unfortunately, seem prepared to accept only an absolute, whether that be failure or success. Thus, the fish becomes "their patriarch, / Dreadfully mild in the half-dark." Mildness, realism, and stoicism are challenges to the passions of love, not because they refute love, but because they mollify the melodrama of romantic passion. Once one accepts that one's individual fate is simply part of "the still and tilted track / That bears the zodiac," then the riddle of existence ceases to be troubling, and instead becomes a condition for happiness.

BIBLIOGRAPHY

Labrie, Ross. *Howard Nemerov*. Boston: Twayne Publishers, 1980.

Meinke, Peter. *Howard Nemerov*. Minneapolis: University of Minnesota Press, 1968.

Temple Cone

GRAHAM, JORIE (1950–) Jorie Graham draws on a LYRIC POETRY tradition that includes T. S. ELIOT's meditations on time and transcendence, WALLACE STEVENS's rhythmic and imagistic richness, and ELIZABETH BISHOP's descriptive acuity. She scrutinizes the flux of phenomena that comprises the perceivable world, as well as the ways in which we attempt to understand it. Meditating on large philosophical problems and their everyday effects, Graham explores the relations of mind and body, materiality and spirituality, subjectivity and objectivity. In lavish and complex poems that dramatize the difficulties of their own making, she scrutinizes the very processes of looking and describing that she employs. She is attentive to the gaps, delays, and distances inherent in perception. In a statement that characterizes Graham's poetic stance, the speaker of her poem "Opulence" (1993) describes her study of an amaryllis blooming as a "stringent self-analysis— / a tyranny of utter self-reflexiveness."

Born in New York City, Graham was raised in Italy and educated at the Sorbonne. In her twenties, she moved to New York to study filmmaking but decided to pursue writing instead, studying at Columbia University and the University of Iowa Writers' Workshop. Her poetry collection *The Dream of the Unified Field* was awarded the Pulitzer Prize in 1996. She has taught at the Iowa Writer's Workshop and Harvard University.

Graham's early work reflects her cosmopolitan upbringing. In "I Was Taught Three" (1980), the speaker's recognition of herself as an "I" coincides with her awareness of the Italian, French, and English names for the chestnut tree outside her window. Many poems in her early books are set in European landscapes, chapels, and museums and engage the challenges of this aesthetic and historical legacy in taut, honed images. Adopting a more expansive and edgy form in such poems as "Self Portrait as Apollo and Daphne" and "Orpheus and Eurydice" in *The End of Beauty* (1987), Graham reimagines mythological characters to stage and interrogate conflicts within the self. Her major work, especially in *Region of Unlikeness* (1991) and *Materialism* (1993), examines and challenges conventions for point of view, voice, narrative, and closure. In these volumes Graham exploits the tensions of what Willard Spiegelman calls her mode of "fugal intertwining" (274), a process of repeating and varying anecdotes, images, and motifs. In her most recent books, these meditations assume a darker skepticism as Graham turns to the eros and violence that ensnare a fractured, fatigued, postmodern imagination.

Graham confronts large themes of beauty, history, and desire through the minutiae of lived experience. As she grapples with the underpinnings of the lyric enterprise, Graham explores the complex ways we perceive and experience the world.

BIBLIOGRAPHY

Jarman, Mark. "The Grammar of Glamour: The Poetry of Jorie Graham." *New England Review* 14, no. 4 (1992): 251–261.

Spiegelman, Willard. "Jorie Graham's 'New Way of Looking.'" *Salmagundi* 120 (fall 1998): 244–275.

Vendler, Helen. "Jorie Graham: The Nameless and the Material." In *The Given and the Made*. Cambridge, Mass.: Harvard University Press, 1995.

Barbara Fischer

GREGER, DEBORA (1949–) Debora Greger's cosmopolitan poetry offers lively explorations of the human-made inheritance from the past, especially the history of art—painting, sculpture, tapestry, literature. Yet she treats, as well, such equally intentional but less often celebrated cultural icons as a gift shop in the cellar of the John Keats house, Holiday Inns, and the nuclear research facility at Hanford, Washington, where her father worked. Her poetry is richly and often wittily allusive, descended from the MODERNISM of EZRA POUND and T. S. ELIOT, and reminiscent of the style of JAMES MERRILL, whom Greger admired. Occasionally her language may seem overwrought, but far more often her excellent ear provides great pleasure. The complex syntax and rhythms characteristic of her poems enforce their meditative pace. The regularity of her unrhymed stanzas—her most frequent pattern, whether couplets, tercets, or quatrains—provides strong formal structure, with or without regular meter.

Born in Walsenberg, Colorado, Greger was raised mostly in Richland, Washington. She has published seven volumes of poems, the first, *Movable Islands*, in 1980. She has received a number of fellowships and in 1987 won the Lavan Younger Poets Award from the Academy of American Poets.

Greger's poems confront the boundary between the world humans have made and the world of raw matter that precedes us. She reminds us that we live in the former, the world of interpretation, no matter how we may long for plain and direct experience. Moments of fully realized direct experience may be "movable island[s] of joy" ("Crossing the Plains" [1980]), but if we speak of them at all, the experience recedes into a frame of interpretation and arrangement. Fictions, history, memory—these are the forms we give to our experience almost instantaneously. All too quickly, as in "Queen of a Small Country" (1986), it is "as if the present / were already being told in another person." These "perfected" narratives become equivalent to landscape and architecture: They are the places where we live.

Greger's work suggests indeed that these shaping acts of fiction-making may be what best defines and sustains us. One way of making that point is to allude to Scheherazade, the character in the *Arabian Nights;*

who staves off her own murder by enthralling a tyrant with stories, an act figuratively represented in the title poem of Greger's third book, *The 1002nd Night* (1990). She does it another way in "A Return to Earth" (1996) by representing the grandeur and precariousness of all human making in the boundary city of Venice, "a city afloat on a promise of nothing / from an unforgiving sea." Humans have their own ways of creating—in her volume *God* (2001), an ironic deity has retired to Florida and muses upon (and is amused by) our parallel or substitute creations—and Greger's poetry both questions and celebrates them.

BIBLIOGRAPHY

Collins, Floyd. "Mythic Resonances." *Gettysburg Review* 11, no. 2 (summer 1998): 344–361.

Greger, Debora. "The New New Poetry Handbook." In *Where We Stand: Women Poets on Literary Tradition,* edited by Sharon Bryan. New York: Norton, 1993.

———. "Out of the Woods." *Southwest Review* 83, no. 2 (1998): 157–163.

William Waddell

GREGG, LINDA (1942–) Linda Gregg has been called by Czeslaw Milosz "one of our best poets" (127), and JOSEPH BRODSKY, on the jacket of her book *Sacraments of Desire* (1991), described her poetry's "blinding intensity," which "stains the reader's psyche the way lightning or heartbreak do." The voice in this poetry speaks with an almost classical reserve even as it probes moments of ecstasy, exile, suffering, and loss in places of "sand and dirt, rocks / and heat, life and death" ("There is No Language in This Country" [1991]). The speaker's eye gazes on bamboo, thistle, and pain with nearly clinical powers of perception and precision shared by poets like LOUISE GLÜCK, ELIZABETH BISHOP, H. D., and Emily Dickinson. Thus although influenced by feminist poetics and committed to exploring existential questions from a woman's perspective (as in, for example, "Not a Pretty Bird" [1999]), her poetry often has less in common with the autobiographical CONFESSIONAL modes than with a more restrained, often imagistic, even philosophical poetics.

Born in Suffern, New York, Gregg grew up in bucolic Marin County, California. She has traveled extensively, and much of her poetry finds its settings in far-flung places including Greece, where Gregg and her former husband, JACK GILBERT, lived for several years. She has taught at Princeton University, the University of Iowa, the University of Houston, and the University of California, Berkeley, and she has been the recipient of the Jerome J. Shestack Poetry Prize (1999), a National Endowment for the Arts grant (1993), a Whiting Award (1985), and a Guggenheim Fellowship (1983).

Crafted out of intense moments of feeling and observation, Gregg's language is at once ardent, austere yet agile and musical. The poems are compact, with life cut down to its essentials—a woman hanging up clothes, someone cutting bread, stone steps lit by the Moon. As the poetry tends toward solitude and contemplation, her language tends toward simplicity and purity. The frequent nominative fragments reduce language to an almost ascetic noticing and naming—"Sun in the air above water. / Sunlight on a rock wall." ("Heavy with Things and Flesh" [1999])—and the use of the verb *be* rather than verbs of action. Things appear in bright light as though announcing their being in the world—intently, visually, as in the poem "Greece When Nobody's Looking" (1991): "The earth bleached pale by two thousand years. / Poppies and weeds blooming in the tough fields." Ordinary facts are trimmed to an essential mystery and take on mythic tones.

Yet the voice invests the landscape with emotion. In "Glistening" (1991), the speaker has poured water over her body and says: "I stand there a long time with the sun and the quiet, / the earth moving slowly as I dry in the light." "Wrapping Stones" (1999) begins with the speaker lamenting lost love and compares love to "the salmon that have not come back." All of Gregg's work casts its eye unflinchingly upon life's fierce realities and tells in chiming phrases of both the loss and the beauty found there.

BIBLIOGRAPHY

Logan, William. "The Way of All Flesh." *New Criterion* 18, no. 10 (June 2000): 63–73.

Milosz, Czeslaw, Introduction to *A Book of Luminous Things : An International Anthology of Poetry,* edited by Milosz. New York: Harcourt, Brace, & Co. 1998.

Peter Rennick. "What Poetry Demands: The Spiritual Journey of Linda Gregg." *Hayden's Ferry Review* 26 (spring/summer 2000): 39–55.

Michael Sowder

GRENIER, ROBERT (1941–) Robert Grenier's poetry explores the textuality of language by drawing attention to words and even letters as material objects. Sparsely arranged on the page, Grenier's early, minimalist work transforms everyday experience into language games, as with these brief, untitled poems: "if raining it's raining" (*Sentences Towards Birds* [1975]), "AWW // Nobody talks at work" (*CAMBRIDGE M'ASS* [1979]), and "WHAAT // someone walking" (*OAKLAND* 1980). Each poem's playful enactment of the aural and visual texture of words frees language from its utilitarian function as a mere vehicle of communication. Building on the poetics of WILLIAM CARLOS WILLIAMS, GERTRUDE STEIN, LOUIS ZUKOFSKY, and ROBERT CREELEY, Grenier rejects the romantic tradition of transcendence for a poetics of materiality, applying Williams's famous dictum, "no ideas but in things," to language itself as the poem's most immediate object.

Born in Minneapolis, Grenier received a bachelor's degree from Harvard in 1965, where he won the Harvard Monthly Prize for most promising writer in ROBERT LOWELL's advanced writing course. In 1966–67, while pursuing an M.F.A. at the Iowa Writers' Workshop, Grenier traveled to France and England on an AMY LOWELL Travelling Scholarship. Grenier has made the San Francisco Bay area his home since the late 1960s, and he has twice been awarded a National Endowment for the Arts Fellowship (1980 and 1985).

In 1971 Grenier cofounded with BARRETT WATTEN *This* magazine, which proved to be an "originary moment" in the development of the LANGUAGE SCHOOL, in the words of BOB PERELMAN (38). In the first issue, Grenier famously declared "I HATE SPEECH," a statement aimed at the then-dominant "workshop voice poem" practiced at Iowa (Perelman 43). During this period Grenier expanded his material focus to include the tools of writing, from his IBM Selectric typewriter, with its Courier font, to the medium of the book itself. Grenier's inscription of the entire writing process culminated in *Sentences* (1978), a collection of 500 poems printed in Courier on 5 x 8 index cards loosely stacked in a collapsible box. As the cards are unpaginated, readers are free to create their own order of reading. *Sentences*'s nonhierarchical structure requires of the reader a more active role in the production of meaning, a move that ostensibly democratizes the relationship between reader and writer.

In the late 1980s, Grenier's interest in everyday materiality led to his abandonment of print altogether for the "scrawl": four-color handwritten poems that, upon first viewing, resemble a child's drawings. Perplexing both critics and peers alike, the scrawl poems stand at the edge of articulation. According to RON SILLIMAN, the scrawl extends Grenier's attention to particulars into the realm of the microscopic: "This is as close to the origin of thinking/feeling as we are ever likely to find ourselves in a poem" (59).

BIBLIOGRAPHY

Perelman, Bob. "Here and Now on Paper: The Avant-garde Particulars of Robert Grenier." In *The Marginalization of Poetry: Language Writing and Literary History,* by Perelman. Princeton: Princeton University Press, 1996, pp. 38–57.

Ratcliffe, Stephen. "Grenier's 'Scrawl.'" *Listening to Reading.* Albany: State University of New York Press, 2000, 119–132.

Silliman, Ron. "'thought or feeling forming.'" *verdure* 3–4 (2001): 57–60.

Tim Shaner and Michael Rozendal

GROSSMAN, ALLEN (1932–) Allen Grossman writes in a style at once prophetic and personal, influenced by Walt Whitman, HART CRANE, ALLEN GINSBERG, and William Butler Yeats (on whom Grossman has written criticism). Grossman believes that poetry is the medium of individual people, through which the "countenance" described in the poem may become immortal: Poetry makes people "present to one another" by showing them as "capable of love," and the poem is not about the poet, but about the poet's beloved, whose countenance it represents. Poems facilitate relationships that "give and obtain the world simultaneously"; they take part in a dialogue that creates its subject (*The Sighted Singer*).

Grossman was born in Minneapolis. He received a doctorate from Brandeis University in 1960 and remained there as a professor. He taught as a visiting professor in Israel at the Universitat HaNegev and as the Andrew W. Mellon Professor of the Humanities at Johns Hopkins University. His first book of poetry, *A Harlot's Hire,* was published in 1959. The many honors and fellowships he has received include: three Pushcart Prizes (1975, 1987, and 1990) and the Bassine Citation of the Academy of American Poets (1990). In 1993 he was elected a fellow of the American Academy of Arts and Science.

Grossman's poetry is at once intensely personal, focusing on his own life and the lives of his parents, and philosophical, addressing existential and historical problems. Poems, such as "The Loss of the Beloved Companion" (1979) and "A Little Sleep" (1982), build on Walt Whitman and Ginsberg in examining the union of the sexual and corporeal self, where "sex and imagination are one" ("The Loss of the Beloved Companion"). Resting more in ideas than in images, his poems explore states of being: He is interested in how spirit is expressed in the human body and the fate of the dead. Jewish and Homeric imagery blend with the physical details of the human body to represent a world populated by family, lovers, and angels. His poetry contains an element of lamentation—for the dead, for the unborn, for the impossible. It draws upon modern poets for its concerns with the nature of reality and upon the reactions and conditions of his own body for its images.

Grossman's parents, Louis and Beatrice, appear in his poems as both emblems of the poet's origins and warnings of his eventual fate. The five-part poem "Poland of Death" (1988) superimposes Louis's death onto a picture of the Holocaust. While Louis Grossman died in America, his ghost joins the ghosts of the Jews who died in the concentration camps. This blending of the private (the death of the poet's father) and the larger metaphysical-historical concern (the fate of the victims of the Holocaust) is typical of Grossman's work. The physical particulars of the body reflect and explain the otherwise unknowable spiritual world.

BIBLIOGRAPHY

Bromwich, David, "Prophetic Dreaming." *Parnassus* 8, no. 1 (1980): 144–149.

Durante, Janice Floyd. "A Conversation with Allen Grossman." *Boulevard* 6, nos. 2–3 (fall 1991): 71–83.

Grossman, Allen, with Mark Halliday. *The Sighted Singer: Two Works on Poetry for Readers and Writers*. Baltimore: Johns Hopkins University Press, 1992.

Stern, Gerald, "Grossman's Lament." *American Poetry Review* 21, no. 4 (July–August 1992): 7–12.

Rachel Trousdale

GUEST, BARBARA (1920–2006) Barbara Guest is an erudite, cosmopolitan poet, whose sensibility is at home in the byzantine coils of art's complications. Her work shares WALLACE STEVENS's propensity to investigate the movement of the lyric imagination as it both creates and exceeds reality. Each Guest poem meditates on the process of its composition and is highly conscious of the vision it constructs, but this makes the work more elusive than clear. Guest is a NEW YORK SCHOOL poet and continues this group's project of translating modern visual art's subversion of ordinary perception into literary forms. It is particularly in modern painting that Guest finds and expresses her commitment to the aesthetic. Painting is an inextricable part of her LYRIC POETRY's complicated and witty style; it inspires the fluidity of Guest's metaphorical transformations as well as her inventive use of space, focus, and line. Guest has stated that, as a young poet, painting gave her a sense of "being unconfined to a page" (190), and her lyrics—whether scattered and fragmented or densely built—move into worlds confined only by their commitment to innovative perception. But for all her innovation, Guest never relinquishes the lyric's potential for beauty; she simply reimagines the possibilities of its appearances. Guest's sustained attention to reinventing the lyric has influenced the work of such poets as MARJORIE WELISH, ANN LAUTERBACH, and MEI-MEI BERSSENBRUGGE.

Guest was born in Wilmington, North Carolina, and spent her childhood in Florida and California. After graduating from the University of California, Berkeley, she settled in New York City and connected with the emerging New York school and the painters of ABSTRACT EXPRESSIONISM. Guest's poem "History" (1962), which is dedicated to FRANK O'HARA, captures the sense of possibility alive within the New York school's playful and adventuresome camaraderie. Guest has been the recipient of many prestigious awards. In 1989 *Fair Realism* won the Lawrence J. Lipton Prize, and in 1993 her collection *Defensive Rapture* won the San Francisco State University Poetry Center Book Award. Guest has received two Americas Awards for the best collections of poetry: her *Selected Poems* won in 1995, and *Quill, Solitary APPARITION* won in 1996. In 1999 Guest was awarded the ROBERT FROST Medal by the Poetry Society of America.

Guest has collaborated with a number of visual artists, producing books that call attention to her work's porous flexibility and its careful, sensitive responsiveness to pictorial forms. An early poem entitled "Heroic Stages" (1962), dedicated to the painter Grace Hartigan, attests to Guest's talent for finding her work's lyric contours within the imaginative landscape of another. Typical of Guest's witty and indirect critiques, "Heroic Stages" qualifies as a poem of feminist subversion, as the "heroics" of abstract expressionism were announced in the art world in explicitly masculine terms. Guest renders—and celebrates—multiple aspects of Hartigan's heroism: its continually elusive transformations, its risky remapping of the world. Guest compares the poets, who are "held to the routes by the tender-eyed peasants," to the painters "who have drawn deep lines on the globes." For Guest, painting and the lyrics that follow painting's heroic lead have the power to make the world and the self, as Welish has said, "complicated with potentiality" and "interestingly fictional" (562).

Like JOHN ASHBERY and O'Hara, Guest draws freely—and often surprisingly—from literature, art, and philosophy, as well as from pop culture, creating juxtapositions that shine with surprise and unveil the odd, the touching, and the elegant existing just at the edge of the ordinary. In a long poem entitled "A Handbook of Surfing" (1968), Guest delves into California beach culture with a combination of lyrical sophistication and biting sarcasm. Her collection *The Countess of Minneapolis* (1976) devotes itself to discovering the possibilities for linking the everyday rhythms of the American Midwest to the regal desires for romance.

For all its emphasis on fictional experiments and shifting personas, Guest's work maintains ties to the real. The first two lines of "Fair Realism" (1989) describe a swift and far-fetched transformation, but the stanza settles into sobriety with the statement "an emphasis falls on reality." The poem moves back and forth between images that suggest a comforting reality and those that suggest the artifice of artistic representation. Guest's poem shows that these distinctions cannot be sustained, as they are continually meeting and transforming one another in language. Just the same, the poem does acknowledge both the emotional and compositional necessity of realism, however perceived or defined, as it is "part of the search, the journey / where two figures embrace."

Guest's work is dense with journeys, foreign lands, borders, departures, and arrivals, but these are images for the process of finding the place where the sensuality of the world and the engaged, imaginative intellect meet. In "Dissonance Royal Traveler"(1993), Guest investigates the compositions that arise as the mind tries to understand the abstraction of music; this process "loosens" "the hoof of the earth" from its "garrison." Readers brave enough to follow Guest into the shifting map of her poetry will see a world unleashed into its imaginative potential.

BIBLIOGRAPHY

DuPlessis, Rachel Blau. "The Gendered Marvelous: Barbara Guest, Surrealism, and Feminist Reception." In *Scene of My Selves: New Work on the New York School of Poets,* edited by Terrence Diggory and Stephen Paul Miller, 189–213. Orono, Maine: National Poetry Foundation, 2001.

Guest, Barbara. "The Forces of the Imagination." In *American Women Poets in the 21st Century: Where Lyric Meets Language,* edited by Claudia Rankine and Juliana Spahr. Middletown, Conn.: Wesleyan University Press, 2002, pp. 189–191.

Lundquist, Sara. "Implacable Poet: Purple Birds: The Work of Barbara Guest." In *American Women Poets in the 21st Century: Where Lyric Meets Language,* edited by Claudia Rankine and Juliana Spahr, 191–217. Middletown, Conn.: Wesleyan University Press, 2002.

Welish, Marjorie. "On Barbara Guest." In *Moving Borders: Three Decades of Innovative Writing by Women,* edited by Mary Margaret Sloan. Jersey City: Talisman House, 1998, pp. 561–565.

Kimberly Lamm

GUNN, THOM (1929–2004) Anglo-American poet Thom Gunn's finest poems are formal masterpieces that elegantly balance emotion and reason in a chaste, plain style, although their subjects are rarely chaste or plain. Gunn inherited from William Shakespeare, John Donne, Fulke Greville, and Ben Jonson the dexterity to handle contemporary subject matter in traditional, formal verse, and from Thomas Hardy, YVOR WINTERS, and ROBERT DUNCAN, he learned to evaluate his experience rationally and expand the range of verse.

Gunn was born in Gravesend, England. At Cambridge, he attended F. R. Leavis's lectures and wrote *Fighting Terms* (1954). British critics connected Gunn with Philip Larkin and others who became known as part of "the Movement": These poets displayed a distaste for romanticism and MODERNISM; eschewed rhetoric, symbolism, and allusion in favor of urbanity, rationality, and emotional restraint; and wrote using traditional forms. In 1954 Gunn received a Stegner Fellowship at Stanford University and studied under Winters. Gunn received an M.A. at Stanford and taught at the University of California, Berkeley, until 2000. Gunn's many awards include the Lenore Marshall Poetry Prize (1992) and a Lila Acheson Wallace/Reader's Digest Award (1992). His criticism has been collected in *The Occasions of Poetry* (1982) and *Shelf Life* (1993).

Gunn himself called *Fighting Terms* overly studious and literary, but its depiction of love as a series of military maneuvers or a game of cynical poses struck readers and critics. These formal poems with their plain-style sententiae (striking, often highly moral sayings) more closely resembled Renaissance verse than the incipient CONFESSIONAL and DEEP IMAGE modes. In "A Mirror for Poets," Gunn expresses nostalgia for the violence, misery, and politics of Elizabethan England, when there were "Wheels, racks, and fires / In every writer's mouth and not mere rant."

The Sense of Movement (1957) explores self-fashioning in a world without meaning. In "Lines for a Book," Gunn sides with history's "toughs"—"those exclusive by their action / For whom mere thought could be no satisfaction." In "On the Move," a motorcycle gang in goggles and leather jackets has "donned impersonality" and overcome existentialist doubt through force of will. They combine instinct with pose, and though restlessness may never lead to wisdom, Gunn writes that in "a valueless world," one becomes "both hurler and the hurled, / One moves as well, always toward, toward." Poets, he argues, are the toughest toughs. In "To Yvor Winters, 1955," Gunn compares Winters's training of dogs to his training of poets with a "boxer's vigilance." In Winters, power, an "exercised intelligence," keeps "both Rule and Energy in view, / Much power in each, most in the balanced two."

My Sad Captains (1961), which marks Gunn's transition away from strictly formal verse, begins with "In Santa Maria del Popolo," whose speaker waits for the Sun to light Caravaggio's painting *Conversion of St. Paul* and finds Saul's arms outstretched, "Resisting, by embracing, nothingness." "Innocence" explores a soldier's "Courage, endurance, loyalty, and skill" as he disinterestedly watches a Russian partisan burn in his boots. In the first section, Gunn writes in traditional metrical verse, but in the second he turns to rhymed and unrhymed syllabic verse (where the number of syllables per line is fixed but the accents vary). The nine syllable lines of "Waking in a Newly Built House" announce the change of style, if not of theme. The speaker's perception of things is a calm awareness of "their precise definition, their fine / lack of even potential meanings."

From the 1960s through the 1980s, Gunn wrote primarily in free verse. *Touch* (1967) contains "Misanthropos," a poem about "the last man" to survive a nuclear holocaust. In *Moly* (1971), which Gunn considered his best book and most critics consider his worst, Gunn wrote poems—in metrical verse—about taking LSD. In "Street Song," which draws on Elizabethan ballads, a drug dealer entices customers to sample his wares, promising them power and access to a different world: "I'll get you anything you need," he sings, *"Keys lids acid and speed."*

Gunn first used explicitly homosexual subject matter in *The Passages of Joy* (1982); his sexuality appeared disguised in *Jack Straw's Castle* (1975), which includes the beautiful love poem in rhymed quatrains "The Bed," a poem about an inept hustler at a gay bar ("Fever"), and "The Geysers," about hot springs in California. Some critics, such as Donald Davie, who praised Gunn's stoic examinations of modern life in traditional verse, attacked him for what they saw as abandoning his craft for contemporary informality and decadence. However, Gunn's experiments in style and subject matter helped prepare him to chronicle the tragedies and social changes of the 1980s and 1990s in some of the most technically and emotionally realized writing of his career.

In *The Man with Night Sweats* (1992), Gunn explores the pleasures of his domestic reality alongside the social ravages of AIDS. In "The Hug," Gunn celebrates friendship, not romantic love, between two men who fall asleep, drunk, and wake in a "secure firm dry embrace." The book contains excellent epigrams, including "JVC," written in memory of J. V. CUNNINGHAM. In exquisite elegiac verse, Gunn explores the dignity of men facing AIDS, as in "The J Car." "In Time of Plague" considers the historical coincidence of desire and death. In the heroic couplets of "Courtesies of the Interregnum," Gunn expresses guilt and relief for being "Excluded from the invitation list / To the largest gathering of the decade." Gunn continues to explore aspects of his life in formal and free verse in *Boss Cupid* (2000). In "Saturday Night," Gunn remembers the gay club scene of the 1970s and "Stepping out hot for love or stratagem." He regrets that the "Dionysian experiment" never built a new utopian city, but it was, at least, an attempt to translate "common ecstasy" into a "paradisal state / Against the wisdom pointing us away."

Gunn's reputation now rests on his poems about AIDS, but he will continue to be read for his formal mastery and for his rational stoicism and deeply felt emotions.

BIBLIOGRAPHY
Davie, Donald. *Under Briggflats*. Berkeley: University of California Press, 1989.
Gunn, Thom. *Thom Gunn in Conversation with James Campbell*. London: BTL, 2000.
Morrison, Blake. *The Movement: English Poetry and Fiction in the 1950s*. New York: Oxford University Press, 1980.

Richard E. Joines

GUNSLINGER EDWARD DORN (1968–1975) "A pageant of its time" is how EDWARD DORN described *Gunslinger* (qtd. in Elmborg 1), his book-length poem written during the Vietnam War years that both reflects and critiques the era. Dorn incorporated into the poem a broad cultural mix of the 1960s and 1970s in chronicling the episodic adventures of the somewhat mysterious, mock heroic *Gunslinger* on a journey through the American Southwest, ostensibly to find the eccentric billionaire Howard Hughes. In the process Dorn parodies and refashions the myth of the West, playing on its promise of freedom and its ongoing economic exploitation while exposing and imploding myths of American individualism, Western rationalism, and their corollary philosophical and economic systems. *Gunslinger* follows in a tradition of long American poems with a focus on place, including WILLIAM CARLOS WILLIAMS's *PATERSON* and the *MAXIMUS POEMS* of CHARLES OLSON (see LONG AND SERIAL POETRY). Dorn was crucially influenced by Olson while a student at Black Mountain College during the time Olson served there as rector; influence from the BLACK MOUNTAIN SCHOOL and Olson can be seen in Dorn's "open field" verse, its lines freed from rigid forms, to be shaped by their content, his use of fragmentation and juxtaposition, the citation of historical sources, the poetry's difficult allusive and personal meanings, and its interest in non-Western cultures. Dorn, however, is especially eclectic in his sources and ambiguous in his tone, and he destabilizes character and narrative in ways not seen in earlier poetry.

Dorn's use of language in the work is manic and whimsically creative, with the kind of puns, personal jokes, and striking phrases to be found in his other poetry. This linguistic inventiveness is evident starting with characters' names, which, as with the Gunslinger himself, are cartoonish and sometimes playfully stereotypical. Characters that initially accompany the Gunslinger include his talking horse Claude Levi-Strauss, named for the noted anthropologist, a saloon keeper and madam called Lil, and a character known as "I." Along the way, the hitchhiker Kool Everything, a 1960s hipster traveling with a barrel of LSD, Dr. Jean Flamboyant, a caricature of an academic, and Taco Desoxin and Tonto Pronto, Hispanic and Native American characters, are added. A lack of quotation marks or other attribution makes following who is speaking sometimes difficult, and characters also sometimes change names for poetic and philosophical reasons, such as to question the impulse of naming or to undermine assumptions about characters and narrative sequence.

Dorn's use of a mix of high and popular culture sources in *Gunslinger* is one of the poem's most distinctive characteristics. Often called a mock epic, *Gunslinger* alludes to John Milton's *Paradise Lost* (1667), Virgil's *Aeneid* (17 B.C.), Lord Byron's *Don Juan* (1819–24), Alexander Pope's *The Rape of the Lock* (1714), and other 18th-century satire, while also citing and parodying poets and writers from William Shakespeare,

William Blake, Walt Whitman, T. S. ELIOT, and EZRA POUND to James Joyce, JACK KEROUAC, and Carlos Castaneda. Arcane scientific and philosophic references abound to thinkers, such as Martin Heidegger and Levi-Strauss. Written during a time when popular culture was becoming a powerful force (and the Western a popular genre), the poem frequently cites contemporary culture, from advertising and drug lingo to television game shows and the comedy *Mr. Ed* to the Beatles and the Rolling Stones. This use of popular culture has prompted Marjorie Perloff to contend that one of the primary concerns in *Gunslinger* is "the archaeology of mass-produced myths" and that the poem thus has "more in common with Pop Art" than with the personal LYRIC POETRY prevalent in America at the time (vii). This self-aware and often parodic use of eclectic sources reveals the poem as one making a transition to a more postmodern style of poetry; its mix of satirical and serious intent, its resistance to conventional or consistent meaning, and its use of multiple font styles and sizes call attention to the poem as a material object and as a text per se, other hallmarks of postmodern work. These same qualities can also present formidable barriers for readers, making the poem difficult to interpret on initial readings.

The character of the *Gunslinger* first appeared in Dorn's "An Idle Visitation" (1967). Most of that poem was incorporated into book I of a longer work entitled *Gunslinger,* published in 1968, at the height of the Vietnam War. The complete poem eventually grew to contain four books and a fifth part called *The Cycle,* each written in a sustained burst of activity and each reflecting its different times and Dorn's changing poetic practices and experiments. Collected into one volume in 1975 as *Slinger,* a new complete edition of the poem was published in 1989 as *Gunslinger.*

Travel is a common theme in Dorn's poetry, and the poem addresses both geographic and ontological journeys. The Gunslinger and his companions move across the Southwest, a transition symbolic of an authentic indigenous culture dangerously exploited by capitalistic interests; they travel between actual places, such as Mesilla, the absurdly named Truth or Consequences, and the geographical oddity of the Four Corners area, and fictional locations, such as Universe City, a pun on university. Questioned about the trip in book I, Claude replies that they will move "Across / two states / of mind." Dorn here creates both visual and verbal humor, placing "Across" literally across the page at its right-hand margin, and plays on two meanings of "states." The character "I" is shown to travel the greatest philosophical distances. He starts the journey literally embodying the mythological unified self of Western philosophy, trusting in logic and rationality, initially attempting to find the "meaning" of events, for which he is repeatedly mocked. When "I" dies in book II, he is embalmed with LSD, symbolizing an alternative way of experiencing reality, which exposes to him the limitations of the Western worldview. By book IIII (the title itself a pun on "I"), he is transformed, now castigating Western logic: "Entrapment is this society's / sole activity, I whispered / and Only laughter can blow it to rags."

Dorn's ambivalent fascination with powerful, questing characters is seen in his use as villain the eccentric entrepreneur Howard Hughes, characterized as "hustling the future" with an exploitative, imperialistic attitude implicitly linked to the war. Using informal diction to convey deflating humor, Hughes is described with animal imagery as "proud, brother, as a dog / With two tails," his face sporting reptilian "slick lids." Hughes uses language and vague "data banks" to control those under him, symbolizing sinister hidden electronic and media powers. Underscoring this deviousness is the change of his name within the poem to Rupert, then Robart (literally, rob art).

In the end the Gunslinger is no epic hero, as he sleeps through the potential confrontation with Hughes, and the poem ends anticlimactically with the characters dispersing. The ending reflects Dorn's own growing pessimism over the effectiveness of the counterculture as a political force and foreshadows his later more cynical poetry. In its time and after, however, Dorn won new readers and a measure of fame with the unique, hip *Gunslinger.*

BIBLIOGRAPHY

Elmborg, James K. *A Pageant of its Time: Edward Dorn's Slinger and the Sixties.* New York: Peter Lang, 1998.

Foster, Thomas. "Kick[ing] the Perpendiculars Outa Right Anglos': Edward Dorn's Multiculturalism." *Contemporary Literature* 38 (spring 1997): 78–105.

Jenkins, Grant. "Gunslinger's Ethics of Excess Subjectivity, Community, and the Politics of the Could Be." *Sagetrieb* 15, no. 3 (winter 1996): 206–242.

Perloff, Marjorie. Introduction to *Gunslinger*, by Durham, N.C.: Duke University Press, 1989, pp. v–xvii.

Sue Barker

GUTHRIE, RAMON (1896–1973) After bringing out six books between 1923 and 1929, including two novels, Ramon Guthrie descended into relative poetic silence for 30 years. When his poem *MAXIMUM SECURITY WARD* appeared in 1970, he was 74 years old. His work might be seen as the last flowering of MODERNISM, showing the influence of EZRA POUND and T. S. ELIOT, and paying homage to WALLACE STEVENS, WILLIAM CARLOS WILLIAMS, and Pound.

Although his early biographical information is mostly unverified, Guthrie's life seems to have been eventful. Born in New York, he was brought up in poverty in Hartford, Connecticut, after his father deserted the family. He served during World War I, first as an ambulance driver, then as a machine-gunner in the aviation section signal corps. He survived a plane crash, shot down four enemy planes, and received a Silver Star and two citations for bravery. When the war ended he studied at the Sorbonne. In Paris he met Marguerite Maurey, who would become his wife in 1922. From the 1920s on, the Guthries spent part of each year in France and part in America. He was made an Officier of the French Academy (1949), and later Officier dans l'ordre des Palmes Academique (1963). In 1970 he was awarded the Marjorie Peabody Waite Award of the National Institute of Arts and Letters.

In his first two volumes, Guthrie used traditional meters and medieval French personae. The title of the first, *Trobar Clus* (1923), is a Troubadour term for a style characterized by twisted syntax and deliberately obscure diction. The second, *A World Too Old* (1927), includes a few poems from the first book, as well as others of similar style and subject matter. From 1930 to 1963, Guthrie taught French at Dartmouth College, publishing only an occasional poem.

At the instigation of the scholar M. L. Rosenthal, Guthrie put together the manuscript for *Graffiti* (1959). *Graffiti* retains some of the jaunty allusiveness of his earlier poetry, but it adopts a more flexible and colloquial style. In "Ezra Pound in Paris and Elsewhere," Guthrie uses the formulation, "and yet" followed by three dots, " . . . there *are* no gods, sere Herakles // And yet. . . ." In *Maximum Security Ward,* "as yet" becomes a catch phrase for the mystery of hope.

Asbestos Phoenix (1968) shows Guthrie working in his own style with full confidence, writing musical free verse that alludes to French literature and culture, classical mythology, and quantum physics, among other things. Though often wry and witty, the poems suggest a longing for transcendence in a world that defeats our hopes.

Guthrie began his masterpiece during a time when he was being treated for cancer. He transformed his hospital ward into *Maximum Security Ward* and in this book created a coherent vehicle for expressing a sensibility shaped by post–World War I angst, joy in life, and an innate toughness of mind.

BIBLIOGRAPHY

Diller, George E., ed. *Ramon Guthrie Kaleidoscope.* Hanover, N.H.: Stinehour Press, 1963.

Thomas Lisk

H

HACKER, MARILYN (1942–) When Marilyn Hacker began publishing her poetry in the late 1960s, free verse had become the poetic standard (see PROSODY AND FREE VERSE). The rise of MODERNISM had led to a rejection of received forms by many poets. Hacker's formalism was further complicated by the belief of many in the women's movement that only a rejection of the male poetics of formalism would enable a woman writer to find her own voice (see FEMALE VOICE, FEMALE LANGUAGE). That Hacker, a lesbian and social activist, chose to embrace rather than reject what was then viewed as a "masculine" use of the language was courageous, and this act inspired many women poets who came after her.

Born in New York City, Hacker attended the Bronx High School of Science, skipping her senior year to enroll in New York University at 15. She left college and married the science-fiction writer Samuel Delany in 1961, later returning to graduate in 1964. Hacker and Delany had one child, Iva, about whom Hacker has written with grace and beauty; they subsequently divorced. Hacker's first book of poetry, *Presentation Piece* (the 1973 Lamont Poetry Selection of the Academy of American Poets), was published in 1974 and won the National Book Award. The author of nine books of poetry, Hacker has served as editor for a number of publications, including the feminist journal *13th Moon* (1982–86) and *Kenyon Review* (1990–94), and has translated the contemporary poetry of Venus Khoury-Ghata and Claire Malroux from the French into English. Among her numerous other awards are the Lenore Marshall Literary Award in poetry (1991 and 1995) and the John Masefield Memorial Award (1994). Hacker has taught at a number of colleges and universities, including Brandeis, Barnard, Columbia, and the City College of New York.

In her sonnet sequence *Separations* (1976), Hacker directly addresses her use of received poetic forms. In "Sonnet VI," rhyme is her "homely lover" and meter the sound of this lover's boots that "scuff up the stairs." In the sonnet's final couplet, Hacker imagines that others may some day come to love her "homely lover" too. In "Ballad of Ladies Lost and Found" (1985), Hacker demonstrates how received form can be reclaimed by women writers. Hacker's poem is a witty response to François Villon's "The Ballad of Dead Ladies" (1461) and answers that poem's *ubi sunt* theme ("where are those who have passed now?") by showing that the women have always been here, not dead but lost, because they were overlooked. In Hacker's poem the women are found through the poet's act of naming each of them within the verse: "Make your own footnotes; it will do you good," Hacker writes, telling women to continue to name themselves, to place themselves in the world so that they do not become lost—or unheard.

BIBLIOGRAPHY

Campo, Raphael. "About Marilyn Hacker." *Ploughshares* 22, no. 1 (spring 1996): 195–199.

Finch, Annie, and Marilyn Hacker. "An Interview on Form." *American Poetry Review* 25, no. 3 (May/June 1996): 23–27.

Wendy Galgan

HADAS, RACHEL (1948–) Rachel Hadas combines both traditional and postmodern poetic forms with a background in classical Greek, infusing commonplace topics with elegiac and transformational elements (see PROSODY AND FREE VERSE). Her poems deal with universal issues of mortality, metamorphosis, and rebirth but also include personal moments of emotional vulnerability. Hadas has been influenced by JAMES MERRILL, who turned away from the MODERNISM of T. S. ELIOT to a poetics of transcendence.

Born and raised in New York City, Hadas, the daughter of a renowned classics scholar, studied the classics at Harvard and then spent four years in Greece, developing friendships with poets Merrill and Alan Ansen. Her arrest, trial, and subsequent acquittal for the arson of an olive oil press prompted her return to America for graduate study at Johns Hopkins (M.A., 1977) and Princeton (Ph.D., 1982). Her awards include a number of fellowships and a prize in literature from the American Academy and Institute of Arts and Letters (1995). She has taught at Columbia, Princeton, and Rutgers Universities, as well as at the Sewanee Writers Conference.

Her lifelong interest in Greek culture has permeated her poetry, supplying a variety of classical elements, and has led to translations of Euripides, Seneca, Tibullus, and Konstantine Karyotakis, while her involvement in the intellectual life of New York City has contributed important personal topics. Christopher Benfey has called Hadas "an urban poet and an urbane one" and compared the poems in *Pass It On* (1989) to RANDALL JARRELL's late poetry (406). Assuming the voice of an educator who passes on knowledge, she incorporates personal memories of her father as well as her own teaching experiences. One poem, "Teaching Emily Dickinson," reveals her students' reactions: "She sings the pain of loneliness for one. / Another sees a life of wasted youth."

In an anthology of poems by both AIDS students and herself, *Unending Dialogue: Voices from an AIDS Poetry Workshop* (1991), and in her own later volume, *The Empty Bed* (1995), Hadas gained recognition for poetry dealing with issues of mortality. Her elegies suggest that the void caused by death can somehow be mitigated by language. In "Literary Executor" (1995), she emphasizes the incompleteness of death as having "no closure" and shows poetry as an "unfinished business," which fosters rebirth.

Hadas's poetry situates miracles or transformations in the midst of everyday experiences. As she says in "Fleshly Answers" (1998), "We are passing through the world. / This is some of what it does to us."

BIBLIOGRAPHY

Benfey, Christopher. "From the Greek." *Parnassus* 16, no. 2 (1991): 405–414.

Clark, J. Elizabeth. "An Interview with Rachel Hadas." *Minnesota Review* 55–57 (2002): 80–83.

Helle, Anita. "Elegy as History: Three Women Poets 'By the Century's Deathbed.'" *South Atlantic Review* 61, no. 2 (spring 1996): 51–68.

Joyce C. Smith

HALL, DONALD (1928–) Donald Hall's poetic career, including 14 published volumes, has been a series of experiments in the extent to which he would achieve detachment. Hall's evolving confidence in his capacity for engagement appears in his movement toward a poetry of experience that ultimately makes few claims upon obscure psychological motivations or disconnected visual phenomena. Whereas in many of his earlier works Hall's preoccupation with poetic craft generates an impression of diffidence or even anxiety, he later finds that the comfort of subjectivity enables him to speak effectively in the cogent voice that characterizes his prose writings. Though his first poems were imitations of Edgar Allan Poe, Hall quickly developed sensitivity to the dangers of excessive influence, and his own poetic practice avoids evidence of direct influence. Though wishing to be his own man in terms of poetic originality, Hall is a great practitioner of poetic cooperation, and one of the major phases of his creative life was his marriage to the poet JANE KENYON. Other significant associations have been with ROBERT BLY and JOHN ASHBERY, along with YVOR WINTERS and THEODORE ROETHKE.

Hall was born in Hamden, Connecticut. He attended Harvard University, where he took courses from JOHN CIARDI and ARCHIBALD MACLEISH. Later he studied at Oxford, where he received the Newdigate Prize (1952) for poetry. In 1953 he became poetry editor for the

Paris Review, in which he began a series of interviews with distinguished writers, himself interviewing EZRA POUND, T. S. ELIOT, and MARIANNE MOORE. Since then his long poetic career has earned him numerous honors, including the Lenore Marshall Award (1986), the National Book Critics Circle Award (1988), the ROBERT FROST Medal from the Poetry Society of America (1990–91), and the Ruth Lilly Poetry Prize (1994). He has also won a Caldecott Medal (1980) for children's literature, and he has twice been poet laureate (1984–89 and 1995–99) of the state of New Hampshire. In 2006, he was elected the U.S. poet laureate.

In 1955 Hall published *Exiles and Marriages,* a book of poems which was well received by critics, establishing him in the literary, academic world as a young poet of promise. The poem "Epigenethlion: First Child," which includes the lines beginning "My son, my executioner," is still Hall's most famous poem. In the light of his later career, the relatively strict formality and laconic frankness of these lines, resembling the work of A. E. Housman more than that of any American contemporary, almost seems to be the work of a different poet. Still the poem reflects the profound impact of fatherhood, the implications of which engage Hall's wit and imagination to good effect. The poem employs the witty "conceit" of 17th-century metaphysical poets in its elaborate pun on "executioner" (a fearsome term usually referring to a hangman) and "executor" (one who makes sure that a will is put properly into effect), words sometimes used interchangeably until the 19th century. The speaker calls his baby "our instrument" and tells the child, "Your cries and hungers document / Our bodily decay."

Hall's *A Roof of Tiger Lilies* (1964) signaled a new poetic phase, one in which the poet sought to generate images and effects that would enable the reader to explore the possibilities of the prerational realm of consciousness. In 1972 Hall married Kenyon, who persuaded him to give up his professorship at the University of Michigan and move to his grandparents' old house in rural New Hampshire. This decision had a powerful effect on his subsequent work, as it reestablished his connections to his family's past and to his own childhood. By 1978 Hall, newly energized by reading Walt Whitman, had resumed his poetic engagement with experience, and, in *Kicking the Leaves* (1978), he tacitly endorses Whitman's commitment to personal expression via a narrative or anecdotal voice. Living in the old farmhouse and writing for a living, Hall developed confidence in his own poetic voice. By the time Hall published *The Happy Man* (1986), his poetry had reached a new level of critical acceptance, and, two years later, Hall's next poetry collection *The One Day* (1988) met with enthusiastic reviews. *Old and New Poems* (1990) continued the tradition of the personal poet making his art from experience, as did Hall's next book *The Museum of Clear Ideas* (1993). Having adjusted very well to his literary life in the New Hampshire farmhouse, Hall became more productive than ever. After nearly 20 years of this life, however, Hall's tranquil existence was interrupted by the discovery that his wife had leukemia, and he devoted his energies to her until her death in 1995.

After Kenyon's death, Hall sought the consolation of his poetic art. In *Without* (1998), he published a moving poetic account of his experiences during Kenyon's physical decline. In *The Painted Bed* (2002), Hall has continued to write of the changes that his life underwent as a result of her death, but here he shows signs of coming to terms with grief and with age. His acceptance of these realities is set out in the poem "Affirmation" (2002), in which, after enumerating, in the present tense, as though they were universal truths, the disappointments and failures of life, Hall concludes, "it is fitting / and delicious to lose everything." Although Hall's poetic works may eventually come to be regarded as less significant than his prose, his poetry consistently reflects intelligence, sensitivity, and insight and, taken as a whole, reflects a remarkable personal journey through the obstacle course of his era's professional and imaginative challenges.

BIBLIOGRAPHY

Cramer, Jeffrey S. "With Jane and Without: An Interview with Donald Hall." *Massachusetts Review* 39, no. 4 (winter 1998–1999): 493–511.

McDonald, David. "Donald Hall—Interview." *American Poetry Review* 31, no. 1 (January/February 2002): 17–20.

Truesdale, Vance, with Meredith Walker. "'I do it all because I love to do it': Donald Hall at Clemson." *South Carolina Review* 21, no. 1 (fall 1989): 23–32.

Robert W. Haynes

HAMILL, SAM (1943–) Like others in the generation of American poets born in the 1930s and 1940s, Sam Hamill practices free verse (see PROSODY AND FREE VERSE), usually writing short lyrical poems (see LYRICAL POETRY). He belongs to a tradition of late 20th-century poets who were strongly influenced by classical Chinese and Japanese verse, among them GARY SNYDER and Lucien Stryk. His translation of Lu Chi's *Wen Fu: The Art of Writing* (1987) summarizes the principles of his own poetics, while his mid-length elegy "Requiem" (1984) indicates the pivotal influence of KENNETH REXROTH. Combined with his appreciation for tradition is a powerful radicalism, more evident in his prose and grassroots political endeavors.

Hamill was born probably somewhere in northern California, left by his father with an adoption agency, and raised on a farm in Utah. He joined the U.S. Marine Corps, spending time on Okinawa, where he became a Zen Buddhist and a conscientious objector. His first collection, *Heroes of the Teton Mythos,* was published in 1973 by Copper Canyon Press, an independent publishing house that he had helped found a year earlier. Hamill's *Destination Zero: Poems 1970–1995* received a Pushcart Prize following its publication in 1995. In 2003 Hamill garnered significant media attention by editing an anthology-as-protest against the American invasion of Iraq, *Poets against the War,* for which he received more than 13,000 submissions. A prolific poet, Hamill is also an essayist and translator from ancient Greek, Latin, Japanese, and Chinese.

His collection *Petroglyphs* (1976) and *Triada* (1978), a book-length poem blending elements of American history and American Indian myth, engage broad cultural and historical themes, addressing, for instance, a young nation's failure to abide by its own principles as it expanded westward, marginalizing and absorbing indigenous cultures. Along the same lines, the poems elegize a loss of respect for the land. Starting with *animae* (1980), Hamill's poetry turns inward, addressing such themes as the relations between men and women and the poet's own masculinity. As his work progresses, Hamill weaves his historical, natural, and aesthetic perspectives into a unified vision.

"Requiem," which Kevin Walzer claims "may be Hamill's single finest poem" (139), maintains that as long as we live, as "long as the tongue can open to the vowel," it remains the poet's responsibility to praise the beauty of the world. For when we stand at death's door, ready to pass into the "other world," we will "suddenly know the earth." As Hamill explains in "Cloistered" (1987), "to know and not to speak / is the greatest grief." In clipped, tender lines, often as solemn as scripture, Hamill's verse satisfies this dual duty of witnessing and praise.

BIBLIOGRAPHY

Shenoda, Matthew. "A Life in Poetry: Sam Hamill." *Bloomsbury Review* 21, no. 6 (November–December 2001): 3–30.

Stryk, Lucien. "Why Zen?" *American Poetry Review* 22, no. 6 (November–December 1993): 25–26.

Walzer, Kevin. "A Radical Classicist: The Poetry of Sam Hamill." In *The Resurgence of Traditional Poetic Form and the Current Status of Poetry's Place in American Culture.* Lewiston, N.Y.: Edwin Mellen Press, 2001.

Jeffrey Encke

HARJO, JOY (1951–) Storyteller, musician, and poet, Joy Harjo is known for a style that juxtaposes the present, past, and future. Although spoken by a lyric "I," her poetry challenges the limitations of personal LYRIC POETRY, as well as stereotypical views of Indians (the name *Harjo* refers to American Indians) and of the nature of reality. The "American Indian consciousness" through which she writes, "has to do with a way of believing or sensing things. The world is not disconnected or separate but whole. All persons are still their own entity but not separate from everything else" (Bruchac 22). Among those she names as poetic influences are GALWAY KINNELL, CAROLYN FORCHÉ, AUDRE LORDE, JUNE JORDAN, SIMON ORTIZ, and especially LESLIE MARMON SILKO (Coltelli "Circular Dream" 68).

Harjo, a member of the Muscogee tribe, was born in Tulsa, Oklahoma. She later moved to the Southwest to attend the American Institute of Indian Arts in Santa Fe, New Mexico. She earned a B.A. in poetry at the University of New Mexico in 1976 and an M.F.A. in creative writing at the University of Iowa in 1978. Harjo published her first full-length collection, *What Moon Drove Me to This?,* in 1979. In 1990 *In Mad Love and War* received an American Book Award and the

Delmore Schwartz Memorial Award, and *The Woman Who Fell from the Sky* (1994) won the Oklahoma Book Arts Award. In 1991 she received the Josephine Miles Award for excellence in literature. She has received a number of other honors.

For Harjo, time is a "mythic spiral," as she refers to it in "Hieroglyphic" (1990). Actual events, communal history, and stories share equal importance in revealing her major themes: the struggle of American Indians, people's relationship with the natural world, the importance of belonging to place, identity, loss, and especially the relationship among all beings, things, and ideas (Coltelli "Introduction" 8). In "The Myth of Blackbirds" (1994), Harjo brings together various realities and times to create a spiral of experience: There is a journey she and her friend make in the present to a "brutal" Washington, D.C., the story of a "man from Ghana, who wheeled our bags" and who "loves the poetry of the stars," as well as "the ancestors who became our grandparents" and the mythic "blackbirds who are exactly blackbirds." By repeating and juxtaposing such images, Harjo creates poetry that is both timely and timeless. The "man from Ghana" and the "brutal city" are recognizable as present-day images but also become mythic when set alongside the ancestors and the blackbirds. Harjo often brings several important themes together in a single poem—to, as Janice Gould says, "transcend [the] ordinary world, to name, in language that seems almost sacred, that visionary land to which she travels, of which her extraordinary awareness is so much a part" (10).

BIBLIOGRAPHY

Bruchac, Joseph. "The Story of All Our Survival." In *The Spiral of Memory: Interviews,* edited by Laura Coltelli, 20–35. Ann Arbor: University of Michigan Press, 1996.

Coltelli, Laura. "The Circular Dream." In *The Spiral of Memory: Interviews,* edited by Coltelli. Ann Arbor: University of Michigan Press, 1996, pp. 60–74.

———. Introduction to *The Spiral of Memory: Interviews,* edited by Coltelli. Ann Arbor: University of Michigan Press, 1996, pp. 1–13.

Gould, Janice. "American Indian Women's Poetry: Strategies of Rage and Hope." *Signs* 20, no. 4 (summer 1995): 797–816.

Barbara J. McGrath

HARLEM GALLERY MELVIN TOLSON (1965)

Harlem Gallery is a poem in 24 cantos (parts), written by MELVIN TOLSON, and divided according to the Greek alphabet. The book-length poem is told through a narrator, called "Curator." Themes include social revolution through art and ironies of racial identity. KARL SHAPIRO has called *Harlem Gallery* the lyrical answer to T. S. ELIOT's *The WASTE LAND,* because the poem describes the problems and social woes that plague the America that Tolson sees. Shapiro notes that *Harlem Gallery* has been described as a comic poem, slapstick, crude, and funny: "It is massive, a kind of Odyssey of the American Negro, that like other works of its quality in the past, will turn out to be not only an end in itself but the door to poetry that everyone has been looking for" (14). RITA DOVE says, "the whole of Harlem Gallery, in fact, is very much like the mythic 'bad man' heroes in black oral tradition"; she calls Tolson's hero "the archetypal black artist" (xxi).

The poem originally was written as "Harlem Gallery: Book 1, The Curator," the first book in a five-volume history of the black man in America. Tolson died before the volume was finished. The book evolved from *A Gallery of Harlem Portraits,* which Tolson wrote in 1930. "Book II: Egypt Land" was planned to be a delineation of slavery. "Book III: The Red Sea" was to be an analogy of the Civil War. "Book IV: The Wilderness" was to discuss Reconstruction, and "Book V: The Promised Land" was to be the arrival to America of the black man.

The Curator, akin to Ralph Ellison's protagonist in *Invisible Man* (1952), is a black intellectual ex-professor of art who introduces the reader to the highbrows, middlebrows, and lowbrows, a description of the class systems in society. The Curator is nameless, a way of criticizing the role of the intellectual in the black community. Tolson condemns both black intellectuals and black bourgeoisie (middle-class) for disassociating themselves from their folk background, and so-called black values, opting instead to assimilate into white American society. The Curator witnesses daily activities of black middle-class cultural figures. Another character, Dr. Nkomo, and the Curator learn about black Americans in a white-dominated society. Through their journey, the reader is introduced to three artists: John Laugart, a half-blind destitute painter; Hideho Heights, the poet laureate of Harlem; and Mister Starks, the conductor of the Harlem Symphony Orchestra.

The first five parts of *Harlem Gallery,* Alpha through Epsilon, set the tone for the themes of exploration into the everyday life of black America and the role of the black artist in white American society. The next four parts, Zeta through Iota, reveal philosophical commentaries on the subjects of art, the gap between the races, and what is considered happiness for black Americans, as told by Curator and Dr. Nkomo. Following is Kappa through Xi, focusing on the colorful character Hideho Heights. The next two parts, Omicron and Pi, are reflections about art, historical figures, and biblical passages. The last four parts, Phi through Omega, "reflect on art and the problem of the black artist," Joy Flasch reports, noting that this portion of the poem "recalls the enslavement and suffering of Africans brought to America and issues a warning to the white man to beware of the power of the black minority in this country" (126). *Harlem Gallery* concludes with the Curator meditating on the state of the black artist and his survival in a white-dominated society.

The formatting of the poems runs according to what is described as Tolson's "S-Trinity of Parnassus" notes Flasch (102): sight, sound, and sense. *Sound* refers to the oral nature of the poem, as Tolson intended his work to be read aloud, *sense* to the meaning and the sensory aspect of language, while *sight* entices the reader to examine closely the style in which the lines are written. Also commenting on this style of writing, Dove maintains that "with allusions to Vedic gods and snippets in French and Latin, much of *Harlem Gallery* is fused with street jive and language told in folk tale" (xxi).

The first manuscript of the poem was written in free verse, deviating from the American standard of iambic meter (see PROSODY AND FREE VERSE), modeled after EDGAR LEE MASTERS's *Spoon River Anthology*. Following two decades of failing to publish his work, Tolson rewrote the piece, patterning it after the style of such writers as Eliot, EZRA POUND, and William Butler Yeats. The vignettes, make use of alliteration and allegories, while paying homage to black vernacular "with mimicry, exaggerated language, spontaneity and the persona of the braggadocio" (Dove xxii). For instance, the poem's seventh canto, "Eta," employs black speech to describe a furor that is wreaking havoc on the black American community: "The black widow spider gets rid of her man / gets rid of her daddy as fast as she can."

Robert Spector, in his review of *Harlem Gallery* on the occasion of the book's debut in 1965, said that there is a "somethingness that stirs in all [of Tolson's] characters: desires, ambitions, frustrations and failures" (29). There are several theories about the title. There is the play on *peanut* gallery, for instance—a term given to the cheaper balcony seats in a movie theater where black Americans were forced to sit. And there is the proselytizing of the notion that an art gallery is a symbol of the series of portraits and faces that humans wear, oftentimes disguising who they really are. Throughout this epic journey of black American life, as Shapiro calls *Harlem Gallery* (15), Tolson continues to employ his unique style of storytelling. He struggles, through the narratives of the artists in the gallery, to tell the plight of black America, showing that he feels misunderstood by the one group to whom he dedicates his works—all black writers.

BIBLIOGRAPHY

Dove, Rita. Introduction to *"Harlem Gallery" and Other Poems of Melvin B. Tolson,* edited by Raymond Nelson, xxi–xxii. Charlottesville: University Press of Virginia, 1999.

Flasch, Joy. *Melvin B. Tolson.* New York: Twayne, 1972, pp. 102, 126.

Shapiro, Karl. Introduction to *Harlem Gallery: Book I, The Curator.* New York: Twayne, 1965, pp. 14–15.

Spector, Robert Donald. "The Poet's Voice in the Crowd." *Saturday Review* (7 August 1965): 29.

Yvette R. Blair

HARLEM RENAISSANCE, THE (1919–1934) Between 1919 and 1934 African-American artists flocked to New York City, specifically to Harlem. This era was to become one of the most prolific periods of African-American writing. What Alain Locke called in 1925 a "New Negro Movement" was later defined by historians as the Harlem Renaissance. Among the poets who gained popularity during this era were LANGSTON HUGHES, CLAUDE MCKAY, COUNTEE CULLEN, JEAN TOOMER, Arna Bontemps, Anne Spencer, Gwendolyn Bennett, Helene Johnson, Angelina Weld Grimké, and JAMES WELDON JOHNSON. Many leading fiction writers also emerged during this period, including Zora Neale Hurston, Rudolph Fisher, Jessie Redmond Fauset, Nella Larsen, and Wallace Thurman. Moreover many of the poets of this era also wrote fiction. The Harlem Renaissance also included the creative works produced by brilliantly talented, prolific dancers, musicians, visual artists, and photographers.

Several conditions enabled this renaissance: Booker T. Washington's death, World War I, deteriorating southern racial conditions, greater publishing opportunities, and Marcus Garvey's influence on racial pride. When Booker T. Washington, a former slave and founder of Tuskegee Institute, died in 1915, W. E. B. DuBois, the first African American to take a Ph.D. from Harvard and one of the principal organizers of the National Association for the Advancement of Colored People (NAACP), replaced him as the principal spokesperson for African Americans. Although he held tremendous respect for Washington, DuBois disagreed strongly with his conciliatory attitude toward racial injustice in the South. DuBois endorsed more urgent demands for social change.

When World War I ended in 1918, returning black soldiers, especially those who had been recognized in France for their heroic achievements, were angered by racial conditions that remained unchanged in the United States. When in 1917 Woodrow Wilson proclaimed U.S. involvement in the war as a means to make the world safe for democracy, many African-American soldiers had felt certain that U.S. discrimination would be dismantled. Confronted by the same racial injustice and violence they left, many black veterans joined their anger with a rising spirit of unrest that was beginning to pervade the country.

Racial conditions in the South were becoming unbearable for African Americans, especially in rural areas. Workers faced unfair sharecropping arrangements, lynching, and segregation, as well as inferior schools and living conditions. Many began moving north with the hope of finding greater economic opportunity in the industrial cities of New York, Chicago, Cincinnati, Indianapolis, and Pittsburgh. Soon African-American professionals followed. This huge influx of African Americans to the North became known as the Great Migration. Many of these people settled in Harlem, which was rapidly becoming known as a center for artistic opportunity.

In his essay "The New Negro," Alain Locke, the first African-American Rhodes scholar, attempted to direct the spirit of unrest he saw rising in many black communities as a result of these changing conditions. Riots were breaking out across the country. McKay's famous sonnet "If We Must Die" (1919) addresses this revolutionary spirit: "If we must die, O let us nobly die, / . . . Pressed to the wall, dying but fighting back!"

Locke's solution was the creation and display of talented art, which would become the black ticket into the social fabric of white America. Placing the future in the hands of young artists like McKay, Locke charged them to produce the uncompromising art essential to the reconstruction of African-American identity. Johnson agreed that "nothing will do more to change [the] mental attitude and raise his status than a demonstration of intellectual parity by the Negro through his production of literature and art" (9).

In this art blacks would be more authentically represented. No more minstrel figures, such as the mammy and coon, comic grotesque figures that represented black females as asexual nurturers and black males as comic buffoons. *Crisis,* a publication of the NAACP, as well as *Opportunity,* the publishing arm of the Urban League, held writing contests to inspire young artists. Other outlets included the black socialist publication the *Messenger,* and white publishers and patrons who became more receptive to black art as well.

A variety of styles and literary devices, including dialect, strict standard English, high and low culture, parody, irony, and satire, fill the pages of Harlem Renaissance writings, creating a window into the rich diversity of perspectives alive in African-American communities. Yet artists continued to debate the best way to represent blacks, which classes to foreground in their work, and whether or not to use dialect. In addition writers struggled against the mean-spirited images of blacks as promiscuous. Some artists considered downplaying the theme of sexuality, which, when used unwisely, could only fuel the harmful effects of this stereotype. Others, like Hughes, insisted that artists must not be servants to outside approval. In his famous essay "The Negro Artist and the Racial Mountain" (1926), Hughes responds to a fellow artist's dismissal of his own culture in favor of uncritical acceptance of white Western culture as standard. Declaring the artist's inability to realize full creative potential without respect for his own culture, Hughes issues a bold mandate to all young black artists:

> We younger Negro artists who create now intend to express our individual dark-skinned selves without fear or shame. If white people are pleased we are glad. If they are not, it doesn't matter. We know we are beautiful. And ugly too. . . . If colored people are pleased we are glad. If they are not, their displeasure doesn't matter either. We build our temples for tomorrow, strong as we know how, and we stand on top of the mountain, free within ourselves. (309)

Toomer was the first artist to enjoy widespread critical acceptance of his first work, *Cane* (1923), success that charged the confidence of other Harlem Renaissance writers. The collection, containing a novella, poetry, and short fiction, as well as drawings, is most noted for its focus on the strength and beauty of rural black women, such as Fern. In his free verse Hughes treats themes of black pride, black unity, racial violence, black poverty, black womanhood, African heritage, and integration. He also transcribed blues, jazz, and gospel into poetic verse. Such innovation gained him the reputation of "poet laureate of the Harlem Renaissance." In one of his most famous poems, the musician and his sounds come alive on the page: "Thump, thump, thump, went his foot on the floor. / He played the chords then he sang some more." Johnson explored the sermonic tradition in his poetry, maintaining black verbal art forms, while McKay and Cullen cast their poetry in the traditional form of the sonnet. Cullen, perhaps more closely aligned with European-inspired poetic verse, nonetheless indulged in social protest with his poems "HERITAGE" (1925) and "Yet Do I Marvel" (1925), which questions God and the paradox of a black poet: "Yet do I marvel at this curious thing; / To make a poet black, and bid him sing!" Although Bontemps once collaborated with Hughes on a literary project, his poetry, influenced by his religious upbringing, is meditative and spiritual with a deep sense of racial pride.

While the movement often seemed to be dominated by men, women also managed to leave their enduring mark on the poetry of the era. Georgia Douglas Johnson attended to racial themes, yet was equally drawn to romanticism, sentimentalism, and issues concerning the human condition. Angelina Weld Grimké treated racial themes with a lyric sensibility. Much of Anne Spencer's work is concerned with gender more than race. Race-conscious Gwendolyn Bennett wrote lyrics that focused on the "grace and loveliness" of the descendants of Africans (Gates 1227). Helene Johnson was described as "one of the younger group who has taken . . the 'racial' bull by the horns" (Johnson 279).

Other important writers of the period include Eric Walrond, STERLING A. BROWN, and Dorothy West. Walrond wrote of his experiences as a West Indian in Harlem, Brown continued Hughes's emphasis on the poetics of blues culture, and West examined the wealthy class of blacks, writing and publishing well into her nineties.

In opposition to the radical modernist movement and such poets as EZRA POUND and T. S. ELIOT, Harlem Renaissance poets did not view the entire modern world as a wasteland (see *The WASTE LAND*). Instead a sense of optimism pervaded their work, unlike the fatalism and pessimism found in many works of MODERNISM. Like blues music, the poetry transformed hopelessness with love and laughter, the words and images infused with the power of persistence.

Historians David Levering Lewis and Nathan Huggins argue that the Harlem Renaissance failed in its mission to challenge inequitable conditions for blacks in North America through art. Literary critic Houston A. Baker, Jr., disagrees: He insists that such faith in the power of art could be "a mark of British and American modernism," but that British and white American scholars would dismiss such efforts by labeling the movement a failure (14). Certainly if the success of the movement can be gauged by its influence on generations to follow, the Harlem Renaissance was a tremendous success. Not only did the movement have an impact on individual artists, but the BLACK ARTS MOVEMENT of the 1960s looked to the Harlem Renaissance for guidance and direction.

BIBLIOGRAPHY

Baker, Houston A., Jr. *Modernism and the Harlem Renaissance.* Chicago: University of Chicago Press, 1987.
Gates, Henry Louis, Jr., et al., eds. "The Harlem Renaissance." *Norton Anthology of African-American Literature.* New York: W. W. Norton, 1997.
Hughes, Langston. "The Negro Artist and the Racial Mountain." In *Voices from the Harlem Renaissance,* edited by Nathan Huggins. New York: Oxford University Press, 1995.
———. "The Weary Blues." In *Norton Anthology of African-American Literature,* edited by Henry Louis Gates, Jr., et al. New York: W. W. Norton, 1997.
Johnson, James Weldon, ed. *The Book of American Negro Poetry.* New York: Harcourt, Brace & World, Inc., 1922.
Karenga, Maulana. *Introduction to Black Studies.* Los Angeles: Kawaida Publications, 1982.
Lewis, David Levering. *When Harlem Was in Vogue.* New York: Oxford University Press, 1981.
McKay, Claude. "If We Must Die." In *The Book of American Negro Poetry,* edited by James Weldon Johnson. New York: Harcourt, Brace & World, 1922.
———. *A Long Way from Home.* New York: Lee Furman, 1937.
Toomer, Jean. *Cane.* New York: Liveright, 1923.
Zinn, Howard. *A People's History of the United States.* New York: HarperCollins, 1980.

Judy Massey Dozier

HARPER, MICHAEL S. (1938–) Michael S. Harper is an African-American poet whose work is influenced not only by other writers, such as STERLING A. BROWN, ROBERT HAYDEN, and Ralph Ellison, but also by jazz and blues, especially the music of John Coltrane and Charlie Parker. Harper says he resisted traditional forms (see PROSODY AND FREE VERSE), because metrical verse "forced an accommodation to the mechanics of the count." Instead, the rhythm of his poems is modeled more after jazz and the way its "music was announced . . . in the auditory registers of phrasing" ("Afterword" 371–372). Harper's poetic language is uniquely conversational and musical.

Harper was born in Brooklyn, New York. He studied at the Iowa Writers' Workshop and in 1970 joined the faculty of Brown University. *DEAR JOHN, DEAR COLTRANE,* his first book of poetry, was published in 1970 and was nominated for the National Book Award. He received the Black Academy of Arts and Letters Award for poetry (1971) and the Melville-Cane Award from the Poetry Society of America in 1977. Additional honors include the ROBERT HAYDEN Poetry Award from the United Negro College Fund (1990), the National Institute of Arts and Letters Creative Writing Award (1972), a Guggenheim Fellowship (1976), and a National Endowment for the Arts grant (1977). He was selected as the first state poet of Rhode Island (1988).

Although Harper's point of view is very personal, cultural issues of black America are the primary subject of his body of work. Several poems recount incidents of racism, not only against blacks but also against Hispanics and American Indians. Other poems are tributes to Coltrane, Parker, Bud Powell, Bessie Smith, and other musicians. A strong sense of family informs many of Harper's poems, particularly the poignantly rendered poems about the death of his newborn son. In "Reuben, Reuben" (1970), Harper shows how music can be a salve for those in pain. His son's death leaves the speaker in a forlorn state, with "a pickle of hate / so sour" that he cannot access song or melody. For solace he reaches out for music. He finds that jazz provides comfort and something else. Where there is emptiness, "the music, *jazz,* comes in," giving voice and expression to the speaker's unutterable grief. In his willingness to address difficult social issues in a strikingly personal way, Michael Harper plays an important role in moving poetry forward. He chose the cadence of everyday language and music over the metrics of traditional verse, creating a poetic language that is true to the world he portrays.

BIBLIOGRAPHY

Harper, Michael S. Afterword to *Songlines in Michaeltree: New and Collected Poems.* Urbana: University of Illinois Press, 2000, pp. 371–372.
———. "Don't They Speak Jazz?" In *The Generation of 2000: Contemporary American Poets,* edited by William Heyen, 89–92. Princeton: Ontario Review Press, 1984.

Stepto, Robert B. "After Modernism, After Hibernation: Michael Harper, Robert Hayden and Jay Wright." In *Chant of Saints: A Gathering of Afro-American Literature, Art, and Scholarship,* edited by Michael S. Harper and Robert B. Stepto, 472–476. Urbana: University of Illinois Press, 1979.

Linda Levitt

HARRYMAN, CARLA (1952–) A key participant in West Coast LANGUAGE writing, Carla Harryman's work incorporates elements of poetry, prose, philosophy, theater, and popular culture. Harryman delves into how consciousness comes into being. Megan Simpson writes that Harryman "has explored narrative transgressions in the Freudian plot, fairytale, pornography, children's stories, and games." For Harryman it may be possible to "construct, alter, reawaken cultural practice by picking up threads that have been neglected or underused as well as by charging into the unknown" (Simpson 516).

Harryman was born in Orange County, California, and educated at the University of California, Santa Barbara, and San Francisco State University. In San Francisco she edited the journal *Qu* and cofounded Poets' Theater (1978–84). She has received awards from the Detroit Arts Fund (2001), the Fund for Poetry (1992, 1994, and 1999), and the Wallace Alexander Gerbode Foundation (1993), among others. Her dramatic work has been performed in a variety of venues, including *Memory Play* at the LAB, San Francisco (1994), and *Performing Objects Stationed in the Sub World* at Oxford Brookes University (2001) and Zeitgeist Theater in Detroit (2002). She has taught at Wayne State University.

Through conceptualizing a "bridge" or "middle," Harryman questions the philosophical distinctions between reason and instinct, human and animal, external and internal. Her texts may reveal a comic, ironic, or surreal edge. In "Typical Domains" (1995) she writes, "Of course I think about sex a lot more than I should. / One evening I put one foot in the clear water. A fish rose to the surface and said, / 'Euphoria never lasts.'"

Poetry and prose interweave in a fantasy concerning sexual knowledge and its conventions. When the speaker "tests the water," she is warned of the temporary nature of its pleasure by symbolic fish, which fittingly expire. The speaker's subsequent "falling" is associated both with the "swoon" and with acquiring knowledge from the pool. The final line, "A conservative make," contextualizes the act of "making out" with the human-made. While Harryman questions the naturalness of such sexual knowledge, she poses the possibility of an area beyond the social, which might be bridged by writing. Often playfully intertextual and formally adventurous, Harryman's writing challenges the reader to reconsider the boundaries of the poem.

BIBLIOGRAPHY

Harryman, Carla. Interview by Megan Simpson. *Contemporary Literature* 37, no. 4 (winter 1996).

Simpson, Megan. *Poetic Epistemologies.* Albany: State University of New York Press, 2000.

Ann Vickery

HASS, ROBERT (1941–) While Robert Hass's work has, from the start, been blessed with great popularity, the praise his work has garnered has not always been unmitigated. When his first book of poetry, *Field Guide,* appeared in 1973 as part of the prestigious Yale Series of Younger Poets, it received much acclaim. However, the book has since been criticized from two very different angles. Ira Sadoff, for example, wrote in the *Chicago Review* that the book "tapped Hass's power of observation carefully and engagingly" but that he nevertheless had reservations about the book "stemm[ing] from some sense of chilliness that seemed to pervade a number of the poems, as if [they] were wrought by an intellect distant from its subject matter" (134). In Robert Miklitsch's *Hollins Critic* article on Hass, though, the book is found most wanting when it is least intellectual: "Hass's imagination," claims Miklitsch, "is essentially discursive and meditative" (3). If Sadoff sees in Hass's book an IMAGIST-influenced poetry marred by intellectual distance, Miklitsch sees an intellectual poetry too often reined in by mere description. Both critics are right in seeing Hass as a poet who combines the imagistic and sensuous with the intellectual and speculative. In fact it is through this ability to hold the intellectual and the sensuous side by side, in tension with one another, that Hass achieves his significance in American poetry.

Hass was born in San Francisco; with the exception of a few years in upstate New York, he has lived in the Bay Area his entire life. He was a student at St. Mary's College of California, from which he received his B.A. in 1963. He continued his studies at Stanford, from which he received his M.A. and Ph.D. in English literature in 1965 and 1971, respectively. At Stanford he was active in the student protest politics of the Vietnam era's antiwar movement, and he remained involved with the movement after taking his first academic appointment at the State University of New York, Buffalo, where he taught from 1967 to 1971. Later teaching appointments included St. Mary's College (1971–89) and the University of California, Berkeley (1989 to the present). Hass served two terms as United States poet laureate (1995–97). While best known as a poet, Hass has in many ways fulfilled the ideal of the man of letters, writing essays and reviews and editing. In fact he has received a National Book Critics Circle Award for the critical essays he gathered together in *Twentieth Century Pleasures* (1984).

In his foreword to *Field Guide,* STANLEY KUNITZ claims that "Hass's poetry is permeated with the awareness of his creature self, his affinity with the animal and vegetable kingdoms, with the whole chain of being" (xii); many of the poems celebrate the animal sensations. In addition to its strong emphasis on the "creature self" and the physical world, *Field Guide* takes up language itself as one of its great themes. The poems often concern themselves with proper names, sometimes to stress their transience: "some days it's not so hard to say / the quick pulse of blood," writes Hass at the end of "Graveyard at Bolinas" (1973). At other times, though, Hass implies that names can be reassuring, giving us the illusion of control over that which is named.

Praise (1979) continues Hass's meditations on the relationship of language to experience. The volume contains two of Hass's most celebrated poems, "Meditation at Lagunittas" and "Picking Blackberries with a Friend Who Has Been Reading Jacques Lacan," both of which question the relationship of words to things. These two poems are notable for the way they incorporate complex ideas of language from structuralist and poststructuralist linguistics without resorting to jargon or arid diction. It is characteristic of Hass's particular virtue as a poet that he finds a way to balance philosophical sophistication with lush, specific description.

Ten years after *Praise,* Hass published his third collection of poems, *Human Wishes* (1989). Many of his characteristic themes, including landscape and the relationship of words and things, appear again, but the book is formally quite different from his earlier work. Many of the pieces take the form of prose poems, for example. Others, such as "Berkeley Eclogue," feature interruptions by an unidentified interlocutor who seems, at times, to be interrogating the speaker of the poem, breaking into the narrative with questions, such as "What for?" and "And then what?" More striking, though, is the way in which some of these poems take Hass's questions about whether or not language can accommodate experience a step further by deliberately shattering narrative continuity and the consistency of perspective and statement.

Like *Human Wishes,* Hass's fourth book, *Sun under Wood,* contains both poems and prose poems, and, as in *Human Wishes,* the poems of *Sun under Wood* often contain the voices of interlocutors. "Faint Music," for example, begins with the line "Maybe you need to write a poem about grace," while "Interrupted Meditation" consists of a dialogue between the speaker and an older man who shares many characteristics with Hass's longtime friend and collaborator Czeslaw Milosz. Some of the most important poems in *Sun under Wood,* though, return to that great perennial theme of Hass's poetry, language: "English: An Ode," for example, uses etymology to explore both the history and the politics of English as it becomes a global language. From *Field Guide* through to his most recent work, Hass never feels that language is simply the poet's medium: It is his topic—and his muse.

BIBLIOGRAPHY

Gander, Forrest. "Robert Hass." *Dictionary of Literary Biography.* Vol. 105, *American Poets since World War II,* edited by R. S. Gwynn. Detroit: Gale Research, 1991, pp. 104–113.

Kunitz, Stanley. Foreword to *Field Guide,* by Robert Hass. New Haven, Conn.: Yale, 1973, pp. xi–xix.

Matthias, John. "Reading Old Friends." *Southern Review* 22 (spring 1986): 391–406.

Miklitsch, Robert. "'Praise,' the Poetry of Robert Hass." *Hollins Critic* 17, no. 1 (February 1980): 2–13.

Sadoff, Ira. "Robert Hass's 'Praise.'" *Chicago Review* 31, no. 3 (winter 1980): 133–136.

Robert Archambeau

HAYDEN, ROBERT (1913–1980) Robert Hayden once declared, "Nothing human is foreign to me" (114), and his poetry demonstrates the extent of this reach. Hayden's voice ranges from an ex-slave ("A Letter from Phillis Wheatley" [1978]) to a white man reflecting on lynching blacks ("Night, Death, Mississippi" [1962]) to someone considering the complicated operations of love ("THOSE WINTER SUNDAYS" [1962]) to a visitor from outer space evaluating the conditions of contemporary America (*American Journal* [1978]). Hayden is much more interested in people and places than in ideas or abstract concepts, and his poems often focus on folk themes, figures from African-American history, and the ordinary human needs that art can fulfill. Hayden's language is unpretentious yet unfailingly accurate, and he has the uncommon ability to disguise craft as spontaneity. Hayden's style is generally restrained, and he is assiduous in his attentiveness to verbal detail: In this, he owes something to W. H. AUDEN, with whom Hayden studied while a graduate student. Other early models for Hayden's poetry include CARL SANDBURG, EDNA ST. VINCENT MILLAY, JEAN TOOMER, HART CRANE, LANGSTON HUGHES, and COUNTEE CULLEN. This admixture indicates Hayden's inclinations toward both formalism and innovation, toward high culture as well as folk, and it creates a poetry that, as he would have wished, defies easy categorization.

Hayden was born in Detroit, Michigan, and named Asa Bundy Sheffey. His eyes were damaged at birth; he suffered from severe nearsightedness his entire life. Before he was two years old, his birth mother turned him over to the care of her neighbors, the Haydens, a devout Baptist couple who renamed the boy Robert Earl and raised him (though they never legally adopted him). Hayden graduated from Detroit City College (1936) and received an M.A. from the University of Michigan (1946). He taught at Fisk University (1946–69) and at Michigan (1969–80). By the time Hayden began teaching at Michigan, his renown was quietly extensive, both in the United States and abroad: In 1966 he had received the Grand Prize in poetry at the First World Festival of Negro Arts in Senegal, and from 1976 to 1978 he served as poetry consultant to the Library of Congress, a position that would later be known as poet laureate of the United States.

As a poet Hayden came into his own after the periods of MODERNISM and the HARLEM RENAISSANCE and yet before the advent of the BLACK ARTS MOVEMENT. Due to timing and temperament, Hayden's poetry was, in many ways, at odds with the latter group, and he aspired, like Cullen before him, to be known not as a black poet but simply as a poet. His most common subjects are related to African-American history and experience—as in "Middle Passage" (1962) and "Mourning Poem for the Queen of Sunday" (1962)—and he declared in his famous sonnet "Frederick Douglass" (1962) that the title figure should be remembered "not with legends and poems and wreaths of bronze alone, / but with the lives grown out of his life." Yet he was criticized by many in the Black Arts movement for his dedication to aesthetic values and for what some perceived as his racial conservatism or indifference to political matters. Hayden never denied the importance of race—for himself or for American society—and he consistently denounced and worked to remedy racial injustices. He bristled, however, at the attempt to "delimit poets, to restrict them to the political and the socially or racially conscious" (120). He continued, "I can't imagine any poet worth his salt today not being aware of social evils, human needs. But . . . I resist whatever would force me into a role as politician, sociologist, or yea-sayer to current ideologies" (120).

Hayden's concept of poetry was much broader than one that would identify verse as nothing more than a tool for political change. He described poetry as a form of prayer or worship, and for him it was an affirmation of the need to blend spirituality with work: "[T]he truly revolutionary poets are always those who are committed to some integrative vision of art and life" (Hayden 70). This "integrative vision" follows, in part, from his Baha'i faith, which Hayden espoused as an adult, and it is seen in such poems as "Words in the Mourning Time" (1970), "Monet's 'Waterlilies'" (1970), "The Peacock Room" (1972), and "The Tattooed Man" (1978). Like most of Hayden's poems, these are reflective but begin with and remain linked to a particular place or person. These meditations allow him to witness the mingling of the familiar and the mysterious, as "The seen, the known / dissolve" in the present and become part of that which "forever is" ("Monet's Waterlilies"). But if art offers a momentary reprieve, it always returns us to life, with all its violence and uncertainty, and to ourselves. Still, art makes it possible for Hayden, as he laments the assassinations of Martin Luther King, Jr., and Robert Kennedy, to understand that their deaths, like all of our griefs, are part of the "process" by which "our humanness must be achieved" ("Words in the Mourning Time").

Although Hayden was active as a professional poet for more than 40 years, the demands of his teaching schedule and his commitment to revision made for a relatively small body of published work. Ten volumes of Hayden's poetry have been published, the most readily available of which is *Collected Poems* (1985, 1996). He also edited several poetry collections, and the introductory essays to them, along with other writings and interviews, are included in *Collected Prose* (1984). In all of Hayden's work, we see the imprint of the "humanness" toward which he strove, as well as evidence that as individuals we are "smaller than myth" ("Astronauts" [1978])—the poems and stories that we create—but that collectively we are much more.

BIBLIOGRAPHY

Goldstein, Laurence, and Robert Chrisman, eds. *Robert Hayden: Essays on the Poetry.* Ann Arbor: University of Michigan Press, 2001.

Hayden, Robert. *Collected Prose.* Ann Arbor: University of Michigan Press, 1984.

Williams, Pontheolla. *Robert Hayden: A Critical Analysis of His Poetry.* Urbana: University of Illinois Press, 1987.

Jeannine Johnson

H. D. (HILDA DOOLITTLE) (1886–1961)

For many years, H. D.'s critical reputation suffered, largely because her initial success as part of an early 20th-century literary movement overshadowed her later work and more important themes. The poems of her early career epitomize the tenets of the IMAGIST SCHOOL. In her middle career she was criticized for growing beyond that movement, despite a similar move away by its cofounder and staunchest advocate, EZRA POUND; in her later years she was overlooked for maintaining within her poetry too many elements of imagism. However, over five decades of work, she provided a large scope and represented, as part of and in addition to an attempt to establish a voice for women, a truly modernist vision: a reaction against Victorian life, the recognition of a fragmented modern age, and a return to myth to establish meaning in that new age (see MODERNISM).

H. D. was born Hilda Doolittle, the only surviving daughter of Dr. Charles Leander Doolittle and Helen Eugenia Wolle Doolittle, in Bethlehem, Pennsylvania. Her mother was a musician and was active in the Moravian Church. Her father was an astronomer and mathematician who was eventually appointed director of the observatory at the University of Pennsylvania. This combination of influences—art concatenated with symbols, rituals, and secrecy from her mother's side and with science from her father's—were perhaps the strongest forces working to create the poet H. D. would become. In Philadelphia she met Pound; the two were briefly engaged to be married, but the greater effect of Pound upon H. D. was to encourage her expression through poetry. H. D. was also introduced to WILLIAM CARLOS WILLIAMS during this time. In 1911 she sailed to Europe and never returned to the United States to live. Through Pound she met other poets and authors, including F. S. Flint and Richard Aldington; they soon formed the imagist movement. In 1912, while sending out her first three poems for publication, Pound launched Hilda Doolittle's new persona (and career) by scratching at the bottom of one page "H. D., Imagiste." She won the Guarantors Prize from *Poetry* magazine in 1915 and the Libre Prize from the *Little Review* in 1917. H. D.'s poems of these early years epitomized the tenets laid down by the imagists; "Oread" (1914), one of her more frequently anthologized poems, exhibits the concrete, concentrated, musical line of the imagist poem: "Whirl up your pointed pines . . on our rocks." It was by this standard that H. D. was judged—at first enthusiastically, but progressively less so—for the rest of her career. At the end of her life, though, a new appreciation began after she received the Brandeis University Creative Arts Award for poetry in 1959 and the Award of Merit Medal for poetry from the American Academy of Arts and Letters in 1960. The ensuing feminist movement of the 1970s and increased critical attention in the 1980s cemented H. D.'s place in American poetry.

In addition to establishing H. D.'s renown, her early experience with imagism gave her the discipline with which to control the excesses of her emotions and distill them into a tightly crafted poetry that probably could not have existed without that discipline. In these and later poems, H. D. employs Greek myth to channel her emotional responses to nature and to attempt to unify a fragmentary modernist existence, but also as a poetic mask behind which the person/poet hides. Her poems of the 1910s, especially those found in her first volume, *Sea Garden* (1916), employ imagery from the natural world and Greek place-names and on H. D.'s memories of the gardens near the American home of her youth. They also explore the individual consciousness and are structured on polarities and dualisms, such as hardness and softness, darkness and light, land and sea, lightness and weight. These opposites point toward the dualisms in H. D.'s own life and in the work that followed this period.

The years during and immediately after World War I brought an end to the formal imagist movement and the first phase of H. D.'s poetry. After a series of personal tragedies and traumas, she began to refocus upon the role of women and her own identity as a woman. "Helen" (1923) is representative of this period, presenting an alternate view of the woman who, according to misogynist myth, began the Trojan War. "All Greece hates" Helen, though they worship her beauty; they see only "God's daughter, born of love / the beauty of cool feet." Forgetting that she is not born of "love," but of Zeus's rape of Leda, these Greeks lust after her and wish her dead in the same moment. For the brutality of war, they blame the woman. Like some of H. D.'s earlier work, the poems of this period recall Euripides and Sappho, but they go further in masking the poet behind myth so as better to express the personal, albeit obliquely.

The collection *Red Roses for Bronze* (1931) was a personal and critical disappointment. H. D. turned to fiction and cinema in the early 1930s when the well of poetry dried up. These influences, combined with H. D.'s interests in the occult and psychoanalysis (she was a student and patient of Sigmund Freud), helped H. D. formulate her new destiny as a kind of poet-prophet and provided her with the inspiration for a resurgence in poetry during the 1940s. The greatest expression of this new energy came in *The Walls Do Not Fall* (1944), an evocation of the horrors of World War II. In this long poem, the speaker, walking through bomb-ripped downtown London, must attempt to ascertain meaning—if it can be found—amid the destruction: "thoughts stir, inspiration stalks us / through gloom." Within this new wasteland lies a spirit of regeneration, perhaps analogous to H. D.'s own personal poetic flowering after the relative dormancy of the 1930s. Though battered, *"Still the walls do not fall,"* and the possibility of transcendence for the poet and people lingers on the horizon: "we are voyagers, discoverers . . . possibly we will reach haven, / heaven." *Tribute to the Angels* (1945) and *The Flowering of the Rod* (1946) continued the theme of triumph over death through the power of love as a spiritual force for peace (these were collected together with *The Walls Do Not Fall* into *Trilogy* in 1973).

For H. D., survival and transcendence are found in the figure of the woman, and she continued to explore a new role for women in the myths that made up much of her poetry. To this figure she devoted much of her energy in the 1940s and 1950s, culminating in her epic poem, *HELEN IN EGYPT* (1961). Based on an obscure alternative tale of Helen of Troy, H. D. weaves elements of her own life, including love, wartime experience, mysticism, psychological analysis, and the search for identity, into a tapestry that accomplishes a modern, feminist revision of the male-centered Greek epic story. Echoing her earlier poem, she begins with "Helena, hated of all Greece," the woman who is seen as the cause of so much misery and destruction. This Helen, though, is brought to Egypt by Zeus (rather than remaining in Troy), and the quest to understand why this has happened eventually becomes a search for self-understanding, an answer to the question—"Helena? Who is she?" In the three sections of the poem, Helen begins by investigating temple hieroglyphs, enters into a liaison with dead Achilles, brought back by her power, and then relives her life with Paris. Discovering that "she herself is the writing," that she is the hieroglyph in need of deciphering, Helen eventually reaches that understanding of herself. Seemingly the poet H.

D. has come to that point as well, reconciling the oppositions in her own life, and presents Helen as a model for all those persons (women in particular) who are engaged in such a search.

Today H. D. remains, closely identified with the imagist movement. However, much critical attention also is focused on the mature work that employs certain aspects of imagism but then goes beyond the single, concrete image to a more extensive exploration of the changing roles of women in the 20th century, the origins and meaning of the poet's and readers' identities and psyches, and all of our places within a fragmented, modern society. For the most part, she accomplishes this through a thoroughly modernist recasting of the Greek classics. Her readers, especially women, other poets, especially American poets, and those exploring the dualities of their own identities can look to H. D.'s poems to find a kindred soul.

BIBLIOGRAPHY

Friedman, Susan S., and Rachel Blau DuPlessis, eds. *H. D. Centennial Issue. Contemporary Literature* 27, no. 4 (1986). [Special Issue]

Guest, Barbara. *Herself Defined: The Poet H. D. and Her World.* New York: Doubleday, 1984.

Robinson, Janice S. *H. D.: The Life and Work of an American Poet.* Boston: Houghton Mifflin, 1982.

Joseph Schaub

HECHT, ANTHONY (1923–2004) Anthony Hecht is known for elegant and formal verse that refuses to settle for easy answers as it both confronts the bleakest moments in human experience and acknowledges the unexpected bounties of nature. Hecht's poetics stem from a New Critical, or formalist, tradition (see FUGITIVES/AGRARIANS and NEW FORMALISM) associated with JOHN CROWE RANSOM, ALLEN TATE, and W. H. AUDEN. Such poetry is often characterized by unresolved ambiguities, surprising juxtapositions, and the use of personae, or "screens," through which a poem's meaning is mediated. Hecht's continued embrace of traditional meters and forms is consistent with his statement in *On the Laws of the Poetic Art* (1995) that a poem "must rely on more than the strength of its convictions. It will have to persuade us that those convictions were arrived at under the pressure of long thought, and were expressed with an artfulness that took into account that almost nothing in this world can be simplified into good and bad, right and wrong" (58). Hecht's poetry, typical of the late 20th century, wrestles with questions of goodness and morality in a post-Holocaust world that cannot be navigated successfully with simple answers.

Hecht was born and raised in New York City. He decided to become a poet during his first year of studies at Bard College when his instructor, Lawrence Leiter, introduced him to the works of poets, such as Auden, T. S. ELIOT, Dylan Thomas, and WALLACE STEVENS. Hecht received a B.A. in 1944 and served in the army from 1943 to 1946. His experiences in infantry and counterintelligence during World War II strongly affected his sense of the world, as is reflected in much of his poetry dealing with wartime themes. Upon returning to the United States, Hecht studied under Ransom at Kenyon College and then under Allen Tate in 1947. Hecht's first book, *A Summoning of Stones,* was published in 1954, and his next book of poetry, *The Hard Hours,* won the Pulitzer Prize for poetry in 1968. Hecht subsequently published more volumes of poetry, in addition to works of translation and literary criticism. He has won numerous fellowships and awards, including the Bollingen Prize in poetry (1983).

Hecht's oeuvre is marked by its versatility of subject matter and approach. Perhaps his most memorable poems are those that peer unflinchingly at the horrors of World War II and the Holocaust. "More Light! More Light!" (1967), for example, juxtaposes a 16th-century burning at the stake with a 20th-century narrative: When a Pole refuses a Nazi's order to bury alive two Jews, the Nazi has the Jews begin to bury the Pole alive, thus coercing the Pole's cooperation. The poem's despair rests in the crumbling of any moral stronghold; no one in the poem remains innocent, and no moment of hope or transcendence offers a way out of the situation. Instead the poem sets the roles of victim and oppressor into a tension that is never resolved. Narrated in a matter-of-fact style that does not offer commentary on the events, the poem nonetheless provokes an emotional yet reflective response.

Other poems, though not always as shocking, continue to negotiate the line at which innocence begins to disintegrate and slip into a dark side that cannot be ignored. "A Hill" (1967) moves from a crowded Italian piazza into a vision of a desolate hill upon which the speaker remembers gazing for hours in the midst of winter. Descriptive details of the vision, from trees resembling "old ironwork gathered for scrap" to "a piece of ribbon snagged on a hedge," work together to suggest that traditional signs of life or comfort are merely useless remnants of a crumbling and futile civilization. Even after the vision is gone, the "plain bitterness" of it haunts the speaker. "The Deodand" (1979) also upsets a state of naïve comfort by introducing unresolved complexities. The poem meditates on a Renoir painting that depicts women playing dress-up with Algerian clothes. This seemingly innocent scene, the poem implies, is one that relies on colonial exploitation and the torture of a French legionnaire, the latter described vividly so as once more to complicate positions of victim and victimizer. Hecht's poetry offers such juxtapositions again and again, moving toward a morality that neither hides from evil in a false sense of security nor sharply delineates the good from the bad; instead, implications of various positions are vigilantly played out in an attempt to depict truthfully the complexities of life.

This is not to suggest, however, that Hecht's poetry presents itself as the final word on any topic. Instead, through humor, the use of detailed situations, and a tendency to ruminate on other works of art, Hecht's poetry constantly reads the world afresh and suggests that these readings too will give way when pressed. "The DOVER BITCH" (1967), a poem often anthologized alongside Matthew Arnold's "Dover Beach" (1867), exemplifies these tendencies. A man speaks about the woman addressed in Arnold's poem, but his take on her is much more earthy and less traditionally poetic than is Arnold's, demonstrating the way many of Hecht's poems "deflate a certain type of rhetoric, searching out and exposing the false and phony, puncturing the heroic gesture" (Hirsch 54). Although the woman does not speak in either poem, the casual tone of the speaker in Hecht's poem allows Hecht to criticize Arnold's use of her as "a sort of mournful cosmic last resort" (54) without himself using the woman as a passive source of comfort in a disappointing world.

Through his long career, Hecht has used formal meter and language to structure concrete, often narrative, treatments of wide-ranging subjects, regularly returning to the most difficult questions of living responsibly in a world that seems rarely to offer truly ethical choices. Often focused on everyday matters, Hecht's poetry attends to that which is jarring or extraordinary, but which is nonetheless usually ignored.

BIBLIOGRAPHY

German, Norman. *Anthony Hecht.* New York: Peter Lang, 1989.

Hirsch, Edward. "Comedy and Hardship." In *The Burdens of Formality: Essays on the Poetry of Anthony Hecht,* edited by Sydney Lea, 53–61. Athens: University of Georgia Press, 1989.

Laurie McMillan

HEJINIAN, LYN (1941–) Lyn Hejinian is associated with the LANGUAGE SCHOOL, a community of writers partly established in the San Francisco Bay area in the mid-1970s interested in how language creates meaning. Her poetry challenges conventions of language and struggles with questions, such as "How can we know anything?" Hejinian's innovative use of language explores the processes of human thinking and is influenced by the work of the American avant-garde writer GERTRUDE STEIN.

Hejinian was born in San Francisco, California. She graduated from Harvard in 1963—the first year that women were given Harvard degrees. In 1968 she returned to the West Coast, where her first books of poetry were published in the 1970s. She has been the editor and publisher of Tuumbra Press and since 1981 the creator and coeditor (with BARRETT WATTEN) of *Poetics Journal.* Her translations of the Russian poet Arkadii Dragomoschenko (and his translations of Hejinan's poetry into Russian) have received critical praise. Among many honors, she has received an award for independent literature by the Soviet literary organization Poetics Function (1989) and a fellowship from the Academy of American Poets for distinguished poetic achievement at midcareer (2000).

Hejinian's work deliberately challenges the reader's expectations: Her prose looks like poetry, her poetry like prose. Her writing relies on quirky juxtapositions and repetition to mimic the path of the mind thinking, and her sentences require an associative, not logical, mode of thought. Prevalent themes in Hejinian's work involve finding strangeness within the familiar. For example, in *The Cell* (1987), Hejinian writes, "It is the writer's object / to supply the hollow green / and yellow life of the / human I," using unlikely pairings of nouns and adjectives to excite the human "I"/eye. She also explores the influences of writing on the subjective speaking "I" in an effort to describe the role of language in the construction of the self.

In *My Life* (1987), her best-known work, Hejinian reworks traditional forms of autobiography. The original prose poem, written when Hejinian was 37, comprised 37 sections, each containing 37 sentences. The more recent version, updated when Hejinian was 45, expands the poem to 45 sections of 45 sentences and reflects Hejinian's belief that writing, like the self, exists in a continual state of development. *Oxota: A Short Russian Novel* (1991) invokes the 14-line sonnet form and is based on Hejinan's own travels in Russia. Her experiments with odd juxtapositions and the visual layout of language on a white page can be seen in *Writing Is an Aid to Memory* (1978).

BIBLIOGRAPHY

Altieri, Charles. "Lyn Hejinian and the Possibilities of Postmodernism in Poetry." In *Women Poets of the Americas: Toward a Pan-American Gathering,* edited by Jacqueline Vaught Brogan, 146–155. Notre Dame, Ind.: University of Notre Dame Press, 1999.

Jarraway, David R. "My Life through the Eighties: The Exemplary LANGUAGE of Lyn Hejinian." *Contemporary Literature* 33. no. 2 (summer 1992): 319–336.

McCaffery, Larry. "A Local Strangeness: An Interview with Lyn Hejinian." In *Some Other Frequency: Interviews with Innovative American Authors.* Philadelphia: University of Pennsylvania Press, 1996, pp. 121–145.

Terry Lynn Pettinger

HELEN IN EGYPT H. D. (1961) Second only to her masterful *Trilogy* (1944), *Helen in Egypt* is H. D.'s most complex and innovative work, taking prominent part in the revival of epic usually associated with the long poems of EZRA POUND and WILLIAM CARLOS WILLIAMS (see LONG AND SERIAL POETRY). From her earliest IMAGIST lyrics, H. D. fuses modernity with the gods and heroes of ancient Greece. Her resuscitation of Hellenistic mythology coincides with similar efforts by D. H. Lawrence and Pound to cultivate a classical heritage for modern poetry, to "make it new" (to use Pound's famous phrase) by realigning the discontinuity and fragmentation of contemporary culture with the cycles of ancient myth (see MODERNISM). As with T. S. ELIOT and WALLACE STEVENS, a deepening spiritual awareness attends H. D.'s mature poetry as she moves beyond imagism. Her sparse line partakes in the modernist rebellion against verbosity, and her verbal precision influenced poets like ROBERT LOWELL and SYLVIA PLATH, whose early verse draws its dense symbolism and condensation from such poems as *Helen in Egypt* and *Trilogy. Helen in Egypt* employs the medieval form of *prosimetrum,* alternating prose and verse segments, which allows the poet more control and structure over the modulations of free verse than later practitioners, such as CHARLES OLSON and LOUIS ZUKOFSKY, exercised.

Published shortly before H. D.'s death, *Helen in Egypt* represents the culmination of nearly 30 years of thought. As with *Trilogy,* she originally planned only the first part, "Palinode," but Helen's "theatre of reverie" grew to epic proportions (Twitchell-Waas 11), and H. D. completed sections two and three, "Leuké" and "Eidolon," by 1954. *Helen in Egypt* elaborates a brief fragment by Stesichorus of Sicily, a Greek poet whose palinode (an ode of "apology" or "reversal") contends that the gods mystically transported Helen into Egypt during the Trojan War; the Helen for whom the Trojans and Greeks fought was an illusion. On a literal level, H. D.'s poem reclaims Helen's own feminine voice, lost amid contending patriarchal mythologies, and represents the heroine's attempt to understand her simultaneous existence as illusion and reality. "What flame over Troy," she asks; "was I ever there?" Allegorically the poem traces the awakening of a poetic consciousness as it grapples with symbolic manifestations of the divine. Helen awakens from "dream or trance" in part 1, moves "as one in a dream" in part 2, and proclaims in part 3: "I am awake. I see things clearly."

The poem follows Helen's attempt to unravel the mystery of an erotic encounter with Achilles on a desolate

Egyptian shore, where the lovers share in a mystic union, accompanied by a visionary "flash in heaven . . . that blinds the sun." In H. D.'s symbology Egypt represents hermetic mystery, and Helen's contact there with the "Dark Absolute" of love and death is an intersection of time and timelessness, a mystery containing the secrets of the "indecipherable Amen-script," the living hieroglyphs which would reveal its personal and universal meaning. Despite Helen's efforts to forget it, the riddle of this meeting persists: She wonders, "Must I forever look back?" Haunted by the portent of her vision, Helen travels from Egypt to Leuké, the white island where the aged Theseus helps her to decipher her own mind, a living hieroglyph, by integrating myth and memories of past lovers into a single reborn creative consciousness: "My Psyche, disappear into the web." "All myth," Theseus tells her, "the one reality, dwells here," and with the figurative rebirth of Leuké—"her island, her egg-shell"—Helen assays to "bring the moment and infinity together in time," to read the riddle of the psyche. For H. D. Greece symbolizes the intellect, and, under the spiritual aide of Theseus, Helen brings the scripts of her memories under the light of consciousness. As she prepares a return to Achilles, her inward struggle finally transcends the self's narcissistic maze, what she calls "the threat of Labyrinth." Her entreaty for reunion with Achilles—"There is one prayer, may he find the way"—culminates in an empathetic vision of vulnerability and love. Following this liberation from the self's labyrinth, the poem's third section traces Helen's successful attempt to reconcile herself and Achilles, to interpret the intricacies of the "one image, one picture" that embodies their mystic union.

If the Helen of "Palinode" is paralyzed by visionary awe, and Theseus's Helen undertakes an intellectual analysis, then "this third Helen," H. D. reveals, "is concerned with the human content of the drama." Beyond the intellect's sovereignty, the third part reasserts the mystery of the timeless "Absolute" and its incarnations in the particularity of personal history, the human content. Finally able to discern the interlocking patterns of universal myth and individual memory, Helen finds that "the simple path refutes at last the threat of Labyrinth" and yields "the clue to the rest of the mystery." H. D. suggests that the human condition, neither transcendent nor intellectual but "numb with memory," is irreducible to vision or intellect and that self-knowledge only comes by discerning the complex mysteries that link us to other people and to the past.

Like Wordsworth's *The Prelude* (1805), the modernist epic's great precursor, *Helen in Egypt* records the growth of a poet's mind. H. D.'s vision of unity is unrivaled by her modernist contemporaries, who often emphasize frustration and alienation. Her interest is spiritual redemption and renewal, but unlike Lawrence's and Eliot's promethean and ascetic extremities, H. D.'s vision recognizes our psychological vulnerability. Although H. D.'s insistence on unity is at odds with much of contemporary literary and cultural theory, her focus on eros and the recovery of a "lost" voice prefigures feminist thought and the contemporary revision of historical narratives. *Helen in Egypt* stands among the most complete and complex of the modernist long poems, representing the crowning achievement of H. D.'s poetic and spiritual vision.

BIBLIOGRAPHY

DuPlessis, Rachel Blau. *H. D. The Career of That Struggle.* Bloomington: Indiana University Press, 1986.

Friedman, Susan Stanford, ed. *Signets: Reading H. D.* Madison: Wisconsin University Press, 1990.

Twitchell-Waas, Jeffrey. "Seaward: H. D.'s 'Helen in Egypt' as a Response to Pound's 'Cantos'." *Twentieth Century Literature* 44, no. 4 (1998): 464–483.

Anthony J. Cuda

HELLER, MICHAEL (1937–) Michael Heller has been publishing poetry and establishing himself as a sort of modern-day, poetic Spinoza. His work is influenced equally by Jewish tradition and mysticism as by philosophy in the poststructuralist mode. Early influences on Heller's poetry include GEORGE OPPEN, CARL RAKOSI, and LOUIS ZUKOFSKY of the OBJECTIVIST SCHOOL, and Heller's work carries on this legacy. Heller's other principal influence is the secular, German-Jewish philosopher Walter Benjamin.

Heller was born in New York City but spent a part of his youth in Miami. His poetic approach is informed by his descent from a distinguished line of Polish rabbis, as well by the nonreligious household in which he was raised. Heller's first full-length volume of poetry was *Accidental Center* (1972), followed by *Knowledge* (1979), which includes the notable sequence "BIALYSTOK STANZAS"; other volumes followed, including the memoir *Living Root* (2000). Heller has received a number of awards and honors, including the Alice Fay Di Castagnola Prize from the Poetry Society of America for his critical work on the objectivist poets, *Convictions Net of Branches* (1985).

"Like [Charles] Reznikoff," Burt Kimmelman has written, "Heller has also explored his Jewish heritage, at the heart of which lies the concept of textuality" (111). Heller expresses his sense of Jewish culture and influence as follows: "The history of the Jews as given in the Pentateuch, half-'fact' and half 'fiction' or 'legend,' establishes primarily, via this very indeterminacy, the possibility of being endlessly rethought" (*Living Root* 33). Beyond the specifically Jewish, Heller's work struggles with the growing divide between language and experience, teasing out the relationships between spaces and emotions. In the title piece of *In the Builded Place* (1989), Heller uses the setting of New York, which the poet dubs a "broken world," fragmented both on the level of vision and being, to interpolate romantic love. The speaker and his lover "are joined as one in the street-lamp's light, / A corrosive light: dissolve, dissolve." Heller would claim that what's most fragile and alive in love is also what's most open and alive in one's use of language," Thomas Gardner has commented on this poem. "[B]oth follow from a skeptical acknowledgment of limits, an acceptance of the fact of isolation" (93). These limits can also be seen in such a poem as "The American Jewish Clock" (1989), in which Heller depicts his immigrant grandfather, once named "Zalman," now called "Solomon," and his failure to assimilate with American culture: "In the vast / benumbed space of us, a little more sound to place him"; the empty sound, the extra syllable in his Americanized name, lengthening and legitimizing, it serves as an iconic reminder of his roots, instead of his new life.

Heller has stated that he wants the influence of his poetry to be "widest, total, [and] transformative": "Poets are the Cosmic Monsters and fascists of language, or they are irrelevant" ("Interview"). Heller's quest for wideness, totality, and transformation continues to the present day, as he sets himself a course to balance linguistic control and the urge to surrender to the events of his time.

BIBLIOGRAPHY

Gardner, Thomas. "'Speaking the Estranged of Things': On Michael Heller." *Talisman: A Journal of Contemporary Poetry and Poetics* 10 (fall 1993): 92–95.

Heller, Michael. Interview by J. M. Spalding, *Cortland Review*. Available online. URL: www.cortlandreview.com/features/october98. Downloaded March 2007.

———. *Living Root: A Memoir*. Albany, New York: State University of New York Press, 2000.

Kimmelman, Burt. "Michael Heller." In *Dictionary of Literary Biography*. Fourth Series. *American Poets since World War II*, edited by Joseph Conte, 108–119. Detroit: Gayle Research, 1996.

Andrew E. Mathis

"HERITAGE" COUNTEE CULLEN **(1925)** COUNTEE CULLEN's poem "Heritage" was first published in the special March 1, 1925, issue of *Survey Graphic* magazine edited by Howard University philosophy professor Alain Locke. Later that year, the *New Negro*, an expanded version of the March *Survey Graphic*, reprinted the poem. In between these two HARLEM RENAISSANCE landmarks, Cullen's first book, *Color*, was published. *Color* features a version of "Heritage" that is 26 lines longer than the *New Negro* version, with the stanzas reordered, the punctuation drastically altered, and a dedication to his close friend Harold Jackman added. By and large, the *Color* text has been the source for subsequent republications of "Heritage."

Immediately celebrated, "Heritage" was anthologized nearly a dozen times once it appeared in the 1931 second edition of JAMES WELDON JOHNSON's *The Book of American Negro Poetry*. Despite its canonization "Heritage" is a somewhat controversial work. Some readers consider it derivative of white primitivist writing that romanticized and celebrated a supposedly natural world antecedent to western European ideas of civilization. But for others the poem presents a more profound reflection on African-American identity.

For writers, such as the novelist Nella Larsen, who used it as an epigraph for her novel *Passing* (1929) and the activist intellectual W. E. B. DuBois, who used it in his examination of race in *Dusk of Dawn* (1940), the italicized refrain that concludes the first and third stanzas became an archetypal interrogative: "*What is Africa to me?*" The repetition of the query and the use of frequent rhetorical questions suggest that the long poem is more interested in earnest meditation on modernity than in unproblematic resolution.

The 128-line poem is composed of 61 rhyming couplets, but two rhyming triplets, both set in the middle of stanzas, and the variation in stanza length, suggest something other than a conventional inquiry. Like the poet, the reader may "find no peace" in the lines of "Heritage."

Even references to the "primal" and the "savage" that might be associated with racist literary descriptions of Africa are used by Cullen to establish a sophisticated contrast with the poet's modern predicament. A reference to "Jungle boys and girls in love" contrasts with philosophical inquiry about the past: "What is last year's snow to me / Last year's anything?" The speaker tries to recognize himself in the romantic image of lovers but sees only a past symbolized by vanishing snow, the memory of which remains intangible.

In its lyrical exploration of African-American identity, "Heritage" remains an important work of the Harlem Renaissance. The poem assimilates popular racial iconography as it explores the poet's predicament.

BIBLIOGRAPHY

Kirby, David. "Countee Cullen's 'Heritage': A Black 'Waste Land.'" *South Atlantic Bulletin* 36, no. 4 (1971): 14–20.

Powers, Peter. "'The Singing Man Who Must be Reckoned With': Private Desire and Public Responsibility in the Poetry of Countee Cullen." *African American Review* 34, no. 4 (2000): 661–678.

Ira Dworkin

HIP-HOP POETRY See CARIBBEAN INFLUENCES; POETRY IN PERFORMANCE.

HIRSCH, EDWARD (1950–) Edward Hirsch's eclectic influences range from the intelligence of WALLACE STEVENS to the English romantic concern with emotion, from the inclusive sympathy of Walt Whitman to Federico García Lorca's exploration of the irrational. Comfortable with both free and formal verse (see PROSODY AND FREE VERSE), Hirsch has called the aesthetic dichotomy between the two "a large mistake in American poetry" (Marshall 57) because poets need access to the range of possibilities offered by language.

Born in Chicago, Hirsch has published six books of poems and three books of prose. His first collection, *For the Sleepwalkers* (1981) won the Lavan Younger Poets Award (1983) and the Delmore Schwartz Memorial Award (1985). He received a National Book Critics Circle Award (1987) for his second collection, *Wild Gratitude* (1986). Other major honors include a Rome Prize (1988) and a MacArthur Fellowship (1998).

Hirsch has said that "someone else's experiences make available your own feelings" (Suarez 63). He applies this philosophy by taking on personae that range from blue-collar workers to well-known writers. In *On Love* (1998), for instance, Hirsch speaks in formal verse through such figures as Ralph Waldo Emerson, Denis Diderot, and Tristan Tzara, a diversity that illustrates the breadth of his learning. These poems also reveal the poet's own voice behind the masks. They are, as James Longenbach notes, "not so much spoken by different figures as written out of an overwhelming sympathy for different sensibilities, foreign selves" (160).

Lament and praise, Hirsch has said, are two fundamental poetic impulses. His frequent return to the topic of insomnia permits him to engage in both. Darkness affords an opportunity for the elegiac in "Four A.M." (1994), which describes that hour as "nausea at middle age" and "the very pit / of all the other hours." But the coming of morning in "Dawn Walk" (1986) sparks thanks "to the soothing blue gift / Of powdered snow!" His poems struggle to balance a desire for transcendence with a concern for individual suffering. Although he has called poetry "similar to prayer" (Mariani 56), his need to return always to the difficult work of ordinary living is expressed in "Earthly Light" (1994), which concludes that "it is not heaven / but earth that needs us" because Earth is "so fleeting, so real."

Hirsch's poetry reaches beyond the self but not beyond compassion for humanity's many selves. Disciplined by form and painstaking craft, his poetry grounds itself in the difficult pleasures of understanding and connecting with other people.

BIBLIOGRAPHY

Longenbach, James. "Edward Hirsch: Eating the World." *Yale Review* 86, no. 3 (1998): 160–173.
Mariani, Paul. "A Conversation with Edward Hirsch." *Image: A Journal of the Arts and Religion* 28 (2000): 52–69.
Marshall, Tod. "The Question of Affirmation and Despair: An Interview with Edward Hirsch." *Kenyon Review* 22, no. 2 (2000): 54–69.
Suarez, Ernest. "Edward Hirsch." *Five Points: A Journal of Literature and Art* 4, no. 2 (2000): 58–74.

Bryan Walpert

HOFFMAN, DANIEL (1923–) Daniel Hoffman's poetry has an unobtrusive iambic flow, often with rhymes, which echo those of William Butler Yeats, but Hoffman's song is closer to speech. Conflicting emotions in his poems are often comprehended through visual imagery. Hoffman's work also has affinities with that of William Jay Smith and STEPHEN DUNN.

Hoffman was born in New York City. His first book, *An Armada of Thirty Wales* (1954), was selected by W. H. AUDEN for the Yale Series of Younger Poets. He has been chancellor of the Academy of American Poets (1972) and a consultant to the Library of Congress (1973–74); among other honors he has received a Memorial Medal from the Hungarian PEN (1980) for his translations of Hungarian poetry.

Hoffman's themes center around the conflicts of individuality in the context of group pressure, as in the title poem of *The Center of Attraction* (1974). An impromptu crowd has gathered to see if a man will jump to his death from a bridge pylon. A few urge him to go ahead. The man lights a cigarette, looks down on the crowd, "and sprinkles / Some of his ashes upon them." He starts climbing down. The crowd immediately loses interest and disperses: "It was his aloneness that clutched them together. / They were spellbound by his despair." In "The City of Satisfactions" (1963), an individual in the comfort of a train "Laved in the superdome observation car by Muzak" speeds toward the "City of Satisfactions." The train stops by a siding in the desert. The area is messy, and he sees a stone, a box, a lid, and a casket. Before getting back on the train, the speaker muses, "If only I could make this broken top / Fit snug back on this casket." The speaker is isolated by his own discontent and luxury. In "The Poem" (2000), a poem arrives, having "stumbled across the harsh / Stones, the black marshes." Hoffman's singing transforms a distant barbarity into knowledge and luminosity.

BIBLIOGRAPHY

Olson, Ray "Daniel Hoffman. Beyond Silence: Selected Shorter Poems, 1948–2003." *Booklist* (April 1, 2003): 1369.
Sylvester, William. "Barbarous Knowledge, Daniel Hoffman." *College English* (1970): 62–68.
———. "Daniel Hoffman's Poetry of Affection." *Voyages* (winter 1970): 110–119.

William Sylvester

HOGAN, LINDA (1947–) Following the American Indian tradition of storytelling and myth-weaving, Linda Hogan's writings reflect the traditional, indigenous respect for and affiliation with animals, land, and plants. Hogan, a novelist and essayist as well as poet, is a contemporary voice of American Indian concerns. Hogan is deeply rooted in the natural world; the health of the environment is her main interest, and her poetry focuses on issues ranging from endangered species and wildlife rehabilitation to nuclear testing. She also explores science, spirituality, ritual, and genocide with a decidedly feminist, matriarchal voice (see FEMALE VOICE, FEMALE LANGUAGE). Her poetry is significant in that it joins such voices as Louise Erdrich's and LESLIE MARMON SILKO's in bringing the noteworthy concerns of a traditionally oral and underrepresented culture into mainstream verse.

Born in Colorado, Hogan grew up in Oklahoma and Colorado. From a military family, she moved around and did not grow up within the Chickasaw Indian community so important to her work. The first in her family to attend college, she also received an M.A. at the University of Colorado in 1978. Her poetry includes *Calling Myself Home* (1979), *Daughters, I Love You* (1981), *Eclipse* (1983), *Seeing through the Sun* (1985), which won the 1986 American Book Award and the Juniper Prize, *Savings* (1988), and *The Book of Medicines* (1993), winner of the 1993 Colorado Book Award. Her award-winning fiction includes two volumes of short stories and two novels. Her other honors include the Lannan Foundation Award for poetry (1994), a Guggenheim grant (1990), a National Endowment for the Arts Fellowship (1986), the D'Arcy McNickle Tribal Historian Fellowship (1980), and a Lifetime Achievement Award from the Native Writers' Circle of the Americas (1998). In 1980 Hogan was honored with a community service award, indicative of her commitment to combine community and environmental concerns. Her primary project is called "River of Words," which seeks to foster responsible stewardship of the environment by blending empirical lessons in painting, writing, and ecology for school-age students.

Hogan's identification is as a tribal member—not an individual. She positions herself as spokeswoman of communally held tribal stories. For her the dead and the living form a continuous chain of existence across time. As she says of a miscarried child in "Crossings" (1993), "he was already a member of the clan of crossings." Hogan also envisions the continual presence of the dead in "The Grandmother Songs" (1993) when she says, "once, flying out of the false death of surgery, / I heard a grandmother singing for help." Hogan's work is wary of a white culture whose science risks damaging the continued existence of the human race. In poems, such as "Mountain Lion" (1993) and "The Fallen" (1993), Hogan links deaths of American Indians to the destruction of animal species. Such potential annihilation leads Hogan to explore fertility and sexual reproduction in the rich and complex language that is indicative of her concern for both the physical and emotional environments.

BIBLIOGRAPHY

Alaimo, Stacy. "Skin Dreaming." In *Ecofeminist Literary Criticism: Theory, Interpretation Pedagogy*, edited by Greta Gaard, and Patrick Murphy, 123–138. Urbana: Illinois, 1998.

Coltelli, Laura. *Winged Words: American Indian Writers Speak*. Lincoln: University of Nebraska Press, 1990.

Salita S. Bryant

HOLLANDER, JOHN (1929–) John Hollander is often referred to as a difficult poet whose work is packed with allusions. His poems display a remarkable knowledge of prosody (see PROSODY AND FREE VERSE). In his wit, inventiveness, and capability with a range of complex verse forms, Hollander's poetic practice shows the influence of W. H. AUDEN. He is often linked to formalist poets who were his contemporaries, such as ANTHONY HECHT and JAMES MERRILL, and his interest in poets from the 17th century—he edited the *Selected Poems of Ben Jonson* (1961)—clearly informs his writing.

Hollander was born in New York City. After receiving his A.B. and M.A. from Columbia University, he earned a Ph.D. from Indiana University in 1959. Auden chose Hollander's first book, *A Crackling of Thorns*, for the Yale Series of Younger Poets in 1958. Hollander won *Poetry* magazine's Levinson Prize in 1974 and the Bollingen Prize in 1983. He has received many other honors, including a fellowship in 1990 from the MacArthur Foundation.

Hollander's poems employ a voice that is philosophical and reflective, often engaging paradoxical themes. In "The Great Bear" (1958), for example, he considers his inability to see a bear in the constellation Ursa Major as a sign that the universe has no meaning, concluding, "If it were best, / Even, to have it there . . . there still would be no bear." *Visions from the Ramble* (1965) describes the speaker's childhood and the present, in what RICHARD HOWARD considers a key theme in Hollander's work, "a contradiction between remembering and forgetting . . . between, in its largest accommodation, life and death which affords only *in the poem* a moment of release" (241). The poems, however personal, never seem CONFESSIONAL; the craft is more important than being self-revealing or shocking.

The commitment to the poem itself, often evident in a precision of form, has always been crucial to Hollander's work. His knowledge of prosody is evident in *Rhyme's Reason* (1981), his primer on poetic forms, and his concern with the look of a poem on the page appears in *Types of Shape* (1969), in which the poems embody the objects they describe, such as a lightbulb or a cat (see VISUAL POETRY).

Hollander's carefully written, thoughtful verse deals with everyday events through a range of allusions and difficult formal techniques. In his work the craft of the poem highlights the poem and hides the poet.

BIBLIOGRAPHY
Howard, Richard. "John Hollander: Between the Deed and the Dream Is the Life Remembered." In *Alone with America: Essays on the Art of Poetry in the United States since 1950.* New York, Atheneum, 1980, pp. 238–275.
Lehman, David. "The Sound and Sense of the Sleight-of-Hand Man." *Parnassas: Poetry in Review* 12, no. 1 (fall/winter 1984): 180–212.

Gary Leising

HOLLO, ANSELM (1934–) Anselm Hollo has been an important experimental poet in the second half of the 20th century. His work was influenced by the BLACK MOUNTAIN poets, especially CHARLES OLSON and ROBERT CREELEY, and he was a major influence on the LANGUAGE group that included the poets CHARLES BERNSTEIN, BRUCE ANDREWS, and RON SILLIMAN. Hollo's poetry is filled with the unexpected; each poem is a singular event, as he states, an "emotional, intellectual entity" (Bielyi 270). His playfulness with form and his stress on the emotional and intellectual aspects of poetry, combined with his many years of teaching, reading, and traveling, have given him a wide international audience.

The son of a translator and university professor, Hollo was born in Helsinki, Finland. He was educated in Finland and the United States, where he was an exchange student in Cedar Rapids, Iowa. In 1966 he immigrated to the United States and has remained here since. He has published more than 30 volumes of poetry, including *Sojourner Microcosms: Poems New and Selected 1959–1977* (1977), and he is an award-winning translator from and into Finnish, Swedish, German, French, and Russian. He is also a journalist. His awards include a National Endowment for the Arts Poet's Fellowship (1979), the Finish Government Prize for translation of Finnish literature (1996), and a GERTRUDE STEIN Award for innovative poetry (1996).

Hollo's poetry is filled with energy and the unexpected. Humor, both whimsical and satirical, abounds in his work. His poetry is playful in form and subject—versatility is one of his assets—and throughout his work he displays an open spirit and tolerance for many experiences. He captures lyrically the details of the everyday and its moments of perception. ROBERT GRENIER once called Hollo's poetry "erratic, comedic, 'tribal,' and profound" (216). This description captures Hollo's evocation of mythic elements, comedy, and his almost surreal vision of human life, which, even though it appears as otherworldly at times, always remains grounded in everyday language. For example, in "when you met him he was a man" (1995), a man becomes a "postage stamp"; this is a world where "mice fall from the sky." This poem shifts rapidly and unexpectedly, following the poet's mind through humor, random thought, and historical references. As in all of his poetry, Hollo gives each poem its own form as it traces the unconscious.

BIBLIOGRAPHY
Alpert, Berry. "Anselm Hollo: An Interview." *Vort* 2 (1972): 2–20.
Bielyi, Sergei, and Anton Hofman. "Anselm Hollo." In *Contemporary Poets.* Vol. 9. Detroit: Gale Research, 1983, p. 270.
Grenier, Robert. "I Had No Idea." *Sulfur* 23 (spring 1988): 216.

William Allegrezza

"THE HOLLOW MEN" T. S. ELIOT (1925) From its two epigraphs to its profoundly bleak conclusion, T. S. ELIOT's "The Hollow Men" offers a study of men whose lack of conviction in life has made them spiritual scarecrows. For Eliot, political depravity, nihilism, and a dread of death and eternity will either create or reflect a moral indecision that prevents people from ever acting with individual conviction, a precondition for becoming an authentic person. Speaking in the persona of men who "grope together / And avoid speech," Eliot evokes those souls who are stuck in Limbo because neither Hell nor Heaven found in them enough spiritual life to lay claim to.

According to T. S. Pearce, "The Hollow Men" began as the remaining fragments from the first draft of *The WASTE LAND* (50), and both poems share in a vision of the modern world's spiritual desolation. Yet as J. Hillis Miller observes, the cultural texture of the latter poem disappears in the former, largely as a way of reflecting the vacuity and nonentity of the speakers. Still, Eliot does use two epigraphs to characterize the spiritual hollowness he depicts. The first epigraph comes from

Joseph Conrad's novel *Heart of Darkness;* it is spoken by one of the natives who live under the thrall of Kurtz, a white, renegade trader who has been corrupted by the lure of absolute power in the Congo. The second is a reference to Guy Fawkes, a Roman Catholic convicted and executed for his part in the 1605 Gunpowder Plot to assassinate King James I and later burned in effigy during an annual celebration. For Eliot, Kurtz and the effigy of Fawkes represent men whose whole character has been eroded by lust for power, though it is worth noting that Fawkes himself, as opposed to his caricature, represents the individual whose principles, for right or wrong, drove him to the sort of passionate decision and action that offers spiritual salvation.

The poem is broken into five sections, each in irregularly rhymed FREE VERSE with numerous instances of anaphora that generate chantlike rhythms and further suggest the undifferentiated group personality of the plural narrator, even when only a single individual is speaking. The first section introduces the speakers, those who are remembered "not as lost / Violent souls, but only / As the hollow men." The second section, spoken by a single voice, reveals the terror such hollow men feel in the presence of those who act from conviction. The third section describes the Limbo the hollow men inhabit, where religious faith, desire, and human tenderness terminate in empty gestures, as "Lips that would kiss / Form prayers to broken stone." The fourth section evokes the blindness of these men, who move as isolated individuals within a group, unable to communicate with each other and consigned to live without hope of love or even "the perpetual star / Multifoliate rose / Of death's twilight kingdom." The fifth and final section parodies the children's rhyme sung on the annual celebration of Guy Fawkes Day, and it is linked typographically with a fragmentary excerpt from The Lord's Prayer, "For Thine is the Kingdom," an utterance the hollow men are ironically unable to complete by the close of the poem for they belong to neither the Hell nor the Heaven that compose God's Kingdom. For these souls, whom critics have variously identified as apostates, intellectuals, moral relativists, or simply the mass man of the secular, modern world, the Day of Judgment will pass over them in an ironic mirroring of their lifetime of indecision. *"This is the way the world ends,"* they chant three times in bitter imitation of the Trinity, *"Not with a bang but a whimper."*

In keeping with his theory of the "objective correlative," or the way a set of words and images evoke rather than describe an emotion, Eliot evokes the theme of hollowness through desert imagery and poignantly limited diction. Like many of Eliot's poems, "The Hollow Men" takes a desert landscape as its setting, using it to reflect the interior nature of the men he evokes; "This is the dead land," they say, "This is cactus land." Images of dryness, emptiness, and death pervade the poem, reflecting the souls of the men whose "dried voices, when / We whisper together / Are quiet and meaningless." The poem is narrated by a plural persona that represents all men whose principles, good or bad, have never been strong enough to make them fully human; even when the narration shifts to the first person singular, the "self" is not differentiated, but remains without identity, selfhood, or individual conviction. By means of a pun ("Eyes" for "I's"), Eliot suggests that the hollow men so lack identity that they cannot even regard those with a sense of self; one of the men observes how "Eyes I dare not meet in dreams / In death's dream kingdom / These do not appear." To act on one's principles is to inhabit a sort of Paradise; for Eliot's speakers, the world is a Limbo where the lack of conviction and action is mirrored in a paucity of language.

BIBLIOGRAPHY

Bush, Ronald. *T. S. Eliot: A Study in Character and Style.* New York: Oxford University Press, 1984.

Kirk, Russell. *Eliot and His Age: T. S. Eliot's Moral Imagination in the Twentieth Century.* Peru, Ill.: Sherwood Sugden & Co., 1971.

Miller, J. Hillis. *Poets of Reality: Six Twentieth-Century Writers.* Cambridge, Mass.: Harvard University Press, 1965.

Pearce, T. S. *T. S. Eliot.* New York: Arco Publishing Co., 1969.

Temple Cone

HOLMAN, BOB (1948–) Bob Holman has been hailed as "Ringmaster of the Spoken Word" and "the dean of the scene" by the *New York Times* (Richardson B2); he once called himself "Plain White Rapper" (Holman). His commitment to the oral traditions and pleasures of the spoken word have given his work the eclectic feel of hip-hop, dada poets, rap, shamanism, and stand-up comedy all intertwined (see POETRY IN PERFORMANCE). Bluntly political and uncompromisingly direct, Holman's work challenges notions of poetry as a rarefied commodity of the intellectual community and insists upon the relevance of poetry to lives lived outside of ivory towers. Holman's efforts to encourage the craft and art of the spoken word have resulted in his popularization of poetry slams, his productions of Public Broadcasting System's *Words in Your Face* and *The United States of Poetry,* and his cofounding of the poetry record label Mouth Almighty/Mercury Records.

Holman was born in LaFollette, Tennessee. He has taught at Bard College, and he founded the Bowery Poetry Club in New York City. He is perhaps one of America's most active poets and has traveled the world performing his work and supporting the work of other spoken-word artists. As well as producing seven books, two edited anthologies, and numerous CDs, he has won three Emmy Awards (1988 and 1992), been nominated for a Grammy Award (1999), and hosted several Internet sites dedicated to spoken word performances and poetry.

Holman's poetry is specifically intended to be heard. His insistence upon poetry as a sensory experience, rather than an intellectual one, gives his work an immediacy that changes from one work to the next in an extremely articulate, emotional, and rhythmic stream of consciousness. Holman's oeuvre is not focused on a singular theme, nor can it be argued that it embodies a governing dictum, other than poetry is to be enjoyed, not endured. Indeed "Poem 3/2" (1990), begins, "There's No Big Message except hope you've had a good time while reading this."

"The Death of Poetry I" (1990) starts by lamenting the elevation of poetics to an elitist art form: "It sucked itself into the coffin spasm. . . . It was enforced tradition of emptiness"; the poem ends by celebrating the return of a democratic poetic performance accessible to everyone: "Hey, amigos, let's go for it / Right out here in public." Holman's work refuses literary hierarchies, dismisses convoluted metaphors, and erodes notions of what is, and what is not, poetry. There is something of the passion of the streetcorner prophet about Holman's work, an insistence that a poet, any poet, is simply someone with something to say and the courage to say it clearly.

BIBLIOGRAPHY

Foster, Edward Halsey. "Bob Holman, Performance Poetry and the Nuyorican Poets Cafe." *Multicultural Review* 2, no. 2 (1993): 46–48.

Gioseffi, Daniela. "An Interview with Bob Holman: 'Mouth Amighty' on the Cutting Edge of Multiculturalism's Future." *Voices in Italian America* (spring 1998): 1–10.

Holman, Bob. "Bob Holman, Plain White Rapper." *Morning Edition.* National Public Radio, 1989.

Richardson, Lynda. "A Poet (and Proprieter) Is a Beacon in the Bowery." *New York Times,* 12 November 2002, B2.

Kathryn Ferguson

HOLOCAUST CHARLES REZNIKOFF (1975)

CHARLES REZNIKOFF'S *Holocaust* is a long narrative poem about the Nazi extermination of the Jews, divided into 12 sections that recall the traditional 12 books of the classical epic (see NARRATIVE POETRY and LONG AND SERIAL POETRY). Like the traditional epic, *Holocaust* contains not only the history of a single person but also of an entire culture. In addition, also like most epics, *Holocaust* recounts a journey into the underworld; indeed, one may say that all the action of *Holocaust* takes place in a very real hell, the territory and institutions controlled by Nazis. Unlike an epic, however, *Holocaust* contains little heroic behavior, although it honors a great deal of suffering and courageous endurance. Unlike *The Iliad,* it records no victory, although its last pages foreshadow the defeat of the Nazis as they retreat from advancing Russian troops. Unlike *The Odyssey* or *The Divine Comedy,* it presents no return home, and unlike *The Aeneid* or *Paradise Lost,* it celebrates no founding of a new people.

Holocaust grows out of two of Reznikoff's long-standing concerns. The first is his concern as a Jewish American with the fate of the Jews and what he sees as a dying Jewish culture. In 1921 Reznikoff published his verse play *Uriel Accosta* about a Portuguese Catholic of Jewish ancestry, who returns to Judaism but finds himself at odds with both the Inquisition and the rabbis. For Reznikoff, Accosta, as the novelist and poet Paul Auster has observed, was "neither wholly assimilated nor fully unassimilated, [but occupied] the unstable middle ground between two worlds" (156). Thus in producing a book-length poem detailing Nazi attempts to exterminate the Jewish people, Reznikoff pursued themes that had concerned him from the beginning of his writing career. Reznikoff's other concern, which finds its fruition in *Holocaust,* is with long documentary works that record, in objective terms, social injustices. His multivolume *Testimony: The United States* (1965, 1968, 1978, 1979) recounts from legal records incidents occurring between 1885 and 1915.

Reznikoff's methods in *Testimony* and *Holocaust* are derived from at least three sources: his brief training as a reporter, his involvement with other OBJECTIVIST writers, and his work as a lawyer and as a writer for *Corpus Juris,* an encyclopedia of law for lawyers. In 1910 he entered the newly established school of journalism at the University of Missouri. He left after a year, but his training in journalism certainly reinforced his tendency to stick to the facts. By 1930 he had met LOUIS ZUKOFSKY, GEORGE OPPEN, and CARL RAKOSI, with whom he formed the objectivists, a group of writers united by their Jewish background, left-wing politics, and desire to use language as an object with certain physical and historical properties. In 1912 Reznikoff entered New York University's law school and passed the bar in 1916, but he was not interested in practicing law. In 1928 he began work at *Corpus Juris,* where for several years he summarized law cases. According to Reznikoff's wife, Marie Syrkin, "He worked painstakingly examining the minutiae of a case and phrasing his analysis not on the prescribed legal jargon but 'accurately' according to his own standards" (45).

These three influences informed Reznikoff's austere style, which is at once meticulously accurate and fully colloquial. Reznikoff typically limits his narratives to the sort of testimony allowed in courts of law—that is, to what people saw, heard, and did. He limits references to states of mind. Reznikoff was assisted in achieving this distance by taking incidents from the U. S. government's records of the Nuremberg Military Tribunals and the trial of Adolph Eichmann in Jerusalem. Yet the effect of such restraint is not dispassion. For example, part VIII, "Children," opens with a report on two freight cars filled with children arriving at a death camp and explains how "young men sorting out the belongings of those taken to the gas chambers / had to undress the children—they were orphans." The young men then took the children "to the 'lazarette'" where they were shot by the German Schutzstaffel (SS). Reznikoff refuses to speculate on the psychological state of the children, the young men who are "sorting out the belongings," or the SS men who shoot the children. He leaves details unexplained: Why were the children shot instead of gassed? Yet such writing is far from purely factual. He emphasizes the hypocrisy of the Nazi concern for children by placing the word *lazarette,* a diminutive French term for a children's washroom, in quotation marks to highlight the unsuitability, of the word to disguise blood-bath reality. He carefully separates with dashes the fact that the children were orphans, not to evoke greater sympathy but to explain why male prisoners who were usually relegated to "sorting out belongings" had been reassigned to "undress the children." Presumably had they not been orphans, their mothers would have undressed them for their executions.

Reznikoff's restraint emphasizes the indescribable cruelty and horror of the Nazi atrocities. It suggests that there is no way to imagine the feelings of those involved—not the SS men, not the children, and least of all the young men assigned to undress the children before they were sent—as those young men surely knew they would be—to their deaths. Any attempt to articulate more than the facts would falsify the horror with melodrama. To dress the narrative in anything other than the objective language of ordinary speech would deflect attention from the crimes and thereby mitigate the offenses. Reznikoff understood that, to transform testimony into poetry, he had to employ techniques so subtle they would disappear to all but the most attentive readers.

BIBLIOGRAPHY

Auster, Paul. "The Decisive Moment." In *Charles Reznikoff: Man and Poet,* edited by Milton Hindus, 151–165. Orono, Maine: National Poetry Foundation, 1984.

Hindus, Milton, ed. *Charles Reznikoff: Man and Poet.* Orono, Maine: National Poetry Foundation, 1984.

Rothchild, Sylvia. "From a Distance and Up Close: Charles Reznikoff and the Holocaust." In *Charles Reznikoff: Man and*

Poet, edited by Milton Hindus, 289–296. Orono, Maine: National Poetry Foundation, 1984.

Shevelow, Kathryn. "History and Objectification in Charles Reznikoff's Documentary Poems, *Testimony* and *Holocaust*." *Sagetreib* 1, no. 2 (1982): 290–306.

Syrkin, Marie. "Charles: A Memoir." In *Charles Reznikoff: Man and Poet,* edited by Milton Hindus, 37–67. Orono, Maine: National Poetry Foundation, 1984.

David Bergman

"HOME BURIAL" ROBERT FROST (1914) "A *faux pas de deux*" is how Nobel laureate JOSEPH BRODSKY describes the grief-filled conflict of ROBERT FROST's "Home Burial," a long narrative poem in BLANK VERSE dramatizing the interaction between a husband and wife in the aftermath of their infant son's death. First published in Frost's groundbreaking collection, *North of Boston* (1914), the poem transforms the setting of a rural New England farmhouse into a dramatic stage, where the characters' movements up and down a central staircase embody their marital strife and the eventual breakdown of their relationship in the wake of their failure to communicate their grief over the child's death. Indeed, "Home Burial" is as much about what men and women cannot say or do for each other amid grief as it is about their capabilities.

The poem's themes of separation and misunderstanding are tied to the ways the main characters interact with the setting, principally the house steps, a window overlooking the child's grave, and a door leading from the house. As Richard Poirier observes, "(T)he husband and wife have become so nearly inarticulate in their animosities that the feelings have been transferred to a vision of household arrangements and to their own bodily movements" (125). The scene opens with the wife, Amy, looking out a second storey window at her son's grave as she descends the stairs, presumably to leave her home for a friend's; her husband meets her on the steps, and Frost immediately links the man's speech and his desire to see (both literally and metaphorically) with his forward, almost aggressive movement: "He spoke / Advancing toward her: 'What is it you see / From up there always—for I want to know.'" The wife shrinks under his advance, and after noticing the window reveals the family cemetery where the child is buried, he claims to see what she sees, implying that he understands her feelings. But if this moment is one of sympathetic identification, it is also an act of domination. Sight becomes a way of framing and limiting what is mysterious and uncontrollable (just as the window frames and isolates the cemetery scene), while the husband's tone and posture are triumphant. His control of the situation, moreover, is underscored by the fact that the family cemetery houses his ancestors, not his wife's, which explains her apparent unease in her own home.

But the wife's reaction indicates her desire to resist such domination and to force her husband to relinquish some emotional control, so that he may feel as powerless as she does, and perhaps may reach a clearer understanding. When he reaches the second floor landing, she slips away, runs down the stairs, and with her hand ready on the door, condemns him for the apparent insensitivity of having dug his own child's grave and spoken of it like any other household project. From the moment the wife slips free of her husband's grasp, the couple is forced into a difficult balance as they conflict over different ways of grieving, of responding to trauma and meaninglessness, and over the basic issue of what it means to communicate. In her criticism of the husband's perceived insensitivity, the wife rejects her husband's efforts at emotional compromise and sees his actions and later statements as emotionally barren, while he struggles to understand why she needs to communicate her grief and why she seems to keep her anguish over the child's death fresh. Early in the poem, the husband dominates through the dialogue, but his uncompromising effort to encapsulate his wife's thoughts and feelings, to understand them as if by force, undercuts the moral grounding of his position. But in the second half of the poem, the verbal control shifts to the wife after the husband's outraged remark that "(I)t's come to this, / A man can't speak of his own child that's dead." Ironically, she sees his remark as the figurative truth, in that he can't speak of the trauma properly, while he sees it as the literal truth, both because she won't accept his remarks but also because he, as a man, has articulated his grief in nonverbal ways.

When Amy describes the sight of her husband digging the grave, "Making the gravel leap and leap in air,

/ Leap up, like that, like that, and land so lightly / And roll back down the mound beside the hole," she fails to notice the significant expense of energy that has gone into this digging, energy spent not to make the labor more efficient, but for the man to purge himself of grief and sorrow. What is problematic about this form of grieving is that it is essentially private and noncommunicable; his wife cannot share in it, and so feels abandoned. Even when such grief gives way to speech, the sort of speech it employs is shaped and ordered. When the husband returned from digging his child's grave, he not only compared it to other farm projects, but he spoke of it in proverbial terms: "I can repeat the very words you were saying," the wife tells him, "'Three foggy mornings and one rainy day / Will rot the best birch fence a man can build.'" While at first the man's speech seems unfeeling, considered poetically it seems a classically toned lament for the inevitable doom that culminates all human labors, whether the building of fences or the raising of children.

Frost himself often noted that poetic form was "a momentary stay against confusion" ("Figure," 777). In the midst of the chaos caused by so great a trauma as the death of a child, control is crucially important for the husband, and it is manifest in his work and his speech. But such an attempt to control the emotional turbulence of these events is ultimately solitary; it relieves the husband, perhaps, but not his wife, and she cannot bear such loneliness. "Friends make pretence of following to the grave, / But before one is in it, their minds are turned," she laments. "But the world's evil. I won't have grief so / If I can change it." He wants her to share her grief with him, and not take it to others as she has in the past, but once again his motives are mixed; certainly her seeking comfort from others is a rejection of his love, but it also threatens his masculine self-image as the sole provider and comforter in her life.

Both characters' motives and flaws are portrayed with unflinching accuracy, and the way Frost wrenches the reader's sympathies between these two grieving figures gives "Home Burial" its peculiar dramatic power. Many critics and biographers have noted that the poem draws upon Frost's own experience of a child's death, for Frost and his wife Elinor lost their first-born child, Elliott, in 1900, and they suffered great grief and anger in the aftermath. Frost himself said that the poem's inspiration came from the separation of his wife's sister from her husband following the death of their first child. Yet he also acknowledged that after Elliott's death, Elinor claimed that "she knew then that the world was evil" ("Indispensable," 227), a sentiment Amy echoes verbatim. Such a shattering of illusion makes "Home Burial" a quintessential MODERNIST poem, and one of Frost's greatest. Its origins in grief belie the image of unblemished marital bliss often associated with the Frosts; its domestic drama annihilates the pastoral illusion created by much of the literature about rural America; and its probing investigation of the ways that language can fail reveals the profound alienation caused by the modern world and the terrible difficulty of maintaining our human bonds.

BIBLIOGRAPHY

Brodsky, Joseph. "On Grief and Reason." In *Homage to Robert Frost,* edited by Joseph Brodsky, Seamus Heaney, and Derek Walcott, 5–56. New York: Farrar, Straus & Giroux, 1996.

Frost, Robert. "The Figure a Poem Makes." In *Robert Frost: Collected Poems, Prose, & Plays,* edited by Richard Poirier and Mark Richardson, 776–778. New York: The Library of America.

Grenier, Donald J. "The Indispensable Robert Frost." In *Critical Essays on Robert Frost,* 220–240, edited by Philip L. Gerber. Boston: G. K. Hall & Co., 1982.

Poirier, Richard. *Robert Frost: The Work of Knowing.* New York: Oxford University Press, 1977.

Temple Cone

"HOUSEWIFE" ANNE SEXTON **(1962)** One of the most common and unnoticed aspects of ANNE SEXTON's poetic technique is the reinvestment of clichés with meaning. Paying close attention to details usually overlooked, Sexton examines apparently tired phrases, and in this way she revitalizes commonplace situations and people. "Housewife" is a pure illustration of this. Beginning with the term *housewife,* Sexton investigates the way in which women become married to houses rather than to their partners, another manifestation of a psychological double bind that is universal for women.

The subject of the woman defined by her relationship to her husband and home was imbued with eroticism by

WILLIAM CARLOS WILLIAMS in his "The Young Housewife" (1916). Seen by the poet, the housewife is an object of amorous curiosity. But in Sexton's poem, the external, objective view moves inward. Williams's speaker passes by the housewife, but in Sexton's poem readers move from the sociological, objective observation about "some women" to the universal and empathic understanding that all women share a similar situation. The distance between the housewife and the speaker diminishes as the poem moves from the extreme example of the obsessive housewife to encompass all women and all relationships. Furthermore the point that "A woman is her mother" is glossed by the conclusion as "the main thing," as if this were the central truth of female reality. The fact that women do not marry their fathers, or their mothers, but actually *become* their own mothers, incorporating their nurture and caring in an existence alienated from others, is a universal truth here.

In a simple 10-line, 60-word poem, to move from the comic figure of the ingenuous and compulsive housecleaner to the assertion of the discovery of a major truth seems initially eccentric. However, the poem reveals a logical and inevitable progression.

The phrase "some women marry houses" is the first in a series of surprising turns in this poem. Beginning with the assumption that women marry houses, not men, Sexton moves seamlessly into understanding that the housewife is searching for identity and protection. As the lines become longer and more discursive, they reveal the attraction in this attachment: The house's "skin" shields the housewife from the outside world, from danger and individuality. The skin encloses the romantic and vital "heart" and the sensual and communicating "mouth." But the extended metaphor grows less appealing, more graphic: A pun of "liver" refers to the house inhabited by people, "livers," and the indelicate organ of bile. A less-balanced metaphor of "bowel movements," however, reduces the house to a rigid mechanical frame for the woman. The house becomes an enlarged version of the mother from whom the woman first learned love, the one who protected her from invasion but also imprisoned her, thus preventing her from actual human contact.

In this model there is neither need nor possibility of masculine relationship and support. Men become mere invaders, fulfilling their Freudian role of marrying their mothers, but female existence is dominated by maternal incorporation. Whether or not a woman is a housewife, within the framework created by the poem, her identity is determined by this psychological truth.

BIBLIOGRAPHY

Alkalay-Gut, Karen. "Sexton, 'Housewife.'" *Explicator* 47 (winter 1989): 52–54.

Bixler, Francis. *Original Essays on the Poetry of Anne Sexton.* Conway: University of Central Arkansas Press, 1988.

Karen Alkalay-Gut

HOWARD, RICHARD (1929–) Richard Howard brings to poetry a subtlety of psychology, richness of language, sensitivity to social structure, and density of cultural reference of the sort to be found in the prose work of Henry James, whose travel writing he edited. His formidable talents make his work quite demanding and have led to its being ignored and misunderstood. While it is true that Howard makes few concessions to the uninformed, he never parades learning for its own sake. Similarly while the work assumes a cosmopolitan sophistication, it is filled with passion; one of his interests is the manner in which erotic desire finds its way into the least likely of places and takes the most unexpected of forms. Formally complex, his poems' intricate structures mirror the complexity of thought and character. Many of his poems are dramatic monologues, and Robert Browning is his clearest influence, but his use of syllabics and complex allusions owe their debt to MARIANNE MOORE.

Adopted by a well-to-do German-Jewish family in Cleveland, where he was born, Howard attended Columbia University and the Sorbonne. Taught French as a child, he has become one of the most respected translators of French, with more than 150 titles to his credit, as well as the 1983 American Book Award for his translation of Charles Baudelaire's *Les fleurs du mal.* In 1982 the French government designated him a Chevalier de l'Ordre National de Mérite for his service to French literature. Howard's concern for continental thought and writing has not meant that he has ignored the American scene. His monumental study *Alone with America* (1969, 1980) examines the major poets who have emerged in the United States since 1950. He was awarded a MacArthur Fellowship in 1996 and served as president of the PEN American Center (1978–80). He was awarded a Pulitzer Prize in 1986.

Much of Howard's poetry has taken the form of dramatic monologues and dialogues, but even his more personal lyrics involve a conversation with the world. Some of the speakers in his poems are famous personages of the past. *Untitled Subjects* (1969), for which he won the Pulitzer, contains the voices of Sir Walter Scott, John Ruskin, and William Thackery. But we also hear in his poems from an unnamed secretary, an anonymous vicar, the daughters of John Milton, a nanny, various wives, and a royal taxidermist. In "The Masters on the Movies" (2002), he imagines what Henry James, Joseph Conrad, and others who lived before motion pictures became an industry would make of this alternative narrative form. "The Masters on the Movies" suggests the kind of free-floating dialogue between personality, history, and culture that is Howard's continual delight and obsession. Such a meditation presupposes a past that is in constant contact with the present, a sensibility in which the canonical crosses and converses with the coarse and common. Howard's James, who died in 1916, having seen Bette Davis in *Now, Voyager,* released in 1942, wryly alludes to the film's concluding lines: "we don't reach the sun, we shall at least / have been up in a balloon."

BIBLIOGRAPHY

Haughton, Hugh, and Adam Phillips. Introduction to *Selected Poems of Richard Howard.* London: Penguin, 1991, pp. vii–xvi.

Summers, Claude, and Ted-Larry Pebworth. "'We Join the Fathers': Time and the Maturing of Richard Howard." *Contemporary Poetry* 3, no. 4 (1978): 13–35.

David Bergman

HOWE, FANNY (1940–) Associated with the LANGUAGE SCHOOL in contemporary poetry, Fanny Howe is recognized as an innovator in the analytic lyric, a type of experimental poetry that does not abandon the lyric form (see LYRIC POETRY). Her poetry is concerned with questions of spirituality and grace in a modern, material world; she deftly balances abstract, encoded language and a moral vision firmly rooted in lived experience. Commenting on her development as a poet, Howe has written, "The language of the other—the sound of what is only half-understood, always out of context, not mine . . what you might call Mystification—became a hidden credo of mine . . . [t]he paradigm . . was the essence of code, of hiddenness." ("Artobiography" 197). She has been compared to Emily Dickinson for her compressed, metaphysical lyrics and to her contemporary RAE ARMANTROUT for her use of experimental, abstract language to explore political themes, occasionally concerning gender and sexuality, but also dealing with poverty, violence, and religious faith.

Howe was born and raised in Cambridge, Massachusetts. Her mother was an actress and playwright at the Abbey Theater in Dublin before starting the Poet's Theater in Cambridge; her father was a law professor at Harvard University and a civil rights activist. Her sister, SUSAN HOWE, is also a poet. Fanny Howe has published more than 14 books of poetry and numerous works of fiction, including several novels for adolescents. She has received two National Endowment for the Arts grants (1970 and 1991) and was chosen to be a fellow of the Bunting Institute at Radcliffe College in 1975.

Howe writes frequently about the desire for paradise and for an end to all forms of human oppression, elaborating in a statement on her poetics: "Words which consciously aspire to the future are heightened by the desire to rise above, be free of, the tyranny of history. They aim for a heightened place—a paradise" ("The Ecstatic"). Her 1986 collection, *Introduction to the World,* comprises a series of untitled, 10-line meditations on morality and spiritual awareness, all constructed of self-consciously chance or arbitrary language. She combines, as she writes in the prefatory prose poem, "Wishes," "chance with deliberate choice. . . . Lines as branches, us all swinging from." The culminating effect of this strategy is not one of technical play merely for its own sake, but rather of a singular austerity, a kind of metaphysical purity, arrived at through the sheer presence of language. She closes the collection, "freedom is synonymous with less, not more" ("After-Thoughts"), arguing ultimately for an existence purged of human-made excesses.

In this and other collections of her poetry, Howe's meticulously crafted and compressed writings often blur accepted boundaries between poetry and prose, and the reader thus experiences in multiple registers the poet's profound moral vision.

BIBLIOGRAPHY

Howe, Fanny. "Artobiography." In *Writing/Talks,* edited by Bob Perelman, 192–206. Carbondale: Southern Illinois University Press, 1985.

———. "The Ecstatic." *Ironwood* 24 (1984): 17–20.

Vickery, Ann. "Finding Grace: Modernity and the Ineffable in the Poetry of Rae Armantrout and Fanny Howe." *Revista Canaria de Estudios Ingleses* 37 (November 1998): 143–163.

Amy Moorman Robbins

HOWE, SUSAN (1937–) Susan Howe is associated with the LANGUAGE SCHOOL of poetry. Her work is opaque, complex, and multifaceted, distrustful of language as a structure, yet fascinated with words and the printed page. Howe claims the work of CHARLES OLSON influenced her interest in writing poetry, although her work compares in complexity with another Language poet, LYN HEJINIAN, and Howe's emphasis on extraverbal visual layout of her poems links her work with that of Language poet CHARLES BERNSTEIN.

Howe was born and grew up in Cambridge, Massachusetts. Her father was a liberal-leaning law professor at Harvard. Her mother had an interest in drama, which influenced Howe to attempt a theater career after high school. She has described herself as a failure in the theater, turning then out of desperation to art school at the Boston Museum School of Fine Arts, from which she graduated in 1961. Howe pursued an art career, moving to New York in 1964 and working in a variety of media, based primarily on collage techniques. The energy and experimentation of the New York downtown art scene in the 1960s influenced her work, especially the interest shown by minimalist and conceptualist artists in writing as an adjunct to their art.

Howe turned to the genre of artists' books, handmade works that treat books as visual objects rather than collections of print. Her artists' books combine images with lists of words. In the late 1960s she was introduced to Olson's poetry by her younger sister, FANNY HOWE, also a practicing poet. In 1988 she began to teach poetry at a variety of universities.

Howe's visual arts background has affected her poetry. She shows special concern for the appearance of words on the page (and has lamented the difficulties of finding a publisher willing to take seriously her precise placement of words). Howe uses character formatting and spacing carefully, as in this example from *Defenestration of Prague* (1983):

E n d l e s s PROTEANL i n k a g e s

The spacing between the letters of the first and last words suggest they are currently in flux, perhaps spreading outward from the center like the edges of the universe. Yet the conjunction between the middle word and the first letter of the last word emphasizes links that remain in the midst of flux.

Sometimes Howe crosses out a word but allows it to remain, crossed out, in the poem. At other times, two words appear superimposed, one over the other, or crowded closer together than normal so that the space between lines is truly diminished, causing a distortion in the separation between the two words; they verge toward becoming a single sign, rather than two. The idiosyncratic spacing and alignment resemble the poetry of E. E. CUMMINGS, though Howe's work is never merely typewriter trickery (a criticism that has been leveled at the work of this older poet).

In her most experimental poems, instead of evenly spacing all of the lines horizontally, Howe arranges words and lines to cross over other words and lines at unexpected angles. This is especially apparent in *The Bibliography of the King's Book; or, Eikon Basilike* (1989); portions of the poem "break out of all form completely," Howe says, resembling advanced algebraic formulas or visual art (Foster 24). Indeed some of these more overtly visual poems create structures similar to those of the earlier abstract-expressionist and minimalist painters with whom Howe interacted in New York in the 1960s (see ABSTRACT EXPRESSIONISM and VISUAL POETRY). For one page of *Eikon,* scattered lines of text cross the page much like Jackson Pollock's drips of paint on a canvas; the page opposite is the exact same poem, but turned upside down.

Many of these visually experimental works are not meant to be read aloud, yet Howe does do readings and is highly attuned to the aural nature of poetry, as suggested by one of her book titles, *Articulation of Sound Forms in Time*. In fact, in the late 1970s Howe hosted a radio program on poetry, featuring readings by and conversation with other poets. By the late 1990s some of her work had become available on the World Wide Web, in both visual and aural forms.

Another characteristic of Howe's poetry is its involvement with previous historical and literary documents. Howe often reacts to preexisting texts or incorporates those texts into her work. This appropriation allows both Howe's voice and the voice of the earlier writer to be heard. The poet with whom Howe feels the greatest bond is Emily Dickinson, whose work she greatly admires. Howe's *My Emily Dickinson* (1985) was her effort to meet the long-deceased Dickinson in the virtual space of writing. Howe went a step further in *Melville's Marginalia* (1989), which reacts to notes Herman Melville wrote in the margins of another author's book.

Howe's interest in working from preexisting documents has centered around work by American authors: Dickinson, Melville, and Mary Rowlandson's captivity narrative, for example. She has spoken of an interest in an American voice, though she has also explored her Irish background.

Tempering Howe's experimentation and interest in history is an awareness that can only be described as feminist, though Howe avoids that label. This awareness shows itself in skepticism of the validity of the literary canon, in an understanding that historical documents tend to erase women, and in her affinity for Emily Dickinson. Women, she says, find themselves in the gaps and spaces of history and literature. Thus when Howe adds that her own work is equally concerned with gaps and spaces, she implies that gender is central to her poetry (see FEMALE VOICE, FEMALE LANGUAGE).

Combined, all these elements of Howe's poetry force her audience to read between the lines.

BIBLIOGRAPHY

Foster, Edward. "An Interview with Susan Howe." *Talisman: A Journal of Contemporary Poetry and Poetics* 4 (spring 1990): 14–38.

Howe, Susan. "Fragments toward Autobiography." Available online. URL: www.english.uiuc.edu/maps/poets/g_l/howe/autobio.htm. Downloaded March 2007.

Perloff, Marjorie. "'Collision or Collusion with History': Susan Howe's *Articulation of Sound Forms in Time*." In *Poetic License: Essays on Modernist and Postmodernist Lyric*. Evanston, Ill.: Northwestern University Press, 1990, pp. 297–310.

Sam McBride

HOWL **ALLEN GINSBERG (1956)** Seized by United States customs agents in 1957, banned, and labeled obscene by the federal government, ALLEN GINSBERG's *Howl* is a poem and a book as well as a moment in American literary history. *Howl* is exactly what the poem's title indicates: an unrestrained, mournful, instinctive exclamation. It is a cry of rebellion and a reaction against the military-industrial complex that the Eisenhower administration both warned against and presided over. *Howl* draws on traditions of prophetic and CONFESSIONAL poetry to communicate its themes of apocalypse and redemption. In the introduction to *Howl,* WILLIAM CARLOS WILLIAMS writes, "Poets are damned but they are not blind, they see with the eyes of angels." Ginsberg openly embraced the idea of poet as visionary and bardic martyr. He found inspiration for *Howl* in the legacy of the British romantic poet William Blake, as well as the long lines and scatological imagery of Walt Whitman and the spontaneous poetics of JACK KEROUAC. True to the bardic origins of poetry, *Howl* is meant to be read aloud and looks to the meter and timing of jazz to achieve its effect. Ginsberg's poetry shocked and disrupted the comfortable, stable, predictable verse preferred by the New Critics and challenged white middle-class values of suburbia, consumerism, and heterosexuality (see FUGITIVE/AGRARIAN SCHOOL). For its subject matter and for its unpredictability, some critics have argued that *Howl* is not poetry, and even if one were to consider it a poem, it should certainly not become part of the American Canon—a set of texts that can be said to define the cultural values of a nation. In spite of criticism, *Howl* galvanized an undercurrent in post–World War II America. Its popularity and its influence continue into the 21st century.

In all, *Howl* consists of three major sections and a footnote. The entire poem pivots at the brink of madness and pulls redemption from insanity. The opening section of the poem elevates the artistic intensity of

BEAT figures, such as Kerouac, Neal Cassady, and William S. Burroughs to a spiritual level. Art is equated with salvation, and the terror of the cold war doctrine—MAD (mutual assured destruction)—is ever present. The stanzas evoke images of isolation, disillusionment, rebellion, ecstasy, and sexuality. Images collide as ghostly figures listen to the "crack of doom on the hydrogen juke box" and burn cigarette holes in their arms to protest the "narcotic tobacco haze of Capitalism."

The second section of the poem begins with a question: "What sphinx of cement and aluminum bashed open their skulls and ate up their brains and imagination?" Ginsberg's answer is Moloch, who is elsewhere mentioned in the First Book of Kings in the Old Testament as a false god to whom the young were sacrificed. Just as the consistent pattern of the first section is "who" plus a verb ("who vanished," "who wandered," "who lit," "who studied"), the name Moloch organizes each stanza in the second section and is the metaphor with which Ginsberg names and locates the objects of his rage. The first section relies on long lines to the point of breathlessness; the stanzas of the Moloch section are equally long, but the rhythm is truncated with exclamation points. As emotions intensify, Moloch transforms from sphinx to monster with a "cannibal dynamo" for a breast and a "smoking tomb" for an ear. As in the first section, the resistance to post–World War II conformity and cold war politics is clear. The fate of Moloch and its victims is prophesied to be a "cloud of sexless hydrogen." By the end of the second section, madness is the poet's only recourse from the influence of society and the devouring energy of Moloch. The final short phrases communicate more hysteria than reason: "the wild eyes! the holy yells!"

The third section of the poem commemorates Ginsberg's friend Carl Solomon—to whom the poem is dedicated. The rhythm shifts from exclamation to incantation: The phrase "I'm with you in Rockland" is not only the organizing principle here but also a counterpoint to the images of isolation in the first section and the ranting madness of the second. With the exception of the direct address greeting, "Carl Solomon!," in the first line, the staccato rhythms and exclamation points disappear. Section three contains no punctuation other than the measured pause of the reader's own breath. Its rhythm is the gentle rocking of a child and the soothing of nerves. Protest is presented in absurd, almost humorous fashion as the poet and Solomon hug and kiss the United States as if it were a child with a cough.

The movement from beat to beatitude is a consistent theme in much of Beat Generation poetry. The final section, "Footnote to Howl," signals the ascent from madness and transforms lament into exaltation via the refrain, "Holy." The poet as prophet is most powerful when prophesying the apocalypse, and the poem closes with joyous images of redemption. The poet, the Muse, and her followers have come out on the other side of madness and everything is holy: "Holy the bop apocalypse."

Many of the famous excerpts from *Howl* are found in the first section, but to read only this section is to understand only half the apocalypse and none of the redemption. In his annotations to *Howl,* Ginsberg quoted the Greek philosopher Pythagoras, who wrote, "When the mode of the music changes the walls of the city shake." Ginsberg challenged his audience as readers, as human beings, as citizens, and as a culture. He asked that readers shake their cities not only with poetry and madness, but also with tenderness and honesty. His vision was ultimately one abounding with great love and resilient hope.

BIBLIOGRAPHY

Lardas, John. *Bop Apocalypse.* Chicago: University of Illinois Press, 2001.

Tytell, John. *Naked Angels.* New York: Grove Weidenfeld, 1976.

Frank Gaughan

HUGHES, LANGSTON (1902–1967) Langston Hughes is best known as a HARLEM RENAISSANCE poet whose lyrics celebrate and document 20th-century African-American life. Committed to expanding poetry's capacity to promote racial justice, his work consistently spoke to and communicated with people left to the margins of literary and political representation. In *The Big Sea* (1940), the first of his autobiographies, Hughes articulates his belief that literature should be a direct engagement with people: "[T]here came a time when I believed in books more than in people—which of course, was wrong" (332). An immensely prolific writer, Hughes worked in a variety of literary genres: poetry, plays, autobiographies, essays, short stories, novels, and musicals. Hughes's voice—familiar, direct, and appealing—remained consistent throughout his astonishing literary output. And yet his poetic persona had a supple flexibility, as a wide variety of characters speak and sing in his lyrics. In the work that draws on dialect and folk performance, one can hear the echoes of Paul Lawrence Dunbar, whom Hughes read and emulated as a child. Hughes also shared Walt Whitman's faith in poetry's potential for recording history and inspiring a democratic and inclusive American culture. Sympathetic and musical portrayals of working people demonstrate the influence of CARL SANDBURG, whose work Hughes greatly admired. Hughes's use of jazz syncopation as a compositional principal was encouraged by the active rhymes and rhythms of VACHEL LINDSAY's poetry.

As a cultural icon and a literary ambassador, Hughes was a crucial role model for young artists. He provided practical and moral support to younger poets, such as RUSSELL ATKINS and AMIRI BARAKA, among many others. His incorporation of themes and techniques from jazz and the blues paved the way for such poets as Sherley Anne Williams and MICHAEL S. HARPER, who weave together jazz rhythms and political critique. In 1964 Hughes edited the anthology *New Negro Poets: USA,* marking his dedication to keeping the canon of African-American literature open to innovation and change.

Hughes was born in Joplin, Missouri. His father moved to Mexico early in his life and became a businessman and landowner there. Following his father's departure, his mother moved Langston to the home of his grandmother in Lawrenceville, Kansas. His grandfather had been an abolitionist and Republican politician. Hughes's mother had to travel to find work; as a result, Hughes had an itinerant, often impoverished childhood, attending school in Topeka, Cleveland, and Lincoln, Illinois. A poet and amateur actress, his mother fostered Hughes's enthusiasm for literature and theater. He recalled, "My mother used to take me to see all the plays that came to Topeka like *Buster Brown, Under Two Flags,* and *Uncle Tom's Cabin.* We were very fond of plays and books" (325). Hughes's talents were recognized early. In high school he published verse and short stories in *Central High Monthly Magazine* and the *Belfry Owl,* became editor of his high-school annual, and was elected class poet. Many of his fellow classmates were children of European immigrants; they exposed him to left-wing periodicals, such as the *Liberator* and the *Socialist Call,* as well as European philosophers, such as Frederich Nietzche, and writers, such as Guy de Maupassant.

After graduation, Hughes spent an unhappy year with his father. As his train to Mexico crossed the Mississippi, Hughes composed "The NEGRO SPEAKS OF RIVERS," which was published in W. E. B. DuBois's journal the *Crisis.* Hughes was 19 years old, and "The Negro Speaks of Rivers" marked the beginning of a distinguished writing career. In 1926 Hughes wrote "The Weary Blues," which won the first prize in poetry in *Opportunity* magazine's literary contest. After meeting such Harlem Renaissance stars as Alain Locke, Arna Bontemps, Zora Neale Hurston, and Carl Van Vechten (who helped him arrange a book contract), Hughes published *The Weary Blues* (1926), and his landmark manifesto "The Negro Artist and the Racial Mountain" (1926).

Hughes's talent and productivity were consistently recognized with awards and honors. With the success of his novel *Not without Laughter* (1930), Hughes received a Harmon Foundation Medal. In 1936 Hughes won a Guggenheim Fellowship, in 1941 a Rosenwald Fund Fellowship to pursue playwriting, in 1946 an award for distinguished service as a writer from the American Academy of Arts and Letters, and in 1960, in the midst of the Civil Rights movement, received the Spingarn Medal, the highest award of the National Association for the Advancement of Colored People (NAACP). A year later he was inducted into the National Institute of Arts and Letters.

"The Negro Speaks of Rivers" (1921) is one of Hughes's finest poems. Arnold Rampersad writes that, with this poem, "the creativity of Langston Hughes . . . suddenly created itself" ("Origins" 180). It is a deeply affirmative poem, and Hughes recalls that before writing it, "I had been thinking about my father and his strange dislike of his own people" (351). This poem foresees Hughes's role as a celebrated figure in the Pan-

African movement, as the speaker describes his involvement in and proximity to the great rivers of Africa (the Congo, and the Nile) as well as the Euphrates and the Mississippi. The poem is built through a series of repetitions and the expressive refrain, "My soul has grown deep like the rivers." Hughes orchestrates the image of the river with ease and elegance; it is a figure for the spirit, suffering, and achievement that resonates in the land and history of African people. "The Weary Blues" (1925), another infectious poem from Hughes's early body of work, describes the emotional effect of hearing a blues musician play on Lenox Avenue in Harlem. As the poem progresses and enacts the slow melancholic cadence of the blues, the musician's song and the poet's lyric become one. Near the end of the poem, a couplet attests to the song's dramatic effect: "And far into the night he crooned that tune. / The stars went out and so did the moon."

While Hughes was primarily a poet of joy, as his poetry developed it identified specific sources of injustice and delved further into anger. The poem "Mulatto" (1926) begins with the reprimand, *"I am your son, white man!"* A condensed drama, the poem enacts the hateful epithets and denials the boy receives in response to his declaration, incorporating lines that voice the white man's objectifying views of black women: "What's a body but a toy?" In *The Big Sea* (1940), Hughes describes working on "Mulatto" every night for an entire summer and reading the poem at JAMES WELDON JOHNSON's home. Listeners were moved and considered it a breakthrough in Hughes's work (Rampersad 394). In the 1930s, aspects of Hughes's work began to change as events, such as the Scottsboro trial, in which a group of black teenagers was wrongfully accused of raping a white woman and sentenced to death, and the Spanish civil war, emphasized the necessity of direct and radical political action. Poems, such as "Good Morning Revolution" (1932), which was published in *New Masses*, announced Hughes's commitment to Marxist ideals: In this poem revolution is personified as a friend who will help workers own the means of production, therefore eliminating hunger and greed, instability and oppression. "Goodbye Christ" (1932) is perhaps Hughes's most controversial poem. It condemns Christ as an outmoded and fictitious figure that has been oversold to those who wield power through influence and violence. In Christ's place, he will insert "A real guy / Marx Communist Lenin Peasant Stalin Worker ME—." When the poem appeared without his permission in the *Saturday Evening Post* in 1940, it not only inspired controversy but protests too. Later, under pressure from the forces of McCarthyism, a period of anticommunist suspicion in which many people were questioned about their political affiliations before Senator Joseph McCarthy's committee on subversive activities, Hughes renounced "Goodbye Christ" as a youthful mistake.

Yet he did not renounce poetry. In fact when asked to testify before McCarthy in 1953, Hughes had recently published one of his strongest and most innovative poetic works, *MONTAGE OF A DREAM DEFERRED* (1951). An elegant and panoramic epic of urban black life, *Montage* displays Hughes's sharpened call and response skills, his full repertoire of lyrical voices and styles, and his knowledge of modernist literary movements, such as the work of those in the IMAGIST SCHOOL (see MODERNISM). The rhymes in *Montage* spark with wit; the rhythms are interjected with bitterness of unrealized dreams. A sensitive portrayal of voices embedded in a specific place and time, *Montage* is played for the ears of all Americans, as it continually asks: "Ain't you heard" of our "dream deferred"?

Deliberately accessible but deceptively simple, Hughes's work reveals the complexities particular to composing a life within the socioeconomic frames of racism and insists upon the importance of African Americans' contributions to and participation in American literature, art, and history.

BIBLIOGRAPHY

Hughes, Langston. *The Big Sea: An Autobiography by Langston Hughes.* In *The Langston Hughes Reader: The Selected Writing of Langston Hughes.* New York: George Braziller, 1958, pp. 317–398.

Rampersad, Arnold. *The Life of Langston Hughes. Volume 1: 1902–1941, I, Too, Sing America.* New York: Oxford University Press, 1986.

———. *The Life of Langston Hughes. Volume II: 1941–1967.* New York: Oxford University Press, 1988.

———. "The Origins of Poetry in Langston Hughes." *Modern Critical Views: Langston Hughes,* edited by Harold Bloom. New York: Chelsea House, 1989, pp. 179–189.

Trotman, C. James, ed. *Langston Hughes: The Man, His Art, and His Continuing Influence.* New York: Garland, 1995.

Kimberly Lamm

"HUGH SELWYN MAUBERLEY" EZRA POUND (1921) EZRA POUND often referred to his experimental persona poem "Hugh Selwyn Mauberley" as a popularization of another persona poem he wrote in critique of World War I, "Homage to Sextus Propertius" (1919), which set poetic lyricism in conflict against the corruption of empire and wartime jingoism. The latter used relatively familiar classical allusions in the manner of T. S. ELIOT's poem "The LOVE SONG OF J. ALFRED PRUFROCK." But in keeping with Pound's project of getting history, culture, economics, and society into poetry, "Hugh Selwyn Mauberley" draws on an even wider range of allusions in its satire of the philistine culture of modern America and England, "an old bitch gone in the teeth." Broken into a number of separately titled sections, some with sections of their own, "Hugh Selwyn Mauberley" juxtaposes and contrasts a range of voices, dealing with such subjects as patriotic cant, the danger to art of consumerism, the rejection of Pre-Raphaelite art, and the degradation of such high values as the Good and the Beautiful. In its challenging experimentalism, "Hugh Selwyn Mauberley" offers Pound's critique of his age and a model for reviving it artistically.

The two-part poem features a number of portraits of different literary types, many of them satirical attacks on bourgeois art. Influenced by the dramatic monologues of the Victorian poet Robert Browning, Pound wrote several of the sections in "Hugh Selwyn Mauberley" in the voices of different fictional personae, or "masks"; in other sections, Pound narrates in a disembodied, culturally erudite voice that seems to resemble his own. For instance, in the opening poem, "E. P. Ode Pour L'Election De Son Sepulchre," Pound describes a man who "strove to resuscitate the dead art / Of poetry; to maintain 'the sublime' / In the old sense. Wrong from the start." Along with the initials "E. P.," this description seems a portrait of Pound himself in 1920, when he left for Paris after London had failed to become the artistic capital he had predicted, though Hugh Kenner advises "against the too-easy supposition that Pound found in *Mauberley* an eloquence of disillusion" (169).

Most of the personae and types described, however, are distinct from Pound. In one section, he praises the figure of the great stylist, "Unpaid, uncelebrated," who "exercises his talents / And the soil meets his distress" (Pound seems to have had in mind the Irish poet W. B. Yeats, whose work Pound promoted from early on), while in another he excoriates "Mr. Nixon," the careerist writer who crassly advises Pound to "Butter reviewers" and admits "I never mentioned a man but with the view / Of selling my own works." In addition to these individual types, Pound shows his sympathy for anti-Victorian literary groups that were overlooked by the mainstream audience, including the Pre-Raphaelite Society in England and the Rhymers' Club in Ireland, while capturing the dejection of the post–World War I era among those who "walked eye-deep in hell / believing in old men's lies, then unbelieving / came home, home to a lie."

The voice that narrates most of the poem proves both erudite and irascible, mixing colloquial and vulgar phrasings with complex cultural references and details from Pound's own artistic circles to create a sort of intellectual shorthand that proves both incredibly dense and explosively apropos. For instance, J. T. Barbarese notes Pound's use of an obscure, but for the learned reader, remarkably effective, multilingual pun in section III of the first part. Condemning the present artistic era as 'an age of tin,' Pound quotes the Greek poet Horace, who asked "What god, what hero, what man shall we loudly praise?" In Greek, Horace's question *tin andra, tin heroa, tin theon,* uses an article (*tin*) that is homophonic with the English word *tin.* Not only has Pound emphasized the shoddiness of much present-day art, but he has also suggested, as Barbarese writes, that "Pindar's poem is a prayer that upon transliteration is absurdly lost in its modern 'equivalents'" (313). In this and many other such passages, Pound's intellectual, artistic, and often private references threaten the poem with obscurity, though proponents might argue that such difficulty is precisely the poem's way of resisting the easily consumable realism that, for Pound, made the early 20th century an age of tin.

At the heart of "Hugh Selwyn Mauberley" is a demanding critique of the current state of art, as well as a program for its recuperation and for society's recuperation through it. Since the modern era is "Unable in the supervening blankness / To sift TO AGATHON from the chaff" (TO AGATHON is Greek for "the Good"), Pound must supply an appropriately modern instrument for understanding goodness and beauty, the seismograph, which measures the slightest to the most earth-shattering vibrations. Pound's own sensitivity to the flow of history makes him a powerful critic of World War I's abuses of nationalism, and it is in "Hugh Selwyn Mauberley" that Pound first begins trying to work out in poetry an economic theory of history. His cries against "usury" reflect his criticism of the economic motivations for World War I, as well as his growing interest in Social Credit theory, though they also foreshadow Pound's later anti-Semitic invectives and his misguided support of Benito Mussolini during the Second World War. The range of vibrations a seismograph can record is also reflected in the variety of Pound's juxtaposed materials, which include obscure references, powerfully straightforward pronouncements, ironic monologues, and passages of delicate lyric beauty. Though a dejected Pound warns that "a tawdry cheapness / Shall outlast our days," his closing image suggests that the philosophical ideals that brought greatness to past societies might still be attainable in the modern, technological world. Describing "The face-oval beneath the glaze" of an Italian Renaissance medallion, Pound notes that it is "Bright in its suave bounding-line, as, / Beneath half-watt rays, / The eyes turn topaz," a figure for the lyrical, multivalent poetry Pound believed could save society.

BIBLIOGRAPHY

Barbarese, J. T. "Ezra Pound's Imagist Aesthetics: *Lustra* to *Mauberley*." In *The Columbia History of American Poetry*, edited by Jay Parini and Brett C. Miller, 284–318. New York: Columbia University Press, 1993.

Casilo, Robert. "Pound and Mauberley: The Eroding Difference." *Papers on Language and Literature: A Journal for Scholars and Critics of Language and Literature* 21, no. 1 (1985): 43–63.

Espey, John. *Ezra Pound's Mauberley: A Study in Composition*. Berkeley: University of California Press, 1974.

Kenner, Hugh. *The Poetry of Ezra Pound*. Lincoln: Bison Books–University of Nebraska Press, 1985.

Longenbach, James. *Stone Cottage: Pound, Yeats, and Modernism*. New York: Oxford University Press, 1988.

Temple Cone

HUGO, RICHARD (1923–1982) Although he started his writing career relatively late in life, Richard Hugo became distinguished as one of the preeminent poets of the American Northwest. After studying (along with DAVID WAGONER) under THEODORE ROETHKE at the University of Washington in the late 1940s, Hugo wrote several books of what became known as the CONFESSIONAL style of poetry. His first book of poems, *A Run of Jacks* (1961), published when he was 38 and working as an executive at the Boeing Company, established him as poet who, with intense psychological acuity, captured the lonesome emptiness of the rural Northwest. It was largely on the basis of its success that in 1964 he was invited to become professor of English and creative writing at the University of Montana, where he remained on the faculty until his death.

Hugo was born in Seattle, Washington, and grew up in an area on the southwest outskirts of town near the Duwamish River called White Center. When he was only 20 months old, his teenage mother abandoned him to be raised by his maternal grandparents, who were stern and reserved Lutherans. He joined the U.S. Army Air Corps six months after Pearl Harbor was bombed and flew 35 bombing missions in Italy before 1945. After the war he attended Roethke's poetry seminars and began to amass a body of work that would later be incorporated into his early books of poetry. He entered psychoanalysis in 1955, through which he discovered techniques to help solidify his own approach to poetry, such as returning to childhood experiences for the source of adult anxieties. In 1981 the Academy of American Poets awarded Hugo the Edgar Allan Poe Fellowship for distinguished poetic achievement. He was twice nominated for the National Book Award and was once runner-up for the Pulitzer Prize.

Hugo was haunted in his adult life by the austerity of his childhood, and his dysfunctional relationship with his grandmother produced recurrent anxiety throughout his life regarding women. In such poems as "The Milltown Union Bar" (1973), Hugo charts a psychological progression from a displaced childhood to an uneasy adulthood, where the only comforts are alcohol and the honest camaraderie of fellow drunks. Hugo repeatedly balanced the grimness of his vision with the promise that suffering is made more tolerable through community. Hugo was also a regional poet. His work is often compared to that of William Wordsworth, although the intensity of Hugo's investigations into his feelings has been described as more postmodern than romantic. In any case his poetry successfully captures the fractured spirit of the Pacific Northwest and the Big Sky country of Montana—its provincial sensibility, the lonesome starkness of its landscape, and the desperate lives of its inhabitants are all presented against a backdrop of inimitable and sublime natural beauty. His most famous and most often anthologized poem, "Degrees of Gray in Philipsburg," is emblematic of his talent for well-crafted and self-conscious poetry about destitute and defeated people living in dying western towns. Lines such as "The last good kiss you had was years ago" and "the tortured try of local drivers to accelerate their lives," tersely capture the gritty reality of the rural West. In spite of the somber and existentialist overtones of this poetry, the view is not altogether dismal; throughout Hugo's work there persists the notion that sympathetic relations with other people can be redemptive, as illustrated in these lines from "Indian Girl" (1975): "We touch each other by forgetting stars in taverns, / and we know the next man when we overhear his grief."

Hugo called his approach "psychogenic," by which he meant that the poem should originate from, and be a reflection of, the self confronting its surroundings and struggling to make sense of feelings inspired by the world. His poetry is more largely governed by *feeling* than by imagery, metrics, or any kind of systematic precision, and it is for this reason often classified as postmodern. A later poem, "Note to R.H. from Strongsville" (1977), is one of the best illustrations of Hugo's self-conscious method of wrestling with demons in order to produce a poem that captures an emotional state of mind: "When I'm alone, no sound, the vodka / and the room begin a roaring of their own." In "Second Chances" (1980), another poem from the same collection, Hugo documents psychological problems he experienced that persisted after he became famous.

Hugo died of leukemia and is buried in St. Mary's Cemetery in Missoula, Montana. His epitaph is taken from a poem called "Glen Uig" in his collection *The Right Madness of Skye* (1980): "Believe you and I sing tiny and wise and could if we had to eat stone and go on."

BIBLIOGRAPHY

Allen, Michael S. *We Are Called Human: The Poetry of Richard Hugo.* Fayetteville: University of Arkansas Press, 1982.
Holden, Jonathan. *Landscapes of the Self: The Development of Richard Hugo's Poetry.* New York: Associated Faculty Press, 1986.
Hugo, Richard. *The Triggering Town: Lectures and Essays on Poetry and Writing.* New York: Norton, 1979.
Pinsker, Sanford. *Three Pacific Northwest Poets: Stafford, Hugo, and Wagoner.* Boston: Twayne, 1987.

Aaron Parrett

"HUMPBACKS" **Mary Oliver (1984)** In her FREE VERSE LYRIC "Humpbacks," the American nature poet MARY OLIVER describes humpback whales breaching off the coast of Cape Cod, "(c)arrying their tonnage of barnacles and joy," an event that delivers the speaker into a state of spiritual ecstasy. Annette Allen has described Oliver's poetry as a "passionate attention to the natural world which [one] sees as the source of revelation about ultimate things," and in this poem Oliver parallels the humpbacks' passage between two worlds (water and air) with the speaker's own passage from the physical world into the spiritual and back again.

The poem is set off Cape Cod, with the speaker (presumably Oliver herself) on a whale-watching expedition. Referring to the ocean around her as "this country / of original fire," Oliver prepares us for a vision of the natural world that resonates with transcendent significance. Thus, when the speaker sees the humpback whales leaping and falling back into the ocean, they become for her figures of innocence and imagination, and when she thinks of their whale songs, they embody the mysterious spirit of music and poetry. Noting that "The sky, after all, stops at nothing, so something has to be holding / our bodies," Oliver introduces the central, Emersonian paradox of the poem. By being mortal and limited, the natural world prevents living beings from experiencing transcendence completely, yet it is also the means of achieving that transcendence, and Oliver ties this paradox to the image of whales breaking out of the sea to fly for a moment before crashing back into it.

The middle stanzas of the poem chart the movement of three whales off the bow of the boat. As Oliver describes the way "they smash through the surface, someone begins / shouting for joy and you realize / it is yourself as they surge," she employs a subtle enjambment to show how the speaker experiences the paradox of transcendence. The speaker loses her identity in the excitement of the moment, for she is so jubilant she does not even realize she is shouting, but she simultaneously recovers her identity through a sense of unity with the three whales, upon which she projects herself imaginatively as they breach the surface. Oliver's focus on the number of whales here is not accidental; they form a sort of naturalized Christian Trinity, which testifies to the potential for personal salvation that union with nature can offer. Such a condition is not permanent, for we fall back into the mortal, natural world, but the temporary separation that one feels for that other world induces longing, not despair. Oliver offers a haunting image that suggests the universality of this desire for connection when she writes that "I know a whale that will come to the boat whenever / she can, and nudge it gently along the bow / with her long flipper."

In spite of Oliver's transcendent vision of nature, critic Vicki Graham cautions against the limited relationship with "the other," or that which is not oneself (in this case, nature), that such a vision possibly entails. Graham writes that "Split into a rigid duality, the self is not porous; it cannot take the other into itself nor can it flow outside its own boundaries. Privileging the body reinforces oppositional thinking and blocks rather than enables immersion in the other." But Oliver's poem seems written out of an understanding of the differences between spirit and body, between humans and nature, which can be overcome, even transcended, but which must be acknowledged. Such an understanding has also great ecological import, as Carolyne Wright observes in her review of Oliver's Pulitzer Prize–winning volume *American Primitive;* Wright notes that Oliver's poems "evoke a sense of the fragility of species, even if they are not directly threatened by human predation." Ultimately, if Oliver posits a dualistic split, it is in the service of demonstrating how the experience of nature's beauty and fragility can transcend that split. The lyric experience of "Humpbacks" reminds us that nature is a place "where everything, / even the great whale / throbs with song."

BIBLIOGRAPHY

Allen, Annette. "Mary Oliver." *Encyclopedia of American Literature.* Edited by Steven R. Serafin. New York: Continuum Publishing Company, 1999. *Modern American Poetry.* Edited by Edward Brunner. 2002. Southern Illinois University at Carbondale. Available online. URL: http://www.english.uiuc.edu/maps/poets/m_r/oliver/oliver.htm.

Graham, Vicki. "'Into the Body of Another': Mary Oliver and the Poetics of Becoming Other." *Papers on Language and Literature* 30, no. 4 (1994): 352–372. Available online. URL: http://www.english.uiuc.edu/maps/poets/m_r/oliver.about.htm.

Wright, Carolyne. "Review of *American Primitive.*" *Prairie Schooner* 59, no. 3 (1985): 108–112.

Temple Cone

"HURT HAWKS" Robinson Jeffers (1928)

Throughout his career, Robinson Jeffers espoused a philosophical attitude he called "Inhumanism," which takes the harsh, sublime beauty of nature for reality's ultimate truth. In "Hurt Hawks," Jeffers dramatizes this vision through an injured hawk's struggle to survive and through the speaker's subsequent mercy-killing of it. While some critics view the poem as nihilistic, Jeffers in fact praises the hawk's purity of purpose, its will to power, as well as the harsh reality that will not let it survive injured and imperfect. The perfection demanded by "The wild God of the world" gives life its meaning, and Jeffers warns that other sources of value, whether religious, social, or political, bring only weakness, distraction, and spiritual death: "You do not know him, you communal people, or you have forgotten him."

In the poem's first section, the speaker describes a hawk whose injured wing prevents it from flying and thus from fulfilling its purpose as a bird of prey. Writing in alternating long and short lines that recall Walt Whitman's "Song of Myself," Jeffers, like Whitman, projects himself imaginatively into the life around him in order to understand the divine cosmos. Here, Jeffers imagines the psychological injury the hawk endures, and finds it more damaging than the physical injury: "He is strong and pain is worse to the strong, incapacity is worse." The speaker personifies the hawk, equating its experience with the existential crisis of a human being's death, a personification that indirectly redeems the humankind Jeffers earlier critiqued, suggests Gilbert Allen: "By remembering our mortality, which our everyday selves deny, we can become more like the hawks with whom we share it" (65). Exposure to the reality of death enables human and hawk alike to comprehend life as a divine (though nonreligious) force.

Having kept the hawk's situation at a literal distance in the first section, the speaker realizes in the second section that he must deal with the hawk directly: "I'd sooner, except the penalties, kill a man than a hawk," he claims, "but the great redtail / Had nothing left but unable misery." Tim Hunt argues that this claim "initiates the mix of anguish, guilt, and awe that should remind us that there are two hurt "hawks" in this poem" (7): the hawk and the speaker who accepts responsibility for killing it. In keeping with Inhumanism's centering of value in the dynamics of the natural world, Jeffers counters his own preference to protect nature in order to enact the harsh perfection nature demands. The poem's elevated tone and psalm-like rhythms suggest this act is in harmony with nature, restoring a balance that disappeared with the hawk's crippling. Thus, the speaker's "gift of lead twilight" is not mercy, but completion and fulfillment, what Robert Zaller calls the gift of "essential freedom" (213). In the poem's final image, the hawk's body falls away and its spirit soars, "unsheathed from reality," a terrifying yet sublime version of the myth of the phoenix, wherein the bird is restored to nature's savage and graceful cycles.

BIBLIOGRAPHY

Allen, Gilbert. "Jeffers and Yeats." In *Robinson Jeffers and a Galaxy of Writers,* edited by William B. Thesing, 60–68. Columbia: University of South Carolina Press, 1995.

Hunt, Tim. "Introduction." In *Robinson Jeffers and a Galaxy of Writers,* edited by William B. Thesing, 1–10. Columbia: University of South Carolina Press, 1995.

Zaller, Robert. *The Cliffs of Solitude.* New York: Cambridge University Press, 1983.

Temple Cone

I

"THE IDEA OF ORDER AT KEY WEST"

WALLACE STEVENS (1936) The poetry of WALLACE STEVENS often takes as its theme the question of human epistemology—the study of what we know and how we know it. This question is central to 20th-century poets, most particularly to the so-called high modernists (see MODERNISM). "The Idea of Order at Key West" approaches this question by meditating on the problem of mimesis, or whether or not art can successfully imitate and represent reality. Above all the poem questions the relationship between human language and nature.

The poem is written in blank verse (unrhymed iambic pentameter), which is well suited to philosophical meditation, because it is the closest in rhythm and meter among traditional verse forms to natural English speech. The speaker of the poem begins by describing a woman walking along the shore of Florida's Key West and singing a song of the sea. But from the first line the speaker insists that the woman's song does not accurately represent the sea, because human sounds and language cannot imitate the nonhuman sounds and rhythms of the ocean. Her song contains words that seek to imitate the sea, but the sea remains alien and inscrutable.

Stevens proposes that because language is a human invention, attempts to represent the natural world through language are merely artifice, a type of deception through which humans attempt to organize and control what they cannot truly perceive or understand. For all her attempts to reach out to the sea and commune with it, the singer finally and inevitably manages only a human impression of the sea.

The last two stanzas of the poem introduce an imagined interlocutor, whom the speaker questions. He asks why those walking along a quay, illuminated by the lights of boats in slips, perceive the sea to be divided in quadrants of light, as if the never-resting ocean could be so contained and organized. In answer, the speaker concludes that humans have a "rage for order," an uncontrollable desire to master and recreate the natural world in their own image and according to their own perceptions.

Although this need for order prevents human beings from reproducing the world of nature, Stevens calls the rage "Blessed." The singer's attempt to order the sea enables her to sing "beyond the genius of the sea"—that is, to transcend nature and become the maker of a world in sound and language that is uniquely human. As critic Harold Bloom writes, the poem is finally equivocal and ambivalent about the relationship between art and nature: It "affirms a transcendental poetic spirit yet cannot locate it, and . . also remains uneasily wary about the veritable ocean" (104).

BIBLIOGRAPHY

Bloom, Harold. *Wallace Stevens: The Poems of Our Climate.* Ithaca, N.Y.: Cornell University Press, 1976.

Cook, Eleanor. Poetry, *Word-Play, and Word-War in Wallace Stevens.* Princeton, N.J.: Princeton University Press, 1988.

Edwin J. Barton

I DON'T HAVE ANY PAPER SO SHUT UP, (OR, SOCIAL ROMANTICISM) **BRUCE ANDREWS (1992)** *I Don't Have Any Paper* strongly displays BRUCE ANDREWS's avant-garde conviction that political art, in order to effect social change, must forcefully alter the reader's consciousness while simultaneously inviting her or his active participation. An embodiment of LANGUAGE SCHOOL philosophy involving the materiality of language, the poem contains syntactical and semantic disruptions, shocking colloquial phrases, and ironic juxtapositions. As much thematically concerned with politics as with enacting social critique, *I Don't Have Any Paper* aims at the radical kind of writing Andrews believes possible only when one accepts the notion that language is not pure, or transparent, but reflects dominant political ideologies. The broken-up rhythms and irregular lines work, much like the poetry of CHARLES OLSON, to shift focus to how language constructs one's perception of the world; yet, as in the poems of CLARK COOLIDGE, these techniques simultaneously underscore the arbitrariness of language and its connection to ongoing political abuses.

Comprising 100 experimental prose poems (see PROSODY AND FREE VERSE), each about three pages in length, *I Don't Have Any Paper* is often cited as Andrews's most accessible work; the volume is also noted for its aggressive, at times hostile, tone. With such titles as "America Shops," "Communism Is a Morale Problem," and "This Unity Sounds Posturepedic to Me," *I Don't Have Any Paper* uses wordplay to reveal the hypocrisy and vacuousness of consumer culture, as well as to underscore the fragmented nature of national identity. Andrews employs parody to illustrate how political beliefs reveal themselves in everyday speech; he frequently combines sexual and scatological puns with financial jargon, and he rewrites popular slogans to expose imperialist desires for blind gratification. Phrases, such as "Sink the boat people!" ("Help Defeat Your Country"), "Tear-gas the middle class. Blonds have more enemas" ("Learn to Be Dispensible"), and "'Control the budget & you have them by the predestined—" ("Oh, Glaze Me Big!"), attack American values, exposing them as contributors to and perpetuators of oppression.

By means of ironic pronouncements, Andrews's speaker takes on the voices of those in power in order to expose abuses. In addition, as BOB PERELMAN points out, Andrews's poems illustrate the philosopher François "Lyotard's archetypal command to postmodern intellectuals to 'wage a war on totality'" (10), to refuse a singular point of view. Andrews therefore denies to readers the central perspective associated with a traditional, unified narrative—one that promotes the speaking self above all else. As Andrews sees it, this is a privileging of the white male perspective and historically has served to erase expressions of race, gender, and class difference.

BIBLIOGRAPHY

Perelman, Bob. "Building a More Powerful Vocabulary: Bruce Andrews and the World (Trade Center)." *Arizona Quarterly:* 50, no. 4 (1994): 117–131.

Megan Swihart Jewell

IGNATOW, DAVID (1914–1997) David Ignatow's poetry speaks for the common people. Walt Whitman was an especially strong influence on Ignatow, although, to some extent, this influence is indirect, via the intermediate force of WILLIAM CARLOS WILLIAMS.

Ignatow knew and corresponded with many American poets, among them Williams, CHARLES REZNIKOFF, GREGORY CORSO, CHARLES OLSON, ALLEN GINSBERG, LOUIS ZUKOFSKY, ROBERT CREELEY, DENISE LEVERTOV, and HARVEY SHAPIRO. Like Whitman and his many followers, Ignatow strove for simplicity and personal immediacy, usually assuming the pose of the common, unliterary observer. And, again like Whitman and Williams, he sought for his effects through a deceptive simplicity and surprising paradox. His numerous works, strongly autobiographical, deal with social as well as personal issues in quietly meditative free verse.

Ignatow was born in Brooklyn, New York, and spent practically all his life in the New York metropolitan area. Ignatow worked for a time as a journalist with the Works Progress Administration (WPA) Federal Writers' Project. His first collection of poetry (*Poems*) appeared in 1948. In a career that lasted more than 50 years, Ignatow authored 17 books and served as editor for various literary journals. He taught in several institutions of higher learning in the United States (including the New School for Social Research, Southampton

College, Columbia University, and York College of the City University of New York). He received several honors during his career—two Guggenheim Fellowships (1965 and 1973), a National Institute of Arts and Letters Award (1964), and the Bollingen Prize (1977).

Of particular interest in *The Gentle Weight Lifter, Say Pardon* (1961), and *Figures of the Human* (1964) is Ignatow's emphasis upon the poetic parable. *Rescue the Dead,* Ignatow's 1968 collection, revealed his interest in the serious themes of social reform, family relationships, and human kinship with nature. In *Facing the Tree* (1975), *The Animal in the Bush* (1977), and *Tread the Dark* (1978), he examines death and the art of poetry. Later collections include *Whisper to the Earth* (1981), *Leaving the Door Open* (1984), *Shadowing the Ground* (1991), and *Against the Evidence: Selected Poems, 1934–1994* (1993). *The Notebooks of David Ignatow* was published in 1973, and *The One in the Many: A Poet's Memoirs* in 1988.

Because Ignatow, like Whitman, lived most of his life in New York City, and because he was stamped indelibly as a New Yorker, he observed that in many of his poems the style of his writing demanded "receptivity to anger, sarcasm, satire, brutality, indifference and anguish, anguish with which all is presented." (Terris "Preface" ii). The posthumous volume *At My Ease* (1998) contains numerous poems that depict city life—weaving in and out of taxis, subways, and crowds, meditating on chance meetings, and observations of strangers' work—all reminiscent of Whitman's *Leaves of Grass.* In a 1956 poem, "For Walt Whitman," Ignatow coyly compares his own emotional and poetic life to that of his model, taunting Whitman for being someone who might not like, when riding on a subway train, to be "pushed out / by your camerados." Basically, as Ignatow confesses to Whitman, the younger poet feels that his life "betrays" the older poet. In another poem, "Walt Whitman in the Civil War Hospitals" (1990), Ignatow attempts to empathize with Whitman's sufferings as he transmutes the hospital experiences into meaningful poetry, accepting—with praise—the inevitability of death.

Ignatow deliberately strove to avoid a "literary" style. Shapiro, close friend and fellow New Yorker, says, "I remember his early manuscripts and can't recall ever seeing a poem that came out of someone else's book, that came out of literature" (28). His exaltation of the pedestrian and the ordinary are closely akin to what Whitman critics often call "the glory of the commonplace" (Aspiz 105).

Ignatow's son, David, was an institutionalized schizophrenic, which caused his father great anguish, as portrayed in "Sunday at the State Hospital" (1970). When visiting in the mental hospital, the son cannot manage to eat the food the father has brought for him. The poet's "past is sitting in front of" him, unable "to bring the present to its mouth." Another sort of anguish is displayed in "Play Again" (1970), a poem written in response to the report late in 1962 in the New York newspapers of a nine-year-old child being raped on a roof and hurled 20 stories to the ground. The poet's outrage is held in check through the use of fantasy, the desire that the child can once again play—not on a roof, but on a stairway: "When we played it was to love each other / in games." Here, as elsewhere in his poetry, the poet exposes a tenderness amid the brutalities of modern city life.

BIBLIOGRAPHY

Aspiz, Harold. "The Body Politic in *Democratic Vistas.*" In *Walt Whitman: The Centennial Essays,* edited by Ed Folsom, 105–119. Iowa City: University of Iowa Press, 1994.

Moran, Daniel Thomas. "With Ignatow at Whitman's Birthplace." *Starting from Paumanok: Newsletter of the Walt Whitman Birthplace Association* (spring 1998): 1.

Shapiro, Harvey. "Tribute to David Ignatow." *Poetry Society of America Journal* 58, no. 1 (spring 1998): 28–29.

Terris, Virginia R. Preface to *At My Ease: David Ignatow's Uncollected Poems of the Fifties and Sixties,* edited by Terris. Rochester, N.Y.: BOA Editions, 1998, p. ii.

———., ed. *Meaningful Differences: The Poetry and Prose of David Ignatow.* Tuscaloosa: University of Alabama Press, 1994.

James T. F. Tanner

"I GO BACK TO MAY 1937" Sharon Olds **(1997)** The CONFESSIONAL tendencies of Sharon Olds's poetry provide her a rich poetic conceit in "I Go Back to May 1937." Punning on the colloquial phrase 'go back,' which means both 'date back' and 'revisit,'

Olds tells her autobiography not through the details of her own past, her youth, her birth in 1942, or even her conception, but through a moment shortly before her parents married in May 1937. The frequent anaphoras beginning her FREE VERSE lines create an incantatory rhythm similar to the rhythms of ancient Hebrew poetry, and like those works, Olds's poem investigates the close ties of the present with the past. Olds suggests that human identity is inevitably composed of the faults of earlier generations, and that the mistakes of the parents are visited upon the children. But Olds wrestles a surprising conclusion from this realization, for she declares that existence itself is worth almost any degree of suffering, and while her vision is by no means conventionally uplifting, it is a powerful expression of the basic desire to survive.

Olds narrates in cinematographic fashion, as if she were rewinding the past and freezing one frame in the film of history in order to analyze its imagery. The poem's setting hints ominously at the parents' future relationship, which Olds links to the figurative violence pervading the college setting, from courtyard tiles that resemble "plates of blood" to the wrought-iron gate rearing "its sword-tips black in the May air." Both parents are characterized as dangerously naïve and unformed, the mother's face "blank," the father's "blind," and their bodies identically described as "pitiful beautiful untouched." For Olds, such innocence is equated with willful ignorance, and though "all they know is they are / innocent, they would never hurt anybody," she wants desperately to stop their marriage, to warn them that "you are going to do bad things to children, / you are going to suffer in ways you never heard of, / you are going to want to die."

Olds's poem offers an unflinching look at the psychological casualties of an ordinary, bourgeois marriage. While her tone is angry, it is also controlled, and the dramatic arc of the poem follows not only the speaker's condemnation of her parents' future actions, but also the speaker's growing realization that "I want to live." In an essay otherwise critical of the control Olds exhibits over her psychologically messy subjects, Kenneth Lincoln usefully observes that "Olds's poetic grist is generated from a savage purism. . . . Hers is a combination of repression and obsession, a fear of the untamed and a fixation on the good-with-bad" (333). This "savage purism" results in the speaker's refusal to undo her own creation, however masochistic the life it results in may (and will) become; thus, it is an expression of the utmost desire for survival. For Olds, the only way to bear such certain misery is to bear authentic witness to it, as she has been doing throughout the poem and as she will do once she is born, for as she says, "Do what you are going to do, and I will tell about it." Telling, or writing poetry in Olds's case, becomes the only thing that can cleanse the poet of the suffering she has endured, suffering that is ironically the very condition that made the creative act of poetry necessary.

BIBLIOGRAPHY

Flint, Roland. "A Way of Knowing." *Poet Lore* 83, no. 1 (1988): 39–44.

Holden, Jonathan. "American Poetry: 1970–1990." *A Profile of 20th Century American Poetry,* edited by Josh Myers and David Abjohn, 254–274. Carbondale: Southern Illinois University Press, 1991.

Lincoln, Kenneth. "Primal Mom: Olds." In *Sing with the Heart of a Bear: Fusions of Native and American Poetry, 1890–1999,* 330–340. Berkeley: University of California Press, 2000.

Temple Cone

"I KNEW A WOMAN" THEODORE ROETHKE (1958) THEODORE ROETHKE's witty poem "I Knew a Woman" takes as its primary metaphor the choreographed dances or odes of classical tragedy in order to depict the speaker's youthful intimacy with the eponymous woman. Numerous puns and the prevailing metaphor of the dance hint, sometimes overtly, at the sexual dalliance between the speaker and the woman, but the poem is more than a rake's exercise in double entendre. The repeated allusions to Greek dramatic poetry, and indirectly to the Elizabethan poets whom Roethke admired, suggest that the poem is an expression of Roethke's own sensual relationship with literature and of the ways that literature plays itself out upon the reader's body.

In classical Greek tragedy, individual actors playing major roles were joined on stage by a chorus composed of multiple anonymous actors who would recite or chant their lines in unison while moving back and forth across the stage in a stylized dance that harkened back to tragedy's roots in religious ceremony. This dance or ode featured three stage directions: the *strophe* (which is also a term for *stanza*), the *antistrophe,* and the epode, which are translated into English as *turn, counter-turn,* and *stand.* Roethke uses these translated literary terms to describe the movements of his dance with the woman, so that their sexual "dance" is masked by a series of puns. But when Roethke writes that "Of her choice virtues only gods should speak, / Or English poets who grew up on Greek," he is also suggesting an intellectual playfulness, a dalliance with poetry itself that can be as full of movement and intimacy as an actual dance.

For one sensitive to double entendres, the poem is racy, almost bawdy. As Karl Malkoff notes, "Even lines easily passed over have hidden sexual connotations." "I nibbled meekly from her proferred hand," Roethke remarks, suggesting at first a tutelary relationship between the speaker and this woman, unless the image is taken literally. Later in the poem Roethke's colorful language intensifies: "Love likes a gander, and adores a goose," he exclaims. And in one of the parenthetical asides that conclude each stanza, he makes puns on the term for a sexual purveyor, *rake,* and on a Scottish expression for intercourse: "(But what prodigious mowing we did make)."

But just as "when she moved, she moved more ways than one," so too the poem moves in various ways. As a result of the numerous allusions, the poem expresses sensual love for literature that the speaker appears to have learned through his relationship with this woman. Thus, as Richard Alan Blessing observes, "(T)he woman, by her movement, becomes a kind of Muse whose turn and re-turn serve as inspiration for the poet's turns of language." The ambiguous meaning created by the numerous puns creates the dance of the central theme, which is about the sensuousness and sensuality of the intellect and the potential for ideas in any experience of the physical. Although his particular focus is on the multiple layers of sexual punning in the poem, Blessing rightly notes that "(A)mbiguity begets ambiguity; a pun in one line creates, in a dynamic and organic way, alternate readings in another, in others." "I'm martyr to a motion not my own," Roethke writes, and the lines weave together the Elizabethan use of "little death" for orgasm with the romantic idea of poetic inspiration as an external energy that moves the poet to create. In "I Knew a Woman," Roethke, a noted instructor of creative writing in his time, not only teaches the reader about the sensuous pleasures of reading poetry but also how that pleasure is inspired by (and perhaps can even inspire) delight in the human body.

BIBLIOGRAPHY

Blessing, Richard Alan. *Theodore Roethke's Dynamic Vision.* Available online. URL: www.english.uiuc.edu/maps/poets/m_ r/roethke/woman.htm.

Malkoff, Karl. *Theodore Roethke: An Introduction to the Poetry.* Available online. URL: www.english.uiuc.edu/maps/poets/m_r/roethke/woman.htm.

Temple Cone

"I KNOW A MAN" ROBERT CREELEY (1957)

The dialogue between the unnamed, loquacious narrator and his pseudonymous friend John in Robert Creeley's free verse poem "I Know a Man" reflects Creeley's view that language is a form of life, not simply a means of describing lived reality. Yet the poem also dramatizes Creeley's belief, voiced again and again in interviews with the poet, that the life of language must be shared in community with other beings to avoid the dangerous egotism of pure subjectivity. In the blunt, conversational diction and rhythms characteristic of the BLACK MOUNTAIN SCHOOL, Creeley challenges the notion of the well-wrought poem, which creates the illusion of control over the chaos of reality even as it tries to represent it.

The poem follows a deceptively simple narrative. The narrator recounts a conversation with a friend about the uncertainty of existence, which ended with the narrator suggesting they "buy a goddamn big car" and the friend telling the narrator to "watch / out where yr going." But Creeley complicates the psychological and thematic background of this narrative in numerous ways, troubling the illusion of control which the ego and the well-wrought lyric both seek. Creeley's skillful use of enjambment breaks the lines, not on end-stops, but across syntactical units, simultaneously fragmenting the grammatical sense of the poem and accelerating its pace. "As I sd to my / friend," Creeley begins, and the separation of the possessive pronoun "my" from "friend" signals that the narrator's subjectivity, his sense of being a self, has overwhelmed his ability to connect with other individuals. For Creeley, genuine communication is "mutual feeling with someone, not a didactic process of information" (Wagner, 174), and the absence of such mutual relationships actually endangers the individual self. Creeley emphasizes this alienation by withholding the friend's true name, suggesting either that he has not learned it, that he does not care what it is and so projects his own choice of name, or that he is concealing it (the latter claim supports the possibility that the friend is not a separate entity, but an aspect of the narrator's own psyche).

Such egocentric separation is further manifest in the narrator's incessant speech; "I am / always talking," the narrator admits, and this barrage of speech prohibits him from entering the silence in which he could hear another's voice, and so make an interpersonal connection. Ironically, because the entire poem is the narrator's spoken recollection, his "talking" can be equated with poetry itself, which suggests a very critical stance towards the absolute subjectivity of lyric poetry. Yet Creeley does not dismiss the narrator's talking out of hand, since it is his only means of countering the fact that "the darkness sur- / rounds us." The narrator seeks verbal connection as a counter to the loneliness of the void, though his incessant speech threatens that goal. The critic Charles Altieri notes that the poem's vague language dramatizes this breakdown between the human self and the world around it. Faced with meaninglessness, Altieri writes, "The only reply is the one John gives—keep your eye on experience; live in it and avoid the purely verbal universe" (175). Bruce Jackson balances the existential bleakness of Altieri's reading with a more comical vision of the narrator as chatterbox, an image closer to Creeley's own good-humored loquacity. "(W)hen Creeley read the poem," Jackson writes, "he put the long caesura after 'drive,' so what the friend said was 'for / christ's sake, look / out where yr going,' just what anyone might say to someone who was walking beside him on the street, mouth running a mile a minute . . and in the process of talking maybe missing the curb, maybe not seeing a lamppost or garbage can or steel grille sticking up around the base of a tree."

This element of humor in Creeley's poem is less often discussed than the ideas about language and control, but it is connected to his emphasis on relationships. Lyric closure, linguistic facility, and subjectivity suggest the possibility of either literal or psychological control of the chaos of life, but the possible car crash looming at the end of the poem suggests otherwise. Instead of control, Creeley suggests, one can possess alertness, which he commands from the reader in tones alternately brash and cajoling, and which he teaches through the careful play of his skillfully enjambed free verse. While the reader may seek the "goddamn big car" of meaning and meaningfulness offered by the well-wrought lyric, Creeley's poem, like the friend, warns instead to "look / out where yr going."

BIBLIOGRAPHY

Altieri, Charles. *Enlarging the Temple: New Directions in American Poetry during the 1960s.* Lewisburg, Pa.: Bucknell University Press, 1979.

Creeley, Robert, and Bruce Jackson. "'I Know a Man': On the Subject of Company." Buffalo Report. Available online. URL: http://buffaloreport.com/2005/050405.creeley.company.html. Downloaded March 2007.

Wagner, Linda, and Lewis McAdams, Jr. "The Art of Poetry X: Robert Creeley." *The Paris Review* XI (1968): 155–187.

Temple Cone

IMAGIST SCHOOL (IMAGISM) *Imagism* is a term associated with an eclectic group of English and American poets working between 1912 and 1917, among them some of the most important writers in English of the first half of the 20th century: EZRA POUND, AMY LOWELL, WILLIAM CARLOS WILLIAMS, H. D. (Hilda Doolittle), D. H. Lawrence, Ford Madox Ford, and Richard Aldington. Never a wholly American movement, imagism nevertheless had a dramatic effect on several subsequent generations of self-consciously American writers and poets, perhaps most directly on those associated with the OBJECTIVIST and BLACK MOUNTAIN SCHOOLS of poetry. Even poets not formally associated with imagism, such as T. S. ELIOT, CONRAD

AIKEN, MARIANNE MOORE, and WALLACE STEVENS, or overtly hostile to aspects of imagist aesthetics, such as ROBERT FROST, benefited indirectly from the imagist school's formal experimentation and widespread critical success.

The history of imagism has two relatively distinct phases. The first is associated with Pound, who led the movement from 1912 until 1914, when he essentially abandoned it to devote himself to championing vorticism, an English version of Italian futurism, centering on the work of the artist and poet Wyndham Lewis and the sculptor Henri Gaudier-Brzeska. Imagism's second phase, which Pound labeled "Amygism" in resentment over his loss of control of the movement, is associated with Amy Lowell and spans roughly the years 1915 to 1917. After 1917 most imagist principles were so widely dispersed and accepted (and badly imitated) within the Anglo-American literary community that the movement, never very cohesive to begin with, made way for more radical avant-garde practices.

Imagism emerged from Pound's involvement in London with a Poets' Club that began meeting formally under T. E. Hulme in 1908. By 1909 the club had been reconstituted as the "second" Poets' Club by Hulme and F. S. Flint, and it included Pound as well as Ford Madox Ford. Although the first reference in print to "Les Imagistes" occurred in 1912 in *Ripostes,* a collection of Pound's poems, the term actually refers to what Pound calls "a forgotten school of 1909," or the second Poets' Club, which he explicitly identifies as "a school of Images" (59).

This imagist school owed much philosophically to Hulme, who is today best remembered as a neoclassical aesthetician, disciple, and translator of the French philosopher and Nobel laureate Henri Bergson. Hulme railed against what he understood to be a prevailing cultural romanticism, which in social philosophy encouraged sentimental optimism concerning the ultimate perfectibility of humankind and which led, in turn, to art that was soft and weakly expressive. In its place he advocated poetry built around the "hard, dry image," along with a view of human beings as finite, fallible, and corrupt. This view would later strike a chord in members of the post–World War I Lost Generation, and it can be seen in the interwar themes of such major novelists as F. Scott Fitzgerald and John Dos Passos.

Following Hulme, the imagists aimed to strip away poetry's tendency toward dense wordiness and sentimentality and to crystallize poetic meaning in clear, neatly juxtaposed images. This crystallization is nicely exemplified by Hulme's poem "Autumn" (1909, published 1915) in which the Moon, the stars, and the images of different faces attached to them become vehicles for questioning the value of modern, urban life:

> A touch of cold in the Autumn night—
> I walked abroad,
> And saw the ruddy moon lean over a hedge
> Like a red-faced farmer.
> I did not stop to speak, but nodded,
> And round about were the wistful stars
> With white faces like town children.

Given its subject matter, the poem remains, in typical imagist fashion, notably free from the kind of tone and rhythmic constraints characteristic of related works by, say, A. E. Housman, an English poet whom Pound would later satirize in his poem "Song in the Manner of Housman" (1911).

The connections in Hulme's poem and elsewhere to William Wordsworth and especially to William Blake are obvious and remain somewhat ironic, given the depth of Hulme's hostility toward romanticism more generally. However, as John Gage has noted in his study of imagist poetics, the imagists maintained links "not only with romantics such as [Percy Bysshe] Shelley or even Blake, but also with the more conservative aestheticists of the Victorian generation, against whom they were in ostensible revolt" (17). Other early and more radical influences on the imagists included the symbolist poets, classical Greek and Roman poetry, and Chinese and Japanese verse forms, in particular the haiku, or *hokku.*

The "image," of course, remained central to imagist theory and practice throughout the existence of the movement and developed principally, though partially, from Hulme's reading of Bergson's metaphysics. In Hulme's translation of Bergson's *Introduction to*

Metaphysics, Bergson proposes that the convergence of images allows one to peer behind the veil of language and thus to experience things as they really are. Bergson's and Hulme's ideas helped Pound refine his understanding of the image in poetry. In his celebrated essay "A Few Don'ts by an Imagist" (1913), Pound somewhat abstractly defines the image in almost photographic terms as

> that which presents an intellectual and emotional complex in an instant of time. . . . It is the presentation of such a "complex" instantaneously which gives that sense of sudden liberation; that sense of freedom from time limits and space limits; that sense of sudden growth, which we experience in the presence of the greatest works of art.

Perhaps nowhere is this sense of freedom more perfectly realized than in Pound's own work "In a Station of the Metro," a poem which the critic J. T. Barbarese has termed imagism's "enabling text" (307).

The compactness and immediacy of Pound's poem recall the three imagist principles agreed to by Pound, H. D., and Richard Aldington in 1912:

> 1. Direct treatment of the 'thing,' whether subjective or objective.
> 2. To use absolutely no word that does not contribute to the presentation.
> 3. As regarding rhythm: to compose in sequence of the musical phrase, not in sequence of a metronome. (Pound "A Retrospect" 4)

This last principle draws attention to the fact that "In a Station of the Metro," and indeed nearly all of the works produced by poets who thought of themselves as imagists, were written in "vers libre," or free verse: poetry in which rhyme may or may not be present but in which cadence is valued more highly than meter (see PROSODY AND FREE VERSE). The commitment of the imagists to free verse followed from their desire to escape from more metrically formal modes of French versification attempted by symbolist poets, such as Arthur Rimbaud and Jules Laforgue.

Pound used his role as foreign correspondent for Harriet Monroe's literary magazine *Poetry* to advance the imagist cause. Monroe herself initially supported Pound's ambitions and proved willing to make available to her readers the very best work of this new school, along with relevant explanatory criticism, with a view to expanding the tastes of America's literary establishment and introducing them to European developments in the poetic and other arts. Monroe published work by many of the imagists Pound brought to her attention, perhaps most notably H. D., whose "Three Poems" can be found in *Poetry*'s January 1913 issue and are attributed somewhat grandly to "H. D., Imagiste," an appellation created by Pound.

It was in the pages of *Poetry* that Lowell first became acquainted with imagism, and the experience of reading H. D.'s poems profoundly altered the way in which she understood herself. In Jean Gould's words, "the revelation of Amy's own identity came over her in a great surge: *She* was an *Imagiste,* too! This was the sort of poetry she had been unknowingly striving to write. It was startlingly clear to her that she was born *Imagiste*" (113). The realization of this affinity with imagism drove Lowell to make contact first with Monroe, whom she persuaded to publish some of her work, then later with Pound in London.

Both strong personalities, Pound and Lowell initially found much in common in their approach to poetry, although differences between them soon became clear. Lowell particularly objected to Pound's relatively weak commitment to imagism per se, to his tendency to champion serially one avant-garde movement after another, rather than consolidating and then evolving as an artist within a single movement over time. During her visit to England in 1914, Lowell found Pound surprisingly detached from imagism and so immersed in vorticism that her questions about the former were met variously with rudeness and indifference.

Taking the initiative, Lowell decided to publish an anthology of imagist verse, one that would extend the movement beyond what she perceived as the rather introductory point it had reached with Pound's edited volume *Des Imagistes* (1914). The result of Lowell's efforts was the first of a series of three collections of verse, each entitled *Some Imagist Poets,* which brought together a heterogeneous group of writers and which appeared, respectively, in 1915, 1916, and 1917. In the 1915 collection, Lowell was careful to distance herself from Pound, who, she implied, had distorted imagism by making it too much in his own image.

What is striking in Lowell's presentation of imagism is her determined anglicization of the movement. Gone from the imagist lexicon are such francophone terms as *imagisme* and *vers libre,* and in their place rest their English-language equivalents: *Imagism, free verse,* and *unrhymed cadence.* Gone too is Pound's emphasis on concision, for, as several critics, have noted of Lowell, "although Imagism was congenial to her penchant for noticing her surroundings, the Imagist stress on conciseness was quite antipathetic to her temperament. Whatever Miss Lowell's virtues, succinctness, except sometimes in repartee, was not among them" (Flint 25). Indeed Lowell's regular failure to adhere to the second of Pound's 1912 strictures noticeably marks (some would say mars) her contributions to 1915's *Some Imagist Poets* and is most striking in her contributions "The Travelling Bear" and "The Letter." Pound read these works as indicative of Lowell's lack of discipline as a poet and, consequently, of her failure as an imagist.

Pound ultimately had very little at stake in his bickering with Lowell, although he launched a series of attacks on her and her publisher just prior to the publication of her first imagist anthology. He, and indeed poetry more generally, had moved on. Imagism would remain a viable "project" throughout the war years, and a touchstone for poets for some time after that, but by 1930 the movement was unequivocally dead. In 1930 the house Chatto and Windus published the retrospective *Imagist Anthology* 1930, edited by Glenn Hughes and Ford Madox Ford, which again brought together the work of Aldington, H. D., Fletcher, Flint, James Joyce, Lawrence, and Williams. The anthology was an anachronism, and Pound attacked it violently, referring to it in a letter as "Aldington's Imagist mortology 1930" and dismissing it as "20 ans apres." But Pound's attack cannot mask imagism's profound importance. It proved to be one of the most deeply transformative literary movements of the early 20th century, and without it so much of what we now take for granted as poetry would be, quite literally, unimaginable.

BIBLIOGRAPHY

Barbarese, J. T. "Ezra Pound's Imagist Aesthetics." In *The Columbia History of American Poetry,* edited by Hay Parini and Brett C. Miller, 284–318. New York: Columbia University Press, 1993.

Bergson, Henri. *An Introduction to Metaphysics.* Translated by T. E. Hulme. New York: G. P. Putnam's Sons, 1912.

Flint, F. Cudworth. *Amy Lowell.* Minneapolis: University of Minnesota Press, 1969.

Gage, John. *In the Arresting Eye: The Rhetoric of Imagism.* Baton Rouge: Louisiana State University Press, 1981.

Gould, Jean. *Amy: The World of Amy Lowell and the Imagist Movement.* New York: Dodd Mead, 1975.

Grieve, Tom. "Imagism Revisited." *West-Coast-Line* 27, no. 3 (winter 1993–94): 110–130.

Hulme, T. E. "Autumn." *Ripostes,* edited by Ezra Pound. London: Elkin Mathews, 1915, p. 60.

Kenner, Hugh. *The Poetry of Ezra Pound.* Norfolk, Conn.: New Directions, 1951.

———. *The Pound Era.* Berkeley: University of California Press, 1973.

Pound, Ezra. "A Few Don'ts By An Imagist." *Poetry* 1, no. 6 (March 1913): 198–206. Reprint, "A Retrospect." *Literary Essays of Ezra Pound,* edited by T. S. Eliot, 3–14. New York: New Directions, 1968.

———. *Literary Essays of Ezra Pound,* edited by T. S. Eliot. New York: New Directions, 1968.

———. "A Retrospect." *Pavannes and Divisions.* New York: Knopf, 1918. Reprint, *Literary Essays of Ezra Pound,* edited by T. S. Eliot, 3–14. New York: New Directions, 1968.

Pratt, William, and Robert Richardson, eds. *Homage to Imagism.* New York: AMS, 1992.

Adam Muller

"IN A DARK TIME" THEODORE ROETHKE (1964) Theodore Roethke's "In a Dark Time" is the first poem in his "Sequence, Sometimes Metaphysical," a series of poems in which Roethke breaks through the limits of reason to achieve a visionary experience in which "The mind enters itself, and God the mind." Self-fulfillment through self-transcendence is Roethke's final aim, and though the poem is not strictly CONFESSIONAL in nature, its frequent references to madness as a metaphor for and perhaps a means of breaking free of the constraints of reason often seem to reflect the poet's own experiences with manic-depression. Denis Donoghue remarks that for Roethke, "The self, the daily world, reason, meant bondage; to come close to God you had to break through. These things were never the medium of one's encounter with God, always obstacles in its way" (230). The "dark time" the speaker endures is his own 'dark night of the soul' or purifying crisis of faith, though in this instance it is faith in the imagination that is challenged and finally affirmed.

Claiming that "I know the purity of a pure despair," Roethke pursues his own imaginative divinity through the desperately pure poetic music of "In a Dark Time." Written in rhymed sestets, the poem displays Roethke's beautiful sense of sound, particularly in its rich internal rhymes and its frequent assonance, consonance, and alliteration, which make surprising associative links between quite divergent ideas. For instance, Roethke exclaims, "Dark, dark my light, and darker my desire," contrasting the heavily emphasized darkness with "light" and "desire," whose long vowels are linked by assonance and echo in the lines that follow, when Roethke writes that "My soul, like some heat-maddened summer fly, / Keeps buzzing at the sill. Which I is *I*?"

Nature frequently provides the mirror in which Roethke might find his own recreated image, for he claims that "I hear my echo in the echoing wood," but the speaker cannot rest content with that simple, pantheistic identification. Restlessly searching the space between reason and nature, Roethke claims that "The edge is what I have," a recognition that self-transcendence can only be achieved through opposition to all definable positions. It is an insight that comes to Roethke from the romantic visionary poet William Blake, who wrote in *The Marriage of Heaven and Hell* that "Without Contraries is no progression" (86). Such opposition to reason, to conventional ideas of the self in society, and even to conventional poetics, will surely lead to condemnation from the masses, Roethke realizes. "What's madness but nobility of soul / At odds with circumstance?" he asks, realizing that only through what may be conventionally called "madness" can one achieve "Death of the self in a long, tearless night, / All natural shapes blazing unnatural light."

Critic John Hobbs writes that the poem's recurrent paradoxes, particularly the paradox of a clarifying darkness, can only be understood in a mystical context, and even then only by sharing "the poet's mental states directly rather than contemplating them in clear, logical sentences" (58), though he goes on to make an analogy between mystical ecstasy and poetic inspiration. The poet and the mystic alike share in an archetypal primitivism residing below the modern, rational consciousness, a lair and layer of the psyche where mortal existence and the natural world are exalted. In this psychological space, so much like the mind of God, resides every image, and they flow together in "A steady storm of correspondences!" "In a Dark Time" celebrates the poet-mystic as one whose vision sweeps together all aspects of the world into a marvelous, transforming conflagration so that, as Roethke exclaims, "The day's on fire!"

BIBLIOGRAPHY

Blake, William. *Blake's Poetry and Designs,* edited by Mary Lynn Johnson and John E. Grant. New York. W. W. Norton & Co., 1979.

Donoghue, Denis. *Connoisseurs of Chaos: Ideas of Order in Modern American Poetry.* New York: The Macmillan Company, 1967.

Hobbs, John. "The Poet as His Own Interpreter: Roethke on 'In a Dark Time.'" *College English* 33, no. 1 (1971): 55–66.

Temple Cone

INEZ, COLETTE (1931–) Colette Inez can be viewed as belonging to the CONFESSIONAL school of poetry, as much of her work draws on her life experiences; however, she also examines more universal themes, such as the formation of identity and the understanding of womanhood. Inez's poetry has been praised for what Thomas Lask calls her "adventuresomeness" in selecting subject material (29). She was influenced as a child by the rhythm of religious songs and her reading of Emily Dickinson, and words themselves became of great importance to her. Her use of free verse allows her to experiment with their sounds (see PROSODY AND FREE VERSE).

Inez was born in Brussels, Belgium, and raised in a children's home; her father, an American priest, and her mother, a French archivist, could not marry, and neither parent wanted to acknowledge Inez's birth. At the age of eight, Inez was brought to America to be raised by a couple in New York. However, they were indifferent parents, and their alcoholism and marital problems created additional problems for Inez. Inez's struggle to overcome her childhood profoundly influences her poetry. She has received numerous awards for her work, including a Pushcart Prize in 1986–87 and the Reedy Memorial Award from the Poetry Society of America in 1972.

Many of Inez's poems explore her parents' illicit liaison and their abandonment of her as well as the difficulties she experienced in her American foster home. Inez tries to understand the choices her parents made and how their decisions have influenced her identity and choices. However, in her search for understanding and ultimately acceptance of her childhood, Inez does not present herself as victim. Rather she "speaks with poise and measure," according to Robert Schultz (154), from the perspective of an adult. In the title poem from her second book, *Alive and Taking Names* (1977), she proclaims: "I am well, sound, hale, cross referenced with fit, / snuffling the morning air, alive and taking names," suggesting that she has overcome her early disadvantages. Inez examines other, more universal ideas in her work as well. For instance, she believes, as Jim Gorman writes, that "the 'female' experience is culturally, socially, and even organically unique" (222). Not surprisingly, birth, abortion, and female sexuality therefore figure prominently in her poetry. In "The Rape of Arethusa" (1972), for example, she describes the sexual abuse of a woman: "Her thighs / . . . buckle and spread; / he prods." Inez shows that women may not only be exploited for their sexuality but may also draw strength from it (see FEMALE VOICE, FEMALE LANGUAGE).

Inez's verse is polished and compelling. Though she draws heavily from her own life, her poetry explores issues that are widely accessible. Her enthusiasm for life and the world around her are conveyed in her poetry with a clear and powerful voice.

BIBLIOGRAPHY

Gorman, Jim. "An Interview with Colette Inez." *Parnassus* 7, no. 1 (1978): 210–223.

Lask, Thomas. "Voices from the Distaff Side." *New York Times,* 18 August 1972, 29.

Schultz, Robert. "Family Life" *Hudson Review* 42, no. 1 (spring 1989): 154–155.

Kelli Murphy

"IN JUST-SPRING" E. E. CUMMINGS (1923)

E. E. CUMMINGS's "in Just-spring," one of his most popular poems, is derived mainly from imagism in that its main purpose is to re-create, in as few words as possible, the sensual particulars of a lyrical moment (see IMAGIST SCHOOL)—but it also introduced much of the technical innovativeness, particularly with regard to the placement of words on the page, that Cummings pioneered and accomplished more than any other American modernist poet (see MODERNISM). First sketched as an exercise for a class at Harvard at a time (about 1914) when free verse excited undergraduates but was discouraged by professors, the poem captured the poet's childhood memories of a street that flooded in spring each year—at the same time that a balloon-seller began showing up, blowing his whistle.

Cummings made many changes in the poem before its publication that greatly illuminate the how and why of his technical innovations. First he changed all the 1916 version's capital letters, such as those beginning the names of children, to lowercase, then capitalized two other letters—the beginning of his practice of using capitalization for emphasis only. He also removed all commas and periods. To better "punctuate" his "score," he broke his stanzas into smaller ones, some but a line in length. Those lines he also frequently shortened, some of them to a single word apiece. More than once, too, he spread his lines out, as when he appropriately prolonged line 4 to "whistles far and wee."

Cummings cut his very first line from "In just-Spring" to "in Just-" to make his reader quickly aware of being in a poem that requires careful, slow reading—and to accentuate how abruptly arrived the scene is in spring. By chopping "mud-luscious" in the same manner, he gave "mud-" time to convey ugliness before its transformation to what mud is delightfully to most children.

Perhaps Cummings's best changes were his condensations of "Bill and Eddy" to "eddieandbill" and "Betty and Isabel" to "bettyandisbel" to show onomatopoetically, through spelling rather than sound, the inseparability and energy of Eddie and Bill and Betty and Isabel (with "isbel" also, of course, suggesting the child-world the poem is from, where names are sometimes only partly pronounced and often misspelled). Also important was Cummings's improvement of "ooze-suave" to "puddle-wonderful," a near-perfect poetic compound word, along the lines of "Just-spring," with its multiple meanings of *just.* Through such techniques and well-chosen imagery, especially that which gradually reveals the true identity of the balloon-seller (as the god Pan), Cummings achieved a marvelous celebration of childhood—and of spring, and the immortal, rather than old, goat-footed, rather than lame, archetypal figure at its core.

BIBLIOGRAPHY

Kennedy, Richard S. *Dreams in the Mirror.* New York: Liveright, 1980, 24–25, 97.

Lindroth, James R., and Colette Lindroth. *The Poetry of E. E. Cummings.* New York: Monarch Press, 1966, pp. 26–28.

Bob Grumman

"IN MEMORY OF MY FEELINGS" FRANK O'HARA (1958) FRANK O'HARA started "In Memory of My Feelings" on what he believed to be his 30th birthday, June 27, 1956—he was born in March, less than nine months after his parents' wedding, and never knew his real birth date—and finished it four days later, having left paper in his typewriter so that he could return to it immediately without having to interrupt his inspiration. The speed and spontaneity of this procedure is not only typical of O'Hara's practice but is also reminiscent of JACK KEROUAC's somewhat concurrent experiment (unpublished until 1957) with the scroll on which he typed *On the Road* in 20 days during April 1951. The poem is dedicated to Grace Hartigan, a painter and one of O'Hara's muses, but is neither about her nor for her. It is an address to her, in five parts of 33 to 44 lines each, through which O'Hara deals with identity in general and his own in particular.

The poem obviously is influenced by SURREALISM in its mass of disparate references, but it is a surrealism coexisting with O'Hara's clearly articulated experiences that surface just often enough. It mentions real events, such as staying at the Y in Chicago with Jane Freilicher, and real things, such as the Hartigan paintings for which O'Hara modeled. These events and things, however, are complicated by an awareness of the numerous "naked selves" making up the various aspects of personality; thus the poem tries to mediate between the real self, the one created by experience, and the desired self, the one created by imagination, bridging the distance between who we are and who we wish to be.

O'Hara uses recurring images of people and things from his own life in order to anchor the poem: "the hunt . . nautical references . . . circus animals, exotic locales . . . and romantic characters" (Perloff 142); these images help to make sense of the historical continuum evident in the poem's universality. All of human experience is here, from time and geography, in O'Hara's claim to be everything from "a baboon eating a banana" to "a Chinaman climbing a mountain." In keeping with its name, the poem is about feeling, and "what matters is not what happened but how one felt or feels about it" (Perloff 142). "The serpent in their midst," who must be saved at the poem's conclusion, is O'Hara himself—the snake being his frequently used totem figure. In this way, self preservation surfaces to reconcile the splintered self by resolving the jumble of impressions.

BIBLIOGRAPHY

Gooch, Brad. *City Poet: The Life and Times of Frank O'Hara.* New York: Knopf, 1993.

Perloff, Marjorie. *Frank O'Hara: Poet among Painters.* New York: George Braziller, 1977.

A. Mary Murphy

"IN MEMORY OF W. B. YEATS" W. H. AUDEN (1940) Representative of W. H. AUDEN's middle style, which was heavily influenced by the Freudian idea of art as a means of healthy psychological catharsis, Auden's "In Memory of W. B. Yeats" is at once an elegy for the great modern Irish poet, W. B. Yeats, and an ARS POETICA articulating the limited political but spiritually maximal function of poetry. The poem commemorates Yeats's death in 1939, a date that rings with additional historical and personal significance for Auden, for it was the year that the Second World War began and the year that Auden immigrated to the United States, where he would later take up permanent citizenship. Thus, the theories of art which the poem articulates are meant to be considered in an atmosphere of war and exile or immigration; in Auden's most oft-quoted line, "Poetry makes nothing happen," the poem simultaneously articulates the limitations of poetry and, within that limited frame, its immense spiritual significance for humankind.

Written in three parts, the elegy first depicts the day of Yeats's death in January 1939, then considers how Yeats's character flaws relate to the limited nature of poetry itself, then explores the significance of poetry in the life of humankind. The first part features many of the hallmarks of Auden's voice—urbane irony, elegant rhythms, diction and imagery drawn from the modern world, and well-turned, memorable phrases. "He disappeared in the dead of winter," Auden announces simply at the opening, and the winter imagery of the first section suggests the frozen misery the world faced at the end of the 1930s, as Germany was pressing toward a war with the rest of Europe. Auden ascribes to Yeats's death great symbolic significance, for having revered Yeats as a poet who wrote in musical phrases of the flaws and strengths characteristic of the human condition, Auden now finds "all the instruments agree / The day of his death was a dark cold day." Here, the emphasis on darkness is highly figurative, suggestive of political, historical, even spiritual darkness, though the repetition of *day* offsets this pessimism, suggesting that Yeats's poetry might serve as light to that metaphorical darkness.

Auden represents Yeats's physical body as both his human form, the full corpus of his poetry, and as a figure for Ireland itself. Like the country of Ireland, Yeats's body was subject to passions, revolts, and uprisings, and after his death, Ireland itself will be preserved in the body of his poetry. Yeats's poetry itself will be preserved and scattered, like the torn limbs of the original lyric poet, Orpheus, or of the fertility god, Osiris, among those who live to read it. "Now he is scattered among a hundred cities," Auden writes, and he praises the subtle but important influence Yeats's work had on the ordinary world around him.

This focus on the function and even the utility of Yeats's work carries over into the second section of the poem, where Auden meditates upon the origins of poetry in trauma (whether political, spiritual, or personal). Poetry is a nonutilitarian creation, surviving "In the valley of its saying where executives / Would never want to tamper." Critic Patrick Deane notes that this assessment of poetry's political efficacy is characteristic of Auden's later writings, after the political idealism of his earlier work: "art, when completed, becomes in a sense detached from history and cannot 're-enter history as an effective agent'" (175). Yet although Auden claims that it "makes nothing happen," he also counters that poetry is "a way of happening, a mouth," and in so doing he notes that poetry creates a world of its own inhabiting, a sensuous world in which men can live and be whole.

This concern with health and fulfillment is what Auden values in Yeats's poetry, and it is the gift that lives beyond the foibles of Yeats's own life, in fact beyond the flaws of all human lives. Auden goes on to associate these qualities with the French poet and novelist Paul Claudel and the English poet and novelist Rudyard Kipling, believing that their artwork redeems them. The issue of the redeeming power of art is particularly crucial in this section, because it is here that Auden addresses the rising tide of war in Europe, citing as its source "Intellectual disgrace" and the freezing of pity. And yet, in the midst of this political despair, and perhaps even because of it, poetry happens. For Yeats, it happened during the conflicts of the Anglo-Irish War and the Irish civil war of the 1920s; for Auden, it is the growing shadow of German aggression. In spite of war and man's constant failing of his fellow man, Auden bids the spirit of Yeats to "Still persuade us to rejoice."

In the final stanzas of the poem, Auden invokes the spirit of Yeats and calls upon his poetry to show humankind how it might confront the troubles of the modern world with uplifted spirit. Auden's language is filled with paradoxes as he urges, "In the deserts of the heart / Let the healing fountain start," ultimately entreating Yeats to "In the prison of his days / Teach the free man how to praise." Writing about the latter, final couplet, Edward Callan observes that it is "one instance of the type of analogy [Auden] liked to draw between vitality arising from imposed restraint in the making of a poem and from the natural limitations of a free man" (17). Thus, Auden's final entreaties, which are implicitly statements of faith in the power of poetry, are as much about his own work as Yeats's. Auden believes that poetry can heal the heart in the midst of the modern wasteland and can rescue us from the prison of history by showing us how to praise the world in spite of its political calamities. It is this understanding of the complexities of modern history, and the lasting belief that art can address and lead us through them, that has made Auden's poem a still-powerful anodyne for the troubles caused by political strife today.

BIBLIOGRAPHY

Callan, Edward. *Auden: A Carnival of Intellect.* New York: Oxford University Press, 1983.

Deane, Patrick. "'Within a Field That Never Closes': The Reader in W. H. Auden's 'New Year's Letter.' *Contemporary Literature* 32, no. 2 (1991): 171–193.

Temple Cone

"IN THE WAITING ROOM" ELIZABETH BISHOP (1971) This autobiographical poem published in ELIZABETH BISHOP's last book, is about a girl on the verge of maturity, "three days" short of "seven years old." ROBERT LOWELL wrote comparable poems about his childhood, but "In the Waiting Room" has too much respect for art's power over circumstance to fit into Lowell's usual genre of CONFESSIONAL POETRY. Bishop's poem is best understood as a relative of WALLACE STEVENS's meditations on art or as a skeptical re-creation of two traditional schemes of human development: the growth of the poet's mind in William Wordsworth's work and the progress of the Christian soul in the poem Bishop herself paired with "In the Waiting Room," George Herbert's "Love Unknown" (1633). "In the Waiting Room" turns disorientation into insight, though the insight is laced with despair.

The instrument of young Elizabeth's epiphany is the *National Geographic* magazine that she reads as she waits for her aunt at the dentist's office. Pictures and words that blur conventional distinctions between the familiar and the alien play upon her mind until, with a start, she recognizes that her aunt's "*oh!* of pain" coming "from inside" is "*me.*" All insides, all appearances of familiarity, she realizes, are, in truth, not insides but an anguishing outside—alienation: Domestic spaces are fictions that conceal the fact of the unknown. The realization dizzies and terrifies her, but it also inspires her first self-conscious artistry. Clinging to what David Kalstone calls the "life-jacket" of "observation" (34)—a shy look at grown-up bodies and a precise phrase, "how 'unlikely'"—she defends herself against the inscrutable with her own primitive fictions. When her vertigo passes, she has been born as a creative being, someone knowingly involved in the "War"—not only World War I, a political struggle to forge community, but also a private version of that conflict: in ROBERT PINSKY's words, "the war of the poet to work on the world of things and people as much as that world works on her" (7).

The "War" finds expression in the form of "In the Waiting Room." Flat, lulling language muffles the shock of revelation. The poet's savvy viewpoint passes into and out of the child's baffled one. The poem exemplifies Bishop's ideal, described by DAVID LEHMAN as "an art that feeds on what might otherwise consume it, that thrives on loss, that welcomes limits in order to transcend them" (68). Such an art offers make-believe security, not security itself: a waiting room, not a home.

BIBLIOGRAPHY

Kalstone, David. *Five Temperaments.* New York: Oxford University Press, 1977.

Lehman, David. "'In Prison': A Paradox Regained." In *Elizabeth Bishop and Her Art,* edited by Lloyd Schwartz and Sybil P. Estess, 61–74. Ann Arbor: University of Michigan Press, 1983.

Pinsky, Robert. "The Idiom of a Self: Elizabeth Bishop and Wordsworth." *American Poetry Review* 91, no. 1 (January–February 1980): 6–8.

Shaileen Beyer

IRBY, KENNETH (1936–) Kenneth Irby has been broadly influenced by such postmodern masters as CHARLES OLSON, ROBERT DUNCAN, and LOUIS ZUKOFSKY, as shown in a broad range of poems that are formally complex and grammatically idiosyncratic while not swerving from a tone that is deeply personal. But a much deeper influence has been his affinity for, and immersion in, the midwestern plains where he has spent most of his life. In an interview Irby said that his poetry partakes of a "Great Plains Mysticism" concerned with evoking the poet's spiritual, intellectual, and emotional relationship to the region (Bartlett 108). His poem "The Grasslands of North America" (1977), for example, rhapsodizes on the sensation that the poet gets each time he enters this homeland region. It seems to him that he is entering it again for the first time, every time.

Irby was born in Bowie, Texas, and was educated at the University of Kansas, Harvard, and the University of California, Berkeley. After serving in the army from 1960 to 1962, he began to publish small editions of his poetry and eventually produced 24 books, chapbooks, and broadsides. Best received among these include *Catalpa* (1977) and *Call Steps: Plains, Camps, Stations, Consistories* (1992). Fellow poets have often remarked on Irby's reticent nature and how he rarely acts forcefully to advance his career, although they all agree that he deserves to be better known, especially among working poets. Irby has taught at the University of Kansas, Lawrence, and has received several awards and fellowships.

Irby's lines are typically varied in length and made musical by the skillful use of consonance, assonance, and internal rhyme. Though the length of the lines often follows the principles of Olson's "breathed" meter (see ARS POETICAS and the BLACK MOUNTAIN SCHOOL), Irby's poems do not have a signature appearance on the page. Instead the subject matter usually determines the overall form of the poem. Another highly significant characteristic of Irby's poetry is his use of grammatical unorthodoxy, like GERTRUDE STEIN, in order to highlight particular words in unfamiliar contexts. One method he uses is the inverted phrase, such as in an untitled poem from *Catalpa* (1977), which reads, in part: "the longer I live the more people I know / are dead, the more the crossing of that line."

BIBLIOGRAPHY

Bartlett, Lee. "Kenneth Irby." In *Talking Poetry: Conversations in the Workshop with Contemporary Poets.* Albuquerque: University of New Mexico Press, 1987, pp. 107–124.

Bromige, David. "Ken Irby's Catalpa." *Credences: A Journal of Twentieth Century Poetry and Poetics* 3, no. 1 (February 1979): 101–103.

Kelly, Robert. "On Irby." *Credences: A Journal of Twentieth Century Poetry and Poetics* 3, no. 1 (February 1979): 121–127.

Michael Van Dyke

"I SING OF OLAF GLAD AND BIG" E. E. CUMMINGS (1931) E. E. Cummings's "i sing of olaf glad and big" narrates the experience of an American soldier who becomes a conscientious objector, is tortured for his beliefs by his fellow soldiers, and dies in prison. The poem is written with a doggerel meter and often formal syntax as if to imitate "a Victorian moralistic tale about a naughty boy who mistreats a kitten" (Kennedy, 76), but the cruelties perpetrated by Olaf's fellow citizens in the name of patriotic duty are savaged by Cummings's irony. Based partly on an imprisoned conscientious objector whom Cummings met briefly in the army in 1918, partly on Cummings's knowledge of what happened to such individuals in prison, "i sing of olaf glad and big" is a devastating critique of the violence of patriotism and a poem of praise for those with the courage to abide by their principles.

"i sing of olaf glad and big" begins with Cummings's echoing the opening of the Roman poet Virgil's epic, *The Aeneid.* But where Virgil praised a hero's adventurous founding of a civilization, writes Gary Lane, "Olaf embraces an integrity of private rather than public convictions; acknowledging only his personal sense of truth rather than merging his will with the gods'" (39). Throughout the poem, Olaf speaks only in order to reject what he perceives to be the unjust demands of his community, saying that "there is some s. I will not eat." These rejections undermine the communal values that lie at the heart of epic heroism, and they cement Olaf's status as an antihero or outsider. Cummings characterizes Olaf as a man "whose warmest heart recoiled at war," who remains serene throughout his physical abuse and "responds, without getting annoyed / 'I will not kiss your f.ing flag.'" Thus, even at a linguistic level, Olaf's conscience remains true to itself; as Lane notes, "Olaf avoids the polite Latin that in our century has time and again been used to justify atrocity" (41).

Ultimately, such an anti-institutional individual cannot survive in a democracy whose "kindred intellects evoke / allegiance per blunt instruments." For

Cummings, the defenders of America have become as ideologically tyrannical as the Soviet Union they claim to oppose, leading Brian Docherty to argue that "America and Russia are two faces of the same coin as far as [Cummings] is concerned" (124). As the poem proceeds, the abuses of power move up the chain of command, through "an host of overjoyed / noncoms (first knocking on the head / him)" to "our president," until the entire society is indicted in the treatment of Olaf. Having himself been imprisoned during World War I under false charges of espionage and authentic charges of refusing to say he hated the Germans, Cummings finds in Olaf an ideal of conscience and courage to which he can aspire and from which modern America has fallen, "because / unless statistics lie he was / more brave than me: more blond than you."

BIBLIOGRAPHY

Docherty, Brian. "e. e. cummings." In *American Poetry: The Modernist Ideal,* edited by Clive Bloom and Brian Docherty. New York: St. Martin's Press, 1995.

Lane, Gary. *I Am: A Study of E. E. Cummings' Poems.* Lawrence: University Press of Kansas, 1976.

Sawyer-Lucanno, Christopher. *E. E. Cummings: A Biography.* Naperville, Ill.: Sourcebooks, 2004.

Temple Cone

"I WENT INTO THE MAVERICK BAR"

GARY SNYDER (1975) By concluding with a line that borrows the title of Lenin's major work on socialist revolution, GARY SNYDER's "I Went into the Maverick Bar" announces the revolutionary impulse behind the "real work" of all his artistic and political endeavors. Occasioned by Snyder's involvement in a political action against violations of Native American rights and environmental law, the poem describes a New Mexico country-and-western, where Snyder encounters people whose cultural, moral, and political beliefs stand at polar opposites from his own. Evoking the increasing political divide between conservatives and liberals in the United States in the 1970s, Snyder nevertheless experiences a moment of insight when he realizes his human kinship with "That short-haired joy and roughness" and his need to reach them across an ideological divide.

In an interview with Bill Moyers, Snyder explained that he was traveling through Farmington with members of the Black Mesa Committee to witness and protest strip-mining that was taking place on Native American lands, and he characterizes the town as "a Texan town full of Texan coil and oil people, and it was considered at that time a pretty heavy town to go through" (366). Snyder's countercultural identity and his overtly liberal political purposes would thus have offered a major point of conflict, and in "I Went into the Maverick Bar," the mood of antagonism is immediately evident, for the speaker says that "My long hair was tucked up under a cap / I'd left the earring in the car." But the speaker goes in, nevertheless, his boldness marked by his choice of drink, "double shots of bourbon / backed with beer," and suggesting both his opposition to the values of those who frequent the bar and his desire for confrontation.

In the second stanza, Snyder surveys the bar and finds nothing he likes or with which he can identify. The cowboys wrestling with each other suggest a superficial form of bonding at odds with Snyder's views on intimacy; the waitress's xenophobia would offend Snyder's personal, anthropological, and religious interest in world cultures; and the country-and-western song "We don't smoke Marijuana in Muskokie" contrasts sharply with the BEAT generation's willingness to experiment with drugs as a means of stimulating and elevating consciousness. But Snyder's hostility, which is opposed to but strangely similar to the unaccepting mood of the bar itself, is reduced in the third stanza when he watches a couple dance "like in High School dances / in the fifties," and Snyder finds himself recalling his own past, when he worked as a trail-crew member in Oregon. Reflecting upon his shared experience of laboring in the natural world, Snyder experiences what in Zen Buddhism is called *satori,* or a sudden, incommunicable experience of enlightenment. Thinking of America, of all its lands and peoples, Snyder realizes "I could almost love you again."

But that "almost" proves an important qualifier. Having left the Maverick Bar and "[come] back to myself," the speaker finds his own causes reaffirmed under the light of the "tough old stars." Lawrence Buell sees this pattern of lapse and reaffirmation in Snyder's work as a sign of "the heroic difficulty of achieving a thoroughgoing redefinition of the self in environmental terms" (167). Yet Patrick D. Murphy finds this moment a confirmation of the differences between Snyder and the bar patrons and of the need to continue "the real work" that is taking him through Farmington. Regardless, when Snyder concludes by quoting the title of Lenin's work on Marxist revolution, *What Is to Be Done?,* he confirms the revolutionary nature of his own project of "becoming native in your heart . . . [and] accepting citizenship in the continent itself" (Moyers, 367). For Snyder, the nonhuman world and the human world exist within each other; to forget this relation is to destroy nature, and by extension, the human species. The real work is of love, a love that goes beyond what Snyder "almost" feels for America again.

BIBLIOGRAPHY

Buell, Lawrence. *The Environmental Imagination: Thoreau, Nature Writing, and the Formation of American Culture.* Cambridge, Mass.: The Belknap Press of Harvard University Press, 1995.

Moyers, Bill. "Gary Snyder." In *The Language of Life: A Festival of Poets,* 356–74. New York: Doubleday, 1995.

Murphy, Patrick D. *Understanding Gary Snyder.* Columbia: The University of South Carolina Press, 1992.

Temple Cone

J

JACOBSEN, JOSEPHINE (1909–2003) Josephine Jacobsen's quiet, formal poetry deals with the problems and anxieties of humanity, but beneath that is a profound sense of optimism, based on her deeply held Roman Catholic beliefs, which include a fervent certainty in an afterlife. In her subjects and language, her poems claim what she described as "high ground." She wrote, as she remarked, "in a formal idiom and elevated tone" (338). Influenced by ROBERT FROST and T. S. ELIOT, many of her nature poems have a steady focus and observation comparable with ELIZABETH BISHOP; they could also be reflexive and reflectively literate, as typical of MARIE PONSOT.

Jacobsen was born in Coburg, Ontario, Canada, and was raised in Baltimore. Her first poem was published when she was 10, but she did not achieve widespread recognition until her sixties. Her first book, *Let Each Man Remember,* was published in 1940. She was appointed in 1971 consultant in poetry to the Library of Congress. She was inducted into the American Academy of Arts and Letters in 1994. She received the Shelley Memorial Award from the Poetry Society of America in 1994 and in 1997 its highest award, the Robert Frost Medal for lifetime achievement in poetry.

Jacobsen's poetry has a muscular beauty and a deeply appealing seriousness. Her use of vernacular speech is exceptional, and her dramatic sense is keen. Her poems revere the world with its birds, bees, flowers, marriage, family bonds—often heightened by a wise sense of reckoning with death as a supreme fact. MARILYN HACKER has observed that Jacobsen is "a compassionate and unsparing participant in the human predicament she observes. Her poems are extraordinary instances which reverberate with imagination while eliciting new awareness in the conscience" (213).

In "Pondicherry Blues" (1979), Jacobsen re-creates the death of an old woman, in a slightly formal and chillingly effective way, using a form that moves between the tone of Philip Larkin and W. H. AUDEN and a spoken blues: "She troubled herself about her soul, / yes, she was concerned about her soul," but the priest she calls for, whom she has earlier exasperated with tiresome academic questions of the nature of sin, has no time for Mrs. Pondicherry. Instead he chooses to spend his time tending to the lonely and the poor of his parish. The poem concludes with the priest not making her last rites, and "she stopped her breath in a lonesome slum of death / that dark trashy street of death." Jacobsen's work demonstrates that enduring poetry is not spun of mere craft but a kind of auditory earnestness, a preference for depth and precision over sheer charm and beauty.

BIBLIOGRAPHY

Jacobsen, Josephine. "Lion under Maples." In *The Instant of Knowing,* edited by Elizabeth Spires. Ann Arbor: University of Michigan Press, 1997, pp. 336–339.

Hacker, Marilyn. "Editor's Shelf." *Ploughshares* 21, no. 68 (winter 1995–96): 213.

Gerald Schwartz

THE JACOB'S LADDER DENISE LEVERTOV **(1961)** Within a year of seeing herself grouped by Donald Allen among the BLACK MOUNTAIN poets of *The New American Poetry 1945–1960* (see POETRY ANTHOLOGIES), DENISE LEVERTOV began, with the publication of her fourth volume of poetry, to dislodge herself from such affiliations. The poems of *The Jacob's Ladder* are not projective (kinetic and defined by breath), ideogrammatic (registering an idea through an accumulation of its isolated attributes), or austere. They constitute not an "open field" of verse, as CHARLES OLSON advocated in his essay "Projective Verse" (see ARS POETICAS), but, as in the title of one of the poems, "a common ground." Upon this ground friends meet, beneath it kin are buried, from it words sprout into sustenance, "to be eaten / in common, by laborer / and hungry wanderer." Though the influence of WILLIAM CARLOS WILLIAMS's vernacular idiom and ROBERT CREELEY's scrupulously inward attention persist, Levertov is here more concerned with sketching an eastern European Jewish genealogy. The poem ascends the Jacob's Ladder in the volume's title poem. Boris Pasternak, Osip Mandelstam, the rabbi Judah Loew, and Martin Buber's *Tales of the Hasidim* are reverently evoked and quoted. The invisible yet tangible presence of a fostering heritage, part Jerusalem, part Crimea, sustains the poet in "Song for a Dark Voice": "Your arms / hold me from falling." In "Come into the Animal Presence" and "The Presence," the presence switches from animal to spiritual. In "A Solitude," the transition is from human to angelic, enacted while leading a blind man out of the subway; the tunnel too can serve as a Jacob's Ladder.

An anxiety courses through the book: Will the poet overlook what, in "From the Roof," she calls "the Hidden Ones"? In "The Presence" she worries, "Will you know who it is?" In "From the Roof" the Logos orders both the urban landscape and the poet's move to a new apartment within it. "Design" is a word used without a hint of ROBERT FROST's quandary (see "DESIGN"). "The Thread" turns out not to be bridle or noose but spring of spiritual action. Beyond the poet's powers of reason, but tangibly within her being, this fine elastic "net of threads" is ancestral legacy at its most durable and like the mythical Ariadne's clue, a reliable means of deliverance. Its tugs inspire not fear "but a stirring / of wonder." One tug presumably allows her to commune with the Russian poet in "In Memory of Boris Pasternak," where the natural and contrived world conspires to communicate intimations of immortality. A butterfly becomes a word emanating from the recently deceased poet.

The book provides many mutations of thing into word and word into thing. Their proximity is another ancestral legacy. "The Necessity" suggests that in words force inheres: every element of "speech a spark / awaiting redemption." The world is legible. The prefatory poem, addressed "To the Reader," assures us that "as you read / the sea is turning its dark pages." Nature "poises itself to speak."

With its personal meditations on childhood in England, on the Judaism of her paternal forefathers (one, Schneour Zaimon, was a Russian rabbi), and on mystic premonition (the Welsh mystic Angel Jones of Mold was a maternal forefather), *The Jacob's Ladder* situates Levertov well outside the range of the Black Mountain poets with whom she had been linked. Like Paul Celan, whose poetry her own work would increasingly resemble, Levertov would invoke, and be guided by, the precedent of Mandelstam (the subject of the first part of "Deaths") over the voices of her adopted homeland.

BIBLIOGRAPHY

Colclough Little, Anne, and Susie Paul, eds. *Denise Levertov: New Perspectives.* West Cornwall, Conn.: Locust Hill Press, 2000.

Gelpi, Albert, ed. *Denise Levertov: Selected Criticism.* Ann Arbor: University of Michigan Press, 1993.

Andre Furlani

JARMAN, MARK (1952–) An important figure in the New Narrative branch of the group identified as the NEW FORMALISTS, Mark Jarman consistently produces both LYRIC and NARRATIVE POETRY in traditional and open forms. In the 1980s, Jarman (along with ROBERT MCDOWELL) provided narrative poets with a place to publish via the controversial literary magazine, the *Reaper* (see POETRY JOURNALS). Jarman and McDowell not only published poets as varied as DANA GIOIA and JORIE GRAHAM but also spearheaded a revival in narrative poetry; the magazine was "devoted specifically to reviving narrative" (Walzer 5). Jarman also has published a landmark anthology of New Formalist poets, *Rebel Angels: 25 Poets of the New Formalism* (1996).

Jarman was born in Mount Serling, Kentucky. His father, an Episcopalian minister, relocated the family to Kircaldy, Fife, Scotland, and finally settled in California. Jarman received a B.A. from the University of California, Santa Cruz, where he studied with Raymond Carver, then received an M.F.A. from the Iowa Writers' Workshop. Jarman's *The Black Riviera* (1990) won the 1991 Poet's Prize, and his *Questions for Ecclesiastes* won the 1998 Lenore Marshall Poetry Prize and was a finalist for the National Book Critics Circle Award. Since 1983 he has been a professor of English at Vanderbilt University.

Jarman's early work in the collection *North Sea* (1978) is clearly lyric; however, by the time he published *Far and Away* (1985), Jarman's poems had begun to take on a more lengthy, open narrative form (Walzer 87). The major theme in Jarman's work is Christian faith despite the silence of God. His poems, Richard Flynn writes, speak of a "rejection of rote faith in order to find poetic faith, more sacred because it is more hard won" (158). His poems reject traditional faith and challenge orthodox Christianity's idea of an unchanged, fixed deity.

In "Unholy Sonnet 9" (2000), Jarman twists the conventional as he describes the first moments of an airline crash: "Someone is always praying as the plane / Breaks up." As the people aboard fall from the craft, "Out of their names," Jarman makes God's absent presence known in his description of "the living sky." The God in this poem may exist, but his silence is keenly felt, as it is in "Questions for Ecclesiastes" (1997), when an aging preacher must comfort parents whose daughter has committed suicide: God might "have shared what he knew with people who needed / urgently to hear it" but instead "kept a secret."

Jarman's other poetry titles include *The Rote Walker* (1981), *Iris* (1992), and *Unholy Sonnets* (2000). In 2001 he published a book of essays, *The Secret of Poetry*. As a poet and critic, Jarman continues to be an important figure in the revival of narrative poetry in American verse.

BIBLIOGRAPHY

Flynn, Richard. "Mark Jarman." *Dictionary of Literary Biography*. Vol. 120, *American Poets since World War II*, edited by R. S. Gwynn. Detroit: Gale Research, 1992, pp. 156–161.

"Jarman, Mark," Academy of American Poets. Available online. URL: http://www.poets.org/poets/poets.cfm?prmID=94. Downloaded March 2007.

Walzer, Kevin. *The Ghost of Tradition*. Ashland, Oreg.: Story Line, 1998.

Jeff Newberry

JARRELL, RANDALL (1914–1965) Randall Jarrell—a poet of war, childhood, dream, and fantasy—evokes a fluidity of experience and a sense of the self as changeable, reminiscent of Marcel Proust. Although Jarrell was influenced by poets W. H. AUDEN, ROBERT FROST, and especially Rainer Maria Rilke, Jarrell's own distinct voice becomes increasingly apparent with each succeeding volume he published. Besides being a significant poetic voice of the mid-20th century, he was a beloved teacher (primarily at the Woman's College at the University of North Carolina), a feared but admired poetry critic, a social critic, and an author of children's stories and an academic novel, *Pictures from an Institution* (1954).

Born in Nashville, Tennessee, he lived through the depression and spent his early adulthood during World War II, briefly as a pilot, but mainly as a trainer of pilots. Despite his education at Vanderbilt University and his respect for the southern Agrarians (see FUGITIVE/AGRARIAN SCHOOL), Jarrell expressed his urban egalitarian sensibility. Among the many awards and honors he received were the Guggenheim Fellowship in poetry (1946) and the National Book Award for *The Woman at the Washington Zoo* (1961).

"With the self-consciousness of the artist, Jarrell approaches [the] problem of identity, subjects it to poetic examination" (152), writes critic Sister M. Bernetta Quinn. The progression of Jarrell's books of poetry reflects not only his growing artistic maturity, but also his deepening concern with this problem. Despite echoes of other poets evident in *Blood for a Stranger* (1942), this first volume reveals feelings of alienation from the self and others so evocative of the years preceding World War II. *Little Friend, Little Friend* (1945) deals with the depersonalization of war and an indomitable human spirit that sometimes survives despite seemingly insurmountable odds. In *Losses* (1948), Jarrell considers how the metamorphosis in fantasy offers escape from a merciless external world and an irrational internal self.

Jarrell's immersion in fantasy, psychology, and philosophy becomes evident in *The Seven League Crutches* (1951), as the poet explores the self-transformation that is at the heart of fairy tale, folktale, and psychoanalysis. In *The Woman at the Washington Zoo* (1960), Jarrell looks further inward through personae (invented voices serving as masks for the author). Jarrell continues this inward turning in *The Lost World* (1965), as the child inside the man—often Jarrell's own troubled past—is resurrected to retrieve lost vitality and faith, to reform his life by repossessing his early years. The terza rima structure and tripartite form of "The Lost World" (1965) echoes Dante's *Divine Comedy,* for Jarrell's protagonist, like Dante's, is undergoing a spiritual journey that takes him to a kind of nether world, where the significant former beings he encounters are his earlier selves reflecting his youthful experiences and fantasies.

Throughout his work, Jarrell explores dualisms. His concerns include the urge for mother as protector ("Bats" [1965]), the maternal home ("Windows" [1960]), and the womb ("A Little Poem" [1942]), as well as his antipathy for the sinister female principle (as in "Cinderella" [1960], "The House in the Wood" [1965], and "In Nature There Is Neither Right nor Left nor Wrong" [1965]). As Jarrell turns to examine that "small, helpless, human center" ("The Old and the New Masters" [1965]), the child remains the uniting, vulnerable "center" of value in opposition to a mechanical and rationalistic vision. In the overtly lighthearted "Deutsch Durch Freud" (1960), Jarrell compares intuition, reverence for language, and the restorative power of art ("Trust, and Love, and reading Rilke") to "hard-eyed Industry / and all the schools dark Learning." The protagonist in "The Woman at the Washington Zoo" (1960), trapped within a self-perpetuated "cage" that she has created out of her dull official life, seeks to liberate herself by affirming her connection with the animal world. "Change me, change me!" is her plea for a fairytale-like metamorphosis achieved by a magical intimacy between the male principle, given concrete form in the vulture, and the woman repressed inside her. Jarrell's five-line tour de force, "The DEATH OF THE BALL TURRET GUNNER" (1945), reveals the conflict between the dehumanization of technologically sophisticated warfare and the precarious human center embodied in the gunner of the aircraft. The final delivery of this figure—after two symbolic births in which he remains a fetus, a mere potentiality—grotesquely merges with the sexual consummation that resulted in his conception: "They washed me out of the turret with a hose."

Filled with sudden shifts from the comically prosaic to the romantic, "A Girl in a Library" (1951) pits the literary, reflective, Prufrockian speaker against the girl he is tenderly observing (see "The LOVE SONG OF J. ALFRED PRUFROCK"). Although she is distracted by her mundane school assignments and her own mediocrity, she retains, unbeknownst to herself, an enchanted and archetypal identity. Reminiscent of Jarrell's transformations of artworks into poetry—such as Durer's engraving in "The Knight, Death and the Devil" (1951) and Breughel's painting in "The Old and the New Masters" (1965)—in "The Bronze David of Donatello" (1960) Jarrell uses the statue as a metaphor for death, not as a negation of individual identity, but as a resolution of struggle, an achievement of tranquility, an ennobling deference to the great universal design.

While Jarrell's technical virtuosity is unmistakable, his syntax is most frequently straightforward and his diction simple, suggesting the rhythms and idioms of speech. Jarrell avoided catering to fads of the day, emphasizing instead continuing standards of excellence. Despite what critic M. L. Rosenthal calls the poet's "depressive transcendence" (25), Jarrell's work, balanced with wit and humor, provides an unflinching evocation of the reality of human suffering and the concomitant urge—often thwarted—to redeem that suffering.

BIBLIOGRAPHY

Burt, Stephen. *Randall Jarrell and His Age.* New York: Columbia University Press, 2003.

Pritchard, William H. *Randall Jarrell: A Literary Life.* New York: Farrar, Straus & Giroux, 1990.

Rosenthal, M. L. *Randall Jarrell.* Minneapolis: University of Minnesota Press, 1972.

Quinn, Sister M. Bernetta. "Metamorphosis in Randall Jarrell." In *Randall Jarrell 1914–1965*, edited by Robert Lowell et al., 139–154. New York: Farrar, Straus & Giroux, 1967.

Doris Zames Fleischer

JEFFERS, ROBINSON (1887–1962) Robinson Jeffers was of the same generation as EZRA POUND and T. S. ELIOT, but he abjured the modernist poetics of symbolism and imagism (see IMAGIST SCHOOL and MODERNISM). He would not operate "in fear of abstraction," as Pound had dictated; accordingly his poetry does not shy away from general statement and political opinion, in concert with intense, often violent descriptions of the natural world. In his introduction to *Roan Stallion, Tamar, and Other Poems* (1935), Jeffers labeled his contemporaries "followers of [Stéphane] Mallarmé," bent on "renouncing intelligibility to concentrate on the music of poetry. . . . [I]deas had gone, now meter had gone, imagery would have to go; then recognizable emotions would have to go; perhaps at last even words might have to go" (ix). Removed from east-coast poetic milieux, Jeffers lived as a rugged outdoorsman in California, where he built himself and his family a stone tower, featured often in his work.

Jeffers was born in Pittsburgh. His father, a professor of theology, gave him a rigorous and varied education. He learned Latin, Greek, and Hebrew while still a child and went to boarding schools in Germany and Switzerland. He attended the University of Western Pennsylvania, Occidental College, the University of Zurich, and the University of Southern California, studying, in addition to classical and literary subjects, philosophy, medicine, and eventually forestry. He became a popular poet during the 1920s, and his translation of *Medea* was a success on Broadway in 1948, but his isolationist position during World War II earned him disparagement, and New Critical reading practices served his work poorly, lacking as it does verbal ambiguity and irony. Nevertheless he won the Pulitzer Prize in 1954 for *Hungerfield and Other Poems*. Some readers see his poetry as a valuable alternative to high modernism, some read him as an important religious poet, and others find in his work a prescient unease about environmental degradation. Jeffers is also valued as a California poet, whose perspective from the Pacific allowed him, in the words of ROBERT HASS, to "tell his culture bitter truths" it often did not wish to hear (xxxi).

Jeffers wrote long poems (based on Greek tragedies) and short lyrics; the LYRIC POETRY is generally considered his better contribution. His lyric speaker is characteristically solitary, meditating outdoors on the contrast between the calmness, indifference, beauty, power, and longevity of natural phenomenon and human vulgarity, turmoil, ugliness, self-indulgence, triviality, and pain. These poems illustrate a philosophical and ethical attitude Jeffers dubbed "Inhumanism, a shifting of emphasis and significance from man to not-man" (Preface xxi). The poems' titles are likely to name animals (most particularly birds of prey) or places: "Pelicans," "Hurt Hawks," "Love the Wild Swan," "The Cruel Falcon," "The Beaks of Eagles," "Vulture," "Skunks," "Birds and Fishes," "Roan Stallion," "Point Joe," "Continent's End," "Tor House," "Cawdor," "New Mexico Mountain," "Carmel Point," "Red Mountain." The former concentrate on the fate of animals, appreciative of their physical particularity, their elegance, ferocity, and dignity. The latter spread out a wilderness landscape panoramically, linking land and ocean to the entire cosmos, trying to portray human presence as a minor folly. The ocean fills the poetry as an emblem of the incontrovertibly real, ultimately (and, to Jeffers, fortuitously) impregnable to the most subtle and persistent imagination. Similarly, everywhere in Jeffers's work, the hard and lovely fact of rock serves as a trusted reminder of the endurance of physical reality.

Indeed he held an unapologetic notion of the real as a vital element of poetry. In "Birds" (1925), for instance, he calls all raucous birds to surround his composing self because a poem "needs . . . multitudes of thoughts, all fierce, all flesh-eaters, musically clamorous." This verse is built of hard alliteration and harsh assonance, propelled by deliberately awkward phrasing and lineation. Well schooled in the merciless beauties of nature, Jeffers turns his unflinching gaze and vivid, abrasive language toward the realities of world war: "Not a few thousand but uncounted millions, not a day but years, pain, horror, sick hatred; / Famine that dries the children to little bones and huge eyes; high explosive that fountains dirt, flesh and bone-splinters" ("Calm and Full the Ocean" [1948]). Such atrocities earn his sorrowful anger, but not his surprise—he bluntly and frequently asserts disbelief in human integrity or wisdom. His consolation is almost invariably that humanity will amount to no more than a brief virulent cancer that will consume itself, giving way to more dignified biological and geological phenomena. The earth will ultimately be cleansed of the ugly menace that human beings are to themselves and to nature. Indeed, in "Vulture" (1962), Jeffers anticipates his own death as a delivery to animality and to "enskyment" from troublesome humanity.

To KENNETH REXROTH in 1957, this attitude amounted mostly to "childish laboring of the pathetic fallacy . . . high-flown statements indulged in for their melodrama alone" (205). In 1982 the Polish poet Czeslaw Milosz, exiled to California, confessed, "I fumed at [Jeffers's] naïveté and his errors, I saw him as an example of all the faults peculiar to prisoners, exiles, and hermits." But Milosz continues, "his spirit, perhaps reincarnated in the gulls . . . flying over the beach in majestic formation, challenged me to wrestle, and through its courage, gave me courage" (273).

BIBLIOGRAPHY

Hass, Robert. Introduction to *Rock and Hawk: A Selection of Shorter Poems*, by Robinson Jeffers. New York: Random House, 1987, pp. xv–xliii.

Jarman, Mark. "Robinson, Frost, and Jeffers and the New Narrative Poetry." In *Expansive Poetry: Essay on the New Narrative and the New Formalism*, edited by Frederick Feirstein. Santa Cruz, Calif. Story Line, 1989.

Jeffers, Robinson. Introduction to *Roan Stallion, Tamar, and Other Poems*, by Jeffers. New York: Modern Library, 1935, pp. vii–x.

———. Preface to *The Double Axe and Other Poems*, by Jeffers. New York: Liverright, 1977, pp. i–xxii.

Milosz, Czeslaw. "Robinson Jeffers." In *Centennial Essays for Robinson Jeffers*, edited by Robert Zaller, 268–273. Newark: University of Delaware Press, 1991.

Rexroth, Kenneth. "In Defense of Jeffers." In *Critical Essays on Robinson Jeffers*, edited by James Karman. Boston: G. K. Hall, 1990, pp. 205–206.

Sara Lundquist

JOHNSON, JAMES WELDON (1871–1938)

James Weldon Johnson personifies the definition of a poet who is a spiritual and political leader. Prophetic, inspirational, and rhetorically elegant, Johnson's poetry resonated in American public life. His poem "Lift Every Voice and Sing" (1900), written to celebrate Abraham Lincoln's birth, became popularly known as the "Negro National Hymn." "Fifty Years" (1913) commemorates the 50th anniversary of the Emancipation Proclamation: It looks back to slavery and pronounces the rightful claim of African Americans to American citizenship. Johnson served, as Arna Bontemps wrote, as the "philosophical onlooker" of the HARLEM RENAISSANCE and rooted the younger generation of poets in a collective tradition by including their work in *The Book of American Negro Poetry* (1922), the first anthology of its kind (vii). As both an editor and a poet, Johnson's work marks a transition away from dialect as the primary characteristic of African-American poetry. In the introduction to the anthology that spans work from Paul Laurence Dunbar to Helene Johnson, he calls for a form "that will express the racial spirit" but is "freer and larger than dialect" (41). Johnson's poetry, which draws from dialect and the more typical features of the 19th-century lyric, insists upon both the continuance and transformation of the African-American oral tradition.

Johnson was born in Jacksonville, Florida. In 1894 he graduated from Atlanta University and gave the valedictory speech, "The Destiny of the Human Race." He would go on to become a poet, journalist, translator, musician, diplomat, educator, novelist, and lawyer. His commitment to civil rights links the wide range of his professional callings. In 1901 he was almost lynched in Jacksonville Park and decided to move to New York. He served as the director of the National Association for the Advancement of Colored People (NAACP) (1920–30) and enacted many firsts; among them, he was the first African American to be admitted to the Florida bar, and he was New York University's first African-American professor. His dedication and literary vision were recognized with many honors. In 1925 he received the NAACP's Spingarn Medal for *God's Trombones: Seven Negro Sermons in Verse*, a book of poetry that translates folk sermons of black preachers into written form; Johnson also received a 1928 Harmon Award, and in 1929 Johnson was awarded a Julius Rosenwald Fellowship to write *Black Manhattan,* a history of African Americans in New York City.

"O Black and Unknown Bards" (1935) is an ode to the artists who created spirituals and songs during, and despite, slavery. W. E. B. DuBois described this body of work as "The Sorrow Songs," in which "the soul of the black slave spoke to men" (204). Emblematic of Johnson's poetic work, the speaker is an incredulous and admiring envoy, transcribing these oral pieces into written form, carrying the work into the present, and insisting that they are not forgotten. By describing the poets as "bards" and drawing on a repertoire of images and tropes from the romantic tradition, Johnson places these songs in the canons of Western poetry without sacrificing their experiential and historical specificity. "O Black and Unknown Bards" attests to the work's power to transcend time and transform a people. These slave songs "still live" because the poets "sang a race from wood and stone to Christ." Johnson's poetry envisions an emancipated future inspired by the songs that bear witness to and transcend America's enslaved past.

BIBLIOGRAPHY

Bontemps, Arna. Introduction to *The Autobiography of an Ex-Coloured Man,* by James Weldon Johnson. 1912. Reprint, New York: Hill and Wang, 1960, pp. v–ix.

DuBois, W. E. B. "The Sorrow Songs." In *The Souls of Black Folk.* 1903. Reprint, New York: Penguin Books, 1989, pp. 204–216.

Johnson, James Weldon. *The Book of American Negro Poetry.* Orlando, Fla.: Harcourt Brace, 1922.

Wilson, Sondra Kathryn. "James Weldon Johnson." *Crisis* (January 1989): 48–71, 117, 118.

Kimberly Lamm

JOHNSON, RONALD (1935–1998) While Ronald Johnson was influenced by LOUIS ZUKOFSKY and the BLACK MOUNTAIN SCHOOL, especially CHARLES OLSON, he is unique in the visionary character of his poetry, most fully manifested in his long poem, *ARK,* which took him 20 years to write. The technical innovation of his work, combined with the insistent strength of his insight into nature, language, and science, has established Johnson's position as one of the most original and compelling poets of the late 20th century.

Johnson was born in Ashland, Kansas. On the G. I. bill, he went to Columbia University in New York City, where he met JONATHAN WILLIAMS, the founder of the Jargon Society, which published Johnson's first book, *A Line of Poetry, A Row of Trees* (1964). After graduating in 1960, Johnson moved with Williams to Great Britain, where a walking tour inspired *The Book of the Green Man,* one of the American Library Association's Notable Books for 1967. In 1971 Johnson was writer-in-residence at the University of Kentucky and in 1973 held the THEODORE ROETHKE Chair for Poetry at the University of Washington. In 1983 he received the National Poetry Series Award and in 1994 was the Roberta Holloway Poet at the University of California, Berkeley.

ARK is Johnson's most fully realized work; he brilliantly combines his early interest in concrete poetry and collage with his quest to understand the shape of being, the "compass beyond confines / music of the spheres solved, / mosaic of Cosmos." Using the myth of Orpheus as a guiding structure and collaging texts as diverse as Tory Peterson's *A Field Guide to Western Birds* (1961) and Milton's *Paradise Lost* (1674)—much like "found materials" are embedded in the *Watts Towers* sculptures in Los Angeles, an inspiration for *ARK*—he sought to create an ahistorical poem: "a structure rather than diatribe, artifact rather than argument, a veritable shell of the chambered nautilus, sliced and polished, bound for Ararat unknown" ("A Note" 274–275). After *ARK,* Johnson wrote "Blocks to Be Arranged in a Pyramid" (1996), a memorial to AIDS victims in San Francisco, and *The Shrubberies* (2001), which were written during the last five years of his life in Topeka, Kansas. *The Shrubberies,* while ostensibly concerned with the idea of gardening and its attendant themes of growth, death, and exile, particularly humanity's exile from the Garden of Eden, addresses not only the minutiae of the natural world, but the nature of language, vision, and even existence itself; in that book Johnson questions if he will live beyond the 20th century and wonders if he will then be able "to part the night of orbs in galaxy / the congeries of word and light" ("Form").

BIBLIOGRAPHY

Johnson, Ronald. "A Note." *ARK*. Albuquerque, N.Mex.: Living Batch Press, 1996, pp. 274–275.

O'Leary, Peter. "Quod Vides Scribe In Libro." In *To Do As Adam Did: Selected Poems of Ronald Johnson*. Jersey City, N.J.: Talisman House, 2000.

Stratton, Dirk. *Ronald Johnson*. Boise, Idaho: Boise State University Western Writers Series, 1996.

Selinger, Eric Murphy. "Ronald Johnson." In *Dictionary of Literary Biography*. Vol. 169, *American Poets since World War II*, edited by Joseph Conte. Detroit: Gale Research, 1996.

Marcella Durand

JORDAN, JUNE (1936–2002) "The creation of poems," June Jordan said, is "a foundation for true community; a fearless, democratic society" (qtd. in Muller 3). One of the most prolific African-American writers, with more than 25 published books, Jordan regarded poetry as her primary calling, although her works also include plays, essays, memoirs, and children's books. A contemporary of AMIRI BARAKA, NIKKI GIOVANNI, and AUDRE LORDE, Jordan's early poetry reflects many of the concerns of the BLACK ARTS MOVEMENT. Since the 1970s her writing has come to explore more broadly the conditions necessary both to attain and to maintain "freedom" for everybody, regardless of race, gender, class, nationality, or sexual orientation, while at the same time staying committed to the expression of her individual vision. In a 1977 essay, Jordan wrote: "I should trust myself in this way: that if I could truthfully attend to my own perpetual birth . . then I could hope to count upon myself to be serving a positive and collective function, without pretending to be more than the one Black woman poet I am" (126).

Jordan was born in Harlem, New York City, to Jamaican parents and grew up in Brooklyn. Educated at Barnard College and the University of Chicago (1953–57), she started to teach English and creative writing in 1966—first at City College, the City University of New York, where ADRIENNE RICH, Lorde, Toni Cade Bambara, Barbara Christian, and Addison Gayle, Jr., were colleagues and friends, then at Sarah Lawrence College and the State University of New York, Stony Brook. She taught African-American studies and women's studies at the University of California, Berkeley, where she founded Poetry for the People in 1991. She described this as "a marvelous adventure in democracy and education" (Muller 3): It encourages students to become poets and to carry their commitment to "the power of the word" into the surrounding communities (Muller 4). Jordan's honors include a Prix de Rome in environmental design (1970–71), a National Endowment for the Arts Fellowship (1982), and a Lila Wallace Writers Award (1995). In 1998 Jordan received the Student's Choice Louise Patterson African-American Award for most outstanding African-American faculty at Berkeley.

From the beginning of her career, Jordan's writing was dedicated to exploring the possibilities of community building through art. Her "most fundamental commitment," according to Peter Erickson, was to "a rigorous scrutiny of democracy that focuses not only on its history of exclusions, but also on its potential for expansion" (132). As a poet—and as a novelist, essayist, activist, and teacher—Jordan addressed a wide spectrum of personal and political concerns. Her early work shows a strong commitment specifically to black issues and explicitly addresses an African-American audience. Her first book, *Who Look at Me?*—a poem illustrated with representations of African Americans in visual art—was published in 1968; it was followed in 1971 by the first novel to be written entirely in Black English dialect, *His Own Where*. Since the 1970s Jordan's explorations into what "freedom" and "democracy" can and should mean to the individual and her or his communities have come to include, more broadly defined, the perspectives of "minoritized" groups in the United States, as well as international concerns: the situations in South Africa and in Lebanon in the 1980s, the war in Yugoslavia in the 1990s, and the plight of the Palestinian people. Important collections that include poems with a wide thematic variety are *Things That I Do in the Dark* (1977) and *Naming Our Destiny* (1989). Jordan was also a regular columnist for the *Progressive* from 1989 to 1997; *Soldier*, the autobiography of her childhood years, appeared in 2000. Despite her long career as a poet and her public visibility, however, Jordan's work has not yet received the sustained critical attention it deserves.

Regardless of some clear thematic and stylistic developments, Jordan's poetry is characterized by, as Jacqueline Brogan observes, "recurring themes and motifs of love and desire, of family, of social injustice, of suffering, and of joy" (200). In "Who Look at Me" (1968), a poem dedicated to the poet's son, the speaker sees herself "stranded in a hungerland / of great prosperity." This notion of the inherent contradictions and tensions between democratic ideals and social and political realities is one of the constants in Jordan's work. The position of the poet, however, is anything but static or passive. "Poem about My Rights" (1977), which Jordan described as both a "conceptual [and] emotional breakthrough" for herself and which is possibly her most anthologized poem, moves the speaker from being "stranded" to an active role characterized by defiance and self-confidence in the face of continuing violence (Quiroz n. p.): "I am the history of the rejection of who I am [but] / I am not wrong: Wrong is not my name / My name is my own my own my own." While vigilance might be necessary, she argues, paralyzing fear should not be: "I / invent the mother of the courage I require not to quit," the speaker says in "War and Memory" (1989). Throughout her work, Jordan's goal is to achieve connection, community, and love: "I will make myself a passionate and eager lover in response to passionate and eager love / I will be nobody's fool" ("Resolution # 1003" [1994]).

BIBLIOGRAPHY

Brogan, Jacqueline Vaught. "From Warrior to Womanist: The Development of June Jordan's Poetry." In *Speaking the Other Self: American Women Writers,* edited by Jeanne Campbell Reesman, 198–209. Athens: University of Georgia Press, 1997.

Erickson, Peter. "After Identity: A Conversation with June Jordan and Peter Erickson." *Transition* 63 (1994): 132–149.

Jordan, June. "Thinking about My Poetry." In *Civil Wars.* Boston: Beacon Press, 1981, 122–129.

Muller, Lauren, et al. *June Jordan's Poetry for the People: A Revolutionary Blueprint.* New York: Routledge, 1995.

Quiroz, Julie. "'Poetry Is a Political Act': An Interview with June Jordan." *ColorLines* 1.3 (winter 1999). Available online. URL: www.arc.org/C_Lines/CLArchive/story1_3_05.html. Downloaded March 2007.

Stefanie Sievers

THE JOURNALS **PAUL BLACKBURN (1975)** *The Journals,* comprising most of PAUL BLACKBURN's final poems, is a milestone in the history of literary innovation, beyond the open-field poetry of the BLACK MOUNTAIN SCHOOL and, earlier, the free verse of the IMAGIST SCHOOL (see PROSODY AND FREE VERSE). Blackburn wanted to create open-ended occasions out of ordinary, everyday experiences, thereby shaping a form that appeared to be, paradoxically, formless. He rejected traditional poetry's point of view, which saw certain historical events as grand or monumental and others as inconsequential and which, accordingly, insisted that poetry follow rhetorical principles of argument first established in classical times and later reaffirmed in the Renaissance. He replaced syllogism with juxtaposition or contingency, logical deduction and inference with the "logic" of experience, such as what a person sees or hears, and he relied on nouns and verbs, not adjectives and adverbs, and on metonyms, not metaphors or symbols. Likewise Blackburn avoided standard meters and employed irregular spacing of words, characteristic of EZRA POUND, CHARLES OLSON, and others. His demonstration that words could be used for their visual effects, often in conjunction with graphics, influenced later VISUAL POETRY, such as ARMAND SCHWERNER's *The Tablets.* Robert Buckeye notes how Blackburn's "use of juxtaposition . . . equalizes the elements of the poem: one thing, no matter how different, is just next to another" (157). Blackburn's visuality might also have been influenced by downtown Manhattan painting during a period in the 1950s and 1960s when poets later to be grouped in various schools—BEAT, Black Mountain, and NEW YORK—were intermingling with each other, as well as with painters and musicians.

Two other poets to be associated with *The Journals* are WILLIAM CARLOS WILLIAMS and ROBERT CREELEY. In its attention to the details of daily life, Blackburn's poetry embraces and extends Williams's dictum, "no ideas but in things," a plea to ground poetry in concrete images, and provides another version of the precision celebrated in Creeley's lines, "and and becomes // just so" in his homage to Williams ("For W.C.W" [1963]). Yet Blackburn aims for a new kind of poetry, as if the poem were a painting that refuses its frame; his is not simply the collage technique Pound made famous in

The CANTOS. Blackburn's work can also be thought of within the context of CONFESSIONAL POETRY—wherein the poet's life is available for viewing, the doors of his home flung open. In this regard, these poems are similar to the work of the New York school, especially FRANK O'HARA's. As Peter Baker has commented, "So little [may] apparently [be] going on in [a Blackburn] poem that it may seem beneath our notice" (44); still, the experience of reading it is palpable as momentary occurrences become events and then rituals, just as in O'Hara's "I do this, I do that" poems, which note otherwise unimportant details in a person's day. Creating the impression of relaxed candor, Blackburn is able, ultimately, "to resist the pull toward transcendence that the romantic and American post-romantic traditions have forced on several generations of poets, readers and interpreters" (52).

On the other hand, this apparent spontaneity is hard won. Blackburn's poems, Gilbert Sorrentino observes, "are journals only in that they purport to follow the events of the last four years of the poet's life, but the selection of the important elements out of the sea of experience . . . is rigorously formal" (103). Each poem has actually been worked by Blackburn to great effect. "AUG/22. Berkeley Marina," for instance, begins with a simply contrasting observation: The day is cold and the sun is bright, the strong

> wind holding the flags out
> flap/flap

as the poet's eye alights on the legs of his wife while she is exercising on the deck of their swaying boat. The couple is perfectly composed, recalling "the 3 graces & the 4 dignities" of ancient Chinese philosophy, which Blackburn sets out on the page as two lists placed beside one another, each encased within a simply drawn rectangle: "grace of word, / of deed, / grace of thought," and, "standing // sitting / walking // & lying down." How are these to be read? There is to be no prescribed method. What is important, however, are the two people "at peace" with the world. In this poem, language, in and of itself, and phenomena, the world taken in by the poet, seamlessly merge as one through the graphics on the page.

Another key aspect of *The Journals* is its examination of dying. Blackburn learns that he has terminal cancer. His characteristic frankness becomes especially memorable when chronicling physical deterioration as the world begins to slip away. He is direct and graphic. "27. VI. 71," for example, records a morning's thoughts, beginning with the exclamation "sundaysundaysundaysundaysunday" and then the observation of the essential elements of the day: "empty walks," a "single bird," a "blue sky." The enumeration leads to a crisis; the phrase "EMPTY AND ALIVE" is repeated three times going down the page. Blackburn notes how his simplest acts—fastening his belt, washing, writing in his diary—are made difficult by pain. Yet this pain, in an apparent contradiction, makes the present vibrant. He notices "the promise of death" in the daylight spilling across the objects in his room; with the "window open, the day comes in, o fade the carcinoma." This blending of diction is remarkable—the contemporaneity of "carcinoma" juxtaposed with the romantic apostrophe "o fade." Finally, there is a bitter turn as he struggles to slip out of death's trap, when he parodies the song "The Girl on the Flying Trapeze": The cancer "floats thru the blood / with the greatest of ease. the pain goes and comes again."

In *The Journals,* no other but the present moment exists, fleeting yet permanent. The typical Blackburn poem, Baker has noted, "stands outside of time while foregrounding time itself" (45), an effect resulting in *The Journals*'s formless formality, which was a breakthrough in new verse possibilities. Blackburn's contribution is utterly original, as well as a stage in the evolution of experimental poetry. "We hear the echo in Blackburn," Joseph Conte writes, "of Olson's statement in 'Projective Verse': 'One perception must immediately and directly lead to a further perception' [see ARS POETICAS]. The poetry of process is opposed to the notion of progress, and in Blackburn . . . we hear a denial of telos, closure, or climax—'any sense of an ending'. Each arrival signals a new departure" (48–49). Gloriously unrestricted, seemingly at loose ends, *The Journals* created, for later poetry, a new aesthetic sense of what a poetic statement could be. This posthumous work culminated the poetic project that had consumed Blackburn throughout his adult life, representing the ultimate refinement of his technique and the distillation of his vision.

BIBLIOGRAPHY

Baker, Peter. "Blackburn's Gift." *Sagetrieb: A Journal Devoted to Poets in the Imagist/Objectivist Tradition* 12, no. 1 (spring 1993): 43–54.

Buckeye, Robert. "'Rock, Scissors, Paper.'" *North Dakota Quarterly* 55, no. 4 (1987): 153–161.

Conte, Joseph M. "Against the Calendar: Paul Blackburn's Journals." *Sagetrieb: A Journal Devoted to Poets in the Imagist/Objectivist Tradition* 7, no. 2 (1988): 35–52.

Sorrentino, Gilbert. "Paul Blackburn ('Singing, Virtuoso: *The Journals*, edited by Robert Kelly')." In *Something Said: Essays by Gilbert Sorrentino.* San Francisco: North Point Press, 1984, pp. 103–113.

Burt Kimmelman

"THE JOURNEY OF THE MAGI" T. S. ELIOT (1927) The first and most anthologized of T. S. ELIOT's "Ariel Poems," "The Journey of the Magi" recounts the travels of the three Jewish magi to Bethlehem to witness the birth of Jesus Christ. Eliot's version lacks many of the familiar details of the Nativity story, such as the rare gifts and the guiding star, and its matter-of-fact tone suggests a limited understanding of the events witnessed. Eliot narrates from the persona of one of the magi, who can no longer abide by his former beliefs, but cannot accept and embrace the newly revealed truth, either, acknowledging at the end that "I should be glad of another death." By narrating the Nativity story in a modern voice characterized by colloquialism and ennui, Eliot provides a bridge between the secular 20th century and the original Christian world. The narrator's lack of belief reflects the challenge of faith, though his neutrality also evokes the profound choice the Incarnation offered, thus restoring its strange, even disturbing character as a way of reinvigorating faith and awe.

For a poem that tries to strip away the familiar details of the Nativity story, "The Journey of the Magi" is richly allusive. As Robert Crawford explains, the poem is based on a version of the Nativity tale told by Lancelot Andrewes, the Anglican minister who oversaw the translation of the King James Bible, and Eliot's style often imitates Andrewes's own. E. G. Burgess writes of how the magi, commemorated in Christmas carols as kings, were in fact priests of the cult of Zoroaster, who prophesied the birth of Christ in Bethlehem 600 years before, which accounts for the speaker's understated admission, after finding the stable of Christ's birth, that "it was (you may say) satisfactory." Michael Dean, among others, finds the poem not only alludes to the Nativity, but also forecasts the ministry, crucifixion, and resurrection of Christ (9). Eliot also alludes to a number of pagan traditions, including the fertility rites described in Charles Frazier's *The Golden Bough.* While these many layers of allusion clearly serve to enhance the meaning of the poem, they contrast with the narrator's claim that "there was no information." The narrator's ignorance or uncertainty about the allegorical significance of the scenes he witnesses, particularly those described in the second stanza, restores a sense of the unknown to events familiar to a 20th-century Western reader. Thus, Eliot dramatizes the early years of Christianity to evoke the essential mystery of Christ, which is a precondition for authentically experiencing the paradox of belief.

The opening lines, which evoke the writings of Lancelot Andrewes, depict a journey through the desolation of winter toward Bethlehem to witness the birth of the savior. By means of this desert setting, which both evokes the setting of his poem *The WASTE LAND* and counters its nihilism, Eliot characterizes salvation as attainable only through suffering. "There were times we regretted / The summer palaces on slopes, the terraces, / And the silken girls bringing sherbet," the speaker acknowledges, disavowing the cultural pleasures that delayed the literal journey to Bethlehem and the metaphorical journey toward salvation. The problems the magi encounter along the way—the mutiny and desertion of their men, hostility from towns they visited, the inadequate shelters they endured—are matched by "the voices singing in our ears, saying / That this was all folly." For Eliot, such challenges reflect allegorically the travails that anyone, pagan or even Christian, would face in pursuit of authentic Christian faith.

Yet the arrival in Bethlehem does not resolve these problems; rather, it reveals a more central, metaphysical conflict that the speaker must attend. Eliot signals the dilemma with his subtle FREE VERSE enjambments, which interrupt the syntax and generate a staggering rhythm and a new emphasis on the act of remembering and recording the events: "And I would do it again, but set down / This set down / This." The miracle of Jesus's incarnation troubles the narrator, for he asks, "[W]ere we led all that way for / Birth or Death? . . . / this Birth was / Hard and bitter agony for us, like Death, our death." Though he has witnessed the miracle of Jesus' birth, the speaker is even more troubled by his own death and by Death itself, the force that has governed human life since the Fall of Man. That Fall created the necessary condition for salvation, and so is referred to as the *felix culpa* or "fortunate fall," yet for Eliot, the promise of salvation has overshadowed the tragedy and desolation of the fall itself, whether the Fall of Man or the death of Christ, foreshadowed in the image of "three trees on the low sky" which the narrator described upon nearing Bethlehem. Eliot restores the original force of that tragedy, to show the difficulty of accepting Christianity but also to emphasize the glory of Jesus' sacrifice.

"The Journey of the Magi" was written the year that T. S. Eliot converted to the Church of England and assumed British citizenship, and the poem reflects Eliot's concerns about his own faith and his national identity; as Grover Smith observes, "'Journey of the Magi' is the monologue of a man who has made his own choice, who has achieved belief in the Incarnation, but who is still part of that life which the Redeemer came to sweep away." What the narrator says of his return to life after witnessing Christ's birth may have applied equally to Eliot's experience after conversion: "We returned to our places, these Kingdoms, / But no longer at ease here, in the old dispensation, / With an alien people clutching their gods." Such a biographical parallel is rare in Eliot's work, who professed an aesthetic doctrine of impersonality in his writings, but it enhances the remarkable spiritual and psychological experience the poem describes, an experience surprisingly close to the experience of the modern world itself. Having witnessed a miracle, whether the birth of Christ or the radical changes of the 20th century, one struggles and perhaps never comes to accept it, but one can never return to the world that existed before.

BIBLIOGRAPHY

Burgess, E. F. "T. S. Eliot's 'Journey of the Magi.'" *The Explicator* 42, no. 4 (1984): 36.

Crawford, Robert. *The Savage and the City in the Work of T. S. Eliot.* New York: Clarendon Press, 1987.

Dean, Michael. "Eliot's 'Journey of the Magi.'" *The Explicator* 37, no. 4 (1979): 9–10.

Smith, Grover. *T. S. Eliot's Poetry and Plays: A Study in Sources and Meaning.* Available online. URL: www.uiuc.edu/maps/poets/a_f/eliot/magi.htm.

Temple Cone

"JUNK" RICHARD WILBUR (1961) RICHARD WILBUR's witty paean to mass-produced, generic objects, "Junk" uses the poetic line of traditional Anglo-Saxon verse (best-known from the epic poem *Beowulf*) to restore a quality of "thingliness" to the cheaply made, cheaply priced objects that have replaced the craftworks of bygone eras. By calling the reader's attention to "the things of this world" (the title of one of his earlier books of poetry), Wilbur rejects the modern emphasis on functionality and attempts to reinvigorate our appreciation of objects as objects, even the junk objects we customarily discard rather than repair once they have outlived their use. Such a perception, the poem implies, might restore a sense of satisfaction in craftsmanship, and thus of higher value in the world, just as the natural processes of weathering that reduces these junk items to "the glitter of glass-chips" will restore them to the earth, "That the good grain / be discovered again."

Wilbur's choice of form is critical to understanding the poem. The lines are written in an Anglo-Saxon meter, with four stressed beats per line, the first two stressed words separated from the latter two by a midline pause or medial caesura, but linked by alliteration, consonance, or assonance. Such a form gives the lines a rich interconnection and coherence, much like the complex designs of books and armor from the Anglo-Saxon era, even though the lines themselves resemble a rickety cabinet, almost toppled over, due to the way Wilbur emphasizes the caesura by dropping the second half-line below the first.

The mixture of design and shabbiness that Wilbur's lines evoke lies at the poem's thematic heart. Peter Stitt reads this poem and many others of Wilbur's as satire "specifically directed to those who would deny the presence of anything sacramental within the concrete world" [15]. "Yet the things themselves / in thoughtless honor / Have kept composure," Wilbur exclaims. The base materials from which the junk was manufactured seem to endure, and this endurance suggests an essence that no degree of change can affect. In one sense, poorly designed junk is closer to its essence than showy craftworks, because the former's design cannot draw attention from the material. However, Charles Woodward's reading of the poem is less affirming than Stitt's, for he identifies in Wilbur's lines a desire for the illusion of permanence: "Wilbur's theme is not mutability alone . . . but the precariousness of a physical world which is known to be different from what our physical senses tell us it is. . . . Wilbur must praise appearance even as he is being hoodwinked by it" [23].

By the close of the poem, Wilbur promises the decaying junk "shall all be buried / To the depth of diamonds." The final lines offer two allusions that suggest that in the "making dark" of the underground, decay and compression recycle all manmade things, though these material elements can be refashioned, perhaps superbly. "Wayland's work / is worn away," Wilbur warns, referring to the Norse god of metalwork in order to show that change affects everything, even the creations of divine beings. But the dark is also where "halt Hephaestus / keeps his hammer," a reference to the Greek god of metalwork which indicates that although change affects everything, it cannot limit the possibility of creation. And as Wilbur's own transforming vision indicates, the fact of the world's mutability cannot prevent the possibility of its perfection.

BIBLIOGRAPHY

Stitt, Peter. *The World's Hieroglyphic Beauty: Five American Poets.* Athens: University of Georgia Press, 1985.

Woodward, Charles. "Richard Wilbur's Critical Condition." *Contemporary Poetry: A Journal of Criticism* II, no. 2 (1977): 16–24.

Temple Cone

JUSTICE, DONALD (1925–2004) Donald Justice's poems are recognized for their supreme technical skill, impersonality of diction, accuracy of observation, and complexity of thought and sentiment. They offer a remarkable combination of exacting neoclassicism, which he learned during his one-year study with the iconoclastic critic YVOR WINTERS at Stanford, and discreet postromantic lyricism, gained through years of study and teaching at the Iowa Writers' Workshop. Above all, Justice's poems reveal an intense preoccupation with American landscape and people, which makes his work similar to that of EDWIN ARLINGTON ROBINSON and EDGAR LEE MASTERS. At his best, Justice can be as discerning and profound as ROBERT FROST.

Justice was born and raised in Miami, Florida, although he spent a large part of his childhood visiting his grandparents in Georgia. He holds university degrees from Miami, North Carolina, and Iowa, where he received a Ph.D. in writing (at that time, the teaching faculty at Iowa included ROBERT LOWELL, JOHN BERRYMAN, and KARL SHAPIRO, among others). For the next 25 years, Justice himself taught at the Iowa Writers' Workshop, with occasional appointments at other universities. In 1982 he moved back to Florida to teach as the poet-in-residence at the University of Florida, Gainsville. He retired in 1992 and moved back to Iowa City. Justice was the recipient of numerous grants, awards, and fellowships. His *Selected Poems* won the Pulitzer Prize in 1980. He also won the Bollingen Prize (1991) and the Lannan Foundation Award (1996). Some of his earlier individual volumes include *The Summer Anniversaries* (1960), *Night Light* (1967), *Departures* (1973), and *The Sunset Maker* (1987), which also contains stories and a memoir. Subsequent editions of selected and new poems were published in 1991 and 1995. Justice also published two books of essays: *Platonic Scripts* (1984) and *Oblivion: On Writers & Writing* (1999).

Justice's poems are most often recognized for their formal precision, fidelity to experience, and reliance on common speech rhythms. A typical Justice poem is verbally sparse yet imaginatively rich, its language elegant and decorous yet straightforward, if not, at times, brutal in its implications. Justice often displays his extraordinary mastery of traditional poetic forms—the canzone, the pantoum, the sonnet, the sestina, or the villanelle. His poems are as crafted as they are candid, often featuring thematic lucidity and tonal austerity in an attempt to offset their sophisticated structure. Justice's exactitude is not only formal, but also verbal. A sentence, a phrase, or even a single word sometimes introduces a startling nuance to a poem; in one of his most famous poems, "Men at Forty" (1967), the men in question listen to the crickets in the woods behind their "mortgaged" houses. "Elsewheres" (1967) begins with the lines: "Already it is midsummer / In the Sweden of our lives."

In an *Ohio Review* interview, Justice admits he has always followed T. S. ELIOT's dictum from "Tradition and the Individual Talent" that poetry is not an expression of personality but an escape from personality (see ARS POETICAS). He regularly leaves himself out of his poems, speaking in imagined or borrowed voice, and, at times, humbly borrowing ideas from other poets, such as Hans Magnus Enzensberger, Eugène Guillevic, and César Vallejo. Yet there is something uncommonly personal in these simultaneously restrained and confident compositions; Justice's speaking voice is characterized by wryness and wit, propensity for meditation, though not abstract philosophizing, and reliance on well-aimed observation reminiscent of WILLIAM CARLOS WILLIAMS. Justice's poems reflect modern loneliness, nostalgia, isolation, loss, and despair. (Some critics have compared his work to the paintings of Edward Hopper.) As a poet, Justice chooses to portray reality and reality only, no matter how troubling or uncomfortable it may be. Like the subject of his villanelle "In Memory of the Unknown Poet, Robert Boardman Vaughn" (1987), Justice perceives "the boredom, the horror, and the glory of the world" with an unchanging and undiscriminating stare, fulfilling the role that Eliot prescribed to all modern poets.

It is not completely surprising, then, that Justice should explore the extremities of human experience, especially with the concept of insanity, in some of his most famous poems, such as "On a Painting by Patient B of the Independence State Hospital for the Insane" (1952) and "Counting the Mad" (1960). Justice is also one of the most realistic poets in the language, demonstrating a deep interest in specific landscapes and people that are part of these landscapes. In "Variations on a Text by Vallejo" (1973), Justice imagines his Miami gravediggers speaking amongst themselves in Spanish. In "Children Walking Home from School through a Good Neighborhood" (1987), he describes the children as figures held in a glass ball, "One of those in which, when shaken, snowstorms occur; / But this one is not yet shaken." Thus only a circumspect social commentary blends with a genuine portrayal of individual places and people.

Thanks to the poet's imaginative perspective, too, American cities, suburbs, and small towns—these most ordinary of places—instantly acquire a most mysterious aura. Many of these poems are set in the past, going back to the poet's childhood during the Great Depression and adolescence during World War II. Many of them show distinctly southern accents, but they do not idealize the South as much as they offer an intriguing mixture of nostalgia and irony, consistent with the poet's belief that one can feel a certain nostalgia for what one never knew or had.

BIBLIOGRAPHY

Gioia, Dana, and William Logan, eds. *Certain Solitudes*. Fayetteville: University of Arkansas Press, 1997.

———., eds. "Donald Justice Special Feature." *Verse* 8 & 9 (winter/spring 1992): 3–72.

Justice, Donald. "Interview," by Wayne Dodd and Stanley Plumly. *Ohio Review* 16, no. 3 (1975): 41–63.

Piotr Gwiazda

K

KADDISH ALLEN GINSBERG (1957) If *HOWL* was the poem that made BEAT poet ALLEN GINSBERG internationally famous and infamous all at once, *Kaddish,* his long, brutal, and painfully beautiful elegy for his mother, Naomi, made him respected by critics and fellow poets alike. *Kaddish* revealed that Ginsberg was a poet destined to alter significantly the face of midcentury American poetry. Indeed, so influential was the poem for its groundbreaking experiments in style, as well as its graphic portrayal of Ginsberg's troubled childhood with a mentally ill mother, that its composition in late 1957 marks the beginning of the CONFESSIONAL movement in American poetry, later made famous by such writers as ANNE SEXTON, JOHN BERRYMAN, and SYLVIA PLATH. Many critics cite *Kaddish* as the inspiration for ROBERT LOWELL's *Life Studies* (1959), a celebrated work in which Lowell dramatically moved away from carefully crafted poems to mine his own personal traumas in highly experimental forms.

By the time Ginsberg's second collection, *Kaddish and Other Poems,* was published by City Lights Books in 1961, the author was one of the major voices of a national social movement derided by literary critics, government officials, and the media. Even so, such attention on the Beat movement—as vitriolic as that attention often was—made Ginsberg perhaps the most famous living American poet, a position he would continue to hold until his death in 1997. Thus *Kaddish* was welcomed with considerable interest. Its title poem would eventually be recognized as one of the greatest elegies written in English in the 20th century by the very literary establishment that first rejected Ginsberg's poetry as anti-intellectual and amateurish. As he had in previous works, beginning with his breakthrough composing sessions for *Howl and Other Poems,* Ginsberg drew from his own personal experiences, particularly those most painful to confront and admit. During the conformist 1950s, when alternative behavior was seen as a threat by American society, Ginsberg wrote in *Kaddish* about his mother's struggle with mental illness. Ginsberg explored in the poem the ways American society itself fueled his mother's paranoia, destroyed her personality and health with its "medical treatments," and created a society where difference was punished. Ginsberg criticized his comfortable 1950s nation for the pain it had caused him and his family. In style, too, *Kaddish* broke many hard-and-fast poetic "truths." The poem leaps breathlessly between prose and Whitmanesque long-lined verse and between reportage, politics, and metaphysics. It was an attempt to encompass the chaos of midcentury American experience that Ginsberg saw embodied in his mother's tragic life. For him, such experience required new forms, new language, and new metaphors.

Perhaps the most urgent reason for *Kaddish,* however, was that Ginsberg himself feared for his own sanity as he confronted personal demons. What did it mean that he was homosexual? Society in the 1950s argued that such sexual "deviance" was to be treated psychologically. What was one to make of his poetic sensibility? As he notes in the closing sections of the poem, Naomi saw life metaphorically, as an artist might. In other words, Ginsberg explores the very real possibility that he too is losing his mind. The opening line of *Howl* had famously told us that "the best minds of [Ginsberg's] generation [had been] destroyed by madness." *Kaddish* would be Ginsberg's test of his own sanity in a world where those he loved and admired were broken by social pressure or sedated by electric shock treatments.

In *Kaddish* we find a broad-ranging elegy on both Ginsberg's mother, who immigrated to New York's Lower East Side from Russia as a child, and a fallen America. As the poem develops, it is clear that the author blames much of his mother's mental illness on the repressions she and others like her (politically left, Jewish, and female) faced during the years following World War II. Throughout the poem, tracing the author's youth with an increasingly ill mother, her eventual commitment in a mental institution, and the months immediately following her death, Ginsberg describes his growth from fearing his mother to seeing her as the inspiration for his own poetic sensibilities.

Structurally the poem alternates between Ginsberg's familiar long lines and sections of prose. It seems at times, appropriately, a work in progress. Rather than presenting a formal, coherent portrait of his mother, the poem presents a world, a history, in fragments. It also reveals a narrative voice desperate to find sense through memory and language. One perhaps sees in the speaker, and in Naomi herself, the displaced sensibility of the modern artist earlier given shape by T. S. ELIOT in "THE LOVE SONG OF J. ALFRED PRUFROCK." With *Kaddish,* though, we encounter a "Prufrock" damaged so deeply that there may be no hope of return to any form of normal life. Paradoxically, the speaker of *Kaddish* eventually embraces the very qualities and voice that make a social outcast.

Perhaps the author's greatest poetic achievement, Ginsberg's *Kaddish* embodies the shattered American psyche at midcentury. It is graphic and tender, angry and inquisitive: It is a hymn to a country at war with its own conscience.

BIBLIOGRAPHY

Bartlett, Lee, ed. *The Beats: Essays in Criticism.* Jefferson, N.C.: McFarland, 1981.

Foster, Edward. *Understanding the Beats.* Columbia: University of South Carolina Press, 1992.

Stephenson, Gregory. *The Daybreak Boys: Essays on the Literature of the Beat Generation.* New York: Morrow, 1979.

Steve Wilson

KAUFMAN, BOB (1925–1986) Bob Kaufman was a street poet—a people's poet. He was one of the founding architects and living examples of the BEAT generation as a literary, historical and existential phenomenon, although he has come to be overshadowed by his white, formally educated contemporaries ALLEN GINSBERG, JACK KEROUAC, and GARY SNYDER. Kaufman cofounded the significant Beat journal *Beatitudes.* Partly out of choice, partly out of disillusioned resignation and the ravages of street life, he turned his back on the seductions of fame and respectability, implicitly declaring solidarity with the world's anonymous poor. A much-admired extemporizer, he blended his own rapid-fire aphorisms and wisecracks with the considerable store of modernist poetry he had memorized (see MODERNISM). His poetry reworks and defamiliarizes that of Samuel Taylor Coleridge, Federico García Lorca, Tennessee Williams, HART CRANE, LANGSTON HUGHES, and others. In its adventurous imagery, sonorous qualities, and biting wit, Kaufman's poetry shares much with other New World black surrealists Aimé Cesaire, Ted Joans, and Will Alexander, as well as with the jazz-inspired poetry and fiction of AMIRI BARAKA and NATHANIEL MACKEY.

One of 13 children, Robert Garnell Kaufman was born in New Orleans on April 18, 1925, into a middle-class, African-American Catholic family, to a schoolteacher mother and a Pullman Porter father. At 18, Kaufman joined the merchant marines, becoming a prominent organizer in the National Maritime Union primarily based in New York City. When the American Federation of Labor (AFL) and the Congress of Industrial Organizations (CIO) merged in the 1950s, he was purged from the union, a casualty of the McCarthy era. Kaufman left New York City, emerging in San Francisco as a familiar figure on the bohemian literary and street scenes, and reinventing himself as a Beat street poet with a colorful if fictitious legacy—a hybrid Orthodox Jewish and "voodoo" upbringing. He embodied playful but purposeful dissent in his lifestyle and poetry. His poem "Bagel Shop Jazz" was nominated for the Guinness Poetry Award in 1961, and in 1979 he received a National Endowment for the Arts fellowship.

Kaufman's first book, *Solitudes Crowded with Loneliness* (1965), was compiled, edited, and sent off to New Directions publishers by his wife, Eileen Kaufman. Many poems from this period describe the Beat community in all its pathos, humor, posturing, and genuine utopian yearnings. "Bagel Shop Jazz," for instance, describes the wary alliance between "mulberry eyed girls in black stockings," "turtleneck angel guys / Caesar-jawed, with synagogue eyes," and "Coffee-faced Ivy Leaguers"—that is, women, Jewish or Italian Americans, and African Americans—who comprise the fragile community of "shadow people . . . nightfall creatures." Other poems chronicle the ongoing social hassles of being African American; still others are modeled on jazz compositional principles or invoke jazz themes, and many are lyrics that express an intense desire to live beyond one's self or an acute dissociation, epitomized by the title "Would You Wear My Eyes?" *Golden Sardine* (1967) continues many of these themes and experiments with new versions of the long poem, notably the satiric "Caryl Chessman Interviews the PTA from His Swank Gas Chamber." After a difficult three years back in New York City (1960–63), Kaufman returned to San Francisco and abruptly withdrew from public life. The late 1970s witnessed a brief second period of productivity, culminating in the publication of the fragmented and visionary *The Ancient Rain: Poems 1956–1978* (1981). Posthumously *Cranial Guitar: Selected Poems by Bob Kaufman* (1996) was also published.

BIBLIOGRAPHY

Christian, Barbara. "Whatever Happened to Bob Kaufman?" *Black World* 21, no. 12 (September 1972): 20–29.

Damon, Maria. "'Unmeaning Jargon'/Uncanonized Beatitude: Bob Kaufman, Poet." *The Dark End of the Street: Margins in American Vanguard Poetry*. Minneapolis: Minnesota University Press, 1993, pp. 32–76.

Edwards, Brent, Farah J. Griffin, and Maria Damon, eds. *Callaloo* 25, no. 1 (winter 2002). [Special issue, *Recent Takes on Jazz Poetics*, special section on Bob Kaufman.]

Lindberg, Kathryne. "Bob Kaufman, Sir Real, and His Rather Surreal Self-Presentation." *Talisman: A Journal of Contemporary Poetry and Poetics* 11 (Fall 1993): 167–182.

Maria Damon

KEES, WELDON (1914–1955?) Since his disappearance in 1955, Weldon Kees, through the efforts of DONALD JUSTICE, among others, has gathered a small but extremely devoted readership; DANA GIOIA calls it a "cult" (xv). He could easily be named the supreme poet of noir (as his poem "The City as Hero" [1943] might seem to suggest), a poet whose subject matter tends toward the somber, although that label would understate the depth and breadth of an electrifying body of poetry. His signature poems center on a mysterious figure, someone named Robinson. The poem "Robinson" (1947), for instance, shows the hallmarks of Kees's work: an effortless formalism, a close attention to details of character and object, a nihilism that seems unmatched among the poet's contemporaries. Robinson's existence is wholly contingent upon his will to exist ("Robinson alone provides the image Robinsonian"). Robinson's house does not exist when he leaves it, yet the phone rings continually: "it could be Robinson / Calling. It never rings when he is here."

Born in Beatrice, Nebraska, Kees attended several universities, finally graduating from the University of Nebraska. He married a melancholic alcoholic. Kees became an almost maniacally multifaceted artist. He wrote poems, short stories, and essays in art criticism (a novel, *Fall Quarter* [1990], was published posthumously), and he composed and performed jazz piano. He was a painter and a photographer, as well as a collaborator in film and book projects in the social sciences. He accomplished all this while crossing the country, every few years, from coast to coast, in search of his place within his generation.

Many have noted Kees's gifts as a social satirist, but few critics have discussed Kees's poetry of protest. At a time when support for World War II seems, at least in cultural memory, virtually unchallenged, Kees's poetry stands as a grim reminder that even the "good" war involved torture, slaughter, and madness. His eerie sonnet "For My Daughter" (1943), for instance, seems at first to praise a newborn but quickly prophesies her "death in certain war" or a related fate as "the cruel / Bride of a syphilitic or a fool." This unrelenting sonnet is so disturbing that the reader feels a horrified relief at the last line: "I have no daughter. I desire none." As Justice puts it, Kees inscribes "the calm in the face of certain doom" (ix). Thus, while clearly influenced by W. H. AUDEN, Kees's poems achieve a pitch of despair and fatality that even Auden's grimmest poems of war cannot approach.

In the months before his car was found abandoned near the Golden Gate Bridge in 1955, Kees had spoken to his friends about both suicide and escape (to Europe or Mexico under an alias). But he seems, after all, to have left this world, left it the way his poems leave his readers—unanswered, unconsoled.

BIBLIOGRAPHY

Elledge, Jim, ed. *Weldon Kees: A Critical Introduction.* Metuchen, N.J.: Scarecrow Press, 1985.

Gioia, Dana. "The Cult of Weldon Kees." In *The Bibliography of Weldon Kees,* edited by Daniel Gillane and Robert N. Niemi, xv–xxxiii. Jackson, Miss.: Parrish House, 1997.

Justice, Donald. Preface to *The Collected Poems of Weldon Kees,* edited by Donald Justice. Lincoln: University of Nebraska Press, 1975, pp. vii–xi.

Rose Shapiro

KELLY, ROBERT (1935–) First associated with the DEEP IMAGE and American surrealist poets (see SURREALISM), including JEROME ROTHENBERG and Gilbert Sorrentino, in the early 1960s, Kelly gradually developed his own "poetics of personal mythology" (to borrow DIANE WAKOSKI's phrase)—creating his own set of symbolic meanings—in more than 50 books of poetry and fiction between 1960 and 2000. In a 1985 interview, Kelly talked about his early development in these terms: "Some focused through the Black Mountain or the [John] Ashbery [see NEW YORK SCHOOL] and so on. I wanted to stay clear of that. I was continually revivifying myself, I thought with the primitive, with the barbaric, with that which comes from outside the culture and every now and then brings life to it again" ("Nothing" 100). His extensive body of work speaks to how he has revivified himself over and over again.

Kelly graduated Phi Beta Kappa from the City College of New York and began to teach at Bard College in 1961. He has been awarded a National Endowment for the Arts Fellowship (1977), the *Los Angeles Times* Prize for poetry (1980), and membership in the American Academy and Institute of Arts and Letters (1986), among other honors. Long interested in the potential of small literary magazines to advance poetic practice, Kelly was founding editor in the late 1950s and early 1960s of *Chelsea Review, Trobar,* and *Matter,* and has since been intimately associated with such groundbreaking POETRY JOURNALS as *Caterpillar, Los, Sulfur,* and *Conjunctions.*

The deeply personal character of Kelly's poetry, combined with its continual allusion to literary, mythological, and musical sources, makes it a daunting challenge. At the same time, many poems can be disturbing in their intimacy. This apparent contradiction is reconciled after one absorbs the overriding sensibility in his poems—that of a subjectivity estranged from a world that can only be partially grasped through language. The reader must enter into the author's subjectivity to understand the poems, yet language is both the entrance and the obstacle.

In directly referring to this theme, Kelly's poem "Windows" (1995) is framed as a warning, beginning, "Beware the simplicity of windows," and then elaborating on the elusiveness of reality as apprehended through language. Language does not bring us any closer to realities outside of us, though it may seem to. Instead it reinforces our separation while helping us accept it. A few lines later Kelly writes, "Language keeps you in your place." Kelly approaches the world through mythological personae, or through an unstable "I," in order to satisfy his insatiable need (even sexual greed) for what can be found, luscious and real, in the world. He writes of "taking refuge" ("Windows" [1995]) in the world as it presents itself to him, in order to open himself up, in a Buddhist sense, to the world as it really is.

BIBLIOGRAPHY

Kelly, Robert. "Nothing but Doors: An Interview with Robert Kelly," by Denis Barone. *Credences: A Journal of Twentieth Century Poetry and Poetics* 3, no. 3 (fall 1985): 100–122.

———. "Robert Kelly: An Interview on Trobar," by David Ossman. *Triquarterly* 43 (1978): 398–404.

———. "A Rose to Look At: An Interview with Robert Kelly," by Larry McCaffery. In *Some Other Fluency: Interviews with Innovative American Authors,* edited by McCaffery. Philadelphia: University of Pennsylvania Press, 1996, pp. 170–195.

Michael Van Dyke

KENNEDY, X. J. (1929–) Though he is sometimes reviled by critics for being superficial, a writer of "light" verse whose form and treatment of subjects are not complex, the majority of X. J. Kennedy's poems are not superficial but are, instead, "serious" with regard to social commentary. The uncertainty of categorizing Kennedy's poetry may be a result of his use of humor in his social criticism—for some, humor has no place in serious poetry. Perhaps the idea of Kennedy's superficiality is extended further by his adherence to verse forms; his poems are often end-rhymed and follow strict meter. Kennedy may be considered an informal member of the NEW FORMALISM movement. Indeed what he said in 1961 acts as the movement's unofficial motto: "Why should a man learn how to write a decent villanelle . . . when . . he can strew lines on a page any cockeyed way . . and be hailed with the new American poetry? Poems ought to be harder to write than this" (243).

Kennedy was born Joseph Charles Kennedy in Dover, New Jersey. His first collection of poetry, *Nude Descending a Staircase,* was published in 1961 and won the Lamont Award. Since then he has garnered many other prizes and fellowships. Formerly a university professor, he has also edited anthologies and written more than a dozen children's books.

Kennedy may be best described as a chronicler and critic of everyday American culture. His wide-ranging observations display an aptitude for recognizing the significant in the ordinary and, often, the destructive as well. He uses meter and verse in an attempt to formalize themes, such as suicide and loneliness, perplexing subjects not easily contained by structure. In his poems one not only gets a sense of seeing something once hidden, as the form illuminates the content, but also one witnesses the control of the uncontrollable and begins to comprehend the incomprehensible.

The frequently anthologized "In a Prominent Bar in Secaucus One Day" (1961) conveys the themes of disappointment and disillusionment, the recognition of both the American dream gone awry and the ravages of time, through the humorous self-portrait of a woman who attempts, with bravado, to assuage the pain of a rough life by bragging about her experiences, dispensing wisdom all the while. The form here acts to solidify the poem's final adage, the rhyme actually making it memorable *as* adage, as Kennedy describes the consequence of one's attempt to subjugate time: "And [you'll] be left by the roadside for all your good deeds / Two toadstools for tits and a face full of weeds."

As an editor of many textbooks and anthologies used in schools across the country, Kennedy has been a great influence on readers of American poetry. As a poet, his work perpetuates debate on the difference between "serious" and "light" verse.

BIBLIOGRAPHY

Collins, Michael J. "The Poetry of X. J. Kennedy." *World Literature Today* 61 (winter 1987): 55–58.

Goldstein, Thomas. "X. J. Kennedy." In *Dictionary of Literary Biography.* Vol. 5, *American Poets since World War II,* edited by Donald J. Greiner, 394–397. Detroit: Gale, 1980.

Gwynn, R. S. "Swans in Ice." *Sewanee Review* 95 (fall 1985): lxxviii–xxix.

Kennedy, X. J. "Comment: *The New American Poetry.*" *Poetry* 98, no. 4 (July 1961): 242–244.

John R. Woznicki

KENYON, JANE (1947–1995) The pastoral emphasis and New England setting of Jane Kenyon's poetry has invited comparisons to ROBERT FROST and Emily Dickinson. The uncluttered spareness of her work and her interrelated themes of faith, guilt, empathy, and pessimism also place her among that collection of people known as New England poets. Kenyon's own love of John Keats—and his haunted experiences of pain and beauty—also informs her work.

Kenyon was raised in Ann Arbor, Michigan, where she attended the University of Michigan, earning her B.A. in 1970 and her M.A. in 1972. There she met her future husband, the poet and editor DONALD HALL. In 1975 Hall and Kenyon left Michigan to settle in Hall's ancestral home in New Hampshire. Their quiet life together in this rural setting figures prominently in her work. She died of leukemia, at the height of her powers, at the age of 47. Her awards include fellowships from the National Endowment for the Arts and the Guggenheim Foundation, and a PEN Voelcker Award.

Kenyon's aesthetic creed is most easily summed up in her favorite quote of EZRA POUND's: "The natural object is always the adequate symbol." Her fastidious adherence to this principle usually results in poems of understated elegance, such as her conclusion to "Camp Evergreen" (1986): "Now it is high summer: the solstice: / longed-for, possessed, luxurious, and sad." But her effort to pare away can sometimes hobble the poetry, resulting in a failure of invention and the substitution of mere reportage for cohesively linked images. Kenyon herself acknowledged this fault of at least one of her poems, "Three Songs at the End of Summer" (1993), though it appears elsewhere, particularly in her earlier work. As her poetic voice matures, what was occasionally ponderous becomes stately.

Understatement, or even silence, in Kenyon's work can, paradoxically, achieve complex and rewarding moments of empathy. Like many of her pastoral poems, "Frost Flowers" (1987) begins with a speaker who, after having taught a class earlier, is now outside in the dusk observing squirrels and flowers. Without preparation, the following devastating lines arrive: "My sarcasm wounded a student today. / Afterward I heard him running down the stairs." A similar moment occurs in her long poem "Having it Out with Melancholy" (1993), where she movingly records her struggles with recurring depression. The third section of the poem reports a friend's advice: The speaker could escape from depression if she "really believed in God." The speaker's refusal to explain away, contextualize, or otherwise redeem these moments makes them intensely poignant.

There is a narrow consistency to Kenyon's work: walks with the dog, narratives of chastened spirituality, descriptions of nature, and the myriad faces of grief constitute the bulk of her thematic concerns. But while there are more varied and virtuosic poets, few have won the kind of devoted readership that Kenyon enjoys.

BIBLIOGRAPHY

Garrison, Deborah. "Simply Lasting." *New Yorker* (September 9, 1998): 91.

Hall, Donald. "With Jane and Without: An Interview with Donald Hall," by Jeffrey S. Cramer. *Massachusetts Review* 39, no. 4 (1999): 493–510.

Mattison, Alice. "'Let It Grow in the Dark Like a Mushroom': Writing with Jane Kenyon." *Michigan Quarterly Review* 39, no. 1 (2000): 120–137.

Jayme Stayer

KEROUAC, JACK (1922–1969) Jack Kerouac is one of the most mythical figures in American literature, his name and the name of his novel *On the Road* (1957) having the power of invocation even for people who have never read a word he wrote; the names conjure freedom. By comparison, his poetry is obscure, but it is both powerful as poetry and significant as a direct influence on his fellow poets. Kerouac, with ALLEN GINSBERG, GREGORY CORSO, and William S. Burroughs, was at the hub of the mid-20th-century shift in American literary consciousness known as the BEAT generation. When his first poems later published in *MEXICO CITY BLUES* (1959), arrived from Mexico in 1955, his friends who were involved in what became known as the SAN FRANCISCO RENAISSANCE, GARY SNYDER, PHILIP WHALEN, Philip Lamantia, and MICHAEL MCCLURE, in particular, were moved and inspired. Kerouac, "author-catalyst" of the writerly cataclysm that shook America (Ginsberg vi), had a traceable impact on the writing of many others, such as ROBERT CREELEY, AMIRI BARAKA, LAWRENCE FERLINGHETTI, Lew Welch, and ANNE WALDMAN. Bob Dylan pointed to Kerouac's verse as "the first poetry that spoke his [Dylan's] own language" (Ginsberg ii). Ginsberg proclaimed Kerouac "a major, perhaps seminal, poet . . and mayhap thru his imprint on Dylan and myself among others, a poetic influence over the entire planet" (vi).

Jean-Louis de Kerouac was born in Lowell, Massachusetts, the youngest of three children in a French-Canadian family. His cultural origins are important, because of the role religion and language played in his life and his work; his first language was French, and his first and last religion was Roman Catholicism, interrupted by an earnest exploration of Buddhism. The collective force of mother tongue, mother church, and his own mother, Gabrielle, made him maternally fixated. He moved away from his language, his church, and his mother, physically and philosophically, but he always returned closer. Kerouac married three times, arguably had sex with as many men as he did women, and shamefully rejected his only child. Burdened all his life by the weight of his trinity of mother figures and by the early childhood loss of his brother Gerard, Kerouac died an ultraconservative, debilitated alcoholic, living once again with his mother.

"Ti Jean," or "Petit Jean," as he was called within his family, knew early that he wanted to be a writer, but he was also an athlete of promise and went to Columbia in 1940 on a football scholarship; he dropped out after a dispute with his coach. It was not until early 1944 that he met Ginsberg and Burroughs; two years after that, he met Neal Cassady, who became Keroauc's muse and the model for *On the Road's* Dean Moriarty. Already shaped by writers such as Walt Whitman, HART CRANE, and Thomas Wolfe, Kerouac was further affected as a writer by his New York friends, by their ideas, their actions, and their speech, as they were by his. Burroughs explained that "Kerouac was a writer. That is, he wrote" (53); rather than just talk about writing or call himself a writer, he did it, even at the risk of being gored by the life about which he wrote. The fact that he was in a frequent state of sorrow surfaces repeatedly in his poems. He would "suffer / even for bugs" ("Running Through—Chinese Poem Song" [1992]), lament "Oh sad Bodhidharma you were right / Everything we loved disappeared" ("Long Island Chinese Poem Rain" [1992]), admit "I'm just a human being with a lot of / shit on my heart" ("Goofball Blues" [1992]), and wonder why "The story of man . . Should hurt me so" ("Bowery Blues" [1992]). He recorded what went on around him, wrote experimentally, incorporated jazz improvisation into his prose and poetry; Creeley warns that there can be no real understanding of Kerouac's work "if there is not the recognition that this remarkable person is living here, is actual in all that is written" (xiii).

Kerouac is in the work, in all his beauty and in all his despair. He appears in his poems as religious seeker, as sexual debauchee, as little boy, as happy friend, as musical composer, as penitent sinner, as unrepentant sinner. He wrote about everything and believed he had "better be a poet / Or lay down dead" ("San Francisco Blues—42nd Chorus" [1995]). He created a concept of spontaneous composition, which, as Ginsberg explains it, was "the notion of writing and not looking back, not revising, but exhausting the mind by an outpouring of all the relevant associations" (qtd. in Miles 193). Kerouac's stated desire at the very start of his journey as a writer was to make "at least one deathless line" (qtd. in Miles 37). He collaborated with Burroughs on a never-published novel, produced more than 20 other prose works, of which more than a dozen were published during his lifetime, and wrote five books of poetry, of which only one appeared in print before his death. Kerouac's iconographic power in the American consciousness is unsurpassed and secure. His life, as a stream-of-consciousness spontaneous composition alive in his art, is his "one deathless line."

BIBLIOGRAPHY

Burroughs, William S. "Kerouac." *High Times* (March 1979): 53.

Clark, Tom. *Jack Kerouac: A Biography*. New York: Marlowe & Company, 1984.

Creeley, Robert. Introduction to *Book of Blues*, by Jack Kerouac. New York: Penguin, 1995.

Ginsberg, Allen. Introduction to *Pomes All Sizes*, by Jack Kerouac. San Francisco: City Lights, 1992.

Miles, Barry. *Jack Kerouac, King of the Beats: A Portrait*. London: Virgin, 1998.

A. Mary Murphy

KINNELL, GALWAY (1927–) Galway Kinnell is best known for poems that deal with death and the physical dissolution of creatures living in this world. He began as a relatively formal poet (see PROSODY AND FREE VERSE), but he quickly changed his style to one influenced by WILLIAM CARLOS WILLIAMS, which uses a more simple, direct diction as well as a looser line and freer structure. His major theme, death, suggests his romantic tendencies; he views death from a personal perspective and as a return to a primitive, prehuman state of consciousness. His influences include American poets Walt Whitman and Emily Dickinson, as well as

Irishman William Butler Yeats and the German-language poet Rainer Maria Rilke. Along with Ted Hughes and JAMES DICKEY, Kinnell is a great writer of animal poems and is often considered one of the DEEP IMAGE poets along with ROBERT BLY, W. S. MERWIN, LOUIS SIMPSON, MARK STRAND, and JAMES WRIGHT.

Kinnell was born in Providence, Rhode Island. He graduated summa cum laude from Princeton in 1948 and received an M.A. in English from the University of Rochester in 1949. An automobile accident claimed the life of his brother, Derry, in 1957. Later he would attempt to come to terms with this loss in such poems as "Freedom, New Hampshire" (1960). A career as an itinerant poet-in-residence marks Kinnell's teaching résumé, which includes positions at a number of schools, including New York University. His first volume of collected poems, *The Avenue Bearing the Initial of Christ into the New World* (1974) was awarded the Shelley Prize by the Poetry Society of America. Later his *Selected Poetry* (1983) received the American Book Award and the Pulitzer Prize. Kinnell also penned a novel *Black Light* (1965) and has garnered acclaim for his translations of French verse.

What a Kingdom It Was (1960), Kinnell's first book of poems, introduces his concern with death and his sense of death as dissolution of one kind of identity into another, most notably in "Freedom, New Hampshire." While narrating memories from a summer spent with his brother on a farm, Kinnell employs the discovery of a cow's skull as an image of his discovery of death. The poem's conclusion, which includes a dedication to Derry, turns toward the grass that grows over a man's grave. "It is true," Kinnell allows, "That only the flesh dies." The grave and its grass, he argues, can heal what a man suffered, "but he remains dead, / And the few who loved him know this until they die." Though everyone's flesh dies, the poem suggests, there is something that lives on, transformed. The idea of transformation through an experience of death recurs in one of Kinnell's best-known poems, "The BEAR" (1968). Richard J. Calhoun argues that this poem exemplifies one of the poet's strengths, a "facility in his descriptions to be both literal and at the same time symbolic and mythic" (66). Kinnell narrates an archetypal bear hunt in which the hunter leaves a sharpened bone in the bear's food; after the bear eats, it slowly kills him from within. The hunter follows until the bear is dead; then the hunter hacks open the carcass, crawls inside, and sleeps. He dreams about the death of the bear, gaining insight into the ways of nature as he considers elements of a bear's life, such as the mother bear licking clean her newborn cubs. The hunter will, he tells the reader, spend his days "wondering" about "that sick infusion, that rank flavor of blood, that poetry by which I lived." The speaker/hunter here has undergone an initiation into death. Awaking from that sleep, he finds that, as Lee Zimmerman maintains, "poetry is redemption, although it is a terrible one" (126).

Kinnell continued his poetic search for a transformative power of experience in *The Book of Nightmares* (1971), a series of 10 poems, each in seven parts, which was influenced by Rilke's visionary *Duino Elegies* (1923). David Perkins writes that these poems suggest "a possibility in experience . . . that somewhat relieves suffering or gives it a meaning" (577). The poems continue to use nature—for instance, the Moon, a hen, and a black bear—and they are more personal, as we see Kinnell speaking in the role of dutiful father. His reflection on his children and their youth lead him to see "poetic creation as a means of resolving the nightmares of dreams for children and the nightmare of death for adults" (Calhoun 80). In "Little Sleep's-Head Sprouting Hair in the Moonlight" (1971), he places his daughter in her crib after a nightmare, and as she finds sleep again, he anticipates her waking as a kind of rebirth and new awareness, when they will walk out into the world among "the ten thousand things, / each scratched with such knowledge, *the wages / of dying is love.*"

Later Kinnell writes of the loneliness of memories in *When One Has Lived A Long Time Alone* (1990). In "Memories of My Father," he thinks of returning to his father's house and hearing someone—his father or some stranger—singing. The act of singing, Kinnell believes, can give form to one's feelings. Articulating in this way imparts structure to feelings and experience, as his songs in *The Book of Nightmares* may bring some peace to him, the father thinking of the inevitable death of himself and his children. Experience and memory gain permanence. In *The Book of Nightmares,* the grown daughter should treasure the mouth that reminds her *"here, / here is the world."*

BIBLIOGRAPHY

Calhoun, Richard J. *Galway Kinnell.* New York: Twayne, 1992.

Perkins, David. *A History of Modern Poetry: Modernism and After.* Cambridge, Mass.: Belknap Press, 1987.

Zimmerman, Lee. *Intricate and Simple Things: The Poetry of Galway Kinnell.* Urbana: University of Illinois Press, 1987.

Gary Leising

KIZER, CAROLYN (1925–) A gifted translator, critic, and poet, Carolyn Kizer has "earned a secure niche in American letters," according to Elizabeth B. House, through her "celebrat[ion of] the joys of art, friendship, family, and good works" (164). Kizer is considered a member of the Northwest school of poets, along with DAVID WAGONER and RICHARD HUGO, because of their tutelage by THEODORE ROETHKE at the University of Washington. Kizer stands among other powerful American women poets, including ADRIENNE RICH, ANNE SEXTON, SYLVIA PLATH, and DENISE LEVERTOV, who were trained by men but ultimately transcended their early training to write powerfully about their experience as women. Known equally for the tightly crafted, formal voice of her work and for her role as an international ambassador for poetry and poets, Kizer established her reputation for meticulous craft in her first work, *The Ungrateful Garden,* in 1961, subsequently publishing a relatively small body of highly polished and critically acclaimed work.

Kizer was born in Spokane, Washington, the only child of two highly intellectual, politically active parents. Her father was a lawyer, and her mother had earned a Ph.D. in biology from Stanford and studied art and philosophy at Harvard. Kizer bloomed under the procession of distinguished philosophers, literary figures, architects, and planners visiting her parents' home and under the doting attention of her mother, who gave up her career to care for her. Though Kizer had a deep intellectual bond with her father, it is her mother's unceasing encouragement of her creative efforts that she credits with nurturing her writing career; her 1984 volume, *Yin*, contains a prose work, "A Muse," that examines their relationship. As a student at Sarah Lawrence College in the early 1940s, she published a poem in the *New Yorker.* The poem, she later said, was not very good, but it nourished her emerging sense of herself as a writer. Kizer did graduate work at Columbia University and the University of Washington, Seattle, studying under Theodore Roethke there in 1946–47. Married to Charles Bullitt in 1948, Kizer had three children in three years and divorced Bullitt three years later. She married John Woodbridge in 1975. She has held teaching positions at the University of North Carolina, Washington University, Barnard, Columbia, Ohio University, Iowa, and Princeton University. She won a Pulitzer Prize for *Yin* in 1985.

Kizer's dual role as both a poet and an ambassador for poetry is evident in her earliest serious work. During her studies at Columbia in 1945–46, she held a Chinese Cultural Fellowship in comparative literature and she later founded and edited *Poetry Northwest,* 1959–65. She served as a U.S. State Department specialist in Pakistan during 1964 and 1965 and directed literary programs for the National Endowment for the Arts from 1966 to 1970. While holding these offices, Kizer also published several works of poetry, including a book of translations. Her first two volumes, *The Ungrateful Garden* (1961) and *Knock upon Silence* (1965), are viewed, especially through the lens of her later work, as intent on avoiding overt sentimentality, particularly through the use of formal structures, intricate rhyme schemes and verse patterns, distancing language, and grotesque imagery. Often cited as evidence of this tendency is the poem, "The Intruder" (1961), in which a woman rescues a bat from a cat but drops it after finding lice on the bat's wings: "Turning on the tap, / She washed and washed the pity from her hands." "The Great Blue Heron" (1961) is a reflection on nature's indifference, one of her favorite early themes. Kizer was also concerned with the role of government in people's lives, expressing in such poems as "The Suburbans" (1961) and "The Death of the Public Servant" (1961) a preoccupation with institutions' tendencies to inhibit individuality.

Knock upon Silence (1965) contains what is possibly Kizer's best-known work, "Pro Femina," a long piece written in hexameters that examines women's roles, focusing particularly on the struggles of women artists who, unlike men, have "politely debated" freedom of will, have "howled" for it, and "Howl still, pacing the centuries." The poem, which is continued in several later volumes, examines the expectations of women in the past, including "old maids," "self-pitiers," and "sad sonneteers," and is a testament to women's emerging freedom and to the quality of women's art. Kizer's third work, *Midnight Was My Cry* (1971), contains reprints from her first two books and new poems that focus less on nature and more on the political-social circumstances of the late 1960s. Favorably received, the book's new poems dealt with sit-ins, the assassination of Robert Kennedy, and the war in Vietnam.

Kizer did not publish poetry again until 1984, when two volumes, both dealing with women's experience, appeared. *Yin* contains "Fanny," a fictional diary of Fanny Osbourne Stevenson, the wife of the writer Robert Louis Stevenson, which was later added as a continuation of "Pro Femina," because of its focus on women's creativity. Fanny's role as nursemaid to Robert's talent is offset only by her one creative outlet, her beautiful gardens. The second volume, *Mermaids in the Basement: Poems for Women* (1984), focuses specifically on many of the roles women are forced, and choose, to assume. The volume contains reprints of many of Kizer's older poems dealing with women, including "Pro Femina." A book for men followed shortly after, in 1986. In this work, entitled *The Nearness of You,* Kizer reprinted previously published material and works dedicated to writers and men in her life. All three of these later works are viewed as less formal than her earlier volumes, more personal, and more demonstrative of a mature writer.

BIBLIOGRAPHY

Kizer, Carolyn. *Proses: On Poems and Poets.* Port Townsend, Wash.: Copper Canyon, Press, 1993.

House, Elizabeth B. "Carolyn Kizer." In *Dictionary of Literary Biography.* Vol. 169, *American Poets since World War II, Fifth Series,* edited by Joseph Conte. Detroit: Gale, 1996, pp. 157–164.

Rigsbee, David, ed. *An Answering Music: On the Poetry of Carolyn Kizer.* Boston: Ford-Brown, 1990.

Sharon Barnes

KNIGHT, ETHERIDGE (1931–1991)

A central figure in the BLACK ARTS MOVEMENT, Etheridge Knight's poems at once mix the vernacular with formal rhymes and rhythmical features that, in turn, bear strong political, social, and spiritual content. The influences of Walt Whitman, STERLING BROWN, and GWENDOLYN BROOKS exist in his work. Few poets since EDWIN ARLINGTON ROBINSON and EDGAR LEE MASTERS have so adeptly handled moralist poetic portraiture. As with Robinson, he was a poet of the people, a people's poet. And as both a prodigious formalist and a powerful performer, his work has directly affected subsequent generations—particularly members of the NEW FORMALISM and spoken word artists (see POETRY IN PERFORMANCE).

Knight was born in Corinth, Mississippi, one of seven children. After growing up in Paducah, Kentucky, he entered the United States Army in 1947, served in Korea, where he saw active duty, and was discharged in 1957, at which time he began to travel the United States. Having developed a heroin addiction in the army and being led occasionally to support this addiction by crime, Knight was convicted of robbery and placed in the Indiana State Prison in Indianapolis in 1960. Brooks, having seen Knight's work in journals, visited the prison and encouraged Knight's poetry writing. His first book, *Poems from Prison,* bore a foreword by Brooks and was published in 1968 by Dudley Randall's Broadside Press. Knight served as poet-in-residence at several universities and, in addition to being nominated for the Pulitzer Prize and the National Book Award, received, among many other honors, the American Book Award for his 1987 collection *The Essential Etheridge Knight.*

Just as adept writing a ballad as he was writing haiku, Knight's poems hold unusually vibrant combinations of ideas, stories, fables, honesty, anger, praise, destitution, and hope. Influenced by the African-American genre of the "toast," his poems often sketch humorous caricatures of people he had known. A preternaturally strong performer, Knight often left audiences thunderstruck. ROBERT BLY once wrote, "I believe that Wallace Stevens and Etheridge Knight stand as two poles of North American poetry" (108). But because Knight's poems are so intricate and varied, Bly went on to warn of the mistake of making Stevens out to be the complicated, elegant, indirect, and highly artificed pole and Knight the straightforward, natural, and piercing pole. Knight is simply less of an idealist, more of realist, but equally as crafted and inventive as Stevens.

Knight's elegy for Malcolm X, "For Malcolm, a Year After," is a complex attack upon Euro-American politics and aesthetics. In addition to paying tribute to Malcolm X, the poem stands as both an example and an indictment of the white, prim formalist poem, at once embracing and rebuffing the oppressive political and aesthetic artifice in which and against which Knight himself struggled: "And make it rime and make it prim." Poetry may die, as do people, "But not the memory of him."

BIBLIOGRAPHY

Bly, Robert. "Hearing Etheridge Knight." In *American Poetry: Wildness and Domesticity*. New York: Harper & Row, 1990, pp. 101–108.

Gabriel Gudding

KOCH, KENNETH (1925–2002) Along with FRANK O'HARA, JOHN ASHBERY, JAMES SCHUYLER, and BARBARA GUEST, Kenneth Koch was a central figure of the NEW YORK SCHOOL of poets. The New York poets engaged artistically with so-called action painters (especially the pioneers of ABSTRACT EXPRESSIONISM Jackson Pollock, Willem de Kooning, and Larry Rivers), the European avant-garde in general, and French SURREALISM in particular. They wrote subjectively and autobiographically but rejected CONFESSIONAL POETRY'S extremes. Their philosophy of poetry is as much one of rejection of things others did as it is an embrace of their own traits. They wanted a poetry that was not arrogant, not prophetic, not boring. While all of the New York school are, in the words of Geoff Ward, "expertly addicted to witticisms and poetic comedy" (3), Koch is "the most frantically and farcically humorous of all these poets" (7). His poetry is "characterized by spontaneity, erotic high jinx and pathos . . . balanc[ing] outrageous improvisation, allusive intelligence and a sweetly impersonal lyric" ("Columbian").

Koch was born in Cincinatti, Ohio, and served in the United States Army in the Philippines during World War II. Koch, Ashbery, and O'Hara all studied together at Harvard in the late 1940s before migrating to New York; after earning a bachelor's degree in 1948, Koch completed a master's degree (1953) and a Ph.D. (1959) at Columbia, where he joined the faculty in 1959. Koch's long list of recognitions includes the Inez Boulton Prize (1959), the Frank O'Hara Prize (1973), the American Academy of Arts and Letters Award of Merit (1987), the Fund for Poetry's "Contribution to Poetry Award" (1992), the Ingram-Merrill Foundation's Distinguished Work Award (1992), the Bollingen Prize for poetry (1995), induction into the American Academy of Arts and Letters (1996), and the French government's Chevalier de l'Ordres des Arts et des Lettres (2000).

In Koch's work, Ward writes, "the colour and the facetiousness . . . are characteristic of his activities" (8). For example, in "Variations on a Theme by William Carlos Williams" (1962), Koch playfully parodies Williams's disarming confession and justification for eating some plums (found in Williams's poem "This Is Just To Say" [1934]) by variously admitting that he demolished a woman's house, fractured her leg, squandered her money, and "sprayed [the hollyhocks] with lye. / Forgive me." He does the same thing in parodying ROBERT FROST'S "Mending Wall" (1914) in his own poem "Mending Sump" (1960). His parodies may be ridiculous, but they never ridicule; instead they tease in an affectionate way. Likewise Koch writes about human experience and broken relationships, but the poems are never despondent. Instead he ends "Talking to Patrizia" (1994), his poem about a woman who repeatedly abandons the poem's speaker, with the hopeful cry that if the woman returns, "Late isn't anything!" In 1968 critic Stephen Koch found Kenneth Koch's poems "a kind of word-playground, the component parts . . . always pleasant and tasty; filled with . . circuses, red shimmering fish, . . . chugging rusty ships"; he considered the poet himself to be "sometimes insufferably silly . . [but nevertheless] perhaps the most polished wit writing in English."

In "The Art of Poetry" (1975), Kenneth Koch explained that he wanted readers to be somewhat perplexed at the end of a poem, both "Distressed and illuminated, ready to believe / It is curious to be alive." He accomplishes this in "One Train May Hide Another" (1994) by revealing that what we see always conceals something else. The poem is a list of examples of things that block other things: siblings obscuring lovers, noise masking music, and so on: "always standing in front of something the other / As words stand in front of objects, feelings, and ideas." The truly distressing revelation is that the reader cannot get behind all the unconcealed people and things in order to find all the concealed ones. There is always another concealment behind the enlightenment.

Starting with his first book, *Poems* (1953), Koch published 20 books of poetry. He also published six collections of plays, beginning with *Bertha and Other Plays* (1966), described by Stephen Koch as "delicious little dadaistic farces." Koch's other enterprises include eight prose works, among them a novel (*The Red Robins,* [1975]), a collection of short stories (*Hotel Lambosa and Other Stories* [1993]), and manuals for teaching poetry and poetry writing both to children (*Wishes, Lies and Dreams* [1970] and Rose, *Where Did You Get That Red?* [1973]) and to the elderly and infirm (*I Never Told Anybody* [1977]), an opera libretto for Marcello Panni's *The Banquet* (produced in Bremen, 1998), and art gallery exhibitions, in Ipswich and New York, of collaborations with painters. Koch's late poems are perhaps more reflective and contemplative than his early work, but they nevertheless are examples, as Ken Tucker has observed, of "that mixture of earnestness, ebullience and dreamy romanticism that long ago rendered Koch the ageless grad student of the New York School of Poets."

BIBLIOGRAPHY

"Columbian Wins Bollingen Prize," Columbia University Available online. URL: www.columbia.edu/cu/record/record2017.13.html. Downloaded February 2002.

Diggory, Terence, and Stephen Paul Miller, eds. *The Scene of My Selves: New Work on New York School of Poets.* Orono, Maine: National Poetry Foundation, 2000.

Koch, Stephen. "The New York School of Poets: The Serious at Play," *New York Times* (February 11, 1968). Available online. URL: www.nytimes.com/books. Downloaded March 2007.

Lehman, David. *The Last Avant-Garde: The Making of the New York School of Poets.* New York: Doubleday, 2002.

Tucker, Ken. "You Talking to Me?" *New York Times* (June 4, 2000). Available online. URL: www.nytimes.com. Downloaded March 2007.

Ward, Geoff. *Statutes of Liberty: The New York School of Poets.* New York: St. Martin's Press, 1993.

A. Mary Murphy

KOMUNYAKAA, YUSEF (1947–) Yusef Komunyakaa wears a number of hats: southern poet, African-American poet, wartime veteran poet. Influences on his work include COUNTEE CULLEN, MELVIN TOLSON, AMIRI BARAKA, WILLIAM CARLOS WILLIAMS, and T. S. ELIOT. Komunyakaa's poetry shifts in tone from lyrical and grand to streetwise and tough.

Komunyakaa was born in Bogalusa, Louisiana. After graduating high school in 1965 he enlisted in the army and was sent to Vietnam. Between 1969 and 1970 he started writing for the *Southern Cross,* a military newspaper. He left the military in the early 1970s and was awarded the Bronze Star for his journalism. Upon his return to the states Komunyakaa received a B.A. and an M.A. from the University of Colorado (1975, 1978), and an M.F.A. from the University of California, Irvine (1980). Although he self-published two volumes of poetry in the late 1970s, it was not until the 1980s that he reached a broader audience and critical success. He has received many awards for his poetry, notably the Pulitzer Prize and William Faulkner Prize, both in 1994 for *Neon Vernacular: New and Selected Poems* (1993). He has taught at Princeton University.

Coming from a tight-knit southern family, Komunyakaa draws on his family experiences and regional roots. His combat experiences in Vietnam as well as his interest in jazz and African-American history also feed his unique poetic voice. Komunyakaa's journalistic brevity gives a stoic and clean structure to his subject matter, which is usually emotionally complex. "Seeing in the Dark" (1988) paints a troubled picture of soldiers trapped by their skin color, lower-class status, chauvinism, and a war that they must fight but know so little about. Komunyakaa shows the complex relationship between love, sex, powerlessness, and war: "We're men ready to be fused / with ghost pictures." There is a primal energy intermingled with romanticism as soldiers struggle to reconcile their mortality with their disconnection from their homes and loves. Komunyakaa employs sharp line breaks and brevity of language to illustrate the starkness and confusion of the men.

Komunyakaa focuses on the power of humanity and the excavation of complex emotions and truths. Through his individual quest he ends up revealing the stark and often lonely circumstances of everyday people, while also finding the beauty and passion residing there.

BIBLIOGRAPHY

Komunyakaa, Yusef. "Still Negotiating with the Images: An Interview with Yusef Komunyakaa," by William Baer. *Kenyon Review* 20, nos. 3–4 (summer/fall 1998): 5–29.

Stein, Kevin. "Vietnam and the 'Voice Within': Public and Private History in Yusef Komunyakaa's *Dien Cai Dau*." *Massachusetts Review* 36, no. 4 (winter 1995–1996): 541–561.

Suarez, Ernest. "Yusef Komunyakaa." *Five Points: A Journal of Literature & Art* 4, no. 1 (fall 1998): 15–28.

Arto Payaslian

KOOSER, TED (1939–) One of America's finest poets of ordinary life and daily experience, Ted Kooser has recently enjoyed great prestige after years of being considered simply a regional writer. His poetry arises out of the IMAGIST and DEEP IMAGE traditions of WILLIAM CARLOS WILLIAMS, JAMES WRIGHT, and WILLIAM STAFFORD, particularly Williams's interest in the quotidian (Kooser has identified Williams's fiction collection *In the American Grain* as one of the books that has had the most influence on his work), Wright's occasional surrealism, and Stafford's midwestern landscapes. However, in its interest in the lyric's capacity to narrate resonant scenes or incidents from fictional and semiautobiographical characters' lives, Kooser's work comes closest to the poetic community envisioned in EDGAR LEE MASTERS's *SPOON RIVER ANTHOLOGY*. Unabashedly accessible, but tinged with hints at the mysteries that surround human experience, their "delights and shadows," as his Pulitzer-prize–winning volume is titled, Kooser's poetry represents an important chapter in the history of poetry about ordinary American life.

Born in Ames, Iowa, Kooser received his B.S. from Iowa State in 1962, and later took an M.A. from the University of Nebraska. For many years, he worked with Lincoln Benefit Life, a Nebraska-based life insurance company, which Kooser served as second vice president of marketing retiring in 1999. In 1967, he founded Windflower Press, a hand-letter press dedicated to regional poetry. His poetry has received the NEA fellowship in poetry, the Pushcart Prize, the Stanley Kunitz Prize, The James Boatwright Prize, The Society of Midland Authors Prize (twice), a Merit Award from the Nebraska Arts Council, the 2001 Nebraska Book Award for poetry, and the 2005 Pulitzer Prize for Poetry (for *Delights and Shadows*). In 2004, he was appointed the Library of Congress's 13th poet laureate consultant in poetry. He is a visiting professor in the English department of the University of Nebraska–Lincoln.

In a review of Kooser's poetry, Peter Makuck praises the way Kooser "makes imagistic precision convey setting, feeling, and idea as did Bashō, Issa, and other Japanese poets; and, like them, he makes minimal use of the first-person pronoun, usually surrendering the self to what is seen," also noting that Kooser balances his generally elegiac tone with "just enough comic relief" (500). In "Biker," for instance, Kooser describes a man as "he lifts his scuffed boot and kicks at the air, / and the old dog of inertia gets out of the way." Kooser is drawn to the ordinary objects that fill people's lives, personifying them by focusing on the history of their use; in "Bank Fishing for Bluegills," he describes "an empty aluminum boat / as it drifts at the end of its rope" and likens it to "a fat man / who has fished all day and fallen asleep / and is dreaming of when he was a little boy." Above all, Kooser is a skillful portraitist, conveying the fullness of his characters' lives by the most modest of details. In "Carrie," an elegy for his late aunt, a committed though frustrated housekeeper, Kooser writes that "her rag, like a thunderhead, / scudded across the yellow oak / of her little house." Kooser celebrates her difficult devotion to home, writing that "dust / is her hands and dust her heart. / There's never an end to it." Kooser's poetry honors the profound mystery, sadness, and devotion that lie beneath the lives of the most ordinary Americans.

BIBLIOGRAPHY

Makuck, Peter. "Heartlands." *Hudson Review* 58, no. 3 (2005): 498–506.

Temple Cone

KOSTELANETZ, RICHARD (1940–) Richard Kostelanetz, though best known as a critic of literature and culture in general, is a pioneer in the fields of VISUAL POETRY and infraverbal poetry (poetry in which what happens inside words is crucial); the most impressive examples of his efforts were collected in his 1993 volume, *Wordworks*. His influences range from William Blake to GERTRUDE STEIN, Robert Indiana, and JOHN CAGE. Among the many poets who have learned from his example are John Byrum, Jonathan Brannen, Crag Hill, G. Huth, and Bob Grumman.

Kostelanetz was born in New York City, where he still lives. He has spent his life almost entirely as an unaffiliated scholar/artist, receiving fellowships from the Guggenheim Foundation (1967), the National Endowment for the Arts (1976, 1978, 1979, and 1985), and numerous other sources domestic and foreign.

Kostelanetz is unusual as a poet in that he did not branch out from mainstream into "otherstream" poetry but began as a purely visual poet: His first poem, "Tribute to Henry Ford," which he produced at the age of 27, uses uppercase *Ts* and *As* to stand for the Ford company's early 20th-century Model As and Model Ts to create a three-frame snapshot of part of the history of American automobiles.

Among his best visual poems is "Genesis" (1972), a sequence of eight words, each filling a page. It begins with its title, "GENESIS," in large black print. "LIGHT" follows, in larger letters. They are pedestrianly stenciled but white on a black page. This reversal, coming directly after the title page's black on white, gives them a dazzling effect. Moreover they touch each other, so, at first, they seem a fusion of light, rather than a word. Once recognized as a word, however, they near-perfectly express the fully unified, overflowing, bright hugeness of a universe just begun. The rest of Kostelanetz's sequence unfolds with equal finesse.

Kostelanetz is also well known for such "fusional" infraverbal poems as those he calls "strings," which consist of chains of words, each of them (except the first) incorporating the preceding word's last, last two, last three, last four letters. The result is an often strangely resonant blend. The string-fragment, "ideafencerebrumblendivestablishmentertain," from "String-Five" (1979), bubbles with ideas about things people fence with, have differences over, use to "divest" the establishment, and so forth. Another example of his variety of fusional infraverbal poems is "dmionneeryo" ("Spanglish Interweavings" [1992]), which interweaves the word *money* and its Spanish equivalent, *dinero*, to make a text surprisingly high in appropriate connotations, one, for example having to do with the domineering quality of money. He has been equally adept at making suggestive "fissional" infraverbal poems along the lines of "REVERBERATE" (1992), which takes its title-word through "RE," "EVE," "VERB," "BE," "ERA," and "ATE" back to "REVERBERATE."

Beyond these poems and many others based on other infraverbal tactics, Kostelanetz has been in the vanguard in the making of video poems, sound poems, poetic holograms, and almost every other unconventional poetic form known.

BIBLIOGRAPHY

Grumman, Bob. "Segreceptuality." *American Book Review* 17, no. 1 (September–October 1995): 20.

Kostelanetz, Richard. "Person of Letters in the Contemporary World." In *Contemporary Authors Autobiography Series*. Vol. 8. Detroit: Gale Research, 1988, pp. 179–199.

Parker, Peter, ed. "Richard Kostelanetz." In *The Reader's Guide to Twentieth-Century Writing*. New York: Oxford University Press, 1996, p. 410.

Bob Grumman

KUMIN, MAXINE (1925–) Atypically for her generation, Maxine Kumin eschewed the free verse revolution in favor of a reinterpretation of traditional forms (see PROSODY AND FREE VERSE). Kumin has said that she loves the challenge of meter and rhyme and that the rigidity of a set form is what gives her the permission to tackle emotionally charged or difficult topics (74). According to her, W. H. AUDEN "exerted an intellectual and visceral influence" both "in terms of rhyme and scansion, and his ability to compress those gifts into images, to make a metaphor of a thought" (197–198). Over time Kumin developed a looser music distinctively her own, employing slant rhyme, nonce forms, and a colloquial diction. Her work incorporates autobiography; even so, in her poems, the self is not the focus, but a lens through which to view the world. Accordingly she has never been associated with CONFESSIONAL POETRY, despite her close association with ANNE SEXTON, a poet inextricably linked to that movement. While Kumin insists upon the androgynous nature of writing, issues of gender have unavoidably marked her career. Her 1972 collection begins with a series of poems written in a male persona because, at the time, Kumin feared they would not be taken seriously if written in a female voice, while the opening poem of her 1989 collection reports, "I suffer, the critic proclaims, / from an overabundance of maternal genes" ("Nurture"), a complaint she co-opts by celebrating it.

Maxine Winokur was born in Germantown, Pennsylvania. She graduated from Radcliffe College with a B.A. in history and literature and an M.A. in comparative literature. In 1946 she married Victor Kumin and settled in suburban Boston. In 1957 she signed up for an adult education poetry workshop conducted by John Holmes; other members of that now legendary class included ANNE SEXTON, George Starbuck, and Sam Albert. Kumin's collection of poems, *Up Country* (1972), won the Pulitzer Prize in 1973, while *Looking for Luck* (1991) received both the Poets' Prize (1994) and the Aiken Taylor Award (1995). Some of Kumin's many honors include the Ruth Lilly Award (1999), an American Academy of Arts and Letters Award (1980), a National Council on the Arts Fellowship (1967–68), the Eunice Tietjens Memorial Prize (1972), the Levinson Prize (1986) from *Poetry* magazine, and a fellowship from the Academy of American Poets (1986). In 1981–82, she served as consultant in poetry to the Library of Congress, and she served as poet laureate of New Hampshire from 1989–94. She is a former chancellor of the Academy of American Poets, a post she and CAROLYN KIZER resigned in 1998 to protest the sparse representation of women and people of color on the board of chancellors. In addition to the volumes already mentioned, Kumin has published 12 other collections of poetry, beginning in 1961 with *Halfway*, continuing with *The Privilege* (1965), *The Nightmare Factory* (1970), *House, Bridge, Fountain, Gate* (1975), *The Retrieval System* (1978), *Our Ground Time Here Will Be Brief* (1982), *The Long Approach* (1985), *Connecting the Dots* (1996), *Selected Poems: 1960–1990* (1997), *The Long Marriage* (2001), *Bringing Together: Uncollected Early Poems, 1958–1988* (2003) and *Jack and Other New Poems* (2005). Kumin has also published five novels, a collection of short stories, more than 20 children's books (four coauthored with Anne Sexton), four books of essays, and a memoir, and she has taught at a number of universities, including Tufts, Brandeis, Columbia, and Princeton.

Mortality and the counterbalancing thrust for life are the recurrent themes of Kumin's poetry; Kumin's reexamination of these themes is distinguished by the unsentimental steadiness of her gaze. Sometimes dubbed "Roberta Frost," Kumin does share in common with ROBERT FROST the dedication to form, the New England sensibility, and the use of nature as a subject, but Kumin is no feminine derivative of Frost. Perhaps her most striking difference from Frost is her forthright rejection of transcendence. Nature in a Frost poem is emblematic; the woods he stops in, or in which his roads diverge stand in for something beyond themselves, and they are more a landscape of the mind than an actual landscape (see "The ROAD NOT TAKEN" and "STOPPING BY WOODS ON A SNOWY EVENING"). In Kumin's poems, by contrast, nature is always materially there, even when it additionally performs metaphoric work: "The cats clean themselves after the kill. / A hapless swallow lays another clutch" ("The Green Well" [1992]). In ALICIA OSTRIKER's words, "she employs metaphor not to *elevate* but to *articulate* phenomena—in the double sense of expressing them clearly and showing their connections and conjunctions" (qtd. in Grosholz 81). Connections are vital to Kumin's poems, most especially in her "tribal" *poems* (Kumin's term for her many poems on family) and in her expression of the interconnectedness and interdependence of all aspects of the natural world. Kumin is known for her empathetic and unflinching poetry about animals and for her presentation of the human not in contrast to (and therefore somehow free of) nature but as embedded in and inextricable from nature. As she reminds us in "Territory" (1970), "We are not of it, but in it."

More than one critic has highlighted the connection between Kumin's use of set form and her pervading theme of mortality: As mortality pressures and makes precious the life we do have, so the confines of form compel and energize the poetry. Though most often rooted in the local of her New Hampshire landscape, the topics and concerns of Kumin's poetry are global in scope.

BIBLIOGRAPHY

Davison, Peter. *The Fading Smile: Poets in Boston 1955–1960.* New York: Alfred A. Knopf, 1994.

Grosholz, Emily, ed. *Telling the Barn Swallow: Poets on the Poetry of Maxine Kumin.* Hanover, N.H.: University Press of New England, 1997.

Kumin, Maxine. *Always Beginning.* Port Townshend, Wash.: Copper Canyon Press, 2000.

Ostriker, Alicia. *Stealing the Language: The Emergence of Women's Poetry in America.* Boston: Beacon Press, 1986.

Christine Gelineau

KUNITZ, STANLEY (1905–2006) Stanley Kunitz is an important modernist poet whose acute phrasing, keen observation, and emotional and intellectual power have delighted readers for more than 70 years (see MODERNISM). At age 95 he published his 12th book of poetry, *The Collected Poems* (2000), representing in its 154 poems work originally published from 1930 to 1995. In recognition for his work and a remarkable longevity, he was twice appointed the nation's poet laureate (1974–76 and 2000–01). In continuing to write strongly into his eighth and ninth decades, Kunitz joins poets such as William Butler Yeats, Thomas Hardy, and Czeslaw Milosz. Like Yeats especially, Kunitz as seer writes out of a personal, created mythology, as exemplified in "The Wellfleet Whale" (1984).

Kunitz was born in Worcester, Massachusetts, to Jewish Lithuanian immigrants. His father, Solomon Z. Kunitz, killed himself before Stanley was born, and his mother, Yetta Helen Jasspon Kunitz, worked as a dressmaker. At Harvard University, he earned an A.B. in English in 1926 and an A.M. in English in 1927. From 1928 to the 1970s, he worked for the H.W. Wilson Company in New York City, a publishing house. At the age of 38 he went off to war in the United States Army. Kunitz has won numerous prizes for his work, including the Pulitzer Prize in 1959 for *Selected Poems 1928–1958* (1958), a National Book Award for his collection *Passing Through* (1995), the Bollingen Prize (1987), and the National Medal for the Arts (1993).

Kunitz's metaphysical visions of physical nature are often coupled with concrete images and rendered in a declarative, indicative style. For example, "The Science of the Night" (1953) compresses the scientific history of human origins and its mystery to a few short lines addressed to the speaker's sleeping female companion: "We are not souls but systems, and we move / In clouds of our unknowing." The speaker marvels, watching her, at the "long seduction of the bone" that has led her down through her genetic history to this point. His lover and he had their beginnings, physical and spiritual, in the "big bang" represented by Adam's rib bone, literally the stuff of "planetary dust . . . blowing." The tight layering of thought and allusion is typical of Kunitz, a craftsman who melds scientific ideas and myth in crisp images and syntax. Understanding, faith, and science combine to tell readers a little about who they are and where they came from, but just as physicists calculate humanity's position from the "beginning of things" by measuring the shift of perceived light toward the red end of the spectrum, so too the poet calculates the distances that lie between our observation of and participation in the act of love and our grasp of the wonder of it all. He alludes to the red shift in the spectrum by which we see how the universe expands. Life is short, and the time for enjoying the human touch rapidly diminishes. The final three lines of the poem summarize his argument with a deft allusion to John Donne's "A Valediction: Forbidding Mourning" (1633). The lovers are physically together some of the time but emotionally together always, just as the hands of the clock are always united at its center, and as the stiff twin legs of the compass are united in Donne's poem. This use of another poet's conceit illustrates an important aspect of Kunitz' method. Even more to the point, it illuminates a fundamental attitude, a respect for and mastery of the techniques and concerns of a certain type of poetic ancestor, the metaphysical poet.

The simple rhythms and syntax of the final poem in the *Collected Poems* (2000), "Touch Me," convey poignance as the speaker acknowledges the passage of the years since he was a child, remembering, like Wordsworth, what it was to be a child again kneeling to hear the crickets underfoot and the "music pour / from such a small machine." Desire makes that small machine go. Kunitz combines acute observation with the language of his poetic ancestors and makes it new.

BIBLIOGRAPHY

Duncan, Erika. *Unless Soul Clap Its Hands: Portraits and Passages*. New York: Schocken, 1984.

Moss, Stanley, ed. *A Celebration for Stanley Kunitz on His Eightieth Birthday*. Riverdale-on-Hudson, N.Y.: Sheep Meadow, 1986.

Orr, Gregory. *Stanley Kunitz: An Introduction to the Poetry*. New York: Columbia University Press, 1985.

Theodore C. Humphrey

KYGER, JOANNE (1934–) Often categorized as a BEAT poet, but more closely associated with the SAN FRANCISCO RENAISSANCE, Joanne Kyger emerged as the Beat movement itself was beginning to wane in the 1960s. Like many of the Beats, Kyger draws on an assortment of influences, including Buddhist traditions and practices, American Indian and First Nations teachings, and certain strains of New Age philosophies.

Kyger was born in Vallejo, California. In 1957 she left Santa Barbara for the San Francisco Bay area where the *HOWL* obscenity trials were in full swing. There she met JOHN WIENERS, and, through the weekly writing groups that they hosted, ROBERT DUNCAN and JACK SPICER. In 1959 Kyger moved into the legendary East-West House, a communal living project where PHILIP WHALEN, Lew Welch, and JACK KEROUAC were sporadic residents. It was during this time that Kyger also began sitting with Zen master Shunryu Suzuki Roshi, who had come to teach at the Soto Zen Church. In 1960 Kyger joined GARY SNYDER in Japan, where they were married. Following their divorce in 1964, she returned to the Bay Area and published her first book, *The Tapestry and the Web* (1965). She then briefly lived in New York, returned to the San Francisco area, and moved to Bolinas. Through her involvement with local environmental issues, editing a local newspaper, and being a sitting member of the Ocean Wind Zendo, Kyger has maintained an active presence in the Bolinas community. Since its beginnings in the mid-1970s, she has also taught at the Jack Kerouac School of Disembodied Poetics at the Naropa Institute in Boulder, Colorado, and at the New College of San Francisco.

Overall Kyger's poetry resonates with a Buddhist attentiveness. Direct and immediate, her poems are often likened to snapshots in time exploring the experience of *sunyata*, or "no-self": "I am bereft / I dissolve quickly / I am everybody" ("what i wanted to say" [1978]). Yet the self demands to be understood. "Breakfast" (1978), for instance, details a series of moments through the point of view of a poetic voice that gives way to sliding variables between the pronouns "I," "she," and "them" and ends, "I wouldn't go there, into their / minds. . . . thru the mirror one can she see / pine branches." Kyger is one of American poetry's key innovators. Her poetry is of place and community, and it examines a range of themes from identity and radical ethics to spirituality, personal relationships, and national politics. Above all else Kyger's challenge has been attending to the processes of realizing and directly engaging with conditions of existence, "the broad / sweeping / form of being there" ("what i wanted to say" [1978]), through poetry.

BIBLIOGRAPHY

Russo, Linda, ed. "Joanne Kyger Feature," *Jacket magazine* 11 (2000). Available online. URL: www.jacketmagazine.com/11/index.html. Downloaded December 2003.

———., ed. "Joanne Kyger author page," Electronic Poetry Centre at the State University of New York, Buffalo. Available online. URL: http://epc.buffalo.edu/authors/kyger. Downloaded March 2007.

Tonkinson, Carole, ed. *Big Sky Mind: Buddhism and the Beat Generation*. New York: Riverhead Books, 1995.

Jason Morelyle

L

"THE LADY IN KICKING HORSE RESERVOIR" RICHARD HUGO (1973) As scholar Sanford Pinsker observes, RICHARD HUGO's "The Lady in Kicking Horse Reservoir" may rightly be called a revenge poem (78), though the stark beauty of its northwestern setting suggests an equal focus on the relinquishment of vengeance. Hugo himself said of the poem's origin, "I'd had a love affair. The woman dumped me for someone else. I was brokenhearted and vengeful, but cowardly. So in real life I suffered but in the poem I had my revenge—at least early in the poem" (60). In the opening lines, the speaker makes an apostrophe to a woman drowned in the eponymous reservoir, hoping "each spring / to find you tangled in those pads / pulled not quite loose by the spillway pour." But as Pinsker observers, revenge "cannot reach beyond the wounded self, cannot engage deeper seriousness . . . The problem, then, is to transcend the weight of conditions" (80). The wished-for vengeance is mediated by the landscape (Missoula, Montana, where Hugo taught at the University of Montana), which like the drowned woman's body is suffused with violence and abandonment, yet also offers the possibility of a limited rebirth, for in the final stanza, Hugo writes that "The spillway's open and you spill out / into weather, lover down the bright canal / and mother, irrigating crops."

As with many of Hugo's poems, "Lady in Kicking Horse Reservoir" is written in free verse, with irregularly metered lines and regular eight-line stanzas providing a lyric pattern to balance the poem's plainspoken language. The emotional force of the poem, however, derives from the associative play of alliteration, consonance, and assonance throughout. "Not my hands but green across you now, / Green tons hold you down, and ten bass curve, / teasing in your hair," begins the angry speaker, and the sonic similarities of "Not," "now," "down," "green," "ten," "across," "bass," and "teasing" suggest his unconscious, though not actual, complicity in the woman's death. The tension between vengeance and self-control, the admission that "We still love there in thundering foam / and love," puts this poem, as Michael S. Allen notes, "at the center of Hugo's fear of women and his lifelong fight against regression" (101).

This preoccupation opens one of the poem's central themes: the importance of acknowledging failure and grief as a way of achieving psychological wholeness. In the middle stanzas, the speaker remembers a fight he witnessed between two boys, and after "the slapped boy . . . screamed a single 'stop' / and went down sobbing in the company pond," Hugo recalls how "I swam for him all night . . / No one cared the coward disappeared." Pinsker conjectures that the slapped boy is a figure for Hugo himself (81), which suggests that the speaker is not only struggling with his desire for vengeance upon one woman, but with all forms of vengeance, their causes, their psychological consequences, and the possibility of their nonviolent resolution.

It is worth noting that, though partly autobiographical in origin, Hugo's poem is not CONFESSIONAL but is instead occupied with how the speaker's psychological conflicts work themselves out upon the landscape, which itself embodies the dilemmas besetting the speaker's thoughts. Such psychological projection, which the Victorian author John Ruskin called "the pathetic fallacy," Hugo relates to the idea of a "triggering town," wherein the qualities of a particular setting provide a stage for the psyche to play out its conflicts, obsessions, and dreams. The speaker proves bitter and regretful whenever he discusses love and romance, claiming that "All girls should be nicer" and that "My future / should be full of windy gems," and this preoccupation is manifest in the imagery of loneliness and abandonment that saturates the setting. But the landscape also offers images that suggest anger and violence might be acknowledged and defused, rather than acted on; as Allen notes, "The poem is extraordinary in its working out of male fears and in its attainment of masculine tenderness" (101). When Hugo observes that "The far blur of your bones in May / may be nourished by the snow," he admits the possibility that his earlier coldness has preserved the woman's memory, and when he describes Dollys (a type of trout) "teasing oil from whales," the erotic force of the image suggests the speaker's reconciliation with his lover has been achieved through an acceptance of the passion, now lost, that they once felt.

BIBLIOGRAPHY

Allen, Michael S. *We Are Called Human: The Poetry of Richard Hugo.* Fayetteville: The University of Arkansas Press, 1982.

Hugo, Richard. *The Real West Marginal Way: A Poet's Autobiography,* edited by Ripley S. Hugo, Lois M. Welch, and James Welch. New York: W. W. Norton & Co, 1986.

———. *The Triggering Town: Lectures and Essays on Poetry and Writing.* New York: W. W. Norton & Co., 1979.

Pinsker, Sanford. *Three Pacific Northwest Poets: William Stafford, Richard Hugo, and David Wagoner.* Boston: Twayne Publishers, 1987.

Temple Cone

"LADY LAZARUS" Sylvia Plath (1965) Written in the explosive productivity of the last months of Sylvia Plath's life and published posthumously in *Ariel* (1965), this poem is both a promise and a curse. The poem articulates the furious despair necessary to commit suicide, combining the need to get out of life with the energy to act on that need. In October 1962 Plath's long-term mental illness, which had led to previous suicide attempts, was compounded by her new status as a woman scorned by her estranged husband, British poet Ted Hughes. Her upcoming death is already in process in "Lady Lazarus," and according to the poem "it feels like hell" for Plath and Hughes both. The poem defiantly speaks of suicide as an accomplishment, something the speaker can "manage" once per decade. The physical person is objectified down to its component parts—the teeth, the feet, the skin. This poem speaks of death as performance by inviting an audience and rejects the idea of suicide as defeat. "Lady Lazarus" uses suicide as an aggressive act or threat of violence not directed at the self, but at whomever she deems responsible for abandoning her to it, including the listener/reader.

One of the most controversial elements of the poem is Plath's use of the language of the Holocaust experience in order to find a context miserable enough to explicate her own misery. The issue for critics is not whether she makes effective use of the metaphor, but whether she has the right to use it at all. For some, the fact that Plath was of German ethnicity, not Jewish, and North American, not European, makes her flippant references indecent. For others, those facts of ethnicity and nationality are irrelevant: A poet has the right to employ whatever will express what needs to be expressed. Regardless of her debatable right to do so, Plath draws, less than two decades after World War II, on extremely fresh memories of behaviors and events more horrible than mere imagination can conjure. She makes raw use of raw wounds in a poem that needs to be spoken for the harsh diction and clipped lines to do their angry work.

Plath employs a freak-show motif, a step-right-up bluster addressed to "The peanut-crunching crowd." She thus makes a revealing comment about her personal acquaintances, suggesting that they stand around and watch without intervention, that a woman could strip her body off in public (this is extreme striptease) and the mob simply "shoves" closer for a better view. They may think they are seeing a "walking miracle," but the burden of resurrection—and the cost of the poem—is that the Lazarus, the resurrected one, has to face death again. The jaded voice of Plath's speaker is bitingly resentful about being revived and having to do it again, and when she speaks of the cost of intimacy, "the very large charge" for touching her, she knows the price is for the one touched as much as for the one who touches. The speaker's great desire is to be absent from the body, that organism through which all sensation is experienced. Being alive hurts too much, so the Lady Lazarus keeps her promise that "soon, soon" her flesh will be as dead as she is.

BIBLIOGRAPHY

Britzolakis, Christina. *Sylvia Plath and the Theatre of Mourning.* Oxford: Clarendon Press, 1999.

Gubar, Susan. "Prosopopoeia and Holocaust Poetry in English: Sylvia Plath and Her Contemporaries." *Yale Journal of Criticism* 14, no. 1 (spring 2001): 191–216.

A. Mary Murphy

THE LANGUAGE SCHOOL The writers who emerged in the 1970s and have been identified variously as "Language poets," "*L=A=N=G=U=A=G=E* poets" and "so-called Language poets" generally conceive of themselves less as a movement or school than as a loosely knit community of writers who, with a particular intensity from the mid-1970s to mid-1980s, cultivated their own means of literary production and engaged critically in each others' work. Although a diversity of formal and thematic concerns characterize the writings of BRUCE ANDREWS, CHARLES BERNSTEIN, Tina Darragh, Ray Di Palma, ROBERT GRENIER, CARLA HARRYMAN, LYN HEJINIAN, P. Inman, BOB PERELMAN, RON SILLIMAN, BARRETT WATTEN, and Hannah Weiner (just a few of the many Language writers who could be listed), in general, these writers may be said to view lived experience more as a construction of language than as a transparent reflection of it. Language writing extends the tradition of avant-garde poetry exemplified by Donald Allen's groundbreaking 1960 anthology *New American Poetry: 1945–1960* (see POETRY ANTHOLOGIES), which cast a number of poetic groupings (BLACK MOUNTAIN, NEW YORK SCHOOL, BEATS, SAN FRANCISCO RENAISSANCE) decidedly against the mainstream, or "academic," verse of the time. Language writing also revisits the work of neglected modernists (GERTRUDE STEIN, LOUIS ZUKOFSKY, and Velimir Xlebniko, among others) and is often informed by Russian formalist and French poststructuralist theories of language and ideology. Additionally the civil rights and free speech movements, along with the protests against the U.S. engagement in the Vietnam War, provided a stimulus for many of these writers.

While the Allen anthology delineated the major tendencies in avant-garde poetry for several generations of poets nurtured on modernists, such as EZRA POUND and WILLIAM CARLOS WILLIAMS, other tendencies emerged on the 1960s cultural landscape that Allen could not have anticipated. The work of ROBERT CREELEY and CHARLES OLSON became syntactically freer. TED BERRIGAN led a second generation of New York school poets by using a variety of collage techniques in his *SONNETS* that picked up where JOHN ASHBERY's "Europe" and FRANK O'HARA's "Biotherm" left off. OBJECTIVIST poets from the 1930s either returned to writing poetry (GEORGE OPPEN) or garnered attention after years of neglect (Zukofsky). JEROME ROTHENBERG's anthologies reasserted the importance of neglected modernists and poetries from cultures previously dismissed as "primitive" (see ETHNOPOETICS). Something Else Press, founded by Dick Higgins in the wake of the antiart movement Fluxus, included reprints of important works by Stein (*The Making of Americans* [1966], *Geography and Plays* [1968]), and *Lucy Church Amiably* [1969]) in its catalogue. JOHN CAGE and JACKSON MAC LOW introduced chance-based compositional procedures into music and writing, while performance art (see POETRY IN PERFORMANCE), free jazz, and the feminist and BLACK ARTS MOVEMENTS also began to flourish. Such interests worked their way into POETRY JOURNALS and little magazines, such as *Caterpillar* (edited by CLAYTON ESHLEMAN), *Joglars* (edited by CLARK COOLIDGE and MICHAEL PALMER, immediate precursors of Language writing who have generally distanced themselves from group alignments), and *0 to 9* (edited by Vito Acconci and BERNADETTE MAYER, whose workshops at the St. Mark's Poetry Project in the early 1970s were attended by several Language writers). One issue of *Toothpick, Lisbon and the Orcas Islands,* edited by Andrews and Michael Wiater (fall 1973), contained work by a number of writers who would by the end of the decade be known as "Language poets."

In 1971, Grenier and Watten launched *This* magazine out of Iowa City, home of the country's first creative writing M.F.A. program (the Iowa Writers' Workshop) and thus a mainstream poetry establishment through which a number of avant-garde dissidents had passed. *This* 1 (winter 1971) featured a cluster of review-essays by Grenier, whose declaration "I HATE SPEECH" signaled an all-caps challenge to a projective verse rooted in speech and the breath (see ARS POETICAS), while the issue also contained a homage to the recently deceased Olson. Claiming "I want writing what *is* thought / where *feeling* is / *words are born*" (qtd. in Silliman "American" 497), Grenier proposed a poetry of attention to language less as a way to refer to the world and more as a fact of experience in its own right. He also applied such attention to critical writing: His own review of Stein's *Lectures in America* consisted of 14 quotations from her book, one quotation from Creeley, and only five lines of his own commentary—essentially letting her work speak for itself.

If Grenier's review-essays in *This* 1 assumed a more critical stance than most of that issue's poetry, language-centered poetries were nonetheless united with the first critical assessment of the writing in "The Dwelling Place: 9 Poets," a special section Silliman edited in 1973 for *Alcheringa*. Rothenberg, who coedited this ethnopoetics journal with Dennis Tedlock, first put Silliman in touch with Andrews and Bernstein in the early 1970s. This mini-anthology presented writing by Andrews, Barbara Baracks, Coolidge, Lee DeJasu, DiPalma, Grenier, David Melnick, Silliman himself, and Watten. "What connects these writers," Silliman states, is "a community of concern for language as the center of whatever activity poems might be" (Silliman "Dwelling," 118). The exemplary work of Coolidge and Grenier, Silliman argues, "goes after a direct confrontation with language, words," such that "neither the words nor the processes of the poem . . point out or away from the poem itself" (118). Citing Creeley's claim (as Grenier had earlier) that "poems are not referential, or at least not importantly so," Silliman emphasizes that "words are not, finally, nonreferential"; rather, these writers are interested in "diminish[ing] the reference," "the creation of non-referring structures," the "disruption of context," or "forcing the meanings in upon themselves until they cancel out or melt" (118).

By 1977 a Marxist political orientation (certainly manifested in private discussions and correspondence before this time) was added to the focus on language itself. Steve McCaffery gathered essays by Andrews, Bernstein, Silliman, and himself in a forum on "The Politics of the Referent" for Frank Davey's Toronto journal *Open Letter* (summer 1977). For McCaffery the referential aspect of the linguistic sign (that is, that the particular word refers to a particular object or concept) is linked to Karl Marx's critique of the commodity fetish: The meaning of words becomes a product that language users consume naively or in bad faith. Writing that thwarts conventional meaning-making processes thus critiques such consumption, turning the reader from a passive consumer of meaning into an active producer of meaning. Another of Silliman's essays from 1977, "Disappearance of the Word, Appearance of the World," extends this critique of reference to the broader historical development of language use under capitalism.

Many Language writers had also by this time converged geographically around key poetry journals and POETRY PRESSES. Perelman and Watten moved to the San Francisco Bay area by 1974 (bringing with them the magazines *Hills* and *This*, respectively), where Watten's college friend Silliman (who had been editing *Tottel's* since 1970) had joined forces with Yale friends Steve Benson and KIT ROBINSON. The latter's one-shot magazine *Streets and Roads*, 1974, contained work by many of these writers. Shortly thereafter Watten began a reading series at the Grand Piano, a café on Haight Street in San Francisco, and Perelman began a series of poet's talks in his Folsom Street loft. Geoffrey Young and Laura Chester began their press, the Figures, in 1975, and Hejinian began her Tuumba letterpress chapbook series the following year. Each press had nearly 20 titles in its catalogue by the end of 1978, while Watten added nearly a dozen titles under his This Press imprint. Meanwhile a number of writers had arrived in New York City since 1975: Andrews and Lally from a fledgling Baltimore–Washington, D.C., poetry scene, Bernstein (returning) from the West Coast, DiPalma from Iowa City via Ohio. Bernstein began a reading series with Ted Greenwald at Greenwich Village's Ear Inn in 1978, the same year he and Andrews began the journal that would soon name this burgeoning activity.

L=A=N=G=U=A=G=E ran for only four years (1978–81) but served in that time as a clearinghouse of information on writing from both coasts. *L=A=N=G=U=A=G=E* published no poetry per se. Instead a typical issue might have contained a forum on one or two poets or topics, review pieces on new works that typically eschewed evaluation and became new works in their own right, and bibliographies or excerpts from a wide disciplinary range of recent journals. Although many of the publications reviewed in *L=A=N=G=U=A=G=E* were hard to obtain even then, the editors offered readers photocopies at cost. With more than 100 contributors, little aesthetic or political consensus resulted. At times lively debates emerged over the value of nonevaluative reviews, the merits of Cage and the artist Marcel Duchamp, and the efficacy of anarchism and Marxism. Nevertheless the magazine gave an appearance of coherence to the group and thus a point of entry for its critics.

The May 1979 issue of the Bay Area newsletter *Poetry Flash* ran a feature on "*L=A=N=G=U=A=G=E* Poetry" that, in part, charged the group with being overly theoretical, willfully obscure, dogmatic, and elitist. Silliman often became chief defender of the group—and not just in *Poetry Flash.* In the preface to "Realism: An Anthology of 'Language' Poets" in *Ironwood* 20 (1982), Silliman recalled the history of language-centered writing, enumerated the various publications and other activities of the group, outlined the changed circumstances of avant-garde poetry since the 1960s and the shortcomings of the New American poetry, and emphasized the importance of readership, audience, and community. Soon other widely circulated journals began publishing collections of Language writing. Bernstein edited a 50-page "Language Sampler" for the *Paris Review* (issue 86 [1982]) and a 100-page feature of "43 Poets" for *boundary* 2 (volume 14 [1985/6]), while JOAN RETALLACK contributed an omnibus review of recent Language publications to *Parnassus* (volume 12 [1984]). These journals appealed to broadly literary and academic readerships and helped Language writing reach new audiences.

Silliman expanded upon his *Ironwood* defense in the preface to *In the American Tree* (1986). At more than 600 pages, this recently reprinted (2001) anthology remains the most comprehensive primary source for Language writing, even while Silliman lists, beyond the 40 writers it includes, more than 70 additional writers from whom "an anthology of comparable worth" could be drawn (xx). A year later Douglas Messerli edited the shorter *"Language" Poetries* anthology for New Directions, giving the group its first book-length presentation via a trade publisher with ties to the historic avant-garde of Pound and Williams. These two anthologies sparked a new round of debates, which, by this point, included important academic critics, including Jerome McGann and Marjorie Perloff. The mid-1980s also witnessed the appearance of essay collections by Bernstein (*Content's Dream* [1986]), Perelman (*Writing/Talks* [1985]), Silliman (*The New Sentence* [1987]), and Watten (*Total Syntax* [1984]).

Many Language writers continue working today, although the intense group activity has subsided. Perelman's *The Marginalization of Poetry* has begun the process of writing the history of Language writing; a similar activity has taken place in another form, an online collaborative work called "the Grand Piano" (after Watten's reading venue) by nine members of the Bay Area group. Ann Vickery has demonstrated how many of the issues confronted by Language writing were framed quite differently for women associated with the movement. Bernstein, Perelman, and Watten have obtained tenure-track positions in university English departments, spurring some (including Silliman) to suggest that the original antiacademic stance of the group has thus been compromised. At the same time a younger generation of writers has emerged, in some cases out of the very M.F.A. system Language writing rejected. While their work furthers some avenues of investigation opened up by Language writing, these younger writers are less inclined toward polemic.

BIBLIOGRAPHY

Andrews, Bruce, and Charles Bernstein, eds. *The L=A=N=G=U=A=G=E Book.* Carbondale: Southern Illinois University Press, 1984.

Kim, Eleana. "Language Poetry," Readme. Available online. URL: http://hone.jps.net/~nada/issuefour.htm. Downloaded December 2003.
Messerli, Douglas, ed. *"Language" Poetries*. New York: New Directions, 1987.
Perelman, Bob. *The Marginalization of Poetry: Language Writing and Literary History*. Princeton, N.J.: Princeton University Press, 1996.
Silliman, Ron, ed. "The Dwelling Place: 9 Poets." *Alcheringa* 1, no. 2 (1975): 104–120.
———. *In the American Tree*. 1986. Reprint, Orono, Maine: National Poetry Foundation, 2001.
Vickery, Ann. *Leaving Lines of Gender: A Feminist Genealogy of Language Writing*. Hanover, N.H.: Wesleyan University Press, 2000.

Tom Orange

LANSING, GERRIT (1928–2003) Gerrit Lansing's poetics are grounded in notions of gnosis, magic, and transcendence. For Lansing poetry is potentially alchemical, magically transformative, releasing the self from convention into rapture. He is a difficult poet; critics and peers place his work among the most ambitious and engaging of our time. "The writing/riting of poetry is for Lansing a testing of the human imagination against the creative and destructive powers of nature and the universe," writes critic Robert Baker. "It is the most serious of games and should only be played by those who would risk everything, but for those, there are worlds to gain." Lansing has been associated with poets of the Boston Renaissance—ROBIN BLASER, JOHN WEINERS, Stephen Jonas, and others who lived in or near that city in the 1950s and 1960s. ROBERT LOWELL, SYLVIA PLATH, and other CONFESSIONAL writers dominated Boston's poetry landscape at this time, and Lansing and his associates, some of whom were, like him, much influenced by CHARLES OLSON, explored forms of LYRIC POETRY less impregnated with Freudian notions than the work of writers like Lowell.

Descended from old Dutch and English colonial stock, Lansing was reared in a small town near Cleveland, Ohio. He graduated from Harvard in 1949 and received an M.A. from Columbia in 1955. He worked in publishing and bookselling.

Lansing edited two issues of a POETRY JOURNAL, *SET*, in 1961 and 1963. His poetry was collected in *The Heavenly Tree Grows Downward* (1977) and in *Heavenly Tree / Soluble Forest* (1995). Poems in the first book appear in a different order in the second, reflecting his belief that his book (both collections are versions of a single work) evolves into a new form as new poems emerge. He contributed *Analytic Psychology* (1983) to *The Curriculum of the Soul*, a series of short books by poets following a series of subjects outlined by Olson. As "The Soluble Forest," that book now forms the concluding section of *Heavenly Tree / Soluble Forest*. Lansing also collaborated with artists Nora Ligorano and Marshall Reese on *On the Book* (2002).

Much of Lansing's work is overtly sexual: "When then love takes you in hand," he writes in "An Inlet of Reality, or Soul" (1977), "you don't languish in the clover / but make song." His ideal is Walt Whitman's world of "comrades," a world of solitary individuals drawn together in a vortex of joy: "Sex on earth," he claims in "Stanzas of Hyparxis" (1977), "is rhymed angelic motion."

Lansing's poetic project—the gradual unfolding of a magical poetic vision of transformation and transcendence—brought him considerable respect among fellow poets. He is, said ROBERT KELLY, in a blurb on *Heavenly Tree / Soluble Forest*, "the most learned among us, and the most fun."

BIBLIOGRAPHY

Baker, Robert. "The Metaphysics of Gerrit Lansing." *Rain Taxi Online* 23 (fall 2001). Available online. URL: www.raintaxi.com/online/2001fall/lansing.shtml. Downloaded March 2007.
Foster, Edward, ed. *Talisman: A Journal of Contemporary Poetry and Poetics* 15 (winter 1995/96). [The Gerrit Lansing Issue]

Edward Foster

LAST POETS, THE This innovative group of African-American poets exemplifies an African oral tradition in the United States that is particularly a part of African-American poetry (see BLACK ARTS MOVEMENT and HARLEM RENAISSANCE). The group formed on May 19, 1968, at a celebration honoring Malcolm X's birthday in Marcus Garvey Park in Harlem. Original members included Gylan Kain, Abiodun Oyewole, David Nelson, and conga player Nilija. During the 1970s the number of members swelled to include Felipe Luciano, Umar Bin Hassan, Jalal Nurridin, and Suliaman El Hadi. Although the Last Poets were not officially connected to the Black Arts movement, AMIRI BARAKA describes the impetus behind their verse as the same: "Our art describes our past, the middle passage, Slavery, the struggle of the Afro-American Nation! For Democracy, Self-Determination, and the destruction of national oppression and capitalism" (xiii).

Using the rhythm of the conga drum in a "call and response" to emphatic vocal expression, the Last Poets brought poetry to the streets, capturing the attention of large numbers of people uninterested in more traditional forms of poetry. The group focused on black experiences and aimed candid, metaphoric political messages and historical accounts of African-American experiences at a black audience.

Through their art these poets attempted to create a collective consciousness among blacks by directly interpreting the social injustices in their lives and laying the blame at the door of the white power structure. One of the most caustic examples is Jalal Nuriddin's "The White Man's Got a God Complex" (1971), a poem focused on American imperialism, oppression, and white supremacy, in which the killing of various groups ("Indians," "Japanese," "black people") is summed up with this pronouncement: "Enslaving the earth I'm God! / Done went to the moon I'm God!"

The hope for social change was the force behind much of the poetry. Nonetheless the Last Poets did not limit their criticism to the white power structure. They struck blows with their poetic accounts of the effects of drug use with poems such as "Jones Coming Down" (1970), which describes in horrid detail the force of addiction. Using the word *jones* as a euphemism for drug habit, the poem indicts the motivation that propels so many poor, disadvantaged youth into this temporary escape from the blighted conditions of their experiences.

Their early repertoire also included tributes to legendary jazz musicians, such as Charlie Parker, and poetry dedicated to ancestors, black women, black people in general, and the African heritage of African Americans. According to the biographer Kim Green, the Last Poets' mission "is to enlighten you with poems that give Black people roots, purpose, and a beginning other than slavery and shame" (xxix).

The Last Poets, hailed as the forerunners of present-day rap artists, continue to perform.

BIBLIOGRAPHY

Baraka, Amiri. Foreword to *On a Mission,* by Oyewole, Abiodun, and Umar Bin Hassan. New York: Henry Holt, 1996.

Green, Kim. Introduction to *On a Mission.* Oyewole, Abiodum, and Umar Bin Hasson. New York: Henry Holt, 1996.

Nuriddin, Jalal, and Suliaman El Hadi. *The Last Poets. Vibes from the Scribes: Selected Poems.* New Jersey: Africa World Press, 1992.

Judy Massey Dozier

LAUTERBACH, ANN (1942–) Since the mid-1970s Ann Lauterbach has been writing philosophical poetry that explores language's relationship to the tensions between presence and absence, continuity and discontinuity, as well as voice and silence. Her meditative style and intellectual content affiliate her with other discursive poets, such as WALLACE STEVENS and NEW YORK SCHOOL poet JOHN ASHBERY, and her formal and linguistic experimentation suggest the influence of the LANGUAGE poets. Lauterbach also cites Emily Dickinson, GERTRUDE STEIN, and SYLVIA PLATH as relevant feminist precursors to her own poetry (see FEMALE VOICE, FEMALE LANGUAGE).

Born and raised in New York City, Lauterbach completed graduate work at Columbia University in 1967. She spent the next seven years working as an editor at the publisher Thames and Hudson in London before returning to New York, where she directed art galleries in the mid-1970s. Lauterbach has published seven books of poetry, the first, *Many Times, But Then* (1979), and the most recent *Hum* (2005), the title poem of which addresses the 9/11 attacks, using the refrain "The days are beautiful. / The towers are yesterday." She has taught at Bard College and, among her other honors and awards, she received a MacArthur grant in 1993.

For Lauterbach language's ability (or lack thereof) to mediate the contradictions of human experience is responsible for constituting the individual's relationship to notions of truth and reality. She has written, in

"On Memory" (1990), that words "release things from the temporal and spatial settings in the real" (520). At the same time, however, "Words are how we own our knowledge of the now" (521). Thus Lauterbach's poetry goes beyond the mere ungrounding of reality to identify a new kind of knowledge that is actually grounded in the transient and uprooting character of language.

Lauterbach employs three interrelated techniques to walk this delicate line between grounding and uprooting: She foregrounds the importance of prepositions and conjunctions, she uses abstraction to generalize her text so as to require completion by the reader, and she treats form as its own meaning-making device, not merely as an extension of content. All three devices present old relations in new ways and imagine new forms of relation.

These lines from "The Prior" in *And For Example* (1994) demonstrate Lauterbach forging new relations through slippages and abstractions of meaning: "What is it based on what pleasure / what lost in what of your own making—." Not only do the "what's" in these lines lack a clear reference within the poem, they also function simultaneously as both questions and nouns. Furthermore the prepositions multiply the syntactic possibilities of the sentence, forcing the reader to hear both "What is it based on?" and "On what pleasure?" Such referential and syntactic ambiguities make Lauterbach's work a poetry of possibility that demands keen attention and full participation.

BIBLIOGRAPHY

Lauterbach, Ann. "Ann Lauterbach: An Interview," by Molly Bendall. *American Poetry Review* 21, no. 3 (1992): 19–25.

———. "On Memory." In *Conversant Essays: Contemporary Poets on Poetry,* edited by James McCorkle, 519–524. Detroit: Wayne State University Press, 1990.

Schultz, Susan. "Visions of Silence in Poems of Ann Lauterbach and Charles Bernstein." *Talisman* 13 (1994–5): 163–177.

Mitchum Huehls

LEE, LI-YOUNG (1957–) Li-Young Lee asserts that "poetry comes out of a need to somehow—in language—connect with universe mind . . . a mind [he] would describe as a 360-degree seeing" (qtd. in Marshall 130). Lee, a "sound-conscious poet," in Chitra Divakaruni's words, uses a variety of poetic forms in order to hear the frequency under language and seeks "a kind of musical inevitability . . . the way the poems open, the way they disclose themselves" (qtd. in Miller 36). Lee's writing, greatly influenced by teacher and poet GERALD STERN, captures a fragmentary 20th-century aesthetic that derives from memories of displacement, while it also sustains an undertone of spirituality that hearkens back to John Donne, Walt Whitman, and T. S. ELIOT, among others.

Born in Djakarta, Indonesia, of Chinese parents, Lee's childhood was a series of flights and losses. His father—a physician to Mao Tse-tung, as well as a preacher, a university professor, and a political prisoner of Sukarno in Indonesia—fled Indonesia in 1959 with his family to Hong Kong, Macao, Japan, and, finally, to the United States, settling in the Midwest, where he continued to preach as a Presbyterian minister. His mother is a granddaughter of Yuan Shih-kai, a warlord and president of the Republic of China. This remarkable personal and familial history finds itself embedded in Lee's three works of poetry, *Rose* (1986), *The City in which I Love You* (1990), and *Book of My Nights* (2001) and his memoir, *The Winged Seed* (1995). Lee's several honors include New York University's DELMORE SCHWARTZ Memorial Poetry Award (1989) for *Rose,* the Lamont Poetry Selection (1990) for *The City in which I Love You,* and a fellowship from the Academy of American Poets for distinguished poetic achievement (2003).

The search for intention and awareness is common to all of Lee's work, as he draws attention to the universal through the particular, focusing on the figure of his father to mediate these connections. A rose, for example, acts as the central metaphor—a delicate symbol of endurance—that personifies a chorus of family voices in the eponymous poem in *Rose.* In *The City in which I Love You* Lee invokes the Bible's "Song of Songs" (Song of Solomon) to connect the secular with the sacred, the mythical/archetypal with the practical, the ordinary with the rare: "All are beautiful by variety" ("The Cleaving"). In *The Winged Seed,* Lee shapes his family's plight as exiles into a surreal narrative that highlights an endless, immediate present that contrasts memory and history. Lee's allegiance to the familial and the spiritual manifests itself in all of his writings.

Lee's poetic and prose styles demonstrate aesthetic thinking combined with ethical, moral gestures that rise above the cultural and the ideological. For Lee the mission of poets is to witness the invisible, as Tod Marshall writes, "making it revealed in the visible so that everybody can line up and know what they're lining up with . . . lining up with the cosmos that they are" (146).

BIBLIOGRAPHY

Marshall, Tod. "To Witness the Invisible: A Talk with Li-Young Lee." *Kenyon Review* 22, no. 1 (winter 2001): 129–147.

Miller, Matt. "Darkness Visible: Li-Young Lee Lights up His Family's Murky Past with Poetry." *Far Eastern Economic Review* 159, no. 22 (May 30, 1996): 34–36.

Marie-Therese C. Sulit

LEHMAN, DAVID (1948–) A New Yorker by birth, residence, and sensibility, David Lehman is most often associated with the NEW YORK SCHOOL of poets, whose lives and work he has chronicled in books and essays. His poetry evokes the irony and wit of that earlier generation, but it more directly engages the immediacies of everyday life in a media-saturated, technological society where values and relationships grow ever more complex and difficult to articulate. Praised by critic Robert Schultz for his "associative exuberance" and "ear for the jargons which exhibit contemporary truth and folly" (508), Lehman attempts to balance formal stylistic concerns against an impulse toward spontaneity.

The son of Jewish refugees from Nazi-controlled Europe, Lehman was raised in upper Manhattan. He holds advanced degrees from Cambridge and from Columbia University, where he studied with KENNETH KOCH. He has held teaching positions at Cornell, Hamilton, Wells, and the New School University. Among his awards are fellowships from the National Endowment for the Arts (1987) and the Guggenheim Foundation (1989). Series editor of the *Best American Poetry* annual, Lehman has published seven volumes of poetry, including *An Alternative to Speech* (1986), *Operation Memory* (1990), *Valentine Place* (1996), and *The Evening Sun* (2002).

For all their cleverness and wordplay, Lehman's earlier poems address serious matters, such as the Holocaust, the Vietnam War, and the dynamics of love and marriage, often at length, and frequently contained within elaborate variations on received forms, including villanelles, pantoums, and sestinas (see PROSODY AND FREE VERSE). Margaret Holley discerns a distance between the poet and his subjects and states that "this poetry of ultimate seriousness is heavily laced with insouciance" (152), while Wesley McNair observes that the poet's polished craft is nonetheless tuned to "the continual transition and perplexities of postmodern experience" (677).

Inspired by the *LUNCH POEMS* of FRANK O'HARA, Lehman began keeping a daily journal in verse to capture authentically life's quotidian flux, a project that resulted in *The Daily Mirror* (2000) and continued through *The Evening Sun,* in which he writes "I'm taking jazz as / a second language" ("March 23"), and indeed the work exudes jazz's improvisational spirit. The gravity in any given poem can shift from light to heavy in the space of a pun, as when a satirically depicted married couple must ruminate on their estranged condition for hours "before the remorse code / is deciphered, repealed" ("January 12").

Less formally constrained and more overtly personal than their predecessors, these poems casually allude to friends, family, popular music, films, and sports, creating a singular tapestry that vibrantly depicts the idiosyncrasies and contradictions of American life.

BIBLIOGRAPHY

Holley, Margaret. "Myth in Our Midst: The Multiple Worlds of the Lyric." *Michigan Quarterly Review* 32, no. 1 (winter 1993): 150–164.

McNair, Wesley. "Craft and Technique: Four Poets." *Michigan Quarterly Review* 36, no. 4 (fall 1997): 668–682.

Schultz, Robert. "One Retrospective, Four Sequels, and Three Debuts." *Hudson Review* 49, no. 3 (autumn 1996): 503–520.

Fred Muratori

LEITHAUSER, BRAD (1953–) The primary feature of Brad Leithauser's poems is a passion for prosodic experimentation (see PROSODY AND FREE VERSE), and he has lamented what he sees as a decline in "metrical literacy" in American poetry of the last several decades (41). His writing, in which the influences of such poets as DONALD HALL, ROBERT LOWELL, and ELIZABETH BISHOP, as well as Gerard Manly Hopkins and A. E. Housman, may be discerned, displays formal mastery and a meticulous attention to form's possibilities, particularly how form relates to intonation and the sounds and cadences of spoken language.

Leithauser was born in Detroit, Michigan. He graduated from Harvard College and Harvard Law School, and he has written six novels as well as four volumes of poetry and a book of essays. He is editor of the *Norton Anthology of Ghost Stories.* Among the many awards and honors he has received is a MacArthur Fellowship (1983). He has taught at Mount Holyoke College.

An expansive poet who often finds metaphors in mathematics and natural science and rhythms in everything from common speech to songs by George Gershwin, Leithauser writes with a wonderful combination of scholarship, a microscopic eye for detail, and a gentle but incisive sense of humor. A sensuous, naturalistic, frequently pastoral imagery is typical of his poems. In his poem "Small Waterfall" (1998), for instance, he neatly conveys the sense of a little waterfall with short phrases that tumble one into the next, breaking off in midstream and regathering, with rhymes splashed throughout to bring continuity and likeness to the lines, as in: "stumbling on this small, all-but-forest-swallowed waterfall." The poem also exemplifies his interest in correlating natural images and phenomena with the psychic "landscapes" of people, as it goes on to liken the waterfall to his wife, the poet MARY JO SALTER, to whom the poem is addressed, calling both cataract and woman "a thing that flows and goes / and stays, self-propelled and -replacing."

In "Plus the Fact of You" (1995), a seamless interchange of personal and environmental details again creates a sense of the sensuous and the cerebral as interchangeable, as the poem's speaker muses sleepily on a day of hiking and wonders, "Why at night do numbers clamor so," as he finds himself counting his partner's breaths. This interplay, as much as his tireless attention to meter and intonation, is at the heart of what makes Leithauser's work inventive and captivating. Leithauser proves that careful attention to form can liberate and give substance to an image or idea; his poems reveal a genuine delight in images and the tireless connections the mind makes among them.

BIBLIOGRAPHY

Gwynn, R. S. "A Field Guide to Poetics of the '90s," Expansive Poetry and Music Online. Available online. URL: http://home.earthlink.net/~arthur505/cult1096.html. Downloaded March 2007.

Leithauser, Brad. "Metrical Illiteracy." *New Criterion* 1, no. 5 (January 1983): 41–46.

Amy Glynn Greacen

LEVERTOV, DENISE (1923–1997) Denise Levertov is considered a member of the BLACK MOUNTAIN SCHOOL of poets, even though she never attended the college. Her friends CHARLES OLSON, ROBERT CREELEY, and ROBERT DUNCAN influenced her work, but it is WILLIAM CARLOS WILLIAMS whom she most closely followed formally. Her poetry combines public and private experience, dealing with private issues, such as love, solitude, divorce, marriage, and motherhood, as well as with some of the major public events of her times, including the Vietnam and Gulf Wars, nuclear proliferation, environmental degradation, and AIDS. Often praised as a master of free verse (see PROSODY AND FREE VERSE), she stressed the role of craft in poetry, and many of her essays, such as "Some Notes on Organic Form," first published in 1965, have become classics of contemporary poetic theory. Although her poetic voice is simple, it relies on concrete images and clear language to provide insight into everyday experience.

Levertov, originally spelled Levertoff, was born in Ilford, Essex, England. She was the daughter of a Russian Jew who converted to become an Anglican priest. Raised in a bookish home, she was educated privately. Her mother read 19th-century novels and poetry to her, and her father provided her with a religious education. Levertov's desire to become a poet came early. At age 12 she sent T. S. ELIOT several of her poems, and she received from a him a two-page letter of encouragement. During World War II she was a nurse in London, and soon afterward she married the American writer Mitchell Goodman and had a son. Goodman introduced her to Creeley, and she soon came to know Olson, Duncan, and Williams. In 1948 she immigrated to the United States, and by 1955, when she became a U.S. citizen, her poetic style had become Americanized. She served as the poetry editor for the *Nation* (1961, 1963–65) and *Mother Jones* (1975–78), and she also taught creative writing at, among other schools, Drew University, Vassar College, University of California, Berkeley, and Stanford University. Among her awards are the Lenore Marshall Poetry Prize (1976) and the Shelley Memorial Award from the Poetry Society of America (1984). Along with being a poet, an essayist, and editor, she translated works from French and Spanish and was active in political protest.

Her first book, *Double Image* (1946), was published in London and provides an example of the neoromantic tendencies of English poetry of its period. Levertov is remembered primarily for her American works, starting with *Here and Now* (1957) and *Overland to the Islands* (1958). These works contain tightly crafted lyrics that display most of her major themes: love, mysticism, marriage, imagination, inspiration, the poet's craft, and solitude. In many of the poems, she presents domestic situations through fresh viewpoints. For example, in "The Gypsy's Window" (1957), she presents plates, paper roses, and a vase as places where there is "the chance of poetry." Also in these early volumes she presents her concerns with religion. In the tradition of Walt Whitman and Ralph Waldo Emerson, she presents religious ideas through her personal experience. In her early works she displays an agnostic worldview, portraying her mystic visions often through nature or her ancestors. For example, in "Illustrious Ancestors" (1958), she mentions "Angel Jones of Mold, whose meditations / were sewn into coats and britches." Angel Jones, a tailor, connects to the divine through daily events and through physical touch, just as Levertov wishes to do through her poetry. Throughout her work Levertov tied her personal experience closely to the poem's formal qualities, since she believed that form is an expression of perception. In "Some Notes on Organic Form," she states that the poet is *"brought to speech"* by an experience (68), which brings the words of the poem as a perception: "the metric movement, the measure, is the direct expression of the movement of perception" (71).

By the late 1960s Levertov became concerned with the Vietnam War. She wrote poetry, was active in protests, and even traveled to Vietnam along with MURIEL RUKEYSER to present the voice of a writer against the war. Many contemporary critics condemned her work during this period as overly polemical. Even some of her most supportive critical allies, such as Marjorie Perloff, questioned her work. In "Poetry, Prophecy, and Survival," Levertov argues that poetry must deal with the horrors of the period, because the imagination makes the events understandable: "The intellect by itself may point out the source of suffering; but the imagination illuminates it; by that light it becomes more comprehensible" (145). Even in her war poetry, Levertov addresses public experiences through personal perceptions. For example, in "Life at War" (1967), she speaks about her experience of Vietnam: "We have breathed the grits of it in, all our lives, / our lungs are pocked with it." She stresses the personal effect of the war on her and on her imagination. Although her volume *Footprints* (1972) marked a turn away from political poetry as a primary concern, she continued to provide a poetry of witness for the rest of her life, writing about such subjects as El Salvador, the Gulf War, and the nuclear arms race.

With her collections after the Vietnam War, such as *Life in the Forest* (1975), *Candles in Babylon* (1978), *Oblique Prayers* (1981), and *Breathing the Water* (1984), Levertov returned to many of her earlier themes but with looser forms. Through close perception of daily experiences, her later work provides insight into the importance of such acts, but it also presents the mystery inherent within objects. The poet finds God in everyday experience and objects, as in "The Task" (1981): "God's in the wilderness next door / —that huge tundra room, no walls and a sky roof." In these collections Levertov also discusses the importance of inspiration. In "A Poet's View" (1984), she states that to believe in inspiration "is to live with a door of one's life open to the transcendent. . . . The concept of 'inspiration' presupposes a power which enters the individual and is not a personal attribute" (241). These collections contain various explorations of religious belief and doubt, and they point to the major concerns of her later poetry.

Evening Train (1990) signals her last period, in which her work is permeated by Christianity and nature. After becoming a Christian in the 1980s, Levertov explored her preoccupation with religion through prominent Christian figures, such as Caedmon, Saint Peter, Saint Julian, and Saint Thomas Didymus. In "Candlemas" she presents Simeon's experiences: "Simeon opened / ancient arms / to infant light." In this poem Levertov portrays, as she often does in her later poems, the importance of faith and revelation, which she ties to poetic inspiration. Frequently, in her later poems, she explores the mystery of everyday experience, and she also discusses the relation between humans and nature. Much like the British romantic poets William Wordsworth and Samuel Taylor Coleridge, she presents nature as something almost imperceptible that changes us slightly for the better: she attempts to describe this process of betterment.

Ultimately Levertov's poetry is one of communion and witness—to contemporary atrocities and to the divine. Through witness she reminds us what it means to be human; moreover, her close examination of the details of life's pains, successes, beauties, and mysteries point toward an understanding of and provide means of coping with the complexity of life.

BIBLIOGRAPHY

Colclough Little, Anne, and Susie Paul, eds. *Denise Levertov: New Perspectives.* West Cornwall, Conn.: Locust Hill Press, 2000.

Gelpi, Albert, ed. *Denise Levertov: Selected Criticism.* Ann Arbor: University of Michigan Press, 1993.

Levertov, Denise. "A Poet's View." *New & Selected Essays.* New York: New Directions, 1992, pp. 239–246.

———. "Poetry, Prophecy, Survival." *New & Selected Essays.* New York: New Directions, 1992, pp. 143–153.

———. "Some Notes on Organic Form." *New & Selected Essays.* New York: New Directions, 1992, pp. 67–73.

Marten, Harry. *Understanding Denise Levertov.* Columbia: University of South Carolina Press, 1988.

Wagner-Martin, Linda. *Denise Levertov.* New York: Twayne, 1967.

William Allegrezza

LEVINE, PHILIP (1928–) Philip Levine's best-known poetry deals with working-class themes in an industrial setting, frequently the Detroit of his upbringing. Yet, because Levine's verse honors the endurance of the human spirit in the midst of harsh exterior conditions, he could best be described as a poet of humanity in general, endowing the silenced with voices that transcend material circumstance. Influenced by the expansive verse of Walt Whitman and, to a lesser extent, WILLIAM CARLOS WILLIAMS, Levine's early poems contain a carefully controlled, rhythmic energy expressive of personal and collective freedom. Levine's recent poems take on a quiet, conversational tone; they are somewhat less controlled than the climatic chants of his first volumes, and in them fury is replaced with reverence. A characteristic intensity of emotion as well as a subsequent break with traditional forms place Levine among those poets of the late 1950s and early 1960s, including several poets of post–CONFESSIONAL and DEEP IMAGE POETRY, responsible for a second flowering of romanticism in American verse.

Born in Detroit, Levine worked many blue-collar jobs and was educated at Wayne State University. In his twenties, Levine left Michigan to attend the University of Iowa Writers' Workshop, where he was influenced by ROBERT LOWELL and JOHN BERRYMAN. Since then Levine has received various grants while also teaching at California State University, Fresno. He has published 18 collections of poetry. Throughout his career, Levine's work has consistently gained critical recognition in American arts and letters. *Ashes: Poems Old and New* (1979), an exploration of Jewish heritage, earned the first American Book Award for poetry. Levine's newer work continues to gain acclaim: *What Work Is* (1991) received the National Book Award, and *The Simple Truth* (1994) won the Pulitzer Prize.

Similar to the work of many poets who began their careers in the 1950s and early 1960s, the formal character of Levine's early poetry eventually gave way to a looser, more conversational technique. His first volume, *On the Edge* (1963), deals with working-class themes in a tightly controlled iambic pentameter, leading many critics to remark on the incongruence between content and form. Not until the publication of *Not This Pig* (1968), written in free verse, does Levine arrive at what is generally cited as his mature style. In "Animals Are Passing through Our Lives," the speaker is an actual pig that maintains a fierce dignity when facing the blades of the slaughterhouse. The pig's last utterance, "No. Not this Pig," encourages a succinct, yet profound connection to Levine's primary sacrificial animal, the American laborer.

They Feed They Lion (1972) is generally considered most representative of Levine's working-class poetry. Its frequently anthologized title poem grew out of the Detroit riots of 1967. In the poem the colloquial title phrase transforms into a forceful litany as Levine's displacement of the word *lion* signifies the rising anger of those thrust into the industrial North in search of work. Finally, the anger of those who have come "out of the gray hills / Of industrial barns, out of rain, out of bus ride," culminates in release. Here Levine subversively celebrates the communal release of the laborers' rage, "They Lion," otherwise kept in check by the system.

Levine's next few volumes can be loosely characterized as belated elegies dedicated to his father and other close family members. The poems written during this period make a general transition out of anger and rage toward a more compassionate outlook on humanity. One of Levine's most expressive poems from this period is "You Can Have It" (1979). Here Levine's 20-year-old twin brother, made prematurely old by his job at an ice plant, "dies when he sleeps / and sleeps when he rises to face this life." In other words, the brother is physically and spiritually exhausted from his job. Levine employs repetition to sum up the whole of his brother's experience; "You can have it" is the poem's refrain.

While continuing to focus on the importance of memory, Levine's recent verse more explicitly tests the ability of language—particularly poetic language—to capture middle- and working-class experience. As a result, his poems have become increasingly more accessible. *A Walk with Thomas Jefferson* (1988) and *What Work Is* (1991) continue to address personal memories and American work with free verse narrative. In these volumes, one can also sense Levine's continued investment in the knowledge to be gained from personal experience. In "What Work Is," Levine recalls waiting in line for work outside of the Ford Highland Plant. Frequently addressing his readers throughout, Levine encourages their participation in the shaping of the poem. In his aim to make poetry useful in our daily lives, Levine reminds his readers of the poetic subject matter residing inside of them. As Levine writes about personal memories in "The Simple Truth" (1994), sometimes "they must be said without elegance, meter and rhyme." Though he often displays a certain self-effacement—a skepticism that resembles how one of his characters might regard poetry—Levine's continued devotion to the craft exhibits his faith in the transformative potential of poetry.

BIBLIOGRAPHY

Buckley, Christopher, A. "A Conversation with Philip Levine." *Quarterly West* 43 1996–97: 267–276.

———, ed. *On the Poetry of Philip Levine: Stranger to Nothing*. Ann Arbor: University of Michigan Press, 1991.

Hirsch, Edward. "The Visionary Poetics of Philip Levine and Charles Wright." In *The Columbia History of American Poetry*, edited by Jay Parini. New York: Columbia University Press, 1993.

Megan Swihart Jewell

LEVIS, LARRY (1946–1997) As the title of his last, posthumously published book of poems, *Elegy* (1998), indicates, Larry Levis was a poet occupied with death, memory, the bonds of friendship and love, and the haunting effects of loss. But Levis was by no means a conventional elegist, nor was his conception of death conventional: "And if Death whispered as always in the language of curling / Leaves," he writes in "To a Wren on Calvary," it also speaks "a later one that makes us stranger, / "Don't come *near* me motherfucker." Levis's work chronicles not only lost lives, but also his own blue collar past in California's San Joaquin Valley and the irreparable changes to American culture in the postmodern era. If the surreal imagery of his early poems recalls the DEEP IMAGE lyricism of JAMES WRIGHT and ROBERT BLY, his later work resists easy categorization, demonstrating an idiosyncratic narrative style imbued with existential irony, absurdist humor, contrastingly lush and antipoetic imagery, and what poet David St. John calls "Levis's hope in a desperate tenderness that might rescue us from our notions of oblivion" (176).

Born in Fresno, California, in 1946, Larry Patrick Levis received a B.A. from Fresno State (1968), an M.A. from Syracuse (1970), and a Ph.D. from the University of Iowa (1974). He taught at the University of Missouri

(1974–80), the University of Utah (1980–92), and at Virginia Commonwealth University, where he was professor of English (1992–97). The author of six books of poetry and a collection of short stories, Levis was honored with the United States Poetry Award from the International Poetry Forum (1971), a Discovery Award (1971), a National Endowment for the Arts Fellowship (1973), a Guggenheim Fellowship, the Lamont Poetry Selection award (1976), selection for the National Poetry Series (1981), and a Fulbright Fellowship (1989), which he spent in Yugoslavia.

"The invigoration of conventions is an important aspect [of Levis's work]," says D. W. Fenza, "because he chose to be subversive in ways that, initially, seemed casual, unassuming, and commonplace" (11). Levis's early work is imagistic and often surreal, depicting parts of his personal life and the American landscape to evoke a nihilistic universe in which nevertheless "You go further into the blank paper. / You go past the white smirk of the benign" ("A Poem of Horses"). Violence is an issue that he must come to terms with. In the haunting multisectioned poem "Linnets," Levis imagines his brother killing a linnet at random, an act of cruelty caused only because "You're tired of summer. / You want to stop all the singing. / And everything is singing," then disavows the confessional impetus for poems when he writes that he never had "This brother for whom / you have been repairing linnets all your life." "[I]t is possible I am not Levis," he warns in "The Crime of the Shade Trees." But these early poems fail to engage dialogically with the cultural turbulence of the 1960s and its disappointing aftermath which so occupy Levis's thought in the powerful manner of his work from 1985 onwards.

Levis's later work is richly narrative, though the poems rarely tell a single story; instead, they weave together multiple storylines, various layers of allusions to high and low culture, and deeply philosophical generalizations, often offering only an imperfect image as resolution. "But it's all or nothing in this life; it's smallpox, quicklime, & fire," Levis writes in "At the Grave of My Guardian Angel: St. Louis Cemetery, New Orleans," "it breaks Lincoln & Poe into small drops of oil spreading / Into endless swirls on the water, & I recognize the pattern." Longing religiously for meaning in a universe without any prior meaning, and living in a country where many of the best dreams have failed, Levis nevertheless finds a slow beauty in the world that offers neither false hope nor easy consolation, but a momentary taste of eternity: "We'd better be getting on our way soon, sweet Nothing. / I'll buy you something pretty from the store. / I'll let you wear the flower in your hair even though you can only vanish entirely underneath its brown, implacable petals."

BIBLIOGRAPHY

Fenza, D. W. "The Wish to Be Swept Clean: The Poetry of Larry Levis." *The American Poetry Review* 31, no. 2 (2002): 11–17.

St. John, David. "Afterword." In *The Selected Levis,* by Larry Levis. Pittsburgh, Pa.: University of Pittsburgh Press, 2000: 175–77.

Temple Cone

LINDSAY, (NICHOLAS) VACHEL (1879–1931)

LINDSAY, (NICHOLAS) VACHEL (1879–1931) Vachel Lindsay was a midwestern poet who achieved great fame from 1914 through the 1920s for his rhythmic verse, which he performed with great skill and vigor. In the latter part of the 20th century his work fell out of favor, largely because of racist overtones, particularly in the poem "The Congo" (1914). In the 1990s critics took a more balanced approach to Lindsay's work. He was identified with two other Illinois populist poets whose work also appeared in the Chicago-based magazine *Poetry:* CARL SANDBURG and EDGAR LEE MASTERS.

Lindsay was born in Springfield, Illinois. In 1913 his poem, "General William Booth Enters into Heaven," was awarded a prize as the best poem *Poetry* magazine had published that year, and it became the title poem of his first commercially published book. In 1915 *Poetry* chose "The Chinese Nightingale" as the best poem published that year. In 1929 *Poetry* gave him a special award for lifetime achievement.

During most of his career, Lindsay toured tirelessly across the United States and eventually visited Europe and China. He recited his rhymed and emphatically rhythmic poetry in an expressive way that charmed audiences. In the summers of 1906, 1908, and 1912, Lindsay took walking tours all over the South, Midwest, and West, bartering self-published pamphlets of poetry or reciting his poems in return for room and board. The tours also resulted in two prose books about his experiences. After his poetry brought him fame, his income came largely from his recitations. On December 5, 1931, Lindsay committed suicide by drinking disinfectant.

Lindsay's poetry, typically in short, rhymed lines, is often characterized by sentimentality about children, as for example, "In Memory of a Child" (1914), which ends, "The angels guide him now, / And watch his curly head." Lindsay's populist political views also anchor much of his poetry, such as his poems celebrating Abraham Lincoln and William Jennings Bryan. "When Bryan Speaks" (1915) describes the voice of three-time presidential candidate Bryan as a "strange composite" of the millions of "singing souls / Who made world-brotherhood their choice."

The controversy over "The Congo" centers on the racial stereotyping of Africans in the poem, as in the opening line, "Fat black bucks in a wine-barrel room." W. E. B. DuBois, African-American sociologist and one of the founders of the National Association for the Advancement of Colored People (NAACP), said Lindsay knew only two things about African Americans, "The beautiful rhythm of their music and the ugly side of their drunkards and outcasts" (182). Ironically the emphasis on the African Americans' enthusiasm for rhythm in the poem is echoed by Lindsay's own tendency to emphasize rhythm in his poems, as in the repetition of the line "Mumbo-Jumbo will hoo-doo you." Nonetheless Lindsay was, in some senses, a liberal-minded man widely regarded in his own time as antiracist. In *War Bulletins* (1909), he had attacked racial prejudice, along with greed and urbanization, and DuBois himself had praised the treatment of African Americans in Lindsay's story, "The Golden-Faced People" (1909).

Lindsay "discovered" LANGSTON HUGHES when Hughes, who was serving as a waiter at a banquet Lindsay attended, gave Lindsay some of his poems. Although Lindsay did not know it, Hughes's first book, *The Weary Blues* (1926), had already been accepted for publication by Alfred A. Knopf. Lindsay's enthusiasm for Hughes's writing, however, suggests that Hughes rightly judged Lindsay to be a sympathetic reader. Lindsay's work, while it sometimes chooses style over substance, remains entertaining to read or listen to and is often charming in its spaciousness. His engagement with the race question makes his life and work an interesting study in the complications of the attitudes of his time.

BIBLIOGRAPHY

DuBois, W. E. B., "The Looking Glass: Literature." *Crisis* 12, no. 4 (August 1916): 182.

Lindsay, Vachel. "The Golden-Faced People." *War Bulletin No. 1* (Springfield, Illinois, 1909): 1–4.

Massa, Ann. *Vachel Lindsay, Fieldworker for the American Dream*. Bloomington, Indiana University Press, 1970.

Thomas Lisk

LOBA DIANE DI PRIMA (1973, 1976, 1977, 1978, 1998) When book I (which includes previously published and new sections) of *Loba* appeared in 1978, this serial work was "hailed by many as the great female counterpart to ALLEN GINSBERG's *HOWL* (Clark) (see LONG AND SERIAL POETRY); according to the Jungian analyst Naomi Ruth Lowinsky, the 1998 volume of books I and II belongs "beside Whitman's *Leaves of Grass* and H. D.'s *Trilogy*—poems that transform consciousness" (147), and Jack Foley likewise declares that it "takes its place with other life-challenging, life changing works of the twentieth century: [Ezra] Pound's *Cantos*, [Charles] Olson's *Maximus* [*Poems*], [Gertrude] Stein's 'Cubist' prose."

There is an explicit and expansive gathering of ideas and myths in the work; after all, the mythical Loba is a gatherer, whose "purpose is to collect and preserve" (Clark). The scope of DIANE DI PRIMA's book is vast; the object of *Loba* is to disrupt norms and assumptions in order to create new ways of seeing the female and her roles through an alchemy of myth, to make "a new / creation myth" (part 1), not to revise an old one.

To this end di Prima overturns traditional modes of progression in the poem. Times, places, and figures are thrown into the mix; for the development of an achronic, ageographic strategy; thus "chinook / breezes from Eden" (part 6) locates the paradise garden near the eastern slopes of the Rocky Mountains. *Loba* is anything but linear narrative, anything but predictable. Divided into two books, each consisting of 8 parts (averaging 15 pages each), the structure itself is unpredictable: Some pieces are titled, and some are not: Some of the epigraphs are historical, and some are imaginary (such as that by a Jungian scholar): Some of the text is italic, and some plain: Sometimes the voice speaks to the Loba, sometimes speaks of the Loba, and sometimes is the Loba speaking: Sometimes the Loba doesn't seem to be anywhere around, as di Prima dips into her net and brings up Persephone or Kali or Guinevere or any of the approximately 130 figures she lists in one piece of part 3.

In part 1 the Loba has tidy animal feet; in part 2 she is wearing traditional aboriginal clothing but changes into 1950s teen garb on the next page. In part 1 she has the flaccid breasts of an elderly woman, but in part 2 these breasts have the newness and firmness of youth. In these and other ways, di Prima denies her readers any chance of identifying the female archetype of this poem with any single mythical figure of choice. Although Mary of Nazareth is the focus of part 6, it is clear that Mary is not the archetype, but only a fragment of her; part 15 turns to Kali and delivers a sequence of hymns and prayers. The female in this poem takes as many guises as possible and is as capable of violence and destruction as she is capable of childbirth and nurturing. While the maternal function is not erased, it is placed in a perspective with the other aspects of the female. Through the Loba, the female is shown to be a creature of appetites and possibilities. She is no longer confined to feminine stereotypes or constrained by gender-based strictures. Instead "no *one* / is depicted here" (part 12), nor can she be labelled by the usual terms designated for social and familial relationship roles (part 14)—she is not derivative or dependent or definable. "She is formless / or that She is all forms" (part 15).

Not surprisingly, red, the signature color of women in mythology, has a subtle symbolic value as the female is repeatedly clothed or accessorized in red (part 14), the uterus likened to a precious red stone (part 13), and "ropes of blood cover her breasts and her wide hips / like red flowers" (part 15). To be female is to bleed, and because blood is the sign of woman, di Prima stresses it as the unbreakable connector every woman has with the overarching Woman (part 16). The collective sign of the female is transitory, however. In the lines "Forty years it took / for the napkin to fall from my eyes" (part 3), di Prima refers to menopause, the great hormonal shift that allows for new ways of being for women. In the poem, however, the postmenstrual female discovers that "There is no myth / for this older ample woman" (part 16), and she needs one.

The Loba appears in order to redress the imbalance and to validate the worth of those whose cultural, procreative, and erotic value have been lost. The three-page "Apparuit" in part 14 speaks of the female self as equally able to handle "the spear / the harp the book the butterfly," as a peaceful but not passive self. *Loba* is complicated, perplexing, and demanding; it must be to achieve its goal of rupturing the established order and providing a female-oriented vision.

BIBLIOGRAPHY

Brainard, Dulcy. Review of *Loba,* by Diane di Prima. *Publisher's Weekly* 245, no. 26 (June 29, 1998): 53.

Clark, Audrey M. Review of *Loba,* by Diane di Prima. *Rambles: A Cultural Arts Magazine.* Available online. URL: http://rambles.net. Downloaded March 2007.

Foley, Jack. Review of *Loba,* by Diane di Prima. *Alsop Review.* Available online. URL: www.alsopreview.com. Downloaded March 2007.

Lowinsky, Naomi Ruth. Review of *Loba,* by Diane di Prima. *Psychological Perspectives* 39 (summer 1999): 146–147.

A. Mary Murphy

LOEWINSOHN, RON (1937–) Ron Loewinsohn's poetry consistently acknowledges its debt to major modernist figures, including EZRA POUND, William Butler Yeats, and WILLIAM CARLOS WILLIAMS (see MODERNISM). Loewinsohn grew up in and around San Francisco; as an aspiring beatnik in the late fifties, he knew ALLEN GINSBERG, who wrote an introduction to his first published volume, *Watermelons* (1959), and encouraged Loewinsohn to send the manuscript to Williams, who added his own prefatory letter praising the author's "poetic gift." Loewinsohn credits these two figures with encouraging him to observe daily experience directly in his work and not to strain to produce poetry according to a formula ("Interview"). Nonetheless his modernist-inspired work, while always accessible, is deeply allusive and intertextual, invoking figures from classical antiquity (Ovid, Aristotle), the English (Chaucer, Shakespeare) and the Continental (Stéphane Mallarmé, Paul Valéry) literary canon, anthropology and other physical sciences, and, most often, modernism. His forms and themes range from shorter lyrics (see LYRIC POETRY), employing repetition, run-on lines, and economically selected internal rhymes and treating love, family and American sports and landscapes, to essays that inquire into the nature of poetic form by engaging with the theories of Pound and Yeats.

Loewinsohn was born in Iolio, Philippines, and came to the United States in 1945. Initially rejecting university education, in keeping with BEAT notions of authenticity, he spent his twenties in various printing jobs and hitchhiking across the country until an opportunity to teach at the San Francisco State University Poetry Center launched his academic career. He earned a B.A. in 1967 from the University of California, Berkeley (where he began teaching in 1970), and an M.A. and Ph.D. (in 1971) from Harvard. He received the Poets Foundation Award in 1963 for *The World of the Lie* and the Irving Stone Award from the Academy of American Poets in 1966.

Meat Air: Poems 1957–1969 (1970) collects four previous volumes and other poems and develops Loewinsohn's sense of the imagination's power to transform physical reality, treating poetry as a form of communion, of the word (air) made flesh (meat). In his final published volume, *Goat Dances: Poems and Prose* (1976), his treatment of language's curative powers grows more sophisticated, and more subtly qualified: He writes of "the dark whole made external / in a muddle of words" ("Goat Dance 'Is it when things are most clear'" [1976]). The volume's opening essay, "May I Have This Dance," playfully examines Pound's definition of *logopoeia* as "the dance of the intellect among words," a definition which Lowinsohn says "leaves that dance mostly a metaphor." Accordingly dancing stands for various creative and cognitive processes throughout the volume, which combines domestic scenes tenderly portrayed ("All the possible is in your brown / hair" ["Goat Dance: Is it when things are most clear"]), acute attention to physical detail ("the coronae of the furniture in the early / morning streetlight filtering thru the blinds" (from the same poem), and eruptions of racy, antipoetic language ("O bright tits of the world!" ["Goat Dance: 'You inspire me,' you said"]). At its best Loewinsohn's work appeals in diverse ways: Its exploration of the fluid boundaries between poetry and essays and its erudite engagement with the modernist canon afford intellectual pleasures, while his range of interests and clear style offer lyrical rewards.

BIBLIOGRAPHY

Barrax, Gerald William. "Four Poets." *Poetry* (August 1968): 343–344.

Harrison, Jim. "California Hybrid." *Poetry* (June 1966): 198–201.

Loewinsohn, Ron. Interview by Jesse Wolfe. Berkeley, Calif., 14 June 2002.

Pritchard, William H. "Shags and Poets." *Hudson Review* (autumn 1970): 563–577.

Jesse Wolfe

LOGAN, JOHN (1923–1987) John Logan extended the boundaries of CONFESSIONAL POETRY as practiced by such figures as ROBERT LOWELL. His earlier work was formal but it evolved into a distinctive free verse (see PROSODY AND FREE VERSE). In his early years Logan wrote in a lyrical language that coalesced into religious themes. During his marriage he joined the Catholic Church; after the couple divorced, he left the church, although it continued to inspire imagery that would remain a prominent aspect of his poetry.

Logan was born and raised in Red Oak, Iowa. His first book of poetry, *Cycle for Mother Cabrini,* was published in 1955. He was the recipient of several honors, including the Morton Dauwen Zabel Award from the National Institute of Arts and Letters (1974). During his career Logan was founder and editor of *Choice* until 1980, as well as poetry editor of *Critic* and the *Nation.*

Logan's use of religious imagery and confessional voice found a significant readership. Regarding his first collection, John Fandel writes, "This thin volume has weight. Ten poems, most of them long, create the adjectives: vigorous, keen, refreshing, neat. They also define the term lyrical" (124). Logan relied on his Catholic faith for most of his early poetry, although, in later collections, his poetry centers around the ephemeral nature of youth or, more specifically, lost youth from the perspective of an adult. Patrick Callahan notes that a "favorite theme of *The Zigzag Walk* (1973), for example, is youth's initiation into adulthood. The rite-of-passage is sometimes presented humorously" (642). The poem "Three Moves" from this book demonstrates Logan's ultimate use of religion and concerns about the fleeting moment: For a time the speaker does not remember "The only one who ever dares to call / and ask me, 'How's your soul?'" Here the author is considering his religious background against his life as an older and more experienced adult. The lines concluding this poem are a confession that the speaker does not currently have a priest. A posthumous volume titled *John Logan: The Collected Poems* (1989) includes some of his best known works. His late poetry continues to center around religion and observations of life from the perspective of an adult; notably, in "Chicago Scene," he alludes to the problems of sexual ambiguity that plagued him throughout life: "A boyish drummer [who] ticks his brush" illustrates Logan's confusion and self-imposed guilt for latent homosexual urges he discovered as an adult.

Logan's poetry depicts a divergence from the confessional mode Logan used as a younger poet into a poetics that involved his perspective as an adult looking back on his life, his family and his religious experiences and his current view that life passes quickly.

BIBLIOGRAPHY

Callahan, Patrick. "Tonal Power, Incoherent Rage: Rhetoric in Three Poets." *Sewanee Review* 78, no. 4 (spring 1972): 639–644.

Fandel, John. "Song and Sanctity." *Commonweal* 63, no. 5 (4 November 1955): 124–126.

Christopher Bloss

LOGAN, WILLIAM (1950–) Formally elegant and tonally acerbic, William Logan is associated with NEW FORMALISM, though he claims that form alone cannot render a poem; he once said, "I can read only so much unvaried pentameter, tedious as a minor god, without wanting to be strangled with piano wire" (140). (See PROSODY AND FREE VERSE.) An active reviewer of poetry with a commitment to rigorous art, he recalls the poet-critic RANDALL JARRELL. Logan's poetry is of a piece with his criticism; he examines events and figures from history, science, and art, often judging against the human capacity to better its conditions. Yet he offers compensations for the decaying world: the pleasure of a virtuoso's command of language, an eye for unexpected natural landscapes, and a refusal to sentimentalize human relations.

Logan was born and raised in Boston. In 1980 he spent time in England on an AMY LOWELL Poetry Traveling Fellowship. His first book was published in 1982. In 1988 the National Book Critics Circle awarded Logan a citation for excellence in reviewing and in 2000 made him a finalist for their award in criticism. He has received the John Masefield and Celia B. Wagner Awards from the Poetry Society of America (1991) as well as the Lavan Younger Poets Award from the Academy of American Poets (2000). He has taught at the University of Florida.

Technical complexity and sharp analysis characterize all of Logan's work. His poems are metered and rhymed, though they push against form by rhyming and breaking stanzas irregularly. A common theme to be found in his poems is that of cultural failures of the past standing as figures for a corrupt modern world. Referring to the title of one Logan's books, Henry Taylor remarks, "Many of the poems are meditations on historical examples of "vain empires," whether earthly, spiritual or intellectual" (28). A fierce witness of cultural decay, Logan balances irony with opulent diction and attention to the difficulties of human life.

In "Stereopticon" (1984), Logan contrasts modern photography with the stereopticon, a 19th-century device that created the illusion of solidity by projecting double images, in order to critique a shallow present. He praises a stereoptic image of an Arctic expedition for showing how "the world is not flat, / but round, whole, dangerous." Logan writes not only about history but also from within it. In "Keats in India" (1998), he imagines the romantic poet John Keats surviving tuberculosis to travel to India, where he sees "a fakir strangle a man" and observes the tipping of ceremonial pots in the Ganges, which "sink into eternities of rest." As an antidote to the modern obsession with the self, Logan offers formal rigor and historical perspective.

BIBLIOGRAPHY
Logan, William. "Interview." In *All the Rage*. Ann Arbor: University of Michigan Press, 1998.
Taylor, Henry. "Hints from Hell." *New York Times Book Review* (12 July 1998): 28.

Temple Cone

LONG AND SERIAL POETRY The long poem has been the measure and the lifework of many significant 20th-century American poets. Yet the term *long poem* is a notoriously vague descriptor applied (by poets and critics alike) to poems of vastly different lengths and forms. One can discriminate, however, between those long poems in the 20th century that maintain the organizational structure of the epic and those that adopt the random and incomplete process of seriality. Epic poems by 20th-century poets adapt or renovate forms whose theoretical and structural underpinnings were set in earlier periods. The series, or serial poem, is remarkable for being the long form that is entirely new in 20th-century poetics.

The epic poem remains the classic type and model for the long form in poetry. The modern epic, however, can be distinguished from its predecessors and other types of the 20th-century long poem. The "open" nonnarrative models for the modern epic differentiate it from such earlier works as John Milton's *Paradise Lost* (1674), William Wordsworth's *The Prelude* (1850), and Robert Browning's *The Ring and the Book* (1868–69), which maintain the developmental structure of a narrative (see NARRATIVE POETRY). Yet the modern epic shares with its predecessors the demand for comprehensiveness—not in a narrow sense of a "comprehensive" treatment of a particular subject, because no epic limits itself to a single thematic concern nor claims to have "exhausted" a given subject, but rather in the sense of a complete worldview, a breadth of intellectual range. Classical works, such as Lucretius's *De Rerum Natura* (50 B.C.), on everything from atomism to Zeno, or Ovid's *Metamorphoses* (A.D. 1), with its definitive re-creation of the Greek mythology, offer themselves as models, though neither of these presents an extended narrative with an heroic figure. In fact, Arthur Golding's translation of Ovid (1567) is a primary source for EZRA POUND's reinspiring of classical mythology in *The CANTOS* (1972). The theory of the universe presented in book I of the *Metamorphoses* and Lucretius's treatment of science and philosophy can also be said to anticipate JAMES MERRILL's *The CHANGING LIGHT AT SANDOVER* (1982) or Frederick Turner's *The New World* (1985). Central to the epic, then, whether narrative or otherwise, is its capaciousness; its length is only justified by its breadth. Thus the form demands a complete portrait of the culture (not an excerpt) or a whole system of belief (not a single idea).

The epic in 20th-century American poetry can also be distinguished from other long forms in its desire for "totality." Pound's *Cantos* demand—even if they do not achieve—a coherent synthesis. They posit an authoritarian hierarchy so that Pound's claim for the sponsorship of Benito Mussolini should not be surprising given Virgil's endorsement of the Augustan reign at the conclusion of book VI of the *Aeneid* or given Ovid's reverential treatment of the "Deification of Caesar" in the final book of the *Metamorphoses*. The modern epic is characteristically concerned with "centering," bringing diverse materials into a synthesis. In contrast, dispersal or separation is more characteristic of serial poetry. The modern epic feels compelled to assert complete control over its materials; the series enjoys its own abandonment to the materials of its presentation. In this sense, the series is more appropriate to an increasingly heterodox culture. Totality in the modern epic represents an attempt to realize a grand design upon the world; the postmodern series accedes to the condition of flux, revels in the provisional state of things. The epic, assertive in principle, gives way to the serial articulation of particulars. The series forsakes mythic permanence in the recognition of cultural transience.

An important transitional work between the modern and the contemporary long poem, *The MAXIMUS POEMS* of CHARLES OLSON (1970) elicits praise for, and raises objections to, the method of Pound's *Cantos* as an "ego-system" and of WILLIAM CARLOS WILLIAMS's *PATERSON* (1963) as an "emotional system." Olson establishes these two modern works as "halves" of a job *The Maximus Poems* would encompass and complete. The poem relies upon the superhuman persona (character) of "Maximus," through whom the poet assumes a didactic authority. In its use of the city of Gloucester,

Massachusetts, (like Paterson, New Jersey) as focal point, the local situation provides the major organizational device of *The Maximus Poems.* Olson's use of persona and locale attempts to provide the comprehensiveness and the coherence to which both *The Cantos and Paterson* originally aspired.

Like Pound and Williams, Olson adopts a compositional method of nonnarrative collage of historical and cultural documents in *The Maximus Poems.* Merrill, in *The Changing Light at Sandover,* prefers dramatic structure as the more illustrious conveyance of the epic into the late 20th century with its expansive worldview. The stylistic and structural contrasts between Olson's and Merrill's poems make for a fascinating study. One pictures the disheveled Olson with a day's growth of beard, drinking Johnnie Walker Black straight from the bottle and jabbing at an enormous topographical map of Gloucester tacked to his study wall. His rambling monologue on the arcane details of the early settlement of Massachusetts perplexes his visitors. In contrast, the urbane and wealthy Merrill hosts a séance for the amusement of a small party of friends in the sumptuous dining room of his mansion at Stonington, Connecticut. His guests are amazed by what reveals itself on the Ouija board, under the guise of entertainment. Despite these fundamental differences of style and substance, both poets are obsessed with cosmology, the creation and evolution of the world. Olson summons this theme of the origin of the world by incorporating substantial portions of Hesiod's *Theogony* (eighth century B.C.) and relating its mythology directly to the New World locale that provides the principal landscape and sensibility of the epic. In "Maximus, From Dogtown-I," Olson models his account of the local lore of Dogtown, the "WATERED ROCK," on Hesiod's tale of Gaia and encircling Okeanos. Merrill, for his part, proposes to tell an "old, exalted" story, the "incarnation and withdrawal of / A god." In his masquelike poem, Merrill introduces his own pantheon; in place of Greek deities, we meet the God Biology and his twin Nature, who doubles as Chaos. Both Olson and Merrill aspire to create a world inside their poems; with map or Ouija board, they chart the dimensions of the epic as universal statement.

The epic demands—even if it does not always achieve—a coherent synthesis of its socioeconomic, anthropological, or cosmological materials. In keeping with what used to be called the "argument" of the poem, the modern epic retains a hierarchical superstructure, even if only the pro forma one of the traditional 24 books. Making his own distinctions between a long poem and a serial poem, Sherman Paul employs the word "*long* to cover poems of length that have a structure that encloses them, frames them, guides them" (37–38). An external framework of accepted ideas "both encloses and closes the poem: the *long* poem, as I define it, is a closed poem" (Paul 37–38). The epic poem strives always to be complete. Olson, literally on his deathbed, felt compelled to designate to his literary executor the final poem of *Maximus* so that if the manuscript finally lacked the kind of cohesion to which he aspired, it would most certainly have closure. RONALD JOHNSON constructs his epic, *ARK* (1996), on an architectural model of Beams, Spires, and Ramparts, "based on trinities, its cornerstones the eye, the ear, the mind." Acknowledging a debt to the spiritual triad of Dante's *Divine Comedy* (early 14th century), Johnson's poetics also invoke the essential elements of "sight, sound, and intellection" in LOUIS ZUKOFSKY's 24-part *"A"* (1978). The transept of *ARK* is capped by Johnson's *RAD I OS,* his rewriting of portions of Milton's *Paradise Lost* by excision, beginning with Milton's text and then deleting lines and even parts of words to form a new text. In an entirely different vein, the completion of Merrill's elegant *Sandover* inspired New Narrative works that deploy a wide cast of characters and developed plots (see NEW FORMALISM). VIKRAM SETH's chronicles of the foibles of Bay Area yuppies, *The Golden Gate* (1986), takes the form of a 307-page novel-in-verse.

The serial form in contemporary poetry, however, represents a radical alternative to the epic model. The series describes the complicated manner in which one thing follows another. Its modular form—in which individual elements are both discontinuous and capable of recombination—distinguishes it from the thematic development or narrative progression that characterizes other types of the long poem. The series resists a systematic or determinate ordering of its materials, preferring constant change and even accident, a protean shape and a chance-determined method. The epic systematically creates a world through the gravitational attraction that melds diverse materials into a unified whole. But the series describes an expanding and heterodox universe whose centrifugal force encourages dispersal. The epic goal has always been encompassment and summation, but the series is an ongoing process of accumulation. In contrast to the epic demand for completion, the series remains radically and deliberately incomplete.

The fizzling of several modernist epic poems to cohere or achieve their goals, including *The Cantos* and *Paterson,* and the distaste for the hierarchical structures and belief systems that frame them has led many postmodern poets to serial composition. Poems written in many loosely associated parts also signify the impatience of poets with the short personal lyric demanded by some POETRY JOURNALS. The series, a modular form in which individual sections are both discontinuous and capable of multiple orderings, contrasts the linear causality of most narrative forms; the serial poem is random and polyvalent, accommodating an expanding and heterodox universe. As discussed in Joseph Conte's *Unending Design: The Forms of Postmodern Poetry,* examples in the first half of the century include Williams's *Spring and All* (1923), GEORGE OPPEN's *Discrete Series* (1934), and Zukofsky's *Anew* (1946). The postwar poetics of the BLACK MOUNTAIN SCHOOL and SAN FRANCISCO RENAISSANCE produced several book-length serial poems: the "unbound and uneven" poems of ROBERT DUNCAN's infinite series, *PASSAGES;* ROBERT CREELEY's granular *Pieces* (1969); *The JOURNALS* (1975) of PAUL BLACKBURN; JACK SPICER's books, such as *Homage to Creeley* (1959) and *The Heads of the Town up to the Aether* (1962); DIANE DI PRIMA's multifaceted experimental *LOBA* (1973, 1976, 1977, 1978, 1998); and ROBIN BLASER's open-ended image-nation series so far compiled in *The Holy Forest* (1993).

Among more recent poets, there is Seth and his *Golden Gate.* NATHANIEL MACKEY combines jazz tonalities and Dogon mythology in his "Song of the Andoumboulou" and "mu" series, both open-ended works appearing in multiple volumes after the style of Duncan and Blaser. LESLIE SCALAPINO prolifically explores the shifting, repetitive, and combinatorial form of seriality in *that they were at the beach* (1985) and *Way* (1988). As Lynn Keller observes in *Forms of Expansion: Recent Long Poems by Women,* such poets as RACHEL BLAU DUPLESSIS (in *DRAFTS*) and BEVERLY DAHLEN (in *A Reading*) have turned to serial poems as an alternative to the patriarchal assumptions of culture prevalent in male-dominated epic poetry. The serial poem represents postmodern poetry's most innovative contribution to the long form.

BIBLIOGRAPHY

Bernstein, Michael André. *The Tale of the Tribe: Ezra Pound and the Modern Verse Epic.* Princeton, N.J.: Princeton University Press, 1980.

Conte, Joseph M. *Unending Design: The Forms of Postmodern Poetry.* Ithaca, N.Y.: Cornell University Press, 1991.

Keller, Lynn. *Forms of Expansion: Recent Long Poems by Women.* Chicago: University of Chicago Press, 1997.

Paul, Sherman. *Hewing to Experience.* Iowa City: University of Iowa Press, 1989.

Joseph Conte

LORDE, AUDRE (1934–1992) "I want my poems—I want all of my work—to engage, and to empower people to speak, to strengthen themselves into who they most want and need to be and then to act, to do what needs being done," Audre Lorde once said ("Above" 94). Poetry as a transformative force in the light of continuing oppression was central to Lorde's artistic, moral, and political vision. As a self-defined "Black, lesbian, mother, warrior, poet," Lorde spent her writing career negotiating the implications of this complex identity, trying to find ways to "make necessary power out of negative surroundings" (Lorde "Above" 91). Loosely associated with the BLACK ARTS MOVEMENT in the 1960s, Lorde continued to be a friend and mentor to poet-activists committed to breaking cultural silences, including ADRIENNE RICH, JUNE JORDAN, Pat Parker, Essex Hemphill, and Barbara Smith.

Lorde was born in Harlem to West Indian parents. Educated at Hunter College and Columbia University, she worked as a librarian from 1961 to 1968; from 1968 to 1988 she taught English and creative writing, mainly at the City University of New York. In 1989 she received the American Book Award for her collection of essays, *A Burst of Light.* As writer, educator, and activist, she was always concerned with improving public visibility for women of color, both within the

United States and internationally: In the 1980s she cofounded Kitchen Table: Women of Color Press and Sisterhood in Support of Sisters in South Africa. She also received the Walt Whitman Citation of Merit and was named poet laureate of New York in 1991.

Lorde's 1968 debut poetry collection, *The First Cities*, has been linked to the Black Arts movement; her complete body of work, however, shows an independent, singular voice. In *The Black Unicorn* (1978), written after a journey to Dahomey in 1974, Lorde broadened the mythic scope of her writing to include West African influences. In the 1980s and early 1990s, she continued to hone a lyrical idiom characterized by both its complex and evocative imagery and its exceptional emotional and intellectual courage.

Lorde's poetry encompasses a wide spectrum of themes, from the necessity for self-definition in "Coal" (1968)—"I / Is the total black, being spoken / From the earth's inside"—to the political responsibilities of the writer who promised of her pen, "never to leave it / lying / in somebody else's blood" ("To the Poet Who Happens to Be Black and the Black Poet Who Happens to Be a Woman" [1986]). Whether she expresses her anger at the violence directed at black children who "play with skulls / at school" ("School Note" [1976]) or examines how love between women of different races "means a gradual sacrifice of all that is simple" ("Outlines" [1986]), however, Lorde's overarching vision is, as she expressed it in the essay "Age, Race, Class, and Sex" (1984), to understand "human difference as a springboard for creative change."

BIBLIOGRAPHY

Dhairyam, Sagri. "'Artifacts for Survival': Remapping the Contours of Poetry with Audre Lorde." *Feminist Studies* 18, no. 2 (summer 1992): 229–256.

———. "An Interview with Audre Lorde," by Karla Hammond. *American Poetry Review* (March/April 1980): 18–21.

Lorde, Audre. "Age, Race, Class, and Sex: Women Redefining Difference," in *Sister Outsider: Essays and Speeches by Audre Lorde*. Freedom, Calif.: The Crossing Press, 1984, pp. 114–123.

———. "Above the Wind: An Interview with Audre Lorde," by Charles H. Rowell. *Callaloo* 14, no. 1 (1991): 83–95.

Stefanie Sievers

"LOST SISTER" CATHY SONG **(1982)** CATHY SONG's "Lost Sister" is a compellingly unsettled portrait of the challenges and regrets that characterize the experiences of women in conservative cultures and of women who have immigrated from those cultures. The poem centers on the life of a woman who leaves "the demons, / the noisy stomachs" of an impoverished life in China for America, only to discover how much she longs for the cultural and social grounding of her former home. Like the two parts of the ethnic identity 'Chinese-American,' the poem is broken into two sections, the first detailing the life of women in China, the second dealing with the disappointments of one woman's life in Hawaii. A sense of unease and restlessness pervades the poem, suggesting that for the modern American immigrant, identity is not to be found in either the Old or New World, but instead in the differences separating them, symbolized by the ocean's vast expanse.

"Lost Sister" begins with a LYRIC passage on the significance of jade in Chinese culture as both a name and as a magical stone that controls weather. These linked themes of identity and control exhibit a paradoxical relation, for one cannot exist separate from the other. Song depicts the life of a woman in China as completely circumscribed and controlled by cultural norms, including living at home, footbinding, and filial duty. These conditions signify a loss of freedom, one that is absolute and unavoidable; as Song writes, "To move freely was a luxury / stolen from them at birth." Therefore, to take control of one's life in this culture requires leaving home, and thereby relinquishing one's cultural identity.

In the second section of the poem, Song introduces a woman, "a sister," who has taken the step of seizing control of her life by immigrating to Hawaii, but at the cost of having "relinquished her name, / diluting jade green / with the blue of the Pacific." For her, this cost has proven too great, for she has discovered the endless possibilities represented by the American dream's lack the stable structure and emotional security of her home culture. As if living on the lonely edge of a frontier, she discovers how much she depends upon "(t)he meager provisions and sentiments / of once belonging." This nostalgia does not obscure her memories of life in China, which Song characterizes ambivalently as "a jade link/ handcuffed at your wrist," but it does not allow for satisfaction either. The woman must continue to live in "an ocean in between, / the unremitting space of your rebellion."

When Cathy Song received the Yale Younger Poets Prize for *Picture Bride,* the collection in which "Lost Sister" appeared, her work was widely praised as an expression of Asian-American identity. But Song seems as interested in the problems of creating cultural identity, particularly for women, as she is in expressing it. In "Lost Sister," writes critic Fu-Jen Chen, "The highlighting of a spatial gap between two worlds reveals an anxiety toward the formation of a new identity" (595). This anxiety cannot be resolved; indeed, it is as much the core of the woman's identity as the roles of wife, mother, and daughter are the core of her mother's identity. Compromised thus, neither woman can 'leave footprints' or otherwise have a lasting influence on the world. Yet as Patricia Wallace observes, Song's poems "transform what seems simple or ordinary—including words themselves—by lifting things out of their ordinary settings" (8). By keeping in mind both the experience of the culturally confined woman and of the immigrant, Song invites the reader into a sphere of experience where those categories are fluid, not rigid. As a result, the reader is less likely to be lured by the sentimental nostalgia of the lonely immigrant or the naïve dreams of the native, and thus can begin the difficult but authentic process of forging her own identity.

BIBLIOGRAPHY

Chen, Fu-Jen. "Body and Female Subjectivity in Cathy Song's *Picture Bride.*" *Women's Studies* 33 (2004): 577–612.

Wallace, Patricia. "Divided Loyalties: Literal and Literary in the Poetry of Lorna Dee Cervantes, Cathy Song, and Rita Dove." *Melus* 18, no. 3 (1993): 3–19.

Temple Cone

"LOVE CALLS US TO THE THINGS OF THIS WORLD" RICHARD WILBUR (1955) Since it appeared in his third volume of poetry *Things of This World* (1956), "Love Calls Us to the Things of This World" has been RICHARD WILBUR's most discussed lyric poem (see LYRIC POETRY), including lengthy analysis in a 1964 symposium with RICHARD EBERHART, MAY SWENSON, Robert Horan, and Wilbur himself. As the signature poem of the volume, it is, in Wilbur's words, "a poem against dissociated and abstracted spirituality" (25). A debate between body and soul, the poem argues for the importance of things of the world, rather than abstractions. This poem signals a new phase in Wilbur's career, in which he stresses the need for the imagination to accept, even celebrate, the given world. The poem's title, taken from St. Augustine's *Confessions* (A.D. 400), represents a struggle between dream and reality. Richard Eberhart sees the poem as a conflict between "a soul-state and an earth-state" that the soul must, by necessity, win (4).

Wilbur describes the occasion of the poem as needing to conjure an early morning "scene" in a "bedroom high up in a city apartment-building; outside the bedroom window, the first laundry of the day is being yanked across the sky, and one has been awakened by the squeaking pulley of the laundry-line" (124). The speaker gets up to a world where everything is inhabited with the spirits of angels. The soul, once loath to accept the new day and what it must remember, now accepts the body, with all its imperfections. One of Wilbur's few unrhymed poems, it is divided into two parts, structured as thesis and antithesis. Part 1, as Paul F. Cummins says, "develops the soul's desire by establishing the relationship between the soul and the laundry." The literal wash hung on the line is transformed by angels who fill everything with "the deep joy of their impersonal breathing" (11).

In the countertheme the waking body now has "a changed voice." The desired-for "nothing on earth but laundry" gives way to the soul's acceptance of the body, but now with a sense of loss and regret. That imperfection of earthly existence, Cummins further notes, underlies Wilbur's theory of the difficulty of reconciling sensibility and objects, summed up by Wilbur: "A lot of my poems . . . are an argument against a thingless, an earthless kind of imagination, or spirituality" (50). In the poem the "bitter love" of the soul still wishes for "clean linens on the backs of thieves."

The things of this world, as St. Augustine acknowledged, take on beauty when they are changed through the senses or the imagination. The poem's structure and diction, through the common experience of laundry, have created, in Frank Littler's words, the "paradox of man's finding the spiritual through the actual—the theme of the poem" (53). The playfulness and ease of Wilbur's language in *Things of This World* underlie a serious commentary on the nature of the poetic process. There must be angels in the modern world, Wilbur argues, and the role of poetry is to define "the proper relation between the tangible world and the intuitions of the spirit" (125).

BIBLIOGRAPHY

Cummins, Paul F. *Richard Wilbur: A Critical Essay.* Grand Rapids, Mich.: David B. Eerdmans, 1971.

Eberhart, Richard. "On Richard Wilbur's 'Love Calls Us to the Things of This World.'" In *The Contemporary Poet as Artist and Critic: Eight Symposia,* edited by Anthony Ostroff. New York: Little, Brown, 1964, pp. 4–5.

Littler, Frank. [No Title] *Explicator* 40, no. 3 (1982): 53–55.

Wilbur, Richard. "On My Own Work." In *Responses: Prose Pieces, 1953–1976.* New York: Harcourt Brace Jovanovich, 1976, pp. 115–126.

Gary Kerley

"LOVE IS NOT ALL. IT IS NOT MEAT NOR DRINK." EDNA ST. VINCENT MILLAY (1931) Poet and critic LOUISE BOGAN praised the work of EDNA ST. VINCENT MILLAY for "cutting into the heart of complicated emotion," and such emotion is evident in Millay's sonnet "Love is not all. It is not meat nor drink," from the sonnet collection *Fatal Interview.* Intense, rhythmic, and written in memorable, epigrammatic lines, the poem confronts the complex longing, self-betrayal, and self-fulfillment at the heart of a romance. A masterful formal poet, Millay intertwines her thematic content with the poem's form, and by framing "Love is not all. It is not meat nor drink" as a Shakespearean sonnet, she not only finds a suitable structure for her claims about the inexpressible and enduring nature of love but also calls up a number of literary associations that enhance her claims.

Traditional sonnets, particularly the Petrarchan sonnet, frequently employ the blazon, or listing of the attributes of the beloved. In his sonnet 130, "My mistress' eyes are nothing like the sun," Shakespeare famously wrote a negative blazon, inverting the exaggerated claims of beauty in the Petrarchan blazon with exaggerated claims of his lover's ugliness. Yet Shakespeare's negative blazon does not so much denigrate the lover as suggest how her beauty transcends conventional standards. In "Love is not all. It is not meat nor drink," Millay not only repeats Shakespeare's negations, but inverts the subject of the blazon itself, attending not to the features of her lover, but to the capabilities of love itself. For Millay, love is a type of action, though it is not an action that preserves material well-being, for it offers none of the traditional benefits of material objects: food, drink, shelter, rescue in the midst of accident, or a means of healing. "Yet many a man is making friends with death / Even as I speak, for lack of love alone," writes Millay, suggesting how love preserves some aspect of human nature that is immaterial but nevertheless essential for life.

In the traditional Petrarchan sonnet, a *volta* or "turn" occurs between the opening octet and closing sestet (between the poem's eighth and ninth lines), suggesting an answer to a question or a resolution to a prior concern. In the traditional Shakespearean sonnet, such *voltas* occur between the three quatrains and the final couplet, though there often remains some echo of the Petrarchan *volta* as well. In Millay's "Love is not all. It is not meat nor drink," Millay seems to offer *voltas* in three places: between the sixth and seventh lines, when she stops negating love's material effects to acknowledge its essential value to life; between the eighth and ninth lines, when she begins her long consideration of the many circumstances that might lead her to "sell your love for peace / Or trade the memory of this night for food"; and between the 13th and 14th lines, when she denies the possibility of her own denial, claiming that "It well may be. I do not think I would."

Norman Brittin conjectures that the love sonnets collected in *Fatal Interview,* a collection that "presents a woman's responses to a passionate love affair from first attraction through the ecstasies of consummation to the sorrows of breaking up (because the lover grows cold) and eventually to resignation" (85), were written with Millay's lover George Dillon in mind. But Brittin's claims are inconclusive, and it is worth noting that "Love is not all. It is not meat nor drink" is stripped of the specific biographical references that would come to characterize the work of such CONFESSIONAL poets as W. D. SNODGRASS and ANNE SEXTON. As a result, the emotion Millay evokes transcends individual differences and cuts close to the essence of love.

BIBLIOGRAPHY

Bogan, Louise. *Achievement in American Poetry, 1900–1950.* Chicago: Henry Regnery Co, 1951.

Brittin, Norman A. *Edna St. Vincent Millay.* Rev. ed. Boston: Twayne Publishers, 1982.

Temple Cone

"THE LOVERS OF THE POOR" GWENDOLYN BROOKS (1960) An ironic satire on the egotism and prejudice at the heart of institutionalized charity, GWENDOLYN BROOKS's "The Lovers of the Poor" contrasts the affluent white population of Chicago's North Side suburbs with the poor African-American population of the city's South Side slums. Like many of her poems, "The Lovers of the Poor" shows Brooks's interest in poetic NARRATIVE; in this case, the poem represents a visit by "The Ladies from the Ladies' Betterment League" to a South Side housing project and the ironic interactions that follow. In a building where "Nothing is sturdy, nothing majestic, / There is no quiet drama, no rubbed glaze," a group of white women whom Brooks describes as "Sleek, tender-clad, fit, fiftyish, a-glow, all / Sweetly abortive" are confronted with a scene of unimaginable African-American "Squalor!" But Brooks's images of African-American domestic life, despite their rough realism, reveal a spirit of independence and endurance, "such a make-do-ness," missing from the white women's lives. As the visit progresses, Brooks takes the conventional (and racist) terms of evaluative contrast between whites and blacks—cleanliness and dirtiness, light and dark, —and inverts them, creating parallel contrasts of sterility and fecundity, illusion and reality, rigidity and improvisation. By challenging the motives and underlying values of the nearly sacrosanct institution of private charity, Brooks raises difficult questions about the possibility of racial and economic equality in American society.

The poem is written in irregularly rhymed lines of loose iambic pentameter (although the lines generally have five stressed beats, the number of unstressed beats varies, due to numerous metrical substitutions), and this tension between conventional form and a more prosaic free verse line imitating the patterns of speech is at play in the contrast between Brooks's baroque language ("debonair," "coddle," "plush," "noxious," "largesse," etc.) and the great poverty her setting and imagery evokes. Having already shown her skill at satire and her delight in parody in "The Anniad," a long poem in the tradition of both Virgil's *Aeneid* and Alexander Pope's mock epic *The Dunciad,* Brooks here draws upon the powerful enjambments and elegant diction of John Milton to evoke a hell that the devils must escape (and, ironically, an ugly paradise the devil would alter).

By comparing inventories of items from both white and black households, Brooks effectively associates the physical squalor of the slums with the moral squalor of the mansions. The slums stink of "urine, cabbage, and dead beans, / Dead porridges of assorted dusty grains, / The old smoke, *heavy* diapers," and the women go there hoping to find "The very very worthy / And beautiful poor. Perhaps just not too swarthy? / Perhaps just not too dirty not too dim." This desire to serve only those like themselves undermines their supposed charity, and renders their supposed morality self-serving, timid, and sterile. Brooks associates such character flaws with the homes of the white women, which resemble crypts in their careful presentation of fine, unused artifacts, the only food permitted near them being an expensive, refined appetizer of "turtle soup": "They own Spode, Lowestoft, candelabra, / Mantels, and hostess gowns, and sunburst clocks, / Turtle soup, Chippendale, red stain 'hangings.'"

Yet as much as Brooks satirizes the bloodless lives of the white families, she does not sentimentalize the slums. She notes, for instance, a "soft- / Eyed kitten, hunched-up, haggard, to-be-hurt," and the threat of physical violence, perhaps as revenge for the cruel history of slavery, is suggested by the "swaggering seeking youth and the puzzled wreckage / Of the middle passage." But such qualities are inferred by the white women themselves, given that their point of view dominates the poem. Moreover, with the figure of the "substantial citizeness / Whose trains clank out across her swollen heart," Brooks suggests that out of the wreckage of such places as this might rise individuals of greater emotional and moral character than any who seek to bring them charity. When the women are repulsed by the multitude of "children children children. Heavens!" one cannot help but hear the final exclamation as a statement of their own dehumanized (and dehumanizing) character.

More than a satirical contrast of two cultures, a contrast which often risks caricature, "The Lovers of the Poor" offers an analysis of the powerful need for control underlying the social and economic hierarchies of modern-day America, and the terrible fear motivating that need for control. Brooks describes the women as wearing "The pink paint on the innocence of fear," and when they flee the building, she notes how they want to remove themselves to the safe distance of financial transactions: "Perhaps the money can be posted. / Perhaps they too may choose another Slum!" But in spite of their fears for their security, the women encounter no real threats, only imagined ones, with the greatest anxiety coming from their own consciences, which must ask "What shall peril hungers / So old old, what shall flatter the desolate?" This terrible desire for approval from the poor, who receive financial "largesse" from a social system that has failed them but that has benefited the lovers of the poor, is driven by guilt, for the women "Judge it high time that fiftyish fingers felt / Beneath the lovelier planes of enterprise." For Brooks, such "charity" is equivalent to the bitter, violent forms of racism these women would surely never associate themselves with, even though they exhibit such prejudice when, at the end, they reveal their fear of being tainted simply by proximity with another race as they "Try to avoid inhaling the laden air." "The Lovers of the Poor" proves a devastating portrait of how deeply racism is ingrained into even the most beneficent features of American society.

BIBLIOGRAPHY

Shaw, Harry B. *Gwendolyn Brooks*. Boston: Twayne Publishers, 1980.

Wright, Stephen Caldwell, ed. *On Gwendolyn Brooks: Reliant Contemplation*, 60–65. Ann Arbor: University of Michigan Press, 1996.

Temple Cone

"LOVE SONG: I AND THOU" ALAN DUGAN **(1961)** ALAN DUGAN's best-known poem, "Love Song: I and Thou," overturns the traditional love lyric by ironically depicting marriage as a bad bit of housebuilding ending with a self-crucifixion that cannot be completed without the help of one's partner. With characteristically bitter and sardonic wit, Dugan repeatedly thwarts various conventions of love poetry, from the *blazon,* or description of the beloved's features, to the treatment of the beloved as a means of spiritual salvation. Yet Dugan rescues his love song (and love itself) from complete annihilation by focusing on the agony of this carpentry (and the final self-crucifixion) as an experience willingly undertaken with the cooperation of another person, acknowledging that "This is hell, / but I planned it."

Dugan's irony begins with the title, which suggests love is an equal and intense exchange, the phrase "I and Thou" alluding to the major work of the Jewish theologian and philosopher Martin Buber, who posited that complete selfhood and identity are achieved through a direct and reciprocal relationship with another being. Moreover, the term "Love Song" evokes the great sonnet traditions of Petrarch and Shakespeare, who wrote numerous lyrics devoted to the beauty of their beloveds. Yet the opening free verse line and the images that follow counter expectations of what a love song should say. "Nothing is plumb, level or square," Dugan writes, focusing not on his lover/wife, but on the house he has built, and not on its sturdiness, but on its flaws: "bent nails / dance all over the surfacing / like maggots." If taken as a symbol of their marriage, the house suggests a relationship marked by anguish, for Dugan's ironic Christian references give the house more than a mere resemblance to the cross that was used to torture and kill Christ, though Dugan will claim for himself no such stature: "By Christ / I am no carpenter."

But for as much as Dugan thwarts the conventions of the love lyric, even to the point of devoting nine-tenths of the poem to describing the carpentry and not the beloved, Dugan's poem slyly participates in the tradition of love songs after all. He describes the house in a blazon, or a naming and description of the specific parts, noting its "studs," "joists," "walls," "floors," and "frame-up." Moreover, in a sly allusion to Shakespeare's sonnet "My mistress' eyes are nothing like the sun," where the speaker describes his beloved in terms of how she deviates from conventional standards of beauty, Dugan depicts the house (and thus his love and his marriage) as being perfect in its imperfection: "It settled plumb, / level, solid, square and true / for that great moment." In the end, Dugan must admit, rather acidly, that though he can nail one of his hands to the boards, "I need a hand to nail the right, / a help, a love, a you, a wife." While this expression of love is surprisingly ironic, even bitter, it is perhaps more trustworthy than any declaration of conventional love poetry. Having admitted that he "spat rage's nails / into the frame-up of my work," the speaker has proven his scorn of sentiment and the implicit deceit of lyricism, so that his final admission of dependence upon another is as undecorated and intense an expression of love as the poem's title would lead the reader to expect.

BIBLIOGRAPHY

Boyers, Robert. "The Poetry of Survival." In *Contemporary Poetry in America: Essays and Interviews,* edited by Robert Boyers, 339–347. New York: Schocken Books, 1974.

Gery, John. "'Pieces of Harmony': The Quiet Politics of Alan Dugan's Poetry." In *Politics and the Muse: Studies in the Politics of Recent American Literature,* edited by Adam J. Sorkin, 206–221. Bowling Green, Ohio: Bowling Green State University Popular Press, 1989.

Temple Cone

"THE LOVE SONG OF J. ALFRED PRUFROCK" T. S. ELIOT (1915) T. S. ELIOT'S "The Love Song of J. Alfred Prufrock" is often identified by critics as the first truly modernist poem emerging from Anglo-American MODERNISM. EZRA POUND, who was instrumental in persuading Harriet Monroe to publish it in *Poetry* magazine, commented that it was the best poem he had "seen from an American" and that it was evidence that Eliot "had trained himself *and* modernized himself *on his own*" (qtd. in Ackroyd 56).

The poem, written predominantly in irregularly occurring rhymed couplets of various lengths, is a dramatic monologue in the tradition of 19th-century English poet Robert Browning, in which the speaker—in a state of distress or crisis—reveals more about himself than he appears to intend. Eliot's speaker, J. Alfred Prufrock, addresses an unidentified "you" concerning attendance at an evening party and asks a woman there "an overwhelming question." The ironic characterization of the protagonist Prufrock—who is not a great lover but a timid, self-conscious, and alienated man, a nonentity—is typically modernist. Although Prufrock exhibits the indecision of Hamlet, he knows that he is not a tragic hero—but rather "Almost, at times, the Fool." He is an antihero confronting the sterility and threat of the modern world, unable to act and frustrated by pseudointellectuality and impotence—both his own and that of the women who "come and go / Talking of Michelangelo."

Like Eliot's mature modernist masterpiece *The* WASTE LAND, "Prufrock" utilizes different tonal registers and modes of language as well as a lack of traditional narrative transitions to create the effect of chaos and fragmentation. An epigraph from Dante in the original Italian and allusions to the Bible, Shakespeare, and 17th-century English poet Andrew Marvell are juxtaposed with jarringly modern descriptive language and images: "When the evening is spread out against the sky / like a patient etherised upon a table." Prufrock's self-doubt, his self-awareness, and his failures are played out against an ugly urban backdrop, which mocks his romanticism and a social milieu that devalues his sensitivity and erudition. Despite all this, he experiences and expresses the idiosyncratic and poignant beauty of the yellow fog, the sea, and the singing mermaids he imagines.

BIBLIOGRAPHY

Ackroyd, Peter. *T. S. Eliot: A Life.* New York: Simon and Schuster, 1984.

Hayman, Bruce. "How Old is Prufrock? Does He Want to Get Married?" *CLA Journal* 38, no. 1 (1994): 59–68.

Smith, Grover. "'Prufrock' as Key to Eliot's Poetry." In *Approaches to Teaching Eliot's Poetry and Plays,* edited by Jewel Spears Brooker. New York: MLA, 1988, pp. 88–93.

Melissa Johnson

LOWELL, AMY (1874–1925) Amy Lowell is widely credited with introducing the IMAGIST SCHOOL to America's reading public. Lowell's identification with the movement began with her discovery of the poetry of H. D. (Hilda Doolittle), which inspired a pilgrimage to England and resulted in a number of lifelong friends (and enemies). Lowell embraced the imagists' emphasis on clear, unadorned poetry and soon brought her considerable resources to bear upon its wider dissemination. Lowell's poetry often explored personal themes of thwarted passion, interpersonal conflicts, the stark life of rural New Englanders, and the losses of war (*Men Women and Ghosts* [1916]), as well as more impersonal forces of myths and legends (*Legends* [1921]), and her work took a particular interest in Asian literature and Art (*Pictures of a Floating World* [1919] and *Fir-Flower Tablets* [1921]). In a career that spanned 650 poems, enriched by her sensitivity to sound and sensual imagery, numerous critical works, and a massive biography on John Keats (1925), Lowell undeniably altered the literary landscape of her time.

Lowell was born in Brookline, Massachusetts, into one of the most respected and influential families in New England. She received a private education at home under the guidance of governesses before attending private schools in Boston. Lowell began writing seriously after an inspiring encounter with the famous actress, Eleonora Duse, in 1902, though it was another actress, Ada Russell, who became her life's love. While Houghton Mifflin published her first collection of poems, *A Dome of Many-Colored Glass* in 1912, it was not until she traveled to London in the summer of 1913 to meet EZRA POUND and H. D. that Lowell's poetry began to receive critical attention. Over the next 12 years, Lowell's influence continued to grow, and by 1919 she became the first woman to deliver a lecture at Harvard. In 1924 she won the Helen Haire Levinson Prize from *Poetry,* and in 1926, one year after her death, her book of poems, *What's O'Clock,* was awarded the Pulitzer Prize.

Lowell's desire for poetry to be a spoken art eventually led her to develop a form of free verse she called "polyphonic prose," which she argued wove poetry and prose into one another so that rhythm and cadence, not appearance or strict meter, identified a work as poetic. In the poem "East, West, North, and South of a Man" (1925), Lowell writes, "Pipkins, pans, and pannikins, / China teapots, tin and pewter," inundating the verse with phonic effects. By employing the alliterative effects of the multiple *ps* and *ns* of the first line and *ts* of the second line to the assonance of the multiple short *i* sounds and the lines' overall rhythm and cadence, Lowell argued that her polyphonic prose served as a balance between the strict meter of Victorian verse and what she saw as the less musical free verse forms of her day. While today Lowell's poems and critical prose are overshadowed by those of other modernists, her work's relevance to present-day literary theories has given her a new life beyond her years.

BIBLIOGRAPHY

Benvenuto, Richard. *Amy Lowell.* Boston: Twayne, 1985.
Damon, Foster. *Amy Lowell: A Chronicle.* Hamdon, Conn.: Archon Books, 1966.

Jonathan Stalling

LOWELL, ROBERT (1917–1977) Robert Lowell was a major voice in American poetry in the cold war years, from the end of the Second World War until his death. The endurance of his reputation can be attributed, in large part, to his success in associating personal torment, his so-called CONFESSIONAL subject matter, with the social and geopolitical struggles of the time: the nuclear standoff between the United States and the Soviet Union, the war in Vietnam, and the civil rights struggle. He began as a successor to T. S. ELIOT and ROBERT FROST and matured into a poet of considerable originality and force. SYLVIA PLATH and ANNE SEXTON, both briefly his students, were profoundly influenced by his work. Other poets closely associated with Lowell include Allen Williamson, Frederick Seidel, CHARLES SIMIC, and Michael Hoffman.

Lowell was born in Boston, Massachusetts. His father was a retired navy officer; his mother, Charlotte Winslow Lowell, was descended from Mayflower stock. The IMAGIST poet AMY LOWELL was his cousin, the poet James Russell Lowell his great-great uncle. Lowell oscillated throughout his adult life between escape from his familial and social ties and return to the familiar, protective confines of Harvard and Beacon Hill, an affluent neighborhood in Boston. He endured two years as an undergraduate at Harvard before transferring to Kenyon College, where he became the protégé of the poet JOHN CROWE RANSOM. Through Ransom,

Lowell came in contact with the FUGITIVE/AGRARIAN SCHOOL—principally, ROBERT PENN WARREN and ALLEN TATE—writers who hoped to reclaim southern agrarian experience from what they believed to be northern misunderstanding and reverse bigotry. Also while he was at Kenyon, Lowell befriended the poet and critic RANDALL JARRELL. In 1940 he married the writer Jean Stafford. In effect, by his early twenties, he was taken up by the most influential literary figures of the time, largely on the basis of his charisma and promise.

As early as his first year at Harvard, however, Lowell showed signs of emotional instability. During a manic episode in 1943, he declared himself a conscientious war objector and was briefly imprisoned, an experience he would recall in his much-anthologized "Memories of West Street and Lepke" (1959). His powers of recovery were nearly as prodigious as his literary ambition; that same year saw the publication of his first book, *Land of Unlikeliness.* Three years later *Lord Weary's Castle* established Lowell as the most important young poet in America. His reputation was consolidated when *Life Studies* (1959) was published, with its candid studies of personal crisis and its masterful use of free verse (see PROSODY AND FREE VERSE). The enthusiastic critical reaction to *Life Studies,* and two volumes in a similar mode in the early sixties, *For the Union Dead* (1964) and *Near the Ocean* (1967), ensured professional security even when his personal life was deteriorating in a succession of affairs, drinking bouts, divorces, and manic-depressive breakdowns. The late 1960s saw his immersion in politics, inspired by his opposition to the Vietnam War and his friendship with senator (and fellow poet) Eugene McCarthy. His later years were taken up with a succession of uneven notebook volumes of 14-line poems (*Notebook 1967–68, History* [1973], *For Lizzie and Harriet* [1973], and *The Dolphin* [1973]). Lowell died soon after the publication of a volume of meditations on memory and death, *Day by Day.* He received the Pulitzer Prize for *Lord Weary's Castle* and the National Book Critics Circle Award for Poetry for *Life Studies.*

Lowell's writing falls into several periods. His early work shifts the ground of the high modernist mythic method of Eliot and EZRA POUND from classical Greece and Rome to Puritan New England (see MODERNISM). A wrathful Jehovah, Herman Melville's white whale, and larger than life Puritan and American Indian warriors take the place of Zeus and the Achaeans and Trojans, though the sense of heroic striving in the face of dark fate is more classical than strictly Calvinist. In style the poems derive from early Eliot by way of Ransom; the metrical elegance, the scholarly ambition, and the world-weary tone come from Eliot, while the affinity for American themes shows Ransom's guiding hand. "Mr. Edwards and Spider" (1947) is an early masterpiece in this style: "I saw the spiders marching through the air, / Swimming from tree to tree that mildewed day." The iambic rhythm of these lines is so assured that it carries the mixing of sea and military metaphors and knocks the dust off what heretofore had been a little known chapter in local history: the hellfire sermonizing of Jonathan Edwards. The New England, Puritan, haunted terrain of this and other poems from his first two books would remain Lowell's home ground throughout his career.

The early works mark a transition point in American poetry; Lowell and many poets following him could do nothing but aspire to a repetition of what he had perfected. The disruptions and torment that mental illness brought to Lowell's personal life made the prospect of writing grand meditations on the order of the late Eliot or WALLACE STEVENS untenable. The BEAT poets, led by ALLEN GINSBERG, and the NEW YORK SCHOOL poets, under the sway of FRANK O'HARA, brought pressure to adopt a more conversational and colloquial approach. Lowell's guide, in this respect, was WILLIAM CARLOS WILLIAMS, whose minute, nuanced poems of observation retained a high measure of craft. The result in *Life Studies* was a poetry that embraced the brutal realism of Ginsberg's incantations while avoiding bardic or visionary claims. Lowell's poems achieve a disarming simplicity and candor, but retain the resources of formalist verse, as in these lines from "To Speak of the Woe That Is Marriage" (1959): "My hopped up husband drops his home disputes / and hits the streets to cruise for prostitutes."

Over the years nearly every American poet of any importance has had to contend with *Life Studies* and *For the Union Dead,* either in embracing what Lowell had made or by deliberately turning away from it.

"Waking in the Blue" (1959) and "FOR THE UNION DEAD" (1964) remain two of the most important political poems of the 20th century; "Commander Lowell" (1959) and "My Last Afternoon with Uncle Devereux Winslow" (1959) are among the more important poems of childhood and reminiscence. Lowell's studies of marital troubles, divorce, and mental illness have long been known for their candor in pushing the limits of acceptable subject matter in poetry, but they would not have received such notice without their technical strengths: an epigrammatic concision line by line, exact and psychologically penetrating imagery, and a technical mastery balanced by a measure of ironic and gentle humor. Lowell appears to have shied from the temptation of the "great" that lured Dylan Thomas so often, as well as from the overly modest sense of the particular characteristic of Jarrell's melancholy late poems. Unfortunately Lowell could not sustain work at this level. Among the sonnets he produced in such volume for 10 years there are a few moving portraits—"ROBERT FROST" (1969) and "Ezra Pound" (1969) most notably—but for the most part they show a falling-off of vision and control. His last book, *Day by Day* (1977), somewhat redeems this late fondness for discursive, autumnal rumination. The poems break free of the previous 14-line restraint, and although the lines tend to meander rather than accumulate or build, the presence of death lends them an expressive coherence of mood.

Lowell can perhaps be compared with the English romantic Samuel Taylor Coleridge in personality and the arc of his life. Both were damaged and sad, their talents only partially realized, yet each was magnificent within his limitations. Like Coleridge, Lowell was a loyal and helpful friend, an unstinting conversationalist, and a great encourager of young talent. In his "Epilogue" (1977), he characterized his work as "heightened from life, / yet paralyzed by fact." The truth of this has been weighed and struggled with by succeeding generations of poets.

BIBLIOGRAPHY

Bell, Vereen. *Robert Lowell: Nihilist As Hero.* Cambridge: Harvard University Press, 1983.

Williamson, Allen. *Pity the Monsters: The Political Vision of Robert Lowell.* New Haven, Conn.: Yale University Press, 1974.

Yenser, Stephen. *Circle to Circle: The Poetry of Robert Lowell.* Berkeley: University of California Press, 1975.

Christopher Moylan

LOWENFELS, WALTER (1897–1976) Walter Lowenfels is perhaps most recognized as the editor of POETRY ANTHOLOGIES, such as *Poets of Today* (1964) and *Where Is Vietnam?* (1967). These collections introduced many new voices into the poetry landscape and cemented poetry's value as political speech in the 1960s and 1970s. Equally important are his own 12 collections of poetry, the best known of which is *Some Deaths* (1965). His work as an editor and author share themes of opposition to oppression and a commitment to poetic experimentation. Lowenfels's work emerges out of MODERNISM.

Lowenfels was born in New York City. He published his first collection of poetry, *Episodes and Epistles* in 1925 and fled to Paris the following year to pursue a writing career. Following the publication of *Steel 1937* (1938), Lowenfels did not write poetry for the next 15 years. During this period he edited the *Daily Worker*, a Communist newspaper based in Philadelphia. His association with the Communist Party led to charges in 1953 of conspiring to overthrow the government (in 1957 the charges were overturned due to lack of evidence). Lowenfels, who had resumed writing poetry during his trial and subsequent incarceration, marked his return to the world of poetry with the publication of *The Prisoners* (1957). It was during this period that he began editing anthologies of avant-garde poetry.

Lowenfels's early poems owe a great debt to modernist poets, such as T. S. ELIOT. Images and themes that appear in work from throughout his career are those of industry, commerce, and the struggle of labor against oppression. His middle and later poems are often characterized by wordplay, social commentary, and allusions to contemporary and historical events. An exemplary poem from Lowenfels's middle period is "Steel 1937" (1938), whose title refers to efforts to unionize small steel producers. He writes that beneath the surface of the earth "coal and iron lie and the men. Scratch it and you'll find / a geography of lies."

Lowenfels is notable for playing a role in many historically significant artistic groups in the 20th century.

Beginning his career as an American exile in Paris and later becoming a McCarthy-era target, Lowenfels went on to shape the landscape for the next generation of avant-garde poets.

BIBLIOGRAPHY

Bonosky, Phillip. "The Life of Walter Lowenfels." *Political Affairs* 75, no. 6 (1996): 16–20.

Lewis, Joel. Introduction to *Reality Prime: Selected Poems*, edited by Lewis. Jersey City, N.J.: Talisman House, 1998.

Jason Stumpf

LOY, MINA (1882–1966) Mina Loy was among the first poets writing in English to register the impact of the early European avant-garde (see EUROPEAN POETIC INFLUENCES), particularly the work of GERTRUDE STEIN and the Italian futurists. During the 1910s and 1920s, Loy used a combination of linguistic experimentalism and a razor-sharp satiric wit to challenge conventional aesthetics and social mores, attacking especially the sentimental attitudes toward women. Although very different in tone, Loy and MARIANNE MOORE represented for fellow poets the cutting edge of antiemotional and intellectual modernist poetry (see MODERNISM). EZRA POUND initially coined the term *logopoeia*, "poetry that is akin to nothing but language, which is a dance of the intelligence among words and ideas" (424), to describe the new poetry being produced by Loy and Moore.

Born in London, Loy originally pursued a career as an artist, which in the years prior to World War I brought her into contact with various avant-garde circles on the Continent, particularly the futurists, whom she credited with instigating her mature poetry. She spent much of the war in New York, where she was active in the most experimental artistic and literary circles and published her stunning early sequence of poems "Songs to Joannes" (1917). Throughout most of the 1920s and 1930s, Loy was a striking figure in the heyday of the expatriate bohemian community in Paris, where she published her collection, *Lunar Baedeker* [*sic*] (1923). Returning to New York, Loy lived increasingly in isolation, writing but rarely publishing poems and constructing artworks, using found materials, depicting street people.

Loy's deliberately artificial syntax, irregularly rhyming free verse, and unusual, highly unsentimental vocabulary create an intellectual and antiexpressive poetry drained of conventional lyric emotion. Although Loy's futurist-inspired manifestos express an expansive sense of liberation, her poetry is typically satiric: A corrosive questioning of respectability combines with a strong empathy for society's victims and rejects. However, underlying a hard verbal surface is an intense spiritual longing, which became increasingly pronounced in her later art and poetry.

"Songs to Joannes" (also published as "Love Songs") sardonically examines a failed affair in a highly compressed and elusive manner. The notorious image—"Pig Cupid his rosy snout / Rooting erotic garbage"—exemplifies the poem's mocking of conventional love poetry and romantic fantasy, which are revealed as grounded in instinct and sexuality. The ambitious long poem, *Anglo-Mongrels and the Rose*, written in the mid-1920s, mythologizes Loy's own upbringing and family in order to analyze the cultural effects of psychological repression. The poem dissects the consequences of the mind's denial of the body at both the personal and cultural levels in relation to sexuality, imperialism, aesthetics, and religion.

BIBLIOGRAPHY

Burke, Carolyn. *Becoming Modern: The Life of Mina Loy*. Berkeley: University of California Press, 1996.

Pound, Ezra. *Selected Prose 1909–1965*, edited by William Cookson. New York: New Directions, 1973.

Shreiber, Maeera, and Keith Tuma, eds. *Mina Loy: Woman and Poet*. Orono, Maine: National Poetry Foundation, 1998.

Jeffrey Twitchell-Waas

LUNCH POEMS **FRANK O'HARA (1964)** FRANK O'HARA's practice of dashing off poems anywhere, any place, any time, is the premise for *Lunch Poems*, his fifth book. The project was proposed by LAWRENCE FERLINGHETTI, whose City Lights Books published the collection once O'Hara finally prepared and submitted the manuscript (see POETRY PRESSES). The process took a number of years, since O'Hara was not particularly ambitious about publication; thus the 37 poems included in *Lunch Poems* sample more than a decade of work. Among these poems ostensibly composed during O'Hara's lunch hours are "The DAY LADY DIED" and an untitled poem which, in typical O'Hara fashion, begins in response to some immediate event, in this case quoting a newspaper headline declaring, "Lana Turner has collapsed!"

Francis Hope dismisses *Lunch Poems* in a single paragraph by concluding, "there's not much reality in these sandwiches—only the puppyish charm of occasional good impromptus" (688). Hope condemns O'Hara's poems for not being scholarly and crafted by revision, the very things O'Hara and other NEW YORK SCHOOL artists eschewed. In fact, O'Hara's technique was to use the impromptu, the spontaneous, and the common to create a charming intimacy. Raymond Roseliep employs stronger language in his assessment of these poems, complaining of the "wearisome cataloging of personalia" and "naughty-little-boy-sayings" (326) that offended him, things characteristic of American poetry after World War II and not just O'Hara's idiosyncratic province. The fundamentals of O'Hara's work elicit a more generous response from Gilbert Sorrentino, who notes the "grace and skill" with which O'Hara navigates a world that is "all fun and games, laughter, *la dolce vita;* even the wretched and miserable segments of it are etched in a fine chiaroscuro of wit" (19). The "brisk and brilliant world" Sorrentino identifies is abundantly evident in *Lunch Poems* (19).

A prime example of this speed and clarity is the compressed progression through time and space in the 11-, five-, and six-line stanzas of "Mary Desti's Ass" (1961). The poem's diverse occasions take place all over North America, Asia, and Europe, involving specific dancers, composers, and poets, but most of all "you" and "I" are the players in these events. The speaker encounters a friend's mother who is recently returned from Turkey, passes judgment on assorted American cities, and includes unknowns among the noteworthy who participate in the whimsical serial. There are pleasant and unpleasant episodes in this poem, which help it maintain contact with the concrete reality of the average person's world, and the finest images in the piece articulate these opposites. While one experience is "like being pushed down hard / on a chair," elsewhere life is balanced by "love sneaking up . . . through the snow." It is this careful touch that saves *Lunch Poems* from being pedestrian and prosaic.

BIBLIOGRAPHY

Hope, Francis. "Suffer and Observe." *New Statesman* (30 April 1965): 687–688.

Roseliep, Raymond. "From Woodcarver to Wordcarver." *Poetry* 107 (February 1966): 326–330.

Sorrentino, Gilbert. "The New Note." *Book Week* (May 1, 1966): 19.

A. Mary Murphy

LUX, THOMAS (1946–) Thomas Lux combines the wit typical of the NEW YORK SCHOOL with a rigorous eye for line and phrase. In his later work, especially, he captures ordinary things—rabbit tracks in fresh snow, an abandoned jar of maraschino cherries on a refrigerator shelf—and brings them to life in a vivid and unusual way. Like his contemporaries Bob Hicok and BILLY COLLINS, Lux captures the complexities of postmodern life in poems that sparkle even as they pack a serious punch.

Lux was born in Northampton, Massachusetts, and holds degrees from Emerson College and the University of Iowa. His first collection of poems, *The Land Sighted,* was published in 1970. Lux has taught at Sarah Lawrence College and the Georgia Institute of Technology. He received the Kingsley Tufts Award for *Split Horizon* in 1994; his *New and Selected Poems, 1975–1995* was a finalist for the 1998 Lenore Marshall/*Nation* Poetry Prize, and it was a finalist for the *Los Angeles Times* Book Award in poetry (1995). He has also been awarded a number of fellowships.

Before he became successful in his writing and teaching careers, Lux worked as a dishwasher and a night watchman, among other positions. Some of his poems reflect the realities of manual work—such as "Cows" (1994), set on the dairy farm where Lux grew up. "What I should be doing is working in a box factory in my hometown or the Elastic Web factory, where my whole family worked," he has said. "Given where I come from, I probably shouldn't be a poet. So I think I'm lucky." (Moore 65–66). He has also said that "good poetry can be accessible and clear and lucid and still be highly original and fresh and powerful." (Interview by Spalding). Although his first two books were heavily influenced by SURREALISM, he finds the style now "too arbitrary, and . . . kind of lazy. It doesn't pay enough attention to the musical elements of poetry" (Interview by Spalding).

Lux's work flows from his respect for the craft of working with words. His poem "An Horation Notion" (1994) tells readers that writing is a craft, neither a God-given talent nor a thunderbolt of inspiration: "You make the thing because you love the thing / and you love the thing because someone else loved it / enough to make you love it." Lux's poems are expressions of his love of words and his fascination with the varied characters and things that populate our world.

BIBLIOGRAPHY

Lux, Thomas. "Interview with Thomas Lux," by J. M. Spalding. *Cortland Review* 8 (August 1999). Available online. URL: www.cortlandreview.com/issue/8/lux8i.htm. Downloaded March 2007.

———. Untitled Interview with Thomas Lux, by B. C. Cohen. *Violet Crown* 1, no. 1 (September 2002). Available online. URL: www.violetcrown.net/text/newinterview.html. Downloaded March 2003.

Moore, Judith. "Thomas Lux." *San Diego Reader* 26, no. 22 (May 29, 1997): 65–66.

Rachel Barenblat

"LYING IN A HAMMOCK AT WILLIAM DUFFY'S FARM IN PINE ISLAND, MINNESOTA" JAMES WRIGHT (1963) Featuring one of the most argued-about final lines in American poetry, JAMES WRIGHT's "Lying in a Hammock at William Duffy's Farm in Pine Island, Minnesota" has been called variously the quintessential DEEP IMAGE poem, a critique of American culture, an immoral expression of nihilism, and a midwestern pastoral of classical Chinese grace and elegance. In a sense, the poem has spawned these varied readings because of its simple descriptiveness: the poem is a series of declarative sentences detailing images of an ordinary midwestern farm perceived from a hammock. The language of these descriptions is precise and realistic but metaphorically evocative, as when Wright describes a butterfly "blowing like a leaf in green shadow." As a result, the poem seems to hint at deep metaphysical truths without dwelling on a philosophical exposition of them, until the final, deceptively ambiguous line.

Of the six sentences that comprise the poem, the first three open with prepositional phrases that locate the images the speaker describes: "Over my head," "Down the ravine," "To my right." The images themselves are pastoral, suggesting tranquility and a sense of peace and ease brought about by the speaker's proximity to the natural world. He sees "the bronze butterfly, / Asleep on the black trunk," an image which recalls the Western use of the butterfly as a symbol of metamorphosis, but also the 18th-century Japanese poet-painter Buson's famous haiku: "On the hanging bell, / staying while he sleeps– / a butterfly." While these first three sentences (which comprise 10 lines of the 13-line poem) are largely focused on the poet's description of the farm setting, the complete absence of personal expression, of statements about the speaker's frame of mind, becomes a conspicuous absence, leading us to consider the state of mind that does not comment on itself, but on its surroundings. In this way, Wright's poem exemplifies what he himself praised in Asian poetry, the ability to "deal with the most commonplace of scenes and occasions, and to fill them with clear feeling and with the light of the imagination" (125).

In the last three lines, each of which is a single sentence, the poem's dramatic crisis occurs. As R. J. Spendal notes, the central conflict of the poem is "the opposition between an impulse to change and the failure to do so." The speaker leans back in the hammock "as the evening darkens and comes on," with the image of evening suggesting both mortality and comfort, but ultimately a resolution to whatever conflicts the speaker has faced. The speaker provides one last image in the penultimate line—"A chicken hawk floats over, looking for home"—that implicitly comments on his own situation. Where the butterfly earlier symbolized the possibility of metamorphosis, here the chicken hawk, whose piercing but unadorned cry is not unlike Wright's own unadorned style, symbolizes the speaker's unfinished quest. Like the hawk, the speaker appears to be looking for home, for a sense of connection to a particular place, a connection that promises self-unification.

In the final line, the speaker says, "I have wasted my life," and this utterance has brought the poem more notoriety than perhaps is warranted. In various interviews, Wright himself expressed exasperation at the negative response the line prompted; in one interview, he rejected the claim that the line was nihilistic or moralizing in tone, suggesting instead that it was "a religious statement . . . perhaps I've been wastefully unhappy in the past because through my arrogance or . . . my blindness, I haven't allowed myself to pay true attention to what was around me" (184).

BIBLIOGRAPHY

Spendal, R. J. "Lying in a Hammock at William Duffy's Farm in Pine Island, Minnesota." *The Explicator* 34, no. 64 (1976): pp. 64–65.

Wright, James. "Poetry Must Think: An Interview with Bruce Henricksen." In *Collected Prose: James Wright,* edited by Annie Wright, 172–190. Ann Arbor: University of Michigan Press, 1983.

Wright, James. "Some Notes on Chinese Poetry." In *Collected Prose: James Wright,* edited by Annie Wright, 123–125. Ann Arbor: University of Michigan Press, 1983.

Temple Cone

LYRIC POETRY The lyric is one of the primary poetic forms, which also include NARRATIVE and dramatic. The 20th-century American lyric poem itself takes on various forms, including the traditional elegy, sonnet, ode, song, as well as original types and styles. American lyric poetry has roots in the medieval song and ancient Greek poetry. Sappho, the sixth-century B.C. poet who shaped the lyric poem, influenced 20th-century writers, such as AMY LOWELL and H. D. Ancient lyric poetry was often set to music; the word *lyric* is derived from the Greek word for "lyre." Lyric poetry has never dwindled much in popularity. In the 20th century, it has often addressed feminist, racial, and other social concerns.

Much of the lyric poetry of the 20th century did not change a great deal in definition or form from the ancient poetry. Like the ancient lyric poems, 20th-century American lyric poetry emphasizes thoughts and emotions, often the poets' own suffering. The lyric poem still most frequently takes the form of a brief, highly personal monologue, often written in the first-person, dealing with a single person or situation, rather than a story involving multiple characters or events. The speaker of a lyric poem might address herself or himself, another person, a group of people, an object, a reader, or nobody. A large portion of American 20th-century poetry can be considered lyrical.

American lyric poetry dates back to Anne Bradstreet and Edward Taylor, 17th-century American poets, although lyricism was not characteristic of the poetry written at that time. The 19th century produced numerous lyric poems in American literature by poets including Emily Dickinson, Walt Whitman, Edgar Allan Poe, William Cullen Bryant, and Ralph Waldo Emerson. These poets had great influence on the lyric poetry of the following century.

Most 20th-century American poets wrote some lyric poetry, including ALLEN GINSBERG, JAMES MERRILL, DAVE SMITH, and JORIE GRAHAM. Major lyric poets of the 20th century included most of the IMAGISTS, T. S. ELIOT, as well as other poets, such as LANGSTON HUGHES, RITA DOVE, EDNA ST. VINCENT MILLAY, and ROBERT FROST. The blues, jazz, folk lyrics, and black spirituals of American music are also an important part of the lyric tradition.

Three traditional forms of lyric have been particularly popular in 20th-century American poetry. The first, the elegy, stems from Greek and Roman poetry covering a variety of subject matter. Ancient elegies followed a particular form: couplets consisting of a hexameter and pentameter line, respectively. The contemporary elegy, a somber poem usually written in remembrance of someone, with no particular meter or form, evolved from the 16th-century English elegy. The elegy may mourn a single person, a group of people, or humanity in general. ROBERT LOWELL's "The Quaker Graveyard in Nantucket (For Warren Winslow, Dead at Sea)" (1946) is a seven-stanza elegy for his cousin, which was inspired by Herman Melville (the poem was originally titled "To Herman Melville"). THEODORE ROETHKE, a friend of Lowell, also wrote elegies, such as "Dying Man" (1955), in memory of William Butler Yeats, and "Elegy for Jane" (1953). Millay's "Memorial to D.C." (1918) is a short poem mourning the death of a child. CONRAD AIKEN's "Crepe Myrtle" (1949), an elegy for Franklin D. Roosevelt, W. H. AUDEN's "In Memory of W. B. Yeats" (1940) and "In Memory of Sigmund Freud" (1940), and IRVING FELDMAN's "The PRIPET MARSHES," (1965), an elegy for the Holocaust victims, are also examples.

The second traditional form of lyric, the 14-line sonnet, originates from medieval songs. Many 20th-century sonnets have retained the respective forms and typical subject matter produced by Petrarch and Shakespeare in the 14th and 16th centuries. GWENDOLYN BROOKS's "The Sonnet-Ballad" (1949) and COUNTEE CULLEN's "Yet Do I Marvel" (1925) are examples of the Shakespearean sonnet form. In 1944 Brooks won the Midwestern Writers Conference prize for her sonnet, "Gay Chaps at the Bar," part of a sonnet sequence about World War II. In style, "Gay Chaps at the Bar" conforms to Shakespearean (three four-line stanzas and a closing couplet) and Petrarchan (an eight-line section and a six-line section) forms, albeit loosely. Other poets have deviated from the common structure and created their own forms. Robert Lowell published three collections of unrhymed sonnets in 1973: *For Lizzie and Harriet, The Dolphin,* and *History*. Other 20th-century poets who have written sonnets include EDWIN ARLINGTON ROBINSON, MARK JARMAN, ADRIENNE RICH, MARILYN HACKER, and Elinor Wylie, whose sonnets are often considered her best work.

The ode, also with roots in the ancient Greek choral songs by such poets as Pindar and Horace, has, like the elegy, undergone a transformation in form and subject matter. The ode is a long, usually formal poem and was popular with 19th-century English poets, such as John Keats and Percy Bysshe Shelley. Usually a poem celebrating something, the contemporary ode is well represented by James William Applewhite, Jr.'s "Ode to the Chinaberry Tree" (1986), WALLACE STEVENS's "The IDEA OF ORDER AT KEY WEST" (1934), DONALD JUSTICE's "Ode to a Dressmaker's Dummy" (1991), and "ODE TO THE CONFEDERATE DEAD" (1928), one of ALLEN TATE's best-known poems. Tate's poem, a meditation in a Confederate graveyard, recalls the ancient Pindaric odes, though Tate's poem speaks at a much more personal level.

The forms described above constitute popular forms of 20th-century American lyric poetry, yet modern lyric poetry is not limited to them. Similarly while many of the lyric poets of the 20th century conformed to traditional lyric forms and subjects, some poets created new styles and forms and departed from traditional subject matter as well. For instance, poets, such as Frost, while practicing well-known forms, such as the sonnet, also developed their own lyric styles and forms. Frost, one of the foremost American lyric poets of his time, is known for his craftsmanship and ability to write both blank verse and rhymed verse. Many of his poems imitate vernacular speech while following a rigid structure concerning rhyme and rhythm.

Traditionally lyric poetry is nonpolitical and nonhistorical. Yet many poets wrote about both political and historical subjects in their lyric poetry. Hughes, for example, incorporates political meaning into his poetry. "The NEGRO SPEAKS OF RIVERS" (1921) is considered a lyric, because of the emotional first-person voice, yet the poem contains overtones of racial issues not usually found in lyric poetry, as does his "Let America Be America Again" (1936). The first-person voice, common in his poetry, often speaks for the collective whole of African Americans.

Lowell, who was sentenced to prison as a conscientious objector to military service during World War II, emphasized history and politics in his poetry in an attempt to come to terms with the events of the wars of the late 20th century. While most of his poetry is lyrical, much of it also contains political overtones, such as "July in Washington" (1964), which describes the "elect, the elected" arriving as "bright as dimes," but dying "dishevelled and soft." Lowell was influenced in his writing by a number of other lyric poets, including Robert Browning, Frost, and WILLIAM CARLOS WILLIAMS.

The lyric poem has been written in a variety of styles by a cross section of 20th-century American poets. The 20th century produced traditional forms and styles of lyric poetry in addition to taking new directions with subjects and styles. Many of the foremost poets of the century earned recognition through their lyric poetry. Lyric poetry will always continue to be a major form of poetry that speaks personally to the reader.

BIBLIOGRAPHY

Jefferys, Mark., ed. *New Definitions of Lyric: Theory, Technology, and Culture.* New York: Garland, 1998.

Johnson, W. R. *The Idea of Lyric: Lyric Modes in Ancient and Modern Poetry.* Berkeley: University of California Press, 1982.

Pinsky, Robert. *The Situation of Poetry: Contemporary Poetry and its Traditions.* Princeton, N.J.: Princeton University Press, 1976.

Rosenthal, M. L. *The Modern Poetic Sequence: The Genius of Modern Poetry.* New York: Oxford University Press, 1983.

Sigrid Kelsey

M

MACKEY, NATHANIEL (1947–) Nathaniel Mackey is among the most prodigious and versatile African-American writers, practicing a unique open form that draws from the OBJECTIVIST and BLACK MOUNTAIN SCHOOLS, CARIBBEAN POETIC INFLUENCES, and the BLACK ARTS MOVEMENT. His poetry is closely connected with improvisational and spontaneous music. It explores and celebrates traditions and mythologies of the African diaspora that are largely marginalized in American culture. A literary nomad who invokes and channels descendants of spirits that inhabit the world, Mackey frequently makes references to Dogon cosmology (from West Africa), continental jazz, and Caribbean ritual in his work. His poetry will often unite, even within the course of a stanza, completely unconventional references with fluidity and lyricism. His collections are transcontinental maps that hold and cross-reference many narratives outside dominant cultural forms.

Mackey was born in Miami, Florida, and raised in California before attending Princeton and Stanford Universities. His first collection, *Eroding Witness,* was published in 1985; besides poetry, he has published three volumes of fiction and a book of criticism. Mackey has been editor of the journal *Hambone;* he also coedited the anthology *Moments Notice: Jazz in Poetry and Prose* (1993). In 2001 he became a chancellor of the Academy of American Poets.

Along with individual works, Mackey has authored an ongoing series of poems entitled *Song of the Andoumboulou* (1977–present), named after the unfinished beings of the Dogon. These poems are emblematic of Mackey's work, an excursion that the author will not bring to a conclusion, opting for hopeful (if fretful) pursuit of originality. This postmodern choice of serial incompletion offers the possibility that in seeking and representing difference or newness, a change in worldly circumstance will follow (see LONG AND SERIAL POETRY). These poems, spiritual-psychic locations, move along a highly developed web, "wrestling with / sound" that is inclusive and unreduced. Words, for Mackey, are blocks to be carved and reshaped while advancing content: "Sat on a / train crossing adverse / heaven. Raz they called / it, fractured masses . . . / Arz it / could've easily been, more / likely Zra, Zar the / asymptotic arrival we / glimpsed, / 'Not yet' yelled at every / stop." The poem continues, "Raz / with an *e* on the / end. A way of / spelling, a spell if / by *e* we meant / exit." This passage is indicative of Mackey's unusual, chordal treatment of words, which reflect the malleability of language. Thematically it shows Mackey's attention to an endless pursuit of something beyond what is present.

Mackey's poetry illustrates that there is progress to be made and boundaries to be crossed by people interested in cultural inclusion. The complexity of his work indicates that exploring the truth of history and density of humanity is a challenging, rough, and potentially endless ride.

BIBLIOGRAPHY

Foster, Ed, ed. *Talisman* 8 (1992). [Special issue on Nathaniel Mackey].

Rowell, Charles, ed. *Callaloo* 23, no. 2 (2000). [Special issue on Nathaniel Mackey].

Christopher Funkhouser

MACLEISH, ARCHIBALD (1892–1982)

Archibald MacLeish wrote poems reflecting on the timeless paradoxes of being human: He also acted as a Socratic voice, pricking the consciences of his fellow citizens, and he was perhaps the only poet of the early 20th century who grasped and wrote about the modern revolution in physics, the space-time continuum, and the four-dimensional universe. Considered a major modernist poet of the generation following EZRA POUND and T. S. ELIOT (see MODERNISM), MacLeish, with his sensitivity to technique and his lyrical gift, expressed common existential anxieties of the time. No poem has expressed the modernist sense of art so well as "Ars Poetica" (1926), with its signature statement: "A poem should not mean / But be."

MacLeish was born and raised in Glencoe, Illinois. He won three Pulitzer Prizes: in 1932 for the narrative poem *Conquistador* (see NARRATIVE POETRY), in 1953 for *Collected Poems: 1917–1952* (which won a National Book Award and the Bollingen Prize in that year), and in 1959 for his verse-drama *J. B.*, based on the *Book of Job*. In 1965 he received an Academy Award for his work on the screenplay of *The Eleanor Roosevelt Story*. He was appointed by President Franklin D. Roosevelt to serve first as librarian at the Library of Congress and later as director of the War Department's Office of Information.

MacLeish's poetry presents a rare wholeness of vision throughout his long career, reiterating the value of the real, the tangible experience of one's impressions and sensations. He distrusted abstractions, in the political arena no less than in the aesthetic. Unlike Pound and Eliot, he did not write for posterity nor for an elite, writing instead as one person to another, specifically as an American. "The poet's best work is elegiac," as DONALD HALL has remarked, "with a special rage for emptiness, for blank faces at the edge of the void. While we fear or dread annihilation, [MacLeish's] lines make their music" (122). In the one-sentence sonnet "The End of the World" (1926), which ends with the lines "There in the sudden blackness the black pall / Of nothing, nothing, nothing—nothing at all," MacLeish depicts our sense of dispossession, in which there are no answers to the ceaseless unfolding mysteries, and exhorts us to rely on the power of the spiritual within our own minds.

With its images able to be experienced directly, MacLeish's poetry pins down instances of the emotion rather than analogues of it, making us believe more than we can prove of the future of the human race, namely that we can make a future, shape a destiny. In the midst of often incredulous and cynical times, his achievement lies in the new ways he found to state what we have always known.

BIBLIOGRAPHY

Donaldson, Scott. *Archibald MacLeish: An American Life*. Boston: Houghton Mifflin, 1992.

Hall, Donald. *Their Ancient Glittering Eyes: Remembering Poets*. New York: Ticknor & Fields, 1992, p. 122.

Gerald Schwartz

MAC LOW, JACKSON (1922–2004)

Jackson Mac Low is among the most innovative and prolific poets of the 20th century. He is best known as a poet who employs chance operations and other deterministic compositional procedures (see CYBERPOETRY). That is, he frequently writes by letting objective and impersonal guides or systems determine what he will write. However, Mac Low also has written traditional sonnets, political, occasional, and CONFESSIONAL verse in a diverse body of work that continues to baffle and inspire his contemporaries, ROBERT CREELEY, JEROME ROTHENBERG, and ARMAND SCHWERNER among them. Influenced by Buddhism, pacifist anarchism, and the modern LYRIC POETRY tradition extending from Walt Whitman and CARL SANDBURG to EZRA POUND and GERTRUDE STEIN, Mac Low has also composed music and theatrical works, worked as a painter, film, and video artist, and performed individual and collaborative works, often with his wife, the artist and poet Anne Tardos. Taken as a whole, Mac Low's work reorients readers' assumptions about free will, conscious authority, and the individual ego.

Mac Low was born in Chicago, Illinois. He studied philosophy with Paul Goodman and other "Chicago Aristotelians," a group of philosophers and critics whose views contrasted to the coterminous New Criticism (see FUGITIVE/AGRARIAN SCHOOL), at the University of Chicago. In 1943 Mac Low moved to New York City, eventually earning a bachelor's degree in classical languages at Brooklyn College (1958). In the meantime he had worked as poetry editor for the pacifist-anarchist magazines *Why?/Resistance, Retort,* and, later, *WIN* (Workshop in Nonviolence [1966–75]). In the mid-1950s, Mac Low studied Zen and Kegon Buddhism with Dr. D. T. Suzuki at Columbia University and attended JOHN CAGE's course in experimental music. Mac Low has performed his poems—often devised as musical/theatrical scores—since 1960, when the Living Theater produced his *The Marrying Maiden: a play of changes.* The title refers to the oracle used to compose the piece, the *I Ching,* or *Book of Changes,* the same oracle Cage used to compose certain of his musical pieces, including his soundtrack for Mac Low's "play." Mac Low's first major poetry collection, *Stanzas for Iris Lezak,* was published by Dick Higgins's Something Else Press in 1972. The works in the collection are among the first composed by means of Mac Low's innovations in procedural, chance-deterministic methods. Other collections of poetry particularly suitable for staged performances followed, among them *Words nd Ends from Ez,* a methodical lyric revision of Pound's epic *The CANTOS,* taking the iconoclastic "spirit of Pound" to a logical extreme. Between 1966 to 1994, Mac Low taught at New York University, Temple University, and the Naropa Institute, among other institutions, and performed and exhibited works in various media from New Zealand to Germany, Japan, France, Sweden, and across the United States. In 1994 his *42 Merzgedichte in Memoriam Kurt Schwitters* shared the America Award for literature for a book of poetry published in that year. Other significant awards, fellowships, and grants have included those from the National Endowment for the Arts (1979), the Guggenheim Foundation (1985), and the Tanning Prize from the Academy of American Poets (1999).

Mac Low's work takes MODERNISM's formal innovations in verse to the level of meaning-making in language itself. From 1954, having already produced a significant body of work in traditional, free verse and cubist forms (see PROSODY AND FREE VERSE), Mac Low began composing via chance-deterministic methods, often devising poems from randomized linguistic units (permuting words or strings of words) culled from "source texts"—whatever he happened to be reading at the time. The motives for composing in this unusual manner, within a poetic tradition and deeply invested in the personal expression of the author, were based in part on interpretations of Zen Buddhism, which advocate circumventing the individual ego so that one's work might lead to the enlightenment of others. Mac Low developed three approaches based on such motives: intentional, quasi-intentional, and nonintentional.

Each approach is defined by the degree to which the author is able to foresee the results of the process of composition, on the one hand, and the performance (including silent reading) on the other. One of the results of using strict compositional methods is that Mac Low is meticulously responsible for his prosody and other formal measures, while performances frequently allow a great deal of initiative to the performers. Nonintentional and quasi-intentional works have contributed toward making Mac Low a primary influence on the linguistic experiments of the LANGUAGE SCHOOL in the 1970s and 1980s.

His later, "intuitive" works, often created, as he has said, "from the liminal area of the mind," point to a fourth method that does not prioritize "intention" in general (Mac Low). These later works produce rich cadences demanding a full and equal attention to language. This attention is signaled by scoring the poetic line with spaces to indicate pauses, hyphenation, and accents, as in this line of verse: "Finding your own level of héll with cultural signifiers-glowing-in-the-lámp-light" ("Finding Your Own Name *{Forties 154}*" [2001]). There is no ultimate religious message in Mac Low's work, implicit or explicit. Instead, he discloses how language permeates the individual ego with the social exigencies of the world that makes the idea of the ego possible in the first place.

BIBLIOGRAPHY

Hartley, George. "'Listen' and 'Relate': Jackson Mac Low's Chance-Operational Poetry." *Sulfur* 23 (fall 1998): 189–203.

Mac Low, Jackson. "Response to Piombino." Available online. URL: http://epc.buffalo.edu/authors/maclow/piombino.html. Downloaded March 2007.

Quasha, George. "A Concrete Dialog with Myself on, and for, Jackson Mac Low." *Paper Air* 2, no. 1 (1980): 55–63.

Retallack, Joan. "______:______" In *Festschrift for Jackson Mac Low's 75th Birthday, Crayon* (Fall 1997): 87–97.

Taylor, Henry. "Jackson Mac Low: Gristlier Translations, Arcane Pronouns." In *Compulsory Figures*. Baton Rouge: Louisiana State University Press, 1992, pp. 245–266.

Patrick F. Durgin

MADHUBUTI, HAKI (DON L. LEE) (1942–) Formerly Don L. Lee, Haki Madhubuti is a poet, educator, essayist, and literary critic whose work emerged out of the 1960s' BLACK ARTS MOVEMENT. Madhubuti read poetry in bars and out on street corners, punctuating his words with sound and rhythm. He was determined to bring poetry to the people, insisting, "Language in the context of the working poem can raise the mindset of entire civilizations, speak to two year olds and render some of us wise" (14). His lines were simple and direct, forging a black aesthetic that might be embraced by blacks who held little interest in the dense allusions of traditional poetic lines.

Born in Little Rock, Arkansas, and raised in Detroit, he settled in Chicago, where he founded Third World Press and established the Institute of Positive Education New Concept School and its publication, *Blacks Books Bulletin*. He also became one of the first members of the Organization of Black American Culture (OBAC). Widely anthologized and the author of more than 20 books, Madhubuti has been a professor of English and director emeritus of the GWENDOLYN BROOKS Center at Chicago State University.

During the 1960s Madhubuti, like many of his contemporaries, began to employ the vernacular in his poetry, "experimenting with vocabulary, spelling, punctuation, and line breaks" and using "a variety of first-person narrative stances" as Eric Weil has observed (234). A revolutionary writer who insists that social change must stand at the forefront of the writer's mission, Madhubuti's themes have ranged from tributes to Steve Biko, Malcolm X, and others to criticism of the Vietnam War and the importance of loving relationships.

In "White on Black Crime" (1984), Madhubuti highlights the effect of widespread unemployment. The speaker follows an unemployed master welder, "milton washington," who wanders the streets, looking "in garbage cans, leaving well lit allies," and pulling his carts, "eyes glued southward long steppin homeward." The speaker tracks washington's journey from his commitment to American patriotism to his disillusionment with the government's indifference to the plight of his family. Madhubuti highlights this inattention to certain classes of the population, while warning of the response of people who feel they have nowhere to turn.

Madhubuti's well-crafted poetry continues to mesmerize and transform with a blend of humor, realism, and rhythm.

BIBLIOGRAPHY

Madhubuti, Haki. *Earthquakes and Sunrise Missions*. Chicago: Third World Press, 1984.

Weil, Eric A. "Personal and Public." In *The Furious Flowering of African-American Poetry*, edited by Joanne V. Gabbin. Charlottesville: University Press of Virginia, 1999.

Judy Massey Dozier

MAJOR, CLARENCE (1936–) As poet, novelist, lexicographer, anthologist, essayist, editor, teacher, and painter, Clarence Major resists categorization. For instance, as editor of *The New Black Poetry* (1969), a volume often associated with the BLACK ARTS MOVEMENT, Major stayed "firmly away from any notion that art needed to be a conscious instrument of social or political change" (Rowell 672). Fiercely individualistic, but not solipsistic, Major's writing "weld[s] a complex modern diction to a constant historical consciousness" (Howe 69).

Born in Atlanta, Major grew up in Chicago. At 17 he studied painting at Chicago's Art Institute and later entered the United States Air Force, serving for a few years (1955–57). Major's 1954 pamphlet of poetry titled *The Fires That Burn in Heaven* was followed by publication in magazines and reviews throughout the next decade. After editing *Coercion Review* from 1958–66, Major moved to New York and worked as associate editor of the *Journal of Black Poetry* until 1970. Major's *Configurations: New and Selected Poems, 1958–1998* was a finalist for the National Book Award in 1999. His poem "The Funeral" won the 1976 Pushcart Prize. He received the National Council on the Arts Award in 1970 for the poetry collection *Swallow the Lake*. The short story "My Mother and Mitch" also won a Pushcart Prize in 1989. The novel *My Amputations* won the Western States Book Award in 1986.

Bebop and blues music are notable influences in his poetry, but Major is a self-described "visual thinker" (670). He sees painterly perspective and narrative point-of-view as interconnected, and his poems are often concerned with revealing their speakers' perspectives, as in the collection *Swallow the Lake* (1970). *Surfaces and Masks* (1988) is richly allusive, referring to famous pictorial art, as well as to literary and social history. This collection demonstrates both Major's sardonic wit and sharpening sense of the dependence of Western cultural traditions upon the presence of the ironically invoked "cultivated Negro": as Major suggests, "Behind every closed window / on the Grand Canal, Othello and Desdemona" ("I" [1988]).

Major's concerns with music, visual culture, and erudition, and their relationship to racist practices, are most pointedly addressed in his stunning long poem *The Slave Trade: View from the Middle Passage* (1994). Here a contemporary speaker possessed by the spirit of Mfu, an African man who drowned himself during the Middle Passage rather than submit to slavery, relates Mfu's story by reference to a series of famous paintings and cartoons. As Othello's spirit shapes the Venice of *Surfaces and Masks*, Mfu's channeled testimony forces a consideration of the ways in which the world continues to be shaped by the events, the logic, and the culture of the slave trade.

Major's individualistic and experimental poetry forces a new, often uncomfortable examination of culture and history.

BIBLIOGRAPHY

Bell, Bernard. *Clarence Major and His Art: Portraits of an African-American Postmodern Artist*. Chapel Hill: University of North Carolina Press, 2000.

Howe, Fanny. "Clarence Major: Poet and Language Man." *Black American Literature Forum* 13, no. 2 (1979): 68–69.

Major, Clarence. "An Interview with Clarence Major," by Charles H. Rowell. *Callaloo* 20, no. 3 (1998): 667–678.

Danielle Glassmeyer

MANDELBAUM, ALLEN (1926–)

Allen Mandelbaum's poetry places him in the mainstream of MODERNISM. Though not lavishly experimental, his verse possesses the allusive density of T. S. ELIOT, the bardic voice of EZRA POUND, the verbal playfulness of WALLACE STEVENS and James Joyce, and the terse, short-lined utterance of WILLIAM CARLOS WILLIAMS. Like some of his modernist precursors, his distaste for his times drives him to seek order and renewal in tradition, and his career as a translator and his deeply rooted Judaism supply him with ceaseless inspiration. "Time," writes Mandelbaum in the introduction to his translation of *The Aeneid* (1971), "with all its density, does not disappear; but it seems to heighten and not to muffle the words of the past addressing us" (xiv).

Heightening "the words of the past" has been Mandelbaum's life's work. The son and grandson of orthodox rabbis, Mandelbaum was born in Albany, New York. He graduated from Yeshiva University at 18 and received his M.A and Ph.D. from Columbia University. He has taught at several universities, including the City University of New York, Wake Forest University, and the University of Torino in Italy. Along with publishing five books of his own poetry, Mandelbaum established his reputation as an important contemporary translator through several translations of classical, medieval, and modern poets. Among his many awards and fellowships, Mandelbaum received the National Book Award for his translation of *The Aeneid* (1972) and was a finalist for the 1994 Pulitzer Prize for his translation of *The Metamorphosis*.

Indeed one can trace the theme of "translation" throughout Mandelbaum's own poetry. In his shorter lyrics and his longer poem sequences, *Chelmaxioms* (1978) and *The Savantasse of Montparnasse* (1988), Mandelbaum reworks classical motifs, such as the epic narrator, the hero, and the journey and quest, for the modern reader. As it bridges the centuries, Mandelbaum's poetry also blends classicism, Christian humanism, Jewish thought, and modern philosophy. Not only time and tradition, but the vastness of the world is translated into an eternally present "here" in Mandelbaum's global vision. Several forms of translation can be seen in this line from "The Civil Sea" (1967): "Arm in (iron) arm (s), Aeneas / and Augustine / sink within /

the wake of twenty centuries." Here literary allusions and the motif of the sea journey translate the present into the universal, assonance and alliteration translate words into music, and wordplay and punning translate the highly serious into the paradoxical and humorous.

Mandelbaum's poetry challenges the casual reader: Its conceptual density and its scholarly weight can drive even the most erudite to the "Notes" appended to each of his books. Nevertheless Mandelbaum's poetry, especially such sequences as *Chelmaxioms* and *The Savantasse of Montparnasse,* never fails to broaden our vision by immersing us in classical and Judaic traditions while delighting us with wit and wordplay.

BIBLIOGRAPHY

Mandelbaum, Allen. "Introduction." *The Aeneid.* Translated by Allen Mandelbaum. Berkeley: University of California Press, 1971, i–xviii.

Moore, Richard. Review of *The Savantasse of Montparnasse,* by Allen Mandelbaum. *American Book Review.* 10 (January/February 1988): 14.

Weinfield, Henry. "Allen Mandelbaum." In *Contemporary Jewish-American Dramatists and Poets: A Bio-Critical Sourcebook,* edited by Joel Shatzky and Michael Taub, 382–389. Westport, Conn.: Greenwood Press, 1999.

Dennis D. McDaniel

MASTERS, EDGAR LEE (1869–1950) Edgar Lee Masters, among the founders of the Chicago Renaissance (which included Theodore Dreiser, CARL SANDBURG, and VACHEL LINDSAY, with whom he associated), was a leading poet of naturalism and regionalism during the early 20th century. Also a novelist, playwright, essayist, and biographer, Masters is best known for his poetry. His most celebrated work, the *Spoon River Anthology* (1915), comprises more than 200 poems. Already a published poet, Masters was to become a prolific writer, but this collection remained his masterpiece.

Born in Garnett, Kansas, Masters spent most of his formative years in the Illinois towns of Petersburg and Lewistown, nearby the Spoon River, which provided many of the surroundings reflected in his work. Masters became a lawyer in 1891 and worked in his father's law practice. After a year Masters moved to Chicago, where he remained until 1923. There he wrote essays, plays, and poetry, often under pseudonyms, fearing that literary aspirations would damage his successful law career. Shortly after his success with the *Spoon River Anthology,* he gave up law to devote himself to writing. Masters received several literary awards, including the Helen Haire Levinson Prize from *Poetry* magazine (1916), the National Institute and American Academy of Arts and Letters award in literature (1942), a Poetry Society of America Medal (1942), and an Academy of American Poets Fellowship (1946).

Masters's early poetry follows conventional forms and deals with traditional topics (see PROSODY AND FREE VERSE). The *Spoon River Anthology* poems depart from this, presenting brief, free verse portraits of inhabitants of the Spoon River cemetery. The monologues provide honest, sometimes bitter or pathetic glimpses of life in a small midwestern town. For example, Knowt Hoheimer laments: "When I felt the bullet enter my heart / I wished I had staid home and gone to jail." The book, almost an instant success, received mixed reviews. Contemporary poets EZRA POUND and Sandburg praised the volume, while AMY LOWELL criticized it. Some held that it was too realistic, and that it contained inappropriate poetic matter.

Subsequent to *Spoon River,* Masters published poetry, plays, and essays, none meeting with his initial success. His second volume of poetry, *The Blood of the Prophets* (1905), received little recognition, as did most of his later publications. *The New Spoon River* (1924), a sequel to the first, is usually considered his second most important work. Masters's later work was criticized as being hastily published, serving as a vehicle to express his own political thoughts and opinions. Masters published 53 books during his lifetime, but will always be known as the "Spoon River poet."

BIBLIOGRAPHY

Russell, Herbert K. *Edgar Lee Masters: A Biography.* Urbana: University of Illinois Press, 2001.

Sigrid Kelsey

MATHEWS, HARRY (1930–) Harry Mathews is better known as a novelist than as a poet, but in both guises he has exerted a decisive influence on the experimental tradition in American letters. In the late 1950s and early 1960s, Mathews became close with many of the key figures in the NEW YORK SCHOOL of poetry, especially JOHN ASHBERY, who led him, Mathews writes, "to discover the possibility of 'MODERNISM'—a world where I was allowed and in some sense obliged to invent what I wrote" ("Autobiography" 137). Since the early 1970s, Mathews has been associated with OuLiPo, or Ouvroir de littérature potentielle (Workshop of potential literature), a French group of writers and mathematicians dedicated to exploring the use of formal constraints in the writing of novels and poems. As the only American member of the group, Mathews has functioned as a cultural emissary between the French and American avant-gardes.

Mathews was born and raised in New York City and attended Princeton and Harvard, where he earned a degree in music in 1952. Between 1953 and 1978 he lived in various European locales, spending most of his time in Paris. From 1961 to 1963 he edited the legendary magazine *Locus Solus,* along with Ashbery, KENNETH KOCH, and JAMES SCHUYLER. In 1973, after befriending the French novelist Georges Perec, Mathews was asked to join OuLiPo. Mathews received a National Endowment for the Arts grant in fiction writing in 1981 and an award for fiction from the American Academy of Arts and Letters in 1991. His novel *The Journalist* won the America Award for fiction in 1994.

In his early poetry, represented in the volumes *The Ring* (1970) and *The Planisphere* (1974), Mathews exhibits a comic SURREALISM and a mercurial range of tones, from breathless exuberance to solitary despair. The poems tend to cohere thematically rather than as narrative situations. For example, "Deathless, Lifeless" (1971) meditates on a loosely related set of images of human death and separation and on their analogues in the natural world: "Someone who is complete became the fragment," "Oaks erect themselves as casually."

After joining the OuLiPo, Mathews became increasingly preoccupied with formal experimentation. The poems that make up *Trial Impressions* (1977) consist entirely of contemporary variations on a love lyric by the Elizabethan poet John Dowland: "Deare, if you change, Ile never chuse againe" becomes "Deep, if you charge, I'll never chug again" and "If you break our breakfast date, I'll go begging in Bangkok." Mathews has called the sequence "an experiment in discovering how formal pretexts lead into intimate experiences" ("Autobiography" 160). The phrase neatly sums up his continuing poetic project. The elaborate surface constructions of Mathews's poems repeatedly reveal themselves as attempts to articulate the deep truths of desire and loss by oblique means.

BIBLIOGRAPHY

Mathews, Harry. "Autobiography." In *The Way Home: Collected Longer Prose.* London: Atlas Press, 1989.

———. "An Interview with Harry Mathews," by Lytle Shaw. *Chicago Review* 43, no. 2 (spring 1997): 36–52.

———. Preface to *A Mid-Season Sky: Poems 1954–1991.* Manchester: Carcanet Press, 1992.

O'Brien, John, ed. *Review of Contemporary Fiction* 7, no. 3 (Fall 1987). [Harry Mathews Issue]

Damian Judge Rollison

MATTHEWS, WILLIAM (1942–1997) Associated with DEEP IMAGE POETRY, William Matthews received much praise for his ability to apply intelligence, wit, irony, and, often, a conversational tone to such recurrent themes as loss, the workings of the mind, and the passing of time. He once remarked, "[W]riting poems was the first time I ever learned to play. When I discovered I could play and be serious at the same time, it was terrific" (33).

Matthews was born in Cincinnati, Ohio, and published his first full-length collection, *Ruining the New Road,* in 1970. His honors included National Endowment for the Arts Fellowships (1975 and 1984), a Guggenheim Fellowship (1980), and a National Book Critics Circle Award in 1995 for his collection *Time & Money.* He served as president of Poetry Society of America, served on the literature panel of the National Endowment of the Arts, and taught at several universities.

Comfortable with free verse and, particularly in later poems, structured form (see PROSODY AND FREE VERSE), Matthews applies intelligence, irony, and a sense of sentence rhythm to subjects ranging from lust to famous last words, Verdi to vasectomies. Critics note that Matthews's work gains a complexity by simultaneously addressing two opposed ideas: "gain and loss are natural partners, as are birth and death," Allen Hoey suggests, noting the twin themes of the titles of such collections as *Rising and Falling* and *Time & Money* (118). In addition, DONALD REVELL has observed that Matthews "skillfully avoids reductiveness just as he avoids the maudlin self-awareness to which CONFESSIONAL poets often succumbed" (123).

Matthews frequently writes about such passions as basketball and jazz, connecting them to a broader sense of the melancholy that accompanies change. In "The Blues" (1989), he links his boyhood music lessons to emotional ones: "I knew the way music can fill a room, / even with loneliness." Known for his love of puns and quips—he titled one poem "The Penalty for Bigamy Is Two Wives" (1982)—his sharp wit serves an emotional depth and resonance. In "Dead Languages" (1995), a poem characteristic of his interest in language itself, Matthews moves from a list of amusing etymologies that show how language changes without our knowing it ("Yes, *senile* / and *Senate* 'grew' from the same 'root'") to an understanding that we too experience subtle, unexplainable changes: "we led our lives / or they led us, and how would we know which?"

At his best, Matthews used his carefully crafted verse, his attention to the slippages of language, and his cultivated wit and erudition to provide perspective on loss and change, offering pleasures to the mind while plumbing the human heart.

BIBLIOGRAPHY

Hoey, Allen. "Love & Work." *Shenandoah* 48, no. 3 (1998): 110–121.

Matthews, William. "Talking about Poetry: An Interview with William Matthews." [Interview by Wayne Dodd and Stanley Plumly (on April 12–13, 1972 in Athens, Ohio)]. *Ohio Review* 13, no. 3 (1972): 33–51.

Revell, Donald. "'The Deep En-leaving Has Now Come': Ammons, Matthews, Simic, and Cole." *Ohio Review* 41 (1988): 116–132.

Bryan Walpert

MATTHIAS, JOHN (1941–) John Matthias's poetry is as grounded in British traditions as it is in American culture. While his work has been influenced by major American poets, including ROBERT DUNCAN and EZRA POUND, it is also very much influenced by the work of the Welsh poet David Jones. Like Pound and Jones, Matthias is deeply concerned with giving language the weight of its lost historical and philosophical connotations. In fact, one of Matthias's most important contributions to poetry is the way he takes language and imbues it with a richness of association, often by writing about found texts in the context of the history and landscape from which they came. The critic Vincent Sherry notes the power this kind of activity can have for readers at a time when so many of the stories once considered central to Western civilization have lost their immediate familiarity. "Matthias," writes Sherry, "offers from his word-hoard and reference-trove the splendid otherness of unfamiliar speech; on the other hand, this is our familiar tongue, our own language in its deeper memory and resonance" (145).

Born in Columbus, Ohio, Matthias attended Ohio State University, then went on to study English literature at Stanford in 1963. While there he was a member of a group of young poets studying under YVOR WINTERS, a group that included two future U.S. poets laureates, ROBERT PINSKY and ROBERT HASS. Deeply involved in the anti–Vietnam war movement and drawn toward the countercultural world of San Francisco, Matthias nevertheless left the Bay Area in 1966 to write poetry and pursue his studies in England. A professor as well as a poet, Matthias began teaching at the University of Notre Dame in 1967. He has published eight books of poetry, as well as translations from Swedish and Serbian, and has edited two books on Jones.

Matthias's poetry is driven by three sets of contrary impulses. In the poems of his first three books (*Bucyrus* [1970], *Turns* [1975], and *Crossings* [1979]), for example, we find Matthias pulled toward political activism, on the one hand, and a playful aestheticism, on the other. In "The Stefan Batory Poems" (1979), he even says of himself that "Prospero whispers in one ear / And Lenin in the other." Another tension in his work comes from the conflict between the desire to write lucid, personal lyrics and the attraction of arcane reference and formal experimentation. A further set of contrary impulses in Matthias's work is the pull toward the geographic particularities of places where he has lived (especially England) and the lure of the imaginative work of artists from long ago and far away: He is simultaneously a poet of place and a profoundly intertextual poet, writing about landscapes and making use of the texts associated with those landscapes. "Northern Summer" (1984) and "A Compostella Diptych" (1991) are exemplary poems of this kind. These contradictions do not make for incoherence, however: It is through orchestrating them into a music of his own that Matthias defines his singular place in American poetry.

BIBLIOGRAPHY

Archambeau, Robert, ed. *Word Play Place: Essays on the Poetry of John Matthias.* Athens: Ohio University Press/Swallow Press, 1998.

Hooker, Jeremy. *The Presence of the Past: Essays on Modern British and American Poetry.* Bridgend, United Kingdom: Poetry Wales Pres, 1987, pp. 97–105.

Sherry, Vincent. "The Poetry of John Matthias: Between the Castle and the Mine." *Salmagundi* 65 (fall 1984): 132–145.

Robert Archambeau

MAXIMUM SECURITY WARD **RAMON GUTHRIE (1970)** *Maximum Security Ward,* published when RAMON GUTHRIE was 74 years old, is one of the last masterpieces of MODERNISM. In this work Guthrie echoes the allusiveness and renaissance humanism of EZRA POUND'S *The CANTOS,* the voices of T. S. ELIOT'S *The WASTE LAND,* and WALLACE STEVENS'S (and Eliot's) obsession with the loss of religious certainty. Like *The Cantos* and CHARLES OLSON'S *MAXIMUS POEMS, Maximum Security Ward* is a long poem made up of smaller individual poems (see LONG AND SERIAL POETRY).

Although *Maximum Security Ward* is a poem of many voices, the dominant one is that of Guthrie's own persona, identified with Merlin, Marsyas, Ishmael, and others who dared to defy the gods. It is a witty, self-conscious, mocking, and tender voice, trying to find a moral center without God and believing in love even in the face of painful death. The voice is given authority not only by the immediate suffering of cancer treatment in an intensive care ward he mockingly calls the Maximum Security Ward, but also by the human suffering caused by the series of wars that mutilated the 20th century. The poem suggests that life teases us with the possibility of beauty, justice, and liberty, only to defeat us in the end by taking away all three. But life does not just tease us, the poem goes on to say, but leaves us to create and affirm meaning, in spite of our ultimate destruction.

Characteristics of the poem include the elements of modernism that Guthrie took from Pound and Eliot (in addition to the love of the medieval Provençal troubadors), allusions to contemporary science played against mythic references, and a reliance on fragments and quick cuts similar to cinema clips or voices on a radio. All these help to give a sense of the upheaval that followed World War I through World War II, the Korean War, and Vietnam. A key theme is embodied in the line "Human I never would have chosen to be," which appears several times, including in "This Stealth," where he says that even though he would not choose to be human, he respects that humans, in spite of "all frustration," try to "push . . . beyond" their limitations. Angry at Christianity's self-righteousness and America's paternalism, Guthrie nonetheless believes in righteousness, as embodied in "lovers of liberty, beauty, justice" ("And the Evening and the Morning"). Those three touchstones—liberty, beauty, and justice—make Guthrie's work less evasive than Eliot's or Stevens's and more sharply focused than Pound's.

A poem about a man dying of cancer may sound depressing, but *Maximum Security Ward* is an exhilarating and uplifting book, full of honest emotion and wonderful fun, with a tight network of cross-references and allusions.

BIBLIOGRAPHY

Gall, Sally. *An American Classic: Ramon Guthrie's Maximum Security Ward.* Columbia: University of Missouri Press, 1984.

———., and M. L. Rosenthal. *The Modern Poetic Sequence: The Genius of Modern Poetry.* New York: Oxford University Press, 1983.

Hadas, Rachel. "Eloquence, Inhabited and Uninhabited." *Parnassus* 12, no. 1 (fall–winter 1984): 133–153.

Thomas Lisk

THE MAXIMUS POEMS **CHARLES OLSON (1960–1983)** CHARLES OLSON'S *The Maximus Poems* articulates an image of "man" through a form of mapping that navigates human uncertainties. Constructing an alternative to political and social life during the 1950s and 1960s, Olson's postmodern ethos projects a familiarity with the human body from which, Olson feels, modern man has become estranged. His aim is to merge the mental and the physical landscapes through passionate acts of attention. Avoiding both sentence and paragraph, he employs fragmentary allusions to an eclectic range of texts that resonate with his purpose. Two volumes of this multivolume poem were published during Olson's life: *The Maximus Poems* (1960) and *The Maximus Poems, IV, V, VI* (1968). *The Maximus Poems: Volume Three* (1975) was published posthumously. The standard text, including previously unpublished fragments, is *The Maximus Poems* (1983), edited by George Butterick. As the poem evolves, an exceptional political vision becomes the tragedy of an isolated visionary. *The Maximus Poems* is arguably the most significant American poem of epic proportions other than *The* C*ANTOS* of EZRA POUND, the poem to which it is most often compared (see LONG AND SERIAL POETRY).

Set largely in Gloucester, Massachusetts, the forward motion of *The Maximus Poems* maps a time-space complex, modeled on the quantum-mechanical view of the universe, and folds inner experience with the poet's sense of place in the world. Olson is insistent about the need for the whole organism to experience direct and immediate perceptions. Maximus, the heroic antagonist, envisions a polis, or ideal city, heeding a necessity "to write a Republic." Here, in a gesture typical of Olson's method, ethical and nautical senses of "write" and "right" pun thematically. Hopes for practical, social success of his project diminish during the years of its composition; nonetheless the poems maintain a visionary quality until reaching the cryptic flatness of the final words, "my wife my car my color and myself."

In the first entry in the larger scheme of poems that make up *The Maximus Poems,* composed in 1950 as one of several "letters" addressed to his contemporaries, Maximus urges the citizens of Gloucester, especially the young, to embrace change. Olson introduces the dominant thematic chord: "love is form, and cannot be without / important substance." This intensity reflects his long-term private correspondence with the writer Frances Boldereff, whose ideas inspired him at crucial turning points. In 1953, after having revised his landmark 1950 essay "Projective Verse" (see ARS POETICAS), Olson returned to the poem with a renewed sense of purpose and method. The page now reflects Olson's visual sense of how words come over into speech when the individual is freed from self-consciousness. For instance, William Stevens, an early shipbuilder, embodies the poetic fact that measurements consonant with the sense of touch are crucial to achieving poetic purpose. Stevens is the first Maximus, or alter ego of the narrator. In the entry "Tyrian Business," Olson himself becomes Maximus and learns "how to dance / sitting down," the breath projecting the kinetic motion of thought. Speaking now with a less rhetorical voice, the poet inhabits the poem. Additionally historical facts have established an objective basis for investigating heroic archetypes and projecting authentic engagement with the environment, as exemplified both by the accomplishments of those colonial-era settlers that Olson considers to have been heroic and by the lore and life styles of American Indians. For Olson the Puritan settlement of New England signifies a perversion of newly discovered material wealth, while seafaring figures, like Juan de la Cosa, represent a realistic and pragmatic relation of person to space conceived as inescapable fact to which the ego must adjust its motions. To Olson's sensibility, projecting a landscape on a map of human possibilities requires firsthand experience. Similarly evidence from the history of the fishing trade and American Indian folklore testify to methods of living in physical and spiritual accord with the earth.

In *The Maximus Poems, IV, V, VI* (1968), the cosmological sweep of the undertaking emerges. Engagement with the archetype of the hero engenders a spiritual order of discoveries. Both American Indian and the earliest Indo-European materials enter the fabric of the poem as Maximus/Olson becomes a reflection of the heroic archetype developed by psychologist Carl Jung, *homo maximus.* Olson's use of Jung fuses with his reading of the philosopher Alfred North Whitehead and his association of ego-transformation with spiritual and physical self-knowledge. Figures that join birth with death and the sea with the land record Olson's sense of becoming one with his mortality. Intoned to refrains from Hesiod's *Theogony* (eighth century B.C.), "Maximus from Dogtown—I" enacts a ritual death of the hero, embraced by the mother. The figure is a transformation of Our Lady of

Good Voyages, who in the first letter cradles, not the Christ Child, but a ship "of uncertain sex." The exploration of the landscape associated with the mother's body reveals a questionable masculinity, reflecting Olson's private uncertainties. In the Gravel Hill section of *Maximus,* outside and inside surfaces, indeed, the very body and method of the poem, merge. Enyalion, a wounded, perhaps castrated type of the god Mars appears first in this context. He will become the poet's alter-ego in the concluding volume.

The mapping of landscape, figure, and enduring pattern is crucial to "Maximus's success in finding a coherent order," Don Byrd has observed, "despite his initial failure to make Gloucester itself cohere" (86). Relations among major themes enact Olson's dream-inspired response to a sentence from *The Secret of the Golden Flower,* a ninth-century Chinese work of alchemy: "that which exists through itself is called meaning" (qtd. in Clark 280–281). Similar themes and images map an intensity of transformative moments, for instance, the image of a "Black Chrysanthemum" and "the flower" that "grows down the air of heaven," near the opening of *The Maximus Poems: Volume Three,* a volume that also contains graphically compelling pages, as words arranged in roseate patterns. In *The Maximus Poems,* the honesty with which the poet portrays both illumination and, finally, a faltering sense of self-worth touches with acute relevance on contemporary struggles with subjectivity, even though some readers have raised questions about Olson's gender-bias and personal arrogance. Olson's commitment to meaning and method has influenced a wide range of poets, including ROBERT CREELEY, ROBERT DUNCAN, and others associated with BLACK MOUNTAIN College; ALLEN GINSBERG, ROBIN BLASER, JOHN WIENERS, and others associated with SAN FRANCISCO RENAISSANCE or BEAT poetry; and contemporary writing like that of SUSAN HOWE, BARRETT WATTEN, RON SILLIMAN, and others associated with LANGUAGE-centered writing.

BIBLIOGRAPHY

Butterick, George. *A Guide to* The Maximus Poems *of Charles Olson.* Berkeley: University of California Press, 1978.

Byrd, Don. *Charles Olson*'s Maximus. Chicago: University of Illinois Press, 1980.

Clark, Tom. *Charles Olson: The Allegory of a Poet's Life.* New York: Norton, 1985.

Olson, Charles. *Collected Prose.* Berkeley: University of California Press, 1997.

Stein, Charles. *The Secret of the Black Chrysanthemum.* New York: Station Hill, 1987.

Don Wellman

MAYER, BERNADETTE (1945–)

Bernadette Mayer is a foremost experimental poet in the NEW YORK SCHOOL tradition. Her work strives for an inclusiveness of quotidian experience, dream materials, memories, and records of consciousness. She writes in a wide range of forms, from more recognizably poetic structures, such as sonnets, to long prose texts, such as journals and extended epistolary sequences. Through her teaching at the St. Mark's Poetry Project in New York in the early 1970s (see POETRY INSTITUTIONS), she helped bring together many of the poets who would later form the LANGUAGE SCHOOL.

Mayer was born in Brooklyn, New York. Her early life was marked by the deaths of both her parents by the time she was 14. She attended the New School for Social Research (B.A., 1968) and has taught widely in New York and various places in New England. She had children with poet LEWIS WARSH, with whom she edited the United Artists book series. She received a National Endowment for the Arts grant in poetry in 1979.

One of Mayer's experimental projects, widely seen as an early example of POETRY IN PERFORMANCE, called "Memory" (1972), combined photography and taped narration. Originally a gallery installation in New York, the text was published as *Memory* (1975). In this work Mayer shot one roll of color film every day during the month of July 1971, accompanied by a taped narration. In *Studying Hunger* (1975), Mayer states: "I had an idea before this that if a human, a writer, could come up with a workable code, or shorthand, for the transcription of every event, every motion, every transition of his or her own mind, & could perform this process of translation on himself, using the code, for a 24-hour period, he or we or someone could come up with a great piece of language/information" (7). Mayer's experimental aesthetic is on display here, breaking down formal distinctions between poetry and prose, with the aim of inclusiveness in recording states of consciousness.

The book-length poetic text *Midwinter Day* (1982) was written on a single day, December 22, 1978, in Lenox, Massachusetts. Mayer's lyric voice here ranges from "Wisdom's gray sky remembers" to "Staying in / And sex is memory's intensity." Peter Baker has written of this work: "Suspending final or totalizing judgments, the text would remain open past the point of critical evaluation, inviting endless readings and active writings, where 'writing' includes much more than composing poetry" (161).

A collection of Mayer's shorter poems and selections from the longer works was made available in *A Bernadette Mayer Reader* (1992). Her highly colloquial voice can be seen in the "Sonnet" that begins, "You jerk you didn't call me up," and proclaims, "I'm through with you bourgeois boys." The collection also includes some of her translations from Catullus and the *Greek Anthology*, a group of 6,000 poems written between the seventh century B.C. and A.D. 10th century, indicating something of the range of this American original.

BIBLIOGRAPHY

Baker, Peter. "Language, Poetry and Marginality." In *Obdurate Brilliance: Exteriority and the Modern Long Poem.* Gainesville: University of Florida Press, 1991, pp. 150–161.

Mayer, Bernadette. *Studying Hunger.* Berkeley, Calif.: Big Sky, 1975.

Shapiro, David. "A Salon of 1990: Maximalist Manifesto." *American Poetry Review* (January/February 1991): 37–47.

Peter Baker

MCCLATCHY, J. D. (1945–) J. D. McClatchy has successfully been a writer, editor, critic, teacher, and political representative. Not only has McClatchy been viewed as an important writer since his first book of poems in 1981, but he has also been influential as the editor of the *Yale Review.* He has edited poetry anthologies and published two collections of critical essays. He has taught at Yale, Princeton, the University of California, Los Angeles, and Columbia, and has been chancellor of the Academy of American Poets. McClatchy's poems, like those of many of his postmodern colleagues, are lyrical versions of NARRATIVE POETRY (poems that tell a story or capture a moment through some form of personal expression) and largely free verse. They are remarkable for their elevated language and subject matter, the latter often containing elements of CONFESSIONAL and metaphysical poetry. The contemplative tone of his work shows the influence of YVOR WINTERS and the early work of JAMES MERRILL and ROBERT PINSKY.

McClatchy was born in Bryn Mawr, Pennsylvania. He is the author of five books of poetry: *Scenes from Another Life* (1981), *Stars Principal* (1986), *The Rest of the Way* (1990), *Ten Commandments* (1998), and *Hazmat* (2005). Aside from his poems and essays (*White Paper* [1989] and *Twenty Questions* [1998]), he has also written four opera libretti, including *Emmeline* (1996), commissioned by the Santa Fe Opera. He is the recipient of many honors, including the Witter Bynner Award for poetry from the American Academy of Arts and Letters (1985).

McClatchy's work often displays a compacted language and verbal virtuosity that he describes as the "knotty lyric" (qtd. in Bloom 330). The poem "Sniper" (2002), for example, begins with a sentence that combines rich sound qualities with a vernacular verisimilitude: "The geedee cannon cockers with their illumes / And boom-boom arty always miss the point." Here "boom-boom arty" refers to exploding artillery; the authentic sound of this phrasing lends a sense of immediacy to the poem. Although his poems are typically free verse, he does occasionally experiment with a more formal structure. He uses varying rhyme schemes and forms, including the *pantoum*, a Malayan poem similar to the French villanelle.

McClatchy's recent book of poems, *The Ten Commandments*, is organized according to God's moral instructional manual, delivered via Moses. Within this frame, McClatchy waxes upon all manner of rule and custom in the personal, social, and philosophical realms and "encompass[es] the range of human pleasures and failings" (Christian). The poem "My Mammogram," for example, is composed of five sections, each sporting four stanzas: two rhyming quatrains and two rhyming tercets. The theme of the poem is very personal and does not cringe from intimate details, such as "useless, overlooked / mass of fat" (17). But, perhaps more important, in the final section, the speaker seems to bow his head in resignation and accept that life is a sometimes "farcical" slippery slope and that a person's various body shapes and stages are only "disguises" for the soul's last laugh.

Like his metaphysical predecessors and contemporaries, McClatchy often seeks the kernel of truth or wisdom embedded in an emotionally imbued situation. McClatchy's work, both his concentrated free verse and formal poems, seems to suggest that not only life's spectrum of glories and disappointments, but also the quiet moments between them, are worthy of examination.

BIBLIOGRAPHY

Bloom, Harold, and David Lehman, eds. *The Best of the Best American Poetry*. New York: Scribner, 1998.

Christian, Graham. "Laws of Gravity." *Boston Phoenix* (March 30, 1998). Available online. URL: www.desert.net/ww/03–30–98/boston_books_1.html. Downloaded December 2003.

Ellmann, Richard, and Robert O'Clair, eds. *The Norton Anthology of Modern Poetry*. 2d ed. New York: Norton, 1988.

Michael Kuperman

MCCLURE, MICHAEL (1932–) Michael McClure was only 23 when he read his poetry at the Six Gallery in San Francisco and, along with ALLEN GINSBERG, among others, helped initiate the BEAT movement. Since that time he has written more than 40 volumes of poetry, fiction, essays, and plays and continues to experiment with POETRY IN PERFORMANCE, including his collaborative work with the keyboardist Ray Manzarek (previously of the rock band the Doors). McClure's work has been consistently experimental, with an aim toward communicating thought and emotion in as visceral and physical a manner as language will allow.

McClure was born October 20, 1932—"the same day as Rimbaud" (McClure *Ghost Tantras,* 109)—in Marysville, Kansas, and grew up in Seattle, where he developed an interest in wildlife and the environment. He moved to San Francisco in 1954, enrolled in ROBERT DUNCAN's poetry workshop at San Francisco State University, and published his first book of poems, *Passage,* in 1956. Like GARY SNYDER, McClure shows a deep concern with nature in his poetry, but McClure's main interests lie less in a descriptive poetry of natural scenery than in the mammalian consciousness he believes is dormant in all human beings. His work has received many honors, including a Guggenheim Fellowship (1973) and distinguished lifetime achievement in poetry award from the National Poetry Association (1999).

A primary motive of McClure's art is the discovery of the materiality of consciousness. This theme manifests itself in the way he typographically centers his poems so that they are "allowed . . . to have a body language on the page" (McClure *Huge Dreams* 168), and in his development during the 1960s of his poetic "beast language," a mode of writing that attempts to convey the very gestures of vocal expression by transcribing vocal sounds without using recognizable words. For example, these two lines from *Ghost Tantras* (1964), his first extended exploration of beast language, convey desire: "NOH. NAH-OHH / hroor. VOOR-NAH! GAHROOOOO ME" (58).

With the license provided by CHARLES OLSON's reconception of the poetic line in terms of the poet's breath (see ARS POETICAS), McClure developed an approach to poetry that conceives of his media (written text, performed word) as an enactment and extension of the poet's own physical presence. McClure's *Meat Science Essays* (1963) marked a turning point in his environmental politics and ultimately in his poetics; the predominant aim of his work from this point on became to "revolt against habitual ways of feeling and action" for the sake of " more direct gestures" (McClure 43).

BIBLIOGRAPHY

Kahn, Douglas. *Noise Water Meat*. Cambridge, Mass.: Massachusetts Institute of Technology Press, 1999.

McClure, Michael. *Meat Science Essays*. San Francisco: City Lights Books, 1963.

———. *Ghost Tantras*. San Francisco: City Lights Books, 1964.

Phillips, Rod. *"Forest Beatniks" and "Urban Thoreaus."* New York: Peter Lang, 2000.

Jason Camlot

MCDOWELL, ROBERT (1953–) Robert McDowell is considered a pioneer in the New Narrative movement in contemporary poetry (see NEW FORMALISM). His keen sense of poetic formalism led him to reevaluate American poetry in the wake of modernist and postmodernist free verse lyrical experimentation (see MODERNISM). As a cofounder with MARK JARMAN of the magazine the *Reaper,* established in 1980, McDowell revived NARRATIVE POETRY and thereby created significant awareness of this medium of expression. Arguing that "poetry, more than ever, is harnessed by and subordinated to its criticism" (Jarman and McDowell 4), he challenged the status quo of American literary criticism by stressing the importance of narrative verse. McDowell is best known for his narrative poetry in loose iambic lines. The critic Kevin Walzer has observed that his "poems draw on, without simply imitating, the example of the three twentieth-century masters of narrative verse: ROBERT FROST, ROBINSON JEFFERS, and EDWIN ARLINGTON ROBINSON" (63). The dominant themes appearing in his poems include American society, culture, and history; the family; and the complexity of familial and conjugal relationships. Using deftly constructed plots presenting everyday characters leading ordinary lives, McDowell's engaging narrative shows how small yet significant moments can alter one's life.

Born in Alhambra, California, McDowell's formal education at the University of California, Santa Cruz, (1971–74) and Columbia University (1974–76) culminated in six years of teaching at Indiana State University, Evansville, where in 1980 he colaunched the *Reaper.* In 1985 he founded Story Line Press and in 1987 published his first collection of poems, titled *Quiet Money,* followed by *The Diviners* (1995), then *On Foot, In Flames* (2002). He is actively involved in criticism, editing such works as *Poetry after Modernism* (1991).

The sense of narrative in all of McDowell's work is palpable. In the single narrative poem "The Diviners" (1995), McDowell presents the struggles of a California family over the span of two generations. We witness Tom, the only son, growing up in a family plagued by alcoholism. Trying to find some meaning in his life, since "Tom's sense of loss and pain won't dissipate," he finally escapes to Ireland after his father's death. In "The Pact" (1994), McDowell explores the theme of forgiveness and redemption, showing how the main character, John-Allen, betrayed by his wife, Sarah, comes to terms with her deceit.

McDowell's narrative poems engage at many levels. His imaginative story lines craft intricate plots and subplots that expose his characters' strengths and weaknesses. Ultimately, though, his poems present a larger and more significant vision of humanity as a whole.

BIBLIOGRAPHY

Gwynn, R. S. *New Expansive Poetry.* Ashland, Oreg.: Story Line Press, 1999.

Jarman, Mark, and Robert McDowell. *The Reaper Essays.* Brownsville, Oreg.: Story Line Press, 1996.

Walzer, Kevin. *The Ghost of Tradition—Expansive Poetry and Postmodernism.* Ashland, Oreg.: Story Line Press, 1998.

Nicolas Fernandez

MCGRATH, THOMAS (1916–1990) Thomas McGrath represents the powerful convergence of the personal and the political in verse. An eccentric mix of pastoral and BEAT radical sensibility, his poetic voice is rooted in the American soil and spirit and speaks out against economic and political injustice. DONALD HALL has called McGrath the best American poet of public denunciation and invective (qtd. in Whitehead 90–91). Far from being merely denunciatory, however, his verse projects the optimism of cultural healing. Attempting to refashion the American perspective on community, work, and nation, McGrath summons us back to a cultural wholeness out of what he sees as the devastation of capitalist corruption. Propelled by an active imagination assuming myriad shapes, his poetry is marked by formal, linguistic, and stylistic unpredictability, from haikulike poems in *Passages toward the Dark* (1982) to his freewheeling, six-beat-lined epic *Letter to an Imaginary Friend* (1970).

McGrath was born near Sheldon, North Dakota, to Irish-Catholic homesteaders. As a child he labored on steam rigs with migrant Wobbly labor crews, exposed to an often violent labor unrest that became the source of his visionary poetry's working-class consciousness. In spite of his family's financial hardship, he studied at the University of North Dakota, Louisiana State University, and, with a Rhodes scholarship, New College, Oxford. McGrath held many jobs throughout his lifetime: union organizer, documentary-film writer, soldier in the Aleutians during World War II, editor and founding-editor, respectively, of *California Quarterly* and *Crazy Horse,* and college teacher in Maine, New York, North Dakota, Los Angeles, and Minnesota. In the 1950s he was called before the House Un-American Activities Committee and blacklisted as a communist, an event that sharpened his socialist resolve. Despite his leftist leaning, he was awarded a number of prestigious prizes during his lifetime. In 1990 he was presented the distinguished achievement award by the Society for Western Literature.

Beginning with *Longshot O'Leary's Garland of Practical Poesie* (1940), the book with which he first achieved recognition, McGrath tried to create a poetry in which private reminiscence mirrors the often tumultuous unfolding of social and political history. Autobiographical moments are never merely CONFESSIONAL in his work; they also reflect the universal: The memory of a foreman's swing at a seasonal farm laborer, for example, effects the collapse of American community and shared labor in the wake of industrial corporatism. But if McGrath's poetry seethes with anger at what is lost to the profit and exploitation of modern America—tradition, family, compassion—he counters this rage with redemptive, visionary alternatives. Work, love, poetry, and, above all, the human imagination represent, for McGrath, the ultimate remedies for an ailing America; vivid, shamanistic dream-visions serve as liberating forces for social and political revolution.

McGrath's expansive range of tone shifts from didacticism to eloquent lyricism to satiric wit. His vocabulary, including neologisms that Reginald Gibbons calls "glossological wonders" (Gibbons and Des Pres 10), mingles patois, slang, and the tall tale with a more traditional "poetic" voice: Packy O'Sullivan of New York shipyard fame interrupts a reflective passage in *Letter* to sputter, "Doublebarreled shitepoke sheepcroakes, swillbelly like a poison pup!" Compounding these vocal pyrotechnics are images of hyperbolic exaggeration and distortion. Into a worker's rainy-day breakfast strides the beautiful Jenny, apotheosized by *Letter*'s exhausted workers: "Jenny! / Entering, the light swarms around her!" Wild, extravagant, and excessive, McGrath's world is stunningly fantastical, brimming with possibility. Infused with a carnivalesque energy, his verse showcases new and dizzying perspectives that upend "official" culture and lend credibility to his own insurrectionary politics.

McGrath's poetry is, above all, a call to action, to social apocalypse. Its linguistic puns, inversions, and echoes contribute to the imperative for newness and movement. In McGrath's masterpiece, *Letter to an Imaginary Friend,* this new order is inspired by Hopi prophecy. A personal and political journey to an American utopia, *Letter* is characteristically chaotic and disorderly, moving geographically between North Dakota, Louisiana, New York, California, Alaska, and Greece and stylistically between hard, biting parody, bawdy humor, and dreamy self-expression, as well as between the lilt of local Irish idiom and the invective of communist agitation. Written over 30 years and adopting the forms of autobiography, Catholic sacrament, and American political history, the epic ends in the fiery blaze of the Kachina, the Hopi blue star that signals the Saquadohuh, or Fifth World, which is to emerge from the dark womb of the earth. Part 4's apocalyptic dream vision, in which the speaker roars through myriad hallucinatory realms to arrive at this new order of solidarity, shared labor, and love, exemplifies McGrath's embracing of violence and chaos as tools to reshape a world gone mad. His poetry surges with fury for the America that once was and, if this fury is turned to productive use, can be again.

BIBLIOGRAPHY

Gibbons, Reginald, and Terence Des Pres, eds. *Thomas McGrath: Life and the Poem.* Urbana: University of Illinois Press, 1992.

Stern, Frederick C., ed. *The Revolutionary Poet in the United States: The Poetry of Thomas McGrath.* Columbia: University of Missouri Press, 1988.

Whitehead, Fred, ed. "The Dream Champ" *North Dakota Quarterly* 50 (fall 1982). ([Special issue devoted to Thomas McGrath]).

Reid Cottingham

MCKAY, CLAUDE (1889–1948) No single poet, with the possible exception of LANGSTON HUGHES, did more to bring attention to the literature of the HARLEM RENAISSANCE than poet and novelist Claude McKay. Despite his strong association with the movement, McKay insisted that his poems should speak to all people, not just to African Americans. This attitude and his attention to poetic craftsmanship evoke the tension between the demands of racial pride and intellectual autonomy that fueled the creative energies of his African-American contemporaries. While he later distanced himself from the Harlem literary scene, the independence, breadth, and scope of McKay's writings made him a crucial reference and influential figure for writers in the later Civil Rights movements.

McKay was born to relatively wealthy parents of Jamaica's peasant class. This almost middle-class status provided him with early intellectual mentors, including a schoolteacher older brother and an influential British folklorist, both of whom directed the budding poet's studies of classical and romantic literature and philosophy. After the 1912 publication of two volumes of juvenile poetry in Jamaica, McKay migrated to the United States, where he studied at both the Tuskegee Institute and Kansas State University until 1914. He followed his studies with a series of menial railway jobs that led him to New York and the publication of his 1922 volume of poetry, *Harlem Shadows,* which critics now hail as the first great literary achievement of the Harlem Renaissance (Barksdale 490). McKay used the earnings from this work to fund extensive travels throughout Europe, North Africa, and the Soviet Union, where he became a world symbol of the African-American literary left. As the vibrancy of the early Harlem Renaissance faded, so did McKay's poetic output. He ultimately resolved the internal struggles seen throughout his poetry through a 1944 conversion to Roman Catholicism.

Many of McKay's poems reflect nostalgically on the island life and folklore of Jamaica; however, he made his reputation with verse that unsparingly confronts the injustice and rage generated by race relations in the United States. Eschewing the free verse style favored by Hughes and other jazz-age poets, McKay reserved the elegant structure of the sonnet for his most militant ideas and images (see PROSODY AND FREE VERSE).

In his most widely anthologized poem, the sonnet "If We Must Die" (1919), McKay elevates the African American's plight with a plea for nobility. The poem's central metaphor compares the African-American experience to fighting off a pack of dogs and calls for determined and noble resistance so that "even the monsters we defy / Shall be constrained to honor us though dead!" This rhetoric of resistance and human dignity makes McKay's message resonate as succeeding generations discover the power of his verse.

BIBLIOGRAPHY

Barksdale, Richard, and Kenneth Kinnamon. "Renaissance and Radicalism: 1915–1945." In *Black Writers of America: A Comprehensive Anthology*. New York: Macmillan, 1972.

Hart, Robert C. "Black-White Literary Relations in the Harlem Renaissance." *American Literature* 44, no. 4 (January 1973): 612–628.

Keller, James R. "A Chafing Savage, Down the Decent Street." *African American Review* 28, no. 3 (autumn 1994): 447–456.

William F. Hecker

"MEDITATION AT LAGUNITAS" ROBERT HASS **(1979)** Drawing on the language of contemporary critical theory, images from his native Northern California, and memories of a distant love affair, ROBERT HASS's "Meditation at Lagunitas" illuminates the fullness and emptiness of human experience. The poem is vibrantly self-conscious, not only exploring the intersections of language and physical experience but also meditating upon its own efforts to find such an intersection. But Hass is no thin-blooded philosopher. In tones at once ironic, humane, and praising, he explores issues of meaning and connection in his own life, as a friend, a sexual lover, and an observer of the natural world.

In an essay on the poet ROBERT CREELEY, Hass wrote of how the popularization of Jacques Lacan's *Ecrits* in the United States had a revolutionary effect in the 1960s, and "Meditation at Lagunitas" is haunted by Lacan's ideas about language (another poem from the same collection, *Praise,* is titled "Picking Blackberries with a Friend Who Has Been Reading Jacques Lacan"). According to Lacan, the meaning or significance of words is arbitrary, not derived from some essence, so that language both generates and is generated by the desire to cross this gap between word and world. In a quiet philosophical tone all the more devastating for its refusal to lament, Hass both voices and submits to the Lacanian idea that "because there is in this world no one thing / to which the bramble of *blackberry* corresponds, / a word is elegy to what it signifies." For a poet as wedded to the physical world as Hass, the failure of language to connect to and embody the world threatens existence itself; he fears that "talking this way, everything dissolves: *justice, / pine, hair, women, you* and *I*." Such anxiety strikes at the heart of Hass's earlier poetry; writing about Hass's development, Sydney Lea observes that "The quintessentially human act of [his first book] *Field Guide,* naming, cannot call such blessings into existence for himself" in the book *Praise* (575).

Yet Lea notes that Hass's poetry remains skeptical of all absolute philosophical claims, suggesting that "no prescribed attitude or world view *can* be pure truth" (575). Thomas Gardner argues that "Meditation at Lagunitas" persistently erodes all claims to the truth, even Hass's own. Although he is troubled by his friend's Lacanian ideas, Hass undercuts them by describing his friend's voice as a "thin wire of grief"; he even questions the sincerity of his love affair, suggesting that it was simply a way of avoiding the "endless distances" created by the longing to feel united with the world. Still, it is precisely this skepticism that allows Hass to traverse distance and separation and be truly immersed in the moment. Having admitted that his love affair "had hardly to do with her," and that "I must have been the same to her," Hass turns to memory as a source of solace. His particular memories of the woman, "the way her hands dismantled bread, / the thing her father said that hurt her, what / she dreamed," establish a ground of presence that cannot be undercut, because memory by its very nature acknowledges the passage of time. Paradoxically, by embracing the ephemeral nature of the world and the inadequacy of language, Hass is able to sing, not an elegy, but a song of praise for the world he tries to represent: "There are moments when the body is numinous / as words, days that are the good flesh continuing."

BIBLIOGRAPHY

Doody, Terrence. "From Image to Sentence: The Spiritual Development of Robert Hass." *American Poetry Review* 26, no. 2 (1997): 47–56.

Gardner, Thomas. *Regions of Unlikeness: Explaining Contemporary Poetry*. Lincoln: University of Nebraska Press, 1999.

Hass, Robert. "Creeley: His Metric." In *Twentieth Century Pleasures*. Hopewell, N.J.: Ecco Press, 1984: 150–60.

Lea, Sydney. "A Matter of Conscience." *Nation* 228, no. 19 (1979): 574–75.

Temple Cone

"MEDUSA" LOUISE BOGAN (1923) The dominant idea of LOUISE BOGAN's early poem "Medusa" is balance, though critics have differed in treating that balance as the symmetry of artistic mastery, the poise of psychological discipline, or the inertia of emotional paralysis. Bogan speaks through the persona of an individual who is either metaphorically or literally petrified, a state of existence linked to the poem's title, which alludes to the Greek myth of Medusa, the hideous, serpent-haired monster whose gaze could turn any being it touched to stone. Tonally, such an allusion might suggest such modern conditions as alienation, spiritual paralysis, and emotional frigidity, but the images of suspended time with which Bogan concludes the poem invite a contrary response to the fixed, unchanging scene she describes, a response that praises the preservation of the mortal world.

The poem is written in loosely metered ballad stanzas, an ironic choice of form because the narrative Bogan tells is not linear and unfolding, but static; as the speaker says, "This is a dead scene forever now. / Nothing will ever stir." The scene is of a house in a wooded area, its semirural domesticity recalling such Renaissance country house poems as Ben Jonson's "To Penshurst" and Andrew Marvell's "Upon Appleton House." Through a series of precise visual images, the speaker recalls seeing Medusa's image in a window, "The stiff bald eyes, the serpents on the forehead / Formed in the air," following it with a description of the world around her after her (presumed) petrification. Malcolm Cowley links this petrification to the experience of art, claiming that for Bogan, "art is fearful as well as beautiful; it is the Gorgon's head that can forever fix an evanescent landscape" (58). Carol Moldaw finds a similarly terrible power in the operations of psychological introspection, arguing that the poem "exemplifies the entrapment that results from confrontation with the other self. In the poem it is not, as in the myth, just the viewer who turns to stone; the entire perceived world is paralyzed" (188).

Bogan's response to this condition remains ambivalent throughout; "I shall stand here like a shadow / Under the great balanced day," she says, and it is unclear whether she regrets or rejoices that she has forsaken fleetingness for permanence. The penultimate stanza suggests the eternally unchanging urn paintings in John Keats's "Ode on a Grecian Urn," in which Keats shows that one of the primary effects of art is to arrest change for the sake of immortality, but at the cost of completion and fulfillment. Where her MODERNIST contemporary, WALLACE STEVENS, had rejected this permanence in his major poem "SUNDAY MORNING," Bogan maintains equal and conflicting attitudes toward it; thus, she writes that "The water will always fall, and will not fall, / And the tipped bell make no sound." For Paul Ramsey, this moment of poise is the great aesthetic effect of the poem; he writes that "[Bogan], like Medusa, fixes motion; unlike Medusa, she does not stop motion. If one fixes motion so that it stops, one has not fixed *motion;* one has usurped its place. . . . 'Medusa,' which is about the startlingness of stopped motion, is itself active and changeless, each note struck and heard" (124). Startling as well is the classical terseness of Bogan's lyric voice, which refuses to embrace art either as immortal or ephemeral, so that the poet ultimately must face the mortal world with only her composure for support.

BIBLIOGRAPHY

Cowley, Malcolm. "Review of *Poems and New Poems.*" In *Critical Essays on Louise Bogan,* edited by Martha Collins, 58–59. Boston: G. K. Hall & Co, 1984.

Moldaw, Carol. "Form, Feeling, and Nature: Aspects of Harmony in the Poetry of Louise Bogan." In *Critical Essays on Louise Bogan,* edited by Martha Collins, 180–194. Boston: G. K. Hall & Co, 1984.

Ramsey, Paul. "Louise Bogan." In *Critical Essays on Louise Bogan,* edited by Martha Collins, 119–28. Boston: G. K. Hall & Co, 1984.

Temple Cone

MEINKE, PETER (1932–) Peter Meinke is sometimes associated with the NEW FORMALISM movement of the 1980s but is a practitioner of both formal and free verse poetry (see PROSODY AND FREE VERSE): "I have a general theory that every poem has its ideal shape, whether free verse or formal," he says (58). Meinke's formal verse often feels, at first reading or hearing, like free verse, and his free verse often feels formal, if misleadingly conversational. His later poems continue an early use of space and line breaks in place of standard punctuation.

Meinke was born and raised in Brooklyn, New York, and has lived in Florida since 1966. Among his many awards are the Olivet National Sonnet Prize (1966), two National Endowment for the Arts Fellowships (1974 and 1989), Poetry Society of America awards (1976, 1984, and 1992), and the Southeast Booksellers Association Best Book of Poetry of the Year Award in 2001, for *Zinc Fingers.* His first book of poetry, *The Night Train and the Golden Bird,* was published in 1977. He was professor of literature and director of the writing workshop at Eckerd College from 1966 to 1993.

As Andy Solomon observes, Meinke forms "a constant web of interconnections between the most common events and objects and the lining of the human heart" (6D). Like Emily Dickinson, Meinke uses small and unassuming objects and moments to illuminate larger truths about our lives. In "Azaleas" (1978), he uses the flowers as "humorous examples / of human hubris" and as connections to the "deep wilderness of the soul."

Like the romantic poets, Meinke's work is easily accessible, but it also shares the intertextuality of modernist and postmodernist poets (see MODERNISM). Titles and themes, such as "Advice to My Son" (1965), "In Gentler Times" (1966), and "Uncle Jim" (1986) invite even the most intimidated reader to read further. One does not need to understand the allusions in poems, such as "A Meditation on You and Wittgenstein" (2000), "Mendel's Laws" (1981), and "Scars" (1996), to appreciate the poems themselves, but those who recognize the references to art, science, and history find further depth in Meinke's poems. The first stanza of "Scars" introduces a boy who worships his father in a fairly ordinary way: "When I was young I longed for scars / like my father's"; these scars are "the best . . . on the block." The last stanza compares the father to Laius, a character from the myth of Oedipus, a move that gives a classical twist to a simple story.

BIBLIOGRAPHY
Byrd, Gregory. "Aesthetics at the Southernmost Point." *Mississippi Quarterly* 52, no. 2 (spring 1999): 287–294.
Meinke, Peter. "Essay on 'Zinc Fingers.'" *Literary Review*. 44, no. 1 (fall 2000): 57–59.
Solomon, Andy. "Meinke Sheds Light through Small Windows." *St. Petersburg Times,* August 27, 2000, 6D.
Trakas, Deno. "Peter Meinke." In *American Poets since World War II*. Part 2: L–Z. Vol. 5 of *Dictionary of Literary Biography,* edited by Donald J. Greiner. Detroit: Gale, 1980, pp. 41–45.

Gregory Byrd

MELTZER, DAVID (1937–) David Meltzer classifies himself as a "second generation Beat" poet (Hawley and Charters). When he slid into the scene in 1957, LAWRENCE FERLINGHETTI had already published ALLEN GINSBERG's *HOWL,* and JACK KEROUAC's *On the Road* had reached classic status. But the accomplishments of his predecessors have not prevented him from finding his niche. In nearly 50 years on the West Coast poetry scene, Meltzer has written copious volumes of poetry and novels and edited seminal collections of interviews with his first-generation BEAT compatriots. He has also become very well known for his historical treatments of jazz, the medium that gave him his start.

Meltzer was born in Rochester, New York, to parents who both made their livings as classical musicians. From an early age, the young Meltzer was on stage, singing with various children's groups, both on the East Coast and in California. This early musical training served him well when he began reading his poetry at the Jazz Cellar, a North Beach hangout favored by Beat poets, including Ferlinghetti and KENNETH REXROTH. Rather than a strict reading, Meltzer would improvise, much like the musicians who backed him up: "I'd scribble out an outline of a poem. . . . There would also be written verses as anchors for areas when I improvised, created lyric (or poem) on the spot—in context with the music & the idea of the poem" (qtd. in Hawley and Charters).

His early verse mirrors this environment. Short, syncopated rhythms, one- and two-word sentences, brief splashes of words on a page like trumpet blasts characterize his work: "units of 4. / In thought. Instrumental" ("Free Jazz [Atlantic 1364]/for CC" [1975]). Much of Meltzer's poetry is inseparable from this era. It bounces back and forth from bebop brevities to free verse that dwells on family, music, the Kabala—whatever topic occupies his mind while the pen occupies his hand: "Rainbow lozenge light prismatic / wobble across cheap scroll Buddha" ("More on the Art" [1975]); each word an image that depicts the dreams in his sometimes nightmarish reality.

It is not until *No Eyes: Lester Young* (2000) that Meltzer pursues any one topic relentlessly. This book was inspired by a photograph of the great saxophonist with his horn, sitting on the bed of the rundown hotel room in which he later died. Meltzer turns one snapshot of "Prez" into a staccato series of loving portraits of a musician who "rejects bruise / accepts blue" in a world not ready for him. Each untitled poem is closed with a fermata, the musical symbol that denotes an elongation of a piece's final note—a reminder that the poem, as well as its subject, has come to an end.

BIBLIOGRAPHY
Hawley, Robert, and Ann Charters. "David Meltzer." In *Dictionary of Literary Biography*. Vol. 16, *The Beats: Literary Bohemians in Postwar America,* edited by Anne Charters, 405–410. Detroit: Gale Group, 1983.
Kerdian, David. *Six Poets of the San Francisco Renaissance: Portraits and Checklists.* Fresno, Calif.: Giliga Press, 1967.
Kirsch, Jonathan. "West Words; Edgy Conversations Get to Heart of Beat Generation." *Los Angeles Times,* June 13, 2001, 5:1.

Aimee Fifarek

MENASHE, SAMUEL (1925–) Samuel Menashe was largely unknown in America for most of the 20th century. His short, meditative poems draw heavily on the roots of words, and he has likened them to mathematical problems best solved with economy and precision. While he has been compared to the IMAGISTS and to Emily Dickinson, he once wrote, "I never thought of anything I read—either on my own or in school—as a literary model" (234). He has not written criticism, taught poetry, or edited, and his influence has been limited, though he has drawn praise from several prominent critics, including Donald Davie, Hugh Kenner, and Stephen Spender. For most of his career, his reputation has remained greatest in England, though this oversight was corrected in 2005 when Menashe received the first-ever Neglected Masters Prize from The Poetry Foundation.

Menashe was born in New York City and learned Yiddish and English by the age of three. In 1943 he trained at Fort Benning, Georgia, and fought in France, Belgium, and Germany during World War II. Under the G.I. Bill, he attended the Sorbonne and received his doctorate at age 24, completing his thesis, in French, on the religious and mystical origins of poetry. His first book, *The Many Named Beloved,* was published in London in 1961. His poems were included in *Penguin Modern Poets,* Volume 7 (1966), and his other books are *No Jerusalem But This* (1971), *To Open* (1974), *Collected Poems* (1986), and *The Niche Narrows: New and Selected Poems* (2000). In 1999 he was one of 21 poets featured in the PBS broadcast *Fooling with Words.*

His spare style has been influenced by the Bible, and his poems are religious but not dogmatic. His main themes are the relationship between the spiritual and the material and between the eternal and the fleeting. As Donald Davie has written, Menashe speaks "at a linguistic and cultural crossroads" (108), where his intersecting concerns are English, French, American, and Jewish. In "My Mother's Grave" (1971), he describes Jerusalem as having a wall made of skeletons ("Bones / Are mortar") and a street held together by dust. Both the speaker and the city thus share bereavement and exile.

Barry Ahearn has commented that Menashe "finds in everyday scenes the materials for extended vision" (297), and he often accomplishes this through the use of rhyme, emphasizing not only the sounds but the physical relationships between words, as would a verbal ideogram. In "The Niche Narrows" (2000), possibly Menashe's ARS POETICA, he describes a scene of paring away toward the essential, where one becomes gradually thinner "Until his bones / Disclose him." As with most of his work, the tone here is a synthesis of celebration and elegy.

Menashe's poems ask for revelation in the physical world. His prayerful deployment of concrete language always calls into question the primal meanings of words, challenging the reader to suspend ordinary association.

BIBLIOGRAPHY

Ahearn, Barry. "Poetry and Synthesis: The Art of Samuel Menashe." *Twentieth Century Literature* 2 (summer 1996): 294–308.

Davie, Donald. "The Poetry of Samuel Menashe." *Iowa Review* 3 (1970): 107–115.

Menashe, Samuel. "Samuel Menashe 1925–." *Contemporary Authors: Autobiography Series,* Vol. 11, edited by Mark Zadrozny, 223–239. Detroit: Gale Research, 1990.

Christopher McDermott

"MENDING WALL" ROBERT FROST **(1914)** A regionalist in the tradition of EDGAR LEE MASTERS and EDWIN ARLINGTON ROBINSON, ROBERT FROST stands with WILLIAM CARLOS WILLIAMS as one of MODERNISM's few rural sages. He pits ritual against reason in "Mending Wall," a blank verse meditation on the darker side of humanity's ostensibly civil traditions (see PROSODY AND FREE VERSE). Each year the poem's speaker joins his neighbor to repair a stone wall that separates their property. It seems an innocent tradition, but Frost hints at underlying problems from the outset: "Something there is that doesn't love a wall," he writes, "[T]hat sends the frozen-ground-swell under it," thereby dislodging its rocks. As the imagery implies, that "something" is ice or frost; by punning on his own name, Frost expresses a distinctly modern ambivalence toward such barriers and what they represent. His language is calculated to emphasize that while he does not hate a wall, destroying a fence is a more social act—a couple, he notes, can walk through the gaps in a broken wall—than rebuilding one. In light of these opening lines, the neighbors' annual get-together seems to stem, ironically, from a rather antisocial impulse.

In addition to being unsociable, the poem's title task ("mending") also seems irrational. Although Frost's speaker is the one to initiate the yearly march, he reflects aloud on its unreasonableness. When his neighbor answers simply, "Good fences make good neighbors," the speaker finds that explanation not only ill founded but also slightly barbaric, a remnant of darker ages. The tradition that Frost initially describes as a sort of game becomes, by the end of the poem, emblematic of an ignorant and outdated mysticism. The boulders balance as if by magic, and the elderly farmer appears a sort of ancient barbarian, a brute who "moves in darkness . . . / Not of woods only and the shade of trees." Enveloped in the dimness of ritual, he simply repeats the old adage without question. In contrast, Frost's more enlightened speaker questions the ritual wall-mending—its origins, its purposes, its effects. Like the preeminent theorists of literary modernism, Frost associates tradition with incivility and even danger.

The poem would not, however, be truly modern if these simple binaries—social/antisocial, rational/irrational, traditional/new, and so on—were not significantly complicated by Frost's craftsmanship. For example, the speaker acknowledges his own mischievously teasing mood, and his one-sided banter with the stolid old farmer eases the poem's heavy social and literary implications. Frost's speaker is an extraordinarily imaginative person who, as his references to elves and stalking apple trees suggest, finds at least some pleasure in the irrational. The wall-mending ritual engages the speaker's sense of fun despite his modern wariness, and, in the final analysis, ambivalence reigns in Frost's New England.

BIBLIOGRAPHY

Lentricchia, Frank. *Robert Frost: Modern Poetics and the Landscapes of Self.* Durham, N.C.: Duke University Press, 1975.

Richardson, Mark. *The Ordeal of Robert Frost: The Poet and His Poetics.* Urbana: University of Illinois Press, 1997.

Betsy Winakur Tontiplaphol

MERRILL, JAMES (1926–1995) James Merrill was a remarkably accomplished and always surprising poet. Beginning with a rare mastery of form and language, displayed in highly wrought creations, he gradually relaxed his manner, enabling it to mimic the vagaries and vicissitudes of habitual experience. But a mere imitation of life was never his poetic object. Instead he was engaged throughout his long and successful career in the crucial task of translating life into art, or perhaps of salvaging through art what is meaningful and precious in the waste of experience. His chief precursor in this task was the modern novelist Marcel Proust, but Merrill was also influenced by the later occultist poetry of William Butler Yeats and by the meditational sequences of WALLACE STEVENS. In the preceding generation of American poets, the work of both ELIZABETH BISHOP and ROBERT LOWELL instructed Merrill in the use of autobiographical material (especially from childhood) approached from psychological viewpoints; he pointed to Bishop in particular as a key influence on the final maturation of his urbane yet intimate poetic voice. As a formalist poet, he was influenced most immediately by the daunting example of W. H. AUDEN and, further back in the tradition, by the perfected 18th-century heroic couplets of Alexander Pope and the 17th-century suave pastorals of Andrew Marvell.

Merrill was born in New York City, the son of the famous financier and cofounder of the Merrill-Lynch brokerage firm, Charles Merrill, and his second wife, Helen Ingram, both of whom were originally from Florida. His parents divorced when Merrill was 13, a traumatic experience that he renders and ponders repeatedly in his poetry. Merrill attended Amherst College, where he studied with Ruben Brower, met ROBERT FROST, and wrote a senior thesis on metaphor in Proust's great novel *Remembrance of Things Past.* His first commercially published book (two earlier books had been privately printed), *First Poems,* appeared in 1951 and received generally favorable and even envious reviews. In 1955 Merrill moved from New York City to the small coastal town of Stonington, Connecticut, where he lived, off and on, with his companion David Jackson for the rest of his life. From 1959 to 1979 he and Jackson spent a part of each year in a house in Athens, and thereafter they wintered mainly in Key West, Florida, where Jackson bought a home. In 1956 Merrill used a portion of his inherited wealth to fund the Ingram Merrill Foundation, which provides money in support of the arts and artists. In addition to poetry, Merrill also wrote two novels, the first of which, the semiautobiographical *The Seraglio,* was published by Knopf in 1957. His second novel, *The (Diblos) Notebook* (1965) was a finalist for the National Book Award in fiction. In 1966 his fourth book of poems, *Nights and Days,* won the National Book Award in poetry. He went on to receive many poetry awards, including the Bollingen Prize (1973), the Pulitzer Prize (1976), a second National Book Award (1978), the National Book Critics Circle Award (1982), and the first Bobbitt National Prize for poetry awarded by the Library of Congress in 1988. He died of a heart attack, having been weakened by a struggle with AIDS.

Taken as a whole, Merrill's creations form an elaborately detailed and multilayered autobiography. In his longer narrative sequences, he merges the autobiographical instinct of contemporary poetry and of his self-proclaimed precursor, Proust, with a complex symbolic system worthy of Dante, William Blake, or William Butler Yeats. In the poem "Scenes of Childhood," the poet describes watching an old home movie with his mother, in which the much younger mother and her toddler son are joined on the screen by the ominous shadow of the inept father-cameraman—at which point the film jams and catches fire. Following this symbolic apocalypse, the poet's resigned, bemused mother goes up to bed, bidding her son "pleasant dreams." Later, as he sits pondering his father's life and death and his own inheritance, he hears his mother's labored breathing upstairs, which he describes as the sound of life "escaping into space." This last word then turns his attention heavenward, to the night sky and its Milky Way of stars, which he imagines as the shed skin of the primal serpent, whose symbolic presence in the world he interprets as proof of the continued existential quandary shared by all who have unwittingly arrived on life's stage as "heroes without name or origin." With its deft, allusive, condensed argument and its surprising, weighty conclusion, the poem is a typically strong Merrill narrative performance, weaving coy allusions to tradition and myth into a witty, touching, CONFESSIONAL depiction of the primal family drama (see NARRATIVE POETRY).

Merrill's most elaborate version of the existential drama is his elaborate mock-epic trilogy, *The* CHANGING LIGHT AT SANDOVER, in which he merges the confessional and mythic modes through the metaphorical device of the Ouija board, at which he and Jackson sat (in real life) for nights and years on end, conjoining the living and the dead, life and art, experience and myth. Critical sentiment concerning the trilogy's success as a modern epic and regarding its relation to Merrill's work as a whole is sharply divided. But the vast sweep and detailed complexity of the poem's imaginative landscape—not to mention the astounding technical virtuosity displayed throughout its nearly 600 pages—confirm Merrill's status as one of the dominant poetic figures of the last half of the 20th century, one of those most likely to be remembered in centuries to come.

BIBLIOGRAPHY

Adams, Don. *James Merrill's Poetic Quest.* Westport, Conn.: Greenwood Press, 1997.

Kalstone, David. *Five Temperaments.* New York: Oxford University Press, 1977.

Materer, Timothy. *James Merrill's Apocalypse.* Ithaca, N.Y.: Cornell University Press, 2000.

Yenser, Stephen. *The Consuming Myth.* Cambridge, Mass.: Harvard University Press, 1987.

Don Adams

MERTON, THOMAS (1915–1968) Arguably the most important Catholic author of the century, the Trappist monk Thomas Merton is best known for the autobiography of his youth and conversion, *The Seven Storey Mountain,* and for his numerous books on such diverse topics as Zen and Tibetan Buddhism, nuclear disarmament, Catholic meditation, and the Vietnam War. But he also wrote poetry prolifically throughout his career, tapping into the modernist aesthetic of such poets as EZRA POUND and LOUIS ZUKOVSKY, while also engaging in the religious meditations of poets such as William Blake, Gerard Manley Hopkins, and Czeslaw Milosz.

Merton was born in Prades, France, the son of two painters who were deeply interested in the experimental arts. His adolescence was wild and unruly, but while attending Columbia University, Merton converted to Catholicism, and in 1941 entered the Abbey of Gethsemani in Kentucky, a community of Trappist monks, the most ascetic Roman Catholic monastic order. During the next 27 years, he remained part of the Trappist order and even lived as a hermit at Gethsemani, though he also traveled widely and wrote extensively, at times clashing with the head of his order.

Merton's early poems are marked by a striking blend of meditative poise, humor, and energy. In "Evening," for instance, he writes that "where blue heaven's fading fire last shines / They name the new come planets /

With words that flower." These qualities continue throughout his career, but as Merton became increasingly involved in social activism, his own work joined themes of praise for creation and quietism with a more direct voicing of political and social responsibility. Addressing the increased American involvement in the Vietnam conflict, Merton declares that "(I)n the middle of this murderous season/ Great Christ, my fingers touch Thy wheat," and he asks for Christ to "Surprise this earth, this cinder, with new holiness!" ("*Senescente Mundo*").

Over the course of his life, Merton became increasingly open to Eastern religious influences, particularly Taoism and Zen Buddhism, and in his poetry, his Catholic ethic and American expressiveness become wedded to an open, empty acceptance of the world. In "Elias—Variations on a Theme," he writes of the prophet Elias or Elijah, who prophesied the coming of Christ: "Elias becomes his own wild bird, with God as his center, / His own wide field which nobody owns." In reviews of Merton's poetry, ROBERT LOWELL warned that the phenomenon of Merton's biography sometimes threatened to overwhelm his actual poetry, but he also called him "easily the most promising of our American Catholic poets," and continued interest in Merton clearly supports that judgment.

BIBLIOGRAPHY

Lowell, Robert. "The Verses of Thomas Merton." *Commonweal* 42 (1945): 240.

Temple Cone

MERWIN, W(ILLIAM) S(TANLEY)

(1927–) A prodigious poet and acclaimed translator, W. S. Merwin's distinguished career follows the ambitious literary projects of his modernist predecessors T. S. ELIOT, EZRA POUND, and WILLIAM CARLOS WILLIAMS (see MODERNISM). In more than 15 books of poetry and five books of prose, Merwin's theme, especially as it develops in the later phase of his work, is the postmodern problem of finding language that can offer an adequate and just account of the world. The insistent and—as some critics have described it—distant voice in Merwin's poems is essential to an understanding of the generation of American poets that includes such authors as JOHN ASHBERY, ROBERT CREELEY, ALLEN GINSBERG, GALWAY KINNELL, JAMES MERRILL, ADRIENNE RICH, GARY SNYDER, and JAMES WRIGHT.

Born in New York City in 1927 and raised in Union City, New Jersey, and Scranton, Pennsylvania, Merwin was educated at Princeton University, where he studied with the influential poet-critics JOHN BERRYMAN and R. P. BLACKMUR. Merwin spent an additional year at the university studying Romance languages before living and working in France, Spain, Majorca, and England. He has lived and worked in Mexico, New York City, the southwest of France, and the Hawaiian island of Maui. His awards include the 1971 Pulitzer Prize, the 1979 Bollingen Prize, the 1998 Ruth Lilly Poetry Prize, the 1994 Tanning Prize from the Academy of the American Poets for outstanding and proven mastery in poetry, the 2003 Harold Morton London Translation Award, and the 2005 National Book Award.

Merwin's first book, *A Mask for Janus,* received the 1952 Yale Series of Younger Poets Award. In his foreword to the collection, W. H. AUDEN calls attention to Merwin's intimate knowledge of poetic tradition and myth. Critics praised Merwin's formal range in the poems written between 1947 and 1958 and now collected in *The First Four Books of Poems* (1975). The 1960s and 1970s mark a period of transition. In the work collected in the *Second Four Books of Poems* (1993), Merwin develops and expands his thematic and formal range. Carefully chosen line breaks, variable use of caesura, evocative rendering of the spoken word, and movement away from punctuation—these formal characteristics are simply the most visible qualities of Merwin's poems from this middle period. Merwin, in describing the difference in these poems, says that "it might be more to the point to say that whatever may provide their form is less apparent" (1).

Merwin's poems require careful listening for what might best be called the "shape" of a speaking voice. Although the seductive rhythms and allegorical impulses of the poems have baffled many of his readers, the inscrutable presence of Merwin's speakers nevertheless registers the struggle to reconcile the public and the private dimensions of experience. "My own life in the sixties," Merwin explains, "seemed to be made of contradictions: City life and rural life; Europe and

America; Love of the old and a craving for change; Public issues and a disposition to live quietly" (2).

One of Merwin's abiding concerns is the relationship between aesthetic and moral issues. Eschewing the impulses of didactic poetry, Merwin hews to the responsibility of the poet who has "no choice but to name the wrong as truthfully as he can, and to try to indicate the claims of justice in terms of the victims he lives among" (*Regions* 291). As early as *The Lice* (1967), Merwin holds human culture accountable to the delicate and sustaining web of life, as in the speaker's haunting address to a grey whale in the poem "For a Coming Extinction." His devotion to nature is shaped by a profound engagement with the contradictions of human culture—a concern with the contours of human desire and its, at times, unacceptable costs.

Through the 1990s Merwin assembled a testimonial to personal and cultural loss: in the elegiac prose of *The Lost Upland* (1992), in the intricate sequences of poems in *Travels* (1993) and *The Vixen* (1996), and in the 300-page narrative-in-verse of 19th-century Hawaii *The Folding Cliffs* (1998). In *The River Sound* (1999), nature's persistence appears as an antidote to human and ecological loss. In the lyric "The Gardens of Versailles," the human impulse to shape nature points to the diminishment of the natural world under the imposition of "form's vast claim." However, the final lines of the poem intimate that despite this rage for order, the presence of the river remains, tenaciously, in "the sound of water falling."

The origin of a poem, Merwin has said, is "a passion for the momentary countenance of the unrepeatable world" (5). The destiny of a poem, it might follow, is to awaken a fuller recognition of the self within the all-too-fragile and quickly passing frame of our lives. Merwin's poems urge us to affirm a wider sympathy with the nonhuman world of nature. And yet, in the opening of "Testimony" (1999), Merwin admits his uncertainty over how the pain of "learning what is lost / is transformed into light at last." Merwin's poems, brilliant flashes of illumination, remind us of the existence of something more substantial—hope.

BIBLIOGRAPHY

Brunner, Edward. *Poetry as Labor and Privilege: The Writings of W. S. Merwin.* Urbana: University of Illinois Press, 1991.

Frazier, Jane. *From Origin to Ecology: Nature and the Poetry of W. S. Merwin.* Teaneck, N.J.: Fairleigh Dickinson University Press, 1999.

Hix, H. L. *Understanding W. S. Merwin.* Columbia: University of South Carolina Press, 1997.

Hoeppner, Edward Haworth. *Echoes and Moving Fields: Structure and Subjectivity in the Poetry of W. S. Merwin and John Ashbery.* Lewisburg, Penn.: Bucknell University Press, 1994.

Merwin, W. S. "Preface." *The Second Four Books of Poems.* Port Townsend, Wash.: Copper Canyon Press, 1993, pp. 1–5.

———. "to name the wrong." *Regions of Memory: Uncollected Prose, 1949–1982,* edited by Cary Nelson and Ed Folsom, 291–292. Urbana: University of Illinois Press, 1987.

Nelson, Cary, and Ed Folsom, eds. *Regions of Memory: Uncollected Prose, 1949–1982,* by W. S. Merwin. Urbana: University of Illinois Press, 1987.

———. *W. S. Merwin: Essays on the Poetry.* Urbana: University of Illinois Press, 1987.

Mark C. Long

MEXICO CITY BLUES JACK KEROUAC (1959)

JACK KEROUAC's personal note on the title page of *Mexico City Blues* declares his wish "to be considered a jazz poet," and the poem's 242 choruses are invested with a musicality and improvisational quality that answer his wish. As with musical compositions, each movement of this book-length poem is independent, but the piece is more fully comprehensible and purposeful when taken in its entirety. The 242 choruses contain allusions to a vast range of experiences, from Kerouac's life: "I was the first crazy person / I'd known" ("88th Chorus"), from literature: "F. Scott Fitzgerald . . . Who burned his Wife Down" ("30th Chorus"), and from religion: "Nirvana? Heaven?" ("199th Chorus"). The poem's private set of references is typical of the BEAT poets, writers associated with this radical shift in American poetry in the mid-twentieth century who often looked outward for experience, then immediately recorded personal responses to everything (unconcerned with social respectability). The more a reader knows about the poet, in this instance, the fuller the understanding of the poem because the background explains the importance of otherwise obscure or confusing places, names, and events. It certainly helps to explain what Charlie Parker and Buddha are doing in the same poem, indeed in the same chorus ("239th Chorus").

Mexico City Blues was written in three weeks, largely influenced by marijuana and morphine, in Mexico City during August 1955. Along with his personal writing philosophy of "spontaneous composition"—writing down experience and impression unmediated by reflection—the only structural rule Kerouac set for himself was that each chorus had to fit on a single page in his notebook (Jones 141), but he occasionally sidestepped this restriction merely by picking up where the page length had stopped him in the next chorus, virtually midsentence or mididea. Some portions of the poem are simple transcriptions of the musings of Kerouac's neighbor, Bill Garver, a morphine addict he had known in New York. But the book is primarily an exercise in creative self-analysis done by a profoundly talented man with profoundly powerful demons.

The poem's rhythms are jazz rhythms, and a nonstop reading of the poem emphasizes the beat of Kerouac's verse as it affects the delivery of the words and lines. The occasional digression into "scat," nonsensical and wordless jazz sound play, provides Kerouac with a respite from the intensity of the issues with which he deals throughout. By providing this natural bridge, designed for the particular musicality of the poem, Kerouac conceals his momentary retreats from the subject matter (essential to the poet's ability to continue) as a change of pace rather than an explicit break. In the poem Kerouac records his attempt to resolve the major issue of his life: the death of his older brother in childhood. This event complicates the Roman Catholic Kerouac's religious seeking, his alcoholism, and his problematic relationship with his mother and, to a lesser extent, with everyone else he knew.

These psychological by-products of early childhood loss are wound together in *Mexico City Blues,* as the language of Buddhism provides Kerouac with both hope for spiritual and mental relief and pleasure for the ear. The critic James T. Jones explains that "the religious motif also connects autobiography to the most important theme of the poem, Kerouac's exploration of the concept of *anatta,* the possibility of annihilating self" (33). The "211th Chorus" ends with perhaps the deepest desire of Kerouac's heart: liberation from "that slaving meat wheel / and safe in heaven dead."

The seeming discontinuity of the choruses, leaping as they do from subject to subject in a stream-of-consciousness fashion, is resolved when they are placed within the framework of Kerouac's life. He found in these poems a way to articulate "personal conflicts into poetic tension [through] his combination of lyric and narrative, cumulation and repetition, language spinning and ideas, in a metaphorically musical structure" (Jones 165). *Mexico City Blues* is a kind of Beat generation variation on the tradition of King David's psalms, full of confidence, doubt, longing, and joy, dealing with spiritual and corporeal things, by a 20th-century romantic psalmist.

ALLEN GINSBERG, who embraced what he called Kerouac's "spontaneous bop prosody" (Miles 317) and whose poem *HOWL* was written the same year as *Mexico City Blues,* approached LAWRENCE FERLINGHETTI, at City Lights Books, to publish Kerouac's book (see POETRY PRESSES). Although Ginsberg even offered to pay the costs out of his own royalties from *Howl and Other Poems,* Ferlinghetti rejected the manuscript. Ginsberg finally approached Grove Press, which published the book in 1959. The book received such a blistering response by KENNETH REXROTH that more congenial reviews by ROBERT CREELEY and ANTHONY HECHT were unable to redress the harm. Rexroth's opinion was scathing: When Kerouac had written previously about "jazz and Negroes, [he had concentrated on] two subjects about which he knew less than nothing," Rexroth claimed, and he did the same thing with Buddhism and drugs in *Mexico City Blues* (14). Even so, in spite of his unconcealed derision, Rexroth admitted that the book exhibits a "terrifyingly skillful use of verse, the broad knowledge of life, the profound judgements, the almost unbearable sense of reality" one expects from Kerouac (14). Certainly this poem skillfully and beautifully communicates Kerouac in all of his simultaneous vulnerability and confidence.

BIBLIOGRAPHY

Jones, James T. *A Map of Mexico City Blues: Jack Kerouac as Poet.* Carbondale: Southern Illinois University Press, 1992.

Kerouac, Jack. *Book of Blues.* New York: Penguin, 1995.

Miles, Barry. *Jack Kerouac, King of the Beats: A Portrait*. London: Virgin, 1998.

Rexroth, Kenneth. "Discordant and Cool." *New York Times Book Review* (November 29, 1959): 14.

A. Mary Murphy

"MIDDLE PASSAGE" ROBERT HAYDEN (1962)

Assembled from various historical accounts, speeches, and documents, ROBERT HAYDEN's best-known and perhaps greatest poem, "Middle Passage," is an epic in miniature about the 19th-century African slave trade that also speaks to the abiding effects of slavery in modern America. Narrating through a range of voices, Hayden depicts the horrifying conditions slaves endured on the Middle Passage, while also condemning the hypocrisies of religion and political liberalism that permitted such injustices to continue. The title suggests slavery's effects continue even in the middle of the 20th century, yet it also reflects Hayden's belief that America is journeying toward personal freedom and racial justice, a belief embodied in the figure of Cinquez, the leader of a revolt of African slaves aboard the Spanish slave ship *Amistad.*

Hayden originally wrote "Middle Passage" as the opening section of a collection of poems he began in the early 1940s titled *The Black Spear,* prompted by Stephen Vincent Benét's claim in *John Brown's Body* that a black poet, not a white one, would have to write "[the] black-skinned epic, epic with the long black spear" (Hayden, 162) of African-American history. Although Hayden eventually abandoned *The Black Spear* project, he revised "Middle Passage" within the demands of high modernist style practiced by such poets as EZRA POUND, T. S. ELIOT, and HART CRANE (see MODERNISM), including the use of historical documents, a collage structure without evident transitions, a floating narrative voice, and obscure but sonorous diction.

Like many modernist long poems, "Middle Passage" inverts the conventions of epic poetry, including the quest-journey, the cataloguing of ships, and the presence of the gods, in order to depict a "voyage through death / to life on these shores" where conditions will differ little from the misery inside the ships' crowded slave-holds. Epic poetry embodies imperialist ideals, which for Hayden are responsible for every aspect of the Middle Passage, from the sale of Africans by rival tribesmen lured by European goods to the cruelties of Spanish slave traders and finally to the hypocrisy of an American democracy built by slave labor. But for Hayden, the integration of history into poetry was less an end than a means to an ultimate goal, the creation of an affirming racial myth.

The first section of the three-part poem is multivocal in its narration. Hayden juxtaposes a catalogue of ironically hopeful-sounding ships' names; lines from a hymn entitled "Jesus, Savior, Pilot Me"; a parody of lines about shipwreck from Shakespeare's play *The Tempest;* an allusion to Samuel Taylor Coleridge's poem about the sufferings of a wanderer at sea, "The Rime of the Ancient Mariner"; ship's log accounts of the horrid conditions the slaves endured, including an outbreak of blindness that spread to the crew; a crewmember's anxious thoughts; and finally a legal deposition concerning the burning of a slave vessel and the deaths of all the slaves within. Like the structure of T. S. Eliot's *The WASTE LAND,* Hayden's collage disorients the reader, though Hayden's more limited range of references helps clarify and intensify the moral crime of the Middle Passage. Hayden withholds his own ironic narrative voice here, letting the accounts of slaves who "went made of thirst and tore their flesh / and sucked the blood" and "leaped with crazy laughter / to the waiting sharks, singing as they went under" speak for the monstrous hypocrisy of those who pray for "safe passage to our vessels bringing / heathen souls unto Thy chastening."

The second section is a dramatic monologue spoken by a retired slave trader to a younger man. In it, the speaker recounts how the Africans themselves, particularly one called King Anthracite, could be induced by the cheap goods offered by European traders to capture neighboring tribesmen and sell them as chattel, "traps / of war wherein the victor and the vanquished // Were caught as prizes for our barracoons." Such a negative portrait, along with Hayden's allusions to works of European literature that in fact demonstrate an awareness of European immorality (like Coleridge's "The Rime of the Ancient Mariner"), challenges the essential racial myth Hayden is working to create. Race alone cannot be linked to the struggle for liberty, so a universal myth is needed, but such a myth risks concealing and devaluing the particular features of the African-American experience.

In the final section, Hayden returns to his earlier multivocal narration, juxtaposing a distant, ironic narrative voice with further parodies of *The Tempest* and a long deposition by an angry survivor of the *Amistad* revolt. In 1839, a group of Mendi African slaves aboard the Spanish ship *Amistad* (meaning "friendship"), led by one named Cinquez, rose up against and killed all but two members of the ship's crew. Later apprehended by the U.S. Navy off the coast of Long Island, Cinquez and the other Africans stood trial for mutiny, but backed by Abolitionist supporters, they defended themselves by claiming status as victims of kidnapping, not slaves. During the trial, Cinquez was portrayed publicly as a "noble savage," and the Supreme Court's decision to free the Africans and return them to Mendiland was seen as an important early step in the abolition of slavery. However, in the slave trader's deposition, which constitutes much of the third section, Hayden refuses to permit self-righteousness about America's role in the cause of liberty and emancipation. The slave trader challenges "you whose wealth, whose tree of liberty / are rooted in the labor of your slaves" with their own hypocrisy, asking why the Abolitionists, led by John Quincy Adams, "speak with so much passion of the right / of chattel slaves to kill their lawful masters." For Hayden, the work of racial justice cannot afford to congratulate itself midway.

In the slave trader's deposition, Hayden finally introduces the figure of Cinquez, the hero of this ironic epic. Continuing his inversion of epic conventions, Hayden represents Cinquez only indirectly and even then only briefly. He is first characterized by the slave trader as "that surly brute who calls himself a prince," then by Hayden himself, who calls Cinquez freedom's "deathless primaveral image, / life that transfigures many lives." This absence of characterization has aroused significant critical dispute about the success of Cinquez as a figure for personal and racial liberty. Earlier critics like Fred Fetrow find the indirect account effective, argue that it evokes the larger-than-life (and therefore inexpressible) status that in fact enables Cinquez, as the symbol of the struggle for freedom, to transfigure many lives. But later critics like Jon Woodson have argued that Cinquez's absence from the scene represents a failure of such transfiguration. For them, Hayden avoids discussion of how to resolve America's past and present moral conflicts, its "life upon these shores," shifting instead to a symbolic mode that treats Cinquez as an inspiring but ultimately silent icon. No consensus has been reached, though Woodson suggests that Hayden's multiple revisions of the conclusion of "Middle Passage" suggests his dissatisfaction with Cinquez's symbolic status. Yet this debate highlights a continuing question: whether to define liberty variously for different identity groups acting in history, or to define it as an abstract ideal in which all individual struggles are subsumed. It is the question of how America defines itself.

BIBLIOGRAPHY

Fetrow, Fred. *Robert Hayden*. Boston: Twayne Publishers, 1984.

Hayden, Robert. *Collected Prose,* edited by Frederick Glaysher. Ann Arbor: University of Michigan Press, 1984.

Williams, Pontheolla T. *Robert Hayden: A Critical Analysis of His Poetry*. Urbana: University of Illinois Press, 1987.

Woodson, Jon. "Consciousness, Myth, and Transcendence: Symbolic Action in Three Poems on the Slave Trade." In *The Furious Flowering of African-American Poetry,* edited by Joanne V. Gabbin, 154–168. Charlottesville: The University of Virginia Press, 1999.

Temple Cone

MILES, JOSEPHINE (1911–1985) In her scholarly work, *Poetry and Change* (1974), Josephine Miles writes, "The poet is a person in place and time, sharing in a language, participating in a culture" (3). Miles's body of work reflects a mind engaged in the 20th century, from her poetry's distinct MODERNISM to her later involvement in the social movements of the 1960s. The colloquial language in which her poetry delights demonstrates her immersion in the everyday life of her era, but the precision of her diction and the dispassion of her voice reveal the painstaking mind of the scholar. Like Emily Dickinson, Miles displays an often comic self-examination; like WALLACE STEVENS or E. E. CUMMINGS, she plays with words and syntax to disorient and delight.

Miles was born in Chicago but spent most of her life in California. She received an M.A. and Ph.D. from the University of California, Berkeley, where she subsequently taught. Her students included A. R. AMMONS, WILLIAM STAFFORD, ROBIN BLASER, JACK SPICER, and DIANE WAKOSKI. A mentor and teacher to BEAT poets, Miles has been called a "precursor" (Knight 7). A prolific scholar, Miles published more than 10 scholarly books and more than 15 collections of poetry. Her *Collected Poems: 1930–1983* won the Lenore Marshall/*Nation* Prize (1983) and was a finalist for the Pulitzer Prize (1983). She received many other awards and fellowships, including one from the Academy of American Poets (1978).

Miles's lyrics are often short, terse observations of a detached, acerbic, scholar: "The gang wanted to give Oedipus Rex a going away present / He had been a good hard-working father and king" ("Oedipus" [1960]). She might also report and reflect on overheard conversation: "Said, Pull her up a bit will you, Mac, I want to unload there. / Said, Pull her up my rear end, first come first serve" ("Reason" [1955]). In her later work, she comments on current events, yet she connects them to her life: "This was a dark year for Spiro Agnew; / It was a dark year for me too" ("Sleeve" [1979]). In all her work, there speaks the voice of one who loves the poetry of the common American idiom and who can perceive the complexity in the most common American experience.

BIBLIOGRAPHY

Knight, Brenda. "Josephine Miles: Mentor to a Revolution." In *Women of the Beat Generation: The Writers, Artists, and Muses at the Heart of a Revolution*. Berkeley: Conari Press, 1998, pp. 39–45.

Miles, Josephine. *Poetry and Change: Donne, Milton, Wordsworth, and the Equilibrium of the Present*. Berkeley: University of California Press, 1974.

Dennis McDaniel

MILLAY, EDNA ST. VINCENT (1892–1950) Edna St. Vincent Millay was a singular phenomenon in American literature of the early 20th century. She was a star whose books sold in numbers more often associated with fiction than poetry and whose speaking voice and magnetic personality gave her an irresistible appeal in both her public and private lives. She was encouraged early by SARA TEASDALE and the critic Louis Untermeyer, but Millay's literary acquaintanceship primarily included publishers and minor poets rather than the other major writers of her time; hers was an art more influential than one influenced by her contemporaries. While her career coincides with the IMAGIST SCHOOL, she is not an imagist poet in any strict sense of community or practice. During the 1920s she wrote plays produced by the Provincetown Players in New York, as did Sherwood Anderson, Djuna Barnes, E. E. CUMMINGS, Susan Glaspell, Eugene O'Neill, WALLACE STEVENS, and WILLIAM CARLOS WILLIAMS. She was significant enough to share a stage with ROBERT FROST and CARL SANDBURG, and her prominent position allowed her to exercise advocacy on behalf of other poets. Millay once declared ROBINSON JEFFERS "the best poet in America" (Milford 330), and in the 1930s she annually advised the Guggenheim Foundation on how best to grant its fellowships. She recommended E. E. Cummings (whom she believed had "a pretty big talent in pretty bad hands" [qtd. in Milford 370]) and LOUISE BOGAN in 1933; CONRAD AIKEN, KAY BOYLE, and WALTER LOWENFELS in 1934; and in 1938 she rejected MURIEL RUKEYSER, whose writing on social issues Millay felt made for poor poetry.

Millay was born in Rockland, Maine, the eldest of three daughters; her irresponsible father was asked to leave by the time she was eight. The girls were raised by their practical mother, a nurse, whose work absences were so frequent and prolonged that the children often were left to their own devices. The all-female family existed in relentless poverty. For her 12th birthday, Millay received a subscription to a children's publication called *St. Nicholas* and began writing seriously, submitting pieces for its editor's consideration. By the time she was 18 and too old to enter any more writing contests, she had won every award the magazine offered. In high school she acted in school plays, played the piano in recital, edited the school paper, and wrote. In 1912 she submitted the poem "Renascence" to a competition, *The Lyric Year*'s selection of the year's 100 best poems. Her poem placed fourth and therefore was awarded no prize money. Ironically this fact garnered the poem more attention than it might have had the poem won. Critics extolled the virtues of "Renascence" and its writer. Millay was rewarded with the attention and patronage of Caroline Dow, who organized sufficient financial support to send her to college. Millay chose Vassar (1913–17). She also chose to have no children, and although she married, hers was not a conventional marriage. Eugen Boissevain took care of her from the time they married in 1923 until his death in 1949, managing their lives so that she was free to immerse herself in living and writing. Millay won the Pulitzer Prize for poetry in 1923, the Levinson Prize in 1931, and the Gold Medal of the Poetry Society of America in 1943. She was elected to the National Institute of Arts and Letters (1929) and the American Academy of Arts and Letters (1940).

From her earliest poems, Millay's work displays a freshness of image, a depth of emotional loss, and a cynicism about love. In "Thursday" (1923), she expresses surprise at a rejected lover's dismay, wondering at the assumption that what was love on Wednesday will still be love the following day—unusual to hear in a woman's voice because of the traditional myth of woman's constancy. Millay showed no interest in a pedestrian life of decorum; in an untitled quatrain she declared, "My candle burns at both ends; / It will not last the night" (1923). Millay's originality is clearly expressed in "Spring" (1923), in which she argues against poems exuberantly praising the season simply for its existence. All of the beauties of spring taken together are not enough to justify life, which the poem compares to "an empty cup, a flight of uncarpeted stairs"; she is unimpressed and unrelieved that every year spring "Comes like an idiot, babbling and strewing flowers." The jaded voice and bravado of many of her poems are counterbalanced by the extraordinary longing articulated in others. Her sonnets (see PROSODY AND FREE VERSE), a form she consistently employed from the time she was 15, variously express sexual desire uncomplicated by emotional involvement but complicated by gender norms ("I, being born a woman and distressed" [1923]), make a case for love as one, but not the only or most necessary, of the necessities of life ("Love is not all: it is not meat nor drink" [1931]), condemn a world inactive in the face of fascist expansion ("Czecho-Slovakia" [1939]), and chart her history as a woman. In these poems she is stricken with love, by turns abandoned and abandoning, and she wrestles with mortality, her own and that of those she loved.

Millay published 25 books between 1917 and 1949, primarily writing poetry, but also fiction, drama, and an opera libretto. Her later poems are not held in the high regard her early work enjoyed, and Millay herself occasionally feared she had lost her gift. Critics sometimes wondered if perhaps she had been too eagerly lauded as a major poet at the start of her career. Her late poems are often politically motivated propaganda rather than passionate love lyrics, and this change of focus may have caused a reassessment of her body of work in more recent times. Whatever one might think of her political statements, there is no denying the emotional power of her LYRIC POETRY.

BIBLIOGRAPHY

Brittin, Norman A. *Edna St. Vincent Millay*. Rev. ed, Boston: Twayne, 1982.

Freedman, Diane P. *Millay at 100: A Critical Reappraisal.* Carbondale: Southern Illinois University Press, 1995.

Milford, Nancy. *Savage Beauty: The Life of Edna St. Vincent Millay*. New York: Random House, 2002.

Thesing, William B., ed. *Critical Essays on Edna St. Vincent Millay*. New York: G.K. Hall, 1993.

A. Mary Murphy

"MINIVER CHEEVY" EDWIN ARLINGTON ROBINSON (1910) Although in many ways a poet of the 19th century, EDWIN ARLINGTON ROBINSON is an important transitional figure whose poems inspired many 20th-century poets. "Miniver Cheevy" is the first American poem to express dissatisfaction with the modern age by satirically contrasting it with earlier eras. In this sense the poem anticipates T. S. ELIOT's *The WASTE LAND* (1922) and EZRA POUND's "Hugh Selwyn Mauberley" (1920). Although Robinson's poem engages the perception of difference between the present and the past mostly for comic purposes, it provides an example of 20th-century poets' sense of attenuated cultural and artistic life in the modern age.

The speaker of the poem subtly delineates Miniver's situation, which, as Wallace Anderson points out, is suggested by the word *vagrant* and the phrase "on the town," meaning "to be supported by the town, a charity case. Miniver . . . is the town ne'er-do-well, the town loafer" (107). But Miniver perceives his condition as a cruel accident of fate. He believes that had he been born to an earlier age, he would have known romance and created art. Instead his untimely and prosaic existence is a burden that he must bear tragically but philosophically. While presenting Miniver's appraisal of his situation, the poem provides no support for his opinion; rather, it undermines Miniver's false sense of martyrdom with exaggerated diction, and excessive repetition.

The first stanza of the poem initiates the ironic tone. Hyperbolic verbs, such as "assailed," expose Miniver's notion that he is a kind of romantic sufferer. Moreover the final line is deliberately truncated so that the solemnity of the rhythm is undercut: "He wept that he was ever born, / And he had reasons." In the third stanza, feminine rhymes (ending in unstressed syllables,) give a humorous, mock-heroic tone to Miniver's fantasies about living in the legendary ages of King Arthur or the Trojans ("Priam's neighbors"), of whom he dreams while "resting" from his decidedly less than Herculean "labors." When rhymed with "labors," "neighbors" not only sounds comically forced and stilted but also echoes the melodramatic falling rhythm.

The concluding stanzas more directly mock Miniver's self-pity. In the penultimate stanza, the repetition of the verb "thought" sarcastically undermines Miniver's self-commiseration. As Anderson notes, "the addition of the fourth 'thought' changes the tone of the stanza entirely, making it absurd" (107). The last stanza provides Miniver's convenient excuse for drowning his sorrows in alcohol: He was born to the wrong time. The rhyming of "thinking" and "drinking" suggests not only that his drinking comes from thinking about his fate but also that his drinking influences his thinking, his bathetic delusion of being destined to languish in a fallen era.

BIBLIOGRAPHY

Anderson, Wallace. *Edwin Arlington Robinson: A Critical Introduction.* Boston: Houghton Mifflin, 1967.

Barnard, Ellsworth. *Edwin Arlington Robinson: A Critical Study.* New York: Macmillan, 1952.

Edwin J. Barton

"MOCK ORANGE" LOUISE GLÜCK **(1985)** A post-CONFESSIONAL meditation on the psychological burden of mind-body dualism, Louise Glück's "Mock Orange" associates an olfactory image, the almost overwhelming fragrance of the mock orange shrub, with the idea that mind and body can be unified, a myth that Glück claims is at odds with the fragmentary reality of human existence in the postmodern world. The poem dramatizes the painful discovery that our physical selves and our intellects and emotions can never interact harmoniously, but are always split "into the old selves, / the tired antagonisms" of mind and body, the dualism at the heart of Western culture. Dan Bogen notes that the poem "disturbs not because it is idiosyncratic but because it defines something we feel but rarely acknowledge; it strips off a veil" (53). Yet for Glück, the categories of mind and body are themselves problematic, contributing to a divisive attitude toward the experience of existence. Glück's analysis of this dualism is thus decidedly feminist in character, criticizing not only traditionally Western, male-centered solutions to the dualistic split (such as Descartes's *Cogito ergo sum,* which links intellect to existence), but the categories themselves, by comparing their effects to the pain of unwanted sexual intercourse and its "low, humiliating / premise of union."

The speaker opens in medias res with an enigmatic assertion, "It is not the moon, I tell you." While the poem is not obviously a dramatic monologue, in which the speaker addresses a second, silent character, an earlier conversation has clearly taken place, and the speaker is now responding to someone else's identification of the moon as the cause of her anxiety about the nature of the self. Because the moon traditionally symbolizes femininity, the body, and the emotions, it appears the silent character has identified emotion and physicality as sources of the speaker's anxiety about selfhood, while also implying that the intellect may provide a remedy. But the speaker rejects this analysis, locating her anxiety not in the moon but in the overpoweringly fragrant aroma of the mock orange bush, a smell that Glück finds sickening because it is pervasive and invasive. The speaker likens this invasiveness to the sexual act, which she finds forced and painful because it is experienced as a violation of her person.

Glück's rejection of sexuality here is more than just personal; she likens the pervasive scent of the mock orange to the equally pervasive idea that sex is an experience of union, a myth the speaker challenges. A kiss, the speaker suggests, simply seals shut a woman's mouth, preventing her from speaking and expressing herself. Discussing *The Triumph of Achilles,* in which this poem first appeared, poet EDWARD HIRSCH notes that "[S]exual union is equated with muteness, with a frightening silence, a loss of self. She treats erotic need and desire as a mockery of the struggle to create a distinguishing and integral self" (35). The idea that a woman needs a man to experience union, that the emotions need the intellect, or that union itself is desirable, is a myth that depends on those same divisive categories of mind and body that it claims to overcome: "We are made fools of," the speaker laments, "And the scent of mock orange / drifts through the window."

But the speaker refuses to give in to the despair she so clearly feels. "How can I rest?" she asks, and she seems to charge herself with the task of feeling discontent clearly so that she can see the truth clearly: that Western traditions of mind-body dualism are related to Western history of gender bias, to a loss of power, control, and sense of authentic self. For Glück, the Western idea that emotion and the body are opposed to the intellect is a myth whose widespread acceptance has sickened her and prompted her to rebel. The poem is a powerful renunciation of gendered power and of the tyranny of the intellect, but it also articulates a philosophically ambitious quest: to see the self not as the sum of body and mind, but as a bodily mind and an intellectual body.

BIBLIOGRAPHY

Bogen, Don. "The Fundamental Skeptic." *The Nation* 242, no. 2 (1986): 53–54.

Hirsch, Edward. "The Watcher." *American Poetry Review* 15, no. 6 (1986): 33–36.

Temple Cone

MODERNISM To most critics, modernism encompasses a relatively short time in the early 20th century, from approximately 1910, just before World War I, to the beginning of World War II, although some critics believe that the movement began in the late 19th century and continued until 1965. The movement began in Europe, but Americans, especially expatriates, played major roles in it. The modernist period was particularly innovative. Modernism is often considered to include all the "isms" of this era—imagism (see IMAGIST SCHOOL), cubism, dadaism, abstractionism (see ABSTRACT EXPRESSIONISM), and so on—and to mark a sense of cultural crisis and radical rupture with the past that became the hallmark of certain artists, literary and otherwise, who created work in the wake of World War I and the early 20th century advancement of industrialization. Regarding modernist ideals of poetic language, EZRA POUND, one of the most important figures of this movement, would issue the famous exhortation to "make it new." The modernist writers do just that: They "make it new," because, for them, this new world could only be adequately reflected in the most innovative paradigms and modes of expression.

Key characteristics of modernist writing include a movement away from realism into abstractions; a deliberate complexity, even to the point of elitism, forcing readers to be very well-educated in order to read these works; a high degree of aesthetic self-consciousness; questions of what constitutes the nature of being; a breaking with tradition and conventional modes of form, resulting in fragmentation and experimentation; and, finally, the privileging of irony. As a result, poetry written in the modernist mode was often impersonal, cosmopolitan, highly learned, and skeptical. To add to this already complicated picture, modernism contained contradictory elements: It proclaimed democracy while holding to certain elitist ideals, such as the level of education the reader needed in order to understand the works, and it was both traditional and antitraditional, searching for order through the use of cherished myths (which can be seen in Eliot's references to the classical world, for example) while at the same time using fragmentary, nontraditional forms.

Numerous cultural forces worked to create the modernist movement in poetry, although modernist artists responded to these forces in various ways. At the beginning of the 20th century, many artists perceived problems with the ideals of the movements that preceded modernism: romanticism, Victorianism, and

Edwardianism. Romanticism's philosophies of pantheism and transcendence no longer seemed to cohere for those who had to cope with the technologies of industrial modernization. In addition, romanticism's more moderate expression and valuation of nature—the rural, agricultural, and traditional—as opposed to culture and art seemed inadequate to express a sense of loss and new beginnings. Victorianism and Edwardianism also proved inadequate: The first seemed too morally earnest, complacent, and, at times, overly squeamish about sexual matters; the second, a reaction to its predecessor's conservatism, began to doubt authority, but not always very deeply. After the Edwardian period, the movement to the ideas of modernism seemed almost inevitable.

As the philosopher Jurgen Habermas states, modernity "revolts against normalizing functions of tradition; Modernity lives on the experience of rebelling against all that is normative" ("Modernity," 162). In the wake of the apocalyptic sense of a new century and the cultural crisis brought on by World War I, Western notions of superiority came into question. In addition, long-held precepts of the Renaissance and Enlightenment models of reality, all encompassing beliefs that humans were essentially good and could perfect both themselves and their societies, were beginning to collapse, and the value systems underlying American society—those of God, country, and capitalism—also faced challenges on almost all fronts. Large-scale migrations from rural areas to urban centers, along with technological change, also caused feelings of cultural dislocation.

The American poets associated with the modernist movement include T. S. ELIOT, Pound, GERTRUDE STEIN, and H. D., all expatriates, as well as WALLACE STEVENS, MARIANNE MOORE, HART CRANE, and WILLIAM CARLOS WILLIAMS. In the British Isles, the primary modernist poets are William Butler Yeats, W. H. AUDEN, Stephen Spender, Edith Sitwell, Cecil Day-Lewis, Louis MacNeice, and Dylan Thomas. Even Gerard Manley Hopkins, the English Jesuit whose poetry was published posthumously in 1918, was seen as a modernist; his proclamations of doubt and despair, and his wrenching of the sonnet form and theory of inscape (in brief, the aesthetic principle that the individually distinctive form of an object reveals its rich singularity) pointed to a key modernist contradiction: a simultaneous break with and embracing of the past.

Modernism also reflects an awareness of new psychological theories propounded by Sigmund Freud and Carl Jung, the historical-cultural theories of Karl Marx, the philosophical theories of Frederich Nietzsche, and the iconoclastic, evolutionary theories of Charles Darwin. These new and radical concepts offered so-called master narratives, such as Marx's ideas on the dynamics of capitalism, which sought to explain history and produce a new sense of historical consciousness. All of these new ideas worked to undermine long-held assumptions about language, culture, religion, and reality, which aided in the creation of the "modernist self" prevalent among literary artists of this movement: self-conscious, nihilistic, fragmented, cynical, alienated, detached, the creator as opposed to the preserver of culture, innovative. This new sense of self gave the modernist writers a heightened sense of purpose, even as their responses to the cultural crises were highly individual.

In particular, the psychologies of Freud and Jung deeply affected modernist writers, who focused on the unconscious mind, concerning themselves with the inner being more than the social being and looking for ways to incorporate these new views into poetry. The new theories of the unconscious led the modernist writers to look inside themselves for their answers instead of seeking truth, for example, through formal religion or the scientific presuppositions that realism and naturalism rested upon. In turn, these poets created a solipsistic, self-conscious imagination that insisted on having a general frame of reference in itself.

The modernists were highly conscious that they were being modern—that they were "making it new"—and this consciousness is manifest in the modernists' radical use of a kind of formlessness; their work thus utilized collapsed plots, fragmentary techniques, and stream-of-consciousness point of view. The modernists also sometimes used associative techniques, a collection of seemingly random impressions and allusions with which readers are expected to make the connections on their own; this technique was meant to convey the creative potential of the unconscious and the pressure of the unspoken on the spoken. Eliot's *The* *Waste Land* is arguably the greatest example of this allusive manner of writing; it includes a variety of Buddhist, Christian, Greek, Judaic, German, and occult references, among others.

Some of the most exciting and innovative modernist work was done in poetry, and the key poets, Eliot and Pound, were also leading critics and promulgators of modernist theories. Pound is perhaps best known for his editing of Eliot's work and for functioning as a catalyst for the modernist movement. At Pound's urging, Harriet Monroe of the Chicago magazine *Poetry* published "The Love Song of J. Alfred Prufrock." This poem, published in 1915, when the poet was still a young man, conveyed a sense of futility and sterility through a stream-of-consciousness, fragmented form. It became the model modernist poem. Pound, in encouraging its publication (Monroe was at first reluctant to publish it, since she wanted it to end on a triumphant note), noted that Eliot had "actually trained himself *and* modernized himself on *his own*" (qtd. in Litz 956). *The Waste Land* was published in 1922, considered to be the apex year of the modernist movement. Brilliantly aided by Pound's careful editing, *The Waste Land* reflects a number of modernist characteristics: despair, a desire for assurance and certainty, fragmentary form and stream-of-consciousness style, in addition to its multiple allusions and perspectives.

Although modernism was a highly innovative movement, it can be accused of not being quite so egalitarian as its proponents might claim. Critic Andreas Huyssen hints at high modernism's elitist project: "Modernism constituted itself through a conscious strategy of exclusion, an anxiety of contamination by its other: an increasingly . . . engulfing mass culture" (vii). This concern for contamination led modernist writers to disregard shared conventions of meaning, making many of their supreme achievements, such as most of Eliot's poetry, especially *The Waste Land,* and Pound's *The Cantos,* inaccessible to the common reader. For Eliot, who, along with Pound, was the most important critic of the movement, this abstruseness was necessary to prevent a literature from heading down the slippery slope of populism. In addition, those in the forefront of modernism were often educated at elitist institutions and came from wealthy backgrounds: Eliot, the pampered youngest son of an upper-middle-class family, was educated at Harvard and Oxford; Pound, H. D., and Williams, a medical doctor, at the University of Pennsylvania; Stein at Radcliffe; and Stevens at Harvard. Furthermore the sometimes radical political inclinations of some of these poets have provoked much critical commentary; critics tend to link these tendencies to the poets' elitist backgrounds. From the fascism of Pound to the conservatism of Eliot and Yeats, modernist writers seem, at times, to have enclosed themselves in a glass cage, far from the teeming masses.

In short, modernists sought to break with the past. While their movement was resistive, a reply to a world considered to be a spiritual and moral wasteland, the modernist rebellion did not extend to an outright rejection of all belief systems. Modernists still believed it possible to "shore up these fragments against ruin," as Eliot famously notes at the conclusion of *The Waste Land.* Meaning may or may not exist in the natural world, but the modernist writers saw themselves as making meaning out of their art, even as they created their own ordering principle.

BIBLIOGRAPHY

Berman, Art. *Preface to Modernism.* Urbana: University of Illinois Press, 1995.

Habermas, Jurgen. "Excerpt from 'Modernity—An Incomplete Project.'" In *Postmodernism: A Reader.* London: Edward Arnold, 1992, pp. 160–170.

Huyssen, Andreas. *After the Great Divide: Modernism, Mass Culture, Postmodernism.* Bloomington: Indiana University Press, 1986.

Kenner, Hugh. *A Homemade World: The American Modernist Writers.* Baltimore: Johns Hopkins Press, 1975.

Litz, A. Walton. "Ezra Pound and T. S. Eliot." In *Columbia Literary History of the United States,* edited by Emory Elliot, 947–971. New York: Columbia University Press, 1988.

Longenbach, James. "Modern Poetry." In *The Cambridge Companion to Modernism.* New York: Cambridge University Press, 1999, pp. 100–130.

Stephanie Gordon

"MONET'S 'WATERLILIES'" **Robert Hayden** **(1970)** Robert Hayden's "Monet's 'Waterlilies'" stands out among ekphrastic poetry, or poems about works of art. With 14 lines, it evokes the sonnet tradition, insisting that viewers must lovingly engage works of art to achieve personal transformation. It was originally published in a collection titled *Words in Mourning Time,* the title of which indicates the volume's preoccupation with the tumult and strife of its era, as well as the clear cathartic function of the poems. As Fred Fetrow notes, Hayden "concludes the cryptic descriptions of chaotic moral disorder not with dire prophecy or self-righteous clucking, but instead with a note of hope, a statement of desperate faith" (28). Challenging "the vagaries of life [with] the permanence of art" (28), Hayden discovers in this impressionist masterwork an injunction to restore to the world a sense of opportunity and hope.

The narrator begins the poem not with the painting, but with this observation: "Today as the news from Selma and Saigon / poisons the air like fallout." Hayden thus recalls a historical moment (March 1965) when country and world seemed to lack critical moral governance, when innocent citizens could be harmed by racism, by war, or by nuclear weapons, and these complications seem to poison the air. But the speaker refuses to drift into mere complaint about social and world conditions, turning his attention instead to this painting of waterlilies.

In the second stanza, the speaker introduces the eponymous painting, stating that "I come again to see / the serene great picture that I love." The speaker has come literally "for the purpose of seeing"; that is, to have a pleasurable aesthetic experience. But the significance of the word *love* must be examined closely. If the conventional view holds that aesthetics is inherently nonpolitical, then the opening lines redefine this enthusiasm with a political and moral gravity that moves the painting beyond the realm of "mere art." The speaker has not simply "come again to see" the painting as a pleasant escape, but to be able to see the painting while keeping in mind the negative news from the opening, as if something had been missing from earlier viewings that current events now fulfill. Indeed, the complex meter of the fourth line seems to hint at an order heretofore unglimpsed. If the first stanza introduces an ethical dilemma into aesthetics—how to view a work of art, ostensibly amoral, while maintaining social consciousness, itself antithetical to the release art provides—then the following stanza hints that one cannot truly approach art without bringing before it an awareness of the world.

Hayden's use of *Here* as an anaphora fixes the audience within the painting, but also with the historical moment in which the speaker views it. To understand a painting, therefore, one must attend to the artwork and to the complex reality in which one exists while viewing it. The assertion that "Here space and time exist in light" points to a harmony missing from the external world, and the speaker goes on to equate the viewing of the painting with an act of faith—"in light / the eye like the eye of faith believes." To view a painting is literally to exercise faith, since a canvas is only a two-dimensional representation of three-dimensional reality, but Hayden hints at a deeper faith. One approaches a work of art with the hope religious faith can bring, and one expects to find goodness and order that might counter the meaninglessness of life.

By viewing the work of art, then one re-envisions the world. In the painting, "The seen, the known / dissolve in iridescence, become / illusive flesh of light." This iridescence calls to mind the rainbow as both a symbol of the imagination and of resurrection, suggesting that art allows humans to live again with a sense of imagination and empathy the news cannot provide. The painting, by transforming the viewer's known world, expands the consciousness to a consideration of the world of possibilities ("that was not"), of the historical past ("was"), and of enduring, transcendent realities ("forever is"). This imaginative transformation has a necessary political component; one cannot be truly illuminated without returning to the historical world, clothed in the "flesh of light." The viewer's consideration of moral and political issues in the presence of amoral art is important, because it prevents the solipsism of "art for art's sake" and reminds the viewer of the need to remain engaged with society.

Hayden's poem never loses sight of either the political or the aesthetic realms, and what allows this unifying vision is the clarity granted by light itself, which Monet's painting conveys; as Fetrow notes, "Beyond comfort and sensual gratification, Hayden also always seeks truth" (120). "Here is the aura of that world /

each of us has lost," Hayden writes, "Here is the shadow of its joy." *Aura* (Greek for breath) and *shadow* both suggest mere mimetic representation, and for a moment the painting seems just a copy of the beautiful world that is being threatened by the historical calamities of the day. But aura and shadow must have a source; they cannot exist independently. The interaction of light with an object creates them, and they highlight their source. The metaphorical light, which dissolves "(t)he seen, the known" in the painting, which illuminates the mind of artist and viewer, is the imagination. If one truly looked in the shadow and traced back the light of imagination, Hayden suggests, the path to that lost paradise would be found.

BIBLIOGRAPHY

Fetrow, Fred. *Robert Hayden.* Boston: Twayne Publishers, 1984.

Temple Cone

MONTAGE OF A DREAM DEFERRED

LANGSTON HUGHES (1951) *Montage of a Dream Deferred,* a book-length poem set in Harlem, uses multiple voices and a jazz bebop structure to explore the joys and sorrows of postwar city life, while echoing LANGSTON HUGHES's ubiquitous phrase "dream deferred" throughout its pages. In this poem, which consists of a series of 87 short pieces designed to resemble a complex musical composition, Hughes demonstrates his continued interest in using African-American popular music as a source of rhythm and structure; indeed, the influence of the blues tradition in his poetry dates from his first published volume, *The Weary Blues* (1926). In his determination to make a new kind of poetry for the masses, using fresh and original language and contemporary poetic forms, Hughes can be linked philosophically with poets of the IMAGIST SCHOOL, such as EZRA POUND, and with the Walt Whitman-influenced writers of the Chicago Renaissance, such as CARL SANDBURG and VACHEL LINDSAY.

However, as Robert O'Brien Hokanson reports, critics have noted that Hughes's particular contribution to MODERNISM lies in "his ability to combine a modern consciousness with an abiding racial consciousness" (79). In doing so Hughes seeks to incorporate African and African-American traditions of myth, music, and culture into his poetry rather than the European models used by his modernist contemporaries. In common with other writers associated with the HARLEM RENAISSANCE, such as STERLING BROWN and Zora Neale Hurston, Hughes's poetic practice reflects his commitment to adapting black dialect and the black folk experience for artistic use. For Hughes this project has intellectual, political, social, cultural, and literary implications, and indeed *Montage* reflects the extent to which, as Steven C. Tracy contends, "Hughes merged the African-American oral and written traditions, exploiting conventions, techniques, and the goals of both to achieve a poetry that is intellectually stimulating, sociopolitically responsible, and aesthetically pleasing both as folk poetry and literature" (2).

Montage with its "boogie-woogie rumble," demonstrates Hughes's interest in the performative nature of poetry (see POETRY IN PERFORMANCE), and the piece lends itself to his practice during this period of staging public readings accompanied by a jazz band. By adapting the structural characteristics of bebop to the poetic form, Hughes created a poem rich with the nuances of this challenging new musical genre. While Walter C. Farrell, Jr., and Patricia A. Johnson argue that the influence of bebop composition allowed Hughes to create in *Montage* a new form of poetry, "a series of short poems or phrases that contribute to the making of one long poem" (61), Hokanson goes further to suggest that just as bebop represents a rebellion against the mainstream jazz tradition, *Montage* reflects the unrest Hughes observed in the postwar African-American urban community (64). As Hughes describes it in his introductory note, the poem's rhythm is "punctuated by the riffs, runs, breaks, and disc-tortions of the music of a community in transition" (387). Bebop words and rhythm are also present in the use of exclamatory jive slang phrases that end several poems, including the opening piece, "Dream Boogie": *"Hey, pop! / Re-bop! / Mop! / Y-e-a-h!"*

The poem's language is enriched by the variety of voices that touch on a variety of subjects, many common to blues music that also specifically reflect Hughes's views on urban social and economic issues and on the "dream deferred," which symbolizes the promise without fulfillment repeated throughout the work. The ironies of postwar economics are expressed in several poems that recall wartime prosperity with nostalgia even as they acknowledge war's sorrow; in "Green Memory," the speaker calls the war a time "when money rolled in / and blood rolled out," while in the piece called "World War II," the war is called a "grand time," even though the poem ends with the "Echo: *Did / Somebody / Die?*" The hope of postwar prosperity has been dashed and little progress made, as apparent from the speaker who complains that although the war allowed him to get off relief, now he is "almost back in the barrel again." In these poetic narratives landladies overcharge and renters land in jail when they protest unlivable housing conditions, girlfriends ask, Can you *"love me, daddy / and feed me too?,"* and the speaker in "Blues at Dawn" is so close to despair that he says, "If I recall the day before, / I wouldn't get up no more." Despite expressions of dismay and difficulty, however, *Montage* shines with brief moments that extol the excitement of city life: A "Parade" becomes a "chance to let / the whole world see / old black me!," and a Harlem night inspires an impulse to take the "neon lights and make a crown." Finally, with the chilling recognition that "there ain't no Ku Klux / on a 133rd," Hughes reminds his readers that despite its drawbacks, Harlem offers African Americans a safer alternative to the lives of violence and oppression they lived in the South.

Although versions of the poem published after the original 1951 edition have altered the original format and typography and thus diminished its presentation as a single long poem, its title serves to emphasize the work's montage composition of juxtaposed images and shifting perspectives. While this structure may be linked to other modernist literary projects that used collage techniques, Hughes's strategy signals also his alignment with significant developments in African-American music and culture. John Lowney acknowledges that even as *Montage* "invoked a polymorphous African American musical tradition familiar to readers of Hughes's earlier blues and jazz poetry, it summons this tradition through bebop's more defiant postwar mood" (358). *Montage of a Dream Deferred* throbs with the beat of its time and place.

BIBLIOGRAPHY

Farrell, Walter C., Jr., and Patricia A. Johnson. "Poetic Interpretations of Urban Black Folk Culture: Langston Hughes and the 'Bebop' Era." *MELUS* 8, no. 3 (1981): 57–72.

Hokanson, Robert O'Brien. "Jazzing It Up: The Be-bop Modernism of Langston Hughes." *Mosaic: A Journal for the Interdisciplinary Study of Literature* 31, no. 4 (1998): 61–82.

Hughes, Langston. Introductory Note to *The Collected Poems of Langston Hughes,* edited by Arnold Rampersad and David Roessel. New York: Vintage, 1994.

Lowney, John. "Langston Hughes and the 'Nonsense' of BeBop." *American Literature* 72, no. 2 (2000): 357–386.

Tracy, Steven C. *Langston Hughes and the Blues.* Champaign: University of Illinois Press, 1988.

Jacqueline O'Connor

MOORE, MARIANNE (1887–1972) Marianne Moore's poetry combines precise visual observation, moral questioning, eclectic erudition, and verbal play together with fastidious attention to metrical and graphic shape in a way that makes her one of the most singular poets of the 20th century. Her work, while distinctly modernist in its method and presentation (see MODERNISM), is not easily classified into any single school or trend in American poetry. Although connected early in her career with the IMAGIST SCHOOL, and later adopted by LOUIS ZUKOFSKY as an OBJECTIVIST, much of her work takes on questions of ethics and abstract intellectual thought not normally associated with those movements. Contemporary poets of the NEW FORMALISM claim Moore as an influence, though her emphasis on the materiality of language and on the function of words outside of the symbolic order also anticipate the LANGUAGE SCHOOL of the late 20th century.

Moore was born in Kirkwood, Missouri. She spent her first years in the house of her grandfather, a Presbyterian minister, together with her mother and older brother. After her grandfather's death in 1894, the family moved first to Pittsburgh, then to Carlisle, Pennsylvania, where they lived for 20 years. Her relationships with her brother and her mother were the most important ones in her life, both personally and artistically. Moore received many awards and prizes over the course of her career, including the *Dial* Award in 1924, a Guggenheim Fellowship in 1945, and the Bollingen Prize for poetry, a National Book Award, and the Pulitzer Prize for poetry for the publication of her *Collected Poems* in 1951. She was a member of the National Institute of Arts and Letters and the American Academy of Arts and Letters.

After graduating Bryn Mawr College in 1909, Moore returned to Carlisle and taught at the Indian School there for several years. During this time she followed the latest developments in art and culture through voracious reading of magazines and research trips to libraries. On a trip to Britain in 1911, she bought EZRA POUND's *Personae* and *Exaltations* (an entry in a college notebook reads "Ezra Pound—at all costs!!"), and the next year she visited the Library of Congress, where she read Wyndham Lewis's and Pound's magazine *Blast*. Her first major publications happened in 1915—in the *Egoist* in London and in Harriet Monroe's *Poetry* and Alfred Kreymborg's journal *Others* in the United States.

Moore's first book, *Poems*, was published in London in 1921 by H. D., her partner Winifred Ellerman (known as "Bryher"), and Richard Aldington. It consists largely of the poems that had been submitted to the aforementioned journals and was apparently prepared without Moore's knowledge. In 1924 Moore's first American book, *Observations*, was published. It was on the strength of this book and her many magazine publications that Moore was awarded the *Dial* magazine's award in 1924. In 1925 she would become the *Dial*'s editor, a position she would hold until it ceased publication in 1929. When the magazine folded, Moore and her mother left Manhattan for Brooklyn, where she would live for the next 36 years.

In 1934 Moore met ELIZABETH BISHOP, then a student at Vassar who first approached her as a mentor, but who would become a very close friend. Moore's *Selected Poems* was published in 1935 (with an introduction by T. S. ELIOT). After the publication of *What Are Years?* in 1941 and *Nevertheless* in 1944, Moore turned her energies toward a novel she had begun in the 1930s entitled *The Way We Live Now*, which was never published. In 1945, encouraged by W. H. AUDEN, Moore began a translation of the *Fables of Lafontaine*. Her translation is distinguished by the painstaking attempt to render in English the metrical patterns and rhymes of the original French. The project took eight years to finish, and it was published in 1954.

The appearance of Moore's *Collected Poems* in 1951 began a period of great celebrity. Through the 1950s and early 1960s, Moore appeared in many magazines and newspapers wearing her trademark tricorn hat and cape. In 1956 she wrote a poem celebrating the Brooklyn Dodgers' appearance in the World Series called "A Hometown Piece for Messr's Alton and Reese" that was printed on the front page of the *New York Herald Tribune*. This moment signaled a definite shift into occasional verse (poetry that results from the observance of various events) that accelerated in her later years. In 1955 she published her first collection of prose writing, *Predilections*. These were followed by more poetry: *Like a Bulwark* (1956), *O to be a Dragon* (1959), and *Tell Me, Tell Me* (1966). Her *Complete Poems* were published in 1967, though a subsequent edition of the book published in 1981 incorporates revisions made by Moore up to the time of her death in 1972.

Much of Moore's poetry resists the CONFESSIONAL or revelatory moment, choosing instead to question the authority inherent in the position of the author by evocatively arranging fragments of text that she found in her reading or in conversation in a manner analogous to a visual collage. Her principles of arrangement include exacting attention to the metrical and visual layout of lines and stanzas, as well as to their rhyme patterns. This method results in rapid shifts in perspective and tone that can be disorienting, but, at their best, they can create a carefully arranged atmosphere for contemplation. In her poem "When I Buy Pictures" (1921), the speaker singles out those objects ("an artichoke in six varieties of blue; the snipe legged / hieroglyphic in three parts") that are "'lit with piercing glances into the life of things'" (a quotation spliced into the poem from a 1919 treatise on the Old Testament) and "acknowledge the spiritual forces which have made it." This attention to the beauty of natural objects or well-made things and the spiritual force behind them is characteristic of Moore's work throughout her career.

Moore's sometimes abrupt juxtaposition of images is accentuated by the typographical arrangement of her poems—line breaks and indents whose importance was as much visual as metrical, as in "The FISH" (1921), in which fish swimming among objects in the sea discover interesting finds, including a "mussel" that is

opening and shutting itself like
an
injured fan.

In Hugh Kenner's 1975 collection of essays on American modernist writers, *A Homemade World,* he describes the stanza these lines come from as "exhibit[ing] an archaic disregard of the mere things human desire does with sentences" (99). Instead the lines show Moore's attention to visual arrangement, as exaggerated or enhanced by her preference for composing poetry on a typewriter.

For Kenner, Moore's aesthetic connects the visual to the verbal through puns that are more associative than explicit: "Moore's poems deal in many separate acts of attention, all close-up; optical puns, seen by snapshot, in a poetic normally governed by the eye, sometimes by the ears and fingers, ultimately by the moral sense" (92). In "The Pangolin" (1941), for example, she describes an exotic, scaled animal as having "scale / lapping scale with spruce-cone regularity" and as being a "near artichoke with head and legs," "Leonardo da Vinci's replica."

Marriage, a long poem published as a chapbook by Moore's friend Monroe Wheeler in 1923, is a high point of her collage style, juxtaposing text from such wide-ranging sources as the 17th-century essays of Francis Bacon, a *Scientific American* article, and an offhand comment from Pound. Much of the poem uses these diverse fragments to present Adam and Eve as avatars of male and female views of marriage, yet the poem ends with the image of a statue of Daniel Webster in Central Park, the motto carved into its base: "'Liberty and union / now and forever.'" Webster's words, which come from a famous 1830 speech defending the rights of the federal government against the claims of secessionists, are pulled from their original context to become a perfect expression of the balance of individual liberty and shared union that is at the heart of marriage.

Moore's impulse to represent the world is always connected to a religious responsibility to praise truthfully through description, without self-aggrandizement, yet always striving toward a spiritual truth. Even "Marriage," which actively questions the traditional gender roles assigned to husbands and wives, also struggles to find a new law on which that relationship can be based. This struggle takes the form of a wide-ranging search across many disciplines and fields of inquiry and ends with the surprising but perfect image of an American icon. For Moore, the pursuit of the genuine produces an aesthetic at once profoundly modest and lapidary, erudite and immediate.

BIBLIOGRAPHY

Costello, Bonnie. *Marianne Moore: Imaginary Possessions.* Cambridge, Mass.: Harvard University Press, 1981.

Engel, Bernard F. *Marianne Moore.* Rev. ed., Boston: Twayne, 1989.

Heuving, Jeanne. *Omissions Are Not Accidents: Gender in the Art of Marianne Moore.* Detroit: Wayne State University Press, 1992.

Kenner, Hugh. "Disliking It." In *A Homemade World: The American Modernist Writers.* Baltimore, Md.: Johns Hopkins University Press, 1975.

Molesworth, Charles. *Marianne Moore: A Literary Life.* New York: Macmillan, 1990.

Michael Barsanti

MORA, PAT (1942–) Pat Mora has been a significant southwestern voice in American literature since the 1980s. Also an essayist, memoirist, and author of children's books, Mora as a poet is interested in the organic poetic line and formal/linguistic play, and she has been influenced by Pablo Neruda, Federico García Lorca, LUCILLE CLIFTON, and MARY OLIVER. Mora's poetry conveys transcendental themes through tightly crafted imagery often rooted in the southwestern desert landscape and its inhabitants. A bilingual, bicultural feminist from a city where the Rio Grande marks the U.S.–Mexico border, Mora ponders rivers and borders, both literal and metaphorical, and her free verse is infused with Spanish words and phrases (see PROSODY AND FREE VERSE).

Mora was born and raised in El Paso, Texas. In 1985 and 1987 she was honored with the Southwest Book

Award for two collections of poems, *Chants* and *Borders,* respectively. In 1986 she received a Kellogg National Leadership Fellowship to study ways of preserving culture (a recurrent theme of her poetry), and in 1994 she received a National Endowment for the Arts Creative Writing Fellowship in poetry. Two of her books of poetry for children have also received awards.

Women are central to Mora's work, and they are portrayed in complex detail, whether they are like "Elena" (1984), an immigrant who tenaciously struggles to learn English ("for if I stop trying, I will be deaf / when my children need my help"), or like Carmen, the feisty octogenarian sacristan of *Aunt Carmen's Book of Practical Saints* (1997), whose prayer to the Good Shepherdess implores, "Madre Mia, teach your cranky Carmen the practicality / of beauty, its joyful mystery necessary as bread." Voice—be it raised or silenced, of landscape or of people, in Spanish or in English or both—is a dominant motif for Mora, leading to close attention to sound imagery and suggesting how important listening is to knowledge. Imagining the stories inherent in the poetry of nature and the nature of poetry, Mora is like the storyteller in "Cuentista" (1995): "She carries a green river / in her arms, a rolling play of light."

BIBLIOGRAPHY

Fox, Linda C. "From Chants to Borders to Communion: Pat Mora's Poetic Journey to Nepantla." *Bilingual Review La Revista Bilingue* 21, no. 4 (September–December 1996): 219–230.

Murphy, Patrick D. "Conserving Natural and Cultural Diversity: The Prose and Poetry of Pat Mora." *MELUS* 21, no. 1 (spring 1996): 59–69.

G. Douglas Meyers

MORLEY, HILDA (1919–1998) Hilda Morley is associated with the BLACK MOUNTAIN SCHOOL of poets, in part because of her affiliation with Black Mountain College, where she lived and taught, along with her husband, composer Stefan Wolpe, from 1952 to 1956. Yet like JOANNE KYGER, another midcentury poet who chose to write poetry outside the establishment and to follow the compelling contours of the spacious page, she is seen as part of a contemporary poetic movement whose practices were more suggestive than definitive.

Morley was born and raised in New York City. She attended various colleges, including University College (London) and New York University, and thereafter she spent many years lecturing and teaching. In the early 1940s Morley was a Hebrew translator for the Office of War Information in New York City; she also translated poems from the Hebrew, winning the L. Lamed Translation Award for *Letters from the Desert* in 1983. Her first book, *A Blessing Outside Us,* prefaced by ROBERT CREELEY, was published in 1976. In 1983 she received a Guggenheim Fellowship and was the first-time winner of the Capricorn Prize (given in recognition of excellence to a poet over 40), awarded for her third book of poetry, *To Hold in My Hand: Selected Poems 1955–1983.*

Morley's work always reflects her experiences; her language is precise and spare, intense and serene. Sensations—visible, tangible, audible—make her lyrics intensely personal. In her poems love and loss are intense forces that shape perceptions of nature, art, and experience. As CAROLYN KIZER has written, "in reading Morley . . . we are wrapped up in seeing, and sensing what we see" (160).

"Curve of the Water" (1988) is a painterly meditation on the shapes and colors in a landscape; it considers the slippery relationship between reality and our ability to perceive and know it. As in other Morley poems, the music and repetition of her language lulls; "water" is a substance that occurs in many ways in the world, as a color (green), a destination, and source (well and harbor). The use of repetition and difference evokes not only the way a landscape compels one to gaze, but also the way the natural world is "at variance to / what we know." The lines "we see them but / they are not held as seen, not kept there / behind the eyes" suggest that to know is not to fix in one place, but to experience again and again. Meditative and evocative, Morley's poems explore the material and sensual world. Her visual poetics creates an apt sense of airiness and movement—freedom of thought.

BIBLIOGRAPHY

Conniff, Brian. "Reconsidering Black Mountain: The Poetry of Hilda Morley." *American Literature* 65, no. 1 (1993): 117–130.

Kizer, Carolyn. *Proses*. Port Townsend, Wash: Copper Canyon, 1993.

Linda V. Russo

MOSS, HOWARD (1922–1987) Howard Moss was an important practitioner of formal verse in the mid-20th century. He also had an uncanny ability to envision nature—and by envisioning it, to transform it into an environment created by humanity—thus bringing it into the realm of civilization; he strove to formalize nature, in keeping with his view of what poetry should be. He once remarked, "What my poems are really about . . . is the experience of hovering between the forms of nature and the forms of art" (29). Moss set an example for his generation among poets who believed in explicit order, as well as for later poets who have identified themselves with NEW FORMALISM. He was also the poetry editor at the *New Yorker* magazine from 1950 until shortly before his death, a position that allowed him influence over much of mainstream American writing.

Moss was born and raised in New York City. In 1942 he won *Poetry* magazine's Janet Sewall David Award for his own poetry. His first book was published in 1946. He was inducted into the American Academy and Institute of Arts and Letters in 1968 and won the National Book Award for poetry for his *Selected Poems* in 1971. His *New Selected Poems* (1984) was awarded the Lenore Marshall/*Nation* Poetry Prize in 1986, a year in which he also received a fellowship from the Academy of American Poets.

All of Moss's work possesses a subtle finish. His early and middle poems are end-rhymed and metered, his later work is freer—but all of it has a striking regularity of meter and tone. The prevalent themes in Moss's work involve fundamental issues, such as change in life, human relationships, loss, and death. He writes ably of "the difficulty of love, the decay of the body, the passing of time, and the inevitability of death," all set against "the inexhaustible beauty of the natural world," as DANA GIOIA has observed (102). He is, in fact, a great elegist who can portray attachment and loss with stunning acuity through graphic simplicity and bitter irony (see LYRIC POETRY).

In "Elegy for My Sister" (1980), he painstakingly details his sister's fatal disease and her struggle to cope with it. Trying to rise from her bed, her leg breaks "simply by standing up"; her bones have been "[m]elted into a kind of eggshell sawdust" by chemotherapy. His metaphors go beyond physical distress to show the plight of the soul. And in "Elegy for My Father" (1954), intense pain, dying, and separation are made vivid through paradox. His father, for example, is freed from life by his pain, a "double-dealing enemy."

Moss's finely crafted verse is matched by his willingness to account for the peripatetic and otherwise insignificant details of living, making them, at times, monumental. In his work the truth peeks out through artifice.

BIBLIOGRAPHY

Bawer, Bruce. "The Passing of an Elegist." *New Criterion* 6, no. 3 (November 1987): 35–37.

Gioia, Dana. "The Difficult Case of Howard Moss." *Antioch Review* 45, no. 1 (winter 1987): 98–109.

Moss, Howard. "Howard Moss: An Interview," by Robert Leiter. *American Poetry Review* 13, no. 5 (September/October 1984): 27–31.

Burt Kimmelman

MOSS, THYLIAS (1954–) Thylias Moss is an important figure in contemporary African-American poetry, a literary descendant of African-American poets LANGSTON HUGHES, ROBERT HAYDEN, and GWENDOLYN BROOKS. Moss is ambivalent about being identified as a representative African-American poet, however, largely because she worries that this could reduce or oversimplify her own work and the works of others identified with this category. Her poetry's breadth spans religion, family, and racism together with references to far more eclectic subject matter. Critic Jabari Asim claims, "[Her] interests are so extensive and varied that readers may exhaust themselves just scrambling to track down the sources of her many allusions" (8).

Moss was born and raised in Cleveland, Ohio, but visits to family members in southern states gave her a keen awareness of the virulent racism most often identified with the South. She has received numerous grants and awards, including a Guggenheim Fellowship (1995) and a MacArthur Foundation Fellowship (1996).

Much of Moss's work presents stream-of-consciousness reflections on life events, characters, and specific objects. Moss is decidedly a free verse poet, and she is primarily concerned with the possibilities of imaginative association apart from regular rhyme or meter: "Only in a few things did I want permanence, consistency, predictability; mine was seldom a yearning for universals" Moss says (305). Moss's poems frequently turn surreal or visionary, but they almost always remain strongly connected to real-world issues or objects. In "Dear Charles" (1993), for example, a rambling prose poem in the form of a letter addressed to a hurricane elicits a response from the masculine hurricane that ties the destructive fury of the tropical storm to the real history of slavery and exploitation in West Africa, the Caribbean, and the Americans. The hurricane speaks, at one point saying, "You know *Charles* ain't no kind of proper African name, but it's the one my patrons give me, the one meteorological overseers picked out."

Moss's relationship with the tradition of modern American poetry is complex and somewhat tense. She has written a response to ROBERT FROST's "STOPPING BY WOODS ON A SNOWY EVENING," "Interpretation of a Poem by Frost" (1991), and another to WALLACE STEVENS's "Thirteen Ways of Looking at a Blackbird," "A Reconsideration of the Blackbird" (1990). Both of her poems insist on the importance of race and gender, elements that are absent from the original poems by the two white male poets. Moss's public praise of GALWAY KINNELL proves that her questioning of the literary canon has not led her to a simplistic dislike of such white, male, acclaimed poets (one such poet, CHARLES SIMIC, was Moss's teacher in the University of New Hampshire's graduate program).

Her free-form poetry reflects her wide-ranging interests in literature, folk life, and American social issues. Moss's use of seemingly unedited language creates a sense of immediacy and unfiltered experience throughout her work.

BIBLIOGRAPHY

Asim, Jabari. "Poet of This World and the Next." *Washington Post,* April 5, 1998, sec. X, p. 8.

Ivry, Sara. "A Fine Line." *New York Times Magazine,* January 7, 2001, p. 8.

Moss, Thylias. "The Generosity of Arpeggios and Ravens." *Michigan Quarterly Review.* 39, no. 2 (spring 2000): 301–306.

Sean Heuston

"MR. EDWARDS AND THE SPIDER" ROBERT LOWELL (1946) ROBERT LOWELL's "Mr. Edwards and the Spider" is a dramatic monologue spoken by Jonathan Edwards, the 18th-century American theologian, author, and minister who sought to revive America's Puritan heritage, to his uncle Josiah Hawley, who committed suicide in 1735. Edwards, who asserted that God's grace alone could avert mankind's absolute damnation, was an important figure for Lowell, who claimed him as an ancestor and even began a biography on him, which, though never completed, provided important material for this and several other poems Lowell wrote about Edwards. Borrowing extensively from Edwards's sermons and prose writings, and employing the complex stanza structure used by the 17th-century Metaphysical poet John Donne in "A Nocturnal on St. Lucy's Day," Lowell recreates Edwards's voice to articulate his own thirst for a perfection attainable only through an absolute abandonment to divine grace.

The opening stanza reveals two sides of Edwards's personality. In the first four lines, Edwards demonstrates a naturalist's calm, detached curiosity about animal life when he observes, "I saw the spiders marching through the air, / Swimming from tree to tree that mildewed day." But in the middle of the stanza, Lowell describes the blowing of the west wind, which signals winter and the death of the spiders. This intimation of the Apocalypse implicit in nature points to that other aspect of Edwards, his ferocious Calvinist vision, which Lowell evokes in a question drawn from Edwards's famous sermon "Sinners in the Hands of an Angry God": "What are we in the hands of the great God?" The question suggests the inapprehensible gulf between God and man, a distance and difference as great as that between man and spider. Yet where Edwards preached this gulf to provoke his worshippers to faith, in Lowell's poem it evokes the anxieties of modern existence. As Bruce Michelson observes, "Lowell's complete Jonathan Edwards ultimately speaks not only an eighteenth-century mind, but a much more modern sensibility as well—detached, scientific, historical, horrified, all at the same time" (145). In early drafts of the poem, notes Michelson, Lowell focused on the hellfire of Edwards's preaching to the neglect of his naturalist's curiosity and his deliberate, systematic theology, a focus that weakened the original last stanza. But with advice from the poet RANDALL JARRELL, Lowell revised the last lines, moving beyond their original harshness and terror to a strangely peaceful acceptance of the truth of mortality and of one's dependence on God.

Like Jonathan Edwards himself, the spider in Lowell's poem is many-faceted. In the opening stanza, the image of floating spiders stands for the delicate, ephemeral beauty of the material world. Later, Lowell treats the spider as a symbol of the vanity of mortal works, suggesting how easily mortal greatness can be brought to ruin when he writes of how "A very little thing, a little worm / Or hourglass-blazoned spider, it is said,/ Can kill a tiger." When Edwards's wrathful Jehovah holds man's soul over "the pit of hell," the soul is as feeble as a spider in its own defense, though Lowell does distinguish between the animal consciousness of the spider, which cannot comprehend its own death, and of man, who can imagine death, the afterlife, and his own distance from God, and so must comport himself accordingly. "[T]his is death," writes Lowell, "To die and know it. This is the Black Widow, death." While it may be surprising that Lowell, a zealous convert to Catholicism in 1941, finds a shared vision with Edwards's Calvinist doctrine of grace, which represents the extremes of Protestantism, both beliefs share a fundamental belief in mankind's fallen state and its utter dependence on God for salvation.

Such considerations are especially important when one considers the dramatic situation of the poem. Lowell's Edwards is addressing his uncle Josiah Hawley, whose suicide in 1735 shook Edwards in the midst of the growing revival of Puritan belief known as The Great Awakening, which was spearheaded by Edwards himself. Here, Edwards calls for Hawley to envision hell by imagining himself burned in "a brick-kiln where the blast / Fans your quick vitals to a coal," then to imagine "the blaze / Is infinite, eternal." Because of the different dates of Edwards's texts which Lowell uses in the poem, it is unclear whether Lowell's Edwards is speaking to his living uncle, and thus is trying to convert him, or to his ghost, and thus is condemning him (while perhaps also expressing some pity), for Edwards's naturalist work *Of Insects* (1719) predates the suicide, while the sermon "Sinners in the Hands of an Angry God" (1741) follows it. Ultimately, however, Hawley's status is secondary to the way that Lowell's infernal imagery indicates the likeness of Jehovah's wrath to Satan's. "Mr. Edwards and the Spider" suggests that the comfort of absolute truth comes with the acknowledgment that one is damned, with no assurance of grace. And for Lowell, whose heavily enjambed iambic lines recall his great forbear, John Milton, if salvation does come, it will be as violent and purifying as the very fires of hell.

BIBLIOGRAPHY

Cosgrave, Patrick. *The Public Poetry of Robert Lowell.* New York: Taplinger Publishing Company, 1970.

Hart, Henry. *Robert Lowell and the Sublime.* Syracuse, N.Y.: Syracuse University Press, 1995.

Mariani, Paul. *Lost Puritan: A Life of Robert Lowell.* New York: W. W. Norton & Company, 1994.

Michelson, Bruce. "Randall Jarrell and Robert Lowell: The Making of *Lord Weary's Castle.*" In *Robert Lowell: Modern Critical Views,* edited by Harold Bloom. New York: Chelsea House Publishers, 1987.

Wiebe, Dallas E. "Mr. Lowell and Mr. Edwards." *Wisconsin Studies in Contemporary Literature* 3, no. 2 (1962): 22–31.

Temple Cone

"MR. FLOOD'S PARTY" E. A. ROBINSON (1920) Many critics and poets hold the short lyric poems from E. A. ROBINSON's book *Avon's Harvest, etc.* (1920) among his best work, with "Mr. Flood's Party" singled out for distinction. Robinson's most characteristic features are evident in the poem: memorable rhythms, a concern for people marginalized within their own communities, evocative names, a familiar landscape made strange by subtly distorted images, and a terrible struggle for love in the midst of loneliness. Sadness about the passage of time and all the losses it entails pervades the mood of "Mr. Flood's Party," but this sadness never lapses into bathos. Instead, it is kept in check by Mr. Flood's somewhat comical, somewhat heroic efforts to find some company in the world, even to the extent of imagining a second moon in the sky and the image of his own self, whom he toasts and welcomes home like a long lost friend.

The poem's narrative is simple: Eben Flood is walking late on the hill above his hometown of Tilbury, possibly on the way back from his still. Under the light of a harvest moon, he holds what amounts to a drunken soliloquy, or perhaps a dialogue, with his imagined self, the subject of which is how the world has changed, and along with the world, himself. The rhyme scheme of the eight-line stanzas recalls that of the ballad stanza, thus emphasizing the poem's narrative qualities and suggesting a thematic focus on misfortune, while the iambic pentameter lines recall the conversational rhythms of Renaissance verse drama. Mr. Flood's movements and gestures during the poem are as expressive as a stage actor's. Robinson describes him as standing "in the middle of the road / Like Roland's ghost winding a silent horn," an ominous allusion to the epic hero Roland's final act before his death, and Robinson notes that Mr. Flood lifts his jug "up to the light" each time he drinks, until the final toast when "He raised again the jug regretfully/ And shook his head, and was again alone."

Yet for all its formal and dramatic qualities, the poem's quiet devastation is felt most forcefully through Robinson's subtle rendering of character. Mr. Flood is an old man, a drunk who carries a jug of alcohol with him on his walk, and a living exile in his hometown, "Where strangers would have shut the many doors / That many friends had opened long ago." For all these estranging qualities, though, he is also a likable figure, one who shows his learning when he quotes Edmund Fitzgerald's *The Rubaiyat of Omar Khayyam* and his gentleness when he sets down his jug "With trembling care, knowing that most things break." Such knowledge suggests Mr. Flood possesses firsthand knowledge of his own fragility, yet that fragility is a condition he strives to overcome, as when he refuses his own nostalgia by saying, "'No more, sir; that will do.'"

For a while, his efforts to cope with what might be called, punning on his name, the ebb and flood of time, prove effective. In response to his loneliness, Mr. Flood not only imagines a second self, but also two moons in the sky, an image that signals both his drunkenness, the unity of his vision (for he sees his own moon and that of his second self), and so great a desire for a "whole harmonious landscape" that Mr. Flood seems to create a second moon for the purpose. These imaginings console Mr. Flood, but they do not completely resolve the loneliness that afflicts him; as ROBERT FROST notes, "One moon (albeit a moon, no sun) would have laid grief too bare. More than two would have dissipated grief entirely and would have amounted to dissipation. The emotion had to be held at a point" (qtd. in Mezey, 236). Such irresolution offers a form of dignity, for it relieves the loneliness without negating it and thereby disproving the absolute effect it has had on Mr. Flood's life.

Ultimately, however, Mr. Flood is a fully realized human being, weak and flawed, and through him Robinson shows that nostalgia for the past, for home and for the connections of community, cannot be withstood. When Mr. Flood gives in to his own desires to sing "For auld lang syne," or "For old long ago," a song by the Scottish romantic poet Robert Burns grieving the passage of time, then the vision of fullness and unity is lost. Robinson does not reject the catharsis or release of the moment, for Mr. Flood sings "Until the whole harmonious landscape rang." Yet such release comes at a price: the loss of balance and control. When he is finished singing, Mr. Flood must confront the fact that "There was not much that was ahead of him, / And there was nothing in the town below." In "Mr. Flood's Party," Robinson has captured the psychological need for poetry, the desire humans have to make their world whole, even though they know it cannot be. The inevitability of that "fortunate flaw" is evident early in the poem. When Mr. Flood begins his conversation with his imagined self, a perfectly timed adverb, "huskily," captures the hesitation, sadness, release, and bravery that comes with this moment of imagined companionship, a moment that would likely end in embarrassment if anyone living had heard him: having invited himself to toast the bird of Time, which is always flying away, he lifts "The jug that he had gone so far to fill, / And answered huskily: 'Well, Mr. Flood, / Since you propose it, I believe I will.'"

BIBLIOGRAPHY

Dickey, James. *Classes on Modern Poets and the Art of Poetry,* edited by Donald J. Greiner. Columbia: University of South Carolina Press, 2004.

Mezey, Robert. ed. "Introduction" *The Poetry of E. A. Robinson.* By E. A. Robinson. New York: Modern Library, 2002.

Temple Cone

MULLEN, HARRYETTE (1953–) Harryette Mullen is a scholar and a poet whose poetry examines the intersection of gender, race, erotics, and the avant-garde. The linguistic and syntactic experimentation of her poetry places Mullen firmly in the avant-garde tradition that stretches from GERTRUDE STEIN to the poets of the LANGUAGE SCHOOL. The racial concerns of her poetry also locate her in the rich tradition of African-American experimental poets, such as Norman H. Pritchard and NATHANIEL MACKEY.

Born in Alabama and raised in Texas, Mullen received a B.A. in English from the University of Texas, Austin. Mullen has taught at Cornell University and the University of California, Los Angeles. She completed graduate work at the University of California, Santa Cruz, in the history of consciousness program, where Mackey directed her dissertation. Mullen has published five books of poetry, the most recent being *Sleeping with the Dictionary* (2002), which was a National Book Award finalist, and a critical work, *Gender, Subjectivity, and Slave Narratives* (1998).

Instead of using figurative techniques such as simile and metaphor, Mullen uses metonymy, anagrams, and puns (which are associative not symbolic) to invite the reader to collaborate in making the text's meaning. For example, the interpretive possibilities in just one line from her Stein-inspired work *Trimmings* (1991) are many: "Girl, pinked, beribboned. Alternate virgin at first blush." This section, about an African-American girl uncomfortably dressed, demonstrates the connections between clothing and gender (the pressure of being "beribboned" can manifest itself in eating disorders that might make her "be rib boned"), clothing and race (being "pinked" not only implies that she is dressed in pink but also that the unwanted clothing is an attempt to make her pass for white), and clothing and sexuality (her "first blush" could be a blush of her cheeks but also her first menstruation or sexual experience).

Although many African-American anthologists do not consider her experimental work to be sufficiently representational of a black voice, Mullen believes that her poetry can usefully address racial concerns while also challenging the categories that make "racial" writing something other than avant-garde or feminist writing. Indeed Mullen's first work *Tree Tall Woman* (1981) employs a stable ethnic voice throughout the collection, but since that volume Mullen's poetry has engaged multiple and fragmented voices. These voices are often not overtly racialized because Mullen's work focuses more on the material words themselves (the fact that they are often puns or anagrams, for instance) than the content to which those words refer. Mullen's poetry represents the convergence of the political and the poetic in innovative forms that enact fruitful alternatives (not just oppositions) to the dominance of identity-based LYRIC POETRY in the contemporary poetic world.

BIBLIOGRAPHY

Frost, Elisabeth. "An Interview with Harryette Mullen." *Contemporary Literature* 41 (2000): 397–421.
Mullen, Harryette. "Solo Mysterioso Blues: Interview with Harryette Mullen," by Calvin Bedient. *Callaloo* 19 (1996): 651–669.

Mitchum Huehls

MUSKE-DUKES, CAROL (1945–) While Carol Muske-Dukes (formerly Carol Muske) certainly engages the world from a feminist perspective, she is not simply a feminist poet. A respected literary critic, she argues that contemporary poetry should move readers "away from chaos, from isolation, divisiveness, away from self-conscious fragmentation" ("Woman"). Such movement, Muske-Dukes claims, is "crucial" for a young poet to develop "an open mind" ("War"). In her poems this open-mindedness results in a compelling combination of progressive politics and aesthetic excellence that inspires the critic Vijay Seshadri to name her "an exemplary citizen both of the world and of the republic of letters" (20).

Muske-Dukes was born in St. Paul, Minnesota. She published her first book of poems, *Camouflage,* in 1975. Her poems are now widely anthologized. Among her awards and honors are the 1979 Alice Fay Di Castagnola Award from the Poetry Society of America and a 1981 Guggenheim Fellowship. She has taught at the University of Southern California.

Even in her earliest poems, Muske-Dukes establishes herself as a poet unafraid to confront the most desolate spaces of the 20th century's social history. Whether writing about a student's reaction to being raped ("China White" [1985]) or her response to a Czech student's self-immolation in protest of the 1968 Soviet invasion of Prague ("Prague: Two Journals 1970, 1990"), her careful craftsmanship offers sympathetic interpretations of even the most dismal facets of the human experience. It is in this very human sympathy that Muske-Dukes presents her poetic vision—a courageous call for poetry to make a difference in the world.

In "At the School for the Gifted" (1997), Muske-Duke's speaker struggles to inspire students to embrace poetry by having them discover verse in the "Cut out camels [that] plodded across the blackboard's high / sill." The students strive to produce poetry befitting their intellectual talents, but fall short, as they are "suspicious / in individual spotlights." Instead of finding satisfaction in inspired flashes of poetic insight, Muske-Duke's speaker and her students find sweetness in the inspired chaos of poetic word and sound association. This commitment to a very American sharing of ideas, inherent in the reading and writing of poetry, marks Muske-Duke as the preeminent spokesperson for both the aesthetic power and the social relevance of contemporary verse.

BIBLIOGRAPHY

Emanuel, Lynn. "The Audience's Audience." *Michigan Quarterly Review* 35, no. 4 (fall 1996): 720–733.

Muske-Dukes, Carol. "War of the Edens," *Boston Review* Available online. URL http://bostonreview.net/BR23.3/muske.html. Downloaded March 2007.

———. "Woman on the Ledge," *Crossroads: The Journal of the Poetry Society of America* Available online. URL: http://poetrysociety.org/journal/articles/muske.html. Downloaded March 2007.

Seshadri, Vijay. "The Neuroses of History." *New York Times Book Review,* February 8, 1998, 20.

William F. Hecker

"MY FATHER IN THE NIGHT COMMANDING NO" LOUIS SIMPSON (1963) Louis Simpson's "My Father in the Night Commanding No" interweaves the libretto of an opera by Donizetti based on a Walter Scott novel, aspects of the Freudian Oedipal conflict, and the image of the hero from Joseph Campbell's anthropology of myth to create a resonant portrait of Simpson's childhood that also captures the complex conflict between art and human relations, imagination and the family. It is, as poet THOM GUNN notes, "a lovely and . . . sinister poem, in which we are continually being put at momentary ease, in familiar surroundings as it were, and continually being made to realize afterwards that we weren't where we thought we were at all" (458). Simpson details a primary conflict between his father, whom Simpson associates with the negativity of ordinary, work-dominated existence, and Simpson himself as a child wanting his father's attentions, whether through play or perhaps an evening story: "My father in the night commanding No / Has work to do." As a consolation, the boy's mother offers him the play of art, whether in the form of an opera recording or a story read aloud, which the boy's imagination embraces. But as the poem progresses, the artistic escape becomes increasingly artificial, and Simpson's poem gradually turns to an indictment of art as an insufficient proxy for close human relations.

Written in stanzas that recall the form of Tennyson's great elegy *In Memoriam* (with the first and fourth and the second and third lines rhyming, respectively), but which truncate the third line and drop the rhyme, the poem opens with a dejected, elegiac mood caused by the alienation associated with the father's "commanding No." Simpson never clarifies what in particular the father has rejected at the start of the poem, but it is clear that his great negativity is an indictment of play and of the imagination itself, which in contrast with "the real world" of work might seem flimsy and unreal. The sense of loss that comes from this rejection so pervades the poem that when the speaker's mother plays a gramophone recording for him, the opera is Donizetti's *The Bride of Lammermoor,* based on Sir Walter Scott's novel about ancient feuds, tempestuous love, and family honor in Scotland, which ironically was the ancestral home of Simpson's father.

The speaker projects himself into the central role of the adventure narratives his mother offers him as compensation for his father's separation, and for a time these satisfy him with "The journey and the danger of the world, / All that there is / To bear and to enjoy, endure and do." The boy as hero recalls Joseph Campbell's "hero with a thousand faces," who must separate himself from his home to seek his destiny in the world, and also the Freudian figure of Oedipus, who must symbolically 'kill' (that is, reject the authority of) his father in order to realize himself as a grown individual. But eventually these fantasies prove unreal to the speaker, and he is troubled by the thought that although he proves that his father's rejection of the imagination is wrong by enjoying it as he does, the characters in these stories "will not change / There, on the stage of terror and of love." The speaker then turns from his remembered childhood to his present state, lamenting of these fictive characters "And you once pretended / to understand them! Shake them as you will / They cannot speak."

Confounded by the failure of art to substitute for the vitality of human relations, Simpson plaintively asks his parents to explain why they did not engage with him as a boy, and his call is echoed by the wind that blows both in the stories and outside the boy's house: "'*Listen!*' the wind / Said to the children, and they fell asleep." Simpson's poem portrays the profound psychological effects of even the slightest childhood experience, and this leads him to question the sufficiency of art as a means of fulfillment. Ultimately, Simpson finds it is not from the everlasting stories, but from the ever-changing people who might share them, that a sense of fulfillment rises. The silence of human voices compels a never-ending cycle of artistic creation, whose sole purpose is to recover that long-lost voice of the parent speaking to the child.

BIBLIOGRAPHY

Campbell, Joseph. *The Hero With a Thousand Faces.* New York: Pantheon Books, 1961.

Gunn, Thom. *The Yale Review* (Winter 1959): 457–458.

Temple Cone

MYLES, EILEEN (1949–) Eileen Myles's writing is firmly established within the lineage of the NEW YORK SCHOOL. Equally vital is her prominence as a high-profile lesbian poet of the late 20th century. She also claims a range of other major influences, including Christopher Isherwood and HART CRANE. Yet Myles's work is independent and original. Her poetry is written in open form (see PROSODY AND FREE VERSE), using a conversational style with brief, columnar lines. Public intent underscores her work. She communicates openly about intimate and personal subject matter, and she manages to revitalize her subjects. Myles upholds her statement, "I've always thought a poet should think big, not small" (qtd. in Richard 26), through constant writing and her efforts to reach audiences and unite multiple communities.

Born, raised, and educated in and near Boston, Massachusetts, Myles moved to New York City in 1974. Her first collection of poems, *The Irony of the Leash,* was published in 1978. She was personal assistant to JAMES SCHUYLER and artistic director of the St. Mark's Poetry Project during the 1980s (see POETRY INSTITUTIONS). Myles has written poetry, fiction, drama, and book and art reviews; she is widely anthologized and has also edited several literary anthologies. In 1992 she engineered a political campaign and was a write-in candidate for president of the United States in 28 states. She has received many honors, including National Endowment for the Arts grants (1989 and 1995) and two Lambda Book Awards, for *The New Fuck You* (1995) and *School of Fish* (1997).

In "How I Wrote Certain of My Poems" (1991), Myles explains that, for her, "life is a rehearsal for the poem" and that she has an obsession with culture (201). Rock'n'roll and the spirit of freedom prevalent in the 1960s provided Myles with permission to forge ahead according to her own inclinations as an artist. In her book *1969,* Myles writes about being at the Woodstock Festival and hearing Jimi Hendrix: "His 'Star Spangled Banner' was the end of America for me. We were through with it" (55–56). Her writing is reality based, playful, and provocative, and she always addresses important human concerns. In the poems Myles personifies herself as a gamut of selves. She is both an immigrant, who explains she was part of "a generation of people who went to / the bars on 7th street and drank" ("Holes" [1991]), and a member of the Kennedy clan, who suggests, "I am not / alone tonight because / we are all Kennedy's" ("An American

Poem" [1991]). Myles is confidently attendant to her immediate surroundings; writing and daily life in New York City, including its inequities and banalities, are deeply connected for her. Her writing is genuine, clear, and purposeful. She is assured in her mission as an active and socially activist poet who characteristically exposes significant human vulnerabilities.

BIBLIOGRAPHY

Durgin, Patrick. "Eileen Myles." In *Dictionary of Literary Biography. American Poets Since World War II,* edited by Joseph Conte. Detroit: Gale Research, 1998, pp. 203–212.

Myles, Eileen. "How I Wrote Certain of My Poems." *Not Me.* New York: Semiotexte, 1991.

———. "Never Real, Always True: An Interview with Eileen Myles," by Frances Richard. *Provincetown Arts* 15 (2000): 24–29.

———. *1969.* New York: Hanuman Books, 1989.

Christopher Funkhouser

"MY LIFE BY WATER" LORINE NIEDECKER **(1968)** "My Life by Water" headlines LORINE NIEDECKER's 1970 book of collected poetry, *My Life by Water: Collected Poems 1936–1968.* Although the poem had been published previously (in *North Central* [1968], by Fulcrum Press), it gained significance in its 1970 publication as the title poem of the last book of Niedecker's poetry published within her lifetime. "My Life by Water" can be seen as autobiographical, not only of poet and place but also of poetics; it demonstrates the culmination of Niedecker's poetic ideals from her earliest OBJECTIVIST short verse to her later experiments in building movements of meaning through poetic sequence. Some of the characteristics commonly associated with Niedecker's work include simple and basic word choice, clarity and purity in aural and visual images, a strong emphasis on the natural world, and irregular stanzaic form. Overarching this is her emphasis on poetic movement; Niedecker was very interested in the ways meanings could turn and shift within a poem through word choice and juxtaposition. "My Life by Water" is an engaging crescendo of these fundamentals.

The poem's first stanza begins with a reassertion of the title and ends with the directive to the reader, "Hear." By choosing to end the stanza with the homonym "Hear," Niedecker introduces "My Life by Water" immediately as a poem of place; through the aural connective of "Hear" and "Here," Niedecker invites the reader to experience both forms of the word at once. She directs the reader's senses to "Hear" the sounds localized in the "Here," which she continues to build throughout the poem. Such wordplays and puns are common in Niedecker's work and are seen throughout this poem. Its title itself evokes a playful ambiguity: "My Life" may be read as an autobiography of "Water" as well as an autobiography of a person "by" or near water. Throughout this work Niedecker finds ways to mix meanings, to invoke more than one sense at a time, and to create a multidimensional experience, one rife with what she once called "the knowledge of everything influencing everything" (86).

As the poem progresses, Niedecker continues to create a sense of "place" through crisp, clear imagery. With only a few words cleverly juxtaposed, Niedecker creates a scene, both visually and aurally, of spring frogs, bending mud boards, and gnawing muskrats. Her word choice is basic and minimally unadorned. The spacing surrounding each word creates a shorthand, giving cues as to pacing, double entendres, and subtle wordplay. One example of this rotates around the center of the poem: "arts and letters." Niedecker creates a rural scene with active sights and sounds: "Muskrats / gnawing / doors / to wild green / arts." The final word, *arts,* however, is broken off from the phrase and given special emphasis by its placement at the beginning of the next line, where it is coupled with its idiomatic partner "letters." Thus the previous line, "to wild green / arts," shifts to "arts and letters."This connective line acts as the poetic nexus, at which the early concrete images of place converge with the abstract language of scholarship. Niedecker brings the reader to experience the fact that her life by water, although rural and outdoorsy, is inexorably linked to the literary. Similarly her scholarship and intellectual pursuits spawn from her surroundings—one cannot exist without the other. This plays into Niedecker's idea that poetry is a liquid form, one that changes and evolves from one reading to the next on the page and in the reader's mind. Niedecker says about this process: "The visual form is there in the background and the words convey what the visual form gives off after it's felt in the mind" (86).

Growing as a poet, Niedecker expanded her ideas regarding language and context when she began to write in the longer, more associative medium of this work: the poem sequence (see LONG AND SERIAL POETRY). Through poetry sequences, Niedecker studied the interconnected movements of a poem. Niedecker's technique of modifying or shifting sentence, as elements are added or subtracted, illustrates this interdependency by focusing on the ever-changing and amorphous nature of language. These movements include the action and agency a poem has on a page (double meanings through strategic punctuation and spacing) and the effect a poem has within the reader psychologically (increasingly layered insights through multiple readings). "My Life by Water" is a tour de force study of constructing and deconstructing meaning; with the advent of each new line and each new word, the experiences of meaning within a poem sequence gets progressively more nuanced.

Showing her poetic roots as well as her ability to move beyond them, *My Life by Water* reflects Niedecker's unique contributions to objectivism and imagism (see IMAGIST SCHOOL). The imagery and spacing of the poem have the well-contained, concrete effects of her earlier work. The double readings and shifting meanings within the poem herald a form of poetics Niedecker called "reflectivism," which focuses on the interconnectedness of words and experience. In a letter to a fellow Fort Atkinson resident and poet, Gail Roub, Niedecker writes, "modern poetry, and old poetry, if its [*sic*] good, proceeds not from one point to the next linearly but in a circle. [It has a] light, a motion, inherent in the whole . . . and awareness of everything influencing everything" (86). Niedecker then goes on to cite the first and last lines of "My Life by Water" as exemplars of these ideals (86).

BIBLIOGRAPHY

DuPlessis, Rachel Blau. "Lorine Niedecker, the Anonymous: Gender, Class, Genre and Resistances." In *Lorine Niedecker: Woman and Poet,* edited by Jenny Penberthy, 113–138. Orono, Maine: National Poetry Foundation, 1996.

Niedecker, Lorine. "Getting to Know Lorine Niedecker," by Gail Roub. In *Lorine Niedecker: Woman and Poet,* edited by Jenny Penberthy, 79–86. Orono, Maine: National Poetry Foundation, 1996.

Judith S. Girardi

"MY PAPA'S WALTZ" THEODORE ROETHKE **(1948)** "My Papa's Waltz," one of the most anthologized and recognizable of Theodore ROETHKE's poems, embodies the poet's emphases on introspection and the anxieties of childhood, which were later to influence CONFESSIONAL POETRY. Originally published in 1948, the poem is somewhat of a departure for Roethke. Many of his works deal with a return to the origins of life and explorations of the subconscious, while "My Papa's Waltz" is a rather traditional and simple poem. Still it takes as its inspiration and subject matter the overriding concern of Roethke's early poetry: the attempt to connect, through the power of memory, the figures of child and father. For most, if not all, of his life, Roethke viewed his father, Otto—who died while Theodore was a teenager—with mixture of fear and love. The father figure in his poetry, then, is often one of awesome, godlike power.

The great conflict in "My Papa's Waltz" involves the ambivalent feelings the grown son has about memories of his father. The speaker recalls a night when the drunken father "waltzed" about the kitchen with the young boy, knocking the kitchen implements off the shelves. Though the father's whiskied breath nearly sickens the child, he clings to his father "like death." The word choice and imagery reflect violence: The father holds the boy's wrist, not his hand, and taps out the dance beat on the son's head; the action of the dance repeatedly scrapes the son's ear against the father's belt buckle. Yet the violence is counterbalanced in other choices of diction and image: the poet chooses to say "we romped," indicating a more playful intent, and the boy clings to his father as they dance their way to the boy's bed, where he will eventually, perhaps, go to sleep.

The presence of a third person in the scene—the boy's mother—reveals another conflict. As the mother watches the two dance, her frown indicates the anxiety and sadness that affects the entire family. While the grown speaker struggles to reconcile his father's abuse with the awe and respect he has for his father, this image of his mother's unhappiness adds more confusion to the understanding he seeks.

Roethke's use of rhythm is an effective tactic for expressing the ambivalent mood of the poem. The dance is fittingly described using a playful iambic trimeter, or waltz time, rhythm. However, the playfulness of the rhythm serves also to further support the ambivalence—should the speaker remember this violence-tinged scene with such a frivolous dance beat? The poem ends with the seemingly benign image of the boy hanging onto his father as he is put to bed, but, as with his own life, the conflict is left unresolved.

BIBLIOGRAPHY

Balakian, Peter. *Theodore Roethke's Far Fields: The Evolution of His Poetry*. Baton Rouge: Louisiana State University Press, 1989.

Kalaidjian, Walter B. *Understanding Theodore Roethke*. Columbia: University of South Carolina Press, 1987.

Joseph Schaub

N

NARRATIVE POETRY Despite the predominance of LYRIC POETRY, narrative poetry has prospered in 20th-century American literature, and its conventions have undergone innovative reconsideration unrivalled since the English romantic era. In contrast to the intense utterance of the lyric, which typically speaks from a single moment in time, conventionally the narrative is a poetic genre that tells a story, binding sequences of events via plot and character. Historically, the narrative subdivides into epics, such as John Milton's *Paradise Lost* (1674), romances, such as Chaucer's *Troilus and Criseyde* (ca. 1385), and shorter ballad forms. But the changes in modes of storytelling, particularly those affected by modernist experimentation with the prose novel, have made it necessary for narrative conventions to change as well.

In the years before MODERNISM, American writers in particular envisioned poetry as fundamentally distinct from story. Walt Whitman transformed epic poetry from the narrative mode to the lyric sequence. Earlier Edgar Allan Poe had contended, in his famous essay "The Philosophy of Composition" (1846), that all poems should be readable in one sitting. These factors, alongside the rising popularity of the prose novel, divided narrative from poetry so that by 1915 modern poets, such as EZRA POUND and H. D., considered the lyric the defining genre of poetry and rarely allowed their early work to include traditional narrative elements. However, as Marjorie Perloff suggests, many poets continued to discover that "to tell a story is to find a way—sometimes the only way—of knowing one's world" (417). To conceive of fragmented events as continuous, with a beginning and an end, is a way for the imagination to endow them with meaning, "to impose its own order on what is," as SYLVIA PLATH observes in her poem "On the Difficulty of Conjuring up a Dryad" (1957). In the face of Whitman's conception of America's expansive, irreducible diversity, American poets have felt the need to refashion the narrative to accommodate their visions of a fragmented and discontinuous modernity. Although some poets continued to use conventional narrative forms, the most interesting innovations have occurred by combining the narrative with the brief, intense character of the lyric.

Modern American narrative poetry falls into two categories. The first is the conventional narrative mode, either in the short form of ROBERT FROST's ironic stories or the epic scope of JAMES MERRILL'S *The CHANGING LIGHT AT SANDOVER* (1982) (see also LONG AND SERIAL POETRY). The second and predominant form is the narrative-lyric, which combines the psychological drama of the lyric with the narrative's descriptive sequence of events. Poems by ELIZABETH BISHOP and RITA DOVE, for instance, typically begin with narrative description and move into meditation, in which the lyric voice realizes a connection between itself and the unfolding story.

CONVENTIONAL NARRATIVE

The reassuring patterns that the conventional narrative offers—a beginning and an end, an authoritative third-person speaker—often invite a wider readership than the difficult diction of the lyric. Though not a predominant mode, the conventional narrative provided a vehicle for modern poets who avoided the experiments of T. S. ELIOT and Pound and turned instead to Thomas Hardy or Henry Wadsworth Longfellow, two precursors to the modern narrative. Frost's narratives in *North of Boston* (1914, 1915) were great popular successes that offered readers scenes of rural life and hardship in clear, everyday speech. "The DEATH OF THE HIRED MAN," which David Perkins has called one of "the finest short narrative poems written . . . in the twentieth century" (241), is composed mostly of dialogue, through which Frost unfolds the tragedy of an old man preparing to die. Forecasting modern innovations in the prose novel, Frost's virtual exclusion of an omniscient narrative voice produces more complex, interesting characters, and the resultant irony and ambiguity haunts his other tales as well, including "A Hundred Collars" (1914, 1915) and the ghostly "Witch of Coos" (1923). Stephen Vincent BENÉT's popular success, *John Brown's Body* (1928), is a long narrative poem that utilizes the conventions of epic, and EDWIN ARLINGTON ROBINSON's Arthurian narratives, *Merlin* (1917), *Lancelot* (1920), and *Tristram* (1927), also found great favor with American readers, with their traditional meters and detached, objective narration (see PROSODY AND FREE VERSE).

Undoubtedly the most successful and sustained narrative poem of the 20th century is *The Changing Light at Sandover,* a poem of some 17,000 lines based on Merrill's experiences with a Ouija board. In three books Merrill invokes poets of the narrative tradition, including Homer, Dante, and W. H. AUDEN to guide him through his sometimes tragic, sometimes comic encounters with the spirits of the dead. The poem observes mainly conventional rhyme schemes and switches between Dantean terza rima and Augustan couplets. *The Changing Light at Sandover* has been heralded as the postmodern generation's epic, encompassing everything from chemical biology to world wars. Merrill's speaker deftly uses repetition and allusion to build his fantastic image of the supernatural universe, as he says: "bit by bit, the puzzle's put together / Or else it's disassembled, bit by bit. Hot pebbles." The speaker reveals that he "yearned for some unseasoned telling found in legends," and in defense of his unusual choice of verse over prose, he asks: "Since it never truly fit, / why wear the shoe of prose? In verse, the feet went bare." Far from detached, Merrill's speaker is enmeshed in the writing of his own poem, consistently reflecting on earlier passages and on the craft of narrative poetry itself. Though composed primarily of long stretches of conventional narration, Merrill's poem also uses the innovations in poetic storytelling form (the narrative-lyric, symbolic logic, reflexive comment on narrative as a genre) that have defined and resuscitated the narrative mode in 20th-century American poetry. Other conventional narratives include ROBINSON JEFFERS's "Roan Stallion" (1924) and *The Double Axe* (1948), RANDALL JARRELL's *Orestes at Tauris* (1948); many of JOHN CROWE RANSOM's poems; ROBERT LOWELL's *The Mills of the Kavanaughs* (1946), Robinson's *Glory of the Nightingales* (1930), ROBERT PENN WARREN's "The Ballad of Billie Pots" (1943), WALLACE STEVENS's "The Comedian as the Letter C" (1923), and the verse segment of Vladimir Nabokov's novel *Pale Fire* (1962).

NARRATIVE-LYRIC

Like the medieval romance, the modern narrative-lyric often employs a single "heroic" central figure, a personage who describes a sequence of events and ruminates on its larger, philosophical significance. In contrast to the traditional third-person grammatical form, the first-person "I" of the narrative-lyric shifts the focus from the events themselves to their meaning for the speaker, who connects them through images that often reveal something about his or her psychological or emotional state. The events need not employ plot nor designate a clear beginning and end. In fact, the speaker assumes the function conventionally fulfilled by plot—a meditating consciousness that connects disparate events, ordering them around its own insights. For instance, Bishop's "IN THE WAITING ROOM" (1976) follows a young speaker to a dentist's office, where she waits for her aunt while looking at magazines filled with photographs of volcanoes and aboriginal women, when there is a sudden sound; from the inner office "came an oh! of pain / Aunt Consuelo's voice." The speaker's mind combines the exclamation of pain, the striking photographs, and the elderly women around her in the waiting room into a realization of her own unique identity and of the feminine and human attributes that "held us all together or made us all just one." Before the poem ends the narrative resumes, but the "slush and cold" of the story have now become symbolic elements of the speaker's changing consciousness. Bishop's fictional narrative isolates a single psychological moment in time in which the speaker discerns an essential connection between the self and community, or storyteller and story.

Other poems, such as JAMES WRIGHT's "Snowstorm in the Midwest" (1971), employ a similar technique, but the narrative element is even further submerged in a symbolic landscape: The poem's speaker steps "into the water / of two flakes. / The crowns of white birds rise." Instead of distinguishing narrative from meditation, Wright's poem combines the two in a series of moving images and symbols, suggesting that the narrative itself is an allegory for the mind's realizations. In her discussion of Wright's poem as exemplary of the return of narrative in postmodern poetry, Perloff writes that the speaker "relives a particular situation or set of events in the past so as to come to terms with . . . the present" (413).

Though he also utilized more conventional narrative form in *The Mills of the Kavanaughs,* Lowell often incorporated narrative elements into his shorter lyrics. His acclaimed "Skunk Hour" (1959) describes a sequence of tangential, unrelated events—a wealthy heiress's downfall, a millionaire's bankruptcy, the speaker's visit to "the hill's skull"—culminating in a morbid insight, which is also the speaker's first and only reference to himself: "My mind's not right . . . / I myself am hell." The meandering narratives of decay and isolation crystallize in the speaker's brief realization, and when the narrative concludes with a description of a mother skunk skulking in the garbage pail, we discern a melancholic continuity of thought despite the seeming disconnections. In his comments on Bishop, which also apply to himself, Lowell sees in the narrative-lyric mode hints of Frost's storytelling technique and WILLIAM CARLOS WILLIAMS's lyric epiphanies, whose "purpose is to heighten or dramatize the description and, at the same time, to unify and universalize it" (77). And Helen Vendler remarks that "even in Lowell's most obscure moments, the presumption of story . . . held fast, no matter how murky the story nor how rapid the utterance" (145). Lowell's more CONFESSIONAL poems in *Life Studies* (1959), such as "My Last Afternoon with Uncle Devereux Winslow" and "Dunbarton," employ similar narrative techniques—lack of plot, quick shifting of scenes, first-person speaker—but emphasize the significance of the story's details by refusing to offer a final unifying moment of realization. Plath's earlier poems, such as "Sow" (1957), "Fable of the Rhododendron Stealers" (1957), and "Blackberrying" (1960), also relate trivial events that move subtly toward a universal insight. In "Sow," the speaker is led on "a tour / Through his lantern-lit / maze of barns" where the speaker's neighbor keeps his prize sow hidden. As the poem closes, the narrative of this labyrinthine quest leads to a "vision of ancient hoghood" and a beast that swills "the seven troughed seas and every earthquaking continent." Plath's brief, hyperbolic story funnels into the ecstatic insight of the lyric, finding common events capable of yielding a visionary wonder.

FRANK O'HARA is another poet who successfully combines narrative and lyric with innovative results. Contrary to Plath's technique, his "I do this, I do that" poems, as he called them (qtd. in Gooch 288), revel in narrating the intimate details of his daily life without universalizing. Rather than move toward meditation, O'Hara's speakers remain concerned with detail and frank honesty, suggesting poetry's inability to impose a single meaning on the apparent formlessness of experience. For instance, "The DAY LADY DIED" (1960), an elegy for jazz vocalist Billie Holiday, narrates a string of seemingly inconsequential "pseudo-events"—a shoe shine, buying a hamburger and milkshake, perusing a poetry magazine "to see what the poets in Ghana are doing these days"—until the speaker glimpses a newspaper headline announcing Holiday's death; he observes that he has begun to sweat and recalls "leaning on the john door in the 5 SPOT [jazz club] / while she whispered a song along the keyboard." Rather than resolve into a single psychological insight, the present-tense narrative remains fluid and descriptive. O'Hara's poem elicits an elegiac pathos (a feeling of sympathy or pity) by accumulating subjective and personal details around a missing central event: the death for which the poem is composed.

Other narrative-lyrics include Dove's sequence in *Thomas and Beulah* (1986), JOHN BERRYMAN's loosely autobiographical *DREAM SONGS* (1969), Williams's fragmented "Spring and All" (1923) and sections of *PATERSON* (1963), Eliot's "Burbank with a Baedeker: Bleinstein with a Cigar" and "Sweeney Erect" (1920), Warren's "Pondy Woods" (1935) and "Kentucky Mountain Farm" (1935), many of DENISE LEVERTOV's volumes, including *The Freeing of the Dust* (1972), ROBERT HAYDEN's "The Dream" (1970), and H. D.'s *TRILOGY* (1944) and *HELEN IN EGYPT* (1961).

BIBLIOGRAPHY

Gooch, Brad. *City Poet: The Life and Times of Frank O'Hara.* New York: Knopf, 1993.

Lowell, Robert. *Collected Prose.* New York: Farrar, Straus & Giroux, 1987.

Perkins, David. *A History of Modern Poetry.* Vol. II. Cambridge, Mass.: Harvard University Press, 1987.

Perloff, Marjorie. "From Image to Action: The Return of Story in Post-Modern Poetry." *Contemporary Literature* 23, no. 4 (1982): 411–427.

Vendler, Helen. *Part of Nature, Part of Us: Modern American Poets.* Cambridge, Mass.: Harvard University Press, 1980.

Anthony Cuda

NASH, OGDEN (1902–1971) Ogden Nash was a humorous poet whose distinctive, playful poetry was very popular during his lifetime and is still frequently quoted. Nash's poems are known for their preposterous rhymes and for their cheerful, affectionate skewering of middle-class American life. His lines deliberately break every metrical rule, exaggerating patterns of speech. His rhymes often depend on new coinages so that "dictionary" rhymes with "fictionary" ("The Eight O'clock Peril" [1935]) and "Calcutta" echoes "butta" and "mutta" ("Arthur" [1940]). While much of the humor of Nash's poetry comes from this sort of linguistic tomfoolery, his subject matter is also funny, consisting of philosophical musings on families, flirtation, animals, money, language, and work. Nash loved Lord Byron and John Keats, and his early poems were imitations of the romantic style, but in his mature work he created a new poetic form.

Nash was born in Rye, New York. After a single year at Harvard and a few odd jobs, he began working at the Doubleday publishing company. During his time there, Nash became acquainted with the New York literati, which resulted in a brief stint as managing editor for the *New Yorker.* His first book of poetry, *Hard Lines,* was published in 1931 and became a best-seller. Sixteen new books followed, as well as many collections of previously published poems. He married Frances Leonard in 1931, and the couple's two daughters, Linell and Isabel, appear frequently in Nash's verse. His other writings include plays, lyrics, and children's books. To his irritation, however, he won no awards.

Nash's wit may be sharp and to the point, as it is in his oft-quoted "Reflection on Ice-Breaking" (1931): "Candy / Is dandy / But liquor / Is quicker." His longer poems contain ruminations on everything from matrimony to airplane engineering. In "Portrait of the Artist as a Prematurely Old Man" (1934), he distinguishes between sins of commission and sins of omission, deciding that the latter kind is worse, because "about sins of omission there is one particularly painful lack of beauty, / Namely, it isn't as though it had been a riotous red-letter day or night every time you neglected to do your duty." Sins of commission are "what you are doing when you are doing something you ortant" (to rhyme with "important"). In Nash's world of lovingly bickering couples and overactive children, these sins are comparatively rare. His interest is in the sins of ordinary life, such as failing to answer a letter or to renew an insurance policy. Nash's humor is based in a detailed and loving observation of everyday truths and foibles, transformed by his eccentric and charming words into poems that simultaneously satirize and praise.

BIBLIOGRAPHY

Stuart, David. *The Life and Rhymes of Ogden Nash.* New York: Madison Books, 2000.

Rachel Trousdale

"THE NEGRO SPEAKS OF RIVERS" LANGSTON HUGHES (1921) The poet's first mature and most recognizable published poem, "The Negro Speaks of Rivers" became an anthem for LANGSTON

HUGHES's life and poetry and the Civil Rights movement in the United States. Hughes is most highly regarded for his poems that utilize blues rhythm, but in this earlier poem he employs a rhythmic structure more akin to the cadences of a gospel sermon. Hughes was interested in capturing the oral traditions of African Americans, and here he fittingly uses a rhythm that represents an important part of black culture and life.

Written while crossing the Mississippi River by train, the poem was published in the African-American journal *Crisis* in June 1921. Although not infused with blues rhythm and written outside of the HARLEM RENAISSANCE, Hughes later included it in his collection *The Weary Blues* (1926), which is now noted as an important part of that literary movement. The poem eventually became so closely identified with Hughes that it was chosen to be read at his funeral service.

Hughes establishes the rhythm of a gospel preacher through his use of repetition of particular words and phrases within a free verse structure. Anaphora (repetition of words or phrases at the start of lines) in the middle stanzas also contributes to the sermonlike quality; "I bathed," "I built," "I looked," and "I heard" begin these lines. The longer lines also recall Walt Whitman's extended lines in *Song of Myself* (1855), establishing the African-American tradition as not only part of the African but also the American traditions.

Thematically the poem speaks of connection and tradition. The speaker links himself to the rivers of the ancient and new worlds. In taking the reader on a tour of these rivers that have been part of his and his ancestors' lives for centuries, he connects his experience—and by extension, that of all African Americans—to the beginnings of the world: first the Euphrates, which flowed through the Garden of Eden, then to Central Africa, at whose heart is the Congo River. Next he makes the connection to one of the great early civilizations: ancient Egypt. Finally, he brings this connection and tradition to America as his thoughts travel down the Mississippi. This American tradition, however, is not one yoked by slavery and death, though it hints at their inextricable tie to African-American experience. The Mississippi is connected to Abraham Lincoln, a reminder of the past injustices of slavery while carrying the promise of freedom. The images of the setting sun, dusk, and the deepness of the rivers and the speaker's soul evoke thoughts of death, but also deathlessness and transcendence; as Arnold Rampersad says, Hughes becomes "the poet who sings of life because he has known death" (1,40).

BIBLIOGRAPHY

Barksdale, Richard K. *Langston Hughes: The Poet and His Critics.* Chicago: American Library Association, 1977.

Rampersad, Arnold. *The Life of Langston Hughes, Volume I: 1902–1941.* New York: Oxford University Press, 1986.

———. *The Life of Langston Hughes, Volume II: 1941–1967.* New York: Oxford University Press, 1988.

Joseph Schaub

NEMEROV, HOWARD (1920–1991) Howard Nemerov has often been described as "deeply divided," which is reflected in his dual devotion to poetry and fiction as well as his incorporation of romantic visions with deep skepticism. Louis Rubin writes that Nemerov's poetry "is unique in its magnificent fusion of idea and emotion in language. He wrote two kinds of poems. One kind was witty, acerbic, satirical [while the other was] lyric, philosophical, meditative" (677).

Nemerov was born in New York City. His sister was the photographer Diane Arbus, who committed suicide in 1971. Nemerov taught at Bennington College and Brandeis University (1966–68), moving to Washington University at St. Louis in 1969. He was a consultant in poetry to the Library of Congress (1963–64) and chancellor of the American Academy of Poets from 1976. Nemerov's many prizes and honors include the first THEODORE ROETHKE Memorial Award (1968), FRANK O'HARA Memorial Prize (1971), the National Book Award (1978), the Pulitzer Prize for poetry (1978) for his *Collected Poems,* and the Bollingen Prize for poetry (1981). He served as poet laureate of the United States from 1988 to 1990.

His *Reflexions on Poetry and Poetics* (1982) uses Menelaus's encounter with Proteus in Homer's *The Odyssey* as the analogy for the role of the artist: "The grasping and hanging on to the powerful and refractory spirit in its slippery transformations of a single force flowing through clock, day, violet, greying hair, trees dropping their leaves, the harvest in which by a peculiarly ceremonial transmutation the grain by which we live is seen without contradiction as the corpse we come to" (220). Nemerov was influenced by the philosopher Owen Barfield, who contended that matter is imbued with consciousness, which in conventional religious terms is expressed in such notions as the earth is the revelation of God. Nemerov strives to depict the inseparability of two kinds of consciousness; The individual poet's mind can never be separated from the consciousness or "mindfulness"—a term used by Barfield to mean "consciousness" or "design"—of things, nor can the inherent mindfulness of things be recognized but for the poet whose mind mirrors them. The mutually exclusive nature of these elements is illustrated in the final lines of "The Blue Swallows" (1967), which explain that the poem itself is not the point; the point is its role in rediscovering the world, "where loveliness adorns intelligible things, / because the mind's eye lit the sun." While it is commonly accepted that the light from the Sun made human life possible, Nemerov reverses the terms to suggest that human origins are mental to the same extent that they are physical. Throughout his poetry Nemerov emphasizes that the role of the poet or artist should be "finding and faithfully reflecting the mindfulness / That is in things, and not the things themselves."

BIBLIOGRAPHY

Bartholomay, Julia. *The Shield of Perseus: The Vision and Imagination of Howard Nemerov*. Gainesville, Fla.: University of Gainesville Press, 1972.

Potts, Donna. *Howard Nemerov and Objective Idealism: The Influence of Owen Barfield*. Columbia: University of Missouri Press, 1994.

Rubin, Louis. "In Memory of Howard Nemerov 1920–1991. *Sewanee Review* 99 (fall 1991): 673–679.

Donna Potts

NEW FORMALISM New Formalism is the name applied to a movement of poets who emerged in the 1980s and 1990s, writing in meter and sometimes in rhyme, reacting against the perceived orthodoxy of the CONFESSIONAL or autobiographical free verse LYRIC POETRY current in POETRY JOURNALS and creative writing programs generally since the 1960s. The movement is also frequently called "Expansive Poetry," for its attempt to broaden the modes, voices, and techniques available to contemporary poetry and for its hope to expand and popularize poetry's reading audience in contemporary American culture. The term *expansive poetry* also includes the New Narrative poets, a closely aligned (and overlapping) group who, as the name suggests, wrote poems (often book-length sequences) that tell stories, fictional or otherwise.

Early essays by New Formalist poets pointed out that current creative-writing education in America, by ignoring or forgetting prosody (the study and technique of writing in meter), severely limited the range of poems or styles in which a young poet could perform. Free verse seemed to be the only model genuinely available to an up-and-coming poet (see PROSODY AND FREE VERSE). Worse, writing-workshop training that emphasized the personal voice over the listening ear left few standards (aside from apt personal expression) for evaluating the tens of thousands of new poems those workshops produced every year—a literary situation that BRAD LEITHAUSER, in his essay "Metrical Illiteracy" (1983), compares both to the search for needles in a haystack and to the well-known image of innumerable "monkeys pecking at typewriters" (149–151). DANA GIOIA, one of the New Formalists' most outspoken writers, was more severe: "this lack of training makes [many young poets] deaf to their own ineptitude," he wrote in a 1987 *Hudson Review* essay (Gwynn 26). The New Formalists' return to meter and rhyme was thus originally a call for new poetry with a greater awareness of its own technique and with a stronger link to the practices of poets before T. S. ELIOT, WILLIAM CARLOS WILLIAMS, and EZRA POUND. New Formalism's first task was to differentiate itself from the dominant style of the time, and the most obvious difference here was the New Formalists' use of meter and traditional forms, such as the sonnet.

However, as any of the New Formalists would acknowledge, formal poetry was still being practiced by several well-known and well-respected figures from a previous generation: Such poets as ANTHONY HECHT, RICHARD WILBUR, and JOHN HOLLANDER, had risen to prominence in the 1950s, before the domination of autobiographical free verse that Gioia and Leithauser argued against. From the beginning, some of the New

Formalists (Leithauser, J. D. McClatchy, Mary Jo Salter, or Gjertrud Schnackenberg, for example) seemed to draw directly on the classicist strategies of this previous generation, preserving a certain cautious tone, academic distance from their subjects, and an admiration for high culture (Breslin 144–145). Others among the New Formalists adopted a stance toward received culture that would be identified as typical for the movement. In his essay "What's New about the New Formalism?" (1988), Robert McPhillips argues that the chief innovations of the New Formalists are an acceptance of popular culture, vernacular diction, and direct (not distanced) depiction of emotion: "If the [New Formalist] poem concerns cultural objects, they are likely to be from popular culture and to be indigenously American," for instance, Charles Martin's trip to a Brooklyn aquarium or Dana Gioia's "Cruising with the Beach Boys" (160–163). By avoiding the high Eurocentric culture and the sometimes arch conceits or diction of the 1950s formalists, this wing of the New Formalism hoped to create a more accessible poetry, to "revers[e] poetry's declining importance to the culture," as Gioia puts it, by reaching out to the general American reader (Gwynn 23)—not the "mass audience of television or radio," exactly, but the segment of the general public that still enjoys "serious novels, film, drama, jazz, . . . and the other modern arts" (*Can Poetry Matter* 249). The New Formalists, to regain an audience alienated not only by the high culture of a Hecht or Hollander but also by the abstruseness of a John Ashbery or Jorie Graham (to say nothing of the deliberate alienations struck by the Language poets), kept their language direct and their allusions recognizable. "Rather than be bards for the poetry subculture," as Gioia puts it, "they aspired to become the poets for an age of prose" (249).

Certainly the New Formalists drew criticism from many sides, as their essays (though not their poems) were often polemic and dismissive of the virtues of much contemporary poetry. Frequently these attacks portrayed meter itself as a sort of ancient fascism, "artificial, elitist, retrogressive, right-wing, and . . . un-American" (Can Poetry Matter 32), as if the regular alternation of stressed and unstressed syllables or the decision to break every line after five beats somehow encoded a political message. These blanket arguments against form or formalism generally misunderstand both the politics of the New Formalism (if such a diffuse movement can be said to have a single politics) and what it is to practice writing in form. When Ira Sadoff writes, for example, that New Formalism is too "univocal," because in a multicultural society "our poetries are enriched by otherness, by many different . . . varieties of meters" (8), he seems to be accusing iambic meter of a kind of tyranny, when the New Formalists as a group do their best to use as many meters as English will bear. (If iambs or iambic meter are dominant in their work, it is because that measure is well suited to the language, not because it somehow exerts a conservative domination over the language. Language precedes meter in any sensible account of prosody.) However, Sadoff seems to be more reasonable when he suggests that "poems that privilege sound and meter are conservative . . . because they decontextualize poetry": That is, by making formal exactness or beauty an end in itself, formalists run the risk of writing in a kind of social isolation that, Sadoff argues, may keep them from being politically responsible (7). This is a reasonable argument, but only to the extent that a poem becomes rarefied on its way to being a finished work of art—and this is clearly a criticism that could be turned against many free verse poets as well as against Leithauser or James Merrill (whom Sadoff inappropriately lists among his "neo-formalists"). Still, the social "decontextualization" of the work of art may be the shadow side of the value of civility implicit in writing in meter, the "premium not only on technique, but on a larger cultural vision that restores harmony and balance to the arts" (Jarman and Mason xviii–xix): Critics, such as Sadoff, might see this restored harmony as a loss of necessary discord.

Paul Breslin, in a more convincing critique, writes that the poets of the New Formalism, as they invoke the Beach Boys rock group or personal ads (as in Vikram Seth's novel-in-verse *The Golden Gate* [1986]) "are inclined to take white middle-class life too readily as the universal" (145). This is a difficult criticism for the New Formalists to answer, for if they write from popular culture or a popular idiom, the populace on which they draw is most generally their own, and a number of the more prominent New Formalists hold Ivy League degrees. To invoke the working-class southern childhood of Andrew Hudgins (*The Glass Hammer* [1994]) or the lesbian love sonnets of MARILYN HACKER is not really an answer to Breslin's criticism, except to show that writing in traditional forms neither precludes nor excludes the writing of other voices or other lives. It may be true, however, that the New Formalists' search for a popular audience has led many of them to accept popular culture too readily "as 'the' established culture" (Breslin 145).

Still, as the scope of the New Formalist movement becomes clearer, it becomes much less possible to identify a single taste or technique for the group, which includes both high and low culture, both strict and loose metrists, and poets from many different backgrounds. "A mistake made by nearly everyone who has written about the New Formalists," Keith Maillard writes in a 1995 essay, "is to claim a common ground for them. . . . it is impossible to find any such shared aesthetic; they are a wonderfully diverse lot" (53).

This diversity is clear in the anthology *Rebel Angels: 25 Poets of the New Formalism* (1996), which MARK JARMAN and David Mason edited for Story Line Press (a publisher that has consistently supported and published the New Formalists). Jarman and Mason include "poets who are chatty and elegiac, satirical and gently moving, [whose] range of subjects and forms has already done much to restore vitality to the art" (Jarman and Mason xix), and although this last claim may seem overstated, the strength of the anthology largely bears it out. *Rebel Angels* is an impressive collection, but it also gives shape to a group of poets whose numbers had been heretofore variously determined by the attention of individual essayists. It includes such prominent voices as Gioia, Leithauser, Martin, Salter, Hacker, RACHEL HADAS, and MOLLY PEACOCK, although it does not include Schnackenberg or McClatchy. The anthology also gives a place to such underacknowledged poets as RAFAEL CAMPO, Wyatt Prunty, and Andrew Hudgins, as well as to young poets who at that time had published only a single book, such as Rachel Wetzsteon, Elizabeth Alexander, and Greg Williamson. Jarman's and Mason's work is excluded, as are a number of the women in ANNIE FINCH's more extensive *A Formal Feeling Comes: Poems in Form by Contemporary Women* (1994), also from Story Line Press. Between the two anthologies, however, a very strong case is made for the resurgence of writing in form in the final decades of the 20th century.

It is still too early to say with certainty what place the New Formalism will have in the history of American poetry. One measure of the movement's success, as Maillard suggests, "can be seen in the . . . increasing number of young poets writing formal verse" (68). Recent books of truly startling quality by poets, such as Philip Stephens (*The Determined Days* [2000]) and Greg Williamson (*Errors in the Script* [2001]), suggest that some of the best poetry of the early 21st century will be written in traditional meters or forms. However, American poetry is still so various, so catholic of taste and democratic of spirit, that it would be impossible to ascribe ascendancy to any one movement or to draw conclusions about the direction of poetry in the coming century.

BIBLIOGRAPHY

Breslin, Paul. "Two Cheers for the New Formalism." *Kenyon Review* 13, no. 2 (spring 1991): 143–148.

Finch, Annie, ed. After New Formalism: Poets on Form, Narrative, and Tradition. Ashland, Oreg.: Story Line Press, 1999.

———, ed. A Formal Feeling Comes: Poems in Form by Contemporary Women. Ashland, Oreg.: Story Line Press, 1994.

Gioia, Dana. *Can Poetry Matter?: Essays on Poetry and American Culture.* St. Paul, Minn.: Graywolf Press, 1992.

Gwynn, R. S., ed. New Expansive Poetry: Theory, Criticism, History. Ashland, Oreg.: Story Line Press, 1999.

Jarman, Mark, and David Mason, eds. Rebel Angels: 25 Poets of the New Formalism. Ashland, Oreg.: Story Line Press, 1996.

Sadoff, Ira. "Neo-Formalism: a Dangerous Nostalgia." *American Poetry Review* 19, no. 1 (January/February 1990) 7–13.

Isaac Cates

THE NEW YORK SCHOOL

The New York school of poetry was an innovative group of poets made up principally by FRANK O'HARA, JOHN ASHBERY, BARBARA GUEST, JAMES SCHUYLER, and KENNETH KOCH. Their poetry was experimental, philosophical, staunchly antiestablishment, and antiacademic. The group began writing in the 1950s and is closely associated with a similarly named movement in painting alternatively called ABSTRACT EXPRESSIONISM or action painting. The name New York school is a result of an aesthetic sensibility and writing style, more than simply a location, although all five poets did live in New York City at some point during their formative years as writers. Their poetry is steeped in the facts, events, and objects of everyday life, and it is characterized by an impulse to blur the boundary between art and life; in writing poetry that includes the discourse and details of normal human interaction, the poets conflated the differences between what is normally considered material for art and what people experience in day-to-day existence. They are also noteworthy for appropriating various aspects of French SURREALISM and French symbolism; they especially employed typically surrealistic juxtapositions, which tended to be combined with whimsical observations of daily human behavior and speech. Their use of ironic gestures coupled with an often casual, informal tone and style created a unique tension that characterizes their distinct poetic sensibility.

The term New York school was supposedly coined by John Bernard Myers, the director of the Tibor de Nagy Gallery in New York City, in an effort to connect the increasingly popular abstract expressionist painters with the then-emerging poets who were also working in New York at the time. Both groups frequently collaborated on projects or shared and argued about ideas regarding art, politics, and philosophy. The characteristics associated with the label—the New York school—emerge first and foremost from the poets' antitraditionalist aesthetic and highly experimental style. Taking the lead from such painters as Jackson Pollock, Willem de Kooning, and Robert Motherwell and, later, a second generation of painters—Fairfield Porter, Jane Freilicher, Nell Blaine, Grace Hartigan, Larry Rivers, Robert Rauschenberg, and Jasper Johns—these poets strove for artistic change by proclaiming poetry to be a process, not simply a product.

The poets never collaborated together on a manifesto, nor did they construct any kind of formal school or program, but they did create a very close-knit community of writers and painters who shared a variety of strong convictions. They also lived an alternative lifestyle, which differed greatly from the dominant conservative culture of the time. Three of the five poets in the core group were homosexual (Ashbery, Schuyler, O'Hara), and all of them, in different degrees, explored culturally dominant conceptions of masculinity. Moreover, like the abstract expressionists, the poets became increasingly interested in the surface and medium of the work of art. In other words, they began to think that the language of the poem—its sounds, structures, forms, interactions of words, and textures—should be just as important as any attempt to create meaning. This was a radical departure from the mainstream poetry being practiced at the time (by academic poets, such as ROBERT LOWELL, ALLEN TATE, and JOHN CROWE RANSOM), and it was also a significant departure from their peers, such as the BEATS and the BLACK MOUNTAIN SCHOOL, who were engaged in other experimental poetic movements. The New York school was different, because it created an emphatic shift away from the supposed meaning of the poem and toward an interest in the materiality of language.

The New York school had a tremendous influence on poets of future generations who have come to share a similar sensibility and style. Some of the poets who are considered to be part of the second generation of the New York school include RON PADGETT, BILL BERKSON, TED BERRIGAN, and Joe Brainard. Other poets who are sometimes associated with the New York school include ANNE WALDMAN, HARRY MATHEWS, Edwin Denby, Kenward Elmslie, ALICE NOTLEY, BERNADETTE MAYER, EILEEN MYLES, and Tony Towle. *Locus Solus,* alternately edited by Schuyler, Ashbery, and Koch, was the primary literary magazine that came to represent the aesthetic flavor of the first generation.

The impact of the New York school has been wide and varied. This group has been considered the precursor to various postmodern movements in poetry, especially LANGUAGE poetry. In particular, the notion that anything in life is material for a poem, ranging from pop culture images and events to daily thoughts and routines, emerged with the poetry of the New York school. What are often called Frank O'Hara's "I do this, I do that poems" (qtd. in Gooch 288), which note the everyday details of the poet's life, exemplify this blending of the mundane with the structure and language of a poem. In one of O'Hara's poems entitled simply "Poem" (1950), the speaker proposes to an interlocutor that they go for a stroll in inclement conditions: "if it rains hard on our toes / we'll stroll like poodles." The playful language here is typical. Like O'Hara, many of the poets in the New York school seem comfortable using a collage of thoughts, actions, and details from their daily experience in ways that may be surreal and complex or direct and straightforward.

Ultimately the poetry of the New York school is difficult to characterize, because it contains a tremendous variety of styles, themes, and methods. Ashbery's poetry, for example, is often characterized as oblique, indeterminate, and periphrastic; it may have no sense of an ending, and it perpetually circumnavigates thoughts and images. His poetry is akin to the movement of consciousness itself, whereby the mental process and language serve to complicate perception and understanding, rather than creating any kind of determinate conclusions. O'Hara's poetry can be an intriguing mixture of surrealist juxtapositions, but, at other times, it contains a very casual discourse with a conversational style that seems like a letter written to a friend. Like O'Hara, Schuyler is known for his conversational style and charm, and he is perhaps the most lyrical and musical of the group. Guest's language is full of tonal complexity that is often rendered through shifts in sound and syntax rather than content. Koch's poetry is replete with wit and humor, and it tends to be more narrative and direct than that of the other writers of the group.

All the same, there are some common characteristics. The most significant of these is the poetry's sense of a process, in which a work tends to emphasize its own methods, procedures, and strategies, rather than simply the end result. In other words, the poem becomes a revelation of its own process as a specific kind of discourse, and not simply a finished product. This strategy fits effectively with the content of the poem, which is often tied to the events of everyday life. The poetry is written while seemingly moving and observing, whether through reality or through the flux of consciousness. In the poetry there exists a strong interest in intellectual and philosophical ideas, ranging from philosophical movements, such as existentialism, phenomenology, transcendentalism, and radical empiricism, to poetic trends, such as romanticism, imagism (see IMAGIST SCHOOL), and objectivism (see OBJECTIVIST SCHOOL). However, ultimately it is the concrete and material connection to the everyday—direct human experience and language—that is the source of a poem's unfolding. O'Hara describes this impulse in "Personism: A Manifesto" (1961): "I'm not saying that I don't have practically the most lofty ideas of anyone writing today, but what difference does that make? they're [*sic*] just ideas. The only good thing about it is that when I get lofty enough I've stopped thinking and that's when refreshment arrives" (498). This "refreshment" can be characterized by a poetry that resists traditional forms and poetic devices, such as end-rhyme, meter, alliteration, and even metaphor (see PROSODY AND FREE VERSE). Even when most oblique, as in Ashbery and Guest, the poetry of the New York school stays grounded in the materiality of language.

New York school poetry is, most of all, sympathetic to the visual arts from which it draws its inspiration; indeed, the materiality important in abstract expressionism—its foregrounding of paint itself—is an obvious shared aesthetic. The five core poets, except for Koch, wrote extensively about art, especially painting. O'Hara and Schuyler wrote for *ARTnews* and both became curators at New York's Museum of Modern Art. Guest and Schuyler were both associate editors at *ARTnews,* and Ashbery established a career as an art critic, writing for *ARTnews, Art in America, Newsweek,* and the Paris *Herald Tribune*. The influence of painting is evident in their poetry through a shift in attention from symbolism, metaphor, and signification to the actual operations and materials required to write a poem. Like a painter's interest in the canvas, paint, and individual brush strokes, these poets became interested in calling attention to their own basic materials—words, phrases, images, sentences, and the white space of the page itself.

Schuyler wrote, in 1959, that "New York poets, except I suppose the color blind, are affected most by the floods of paint in whose crashing surf we all scramble" (qtd. in Lehman *Beyond* 2). A painterly poetics in this sense can be, on the one hand, involved in creating a vivid picture with intense sensory detail, concrete imagery, tonal complexity, and multivalent coloration, and, on the other hand, a poetics that is interested in detaching language from its meaning. Like the abstract expressionists who stopped using lines and color to represent things or objects, and who began visualizing the canvas as an arena in which to act out a process detached from verbal or linguistic logic, these poets began to regard writing as an activity that always refers to itself in some way and poetry as a type of collaboration with life and language. The poets, however, faced an additional paradox that the painters did not: They were working with language, the terms of which are abstract and inherently denotative. The New York school poet must turn the signifying quality of language against itself and must do so in a concrete and visual way. The images and details the New York school poets created often subordinated or even abandoned referent and meaning in favor of texture, sound, or linguistic gesture. Ashbery is perhaps most notable in this regard, as can be seen in the following excerpt from "Our Youth" (1962): "Of bricks . . . Who built it? Like some crazy balloon / Of bricks . . . Who built it? Like some crazy balloon . . . / When love leans on us." The words create a tension that invigorates the possibilities of language by challenging causality and referentiality. Guest writes similarly in her poem "An Emphasis Falls on Reality" (1989): "Cloud fields change into furniture / furniture metamorphizes into fields."

The poetry of the New York school was pivotal to the American literary landscape of the 20th century, because of its liberating effects on poets who could now consider a greater range and kind of material appropriate for poetry, as well as the way in which this material could be expressed. These poets demonstrated that colloquial discourse was a viable and effective means for expressing daily emotions and thoughts, as well as for expressing deeper imaginative and metaphysical challenges, such as identity formation and consciousness. This movement demonstrated that almost anything, including the mundane and ordinary, could be made exciting and intriguing within the margins of a poem.

BIBLIOGRAPHY

Gooch, Brad. *City Poet: The Life and Times of Frank O'Hara.* New York: Knopf, 1993.

Lehman, David. *The Last Avant-Garde: The Making of the New York School of Poets.* New York: Doubleday, 1998.

———, ed. *Beyond Amazement: New Essays on John Ashbery.* Ithaca, N.Y.: Cornell University Press, 1980.

O'Hara, Frank. "Personism: A Manifesto." In *The Collected Poems of Frank O'Hara,* edited by Donald Allen. Berkeley: University of California Press, 1995, pp. 498–499.

Ward, Geoff. *Statues of Liberty: The New York School of Poets.* New York: St. Martin's Press, 1993.

Watkin, William. *In the Process of Poetry: The New York School and the Avant-Garde.* Lewisburg, N.Y.: Bucknell University Press, 2001.

Mark Tursi

"NEXT TO OF COURSE GOD AMERICA I"

E. E. CUMMINGS (1926) Exemplifying his formal mastery and penchant for political satire, E. E. CUMMINGS's Shakespearean sonnet "next to of course god america i" employs a pastiche of clichéd slogans and lines from American national anthems to undercut patriotic jingoism and question the motives of ardent nationalists. Cummings uses cliché the way the Cubist painters he admired used ready-made materials like newspapers in their paintings, rethinking the content of familiar objects and ideas by placing them in a new, unfamiliar context. In the case of "next to of course god america i," this new context is a speech, perhaps even a lecture, given by a self-righteous patriot whose language is a fragmentary mix of American slogans, noisy invective, debased aesthetic theory, and slang. No one type of language discredits him more than another, but his speech's fragmentary nature signals an incompleteness in his thought, and thus becomes the basis of Cummings's critique of a single-minded nationalism that will accept any loss of life to maintain the illusion of the glory of war.

"next to of course god america i" experiments with the sonnet form. The poem is heavily enjambed, with only one end-stopped line, suggesting the hurriedness of the narrator's speech, as if he feared the illogic of his ideas and thus was trying to prevent their interruption. Such enjambments partly conceal the rhymes, so that Cummings sets in conflict the poem's formal, considered structure with the speaker's vague, thoughtless diction. And although it is a Shakespearean sonnet, the poem echoes and inverts the division of the Petrarchan sonnet into an eight-line octet and a six-line sestet with an intervening *volta,* or turn, from problem to resolution; here, the speaker moves from patriotic fervor to a question, "why talk of beauty," which he can only answer with a rhetorical question, "what could be more beaut- / iful than these heroic happy dead / who rushed like lions to the roaring slaughter."

The sonnet's final six lines address the issue of modern warfare and patriotic fervor. While the speaker praises the dead soldiers who "did not stop to think they died instead," Cummings ironically undercuts the speaker's logic by having him conclude with a non sequitur, "then shall the voice of liberty be mute?" Having dismissed discussions of beauty and having praised fatal, unthinking obedience to duty, the speaker here presents himself as the sole voice of liberty, a seizure of absolute power at odds with the nature of liberty itself. Yet Cummings indicates the instability of such absolutism by dramatizing the speaker's anxiety about his own righteousness. The first 13 lines, which constitute the speaker's entire speech, are a single sentence crammed with simplistic slogans and turns of illogic. But in the final line, Cummings omits the terminal period when he writes that "He spoke. And drank rapidly a glass of water," suggesting the speaker has only paused for refreshment before beginning his verbal barrage again, for fear of having his unsound platform questioned. As "next to of course god america i" shows, however, such jingoistic patriotism always works against itself, its disorderly assemblage of sayings a sure sign of its inherent lack of meaning.

BIBLIOGRAPHY

Friedman, Norman. *E. E. Cummings: The Art of His Poetry.* Baltimore: Johns Hopkins University Press, 1960.

Kennedy, Richard S. *E. E. Cummings Revisited.* New York: Twayne Publishers, 1994.

Kidder, Rushworth M. "Cummings and Cubism: The Influence of the Visual Arts on Cummings' Early Poetry." *Journal of Modern Literature* 7, no. 2 (1979): 255–291.

Pagnini, Marcello. "The Case of Cummings." *Poetics Today* 6, no. 3 (1985): 357–373.

Temple Cone

NIEDECKER, LORINE (1903–1970) A poet of the OBJECTIVIST movement of the 1930s, Lorine Niedecker is known for her use of pristine images, minimalist technique, and subtle wordplay. A rural poet, Niedecker was nevertheless cosmopolitan in her literary connections. Her best-known and most artistically intimate correspondence was with the objectivist poet LOUIS ZUKOFSKY. Through Zukofsky, she met such poets as WILLIAM CARLOS WILLIAMS, GEORGE OPPEN, CID CORMAN, and CARL RAKOSI.

Lorine Faith Niedecker was born in Fort Atkinson, Wisconsin. She spent most of her life in a cabin by the Rock River along the shores of Lake Koshkonong on Black Hawk Island. Niedecker is frequently referred to as a poet of "place," because of her strong connection and frequent poetic use of the people and environs of her home. She was not widely known during her lifetime, but those who knew and appreciated her work were loyal in their support. In 1946 she published her first book-length publication of poems, *New Goose.* Her next book, *My Friend Tree,* appeared in 1961. Only five books of Niedecker's poetry were published in her lifetime, the last one, *My Life by Water,* just months before her death.

Niedecker's poetic themes are diverse and far-reaching. Her work ranges from poems of geology and natural history to poems of historical figures and current events. The subject that seemed to inspire her most was the lake country she lived in and the small town "folks" around her. From 1944–50 she worked as a copy editor for *Hoard's Dairyman,* and she calls upon this experience in her 1950 poem "In the great snowfall before the bomb" (1961). Here she gives a detailed description of her experience in the working world, in a voice that balances the line between dismissal and admiration. "I worked the print shop / right down among . . . the folk from whom all poetry flows." Keeping with the objectivist tradition, Niedecker worked to capture and report accurately the folk speech and natural rhythms of the Fort Atkinson people and landscape. She wanted to present life as it was, stripping away all modifiers that could bias or sentimentalize the people or places around her. In the final stanza to this poem, she discusses not only the process of writing poetry, but also its effect in her life as a medium of appreciation and isolation. She wonders, what would people "say" if they were aware that "I sit for two months on six lines / of poetry?"

Niedecker, like other objectivist poets, believed that excessive verbiage could obfuscate or worse yet compromise meaning within a poetic work. Because of this, Niedecker's poems are often short and focused as they capture a person, place, moment, or emotion and hold it suspended in time with a gemlike integrity. Toward the end of her life, Niedecker began to string her short poems together to form larger poem sequences. This poetic form encompasses some of her best work, setting her clear images and concentrated ideas within a larger context, while still keeping verbiage sparse.

The beginning poem in Niedecker's sequence *Thomas Jefferson* (1970) displays these characteristics. This short segment focuses on the difficulties of political life by relating a fleeting but impassioned thought as Jefferson is caught between his role as husband and patriot. "My wife is ill!" he says, and yet he must await "a quorum." The forceful clause that begins the sequence clearly sets the stage not only in content (Jefferson's wife is sick), but also of pace and tone (Jefferson is concerned and alarmed by his wife's condition). The image of Jefferson sitting dutifully in a room while feeling internally trapped by circumstance is made very clear in this short verse of four lines. Yet the situation is not overdrawn or sentimentalized. As critic Paul G. Hayes says: "Such is all Niedecker's poetry: never rhapsodic, always spare, clear, honest, distilled to an irreducible base" (67).

Despite the lack of recognition in her lifetime, interest in Niedecker's poetry continues to grow. Her poems are consistently anthologized, and scholarship around her seemingly simple but often enigmatic works is increasing. Niedecker was involved in some of the most philosophically and technically innovative shifts in modern poetry (see MODERNISM). She used poetry and language as a meeting and meshing place for psychology, history, science, and art.

BIBLIOGRAPHY

Hayes, Paul G. "'At the Close—Someone': Lorine's Marriage to Al Millen." In *Lorine Niedecker: Woman and Poet,* edited by Jenny Penberthy. Orono, Maine: National Poetry Foundation, 1996, pp. 65–77.

Penberthy, Jenny, ed. *Lorine Niedecker: Woman and Poet.* Orono, Maine: National Poetry Foundation, 1997.

Judith S. Girardi

"90 NORTH" RANDALL JARRELL (1942) RANDALL JARRELL's devastating "90 North" expresses, with heartbreaking anguish, the insurmountable difficulty of articulating meaning in a metaphysically chaotic world. Like much of Jarrell's work, "90 North" focuses on the twinned experiences of despair and desperation. The poem recounts the speaker's nighttime dream of arctic exploration, a mental journey toward what is "really my end," that ultimately discovers that "my world spins on this final point / Of cold and wretchedness." For Jarrell, the barren cold of the North Pole figures the accident and disorder of existence, both the individual's and the world's. Confronted by the "berg of death" waiting at the terminus of every life, the speaker waivers on the edge of nihilism but wrings from it the stoic consolation of describing the void truthfully.

In the opening scene, the speaker goes to bed wearing a flannel gown, an image of warmth and security, but in view of the metaphorical darkness and cold pervading the poem, Jarrell seems to be undermining any possibility of metaphysical comfort derived from the material world. He recounts his dream-journey to the North Pole, eponymous point of 90 degrees north, where "the flag snaps in the glare and silence / Of the unbroken ice," but the desolate landscape proves only that the journey can never reach a satisfying conclusion: "And now what?" Jarrell asks, "Why, go back. // Turn as I please, my step is to the south." When the speaker wakes, he realizes the dream-journey was a child's fancy, a narrative taken from cloud-cuckoo-land that proves untenable in adult reality, where "I die or live by accident alone— // Where, living or dying, I am alone." Charlotte Beck claims this realization signals "the journey from childhood to maturity, which bring the speaker to a sense of knowledge without wisdom" (196), though the repetition of "alone" in these lines (the only two line endings to repeat in the poem) signals a darker epiphany than Beck may be acknowledging. For Jarrell, man is abandoned to existence and must endure without guidance or purpose. Yet in the face of this desperate nihilism, the speaker can still express one remaining truth that does not smack of illusion, albeit through a series of terrifying syllogisms: "nothing comes from nothing, / The darkness from the darkness. Pain comes from the darkness / And we call it wisdom. It is pain."

Florian Hild finds in these closing lines a powerful, even consoling stoicism: "By refusing to go beyond tautological assertions, Jarrell . . . [urges] readers to attend to the world before them in all its nonunifying and complex aspects" (140). Stephen Burt in fact sees the poem as an expression of lonely self-dedication to the work of poetry, though he acknowledges that Jarrell is equally focused on "a dilemma central to that vocation: loneliness, in various guises, constitutes the problem, and the 'pain,' that the poems wish to remedy" (24). Ultimately, Jarrell is offering an unflinching look at the loneliness and unease of the individual self in the modern world, divested of all the systems of meaning that once brought order to the universe, but striving nevertheless to wring some order from "the ignorant darkness."

BIBLIOGRAPHY

Beck, Charlotte H. "Unicorn to Eland: The Rilkean Spirit in the Poetry of Randall Jarrell." In *Critical Essays on Randall Jarrell,* edited by Suzanne Ferguson, 191–202. Boston: G. K. Hall & Co., 1983.

Burt, Stephen. *Randall Jarrell and His Age.* New York: Columbia University Press, 2002.

Hild, Florian. "Randall Jarrell and Ludwig Wittgenstein: Poetic Philosophy." In *Jarrell, Bishop, Lowell, & Co.: Middle-Generation Poets in Context,* edited by Suzanne Ferguson, 126–144. Knoxville: The University of Tennessee Press, 2003.

Temple Cone

"NOTES TOWARD A SUPREME FICTION" WALLACE STEVENS (1942) Despite the provisional nature of its title, "Notes toward a Supreme Fiction" contains WALLACE STEVENS's most sustained and significant comment on his poetics, and it marks an important expression of modern humanist thought. In it, Stevens relates some of his neo-romantic ideas about the sublime—yet fully human—heights of experience and understanding that are available to us through poetry. The poem certifies that while our everyday understanding of life is imperfect, poetry can point to a truth about the human condition that goes beyond the ordinary. This is a truth that is "Venerable and articulate and complete," even if it is accessible only in our temporary experience of the poem.

To be sure, "Notes" has many concerns beyond poetry, and it would be inaccurate to characterize it as nothing more than a statement of literary philosophy. Nevertheless it is illuminating to focus on the poem's self-reflexive qualities. "Notes" begins with an eight-line prologue in which, according to Harold Bloom, the poet declares his love for his poem, indicating that this is an emotional as well as an intellectual project for Stevens (168). The poet also affirms his belief that we can comprehend and find satisfaction in the poem's "vivid transparence," a vital and vibrant truth that comes to us without mediation. However, the certainty of the prologue is short-lived, and the poet's confidence in completely revealing this truth dissolves as the work progresses. We might have expected as much, since the title promises nothing more than some loosely unified "notes" that are aimed "toward" something which Stevens is reasonably sure exists but that ultimately remains elusive.

Stevens names this goal the "supreme fiction." This destination marks not only our encounter with it—or with "the first idea"—but also the means by which we experience it. When Stevens speaks of a "fiction," he does not mean to suggest that this ideal is unreal or untrue. Instead, taking advantage of the word's Latin root, Stevens uses "fiction" to emphasize that this is something constructed, arranged, or, to use one of his terms, "confected." Still although the supreme fiction is something that is made, it is not made up: The supreme fiction constitutes "the real," and its "poem refreshes life so that we share, / For a moment, the first idea." As a guide to a truth which we intuit with a faculty beyond rationality, the supreme fiction is, in part, a humanist substitute for religious faith. However, the poet looks to produce this supremity, or what he calls "The final elegance, not to console, / Nor sanctify, but plainly to propound." In other words, whereas for Stevens conventional religion aims to provide solace or to transform the mundane into something divine, the poem of the supreme fiction intends only to reveal that the human sphere is profound and sufficient unto itself.

BIBLIOGRAPHY

Bloom, Harold. *Wallace Stevens: The Poems of Our Climate.* Ithaca, N.Y.: Cornell University Press, 1976.

Kermode, Frank. *Wallace Stevens.* New York: Grove Press, 1961.
Vendler, Helen. *On Extended Wings: Wallace Stevens' Longer Poems.* Cambridge, Mass.: Harvard University Press, 1969.

Jeannine Johnson

NOTLEY, ALICE (1945–) Alice Notley's poetry attempts, in her words, to "re-center" the "I," to find how, in the wake of postmodernist criticism, one can situate the first person at the center of a poem ("Small"). She has also insisted on full freedom to speak with a woman's voice, including during an interview published in *Talisman* (2002): "[I] never identified with a poetics outside myself really. Partly I had such trouble with the concept of the [poetic] line. . . . As I've said so many times, it seemed so male-owned" (531). Although her poetics are uniquely her own, WILLIAM CARLOS WILLIAMS, PHILIP WHALEN, and TED BERRIGAN, in their respective ways showed the route to the independence that is Notley's trademark.

Notley grew up in Needles, California, in the Sonoma Desert. She graduated from Barnard College in 1967 and two years later received an M.F.A. from the University of Iowa's Writers' Workshop, where she met Berrigan, her future husband. They had two sons, Anselm and Edmund, both now established poets in their own right. Notley and Berrigan settled in New York's Lower East Side in 1976, where she was soon recognized as a major figure in the second generation of the NEW YORK SCHOOL. Berrigan died seven years later, but Notley remained in New York until 1992, when she moved to Paris with her second husband, the British poet Douglas Oliver. Her long poem *Mysteries of Small Houses* received the Los Angeles Times Book of the Year Award in 1998, and in 2002 she received an American Academy of Arts and Letters Award, the Griffin Poetry Prize for her long poem *Disobedience,* and the Shelley Memorial Award of the Poetry Society of America.

In *The Descent of Alette* (1992), Notley uses quotation marks to isolate and emphasize words as spoken units: "it smelled of mice," "smelled of warm fir" "& meek blood." Drawing on Notley's dreams, the poem concerns a "descent" into mythic depths where a domineering man, the tyrant, must be deposed. A woman's epic (a genre traditionally reserved for men), the poem was originally published in Notley's and Oliver's *The Scarlet Cabinet* (1992). Reissued in 1996, it has become an important work in the feminist poetic canon.

Notley's *Selected Poems* (1993) brought together a massive range of innovative writing, from *165 Meeting House Lane* (1971) to *At Night the States* (1988). *The Descent of Alette* was followed by *Mysteries of Small Houses* (1998) and *Disobedience* (2001). "It's necessary to maintain a state of disobedience against . . . everything," Notley said in a lecture at King's College, London, in 1998 ("Poetics"). Her poetry is always evolving, always finding new forms and material. Disobedient to all traditions, it is among those most closely watched by avant-garde poets and critics today.

BIBLIOGRAPHY

McCabe, Susan. "Alice Notley's Epic Entry: 'An Ecstacy of Finding Another Way of Being.'" *Antioch Review* (summer 1998): 273–280.
Notley, Alice. "An Interview with Alice Notley," by Edward Foster. *Talisman* 23–26 (2002–2003): 506–515.
———. "Small Houses Rebuilt with Musical Glue: A Word-by-Word with Alice Notley," by Maureen Holm. Available online. URL: http://www.geocities.com/LyricRecovery/alice_notley.htm. Downloaded March 2007.
———. "The Poetics of Disobedience," Electronic Poetry Center. Available online. URL: http://wings.buffalo.edu/epc/authors/notley/disob.html. Downloaded March 2007.

Edward Foster

"NUMBERS, LETTERS" AMIRI BARAKA (LEROI JONES) (1969) First published in *Black Magic* (1969), "Numbers, Letters" appeared during AMIRI BARAKA's black nationalist period of the late 1960s and early 1970s, when he was one of the leading figures in the BLACK ARTS MOVEMENT. However, Baraka included "Numbers, Letters" in the section of *Black Magic* entitled "Target Study: 1963–1965" and so identified the poem with the crucial phase of his personal, artistic, and ideological development that preceded his nationalist period. Between 1963 and 1965, Baraka gradually severed his personal and professional ties with the white bohemian subculture of Greenwich Village and began to view the black community of Harlem as his proper home. Self-consciously autobiographical, "Numbers, Letters" is a meditation on the black writer's relationships to white America and black America.

Baraka recalls in his 1984 autobiography that after leaving Greenwich Village for Harlem in March 1965, he felt as if he were "Back in the homeland to help raise the race" (*Autobiography* 295). Yet, as he readily admits, his nationalist ardor was tinged with guilt. The speaker of the autobiographical fragment "Words" (1967) confesses, "I live in Harlem . . . and suffer for my decadence which kept me away so long" (*Tales* 89). Similarly in "Numbers, Letters," Baraka emerges as a black intellectual who has recently returned, guiltily, from the decadent world of white bohemia. Baraka clearly regards his sojourn in bohemia as an act of race-treason, and, in a grotesque gesture of self-condemnation, he takes himself to task for having associated there with white women and gay men.

Struggling with these menacing feelings of guilt, Baraka attempts to find a form of expression, a system of "Numbers" and "Letters," appropriate to his nascent black identity. In "Square Business" (1961–63), another poem from *Black Magic,* the speaker complains that white people "own" both "language" and "numbers," but he adds (mysteriously) that black people own the "strong" numbers. By contrast, in "Numbers, Letters," Baraka stakes a claim upon language. He resolves to say what he means and to "be strong / about it." However, Baraka does not clearly identify the source of this "strong" black language. Is this language grounded in any personal or cultural history? On the one hand, Baraka suggests that the past forms the foundation for his new idiom. His art is an expression of "all the things that make me, have formed me, colored me." On the other hand, he intimates that the present is the true basis of this idiom. The history that matters is "today." Epitomizing a recurrent paradox in Black Arts writing, Baraka conceives of authentic black identity and language as both historically conditioned and strictly of the moment.

BIBLIOGRAPHY

Baraka, Amiri. *The Autobiography of LeRoi Jones.* Chicago: Lawrence Hill, 1997.

———. *Tales.* Grove: New York, 1967.

Sollors, Werner. *Amiri Baraka/LeRoi Jones: The Quest for a "Populist Modernism."* New York: Columbia University Press, 1978.

Matthew Calihman

NYE, NAOMI SHIHAB (1952–) Naomi Shihab Nye, poet and children's author, writes about conciliation. Nye writes as Swiss/German-American-Palestinian, Texan, wife, mother, and teacher (of both children and graduate students). WILLIAM STAFFORD has been a major influence on her work. Nye's writing focuses on ordinary experiences and the importance of surpassing the ordinary. Her poetry draws from Mexican-American neighbors in Texas, Arab-American perspectives, and other cultural traditions.

The daughter of an American mother and a Palestinian father, Nye grew up in St. Louis and Jerusalem and has spent her adult life in San Antonio. Nye has worked as a journalist and has taught at the University of Texas, Austin. Her poetry has been featured on National Public Radio's *The Writer's Almanac* and *A Prairie Home Companion,* and on PBS *The Language of Life* and *The United States of Poetry.* Nye's many honors include fellowships from the Library of Congress (2000) and the Lannan Foundation (2002). She won the National Poetry Series prize for *Hugging the Jukebox* (1982) and was a National Book Award finalist (2002) for *19 Varieties of Gazelle.*

The scope of Nye's work is global. Common human characteristics and universal acceptance are her major themes. Nye often illustrates these through her own life. In her autobiographical novel *Habibi* (1997), Nye presents the meeting of displaced Americans, newcomers to Palestine, and Palestinian villagers. Tensions in the meetings are removed through the nurturing of mutual acceptance and mutual experience.

Nye promotes self-questioning. In "Words to Sit In, Like Chairs" (2002) she asks, "If people . . . could use words instead of violence, how would our world be different?" (159). Much of Nye's poetry deals with how to reconcile belonging to more than one ethnic or national group. In "Half and Half" (1998), soup is made by a woman with "what she had left / in the bowl, the shriveled garlic and bent bean. / She is leaving nothing out." To leave nothing out is Nye's prescription for living. Her overriding principle, in life and in her writing, is acceptance.

BIBLIOGRAPHY

Moyers, Bill, et al. *The Language of Life.* Garden City, N.Y.: Doubleday, 1995.

Nye, Naomi Shihab. "Talking with Poet Naomi Shihab Nye," by Lisa Suhair Majaj. *Al Jadid,* 2, no. 13 (1996).

———. "Words to Sit in, Like Chairs." In *911: The Book of Help: Authors Respond to the Tragedy,* edited by Michael Cart. Chicago: Cricket Books, 2002.

———, and Neil Conan. "Do We Need Poetry?" *Talk of the Nation.* National Public Radio. December 10, 2001.

Freda J. Fuller-Coursey

O

OBJECTIVIST POETRY The term *objectivist* was coined by LOUIS ZUKOFSKY in 1930 for "'Objectivists' 1931," a special issue of *Poetry* for which he served as guest editor. Of the many poets included in that issue and in its follow-up anthology, *An "Objectivists" Anthology* (1932), the poets now most often associated with the label are Zukofsky, GEORGE OPPEN, CARL RAKOSI, CHARLES REZNIKOFF, and (sometimes) the Englishman Basil Bunting. LORINE NIEDECKER, a Wisconsin poet, is also often included among the objectivists. The four core members of the objectivists—Oppen, Rakosi, Reznikoff, and Zukofsky—were all Jewish, urban, intensely intellectual, and (except Reznikoff) politically left-wing, and their poetry reflects these backgrounds and inclinations. These poets, who all began seriously writing and publishing in the 1920s and 1930s, remained largely unknown until the 1960s; since then they have received increasing critical attention and have been recognized as an important set of influences on more recent poetic movements, including many of the poets anthologized in Donald Allen's *The New American Poetry* 1945–1960 (1960) and, later, the LANGUAGE SCHOOL (see POETRY ANTHOLOGIES). The objectivists, it can be argued, are a crucial bridge between the high MODERNISM of T. S. ELIOT and EZRA POUND and the postmodernism of these more recent movements. In large part because of their steadfast adherence to poetry's truth-telling ambitions, the objectivists' work stands as an important model of how political and ethical concerns can be incorporated into a poetry of formal experimentation.

The most important statement of objectivist poetics is Zukofsky's essay "Sincerity and Objectification: *With Special Reference to the Work of Charles Reznikoff*," first published in "'Objectivists' 1931." In this essay he lays out the fundamental principles of his own poetic practice: The poet ought to compose always with "sincerity," the most scrupulous attention both to the objects and events about which he writes and to the particulars of his own language, and the finished poem ought to exhibit "objectification," an object-like, tangible form as if language were material. In these principles objectivist poetics goes beyond the imagism of Ezra Pound, which prescribed rules for dealing with images and using language but largely failed to discuss the finished form that the poem ought to assume (see IMAGIST SCHOOL).

Zukofsky's theory deeply influenced some of the poets among the objectivists, particularly Oppen, Rakosi, and WILLIAM CARLOS WILLIAMS; others of them, less closely associated with objectivism, including Reznikoff and KENNETH REXROTH, seemed largely oblivious both to the theory and to the overall label. Indeed while Zukofsky seemed to view the objectivist "movement" for some years as a useful marketing device for his and his friends' poetry, he was well aware that the objectivist poets were by no means a coherent group or school: He had arrived at the critical terms "sincerity" and "objectification" without consulting the other poets included in the *Poetry* issue, and he would always insist that there was no such thing as "objectivism."

Charles Reznikoff's poetic style was largely formed before he came in contact with Zukofsky and the other objectivist poets, and he interpreted Zukofsky's term *objectivist* as referring not so much to the shape that the poem ought to take as to the poet's stance toward reality: Reznikoff's own poetry, deeply influenced by training in law, often takes the form of objective testimony, as in his long poems *Testimony* (1975) and *HOLOCAUST* (1975), which draw directly upon court transcripts (see LONG AND SERIAL POETRY). His short poems are notable for the laconic, precise manner in which they present both moments of interpersonal emotion and the varied tableaux of the Manhattan streets that Reznikoff walked obsessively.

Rakosi's work is often far more playful, sometimes even "light," than that of his companions. He began writing much under the influence of the imagists and WALLACE STEVENS, though his association with Zukofsky turned his work in more angular, compressed directions. While his early work is often biting and startling, the poems Rakosi wrote after his return to poetry in 1965 are more relaxed, gentle, and good-humored, often taking the form of a loose series, such as "Americana" (1967–86). The progression of his career is largely obscured in his *Collected Poems* (1986), for which Rakosi rearranged and often revised his earlier work, but is clear in *Poems 1923–1941,* which Andrew Crozier edited in 1995.

The Wisconsin poet Niedecker was inspired to get in contact with Zukofsky when she read the "'Objectivists' 1931" issue of *Poetry,* and she and Zukofsky shared an almost four decades-long friendship and correspondence. Her poetry, which began with experiments in SURREALISM and modifications of the forms of nursery rhymes, has much in common with Zukofsky's in its striking images, juxtapositions of language, and short lines. In the last decades of her life, she wrote a number of major sequences revolving around various historical figures and around the history and geology of the American Midwest. While she remained largely isolated from the other objectivist poets, her work (like Zukofsky's) was championed and published by CID CORMAN, editor of *Origin* magazine (see POETRY JOURNALS), and JONATHAN WILLIAMS, editor of the Jargon Press (see POETRY PRESSES), in the 1960s.

Oppen and Zukofsky, though they renewed their friendship in the late 1950s, when Oppen returned to New York after a decade living in Mexico, eventually broke with one another. One reason for their estrangement was their attitudes toward difficulty in poetry. Both men had written dense and oblique LYRIC POETRY in the early 1930s, but Zukofsky's work—in particular his long poem "A"—grew more and more obscure over the course of its composition and serial publication. While Zukofsky was capable of writing lyrics of great beauty and limpidity, he was also enamored of complex forms and recondite reference. As *"A"* moves into the second half of its 24 sections, the poem seeks to wind in more and more information, doing so in more and more oblique, "coded" manners. Zukofsky saw this merely as an extension, a following-through of his objectivist rhetoric of the early 1930s. His goal was to make the poem a continually "musical" object, and to do so he experimented with various forms derived from classical music. Early parts of *"A"*, for instance, imitate the form of the baroque fugue, often to dizzying lengths, while *"A"*-13 is a formal imitation of the rhythms of one of Bach's partitas for solo violin.

Oppen's later work is also difficult, but his difficulty stems not from the complexity of formal devices or the variety of literary, historical, philosophical, and personal references, as in Zukofsky, but from the gravity of the philosophical and ethical issues with which his poems seek to grapple. Oppen's later poetry is obsessed with problems of communication and community and derives much of its weightiness from his reading of the pre-Socratic philosophers and the 20th-century German philosopher Martin Heidegger. For Oppen, the issue of difficulty in poetry was ultimately an ethical matter. Oppen felt that the obscurity of Zukofsky's poetry was a mere superficial complexity, a screen by which Zukofsky could repel the casual reader, while his own poetry, in contrast, dealt with inherently difficult problems.

While there is no single objectivist "style" shared by all the poets associated with the name, there are a number of characteristics that their poetries share. They all tend to write free verse (though Zukofsky and Niedecker experimented with forms derived from traditional meters and rhyme schemes). They are intensely aware of what Zukofsky calls "historic and contemporary particulars" (*"A"*-24, 1978) including both the political and the historical implications of whatever they might be writing about. (Indeed Oppen, Zukofsky, and Rakosi worked on behalf of Communist Party causes during the 1930s and remained politically aware throughout their lives.) And, perhaps most importantly, they write in conscious opposition to establishment verse culture: the refined formal verse promoted by the poets and critics of the New Criticism during the 1940s and 1950s (see FUGITIVE/AGRARIAN SCHOOL), and later what was perceived as the limp, personal, diaristic verse promoted by American creative writing programs.

And while the term *objectivist* can only with difficulty be used as a stylistic description of these poets' work, the objectivists share certain fundamental stances toward the world and the poem. All of them insist upon the utmost precision in the use of language and the most careful adherence to the facts of perception. This is what Zukofsky calls "sincerity," what Oppen means when he says that "the poem is concerned with a fact which it did not create" (2), and what Reznikoff intends when he relates the poet's words to the sworn testimony given in a court of law. The objectivist poets, then, share a sense that the relationship of the poem and the world must be in some sense a relationship of truth—an ethical relationship. They may not write in superficially realistic styles, but their work always bears an ethical responsibility to the real as perceived and experienced.

After the publication of the "'Objectivists' 1931" came *An "Objectivists" Anthology,* which was published by To Publishers in 1932. To was a short-lived imprint run by Oppen and edited by Zukofsky himself, and it folded soon after, having printed books by Williams and Pound in addition to the anthology. In 1933 Oppen, Reznikoff, Zukofsky, and Williams combined to start the Objectivist Press, a cooperative venture which would publish self-funded volumes. The Objectivist Press printed books by Williams, Reznikoff, and Oppen before it too folded. (The imprint was briefly revived by Zukofsky's wife, Celia, in 1948 to publish his anthology *A Test of Poetry.*)

Whatever momentum the objectivist movement had initially generated among its participants was largely dissipated over the 1930s, and the objectivist poets drifted out of touch with one another; Rakosi and Oppen, in fact, completely abandoned writing poetry for some years. The name, however, was revived in the early 1960s when James Laughlin's New Directions Publishers, in collaboration with the *San Francisco Review,* began publishing books by Oppen, Rakosi, and Reznikoff, and in 1968 L. S. Dembo, editor of *Contemporary Literature,* conducted a series of interviews with Oppen, Rakosi, Reznikoff, and Zukofsky that helped to solidify the critical association of the four poets as "objectivists." (While Oppen, Rakosi, and Reznikoff accepted their rediscovery under this banner with good grace—and perhaps bemusement—Zukofsky would have nothing to do with a revived objectivist movement. He considered himself to have moved beyond that moment in his career, and he repeatedly refused invitations to appear with the other three poets on "objectivists" programs.) Since Dembo's interviews there has been increasing critical attention paid both to the poets individually and to their collective achievements.

Quite apart from their critical reception, the objectivists have proved an enduring influence on important contemporary American poets, including ROBERT CREELEY, CHARLES BERNSTEIN, RACHEL BLAU DUPLESSIS, MICHAEL HELLER, DAVID IGNATOW, ROBERT KELLY, SHARON OLDS, MICHAEL PALMER, JEROME ROTHENBERG, ARMAND SCHWERNER, HUGH SEIDMAN, HARVEY SHAPIRO, and JOHN TAGGART. They have also been significant to a number of contemporary French poets, including Anne-Marie Albiach, Claude Royet-Journoud, and Emmanuel Hocquard.

BIBLIOGRAPHY

Dembo, L. S. "The 'Objectivist' Poet: Four Interviews." *Contemporary Literature* 10 (1969): 64–91.

DuPlessis, Rachel Blau, and Peter Quartermain, eds. *The Objectivist Nexus: Essays in Cultural Poetics.* Tuscaloosa: University of Alabama Press, 1999.

Heller, Michael. *Conviction's Net of Branches: Essays on the Objectivist Poets and Poetry.* Carbondale: Southern Illinois University Press, 1985.

McAllister, Andrew, ed. *The Objectivists.* Newcastle upon Tyne, England: Bloodaxe, 1996.

Oppen, George. "The Mind's Own Place." *Kulchur* 10 (summer 1963): 2–8.

Williams, William Carlos. "Objectivism." In *Princeton Encyclopedia of Poetry and Poetics,* edited by Alex Preminger

et al. Princeton, N.J.: Princeton University Press, 1965, p. 582.
Zukofsky, Louis. *Prepositions+: The Collected Critical Essays.* Hanover N. H.: Wesleyan University Press, 2000.
———, ed. *An "Objectivists" Anthology.* New York: To, Publishers, 1932.
———, ed. "'Objectivists' 1931." *Poetry* 37, no. 5 (February 1931).

Mark Scroggins

"ODE TO THE CONFEDERATE DEAD"

ALLEN TATE (1927) "Ode to the Confederate Dead," ALLEN TATE's most anthologized and best-known poem, brought MODERNISM more fully to bear on American poetry, especially in the South, where a pervasive sentimental/romantic poetics was giving way to the agrarian aesthetics of the Fugitives (see FUGITIVE/AGRARIAN SCHOOL). First published in 1927 and revised over the next 10 years, the poem describes, in second-person address, a man who has stopped beside a dilapidated Confederate graveyard. The reader is encouraged to contemplate the scene by observing the many signs and symbols of death and the possibilities of regeneration.

Tate technically and philosophically explained his own poem in an essay entitled "Narcissus as Narcissus" (1968), indicating that the poem was "'about' solipsism or Narcissism, or any other *ism* that denotes the failure of the human personality to function properly in nature and society" (595). The verse is saturated with a stoic yet apocalyptic tone and deals unflinchingly with the conflicting modern themes of nature, history, death, and alienation. The poem responds to what T. S. ELIOT promoted in his prose work, *The Sacred Wood* (1920), employing "depersonalization" and an "objective correlative," which reveals emotion through the removed (often imperative) voice, the specific event, and oddly juxtaposed images.

In Tate's essay "Homage to T. S. Eliot" (1975), Tate claims that he "never tried to imitate [Eliot] or become a disciple" (90). Still a modernist influence pervades the poem, and the debt to Eliot is clear. The fallen, decaying leaves in the first stanza and throughout the poem recall the "grimy scraps / Of withered leaves" that wrap around the feet of the addressee in Eliot's "Preludes" (1917). Tate's startling images of a blind crab, leaping jaguar, and spiders are reminiscent, respectively, of Eliot's "ragged claws" in "The LOVE SONG OF J. ALFRED PRUFROCK" (1915) and the springing tiger and spiders in "Gerontion" (1920). The strangely unpunctuated two-line refrain reappearing four times in Tate's poem echoes Eliot's use of refrains. The abstractions in the poem are as startling as the images: "[S]trict impunity," "casual sacrament," "seasonal eternity of death," "fierce scrutiny," and "rumour of mortality" thicken the first stanza (a nine-line sentence) of the poem with intellectual rigor.

The poem is "agrarian" in that it resurrects the history of the South and tries to restore a sense of stoic pride to the heirs of its troubled past. Yet, doubting memory's comforts, the poet shows restraint in its conclusions about how to proceed in a death-drenched world. The penultimate stanza begins with a suggestion to speak to the mortal predicament, but the stanza ends in a series of bleak questions. Tate finally suggests, "Leave now / and shut the gate." We are left with an image of a serpent who, much like the poet confounded by death, "Riots with his tongue through the hush."

BIBLIOGRAPHY

Eliot, T. S. *The Sacred Wood and Major Early Essays.* Mineola, N.Y.: Dover Publications, 1998.
Tate, Allen. "Homage to T. S. Eliot." *Memoirs and Opinions, 1926–1974.* Chicago: Swallow Press, 1975, pp. 87–91.
———. "Narcissus as Narcissus." In *Essays of Four Decades.* Chicago: Swallow Press, 1968, pp. 593–607.
Underwood, Thomas. *Allen Tate: Orphan of the South.* Princeton, N.J.: Princeton University Press, 2000.

John Poch

"OF BEING NUMEROUS" GEORGE OPPEN

(1968) Published as the central poem in a collection of the same name, "Of Being Numerous" is arguably GEORGE OPPEN's finest poetic achievement. Oppen had wanted to write "a decisive expression of the period," a long poem that would illuminate the existential backdrop to the turmoil of the 1960s (108). But he hoped to do so without engaging in the heroic quest-romance common to epic poetry and without recourse to the didacticism of works produced by such poets as EZRA POUND. This unusual approach to the function of poetry arises from Oppen's desire to be part of a "sincere and public conversation" concerning humanity (82), a desire for which he is greatly admired by contemporary poets across the political and aesthetic spectrum.

"Of Being Numerous" has deep roots in OBJECTIVIST poetics. It is a serial poem constructed out of 40 extraordinarily condensed, quasi-independent sections (see LONG AND SERIAL POETRY). There is no narrative progression, but rather it consists of a sequence of lyric, philosophical investigations that reveal a mind unwilling to fabricate truth when none can be found. Oppen thought the purpose of "Of Being Numerous" was to try to understand humanity as "a single thing"—he was grappling with "the fact of being numerous, without which we are marooned, shipwrecked" (121). The poem examines the distances between people, the relationship between people and place, and the way in which we use language to navigate between people and places. Like Walt Whitman, Oppen uses New York City as the archetype of these relations: It is a city in which the numerous is continually haunted by the "shipwreck / Of the singular" and in which both are forcibly grounded and encompassed by "the mineral fact" of the city, the "impenetrable" matter that provides both bedrock and circumference.

The poem is profoundly dialectical; Oppen scrutinizes opposing concepts (thesis and antithesis) in an effort to reveal how they mean. The singular/numerous opposition, though the most critical, is but one among a number of oppositions that Oppen contemplates in the poem, such as distance/nearness, solidity/evanescence, youth/age, clarity/obscurity, and rootless speech/rooted speech. Unlike other dialectical constructions, however, Oppen's oppositions do not resolve into syntheses that become terms in further dialectics. "Of Being Numerous" does not have a thesis to prove—it is not an argument. Instead the poem brings clarity to the problems with which we are collectively perplexed. Oppen searches for clarity and transparency. "I don't mean that much can be explained," he adds: "Clarity in the sense of silence." *Of Being Numerous* won the 1969 Pulitzer Prize.

BIBLIOGRAPHY

DuPlessis, Rachel Blau. "Objectivist Poetics and Political Vision: A Study of Oppen and Pound." In *George Oppen: Man and Poet,* edited by Burton Hatlen. Orono, Maine: National Poetry Foundation, 1981.

Golding, Alan. "George Oppen's Serial Poems." In *The Objectivist Nexus,* edited by Rachel Blau DuPlessis and Peter Quartermain. Tuscaloosa: University of Alabama Press, 1999.

Oppen, George. *The Selected Letters of George Oppen,* edited by Rachel Blau DuPlessis. Durham, N.C.: Duke University Press, 1990.

Duncan Dobbelmann

O'HARA, FRANK (1926–1966)

Francis Russell O'Hara immersed himself in art of all kinds for all of his adult life. Along with JOHN ASHBERY, BARBARA GUEST, KENNETH KOCH, and JAMES SCHUYLER, all of whom he knew well, he was one of the first-generation NEW YORK SCHOOL poets; he knew many contemporary painters and their work equally well (including the New York school painters, for which the group of poets was named), and internalized the aesthetic of ABSTRACT EXPRESSIONISM. O'Hara worked as an art critic and curator, internationally promoting Jackson Pollock, Willem de Kooning, and Larry Rivers, among others. A prolific poet, O'Hara's practice was akin to the BEAT POETRY of the post–World War II period in its subjectivity and spontaneity, but nevertheless stopped short of outright confessionalism, the American origins of which could be found in Beat poetry and which the New York poets rejected (see CONFESSIONAL POETRY). While the New York poets, in general, "wrote in language that was illogical and often meaningless, O'Hara's particular tone was surrealist, Ashbery's was philosophical, and Koch's was comic" (Gooch 224).

O'Hara was born in Baltimore, Maryland, where his parents had moved to conceal the somewhat premature birth of their child just six months after they were married, a fact which O'Hara never learned; they soon returned to their origins in Grafton, Massachusetts. In 1944 O'Hara enlisted in the navy and served as a sonarman in the South Pacific. The military rationale for his assignment was that his musical training would give him a more sophisticated ear for tonal changes. O'Hara had studied piano through his childhood, and when he entered Harvard on the G.I. bill in 1946, he planned to pursue a career in music performance and composition.

The influence of music can be found in his poems, formally in "phonetic and rhythmic devices modeled on the music of JOHN CAGE and Eric Satie" (Perloff iii), and in the content of such pieces as his birthday poems to Rachmaninoff. O'Hara's life and vocation soon shifted permanently with the death of his father, who had nurtured O'Hara's love of music, in early 1947, during O'Hara's second semester of university. From that moment he composed more poetry than music. Although his formal education gave him a thorough grounding in the history and prosody of English poetry (see PROSODY AND FREE VERSE), he considered himself a prose writer for a number of years, "coming to poetry by way of poetic prose" (131). Following his graduation from Harvard in 1950, O'Hara went to the University of Michigan, where he received his master's degree in 1951. He had gone to Ann Arbor on JOHN CIARDI's suggestion; Ciardi taught poetry composition at Harvard and believed O'Hara should go to Michigan with the goal of winning the Avery Hopwood Major Award in poetry, which O'Hara did win in 1951. He received a Rockefeller Fellowship to serve as playwright-in-residence at the Poet's Theatre in Cambridge, Massachusetts during the first six months of 1956. He published six books of poetry, three plays, and a great many essays and reviews; since his early death several collections of poetry have appeared in print, as have collaborations in the form of poem-paintings with visual artists.

O'Hara's early writing combines his exploration of dada and SURREALISM, abstract expressionism, and vernacular speech "to produce a body of exciting experimental poetry" (Perloff ii). His mature work is likewise a fusion of influences, such as Guillaume Apollinaire, Vladimir Mayakovsky, Rainer Maria Rilke, WILLIAM CARLOS WILLIAMS, and EZRA POUND. Also fundamental to O'Hara's poetry was his need for a muse in order to generate the poems that resulted from his great capacity for friendship, his solid situation as an urban poet of New York, and his endless experiences with his vast circle of friends in his city. "Larry Rivers . . . inspired poems of expressionist pain and dazzling surface, [while] Jane Freilicher and Grace Hartigan . . . inspired poems of almost weightless fondness and affection, [and] Vincent Warren was the first muse to inspire O'Hara to openly gay love poems" (Perloff 330). He was so utterly a city poet that he admitted, "I can't even enjoy a blade of grass unless I know there's a subway handy, or a record store" ("Meditations in an Emergency" [1957]).

The immediacy of his work, written in the moment of impulse, makes for a diaristic content in poetic form that O'Hara described as "simply unmade telephone calls" (qtd. in Gooch 150). His recording of events, most pronounced from 1956 on, resulted in poems that were, in his words, "I do this, I do that" poems (qtd. in Gooch 288)—an echo of James Joyce's practice of recording what went on around him as it happened, with which O'Hara would have been very familiar since he read Joyce devotedly. Among his most well-known poems are "THE DAY LADY DIED" (1964), "IN MEMORY OF MY FEELINGS" (1958), and *LUNCH POEMS* (1964), so called at LAWRENCE FERLINGHETTI's suggestion, because O'Hara wrote them on his lunch hours. Death and unhappy love consistently were events provoking O'Hara to write with a "sentimental directness that set his work apart in style" from the other New York poets, and his poems on the death of James Dean brought popular culture into poetry (Gooch 269). Likewise his poem on the collapse of Lana Turner is a typical example of his journalistic style combined with current events in a uniquely poetic way. In "Lana Turner has Collapsed!" (1964), O'Hara opens with the newspaper headline, then discusses the weather conditions, complains briefly about the traffic that impedes his progress to an appointment, and returns to the headline once he situates it in his day and makes clear that the snow and rain in New York are nothing like the weather in California, where Turner's collapse has occurred. He then indirectly tries to comprehend what could cause such an incident, by remarking that he has exhibited shocking behavior in social settings—but "I never actually collapsed"—and immediately concludes the poem with the endearing plea, "oh Lana Turner we love you get up."

O'Hara wrote not only short lyrics in reaction to current conditions and situations, but also longer retrospective pieces, such as "Lament and Chastisement," a 1948 prose memoir of his navy service, and "Ode to Michael Goldberg ('s Birth and Other Births)" (1960), a poem of early life, in which O'Hara "absorbs the family snapshot into the larger movement of life so as to create a dynamic composition" (Perloff 141); then there is "Memorial Day 1950" (1971), which is full of references to figures in his artistic heritage as well as to his childhood. "Second Avenue" (1960) is O'Hara's longest poem; written during March and April 1953, the poem consists of 11 movements and nearly 500 lines. The piece is full of scenes and descriptions, and it is "O'Hara's most ambitious attempt to do with *words* . . . what the Abstract Expressionists were doing with paint" (Perloff 70). It has the inexplicable surrealist "Grappling with images of toothpaste falling on guitar strings," but also the gently erotic lover "lissome in whispering, salivary in intent" and the echoing of remembered advice of his father to "Leave the men alone, they'll only tease you." "Second Avenue" is an important transitional moment in O'Hara's development, containing everything that is typical of O'Hara stylistically, such as colloquialism, exclamation points, enjambed lines, and unique syntax, and in terms of subject matter, including specific people, the city, and art, just at the same time that he moves away from a French surrealism into an American perception. Critic Marjorie Perloff claims that "Ashbery and O'Hara, like ALLEN GINSBERG . . . have an influence that transcends schools and geographic boundaries" (196); these three are poets who "have taken the contemporary lyric down parallel courses that never quite meet" (xiii). O'Hara's critical reputation was building during his lifetime, but his greater impact was on younger poets, who discovered him early and who learned a poetic freedom from him. Those who read most closely saw the depth that can lie beneath speed and spontaneity.

BIBLIOGRAPHY

Diggory, Terence, and Stephen Paul Miller, eds. *The Scene of My Selves: New Work on New York School Poets.* Orono, Maine: National Poetry Foundation, 2000.

Gooch, Brad. *City Poet: The Life and Times of Frank O'Hara.* New York: Knopf, 1993.

Lehman, David. *The Last Avant-Garde: The Making of the New York School of Poets.* New York: Doubleday, 2002.

Perloff, Marjorie. *Frank O'Hara: Poet among Painters.* New York: George Braziller, 1977.

A. Mary Murphy

OLDS, SHARON (1942–)

Sharon Olds is a CONFESSIONAL poet who has published nine books of poetry since 1980. Emily Dickinson, MURIEL RUKEYSER, ANNE SEXTON, and ROBERT LOWELL are among her greatest influences. Olds uses unadorned language coupled with biting imagery to explore themes of sexuality, family relationships, domestic violence (both physical and psychological), and the body. Although her poems often present images of horror and terror, she nonetheless seeks to allow poetry, time, and reflection to bring us, in Peter Harris's words, "back to health" (262).

Raised in San Francisco, California, Olds attended Stanford University and received a Ph.D. from Columbia University in 1972. Her first book of poetry, *Satan Says* (1980), was published when Olds was 37. *The Dead and the Living* (1984) won the Lamont Poetry Prize and the National Book Critics Circle Award, establishing Olds as one of the best new voices in poetry. Olds is founding chair of the writing program at Goldwater Hospital for the severely physically disabled. She was named New York State poet (1998–2000) and has taught at New York University.

The immersion into the dark, graphic world of domestic violence, alcoholism, and social abuses is a staple of Old's poetry. But she is always accessible and has an intense, urgent voice. "By confronting her own 'darkness' fairly," says Carolyne Wright, "Olds has affirmed the humanity of those who engendered that darkness, and shown herself . . . to be a poet of affirmation" (151).

Olds is successful in moving into the violence of domestic and social abuses and becoming part of the same emotive density as those it would appear her poems seek to criticize. In "Fate" (1992), the speaker discusses her relationship with her abusive, alcoholic father, and we see her transformed from a state of hate to one of understanding, which accepts even his "bad breath" and "slumped posture of failure, his sad / sex dangling on his thigh." There is no inflated language or mannerisms here. In "Photograph of the Girl" (1984), reader and speaker together become part of the same emotive fabric as the poem's subject. To produce this effect, the external image of a beautiful victim of starvation is conflated with happenings invisible to a camera.

As the Russian drought of 1921 takes the girl's life, the reader finally sees that deep in the body "ovaries let out her first eggs / golden as drops of grain."

Olds's poetry explores places unseen, sometimes immediately terrifying and sometimes peaceful and redemptive. Olds explores the violence of the world so that she—and readers—may learn how to forgive.

BIBLIOGRAPHY

Harris, Peter. "Four Salvers Salvaging: New Work by Voigt, Olds, Dove, and McHugh." *Virginia Quarterly* 64, no. 2 (1988): 262–276.

Wright, Carolyne. Review of *The Dead and the Living,* by Sharon Olds. *Iowa Review* 15, no. 1 (1985): 151–161.

Robert Leston

OLIVER, MARY (1935–) Rooted in the tradition of American romanticism, the voice of Mary Oliver has become inseparable from the chorus of 20th-century poets concerned with the natural world, including ROBINSON JEFFERS and THEODORE ROETHKE, W. S. MERWIN and DENISE LEVERTOV, GARY SNYDER and WENDELL BERRY. Nature is the subject of Oliver's work, yet her mystical inclinations do not draw her away from a devotion to the civilized use of language and literature.

Oliver was born in Cleveland, Ohio, and was educated at Ohio State University and Vassar College. *No Voyage and Other Poems,* her first book, appeared in 1963. Her sixth collection, *American Primitive,* won the Pulitzer Prize in 1984, and *New and Selected Poems* received the National Book Award in 1993. Oliver's work has also been recognized with a Lannan Foundation Award (1998), a National Endowment for the Arts Fellowship (1972–73), and a Guggenheim Fellowship (1980–81). Oliver has taught at the Fine Arts Workshop in Provincetown, Massachusetts, Case Western Reserve University, Bucknell University, Sweet Briar College, and Bennington College.

The early work—*No Voyage and Other Poems* (1963), *The River Styx, Ohio, and Other Poems* (1972), *Night Traveler* (1978), *Sleeping in the Forest* (1978), and *Twelve Moons* (1979)—draws on Oliver's midwestern roots. The spare, conversational language of the poems is concerned with landscape, longing, and family. The poems in *American Primitive* are inclined toward transcendence. "I want to lose myself," Oliver says in "White Night," enacting the ritual of reconnecting with nature. In *Dream Work* (1986), *House of Light* (1990), and *White Pine* (1994), Oliver's concerns are with the unknown life around us. As Oliver suggests in a later essay, "The world is not what I thought, but different, and more! I have seen it with my own eyes" (*Winter Hours* 88). The themes of revelation and reverence also distinguish her graceful and meditative prose in *Blue Pastures* (1995) and *Winter Hours* (1999).

"Would it be better to sit in silence? / To think everything, to feel everything, to say nothing?" Oliver asks in her book-length poem *The Leaf and the Cloud* (2000). Such is the impulse of the river and the stone, "But the nature of man is not the nature of silence." The nature of man, Oliver admonishes her reader, is wild and civilized—utterly alive in the flesh, obliged to the devotions of curiosity and respect.

BIBLIOGRAPHY

Bonds, Dianne S. "The Language of Nature in the Poetry of Mary Oliver." *Women's Studies: An Interdisciplinary Journal* 21 (1992): 1–15.

Fast, Robin-Riley. "The Native American Presence in Mary Oliver's Poetry." *Kentucky Review* 12, nos. 1–2 (autumn 1993): 59–68.

McNew, Janet. "Mary Oliver and the Tradition of Romantic Nature Poetry." *Contemporary Literature* 30, no. 1 (spring 1989): 59–77.

Oliver, Mary. *Winter Hours: Prose, Prose Poems, and Poems.* New York: Houghton, 1999.

Mark Long

OLSON, CHARLES (1910–1970) Charles Olson is a towering figure in 20th-century American poetry, figuratively and literally (he was 6'10"), and he used his large stature as a basis for his Maximus persona, as in his monumental work *The MAXIMUS POEMS.* Olson also provides a key link between American poets of an earlier generation, such as WILLIAM CARLOS WILLIAMS and EZRA POUND, and his younger contemporaries, such as ROBERT CREELEY and EDWARD DORN, who would come to be known as members of the BLACK MOUNTAIN SCHOOL. His "Projective Verse" essay (1950) stands as a crucial statement of the poetics of open-field composition (see ARS POETICAS).

Olson was born in Worcester, Massachusetts, though childhood experiences in nearby Gloucester, north of Boston, excited a lifelong fascination with this New England fishing village. He produced an account of his relationship with his postman father in *The Post Office* (1975). Olson attended Wesleyan University (1928–32), earning a B.A. and M.A. He later pursued graduate studies at Harvard and taught there from 1936–39. Among his students was a young John F. Kennedy. Olson's own career in government service (1940–45) was cut short, it would seem, due to his strong support of progressive democrat Henry A. Wallace's presidential candidacy. Olson's entry into the literary field came with his highly original work on Herman Melville, *Call Me Ishmael* (1947). His association with Black Mountain College in North Carolina (1951–56) as its rector created the company of writers who came to be known under this name. He used a 1950–51 Guggenheim Fellowship to study ancient Mayan culture in Mexico. His last significant period of teaching came at the State University of New York, Buffalo (1963–65), where he influenced yet another generation of American writers.

Olson entered his period of poetic maturity relatively late. His first surviving poems, such as "La Préface" (1946), came from the time he was revising his earlier scholarly work on Herman Melville into *Call Me Ishmael* (1947). He provides sociohistorical context for *Moby Dick* through reference to the extreme experiences of suffering of Owen Chase and the crew of the *Essex*, a Nantucket-based whaler rammed and sunk by a sperm whale in 1820. He links the nautical experience of these men to the 19th-century movement west across the North American continent, saying: "I take SPACE to be the central fact to man born in America, from Folsom cave to now. I spell it large because it comes large here. Large, and without mercy" (*Collected Prose* 17). Olson's research included the physical reconstruction of Melville's personal library, leading to his discovery of the genesis of *Moby Dick* in the marginal notations to Melville's copy of *King Lear*. This research fed the historical imagination of his first poems in a way that has come to be recognized as postmodern, a word which he is often credited with using for the first time in its currently accepted meaning. In "La Préface," Olson addresses in a prescient way the meaning of the Nazi concentration camp, calling "Buchenwald new Altamira cave," thereby linking the horrors of the Holocaust to the earliest known human art forms and calling on readers to reflect on the full range of recorded human history. Already highly advanced in his myth thinking, Olson takes the figure of Odysseus as an early persona. He also faces directly the problem of giving meaning to the incomprehensible: "The closed parenthesis reads: the dead bury the dead, / and it is not very interesting" (47).

Also in the immediate aftermath of World War II, Olson instigated an intense literary friendship with Pound, who was being held at St. Elizabeth's Hospital in Washington, D.C., after having been found incompetent to stand trial for treason. Olson's essay "This Is Yeats Speaking" (1946) seeks to provide a hearing of sorts for the incarcerated elder poet. By 1950 Olson had broken off his visits to Pound, due to Pound's unregenerate support for fascist ideology. At this time Olson was contacted by Creeley, leading to an epistolary relationship that changed both of their poetic careers. From Creeley, Olson took the central tenet of his "Projective Verse" essay that "FORM IS NEVER MORE THAN AN EXTENSION OF CONTENT" (*Collected Prose* 240). Olson's letters to Creeley from his archaeological sojourn to the Yucatán Peninsula in Mexico became known as *The Mayan Letters*. Poet and critic NATHANIEL MACKEY has written: "The ancient Maya represented an alternative to the reign of abstraction [Olson] argues against, an orientation that refuses to depreciate the phenomenal world or to take it for granted . . ." (126). Creeley later joined Olson at Black Mountain College.

This intense period of literary activity by Olson saw the publication of some of his most celebrated shorter poems, such as "The Kingfishers" (1950) and "In Cold Hell, In Thicket" (1951). The same period witnessed the germination of Olson's life-long epic-length poem, *The Maximus Poems* (1960–83). The publication of Olson's correspondence with Frances Boldereff has given unprecedented insight into Boldereff's role in helping Olson to attain the multifaceted vision of his ambitious epic. The poem begins with the declaration of the Maximus persona's identity: "Off-shore, by islands hidden in the blood / jewels & miracles, I, Maximus." Olson uses this persona to achieve a complex interweaving of the literary, sociohistorical, mythical, and geological dimensions of the poem. Albert Cook has proposed: "In Olson's critical writings the historical-microscopic, the geographical-millenial, and the archetypal, are reasoned into interdependence over and over again. He angles those interdependences into *The Maximus Poems* in such a way that the images, though 'flat' and in a seemingly linear sequence, transcend the found objects or actions with which they begin" ("Maximizing" 158). By this understanding, the physical location of the poem in Gloucester affords Olson a way of linking place and history. According to Charles Stein, "Geography and historical geology are given primary attention in presenting the human action of the poem" (121). Over time the significance of Olson's achievement in *The Maximus Poems* has come to overshadow the brilliance of his work in shorter forms.

In the course of the later progression of *The Maximus Poems,* Olson's vision becomes more directly personal, based on the self-orienting turn he refers to as *tropos.* Peter Baker has written: "the self-orienting of *tropos* allows Olson to make what he calls the 'LEAP' from the geography of actual place, actual reality, to the comprehensive mythological view that serves as humankind's guide back to that reality" (94). In the second volume of the poem, for example, Olson writes, "my memory is / the history of time." He also writes, "I am making a mappemunde. It is to include my being." Historical memory and the mapping of physical geography merge with the personal vision of the poet. As Don Byrd has argued, "The *maximus* . . . gives evidence of the adequacy and reality of Olson's *own* time, and, in our reading, evidence of the adequacy and reality of our own time. Unlike disciplinary, statistical knowledge, it makes itself available to us . . . by proposing specific concrete acts of knowing" (363). Olson's unique contribution to American poetry of the 20th century was to propose a poetry as well as a poetics that were also and always a way of knowing the world.

BIBLIOGRAPHY

Baker, Peter. "Poetic Subjectivity in Olson's *Maximus Poems.*" In *Obdurate Brilliance.* Gainesville: University of Florida Press, 1991, pp. 94–107.

Byrd, Don. *The Poetics of the Common Knowledge.* Albany: State University of New York Press, 1994.

Cook, Albert. "Maximizing Minimalism: The Construct of Image in Olson and Creeley." In *Figural Choice in Poetry and Art.* Hanover, N. H.: University Press of New England, 1985, pp. 149–166.

———. *Myth and Language.* Bloomington: Indiana University Press, 1980.

Mackey, Nathaniel. "That Words Can Be on the Page: The Graphic Aspect of Charles Olson's Poetry." In *Discrepant Engagement.* New York: Cambridge University Press, 1993, pp. 121–138.

Maud, Ralph. *Charles Olson's Reading: A Biography.* Carbondale: Southern Illinois University Press, 1996.

Olson, Charles. *Collected Prose,* edited by Donald Allen and Benjamin Friedlander. Berkeley: University of California Press, 1997.

———. *Selected Writings,* edited by Robert Creeley, New York: New Directions, 1966.

Stein, Charles. *The Secret of the Black Chrysanthemum.* Barrytown, N.Y.: Station Hill Press, 1987.

Peter Baker

OLSON, TOBY (1937–) Toby Olson's pacing, rhythms, and themes are evocative of ROBERT CREELEY. His conversational approach is reminiscent of DAVID ANTIN's talk poems. And, generally, he shares a poetic kinship with such innovators as JOHN TAGGART and JACKSON MAC LOW. His work shows influences from romanticism's return to nature, MODERNISM's revival of epic tropes, and the NEW YORK SCHOOL's emphasis on speech patterns. Olson engages these traditions while transforming them into his own particular style courageous enough to stare down divorce, socioeconomic politics, carcinoma, immigration policies, and racism in his characteristically breathless cadences.

Merle Theodore Olson was born in Berwyn, Illinois, but there is little evidence of this midwestern beginning in his writing. Perhaps Olson's early disposition toward places and pacing are more easily traced to his days in the United States Navy from 1957–61, during which time he served as a surgical technician. Taking to the sea and water are repeated undercurrents through much of Olson's work, but, even more, the simultaneous skills of diligent observer and precise craftsmanship demanded of surgeons define Olson's relationship to writing. After military duty Olson pursued a B.A. at Occidental College and subsequently a master's degree from Long Island University. He has served on numerous faculties and writer residencies, and he has dedicated his teaching career to Temple University, starting in 1975. He has received a number of fellowships, and his acclaimed novel, *Seaview* (1983), was recognized with the PEN/Faulkner Award for fiction.

Throughout his career, just as ROBERT DUNCAN continuously wrote *PASSAGES* or JOHN BERRYMAN endlessly wrote *DREAM SONGS*, Olson has composed "Standards." In these "Standard" poems, by employing jazz's technique of creating subtle differences through repetition, Olson reminds readers how words—through rhythm, tempo, and cadence—make music. "Standard-9, Just One (Some) of Those Things" (1993) demonstrates how a single memory rolls into other memories, how a dream riffs on the original experience: "these strange conglomerates? . . . / how turn the body off from dreaming?" Since he is a renowned fiction writer as well as poet, it is not surprising that his writing operates fluidly, flowing back and forth across genre divisions, illustrating how memory ebbs between past and present. Olson's most acclaimed novels fall within the detective story genre, and so too his poems grapple with the mystery of memory. Much as a detective collects clues, Olson's speakers collect memories as snapshots which fuse into a collage of dizzying beauty.

As the titles of his most recent collections imply, Olson is interested in how *Human Nature* (2000) remains a process of *Unfinished Building* (1993). Similar to the way a building under construction, complete with external scaffolding, houses the internal hopes of what is to come, Olson's poems avoid enclosures, simple symmetries, and neat conclusions. His speakers set out in each poem to discover where the paths of memory will lead. The goal is not some hidden treasure chest of lyric "truth"; rather it is the search itself which keeps us fascinated. Olson's poems remain standards to be played over and over, each one perpetually building stories and making poetic music that will never be finished.

BIBLIOGRAPHY

Olsen, Lance, and Dennis Barone, eds. *Review of Contemporary Fiction* 11, no. 2 (summer 1991). [Donald Barthelme/Toby Olson Issue]

Owens, Rochelle. Review of *Human Nature*, by Toby Olson. *World Literature Today* 74, no. 3 (summer 2000): 599–600.

Barbara Cole

"ONE ART" ELIZABETH BISHOP **(1976)** "The art of losing isn't hard to master," writes ELIZABETH BISHOP in "One Art," a central poem from *Geography III*, which many critics consider Bishop's greatest book (Kalstone, 251). The poem is a masterful villanelle, its refrains troubled by, yet cheerfully confronting, exile, the desire for home, and the loss of love. It is also one of Bishop's most personal poems, beginning with a catalog of mundane losses and accidents that quickly escalates to a series of disasters, many of them subtle allusions to Bishop's life. In writing of the heartrending difficulty with which poetry moderates grief, Bishop creates an ARS POETICA that highlights the central themes of her work.

In the opening stanza, the speaker tries convincing herself and the audience that one can stoically accept loss as "no disaster." The tone is characteristic of Bishop—casual, comically rather than tragically ironic, and memorable in its phrasings. In the second stanza, the speaker treats loss not as an abstraction but as a common, concrete experience. She begins with the mundane, speaking of "lost door keys" and "the hour badly spent," but these ordinary events foreshadow more devastating losses in the stanzas that follow. The idea that disaster pervades everyday life is crucial to the poem, belying the repeated claim that grief can be mastered gracefully, by art or any other means.

The lost door keys prefigure the disappearance of houses, cities, rivers, a continent, and finally even the idea of home, and by describing these homes with adjectival forms of "love" ("loved houses," "lovely [cities]"), Bishop associates this exile with the loss of personal love. Bishop's biography illuminates "the events that evoke the sense of loss" in the middle stanzas. Her childhood was split between the homes of her maternal and paternal grandparents in Nova Scotia, Boston, and Worcester, Massachusetts, after her father's early death and her mother's institutionalization. During the 1950s, Bishop lived in Brazil with her partner, Lota de Macedo Soares, though Bishop separated from her and left the country in the mid-1960s. Soares's suicide in 1967 seems to shadow the poem, though critic Brett Candish Millier believes that personal conflicts with Bishop's partner Alice Metfessel inspired it more directly (234). Ultimately, Bishop's cool, classical tone keeps these biographical disputes at a distance: her theme is the universal experience of personal loss.

These losses never seem to overwhelm the speaker, or so she would have us believe: "I miss them, but it wasn't a disaster." Speaking of the lost beloved, Bishop's artistic mastery seems too poised to be credible: "Even losing you (the joking voice, a gesture / I love) I shan't have lied." By its close, the villanelle form works ironically against the speaker, its refrains sounding like the speaker's effort to convince herself of her own claims. Faced with total loss, Bishop exclaims that one must "(*Write* it!)," but however therapeutic such expression may be, it is a momentary stay at best, always subject to change (Costello, 2). As poet-critic J. D. MCCLATCHY writes, "The [last] stanza is in danger of breaking apart, and breaking down. In this last line the poet's voice literally cracks" (145). Like any art, Bishop suggests, mastering loss must be practiced continuously, but with only the appearance of mastery a promised result.

BIBLIOGRAPHY

Costello, Bonnie. *Elizabeth Bishop: Questions of Mastery*. Cambridge, Mass: Harvard University Press, 1991.

Kalstone, David, and Robert Hemenway, ed. *Becoming a Poet: Elizabeth Bishop with Marianne Moore and Robert Lowell*. New York: Farrar Straus & Giroux, 1989.

McClatchy, J. D. *White Paper: On Contemporary American Poetry*. New York: Columbia University Press, 1989.

Millier, Brett Candlish. "Elusive Mastery: The Drafts of Elizabeth Bishop's 'One Art.'" In *Elizabeth Bishop: The Geography of Gender*, edited by Marilyn May Lombardi, 233–243. Charlottesville: University Press of Virginia, 1993.

Temple Cone

OPPEN, GEORGE (1908–1984)

George Oppen came to prominence in the early 1930s as part of the OBJECTIVIST SCHOOL. The objectivists were linked to the IMAGIST SCHOOL and were heavily influenced by WILLIAM CARLOS WILLIAMS. In addition to Oppen, the group most notably included LOUIS ZUKOFSKY, CARL RAKOSI, and CHARLES REZNIKOFF. Oppen's distinctive, spare style stayed consistent through the eight books of poetry that appeared between 1934 and 1978. His understated control and economy of phrase also influenced writers and movements as varied as Paul Auster, WILLIAM BRONK, J. H. Prynne, LOUISE GLÜCK, MICHAEL PALMER, and the LANGUAGE SCHOOL.

Oppen was born in New Rochelle, New York, and grew up in San Francisco. After an unhappy time at a military academy, he attended Oregon State University in Corvallis. There he read CONRAD AIKEN's anthology of modern poetry, a pivotal moment in his life. There too he met his lifelong companion, Mary Colby. They quit college and set out, as she put it, to "discover the world" (Mary Oppen 64). Oppen's early work with the objectivists brought him attention, but his later work—after a 20-year silence—brought him awards: the PEN/West Rediscovery Award (1982); lifetime recognition awards from the American Academy of Poets (1980), the National Endowment for the Arts (1980), and the American Academy and Institute of Arts and Letters (1980); and in 1969 the Pulitzer Prize for *Of Being Numerous*.

In 1934 the Objectivist Press published Oppen's *DISCRETE SERIES*, with a preface from EZRA POUND and an appreciative review in *Poetry* magazine from Williams. This slim book demonstrates how his clear and concrete minimalism was won from the verbose style that was still fashionable in the 1920s. The series begins by juxtaposing a pastiche of grandiose sentimentalism—"the world, weather-swept, with which one shares the century"—with his more prosaic choices that are no less profound for being simple. From here his urban lines carry on from Williams and describe the machined cityscape of a New York full of bolts and ships and "Deaths everywhere—."

Discrete Series was followed by three phases of an extended period of silence. First, during the depression, Oppen joined the Communist Party to devote himself to poverty relief work. He needed to do something in the physical, political world that poetry could not affect. In the second phase, he enlisted and fought for the United States Army. Finally, after his return to civilian life and a brief stint in California, he spent 1950–58 with his wife and daughter in self-imposed exile in Mexico avoiding the House Un-American Activities Committee (HUAC) and others engaged in the communist "witch-hunt."

In 1962 Oppen published *The Materials,* which he had begun in 1958 just before leaving Mexico—it was his first new book for almost 30 years. The word *materials* in the title refers both to the physical presence of things in the world and also to the "material" of Marxist "dialectical materialism." In as concrete a way as possible Oppen includes both the tactile world and his tangible experience of the abstract ideas of Marxism in which Hegel's philosophical model of discourse is played out materially through class-structures in the political world. *The Materials* is similar in style to *Discrete Series.* In "Blood from the Stone," Oppen even observes people in the street; the decade of the 1930s "Is still in their lives." In an even more specific movement of identification with his earlier work, Oppen refers to the earlier poem and its era as "our times." The book is a series of poems that brings him up to date, not only from the 1934 *Discrete Series* but also from "'Birthplace: New Rochelle'" to his present situation as a father himself, returning physically and symbolically to "The house / My father's once."

This in Which (1965) confirmed Oppen's return to writing and provided initial versions of title poems for three of his next books ("Of Being Numerous" that was originally titled "A Language of New York," "Alpine," and "Primitive"). It followed *The Materials* in talking about class and, especially in the series "Five Poems about Poetry," about poetry's relation to class structure. For Oppen the interconnectedness of individual and global events is key, and he emphasizes this at the opening of the book through the content and the eclectic epigraphs from Robert Heinlein and Martin Heidegger. Even in the final poem, "World, World—," Oppen criticizes the "medical faddism" of the contemporary obsession with the self and suggests instead that the mystery of existence is an individual who is simultaneously local—"here"—and historical—"More than oneself."

Oppen's next book, *Of Being Numerous* (1968), directly confronted the historical. Returning to the Bay Area after a trip to Europe, he wrote his most obviously polemical collection, including the eponymous title poem "OF BEING NUMEROUS." He espoused multicultural tolerance—the "numerous"—and opposed the Vietnam War—"Ours aren't the only madmen tho they have burned thousands." *Of Being Numerous* was originally called *Another Language of New York,* after the 40-poem series which comprises the bulk of the book—an expanded version of the poem "A Language of New York" from the volume *This in Which.* The ensuing Pulitzer Prize success guaranteed the book a wider circulation than any of his previous work, although the poetry showed no political or formal concessions.

In *Seascape: Needle's Eye* (1972), Oppen concerns himself with the horizon of the Pacific Ocean. This "sea and a crescent strip of beach" and the biblical aphorism that it is as easy for a rich man to go to heaven as for a camel to pass through a needle's eye give the collection its title. *Seascape* is inescapably about the West (215), as the 10 poems in "Some San Francisco Poems" remind us. It marks his return to the place where he grew up and also to his involvement with the younger San Francisco (see SAN FRANCISCO RENAISSANCE) poets and European poets of the late 1960s. Despite its brevity this book deals seriously with history from geographical, political, and theological perspectives, noting the marks of power, history, and even potential salvation, on the Bay landscape—"a kind of redemption / Exposed still and jagged on the San Francisco hills" ("Some San Francisco Poems—4. Anniversary Poem"). This seriousness notwithstanding, Oppen finds grounds for optimism—this is, after all, the needle's eye that, surprisingly, gives access to heaven. In the closing poem "Exodus," he links his poetry directly to his belief in the future. The poem, whose subject matter is already the divine deliverance from bondage, stops unfinished and invites us to read the living future of the children as the continuation of ". . . Miracle / of."

In *Myth of the Blaze* (1975), the "blaze" of the title comes from William Blake's 19th-century blazing "tygers" (the stars in the night sky), and the collection is explicitly involved with the history of writing poetry from the Book of Job to 16th-century Sir Thomas Wyatt, Shakespeare, and Blake right up to Oppen, Reznikoff, and Zukofsky. Oppen's final book, *Primitive* (1978), owes more to his wife, Mary, than any of his previous books, and it is difficult to know how far the early symptoms of Alzheimer's disease affected his writing. Entering his seventies and looking back on a decade since his Pulitzer Prize, Oppen reflects on his achievements as a man, a poet, and a famous poet. Oddly it is the opening of the book that dwells more on his state of life. In both "Disasters" and "To Make Much," respectively, he reflects obliquely on his ebbing vitality: "the desert my life / narrows," and "we are old / we are shrivelled." Although still keenly aware of his failing faculties, in "Populist," he regains some of his hope for the young.

Oppen was a craftsman for whom each poem was a crafted object. The concentration on the object in his early objectivism refers to "the objectification of the poem, the making of an object of the poem" ("Interview" 160), and his writing adhered to this ideal of craftsmanship throughout his career.

BIBLIOGRAPHY

Hatlen, Burton, ed. *George Oppen, Man and Poet.* Orono, Maine: National Poetry Foundation, 1981.

———, ed. *Paideuma* 10, no. 1 (1981). [Special Issue on George Oppen]

Oppen, George. Interview conducted by L. S. Dembo. *Contemporary Literature* 10, no. 2 (1969): 159–177.

Oppen, Mary. *Meaning A Life: An Autobiography.* Santa Barbara, Calif.: Black Sparrow Press, 1978.

Dan Friedman

OPPENHEIMER, JOEL (1930–1988) Joel Oppenheimer was a student of CHARLES OLSON's at BLACK MOUNTAIN College in the 1950s and published in the avant-garde journals *Origin* and the *Black Mountain Review.* While the early influences on his writing came from E. E. CUMMINGS and Don Marquis, it was the poetry of WILLIAM CARLOS WILLIAMS and the instruction of Olson that made him into a successful poet. He appeared in the first section of the now famous *The New American Poetry* in 1960 (see POETRY ANTHOLOGIES and POETRY JOURNALS), along with Olson, ROBERT DUNCAN, EDWARD DORN, and ROBERT CREELEY. The discursive style and his commitment to the open form of poetry, the generation of the form of the poem from inside the act of writing (see PROSODY AND FREE VERSE), make him a Black Mountain poet, but he was a Black Mountain poet who acknowledged the influence of the time and temper of New York City in his writing. While he experiments in using only lower case and no uppercase letters appear from time to time, Oppenheimer's use of these features remains unique in American poetry since 1945.

Oppenheimer was born in Yonkers, New York, and grew up in New York City in a middle-class Jewish family. He discovered his interest in poetry while in high school, but he went to Cornell, then University of Chicago for a technical education before finding Black Mountain College, where he was a student of M. C. Richard, Paul Goodman, and Olson. In 1966 he became director of the St. Mark's Poetry Project (see POETRY INSTITUTIONS). Between 1966 and 1968 he developed a program that grew into the "Poets in the Schools" project, which continues through the present. Between 1969 and 1984 he wrote a regular column for the *Village Voice* on baseball, public issues, and political themes, the news of the city. By 1980, however, he began looking outside of New York for a place to live. In 1982 he secured a position teaching at New England College (he had taught previously at the City College of New York).

Oppenheimer's early books—*The Dancer* (1951) and *The Dutiful Son* (1956)—were published by JONATHAN WILLIAMS, who was also a student at Black Mountain College. The poems from 1959–62, published as *Just Friends/Friends and Lovers* (1980) fill out the record of the early writing. With the publication of *The Love Bit and Other Poems* (1962), Oppenheimer had established a distinctive style built on short lines, frequent enjambment, intricate metrical measures (developments coming from a close reading of William Carlos Williams's poems), and, most of all, lowercase—and no uppercase—letters. He developed a discursive style that allowed all kinds of information to come into the poem even as it maintained multiple points of view in sharp metaphors without a symbolic structure. He called his line the "flat line." The pivotal poem of this early period is "The Fourth Ark Royal" (1959), which talks about the men from the British warship *Ark Royal,* the news of people and events at the Cedar Tavern in New York City, and events in the poet's life.

In Time: Poems 1962–1968 (1969) was Oppenheimer's first book published with a trade publisher, and that was followed by the second, *On Occasion: Some Births, Deaths, Weddings, Birthday, Holidays, and Other Events* (1973). He was now a master of the occasional poem, a poem for a wedding or birth, family things. These poems, such as "The Polish Cavalry" (1970) written after Olson's death, "A Wedding" written on the occasion of a friend's wedding, "For Matthew Dead" written after the death of Paul Goodman's son, and "A Poem for Children" (1970), written in response to the anti–Vietnam War movement and other political movements, all have the features of honoring specific occasions with a patient telling of circumstances and a poetic line supported by finely tuned measures and cadences.

His columns for the *Village Voice* (1969–84) added another dimension to Oppenheimer's writing. He could deal in prose with political movements, mainly the Vietnam War protests, public issues of life in New York, and family affairs, freeing his poetry for meditations on other subjects. The result was a major book of American poetry, *The Women Poems* (1975). He took his lead from ROBERT BLY's book, *Sleepers Joining Hands* (1973), in finding information about the eternal female goddess, but he added his own obsessions about sex and women and his intense personal relationships. *The Women Poems* are a serial poem in which each poem explores one aspect of the central theme, but together they form a sustained, meditative narrative (see LONG AND SERIAL POETRY). By the next major collection, *New Spaces; Poems 1975–1983* (1985), Oppenheimer was moving on to other concerns without forgetting the great value of ordinary events; he was exploring new spaces, as well as new ways in which his poetry could create spaces for living as an imaginative act. "A Village Poem," for example, is a meditation on places and people associated with the Cedar Tavern, such as the artists Franz Kline and Jackson Pollock whom he would meet there: Oppenheimer invokes "history" and says that "it is where the paintings / come from and the poems." Oppenheimer's poetics change complex ideas of history and personal passions into simple grammatical statements. The poems move from line to line smoothly with recurrences of vowel and consonant sounds. And yet the poems turn out to be metrically complex and conceptually profound. Also notable from this collection is the poem "CACTI."

After this large collection smaller books followed, such as *The Uses of Adversity* (1987), a long poem describing the effects of chemotherapy on Oppenheimer's mind and body, naming the chemicals and recording the effects, but with wit and an affirmation of the value of living even as the illness advances. The last poems were published as *New Hampshire Journal* (1994).

Oppenheimer will be remembered as the master of the occasional poem. He will also be known as a poet who celebrated living and the rituals of living and who insisted that life, love, and erotic desires should be celebrated along with marriages, the new season, and deaths. He made simple and graceful statements.

BIBLIOGRAPHY

Butterick, George F. *Joel Oppenheimer: A Checklist of His Writings.* Storrs: University of Connecticut Library, 1975.

Gilmore, Lyman. *Don't Touch the Poet: The Life and Times of Joel Oppenheimer.* Jersey City, N.J.: Talisman House, 1998.

Thibodaux, David. *Joel Oppenheimer: An Introduction.* Columbia, S.C.: Camden House, 1986.

Robert Bertholf

ORR, GREGORY (1947–) Of all the poets influenced by the DEEP IMAGE poetry of ROBERT BLY and JAMES WRIGHT, Gregory Orr has most fully explored the psychological significance of the illuminating image. His lyric style, often autobiographical and more imagistic than metaphorical, is as spare and engaging as that of his predecessors, but is profoundly original in its exploration of the psychology of vulnerability, trauma, and healing. A poet for whom "Saying the word / Is seizing the world," Orr's body of "personal lyric" poetry (his term for the semiautobiographical poetry he both writes and theorizes about) is as psychologically resonant as any autobiographical poetry written today.

Born in Albany, New York, Gregory Simpson Orr lived a bucolic childhood, and the natural world figures importantly in his poetry. When he was 12, he accidentally killed his brother in a hunting accident, tragically repeating his own father's accidental slaying of a childhood friend. A year later, Orr's father, a brilliant, amphetamine-addicted physician, moved the family to Haiti, where he volunteered at an American-run hospital and where, that year, Orr's mother died of complications from a routine surgery. The struggle to recover meaning and psychological wholeness from traumatic events such as these would later become thematically central to Orr's work. After returning to upstate New York, Orr discovered his own poetic aspirations, entered college, and participated in Civil Rights protests in the South, for which he was jailed, beaten, and threatened with death. But even in the midst of such political endeavors, the imagination always proved central for Orr; in "Solitary Confinement," he writes of how "They've taken the SNCC pamphlets / but let me keep a book / of Keats."

Orr received a B.A. from Antioch College (1969) and an M.F.A. in creative writing from Columbia University (1972). His poetry won early acclaim, receiving an Academy of American Poets prize (1970), and over his career Orr has received fellowships from the Guggenheim Foundation and the National Endowment for the Arts (twice), and has been a Rockefeller Fellow at the Institute for Culture and Survival. He has received the Virginia Prize for Poetry (1984) and the American Academy of Arts and Letters Award in Literature (2003). A former poetry consultant for the *Virginia Quarterly Review* (1976–2003), he has been professor of English at the University of Virginia since 1975.

For Orr, lyric poetry can order the chaos of personal experience; his work thus compares thematically with that of his close friend, the poet JANE KENYON, though Orr does not share Kenyon's solacing Christian beliefs. Orr's primary means of ordering chaos is, as Steven Cramer notes, "[F]igurative language [that] evolves away from metaphor, simile, and the totemic emblem to perceived details chosen for their emotional resonance" (232). Though these details are often drawn from the poet's autobiography, Orr's vision of poetry is not CONFESSIONAL, because healing and resolution, not self-expression, are the ultimate purposes of such details. Nor is Orr content with mere autobiography; Hank Lazer notes that Orr finds particular power in the "the story based on myth, on repetition, on resonance, and on a central image" (43). In his memoir, *The Blessing,* Orr writes of how he came to terms with his brother's death by comparing himself to the biblical fratricide Cain: "[S]tories are where human meanings begin. If I were Cain, I knew who I was and where I was situated in the universe" (28). Orr's focus on myth and repetition explains not only the recurrence of mythical figures and motifs in his poems, but also his recent experiments in the villanelle, which Orr considers a vehicle for relieving and maintaining obsessive, apparently unresolvable experiences. As he writes in "Some Part of the Lyric," "[I]ts beauty, / like that of a tear or a globe of dew, / reflects the world it meant to exclude." Preservation of life in a poem, whether of the darkest memories or the gentlest, is the secret to survival and ultimately of immortality for Orr; as he writes in his most recent work, the book-length poem *Concerning the Book That Is the Body of the Beloved,* writing and reading poems "[I]s the reciprocity of love / That outwits death. Death looks / In one place and we're in the other. // Death looks there, but we are here."

BIBLIOGRAPHY

Cramer, Steve. "Poems Will Be Poems." *Poetry* 182, no. 4 (2003): 230–235.

Lazer, Hank. "Gregory Orr: Resources of the Personal Lyric." *The American Poetry Review* 32, no. 6 (2003): 43–51.

Orr, Gregory. *The Blessing: A Memoir.* San Francisco: Council Oak Books, 2002.

Temple Cone

ORTIZ, SIMON J. (1941–) During the American Indian renaissance of the 1960s and 1970s, Simon Ortiz emerged as one of the most influential American Indian writers. Though also a fiction writer, essayist, and filmmaker, he remains best known for his poetry. Ortiz sees his work as that of reclaiming, revitalizing, and demystifying language to enable Native peoples to "come into being as who we are within the reality we face" (27). With a colloquial voice and accessible, usually narrative form, Ortiz revitalizes the oral traditions of his Navaho Acoma heritage, using creation stories, animal voices, and the rhythms of ceremonial songs and chants (see NARRATIVE POETRY).

Born in Albuquerque, New Mexico, Ortiz was raised in an Acoma-speaking family in the village of Deetziyamah. At government and religious schools, he was "socialized" into American culture and became aware of his inclusion in, and exclusion from, that world. His education was completed at Fort Lewis College (1962–63), the University of New Mexico (1966–68), and the University of Iowa's Writers' Workshop (M.F.A., 1969). He has taught at California State University, the University of New Mexico, and Sinte Gleska College in Rosebud, South Dakota. Ortiz works actively for Native interests and has assumed leadership positions in tribal government. He has received a National Endowment for the Arts Discovery Award (1969), an NEA Fellowship (1981), and the Pushcart Prize for poetry (1981).

Ortiz's first collection, *Going for the Rain* (1976), recounts in contemporary settings a traditional journey of awakening manifested through an identification with the land and the Acoma people. *A Good Journey* (1977), his second collection, employs traditional storytelling techniques: personification of animals, multiple voicings, dramatic monologue, quotation, embedded story, and second-person address. He observes, "The only way to continue is to tell a story and that's what Coyote says" (153). In "Telling about Coyote," for example, a traditional speaker explains how coyote created the trouble in the world; coyote (who is described as "existential Man") says, "'Things are just too easy . . .' / Of course he was mainly . . . shooting his mouth." In his third collection, *Fight Back: For the Sake of the People, For the Sake of the Land* (1980), Ortiz commemorates the Pueblo Indian Revolt of 1680. The first part, "Too Many Sacrifices," laments the suffering caused by corporate domination of the land and people; the second part, "No More Sacrifices," is a prose memoir and cultural history interspersed with poems. *From Sand Creek* (1981) retells the story of a 19th-century massacre at Fort Lyons, Colorado, and seeks through storytelling a healing of both Native and European Americans. *After and Before Lightning* (1994) chronicles a winter on the Rosebud Lakota Reservation with poems of celebration and prayers for continued survival.

In all of his work, Ortiz confronts the exploitation and loss suffered by Native peoples, yet he always reaches back, brings forward, and celebrates the old traditions with the aim of healing and renewal.

BIBLIOGRAPHY

Allen, Paula Gunn. *The Sacred Hoop*. Boston: Beacon Press, 1986.

Ortiz, Simon J. *Woven Stone*. Tucson: University of Arizona Press, 1992.

Siget, Andrew. *Simon Ortiz*. Boise, Idaho: Boise State University, 1986.

Michael Sowder

OSTRIKER, ALICIA SUSKIN (1937–)

Alicia Ostriker stands in the company of feminist poet/critics, including ADRIENNE RICH, AUDRE LORDE, and MARGE PIERCY, who helped create—and were influenced by—the United States feminist movement (see FEMALE VOICE, FEMALE LANGUAGE). Ostriker's critical and poetic contributions to American letters are a significant record of an observant, thinking, politically aware woman who examines her experiences in light of the political and social circumstances that surround her. A hallmark of Ostriker's work is her ability to mix personal reflection with political observation. A particularly powerful example of this is *The Mother/Child Papers* (1980), which juxtaposes poems about her family, particularly the birth of her son, with political commentary on the Vietnam War.

Born in Brooklyn, New York, Ostriker grew up in Manhattan housing projects in a working-class Jewish family. Graduating with a B.A. in English from Brandeis University in 1959, Ostriker continued her education at the University of Wisconsin, earning an M.A. (1961) and a Ph.D. (1964). Ostriker has been a professor at Rutgers University since 1965. The author of nine volumes of poetry, two significant works of feminist literary criticism (*Writing like a Woman* [1983] and *Stealing the Language: The Emergence of Women's Poetry in America* [1986]), two groundbreaking works of biblical analysis, and several other works of criticism, Ostriker is the winner of numerous honors and awards, including, for her 1986 collection, *The Imaginary Lover*, the WILLIAM CARLOS WILLIAMS Award of the Poetry Society of America and, for her 1996 *The Crack in Everything*, the Paterson Poetry Award and the San Francisco State University Poetry Center Award.

Reflecting on her experience as a Jewish-American woman of the 20th century, Ostriker's poetry is accessible, conversational in tone, and quick to combine cultural or spiritual critique with observations of her immediate surroundings. In *A Woman under the Surface* (1982), many of the poems, including "The Waiting Room" and "The Exchange," look at women's experiences, the former examining "the fears of the betrayal / Of our bodies" and the latter exploring anger, revenge, and freedom from women's roles. Later works, less formal than her first, continue these themes, examining motherhood, relationships, art, religion, and healing, among other issues, from an unabashedly political and feminist perspective. Especially significant is the final section of *The Crack in Everything* (1996), "The Mastectomy Poems," which chronicle her treatment for breast cancer. Ostriker's ability to artfully enhance her observations of life with insightful political and social critique is a consistent feature of her work.

BIBLIOGRAPHY

Cook, Pamela. "Secrets and Manifestos: Alicia Ostriker's Poetry and Politics." *Borderlands: Texas Poetry Review* 2 (spring 1993): 80–86.

Ostriker, Alicia. "An Interview with Alicia Ostriker," by Katharyn Aal. *Poets and Writers Magazine* 17, no. 6 (November/December 1989): 16–26.

Williams, Amy. "Alicia Ostriker." In *Dictionary of Literary Biography*. Vol. 120, *American Poets since World War II*, edited by R. S. Gwynn. Detroit, Mich.: Gale Research, 1982, pp. 239–242.

Sharon L. Barnes

"O TASTE AND SEE" DENISE LEVERTOV (1964) The title poem in DENISE LEVERTOV's 1964 collection of poetry, "O Taste and See" is a strong statement of her poetics. "The world is / not with us enough," she begins, and her opening lines do more than just allude to William Wordsworth's sonnet ("The World Is Too Much with Us" [1807]); they contradict it and in doing so signal not only Levertov's movement away from the formalism of her poetic predecessors but also her rejection of the classification "New romantic" given to her when she was a young writer. The formalism and conventional style of earlier poets (including her younger self) were challenged by her evolving use of organic form and her development of poetry in which metrical patterns and highly formal diction were discarded in favor of direct utterance and the use of what WILLIAM CARLOS WILLIAMS called the "variable foot," a metrical system based on the rhythm of everyday language rather than the meter of traditional poetry (see PROSODY AND FREE VERSE).

Levertov wants to teach us that when we embrace "all that lives," we embrace the world and all the things within it, things we not only see but also take within our very selves: wind, rain, fruit, color, even the words we speak. Our embrace of "all that lives" means we are totally alive to the experience of life, and, for Levertov, life also means poetry. Everyday experiences inspire the poetry she writes, and the Bible poster the speaker of this poem sees on the subway is, in itself, a reference to this poetry of human experience through its quotation from Psalm 34 ("O taste and see that the Lord is good!"), for the Psalms themselves are poems. "O Taste and See," then, is a poem about the small things that lend our lives grace and beauty because of their quotidian and poetic nature.

The subway poster with its biblical quotation is not the only example of the secularization of religious experience and the experience of human life this represents. Transubstantiation (as in the Christian Mass) here becomes the way in which we are able to face the fact of our eventual death and weave it into our lives, and the fall of Adam and Eve becomes the means by which we can gain the knowledge we need to lead a full and joyfully engaged life. Levertov's use of the fall is also a reference to the romantic poets (who turned to secularized versions of the story of the Garden of Eden as a means of examining human experience), and once again we see that Levertov is signaling a change from the work of her poetic predecessors; while the fall was a morality tale for the romantics, it becomes here a lesson in how to embrace life—a lesson, in other words, in how to taste and see.

BIBLIOGRAPHY

Rodgers, Audrey T. *Denise Levertov: The Poetry of Engagement*. Rutherford, N.J.: Fairleigh Dickinson University Press, 1993.

Wagner, Linda W. *Denise Levertov*. New York: Twayne, 1967.

Wendy Galgan

"OTHERWISE" JANE KENYON (1993) Exemplifying the plain voice, rhythmic control, and emotional vulnerability for which her work was admired, JANE KENYON's "Otherwise" is an autobiographical LYRIC in FREE VERSE which rejects the emotional excesses of CONFESSIONAL poetry for a stoic attitude towards illness and mortality. Written in response both to her lifelong battle with depression and to her husband DONALD HALL's ultimately successful battle with cancer, "Otherwise" explores the ways that nature, the domestic world, and simple habit provide solace and strength during times of happiness and of struggle alike.

The poem alternates between declarative sentences describing the speaker's daily routine, followed by a simple refrain that gains in power as the poem advances. "It might have been otherwise," the speaker says again and again, reminding herself that the accidents and traumas of a life can interfere not only with personal happiness, but with the habits and rituals on which a happy life is built. But Kenyon's careful use of enjambment breaks the repeated sentence across lines, so that its declaration never completely appears on a single line until the very end of the poem, as if Kenyon were using poetic form itself as an incantation against misfortune; ultimately, it is this constant reminder to herself of the possibility of things being "otherwise" that enables Kenyon to grasp the present moment and experience it truly, which is to say, beautifully. "I got out of bed / on two strong legs," Kenyon opens the poem, but "It might have been / otherwise." The routine she describes is simple, ordinary, and peaceful: she eats breakfast, walks with her dog, writes, makes love to her husband, eats dinner, and sleeps. But she is always mindful that this peacefulness not only can be disturbed but also will be disturbed by mortality. Yet such knowledge does not produce despair; instead, it serves as an impetus to embrace the peacefulness and fulfillment of the present moment precisely because it will pass away.

GREGORY ORR notes that in ordinary life, Kenyon had a habit of repeating phrases twice when she spoke, and he claims that this repetition was both a way of making "incantatory blessings" and a sign of her ability "to be both completely present and aware, and at the same time to be, in some sense, 'detached'" (29). Similarly acknowledging the duality in her work, Todd Davis and Kenneth Womack identify the acceptance the poem urges with an "ethics of grace" wherein people are urged to embrace "the ordinary, blessed activity of life through its insistence that we acknowledge that one day the aesthetic and spiritual trappings of our existence will come to an end" (88). The inevitability of that decline is figured in the structure of the poem itself: two stanzas divided between the two halves of the day, hinging on noon and the downward progress of the illuminating sun. But Kenyon counters that inevitability near the close of the poem; as she falls asleep, she plans "another day / just like this day," a wonderfully understated expression of will, even of hubris, given that the preceding poem has meditated constantly on how our plans often end "otherwise." The first stanza is 12 lines in length, and up to this point the second stanza is as well, but Kenyon concludes with a final summary couplet that, by acknowledging the inevitability of her own end (only months after the poem was published in *Constance* (1993), she contracted the leukemia that ended her life in 1995), appears to take control of it as well, so that whatever misfortune or suffering life may afford, she can attend it with grace: "But one day, I know / it will be otherwise."

BIBLIOGRAPHY

Davis, Todd F. and Kenneth Womack. "Seeing into the Light: The Ethics of Grace in the Poetry of Jane Kenyon." In *"Bright Unequivocal Eye": Poems, Papers, and Remembrances from the First Jane Kenyon Conference,* edited by Bert G. Hornback, 87–97. New York: Peter Lang, 2000.

Orr, Gregory. "Our Lady of Sorrows: Some Thoughts on Jane Kenyon." In *"Bright Unequivocal Eye": Poems, Papers, and Remembrances from the First Jane Kenyon Conference,* edited by Bert G. Hornback, 27–38. New York: Peter Lang, 2000.

Temple Cone

OWEN, MAUREEN (1943–) Maureen Owen was an important participant in the "mimeo" (mimeograph copy machine) revolution that fundamentally shaped a second generation of NEW YORK SCHOOL poets. A long-time member of the community of poets associated with the St. Mark's Poetry Project in the Bowery (see POETRY INSTITUTIONS), she served for many years as program coordinator and, in 1969, began publishing an influential magazine, *Telephone,* in the church basement. In 1972 Owen began a series of books—through a press she called Telephone Books—and published, early on in their careers, such notable writers as FANNY HOWE and SUSAN HOWE, and other writers such as Janine Pommy-Vega, Fielding Dawson, and Ed Friedman. Her own collagist poetry, which is inclusive, witty, and vivacious, reflects a personal ethic largely defined by her devotion to a sense of community.

Owen was born in Graceville, Minnesota, and grew up on a farm. Later her father and mother worked as horse trainers on the California racetrack circuit. She studied at San Francisco State University and Seattle University, and she lived in Japan for three years, studying Zen Buddhism. She has taught at Naropa University and at Edinboro University in Pennsylvania. Her first book, *Country Rush,* was published in 1973. In 1979 she was awarded a Poetry Fellowship by the National Endowment for the Arts, and she won the Before Columbus American Book Award for *AE (Amelia Earhart)* in 1984. *American Rush: Selected Poems,* nominated for the *Los Angeles Times* Book Prize, was published in 1998, the same year Owen received a grant from the Foundation for Contemporary Performance Arts.

Owen has consistently written an intriguing quotidian poetry, often diarylike in its form. Many poems move quickly in their attentions, collaging quotes (both literary and conversational), witty anecdotes and exclamations, and vivid descriptions. Blank space incorporated within lines and between words or phrases relays a sense of the connection-across-distance that the various sources suggest. As Fanny Howe has written, her lines are "galactic . . . spaces between starry explosions," such that her poetry "scatters and spreads and stops mysteriously" (79). In "FROM GOSSIP NOTES OF COURT LIFE" (1993), spirited invocations of precious stones—"O Ambivalent Onyx! Reckless diamonds obsessed opal / or Unplumbed tourmaline"—are interspersed with various textual commentaries. In the story of Cinderella, "the slipper is / made of fur but the translator mistook the French / & translated it as being of glass." This poem, like many others, incorporates an awareness of the sexism that permeates literary and cultural contexts: "& now the author / has agreed to define a woman's genitalia as an 'absence.'" Owen's use of cataloging in different poems displays the exuberance for sensual experience that underlies much of her poetry, as in "Dear L" (1973), which begins: "Thanks for the early guided hike down to / the bottom lands through juniper & hawthorn, / grapevine, sassafras, hackberry, honeysuckle."

Owen's vivid poems are graced by her unwillingness to see any details—especially life's small complexities—as unfit material for poetry. Her poems are significant without aspiring to be monumental. There is no estranging distance here; the poem, equal to the life, is full of experience and courageous experimentation.

BIBLIOGRAPHY

Foster, Edward, ed. *Talisman* 21 (winter/spring 2001). [Maureen Owen Issue]

Owen, Maureen. "An Interview with Maureen Owen [with Edward Foster]." *Talisman* 21 (winter/spring 2001): 67–78.

Linda V. Russo

OWENS, ROCHELLE (1936–) An award-winning playwright as well as a poet, Rochelle Owens was one of the few women writers to achieve recognition within the male-dominated circles surrounding BEAT POETRY. In the late 1950s, her idiosyncratic poems caught the attention of the poets GEORGE ECONOMOU and Imamu AMIRI BARAKA (then LeRoi Jones), whose enthusiasm led to the publication of her work in the influential underground magazines *Trobar* and *Yugen.* Soon afterward she received widespread notice for iconoclastic, Off-Off Broadway plays, such as *Futz* (1968) and *Istanboul* (1968). In its subversive themes and linguistic experimentation, her work anticipated the products of the LANGUAGE SCHOOL that would emerge several decades later. Acknowledging the connection, the critic Marjorie Perloff nevertheless asserts that Owens's writing "is *sui generis*" and that "Owens is angrier, more energetic, and more assertive than most of her Language counterparts" (12).

Owens was born in Brooklyn, New York. She attended public schools and the New School for Social Research. She has taught at the University of California, San Diego, Brown University, and the University of Oklahoma. Among her 16 volumes of poetry are *Rubbed Stones* (1994), *New and Selected Poems, 1961–1996* (1997), and *Luca: Discourse on Life and Death* (2001).

Owens's early poems demonstrate the tangibility and volatility of language, employing phonetic misspellings, disjunctive syntax, typographical variations, and unusual juxtapositions to create the sense of the poem as an object wholly separate from other forms of expression and resistant to traditional modes of interpretation. The opening line of "Called Also the Instant" (1961) illustrates the sonorous quality of these experiments: "Become limulus sounded minuted Gradual the silent lumps." Fueled by feminism and radical politics since the mid-1960s, Owens's work explores themes of violence and corrupt authority, as well as "the agonies of living in the 20th century world, and the pain of awareness of apocalypse impending," according to Susan Smith Nash (131). Owens's use of polyphony—multiple voices of historical and archetypal figures conveyed through the speaker's bitter tongue—creates dramatic tension and works to expose the hypocrisy of male-dominated Western culture. Her book-length poem, *Luca,* intersperses narration by Leonardo da Vinci, the model for his *Mona Lisa,* Sigmund Freud, and Freud's patient Flora in order to weave a shifting, disjunctive tapestry in which the myth of exclusively male creative genius ("Sigmund lip-synced") is undermined by the inspirational dynamism of the women.

Owens's poems seem improvisational but, in fact, are carefully orchestrated critiques that strike at the heart of society's conventional wisdom. Nash points out that Owens "constructs poetry that analyzes, dissects, reorders, and recasts underlying beliefs about the nature and goals of poetry" (131).

BIBLIOGRAPHY

Muratori, Fred. "A Curious Kind of Derangement." *American Book Review* 20, no. 1 (November/December 1998): 21, 24.

Nash, Susan Smith. "An Immense and Continuous Splendor: Thoughts on the Poetry of Rochelle Owens." *Talisman* 12 (spring 1994): 129–140.

Perloff, Marjorie. Introduction to *Luca: Discourse on Life and Death,* by Rochelle Owens. San Diego, Calif.: Junction Press, 2001, pp. 9–12.

Fred Muratori

"OX-CART MAN" DONALD HALL (1978) DONALD HALL's "Ox-Cart Man" has the rare distinction of having received the highest American honor given for a children's book, the Caldecott Medal (1980), a distinction all the more impressive because the poem was first published in *The New Yorker* magazine (1977) for a far different audience. While its New England setting and steady, declarative sentences may seem simple, suggesting the pastoral quaintness of folk tales, the poem's simplicity is that of a profound truth clearly expressed. Its five, well-turned FREE VERSE stanzas tell of a farmer who manages to sell, every year, all the goods he has produced and all the equipment he used to produce them. Hall has called this act "Total Dispersal," describing it in an interview as "the thrilling notion of emptying out, getting rid of absolutely everything. It is thrilling because: *Only if you empty the well will the water return to the well*" (232). Such dispersal resembles the creative act itself, with the poem's rich details and engaging rhythms suggesting a parallel between the poet's and the farmer's dependence on the patterns of nature for their survival and fulfillment.

Although the poem evokes the work of a whole year, it is important to note that the action of the poem takes place over just two months, October and November, from the time the farmer gathers his goods for market to the time he begins preparing for the next year's labors. Hall's vivid catalogue of items, including "wool sheared in April, honey / in combs, linen, leather / tanned from deerhide," evokes the four seasons. Indeed, the promise of spring's renewal is suggested right from the opening stanza, when Hall shows the farmer gathering potatoes and "counting the seed, counting / the cellar's portion out." Such counting suggests the farmer's intent to last out the winter and begin his labors again in spring, a plan that speaks of great hope.

"Ox-Cart Man" portrays the cycle of life and the satisfaction of living close to nature, though neither Hall nor the farmer discuss these themes in such abstract terms. In this sense, Hall's poem exemplifies what T. S. ELIOT called the objective correlative, the way in which particular phrases, images, and patterns of images evoke rather than explicitly discuss more general, abstract ideas. For instance, the first three stanzas are each single sentences, but in the fourth stanza Hall writes a single-line sentence, "When the cart is empty he sells the cart," which breaks the stanzaic rhythm and calls particular attention to the emptiness not only of the cart, but also of the farmer himself, who has gradually shed all his possessions. Hall himself has said that the turning point of the poem occurs in the next line, when the farmer sells the ox (Woodruff, 232), because this act rids the farmer not of an object, but of a living being that has been his companion from the start of the poem. Yet the farmer is neither distressed nor lonely, but returns to his home and resumes his labors. Interestingly, in early drafts of the poem, Hall had included an additional stanza at the end describing the return of spring and the regrowth of the crops. But at LOUIS SIMPSON's suggestion, Hall cut this stanza and concluded the poem with the farmer "by fire's light in November cold / . . . building the cart again." By ending the poem this way, Hall suggests that even more fulfilling than a life lived close to nature is a life of making and building. Here the metaphorical connection between the farmer's labors and the poet's work is clear: the cycle of life, like the cycle of the year, draws the poetic laborer into a pattern that sustains him, and will, if he permits, provide a fitting subject for his poems as well.

BIBLIOGRAPHY

Moramarco, Fred, and William Sullivan. *Containing Multitudes: Poetry in the United States since 1950.* New York: Twayne Publishers, 1998.

McDonald, David. "Donald Hall: Interview." *American Poetry Review* 31, no. 1 (2002): 17–20.

Woodruff, Jay, ed. *A Piece of Work: Five Writers Discuss Their Revisions.* Iowa City: University of Iowa Press, 1993.

Temple Cone

P

PADGETT, RON (1942–) Ron Padgett, associated with the so-called second generation NEW YORK SCHOOL, is a primary figure in post–World War II experimental American poetry. In addition to producing a wide range of poetry, essays, and prose poems, Padgett has translated French writers, including Blaise Cendrars, Guillaume Apollinaire, and Paul Reverdy. In a personal interview Padgett expressed literary affinity with "[Frank] O'Hara, [Kenneth] Koch, [John] Ashbery, [James] Schuyler, [Kenward] Elmslie, [Allen] Ginsberg, [Aimée] Cesaire, Kenneth Patchen, Hart Crane, [William Carlos] Williams, [Ezra] Pound, Wallace Stevens, early [T. S.] Eliot, [Federico García] Lorca, [Vladimir] Mayakovsky, [Pablo] Neruda, the surrealists, the dadaists, [Gerard Manley] Hopkins, Apollinaire, [Max] Jacob, [Pierre] Reverdy, [Blaise] Cendrars, [Valery] Larbaud, St-Pol-Roux, [Stéphane] Mallarmé, [Conte de] Lautréamont, [Arthur] Rimbaud, [Charles] Baudelaire, [Walt] Whitman, [Emily] Dickinson, [Friedrich] Hölderlin, [William] Blake, [Ludovico] Ariosto. . . . Let's go back to Aristophanes!" (Padgett/Kane).

Padgett was born in Tulsa, Oklahoma. As a 16-year-old high-school student, he edited the *White Dove Review,* an influential little magazine that published the work of, among others, PAUL BLACKBURN and JACK KEROUAC. Padgett moved to New York City in 1960 to study at Columbia University. While in New York he helped edit and produce TED BERRIGAN's *C* magazine, a crucial organ for New York school poets. He moved to Paris as a Fulbright Fellow in 1965–66, where he "fell in love with the work of the Surrealist predecessors" (qtd. in Eshleman 9). Padgett has won many prizes, including fellowships from the National Endowment for the Arts (1976) and the Guggenheim Foundation (1986) and the Officier dans l'Ordre des Arts et des Lettres from the French Ministry of Culture and Communication (2001).

Although characteristically Padgett's work is highly comedic, it does not avoid serious concerns. His early poems show the influence of FRANK O'HARA's "I do this, I do that" aesthetic, where the poet lists—often in a whimsical and disarmingly informal manner—the routines of a walk in the city or the unfolding of a thought. Padgett's later poetry shows increasing originality and formal daring, as he experiments with prose poems, poem-pictures (often in collaboration with artists, including Joe Brainard, George Schneeman, and Jim Dine), and other multigenre and collaborative works. His poems are populated by characters and language specific to popular culture. Padgett explains this influence: "[M]y upbringing was quite 'normal': toys, baseball, movies, cars, with their attendant vocabularies" (qtd. in Eshleman 8).

The effect comic books had on Padgett's poetry must not be underestimated: In *Great Balls of Fire* (1969), he evokes cartoonlike characters, including "a stupendously terrifying huge grotesque Flower Dog" ("A Careless Ape"). In his book *The Big Something* (1990), one encounters "Dagwood outlines with Blondie disheveled" ("How to Be a Woodpecker").

Nevertheless Padgett's work is always tempered by what DAVID SHAPIRO refers to as "a very uncanny darkness" that keeps it as serious as it is pleasing and hilarious (82). Padgett generates poetry off the sheen of a comic surface.

BIBLIOGRAPHY

Eshleman, Clayton. "Padgett the Collaborator." *Chicago Review* 43, no. 2 (1997): 8–14.

Padgett, Ron. "An interview with Ron Padgett," by Ed Foster. In *Postmodern Poetry: The Talisman Interviews/Interviewed by Ed Foster.* Hoboken, N.J.: Talisman House, 1994, pp. 99–114.

———. Interview with Ron Padgett, by Daniel Kane. New York City. 12 December 1997.

Shapiro, David. "A Night Painting of Ron Padgett." *Talisman* 7 (1991): 82–87.

Daniel Kane

PALEY, GRACE (1922–2007) Although best known for her short stories, Grace Paley was an accomplished poet who wrote poetry for more than half a century. Paley's style is open and casual, written in simple language with little punctuation. This "comfortable" style—something she learned from W. H. AUDEN—and Paley's habit of grounding her poems in her own experiences as a social and political activist, mother, teacher, and writer, create a connection between poet and audience, reader and text. In her poems Paley uses the combination of a sharp ear for dialogue and a concern about larger issues to merge the provincial and the global in interesting ways.

Born to Russian Jewish immigrants, Paley was raised in New York City. She published her first book of short stories, *The Little Disturbances of Man,* in 1959. She was inducted into the American Academy and Institute of Arts and Letters in 1968, and in 1987 she was awarded a prestigious Senior Fellowship by the National Endowment for the Arts. Her first collection of poems, *Leaning Forward,* was published in 1985; her *New and Collected Poems* was published in 1992.

Among the prevalent themes in Paley's work are her connections to family and history, women's issues, time, the city of New York, and, importantly, issues of social justice. In poems that seem to concentrate on simple, everyday events, Paley explores the connections between these events and larger concerns. Affirming the importance of the poet's connection to society, many of Paley's poems are testimonies to what she witnessed in her years as an activist. These poems, which often focus on linguistic events—such as a story told to her as a child or the testimony of an El Salvadoran woman who has lost a son—highlight her conversational style by including various phrases—such as "they said" or "she answered." These powerful poems about social and political issues constitute Paley's most distinctive contribution to American poetry.

"Street Corner Dialogue" (1992), for example, opens with the exclamation "Thank God for the old Jewish ladies / though their sons are splendid with houses"; these are people who can be relied upon to "take our leaflets." She describes a dialogue in which their acceptance signals the promise of a better future. In "Responsibility" (1984), Paley reaffirms her concern with the world's future, stating that it is the poet's responsibility to watch over this world and to "cry out like Cassandra, but be / listened to this time."

BIBLIOGRAPHY

Arcana, Judith. *Grace Paley's Life Stories: A Literary Biography.* Urbana: University of Illinois Press, 1994.

Bach, Gerhard, and Blaine H. Hall, eds. *Conversations with Grace Paley.* Jackson: University Press of Mississippi, 1997.

Clark, LaVerne Harrell. "A Matter of Voice: Grace Paley and the Oral Tradition." *Women and Language* 23, no. 1 (spring 2000): 18–25.

Kimberly Bernhardt

PALMER, MICHAEL (1943–) Michael Palmer is an influential poet of the avant-garde whose work has been associated with the LANGUAGE SCHOOL of poetry. Palmer's work builds on the American modernist poetic tradition of such poets as EZRA POUND, WILLIAM CARLOS WILLIAMS, and GERTRUDE STEIN (see MODERNISM), and his work also has been influenced by the poetry of ROBERT DUNCAN and ROBERT CREELEY. Since Palmer is concerned with how sound and meaning function in poetry, the images in his work are often abstract, and he plays with the slipperiness of the words' meanings. However, Palmer's poems certainly are not meaningless. Echoes of common experience create multiple interpretations that are not directly explained in the poems. According to Palmer his poetry has "a resistance to the static image and, in fact, an invocation of one that is more nomadic and that forces the reader into a somewhat more active mode of reading" (109). Palmer expands on the modernist tendency to break away from narrative or lyrical poems that depend on formal devices (such as meter or rhyme), storytelling (such as the dramatic monologue or CONFESSIONAL lyric), or explanations of political or philosophical positions (see LYRIC POETRY and NARRATIVE POETRY). Instead his work opens up a field of semantic possibilities for the reader.

Palmer was born and raised in New York City. To date, he has published 11 collections of poetry, from *Blake's Newton* (1972) to his most recent collection, *Company of Moths* (2003). Palmer's influence extends beyond poetry, as he also has collaborated with the Margaret Jenkins Dance Company on renowned works of modern dance during the last 30 years. He has received several fellowships, and in 1999 he was elected a chancellor of the Academy of American Poets; in 2001 he received the Shelley Memorial Award from the Poetry Society of America.

In "Untitled (April '91)" (1991) Palmer engages the idea of a narrative in a poem, stating that a narrative demands that one must "paint a flower with a death's head." The combination of "flower" and "death" seems contradictory and subverts the reader's expectations regarding the function of a narrative, that the flower would be related to life or fertility. The poet then writes that the words in the narrative are subject to gravity; therefore, they bend "as if suns would flower as sparks of paint / then fall before the retinal net." In this surreal image, the bending or manipulation of words is compared to suns that bloom in bursts of color before one's field of vision. Palmer's innovative use of language can have the same effect, allowing for the experience of a fresh outlook on the world through the bending—and reading—of words.

Palmer's poetry explores the dichotomy between the personal and the philosophical, creating a destabilizing tension that the reader may find unsettling. However, the controlled uncertainty of his work allows for a response and engagement with language that is at turns sensual, paradoxical, musical, and frequently beautiful.

BIBLIOGRAPHY

Clover, Joshua. "Ghosts in the Arcade." *Village Voice,* May 9, 2000, 78.

Palmer, Michael. "An Interview with Michael Palmer," by Paul Naylor, Lindsay Hill, and J. P. Craig. *River City* 14, no. 2 (1994): 96–110.

Selinger, Eric Murphy. "Important Pleasures and Others: Michael Palmer, Ronald Johnson." *Postmodern Culture* 4, no. 3 (1994). Available online. URL: http://muse.jhu.edu/journals/postmodern_culture/v004/4.3selinger.html. Downloaded March 2007.

J. Andrew Prall

"THE PANGOLIN" MARIANNE MOORE (1936)

While critics disagree over the intent of MARIANNE MOORE's "The Pangolin"—whether its primary attention rests on civic virtue, artistic purpose, or how the world is experienced—almost all agree on its central issues: namely, a concern with art, poetry, and science as a unified investigation of the natural world, the relationship between the animal, human, and spiritual kingdoms, and the importance of "grace" in humanity's betterment of its condition. Such concerns place "The Pangolin" in the modernist tradition, along with such poems as T. S. ELIOT's *The WASTE LAND* (see MODERNISM); moreover, its difficulty of interpretation, formal innovation, and interest in cultural reference lend "The Pangolin" to being placed in the category of modernist masterpiece.

Published first in England as the title poem of *The Pangolin and Other Verse,* "The Pangolin" is one of Moore's most superbly executed animal poems, a topic that dominated her early poems, such as "The FISH" (1935) and "The Paper Nautilus" (1941), as well her later poems, such as "To a Giraffe" (1966). The first five of "The Pangolin"'s nine stanzas focus mainly on the physical characteristics of the pangolin—a long-tailed, scale-covered mammal of tropical Africa and Asia, which has a long snout and sticky tongue for eating ants and termites—and the last four compare these features to "man." In many respects Moore's Puritan sensibility—her reliance on sparse, layered symbolism and her sense that people need to work at virtue—

places a great deal of spiritual weight on the lines, such as "that the outside / edge of his hands may bear the weight and save the / claws // for digging," by pointing out features that suggest prudence and functional necessity. Even when other sections of the poem focus on the "grace" of the pangolin, they do so by focusing on the pangolin's attainment of grace through "adversities" and "con- / versities" so that "grace" for the pangolin is as much a spiritual state as it is an aesthetic one.

And yet the pangolin itself is as much a subject of the poem as any moral lesson. The aforementioned lines clearly foreground the pangolin's physical makeup. This concern with the animal's habits, movements, and physical appearance runs the length of the poem, which covers diet, defensive strategies, characteristics of its skin and tail, and nocturnal wanderings. This material information dominates the poem to such a degree that the pangolin as subject itself and the pangolin as teacher of virtue and grace become parallel investigations. "The Pangolin" in some ways splits the difference between EZRA POUND's high modernist desire for historical and aesthetic instruction and the postmodern interest in objects and words as materials in themselves above and beyond their functions as signifiers. With such a bridge in mind, Moore's mixing of poetry, science, and ethics in "The Pangolin" becomes a way of foregrounding our material environment while being instructed by it.

BIBLIOGRAPHY

Joyce, Elisabeth. *Cultural Critique and Abstraction: Marianne Moore and the Avant-Garde.* Cranbury, N.J.: Associated University Presses/Bucknell University Press, 1998.

McQuade, Molly, ed. *By Herself: Women Reclaim Poetry.* St. Paul, Minn.: Graywolf Press, 2000.

Willis, Patricia, ed. *Marianne Moore: Woman and Poet.* Orono, Maine: National Poetry Foundation, 1990.

Joel Bettridge

"PANTOUM OF THE GREAT DEPRESSION" DONALD JUSTICE (1995) Late in his career, DONALD JUSTICE became increasingly interested in the Great Depression as a subject, claiming that it fascinated him because "It's history—and with feeling. An epic—without heroes. And then there are all the great photographs recording it. You can still see it; it is still vividly there" (Gioia, 45). The worldwide economic downturn, which was triggered by the Wall Street crash of 1929, led to massive unemployment, economic misery, and political turmoil in the United States, which were in turn endured, bravely or resignedly, by the most ordinary citizens. Justice captures "the usual celebrations, the usual sorrows" of that heroless epic in the stylized repetitions of "Pantoum of the Great Depression."

The pantoum form consists of an indefinite number of quatrains that follow a particular pattern: the even lines of one quatrain appear in the same order as the odd lines of the next quatrain, while the odd lines of that first quatrain reproduce in the same order the even lines of the preceding quatrain. In general, the pantoum's lines are repeated verbatim, and though Justice's poem makes some slight word changes, he adheres largely to the form. Typically, the pantoum concludes by repeating the odd lines of the first stanza in reversed order as the even lines of a final quatrain. In "Pantoum of the Great Depression," however, Justice deploys the first stanza's first two lines as the even lines of the final quatrain, followed by a single line that echoes the third line of the first quatrain to devastating effect.

"Our lives avoided tragedy," Justice begins, "Simply by going on and on." Those who survived the Great Depression managed, it seems, through an almost brute stubbornness, and although Justice himself did not suffer the depression's effects, his decision to narrate the poem in the first person plural is crucial to his ideas about that period. James McCorkle argues that "The poem's use of 'we' does not denote universal inclusiveness, but rather it implies a generational difference between those who experienced the Great Depression and those who did not" (184), and the reticence and endurance of that era is enhanced by the pantoum's repetitiousness. Yet for Justice, the depression remains a vivid historical experience, epic in scope but affecting ordinary citizens, and the narrative voice suggests this immediacy. Moreover, even if it is not meant to be inclusive, the narrative voice helps the reader imagine and understand the collective experience of the depression and the way it overshadowed the importance of the individual.

Ironically, Justice finds those who endured the depression most interesting because their lives seem so resistant to the distortions of literature. "We managed. No need for the heroic," Justice writes, ironically adding, "Thank god no one said anything in verse." This tension between unpoetic lives represented poetically provides Justice a rich paradox, one well equipped for depicting the character of this generation of Americans; as James McCorkle writes, the poem "resists any sentimental transcendence of suffering. Instead, Justice portrays a stoicism that originates more out of banality and a fatedness of not knowing any other way to react" (184). Most remarkably, Justice conveys this paradox by means of a variation in the form of the poem. The last quatrain seems to follow the pattern for the conclusion of a pantoum, where the even lines repeat in reverse order the odd lines of the initial stanza. However, in this last quatrain, Justice repeats the poem's very first two lines, then follows the quatrain with a single line that echoes the theme of the poem's third line—"Without end and with little apparent meaning"—but with a distinct wording that reiterates the unpoetic endurance of these people whose lives nevertheless invite poetry. "But it is by blind chance only that we escape tragedy," Justice admits in the penultimate line, before he claims, with a tinge of regret for this rough materialism, "And there is no plot in that; it is devoid of poetry."

BIBLIOGRAPHY

Gioia, Dana. "Donald Justice: An Interview." *American Poetry Review* 25, no. 1 (1996): 37–46.

McCorkle, James. "Donald Justice: The Artist Orpheus." *The Kenyon Review* 19, nos. 3–4 (1997): 180–88.

Temple Cone

PASSAGES **ROBERT DUNCAN (1968–1987)** Written in the mode of the long poem associated with LOUIS ZUKOFSKY'S *"A,"* WILLIAM CARLOS WILLIAMS'S *PATERSON,* and CHARLES OLSON'S *The MAXIMUS POEMS* (see LONG AND SERIAL POETRY). ROBERT DUNCAN'S *Passages* (otherwise known as "the 'Passages' poems") demonstrates a poet's deep commitment to various mythopoetic traditions and his view of poetry as a "grand collage" (Introduction vii). Influenced by EZRA POUND'S *The CANTOS,* H. D.'s spiritualism, and Olson's notion of composition by field (see ARS POETICAS), *Passages* is a significant feature of Duncan's mature work. "Passages 1–30" appear in *Bending the Bow* (1968); "Passages 31–37" appear in *Ground Work* (1984), along with three other unnumbered "Passages," since Duncan stopped numbering them in order to deny a linear coherence. *Ground Work II* (1987) contains an additional 13 "Passages." Intended to be a meaningful part of the individual books in which they were published as well as "the unfolding revelation of a Sentence beyond the work" ("Some Notes" xi), the "Passages" poems are intricately connected to Duncan's other writing. "An Illustration Passages 20," for instance, is also number XXVI of Duncan's other major series *The STRUCTURE OF RIME,* and "Passages 36" is included in a separate set entitled *A Seventeenth Century Suite.*

Passages is a series of poems without end, engaging simultaneously with aspects of history, myth, memory, aesthetics, imagination, and identity. Beginning with an epigraph from the Emperor Julian, which reads, in part, "For the even is bounded, but the uneven is without bounds and there is no way through or out of it," "Tribal Memories Passages 1" introduces the questions of form and formlessness. Romantic in his belief that the artist is one who searches for meaningful patterns, Duncan considers correspondence an immanent characteristic of language, and subsequently he views the field of the poem as something to be yielded to rather than overly controlled. The poems recognize that "Chaos / and the divine measures and orders / so wedded are" ("Transgressing the Real," Passages 27 [1968]), and that "Not one but many energies shape the field" ("Transmissions," Passages 33 [1984]).

Welcoming puns, etymologies, errors, silence, fragments, and disruptions, Duncan "works with all parts of the poem as *polysemous,* taking each thing of the composition as generative of meaning" (Introduction ix). Two notable poems in *Passages* include "The Torso Passages 18," a celebration of homosexual love, and "Up Rising Passages 25," which critiques the United States military presence in Vietnam. Later "Passages" grow more insistent on the dissolution of imaginative boundaries as a way to overcome the darkness of corrupt politics and spiritual stagnation: "There is truly no direction no 'center' to the 'center' our sounding / goes out as we go out no circumference to the 'circumference'" (Untitled [1987]).

Passages mixes poetry and prophecy in an active exploration of the unknown. Focusing on different myths of the past and their continuing influence on the present, Duncan's series favors process over closure and beginnings over endings while acknowledging that each is an inherent part of the poet's creative act.

BIBLIOGRAPHY

Duncan, Robert. Introduction to *Bending the Bow*. New York: New Directions, 1968, pp. i–x.

———. "Some Notes on Notation." In *Ground Work*. New York: New Directions, 1984, pp. ix–xi.

Reid, Ian W. "The Plural Text: 'Passages.'" In *Robert Duncan: Scales of the Marvelous*, edited by Robert J. Bertholf and Ian W. Reid. New York: New Directions, 1979.

James L. Maynard

PASTAN, LINDA (1932–) Linda Pastan is most often recognized for what many consider to be "domestic poetry"—explorations of her roles as daughter, wife, and mother—as well as her fine eye for the nature around her. Her recurring themes of family and nature are lyrically interwoven with her recognition of the cyclical qualities of life, acknowledging this as the source of both life's pain and its wonder: "One exodus prefigures the next" ("Passover" [1971]).

Pastan was born and grew up in the Bronx, New York. Despite her family's hopes that she would pursue a career in medicine like her father, she earned degrees in English and library science in the 1950s from Radcliffe, Simmons, and Brandeis. In 1958 she won *Mademoiselle*'s Dylan Thomas Award, after which she put her writing aside for 10 years to marry and to raise three children. Her first volume of poetry, *A Perfect Circle of Sun*, was published in 1971. Since then she has written 10 additional books of poetry, most recently *Queen of a Rainy Country: Poems* (2006), spent four years as the poet laureate of Maryland (1991–95), and earned a National Endowment for the Arts Fellowship (1972) and several other awards, including the Alice Fay Di Castagnola Award from the Poetry Society of America (1978).

When she began writing poetry as a teenager, Pastan focused on religious and other familial tensions, and this tendency carried over into her published verse. More than a cast of characters, her family members represent natural forces that shape the poet's world, from the baby whose wails of vowels seem to be "calling / for their lost consonants" ("Night Sounds" [1975]) to the stern father who sits, "clearing / his throat of language" ("Silent Treatment" [1995]). These descriptions contrast sharply with the recurring images of her home, set placidly among the trees of rural Maryland, under an "alphabet / of silence" ("Blizzard" [1981]).

Pastan is at her most lyrical when reveling in the intersection of these natural forces and her own relatively brief time on earth. In "Topiary Gardens" (1991), she laments that she will never grow leaves and berries, but she takes as consolation that someday "planted deep underground / [she] too will send up green" that will drape the gravestones sitting unchanging above her. This intertwining of loss with life, sorrow with happiness, imbues her work with a passionate love of the natural cycle. Pastan's poetry has an intimate quality that resonates, as if her words were memories, rather than poems, familiar yet "strangely new, words / you almost wrote yourself" ("A New Poet" [1991]).

BIBLIOGRAPHY

Adelman Ken. "Word Perfect: For Linda Pastan, Revision Is the Purest Form of Love." *Washingtonian* (May 1996): 29.

Nordhaus, Jean. "Linda Pastan: The Heightened Present," The Writer's Center. Available online. URL: www.pre-viewport.com/Home/pastan-e1.html. Downloaded 2000.

Pastan, Linda. "Linda Pastan [Interview with Lisa Granik]." In *Truthtellers of the Times: Interviews with Contemporary Women Poets*, edited by Janet Palmer Mullaney, 82–87. Ann Arbor: University of Michigan Press, 1998.

Aimee Fifarek

PATCHEN, KENNETH (1911–1972) One of the earliest figures associated with the literary BEAT movement, Kenneth Patchen was an avant-garde writer, poet, and artist whose work consistently demonstrated his proletarian roots, as well as his commitments to pacifism, socialism, relentless experimentation with literary form, and radical human consciousness. From 1936 to 1972, Patchen published more than 36 books of poetry, fiction, and drama, including experiments in the antinovel, concrete poetry (see VISUAL POETRY), poetry and jazz (several of his recordings have been released on the Folkways record label), irrational tales and verse, and painting. Strongly influenced by Walt Whitman and William Blake, Patchen's unique aesthetic followed no particular group or style, and, like Blake, he saw his art as the visionary work of a poet-prophet. From his introduction to Blake's *The Book of Job* (1947) also came one of Patchen's many assertions of personal and artistic freedom, a cry for personal liberty that contributed to the ethos of an emerging post–World War II American counterculture: "Do what you want and what you want will make / everybody more beautiful."

The third of five children in a working-class family, Kenneth was born in Niles, Ohio. An excellent student and athlete, Patchen worked two summers in the Ohio steel mills with his father and brother to supplement his college scholarship at Alexander Meilejohn's Experimental College at the University of Wisconsin. Later he studied with his mentor, Meilejohn, at the Commonwealth College in Mena, Arkansas, but Patchen soon became disenchanted with academics and left after one semester. In 1967 he received an award from the National Foundation on the Arts and Humanities for "lifelong contribution to American letters."

Working at odd jobs and traveling in the United States and Canada from 1930 to 1933, Patchen continued his writing. "Permanence," a sonnet, was published in the *New York Times* in 1932. *Before the Brave* (1936), Patchen's first book of poetry, set out his favored themes of love and pacifism in the years leading to World War II. In "Class of 1934," a bitter survey of the prewar political climate, he writes, "Hitler offers / Death Death." As the war churned on, Patchen wrote prolifically and angrily about its destructiveness. His refrain, "To hell with power and hate and war," in "Instructions for Angels" (1945) characteristically precedes an equally fervent call to love and humanity. Refusing the violence and death of battle, the speaker locates instead the life-giving power of his lover, for "in her eyes / Is a country where death can never go" ("All the Roses of the World" [1946]).

In 1959 a surgical accident permanently damaged his spine, and Patchen was bedridden for the remainder of his life. This, however, did not prevent him from continuing to write and paint.

BIBLIOGRAPHY

Nelson, Raymond, *Kenneth Patchen and American Mysticism.* Chapel Hill: University of North Carolina Press, 1984.
Smith, Larry R. *Kenneth Patchen.* Boston: Twayne, 1978.

James Emmett Ryan

PATERSON **WILLIAM CARLOS WILLIAMS (1946, 1948, 1949, 1951, 1958, 1963)** The five books which make up *Paterson* were originally published separately in sequence by New Directions in New York, and WILLIAM CARLOS WILLIAMS had begun work on a sixth at the time of his death in 1963. The poem was published in a single volume in 1963, including the brief fragments of book 6 found among Williams's papers. Because of its epic scope, *Paterson* is grouped among such long American poems as HART CRANE's *The BRIDGE,* T. S. ELIOT's *FOUR QUARTETS* and *The WASTE LAND,* EZRA POUND's *The CANTOS,* LOUIS ZUKOVSKY's *"A,"* and CHARLES OLSON's *The MAXIMUS POEMS* (see LONG AND SERIAL POETRY).

Williams, the most celebrated practitioner of imagism (see IMAGIST SCHOOL), explained his plan and premise for *Paterson* in the poem's "Author's Note," which appeared with book 1 in 1946; he envisioned "a long poem in four parts—that a man in himself is a city, beginning, seeking, achieving and concluding his life in ways which the various aspects of a city may embody" (n.p.). Book 1 brings together Paterson the man and Paterson the city in its opening lines: "Paterson lies in the valley under the Passaic Falls / its spent waters forming the outline of his back," thus personifying the city and sexualizing the river and its falls. Williams subsequently interspersed prose excerpts from personal letters, newspapers, and local histories with his lines of verse. The complete work has been described by Gilbert Sorrentino as "a masterwork of High MODERNISM, an open collage of sustained and exquisite lyrics, fragmented narratives, recollected, revived, and revised history, and a bravura display of bricolage" (261). From the start, fellow poets and critics watched closely and held widely divergent opinions of Williams's "masterwork." RICHARD EBERHART welcomed the second installment as "even more exciting than the first," because "the sense of energy, movement and reality is everywhere present" ("Energy" 4), and ROBERT LOWELL connected the book to the first great icon of American poetry when he declared it to be "Whitman's America, grown pathetic and tragic, brutalized by inequality, disorganized by industrial chaos, and faced with annihilation" (693).

As the first four parts of the sequence progress, earth, air, fire, and water maintain symbolic value at the same time as sets of binaries (including man/woman, city/wilderness, and marriage/divorce) emerge to expand the symbolic framework of the poem. The irony of *Paterson* is that Williams, who always insisted on common speech by and for ordinary people, would write a book so complicated that it requires interpretation by specialists (Eberhart "Image" 5). HAYDEN CARRUTH was bothered that even "at the eighth reading some details of structure and aspects of symbol remain unclear" (331); while a particular symbol appears consistently, its use and meaning are inconsistent (Spears 40). One critic describes book 3 as "some magnificent passages, some silly passages, and a great mass of undigested material" (Spears 42), and he concludes that the third installment is "not only *about* the failure of language; it is a failure of language" (43). Books 4 and 5, published later, also received mixed reviews.

Carruth's mixed feelings about Williams's epic continued with the publication of Book Four, the last line of which reads "the end" because it was intended to be the final segment. While Carruth believed it to be a major moment in American poetry and admired the whole as an "often superlatively good, lyrical meditation," he nevertheless considered Book Four as "less satisfactory" and "less well integrated" than its predecessors (156). JOHN CIARDI and THOM GUNN agree that the subject and meaning of Book Five are never clear, but while Ciardi confesses to being occasionally "baffled," he insists there still is "richness" and "master[y]" in the book (39); Gunn also concedes Williams's "purity of language," but in the end he believes that "whole sequences of *Paterson Book Five* could be rearranged and still mean about as much and as little as they do now" (298). Finally, the reception of the posthumous 1963 edition is harshest of all, perhaps because the venerable Dr. Williams no longer could be touched by the criticism; Christopher Ricks calls it "boring" and an "almost total failure" citing "a complete absence of rhythm, an arbitrariness of line-length, a flatness of diction, a poverty of metaphor" and "appallingly bad prose" (449).

It is impossible to know how to reconcile dismissals such as these with the claim that the book is what another reviewer called a "modern classic," "disarmingly simple in its sharp clarity and intense sincerity of expression" (Wills 415). The "sharp clarity" is found when "the man broke his wife's / cancerous jaw," the "sincerity of expression" heard when "Love is a kitten, a pleasant / thing, a purr."

After taking more than a decade of critical coverage into account, spanning the publication history of the book in its parts, what emerges from among these voices is a consensus that while the book's structure and design are so problematic as potentially to defeat its premise, Williams's lyrical power is unquestionable and his control of the image remains unmatched. This lyricism is evident in *Paterson* when Williams likens a man's thoughts to boughs "from whose leaves streaming with rain / his mind drinks of desire," and it is the grace by which the poem might be redeemed.

BIBLIOGRAPHY

Carruth, Hayden. "Dr. Williams's 'Paterson.'" *Nation* 170 (April 8, 1950): 331–332.

———. "The Run to the Sea." *Nation* 173 (August 25, 1951): 155–156.

Ciardi, John. "The Epic of a Place." *Saturday Review* 41 (October 11, 1958): 37–39.

Eberhart, Richard. "Energy, Movement and Reality." *New York Times Book Review*, June 20, 1948, 4.

———. "The Image of Ourselves." *New York Times Book Review*, February 12, 1950, 5.

Gunn, Thom. "Poetry as Written." *Yale Review* 48 (December 1958): 297–305.

Lowell, Robert. "Paterson II." *Nation* 166 (June 19, 1948): 692–694.

Mariani, Paul L. *William Carlos Williams: A New World Naked.* New York: McGraw-Hill, 1981.

"One Man's River." *Times Literary Supplement* September 10, 1964: 842.

Ricks, Christopher. "Sprawling." *New Statesman* (September 25, 1964): 448–450.

Sorrentino, Gilbert. *Review of Paterson,* by William Carlos Williams. *Review of Contemporary Fiction* 13, no. 2 (summer 1993): 261–262.
Spears, Monroe K. "The Failure of Language." *Poetry* 76 (April 1950): 39–44.
Williams, William Carlos. "Author's Note." William Carlos Williams. *Paterson,* New York: New Directions, 1963. n.p.
Wills, G. Review of *Paterson,* by William Carlos Williams. *National Review* 16, no. 20 (May 19, 1964): 415.

A. Mary Murphy

PEACOCK, MOLLY (1947–) Molly Peacock is an advocate for what is often called "expansive poetry," verse that blends formalist and narrative techniques (see NEW FORMALISM). With the goal of extending poetry's readership by incorporating "novelistic narrative and traditional forms" (Walzer 11), Peacock utilizes rhyme, form, and strict syllabic count to describe and explore life's most trying, tumultuous, and intimate events. She is known for her personal, almost CONFESSIONAL revelations about abusive family relationships, female sexuality, abortion, marriage, and divorce. Influenced by ANNE SEXTON's astonishing revelations, SYLVIA PLATH's intense imagery, and ELIZABETH BISHOP's polished language, as well as by feminist activism of the 1960s and 1970s, Peacock clearly stands out as a poet who speaks dispassionately about her experiences without being deadened by shame or regret.

Peacock was born in Buffalo, New York. She received a B.A. from the State University of New York, Binghamton, (1969) and later was a Danforth Fellow at Johns Hopkins University (M.A., 1977), where she studied with the poets Cynthia MacDonald and RICHARD HOWARD. Peacock's first book of poems among five collections was *And Live Apart* (1980). She has also published a creative nonfiction memoir, *Paradise, Piece by Piece* (1998), and a teaching anthology, *How to Read a Poem—and Start a Poetry Circle* (1999). She has garnered numerous awards, including fellowships from the Ingram Merrill Foundation (1978 and 1988), New York Foundation for the Arts (1985 and 1990), National Endowment for the Arts (1990), Lila Wallace Foundation (1994), and Woodrow Wilson Foundation (1995). Peacock served as president of the Poetry Society of America from 1989–94, during which time she began "Poetry in Motion," a project that mounted hundreds of short poems in New York City subways and became a model for similar programs across the country.

In *Paradise: Piece by Piece,* Peacock acknowledges that formal poems, such as sonnets, "were poems with happy barriers" and that working out formal poetic "puzzles" afforded her creative freedom and emotional safety (140). For example, in "Say You Love Me" (1989), she uses the terza rima form as the grounding for a description of her father's alcoholic rampage and his drunken insistence on love and obedience. In this poem the family interacts through threats and lies. The child may be forced to profess love and may, indeed, love the father. Nevertheless isolation and loss envelop everyone in the household: The telephone didn't ring. "There was no world out there, / so we remained, completely alone." This poem underscores Peacock's commitment to direct, honest communication, which is the basis for personal relationships, family, and community.

BIBLIOGRAPHY

Allen, Annette. "Molly Peacock." In *Dictionary of Literary Biography.* Vol. 120, *American Poets since World War II,* edited by R. S. Gwynn, 243–247. Detroit: Gale Research, 1992.
Rector, Liam. "Molly Peacock." In *Contemporary Poets.* 5th ed. Chicago: St. James Press, 1991, pp. 749–750.
Walzer, Kevin. *The Ghost of Tradition: Expansive Poetry and Postmodernism.* Ashland, Ore.: Story Line Press, 1998.

Diane Warner

PERCHIK, SIMON (1923–) Simon Perchik's poetry reflects the reality of contemporary American life that is a culmination of the past and a continuous struggle for identity. Perchik can best be described as a modernist whose influences include Vincente Aleixandre, Paul Celan, and Pablo Neruda (see MODERNISM). Perchik can capture a moment, a photograph, or a memory in expressive, emblematic words, such as in his depiction of a graveyard whose "notices . . . offer the dead / page after page ("You read these notices . . ." [2000]). The images of Perchik's work starkly erupt from urban concerns about war, existence, and place.

Perchik was born in Paterson, New Jersey. After serving as a pilot in World War II, he earned both a

B.A. in English and a law degree from New York University. In 1964 he published his first book, *I Counted Only April,* and has since published more than 20 chapbooks and books of poetry.

Each word in Perchik's poetry creates a visible and veritable image. The poetry involves such themes as self exploration and the impact of external forces on identity, as seen in war's influence on Perchik. In *Hands Collected* (2000), airplane images parallel the images of birds (these also pervade much of his early poetry), serving both to revive personal memories as a pilot and to link the collective human mind to a flight for poetic freedom. In *Touching the Headstone* (2000), Perchik focuses on the interconnectedness of life and death, allowing the living to touch the past, as emphasized by the title.

Perchik omits all titles from his work, a strategy that resists traditional poetic form and definition and allows for a range of reader interpretations. In a poem beginning "Wherever I turn . . ." (2000), Perchik revisits his past and the war. Images of planes lend a cold, harsh edge to "this yard" that exists as a place of personal history. The yard, representative of memory, history, and experience, is being dug through by "a shovel that won't leave the ground." Perchik further explores moments of human maturity in "It's easy to grow tall . . ." (2000) as he describes the natural transitions of life from a "first born leaf" to icy peaks "taking you with them."

Perchik's substantial gift for crafting poetry is evident in his lucid and concrete language. His precise choice of words solidifies every poem.

BIBLIOGRAPHY

Bennett, Jim. "Simon Perchik: *Touching the Headstone,*" New Hope International Review Online. Available online. URL: www.nhi.clara.net/bs0283.htm. Downloaded December 2003.

Perchik, Simon. "Interview with Simon Perchik," by David Baratier. *Jacket Magazine* 8 (1999). Available online. URL: http://jacketmagazine.com/08/perchik-iv.html. Downloaded December 2003.

Maria D. Lombard

PERELMAN, BOB (1947–) Bob Perelman is recognized as one of the most political, and often the most humorous, of the LANGUAGE poets. From their beginnings at the Iowa Writer's Workshop, Perelman and fellow language poets Michael Waltuch, Tomaz Salamun, and BARRETT WATTEN came to the forefront of poetry's avant-garde by deliberately rejecting the lyrical and personal poetry of the BEAT and NEW YORK SCHOOL aesthetics. Language poets seek to nullify traditional methods of meaning-making by disrupting the standard syntax of language, introducing "self- / doubt and word-doubt" ("The Poet" [1986]) into both the poem and the reader, thus forcing the reader to participate in the creation of the poem.

Perelman was born in Youngstown, Ohio, the second of two children, to solidly middle-class parents. He began attending the Putney School in Vermont at age 12, where he received intensive education in music, poetry, and the classics. Although he originally aspired to be a concert pianist, his admitted lack of technical ability and passion for literature led him to the University of Michigan, where he earned a degree in classics (1969) before going on to the Iowa Writers' Workshop to earn an M.F.A. in poetry (1970) and a Ph.D in English from University of California, Berkeley (1990).

Perelman's poetry has been described by his critics and peers alike as cynical, satirical, and dire. In his poem "Anti-Oedipus" (1986), whose title repeats that of philosophers Gilles Deleuze and Felix Guattari's seminal work (1977), his speaker stops himself from gouging out his eyes, which "deny" the truth they observe, to "see" into a seemingly simple word: "Inside the house (note the word / standing solid, timbered, painted, mortgaged, but that's okay." Perelman's juxtaposition of a modern-day Oedipus tearing out his eyes, so as not to see the truth of his condition, with the linguistic act of seeing the house in a multiplicity of contexts diverts the imagination from the man who will not see to the house, which now seems to hold significantly more meaning.

Language is the true subject of Perelman's poetry. With their endlessly shifting focus and redirections, Perelman's poems constantly emphasize the space between meaning and language. The reader is denied the option of ignoring the usually transparent interface between the "I" who writes "and the you reading (breath still misting the glass) / examples of the body partitioned by the word" ("Binary" [1986]). In recognizing language for what it is, we are also acknowledging that it is our connection, albeit imperfect, to each other. In this way poet and reader become a single entity, entwined in language, comaking a new shared reality at the level of the poem.

BIBLIOGRAPHY

Evans, Steve. "Bob Perelman." In *Dictionary of Literary Biography*. Vol. 193, *American Poets since World War II,* edited by Joseph Conte, 266–281. Detroit: Gale Group, 1998.

Monroe, Jonathan. "'Poetry, Community, Movement': A Conversation, with Bob Perelman, Charles Bernstein, and Ann Lauterbach." *Diacritics* 26 (fall/winter 1996): 196–210.

Aimee Fifarek

"PERSIMMONS" LI-YOUNG LEE **(1986)** Drawing upon the poet's cross-cultural experience as a second-generation Chinese immigrant, Li-Young Lee's "Persimmons" explores the power of imaginative language to negotiate the pitfalls of racism and personal loss and to create a rich, almost sacramental experience of life. The poem associates Lee's experiences as young boy, grown man, son, husband, and artist with repeated but varied images of the persimmon fruit in order to represent the fragmentary pieces that construct a human identity and the way that those pieces can be bound up by a love of the world so great one would eat "all of it, to the heart." In its quiet tone, plain diction, and resonant imagery, the poem recalls the work of the DEEP IMAGE poets, but Lee's particular ethnic narrative and his interlacing of familial love, erotic passion, and sensuous pleasure distinguish the work of this late century master.

Ironically, for a poem so focused on the experience of sweetness, "Persimmons" opens with a moment of intense racism, as Lee remembers his sixth-grade teacher striking him "for not knowing the difference / between *persimmon* and *precision.*" Later, when the teacher brings her class a persimmon to eat, derisively calling it a "Chinese apple," Lee's culturally defined knowledge comes to his aid: recognizing that the persimmon the teacher selected is neither ripe nor sweet, he doesn't eat the fruit, but watches his classmates make faces at its sour taste. Critic Zhou Xiaojing observes that in much of Lee's work, his "bi-cultural heritage helps him escape 'closedness and one-sidedness' in his perceptions and view. His cross-cultural experience helps generate and enrich his poems" (117). The comical outcome of the persimmon tasting suggests that cultural knowledge such as Lee's can lead one away from bitterness and into sweetness, and that poetic "imprecision" can ultimately reveal the truth, if heard and understood by sympathetic ears.

Dispute arises among readers over the extent to which "Persimmons" should be read as representative of one person's cultural experience, as generally representative of cultural experience, or as transcendent of such experiences. In his introduction to Lee's book *Rose* (in which "Persimmons" first appeared), poet GERALD STERN praises Lee's poetry on various points, including "a pursuit of certain Chinese ideas, or Chinese memories, without any self-conscious ethnocentricity, and a moving personal search for redemption" (9). But critic S. G. Yao dismisses Stern's praise as naïve 'Orientalism,' which treats the diversity of Asian and Asian-American cultural experiences as homogenous and monolithic (2); instead, Yao argues, Lee's poem struggles to synthesize Asian and American experience, and this incompleteness is at the heart of the poem's exploration of ethnic hybridity (6–7). Ultimately, however, Lee appears to reconcile these differences in his focus on the human body as a site where transcendent union can occur, whether through sexual passion or sensory pleasure. Thus, the poem is filled with images of weaving, as when Lee writes of confusing the words *wren* and *yarn,* or when he attempts to teach his wife Chinese during a sexual encounter: "Crickets: *chiu chiu.* Dew: I've forgotten. // Naked: I've forgotten. // *Ni, wo*: you and me."

As with many of Lee's poems, the poet's father appears as a powerful figure whose role in Lee's life is simultaneously confessor, comforter, dependent, teacher, and protector. By the end of the poem, Lee remembers his father's blindness, and the way in which the persimmon fruit figures into the men's interactions demonstrates the complexity and richness of their relationship. Having realized that his father is going blind, he gives him a gift of persimmons, "swelled, heavy as sadness, / and sweet as love," and later, when the old man's eyes are "All gone," Lee sits with his father and talks about a scroll painting of "Two persimmons, so full they want to drop from the cloth," a figure for the fullness of both men's lives. The scroll depicts an image which Lee's father painted *"hundreds of times / eyes closed. These I painted blind."* Indeed, through the father's blindness Lee is led to see how the father has never lost the son, and how the son, even after his father's death, will never lose the father. The poem concludes with a moment of profound assurance and consolation as Lee realizes *"Some things never leave a person."*

BIBLIOGRAPHY

Stern, Gerald. "Foreword." *Rose.* By Li-Young Lee. Brockport, N.Y.: BOA Editions, Ltd., 1986: 8–10.

Xiaojing, Zhou. "Inheritance and Invention in Li-Young Lee's Poetry." *MELUS* 21, no. 1 (1996): 111–132.

Yao, S. G. "The Precision of Persimmons: Hybridity, Grafting and the Case of Li-Young Lee." *Lit: Literature Interpretation Theory* 12, no. 1 (2001): 1–23.

Temple Cone

PETERS, ROBERT (1924–) Robert Peters is equally adept in CONFESSIONAL and observational modes of writing, brief, parabolic incantations, and book-length dramatic monologues. Besides being a poet, he is also a noteworthy scholar, critic, dramatist, and fiction writer. His chief influences are THEODORE ROETHKE, ROBERT BLY, and Robert Louis Stevenson, after whom he was named. His project is to find the connections between different poetic movements and, on a larger scale, different genres of writing. His work explores similar meetings of brutality and tenderness, the sublime and the grossly physical, memory and lived experience.

Peters was born and raised in northern Wisconsin. What he would later cite as the beginning of his life as a poet occurred in February 1960 when his four-year-old son Richard died of one-day meningitis. His first book of poetry, *Songs for a Son,* was chosen by DENISE LEVERTOV in 1967 for a series of books she was editing. In 1952 he received a Ph.D. from the University of Wisconsin. He received a Guggenheim Fellowship for the 1966–67 academic year, and in 1974 he received a fellowship from the National Endowment for the Arts. He taught at several universities before finally settling at the University of California, Irvine, where he went on to teach for more than 30 years.

Although Peters sees brutality in the world, he does not try to avoid it. It is instead more important for him to be fully conscious in the face of trauma in order to render it more powerfully in language. He finds redemption in writing. This comes through in his erotic odes to John Dillinger and Robert Mitchum, the secret lusts of his youth. In maturity, having realized his identity as a poet and a homosexual, Peters retains his old longing; the only difference is in his freedom to articulate this longing.

An early work, "Christmas Poem 1966: Lines on an English Butcher-Shop Window" (1968), demonstrates well this willingness to confront—even to celebrate—violence. "O beautiful severed head of hog," Peters begins his catalogue of dismembered animal parts, ending with the almost euphoric exclamation, "I see you all!" To encounter this horror, then to speak of it is itself a triumph.

Pain threatens to destroy even language, as in Peters's poem "the child in the burnt house" (1974). The child "finds his father / charred, dead, huddled," and after escaping from the house, the stars "tell the child to sing. / but he can't do anything." Pain has overwhelmed the child, as it constantly threatens to overwhelm the adult poet. But language yields its own rewards. To speak is to survive.

BIBLIOGRAPHY

Bertolino, James. "Robert Peters: An Appreciation." *Bellingham Review* 10 (spring 1987): 55–56.

Collins, Billy. "Literary Reputation and the Thrown Voice: The Poetry of Robert Peters." In *A Gift of Tongues: Critical Challenges in Contemporary American Poetry,* edited by Kathleeen Aguero and Marie Harris, 295–306. Athens: University of Georgia Press, 1987.

Wakowski, Diane. "Robert Peters." *American Poetry* 2 (winter 1985): 71–78.

Matthew Purdy

PIECES **ROBERT CREELEY (1969)** This controversially obscure sequence of minimalist poems, written in the late 1960s and published in 1969, takes as its subject the question of form: cosmic, national, human, poetic. ROBERT CREELEY's tactics here are elusiveness and inwardness, qualities drawn largely from the influence of CHARLES OLSON, his BLACK MOUNTAIN College friend. In *Pieces,* however, Creeley's voice veers modestly away from the prophetic majesty of Olson's Maximus persona, used in *The MAXIMUS POEMS,* in favor of what Creeley calls "small facts" (3). Responding to Olson's theory of "Projective Verse" (see ARS POETICA), *Pieces* expresses in verse Creeley's engagement with the limits and parameters of poetry itself and his concern with the question of how poetry works. As he told ALLEN GINSBERG, "I cannot define a poem. . . . I cannot tell you what I think a poem is. I think that has to do with the fact that all the terms of consciousness are, at the moment, undergoing tremendous terms of change" (36).

The organization of *Pieces* requires explanation. Of the 73 short poems that constitute the volume, 33 are titled; the rest are listed in the table of contents by their opening line—after the fashion of E. E. CUMMINGS. Many of the poems are extremely brief, seeming to be constructed in the spirit of a haiku or zen koan, as with the enigmatic "So tired / it falls / apart." Creeley has since explained that the writing of the poems was conducted as a daily journal so that the poems are arranged exactly in the order that they were written: "When the time came to publish it, I simply used the chronological sequence of its writing, and let . . . three dots indicate that that was the end of a day's accumulation, and the single dots most usually indicate divisions in the writing as it's happening" (192–193).

Despite such explanations, however, considerable uncertainty remains about where each poem ends and the next begins, particularly since the chronological ordering of the poems results in the theme of one "piece" echoing through the lines of subsequent "pieces." Indeed many of these pages have a calculated rough-draft quality about them, suggesting that they are fragments, shards of a work in progress, unpolished and in disarray. "Mazatlan: Sea," for example, opens with a precisely rhymed couplet, initiating a pair of precisely wrought stanzas ("The sea flat out, / the light far out"), but the concluding fourth and fifth stanzas appear unfinished or perhaps directionless. Sometimes, too, Creeley inserts brief sections of prose between the poems, as did WILLIAM CARLOS WILLIAMS in *PATERSON,* the American poetry sequence that *Pieces* most closely resembles (see LONG AND SERIAL POETRY).

The apparently fragmentary selections in *Pieces* figure importantly in Creeley's insistence not only on the "small facts" of daily life, but also in his understanding of poetic authenticity, which calls for a transcript of perceptions and modes of consciousness that can be documented, although not completely and not always coherently. Following language to the deepest levels of its authenticity through *Pieces* requires a strong resistance, on Creeley's part, to simile and metaphor and a commitment to words as things, as facts themselves. Creeley voices this commitment in a number of indirect ways, but also directly. "I hate the metaphors," he announces, insisting on the reality "of things / in words." If the minimalist verse of *Pieces* lacks perfectionism and retains much of the rough quality of a working notebook, then just as surely it expresses a devotion to the possibility of charting consciousness incrementally through language, even if that consciousness must be advanced haltingly, word by word. The extreme concision of Creeley's word-by-word minimalism here accords with Olson's principle of projective verse, whereby perceptions are recorded sequentially and, in turn, lead to new perceptions. In another sense, however, Creeley—a New Englander by birth and disposition—can be seen as following Ralph Waldo Emerson's notion, in his "Nature" essay (1849), that "words are signs of natural facts." But what marks out Creeley's unique attitude about language is his alignment of pleasure and the materiality of language: "Words / are / pleasure."

As these influences and associations suggest, *Pieces* stands as a contribution to both theory and practice in poetry. As theory it recalls Williams's comment in *Paterson* that there are "No ideas but in things." Creeley's concept of language's materiality adds the concept of time and movement so that, as he indicates in the first poem, "No forms less / than activity." The journal-like structure of *Pieces,* implying "age as form," reinforces this chronological patterning of words; the poems express shards of sequential perception, not only word by word, but also day by day and minute by minute. Addressing the difficulty of mutual human understanding and the radical separation of even highly conscious individuals—"Here I / am. There / you are"—leads Creeley to a conclusion that even when language, as in *Pieces,* is purified of metaphor, its meanings can be accepted and yet not entirely understood.

The poems enlist minimalism in the service of immediacy; each brief line examines an instant: *"Present again / present present / again present / present again,"* with "present" indicating both material presence and the "now," or present tense. Creeley's preoccupation with the poems' ability to remain present in discrete moments resonates with T. S. ELIOT's attempt to work through the problem of time in *FOUR QUARTETS,* particularly his paradoxical notion that "If all time is eternally present / All time is unredeemable." In this sense, like Eliot, Creeley's *Pieces* haltingly works toward a combined theory of poetry and time.

BIBLIOGRAPHY

Creeley, Robert. *Contexts of Poetry: Interviews 1961–1971,* edited by Donald Allen. Bolinas, Calif.: Four Seasons, 1973.

Faas, Ekbert. *Robert Creeley: A Biography.* Hanover, N.H.: University Press of New England, 2001.

Wilson, John, ed. *Robert Creeley's Life and Work: A Sense of Increment.* Ann Arbor: University of Michigan Press, 1997.

James Emmett Ryan

PIERCY, MARGE (1936–) Marge Piercy is one of the 20th century's most prolific and respected feminist writers. Her work shows a commitment to the dream of social change, rooted in personal narratives, the wheel of the Jewish year, and landscapes both urban (Detroit) and pastoral (Cape Cod). The title of one of her favorite poems is "To Be of Use" (1973), and she believes poems should be useful. By this she means not necessarily that poems should be didactic, though many of hers are, but rather "that readers will find poems that speak to and for them" (Piercy xii).

Piercy was born in Detroit, Michigan, to a family deeply affected by the depression. She was the first in her family to attend college, at the University of Michigan; she earned a B.A. in 1957. Winning a Hopwood Award for poetry and fiction (1957) enabled her to finish college and spend time in France, and her formal schooling ended with an M.A. from Northwestern University. Her first book of poems, *Breaking Camp,* was published in 1968. She has won a number of awards, including the Massachusetts' Governor's Commission on the Status of Women Literary Award (1974) and the Sheaffer Eaton–PEN New England Award for literary excellence (1989).

Piercy's activism began with the Civil Rights movement and progressed to the feminist movement. Her lifetime of spiritually motivated social action is a resonant theme throughout her body of work. "This is how . . . coalitions are knit from strands of hair, / of barbed wire, twine, knitting wool and gut," begins "Report of the Fourteenth Subcommittee on Convening a Discussion Group" (1992). Many poems reflect her frustrations with industrialized, patriarchal society and her visions of the better world she aims to help create. Her poems about, for, and to her mother are especially powerful. In "My Mother's Body" (1985), she writes: "This body is your body now, ashes now / and roses, but alive in my eyes." This extended musing on Piercy's complicated connection with her mother is, by turns, angry and compassionate, loving and fierce.

Piercy's early work is marked by short lines and her discovery of feminist theory; her later work shows longer lines, a larger range of imagery, and the influences of country living and her reconnection with Judaism. Piercy's increasing involvement with Judaism is mirrored in its increasing role in her work, especially her collection *The Art of Blessing the Day* (1999). Her work as a whole combines earthy humor, a gift for sacralizing ordinary moments, a strong sense of narrative, and a passion for what in Hebrew is called *tikkun olam,* the imperative to heal the world.

BIBLIOGRAPHY

Mitchell, Felicia. "Marge Piercy's *The Moon Is Always Female:* Feminist Text, Great Books Context." *Virginia English Bulletin* 40, no. 2 (1990): 34–45.

Nowik, Nan. "Mixing Art and Politics: The Writings of Adrienne Rich, Marge Piercy, and Alice Walker." *Centennial Review* 30, no. 2 (spring 1986): 208–218.

Piercy, Marge. Introduction to *Circles on the Water.* New York: Knopf, 1982, pp. xi–xv.

Walker, Sue, and Hamner, Eugenie, eds. *Ways of Knowing: Essays on Marge Piercy.* Mobile, Ala.: Negative Capability Press, 1991.

Rachel Barenblat

PINSKY, ROBERT (1940–) Robert Pinsky's poetry reveals the influence of YVOR WINTERS, the poet and critic under whom Pinsky studied during his graduate school years at Stanford University. Winters's antimodernist poetics and Augustan sensibility were important to Pinsky's development, as was Winters's ideal of an articulate poet-professor. In accordance with this ideal, Pinsky has published three volumes of literary criticism. Pinsky has, nevertheless, always maintained a populist approach in his poetry (which concerns itself with such topics as television, tennis, and his hometown of Long Branch, New Jersey), especially in its insistence on accessible, discursive language, language that embodies what Pinsky has called the "prose virtue" of clarity. This populism has given Pinsky a great deal of visibility in American literary culture.

Born and raised in Long Branch, New Jersey, Pinsky received a B.A. from Rutgers University in 1962. He attended graduate school at Stanford, along with a number of other important American poets, including JOHN MATTHIAS and ROBERT HASS. He received a Ph.D. in 1966 and has taught English literature at several universities. He served as the poetry editor of the *New Republic* from 1978 to 1986 and held a similar position with the online magazine *Slate* starting in 1996. He was the first poet ever to serve three consecutive terms as United States Poet Laureate (1997–2000), following his Stanford classmate Hass in that office. Pinsky has won the American Academy of Arts and Letters Award (1999) and the Howard Morton Landon Prize for translation (1995), among many other honors.

Pinsky's first book, *Landor's Poetry* (1968), celebrates the work of the 19th-century English poet Walter Savage Landor. It is fitting that Pinsky should begin his career with a study of a poet like Landor, since Pinsky's own poetry embodies many of the same qualities of Landor's writing: classical restraint, clarity, and a respect for poetic tradition. When Pinsky writes that Landor is "not an innovator who breaks or abandons traditional forms, but one who exploits, combines, and furthers them" (*Landor*'s 2), he describes not only Landor but also the poet that he himself will become over the next three decades.

Landor also makes an appearance in the long poem "Essay on Psychiatrists," in Pinsky's first book of poems, *Sadness and Happiness* (1975) (see LONG AND SERIAL POETRY). It is a mark of Pinsky's populism that Landor and Euripedes rub shoulders in that poem with figures out of popular culture, such as Rex Morgan, M.D., from the comic strip of the same name. "Essay on Psychiatrists" is also important because it is one of Pinsky's first major experiments with what he calls "discursive poetry": a poetry that allows itself to discuss a topic, to express opinions, to pose and answer questions, and to present ideas abstractly and at length. Like the long poem "Tennis" (also from *Sadness and Happiness*), "Essay on Psychiatrists" divides its topic into parts, examining each in turn in the manner of an expository essay. This may seem like a modest goal, but it was a radical gesture at a time when such slogans as "No ideas but in things" (see WILLIAM CARLOS WILLIAMS) and "A poem should not mean but be" (see ARCHIBALD MACLEISH) had become standards of poetic taste.

The Situation of Poetry: Contemporary Poetry and Its Traditions (1976), Pinsky's next book, can be seen as a kind of manifesto for the poetry Pinsky was writing in *Sadness and Happiness.* While the book is written as a study of several contemporary poets rather than as a polemical essay, it nevertheless makes forceful arguments for discursive, essayistic poetry. Arguing against the antiessayistic qualities of modernist poetry, Pinsky says that "the techniques of imagism, which convey the powerful illusion that a poet presents, rather than tells about, a sensory experience" are "tormented premises" for poetry (see IMAGIST SCHOOL), but that they have become the norm for American poetry in the 1970s (*Poetry* 3). He finds that many of the most popular poets of the time "avoid abstract statement, or at least avoid unqualified commitment to such statement" (155). In *The Situation of Poetry,* he argues that this avoidance of abstract statement truncates poetry's possibilities, while in "Essay on Psychiatrists" he demonstrates the richness of those possibilities.

In *An Explanation of America* (1979), Pinsky makes his most ambitious effort in writing discursive poetry. With the exception of "Lair" and "Memorial," the short poems that open and close the book, the entire volume consists of a single long poem in 12 parts, composed in Pinsky's discursive or essayistic style. Addressing the poem to his daughter, Pinsky sets himself the task of "tell[ing] [her] something about our country, / Or [his] idea of it." While this father-to-daughter address appears intimate and domestic, the poem itself is very much a public act, taking up American history on a grand scale in the manner of ROBERT LOWELL and examining the national character at a time when many Americans shared their president's assessment of the country as suffering through a "national malaise," as Jimmy Carter termed it in a speech earlier that year.

If *An Explanation of America* took up the public side of Lowell's poetics, then Pinsky's next two books of poetry, *A History of My Heart* (1984) and *The Want Bone* (1990) can be seen as taking up the more personal, CONFESSIONAL side of Lowell's work. In the long title poem, as well as in such shorter lyrics as "The Questions" and "The Garden," Pinsky addresses the matter of his own past more directly than ever before. The book appeared in the same year as the translation of Czeslaw Milosz's *The Separate Notebooks* that Pinsky completed with Hass, and Pinsky's renewed interest in memory and the private life shows the influence of his work as a translator of Milosz's meditative writings. While Pinsky's poetic concerns become more private in *A History of My Heart,* his poetic form and diction remain resolutely public, shying away from obscurity and arcane reference.

In the 1980s Pinsky showed interest in the public life of poetry outside of the small world of professional poets and critics. *Poetry and the World,* Pinsky's 1988 collection of critical essays, returns again and again to the question of the place of poetry in the public sphere. "What is, or what would be, a democratic poetry?" he asks at the beginning of "Freneau, Whitman, Williams" (101), and versions of this question animate "American Poetry and American Life," "Poetry and Pleasure," and the volume's title essay. One of Pinsky's projects in the 1980s shows how serious he was about bringing poetry into new, popular contexts: In 1984 Brøderbund Software released the text-based computer game Mindwheel, for which Pinsky did much of the writing and into which he introduced a number of poems from the classics of English literature.

Pinsky's interest in the popular, nonprofessional context of poetry continued into the 1990s, when he used his prominence as poet laureate to launch the Favorite Poem Project, a program in which Americans from all walks of life were asked to record their favorite poems. The project involved many public readings and an extensive Web site, and it eventually led to the publication of the anthology *America's Favorite Poems* (1999), which Pinsky edited along with Maggie Dietz, and to Pinky's study of poetry and democracy, *Democracy, Culture, and the Voice of Poetry* (2002).

It should come as no surprise that a poet concerned with the public life of poetry should be drawn to Dante, who boldly chose to write in the "vulgar tongue" of Italy, as Dante put it. Pinsky's translation of *The Inferno of Dante* (1994) was received with much critical acclaim, and it allowed him to continue the investigations of world religious traditions that he had begun in such poems as "The Figured Wheel" (1997) and "Shiva and Parvati Hiding in the Rain" (1990) and continued in his biography of the biblical King David, *The Life of David* (2005).

Religion is a major topic of Pinsky's two most recent volumes of poetry, *The Figured Wheel: New and Collected Poems* (1996) and *Jersey Rain* (2000), which also revisit other familiar themes, including American public life ("In Memory of Congresswoman Barbara Jordan") and that most perennial of Pinsky's subjects, his early years in New Jersey ("An Alphabet of My Dead"). Pinsky's career path may have led him to the American laureateship, but it has also led him home.

BIBLIOGRAPHY

Archambeau, Robert. "Roads Less Traveled: Two Paths Out of Modernism in Postwar American Poetry." In *The Mechanics of the Mirage: Postwar American Poetry,* edited by Michel Delville and Christine Pagnoulle, 35–48. Liège, Belgium: University of Liège Press, 2000.

Longenbach, James. "Robert Pinsky and the Language of Our Time." *Salmagundi* 103 (summer 1994): 155–177.

Parini, Jay. "Explaining America: The Poetry of Robert Pinsky." *Chicago Review* 33, no. 1 (summer 1981): 16–26.

Pinsky, Robert. *Landor's Poetry.* Chicago: University of Chicago Press, 1968.

———. *Poetry and the World.* Hopewell, N.J.: Ecco, 1988.

———. *The Situation of Poetry.* Princeton, N.J.: Princeton University Press, 1976.

Robert Archambeau

PIOMBINO, NICK (1942–) Nick Piombino is one of the founding members of the LANGUAGE SCHOOL of poets and a particularly important contributor to the theory associated with experimental poetry and aesthetics in the post–Vietnam War era. Piombino demonstrates an important trend in poetics, a blend of writing practices adopted from poetry and more prosaic and speculative forms of writing: an extraordinary emphasis on the philosophical question of what constitutes the literary object. A social worker and psychoanalyst as well as a poet, Piombino has considered the status of a poem as an object for decades, most prominently in his essays.

Piombino was born and has continued to live in New York City. His writing began appearing in the late 1970s. Piombino's major awards include the New York Foundation for the Arts Fellowship in poetry (1990–91) and a Postgraduate Center for Mental Health Author's Recognition Award (1992).

By using techniques associated with the prose poem, Piombino's poetry often looks like prose, and vice versa. The ensuing difficulty the reader may experience is a difficulty to categorize, but such a difficulty can be enjoyed. And in his explorations of the object-status of poetry, Piombino encourages us to read all such writing uncategorically. Poems and essays can be considered, according to Piombino, as equally "theoretical objects," hence the title of his 1999 volume *Theoretical Objects.* From an early essay written with poet Alan Davies, Piombino asserts that the "object state is the blur between the thing and a word. . . . The word itself is at first a thing, then becoming an object representing an object" (38). The implications of language as a blurry "object" carry over into his more recent work, often written as sentence groups broken into discrete verse lines: "Poetry is never satisfied, so it never satisfies. Poetry provokes and will not relent. But it won't intrude either. / Poetry is a chameleon. Poetry changes form faster than perception can follow, so poetry can enlarge perception" ("With Open Arms" [2001]).

Piombino's declarative statements ask readers to question if what they are reading is a poem or an essay. But if it is true that "it never satisfies," the result of such questions is a kind of "blur," a writing that is "faster than perception," and an object that resides more in the reader's mind than in the world outside. By focusing on perception and other psychic phenomena, Piombino's training as a psychoanalyst shines through to augment the literary project of Language poetry with highly original insights into what poetry has been and can be in the future.

BIBLIOGRAPHY

Bernstein, Charles. "The Second War and Postmodern Memory." In *A Poetics.* Cambridge, Mass.: Harvard University Press, 1992, pp. 193–217.

Piombino, Nick, and Alan Davies. "The Indeterminate Interval: From History to Blur." In *The Boundary of Blur*. New York: Roof Books, 1993, pp. 34–42.

Patrick F. Durgin

"THE PLAIN SENSE OF THINGS" WALLACE STEVENS (1954) In contrast with his early poetry, which often delighted in its own baroque designs and splendid play of imagery, WALLACE STEVENS's late poem "The Plain Sense of Things" is committed to revivifying ordinary, objective reality, not through elaborate decoration, but through an intensification of the world as it is. While some critics view this turn to plainness in Stevens's work as a metaphor for artistic exhaustion, which Stevens apparently felt when he began composing the poem (Lensing, 61–62), others hail the effort to make the quotidian feel extraordinary again as a supreme exercise of the imagination. As a key work in his final collection, *The Rock,* "The Plain Sense of Things" reflects Stevens's shift to a more restrained visual palette the better to meditate upon the nature of the poetic imagination itself.

The scene Stevens depicts is sparse, almost ruined, with a dilapidated home and greenhouse and a choked pond. Set in the countryside in late autumn, the poem evokes several literary traditions, including the pastoral, the country house poem, and the romantic nature lyric. But Stevens undercuts each of these traditions through his imagery, which strips away the conventions of scenic beauty by focusing on how the scene fails to meet them, as when he notes that "It is difficult even to choose the adjective / For this blank cold." When Stevens asserts that "The great structure has become a minor house," his claim applies not only to a ruined building, but to all structures of thought whereby humans comprehend their world. For George S. Lensing, "The Plain Sense of Things" exemplifies Stevens's autumnal poetry, or works set in autumn, which feature "the suppression of the imagination," "a return to ignorance," "a sense of discomfiture," and "tropes of reduction" (62). When he writes of how "After the leaves have fallen, we return / To a plain sense of things," Stevens correlates the end of autumn to other existentially resonant endings: the decline of the once vital imagination, the death that ends mortal life, even the end of the world.

In one sense, seasonal imagery naturally implies a cyclic return to the halcyon days of spring and summer, but Stevens does not look ahead to the earth's regrowth. Instead, he attends to the experience of ruin itself, to "A fantastic effort [that] has failed," not to conceal or resolve it, but to show how the imagination can intensify even such a subject as ruin, and make it deeply felt. Stevens can thus claim that "the absence of the imagination had / Itself to be imagined." Indeed, suggests Frank Kermode, the difficulty of imagining the scene at all becomes a quality that can itself characterize the scene, creating "a valid description implying wholeness" (122). When, in the final stanza, a rat rises from the stagnant water to preside over "The great pond and its waste of lilies," Stevens is signaling how far the imagination and human existence can be reduced, yet he balances this reduction by evoking the sense of absolute necessity and aptness conveyed by acts of perfectly realized imagination, even when depicting such ruined scenes as the setting of this poem. As James Longenbach writes, "This act of recovering the ordinary world is not in itself inevitable or necessary—nothing can force us to be like a rat when we have the power to be an old philosopher: we must make the act necessary through the power of perceiving" (303). With imagery and diction more stripped and spare than anything he used early in his career, Stevens simultaneously discusses and demonstrates how it is the power of the imagination itself, not the materials the imagination uses, that provides humankind with a world worthy of its understanding.

BIBLIOGRAPHY

Humphries, David. "A New Kind of Meditation: Wallace Stevens' 'The Plain Sense of Things.'" *Wallace Stevens Journal* 23, no. 1 (1999): 27–48.

Kermode, Frank. *Wallace Stevens.* New York: Chip's Bookshop, 1979.

Lensing, George S. *Wallace Stevens and the Seasons.* Baton Rouge: Louisiana State University Press, 2001.

Longenbach, James. *Wallace Stevens: The Plain Sense of Things.* New York: Oxford University Press, 1991.

Temple Cone

PLATH, SYLVIA (1932–1963) Sylvia Plath is better known for her troubled life than for her poetry. She suffered an early mental breakdown that she fictionalized in *The Bell Jar* (1963), which became a best seller after her suicide. But her poetry deserves more attention than it receives. She is considered a CONFESSIONAL poet, because of the intimate nature of her poetry and because of her relationships with confessional poets ANNE SEXTON and ROBERT LOWELL. Like them, Plath rejects the MODERNISM of EZRA POUND, T. S. ELIOT, and WILLIAM CARLOS WILLIAMS, which emphasizes the abstract and the universal. Instead Plath embraces the deeply personal. But she is not purely autobiographical either. In a 1960 BBC interview she said, "I think my poems immediately come out of the sensuous and emotional experiences I have, but . . . I believe that one should be able to control and manipulate experiences, even the most terrifying" (qtd. in Alexander 305–306). Plath's poetry transcends the term *confessional* through her attention to the craft of poetry and by her filtering of experience through the lens of her own stylized mythology. The "I" in her poems is a persona, or fictional mask, rather than the true voice of the poet. It is a shell to protect an intense, highly sensitive individual who needed to be heard, but not seen too deeply. This dramatic tension between disclosure and omission is a large part of what makes Plath's work so difficult yet so rewarding.

Plath was born in Boston, Massachusetts, to a German immigrant father and a mother of Austrian descent. Her father, Otto Plath, was a professor of German and biology who authored a landmark study on bumblebees. Her mother, Aurelia Schober Plath, had been a student of Otto's at Boston University and was the valedictorian of her class. According to biographer Paul Alexander, Aurelia Plath's strongest desire was to be a writer, but she chose instead to raise a family and to advance the career of her husband. Born of such ambitious and exacting parents, it is not surprising that Plath was a volatile mix of drive and self-doubt. Her father's death when she was eight, of complications from long-undiagnosed diabetes, affected Sylvia profoundly for her entire life. Even then she was driven to write, and she published her first poem in a Boston newspaper at age eight. She won literary prizes throughout high school and pursued a degree in English at Smith College, where she published both prose and poetry in national periodicals. She also won a contest for an internship with *Mademoiselle* magazine in New York. Her experience there precipitated a mental breakdown that resulted in a nearly successful suicide attempt.

Following graduation from Smith in 1955, Plath went to Cambridge University in England on a Fulbright Fellowship. She met the then-unknown British poet Ted Hughes, and after a short courtship, they married and had two children. The union lasted six years; she was estranged from him when she died. The separation provided the catalyst for Plath's best-known poems. In the seven months between the initial breakup and her death, Plath wrote more than 50 poems, most of which she ordered in a manuscript entitled *Ariel and Other Poems* and left on her desk. Published posthumously in 1965, Ariel became one of the best-selling volumes of poetry ever sold in America. Long after her death, Plath's *Collected Poems* (1981) won the Pulitzer Prize in 1982. Other awards and honors include recognition by the Academy of American Poets (1955), the Ethel Olin Corbin Prize (1955), and the Marjorie Hope Nicholson Award (1955).

Arguably Plath's earlier poems are just as accomplished as her later ones, yet not as dire. She published regularly and had a contract with the *New Yorker*. American critics largely ignored Plath's first book, *Colossus and Other Poems* (first published in England in 1961), although the few reviews it received were mildly positive. The title poem visits a lifelong theme of Plath's—her relationship to her father. The speaker is trying to uncover and reassemble a giant stone statue of her father with "Lysol" and "gluepots" ("The Colossus" [1959]). At peace with this project, she shelters in his ear at night. The overall tone is of regret over his absence. Plath wrote many poems trying to exorcise her father's influence. Hughes came to be a father figure, though she resisted her growing dependence on him and she fought against her discomfort with his literary success, which was complicated by his appeal to other women. A late poem, "Gulliver" (1962), seems to be directed toward Hughes, and the overlarge stature of Gulliver is similar to the size of the father in "The Colossus." "DADDY" (1962) is used as a vehicle to vilify her father and Hughes, both of whom she felt had abandoned her. Here Plath uses the conceit of a Jew to express her feelings of powerlessness in the face of "Nazis," but instead of being killed by them, she bests them: "If I've killed one man, I've killed two." Other poems—"The Rabbit Catcher" (1962), "The Jailer" (1962), and "Purdah" (1962)—express more of the helplessness Plath felt at this time when her own death seemed to her the only way to become powerful. In "The Jailer," the speaker has been "drugged and raped" and ends wondering "what would he / Do do do without me," implying that the captor needs her as much as she depends on him for her survival. "The Rabbit Catcher" marks the beginning of the end of Plath's marriage; the speaker identifies with a rabbit caught in a snare and implies that the constriction is killing both people in the relationship.

Toward the end of her life, Plath had difficulty publishing the intense poems she was churning out on either side of the Atlantic. Several of these last poems forecast or perhaps confessed her will to suicide. The erotic energy of "ARIEL" (1962) is focused on a self-destructive "drive / Into the red / Eye, the cauldron of morning." In "LADY LAZARUS" (1962), the speaker implies that her suicides are sideshow curiosities in which she annihilates herself once in every decade for the enjoyment of onlookers, miraculously surviving but suffering. Plath's anger and feelings of victimization merge into a private mythology of retributory suicide in which, through death, the female persona becomes purified and perfected. Her death is revenge on those left behind, though the object is not necessarily to cause them pain. In "Fever 103°" (October 1962), the speaker says, "I am too pure for you or anyone." Death becomes a rejection of the pain the "you" has caused. The last poem she ever wrote, "Edge" (1963), depicts the scene of a suicide in which a mother lies sprawled in "perfection," her two children "coiled as serpents" nearby.

Plath wrote especially poignantly about her children, and her love for them is evident. The speaker in "For a Fatherless Son" (1962) warns her son that he will soon feel an absence in his life, but that for now she loves him for his "stupidity" which represents his innocence and ability to love her, and she calls his smiles "found money." The poems about pregnancy, childbirth, and mothering are among the most unshielded works Plath wrote. Here she lowers her masks and expresses emotion without excessive drama. In "Magi" (1960), "Child" (1963), and "Balloons" (1963), she shows the strength of her love as well as the depth of her dilemma: How can she go on living without contaminating her children with "the troublous wringing of hands" ("Child" [1963])? These mothering poems show ambivalence as well, but they are much more positive and less mediated than her poems of victimization and revenge.

Plath's three major lifelong themes are death, victimization, and motherhood. At the end of her life, these preoccupations merge into a vision of her own death, despite or because of her love for her children, as a way to resolve conflict. Her poems of brutal self-examination helped open the way for poets, particularly female poets, to use their intimate experiences in their work.

BIBLIOGRAPHY

Alexander, Paul. *Rough Magic: A Biography of Sylvia Plath.* New York: Viking Penguin, 1991.

Hall, Caroline. *Sylvia Plath.* Boston: Twayne, 1978.

Meyering, Sheryl L. *Sylvia Plath: A Reference Guide.* Boston: G.K. Hall, 1990.

Wilma Weant Dague

PLUMLY, STANLEY (1939–) Stanley Plumly writes NARRATIVE POETRY in a sensitive, unsentimental voice that recreates moments through images and exploration of memory. His poetry is formalized without being formal; spiritual without being religious. Although his poetry is personally reflective, he is not a CONFESSIONAL poet. Rather by examining polarities—father/son, light/dark, dream/reality—Plumly attains the present moment's personal truth. "It seems to me," Plumly has said, "what a poem does is it . . . transforms, returns, so that we can better *see* experience for what it is and what it means" (404).

Born and raised in Barnesville, Ohio, Plumly completed a B.A. at Wilmington College in 1961 and an M.A at Ohio University in 1968. He was the editor of the *Ohio Review* from 1970–75, a recipient of a Guggenheim grant in 1973, and since 1968 has taught at major universities, among them Columbia and Maryland. He has won many awards, including the 1973 DELMORE SCHWARTZ Memorial Award for his first collection, *In the Outer Dark: Poems* (1970), and the WILLIAM CARLOS WILLIAMS Award for his third collection, *Out-of-the-Body Travel* (1977), which was also nominated for a National Book Critics Circle award.

Influenced by his relationships with his parents, particularly his alcoholic father, Plumly's poems are often set against the background of his Ohio childhood. His poems deal with common situations and are accessible in both content and language. Remarking on *In the Outer Dark,* Anthony Piccione asserts, "Plumly is at his best in the image poem. His is a precise blend of ordinary language and bright new perceptions, couched in a low-keyed voice that speaks to us all" (409). In "The Iron Lung" (1977), Plumly explores the father-son identity through image (the son's face "moons in the mirror," and he dreams he "is wearing [his] father's body"), as well as through affirmation and impossibilities ("So this is the dust that passes through porcelain," and "If we could fold our arms, but we can't"). Plumly explores reality with such verbs as "dreaming," "realize," and "remember." And through phrasal repetition, Plumly creates heredity and regeneration, showing how people cannot escape their or their family's past. Even as Plumley's father plays a major role in his first four books, *Summer Celestial* (1983) exhibits a desire to stop treating memory as past and, through his mother, move toward a present state of ancestry and spirituality. Plumly's poetry unabashedly strives to marry his own experience with his family's, and the outer world of indifference with the interior world of self-definition, hoping to find the shadow of truth residing where the past and present intersect.

BIBLIOGRAPHY
Piccione, Anthony. Review of *In the Outer Dark,* by Stanley Plumly. *Southern Humanities Review* 6, no. 4 (fall 1972): 406–410.
Plumly, Stanley. "Plumly, Stanley (Ross) 1939–." *Contemporary Authors,* Vol. 110, edited by Christine Nasso. Detroit: Gale, 1984, pp. 404–407.

Michelle Bonczek

"THE POEM AS MASK" MURIEL RUKEYSER **(1968)** "No more masks! No more mythologies," pledges MURIEL RUKEYSER in "The Poem as Mask," an influential feminist poem that not only proclaimed the validity of women's issues as fit subjects for poetry but also called for resistance to the imposition of denigrating "myths" upon the lives of women. Self-critical yet movingly lyrical, the poem alludes both to the myth of Orpheus and to Rukeyser's own use of that myth to represent two important events in her life, her childbirth and her subsequent involuntary hysterectomy. In reflecting on the nature of myth, Rukeyser calls for a new form of poetry that can attest authentically to the complexities of women's lives, one in which "the fragments join in me with their own music."

In 1949, Muriel Rukeyser wrote "Orpheus," a long poem composed as a masque, or elaborate entertainment modeled on the poetic masques of the 17th century, in which she narrated her own disturbing experience of childbirth through the tale of Orpheus. In the original myth, the archetypal poet Orpheus tries unsuccessfully to rescue his wife from the dead and is later torn to pieces by the Maenads, who were the followers of Dionysos. Rukeyser found in the rending of Orpheus a parallel to her own experience of childbirth, when she woke from anesthesia to learn her son had been delivered by cesarean section and that she had had an involuntary hysterectomy.

In "The Poem as Mask," Rukeyser writes that Orpheus "was myself, split open, unable to speak, in exile from myself." But as Annette Kolodny observes, the pun on "masque" in the title "The Poem as Mask" suggests Rukeyser's use of the myth concealed rather than revealed the emotional contours of her experience, and in the first stanza of the poem, Rukeyser twice writes that the myth "was a mask." But Rukeyser struggles to reject the myth's compelling narrative, recalling such events as the Maenads "on their mountain, gold-hunting, singing, in orgy" and Orpheus "fragmented, exiled from himself, his life, the love gone down with song." Even at a formal level, the pulsing rhythm Rukeyser creates through her frequent use of caesuras evokes the dance of the Maenads and Orpheus's music at the same moment that she is trying to distance herself from them.

But in the second stanza, Rukeyser reclaims power by negating the myths that have provided a limited and limiting structure for expressing her personal experiences. "There is no mountain, there is no god, there is memory / of my torn life," she writes. For Rukeyser, a woman's personal experiences, whether bodily, emotional, intellectual, or other, are inherently worthy as subjects of poetry, and do not need to be adorned or legitimized by myth. Moreover, Rukeyser rejects such myths for having been handed down through the same patriarchal society that condoned the simultaneous violation of her body, her will, and her human rights through involuntary hysterectomy. This rejection occasions the creation of a new feminist poetry, one whose form remains undetermined, but which is original and powerful, drawing on authentic experience and not derived from the myths and forms of the past. Yet the grandeur suggested by myth, if not the myth itself, remains an inescapable property of poetry, and ironically of Rukeyser's verse as well; in the concluding lines, Rukeyser describes how the new poetry she has called for will receive the sanction of the same mythological poet whom she has just rejected: "Now, for the first time, the god lifts his hand."

BIBLIOGRAPHY
DuPlessis, Rachel Blau. *Writing Beyond the Ending: Narrative Strategies of Twentieth-Century Women Writers.* Bloomington: Indiana University Press, 1985.
Kolodny, Annette. "The Influence of Anxiety: Prolegomena to a Study of the Production of Poetry by Women." In *A Gift of Tongues: Critical Challenges in Contemporary American Poetry,* edited by Marie Harris and Kathleen Aguero. Athens: The University of Georgia Press, 1987: 112–141.
Rukeyser, Muriel. *A Muriel Rukeyser Reader,* edited by Jan Heller Levi. New York: W. W. Norton, 1994.

Temple Cone

"A POEM FOR SPECULATIVE HIPSTERS" LEROI JONES (AMIRI BARAKA) (1964) First published in his second collection of poems, *The Dead Lecturer,* "A Poem for Speculative Hipsters" is the work of AMIRI BARAKA's (then LeRoi Jones's) bohemian period of the late 1950s and early 1960s. Baraka was one of the contributors to *The New American Poetry: 1945–1960* (1960), an influential anthology of postwar experimental poetry (see POETRY ANTHOLOGIES). Like many of the poets included in this volume, he rejected the formalist, or "academic," poetics still dominant in the United States at midcentury. Baraka often insisted that the process of making poetry is far more important than poems themselves and that to confine oneself to regular verse forms is to conclude the poetic process before it begins. Poems thus composed, he thought, are dead artifacts instead of vital expressions of actual life. In the essay "How You Sound??" (1960), Baraka proclaims, "There cannot be anything I must *fit* the poem into." The poetic process, he says, consists of making everything "fit into the poem" (424). "A Poem for Speculative Hipsters," published a few years after this essay appeared, envisions an ideal world in which a poet can create literature in accordance with this principle. The poem recalls an artist's journey to a "forest / of motives," a distant and mysterious sanctuary where art, safe from the impositions of form, can exist as pure process.

Like the journey Baraka imagines, his poem is itself a "speculative" philosophical and aesthetic exercise: an attempt to push thought and art beyond the limits of immediate perception and everyday experience. In a contemporaneous essay, "Hunting Is Not Those Heads on the Wall" (1964), Baraka argues that just as "hunting" cannot be defined in terms of its stuffed and mounted artifacts, "Art-ing" cannot be defined in terms of formally determined, completed works of art (175). Thus the "forest / of motives," devoid of such gross material forms as "owls" and "hunters," appears to be a place where the artist's "motives" or "ideas" exist unto themselves. Baraka contrasts his artist with Connie Chatterley, the heroine of D. H. Lawrence's *Lady Chatterley's Lover* (1928), who emerges in this poem as a figure of mere sensuality and half-hearted political commitment. Yet if the "forest / of motives" is an escape from the entrapments of the material world, it is also a place of absence: Baraka's artist is "*really / nowhere.*" In the end, then, "A Poem for Speculative Hipsters" perhaps anticipates Baraka's later black nationalist and Marxist writing, in which art is not a matter of speculation but a practical form of cultural and social engagement.

BIBLIOGRAPHY

Jones, LeRoi. "How You Sound??" *The New American Poetry: 1945–1960,* edited by Donald M. Allen. New York: Grove, 1960, pp. 424–425.

———. "Hunting Is Not Those Heads on the Wall." In *Home: Social Essays.* New York: Morrow, 1966, pp. 173–178.

Sollors, Werner. *Amiri Baraka/LeRoi Jones: The Quest for a "Populist Modernism."* New York: Columbia University Press, 1978.

Matthew Calihman

"POETRY" MARIANNE MOORE (1921) "Poetry" is remarkable in that it demonstrates the ambiguity of textual authority—MARIANNE MOORE revised the poem throughout her lifetime and supported concurrent publications of different versions. Without one authoritative text to ground any reading of the poem, "Poetry" becomes fluid, mutating over time to reflect Moore's poetic development. Critics count as many as 11 different texts of "Poetry" published between 1919 and 1981, but Bonnie Honigsblum notes four basic versions: a five-stanza version with near consistency of syllabic meter and rhyme; a 13-line version in free verse; a 15-line version with three stanzas, internal rhyme, and a roughly consistent syllabic meter; and a compressed three-line version with a revised five-stanza version attached as a footnote. This 32-line, five-stanza footnote, published in Moore's *Collected Poems* (1967), is the most frequently anthologized version of "Poetry."

Stylistically "Poetry" reads almost like prose, with Moore's typically long sentences, jagged line breaks, and plain diction. Moore characteristically integrates outside quotations into her poems—in "Poetry" she cites Count Lev Nikolayevich Tolstoy and William Butler Yeats. Her inventive juxtapositioning of quotations strengthens her own voice by calling attention to it within a context of external voices.

"Poetry" begins ironically as a poem that takes a derogatory stance towards poetry ("I, too, dislike it"). But poetry here remains ambiguous and undefined. Instead of offering the reader an objective explanation of what poetry is, Moore shifts her focus to the detailed physical effects brought about by reading poetry. She zooms in on particulars, noticing the sensations in her hands, eyes, and hair that indicate a reaction to good poetry. Natural imagery of inverted bats, hefty elephants, and wild horses followed closely by more mundane references to the practical world of business suggests that poetry may exist in the intersection between the practical and the imaginative. Poets are "literalists of the imagination," Moore writes. And if poetry can be found in the stuff of everyday life, Moore's opening indictment of poetry suddenly seems less ironic. The objection, it would seem, is to academic definitions that seek to generalize or intellectualize the particular experience of a strong poem.

Moore's development of her topic alters with alternate versions of "Poetry." The 1924 13-line poem concludes with "enigmas are not poetry," which suggests a plea for lucidity and exactness of language that Moore's own vague opening lines would seem to resist. However, the 1967 shorter three-line text concludes by tersely asserting that poetry is "a place for the genuine," yet offers no concrete definition of the "genuine," leaving the work of identifying it up to the reader. Moore's predilection for multiple variant texts virtually explodes the common notion of the unified authoritative text, and her process serves as a model for such 20th-century poets as DONALD HALL and LYN HEJINIAN, who likewise resist the limitations of textual closure. A text can be returned to again and again with each version in conversation with the others.

BIBLIOGRAPHY

Honigsblum, Bonnie. "Marianne Moore's Revisions of 'Poetry.'" In *Marianne Moore: Woman and Poet*, edited by Patricia C. Willis, 185–222. Orono, Maine: National Poetry Foundation, 1990.

Martin, Taffy. *Marianne Moore: Subversive Modernist.* Austin: University of Texas Press, 1986.

Terry Lynn Pettinger

POETRY AND TRANSLATION Perhaps it should not come as a surprise that a century marked by world wars, ease of travel, economic globalization, and further racial and ethnic diversification of its populace might also see a greater interest in translation by American poets than in previous periods. Poets responded to the globalization of the metropolitan West with an unparalleled production of English-language translations, resulting in a wide variety of forms and theories of translation. Important poets who also translated poetry include ELIZABETH BISHOP, PAUL BLACKBURN, CID CORMAN, LYN HEJINIAN, RICHARD HOWARD, LANGSTON HUGHES, ALLEN MANDELBAUM, GARY SNYDER, ROSMARIE WALDROP, ELIOT WEINBERGER, and RICHARD WILBUR, among others. The present essay will limit its focus to the works of six of the most influential poet/translators, EZRA POUND, AMY LOWELL, KENNETH REXROTH, ROBERT BLY, JEROME ROTHENBERG, and LOUIS ZUKOFSKY.

Ezra Pound initiated a century of American poetry greatly indebted to the bounty of material gathered from around the globe. Pound translated, among others, Guido Cavalcanti from the Italian, Sappho from the Greek, Arnaut Daniel from the Provençal, and Sextus Propertius from the Latin. In his essay "Guido's Relations" (1954), he explains his propensity for altering the target language (the English) in ways that can produce sonorous textures, which evoke the source text's linguistic particularities. He sought to escape the rigidity of Victorian English tradition by enriching his translations with archaic elements of Greek, Latin, and Anglo Saxon. For instance, in his translation of the Anglo-Saxon poem "The Seafarer" (1912), Pound imitates the source text's meter and archaic diction ("mews" for "seagulls," "Nathless" for "nevertheless") and often translates literally ("corna caldast" becomes "corn of the coldest") as well. Yet Pound did not reserve these compositional strategies for translations alone; instead, they inflected his own work with archaic diction and foreign syntax that often evokes strong, nearly sanctified resonances. By making translation into a trope, a metonym for a distant authenticity, the "luminous details" (Pound, "I Gather the Limbs of Osiris," 24) that Pound gathered during his intertextual travels operated as symbols for larger cultural networks of authority. Therefore Pound's poetics can be seen as a product of an expeditionary model of translation, where the poet searches old foreign literature for images and textures that can then enrich and renew the Anglo-American idioms with new clarity, rhythms, sounds, and forms.

While his translations from Western sources were important to Pound's original works, his encounter with Chinese poetry via a manuscript of Ernest Fenollosa left the greatest mark on both his work and, by extension, early Anglo-American MODERNISM. In 1913 Pound received papers of the late Fenollosa, who, up until his death, had been working on a series of translations of ancient Chinese verse and Japanese Noh drama. Once in possession of these decipherings and Fenollosa's romantic translation theories, Pound went on to publish his most popular translation: *Cathay* (1915). But perhaps just as important, Pound was able to locate both the IMAGIST and vorticist literary movements within the classical Chinese tradition. Fenollosa's notes argue that a Chinese character is "a vivid shorthand picture of the operations of nature. . . . The thought-picture is not only called up by these signs as well as by words, but far more vividly and concretely. . . . [T]hey are *alive*" (8–9). He goes on to claim, "Poetic thought works by suggestion, crowding maximum meaning into the single phrase pregnant, charged, and luminous from within" (28). For Pound, Fenollosa's work uncovered a vast and ancient cultural system that could validate the avant-garde in its efforts to revitalize Western civilization.

Yet Pound was not the only poet associated with the imagists to publish translations of East Asian verse. Amy Lowell also made translation an important component of her poetry. While East Asian themes appear even in her earliest work, *A Dome of Many-Coloured Glass* (1912), in such poems as "A Japanese Wood Carving" (1912), her later work begins to show a greater interest in the Far East, typified by her book of verse, *Pictures of a Floating World* (1919). The title is a translation of the Japanese term *ukiyo-e,* which is associated with a form of 18th-century Japanese lacquer prints that Lowell's 174 short, free verse lyrics take as their collective subject. Her later collaboration with the expert on China and translator Florence Ayscough on *Fir-Flower Tablets* (1921) solidified Lowell's prominence as a populist of Asian verse. Even though neither Lowell nor Pound read Chinese and were poorly received by the community of experts on Chinese, their translations helped usher in and popularize the century's interest in poetic translations, Asian verse, and the exoticized East.

Perhaps the most well-known American poet after the imagists to find inspiration from contact with non-Western cultures is Rexroth. He translated from many languages—Latin, Greek, Italian, Spanish, French, Chinese, and Japanese—but he is best remembered for his East Asian translations. His translations resisted Pound's undeniable influences by adopting a more idiosyncratic and willfully colloquial tone: "Every day on the way home from my office, I pawn another of my Spring Clothes" (*One Hundred Poems from the Chinese* [1971]). The substitution of "office" for the more common choice "court" along with the everyday syntax reveals Rexroth's willingness to reframe ancient verse in his modernized personal idiom. Nevertheless his translations often lean toward the direct, clear, and concrete qualities that not only characterize Pound's East Asian translations but had, by midcentury, become quintessentially modernist: "The bright, thin, new moon appears" (*One Hundred Poems from the Chinese* [1971]).

Ever since the publication of *One Hundred Poems from the Japanese* (1955), Rexroth's translations have been widely read, enjoyed, and criticized. Over his long career Rexroth translated several volumes of poetry from both Japanese and Chinese (with a particular concentration on the Tang poet Du Fu), as well as hundreds of tanka (a form of short Japanese verse of generally five lines), and he also composed tanka in English. In fact, one can see numerous references, images, and syntactic translative hauntings throughout his original work, but the most dramatic instance of translation's transposition occurs in his last major work, *The Love Poems of Marichiko* (1978). Rexroth used the guise of translation to write from the voice of a fictive Japanese woman. The poems depict a detailed and exoticized (and often highly eroticized) Japanese world: "The moon sinks into the far off hills. / Dew drenches the bamboo grass. . . . / At midnight the temple bells ring." Unlike Rexroth's own tanka written in

English, however, these poems were first falsely published as translations. The Marichiko series uses a suggestive haiku-like form and Orientalized details to perform an act of ventriloquism suggesting an ultimate fusion of the poet and translator.

In addition, both Robert Bly and Jerome Rothenberg continue to produce a huge volume of foreign poetry in translation and, in turn, reproduce the theory of translation as both a humanistic bridge and poetic necessity. Rothenberg and Bly were associated with a movement of poetry called DEEP IMAGE, a term coined in an essay published in 1961 by ROBERT KELLY. While Bly and Rothenberg may not have agreed on the particulars, they both translated with an intense belief in the ability to bring across complex images through translation. In 1958 Bly, along with William Duffy, began a journal entitled the *Fifties,* which Bly later solo edited as the *Sixties* and the *Seventies* and which focused on presenting translations from both Europe and Latin America. Bly argued that translations were vitally important to American poetry, since American poetry needed the importation of foreign images to keep it alive. To this day Bly remains one of the most voluminous poet/translators working, and his example continues to fuel a near-ubiquitous interest in gathering foreign images through translation. But like the aforementioned poets, Bly is not only interested in translating content; he also employs non-English templates in his own creative work. In his book *The Night Abraham Called to the Stars* (2001), he uses the *ghazal,* an Arabic form of poetry in which the individual strophes, or stanzas, are poems themselves: "My heart is a calm potato by day. . . . // Friend, tell me what to do." Not only does he employ a foreign compositional template (here dialogic, autonomous stanzas), but his imagery reflects a lifetime of reading foreign literature.

Similar to Bly, Rothenberg is still producing both translations and his own creative work, yet Rothenberg is perhaps most recognized for his industrious publications of intercultural anthologies. His latest anthology, *Poems for the Millennium* (1995), coedited with Pierre Joris, is perhaps his most exhaustive contribution yet. While his anthologies are very important to the history of translation and poetry in the 20th century, he is also recognized for his innovative translation strategies. He coined the term *total translation* to describe his translations of Navajo songs entitled *The 17 Horse Songs of Frank Mitchell* (1970), in which he includes nonsense syllables and bends the English phonemes toward the Navaho: "Because I was thn boyngnng raised ing the dawn NwnnN go to her my son N wnn N wnn N nnnn N gahn." His total translations and the field of ETHNOPOETICS that he and the anthropologist/translator Dennis Tedlock initiated with the 1971 publication of *Alcheringa* explored the importance of aurality, or sound, in translating primarily indigenous oral poetry. Robert von Hallberg sees this focus on aurality as a shift to a poetics in which "the objective is a radical contemporaneity. . . . What was emerging was the premise that the body is the basis of language, that sounds made by a speaking body in one locale may be likened to similar sounds made by a speaking body in a distant locale or time" (261).

This development leads us back to what was perhaps the most controversial translation in the 20th century, Zukofsky's *Catullus* (1969), a "homophonic translation" (translating the sounds of the source text into words in the target language that mimic those sounds) of the Latin. While translating from Latin and Greek has been an important genre in its own right for centuries, Zukofsky's translation stands in a category all its own. In his translator's preface Zukofsky states, "This translation of Catallus follows / the sound, rhythm, and syntax of his / Latin—tries, as is said, to breathe / the 'literal' meaning with him" (1). Therefore the source work's textures become a compositional template that selects English words based primarily upon their similarity to the spoken Latin and not their semantic properties. For example, the Latin "*Tondet os. miser a miser / concubine, nuces da*" appears in English as "toned down his *me, sir ah me, sir* / quaint cute boy, now it's the nuts" (61).

Later we see Zukofsky, like so many poets before and after him, apply the textures discovered during his work on translation to his original poetry as well, as in this line from "A"-22 (1975), a section of his long poem "A": "Ye no we see hay / io we hay we see / hay io we see no" (36). For Zukofsky, translation was about discovering new sounds and rhythms more than deep images or exotic details; therefore his work after his homophonic translations plays more liberally with sound and syntax, just as his translations had. The resultant disjointed syntax resembles verse produced through the chance operations (a compositional method based on random sampling) of, say, JACKSON MAC LOW and in turn provides a strong antecedent to the material (visual and aural) poetics of those writing in the tradition that has come to be called LANGUAGE poetry.

In all of the poets discussed here, translation reveals itself to be an intercultural as well as interlinguistic poetic practice. And while translations informed by many of the poets discussed thus far continue to be published, many American poets, especially multilingual ones such as Cecilia Vicuqa and Anne Tardos, are breaking down the formal distinction between translation and writing proper, as well as publishing American poetry in languages other than English. It is safe to say, therefore, that the poetics of translation will continue to play a central role in the poetry of the 21st century.

BIBLIOGRAPHY

Apter, Ronnie. *Digging far the Treasure: Translation after Pound.* New York: Paragon House, 1987.

Fenollosa, Ernest. *The Chinese Written Character as a Medium for Poetry,* edited by Ezra Pound. San Francisco: City Lights Books, 1936.

Huang, Yunte. *Transpacific Displacement: Ethnography, Translation, and Intertextual Travel in Twentieth-Century American Literature.* Berkeley: University of California Press, 2001.

Pound, Ezra. "Guido's Relations." In *Literary Essays of Ezra Pound,* edited by T. S. Eliot. London: Faber and Faber, 1954, pp. 191–200.

———. "I Gather the Limbs of Osiris" (1911). *Selected Prose, 1909–1965,* New York: New Directions, 1973, pp. 21–43.

von Halberg, Robert. "From Translation." *TriQuarterly* (winter 1995): 249–276.

Zukofsky, Louis. Translator's Preface to *Catullus,* translated by Celia Zukofsky and Louis Zukofsky. London: Cape Goliard, 1969, n.p.

Jonathan Stalling

POETRY ANTHOLOGIES In its broadest sense, a poetry anthology is a collection of poems written by a variety of poets. Typically an anthology also contains or is organized by a determining thematic or time-period focus. Thus, on the one hand, we might read the *Norton Anthology of Modern Poetry,* which demonstrates a period but not a thematic unity, or, on the other hand, we might pick up an edition of *100 Love Poems,* which showcases love poems throughout history. Regardless, however, of their determining focus or organization, anthologies are, almost without exception, involved in the work of establishing "representativeness" or the institution of what is called "canonicity." That is, all anthologies, as Jed Rasula declares, "aspire to canonical service" in one way or another (477), and their attempt to construct, maintain, or challenge the literary canon (the list of writers or texts that are considered exemplary) is one of their crucial functions.

Anthologies have existed in the West since at least the Alexandrian period, when Greek scholars began to collect texts of Sappho, Archilochus, Pericles, and other poets of Greek as exemplary instances of either a particular metrical form or poetic content. The anthologist's and anthology's instructional purpose remained, more or less, intact through the years. In the 20th century, however, both the editorship and purpose of anthologies transformed, at least in part, the classroom and became, to a large extent, a primary venue for establishing a way in which poets themselves might develop a map of both contemporary and historical poetry.

Arguably the modern anthology begins in 1914 with EZRA POUND's *Des Imagistes,* which included poems by American- and British-born poets: Pound himself, H. D., Richard Aldington, and F. S. Flint. In large part working against the formal and thematic conservatism of late 19th-century Victorianism, Pound used his collection to advance a very specific sense of the poem, which disavowed established meters and metaphors for a responsive and open poetic form that came to be called "free verse" (see PROSODY AND FREE VERSE). While Pound's anthology initiated an influential, international American presence, he constructed his poetics from Greek, Roman, French, Italian, and Irish traditions and disregarded possible American examples of innovative verse, including the work of Edgar Allan Poe, Emily Dickinson, and Walt Whitman.

In addition to the sense of the poem it explicitly advocated, *Des Imagistes* importantly marked the assumption of the anthologist's role by a poet and the refusal of the anthology's historic impulse, though the instructional and canonical purpose of the anthology remained intact (as much as Pound's editorial practice was essentially polemical and corrective), Pound's effort marked a change in the stake of the anthology through its assumption of the editorial role by a poet and its interest in redirecting public recognition of poetry's history and contemporaneity. Shortly after Pound's gathering, James Weldon Johnson published *The Book of American Negro Poetry* in 1922. While clearly not a direct consequence of Pound's project, Johnson's anthology nonetheless showed the change in the anthology's editorial project and agency. Following Johnson's efforts, Alain Locke (*The New Negro*), Countee Cullen (*Caroling Dusk*), Sterling Brown, Arthur Davis and Ulysses Lee (*The Negro Caravan*) and Langston Hughes and Arna Bontemps (*The Poetry of the Negro, 1746–1949*), all put together collections of African-American literature before 1949. These anthologies were central to the formalization of the Harlem Renaissance and testify to the power of the anthology to affect the sense of both historical and contemporary scene of American poetry. Also these collections established the crucial possibility of the anthology to recognize and gather writing that might otherwise be unavailable to a general readership and significantly affected the map of Modern American literature.

A more direct consequence of Pound's *Des Imagistes* was the circuitously influential *An "Objectivists" Anthology* edited by Louis Zukofsky and printed by Harriet Monroe's *Poetry* in 1931 (see objectivist school). Pound, seeking to facilitate a specifically American participation in and response to the active European production of poetic manifesto and anthology, urged Monroe to grant editorial reign to Zukofsky (see European poetic influences). Publishing himself, Charles Reznikoff, William Carlos Williams, George Oppen, Kenneth Rexroth, and others, Zukofsky's gathering represented a group of poets who, working within explicitly modernist modes, almost entirely resisted the draw to Europe. While more or less overlooked at the time, Zukofsky's anthology has become progressively more important to a sense of an American modernism, documenting the work of poets who assumed and practiced a recognizably modernist writing while remaining in the United States.

Together with such collections as Alfred Kreymborg's *Others* (1916), Harriet Monroe and Alice Corbin Henderson's *The New Poetry* (1917), Louis Untermeyer's *Modern American Poetry: An Introduction* (1919), and Conrad Aiken's *American Poetry 1671–1928* (1928), Zukofsky's and the assorted African-American anthologies offer a rich and varied picture of early 20th-century American poetic production. In addition to focusing attention on both a past and present work of poetry by largely unknown writers, these anthologies articulated a developing sense of a specifically American poetry.

Despite the explosion in the publication of poetry anthologies in the first part of the 20th century, no consensus on what typified modern verse was established. In fact, the very proliferation of publication may have made it impossible for any accord to be reached. Ironically this difficulty of characterizing and canonizing the poetic production of the modernist period defines the post–World War II approach to anthologization.

In 1957 Meridian published *The New Poets of England and America,* edited by Donald Hall, Robert Pack, and Louis Simpson and featuring an introduction by Robert Frost. The anthology was seen by many as the securing claim on the postwar American literary landscape by a younger generation of English and American poets, such as Donald Justice, Robert Lowell, Adrienne Rich, and W. D. Snodgrass. The editors selected largely academic poets working within a tradition of modernist verse and valuing the forms, structures, and craft of such British and American modernist poets as Frost, W. H. Auden, Wallace Stevens, and T. S. Eliot. Three years later, in 1960, and partly in opposition to *The New Poets of England and America, Grove Press published Donald Allen's The New American Poetry, 1945–1961*. Featuring a diverse range of poets—LeRoi Jones (Amiri Baraka) to Helen Adam, Charles Olson to John Ashbery, Robert Duncan to Allen Ginsberg—the anthology offered a very different picture of the poetic landscape and represented exclusively American writers who, unaffiliated with any academic institution and largely unpublished, were considered "outsiders," although Allen grouped individual poets into categories and thus established new "insiders," albeit antiacademic ones. The two texts engaged in a "battle of the anthologies," competing for representativeness and readership.

The stake in this war between the anthologies was twofold. On the one hand, the landscape of contemporary poetry was being disputed; on the other, the character, canon, and continuity of modernist verse was under scrutiny. In his introduction to *Modern Verse in English, 1900–1950* (1950)—an anthology closely linked to The *New Poets of England and America*—ALLEN TATE writes, "The early reception in England of Robert Frost and the enormous international influence of Pound and Eliot and, later, of W. H. Auden, have at last produced an Anglo-American poetry that only by convention can be separated" (qtd. in Rasula 223). Tate's sense of an inseparable synthesis of U.S. and British traditions is echoed in the Hall, Pack, and Simpson anthology, particularly in its amalgamation of British and American poets. Implicit to these anthologies' claim of a poetry of Britain and the United States is a sense that the two countries not only share a literary tradition but also produce an ultimately indistinguishable poetry.

Allen's *The New American Poetry,* in contrast, is exclusively and explicitly American. Aside arguably inseparable from, the formal distinctions of the two collections, this attempt to define "American poets and poetry" crucially differentiates the terms and claims of each anthology. While the Hall, Pack, and Simpson anthology, like its Tate-edited predecessor, insists on an "English language" tradition, the Allen anthology claims a uniquely American writing that depends upon the singular conditions of U.S. history, politics, and general culture. While Pound is a shared poetic exemplar, the Allen anthology, one might say, substitutes Williams for Auden and Zukofsky for Eliot, adding (in no particular order) LAURA RIDING, H. D., Walt Whitman, Emily Dickinson, Herman Melville, GERTRUDE STEIN, Hughes, and others. In the midst of the Hall-Allen poetry war, Robert Kelley and Paris Leary published *A Controversy of Poets* (1965), in which the editors offered a potpourri of writers that crossed camp lines, as Snodgrass was followed by JACK SPICER and JAMES DICKEY by ED DORN. Boldly disregarding partisan tendencies, the anthology attempted to represent the conflicted and complex state of early postmodern American verse. The editorial strategy of Kelley and Leary was not widely adopted, and anthologies—particularly those assembled by poets—largely remained explicitly partisan through the second half of the 20th century.

Allen's anthology published a solely American poetry which, heir to a primarily Anglo Modernism, attempted to establish a characteristically and innovative U.S. postwar verse. This project was taken up most significantly in 1986 with RON SILLIMAN's *In the American Tree.* Like Allen's some three decades earlier, Silliman's editorship served a polemical function. As both the publishing and educational industries proliferated in the 1950s and 1960s, textbook anthologies mushroomed. By 1970 Norton had published its first anthology of poetry and formalized what would become the increasingly dominant purpose of the anthology: to provide the classroom with a fairly stabilized group of Anglo-American poets. Silliman's anthology, however, attempted to deflect an uncritical assumption of a traditional canon and offered a vibrant and oppositional gathering of poets who explicitly put into question the poetic forms and modes prominent in commercial and university publications. Importantly *In the American Tree* made possible a more public appearance of independently published American poets working in an experimental tradition. More recently, Douglas Messerli's *From the Other Side of the Century* (1994) and the Pierre Joris—and Jerome Rothenberg–edited *Poems for the Millennium* (1995) take up Silliman's and others' project of anthologizing innovative and international poets.

These recent attempts to complicate the canon have centered on formally experimental poems and poets and thus, as some critics have pointed out, showcase a very limited range of race and gender. In this way these more adventurous contemporary anthologies showed the same exclusivity as that of more mainstream collections of American verse, such as Helen Vendler's *The Harvard Book of Contemporary American Poetry* (1985) and J. D. MCCLATCHY's *The Vintage Book of Contempo-*

rary American Poetry (1990), both of which offer readers valuable collections of formally conventional poetry directly heir to an Anglo-American High Modernism. Partly in response to the limitedness of these late century collections, anthologies African Americans, women, gays, and other marginalized groups appeared more frequently. *Catch the Fire!!!: A Cross-Generational Anthology of African-American Poetry* (1998), for instance, included Baraka, JUNE JORDAN, SONIA SANCHEZ, and Quincy Trupe, and Florence Howe's *No More Masks!: An Anthology of Twentieth Century American Women Poets* appeared in 1993. *Resurgent: New Writing by Women* (1992), edited by Lou Robinson and Camille Norton, is an important collection of innovative prose-poetry work, and Timothy Liu's *Word of Mouth: An Anthology of Gay American Poetry* (2000), collects the work of vital postmodern gay poets. There is also the annual *Best American Poetry*, edited by DAVID LEHMAN.

In the end any anthology, if only implicitly, makes a canonical claim regarding the poems included. These claims vary wildly, yet are nonetheless central to the anthology's formation. Ultimately the anthology is both an invaluable educational aid and an ideological tool. Teachers, students, and readers of poetry must be both alert to the distinctive advantage of the anthology—to offer access to poems that might not otherwise be read—and be aware and critical of the anthology's motivated, essentializing, and canonizing functions.

BIBLIOGRAPHY

Golding, Alan. *From Outlaw to Classic: Canons in American Poetry*. Madison: University of Wisconsin Press, 1995.

Rasula, Jed. *The American Poetry Wax Museum*. Urbana, Ill.: National Council of Teachers of English, 1995.

Thomas Fisher

POETRY IN PERFORMANCE Poetry in performance is a broad category used to describe the work associated with a wide range of literary movements and trends, including BEAT POETRY, the BLACK ARTS MOVEMENT, the LANGUAGE SCHOOL of poetry, the oral poetics movement, ETHNOPOETICS, rap, slam poetry, fusion poetry, and CYBERPOETRY, and it may include activities as diverse as the private oral recitation of poetry, live and recorded poetry readings, sound poetry (which emphasizes the sound of words, instead of their meaning), and performance art, to list a few. While technically a "poetry performance" can refer to any poetic work in any form, including poems printed on the page, it is more commonly used to describe poetry that is "off the page" and, if not always "on the stage," at least made manifest in a medium or in media other than the printed word. Perhaps most commonly it refers to the oral performance of poetry either as a poem read aloud or recited from memory, which may include body gesture, movement, props, and musical or sound accompaniment and which, as a "performance," represents a public and often politically inflected alternative to the printed poem read silently in solitude. By taking the poem off the page, a poem in performance can call attention to the affinities of poetry with other modes of expression; these affinities suggest different ways poetry can (and should) communicate, alternative venues in which poetry can appear, and new ways that it can have an impact upon the world. Thus poetry in performance is often figured in opposition to more traditional kinds of poetry, and its literary movements often position themselves against poetry as "high art," against white, middle-class, corporate culture, and against poetry's academic institutions.

Preexisting models for the oral performance of poetry in 20th-century America range from the ancient rhapsodists (the wandering poets in the time of Homer) and Brahmanic mnemonists (students who memorized and recited ancient Indian hymns), African, Oceanic, and American Indian oral chant and storytelling, and the Celtic and European bard and minstrel tradition, as well as early 20th-century European avant-garde performances, such as those of dadaist artists in Zurich's once-famous Cabaret Voltaire (see EUROPEAN POETIC INFLUENCES). While these models have been drawn upon in various ways by American poet-performers in order to formulate alternative poetry practices and to make poetry a public, communal, and sometimes a countercultural and radical political activity, the earliest historical examples of the performance of poetry in the United States are found in the primarily educational, yet still community-oriented practice of elocution and drawing-room recitation. Emerging in the 19th-century and persisting well into the first two decades of the 20th, poetry reading and recitation clubs aimed to acculturate and entertain. In the first decades of the 20th century, poets as different as VACHEL LINDSAY and LANGSTON HUGHES gave poetry performances that were legendary even in a period when audiences were used to similar theatrics in performances on vaudeville and in the delivery of church sermons. The recordings of modernist poets T. S. ELIOT, EZRA POUND, and GERTRUDE STEIN, among others, reading their own work, which were released by the Library of Congress and commercial labels, such as Caedmon, in the 1940s and 1950s, represented a break with these earlier practices of popular recitation and introduced the oral performance of poetry as an extension of the expressive work of the avant-garde, high art poet (see MODERNISM). But it was probably not until 1955 and the Six Gallery reading in San Francisco, featuring poetry performances by the likes of MICHAEL MCCLURE, PHILIP WHALEN, GARY SNYDER, and ALLEN GINSBERG's reading of *HOWL* (with JACK KEROUAC cheering them all on) that the true significance of poetry in performance as an antiestablishment, antitraditional gesture materialized in the United States. The Beats took CHARLES OLSON's idea that the limitations of poetry arise from "manuscript, press, the removal of verse from its producer and reproducer, the voice" and developed a poetics rooted in oral performance, drawing upon Buddhist chant, popular folk and protest singing, improvisational jazz, and the political stand-up routines of comics, including Lenny Bruce ("Projective Verse" 22).

While this work of the Beats expressed a loosely defined leftist and environmentalist politics, the poetry performances of the Black Arts movement, starting in the mid-1960s, identified social engagement and black power as defining aspects of its performative aesthetic. From such bases as the Black Arts Repertory Theatre and School, founded in Harlem in 1965 by IMAMU AMIRI BARAKA (LeRoi Jones), the movement was innovative in its use of language (particularly Black English), music, and performance to produce a poetry that emphasized orality and featured a ritual use of call and response between artist and audience coherent in purpose with the community meetings, lectures, and study groups that were held in the same venues as the performances. Fueled by a politically informed anger, Baraka's piece, "Black Art" (1966) suggests the degree to which poetry was conceived by this movement as a gesture of forceful action: "We want 'poems that kill.' / Assassin poems, Poems that shoot guns. Poems that wrestle cops into alleys."

Some of these same performance strategies, as well as the sense of poetry as a vehicle for self-definition through "speaking out" against an oppressive status quo, is also apparent in rap and slam poetry. Rap (also called "emceeing")—speaking in rhymes to the beat of music—draws its roots from the Jamaican DJ "toasting," or speaking live over a music recording, and from the African-American verbal game of one-upmanship called "dozens," in which witty insults (often about "your mama") are exchanged (mainly) between men, the winner being the one who is able to verbally destroy all of his opponents (see CARIBBEAN POETIC INFLUENCES). Rap, which emerged out of the South Bronx section of New York City in the 1970s, shares Black Art performance's sense of language as a weapon of power. The rapper often boasts of his rhyming (and sexual) prowess and answers the stated attacks of his opponents and detractors. Rap is a dialogical verbal performance within the larger art form of hip-hop, which includes deejaying (cutting and scratching a vinyl recording), break dancing and other forms of movement, graffiti art, and specific codes of dress. Rap is one aspect of a multimedia art form.

Slam poetry represents another confrontational and, in this case, explicitly competitive form of poetry performance. Slam poets compete against each other by winning over an audience with work that is entertaining and powerful on a first hearing and by impressing judges who rank and score their performances, the winner being decided through a process of elimination. The slam was born in the mid-1980s in Chicago and quickly spread to the Nuyorican Poets' Café in Manhattan, where a multiethnic field of poets performed work that was typically lively, declamatory, humorous, confessional, vulgar, political, and rantlike in nature. The short length of the slam piece (measured not by lines but by minutes, traditionally three) combined with the need to convey an arresting and persuasive message before an audience in such venues as bars and night cubs has made the slam poem an identifiable genre of poetry in its own right, a genre that has persisted beyond the competitive context of the poetry slam and can still be heard at actual "open mic" and "spoken word" events across North America. Slam-influenced spoken word events continue be a significant site of organization for grassroots, ethnic-based poetry communities. These poetry communities have also been developed as "virtual" communities, gathering in "electronic bars" on the Internet, where the printed word is made to perform in new ways, "deploying new idioms, rhythms, and typographical conventions," as a means of establishing a "poetics of virtual proximity" that mimics spoken word gatherings in the domain of cyberpoetry (Brawley 164, 173).

These grassroots and community-based activities are only tangentially linked to other more theoretically developed experimental and performance-oriented work in the oral poetics, ethnopoetics, sound poetry, Language poetry, and fusion poetry movements. Some primary characteristics of these new approaches poetry (identified in an early essay on the subject by JEROME ROTHENBERG) include a sense of "ethnological continuity," the "breakdown of boundaries and genres," "a move away from the idea of 'masterpiece'" toward a sense of the "transientness" of the artwork, "a new sense of function in art," based on "what it does" in a specific (social or performance) context, "a stress on action and/or process," as well as the blurring of boundaries between artist and audience, between real time and theatrical time, and between transformations that are expressed in a performance and "actual transformations (of the self, of consciousness)" that result from it (12–15). Ethnopoetics originated among poets with an interest in anthropology and linguistics and among anthropologists and linguists with an interest in poetry, such as Rothenberg, DAVID ANTIN, and Denis Tedlock. These poets and critics emphasize the dialogical dimensions of performance and associate the art of poetry with the acts of talking, chanting, or singing, which give shape to proverbs, riddles, curses, laments, prayers, public announcements, and stories.

In sound poetry the conventional hierarchy between vocal sounds and semantic sense is modulated and often reversed, resulting in a poetry that foregrounds words as vehicles of sound and often moves beyond recognizable language to explore the nonverbal, expressive capacities of the human voice. Words become shrieks and squawks, moods are struck through modulations in vocal tone and volume, and rhythmic patterns are developed by alternating guttural grunts and high-pitched yelps. The CANADIAN POETIC INFLUENCE upon American poetry by sound poets, including Bill Bissett and the poetry performance group the Four Horsemen, is worth noting. The work of these Canadian poetry performers and of American poets, including JACKSON MAC LOW and JOHN CAGE, was motivated by a desire "to create a poetry of spontaneous affect" (Bernstein 168–169), and the sound pieces they created were often based on chance operations governing the choice of words, proving that sound has an emotional effect beyond rational meaning and highlighting the human speaking voice as a musical instrument (Morris 129–146).

Not unlike the sound poet, who "practices the deformation of linguistic form at the level of the signifier" (Andrews and Bernstein 89), the writers associated with the Language movement (the name taken from its journal, *L=A=N=G=U=A=G=E,*) approached poetry as a way of placing attention "primarily on language and ways of making meaning, that takes for granted neither vocabulary, grammar, process, shape, syntax, program, or subject matter" (Andrews and Bernstein ix). Thus, counter to spoken word poetry, Language poetry often defies any principle of direct address or dialogue; rather, it performs language in a way that underscores its status as a nontransparent medium of expression. Instead of establishing a sense of community in performance, it articulates a dry skepticism toward community, as CHARLES BERNSTEIN puts it in his essay, "The Conspiracy of 'Us'" (1984): "I don't believe in group formation, I don't like group formation" (Andrews and Bernstein 185).

The recent phenomenon of fusion poetry manifests a conscious awareness of all of these preceding movements, fusing the worlds of the oral and the written and working "with a full awareness of the variety, eclecticism, the wild multiplicities of media and meaning available to any creative imagination in the Infobahn age" (Cabico and Swift 26). In sum, the phrase *poetry in performance* can refer to numerous poetic practices, all of them seeking to enliven poetry by infusing it with other genres and media and by performing it in novel venues.

BIBLIOGRAPHY

Andrews, Bruce, and Charles Bernstein, eds. *The L=A=N=G=U=A=G=E Book.* Carbondale: Southern Illinois University Press, 1984.

Bernstein, Charles, ed. *Close Listening: Poetry and the Performed Word.* New York: Oxford University Press, 1998.

Brawley, Lisa. "The Virtual Slam: Performance Poetry on the Net." *Chicago Review* 40 (1994): 157–163.

Cabico, Regie, and Todd Swift, eds. *Poetry Nation: The North American Anthology of Fusion Poetry.* Montreal, Canada: Véhicule Press, 1998.

Gladney, Marvin J. "The Black Arts Movement and Hip-Hop." *African American Review* 29 (1995): 291–301.

Morris, Adelaide, ed. *Sound States: Innovative Poetics and Acoustical Technologies.* Chapel Hill: University of North Carolina Press, 1997.

Olson, Charles. "Projective Verse." In *Selected Writings,* edited by Robert Creely, 15–26. New York: New Directions, 1966.

Rothenberg, Jerome. "New Models, New Visions: Some Notes towards a Poetics of Performance." In *Performance in Postmodern Culture,* edited by Michel Benamou and Charles Carmello. Madison, Wis.: Coda Press, 1977.

Van Wienen, Mark W. "Vachel Lindsay as Performer," Modern American Poetry: An Online Journal and Multimedia Companion to Anthology of Modern American Poetry, compiled by Cary Nelson. Available online. URL: http://www.english.uiuc.edu/maps/poets/g_1/lindsay/performer.htm. Downloaded October 2003.

Jason Camlot

POETRY INSTITUTIONS Although poetry institutions have existed since the early 20th century, with the advent of writing programs in American universities, these institutions have greatly proliferated, becoming crucial for readers to decide which poets are important. The need for such institutional guidance has grown as poetry itself has fragmented into disparate schools and subcultures. As DANA GIOIA states in his seminal essay "Can Poetry Matter?" (1991), "American poetry now belongs to a subculture. . . . To maintain their activities, subcultures usually require institutions, since the general society does not share their interests" (96, 103). Gioia is referring largely to academic institutions, though other organizations devoted to poetry have also emerged, differentiated from schools of poetry (such as the IMAGIST or the BLACK MOUNTAIN SCHOOL) in this crucial aspect: While the schools are largely initiated and sustained by poets, poetry institutions include critics, poetry-readers, and even nonspecialists, thereby creating effects on a much broader social scale.

The nation's oldest poetry organization, the Poetry Society of America (PSA), was founded in 1910 and once counted among its members ROBERT FROST, LANGSTON HUGHES, EDNA ST. VINCENT MILLAY, MARIANNE MOORE, and WALLACE STEVENS. Unlike other organizations with a more elitist agenda, the PSA has evolved to take the wide dissemination of verse as its purpose. One of its recent endeavors has been the creation of "Poetry in Motion," a campaign that mounts poems on posters in places of public transportation across the country, begun by MOLLY PEACOCK in New York City. Another populist project, launched by ROBERT PINSKY during his term as poet laureate of the United States, the Favorite Poem Project archives and promotes poetry's role in the lives of everyday Americans, irrespective of age, profession, ethnicity, gender, or socioeconomic background.

The largest institution in the country dedicated to poetry is the Academy of American Poets, founded in 1934 by Marie Bullock. While the academy shares some of the breadth and scope of the PSA—having, for example, named April "National Poetry Month"—the organization exists more to support American poets at various stages of their careers. To that end the academy sponsors numerous contests, poetry readings, and poets' residencies, in addition to providing resources for poetry teachers, offering financial support to poetry publishers, and archiving text and audio recordings of established and emerging poets. The academy's pervasive sensibility over the years has been tilted toward LYRICAL and NARRATIVE POETRY not very experimental in structure or disjunctive in voice. Nonetheless, as the most financially sufficient poetry institution in the country, it can be considered the most influential. It has a board of chancellors, composed of preeminent

American poets in the latter stages of their career, and this board is responsible for conferring some of the country's largest literary awards. In 1998 two chancellors, CAROLYN KIZER and MAXINE KUMIN, very publicly resigned to protest the absence of minorities on the board. A longstanding perception exists that the academy is an insular, elitist institution, a kind of old boys' club, and Kizer and Kumin's resignation called attention to the facts that there had never been an African-American chancellor and that the annual academy fellowship had been awarded disproportionately to white males of a certain generation. As a result of this protest, the composition of the board of chancellors has since become more heterogeneous; the 2003 board included NATHANIEL MACKEY, YUSEF KOMUNYAKAA, MICHAEL PALMER, and SUSAN HOWE.

There have been a number of alternatives to the mainstream poetics espoused both by the PSA and the Academy of American Poets. One such institution is the National Poetry Foundation (NPF), created in 1971 by Carroll Terrell, the foremost publisher of scholarly work on EZRA POUND and the Pound tradition, including OBJECTIVIST and, recently, LANGUAGE poetry, as well as an occasional book of verse. The NPF also hosts international conferences on modern poetry. Another nontraditional organization is the Naropa Institute in Colorado, which was founded by Buddhist scholar and artist Chogyam Trungpa Rinpoche on principles that combine contemplative Eastern studies with traditional Western scholastic and artistic disciplines. Inaugurated as the JACK KEROUAC School of Disembodied Poetics by ALLEN GINSBERG and ANNE WALDMAN, Naropa offers academic degrees in poetics with an aesthetic model inseparable from the cultivation of mindfulness and awareness integral to Buddhist ideals of existence. Such principles as synchronicity of body and mind and the need to transcend egoism to arrive at ethical consciousness are thought to be applicable to living and to writing. The writers initially associated with Naropa were considered BEATS, and the kinds of poems produced there today are still influenced by Ginsberg, Waldman, GREGORY CORSO, DIANE DI PRIMA, and LAWRENCE FERLINGHETTI. Naropa also hosts readings and other nonacademic functions.

During the 1930s, Black Mountain College was formed out of a dispute over pedagogy and academic freedom. It did away with such bureaucrats as deans and provosts so that the locus of power resided with the faculty themselves. The school came to be known as a sanctuary for artists, musicians, and writers, both as teachers and students who participated in collective labor, maintenance work, food preparation, and so on. The poet CHARLES OLSON arrived to teach during the 1950s, and others, including ROBERT CREELEY and ROBERT DUNCAN, followed. They were known as the BLACK MOUNTAIN SCHOOL of poets, and while they and the other poets associated with the movement, such as DENISE LEVERTOV and EDWARD DORN, wrote dissimilar kinds of poems, they shared a disdain for baroque, romanticized, end-rhymed poems, seeking instead to use plain-spoken diction to present a view of reality derived from science rather than religion. Though the college became defunct in 1956, its influence was felt deeply by a generation of American artists and writers.

Located in St. Mark's Church in New York City's East Village since 1966, the St. Mark's Poetry Project offers many diverse readings and writing workshops. As JEROME ROTHENBERG relates, "The Poetry Project vortex circa 1967—to which I was witness—included Beat poets, NEW YORK SCHOOL poets, San Francisco poets [see SAN FRANCISCO RENAISSANCE], Black Mountain poets, DEEP IMAGE poets, Midwest & Southwest regionals, Fluxus poets, Umbra poets & so on . . . even—in this unusually most generous of vortexes—academic poets." Demonstrating a commitment to live poetry events, the project offers biweekly readings, marathon readings, and audio archives, including a recording of the only known joint reading between Ginsberg and ROBERT LOWELL. Another institution dedicated to the preservation of live recordings is the San Francisco-based Poetry Center and American Poetry Archives, which was founded in 1954 on the basis of a gift from W. H. AUDEN at San Francisco State University. After the Library of Congress, the center has the largest literary recording archives in the nation, including more than 2,000 original audio, video, and film recordings of poets reading their works. The center also has an extensive reading series.

The tradition of slam poetry began in Chicago in 1986 (see POETRY IN PERFORMANCE), when Marc Smith began a poetry reading series at a jazz club, the Get Me

High Lounge, which gave birth to a phenomenon in which performance is highlighted and judges from the audience assign numerical values to poets' performances. In 1999 Poetry Slam, Inc. (PSI) became a nonprofit organization that oversees an international coalition of poetry slams. Another poetry institution dedicated to slam is the New York-based Nuyorican Poets Café, where performers are often of Puerto Rican, Dominican, or African-American descent. Largely overlooked by academia, slam has created a pantheon of its own stars, who have appeared on such programs as HBO's *Def Poetry Jam* and on Broadway as *Russell Simmons Def Poetry Jam.*

Poets House, cofounded in 1985 by STANLEY KUNITZ, is best known for its vast poetry library, which is free and open to the public. Poets House has more than 40,000 volumes of books, journals, chapbooks, audio tapes, videos, and electronic media, and anyone can find haven in its New York office. Poets House also sponsors public programs, including panel discussions, seminars, readings, and lectures, in such venues as public parks and libraries. More than any other poetry institution, Poets House is dedicated to new poets, as evinced in its annual showcase where the year's new poetry books are gathered, exhibited, and eventually documented in the *Directory of American Poetry Books,* the most comprehensive bibliographic resource for contemporary poetry. Poets House has also forged a partnership with the American Library Association to help increase the presence of poetry in libraries nationwide. Generally Poets House offers a kinder, gentler community than other poetry organizations.

The 92nd Street Y in New York has a broad range of social and cultural programs, of which poetry is just one small part. The Y, started in the 1870s as the Young Men's Hebrew Association, is largely considered the most prestigious venue for a poet to read in in America and generally the kinds of poets who read here, such as Seamus Heaney and DEREK WALCOTT, are at the later stages of their careers. The part of the Y dedicated to poetry, the Unterberg Poetry Center, offers workshops and seminars. Along with the *Nation* magazine and other organizations too numerous to mention, the Y also sponsors an annual poetry contest for poets who have not yet published a book. Past winners of the "Discovery"/ *Nation* prize include MARY JO SALTER, MARK STRAND, GARY SOTO, and LUCILLE CLIFTON.

The Dodge Poetry Foundation, created in Madison, New Jersey, in 1987, emphasizes helping educators incorporate poetry into the classroom. The foundation is responsible for a biennial poetry festival that is the largest in the nation. Since it has such broad popular appeal and takes "getting poetry off the page" as its mantra, the poets who are celebrated in the festival are mainstream in form and sensibility. One of the most noteworthy poetry film documentaries, Bill Moyers's *The Language of Life* takes place at the Dodge Poetry Festival. This documentary consists of interviews of 18 poets, including MICHAEL HARPER, ADRIENNE RICH, NAOMI SHIHAB NYE, and CAROLYN FORCHÉ, and was subsequently broadcast on television, giving poetry one of its largest audiences. Subsequent documentaries with Bill Moyers, such as *The Power of the Word, Sounds of Poetry,* and *RITA DOVE, Poet Laureate,* have been filmed in part at the Dodge Poetry Festival and later broadcast.

Finally, the Electronic Poetry Center (EPC) serves as a hub for resources in electronic poetry and poetics at the State University of New York, Buffalo, as well as on the Web at large. The ambitious goal of the EPC is to provide the widest possible range of resources centered on "digital and contemporary formally innovative poetics, new media writing, and literary programming" ("Intro"). These include curated lists of readings, interviews, audio files, and other digitally archived texts. The EPC also hosts periodic festivals in poetics, with an emphasis on the way the Internet is changing poetic modalities. This emphasis includes hypertext and multimedia, where the use of links, audio, image, and interactivity conspire to create new species of poems (see CYBERPOETRY).

One of the most vital aspects of the EPC is the Poetics Listserv, which is a virtually connected network of poets, the most active and prominent of a number of such electronic poets' communities. The poets who compose the listserv can send e-mail of any variety, be it an announcement of publication, call for submissions, theoretical question, political statement, response to a prior posting, or simply their latest poem, and this e-mail will reach every other member of the listserv. As a result, collaborations and dialogue have been generated among poets residing on other sides of the globe, who might otherwise had no opportunity to encounter each other. On any given day, some hundred-odd poets will post messages to the listserv.

Poetry institutions, in all their different manifestations, are integral to the formation of what is known as a canon in American poetry. From practitioners of NEW FORMALISM to Language poets, nearly every aesthetic school has an organization to help support and to proliferate its ends. The largest institution, however, remains academia, where a majority of poets work when they are not writing. It is not hyperbole to claim that without the sustenance of these institutions, poetry, as we know it, would not exist.

BIBLIOGRAPHY

Gioia, Dana. "Can Poetry Matter?" *Atlantic Monthly* 276, no. 5 (May 1991): 94–106.

"Intro," Electronic Poetry Center. Available online. URL: http://epc.buffalo.edu/intro.html. Downloaded March 2007.

Rothenberg, Jerome. "The History/Pre-History of the Poetry Project," Project Papers. 1996–2002. Available online. URL: www.poetryproject.com/pap_rothenberg.php. Downloaded March 2007.

Ravi Shankar

POETRY JOURNALS Throughout the 20th century, journals have been one of the most important means of disseminating poetry, creating poetic communities, introducing new poets, and encouraging poetry that falls outside of the mainstream. Generally poetry journals have been established to fill a gap in literary publications. The most successful of these journals have made an impact on literary history by promoting a particular style or school of poetry so that even if the journals themselves are not widely distributed, the poets and poetry they endorse become well known and influential.

Poetry journals are often referred to as "little magazines," because of their limited readership. Such publications are distinct from commercial ventures in that they exist not for profit but instead to circulate literature that popular presses will not print. Usually one person or a small group of people oversees the entire publication of a little magazine. While the majority of poetry journals publish, usually, six issues or less before shutting down, many remain in print for decades. Some little magazines are devoted strictly to poetry, but most include a variety of literary and nonliterary works. The aims, contributors, and audiences of these journals vary greatly, often based on poetic school, region, political party, gender, race, class, sexual orientation, or another defining artistic or cultural characteristic. Because poetry journals are generally open to new voices and new styles, they often introduce writers who eventually achieve public recognition. Thus these little magazines, along with POETRY PRESSES and POETRY INSTITUTIONS, encourage diverse poetic practices by challenging dominant modes and moving poetry in new directions. Through the century the role of the little magazine has varied to a degree, but it has consistently been a shaping force in literary studies.

The early part of the century is known as the era of the little magazine, because poetry journals were very important to the publicizing of MODERNISM—its ideas, its major figures, and its literature. Approximately 80 percent of authors who achieved fame between 1912 and 1946 were first published in little magazines. They were specifically useful for the publication of manifestos outlining modernist values. EZRA POUND, for example, defined the IMAGIST SCHOOL in "A Few Don'ts," first published in *Poetry,* and little magazines also carried explanations of futurism, dadaism, vorticism, and other movements. The degree of engagement with modernist ideas varied among the magazines, but almost all contributed to the eventual acceptance of new poetry styles.

Such writers as T. S. ELIOT, Pound, H. D., WILLIAM CARLOS WILLIAMS, MINA LOY, CARL SANDBURG, ROBERT FROST, and MARIANNE MOORE appeared in a number of modernist magazines. Harriet Monroe's *Poetry,* begun in 1912, took a somewhat conservative stance, though it was one of the earliest of the little magazines. It printed a wide range of material and is still one of the most prestigious poetry journals in the United States. In 2003 *Poetry* received a $100 million bequest from Kuth Lilly, heir of a pharmaceutical foundation, making it the richest poetry foundation in the world. The

Dial (1920–29) was slightly less conservative than *Poetry* and was the first publisher of Eliot's *The* WASTE LAND. The *Little Review* (1914–29) printed an eclectic group of writers, as did *Poetry,* but it was more radical, as it "invit[ed] and enact[ed] opinionated debate about the nature and value of art" (Marek 60). Williams began *Contact* (1920–23) to reflect his commitment to formally experimental poetry that also attended to the poet's locale; that is, he sought poetry that seemed distinctly American rather than rooted in European traditions. Alfred Kreymborg's *Others* (1915–19) was yet another radical journal, as it published writing with extreme styles of formal experimentation. While most of the modernist poetry considered important today first appeared in one of these small magazines, there were many other journals of the time doing slightly different sorts of work.

Most of the writers of the HARLEM RENAISSANCE were excluded from the little magazines above, but they created their own venues for poetry, the arts, and politics. The National Association for the Advancement of Colored People (NAACP) started the Crisis in 1910, which published such writers as LANGSTON HUGHES and JEAN TOOMER. The *Messenger* (1917–28) was known for its socialist writing, but it also printed poetry by Hughes, CLAUDE MCKAY, and others. *Opportunity* (1923–49) was the most literary of these three major Harlem journals, and it published work by COUNTEE CULLEN, Paul Lawrence Dunbar, Gwendolyn Bennett, and nearly all of the other important writers of the time. Although African-American poets benefited from little magazines, they still were granted less freedom than their white counterparts, because the Harlem Renaissance journals usually favored poetry with positive portrayals of black culture and minimal formal experimentation.

In the 1920s and 1930s, three major developments occurred in the realm of the little magazine. First, regional small magazines were developed in areas where writers felt underrepresented and misunderstood by northeastern journals. The *Fugitive* (1922–25) jumpstarted the careers of several southern writers, such as ALLEN TATE, JOHN CROWE RANSOM, and ROBERT PENN WARREN, who championed southern nationalism (see FUGITIVE/AGRARIAN SCHOOL). The *Prairie Schooner,* begun in 1927, was developed to represent perspectives from the Midwest, though it now publishes writers from any region. The longevity of the *Prairie Schooner* and the continued introduction of new magazines centered around local perspectives attest to the ongoing importance of region in the little magazine.

In addition, the 1920s and 1930s saw the advent of many political magazines, because of renewed interest in leftist politics. The *New Masses* (1926–48) published political poetry in direct support of class revolution. The *Partisan Review* (1933–2003), however, supported literature that was for and about the working classes, whether or not it encouraged class struggle, finally breaking with the Communist Party in 1936. While proletariat literature is often considered separately from that of the major modernist and Harlem Renaissance writers, all three movements overlapped with one another.

Finally, a number of universities began to sponsor poetry journals to further their own reputations, a trend that continues today with such well-known journals as the *Kenyon Review,* begun in 1939. This tendency has spawned a debate between the independent and the academic little magazines, highlighting the potential merits and drawbacks of each. While independent little magazines may print the most cutting-edge work, they also often print much writing of poor quality; furthermore, they frequently lack funds and support. Academic poetry journals, on the other hand, generally have consistently high standards, but their editorial decisions may be conservative or even subject to censorship, because of a university affiliation. Fortunately both academic and independent journals have proliferated, and both forms can claim significant literary contributions.

By the 1950s, most poetry journals were publishing formalist verse and were associated with universities. However, some writers developed journals specifically to counter the mainstream trends, eventually changing what was accepted as "literary." CID CORMAN's *Origin* (1951–57), one of the first of these, contributed to the eventual legitimization of the BLACK MOUNTAIN SCHOOL, especially the work of CHARLES OLSON and ROBERT CREELEY. Then Creeley buttressed this effort by editing the *Black Mountain Review* (1954–57), originally intended simply to publicize the then-existing Black

Mountain College. The last issue of the *Black Mountain Review* was devoted to the SAN FRANCISCO RENAISSANCE and BEAT POETRY. Other editors were also bringing the schools of poetry together. LeRoi Jones (later known as AMIRI BARAKA) published *Yugen* (1957–63) with Hettie Jones and the *Floating Bear* with DIANE DI PRIMA, encouraging Beat, Black Mountain, and other experimental artists. DONALD ALLEN's *Evergreen Review* (1957–70) also printed poetry from communities across the United States, with the notable publication of ALLEN GINSBERG's *HOWL* (1957). At the same time, the San Francisco Renaissance was particularly encouraged by journals such as *Semina* (1954–64), *City Lights* (1963–78), *Ark* (1947–48), and *J* (1959–62), which printed writing by such poets as KENNETH REXROTH, ROBERT DUNCAN, and MURIEL RUKEYSER. Poets of the OBJECTIVIST SCHOOL, including LOUIS ZUKOFSKY and GEORGE OPPEN, were printed not only in alternative publications but also in established journals, such as *Poetry New York* (1949–). And such writers as JOHN ASHBERY, KENNETH KOCH, FRANK O'HARA, and JAMES SCHUYLER, started journals (*Locus Solus* [1961–62] and *Art and Literature* [1964–67]) to encourage a poetry which came to be known as the NEW YORK SCHOOL. A second generation of New York school poets, including TED BERRIGAN and RON PADGETT, edited journals such as the *World* (1967–) and *C* (1963–67). Of course, many more magazines contributed to the diverse literature of the 1950s and early 1960s, but these are some that proved especially vital in forming communities of writers who might otherwise have slowed in production or been lost in obscurity.

By the late 1960s, new magazines were being published at an astonishing rate for at least three reasons. First the mimeograph machine made publication easier and less expensive than ever before. Second civil rights activism, antiwar protests, and environmental movements fueled the creation of many journals. Finally, foundations, such as the National Endowment for the Arts and the Coordinating Council of Literary Magazines (later renamed the Council of Literary Magazines and Presses), began funding magazines. The boom in little magazines continues today, provoking controversy. Some argue that most magazines have small audiences and publish a large percentage of poor writing: Would not fewer magazines with a larger circulation and better material be preferable? The opposing side answers that having a greater number of magazines allows more opportunities for important writers to emerge, even if most writing does tend toward mediocrity. Furthermore an abundance of magazines appealing to small groups is preferable to a homogenized publication directed toward a mass audience. During this period of rapid growth, such journals as CLAYTON ESHLEMAN's *Caterpillar* (1967–73) printed innovative poetry, while the *New American Review* (1967–) published work by every major poet of the time.

During the 1970s, poetry journals moved in a few directions. On the one hand, poets writing in a personally expressive—though often also political—mode, such as ADRIENNE RICH, were regularly published in mainstream journals. In addition, many journals, such as *Tottels* (1970–81), *Hills* (1973–83), and *This* (1971–82), were precursors to the LANGUAGE SCHOOL of poetry in their attention to the early phases of postmodernism. The signature journal, *L=A=N=G=U=A=G=E* (1978–82), edited by CHARLES BERNSTEIN and BRUCE ANDREWS, included poetry by well-known writers, such as SUSAN HOWE. Lee Hickman's *Temblor* (1985–89) also published innovative poetry, but it had a wider range than journals of the Language school. At the same time, both academic journals, such as the *Southern Review* (1965–) and *boundary2* (1972–), and independent magazines, such as *ManRoot* (1969–) and *Sparrow*, established specializations to shape their publications.

In the 1980s and 1990s, mainstream journals flourished as they printed work by well-known writers as diverse as ROBERT PINSKY, ALICIA OSTRIKER, and NATHANIEL MACKEY. Among these were the *Painted Bride Quarterly* (1973–), *Ploughshares* (1971–), and *American Poetry Review* (1972–), the last of which has boasted a circulation of 17,000. At the same time, other prominent journals continued to print experimental poetics and/or were aimed at underrepresented groups. *Talisman* (1982–), for example, edited by EDWARD FOSTER, has published innovative poetry, such as that by ALICE NOTLEY and WILLIAM BRONK, though it tries to present a range of poetic styles rather than representing a single school. *Callaloo* (1976–) prints African and African-American literature that might not always find an outlet despite increased multicultural awareness. KATHLEEN FRASER began *HOW (ever)* (1983–92) to establish a place for women writers to publish experimental poetry, and the journal was recently reinvented in an online format called *HOW2* (1999–). This move into cyberspace is a trend that has already increased the numbers of little magazines, and it is one that will likely continue. The widespread use of the Internet has allowed the development of CYBERPOETRY and e-zines, publications that are desirable not only because of the low cost and potentially widespread circulation but also because cyberspace offers opportunities for experimenting with form and format that would be quite costly—or even impossible—in a print journal. Like *HOW(ever)*, the *Little Magazine* (1970–), published by the State University of New York, Albany, moved from a print to CD to an online version, partially to take advantage of the multimedia available on the Web. Other online journals, such as *Xcp: Cross Cultural Poetics* (1997–) (also in print form), work to combine experimental poetry, such as that by Baraka or HARRYETTE MULLEN, with unique Internet formats and an international appeal. The *Blue Moon Review* (formerly the *Blue Penny Quarterly* [1994–]) is one of the oldest e-zines and reaches more than 25,000 people. It remains to be seen how the voluminous growth of the e-zine will eventually affect American poetry.

Whether in print or in cyberspace, little magazines continue to flourish in number, though most have a small audience and tend to publish for only a brief period. More than ever before, American poetry journals are sites where local and international interests come together. The local is encouraged as small magazines are developed to fill precise aims. Meanwhile changes in technology have encouraged an international focus: Because all types of poetry are available at all times, networks can be developed across geographical spaces, and people are increasingly reminded of the relevance of global issues. Poetry journals have been crucial in the reception of various poetry movements, and they continue to influence the way in which readers understand poetry of the present and the past.

BIBLIOGRAPHY

Anderson, Elliott, and Mary Kinzie, eds. *The Little Magazine in America: A Modern Documentary History*. New York: Pushcart, 1978.

Golding, Alan. *From Outlaw to Classic: Canons in American Poetry*. Madison: University of Wisconsin Press, 1995.

Hoffmann, Frederick J., Charles Allen, and Carolyn F. Ulrich. *The Little Magazine: A History and a Bibliography*. Princeton, N.J.: Princeton University Press, 1946.

Marek, Jayne E. *Women Editing Modernism: "Little" Magazines and Literary History*. Lexington: University Press of Kentucky, 1995.

Morrison, Mark S. *The Public Face of Modernism: Little Magazines, Audiences, and Reception, 1905–1920*. Madison: University of Wisconsin Press, 2001.

Laurie McMillan

POETRY PRESSES From the beginning of the century, small independent presses have had an important role to play in the championing of poets whose experimentalism made them an uneasy fit at larger publishing houses, whether because the perceived difficulty of their work was seen as too great a marketing risk or because mainstream publishers themselves underestimated the worth of poets who posed a challenge to literary tradition. Indeed Jed Rasula suggests that American poetry is founded on alternative publishing, as typified by Walt Whitman's self-published *Leaves of Grass* (1855) and Emily Dickinson's carefully prepared manuscripts. "The American poetic tradition as such," Rasula writes, "begins with a repudiation of, and by, the dominant media" (412).

In the modernist period (see MODERNISM), such writers as EZRA POUND and GERTRUDE STEIN self-published many of the books on which their reputations now rest. And Pound tirelessly promoted the publication of other important poets and novelists, often in alternative venues. Stein, before the sensation of *The Autobiography of Alice B. Toklas* (1933) led Bennett Cerf to take her on at Random House, had such difficulty securing publication of her genre-defying works, such as TENDER BUTTONS (1914) and *The Making of Americans* (1925), that she and her partner, Alice B. Toklas, printed several of her books in their own Plain Editions, including the important collection *Operas and Plays* (1932).

The loose collective of second-generation modernist poets known as the OBJECTIVISTS founded the important presses To Publishers and the Objectivist Press, which they used to gain exposure for their own poetry; publications of the two presses include *DISCRETE SERIES* by GEORGE OPPEN and *In Memoriam: 1933* by CHARLES REZNIKOFF (Objectivist Press [both 1934]), as well as the work of first-generation poets, such as Pound (*How to Read* and *The Spirit of Romance,* To Publishers [both 1932]) and WILLIAM CARLOS WILLIAMS (*Collected Poems 1921–31,* Objectivist Press [1934]). Perhaps the most enduring influence of Pound on the world of alternative publishing was his advice to James Laughlin, then a student at Harvard, to give up trying to become a poet and found a publishing house. In 1936 Laughlin founded New Directions, a press that became one of the largest independent houses and that made available on a relatively wide scale works by central modernist poets and younger writers, such as KENNETH PATCHEN, GREGORY CORSO, and DENISE LEVERTOV, as well as English translations of Arthur Rimbaud, Charles Baudelaire, Guillaume Apollinaire, and Federico García Lorca.

Perhaps the most important of the smaller presses in the 1950s and 1960s was Grove Press, which in 1960 brought out Donald Allen's watershed anthology *The New American Poetry 1945–1960* (see POETRY ANTHOLOGIES). Allen's book collected emerging poets associated with various poetic "schools": NEW YORK, BLACK MOUNTAIN, SAN FRANCISCO RENAISSANCE, and the BEATS, and helped to define the aesthetic boundaries of experimental poetry in the postwar period and beyond.

Beginning in the 1950s, LAWRENCE FERLINGHETTI'S City Lights Books, an extension of his bookstore of the same name in San Francisco's North Beach, published in its Pocket Poets Series first editions of many of the most important poetic works of the postwar era, such as ALLEN GINSBERG'S *HOWL* and Other Poems (1956) and FRANK O'HARA'S *LUNCH POEMS* (1964). In 1968 John Martin founded what soon became one of the most respected publishers of fine-quality small editions, Black Sparrow Press, in order to publish the work of the iconoclastic Los Angeles poet CHARLES BUKOWSKI; Black Sparrow went on to publish important works by JOHN WIENERS, DAVID ANTIN, EDWARD DORN, ROBERT DUNCAN, and many others, while its Bukowski catalog has become among the most valuable properties in contemporary poetry.

In the 1970s the nascent group that would soon come to be known as the LANGUAGE SCHOOL were highly active in small-press publishing; among the most notable examples is LYN HEJINIAN'S tuumba Press and BARRETT WATTEN and ROBERT GRENIER'S. This Press (which published RON SILLIMAN'S *Ketjak* [1978] and BRUCE ANDREWS'S *Sonnets (Memento Mori)* [1980]). Presses associated with Language poetry published work that pushes against the boundaries of what is usually called "mainstream poetry." Even the so-called mainstream, however, relies heavily on small presses as a venue. There is, for example, Copper Canyon Press, founded in 1972, whose catalog includes W. S. MERWIN, HAYDEN CARRUTH, and LUCILLE CLIFTON. Poetry has been, of course, brought out by major publishing houses, including W. W. Norton and Penguin. Yet other smaller presses have helped give rise to new movements in poetry; NEW FORMALISM (which emerged in the 1980s), for instance, has been strongly associated with Story Line Press, founded in 1984 by ROBERT MCDOWELL, and associated with such poets as MARK JARMAN, ALFRED CORN, and ANNIE FINCH.

If the academy has become, as Alan Golding claims, "the main audience for poetry today" (159), one result has been the increasing importance in recent decades of the academic press. Significant examples of this aspect of the publishing scene include the University of Pittsburgh Press's Pitt Poetry Series, whose catalog includes SHARON OLDS, CATHY SONG, and CAROL MUSKEDUKES, and Wesleyan University Press, publisher of a remarkably wide array of poets, including DAVID IGNATOW, JAMES WRIGHT, JOAN RETALLACK, RAE ARMANTROUT, and YUSEF KOMUNYAKAA. Wesleyan, along with other university presses, such as Johns Hopkins, has done much to keep in print important 20th-century poets, such as LOUIS ZUKOFSKY. Also worthy of note is the National Poetry Foundation at the University of Maine, Orono, whose press makes available an array of hard-to-find editions of 20th-century poetry, as well as the first collected editions of such poets as KENNETH FEARING and CARL RAKOSI.

While perennially struggling with formidable financial obstacles, small presses continue to act as a crucial entry point, introducing new and challenging poetry to the culture at large. It is a measure of the strength of alternative publishing since the 1970s that it would be too difficult to offer a representative list of important presses. While it would be difficult to point to a single publishing house that has shaped the poetic canon as profoundly as did New Directions or Grove at midcentury, as a collective enterprise, small presses have become a permanent feature in the world of contemporary poetry.

BIBLIOGRAPHY

Clay, Steve, and Rodney Phillips. *A Secret Location on the Lower East Side: Adventures in Writing 1960–1980*. New York: Granary Books, 1998.

Golding, Alan. *From Outlaw to Classic: Canons in American Poetry*. Madison: University of Wisconsin Press, 1995.

Rasula, Jed. *The American Poetry Wax Museum: Reality Effects, 1940–1990*. Urbana, Ill.: National Council of Teachers of English, 1996.

Damian Judge Rollison

POETRY PRIZES The 20th century has seen the advent of a great number of prizes for excellence in American poetry, especially in the later decades. Building on the tradition begun by Alfred Nobel, newspaper publisher Joseph Pulitzer established prizes for American journalism and letters in 1917, with the first Pulitzer Prize for poetry being awarded in 1922. Major poetic awards were also established in the first half of the century by large philanthropic organizations, arts journals, literary societies, and prestigious academic institutions. Some, such as the Levinson Award (1914) given by *Poetry* magazine, were established to encourage young writers and to recognize the excellence of specific volumes. Others, such as the Poetry Society of America's Frost Medal (1930) and the Shelly Memorial Award (1929), are given in recognition of excellence of a poet's body of work overall.

Another group of prestigious awards emerged in the 1950s. The National Book Foundation began giving out its awards in 1950, and a few years later the prestigious James Laughlin Award was established by the Academy of American Poets. This is also the time when the American literary landscape was changing. While such poets as CARL SANDBURG and THEODORE ROETHKE were accepting the major awards of the day, poetic movements, such as the BEATS, BLACK MOUNTAIN, and the NEW YORK SCHOOL, were rejecting the traditional literary forms for which these poets were praised. In the famous collection *The New American Poetry* (1960) (see POETRY ANTHOLOGIES), the poets in their biographies do not mention receiving any awards beyond the occasional fellowship. Instead they focus on the people and ideas that influence their poetry.

This emphasis on the personal rather than the institutional was a sign of the changing times. Traditional ideas of good poetry gave way to subjective assessments based on ethnicity, gender, or sexual orientation—the multiculturalism experienced in the late century. The bursting open of the canon made space for the recognition of previously unappreciated poetics. The resurgence of the popularity of American poetry in the last decades of the 20th century was accompanied by a proliferation of prizes to honor the creators. Prizes, such as the Before Columbus Foundation's American Book Award and the Ruth Lilly Poetry Prize offered by the Modern Poetry association, were established in the 1980s and 1990s—some with substantial cash awards. (The purse for the Lilly Prize, for instance, is $100,000.) In the 2001 edition of the *Best American Poetry* series, more than half of the awards cited by the poets in their biographies were established in the last quarter of the 20th century.

There is little evidence to suggest what, if any, effect winning these awards has on a literary career. Some of the traditional awards seem to be little more than academic entitlement programs: Established poets are members of the selection board one year, then awarded winners a few years later. Other first and second book awards, such as the Yale Series of Younger Poets (1973), generally awarded to unknowns, do not seem necessarily to lead the winners to fame and fortune. Few of these winners have become literary stars, with the exception of such poets as JOHN ASHBERY, ADRIENNE RICH, and STANLEY KUNITZ. On the whole, prizes no longer guarantee future literary success—if they ever did.

Today the taste of poets, publishers, and the reading public is much more of a factor in the success of a young poet than the awards he or she might earn. While the academy may continue to recognize its stars and those who follow their paths, it is the popular appeal of poetry today that may be most influential. Individual poems published in literary magazines are the raw material for anthologies, the delivery method of choice today. In such series as the *Best American Poetry,* a first-time poet has as much chance as a veteran of appearing in print next to the likes of an Ashbery or a Kunitz. The opportunities for a poet to share his or her work—through the many poetry journals, online e-zines, or poetry slams available—vastly outnumber those of previous years. Having succeeded without aid of the traditional academic/publishing network, late-century poets have not necessarily needed or craved its accolades.

Some major poetry awards (in order of establishment):

Pulitzer Prize (1922): Nominated by a volunteer jury of five, selected by the Pulitzer Board, and presented by the president of Columbia University, the Pulitzer remains the most prestigious American award in letters. Winners include EDWARD ARLINGTON ROBINSON (1922), SYLVIA PLATH (1982), YUSEF KOMUNYAKAA (1994), and STEPHEN DUNN (2001).

Frost Medal (1930): The Frost Medal and $2,500 are awarded annually at the discretion of the Poetry Society of America's Board of Governors, for distinguished lifetime service to American poetry. Past winners include EDNA ST. VINCENT MILLAY (1943), ROBERT PENN WARREN (1985), and SONIA SANCHEZ (2001).

Shelly Memorial Award (1929): The Shelley Memorial Award of between $6,000 and $9,000 is given by the Poetry Society of America to a living American poet "selected with reference to genius and need" ("Poetry"). Winners include CONRAD AIKEN (1929), GWENDOLYN BROOKS (1975), and ALICE NOTLEY (2001).

Bollingen Prize (1949): The Bollingen Prize, established by Paul Mellon, with a current purse of $50,000, is awarded biennially by the Yale University Library to an American poet for the best book published during the previous two years. EZRA POUND was awarded the first Bollingen prize, despite being incarcerated for treason at the time of the award. Winners include E. E. CUMMINGS (1958), JAMES MERRILL (1973), and LOUISE GLÜCK (2000).

National Book Award (1950): Given to an American poet by the National Book Foundation for the best book of poetry published during the award year. Winners include WILLIAM CARLOS WILLIAMS (1950), ALLEN GINSBERG (1974), and LUCILLE CLIFTON (2000).

James Laughlin Award (1954): Given to a poet for his or her second book already under contract with a publisher, this award includes a $5,000 purse and a promise from the Academy of American Poets to purchase 10,000 copies of the book for distribution to its members. Past winners include DONALD HALL (1955), STEPHEN DOBYNS (1971), AI (1978), and Peter Johnson (2001).

Yale Series of Younger Poets Prize (1973): Awarded to a poet under age 40 by the Yale University Press for her or his first published volume of poetry, past winners include ROBERT HASS (1973), CATHY SONG (1983), and Maurice Manning (2000).

Lenore Marshall Poetry Prize (1975): Awarded by the *Nation* and the Academy of American Poets for the best book of poetry published in the previous year, the award and purse of $10,000 has been given to DENISE LEVERTOV (1976), JOSEPHINE MILES (1984), MARK JARMAN (1998), and WANDA COLEMAN (1999).

Walt Whitman Award (1975): Awarded to an American who has not yet published a book of poetry, this prize includes $5,000, a one-month residency at the Vermont Studio Center, and publication of the poet's first book. Recipients include DAVID BOTTOMS (1979), April Bernard (1988), and John Canaday (2001).

Alice Fay Di Castagnola Award: This memorial award for a manuscript-in-progress of poetry or verse-drama is open only to Poetry Society of America members and carries with it a purse of $1,000. Past winners include LINDA PASTAN (1978), CAROLYN FORCHÉ (1982), and Angie Estes (2001).

American Book Award (1980): Established by the Before Columbus Foundation, this award is bestowed by a panel of writers, editors, and publishers. Its winners include WILLIAM BRONK (1982), Dorothy Barresi (1997), Andres Montoya (2000), and SANDRA GILBERT (2001).

Witter Bynner Poetry Prize (1980): Established by the American Academy & Institute of Arts & Letters, this prize supports the work of a young poet. Winners include FRANZ WRIGHT (1995), MARK DOTY (1997), and Rachel Wetzsteon (2001).

National Book Critics Circle Award (1981): Given to an American author by the National Book Critics Circle for the best book of poetry in the preceding year, past winners include A. R. AMMONS (1981), HAYDEN CARRUTH (1992), and Judy Jordan (2000).

Aiken Taylor Award for Modern American Poetry (1986): This award and $10,000 prize are given by the *Sewanee Review* to honor the distinguished career of an American poet. winners include HOWARD NEMEROV (1986), X. J. KENNEDY (1998), and Frederick Morgan (2001).

Ruth Lilly Poetry Prize (1986): The award and substantial purse ($100,000 in 2001) is offered by the Modern Poetry Association, affiliated with *Poetry* magazine, to recognize the lifetime achievement of an American poet. Winners include CHARLES WRIGHT (1993), WILLIAM MATTHEWS (1997), and Yusef Komunyakaa (2001).

Lannan Literary Awards (1989): This award was established by the Lannan Foundation to honor both established and emerging writers whose work is of exceptional quality. Nominations are made anonymously by the foundation's literary committee. Winners include CID CORMAN (1989), William Bronk (1992), Denise Levertov (1993), and Herbert Morris (2000).

Rebekah Johnson Bobbitt National Prize (1990): This prize of $10,000 is awarded by the Library of Congress every other year for the best published book of poetry. Winners include James Merrill (1990), KENNETH KOCH (1996), and David Ferry (2001).

Kingsley Tufts Poetry Award (1992): This memorial award, offered by Claremont Graduate University, is awarded to a poet who has been published but has not yet reached the pinnacle of his or her career. The award carries a substantial purse ($100,000 in 2001). Previous winners include Susan Mitchell (1993), John Koethe (1998), and Alan Shapiro (2001).

Robert H. Winner Memorial Award: Established to reward original work being done in midcareer by a poet over age 40 who has not yet received significant appreciation, this award brings with it a purse of $2,500. Previous winners include Helen Frost (1993), Liz Waldner (1998), and Jeffrey Franklin (2001).

Wallace Stevens Award (1994): Given annually by the Academy of American Poets to recognize proven mastery in poetry, the award and stipend of $150,000 has recently been awarded to Adrienne Rich (1996), JACKSON MAC LOW (1999), FRANK BIDART (2000), and RICHARD WILBUR (2003).

BIBLIOGRAPHY

"Book Awards FAQ." Academy of American Poets. Available online. URL: www.poets.org. Downloaded March 2007.

"Poetry Society of America Awards Guidelines," Poetry Society of America. Available online. URL: www.poetrysociety.org/psa-awards_gdln.html. Downloaded March 2007.

Rasula, Jed. *The American Poetry Wax Museum: Reality Effects, 1940–1990.* Urbana, Ill: National Council of Teachers of English, 1996.

Aimee Fifarek

PONSOT, MARIE (1921–) Termed a formalist because of her mastery of the sonnet, villanelle, and sestina, Marie Ponsot considers herself an eccentric, having written as much free as formal verse (see PROSODY and FREE VERSE); her poems are always formal, she said in a telephone interview, in the sense that "language generates form" (Interview). Compared with 17th-century John Donne for her metaphysical poems, with James Joyce for her word coinages and puns, and with Seamus Heaney for her connection to the earth, Ponsot can nevertheless be best described as keenly independent.

Ponsot was born and reared in Queens, New York. Her first volume, *True Minds* (1957), was swallowed in the wake of ALLEN GINSBERG's *HOWL.* Living for decades "outside the world of poetry," as she supported seven children by writing for television and radio, teaching and translating, Ponsot maintained the "desire to write poems, not to publish them" (Interview). She won the Eunice Tietjens Memorial Award for poems in *Poetry* magazine (1960). Her second volume, *Admit Impedi-*

ment (1981), did not appear until she was 60. *The Green Dark* (1988) won the DELMORE SCHWARTZ Memorial Poetry Award. Long revered in poetry circles, she came to popular prominence when *The Bird Catcher* (1998) won the National Book Critics Circle Award. *Springing: New and Selected Poems* (2002), featured in a front-page review in the *New York Times Book Review* when Ponsot was 81, includes one uncollected poem from each year between 1946 and 1971. She was awarded the Shelley Memorial Award by the Poetry Society of America and the Phi Beta Kappa Poetry Prize (2002). Ponsot has taught at Queens College of the City University of New York.

Dinitia Smith has written that a "Marie Ponsot poem is a jeweled bracelet, carefully carved, with small, firm stones embedded in it" (E1). Her poems begin with stark assertions, such as "Death is the price of life" ("For A Divorce" [1981]), include puns, such as "I think I've got what I need / In the overhead compartment" ("What Do You Want to Be When You Grow Up?" [2002]), or end in witty aphorisms, such as, "Age is not / All dry rot" ("Pourriture Noble" [1998]). "Late" (1981) is a crown of sonnets (a series in which the last line of each sonnet becomes the first line of the next). The intricate form and the recurring image of her mother's diamond, whose "permanence defies / The dark, in sparkles on this page," demonstrate her signature elegance.

Whether writing about motherhood or metaphysics in colloquial or philosophical diction, Ponsot demonstrates, in David Orr's words, "the exhilarating integrity" (9) of one who insists that poetry is, as Ponsot herself said, "human language at its most triumphant" (Interview).

BIBLIOGRAPHY

Deen, Rosemary. Review of *Springing,* by Marie Ponsot. *Image: A Journal of the Arts and Religion* 35 (summer 2002): 114–116.

Orr, David. "What's Not a Poem Has Been Discarded." Review of *Springing,* by Marie Ponsot. *New York Times Book Review,* April 21, 2002, 9.

Ponsot, Marie. Telephone Interview with Maureen Connolly McFeely. New York City. December 9, 2002.

Smith, Dinitia. "Recognition at Last for a Poet of Elegant Complexity." *New York Times,* April 13, 1999, E1, 3.

Maureen Connolly McFeely

POUND, EZRA (1885–1972) Ezra Pound's battle cry, "Make it new!," became the implied motto for one of the most significant literary movements of the 20th century. MODERNISM found its most fervent advocate in Pound and his numerous poems, essays, tracts, and manifestos, all of which sought to redefine poetry in light of a declining, late Victorian culture. Inspired early in his life by such varied sources as the Troubadours, Homer and the classical Greek canon, Robert Browning, and Confucius, Pound condensed his learning and skills into highly concise and allusive verse. This move toward a rougher, more volatile poetics was, in part, a revolutionary's response to staid societal norms. Pound saw early 20th-century poetry and the culture to which it pandered as rotten and sorely in need of classical revival under the pressure of a modern consciousness. His sense of timing, his shrewd business sense, and his knack for garnering the praise of other artists and important patrons guided him to the foreground of literary modernism in London. Pound helped William Butler Yeats mature, aided in WILLIAM CARLOS WILLIAMS's move toward modernism, promoted ROBERT FROST, and discovered T. S. ELIOT, H. D., James Joyce, and countless others. Had Pound never written a word of verse, he would still command recognition in 20th-century poetry. His own poetry, however—its stoic boldness, dramatic concisions, and haikulike faithfulness to image (see IMAGIST SCHOOL)—still demands attention and study. Pound's sense of his own importance and place in the artistic tradition, along with his later political antics and eventual trial for treason, have catapulted him into both the infamous and glorious position of gatekeeper to literary modernism in the West.

Born in Hailey, Idaho, Pound moved at the age of two with his family to Philadelphia. He attended the University of Pennsylvania before earning a B.A. at Hamilton College (1905). He then continued his work in Romance languages, especially the Provençal of the 12th-century Troubadour poets, and earned an M.A. from the University of Pennsylvania in 1906. Following a Harrison Fellowship from the University of Pennsylvania (1906), which he used to finance a trip to Spain, Pound took a teaching post at Wabash College in Crawfordsville, Indiana. After offering a young burlesque actress shelter for a night, however, he was removed from the college for what was deemed immoral behavior. This inauspicious ending to his American teaching career began Pound's ascendancy in the London literary scene. In 1908 after a stay in Gibraltar and then Venice—where he published his first book, *A Lume Spento* (1908)—Pound went to London. A steady stream of publications followed, both in Europe and America, as well as editorships at premier poetry magazines, such as *Poetry* (1912), the *Little Review* (1917), and the *Dial* (1920). Although he never received the accolades he thought he deserved (and which his contemporaries Eliot, whom he helped edit and revise *The Waste Land*, and Frost did), he eventually won the *Dial* award for poetry (1928), an honorary degree from Hamilton College (1939), the prestigious Bollingen Prize for poetry (1949), and the Academy of American Poets Award (1963).

His estrangement from the United States creates a violent tension in his poetry. In "Hugh Selwyn Mauberley" (1920), he ridicules America for its cultural poverty, referring to his homeland as "a half-savage country." American pragmatism, though, fostered in Pound a predilection for vernacular and crass directness. Indicative of Pound's linguistic range are his diction choices, such as "Guffaw," "Kulchur" instead of "Culture," and "sd" instead of "said." Pound's early poetry, however—from *A Lume Spento, Personae* (1909), and much of the loose translations in *Cathay* (1915)—owes much to Browning's dramatic monologues by historical figures. "Sestina: Altaforte" (1908), the first sestina published in English, for example, is written in the voice of Bertran de Born, a troubadour who is one of the damned in Dante's *Inferno*. The poem exhibits a high degree of technical bravado and talent, and it alludes to many of the themes and formal moves that Pound obsessed over: an artist's being punished for boldness, classical allusion, dramatic personae, and a typically Anglo-Saxon vocabulary. "I have no life save when the swords clash" appears to be a line that fits not just Pound's persona, but Pound himself. Pound's early work attests to his awareness of poetic heritage and his intense study of both Anglo-Saxon and Provençal traditions. His early work only hints, though, at the dramatic shift he would undergo just years later.

The first blatant move toward a modern style—what Pound referred to as "nearer the bone" and "free of emotional slither"—came in 1913 with the publication of "A Few Don'ts by an Imagiste" in *Poetry*. In this short essay, Pound outlined the tenets that would, in various forms, dominate not only his own aesthetic practice but most of the literary tradition of the West for the next half century. Among the initiatives Pound called for were "direct treatment of the 'thing'" and composition "in the sequence of the musical phrase, not in sequence of a metronome." Verse, to Pound at this stage, became more like sculpture, something carved from alabaster, something done with craftsman quality and made to endure. Pound even offered a name for this new aesthetic: imagism. Throughout World War I and immediately following, he continually refined his imagist dicta, escaping any potential stagnation or misuse by lesser artists. Under the banner of vorticism—"a combination of literary high jinks and aesthetic mumbo jumbo" (Tytell 159)—Pound and cohort Wyndham Lewis published *Blast!* (1914). In this vitriolic rant, Pound espoused such themes as an artistic reconquest of culture, political and economic revolution, antiusury, and an ominous anti-Semitism that later led to political turmoil and his arrest. Typical of the bitterness in *Blast!* is his ending denouncement in "Salutation the Third": "Here is the taste of my boot. . . . Lick off the blacking."

Pound's poetic idiom—one that emerged during the war years and took firm hold on him by the time of his departure for Paris in 1920—displays concision, objectivity, and harsh juxtapositions. He forces readers to juggle myriad allusions and cryptic comparisons. In "Hugh Selwyn Mauberley" (1920), the line "Capaneus; trout for facticious bait" places the burden of reconciling the two images on the reader. At his best Pound epitomizes verbal economy and imagistic precision. His rhyming of classical languages with English and his vast knowledge and study of medieval forms and meter still loom large in the English poetic tradition. At his worst, however, Pound can be pedantic and overly allusive, relying on intimidation to force his readership into acknowledging his prowess. His lifelong work, *The Cantos* (1930–70)—a daunting sequence of 117 poems in which Pound attempted an agnostic version of Dante's *Divine Comedy*—still leaves audiences baffled. The poem's Odyssean journey to the underworld, as well as its Dantesque mixture of mythic with contemporary figures, place it strongly in the Greek and Italian traditions Pound admired. Collages of Chinese characters and foreign languages, highly cryptic allusions, and veiled personal and political attacks, however, make *The Cantos* one of the most challenging reads of the 20th century. Though the work still stands as a monument to modernism, the extent to which Pound's *Cantos* succeeds aesthetically is still debated by scholars and poets alike.

While in voluntary exile in Italy in the 1920s and 1930s, Pound's obsession with constructing an artistic utopia led him to fascist politics, harsh anti-Semitic rants, and, ultimately, to anti-American broadcasts during World War II. He vilified Jews and capitalism as the causes of cultural ruin in the West, and he suffered delusions regarding the role both Jews and capitalism played; and he supported overly optimistic economic systems. Ultimately Pound was detained by the American authorities after the liberation of Italy, and he was returned to the United States in 1945 under arrest for treason. Though he was later acquitted on the grounds of mental instability, he spent many years in St. Elizabeth's mental hospital in Washington, D.C., where he received visits from young poets, such as ALLEN GINSBERG and PAUL BLACKBURN. Pound's Bollingen Prize for the *Pisan Cantos* in 1949 finally afforded his friends the opportunity to persuade authorities to release him. They succeeded; Pound was finally freed in 1957 and returned to Italy the following year. Ezra Pound was both admired and despised, idolized and vilified, as the dominant figure of modernism.

BIBLIOGRAPHY

Kenner, Hugh. *The Pound Era.* Berkeley: University of California Press, 1971.

Nadel, Ira B. *The Cambridge Companion to Ezra Pound.* New York: Cambridge University Press, 1999.

Tifany, Daniel. *Radio Corpse: Imagism and the Cryptaesthetic of Ezra Pound.* Cambridge, Mass.: Harvard University Press, 1995.

Tytell, John. *Ezra Pound: The Solitary Volcano.* New York: Doubleday, 1987.

Chad Davidson

"THE PRESIDENTS OF THE UNITED STATES OF AMERICA" JACKSON MAC LOW **(1963)** "The Presidents of the United States of America" demonstrates a trend in mid-20th-century MODERNISM—in line with WILLIAM CARLOS WILLIAMS's dictum, "no ideas but in things"—in a synthesis of compositional methods peculiar to JACKSON MAC LOW. By taking an objective view of poetry's basic building block, language, through a systematic approach to writing, "The Presidents" stands with CHARLES OLSON's *The MAXIMUS POEMS*, PAUL BLACKBURN's *The JOURNALS*, and ARMAND SCHWERNER's *The TABLETS* as an epic experiment in the turn from metaphor to metonymy, from fluid grammatical structures to radical parataxis (setting incongruent elements side-by-side), and from standard free verse layout to visually provocative and disruptive lineation (see LONG AND SERIAL POETRY). Like EZRA POUND's *The CANTOS*, Mac Low's poem builds a "structure of images" out of everyday language, which, in turn, allows the poet to make social and political commentary that transcends the everyday. Frequently performed in the latter half of the 1960s, the poem was not published in full until 1986.

To compose the poem, Mac Low structured images and sometimes irregular stanzas, or strophes, by translating the letters of each U.S. president's name (from Washington to Fillmore) into a word based on each letter's Phoenician meaning. Modern Roman script descends from the Phoenician, and Mac Low's system implies a relation between ancient writing systems and contemporary American social systems. For example, here is the end of the first section, entitled "1789," after Washington's inaugural year. This passage contains images corresponding to the last four letters of "Washington," G (camel), T (mark), O (eye), and N (fish):

> for tho he had no camels he had slaves enough
> and probably made them toe the mark by
> keeping
> an eye on them
> for *he* wd never have stood for anything fishy.

The words and images are thus connected by commentary that implicates Washington in an evil slaveholding system. But the arbitrariness of the image structure also suggests that the public persona of a president, or perhaps any such authority figure, is just as arbitrarily imposed as benevolent and worth following or believing. On the other hand, an awareness of which elements of the poem are imposed by the system and which are not allows Mac Low's own authority to manifest itself transparently.

The cumulative effect of the poem, commensurate with the gradually wilder form it takes on the page, is as incendiary as the repetition of images. This repetition lends ominous semantic weight to ordinary words and images, even as Mac Low's deft treatment of them lends humor to the poem. Though relatively short, "The Presidents of the United States of America" evokes both the epic tradition from Homer through Pound and the burgeoning alignment in the 1960s of avant-garde literary practice with American social dissent.

BIBLIOGRAPHY

Hartley, George, "'Listen' and 'Relate': Jackson Mac Low's Chance-Operational Poetry." *Sulfur* 23 (fall 1998): 189–203.

Taylor, Henry, "Jackson Mac Low: Gristlier Translations, Arcane Pronouns." In *Compulsory Figures*. Baton Rouge: Louisiana State University Press, 1992, pp. 245–266.

Patrick F. Durgin

"THE PRIPET MARSHES" IRVING FELDMAN **(1979)** "The Pripet Marshes" belongs to that genre of poetry that deals with, or bears witness to, the Holocaust. Its final version appears in the center of IRVING FELDMAN's work. Feldman imagines his own family and loved ones on the site of the tragedy. Thinking of his Jewish friends, he seizes "them as they are and transport[s] them in [his] mind to the *shtetlach* and ghettoes," the poem begins. The words *seizes* and *transport*—relating to the Nazis gathering their victims—are used ironically. This imaginative act at first gives the speaker a sense of control. At times he takes a biblical tone. The poet's defeat at the end signifies the utter failure of the artist or, indeed, of the individual to stem the tide of hatred that will soon, like the Pripet Marshes, an area in Eastern Europe overrun by the Germans, engulf his loved ones. Desperately trying to seize his people, the speaker collapses "as though drugged or beaten," stupefied by the prospect of such brutality.

The poem is full of color. Feldman celebrates people, friends, and relatives, whom he imagines in a Russian village moments before the Germans arrive. Frank has the "hair and yellow skin of a Tartar"; there is also "Abbie whose coloring wants lavender," his mother "whose gray eyes are touched with yellow," as well as his "brown-eyed son" and "red-haired sisters." Against the grim and anonymous Holocaust, which annihilated the individual, Feldman evokes character, personality, individuality: One friend is "Sullen," while another is a "moping, melancholy clown." He also includes the names—Marian, Adele, Munji—of those who engage in social activities, "walking the streets, visiting, praying in shul," and "arguing." There is banter and impatience and merriment.

The poem is also full of sound. The speaker's ears "tingle" when he hears voices: Maury's voice "is rapid and slurred," Lottie's voice "flattens every delicacy," Abbie "who, when [he] listen[s] closely is speaking to [him]," and the family is "bantering [its] tenderness away." The emphasis on daily human activity substitutes here for any rumination on nature. The primordial marshes, the nature, is irrelevant to the poet's vision. Of course, the individual is helpless. As the Germans approach on their motorcycles, the speaker cries, "I snatch them all back, / For, when I want to, I can be a god." But the protective mist with which he seeks to cover his people "clouds" his own mind instead. He is overtaken by primordial and voiceless forces. It is the end of civilization. But such is the force of the witness poem, or Feldman's dramatic reinvention of it, that the testimony itself provides transcendence.

BIBLIOGRAPHY

Stiller, Nikki. "On Jewish Poetry in English." In *The State of the Language*. Vol. 2. Berkeley: University of California Press, 1990, pp. 51–60.

Nikki Stiller

PROSODY AND FREE VERSE Traditional English prosody depends on identifying syllables and stresses (or accented and unaccented syllables). To indicate which syllables receive emphasis, the convention is to use an acute accent (´) and for syllables receiving less emphasis to use a breve (˘). The first line of

ROBERT FROST's "Birches" would thus be scanned as follows: "When Í see bírches bénd to léft and ríght." Against this underlying rhythm, which operates throughout the poem, a reader might add less repetitive rhythmic emphasis appropriate to the sense of the passage. *Scansion* is the process of identifying the stressed and unstressed syllables of a particular poem and noting how they are arranged in patterns.

Rhythm and *meter* are not synonymous. Meter is a specific form (or variety of forms) of rhythm; more specifically, meter is an arrangement of syllables that underlies a rhythm. Perhaps the most common form of meter is *iambic pentameter,* in which each line of poetry contains 10 syllables, with every other syllable accented (sometimes a group of syllables will not follow the iambic pattern, yet the majority of groups of syllables do). The line from Frost cited above is an example. Iambic pentameter that does not rhyme is called *blank verse.* Some theorists have argued that rhythm is a subtler term than meter, since it includes sound effects that cannot easily be described by the language used to understand meter.

Free verse is most simply defined as nonmetrical poetry. A subtler definition would note that free verse may have meter and rhyme, though not in a strict, repeated pattern, such as iambic pentameter. The critic Charles Hartman says, "Free verse, like all verse, is prosodically ordered and not aimless" (24). Prosody also includes efforts to explain the irregular rhythms of free verse, as well as the effects of meter and rhyme.

Walt Whitman's *Leaves of Grass* (1855) is the first major work of American poetry to be written in free verse. But, as Chris Beyers explains in *A History of Free Verse,* unmetered verse existed in English and American poetry before Whitman, notably in parts of the King James version of the Bible, in the prophetic books of romantic William Blake, and in the 18th-century work of Christopher Smart. The effect of Whitman's long free verse lines in *Leaves of Grass* was not to be felt strongly until the 20th century, long after Whitman's death in 1892. In the first half of the 20th century, most free verse poets were trying to define their own styles as distinct from Whitman's.

After Whitman's practice came the work and theories of EZRA POUND, WILLIAM CARLOS WILLIAMS, and CHARLES OLSON. Pound wanted to break with the metrical tradition by identifying a more flexible organizing principle—*cadence.* Making an analogy with musical structure, Pound claimed that cadence had been the basis for the rhythms of good poetry since the classical Greeks (Beyers 19).

The word *cadence* comes from the Latin *cadere,* meaning "to fall." It refers to the rise and fall of the voice in speaking, though the term may refer to modulations of tone as well. Most loosely, cadence refers to the rhythmic flow of the whole poem and serves to remind us that traditional prosody is more a matter of how the lines sound when read aloud than of how they appear on the white space of the page. But some 20th-century poets, such as Williams, were concerned with both the sound of verse and the appearance of the poem on the page.

Pound's musical analogy raises the question of *duration,* a concept borrowed from Greek and Latin poetry to interpret the auditory dimension of both metrical and free verse lines. Duration refers to how long it takes to say a particular syllable out loud. In English, however, unlike Greek and Latin, there are no agreed-upon measures of syllabic duration in the practice of poetry. Although linguists analyze duration, there is no fixed vocabulary for discussing specific durations in poetic practice. The lack of such a standard means that a reading of a given line or poem based on the duration of the sounds in the line depends on the highly subjective and variable interpretation of the individual reader.

Pound's idea, "to break the pentameter, that was the first heave," current long before he articulated it in canto LXXXI (of *The CANTOS*), set forth a cause that Pound's friend Williams elaborated on under the term, *variable foot* (Williams 289). Williams claimed that traditional meter was "wholly unrelated to our language" (quoted in Beyers 187). Williams used *variable foot* to describe means other than metrical scansion to determine the length of the poetic line.

Although there is still no agreed-upon way of "measuring" its form, free verse was, through most of the 20th century, the dominant mode or style of poetry. Few notable 20th-century American poets wrote no free verse, and several notable ones wrote only free verse, including ALLEN GINSBERG and MARIANNE MOORE. Many poets, in fact, have written in both metered and free verse forms, including THEODORE ROETHKE and ADRIENNE RICH. It is possible to write in rhyme and not in meter or to use *alliteration* (similar consonant sounds at the beginnings of words), *consonance* (generally, similar consonant sounds), or *assonance* (similar vowel sounds) to provide form in a poem. Pound's famous two-line poem, "In a Station of the Metro," though nonmetrical, used assonance in the words *crowd* and *bough*. Advocates of free verse have argued that such subtleties of sound are more likely in free verse than in metered verse, and considerable artistry is required to achieve them.

Free verse has been studied extensively with the goal of finding a way to indicate the rhythm of free verse lines. Most analysts have been forced to fall back on the examination of stressed and unstressed syllables or to borrow terminology, such as the *phoneme* (an abstract, written entity that corresponds to a sound made in speech) from linguistics. More comprehensive and successful attempts to understand the workings of free verse have taken into account the visual and grammatical as well as the auditory reasons for establishing line breaks.

Enjambment designates the carrying over of sentence syntax from one line to the next. Williams relies heavily on enjambment for his poetic effects. In "Poem" (1934), for instance, which begins "As the cat / climbed over," a single sentence is sustained without punctuation through the 12 lines of the poem. The movement of the sentence thus imitates the cat's smooth climbing over various obstacles, an effect Williams might say would be impossible with rhyme and meter dictating consistency.

The study of the forms of free verse encourages readers to look beyond the regular rise and fall of meter to find more complex and individual elements of order, including grammar and syntax. "In a Station of the Metro," for example, ends each line with a break in the syntax. Each of the two lines of the poem is a grammatical unit, though, interestingly, the poem as a whole is not a sentence but simply the two parallel noun-based phrases, each of which has embedded in it a prepositional phrase.

For most free verse poets, the form of the poem evolves from the inner necessity of the poem's meaning rather than the form being a rigid external pattern that the poem's "meaning" must be made to fit. For example, Olson's formulation in his 1950 essay "Projective Verse" (which he attributes to ROBERT CREELEY), "FORM IS NEVER MORE THAN AN EXTENSION OF CONTENT" (387), echoes Ralph Waldo Emerson's "meter-making argument" in "The Poet" (1844), which influenced Whitman. In other words, for Olson, as for Emerson, content should create form, not be made to fit a preexisting form (see ARS POETICAS.)

Although Williams's application of the term *variable foot* can be confusing, it is at least clear that he was concerned with establishing a standard by which the integrity of the free verse line might be judged. In a given poem, Williams's lines tend to look the same. They are relatively short, often characterized by stair-step indentation, and grouped in threes. Although Williams used enjambment a great deal for various effects of meaning and sound, he started with the syntactical unit (the phrase or clause) as the basis of the line. According to Beyers, "What Williams was after, and what he spent his entire career pursuing, was the *sound* not of *words* but of *meaning*" (216). The sense, or meaning, of the sentences therefore tends to take precedence over the line breaks.

Olson's "Projective Verse"—his theory of "open field" poetics—has often been cited as a seminal document laying out the principles of "composition by field." Olson proposes "projective" verse as a desirable alternative to "closed" verse, "which print bred and which is pretty much what we have had in English & American, and have still got, despite the work of Pound & Williams" (386). Olson argues that "composition by field" makes the poem a transfer of energy "from where the poet got it . . . by way of the poem itself to, all the way over to, the reader" (387).

The basis of Olson's organic conception of form is human breathing. Where a practitioner of traditional prosody, such as Frost, hears in meter the regular orderly rhythm of breath and heartbeat, Olson hears constraint. Olson therefore shifts emphasis from the causal rhythm of meter—against which syntax, tone of voice, duration, and so on are played—to an open form in which syntax, breath pauses in speech, and modulations of meaning and tone become the dominant rhythm of the poem.

For Olson, as for more traditional prosodists, the syllable (or its audible counterpart, the phoneme) "is the king and pin of versification, what rules and holds together the lines, the larger forms, of a poem" (388). Although Olson is not particularly coherent about exactly how the syllable is supposed to work in projective verse, he does explain that "the two halves" (of poetic practice, presumably) are the syllable, which he identifies with "the HEAD, by way of the EAR," and the line, which he identifies with "the HEART, by way of the BREATH" (390).

The line, for Olson, follows Williams's practice of making form, in Olson's words, "an extension of content." Although theories about free verse have often attempted to identify or establish rules by which to judge the form, free verse remains flexible and various in practice. But then, much of free verse has been an effort to inject new energy and complexity into the literary form called "poetry."

BIBLIOGRAPHY

Beyers, Chris. *A History of Free Verse*. Fayetteville: University of Arkansas Press, 2001.

Hartman, Charles O. *Free Verse: An Essay on Prosody*. Princeton, N.J.: Princeton University Press, 1980.

Holder, Alan. *Rethinking Meter: A New Approach to the Verse Line*. Lewisburg, Penn.: Bucknell University Press, 1995.

Olson, Charles. "Projective Verse." In *The New American Poetry 1945–1960*, edited by Donald M. Allen. New York: Grove Press, 1960.

Williams, William Carlos. "Free Verse." In *Princeton Encyclopedia of Poetry and Poetics*, edited by Alex Preminger, Frank J. Warnke, and O. B. Hardison. Princeton, N.J.: Princeton University Press, 1974.

Thomas Lisk

"PSALM" GEORGE OPPEN (1965) The poem "Psalm" is from GEORGE OPPEN's third book, *This in Which*. (1965) The influence of Walt Whitman and an American free verse tradition is evident (see PROSODY AND FREE VERSE), but the strict sense of image and line in the poem comes out of Oppen's IMAGIST and OBJECTIVIST roots. Using vivid images, Oppen describes a pastoral scene following deer as they bed down and graze in their forest home. The scene is interrupted in the last stanza, where the poem's speaker jolts and shocks by suggesting that the leaves in the woods and the deer are "nouns." However, the poem is not cynical—it does not reduce the deer to mere illusions of language—in fact, for Oppen the word *deer* becomes, through the poem, a statement of "faith" in existence.

LOUIS ZUKOFSKY's 1931 essay "Sincerity and Objectification," defining objectivist poetics, begins by focusing on sight and perception: "optics—the lens bringing the rays from an object to a focus" (12). Objectivist poets are concerned not with a scientific or moral objectivity but with a focused artistic vision that makes the poem an object itself. Zukofsky does, however, link formal achievement in poetry with the poet's emotional, artistic, and ethical "sincerity," and this concern also appears in "Psalm," in which the issue of truth itself is primary. "Psalm" opens with an epigraph taken from Thomas Aquinas: *"veritas sequitur esse rerum,"* or "truth follows the existence of things." The relation of truth to "the existence of things" is identified by Oppen—and by the objectivists generally—not so much as an ontological or epistemological one, but rather as a problem of language generally and poetry specifically. The issue for Oppen is how to make a poem that is as real (object-like) and startling as the world "in which" the poem arises. The issue of truth as a predicament of language, not existence, has also been later taken up by postmodern writers, such as the LANGUAGE SCHOOL of poets.

For Oppen, "Psalm," along with the several other poems that open *This in Which*, makes "a prelude, a statement of the metaphysical vision and the anthropocentric—the social as they would say" (Oppen 108). This song, in praise of deer in a forest—"that they are there"—is also an attempt to ground and bring into focus a relation with the world and "anthropocentrically" (Oppen 84) with humanity by way of language. In the space of the poem, the "small nouns" Oppen proclaims in his purview become a cord that can bind us to the world and to each other. The weight Oppen gives to this poem is quite striking. He says in a letter, "P[salm] makes a rather desperate declaration of faith. It is true I can't convince myself that human society will survive long without some such stubborn faith—but that is almost an open declaration of desperation" (84).

"Psalm" is arguably the most visually striking of the poems in *This in Which.* Five four-line stanzas, each with a deeply indented first line, demands unusual attention to the visual appearance of this poem on the page. Oppen's foregrounding of the visual aspect of the material poem causes a switch in focus back and forth from the look of the poem to what the poem "looks at" through words.

BIBLIOGRAPHY

DuPlessis, Rachel Blau and Peter Quartermain. *The Objectivist Nexus: Essays in Cultural Poetics.* Tuscaloosa: University of Alabama Press, 1999.

Hatlen, Burton, ed. *George Oppen: Man and Poet.* Orono, Maine: National Poetry Foundation, 1981.

Oppen, George. *Selected Letters of George Oppen,* edited by Rachel Blau DuPlessis. Durham, N.C.: Duke University Press, 1990.

Zukofsky, Louis. *Prepositions.* Berkeley: University of California Press, 1981.

Alicia Cohen

PURDY, AL (1918–2000) Through his nonconformity and alignment with the working class, Al Purdy went from being an outsider to someone who, through his poetry, has had a great effect on both readers and other writers. His use of everyday language and a lyrical sense of place and history reflect his diverse influences, such as D. H. Lawrence, Bliss Carman, and Walt Whitman. Purdy went from high school dropout, a stint in the Royal Canadian Air Force, and riding the rails to being honored as the grand mentor to a new generation of Canadian poets. Although he was vocal in his opposition to much of U.S. governmental policies, Purdy nonetheless integrated the American poetic vision of Whitman and ROBINSON JEFFERS in his work, even as he often dismissed Whitman.

Purdy was born in Wooler, Ontario. Having left school prematurely, Purdy traveled throughout Canada during the depression, working factory jobs. After six years in the Royal Canadian Air Force, he and his wife settled in Ameliasburg, Ontario. It would be Purdy's home until his death. Although he published his first chapbook in 1944, Purdy did not receive critical and popular acclaim until *The Cariboo Horses* (1965) was awarded the Governor General's Award. Purdy continued to write until 2000, publishing his first novel, *A Splinter in the Heart* (1990). *The Collected Poems of Al Purdy* (1986) won Purdy his second Governor General's Award.

Purdy abandoned conventional poetic forms early on and turned to a more conversational and accessible tone. His interests in history, literature, and the environment created a kind of livable poetry in which the reader is placed within a cultural and geographic context. In "For Robert Kennedy" (1973), Purdy's melancholy, straightforward tone turns lyrically from the towering figure of Kennedy to Purdy's grandfather as a man "newspapers never heard of / but loved for no reason or every reason." Purdy's tenor is that of an equalizer, finding the quiet humanity in the world, big and small.

He struggled to validate a Canadian history that seemed always to exist on the margins of world history. He consciously took on the role of being Canada's poet long before his success reaffirmed it. Many critics have noted that Purdy took much from his American influences, such as JAMES WRIGHT and CHARLES BUKOWSKI, to formulate his own vision of Canadian poetics. Purdy had complex and contradictory relationships with the poetry of CHARLES OLSON, WILLIAM CARLOS WILLIAMS, and EZRA POUND. Yet, over time, the connections between Purdy's vast body of well-crafted, open poems seem to share much in common with these American counterparts.

BIBLIOGRAPHY

MacKendrick, Louis. *Al Purdy and His Works.* Toronto: ECW Press, 1991.

Rogers, Linda, ed. *Al Purdy: Essays on His Works.* Toronto: Guernica, 2002.

Solecki, Sam. *The Last Canadian Poet: An Essay on Al Purdy.* Toronto: University of Toronto Press, 1999.

Arto Payaslian

"THE PURSE SEINE" ROBINSON JEFFERS (1937) The poetry of ROBINSON JEFFERS is best described not as part of a movement but as a search for solitude and a rejection of human-created movements. "The Purse Seine" represents the poet's antimodernist disavowal of civilization. While the modernists saw the height of humanity in civilization, but felt that the golden age was long past and unrecoverable (see MODERNISM), Jeffers felt that civilization had sustained itself, but at the expense of humanity. He believed that the modern world was declining in its relentless pursuit of progress. He also rejected the modernists' break with traditional forms, using instead blank verse in long, narrative poems, and a Whitmanesque free verse in his shorter lyric poems (see PROSODY AND FREE VERSE).

"The Purse Seine" was published in the collection *Such Counsels You Gave Me* at a time when Jeffers was beginning to lose his audience, which had grown weary of his pessimism and seeming misanthropy. Still it captures the main thrust of Jeffers's world view: We are doomed, because we seek comfort and answers in civilization. William H. Nolte describes the poem as "one of his most striking commentaries on the inevitability of the disasters that must follow the separation of man from the earth" (121–122).

The poem is simple and direct, reflecting the poet's typical style. Aside from a single extended metaphor of a fish, it is devoid of symbols. The speaker presents first a scene of sardine fishing boats (the poem is named for a type of fishing net). Because of the natural phosphorescence of the schools of fish, the fishermen must work at night during the dark phase of the Moon. Guided by the glowing of the fish, they place their nets, then haul in their catch. As he watches the trapped fish being drawn closer and tighter together within the net, the speaker describes the scene as both "beautiful" and "a little terrible." The silver glints of the masses of sardines contrast their terror and imminent deaths.

Later, as the speaker looks from a promontory over the lights of the city, he is reminded of the trapped sardines flickering within the net. Humanity has created its own net, called progress, and has become trapped in cities. The net has not closed yet, but it is being drawn tighter. Finally, in a direct address to the reader, the speaker confronts his contemporaries who take exception to what they perceive as mere pessimism in his verse. His is no prophecy of doom; it is simply an observation of the inevitable. The poem states that any enterprise conducted by the mass of flawed humanity will eventually bring about destruction, though the earth will live on.

BIBLIOGRAPHY

Karman, James, ed. *Critical Essays on Robinson Jeffers*. Boston: G. K. Hall, 1990.

Nolte, William H. *Rock and Hawk: Robinson Jeffers and the Romantic Agony*. Athens: University of Georgia Press, 1978.

Joseph Schaub

R

RAKOSI, CARL (1903–2004) Carl Rakosi is best known as one of the original OBJECTIVIST poets, along with LOUIS ZUKOFSKY, CHARLES REZNIKOFF, GEORGE OPPEN, LORINE NIEDECKER, and Basil Bunting, although he is perhaps the least studied. These second-generation modernists sought variously to bring poetic innovation together with social engagement in the depression years of the 1930s (see MODERNISM). From 1940 through 1965, Rakosi gave up writing poetry and devoted himself entirely to a career as a social worker and psychologist. After this long hiatus, Rakosi, with remarkable longevity and wry wit, has been writing in a direct style marked by a tone of sincerity that runs through his diverse reflections on popular culture, metaphysics, and aging. More than any other objectivist poet, Rakosi has explored the psychology and ramifications of the poet as a speaking individual.

Born in Baja, Hungary, Rakosi immigrated to the United States at the age of six to live with his father and stepmother, first in Indiana, then in Wisconsin. At the age of 21, after completing a degree in English at the University of Wisconsin, Rakosi legally changed his name to Callman Rawley to counter some of the antiimmigrant sentiment of the time. As he writes, "For one thing, Rakosi was always being mispronounced and misspelled, but the main reason was that I didn't think that anyone with a foreign name would be hired, the atmosphere was such in English departments in those days" (*Contemporary Authors* 205).

While using Rawley as his professional name, he kept Rakosi as his pen name. Through the late 1920s and 1930s, he dedicated himself to his poetry while attempting to find a career that would both sustain him personally and concretely contribute to others. He spent brief periods in graduate, law, and medical schools before entering a long career as a social worker. Eventually unable to synthesize the need for direct social action with his artistic demands, Rakosi entirely gave up writing poetry. His poetry of the late 1930s contends with this widening personal divide, apparent in "Declaration," (1941) when he affirms, "I shall put my purity away now / and find my art in other men," and in "To the Non-Political Citizen," (1941) which ends "When will you become indignant / and declare yourself / against the wrongs of the people?"

For 25 years Rakosi lived entirely as Callman Rawley, removing himself so fully from poetry that the publisher of his first book, *Selected Poems* (1941), thought that Rakosi had died in Eastern Europe behind the iron curtain. Rakosi published several professional articles as Rawley, but it was only as he neared retirement that Andrew Crozier, a young graduate student who had rediscovered Rakosi's early poetry, contacted him, rekindling his creative output.

One of the influences on his earliest poetry was WALLACE STEVENS; Rakosi remembers being "seduced by the elegance of language, the imaginative associations of words. . . . [He] was involved in a language world" ("Interview" 182). While Rakosi adopted these lush surfaces of language, he could also parody them to some degree with such lines as "All motion blurs the scented yaw of her skirts / (linen like the subsiding of labials, / like the undertow in the veins)" in his series "Domination of Wallace Stevens" (1925).

As Rakosi matured toward a poetry of clear, direct communication that valued subject matter as much as language, he was drawn to the precise images and clipped lines of WILLIAM CARLOS WILLIAMS. In this, Rakosi's most objectivist work, he maintains a sharp edge to his verse and quick attention to detail in description. Like Williams, Rakosi turns this keen perception upon the particulars of urban life. In "Good Prose," (1933) for example, he describes a caged canary as "the sun lights up / the lettuce leaf / between the bars" in brief lines that can read like the pieces of a prose sentence in which each piece is a measured observation or association.

Rakosi also takes Williams's style and turns it to social critique, most notably in his parody of Williams's 16-word poem "so much depends" (also known as "The Red Wheelbarrow" [1923]). Whereas Williams sketched a quiet farm scene centered on a red wheelbarrow, Rakosi in "YES" (1971) recasts the poem in an urban setting, placing the speed of the verse in the context of business executives and excrement. Rakosi's short one- and two-word lines tick by with the insistent pace of an "instant // wrist / watch"; by the end, the precise beauty of image becomes little more than "a clean / bowel."

The quarter-century break in writing divides Rakosi's poetry into two distinct phases (Crozier 13), with the latter characterized by a direct, conversational tone and a broken, two-part line. Still there are some connections between the two halves; as Marjorie Perloff has pointed out, Rakosi continues reworking his earlier poetry throughout his later volumes.

In his second phase, Rakosi blends his modernist form with a more romantic concern for the speaking subject, bringing together his early focus on precise description of objects with an appreciation that "individuality remains avant-garde" (*Collected Prose* 46). A number of separate, often ironic voices work their way through the considerations of history and popular culture in his "Americana" (1967) series, mixing observation with critique in the poems, such as "Coca Cola Sign," (1975) which begins "In this country / the sign outlives America." Rakosi rounds out his extensive later writing with a series of poems reflecting on the personal process of aging, the artistic practice of poetry, and eclectic spiritual meditations.

BIBLIOGRAPHY

Crozier, Andrew. Introduction to *Poems, 1923–1941,* by Carl Rakosi. Los Angeles: Sun & Moon, 1995.

Heller, Michael, ed. *Carl Rakosi: Man and Poet.* Orono, Maine: National Poetry Foundation, 1993.

Perloff, Marjorie. "Looking for the Real Carl Rakosi: Collecteds and Selecteds." *Journal of American Studies* 30 (Aug. 1996): 271–283.

Rakosi, Carl. "Carl Rakosi." *Contemporary Authors Autobiography Series.* Vol. 5, edited by Adele Sarkissian, 193–210. Detroit: Gale Research, 1987.

———. *Collected Prose.* Orono, Maine: National Poetry Foundation, 1983.

———. "Interview with Carl Rakosi." *Contemporary Literature* 10 (spring 1969): 155–159.

Michael Rozendal

RANSOM, JOHN CROWE (1888–1974)

As an essayist, teacher, and poet, John Crowe Ransom was a major influence on American poetry, southern writing, and criticism. He was a founding member of the FUGITIVE/AGRARIAN SCHOOL, which included, among others, ALLEN TATE, ROBERT PENN WARREN, and DONALD DAVIDSON. The Fugitives and the IMAGISTS SCHOOL were the two most influential forces in American poetry in the early part of the 20th century. The imagists tended toward experimentation and individualism, while the Fugitives tended toward classicism and traditionalism. Often Ransom is called a minor poet, since his poetic output was small; however, he is an important figure in the Southern Renaissance, which included such writers as Warren, William Faulkner, and Eudora Welty. As a literary critic, Ransom coined the term New Criticism, which came to describe the dominant critical practice in American universities in the 20th century, and he was otherwise an influential critic and teacher, counting among his students poets RANDALL JARRELL and ROBERT LOWELL.

Ransom was born in Tennessee in 1888, and he grew up in the household of an open-minded Methodist minister. At 15 he entered Vanderbilt University; his primary interest was philosophy. After graduation he studied classics as a Rhodes scholar at Oxford from 1910 to 1913. Upon returning from England, he was appointed to the English department faculty at Vanderbilt. Outside of military service in World War I, he remained at Vanderbilt until departing in 1937 for Kenyon College, where he founded the literary journal the *Kenyon Review*. He was awarded the Bollingen Prize for poetry in 1951 and the National Book Award in 1964.

His first book, *Poems about God* (1919), was written during World War I, but he quickly became disillusioned with the work. During his years with the Fugitives, he published *Chills and Fever* (1924) and *Two Gentlemen in Bonds* (1927), and it is these two collections upon which his reputation rests. By 1927 Ransom ceased writing poetry in favor of criticism.

Ransom's recurring themes are the conflict of the body and the soul, the transience of life, the passing of beauty and love, myth, and tradition. His poems are traditional in form, but his use of language is playful, filled with wit and irony. Often he portrays the particular in delicate situations to attention to the universal. For example, in "Janet Waking" (1927), a young girl learns about death through the death of her pet hen: "It was a transmogrifying bee / Came droning down on Chucky's old bald head." Janet's response is "Wake her from her sleep!" In this poem traditional elements, such as rhyme, are connected with humor to display an experience that everyone knows—the first awareness of death.

BIBLIOGRAPHY

Quinlan, Kieran. *John Crowe Ransom's Secular Faith*. Baton Rouge: Louisiana State University Press, 1989.

Young, Thomas Daniel, ed. *John Crowe Ransom: Critical Essays and a Bibliography*. Baton Rouge: Louisiana State University Press, 1968.

William Allegrezza

RAP POETRY See CARIBBEAN POETIC INFLUENCES; POETRY IN PERFORMANCE.

"THE RED WHEELBARROW" WILLIAM CARLOS WILLIAMS (1923) Although other MODERNIST poems may lay claim to greater canonical importance or influence, few are as widely read, recognized, and discussed as WILLIAM CARLOS WILLIAMS's brief LYRIC, "The Red Wheelbarrow." An IMAGIST poem, it concentrates upon a short series of visual images drawn from an everyday agrarian setting: a rain-slicked red wheelbarrow near some chickens. Nothing literally happens in the poem, though the image itself unfolds grammatically and associatively to articulate a critical philosophical position. Williams writes in the opening lines that "So much depends / upon" this red wheelbarrow, but this claim begs the question "Why?" and the interpretive answers have varied widely. At heart, whether they focus on the poem's symbolism, grammatical constructions, sounds, lineation, or historical significance, these interpretations all seem to acknowledge that the vitality of human life and experience depends upon cultivating a vision of the world that imbues the world with significance.

Much has been made of the linguistic and visual pun Williams makes in the opening lines by using the word *depends*, which connotes reliance or basis, but denotes a hanging attachment. Thus, the lines that follow from the opening stanza depend upon the opening (they literally hang from it), while the poem itself, including its philosophical opening, depends upon (relies or is based upon) the image of the red wheelbarrow and the white chickens. From this initial focus on dependence, any number of readings may arise. The barnyard setting introduces the theme of human connection to nature, while the wheelbarrow itself, as a manmade object, may stand for the means of mediating that relation. The red and white colors may suggest maturation and purity, while the presence of the chickens may indicate a particular feminine presence.

Barry Ahearn argues for viewing the wheelbarrow as an emblem for all human creations, claiming "numbers and the red wheelbarrow do have one thing in common: both are elementary in the sense that civilization depends on them." Hugh Kenner places a similar emphasis on the wheelbarrow and on the poem itself as indicative of the significance of human "making": "Not only is what the sentence says banal, if you heard someone say it you'd wince. But hammered on the typewriter into a *thing made*, and this without displacing a single word except typographically, the sixteen words exist in a different zone altogether, a zone remote from the world of sayers and sayings." Richard R. Frye points to the ontological significance of the wheelbarrow, suggesting that the poem confirms "there is a world to begin with for art to affirm." Peter Baker calls attention to the existential importance of any visual image, connecting "dependence" to Williams's statement in "Asphodel, That Greeny Flower" that "men die miserably every day / for lack / of what is found there [in poems]," while Quentin Youngberg reads the poem as a romantic celebration of nature, noting that "the reader must . . . be aware that the very health of man and the world depends on [the red wheelbarrow's] existence and the unity that results from communion with nature" (153).

Whether or not any, all, or none of these interpretations of the poem satisfy the reader may be beside the point. The poem is equally an ARS POETICA and an *ars vitae* (art of living), for the opening lines call attention to the linguistic concentration that is the hallmark of lyric poetry, and which is analogous to the dense complexities of human existence. Poet X. J. KENNEDY seems to have identified this particular concern with human experience when he relates Williams's claim that "the poem refers to a moment when the poet was 'gazing from the window of the house where one of his patients, a small girl, lay suspended between life and death'" (32). Ultimately, poetic images and poetry itself help us as humans to make sense of how the scattered events of a life relate to each other meaningfully.

BIBLIOGRAPHY

Ahearn, Barry. *William Carlos Williams and Alterity: The Early Poetry*. Modern American Poetry. Available online. URL: www.english.uiuc.edu/maps.poets/S_Z/williams/wheelborrow.

Baker, Peter. *Modern Poetic Practice: Structure and Genesis*. Modern American Poetry. Available online. URL: www.english.uiuc.edu/maps/poets/S_Z/williams/wheelbarrow.

Frye, Richard R. "Seeing the Signs: Objectivist Premonitions in Williams' *Spring and All*." *Sagetrieb* 8, no. 3 (1989): 77–95.

Kennedy, X. J. *Introduction to Poetry*. 6th ed. Boston: Little, Brown, 1986.

Kenner, Hugh. *A Homemade World: The American Modernist Writers*. Modern American Poetry. Available online. URL: www.english.uiuc.edu/maps/poets/S_Z/williams/wheelbarrow.

Youngberg, Quentin. "Williams's 'The Red Wheelbarrow.'" *The Explicator* 58, no. 3 (2000): 152–153.

Temple Cone

REED, ISHMAEL (1938–) Although Ishmael Reed is now better known for his novels than for his poetry, his early verse received considerable attention and acclaim during the 1970s. Influenced by the various experimental poetry movements that developed in the United States after World War II, Reed came of age as a writer in New York City during the 1960s. He was loosely associated with the nationalist BLACK ARTS MOVEMENT, but he criticized its attempt to codify a single black aesthetic. Fascinated by hoodoo, the African-American form of voodoo, Reed developed an idiosyncratic "Neo-Hoodoo Aesthetic" that honored hoodoo's spirit of individual improvisation. The poem "Catechism of d Neoamerican Hoodoo Church" (1970) calls upon the African-American writer to "conjure" the black traditions hidden in American culture but also to "DO YR ART D WAY U WANT." However, even as Reed conceived of this more inclusive black aesthetic, he began to see the interrelatedness of the many distinct cultures comprising the American "multiculture." Since the early 1970s, he has been a prominent advocate of multiculturalism.

Born in Chattanooga, Tennessee, Reed grew up in Buffalo, New York, where he attended the University of Buffalo (now the State University of New York, Buffalo). He lived in New York City from 1962 to 1967 and there helped to build two proto–Black Arts movement institutions, the Umbra poetry workshop (1962–64) and the group's magazine *Umbra* (1963–64). Reed began teaching intermittently once he left New York for the San Francisco area in 1967, at the University of California, Berkeley. As a founding member of the multiculturalist Before Columbus Foundation, which sponsors the American Book Awards, and as a coeditor of *Yardbird* (1972–76) and several other literary magazines, Reed has promoted the work of many underappreciated writers of various cultural backgrounds. His own body of work includes six volumes of poetry: *catechism of d neoamerican hoodoo church* (1970), *Conjure* (1972), *Chattanooga* (1973), *A Secretary to the Spirits* (1978), and *New and Collected Poems* (1988), which was updated with new work in 2006. In 1973 *Conjure* was nominated for both the National Book Award in poetry and the Pulitzer Prize, and in 1998 Reed was awarded a MacArthur Foundation Fellowship.

Like the Black Arts poets, Reed views the making of poetry as a revolutionary activity. Challenging the elitism and racism he perceives in both the Anglo-American literary tradition and traditional accounts of American history, he experiments with such neglected poetic materials as Egyptian mythology, characters and motifs from popular films, 19th-century hoodoo lore, and conversations with everyday people, such as flight attendants and cab drivers. "The Jackal-Headed Cowboy" (1972) imagines the ancient Egyptian god of the dead, Anubis, as an outlaw-hero in contemporary America. Reed's multiculturalist focus is more explicit in "Chattanooga" (1973), in which he pictures his birthplace as the site of many different cultural histories. The poem suggests that this American city, like writing itself, is "something you / Can have anyway you want it."

BIBLIOGRAPHY

Dick, Bruce, and Amritjit Singh, eds. *Conversations with Ishmael Reed.* Jackson: University Press of Mississippi, 1995.

Mackey, Nathaniel. "Ishmael Reed and the Black Aesthetic." *C.L.A. Journal* 21, no. 3 (March 1978): 355–366.

Matthew Calihman

RETALLACK, JOAN (1941–) Joan Retallack's work is most clearly associated with that of JOHN CAGE in its use of chance-operation and audience-centered techniques and with the LANGUAGE SCHOOL of poets in its concern with the materiality of texts—the forms of letters and words on the page. In much of her work, the reader must pay attention to details of typography and seemingly accidental textual inclusions, such as apparent typographical errors.

Retallack was born in New York City. She received an M.A. in philosophy from Georgetown University in 1976, by which time her performance works were appearing at the Corcoran Gallery, the New Playwright's Theater, and other gallery spaces throughout the Washington, D.C., area. *Circumstantial Evidence,* Retallack's first full-length collection, appeared in 1985. It was followed in 1993 by *Errata Suite,* which was selected for the 1994 Columbia Book Award by ROBERT CREELEY. Retallack's other awards include two GERTRUDE STEIN Awards for innovative North American poetry (1993 and 1997) and a grant from the Lannan Foundation (1998–99). Retallack has taught at Bard College.

Retallack has also published numerous critical essays and interviews. *MUSICAGE* is a book-length interview/conversation with Cage. Many of Retallack's critical writings involve what she has termed "poethics," an idea key to understanding Retallack's work. Central to poethics is the concept of the poethical "swerve," which comes about as one relinquishes control of the language. This "swerve" allows the poet to attend to the multiplicity of patterns (typographical and material as well as syntactical and associational) that constitute language and our relationship to it. The interplay between the poet and the language is made available to the reader in what Retallack has termed a "geometry of attention." The poet is no longer dictating terms nor allowing previously constructed terms to dictate meaning. The attentive reader, then, creates her or his own meaning in a complex relationship with the text.

An example of the importance of the reader's role in a Retallack poem can be seen in *Errata Suite.* On page 59, there is a blank space in the text (literally, "——"). Page 60 is a nearly exact repeat of the same text. If the page is held up to a light, the word *time* from page 60 shows through exactly where the "——" is on page 59. Furthermore, the word *time* backwards ("emit," but with a backwards *e*) looks like "omit" (the reversed e looks like an *o*). One cannot know if this is intentional, and it does not matter—the word is there, and it is real. The reader makes of it what she or he will.

Retallack's "poethical wager" is a bet with the future: the possibility that one's work will be influential in ways that one cannot foresee. Retallack's work invites such uncertainty, recognizing it as the opportunity it is.

BIBLIOGRAPHY

Hatlen, Burton. "Joan Retallack: A Philosopher among the Poets, a Poet among the Philosophers." *Contemporary Literature* 42, no. 2 (summer 2001): 347–375.

Lazer, Hank. "Partial to Error: Joan Retallack's *ERRATA SUITE.*" In *Opposing Poetries.* Vol. 2, edited by Hank

Lazer, 70–76. Evanston Ill.: Northwestern University Press, 1996.
Vickery, Ann. "Taking a Poethical Perspective: Joan Retallack's Afterimages." In *Leaving Lines of Gender: A Feminist Genealogy of Language Writing.* Hanover, N.H.: Wesleyan University Press, 2000, pp. 167–178.

Dean Taciuch

REVELL, DONALD (1954–) Donald Revell's poems should expose reality through art in the way a prism reveals the colors of light. However, Revell describes his poetics as an attempt to "unname things" and opposes "anything that seeks to define" ("Better Unsaid" 29). What powers his poems is not formal virtuosity, but "delight"—his sincerity and attention to the world and ability to convey experience (29). Concerned with ethical and political problems, Revell is willing to let them shape his aesthetics. Though influenced by JOHN ASHBERY, Revell cannot be grouped with the NEW YORK SCHOOL of poetry. His books show his desire to experiment with new forms, and to revive old ones.

Revell grew up in New York City. He received a Ph.D. in English from the State University of New York, Buffalo in 1980. In 1991 he married the poet Claudia Keelan. Revell was the editor-in-chief of the *Denver Quarterly* from 1988 to 1994. His first book, *From the Abandoned Cities,* winner of the 1983 National Poetry Series, is characterized by short lyrics and formal poems; however, he soon started to experiment with less conventional structures and abandoned personal issues for larger themes in his next three books, *The Gaza of Winter* (1988), *New Dark Ages* (1990), and *Erasures* (1992). Appalled at the bombastic rhetoric of early century futurism and vorticism (two literary modernist movements advocating an aesthetic of speed, technical innovation, and political violence [see MODERNISM]), which helped spread fascism and communism, Revell undertook to discredit utopian ideologies by helping his generation rebuild poetry after the mass exterminations of the mid-20th century. Although Paul Celan, Samuel Beckett, and other post-Holocaust writers had devised a sparse, pointed rhetoric, Revell chose to "betray the silence" of his predecessors, claiming that poetry needed to return to "the grand gesture, the didactic example," if it were to teach about reality again ("Betraying" 18).

In his most recent work, Revell refuses the formal poetic closure of fixed forms and genres to avoid oversimplifying the real. Poets should ask questions, he says, but not worry about the answers, because "understanding is not necessarily important" ("Conversation"). For Revell, any answer comes short of the truth, and any form comes short of closure. For example, in "Elegy" (1998), Revell discovers that the elegiac genre fails to assuage a mourner's grief. Grief eludes language, and the elegy can only mirror grief's fragmented, elliptical quality: "myself the other / winter even more."

BIBLIOGRAPHY

Baker, David. "Plainness and Sufficiency." In *Heresy and the Ideal: On Contemporary Poetry.* Fayetteville: University of Arkansas Press, 2000.
Revell, Donald. "Betraying the Silence." *American Poetry Review.* 21, no. 5 (1992): 17–18.
———. "Better Unsaid: On Poetic Fragments." *American Poetry Review.* 25, no. 4 (1996): 29–30.
———. Interview/Conversation with Marie C. Jones, University of North Texas, Denton. March 23, 2000.
Schultz, Susan M. "Houses of Poetry after Ashbery: The Poetry of Ann Lauterbach and Donald Revell." *Virginia Quarterly Review* 67 (1991): 295–309.

Marie C. Jones

REXROTH, KENNETH (1905–1982) Kenneth Rexroth's work intersects with a broad range of 20th-century American poetry, poetics, and movements: MODERNISM, the OBJECTIVIST SCHOOL, the SAN FRANCISCO RENAISSANCE, and the BEATS. Yet despite the significant areas of overlap with these poetic movements and personal involvement with various poets associated with them, Rexroth remains somewhat of an anomaly in the poetic landscape—in part, because he positioned himself as the perennial aesthetic, social, and political outsider.

Born in South Bend, Indiana, and raised by a mother with strong feminist and socialist leanings, Rexroth was deeply affected by the progressive politics of his upbringing, and his work bears the imprint of the leftist ideologies that dominated his childhood home.

When his mother died in 1916 and his father died three years later, Rexroth initiated a plan of self-education whereby he dropped out of high school in order to pursue a real education of street politics, books, and writing. Eventually, though, he began to study music and art at the Art Institute of Chicago and the University of Chicago, and his early life was that of the poet, painter, and political activist. His lengthy career has not been without renown; his honors include the Shelley Memorial Award from the Poetry Society of America (1958) and the Academy of American Poets' Copernicus Award (1975).

In 1927, after marrying the painter Andree Schafer, the first of Rexroth's four wives, he moved to California. Largely supported during this period by the Federal Writers Project, Rexroth melded his politics with the California landscape into a poetry that was poignant and played upon a deep emotional register—a point perhaps best exemplified by "Climbing Milestone Mountain, August 22, 1927" (1940), which juxtaposes the 1927 execution of the anarchists Nicola Sacco and Bartolomeo Vanzetti with images of stars over the sierra and reminiscences of Boston and the political events leading up to Sacco's and Vanzetti's infamous arrest, imprisonment, and execution: "We sat up late while Deneb moved over the zenith / And I told Marie all about Boston, how it looked / That last terrible week." "Climbing Milestone Mountain" typifies Rexroth's poetic style of fairly regular free verse lines as well as his tendency to ruminate upon a particular landscape that leads to sociopolitical, philosophical, and spiritual points of view.

After 1927 Rexroth's poetry took a more experimental slant, and in 1931 his work was included in a special issue of *Poetry*, edited by LOUIS ZUKOFSKY, which served as the poetic manifesto of objectivism. "Fundamental Disagreement with Two Contemporaries" (1966), for example, exemplifies Rexroth's early experimentation, and it is remarkable how this poem, in its use of lettering for the sake of visual shaping at the sacrifice of language, is closer to the poetry of the later half of the 20th century than to Rexroth's own later works. Zukofsky also included Rexroth's early experimental work in *An "Objectivists" Anthology* (1932). Yet not long afterward and in a maneuver that was frequently repeated throughout his career, Rexroth distanced himself from the objectivists and abandoned his experimental, cubist-influenced poetry in favor of a more direct and less oblique style. This period was marked by a series of affiliations with various poetic movements, including poets who would figure large in the San Francisco Renaissance and the Beats.

In 1940 *In What Hour,* his first book of poetry, was published. With its sociopolitical critiques of war and environmental themes, the poetry favors a rhetorical stance that borders upon the didactic. In *The Phoenix and the Tortoise* (1944), which was regarded as a "masterpiece" by some critics, Rexroth strikes a balance between social commentary and LYRIC POETRY.

The 1940s not only marked a breakthrough in Rexroth's writing career, it was also a period of immense intellectual development that included extensive study of Japanese and Chinese culture and art and translations of Greek, Chinese, and Japanese poetry—all of which are evident in *The Act of Worldly Wisdom* (1949), as well as the masterful *The Signature of All Things* (1950), which blends pacificism, the spiritual interconnectedness of the natural and the human worlds, and the influence of the late 16th- and early 17th-century German mystic Jacob Bohme (see POETRY IN TRANSLATION). At this time, Rexroth also defines the poet's role in *The Signature of All Things* as "one who creates / Sacramental relationships / That last always."

In the 1950s Rexroth's daughters Mary Delia Andree and Katherine Ann Helen were born. Both became subjects for his poetry—most notably *A Bestiary for My Daughters Mary and Katherine* (1955). Rexroth continued writing throughout tumultuous personal crises, and his critical acclaim grew with his antiestablishment poem "Thou Shalt Not Kill" (1955): "They are murdering all the young me. / For a half a century now, every day." While the poem responds to the death of Dylan Thomas, it clearly embodies the humanist-pacifist ideology that informs all of Rexroth's poetry. The poem demonstrates the degree to which the later poetry, under a more mature and skilled hand, can present a scathing sociopolitical critique that has poetic merit and avoids didacticism.

Publication of *The Collected Shorter Poems* (1966) and *The Collected Longer Poems* (1968) further testified to Rexroth's acknowledged presence within the pantheon of significant American poets. This period included the publications of well-received and popular translations of poets of China and Japan, as well as the masterful and erotic *The Love Poems of Marichiko* (1978), written in a woman's voice. The tenderness and eroticism of the later works of poetry are a natural extension of Rexroth's long poetic career and his preoccupation with love as the force that binds human beings to one another. Rexroth's legacy is his loving documentation of all facets of human life—even its shortcomings—and his desire to eliminate hatred and war through the force of poetry.

BIBLIOGRAPHY

Bartlett, Lee. *Kenneth Rexroth.* Boise, Idaho: Boise State University Press, 1988.

Gibson, Morgan. *Revolutionary Rexroth: Poet of East-West Wisdom.* Hamden, Conn.: Archon Books, 1986.

Hamalian, Linda. *A Life of Kenneth Rexroth.* New York: Norton, 1991.

David Clippinger

REZNIKOFF, CHARLES (1894–1976) There is likely no better example of OBJECTIVIST poetics than the work of Charles Reznikoff. LOUIS ZUKOFSKY acknowledged this in "Sincerity and Objectification," the essay that launched the objectivist venture in 1931: Reznikoff's poetry was "sincere," because it was concerned with "the detail, not mirage, of seeing" (Zukofsky 273). And Reznikoff's poetry embodied "objectification," because it was at "perfect rest," like an object "to which the mind does not wish to add" (Zukofsky 276). Reznikoff was an observer who preferred "thinking with things as they exist" to thinking things into existence (273). His stated preference was for "the pithy, the necessary, the clear, and the plain" ("Early History of a Writer" [1969]), but an uncommon clarity of vision is not benign simplicity. In Reznikoff's poems the subjects speak for themselves; sentimentality is all but excised, and the persona of the poet is nowhere to be found. This extraordinary restraint, coupled with a heightened sense of the poem as a linguistic construct, has made Reznikoff popular among many contemporary poets, such as CHARLES BERNSTEIN and MICHAEL HELLER. Reznikoff was consistently championed by fellow objectivists Zukofsky and GEORGE OPPEN and later praised by such poets as WILLIAM CARLOS WILLIAMS and ROBERT CREELEY.

Reznikoff was born in Brooklyn, the son of Russian Jews who fled persecution. At the age of 16, he set off to study journalism at the University of Missouri. Discovering, however, that journalism concerns itself much more with news than it does with language, he left after only a year. Upon his return to Brooklyn, Reznikoff went to work as a salesman in his parents' millinery business (as documented in *Family Chronicle* [1963]). He soon decided to attend law school; after passing the bar in 1916, he returned to selling hats, a job he enjoyed, because it left his mind free to think about poetry. Heeding the fate of his grandfather, whose legacy of 30 years worth of verse (in Hebrew) had been lost, Reznikoff decided to publish his own work. His first book, *Rhythms,* came out in 1918; many of the books that followed, including the playlets collected in *Nine Plays* (1927), were also self-published. In 1928 Reznikoff began work at a law encyclopedia company; he was fired some years later, because he could not adapt his writing style to the prescribed legalese. He went to Hollywood in 1938 to read scripts and conducted research for a friend in the industry; the improbable combination, however, did not last much longer than a year. His experiences there provided the grist for the posthumously published novel *The Manner Music* (1977). Like most of the objectivist poets, Reznikoff published no poetry at all from 1941 to 1959; during these years he devoted his meticulous attention to editing the *Jewish Frontier* and translating and researching for organizations, such as the Jewish Publication Society. *By the Waters of Manhattan,* a selection of poems published by New Directions in 1962 at the urging of Oppen, finally brought Reznikoff to the attention of a broader public. Though recognition was a long time in coming, he was awarded the Morton Dauwen Zabel Prize by the National Institute of Arts and Letters in 1971.

Reznikoff's legal work, particularly the condensed narratives and minutiae of the case studies themselves, exerted a significant influence upon his writing. While reading the law, he found it "delightful" to "bathe in the clear waters of reason" and to "use words for their daylight meaning / And not as prisms" ("Early History of a Writer" [1969]). In contrast, traditional verse seemed "affected" to him, "fake flowers / In the streets which I walked." The reference to walking here is not accidental. Reznikoff's primary method of research was to roam the streets of New York: In his prime, he walked 20 miles a day. This ambulatory routine provided him with the data for what Bernstein, in his essay "Reznikoff's Nearness," has usefully identified as a poetry of witness. Here an old man "pulls off a bit of baked apple, shiny with sugar, / eating with reverence food, the great comforter" (*Poems* [1920]), and there "Among the heaps of brick and plaster lies / a girder, still itself among the rubbish" (section 69 *Jerusalem the Golden* [1934]). Observations such as these, which have a haikulike burst of incisive clarity, are generally embedded in a long series of similar ones that together constitute a single poem. This serial structure adds to the perceptual detail a wide scope that has the overall effect of subtle social commentary (see LONG AND SERIAL POETRY).

Testimony (1978) perhaps best illustrates Reznikoff's poetry of witness. Using law reports, he distills—sometimes verbatim—events that took place in America during the late 19th century. Characters, such as Gunnysack Joe, "Uz" Waffle, and Dutch Maggie, engage in robbery, land disputes, quarrels, rape, adultery, and prolific amounts of racism and abuse. The reader is immersed in a cascade of trauma mitigated only by nuances in tone that add humor, insight, and mystery. After the painful specificity of previous sections, for example, one six-line section, consisting of a letter exhorting its recipient to "keep things still as a mouse" until he or she arrives to "do up the town" ("Social Life"), leaves one wondering what manner of folly landed the perpetrators in court. Here, as elsewhere in his work, Reznikoff does not privilege the beautiful over the ordinary or even the ugly; instead he attempts to illuminate shared experience. Reznikoff wrote "not for victory" but "for the common sunshine"; he did not seek "a seat upon the dais / but at the common table" ("Te Deum" [1959]).

BIBLIOGRAPHY

Bernstein, Charles. "Reznikoff's Nearness." In *The Objectivist Nexus: Essays in Cultural Poetics,* edited by Rachel Blau DuPlessis and Peter Quartermain. Tuscaloosa: University of Alabama, 1999, pp. 210–239.

Hindus, Milton, ed. *Charles Reznikoff: Man and Poet.* Orono, Maine: National Poetry Foundation, 1984.

Zukofsky, Louis. "Sincerity and Objectification: With Special Reference to the Work of Charles Reznikoff." *Poetry* 37, no. 5 (February 1931): 272–284.

Duncan Dobbelmann

RICH, ADRIENNE (1929–) Adrienne Rich has said that, as a young poet, she used poetry "to write [her]self out of [her] own divisions" (*What Is* 196), and the same could be said for her entire career. Over the years those "divisions" have come in many forms, and while poetry has resolved some of them for Rich, it has also reinforced others. One of the enduring divisions—and one which has served as a renewable source for her work—involves her ambivalent attitude toward poetic language. Early in her career, for instance, Rich felt both empowered and divided from herself as a woman, as she attempted to write in the ostensibly genderless, supposedly universal voice of the male poets she had studied in high school and college (see FEMALE VOICE, FEMALE LANGUAGE). The title of her 1978 collection *The Dream of a Common Language* indicates Rich's desire to find or create a women's lexicon; though in time she found a language that seemed more faithful to her experience, she has never discovered a common language that could reflect and unite the experiences of all women. Rich has also remained divided between feeling that poetry is a powerful tool for creating community and promoting justice, on the one hand, and knowing, on the other, that language alone cannot create social change. Somewhat paradoxically, her poetic production has been, in part, motivated by her doubt about her art. And yet, over a 50-year span, she has published 20 volumes of poetry, in addition to five collections of nonfiction prose. Moreover she has found lasting inspiration in the work of poets as disparate as Emily Dickinson, WILLIAM CARLOS WILLIAMS, WALLACE STEVENS, H. D., W. H. AUDEN, Pablo Neruda, MURIEL RUKEYSER, Anna Akhmatova, and AUDRE LORDE.

Rich was born in Baltimore, Maryland. She graduated from Radcliffe College in 1951, and that same year she won the prestigious Yale Series of Younger Poets Award for her book *A Change of World.* She married Alfred Conrad in 1953, and by 1959 they had three sons. In the 1960s she became increasingly involved in political causes, including the Civil Rights movement, anti–Vietnam War protests, women's rights actions, and the push for gay rights. In 1970, as she was just beginning to identify herself privately as a lesbian, she ended her marriage. For *Diving into the Wreck* (1973), one of her most celebrated collections, Rich won the 1974 National Book Award, which she accepted in the name of all women and on behalf of herself and two other nominees, Lorde and Alice Walker. After living almost her entire life in the northeastern United States, Rich moved to California in 1984.

She has received many awards and honors, including the National Medal for the Arts (1997)—which she refused to accept, citing the U.S. government's insufficient support for the arts—a MacArthur Fellowship (1994), and the National Book Critics Circle Award for *The School Among the Ruins* (2004). Over the years she has taught at several colleges and universities, including Swarthmore, City College of New York, San José State, and Stanford.

Rich's poetry has evolved through several stages, and the style of her best-known writing is quite unlike that of her earliest verse. In her work of the 1950s, the influences of 17th-century John Donne, William Butler Yeats, Stevens, and Auden are apparent, and the poetry largely uses iambic pentameter, rhyme, and regular stanzaic breaks (see PROSODY AND FREE VERSE). Rich's subjects in these poems tend toward the abstract, and her voice is rather detached, emanating from a third-person perspective that is rarely identified as specifically female. She would later chide herself for valuing verse that aims to be "'universal,' which meant, of course, nonfemale" ("When We" 44). However, even then—as in "Aunt Jennifer's Tigers" (1951)—there were signs of the strong feminist voice that would emerge later and define her poetics: As Rich explains it, "poems are like dreams: in them you put what you don't know you know" ("When We" 40).

In the 1960s, for the first time, Rich became familiar with the work of women poets—both predecessors and contemporaries—and her poems, such as "SNAPSHOTS OF A DAUGHTER-IN-LAW" (1963), reflect her burgeoning feminist concerns. They also exhibit her growing belief in the value of using themes drawn from ordinary life and are consistently written in the first person. As the decade progressed, Rich became more attentive to the ways in which language is gendered and politicized, and she laments in "The Burning of Paper instead of Children" (1971) that "this is the oppressor's language // yet I need it to talk to you."

With the poem "DIVING INTO THE WRECK" and the collection of the same name, Rich established herself as a poet of the first rank and continued to explore forces that influence the woman artist. A few years later, in her poems of the skillful collection *The Dream of a Common Language,* Rich displays a more steadily sophisticated and varied hand: These poems, such as "Power," "To a Poet," "Transcendental Etude," and "Cartographies of Silence," demonstrate the accomplishment and range of a poet who can continually renew the "old theme" that "Language cannot do everything," as she puts it in the latter poem. The volume also contains "Twenty-One Love Poems," a remarkable sonnet sequence of unconventional prosody that celebrates lesbian love and reinvents a traditional poetic form to suit a decidedly nontraditional theme.

The subject of lesbian love in itself is an important one for Rich, but it is also significant as one example of the kinds of connection that are possible on what she calls the "lesbian continuum" ("Compulsory" 51). As she explains in her essay "Compulsory Heterosexuality and Lesbian Existence," the lesbian continuum marks a spiritual link between and among all women, regardless of their sexual or affective orientation. This essay marks a refinement of her earlier ideas about a "common language" and presages a change in her concerns: In the 1980s Rich shows less interest in the differences between male and female and in the problems that language poses for women in particular, and she becomes more interested in the differences in "verbal privilege" among women of varying classes and ethnicities ("North American Time" [1986]).

In "Frame" (1981), for instance, the speaker watches from a point of safety as a young black woman is harassed and arrested without cause by police on the campus of a Boston university. Rich recognizes the ways in which race, class, and nationality affect one's voice and one's power, ideas which she considers in her essay, "Blood, Bread, and Poetry: The Location of the Poet" (1986). There Rich acknowledges her advantaged position, as someone who "can write at all" and whose "words are read and taken seriously" (187). She also recognizes that with those privileges comes a responsibility not to presume to speak for others and to "examine the ego that speaks in [her] poems—not for political 'correctness,' but for ignorance, solipsism, laziness, dishonesty, automatic writing" (187).

After Rich's move to California, her sense of the importance of location was heightened. In such poems as "North American Time" (1986), "Dreamwood" (1989), and "An Atlas of the Difficult World" (1991), she engages the metaphor of the map to examine her position, especially as it exists relative to that of her readers. In the final section of "Atlas," she is quite conscious of the ways in which one's place—social, geographical, emotional—affects one's relationships to others. There Rich presents a catalogue of imagined readers who encounter her poetry "late, before leaving the office," "standing up in a bookstore," "in a room where too much has happened for you to bear," or with "a crying child on your shoulder." She repeats the phrase, "I know you are reading this poem," perhaps wishing as much as declaring that it is possible for people in many different situations to find a connection through poetry.

For Rich, it is essential to believe that poetry can create such connections and that it can have some tangible effect on the world. In a recent poem, "Letters to a Young Poet" (1999), Rich names several examples of violence, both large scale (the World War II concentration camp Terezin) and small (the recent suicide of a woman artist). Then, echoing Auden's "In Memory of W. B. Yeats" (1940), she asks the novice whom she addresses, "would it relieve you to decide *Poetry / doesn't make this happen?*" Rich refuses to "decide" that poetry's effect on the world is negligible, even if that belief would ensure that her art cannot be responsible for such atrocities. Whatever limitations poetry has, Rich still believes it has some power to improve our lives, and she turns to it to help her as both a witness to history and a participant in it.

BIBLIOGRAPHY

Cooper, Jane, ed. *Reading Adrienne Rich: Reviews and Re-visions.* Ann Arbor: University of Michigan Press, 1984.

Rich, Adrienne. *Adrienne Rich's Poetry and Prose: Poems, Prose, Reviews, and Criticism,* edited by Barbara Charlesworth Gelpi and Albert Gelpi. New York: Norton, 1993.

———. "Blood, Bread, and Poetry: The Location of the Poet." In *Blood, Bread, and Poetry: Selected Prose, 1979–1985,* 167–187. New York: Norton, 1986.

———. "Compulsory Heterosexuality and Lesbian Existence." In *Blood, Bread, and Poetry: Selected Prose, 1979–1985.* New York: Norton, 1986, pp. 23–75.

———. *What Is Found There.* New York: Norton, 1993.

———. "When We Dead Awaken: Writing as Re-Vision." In *On Lies, Secrets, and Silence: Selected Prose, 1966–1978.* New York: Norton, 1979, pp. 33–50.

Templeton, Alice. *The Dream and the Dialogue: Adrienne Rich's Feminist Poetics.* Knoxville: University of Tennessee Press, 1994.

Werner, Craig. *Adrienne Rich: The Poet and Her Critics.* Chicago: American Library Association, 1988.

Jeannine Johnson

RIDING (JACKSON), LAURA (1901–1991)

Laura Riding was one of the central women writers of the period of MODERNISM, because of her contributions as a poet, her collaborations with Robert Graves on literary-critical works, and their editorial work on the journal *Epilogue* (1935–37), as well as for her writings on poetry's form and function. During Riding's early poetic career, she was a member of the FUGITIVE/AGRARIAN SCHOOL of poets, who praised her poetry's ability to avoid the sentimentality of contemporary female poets, such as EDNA ST. VINCENT MILLAY. Riding's own poetic quest was to find language that illuminated what she called "truth," which, in her own poems, included shunning a reliance on analogy, metaphor, and sensuous language. After the publication of her *Collected Poems* (1938), her meditations on poetry's inability to contain truth ultimately led her to stop writing poems altogether. Although Riding herself was uncomfortable with poets naming her as a literary precursor, such poets as Graves, W. H. AUDEN, and JOHN ASHBERY claim her as a poetic influence.

Laura Reichenthal was born in New York City and attended Cornell University from 1918–21, leaving before completing a degree. In 1927 she changed her name to Laura Riding. Riding's first book, *The Close Chaplet,* was influenced by her friendship with Graves, who invited Riding to come to England with him and his wife in 1926, the same year Riding's first book appeared. Riding and Graves coauthored *A Survey of Modernist Poetry* (1927) and founded the Seizin Press in 1928. Later they moved the press to Deyá, Spain. When the Spanish civil war broke out, Graves and Riding returned to Pennsylvania, where Riding met Schuyler Jackson, whom she married in 1941. Riding received the Bollingen Prize for her contributions to poetry in 1991, the same year she died.

Riding's recurrent subjects in her poetry were the observation of the rift between mind and body, as well as a preoccupation with death as a way to unite to this rift. The evanescence of the sensory world led Riding to believe it did not contain unity, or truth. As she writes in "Truth and Time" (1926), "The succession of fair things / Delights, does not enlighten." In the preface to the reprint of her *Selected Poems in Five Sets* (1970), Riding rejected poetry as her cause, explaining her quest for truth to be a "something" beyond poetry: "My cause is something poetry fails to be—belying its promissory advertisement of itself" (17). Nevertheless one of the lasting values of her poems lies in the inherent tension they display, "excit[ing] some sense of wherein the failure of poetry lies, and some fore-sense of what that something might be" (Preface 17).

BIBLIOGRAPHY

Ashbery, John, "The Unthronged Oracle: Laura Riding," *Other Traditions.* Cambridge, Mass.: Harvard University Press, 2000, 95–121.

Riding Jackson, Laura. Preface to *Selected Poems in Five Sets,* by Laura Riding Jackson. New York: Persea Books, 1970.

Simon, John, "Laura Riding and Her Traveling Circus." In *Dreamers of Dreams: Essays on Poets and Poetry.* Chicago: Ivan R. Doe, 2001, pp. 12–21.

Wexler, Joyce Piell. *Laura Riding's Pursuit of Truth.* Athens: Ohio University Press, 1979.

Jennifer Grotz

RÍOS, ALBERTO (1952–) Since the publication in 1982 of *Whispering to Fool the Wind,* Alberto Ríos has emerged as a leading figure in contemporary Chicano literature. A short story writer and memoirist as well as a poet, Ríos takes a narrative approach in much of his poetry (see NARRATIVE POETRY). His poetic voice is often that of a storyteller, and frequently the stories he tells draw upon his childhood in the border town of Nogales, Arizona. While his early poetry was most notable for his efforts to capture childhood perspectives, much of Ríos's recent work exhibits qualities of SURREALISM in the tradition of magical realism. Ríos's extravagant use of language places him alongside such writers as MARY OLIVER, C. K. WILLIAMS, and JOY HARJO.

Ríos was born in Nogales, Arizona. He studied at the University of Arizona and began teaching creative writing in 1982 at Arizona State University. *Whispering to Fool the Wind* won the Walt Whitman Award from the Academy of American Poets in 1981. His short story collection, *The Iguana Killer: Twelve Stories from the Heart,* won the 1984 Western States Book Award, and his collection of poems, *The Smallest Muscle in the Human Book* (2002), was a finalist for the National Book Award.

Ríos emerged in the 1980s as a leading figure among a new group of university-trained Hispanic writers who made bicultural experiences central to their work. In his poetry he is drawn toward multiple understandings of events, a hallmark of borderland writers who know there are at least two languages for describing any situation. In much of his work, Ríos explores truths of experience that do not conform to rational explanation. As William Barillas notes, "Ríos is a poet of the body's intelligence, of inherent perception and expression in physical gesture and embrace" (116). In Ríos's poem "Advice to a First Cousin" (1985), a grandmother's folk cure for a scorpion bite—placing a live scorpion on the bite—turns into a lesson for surviving in an unsafe world. The poem's speaker is told to watch out for other scorpions who will be smarter and meaner, "the way you must look out for men / who have not yet bruised you."

The magical realism of the Colombian novelist Gabriel García Márquez has had a profound impact on Ríos. From García Márquez, Ríos takes an appreciation of how surrealistic juxtaposition can ultimately be instructive rather than mystifying. In "On January 5, 1984, El Santo the Wrestler Died, Possibly" (1985),

Ríos takes an actual event—the funeral of a costumed Mexican professional wrestler—and uses it as a meditation upon the mythic power of icons, venturing far afield from the funeral itself. Such a poem is an example of what Deneen Jenks sees as "ideas of patience, of moving sideways, of crossing quietly over borders" that is characteristic of Ríos's work (121). Ríos painstakingly explores the significance to be drawn from moments that might be otherwise overlooked.

BIBLIOGRAPHY

Britton, Sheilah. "Discovering the Alphabet of Life," ASU Research. Available online. URL: http://researchmag.asu.edu/articles/alphabet.html. Downloaded March 2007.

Jenks, Deneen. "The Breathless Patience of Alberto Ríos" *Hayden's Ferry Review* 11 (fall/winter 1992): 115–123.

Ríos, Alberto. "Words like the Wind: An Interview with Alberto Ríos, by William Berillas." *Americas Review* 24, nos. 3–4 (fall/winter 1996): 116–129.

Jim O'Loughlin

"RIPRAP" **Gary Snyder (1958)** The 25-line poem "Riprap" registers the Zen-inspired aesthetics of Chinese poetry that Gary Snyder inherited from his modernist predecessor Ezra Pound and his contemporary Philip Whalen, as well as the western landscapes in the poems of Robinson Jeffers and Kenneth Rexroth. "Riprap" is part of a cycle of poems Snyder composed during his stint as a trail crew laborer in California's Sierra Nevada. By the summer of 1955, Snyder had dedicated himself to the study of Chinese language and Buddhism and had abandoned writing poetry. But, as he would write later, "under the influence of the geology of the Sierra Nevada and the daily trail-crew work of picking up and placing granite stones in tight cobbled pattern on hard slab," Snyder found himself writing poems that did not resemble anything he had done before (qtd. in Allen 420–421).

The opening lines, "Lay down these words / Before your mind like rocks," compare the mental activity of arranging words on the page with the physical activity of laying stones on a mountain trail. A celebration of the body and mind at work, the poem begins with the speaker instructing himself on the intentional activity of poetic composition. The activity is not determined by the existing structures of the mind, but rather by the exigencies of constructing a functional pattern, a means of access to new terrain.

The body of the poem opens into a sequence of associations, moving from substantial objects in the world—"Solidity of bark, leaf or wall"—to the cosmological arrangement of the "straying" planets in the universe. The lines, wrestling free from the constraints of syntax, follow the requirements of the poem's associative method. The second controlling analogy in the poem is between the world and "an endless / four-dimensional / Game of *Go*." An ancient Chinese game of strategy, Go involves placing stones on a board to control space and in response to the emergent patterns of the game as it unfolds. The comparison is perfectly appropriate to Snyder's understanding of the ever-changing realm of the phenomenal world.

"Riprap" is the product of a mind sharpened by the hard-edged, sun-splashed natural forms of the high Sierras; its economical structure, moreover, reflects the rhythms of working with stone. Literally the pattern of well-placed stones offers a foothold in otherwise slippery terrain. By analogy, Snyder suggests, the poem provides a similar solidity in the changing order of thoughts as well as things.

BIBLIOGRAPHY

Allen, Donald M., ed. *The New American Poetry, 1945–1960.* New York: Grove Press, 1960, pp. 420–421.

Dean, Tim. *Gary Snyder and the American Unconscious: Inhabiting the Ground.* New York: St. Martin's Press, 1991.

Murphy, Patrick D. *A Place for Wayfaring: The Poetry and Prose of Gary Snyder.* Corvallis: Oregon State University Press, 2000, pp. 43–62.

Mark Long

"THE ROAD NOT TAKEN" **Robert Frost (1915)** "The Road Not Taken" is among the best-known poems of the 20th century. Readers who encounter the poem in high school, perhaps even in college, are likely to hear that it is an expression of the importance of American individualism. Most Americans have probably heard the final lines of "The Road Not Taken" used in such a way: "Two roads diverged in a wood, and I— / I took the one less traveled by." That choice is what is distinctive. It would be a mistake to say that this sort of interpretation—the one generations of American readers have been encouraged to accept—is simply wrong, but ROBERT FROST's letters show that this meaning is not at all what he originally had in mind.

George Monteiro explains that Frost did not personally identify with the poem's speaker; rather he thought of the poem as a private joke about the general indecisiveness of his friend, the British poet Edward Thomas. Thomas's letters to Frost make it clear that, at first, Thomas did not get the joke; he took the poem completely seriously, just as many readers have been encouraged to do (Monteiro 1–3). It is important to note that the poem quickly took on a life of its own, and that Frost certainly did not mention the "private joke" publicly. Instead he apparently recognized the advantage of letting readers interpret the poem in a variety of complex ways.

Richard Poirier claims that "[Frost's] ultimate subject is the interpretive process itself" (xxiii), and the complexities of "The Road Not Taken" support this statement. The poem's speaker describes the two diverging roads in a way that should make readers wonder how different these roads really appeared to be. Although he initially says that one road appeared to be less traveled, he soon mentions that actually the two roads looked very similar and that they were equally covered in fallen leaves on the morning the speaker made his choice. If the roads looked the same, readers may wonder, how can the speaker possibly know that he took the less-traveled road, and how can he know what difference, if any, this choice made? The title further undermines the sense of certainty by mentioning the road the narrator did *not* take, rather than the one that supposedly was so significant for the rest of his life. As Jay Parini points out, "There may well be no road less traveled by" (154).

Frost never publicly disagreed with the conventional interpretation of the poem. He seemed to accept that the poem had taken on a life quite different from his original intent. An example from China emphasizes the poem's potential for very different interpretations. Chinese schoolteachers commonly use the poem to symbolize the exact opposite of American individualism. Instead, in their interpretation, the road less traveled suggests the political road of communist principles and cultural revolution.

BIBLIOGRAPHY

Monteiro, George. "Commentary: 'The Road Not Taken.'" In *Robert Frost: Poems, Life, Legacy*. New York: Henry Holt, 1998.

Parini, Jay. *Robert Frost: A Life*. New York: Henry Holt, 1999.

Poirier, Richard. *Robert Frost: The Work of Knowing*. Stanford, Calif.: Stanford University Press, 1990.

Sean Heuston

"ROBIN REDBREAST" STANLEY KUNITZ (1971)

STANLEY KUNITZ's "Robin Redbreast" is a study of suffering and sympathy that endows nature with religious significance without ever supplanting the natural world that is the poem's actual subject. The poem, a first-person monologue ostensibly spoken by Kunitz, depicts a man's effort to rescue a robin hectored by blue jays. Although the subject is local and personal, as is customary in Kunitz's IMAGE-centered, POST-CONFESSIONAL work, the poem's title calls to mind two legends about how the robin received its red breast. The first legend was that the bird was stained by Christ's blood while trying to remove thorns from his skull during the crucifixion (and becoming injured itself in the process); the other legend holds that the bird's feathers were scorched red from delivering water to the souls of sinners in hell. In the poem, the legend of the bird as one who eases suffering (whether of Christ or of sinners) is picked up by the speaker, who tries to ease the suffering of this bird, only to be wounded himself by the discovery of an older wound afflicting the bird.

Kunitz's poem opens with a simple description of the bird's plain appearance: "It was the dingiest bird / you ever saw," Kunitz writes, and his use of the second-person address functions as an apostrophe, involving the reader directly in the poem and enlisting the reader's sympathy for this bird which has been "friendless and stiff and cold / since Eden went wrong." Kunitz's mention of the Garden of Paradise here is no accident; it calls to mind the religious associations of the robin with Christ, suggesting that the bird itself has suffered from the Original Sin perpetrated there. What motivates the speaker's compassion, and enlists the reader's sympathies, is an implicit identification with the bird's plight. As poet GREGORY ORR notes, "(O)ne of the poem's primary strategies is to identify the bird's situation and the speaker's, [and] we see Kunitz making connections between Eden, the self's desolation and insecurity, and the house image" (27). Indeed, the speaker first sees the bird from his room in a house that is for sale, and such places figure in Kunitz's work as places of misery and discord (his own first marriage, which ended in divorce, having been lived out in a small home in Truro, Massachusetts, which Kunitz later sold).

Finding the bird attacked by blue jays (beneath wild persimmon trees, perhaps a figure for the Tree of Knowledge whose fruit brought about the Fall of Man), Kunitz goes outside to rescue it, and in his act discovers a kinship with the bird. His act fills him with purpose and satisfaction, and he is glad he could offer the bird "my lucky help / to toss him back into his element." But Kunitz's work is more tragic and not so consolingly Christian as this rescue might imply, and when the speaker raises the bird, he sees a hole between the bird's eyes "where the hunter's brand / had tunneled out his wits." Cynthia Davis notes that in this moment, "(N)arrow certainty of meaning is deflated by the glimpse of a 'blue, unappeasable sky,'" a figure for the naturalized, meaningless universe. It is a shocking discovery for Kunitz. The wound implies longstanding human cruelty towards nature, an attitude at odds with the merciful act the speaker has just performed, but in terms of the legend of the redbreast, it also implies an indifference or rejection of salvation and mercy that stuns the speaker. But the poem offers one consolation: one may choose to oppose such cruelty, and in doing so, one may at least try to redeem oneself from desolation. Thus Kunitz both places himself and discovers himself "in league with that ounce of heart / pounding in my palm."

BIBLIOGRAPHY

Davis, Cynthia A. "Stanley Kunitz and the Transsubstantial World." *Literary Review* 24, no. 3 (1981): 413–426.

Orr, Gregory. *Stanley Kunitz: An Introduction to the Poetry*. New York: Columbia University Press, 1985.

Temple Cone

ROBINSON, EDWIN ARLINGTON (1869–1935) Edwin Arlington Robinson is best known for his formal rhyming poems, surprise endings, and characterizations of the human condition not typical of any particular literary movement. With 23 publications ranging in genre from collections to book-length narrative poems (see NARRATIVE POETRY), and in style from villanelles and sonnets to blank verse (see PROSODY AND FREE VERSE), Robinson is perhaps one of the most overlooked and undervalued poets of 20th-century American literature. Influenced by the 19th-century likes of Walt Whitman, Ralph Waldo Emerson, William Wordsworth, and Rudyard Kipling, Robinson's work reflects a transition from the themes and styles of the romantics to those of the modernists (see MODERNISM).

Robinson was born in Head-of-the-Tide, Maine. He lived most of his life in Maine and New York. He studied at Harvard University from 1891 to 1893, although he was a poor student. His first collection of poems, *The Torrent and the Night Before*, was published on his own in 1896. Other publications, including *The Children of the Night* (1897) and *Captain Craig* (1902), soon followed, the former catching the attention of President Theodore Roosevelt, who appointed Robinson to a position in the office of the collector of customs, New York, in 1905. In 1919 the *Outlook* magazine published a celebration issue for Robinson's 50th birthday. It was not until 1921, however, with the publication of his *Collected Poems* and his first Pulitzer Prize, that Robinson finally broke through as a major poet. He won two more Pulitzers, in 1924 for *The Man Who Died Twice* and in 1927 for *Tristram*. His last book, *King Jasper*, was published in 1935, just before his death from cancer.

Robinson's poetry often deals with conflict, such as the opposition between light and dark, particularly within individual characters. With this theme Robinson "took the middle romantic style and put it to uses it had not known. He made it American and he made it Realistic; and incidentally, he made it in an important sense, urban," as Louis Coxe has noted (27–28). Especially at the beginning of the 20th century, Robinson's work portrays a fresh reality that would continue throughout his career.

In his early shorter poems, Robinson explores conflict, through specific forms, such as the villanelle and the sonnet. In the villanelle "The House on the Hill" (1894), he emphasizes that the past is gone and cannot be changed: "The House is shut and still, / There is nothing more to say." In other words, the ghosts of the past may linger, but we should not dwell on the darkness of the past. In the sonnets "Cliff Klingenhagen" (1897), "Thomas Hood" (1897), and "Reuben Bright" (1897), the focus turns to the struggle between light and dark within individual characters. Klingenhagen is a man who will swallow the darkness, represented by wormwood, to save the light, or wine, for his dinner companion. Hood hides his sorrow from the community, yet the community still senses "a weird unrest." And Bright, the friendly butcher, cannot calmly survive the death of his wife, and the darkness appears when he "tore down the slaughterhouse."

In Robinson's poetry, "The twilight warning of experience, / The singular idea of loneliness" ("Isaac and Archibald" [1902]) are often the darkness against which humans must fight. Such is the case for many of the characters in Robinson's medium-length poems, such as "Isaac and Archibald" (1902), "Aunt Imogen" (1902), and "Rembrandt to Rembrandt" (1921). Generally the characters are older and feel alone in life, yet each one comes to realize that he or she is loved and cherished by friends and family—perhaps not as he or she had imagined, but loved nonetheless. Each person must "Forget [her or his] darkness in the dark" and come to the light of living life in the present.

This theme is best expressed in Robinson's long, narrative poems. The movement from darkness to light appears throughout the Arthurian trilogy of *Merlin* (1917), *Lancelot* (1920), and *Tristram* (1927). Ending with the line, "And there was darkness over Camelot," *Merlin* represents the movement into darkness that comes with age. *Lancelot* ends with an alteration and addition to *Merlin*'s lesson: "Where the Light falls, death falls; / And in darkness comes the Light." Once one accepts the darkness and embraces it, he or she can move on toward the light, and the light is a glorious place. The final chapter, *Tristram,* illustrates the glory of the light with Isolt. In the medieval story of the ill-fated love between the knight, Sir Tristram, and the lady, Isolt the Fair, Tristram is sent to bring Isolt to marry his uncle, but on the journey they swallow a potion that binds them forever in eternal love. Many hurdles face the lovers, so they never can be together, and each eventually dies in despair over this lost love. Robinson emphasizes the love of this story by depicting Tristram, who, though alone, contemplates "the white sunlight flashing on the sea." This final image of light in the Arthurian trilogy is the one that Robinson returns to again and again in his long, narrative poems, especially his final two publications, *Amaranth* (1934) and *King Jasper* (1935). The lesson is clear for the reader and the characters, such as Fargo, who finds "The world around him flamed amazingly / With light that comforted and startled him," and the lady Zoë, who "Fled upward through the darkness," out of Jasper's kingdom to live on in the light.

In these poems the movement to light is Robinson's lesson for all. It is a model "for people to come to terms with life on their own account, to find some degree of peace and satisfaction within themselves" (Barnard 233–234). Such a lesson and the amazing expression of it are what make Robinson a great American poet.

BIBLIOGRAPHY

Anderson, Wallace L. *Edwin Arlington Robinson: A Critical Introduction.* Boston: Houghton Mifflin, 1967.

Barnard, Ellsworth. *Edwin Arlington Robinson: A Critical Study.* New York: Macmillan, 1952.

Coxe, Louis O. *Edwin Arlington Robinson: The Life of Poetry.* New York: Pegasus, 1969.

Winters, Yvor. *Edwin Arlington Robinson.* Norfolk, Conn.: New Directions, 1946.

Keri Overall

ROBINSON, KIT (1949–) Known for his participation in the Bay Area LANGUAGE SCHOOL scene of the 1970s and 1980s, Kit Robinson shares with his peers a focus on the ways in which language frames our thoughts and perceptions. Building on the traditions of his modernist and postmodernist predecessors (GERTRUDE STEIN, WILLIAM CARLOS WILLIAMS, and other poets of MODERNISM, as well as the poets of the NEW YORK SCHOOL), Robinson employs strategies, including the non sequitur, which deliberately confuse the unsuspecting reader. "In the Orpheum Building" (1982), for example, opens with the following sentence: "Single story two bedroom dwelling across from / Parts unknown and won't be back and hesitates / To hand over that strongbox." Composed of a series of seemingly unrelated textual fragments, the poem imitates yet subverts the syllogistic logic of conventional discourse. While we come to recognize in its various fragments the language of classified advertisements, scraps of passing conversation, and technical jargon, the text's overall meaning is left open and unresolved. The poem, in refusing to use language as a transparent window through which the world is made both visible and knowable, highlights the ways in which our perception is ordered by the linear structure of the sentence.

Born in Evanston, Illinois, Robinson received a B.A. from Yale University in 1971. He taught in the California Poets in the Schools program from 1977–83, and then he worked as an executive in the information technology industry in and around San Francisco. Robinson's first book, *Chinatown of Cheyenne,* was published in 1974. He has received a number of grants, including one from the National Endowment for the Arts (1979).

Like the double careers of Williams and WALLACE STEVENS before him, Robinson's career as an executive in California's high-tech industry has had an important impact on his poetry. In his poem "The Wig" (1991), he reveals his practice of writing on the job, "of doing a bit of one's private work on company time, of thereby 'personalizing' one's corporate labor." Robinson argues elsewhere that writing on the job grounds poetry in common experience. His sampling of corporate language seeks to "drain specialized language of its isolating productive assurance and exploit it in the expression of human desires" ("Time and Materials" 27). Employing a variety of invented forms, Robinson's poetry is grounded in the poetics of the everyday, from the language of the corporate workplace to domestic meditations to the visual and aural traffic of the commute in between. As he puts it in his afterword to *The Crave* (2002), his poems "skirt the fringes of love and business, form and emptiness, the spaces between things, home and a restless movement from place to place" (119).

BIBLIOGRAPHY

Perelman, Bob. "Language Writing and Literary History." In *The Marginalization of Poetry: Language Writing and Literary History.* Princeton, N.J.: Princeton University Press, 1996. 11–37.

Robinson, Kit. Afterword to *The Crave.* Berkeley, Calif.: Atelos, 2002, p. 119.

———. "Time & Materials: The Workplace, Dreams, and Writing." *Poetics Journal* 9 (June 1991): 21–35.

Strang, Brian. "Presence and Permeability." Review of *Democracy Boulevard,* by Kit Robinson. *Aufgabe* 1 (summer 2001). Available online. URL: http://www.durationpress.com/litmuspress/aufgabe/issue1.htm. Downloaded April 2003.

Tim Shaner

RODEFER, STEPHEN (1940–) "My program is simple," Stephen Rodefer writes, in the preface to his best-known work, *Four Lectures* (1982): "[It is] to surrender to the city and survive its inundation. To read it and in reading, order it to read itself" (7). In declaring the city his muse, Rodefer places himself in a long line of "urban" poets—from first-century B.C. Catullus (84–54 B.C.) to 15th-century François Villon to FRANK O'HARA—who find their text and their audience in the cultural flood of Western capitals. Rodefer's work moves as comfortably in the domain of the spoken and the heard, carrying forward the New American poetry (see POETRY ANTHOLOGIES) emphasis on everyday speech, as in that of the written and the decoded, though sometimes shifting to the broadly ranging investigations of LANGUAGE writing.

Born in Bellaire, Ohio, Rodefer earned a B.A. in art history at Amherst College (1963) and an M.A. in language and literature at the State University of New York, Buffalo (1965), where he studied with CHARLES OLSON; Rodefer earned an M.F.A. at San Francisco State University (1976). Rodefer's first book, *The Knife,* was published in 1965. His translation of Villon (1968) under the pen name Jean Calais received wide acclaim. He has taught at several universities, including the University of California, San Diego, where from 1985–87 he curated the Archive for New Poetry. Rodefer has settled in Paris; there he has worked on moving his poems from the page to the canvas, where he literally paints them.

The canvas of *Four Lectures* is large: "When I say me it's a figure of speech. Just another poet AGOG for foam. / Look at all those f-stops up there. Eventually everything becomes all stars." In stanzas of 15 lines, the poet-persona ventriloquizes a range of tones and discourses—from satiric to amorous, lyrical to didactic—and orchestrates abrupt switches between high art and advertising, street obscenity and literary allusion, with an unerring sense of music. Much of the play occurs by ear—where "foam" slides into "fame," and "poet AGOG" into "demagogue."

Unlike Walt Whitman and his BEAT descendants, Rodefer brings an ironic scrutiny to his materials, distancing the poetry from the very excess that drives it. Moral ambivalence is reinforced through the disjunctions of the "I," direct in its address but hard to locate, an overheard narrator more in the manner of JOHN ASHBERY than Frank O'Hara's expressivist meditations. Rodefer writes, "Though the species is in me, I am neutral" ("Enclosure of Elk" [1991]).

The result is often satirical—"Oh academy, oh gainsville, oh tenured night" ("Daydreams of Frascatti" [1992]), often frankly erotic—"Julie my duck . . . ex sexy gerun / diva, my rue de la main d'or" ("Mon Canard" [1995]), but it is always rooted in the central impulse of a LYRIC POETRY: "love does not / die, that is / the fathomless question" ("Beating Erasers" [1994]).

BIBLIOGRAPHY

Rasula, Jed. "Rodefer's 'Lectures.'" *Poetics Journal* 3 (1983): 87–90.

Rodefer, Stephen. Preface to *Four Lectures.* Berkeley, Calif.: The Figures, 1982.

Ward, Geoff. *Language Poetry and the Avant-garde.* England: British Association for American Studies, 1993.

Jonathan Skinner

ROETHKE, THEODORE (1908–1963) Theodore Roethke's experiments in seeking a language for the incommunicative experience of madness and employing classical poetic structures for explorations of the modern soul influenced an entire generation. SYLVIA PLATH, ROBERT LOWELL, JAMES WRIGHT, DAVID WAGONER, CAROLYN KIZER, and others found in Roethke's poems the language, rhythms, and approach for their own discoveries of the self. His dialogue with great verse as a means of developing individual voice was important to many modern writers. William Butler Yeats, T. S. ELIOT, Emily Dickinson, Leonie Adams, Elinor Wylie, W. H. AUDEN, and Dylan Thomas were his most acknowledged influences.

Roethke was born in Saginaw, Michigan. His childhood amid a greenhouse empire owned by his immigrant family became the source of his cardinal work. The family greenhouses encompassed for Roethke all stages of life, phases of evolution, and range of emotions, they were his personal Eden and the source of all his nightmares. Although kept close to home and sent to the University of Michigan (B.A., 1929), Roethke resisted pressure for a practical legal career, and he escaped to English studies and poetry at Harvard. Despite the depression, he pursued an academic career and from 1931 to 1935 taught at Lafayette College. LOUISE BOGAN (a poetry editor of the *New Yorker*), STANLEY KUNITZ, Rolfe Humphries, and others helped him publish in *Poetry,* the *New Republic,* and the *Saturday Review.* In 1935, after moving to Michigan State University, he suffered the first of numerous breakdowns and was institutionalized for three months. He finished his M.A. at Michigan in 1936 and began teaching at Penn State College, during which time his first book, *Open House* (1941), was published. This was the beginning of a great career, earning him two Guggenheim Fellowships (1945 and 1950), the Eunice Tietjens Memorial Prize (*Poetry* magazine, 1951), two Ford Foundation grants in (1952 and 1959), the Pulitzer Prize for *The Waking* (1954), a Fulbright grant (1955), the Bollingen Prize (1959), two National Book Awards—for *Words for the Wind* (1959) and *The Far Field* (1965)—and the Shelley Memorial Award (1962), among other awards and honors.

A deceptively straightforward CONFESSIONAL work, *Open House* begins Roethke's quest into the possibilities of using consciousness and language to understand the self and the world. Exploring the techniques of his predecessors and mentors, Roethke tries on the styles of others in order to achieve his own goals and explores theories of psychoanalysis and socialization, as well as the possibilities of straightforward expression. But although he finds these styles and theories insufficient, his unique responses were only to be discovered in the coming years.

His reputation as a teacher growing, he was soon invited to Bennington College, where he became friendly with Kenneth Burke. At Bennington he began intense experiments with mysticism, meditation, and concentration. His insistence upon understanding, imitating, and using his experiences of manic depression was dangerous; although aware of this danger, he felt his unique experiences were a vital tool for poetic achievement, finding poetic brotherhood in the romantics William Blake and John Clare. As he says in "In a Dark Time" (1965), "What's madness, but nobility of soul / At odds with circumstance?"

In *The Lost Son* (1948), published a year after he moved to the University of Washington, Roethke shows the results of his mental and poetic risks. He describes the direction in "An American Poet Introduces Himself and His Poems," as going "back in order to go forward," and he reveals the technique of close observation and identification, which leads to loss and subsequent reintegration of the self and was influenced by D. H. Lawrence, upon whom he wrote his M.A. thesis. In the poem "Cuttings," Roethke describes plant cuttings, which appear to die above ground but grow hidden roots. The poem that follows, "Cuttings (later)," is an identification with these cuttings, a first-person experience of rebirth, and an acknowledgment of the consciousness of his quest: "When sprouts break out, / . . . I quail, lean to beginnings, sheath-wet." This "preliterary" style, with its curt, breathless lines, and non sequiturs, are all aspects of the search of the lost son for his true father.

If the poems of *Praise to the End!* (1951) are not initially clear and communicative, it is because they begin in a state of almost pure subjectivity, a complete union with the self, which has no need of external communication. The influences of Yeats's cycles are clear. The developing speaker follows the progress out of the self and into the world, metaphorizing evolution, the mystic way, and psychoanalysis. *The Waking* (1953) and *Words for the Wind* (1958) continue this direction. From an awakening into the world of others in the former book, Roethke explores the subject of love in the latter. His marriage with Beatrice O'Connell in 1953 inspired these moving and intelligent inquiries into the conflicts of love. *Words for the Wind* received the most recognition in Roethke's lifetime, and it won the most prizes. It is significant that this first book about relationships was followed by poems for children, *I Am! Says the Lamb* (1961). *The Far Field* (1964), published posthumously after a fatal heart attack, anticipates death as a unity with the cosmos.

To read the *Collected Poems of Theodore Roethke* (1966) from beginning to end is to follow the determined, methodical quest for a viable poetic identity and simultaneously to experience the possibility of madness at any given moment.

BIBLIOGRAPHY

Blessing, Richard. *Theodore Roethke's Dynamic Vision.* Bloomington: Indiana University Press, 1974.

Burke, Kenneth. "The Vegetal Radicalism of Theodore Roethke." *Sewanee Review* LVIII (winter 1950): 68–108.

Malkoff, Karl. *Theodore Roethke: An Introduction to the Poetry.* New York: Columbia University Press, 1971.

Roethke, Theodore, and Carolyn Kizer. *On Poetry and Craft.* Seattle: Copper Canyon Press, 2001.

Seager, Allan. *The Glass House: The Life of Theodore Roethke.* New York: McGraw-Hill, 1968.

Stiffler, Randall. Theodore Roethke: *The Poet and His Critics.* Chicago: American Library Association, 1986.

Karen Alkalay-Gut

ROGERS, PATTIANN (1940–) Pattiann Rogers's poetry links the intellectual rigors of the scientific method with the possibilities and suppositions inherent in a life based upon spiritual questioning. Often compared with Walt Whitman, Henry David Thoreau, and THEODORE ROETHKE, Rogers notes that for these writers landscape and environment are much more than "picturesque background" (Elliot "Interview" 24). In her work the natural world becomes a "source of self-knowledge and sustenance, a force, an actor, often a determining presence" (Elliott "Interview" 24). Although she takes plants, animals, and forces of nature as her subjects, Rogers is not merely a "nature" poet, nor can her work be identified with any particular American region. Her poems are characterized by an awareness of, and reverent curiosity about, the immensity of things unknowable.

Rogers was born in Joplin, Missouri. When she was 13, her parents joined a fundamentalist Christian sect that followed a literal interpretation of the Bible. Though the sect opposed advanced education, Rogers's parents allowed her to attend the University of

Missouri, where she studied philosophy, astronomy, and zoology, which run counter to the restrictions of religious fundamentalism. Rogers studied creative writing at the University of Houston (M.A., 1981). Her first book, *The Expectations of Light,* was published that same year. Many other titles have followed, including a collection of essays on the art of writing, *Dream of the Marsh Wren* (1999). Rogers has received numerous awards, most notably the Theodore Roethke Prize (1981), five Pushcart Prizes (1984, 1985, 1989, 1991, and 1997) and a Lannan Foundation Award (1991).

Rogers, in a conversation with David Elliott, called scientific terminology "an evocative, musical, beautiful vocabulary," which she believes has been neglected by contemporary poets (19). For example, "The Verification of Vulnerability: Bog Turtle" (1986) contains a description of a turtle's body that combines zoological terminology with poetic simile: The turtle's carapace resembles "beveled wood," and the "hingeless / plastron" becomes a fortified chest, which shields the turtle's heart, or its "particle of vulnerability."

Rogers's poems express the wonder and exhilaration of scientific discovery, and she credits Jacob Bronowski's *The Ascent of Man* (1973), an exploration of scientific thought, history, and art, as having been a tremendous influence on her life and work. Her poetry explores the way scientific study can affect our view of ourselves, our communities, and our world. In "Why Lost Divinity Remains Lost" (1993), the speaker describes her attempts to locate the divine—she searches for enlightenment but her "concentration / is broken by the pattern of leaf shadows" on "the wall." The physical world for Rogers is a sensuous, pleasurable, and, ultimately, life-affirming distraction. She intends for her unique and sometimes difficult material to bridge the gaps between science, literature, and spirit.

BIBLIOGRAPHY

Engelbrecht, Marsha. "Pattiann Rogers." In *Dictionary of Literary Biography,* Vol. 105. *American Poets since World War II,* edited by R. S. Gwynn, 210–214. Detroit: Gale, 1991.

Rogers, Pattiann. "An Interview with Pattiann Rogers," by Richard McCann. *Iowa Review* 17 (spring/summer 1987): 25–42.

———. "'Praise Is a Generative Act': A Conversation with Pattiann Rogers," by David L. Elliott. *Tampa Review* (1999): 19–32.

Diane Warner

ROSENBERG, DAVID (1943–) David Rosenberg is a startling poet of learning, subtlety, and ambition, and his books include heroic translations, commentary, and anthologies. He is in the tradition of EZRA POUND, who insisted that in recovering our archaic, cultural, and theological roots, we may get closest to a sacred matrix. Rosenberg, however, began writing in conjunction with the NEW YORK SCHOOL of poetry, in which a new SURREALISM competed with a parodistic mania and a whimsy of kitsch and culture. But he outgrew this observational bias and has been guided in a complex symbolist journey toward Jerusalem and the origins of the Bible.

Rosenberg was born in Detroit. He studied with ROBERT LOWELL at the New School and with DONALD HALL at the University of Michigan, where he received a B.A. in English (1964) and refined his work. He also met DELMORE SCHWARTZ at Syracuse University, where he received an M.F.A. (1966). After six books of poems were published in Canada, where he worked as an editor, and with his doctorate on GERTRUDE STEIN almost completed, he made a commitment to study Hebrew literature in Israel and the United States, and these studies changed his life. One of his translations is the well-known and controversial *Book of J* (1990), a recovered biblical text. He has taught at many universities and has lectured both nationally and internationally.

Rosenberg's poems are sensual and provocative. He translates the Psalms as blues, maintaining the freshness of American jazz. He continued for many years to create "a poet's Bible," not merely a mistranslation, but a wise and moderate *nigun,* or improvisation. He gave himself up to a lengthy series of testaments concerning Jewish life and art, and he created the influential anthologies on Judaism for his generation: *Congregation* (1987), *Genesis* (1996), *Testimony* (1989), and others. The main theme and stylistic finesse in Rosenberg's poetry and other writings is the mystery of translating and mistranslating. He always plays with the boundaries between an original and a copy, between a sacred poem and its restoration. Eventually, a reader hardly knows whether the text at hand is an original, homage, essay, or fiction. A poem in *The Lost Book of Paradise* (1993) radiates this mystery in lines that might be from a lost Hebrew text or from a very contemporary American one: "[T]he creator" becomes both poet and divinity, bringing the reader "to crawl in a great library / of the natural world, to read / the text of plants." This new poem tries to recreate an old, possibly inverted, sacred poem, to restore a tone from the biblical Song of Songs, and to make readers feel the archaic as something as fresh as a scientific discovery. Immersed in natural and human history, Rosenberg finds in a destroyed forest material for a new Bible. His poems raise a bridge between scientific and linguistic marvels.

BIBLIOGRAPHY

Bloom, Harold. "Translating J." In *The Book of J*, translated by David Rosenberg. New York: Grove Weidenfeld, 1990, pp. 49–55.

Carruth, Hayden. "David's Psalms." *Bookletter Literary Supplement* 3, no. 9 (December 20, 1976): 2.

Hall, Donald. Foreword to *Job Speaks*, by David Rosenberg. New York: Harper and Row, 1977, pp. vii–viii.

David Shapiro

ROTHENBERG, JEROME (1931–) Poet, translator, anthologist, and critic, Jerome Rothenberg is best known for his development of DEEP IMAGE POETRY and his strategies of "total translation." An emphasis on oral performance in poetics coupled with a drive to expand the formalistic legacy of what came to be known as New Criticism (see FUGITIVE/AGRARIAN SCHOOL) has motivated his composite career in ETHNOPOETICS. Influenced by the work of both EZRA POUND and GERTRUDE STEIN, Rothenberg has long labored to revise what he refers to half-ironically and half-seriously as the "great tradition" of Anglo-American MODERNISM (*Pre-Faces* 100). His early efforts in this regard involve the recovery of forgotten modernists, such as MINA LOY, in an important gathering of avant-garde poetry in English, *Revolution of the Word* (1974). This anthology's "Pre-Face" illustrates his reasons for resisting the New Critical style that increasingly dominated American poetry in the 1950s, which he dismisses as "little toughening of Tennyson" and attributes to W. H. AUDEN, ROBERT LOWELL, ALLEN TATE, and RICHARD WILBUR, among others (99). The Pre-Face also, however, illustrates his debt to the experimental modernism that preceded it—and his rationale for recasting that modernism to fit his particular postmodern style. *Revolution* has been supplanted by the innovative *Poems for the Millennium* (1995), a massive two-volume sourcebook, coedited with PIERRE JORIS, which situates 20th-century poetry in a truly global context. For Rothenberg, poetry has been, first and foremost, a process, and in that process the successful poet creates not only his or her poem but also himself or herself. His own poetic development has involved an amplification of the principles of the artistic dada movement in that he regularly experiments with sounds as sounds, with the perceptual and cognitive possibilities offered by repetition, and with the relationship of the primitive and the contemporary.

Rothenberg was born to first-generation Polish-Jewish immigrants in New York City. He launched his career as editor of the small magazine *Poems from the Floating World* (1959–63) and operator of Hawk's Well Press, through which he published important works by ROBERT KELLY, ARMAND SCHWERNER, and DIANE WAKOSKI, as well as his own first volume of poems, *Black Sun White Sun* (1960). But his first publications, significantly, were relatively standard translations of contemporary German poets. As a member of the United States Army, he had been stationed in Mainz, Germany, from 1953 to 1955, after which time he attended Columbia University for graduate work (he had previously earned a B.A. at the City College of New York and an M.A. at the University of Michigan). On the strength of these translations, LAWRENCE FERLINGETTI invited him to prepare a collection of postwar German poetry, *New Young German Poets*, for the Pocket Poets Series, published in 1959 by City Lights Books (see POETRY PRESSES). The poems Rothenberg later culled for inclusion in the widely circulated *Poems for the Game of Silence, 1960–1970* (1971) demonstrate an engagement with the "deep image" that had been sparked by these translations—particularly those of Paul Celan, a German-speaking East European Jew—and exhibit a commitment to the exploration of his own Jewish heritage. They also lay the groundwork for the subsequent contributions to the fields of poetics and ethnology that led him to found the ethnopoetics movement.

With the help of a few close collaborators—particularly the anthropologist Dennis Tedlock and the lyrically gifted NATHANIEL TARN—Rothenberg centered ethnopoetics with *Technicians of the Sacred* (1968), an achronological collection of indigenous North American poems, and consolidated it with *Alcheringa* (1970–73, 1975–80), "the first magazine of the world's tribal poetries" (Rothenberg and Tedlock "Statement of Intention" 1). Rothenberg has taught at a number of schools, including the University of California, San Diego. Over the course of four decades, he has won numerous awards, including the 1982 American Book Award for *Pre-Faces & Other Writings* (1981), and three PEN writing awards (1994, for poetry, 1994 and 2002 for translation).

As his work with the deep image edged toward ethnopoetics, Rothenberg began working simultaneously to preserve traditions even as he distorted or dislodged conventions. Within a decade he was considering how the contemporary poet might fill the role of shaman in the tribal sense, as a holy man and healer. The "minimal" poetry of *Shaking the Pumpkin* (1972) contains a strong element of play and consistently privileges sounds over sense. "The 12th Horse Song of Frank Mitchell (Blue)," a poem in which a sacred singer describes why "Some are & are going to my howinouse [house]," makes clear the use of meaningless syllables and distorted sounds in this tribalized poetics. For this kind of total translation, the unit of composition is an extended breath, and before the poem begins Rothenberg provides a phonetic key to each breath's chanted rhythm: "wnn N nnnn N gahn hawuNnawu nngobaheegwing." Yet individual lines on the page, like these last, gain power only when spoken aloud: "Some are & are gone to my house now naht bahyeee naht— / nwinnng buht nawuNNN baheegwinning."

Throughout his career Rothenberg has emphasized intercultural solidarity and attacked the fashionable postmodern notion that impermeable boundaries separate people, contending instead that the nature of translation "asserts or at least implies a concept of psychic & biological unity" (*Pre-Faces* 93). He has, for more than 25 years, been unsatisfied with a tepid multiculturalism, since poetry, in his view, can strive for an intercultural future. Indeed he has written and translated poems that are meant to matter in the social and cultural lives of readers; many times, and in many registers, he insists, *I will change your mind.* His volume *A Paradise of Poets* (1999) concludes with a statement that encapsulates the theory that underlies this goal: "I do not of course believe that [a paradise of poets] exists in any supernatural or mystical sense, but I have sometimes felt it come to life among my fellow poets, and, even more, in writing—in the body of the poem" (117).

BIBLIOGRAPHY

Lazer, Hank. "Thinking Made in the Mouth: The Cultural Poetics of David Antin and Jerome Rothenberg." In *Picturing Cultural Values in Postmodern America,* edited by William G. Doty. Tuscaloosa: University of Alabama Press, 1994.

Mottram, Eric. "Where the Real Song Begins: The Poetry of Jerome Rothenberg." *Dialectical Anthropology* 2, nos. 2–4 (1986): 171–177.

Rothenberg, Jerome. *A Paradise of Poets: New Poems and Translations.* New York: New Directions, 1999.

———. *Pre-Faces & Other Writings.* New York: New Directions, 1981.

———, and Dennis Tedlock. "Statement of Intention." *Alcheringa* 1, no. 1 (1970): 1.

Selerie, Gavin. *The Riverside Interviews 4: Jerome Rothenberg.* London: Binnacle Press, 1984.

Matthew Hofer

RUDMAN, MARK (1948–) Mark Rudman's poetry takes up the relationships between fathers and sons, history and memory, literary tradition and scholarship. The figures of motion and architecture appear central to his poetics. Rudman composes in a shortened version of the American long poem (see LONG AND SERIAL POETRY), something he calls the "intermediate" poem inspired by William Blake's "The Marriage of Heaven and Hell" (1790) and T. S. ELIOT's *The WASTE LAND* (two important early influences). Increasingly Rudman has attempted "to transpose an American context onto Horace's Roman world" (Rudman "Notes" 201) by writing a series of Horatian palimpsests including such poems as "Against All Odds" (1999) and "In Your Own Time" (1999).

Rudman was born in New York City. He has edited the journal *Pequod* since 1975 and has taught at New

York University since 1984. In 1987 he published By *Contraries* (1987), which was followed by four more collections of poetry. Rudman is also the author of *My Sister-Life* (1983), a translation of Boris Pasternak and winner of the Max Hayward Award for translation (1985), *Robert Lowell* (1983), and *Diverse Voices: Essays on Poetry and Poets* (1993). Rudman's numerous honors include the Academy of American Poets Award from Columbia University (1971) and a National Book Critics Circle Award (1994).

In a 1997 interview, Rudman explains, "A poem is not just a repetition of something everyone knows, in the Ecclesiastical sense. It throws a wrench into the knowledge that preceded it" (125). Rudman particularly wrenches our knowledge of human mourning, memory, and grief. In *The Nowhere Steps* (1990), in which he elegizes his father, he writes briskly, "Mourning is endless." Just when it seems as if recovery is near, grief seems to return: Like a "flash of sunlight on a curb, you're back in the work of grief, overcome." Later in the volume, a child's death spurs him to reflect again on the motion of grief; unable to define it precisely, he calls it "a gap, / [that] the mind can only go around." For Rudman, mourning and grief are not simply experiences to be worked through or overcome; rather they are a constant, uncontainable, and ungraspable reminder of loss. Rudman's sounds further emphasize this endlessness, rolling across the page in a sea of words composed of the letters *s* and *l*.

In *Rider* (1994), Rudman asks, rhetorically, "Is there ever an end to mourning work?" Later, in *The Millennium Hotel* (1996), he writes, "Life is an apprenticeship in mourning," emphasizing the poetic nature of mourning itself—the work of life as Rudman has come to know it. In fact, Rudman's body of writing is itself an apprenticeship in mourning, elegizing not only his personal losses but also history and the memories that constitute it.

BIBLIOGRAPHY

Orr, Linda. "Form and the Father: On Mark Rudman's Poetry." *Agni* 35 (1992): 299–302.

Revell, Donald. "Rose as Decoy, Beauty as Use." *Ohio Review* 53 (1995): 150–163.

Rudman, Mark. "An Interview," by Mark Rudman. *Denver Quarterly* 31, no. 3 (1997): pp. 119–131.

———. "Notes." *Provoked in Venice*. Hanover: Wesleyan University Press, 1999, pp. 201–202.

Aimee L. Pozorski

RUKEYSER, MURIEL (1913–1980) Muriel Rukeyser's poetry shares the ethics of the proletarian, left writers of the 1930s, with whom her early work was associated, and the formal and stylistic experimentation of her contemporaries in literary MODERNISM; her poetics also echoes the work of what is perhaps Rukeyser's single most significant literary influence, the 19th-century American poet Walt Whitman. Rukeyser's earliest poetry also shows the influence of W. H. AUDEN, while as a Jewish woman social activist poet in New York, Lola Ridge is another important predecessor. Late in her career, Rukeyser's work inspired a new generation of women poets searching for a distinctly FEMALE VOICE, FEMALE LANGUAGE, among them ADRIENNE RICH and ANNE SEXTON, who famously referred to her as "Muriel, Mother of everyone" (qtd. in Levi xvii).

Rukeyser was born and raised in New York. She was educated at Vassar College and Columbia University, and she briefly attended Roosevelt Aviation School, an experience informing her first volume, *Theory of Flight* (1935), for which she won the Yale Series of Younger Poets Award. She had one child, a son, William, and was mentor to the American novelist Alice Walker. She taught at Vassar, the California Labor School, and, for many years, Sarah Lawrence College. Although her father's financial difficulties forced her to leave her studies at Vassar, her coverage of the Alabama Scottsboro trial in 1932 for *Student Review* (a literary magazine she founded with classmates ELIZABETH BISHOP, Mary McCarthy, and Eleanor Clark) motivated her lifelong commitment to the struggle for human rights; as a journalist she also covered the silicon mining disaster in Gauley Bridge, West Virginia, and the Spanish civil war. Living in what she referred to as "the first century of world wars" ("Poem" [1968]), Rukeyser was witness to and participant in some of the defining events in the 20th-century quest for social justice. She was arrested in Washington, D.C., for protesting U.S. involvement in Vietnam, and she later traveled to Hanoi; in the 1970s she went to South Korea as president of the American Center for PEN to protest the death sentence of imprisoned radical Catholic poet Kim Chi-Ha, an experience that becomes the subject of the poem "The Gates" (1976). In addition to poetry, Rukeyser wrote biographies, children's books, and plays and published translations of Octavio Paz and Bertolt Brecht. Rukeyser won numerous awards and prizes, among them a National Institute of Arts and Letters grant (1942), a Guggenheim Fellowship (1943), and the Copernicus Award in recognition of her lifetime contribution to poetry (1977).

Considering Rukeyser's association with the labor movement of the early 20th century, the midcentury Civil Rights movement, and the late 20th-century women's liberation movement, KENNETH REXROTH identifies her as simply "a poet of liberty" (qtd. in Kertesz xii). In *The Life of Poetry* (1949), Rukeyser writes of poetry as a liberating practice, saying that "the total imaginative experience [which is the end of Art] will apply to your life; and it is more than likely to lead you to thought or action, that is, you are likely to want to go further into the world, further into yourself, toward further experience" (26). Poetry, for Rukeyser, becomes a form of social activism, and her strongest work—from "The Trial" (1935) to "The Gates"—is in direct response to social injustice.

Fueled by the national zeitgeist, Rukeyser enjoyed a period of renewed literary production amid the social protest and revolution of the 1960s, as, at the same time, many feminists and women poets were coming to regard her—politically, if not aesthetically—as a literary foremother. This regard is evident in that the titles of two POETRY ANTHOLOGIES edited and including work by women during this period—*No More Masks!* (1973) and *The World Split Open* (1974)—refer directly to Rukeyser's poetry. The latter alludes to the poem "Käthe Kollwitz" (1968), in which the poet questions what the effect would be "if one woman told the truth about her life." In this poem Rukeyser identifies her double in the early 20th-century German artist whose haunting black-and-white prints and woodcut images depict suffering caused by war and other social injustices. The poem, separated into five sections, reflects Rukeyser's tendency to group poems into sequences and clusters (similar, in some ways, to those of HART CRANE; his *The BRIDGE* is often likened to Rukeyser's *Theory of Flight,* because it is a modernist poem that uses an object representative of technological progress as a positive image of human potential). Like fellow modernists, including WILLIAM CARLOS WILLIAMS, and their shared literary forebear Whitman, Rukeyser rejects European elitism in the search for a uniquely American literature, and the poetics evident in "Käthe Kollwitz" is one she developed early—a merging of proletarian subject matter with modernist aesthetics—and which remains fairly consistent throughout her career. From her earliest work in *Theory of Flight* to her work in her last volume, *The Gates,* in 1976, Rukeyser's poetry documents and testifies to the struggle for social justice in the 20th century.

BIBLIOGRAPHY

Dickie, Margaret and Thomas Travisano, eds. *Gendered Modernisms: American Women Poets and Their Readers.* Philadelphia: University of Pennsylvania Press, 1996, pp. 264–279.

Herzog, Anne F., and Janet E. Kaufman, eds. *"How Shall We Tell Each Other of the Poet": The Life and Writing of Muriel Rukeyser.* New York: St. Martin's Press, 1999.

Kertesz, Louise. *The Poetic Vision of Muriel Rukeyser.* Baton Rouge: Louisiana State University Press, 1980.

Levi, Jan Heller, ed. *A Muriel Rukeyser Reader.* New York: Norton, 1994.

Rexroth, Kenneth. Foreword to *The Poetic Vision of Muriel Rukeyser,* by Louise Kertesz. Baton Rouge: Louisiana State University Press, 1980,

Rukeyser, Muriel. *The Life of Poetry.* Ashfield, Mass.: Paris Press, 1996.

Maggie Gordon

RUTSALA, VERN (1934–) Vern Rutsala is a prominent Northwest poet and an important voice in western American literature. Starting with the publication of his first collection, *The Window* (1964), his poetry has sought to uncover the intricate relationships in daily lives, with a particular focus on the importance of place. Like the earlier Northwest poet THEODORE ROETHKE, his work finds its substance in exploring regional differences and circumstances. Yet Rutsala's use of locality achieves universal significance through a constant inquiry into shared existential conditions, moments in the routine patterns of our lives when each of us is confronted with the absolute freedom of choice. What the critic Erik Muller calls "a critique of practical living" opens the poems to a range of such concerns with the past and its place in the poet's ongoing life (23).

Born in McCall, Idaho, Rutsala has spent the greater portion of his life in Portland, Oregon, where he teaches at Lewis and Clark College. He has received fellowships from the National Endowment for the Arts (1974 and 1979) and the Guggenheim Foundation (1982). His book, *Little Known Sports* (1994), a collection of prose poems—of which he was an early practitioner, shaping the form for himself in the early 1960s—was the winner of the Juniper Prize, and his most recent book, *The Moment's Equation* (2005), was a finalist for the National Book Award.

A proponent of free verse, Rutsala revels in the subtleties of nuance and phrase associated with the common American idiom (see PROSODY AND FREE VERSE). His work over the years has developed through various phases of experimentation with line length and form, such as in the prose poem collections *Paragraphs* (1978) and *Little Known Sports*. The short, sometimes almost voyeuristic views of the daily world found in *Paragraphs* reinforce the poet's quiet intensity as a discoverer of the hidden workings of everyday life. Two of his most important collections to date are the sequential *Walking Home from the Icehouse* (1981) and *Backtracking* (1985). In these, Rutsala returns to his childhood in order to explore how present-day experiences are informed not only by our personal past but by our memories of a common past.

In "Long Distance" (1985), Rutsala writes, "The only way out is against the law," and against, that is, the comfortable routines our lives create for us. Our relationship to the past is constantly refigured and reformed, and the poet must be prepared to live in this continuum. "The present is all transition," he writes, "each man his own / agent against himself" "Long Distance." In this way, the individual is paramount in Rutsala's understanding of the struggle of life; at some point each must stand alone. And yet, throughout the poems, the poet employs the language of common people, aware of the shared value of their failures as well as of their triumphs.

BIBLIOGRAPHY

Muller, Erik. *Vern Rutsala*. Boise, Idaho: Boise State University, 1998.

George Moore

S

"SADIE AND MAUD" GWENDOLYN BROOKS **(1945)** A ballad dramatizing the difficult life choices facing African-American women, GWENDOLYN BROOKS's "Sadie and Maud" chronicles the very different fates of Maud, who "went to college," and Sadie, who "stayed at home" and "scraped life / With a fine-toothed comb." The poem builds upon the dialectical imagery Brooks developed in "A Song in the Front Yard," where the front yard stands for obedience, duty, and propriety, values clearly associated with assimilation to white social and cultural norms, while the back yard stands for sexuality, play, lawlessness, and freedom, qualities associated with the rejection of mainstream white values and the embrace of an African-American heritage and identity. As critic Harry Shaw notes, "'Sadie and Maud' is concerned with the same dialectic between the high life and no life. It is carried further, and we can see the results of both," adding that, overall, "The tone of the poem is clearly more favorable toward Sadie than Maud" (70).

Although Brooks does not specify that Sadie and Maud are sisters, one cannot help but connect them, largely because their lives seem equally troubled; both women, Eleanor Holmes Norton observes, share an "overriding problem . . . loneliness, a life lacking the chance to develop a relationship with a man or satisfactory family relationships" (61). At first, the poem seems more of a cautionary tale about the dangers of life "in the back yard," since the narrative focuses largely on Sadie's life: her sexiness, her two children born out of wedlock, the resulting family shame, and her poverty. When Sadie dies, she leaves her children "as heritage / Her fine-tooth comb." But the material meagerness of this bequest seems to conflict with the "fineness" of life Brooks ascribes to Sadie: she proves to be "one of the livingest chits / In all the land," and though her children were born out of wedlock, they appear to have lived securely enough at home. Brooks carefully removes any authorial comment on Sadie's life, reporting instead the plain facts of it and how others (but not Sadie herself) perceived its qualities. If Sadie has been troubled by loneliness of a life without satisfactory relationships, as Holmes argues, then she has also struggled to rectify her dissatisfaction.

By contrast, Brooks's assessment of Maud seems much more judging, though that judgment is likewise rendered indirectly. Maud's absence from the middle stanzas of the poem suggests that she was never involved in such shameful activities as Sadie, but it also suggests the emptiness of her own life, which seems to lack any deeds worthy of mention in the ballad. Moreover, whereas Brooks ascribes actions to Sadie ("scraped," "found," "bore"), Maud seems passive, "a thin brown mouse." If Sadie signifies the African-American woman's struggle with loneliness, Maud shows what happens when that woman succumbs. "She is living all alone / In this old house," Brooks concludes, reminding the reader that healthy, satisfying relationships, not property or career or status, ultimately define happiness in life.

The last line of the poem offers a powerful social commentary. "This old house" is a clichéd phrase signifying domestic happiness, but in the context of Maud's unhappy life, it now stands for the way that the promise of America is denied to African-American women, even (or especially) those who conform to mainstream values. Moreover, the demonstrative pronoun "this" suggests the speaker's own presence in the house where Maud lives, alerting us to the dangerous fact that the loneliness and abandonment Maud faces are not unique to her, but are dangers confronting African-American women everywhere in 20th-century America.

BIBLIOGRAPHY

Norton, Eleanor Holmes. "For Sadie and Maud." In *On Gwendolyn Brooks: Reliant Contemplation,* edited by Stephen Caldwell Wright. Ann Arbor: University of Michigan Press, 1996: 60–65.

Shaw, Harry B. *Gwendolyn Brooks.* Boston: Twayne Publishers, 1980.

Temple Cone

SALAAM, KALAMU YA (1947–) Kalamu ya Salaam is best known as a member of the BLACK ARTS MOVEMENT. The fundamental goal of these poets is the liberation of African peoples from forms, images, and subject matters that deny them complete humanity. His poetic style is the epitome of the new black aesthetic critics of the late 1960s. His use of "linguistic liberation"—an aggressive assault upon and refashioning of the English language—attempts to make a foreign tongue speak for a group that the language has traditionally oppressed. As he says in the introduction to the unpublished *A Precise Tenderness,* "I am always interested in propagating and extending the African aesthetic. What makes my poetry 'Black' is much more than subject matter. World-view and structure. Tradition and innovation. Culture and consciousness. All that" (3). Primary aspects of his poetry include the narrative stream of consciousness; linguistic liberation of terms, concepts, and icons; humor/satire; the application of musical rhythms and structures in printed poetry; and didactic text. His work perpetuates the tradition of AMIRI BARAKA, NIKKI GIOVANNI, SONIA SANCHEZ, Hoyt Fuller, Larry Neal, and ETHERIDGE KNIGHT.

Born Vallery Ferdinand III in New Orleans, his first book, *The Blues Merchant: Songs for Blkfolk,* was published in 1969. He is the recipient of the 1995 Louisiana Literature Fellow, a 1997 Mayor Marc Morial's Arts Award, the 1998 Louisiana Endowment for the Humanities Award, and a 1999 Senior Literature Fellowship from the Fine Arts Work Center in Provincetown, Massachusetts. He has also edited some of the most important African-American journals and anthologies to date, including *African American Review, 360 Degrees,* and the *Black Collegian.*

The core of Salaam's poetry is revolution. Explicit and explosive imagery drive his poetry, as he tries to shock the reader from mindless acceptance of mainstream definitions. He also uses juxtaposition, showing the irony or contradiction between verbalized principles and actualized behavior. Salaam seeks to exploit the space between the rhetorical principles and the behavior of the dominant class, which allows space for the oppressed to find their own humanity, beauty and worth. This is seen in "Words Have Meaning / But Only in Context" (1989): "All men are created equal was first said by people who owned slaves / The land of the free was stolen from the native Americans." He demonstrates that terms and meanings are arbitrary, political, and subjectively fashioned and must be manipulated to uncover our metaphoric essence through our actions. In "Sun Song XIII" (1994), he redefines beauty: Beauty is no longer in the eye of language's power brokers, but in the actions of one who is able to rise above life's oppression and grime and shine. At the center of his work is the desire to liberate people of color from a language that has been used to oppress them.

BIBLIOGRAPHY

Ward, Jerry. "Kalamu ya Salaam: A Primary Bibliography (in Progress)." *Mississippi Quarterly.* LI, no. 1 (winter 1997–98): 105–148.

Salaam, Kalamu ya. Introduction to *A Precise Tenderness.* Unpublished, manuscript courtesy of Kalamu ya Salaam, 2001.

C. Liegh McInnis

SALTER, MARY JO (1954–) A distinguishing element of poetry is that a poem's form can signify as much as its vocabulary—a relationship made particularly apparent in the poems of Mary Jo Salter. A superb craftsperson who delights in using form like a jeweler's setting to display every facet of a word or phrase, Salter deftly reveals the universal in personal experiences, objects, and places. Often humorous and poignant at once, her poems have an appealing humility and a sure-footed confidence. Her love of double-meanings and puns is much in evidence (showing the influences of W. H. AUDEN and JAMES MERRILL). She uses her fluency with traditional forms to interpret and reinvent formal poetry, to both playful and solemn effects.

Born in Detroit, Salter was educated at Harvard, where she studied under ELIZABETH BISHOP and Robert Fitzgerald, and at Cambridge University. In addition to five collections of poems, Salter is the author of a children's book. She has received numerous awards, including an AMY LOWELL Poetry Travelling Scholarship in 1996, and she is a coeditor of the *Norton Anthology of Poetry*. Her second collection, *Unfinished Painting*, was the Lamont Poetry Selection for 1988. She has been the Emily Dickinson Senior Lecturer in the Humanities at Mount Holyoke College.

Salter exploits the familiar sounds and rhythms of formal poetry to evoke particular moods; she opens "Chernobyl" (1989) with a familiar, singsong convention from children's storytelling: "Once upon a time / The word alone was scary." Her vocabulary and regular *abab* rhymed lines (a system in which alternating lines rhyme), including many feminine endings, reverberate surprisingly against the poem's grim subject matter to remind us of how quickly disasters become distant stories. In "Elegies for Etsuko" (1989), the suicide of a young friend is treated in a series of poems with structures from villanelle to free verse, creating a formal mirror of the many conflicting responses we have to such losses.

Salter's extensive travels in Iceland, Japan, and France have given rise to numerous poems in which travel and the experience of foreignness become metaphors for movement into different mentalities and perspectives. Craft and art are strong presences in Salter's subject matter as well, and much of her work imagines the lives and preoccupations of artists and inventors, from a sidewalk chalk artist in "The Rebirth of Venus" to Emily Dickinson, ROBERT FROST, and Thomas Jefferson to her own mother, a painter whose work (and death from cancer) occasioned many of Salter's poems. Domestic objects—a refrigerator magnet, the Christmas tree, her father's home movies—are treated with the same care as a painting by Titian.

Uniquely masterful in her exaltation of the daily and the domestic, Salter expresses the correlations among the most mundane objects and experiences with a seemingly effortless interpolation of poetic resonance into everyday life, formalizing it as if to hint that a grand scheme does indeed underpin all human experience.

BIBLIOGRAPHY

Taylor, Henry. "Faith and Practice: The Poems of Mary Jo Salter." *Hollins Critic* XXXVII, no. 1 (February 2000): 1–6.
Whited, Stephen. "Mary Jo Salter." *Book* (March/April 1999). Available online. URL: www.bookmagazine.com/archive/issue3/poetics.shtml. Downloaded February 2003.

Amy Glynn Greacen

SAMPERI, FRANK (1933–1991) Frank Samperi sought the ideal in eternal forms and represented primarily single images in space and time. Particularly Samperi considered the position of "the eternal" in time; similar to the OBJECTIVIST poets, he refused MODERNISM's nostalgic attempt to recover lost time. Instead he focused on "the consciousness of objects *in* time, but removed from their dependence upon time" (Faust 248). Early influences on Samperi's work include LOUIS ZUKOFSKY and CID CORMAN. Samperi shared significant correspondences throughout his life with Corman and THEODORE ENSLIN, as well as the Australian poet Clive Faust, and he admired his contemporary, Robert Lax, for "the Franciscan sensibility of his writing" (Miller and Zurbrugg 12).

Samperi was born in Brooklyn, a city often celebrated through "snapshots" in his poetry. He served in the United States Army in the Korean War from 1953–55. Shortly after his return, he began to publish; his first collection, *Song Book*, appeared in 1960. Samperi subsequently published several extended series of poetry, such as *The Prefiguration* (1971) and *Quadrifariam* (1973).

Samperi's untitled poems are both spiritual and metaphysical: He calls, in *Quadrifariam*, for a "theological" poetics, saying that he writes "for angels" and, consequently, does not "know the practical world." Despite these transcendent ideals, however, Samperi is also concerned with the details of ordinary life—depicting such images as pigeons flocking near a tree, a woman gathering hill flowers, and children in a valley. In *The Triune* (1969), for example, Samperi describes "seeing children in the midst of a valley / the stars wood beyond wood beyond a river." Here Samperi not only renders the layering effect of the natural world, but he also foregrounds the position of the child in this vision. The repetition of "wood beyond" and other phrases gesture to that mysterious "Eternal Form" that lies beyond the pastoral scene, just before the poem proceeds to describe that "Back street / drunk" in the city.

In addition to the tensions between the ideal and the material, as well as life in the country and life in the city, Samperi is also keenly interested in the legacy of the poet and his or her craft. For example, he claims in *Anti-Hero* (1973), that "it is not the writer's job to seek out the latest innovations; he has ancient teachers and with them he silently converses." In silent conversations with his IMAGIST predecessors, Samperi wrote poetry that, like the haiku form, makes minimalist linguistic statements. These statements often only contain one- or two-word lines, forcing confrontation with not only the words, but also the white space of the page that surrounds them.

BIBLIOGRAPHY

Faust, Clive. "Time and Eternity in Frank Samperi's Letters." *Sulfur* 31 (fall 1992): 245–252.

Miller, David, and Nicholas Zurbrugg. Introduction to *The ABCs of Robert Lax*. Devon, England: Stride, 1999, p. 12.

Aimee L. Pozorski

SANCHEZ, SONIA (1934–) Sonia Sanchez began her career during the BLACK ARTS MOVEMENT of the 1960s and 1970s, a period of black nationalist influence over art and politics. Inspired by black cultural nationalism and feminism, Sanchez has written extensively about issues of justice and equality in American society, as a public intellectual and as a poet. Among the poets that emerged from the Black Arts movement, including NIKKI GIOVANNI, HAKI MADHUBUTI, and AMIRI BARAKA, Sanchez may be the most successful at adapting both form and content to reflect her growth as a poet and activist.

Sanchez was born Wilsonia Benita Driver in Birmingham, Alabama, and moved to Harlem as an adolescent. She attended Hunter College, graduating in 1955, and studied poetry at New York University. She has taught at Temple University and has received numerous honors, including PEN writing awards (1969 and 1993) and an American Book Award for *homegirls and hand grenades* (1985).

In 1974 Sanchez published *A Blues Book for Blue Black Magical Women*, which traces the development of a black female consciousness through poetry. The poems evoke the folk spirit of black cultural nationalism through imagery and metaphor, as expressed in the sequence entitled "Part Two: Past," in which she describes African-American hairstyles and music as cultural forms that are blended within American traditions. Through metaphor, she suggests that the "birth" of her braids "cut a blue / song for america."

Sanchez calls attention to trauma, healing, joy, and collective memory as expressed by black cultural traditions and family history, with many poems illustrating the uncertain progress of African Americans toward justice and equality. "Sister's Voice" (1995) describes her brother's internal struggles and eventual death from AIDS, tracing his decline due to drug addiction, limited communication skills ("he specialized in generalize"), and increasing isolation from family, community, and history; ultimately he "denied his father's signature / damned his sister's overture." Stylistically a subtly crafted rhyme scheme recalls the musicality of African-American urban dialect, while the subject matter powerfully conveys the despair and restlessness that can result from unstable relationships with family and community.

Sanchez depicts African-American cultural life realistically and sympathetically. Her rigorous attention to form and idea reminds readers that the art of poetry requires periodic reinvention, if it is to express the continuing struggles of ordinary people for justice, love, and community unity.

BIBLIOGRAPHY

Evans, Mari, ed. *Black Women Writers 1950–1980: A Critical Evaluation*. New York: Anchor Books, 1984.

Quashie, Kevin Everod, Joyce Lausch, and Keith D. Miller. *New Bones: Contemporary Black Writers in America.* Upper Saddle River, N.J.: Prentice Hall, 2001.

David M. Jones

SANDBURG, CARL (1878–1967) Carl Sandburg, one of the most celebrated poets of his generation, was devoted to issues of democracy and the voice of the people in the tradition of Walt Whitman, EDGAR LEE MASTERS, and VACHEL LINDSAY. The author of books of poems, children's books, biographies, and other work, Sandburg was known for celebrating American folk life and for his experiments with language, wherein he attempted to capture the voice of common people. His work experience as a manual laborer, coupled with the vision of the United States he saw in his travels, proved foundational to his later effort at democratic verse.

Carl August Sandburg was born to Swedish immigrant parents in Galesburg, Illinois. Sandburg finished public schooling in 1891, upon his graduation from eighth grade, when he began working a series of labor-intensive jobs, such as harvesting ice and delivering milk. In 1897 he left home aboard a railroad car, choosing the life of a hobo, moving from town to town, and working odd jobs across the Midwest. Through these experiences, he developed a keen sense of "the people" and the great disparities between the wealthy and working class. In 1898 he served in the Spanish-American War. Stationed in Puerto Rico, he wrote letters home that were featured in the local paper. Sandburg's service as a veteran entitled him to receive free college tuition, something he pursued by enrolling in Galesburg's Lombard College upon his return home. From 1902 Sandburg worked for a series of small magazines while he toured the country giving speeches on Whitman and Abraham Lincoln. Sandburg's love of politics played out in work as a journalist from 1909–12, as a city hall reporter, as a secretary for the mayor of Milwaukee, as city editor of the *Social Democratic Herald,* and as a staff writer of the Milwaukee *Leader.* Sandburg won the Poetry Society of America Award (1919 and 1921), the Friends of Literature Award (1934), the Roosevelt Memorial Association Prize for biography (1939), the Pulitzer Prize for history (1940) and for poetry (1951), and the American Academy Gold Medal (1952).

Harriet Monroe, who published some of Sandburg's *CHICAGO POEMS* in *Poetry,* officially introduced him to the world of poetry readers in 1914. Readers and critics alike were captivated by his use of free verse (see PROSODY AND FREE VERSE) in such poems as "CHICAGO" (1914), which coupled innovative form and imagery to introduce the city as a "Hog Butcher for the World" and "City of the Big Shoulders." His use of plain speech in short, descriptive poems, such as "Fog" (1916), which imagines the fog "on little cat feet" appearing "over harbor and city," and his keen attention to developing the voice of working people redefined the American poetic tradition.

Cornhuskers appeared in 1918 to many of the same positive reviews as the *Chicago Poems* (1916), all of which generally noted Sandburg's unusual use of form and his dedication to democratic voices. "Gargoyle" (1918) represents Sandburg's experimentation with clear language: "A fist hit the mouth: knuckles of gun-metal driven by an electric wrist and shoulder. / It was a child's dream of an arm." Three original collections of poems were published in the 1920s, *Smoke and Steel* (1920), *Slabs of the Sunburnt West* (1922), and *Good Morning, America* (1928). Two edited collections of Sandburg's work, Hughes Mearns's *Poems* and Rebecca West's *Selected Poems,* appeared in 1926. Some critics objected to Sandburg's work, calling it prose, but Aldous Huxley defended Sandburg in his 1923 essay "The Subject Matter of Poetry."

From 1926 to 1939 Sandburg devoted himself to researching and writing two massive biographies about Lincoln, the two-volume 1926 *Abraham Lincoln: The Prairie Years* and the four-volume 1939 *Abraham Lincoln: The War Years.* Sandburg's love of Lincoln was reflected in such poems as the 1918 "Cool Tombs," which reflects on the role of death for both the famous, who "forgot the copperheads and the assassin . . . in the dust, in the cool tombs," and ordinary people, who "get more than the lovers . . . in the dust . . . in the cool tombs."

Sandburg's epic *The People, Yes,* a book-length poem on the Great Depression, was published in 1936. Similar to the poems before these, Sandburg's voice meditated on the people, celebrating the possibilities of democratic writing: "These are heroes then—among the plain people—Heroes, did you say? And why not?" Sandburg sought greater understanding of the role of poetry as a source of power through representation.

After 1936 Sandburg worked for a series of newspapers and universities. His poetry moved away from serious social commentary toward work about nature and children. His later poetry consisted of *Bronze Wood* (1941), *Harvest Poems, 1910–1960* (1960), *Six New Poems and a Parable* (1961), and *Honey and Salt* (1963). He also continued as an active Lincoln scholar. In 1959 he gave the annual Lincoln Day address before a joint session of Congress. Sandburg's impressive poetic career stretched to include 22 books of poetry, nine of which appeared posthumously, including collections and reprints of his earlier work, such as *The Complete Poems of Carl Sandburg* (1969 and 1970), and poetry for children.

BIBLIOGRAPHY

Epstein, Joseph. "'The People's Poet.'" *Commentary* (May 1992): 47–52.

Huxley, Aldous. "The Subject Matter of Poetry." In *Collected Essays*. New York: Harper, 1958.

Kostelnick, Charles. "Sandburg, Futurism, and the Aesthetics of Urban Dynamism." *American Poetry* 8 (fall 1990): 46–56.

Niven, Penelope. *Carl Sandburg: A Biography*. New York: Scribners, 1991.

van Doren, Carl. "Carl Sandburg: Flame and Slag." In *Many Minds*. New York: Knopf, 1924. Reprint, Port Washington, N.Y.: Kennikat Press, 1966.

Yannella, Philip R. *The Other Carl Sandburg*. Jackson: University Press of Mississippi, 1996.

J. Elizabeth Clark

SANDERS, ED (1939–) Ed Sanders belongs to the second wave of BEAT poets who came to prominence in the late 1960s. Influenced by ALLEN GINSBERG and first published by LAWRENCE FERLINGHETTI, Sanders' poetry is a hybrid product of the hippie movement and the Beat generation that preceded it. In this respect, he is in the company of activist poets, such as CHARLES OLSON and JOHN WEINERS.

Sanders was born and raised in Kansas City, Missouri. He dropped out of Missouri University in 1958 and traveled to New York City. In 1964 he helped found the poetry-music ensemble the Fugs with Tuli Kupferberg, during a period in which Sanders owned the famous Peace Eye Bookstore in the East Village. Both the Fugs and the Peace Eye Bookstore were cornerstones of the emerging counterculture and were forums for Sanders's poetry. Yet surprisingly, perhaps, Sanders's most famous and best-selling book is *The Family* (1971), a well-documented account of the Manson family murders, written in prose salted with terse poetic commentary on the cataclysm that ended the 1960s. He has received a Guggenheim Fellowship (1983) and a National Endowment for the Arts Fellowship (1987). His book *Thirsting for Peace in a Raging Century: Selected Poems 1961–1985* won an American Book Award in 1988.

Similar to the earlier Beat poetry, Sanders's writing in the 1960s was often overtly political and discussed social issues as a subtext. "We demand the Politics of Ecstasy!" was one of his most memorable mottoes and reflects his participation in the political moments of that turbulent decade. "Hymn to the Rebel Café" (1993), for example, opens with a tribute to the young radicals of the 1960s: "They were planning a revolution / to end want & hunger."

Sanders works in syllabically brief lines, often arranged in chaotic form on the page. He balances the heavy introspection of the poetic impulse with a dose of ribald humor: One of the defining qualities of his work is its tone of sheer irreverence. In his poetry Sanders celebrates nature, the animal urges that propel us, and the organic functions of the body.

In college he was trained in the classics and studied Latin and Greek. The classical influence persists in his poetry. "Under the Quercus" (1993), is composed in Latin and followed by Sanders's translation in English: "*Hic jacet Peeper/ qui anas celerrima et optima erat*" ('Here lies Peeper / who was a duck most swift and fine')." Even more experimental works, such as "Sheep Fuck Poem" (1988), exhibit classical influences. Sanders often punctuates his poetry with hand-drawn hieroglyphs—sometimes reproductions from ancient Egyptian sources, more often of his own invention.

Recently Sanders has devoted himself to the development of what he calls "investigative poetry," or poetry written in the style of investigative journalism, which is a medium that corresponds well to political activism. Sanders has remained active as public reader of poetry—at times, linked to environmentalism—and as a musician, often recording poetry and music together.

BIBLIOGRAPHY

Brooke, Horvath, ed. *Review of Contemporary Fiction* 19, no. 1 (spring 1999). [Ed Sanders Issue].

Sanders, Ed. "Interview with Ed Sanders," by Sean Thomas Dougherty. *Long Shot* 13 (1992): 87–90.

Aaron Parrett

SANER, REG (1931–) Reg Saner is part of a new generation of nature poets. His concerns are not solely with the beauty manifest in wilderness, such as that which surrounds his Boulder, Colorado, home, but rather with the environmental concerns that would make such open spaces sustainable into the future. His free verse poetry continues a line of American romantic poets who descend from Walt Whitman and WALLACE STEVENS (see PROSODY AND FREE VERSE). But unlike Stevens, Saner avoids taking moral sides, preferring instead to present the world as it is in its natural complexity. As a Shakespearean scholar, Saner writes with an understanding of the well-crafted rhythms and wordplay of the Renaissance masters.

Saner was born in Jacksonville, Illinois. He took a Fulbright Fellowship in Florence, Italy, in 1960. His first book, *Climbing into the Roots* (1976), won the Walt Whitman Award. His second collection, *So This Is the Map* (1981), was selected by DEREK WALCOTT for the National Poetry Series Open Competition. His fourth collection, *Red Letters,* was published as part of the *Quarterly Review of Literature*'s 1989 book award. Saner was also awarded the Wallace Stegner Award in 1998 for his long-standing commitment to western American concerns, in both his poetry and essays on nature.

More than a simple regionalist, Saner attempts to capture the open spirit of the West as it was before the displacement of Native peoples. At the same time, he is not an apologist for western expansion, but a poet concerned with the interaction of past and present cultures. Many of his poems bear the titles of western place names, such as "August Evening at Crater Lake" (1976), "Anasazi at Mesa Verde" (1976), and "Reaching Keet Seel" (1987). His Fulbright years in Italy also provided sources for his passion for cultures, in ways contrasting with but also complementing his love of American wilderness. In such poems as "Waking to the Ceiling of an Italian Farmhouse" (1984) and "The Vesuvius Variations" (1983), Saner revels in a thick history of place; these poems are equal in their insights to the western poems. "I need to travel to do my thing," Saner has recently said, "I have to be physically, wherever it is I'm writing about. In a way, I write with my feet" (qtd. in Libid).

In "Road Life" (1982), he further explores this theme of geographical travel as the poet's passage through life. The speaker is called out into the world—"U.S. 36 has always poured possibilities / through your hometown"—only to find it always new—"Because you're a blur making time / like everyone else you've had to reinvent the wheel." Again, in "Skiing Alone near the Divide" (1981), the poet writes of his experience as explorer: The "compass is wind / incessant and westerly." The poet's identity forms through his constant uncovering of natural and cultural places.

BIBLIOGRAPHY

Libid, Jon. "Saner Retires while He Still Has 'Juice,'" Carillon. Available online. URL: www.colorado.edu/Carillon/volume34/stories/6–2juice.html. Downloaded March 2007.

Moore, George. "Essay on Air." *Bloomsbury Review.* 5, no. 9 (June 1985): 12–13.

George Moore

SAN FRANCISCO RENAISSANCE In the two decades following World War II, an overarching reevaluation of art and its purpose occurred. This reconsideration gave rise to a number of identifiable movements and schools worldwide in the same period; even though those movements had some philosophical and aesthetic similarities, each had distinctive qualities that set it apart from the others. In the United States, the postwar period saw the simultaneous emergence of four particular poetic phenomena: the BLACK MOUNTAIN SCHOOL, BEAT POETRY, the NEW YORK SCHOOL, and the San Francisco Renaissance. There is much description and definition that might seemingly fit any or all of these, and there are many individuals whose names legitimately are listed among the notable figures of more than one of them. Warren French, who tends to conflate the Beat and the Renaissance, sets the outer limits of the Renaissance period between the 1944 launch of the first issue of *Circle* and the deaths of KENNETH REXROTH in 1982 and ROBERT DUNCAN in 1988 (xviii), a span of 40 years, but focuses on 1955–1960 as the most significant time. MICHAEL DAVIDSON marks the Renaissance period "from the late 1940s to Jack Spicer's death in 1965" (6) and firmly situates it in the San Francisco Bay area.

One of the reasons for the familial relationship between the so-called Beat generation and San Francisco Renaissance is that the renaissance, the rebirth of poetry in San Francisco, is commonly dated from the incredible moment in October 1955 when the Six Gallery was the scene of ALLEN GINSBERG's first public performance of *HOWL*, undoubtedly one of the most important moments in American poetry; the master of ceremonies that evening was Rexroth, who was a precursor influential in the development of most San Francisco Renaissance poets, some of whom also read at that remarkable event: PHILIP WHALEN, GARY SNYDER, MICHAEL MCCLURE, and Philip Lamantia. JACK KEROUAC was also there, liberally pouring out the wine and musically urging the readers on with exclamations of "Go! Go!" This is the night which prompted LAWRENCE FERLINGHETTI to send Ginsberg the famous telegram, echoing Emerson's to Whitman, welcoming him into his career and asking to publish the poem. The selection of poetry presented that night provides examples of the variety of technique developing in these poets and eventually encompassed by the term San Francisco Renaissance: "a vatic, confessional mode; imagist precisionism; satire and self-projection; surrealism; personalist meditation" (Davidson 4). Robert Duncan, Lew Welch, KENNETH PATCHEN, BOB KAUFMAN, DIANE DI PRIMA, and Lenore Kandel are also among those whose names often appear in assessments of the renaissance, but any version of the list might include up to 30 names, from AMIRI BARAKA and CHARLES BUKOWSKI to Anne Waldman and David Rafael Wang; not surprisingly, due to prevailing 1950s attitudes, there were few women and few minorities.

The diversity of style so evident in the work of these poets is balanced by a common goal and concern. San Francisco Renaissance poets wanted a reborn American romanticism to embody poetry's return from academic institutions to the masses in the streets, to speak in the language of the ordinary person (in the tradition of WILLIAM CARLOS WILLIAMS) rather than of the academy, and to concern itself with populist issues. Although oral performance is integral to their poetic practice (see POETRY IN PERFORMANCE), renaissance poets also found outlets for their work in the pages of such periodicals as George Leite's *Circle* (1944) and, later, Barney Rosset's *Evergreen Review* (1957), and such publishing houses as Rosset's Grove Press, James Laughlin's New Directions, and Ferlinghetti's City Lights Books (see POETRY PRESSES). Ferlinghetti, scholar and poet, has also been described as "that rarest of persons—a practical-minded, visionary businessman" (French x). It took a San Francisco poet-publisher to recognize and promote so readily this poetry of place (although he resisted the strictures of regionally based definitions). The component parts of San Francisco that provided the impetus for the renaissance are its "long history of alternative religions . . . [and] long tradition of political radicalism" (Davidson 11). Critic Michael Davidson's analysis of the period acknowledges, in fact, it stresses, the meld of historical context with cultural conditions that produced this particular poetics of place. Aboriginal and Asian religions, for example, are a major part of that "alternative" mix and help to explain how San Francisco had "escaped the Puritan ethos" (Davidson 11) so dominant in the East. The hybrid culture produced in the Bay Area came up against the diffused disillusionment of the post–World War II generation and thus generated a regionally identifiable response. Only part of this response is a concern shared by the New York Beat and renaissance poets.

By virtue of his dual citizenship in these schools, Ginsberg marks the similarities and differences in Beat and renaissance sensibility. He is the clearest exemplar of the Beats, because his is enormous poetry, relentless and overpowering, often right at the edge of comprehensibility. It sustains an excruciating balance through the constant tension of its (and all Beat and renaissance poetry's) guy-wires: sex, politics, and mysticism—the human body, mind, and spirit. The poems are physical without shrinking from bodily function, intellectual without resorting to theoreticism, and spiritual without reduction to preaching. Although he speaks to the universal, he does it through the particular, explicitly rather than metaphorically. These common aspects, however, do not encompass all of the central concerns of renaissance poets. Ginsberg's decidedly East Coast, urban poetry has no trace of the pronounced and paradoxical urban ecopoeticism of San Francisco. The West Coast was still close enough to its wilderness past and present for the natural world to be an essential thread in the genetics of northern California poetry, and its poets were still affected by that wilderness as much as they were by the city. Kerouac's city-boy inability to cope mentally with the seclusion of Ferlinghetti's cabin in Big Sur or, on Snyder's suggestion, the isolation of a firewatch tower in the Cascades is partially the result of an eastern detachment from nature and is the perfect demonstration of a fundamental difference between the two groups.

Further Davidson points to the characteristics that differentiate the San Francisco poets from each other by identifying their personal literary lineage: the apocalyptic and bardic style of romantic William Blake and Whitman in Duncan, WILLIAM EVERSON, and Rexroth; the biting satire of Guillaume Apollinaire and Jacques Prévert in the café poems of Ferlinghetti; Asian nature poetry and British romanticism in Rexroth, Snyder, Welch, and Whalen; the introspection of Samuel Taylor Coleridge in McClure, Whalen, and Duncan; Surrealism in Philip Lamantia, Duncan, JACK SPICER, Ferlinghetti, Kaufman, and McClure (17). These poets led very individual lives, unlike the somewhat communal Beats, traveling and living apart at great distances for long periods; Snyder spent nearly a decade living in Asia. What unites them is their activist impulse, driven primarily by their environmental conscience and pacificist anarchism and addressing civil rights, gay rights, environmental issues, and American foreign and domestic policy. These poets spoke in the vanguard of social and political movements; Ginsberg, for example, voiced an antiglobalization position long before the term was coined. Davidson reports that, as "early as 1958, Ginsberg was arguing with his father over the need to reject monolithic solutions to world problems in favor of more personal transformations" (29).

Snyder likewise believed in the need for an immediate and local understanding as part of personal development. Ultimately knowing place is essential to knowing self, as the world is "an intense geography that is never far removed from [the] body" (qtd. in Davidson 13). The landscape is part of the person, not something to have dominion over, but something to honor and respect. This is an example of how the multireligious historical background of San Francisco influences local attitude: The earth is not to be conquered and dominated in the way of the Old Testament, but it is to be lived with harmoniously, recognizing that it is not separate, not an adversary. In *Hallelujah Anyway* (1960), a book of picture-poems blending language and image, Patchen writes, "Inside the Flower there is room for every sower," but "The Best Hope Is that one of these days the ground will get disgusted enough just to walk away," because people are so involved with declaring platforms that they neglect the one on which they are physically supported. In "Junkman's Obbligato" (1958), Ferlinghetti knows "The real earthquake is coming. / [He] can feel the building shake" and waits, in "I Am Waiting" (1958), "for forests and animals / to reclaim the earth as theirs." In these ways the poets warn of the dangers of abuse and neglect of the planet at the same time as they underscore the reciprocity inherent in all aspects of place. Any surrounding is more than merely a place to be—it affects the way of being.

Ginsberg would have us put our own "queer shoulder to the wheel" ("America" 1956), whatever kind of shoulder we may have and whatever our wheel might be. The personality and disposition of the San Francisco Renaissance poets varied widely; Thomas Parkinson describes "the genuine vigor and force of Allen Ginsberg . . . the extraordinary wit and hilarity of Lawrence Ferlinghetti . . . the obvious intelligence, learning and decency of Gary Snyder and Philip Whalen, the hard integrity of Michael McClure" (qtd. in French 57). These characteristics and the combination of common speech and oral performance in San Francisco Renaissance poetry create a dialogue between speaker and listener, removing traditional boundaries so that the immediacy and intimacy of the poetry become a personal call to a personal response of experience and activism. By example, the poems model the need both to feel and to act in the body, mind, and spirit.

BIBLIOGRAPHY

Davidson Michael. *The San Francisco Renaissance: Poetics and Community at Mid-Century*. New York: Cambridge University Press, 1989.

French, Warren. *The San Francisco Poetry Renaissance 1955–1960*. Boston: Twayne, 1991.

A. Mary Murphy

SCALAPINO, LESLIE (1947–) Leslie Scalapino's work has made a significant contribution to the understanding of poetry as a process engaged with questions of perception. Her questioning of how "phenomena appear to unfold" aims to create "a perspective that is socially democratic, individual (in the sense of specific) and limitless" (119). She is often identified with the LANGUAGE SCHOOL of writing, and her work's interest in the connections between gender and representation has affinities with that of poets such as BERNADETTE MAYER, LYN HEJINIAN, SUSAN HOWE, and JOAN RETALLACK. Her interest in the interconnections between knowledge and repetition has been more broadly influenced by the work of experimental poets such as ROBERT GRENIER, GERTRUDE STEIN, and ROBERT DUNCAN.

Scalapino was born in Santa Barbara, California, but spent significant parts of her childhood traveling in Southeast Asia. She gained her B.A. from Reed College and her M.A. from the University of California, Berkeley. Her first book, *The Woman Who Could Read the Minds of Dogs,* was published in 1976, and numerous collections, which variously combine poetry, fiction, plays and essays, have followed. She has been the editor of O Books and has also received two National Endowment for the Arts Fellowships (1976 and 1986), a Before Columbus Foundation Award (1988), and a Lawrence Lipton Award (1988).

The central aim of Scalapino's writing has been to make it as close to reality as possible, to do away with the separation of presentation and representation in language. In the recent book-length poem, *The Front Matter Dead Souls* (1996), she describes this aim as a desire, "to bring (actually to be) 'the American grain.'" Scalapino seeks to integrate WILLIAM CARLOS WILLIAMS's desire for an American vernacular with an analysis of how we represent what we are able to understand and witness in public spaces. In another recent book-length poem, *New Time* (1999), this aim results in a detailed social choreography, an attention to who moves and how they move, that makes apparent the social processes by which action becomes meaning: "groups ridiculing for playing, their being outside playing. but / ridiculing the characteristic which is that, their not doing it." The poem challenges the distinctions between thought and appearance and uses this to suggest that "social existence" is comprised of both activity ("playing") and discourse ("ridiculing").

Scalapino's dense and elliptical style aims to disrupt the processes that allow racism, sexism, and poverty to appear natural. Her concern with producing the "real," with pointing out that language both constructs and disrupts social meaning, has been consistently motivated by a critique of social injustice.

BIBLIOGRAPHY

Elizabeth Frost. "Signifyin(g) on Stein: The Revisionist Poetics of Harryette Mullen and Leslie Scalapino." *Postmodern Culture* 5, no. 3 (1995). Available online. URL: http://muse.jhu.edu/journals/postmodern_culture/v005/5.3frost.html. Downloaded March 2007.

Scalapino Leslie. "An Interview with Leslie Scalapino. Conducted by Edward Foster." *Talisman* 8 (1992): 32–41.

———. *How Phenomena Appear to Unfold.* Elmwood, Conn.: Potes and Poets Press, 1989.

Nicky Marsh

SCHNACKENBERG,GJERTRUD (1953–) Gjertrud Schnackenberg is often identified with the NEW FORMALISM movement, including MARK JARMAN and RAFAEL CAMPO. She is a traditional and highly intellectual poet, and her more remote influences extend to Dante, William Butler Yeats, and T. S. ELIOT. Her poems, like theirs, emphasize rhyme, meter, and story, while she seems to pursue a particular interest in the juxtaposition of history, art, and religion.

Schnackenberg was born in Tacoma, Washington. She has been the recipient of numerous awards for her poetry, twice winning the prestigious Glascock Award for poetry while a student at Mount Holyoke College (1974, 1975). She went on to receive the Lavan Younger Poets Award from the Academy of American Poets (1983), among other prizes and fellowships; she has also been made a member of the American Academy of Arts and Sciences (1996).

Schnackenberg's early use of hymn meter (the meter of Emily Dickinson) eventually was replaced by the terza rima (three-line stanzas with interlocking end rhymes) of *A Gilded Lapse of Time* (1992). Although her later work employs several, sometimes looser forms, she remains a formalist. The poem "Imaginary Prisons" (1985) contains lines that seem to encapsulate many of the concerns of Schnackenberg's poetry: history, grief, and writing. As she wrote in that poem, "It isn't history if it isn't written— / It's written here, and written here in memory." The lines draw a connection between history and writing, and their ability in some respects to overcome the tragic aspects of mortality.

Schnackenberg's references and interests seem all-encompassing at times, and her poems are populated by such figures as St. Augustine, Dante, Piero della Francesca, Mantegna, and Osip Mandlestam. Her father was a professor of history, and his presence is much felt throughout her work, perhaps most strongly in her first two books: *Portraits and Elegies* (1982) and *The Lamplit Answer* (1985). *A Gilded Lapse of Time,* her third book, is divided into three sections: One addresses Dante, the second addresses Christ's suffering and resurrection as depicted in Renaissance and Byzantine paintings, and the last addresses the Russian poet Osip Mandlestam, who was to die in one of Stalin's labor camps—the victim, in a sense, of his writing. Schnackenberg's *The Throne of Labdacus* (2000), which won the 2001 Los Angeles Times Book Prize in Poetry, is an extended meditation on the fate of Oedipus. The link between all of these topics is the lineage of families, both personal and poetic, and the consequences of art. The body of Gjertrud Schnackenberg's work forms a record of a poet looking, throughout all time and literature, for her place in the world of poetry.

BIBLIOGRAPHY

Pettingill, Phoebe. "Painful Mysteries." *New Leader* 83, no. 4 (September 2000): 38.

Warren, Rosanna. "A Gilded Lapse of Time—A Review." *New Republic* 209, no. 11 (September 13, 1993): 37–42.

Anna Priddy

SCHUYLER, JAMES (1923–1991) James Schuyler was a central member of what has come to be known as the NEW YORK SCHOOL of poets. His most characteristic poems are strikingly direct and simple, "as clear and satisfying as a glass of water," in the apt words of William Corbett (52). As with the manner of the 17th-century Dutch painter Jan Vermeer, Schuyler's writerly artifice is so complete as to be almost undetectable. Such casually perfect creations seem to have been discovered rather than rendered, implicitly challenging any easy distinction between the natural and the artificial. In his mature work Schuyler found a way to be wholly himself without self-consciousness. In his effort to put his whole self on the page, Schuyler proves his indebtedness and devotion to the model and inspiration of Walt Whitman.

Schuyler was born and raised in Washington, D.C., and East Aurora, New York, near Buffalo. He attended Bethany College in West Virginia from 1941 to 1943 and moved to New York City in the late 1940s, where he lived, off and on, for the rest of his life. His first book, a novel, *Alfred and Guinevere,* was published in 1958. In 1969 his first major collection of poetry, *Freely Espousing,* was published, along with a novel, *A Nest of Ninnies,* cowritten with JOHN ASHBERY. His 1981 book, *The Morning of the Poem,* won a Pulitzer Prize.

In his poem "A Few Days" (1985), Schuyler considers an Ashbery "poem written in two / columns supposed to / be read simultaneously" and comments, "John is devoted to the impossible." Schuyler, by contrast, is devoted to the real: "All things are real / no one a symbol," as he writes in "Letter to a Friend" (1972). DAVID LEHMAN remarks of Schuyler that he is "committed to a vision of things as they are rather than as they might be in some idealized or reconfigured state" (246). Reality, for Schuyler, is its own defense.

Ashbery said of Schuyler that he is "a poet who knows the names for things, and whose knowing proves something" (12). Schuyler's knowing of the names for things, and his insistence upon basing his poetry on such candid naming, spurred him to be truthful about his homosexuality in poetry long before it was the standard to be so. For later gay writers Schuyler's poetics of truthfulness and naturalness provided a way out of the closet of elegant W. H. AUDEN-esque generalizations (in which the beloved is referred to and addressed as an ungendered "you") and away from the hyperbolic confessionalism of ALLEN GINSBERG and his followers (see BEAT POETRY and CONFESSIONAL POETRY).

For Schuyler, homosexuality is yet another of nature's odd blooms. To live is to be natural, and to be natural is to live. Life itself is a miracle, which the poet celebrates in one of his greatest poems, "Hymn to Life" (1974): "The days slide by and we feel we must / Stamp an impression on them. It is quite other. They stamp us."

BIBLIOGRAPHY

Ashbery, John. "Introduction to a Reading Given by James Schuyler." *Denver Quarterly.* (spring 1990): 10–12.

Corbett, William. "Poet of the Present." *Denver Quarterly.* (spring 1990): 49–52.

Lehman, David. *The Last Avant-Garde: The Making of the New York School of Poets.* New York: Doubleday, 1998.

Don Adams

SCHWARTZ, DELMORE (1913–1966) After the publication of his first book, *In Dreams Begin Responsibilities* (1938), Delmore Schwartz became one of the best-known and most highly respected poets of his day. He is often called a poet of "the middle generation"—that is, as Bruce Bawer explains, a group of American poets born between 1913 and 1917 and sharing similar biographical characteristics and literary careers (3–4). Schwartz is usually thought of in connection with his contemporaries RANDAL JARRELL, JOHN BERRYMAN, and ROBERT LOWELL. As poet, editor (of *Partisan Review*), essayist (*The Ego Is Always at the Wheel: Bagatelles* [1986]), playwright (*Shenandoah* [1941]), and literary critic (*Selected Essays* [1970]), Schwartz interacted with nearly every modern American poet from the late 1930s through the 1960s, most notably with ALLEN TATE, KARL SHAPIRO, and HOWARD MOSS. Schwartz was strongly influenced in his early poetry by the MODERNISM of T. S. ELIOT and by the IMAGIST SCHOOL of EZRA POUND, typified for Schwartz in the work of WILLIAM CARLOS WILLIAMS. Schwartz developed his own unique voice—that of an existentialist dealing with the Jewish diaspora—and influenced the direction of contemporary poetry in his examination of the isolated individual consciousness. Schwartz's work is read less in the years since he was writing, and yet his presence has been memorialized in Saul Bellow's fictionalized rendering of Schwartz in *Humboldt's Gift* as well as in a highly acclaimed biography by James Atlas.

Schwartz was born in Brooklyn, New York. After briefly attending the University of Wisconsin, Schwartz received a B.A. in philosophy from New York University in 1935. He undertook graduate studies at Harvard University but left in 1937 without completing his degree. The publication of *In Dreams Begin Responsibilities* led to his appointment as poetry editor of *Partisan Review* in 1939 and to a Guggenheim Fellowship in 1940. In 1955 he would serve as poetry editor for the *New Republic.* He taught at Harvard and several other universities. Following the 1959 publication of *Summer Knowledge: New and Selected Poems, 1939–1958,* Schwartz was awarded the Bollingen Prize for poetry. Both the professional security of academic tenure and the personal happiness of permanent relationships proved elusive for Schwartz. In "The Kingdom of Poetry" (1959), he writes, "poetry is like light, and it is light." In his unabashed love of the transforming power of language—"For Poetry magnifies and heightens reality"—his life as an American poet was devoted to the remorseless pursuit of vision.

Schwartz identified his Eastern European heritage as central to his poetry. He lived in "The shadow of Israel and the shadow of Europe," as he wrote in *Shenandoah.* In "The Ballad of the Children of the Czar" (1938), Schwartz drew upon that heritage, making connections between his own childhood and that of Nicholas II's children. Schwartz's grandfather had served in the czar's army, but Schwartz does not rely upon biographical detail alone to integrate his life into history. The setting is 1916, the eve of the Russian Revolution. The children of Nicholas II play with a bouncing ball in their father's garden while Schwartz sits, "aged two, irrational," in his father's house in Brooklyn. In true imagist fashion (as Atlas observes [134]), the moon that hovers over the czar's children, their bounding ball, and the buttered potato that the two-year-old Delmore eats are united. In the intersection of the individual and history, Schwartz finds tragedy: "the innocent are overtaken, / They are not innocent." All in the poem labor under the inescapable burden of history.

If history brings burdens, philosophy offers little consolation. A student of Alfred North Whitehead at Harvard, Schwartz brought a philosopher's metaphor to bear in one of his most anthologized poems, "In the Naked Bed in Plato's Cave" (1938). The setting is early morning, one in which a car's headlights, not fire (as Plato had depicted in his imagined cavern), illuminate the wall. The sounds of trucks and milkmen and horses' hooves fill the air as morning melts the scene. But if "History is unforgiven" in creating this perpetual scene, there is beauty here too, an elegance in the rendering of a scene in which shadow yields to light and morning distinguishes the features of the room—The light "kindled the looking glass, / Distinguished the dresser and the white wall." The poem, as Bruce Bawer has written, "is the produce of a mind which believed that it can achieve something important by setting one's heart's anguish into the constraining contexts of history, religion, philosophy, and the literary tradition" (121–122). In a poem that utilizes Platonic metaphor, quotes the prophet Ezekiel, and pays homage to Eliot's *The WASTE LAND,* Schwartz has created an enduring image of 1930s America, reminiscent of the paintings of Edward Hopper.

The visual techniques of painting, indeed, influenced Schwartz throughout his career, and this influence is most evident in "Seurat's Sunday Afternoon along the Seine" (1959). In 1945 Schwartz attended a lecture by art historian Meyer Schapiro on the 19th-century French postimpressionist Georges Seurat. Schwartz noted Seurat's technique of pointillism (the use of tiny, brush-worked dots to create patterns) in his painting *La Grande Jatte.* In the technique there are, he noted in his journal, "violations of perspective to gain collective experience" (qtd. in Pollet 268). Schwartz is similarly concerned in his poem with composition, striving, as he also wrote in his notes on the Schapiro lecture, "to make something which is more than itself; which is inexhaustible; which turns into its contrary" (qtd. in Pollet 269). Describing the painting, where "Everyone holds his heart within his hands," Schwartz wonders if "immortality" is possible through art, a task that requires "the labors of Hercules, Sisyphus, Flaubert, Roebling"—the efforts of myth, literature, and engineering. Can we look at this painting and proclaim with Flaubert: *"Ils sont dans le vrai!"* ("Theirs is the right way?") For Schwartz, permanency through art may be possible, but there is no consolation for him: The figures may stretch out their hands, but they are too far away. For the individual poet, a dark vision prevailed. While his own redemption proved impossible, Schwartz rendered eternal verities of beauty and isolation in a unique American vision.

BIBLIOGRAPHY

Atlas, James. *Delmore Schwartz: The Life of An American Poet.* New York: Farrar, Straus & Giroux, 1977.

Bawer, Bruce. *The Middle Generation: The Lives and Poetry of Delmore Schwartz, Randall Jarrell, John Berryman, and Robert Lowell.* Hamden, Conn.: Archon, 1986.

Pollet, Elizabeth, ed. *Portrait of Delmore: Journals and Notes of Delmore Schwartz, 1939–1959.* New York: Farrar, 1986.

———. *Shenandoah.* New York: New Directions, 1941.

Schwartz, Delmore. *The Ego Is Always at the Wheel: Bagatelles,* edited by Robert Phillips. New York: New Directions, 1986.

Norbert Elliot

SCHWERNER, ARMAND (1927–1999) Armand Schwerner is best remembered for his translations and his performances, as typified in his book-length serial poem *The TABLETS* (1999) (see LONG AND SERIAL POETRY). As an avid translator, Schwerner was concerned with the relationship between the spoken and written word and how the transition from one to the other affected the meanings of language (see POETRY AND TRANSLATION). His nonlinear style recreates the fragmented and uncertain nature of experience. Throughout his life Schwerner studied Buddhism, first as a student, and later as a lay priest. This fascination with spirituality, coupled with the difficulties of language, locates Schwerner in a tradition that includes such poets as GEORGE OPPEN, JEROME ROTHENBERG, MICHAEL HELLER, and DAVID ANTIN.

Schwerner was born in Antwerp, left Belgium for France, and, with the Nazi invasion of Europe imminent, finally immigrated to the United States in 1936. He studied French literature at Cornell and Columbia Universities and pursued graduate studies at Columbia in anthropology and literature. He taught at several colleges and universities, including the College of Staten Island, the City University of New York. He received several awards, most notably three grants from the National Endowment for the Arts (1973, 1979, and 1987) and an award for contributions to American literature from the Fund for Poetry (1991). Despite these honors and the production of more than 20 volumes of translations and original poetry, his work rarely received wide critical attention. Much of this neglect owes to the performative nature of his work, and indeed, Schwerner's allegiance to the spoken word is plainly evident in his verse (see POETRY IN PERFORMANCE), since it favors the whimsical nature of speech over the static materiality of written language, as in this excerpt from "the work" (1977): "it's no good it's closed the door is closed the energy / wave's short-circuited impossible not to sing."

That language is essentially transient allows for its volatile behavior, and the meanings given to words are equally unstable. Ultimately the poet owns neither the words nor their meanings. In "sounds of the river Naranjana" (1983), Schwerner writes, "what I hear keeps changing, the flute becomes a garbage truck." The poem goes on to list many common sounds that, when heard at length, come to resemble something else. Therefore a flute over the stereo may, for a fleeting moment, remind one of a sound made by a garbage truck. Likewise words can be used in ways that are incompatible with their traditional meanings, for, as Schwerner asks in *The Tablets,* "What sorts of things store concepts?"

For Schwerner, those concepts often reside in unexpected places. Where one looks for substance, one often finds emptiness—it is amidst this terrain that Schwerner creates his poems. Like the Scholar/Translator, the fictive interpreter of *The Tablets,* Schwerner both creates and is created by the poem he renders, with each undergoing changes as the poem progresses. As in Buddhism, a poem is composed of a series of perceptions, many of which are illusory. Reality is nothing more than an amalgamation of those contingencies we accept as truths, and we accept them, because, in some way, our lives require us to do so. Says Schwerner in Tablet XIX (1976): "magic word floats out of my need for it," and as need creates language, so too is truth created by circumstances. And a truth does not remain a truth for long.

This constant change and shifting creates a palpable anxiety in Schwerner's work. On one hand, Schwerner recognizes values (whether poetic or ethical) as something ever shifting, and his poetry attempts to overturn whatever truths it posits. His poem "blood" (1999) says that writers "'begin in joy and gladness and descend therefrom / into despondency and madness.' or or or or or or." The stereotype of the poet as a brooding and volatile person, who cannot create except in the grip of turbulent emotions, is dispelled by a single word: *or. Or* suggests an alternative, a choice. And where tradition would have us believe poets incapable of writing unless half-crazed by "despondency and madness," Schwerner makes the poet less heroic and, in the process, more human.

The act of becoming human—and taking risks to achieve that end—is a primary goal of Schwerner's poetry. In it, we see the travails of a man performing, as Kathryn VanSpanckeren says, "an unembarrassed surgical examination of living tissues of the mind" (16). This internal investigation is turned outward, as the reader is expected to accompany Schwerner, sharing in his introspection, often risking (mis)understanding along with the author, in a work, which, as Schwerner relates, "allow[s] the reader to fall into the holes again and again" (qtd in VanSpanckeren 31).

In an essay on *The Tablets,* Hank Lazer points out that "particularly if one can resist the lure of using the poem as a site to display one's (personal) craft, mastery, or grace, the poem may become a treasured site for discovery" (150). During his life, Schwerner was many things: a student of Buddhism, a trained musician, a performer, a translator and a poet. These activities exhibit the inquisitiveness present in all of Schwerner's pursuits. By these methods Schwerner learns the patience of effort—this process is growth—and, as Willard Gingerich points out, "the process is never complete, has no *telos* (Gk. *end*)" (20). The end product is a body of work that resists generalizations. Schwerner has very little to say that is easily said. As the poet himself pointed out in *The Tablets*, "The greatest daring is in resisting what comes easily," and his work was neither written nor can it be read without a considerable degree of sacrifice.

BIBLIOGRAPHY
Foster, Edward, ed. *Talisman* 19 (1998). [Armand Schwerner Special Issue.]
Gingerich, Willard. "Sacred Forgeries and Translation of Nothing in *The Tablets* of Armand Schwerner." *Talisman* 21/22 (2001): 18–26.
Lazer, Hank. "Sacred Forgeries and the Grounds of Poetic Archeology: Armand Schwerner's *The Tablets*." *Chicago Review* 46, no. 6 (2000): 142–154.
Schwerner, Armand. "Armand Schwerner: An Interview by Willard Gingerich." *American Poetry Review* 24, no. 5 (1995): 27–32.
VanSpanckeren, Kathryn. "Moonrise in Ancient Sumer: Armand Schwerner's *The Tablets*." *American Poetry Review* 22, no. 4 (1993): 15–19.

Chris Pusateri

"THE SEARCH PARTY" WILLIAM MATTHEWS (1970) "(T)he issue was a human life," asserts WILLIAM MATTHEWS in "The Search Party," a poem that wrestles with its own efforts to transform the search for a missing child into a commentary on the tricky relationship between art and reality. For Matthews, meaningful art has at its core a resistance to the artistic appropriation of experience, although the impulse to make life meaningful by transforming it into art is equally central to his thinking. Exhibiting the conversational voice, the humane intelligence, and the compelling sense of credible narrative that mark Matthews's best work, "The Search Party" confronts the reader with the fact that "you know just where we are, / deep in symbolic woods," but also warns against forgetting the event that inspired the poem.

The poem opens in medias res with the speaker (ostensibly Matthews himself) now questioning his motives as he participates in the search for a lost child. "[W]hat did I fear?" he asks. "I feared I'd find something." Parallel to this search for a child, which leads the speaker deeper into the woods, is another search, "that of art," which attempts to find meaning in "someone else's suffering." Here Matthews seems ready to offer a metanarrative, a story that is not so much about the reality it depicts, but about the art of writing that reality. Yet the poem's dramatic and moral force comes from Matthews's refusal to avoid confronting the actual crisis that triggered the poem: "There was a real lost child," he writes, "I don't want to swaddle it / in metaphor." In a series of apostrophes, Matthews challenges the reader for treating this or any event depicted in art as mere fiction. But rather than alienating the reader, Matthews argues that a more humane impulse lies beneath the desire for art: "Come off it, / you're the one who thought it wouldn't / matter what we found." For Matthews, the reader turns to poetry because, in the world it describes, the search can end as the reader desires—happily. When he reveals that the child was found, still alive, Matthews chides the reader to "Admit you're glad."

Ironically, for as much as Matthews attends to the reality from which literature is drawn, "The Search Party" is still very much about the act of reading and the experience of art. If children tend to read fiction and poetry with all the belief and emotional investment that one usually devotes to the truth, then the discovery of the child at the poem's close is in fact a recovery of the reader's "innocent" experience of art. By repeatedly stating that the story of the lost child indeed happened, Matthews invites the reader to believe in literature again. This invitation is not chicanery; in the wake of such philosophical movements as deconstruction, postmodern readers have grown distrustful of the claims that language and literature have definite meaning. For Matthews, such distrust threatens the capacity for hope and for happiness, not only in literature, but in life itself. Literature enhances life, and a vital sense of life's wholeness gives meaning to literature; as Matthews claims, "I'm in these poems / because I'm in my life."

BIBLIOGRAPHY
Hoey, Allan. "Love and Work." *Shenandoah: The Washington & Lee University Review* 48, no. 3 (1998): 110–121.

Mehta, Diane. "'Passionate and Structured Ignorance': The Poetry of Bill Matthews." *Gettysburg Review* 13, no. 2 (2000): 219–232.

Temple Cone

SEIDMAN, HUGH (1940–) Hugh Seidman is an important heir to LOUIS ZUKOFSKY and the OBJECTIVISTS on one side, and yet his work is also influenced by the Peruvian poet César Vallejo. Seidman joins a direct, unsentimental poetic style with a strong historical sense and social conscience. In both form and content, he plays with perspective, moving from the intensely personal to the universal and back again in an effort to document both subjective experience and the abstract theory, timeless moment, or wider historical context to which it is ironically or tragically juxtaposed. "Scientist of poetry," he writes, "they're burning Newark." ("The Last American Dream" [1970]).

Seidman was born in Brooklyn, New York. In 1969 he won the Yale Series of Younger Poets Award. Since then his poetry has won numerous awards, and his collection, *Selected Poems, 1965–1995,* was chosen as one of "25 Favorite Books of 1995" by the *Village Voice.*

Seidman's primary terrain is that of difficult or conflicted emotion—the personal triumph marred by echoes of global disaster, the joyous new love undercut by memories of loss. In his early work he approaches these subjects through precise, even scientific, dissection of the moment and its feelings. Academically trained in mathematics and physics, he often uses the vocabulary of these disciplines to redefine objects and how they are seen. A heart becomes "the long sought / perpetual engine, entropy zero, here" ("Blood Lord" [1974]). What we sense is the desire of the poet (and humanity) to name and control experience through the discipline of language, poetry, or science, while remaining aware of the impossibility or danger of doing so. In his middle work, he adds an archetypal dimension by making connections to Egyptian, Greek, and other mythologies: "Let the light be the gilt sistrum / Let a waitress be Egypt's sixty centuries" ("Cult of Isis" [1982]). More recently, he has continued to explore these themes but has shifted the balance in his poems toward the personal. One of the strongest series of poems in his work is that exploring his complicated relationship with his parents as they lived, fell ill, and died: "Forgive me if I lift my hand to affirm. / Or is it to question?" ("Did I Say Father?" [1995]), he writes to his father. "But who shall speak for her? / Who shall say her name?" ("The Senile" [1992]), he asks of a mother who remembers nothing due to Alzheimer's.

At his best Seidman combines poetic virtuosity with an eye that creates experiences an almost dizzying change in perspectives, as when a toy bear near a pair of lovers becomes an icon of a benevolent Ursa Major ("Mr. Bear" [1992]). What results is a complex voice that is compassionate, powerful, intelligent, and exacting.

BIBLIOGRAPHY

Joseph, Lawrence. "Pure Song." *American Book Review* (December 1993): 27.
Tillinghast, Richard. "Pleasure and Dazzlement." *New York Times Book Review,* May 1, 1983, 15, 23.
Zavatsky, Bill. "Breaking In and Out of Self." *New York Times Book Review,* December 26, 1971, 6, 15.

Lily Phillips

"SELF-PORTRAIT IN A CONVEX MIRROR" JOHN ASHBERY (1975) *Self-Portrait in a Convex Mirror,* the volume in which the poem by the same name first appeared, won the National Book Award, the Pulitzer Prize, and the National Book Critics Circle Award. The critical and commercial success of the book made it a turning point in JOHN ASHBERY's career. Ashbery's work, in general, is linked with the NEW YORK SCHOOL, a group of poets involved with art in New York in the 1950s and 1960s.

A long free verse poem of six unequal stanzas, "Self-Portrait in a Convex Mirror" is a meditation on the 1524 painting by the Italian Francesco Mazzola (known as Il Parmigianino). The poem's title refers not only to Parmigianino's painting but also to the poem itself, a "convex," or distorted picture of painter and poet. Less elusive than the voice of many of Ashbery's other poems, the speaker of this poem seems to be Ashbery himself. He thinks out loud (or on the page) about the painting; the speaker permits elements from his own biography (and Ashbery's) to appear.

At the beginning of the poem, Ashbery quotes from Giorgio Vasari's *Lives of the Most Eminent Painters, Sculptors and Architects* (1550) to explain that Parmigianino used a half ball of wood rather than a board or canvas as the surface for his painting. The artist then skillfully painted his own youthful self-portrait on the ball so as to represent himself gazing into a convex mirror, a little bit like a funhouse mirror. The result both is and is not an accurate representation of the face, the first of several paradoxes identified in the poem. The unusual painting medium contributes to the oddity of the portrait, creating a surface that appears to have depth, representing a "soul that is not a soul," and seeming to offer an "affirmation that doesn't affirm anything."

"Self-Portrait in a Convex Mirror" focuses on the relationship between time and identity. Art tries to capture the elusive present, but it captures only an image, not the reality. Attempting to stop time, paintings distort fluent reality. Parmigianino's deliberate distortion of his own image gives Ashbery the occasion for a poetic self-portrait, but words possibly represent the fluency of time (and all reality that exists in time) differently and perhaps better than a static visual image. The difference between the visual immediacy of the painting and the flow of the poem enables Ashbery to describe, imitate, and challenge the painting at the same time.

Parmigianino's self-portrait is devoted to portraying the central figure, the painter himself. It therefore seems a pure representation of an identity and a moment. Compared with the painting, the poem seems cluttered by extraneous details and associations. Ashbery chooses not to describe his own face but to try to render the processes of his mind, including thinking, feeling, and sensuous apprehension. Although it takes more time to read Ashbery's poem than to glance at the painting, it could have taken the poet less time to write it than it took Parmigianino to make the painting. The poem therefore represents a more spontaneous image than the painting, though neither is the reality of identity.

In spite of the apparent spontaneity of the poem, it never wanders far from the painting as its subject. In the 1960s and 1970s, Ashbery wrote art criticism for *Art News.* "Self-Portrait in a Convex Mirror" gave Ashbery an opportunity to integrate his poetic skills with his interest in graphic art. The poem thus refers to Vasari and to Sydney Freedberg, an art critic who wrote during Ashbery's lifetime. Although Ashbery is vague about the voices of quotations in many other poems, here he is careful to identify the sources of quotations he uses, as he would be if he were writing prose art criticism.

Parmigianino's painting is an exterior self-portrait and is closed in the sense that it is physically limited by the block of wood on which it is painted. By contrast, Ashbery's poem as an interior portrait is more open. Insofar as it represents the workings of the poet's mind, it could go on as long as his mind does. The figurative accuracy of Parmigianino's self-portrait allows us, hundreds of years later, to think we know exactly what he looked like during the time when he painted the picture. The inner state of the figure in the painting is, however, much harder to understand. The poet can only speculate about the painter's thoughts and feelings as he painted himself. "Reading" the painting creates a poetic self-portrait of which the opposite is true: From the poem, we know what the speaker is thinking and feeling but not what he looks like.

Speculate is an important word because, as Ashbery explains, *speculate* derives from the Latin word for a mirror, *speculum.* The poem is thus a mirror facing a mirror. A mirror offers a reverse image, and in one sense that is what Ashbery's poem offers to the painting. In another sense, a mirror facing a mirror would correct the reversal and actually render a more accurate image by recognizing ambiguities and distortions. For example, the hand the painter holds forth in the painting might be either a shield (a protection) or a greeting (an advertisement).

Parmigianino's painting is an odd experiment, giving Ashbery the occasion for an inclusive meditation on identity. But the painting also frustrates the poet's attempt to penetrate it. The painting is always there to be examined, but, paradoxically, it exists only when living consciousness engages it in "its room, our moments of attention." "Self-Portrait in a Convex Mirror" tries to bridge "the distance between us," the poet and the painter, vision and interpretation, artwork and audience, and, finally, Ashbery and the reader.

BIBLIOGRAPHY

Bloom, Harold, ed. *John Ashbery: Modern Critical Views.* New York: Chelsea House, 1985.

Schultz, Susan M, ed. *The Tribe of John: Ashbery and Contemporary Poetry*. Tuscaloosa: University of Alabama Press, 1995.

Shoptaw, John. *On the Outside Looking Out*. Cambridge, Mass.: Harvard University Press, 1994.

Thomas Lisk

"SEPTEMBER 1, 1939" W. H. AUDEN (1939)

"September 1, 1939," written as Germany invaded Poland, signaled the end of the 1930s era of political activism, at least for W. H. AUDEN, one of the most important political poets of the 1930s. The poem grew to have a significant place in the discussion of what makes a final, canonical version of a poem, as Auden excised one stanza from his *Collected Poems* (1945) and then later repudiated the entire poem. As World War II began, Auden saw, as he wrote in the poem, the "clever hopes" of a "low dishonest decade" dashed, dying as the threat of an evil nurtured by that decade—and, by extension, Auden and his fellow leftists. The poem was also his farewell to England and to himself as an English poet. Ensconced in a "dive . . . on 52nd Street" in New York City, Auden saw Europe from a distance and concluded that while "accurate scholarship" can purport to explain war, the real explanation is that "those to whom evil is done / do evil in return."

The poem as it was published in the *New Republic* in October 1939 and in his 1940 collection *Another Time* rejected old political answers and looked toward humanism in its most famous line, "We must love one another or die." Auden was later to reject the line, then eliminate the stanza in which it appears from his *Collected Poems*. He ultimately categorized the entire poem as dishonest— "I shouldn't have written it," he told Daniel Halpern, "it's a forgery" (137). He had earlier reached the conclusion, justifying the excision of the stanza, that "we must die anyway" (Foreword viii). Joseph Beach questions Auden's judgment here, pointing out that nothing in the stanza is inconsistent with the poet's later philosophy: "The love for another that we must have or die is directly opposed, in the manner of all his Christian writing, to the self-regarding Freudian Eros. . . . [T]here is no better statement of Auden's [subsequent] political and psychological position" (50). The major anthologists of the day, Oscar Williams and Louis Untermeyer, retained the stanza. Today almost every reprinting of the poem includes the stanza.

"September 1, 1939" gained new life after the September 11, 2001, terrorist attacks, as it became widely e-mailed, not just by devotees of poetry. Eric McHenry hails its "prescien[ce]. . . . Zealotry and violence are cyclical—'The habit-forming pain, / Mismanagement and grief: / We must suffer them all again.'"

BIBLIOGRAPHY

Auden, W. H. Foreword to *W. H. Auden: A Bibliography—The Early Years through 1955,* by B. C. Bloomfield. Charlottesville: University of Virginia Press, 1964, pp. vii–ix.

———. Interview with W. H. Auden, by Daniel Halpern. *Antaeus* 5 (spring 1972): 137.

Beach, Joseph Warren. *The Making of the Auden Canon*. Minneapolis: University of Minnesota Press, 1957.

McHenry, Eric. "Auden on Bin Laden," SLATE Available online. URL: http://slate.msn.com/id/115900/. Downloaded March 2007.

Tad Richards

"SESTINA" ELIZABETH BISHOP (1965)

Though born in Worcester, Massachusetts, ELIZABETH BISHOP left at the age of five to live with her maternal grandparents in Great Village, Nova Scotia, after her mother was committed to a mental institution. Bishop never saw her mother again, a loss compounded by the death of Bishop's father when she was just an infant. Though she developed close ties to the Nova Scotia landscape and to her grandparents in the short time she was there (her paternal grandparents returned her to Massachusetts two years later), her early childhood experiences haunted her life and her art. Bishop's great poem "Sestina" recounts a moment from this brief period in Nova Scotia, distilling the experience of trauma and dislocation through a series of richly described and symbolically suggestive images. The poem offers a technically perfect and emotionally gripping instance of how a poet might use form in general, and the sestina in particular, as a way of providing (to quote ROBERT FROST) "a momentary stay against confusion."

"Sestina" depicts a simple domestic scene. Outside the house, it is raining; inside the kitchen, a girl is drawing a house with crayons while her grandmother reads an almanac and makes tea. But this simple scene conceals important, unnamed tragedies, including the loss of daughter/mother (the absence of Bishop's mother creates a generational gap) and the loss of home. Bishop writes that the grandmother is "laughing and talking to hide her tears," while the young girl is drawing "a rigid house/ and a winding pathway." The present losses wind into others, for as she finishes the house, "the child / puts in a man with buttons like tears," suggesting Bishop's own dead father.

Bishop uses the sestina form to articulate the inescapable sense of loss felt by both the girl and her grandmother. The sestina is a medieval French lyric form composed of six sestets, whose end words (or *teleutons*) are repeated in a 6-1-5-2-4-3 pattern based on the line numbers of the preceding stanza, followed by a final tercet called the *envoy,* which places a different teleuton in the middle and at the end of each line. (Thus, the first stanza's teleutons, in order, are *house, grandmother, child, Stove, almanac, tears;* the second stanza's are *tears, house, almanac, grandmother, stove, child;* the third stanza's are *child, tears, stove, house, grandmother, almanac,* etc.) As Bonnie Costello notes, "Its emphasis on nouns heightens the iconicity of the poem and intensifies the image by repetition so that it appears obsessive" (199). In addition, Costello finds the poem suggests "the primer language of the child" (199), a reminder of how Bishop's persistent sense of loss dated back to an early age. For James Cummins, Bishop's stanzas "'mirror' each other in the sestina, something the medievals were obsessed with. This 'mirroring' is essential to the progression of a sestina; and in this case, one way of seeing it work is to look closely at the teleutons, especially 'tears'" (152). Through a careful choice of teleutons, five of which are concrete with the sixth having both concrete and abstract associations ("tears"), Bishop emphasizes the tangibility of loss and grief for both of these people, which must have been devastating, considering the biographical circumstances of the poem.

Yet the poem invites alternatives to this strictly biographical reading. Ryan Lankford argues that if we read both the girl and the grandmother as figures for the adult Bishop, then "Sestina" becomes "a poem about writing itself—about the poet's survey of her past and the absence of answers there" (57). Anne Colwell makes a similar point when she notes that the winding pathway the girl draws figures the twists and turns of the sestina form itself, each creation seeking "a structure in which to embody the otherwise incomprehensible experience" (155). Colwell suggests that all efforts at containing and thereby resolving loss, whether in the form of the sestina, the drawing, or the knowledge of the grandmother's almanac, are destined to fail, yet "Because the poem tries so hard to evade the sense of loss, we will feel it acutely and identify its humanity" (156). By the end of the poem, Bishop achieves a paradoxical form of knowledge, both stoic and imaginative, that can marvel at the profundity of existence and of human love without ever presuming to understand them: "The grandmother sings to the marvellous stove / and the child draws another inscrutable house."

BIBLIOGRAPHY

Costello, Bonnie. *Questions of Mastery.* Cambridge, Mass: Harvard University Press, 1993.

Colwell, Anne. *Inscrutable Houses: Metaphors of the Body in the Poems of Elizabeth Bishop.* Tuscaloosa: The University of Alabama Press, 1997.

Cummins, James. "Calliope Music: Notes on the Sestina." *The Antioch Review* 55, no. 2 (1997): 148–159.

Lankford, Ryan. "Bishop's 'Sestina.'" *The Explicator* 52, no. 1 (1993): 57–59.

Temple Cone

SETH, VIKRAM (1952–) In Vikram Seth's work the elegant formalism typical of Victorian poetry is combined with a contemporary concern for postcolonialism, the only constant being Seth's willingness to experiment with form. From meticulously rhymed sonnets set in modern-day San Francisco to free verse translations of ancient Chinese poets (see PROSODY AND FREE VERSE), Seth has proved elusive and inventive in his approach to poetry. By and large, he is allied with NEW FORMALISM, in the tradition of a poet such as Robert Graves, though his diverse creative output—novels, memoirs, children's books—makes him difficult to classify.

Born in Calcutta, India, Seth graduated from Oxford University (B.A., 1975), then went on to study economics at Stanford, during which time he was also a Stegner fellow in Creative Writing (1977–78). Much of his first book of poems, *Mappings* (1980), comes from this period and includes translations of Chinese, German, and Hindi poets, plus a sense of how Seth felt as a cultural mongrel. The representative poem "Diwali" (1979) is his call to exile, to those "Who are not home at home / And are abroad abroad." After finishing his first book, Seth moved to China to study classical Chinese poetry at Nanjing University. He then hitchhiked home to New Delhi via Tibet, a trip chronicled in the memoir *From Heaven Lake* (1983). Travel also helped gestate Seth's next collection of poems, *The Humble Administrator's Garden* (1985), which are cleverly organized around plants and places. Seth's subsequent effort, *Golden Gate* (1986), confounded genre, as it was billed as a novel, but it is actually an epic poem in the mold of the romantic Lord Byron: a series of 690 rhyming tetrameter sonnets that spins a satirical romance between two San Francisco "yuppies." Seth's next book of poems, *All You Who Sleep Tonight* (1990), delves into darker material, such as the experience of a Nazi concentration camp commandant and a doctor in Hiroshima the day the bomb dropped (see LONG AND SERIAL POETRY). Seth has received a number of awards and honors including, in 2001, the Commander of the Order of the British Empire.

Much of Seth's poetry possesses a graceful, if antiquated craftsmanship. *Golden Gate* is based on Alexander Pushkin's *Eugene Onegin* (1833). The critic Ruth Morse writes, "allusion is at the heart of Seth's style, if not his voice" (140). The poem "Cant" (1990) engages this notion, which begins: "In Cant's resilient, venerable lies / There's something for the artists to take heart." Seth's themes, handled with a formalist's eye and a rhetorician's gloves, include travel, family, heritage, and music. From the sonnets in *Mappings* to the translations of Mirza Ghalib's *ghazals* in *A Suitable Boy* (1994), Seth shows considerable range.

BIBLIOGRAPHY

Currie, Jay, and Michèle Denis. "Hearing a Different Music," January Magazine. Available online. URL: www.januarymagazine.com/profiles/vseth.html. Downloaded March 2007.

Morse, Ruth. "Rooted Cosmopolite: Vikram Seth and 'The Scars of *Middlemarch*'" *Etudes Britanniques Contemporaines* 5 (1994): 139–157.

Ravi Shankar

SEXTON, ANNE (1928–1974) Anne Sexton helped to expand the subject repertoire of CONFESSIONAL POETRY to include issues and experiences specific to women: the fertility cycle, birth, child rearing, objectification, and sexual violence. She is an important figure in the intersection of confessional poetry and feminist poetry (see FEMALE VOICE, FEMALE LANGUAGE). Sexton is associated with ROBERT LOWELL, with whom she studied, and with her friends SYLVIA PLATH and George Starbuck, both of whom influenced her work. W. D. SNODGRASS and MAXINE KUMIN were early mentors and close friends. Sexton's influence can be seen in the work of Plath, as well as SHARON OLDS, ADRIENNE RICH, and other poets interested in women's issues.

Anne Harvey was born in Newton, Massachusetts, and attended boarding and finishing schools in the Boston area. Indications of serious emotional problems began appearing early in adolescence, but her parents resisted placing her in treatment. It was only after a series of affairs threatened her marriage to Alfred Muller Sexton II, with whom she eloped in 1948, that Sexton turned to psychotherapy. Her emotional problems worsened—she was hospitalized with postpartum depression after the birth of her first child, Linda, in 1953, and struggled with breakdowns and suicidal urges thereafter. Treatment, though only intermittently successful in relieving Sexton's depression, did have the benefit of turning Sexton to poetry. In 1957 she followed her doctor's suggestion to write as a form of therapy. A year later she enrolled in Lowell's seminar at Boston University, where she met Plath and Starbuck. Houghton Mifflin accepted her first book, *To Bedlam and Part Way Back* in 1960. In the mid-1960s Sexton became a poet celebrity, accumulating literary awards and academic positions—*Live or Die* (1967) was awarded the Pulitzer Prize—and drawing media attention as a tormented, and attractive, artist. The lines between therapy, art, and personal life were constantly blurred in her work, as they were in her life. Affairs with her teachers, her therapist, and her friends made their way into her poetry, and the public sensation of her poetry stimulated the daring and flamboyance of her life. In what has become a cliché of American celebrity culture, she became more isolated and vulnerable as she became more famous. Divorce, alcoholism, and a gradual loss of self-confidence as a poet left Sexton with few resources to continue her struggle with mental illness. She died by carbon monoxide asphyxiation. In professional terms her career, though fairly short, had been remarkably distinguished. Among her many other honors, she was elected a fellow of the Royal Society of Literature in 1965.

Sexton's verse is characterized by childlike rhyme schemes to suggest regressive states, resourceful use of simile and metaphor, and a reliance on lists, anaphora (the repetition of words or phrases at the beginning of lines), and parallel constructions. Her early poetry is formally constrained; her later work typically is in free verse (see PROSODY AND FREE VERSE). The first stanza of the much-anthologized "You, Doctor Martin" (1960) shows her facility with compressed, associative metaphor and her indebtedness to other poets, in this case, T. S. ELIOT and Lowell: "You, Doctor Martin, walk / from breakfast to madness," she writes, the image fusing the impatient swiftness of his march through the underground tunnel of the hospital with the manic swiftness of her own thought processes. Her vision of the hospital as an underworld of living dead patients "thrusting against / cure" pays homage to Eliot's *The WASTE LAND* while adroitly stepping over the line of good taste to a mad vulgarity.

Lowell, however, is the more important influence on her writing; it would not be entirely unfair to characterize Sexton as his disciple. The narrative line in *To Bedlam and Part Way Back* is clearly indebted to his depictions of hospitalization and recovery in *Life Studies* (1959), as it is to his discursive, colloquial line. Even the geography of her early work is derivative; railing at her "bachelor therapist / who sat on Boston's Marlborough Street" ("Flee on Your Donkey" [1966]), she poaches on her teacher's Beacon Hill terrain. In some respects, however, her work differs importantly from that of Lowell. Her scathing humor and preference for shock over personal examination distinguish her work from the start. One can indulge in the wicked pleasure of her sarcastic characterization of her lover's wife—"She is the sum of yourself and your dream / Climb her like a monument step after step" ("For My Lover, Returning to His Wife" [1967])—or one can withdraw from it, but the brilliance remains. Hers is the brash, wounded voice at the back of the confessional congregation, drawing attention to herself, her pain, and not, as Lowell did so famously, to political and social anguish concentrated in the personal. As critic David Perkins has noted, "Sexton's aim as a poet was to uncover painful, repressed emotions" (595), much in the mode of psychotherapy. This constant focus on the self had its strengths and its drawbacks. Her willingness to explore such highly intimate subject matter as masturbation, incest, menstruation, and child abuse made her something of a pioneer in marking out new subject matter. As a rule, however, Sexton stops short of personal reconciliation or insight: "In this place everyone talks to his own mouth" ("Flee on Your Donkey"), she writes. She refers to a mental hospital, but her despair was more general, haunted by a lapsed Catholic's sense of lost redemption.

Of all the confessional poets, including the Catholic convert (later lapsed as well) Lowell, Sexton comes closest to practicing confession in its primary sense of a public baring of one's faults. She was "born / doing reference work in sin, and born / confessing it" ("With Mercy for the Greedy" [1962]), she writes, but in the absence of God or, just as important to her, a therapeutic authority she could fully believe and respect, her confessions became repetitive dead ends. Sexton was susceptible to criticism for self-indulgence and narcissism as a poet, but in this regard events were in her favor. Plath's suicide in 1963 and the publication soon after of her *Ariel* poems validated the subject matter of women's rage and self-destruction through the undeniable achievement of her expression. Sexton, a more glamorous public figure was left to explore this bleak terrain on her own. Her celebrity increased in the absence of her friend, as did feminist interest in the abject and self-destructive domestic lives of women.

Helen Vendler characterized Sexton's work as "cartoons, malicious and often off target" (301), yet praised the occasional inventiveness of her satire and phrasing.

It is generally agreed that Sexton's control of her materials was uneven, and her rhetorical and technical resources narrowly defined. In her sensibility and technical repertoire she may be closer to BEAT POETRY than to the rigorous intelligence of Plath, the poet with whom she is often associated. In any case, for the reading public, her celebrity as an attractive and publicly self-destructive artist has outweighed the negative assessments of her work, and she remains widely read and consistently anthologized. She was daring, humorous, and brutally honest. Her politically informed and highly personal awareness of the body has grown only more pertinent with the passage of time. Sexton's poetry, like the best popular fiction, reads with swiftness, invention, and sensuality. Hers is an adult and courageous body of work, all the more liberating for its flaws.

BIBLIOGRAPHY

McClatchy, J. D. *Anne Sexton: The Artist and Her Critics.* Bloomington: Indiana University Press, 1978.

Perkins, David. *A History of Modern Poetry: Modernism and After.* Cambridge, Mass.: Harvard University Press, 1987.

Vendler, Helen. "Anne Sexton." In *The Music of What Happens: Poems, Poets, Critics.* Cambridge, Mass.: Harvard University Press, 1988, pp. 300–309.

Christopher Moylan

SHAPIRO, DAVID (1947–) David Shapiro's imaginatively agile and erudite poems make him one of the most eloquent poets of the NEW YORK SCHOOL's second generation. Shapiro wrote the first dissertation on JOHN ASHBERY's work and edited, with RON PADGETT, *An Anthology of New York School Poets* (1970). His work develops the New York school's play between a poem's depth and surface and, like the work of Ashbery and Barbara GUEST, uses painting as a celebrated resource for rendering supple images and the shapes of perception. Shapiro's work as an art critic imaginatively dovetails with his poetry. Words and ideas achieve a surreal and fluid flexibility within the frame of his poems, and definitions slide easily into the unexpected. As Joanna Fuhrman explains, "To read a David Shapiro poem is to enter a space in which 'emotion' is as abstract as theory and an 'idea' is as visceral and tender as the best pop song" (1).

Shapiro was born in Newark, New Jersey; as a child he was immersed in the arts. He recalls, "One of the great influences of my life was my father constantly memorizing Virgil, Shakespeare, Milton, and he had me do the same, as soon as I could speak" (qtd. 1). Before he became a published poet, Shapiro was an accomplished violinist. Thomas Fink writes that his poems "abound" in "subtle, complex, often unpredictable tonal shifts" (1993, 13). At 18 he published his first book, *January: A Book of Poems* (1965). His collection *A Man Holding an Acoustic Panel* was nominated for a National Book Award in 1971. Among a number of other honors, Shapiro has also received the American Academy of Arts and Letters Morton Dauwen Zabel Award (1977).

As the title of his collection *After a Lost Original* (1994) suggests, Shapiro's poems investigate the possibilities for representation when a stable source of reality cannot be found. His work alludes to many artists "who have mischievously concocted ironies about the perils of referentiality" (Fink 1988, 29), though his voice retains sincerity even as his lines take surprising or disjunctive turns. Throughout his work Shapiro experiments with a wide range of styles and devices that are charged with his knowledge of aesthetics and literature.

One of many poems that reflects upon literature's imaginative terrain, "To an Idea" (1983) explores a poet's mind in the act of composition. He begins by articulating, then revising a desire to write out of the experience of possibility that an abstract nothingness represents: "I wanted to start *Ex Nihilo* / I mean a review of sorts." The poem transforms itself into an ode to poetry, which has "carried [him] like mail / From one house to another." Shapiro's work attests to art's potential for taking readers and writers into meaningful uncertainties.

BIBLIOGRAPHY

Fink, Thomas. *The Poetry of David Shapiro.* Madison, N.J.: Fairleigh Dickinson University Press, 1993.

———. "The Poetry of David Shapiro and Ann Lauterbach: After Ashbery." *American Poetry Review* 17 (January/February 1988): 27–30.

Shapiro, David. "Plurist Music: An Interview with David Shapiro," by Joanna Fuhrman, Rain Taxi Review of

Books. Available online. URL: www.raintaxi.com/online/Fall 2002/Shapiro.shtml. Downloaded March 2007.

Kimberly Lamm

SHAPIRO, HARVEY (1924–) The year 2003 marked Harvey Shapiro's 50th anniversary as a published poet. His extensive corpus demonstrates an affinity for an American OBJECTIVIST form, but personalizes it with spare constructions that are used to detail a balancing of everyday urban affairs with the traditions of religious orthodoxy. Shapiro's style is akin to those of WILLIAM CARLOS WILLIAMS, CHARLES REZNIKOFF, and DAVID IGNATOW, as conciseness, detachment, and neutrality are challenged by vivid imagery, which exposes sentiment deeper than the scene itself describes.

Born in Chicago, Shapiro has lived most of his life as a New Yorker, spending many of his young adult years in the jazz clubs of Greenwich Village. After serving in the U.S. Army Air Force in World War II, he earned an M.A. in English from Columbia University. His first volume of poetry, *The Eye,* published in 1953, won the Swallow Press Award the following year. Among other honors he has won a Pushcart Prize for poetry (1982). Shapiro has worked as an editor since the mid-1950s at *Commentary,* the *New Yorker* and the *New York Times,* and he has produced 12 volumes of poetry. He has also edited an anthology, *Poets of World War II* (2003).

Shapiro's poems are notable for their use of concrete imagery that exposes the tensions between the secular, urban cityscape of New York and the Jewish culture that sparks his constant search for existential understanding. Two poems, 35 years apart, demonstrate the constancy of his setting and his exploration, along with a persistent sardonic wit. In "His Life" (1966), Shapiro's voice is emotionally disengaged while also focused, but it is one that does not contain sadness or disappointment: "When he writes about his life / He just rakes it back / And forth." "New York Notes" (2001) offers a tone of whimsical approval and acceptance measured with a knowingness born of patience and experience: On the receiving end of New York sarcasm, Shapiro knows "I am home among my people."

Ignatow finds that Shapiro's works "spring from a dual vision of the poet of disillusionment, and regeneration born from disillusionment. . . . The permanent and immutable are to be found in the processes of life itself of which we are one expression, no matter what form of it we take" (531). This dual vision produces in Shapiro's work, as Michael Collier notes, a "tumult [that acts] as a metaphor for the chaos in our individual lives" (30).

BIBLIOGRAPHY

Collier, Michael. "These Are the Streets." *New York Times Book Review,* September 25, 1994, 30.
Flamm, Matthew. "I Sing the City Electric." *Nation* 258 (June 13, 1994): 839.
Ignatow, David. "The Past Reordered." *Nation* 204 (April 24, 1967): 531–532.
Ray, David. "Harvey Shapiro—An Appreciation." *New Letters Review of Books* 2, no. 1 (1988): 4, 12.

Robert S. Friedman

SHAPIRO, KARL (1913–2000) Karl Shapiro's rise to national prominence after World War II signified a turn away from socially conscious prewar verse and toward the more personal and experiential poetic voices that marked postwar poetry. As Shapiro reacted against what he perceived to be the "paralysis" of high MODERNISM's sterile literary dogmatism, he began to build a poetry that retained the expansive potential of free verse while simultaneously articulating his own southern Jewish perspective (Shapiro 37). His success at articulating his distinctive American experience encouraged other poets to give voice to their own experiences and contributed to the ascendance of the poetry of personal confession (see CONFESSIONAL POETRY). His influence emanated not only from his poetry, but also from his editorship of the magazine *Poetry* (1950–56) and his academic leadership at the University of Nebraska (1956–66) and the University of California, Davis (1968–85).

Shapiro was born in Baltimore. In 1932 he enrolled at the University of Virginia but dropped out during his first year, citing antipathy toward his Russian-Jewish background. His poetry only truly came to maturity after the army drafted him for service in the war. Amidst the notoriously brutal combat in the South Pacific, he wrote and published two critically acclaimed volumes of poetry, winning the Pulitzer Prize for the second, *V-Letter and Other Poems* (1944). After winning this prize, Shapiro served as the consultant in poetry to the Library of Congress from 1947 to 1948. For his *Selected Poems* (1968), Shapiro shared the 1969 Bollingen Prize for poetry with JOHN BERRYMAN.

In addition to the highly personal nature of Shapiro's poetry, his verse demonstrates an intense dedication to poetic craftsmanship. In "Elegy for a Dead Soldier" (1944), he uses traditional closed-form verse to portray the tension of being a soldier fighting for a country that does not fully embrace his Jewishness (see PROSODY AND FREE VERSE). The speaker criticizes his dead American comrade, because "He was ashamed of the down and out" and "Spurned the panhandler like an uneasy doubt." Despite acknowledging his country's social apathy, the speaker still hopes, amid the war's ashes, that the next generation might discover "whole toleration or pure peace." Such poetic resolutions to the problems of his American experience followed Shapiro's poetry throughout his career, even as his work adopted more experimental styles. In *The Bourgeois Poet* (1964), for instance, Shapiro concedes that even middle-class aspirations make up part of his poetic identity: "Your father becomes a businessman so you can get an education and become a writer. You don't want to give up those material things that you just got."

Shapiro's commitment to the craft of verse and the fierce self-analysis of his writing make him one of his generation's most compelling poets. At the center of his tautly written verse lies a profound vision of mid-20th-century American life.

BIBLIOGRAPHY

Hoffman, Daniel. "Constraints and Self-Determination." *Poetry* 114 (August 1969): 336–338.

Shapiro, Karl. *Reports of My Death*. Chapel Hill: Algonquin Books, 1990.

Spender, Stephen. "The Power and the Hazard." *Poetry* 71 (March 1948): 314–318.

William Hecker

"THE SHIELD OF ACHILLES" W. H. AUDEN (1955)

W. H. AUDEN's meditation on the brutal, warlike nature of the modern world, "The Shield of Achilles" is based on Homer's account in the *Iliad* of the Greek god Hephaestos's construction for Achilles of a suit of armor whose rich design and decorations retell the history of the world. Written in alternating seven-line stanzas of rime royal (rhymed ABABBCC) and eight-line stanzas recalling the ballad stanza (ABCBDEFE), the poem operates on a series of contrasts. The main character, Thetis, watches Hephaestos's labors, and Auden creates an ironic conflict between her expectations of beautiful scenes and the images Hephaestos renders instead, of imperial Rome and of the modern world's industry and impersonality. This discrepancy shows the distance between the myth of history and its brutal reality; moreover, Auden suggests, the notion of progress itself is a myth, since the brutal past is scarcely distinguishable from the brutal present. The poem thus exemplifies Auden's vision of poetry as a powerful way to "disenchant and disintoxicate" the reader (*Dyer's*, 27), freeing one from the myths and fictions of history that, for all their beauty, often serve to compound or conceal human misery.

In book XVIII of the *Iliad*, Homer writes of how the goddess Thetis, mother of Achilles, the greatest of Greek warriors, petitioned the god Hephaestos to forge him a new suit of armor to replace the one stripped by the Trojan leader Hector from the body of Achilles's slain friend, Patroclus. In describing the ornate design that Hephaestos works into the armor, Homer relates a world history that encompasses all the ages of man, and by connecting art, history, and war, Homer makes epic poetry a means of exploring the richness of human culture through a narrative of war. In this LYRIC poem, Auden alludes to the Homeric narrative through Thetis's initial expectation of pastoral or bucolic scenes depicting the peaceful interactions of human beings with their natural environment. Instead, Auden produces a set of highly modern and dystopian images rendered in rime royal (the stanza form used by Chaucer in his *Troilus and Criseyde*, and more relevantly, by W. B. Yeats in "Sailing to Byzantium," a poem about escaping the flawed modern world). In Hephaestos's depiction of modernity, the landscape is completely denuded, yet filled with "An unintelligible multitude, / A million eyes, a million boots in line, / Without expression waiting for a sign." This multitude, following the orders of a faceless voice that "Proved by statistics that some cause was just," then marches off to a war they do not believe in, for which their sacrifices are meaningless.

Following her initial disappointment, Thetis begins looking for Hephaestos to include designs of a religious nature, particularly the nature-based religious rites typical of the *Iliad*: "libation" (the pouring out of wine as an offering) and "sacrifice" (the ritual slaughter of prized animals). But the "ritual pieties" Thetis seeks have been replaced, in Hephaestos's image of the modern future, by "barbed wire," "bored officials," sweating sentries, and indifferent crowds, who look upon the torture and execution of "three pale figures . . . led forth and bound / To three posts driven upright in the ground." The image suggests Calvary and Jesus' crucifixion, but Auden's decision not to name the victims of this execution serves a dual purpose. First, it evokes the horror of the crucifixion without naming it specifically, and this historically appropriate anonymity (given that the events of Homer's epics predate Christianity by a thousand years) allows this particular event to stand for numerous other instances of torture and execution that have occurred in the 20th century. Second, the anonymous image also displaces the greater spiritual significance of the Christian sacrifice, suggesting that in the modern world such sacrifice has lost its ultimate meaning and that the victims, Christ in particular, have become nameless and insignificant. As poet ANTHONY HECHT observes, "(T)he three men who are executed . . . are not martyrs; they are, alas, merely victims. All of this has had the effect of making traditional heroism a thing of the past and greatly diminishing the world of human possibility" (437).

By the close of the poem, Thetis searches Hephaestos's work for signs of human intimacy, of the pleasures of sports, dance, and music, but "His hands had set no dancing-floor, / But a weed-choked field." The final scene on the armor depicts not a crowd, but a single individual, a "ragged urchin" whose understanding of human relations is brutal and obscene: "That girls are raped, that two boys knife a third, / Were axioms to him," Auden writes, and we learn that this boy has no idea "Of any world where promises were kept / Or one could weep because another wept." At this moment, Hephaestos walks away, leaving Thetis not only to her own despair at this vision of the future, but to the bitter realization that this brutal world is precisely what her son, "the strong / Iron-hearted man-slaying Achilles / Who would not live long," had desired and created through his warring. The poem is a powerful indictment of modern progress and of the alienation the modern world creates. Hecht writes that "The poem was written in 1952, when the full horror of WWII and its destructive effects were beginning to be appreciated" (427). Auden himself summarizes the thematic import of the poem this way: "A society which was really like a good poem, embodying the virtues of beauty, order, economy, and subordination of detail to the whole, would be a horror" (85). In the wake of a world war motivated in part by fascism's ideals of cultural purity, Auden's poem dismantles the fiction that a society devoted to both war and culture (like Homeric Greece or imperial Rome) is somehow superior to or even different from a society founded simply on war and bloodshed.

BIBLIOGRAPHY

Auden, W. H. *The Dyer's Hand.* New York: Vintage, 1990.
Hecht, Anthony. *The Hidden Law: The Poetry of W. H. Auden.* Cambridge, Mass: Harvard University Press, 1993.

Temple Cone

"SHINE, PERISHING REPUBLIC" ROBINSON JEFFERS (1923) One of ROBINSON JEFFERS's earliest expressions of antinationalist sentiment, "Shine, Perishing Republic" is also an example of the philosophical attitude Jeffers later termed "Inhumanism" and a moving address to the poet's sons, whom Jeffers warns "to be in nothing so moderate as in love of man, a clever servant, an insufferable master." Written in couplets of Jeffers's characteristically long-lined free verse, the poem opens with an invective against 20th-century American imperialism and against the failure of protest to restrain American ambitions. But the speaker eventually assumes a stoic attitude toward this turn in the nation's history, and he accepts corruption as the inevitable outcome for all great empires, while also acknowledging that decay and ruin can lead to a cultural flowering. In spite of his assertion that "life is good, be it stubbornly long or suddenly / A mortal splendor," Jeffers never relinquishes his distrust of humankind in general, and warns his sons not to trust too much the innate goodness of human nature.

Written in the wake of World War I and the excessively punitive Treaty of Versailles (which Jeffers and many others saw as directly responsible for the resuscitation of European conflict in World War II), the poem criticizes modernism's failed narrative of progress, with Jeffers attacking America's "mould of vulgarity, heavily thickening to empire." This disgust arises from Jeffers's staunch isolationism, which peaked during World War II (and for which he was widely criticized), but which he was already espousing in World War I, when he was building by hand the stone cottage and tower on the coast of Carmel, California, which would be his lifelong home and a central subject of much of his poetry. As if to underscore his withdrawal from national and international conflict, Jeffers's criticism of American imperialism lasts only a stanza before he "sadly smiling remember[s] that the flower fades to make fruit, the fruit to make earth." While the valuing of culture in the midst of historical decay may seem misguided to some, it is in keeping with Jeffers's belief that art provides a sense of permanence that contrasts with the flux of history; as he later wrote in the foreword to his *Selected Poems* "[P]oetry is bound to concern itself chiefly with permanent things and the permanent aspects of life" (714). Thus, with this reminder that culture can flourish in the face of historical calamity, Jeffers offers a direct, if somewhat ironic, apostrophe to America: "shine, perishing republic."

But even if Jeffers can accept culture as a compensation for history, he remains distrustful of mankind's motives, and in the latter half of the poem he imparts that distrust as advice to his sons. Jeffers called this philosophical attitude "Inhumanism," and in the original preface to *The Double Axe and Other Poems*, he described it as a belief "based on a recognition of the astonishing beauty of things and their living wholeness, and on a rational acceptance of the fact that mankind is neither central nor important in the universe; our vices and blazing crimes are as insignificant as our happiness. . . . The attitude is neither misanthropic nor pessimist nor irreligious, though two or three people have said so, and may again; but it involves a certain detachment" (719). This Inhumanism is evinced clearly in Jeffers's scorn for humankind in general and large communities in particular, but it is not a cynical or nihilistic attitude, for one may still find beauty and solace in nature: "when the cities lie at the monster's feet there are left the mountains." Jeffers advises skepticism and distrust because a questioning attitude offers the best protection against the snares of liberal ideology ("love of man") that can lead countries into international entanglements and into war, "that caught—they say—God, when he walked the earth."

BIBLIOGRAPHY

Jeffers, Robinson. "Foreword, *The Selected Poetry of Robinson Jeffers* (1938)." In *The Selected Poetry of Robinson Jeffers*, edited by Tim Hunt, 713–718. Stanford, Calif.: Stanford University Press, 2001.

———. "Preface, *The Double Axe and Other Poems* (original version, 1947)." In *The Selected Poetry of Robinson Jeffers*, edited by Tim Hunt, 719–722. Stanford, Calif.: Stanford University Press, 2001.

Temple Cone

"SHIRT" **Robert Pinsky (1990)** Unfolding from a conceit of remarkable power, Robert Pinsky's "Shirt" juxtaposes the language of shirt-making with the history of garment manufacture, depicting famous instances of worker exploitation in order to dramatize the moral burdens associated with our economic lives. As Roger Gilbert notes, "Shirt" is Pinsky's "fullest attempt to locate a common object in history, to see it both as a material presence and as a ghostly embodiment of invisible forces and lives." By naming all the parts of the shirt, like "the collar / Turned in a sweatshop by Koreans or Malaysians," Pinsky makes the reader more attentive to this commonplace material good, and he uses this heightened physical intimacy to establish a greater emotional connection to the manufacturers of such goods, past and present, so that he cannot avoid imagining the sweatshop worker who "fitted / This armpiece with its overseam to the band // Of cuff I button at my wrist." For Pinsky, such imaginings broaden the circle of community and of justice, so that when the poet assumes Adam's power to name the world, he must also assume responsibility for and connection to all that he names.

Throughout the unrhymed tercets of "Shirt" (which evoke the terza rima of Dante's justice-obsessed *Inferno*), Pinsky interweaves the names of shirt parts with the names of textile machines, of the other types of garments produced, and of the different jobs involved in garment manufacture. This process of associative juxtaposition is *metonymy,* and it enables Pinsky to make an argument for economic justice: one cannot dissociate a product from the circumstances of its manufacture, nor from the original production of its materials. To ground these ideas, he also juxtaposes several major historical instances of garment industry abuses and disasters in the poem. The first of these references is to the Asian sweatshops on which much of the present-day global economy depends, and Pinsky tries to individualize the lives of those who toil in them, depicting the workers as "Gossiping over tea and noodles on their break/ Or talking money or politics." Paralleling this treatment of contemporary economic affairs is an initial focus on the visible features of the shirt, particularly the parts enclosing the body, a focus that suggests how individuals in the modern world are bound to far-flung economies. From this point on, the poem's points of focus move back in time, dealing with the less visible aspects of the shirt (including its design and the production of its raw materials) and with earlier garment manufacturers, suggesting how the modern individual is not only figuratively, but literally tied to the past.

Later, reflecting upon the parts of the textile machinery that fashion the shirt, Pinsky refers to the Triangle Shirtwaist Factory fire, which took place in New York City on March 25, 1911. This fire, in which "One hundred and forty-six died in the flames / On the ninth floor, no hydrants, no fire escapes," was seen as a terrible industrial disaster, one which eventually led to major revisions in factory safety standards. Pinsky humanizes this catastrophe by focusing on the eyewitness accounts concerning a few individuals who jumped to their deaths from the building to escape the fire. The pace of the poem slows here, as Pinsky describes the suicidal escape in patient detail, capturing the courage of the man who helped the women leap from the window "As if he were helping them up / To enter a streetcar, and not eternity." (According to Gilbert, this passage, including the simile, comes verbatim from the eyewitness account.) But even this man's courage cannot save him, and as he drops from the window, Pinsky compares him to a falling man from one of Hart Crane's poems (Crane himself committed suicide by jumping from a ship). When Pinsky notes that it is "Wonderful how the pattern matches perfectly / Across the placket and over the twin bartacked// Corners of both pockets," his ironic use of pattern not only calls to mind the shirt's pattern, but repeated patterns of personal and economic history, patterns which can even be found in poetry.

The third industry abuse Pinsky discusses is the history of "The clan tartans // Invented by mill-owners inspired by the hoax of Ossian, / To control their savage Scottish workers." In some ways, this injustice is the most insidious for Pinsky, for it involves the exploitation of workers by means of myth and poetry. In the 1760s, James Macpherson published what he claimed were translations from Scots Gaelic of the tales of Ossian, ancient texts of equivalent cultural status to Homer's epics. But while Macpherson had indeed collected the ancient Ossianic legends, his "translations" were adapted to modern sensibilities and liberally changed the themes to suit Macpherson's own ideas. For Pinsky, the false history of the clans and of their tartan kilts is used to encourage Scottish textile workers to submit to unfair working conditions while manufacturing those same kilts.

The literary reference to Ossian seems to prompt the last and most individualized reference to an individual involved with the manufacture of Pinsky's shirt. In an apostrophe to the Renaissance lyric poet George Herbert, an Anglican minister who dealt with the burdens of religious duty in a poem titled "The Collar," Pinsky writes, "George Herbert, your descendent is a Black / Lady in South Carolina, her name is Irma / And she inspected my shirt." By linking his shirt to Herbert, Pinsky rightly ties his own poetry to the metaphysical tradition, in which poets used well-designed conceits, or extended metaphors, to house powerful and complex arguments. But in a darker fashion, the link implicates Pinsky in the same crime for which Herbert is accused: namely, the history of rape and oppression of colonized peoples. By the poem's close, Pinsky has subtly but powerfully brought into the light of moral awareness the extent to which all people's lives and decisions are woven into the world's history, even those as removed from that world as metaphysical poets.

BIBLIOGRAPHY
Modern American Poetry. "On 'Short.'" Available online. URL: http://www.english.uiuc.edu/maps/poets/m_r/pinsky/shirt.htm. Accessed December 26, 2006.

Temple Cone

SILKO, LESLIE MARMON (1948–)

Although Leslie Marmon Silko is best known as a novelist, her fiction brings together poetry and prose to form a rich, evocative literary voice. As JAMES WRIGHT observes, poems "rise out of the text" of her first novel, *Ceremony* (1977): "[I]t is astonishing," goes a Wright letter to Silko, "to see your mastery of the novel combined with a power of poetry within it" (Silko and Wright, 5). While *Laguna Woman* (1974) is Silko's only published collection of poetry (other publications include poetry, but are mixed genre), poems do indeed rise out of all her texts—whether they are short stories, novels, essays, letters, or screenplays. In the canon of American poetry, Silko—with her emphasis on such subjects as exile, community, interconnections, the land—stands with JOY HARJO, Wendy Rose, SIMON ORTIZ, Wright, GARY SNYDER, Louise Erdrich, and N. Scott Momaday, among other contemporary writers.

Silko was born in Albuquerque, New Mexico, and raised on the Laguna Pueblo reservation. She has won many literary awards, including a MacArthur Foundation Award (1981), a Lila Wallace-Reader's Digest Foundation Writer's Award (1991), a Native Writers' Circle of the Americas Lifetime Achievement Award (1994), and a Lannan Foundation Award (2000).

Usually categorized with other contemporary American Indian writers, Silko suggests that while her contemporaries "are 'rescuing' songs and stories from old Bureau of American Ethnology Reports," she is "working from a more vital source"—that is, directly from oral tradition (191). This "vital source" is grounded in the land and the earth, as well as in stories, legends, myths, and songs that were passed down to her. Dominant themes include the interrelationship between people and the earth, the need to restore balance and harmony, and the circularity of time and space.

The structure of Silko's poetry is perhaps best called organic: "I read [poems] the way I write them: by feeling my way to them" (Silko 23–24). Silko's poems move back and forth across the page, just as the ceremonial dancers sway in "Coyotes and the Stro'ro'ka Dancers," as the storm winds blow in "In Cold Storm Light," as the light on the canyon walls shifts in "Cottonwood *Part One*," or as the "cold water river" runs in "Indian Song: Survival," all poems from her 1981 volume *Storyteller*.

While Silko's fiction has been criticized as overly political and didactic, her poems have retained a purity and leanness, like a "lean gray deer / running on the edge of the rainbow" ("Indian Song: Survival" [1981]).

BIBLIOGRAPHY
Barnett, Louise K., and James L. Thorson, eds. *Leslie Marmon Silko: A Collection of Critical Essays*. Albuquerque: University of New Mexico Press, 1999.
Silko, Leslie Marmon. "Leslie Silko, Laguna Poet and Novelist." In *This Song Remembers: Self-Portraits of Native Americans in the Arts*, edited by Jane B. Katz. Boston: Houghton Mifflin, 1980, pp. 186–194.
———, and James Wright. *The Delicacy and the Strength of Lace: Letters between Leslie Marmon Silko & James Wright*, edited by Anne Wright. Saint Paul, Minn.: Graywolf Press, 1986.

Patricia Keefe Durso

SILLIMAN, RON (1946–)

Ron Silliman, a prolific writer of poetry and criticism since the early 1970s, was one of the founding members of the San Francisco–based LANGUAGE poets. As a Language writer, Silliman's poetry resists what fellow Language writer CHARLES BERNSTEIN calls "official verse culture" (6) and instead is in the tradition of 20th-century American avant-garde poetry.

Born in Pasco, Washington, and raised in Albany, California, Silliman has spent most of his life on the West Coast, especially Berkeley, California. He received his B.A. from Merritt College and did graduate work at San Francisco State University and the University of California, Berkeley. In addition to publishing more than 20 books of poetry and garnering many accolades,

Silliman won a National Endowment for the Arts fellowship in 1979.

Like most Language poets, Silliman is concerned with linguistic problems of representation and reference. Focusing on the relationship between the signifier (the material word itself) and the signified (what the word refers to), Silliman creates writing that treats the materiality of the word, the signifier, as the heart of all meaning-making activity. Silliman claims that the signified has dominated conventional understanding of language, and he associates that dominance with capitalist oppression. He asserts that highlighting the signifier raises a reader's consciousness by illustrating a change in the mode of language production from a capitalist mode, which creates an illusion that language is transparent, to a materialist mode, which calls attention to the language production itself; this change is a form of opposition to capitalism.

To achieve these ends, in *The New Sentence* (1987), Silliman proposes a form of writing that treats the sentence as the fundamental unit of textual meaning. Consequently much of Silliman's creative work consists of mosaiclike prose poems without syntactic links between sentences.

For example, *Tjanting* (1981) is a book-length prose poem that contains one apparent non sequitur after another: "A plausibility. Analogy to 'quick' sand. Mute pleonasm. Nor that either. Planarians, trematodes." Although the reader might guess at associative meanings, there is no necessary meaning or narrative beyond the material words themselves, leaving the reader with an opaque, and problematic, relationship to the words on the page. Furthermore the poem's predetermined form (each paragraph has the number of sentences of the previous two paragraphs added together) constrains meaning and exposes the mode of poetic production. The question remains as to whether this difficult writing makes a difference politically; still Silliman's poetic application of the "new sentence" marks a significant innovation in late 20th-century poetics that has challenged the conventional ways that poems convey meaning to their readers.

BIBLIOGRAPHY

Bernstein, Charles, "State of the Art," *A Poetics*, Cambridge, Mass.: Harvard University Press, 1992, 1–8.

Lazer, Hank. "Opposing Poetry." *Contemporary Literature* 30 (1989): 142–150.

Perelman, Bob. "Parataxis and Narrative: The New Sentence in Theory and Practice." In *Artifice and Indeterminacy: An Anthology of New Poetics*, edited by Christopher Beach. Tuscaloosa: University of Alabama Press, 1998.

Mitchum Huehls

SIMIC, CHARLES (1938–) Charles Simic is one of the most original and prolific voices in contemporary poetry. Born in Belgrade, in the former Yugoslavia, he has written thousands of inimitable poems that bring a distinctly European perspective to American literature. This eccentric un-American perspective remains a recognizable part of Simic's body of work, even though he has lived and worked in the United States his entire adult life.

After he emigrated to the United States in 1954, he received a B.A. from New York University. He served in the army from 1961 to 1963. Since 1973 he has taught creative writing at the University of New Hampshire, Durham. He has received several prestigious awards and fellowships, including the Pulitzer Prize for *The World Doesn't End* in 1990. His numerous poetry volumes include *Dismantling the Silence* (1971), *Classic Ballroom Dances* (1980), *Hotel Insomnia* (1992), *Jackstraws* (1999), and *The Voice at 3 A.M.* (2003). He is also the author of several collections of essays and translations, including, in 1992, *Dime-Store Alchemy*, a book of essays and poems about the work of the modern American visionary artist Joseph Cornell.

Simic's poems offer an unusual mixture of realism and SURREALISM, often refined by an acute sense of the absurd or simple black humor. This is not to say that Simic's poems are not serious. Simic can be funny, gaudy, and witty as a clown, but also incisive, terse, and elliptic as a monk. His poems are concrete and detailed, demonstrating a vast variety of modes and moods. They shun abstraction and often focus on everyday situations and objects, adding to them qualities that become unexpectedly fresh and fitting.

In his early miniaturist poem "Fork" (1969), for example, Simic describes the utensil as the claw of some terrifying primordial bird. In a late poem, "Country Fair" (1991), the opposite takes place. A six-legged dog, billed as the principal exhibit at a country fair, suddenly becomes the most ordinary of dogs: "The dog got the stick and looked back at us. / And that was the whole show." The world created by Simic has all the trappings of reality. It is familiar, because it is human, a world readers recognize but without a consoling sense of relief. Instead the reaction is more like one of unease or self-estrangement.

The most recognizable feature of Simic's poems is that they never take anything for granted. They create their reality out of the most trivial, random, and incoherent parts of life, with a result that is often unsettling, but also unexpectedly profound. His poems achieve transcendence by taking ordinary shortcuts. In 2007, Simic was named U.S. poet laureate.

BIBLIOGRAPHY

Simic, Charles. "Interview with Charles Simic," by Eric McHenry, Atlantic Unbound. Available online. URL: www.theatlantic.com/unbound/interviews/ba-2001-01-10.htm. Downloaded March 2007.

Stitt, Peter. "Charles Simic: Poetry in a Time of Madness." In *Uncertainty & Plenitude: Five Contemporary Poets.* Iowa City: University of Iowa Press, 1997.

Weigl, Bruce, ed. *Charles Simic: Essays on the Poetry.* Ann Arbor: University of Michigan Press, 1996.

Piotr Gwiazda

SIMPSON, LOUIS (1923–) During the 1950s, along with GALWAY KINNELL, DAVID IGNATOW, JAMES DICKEY, DONALD HALL, and, most notably, ROBERT BLY, Louis Simpson began using the individual voice and open form, dismissing the conventions of rhyme, meter, and regular stanzas. Simpson's verse, along with the others, became known as DEEP IMAGE, deploying story lines a reader could actually visualize. Marked by a spiritual intensity and transcendence of the self rather than CONFESSIONAL immediacy, Simpson was influenced by Spanish and Latin American writers, such as Federico García Lorca and Pablo Neruda, especially their surreal association of images (see SURREALISM), as well as the meditational work of THEODORE ROETHKE, with his deep feeling for nature as a vehicle of spiritual transformation.

Simpson, born in Jamaica, the West Indies, won the Pulitzer Prize for his book, *At the End of the Open Road, Poems* (1963). *The Arrivistes* (1949), from his first book, was published while he was living in France. He studied and taught at Columbia University, later teaching at the University of California, Berkeley, as well as the State University of New York, Stony Brook. He has garnered numerous honors and awards, including the Pulitzer Prize for *At the End of the Open Road, Poems* (1963), and the Harold Morton Landon Translation Award for *Modern Poets of France: A Bilingual Anthology* (1998).

Simpson's poems do not simply record situations, events, and people as they appear to an imaginative and skilled poet; rather they locate the conditions shaping the life within: "I am writing poems based in experience and the images are related to the environment," he once said. "When one of these poems works there's no split between inner and outer worlds" ("Simpson" 51). His themes are many and varied: America, its character, spirit, and ethos; war, from the view of an infantry soldier; and the lives that his actual and visualized ancestors led in Volhynia, a part of ancestral Russia. His style is ever-developing: Early adherence to poetic conventions of rhyme, meter, and regular stanzas turned to free verse in the 1950s, and in the 1970s, he began to write NARRATIVE POETRY, convinced it was the form best suited to revelation.

"An Accident" (1997) turns the reality of a car wreck into an intense visualization of progress and materialism gone awry: "Why are the cars slowing up? / An Accident. To rubberneck." The carnage we witness is charged with reality. The persona fuses the poet and his reader, and, using a technique of prose fiction, it creates a narrative poem in much the same way that Anton Chekhov would with prose. Here is Simpson's willingness to make his proxy a participant in the scene, not its documentarian. And, if the speaker notices "gawkers," then those of us who do "rubberneck" are more attentive to the speaker. When the speaker looks at a road ahead, he sees it "either pointing at the sky / or falling off an edge into space." The reader is urgently, plainly taken to the physical frontier of trauma and presented with spiritual choices. As the distractions that the world presents as reality must be understood for what they are and for what they are not, Simpson's poetry moves us to an understanding of this less-than-complete life.

BIBLIOGRAPHY
Simpson, Louis. "Capturing the World As It Is: An Interview with Louis Simpson." *Ohio Review* 14, no. 3 (spring 1973): 35–51.
Turner, Alberta T. *50 Contemporary Poets: The Creative Process. New York: Longman, 1977, pp. 289–292.*

Gerald Schwartz

"SKUNK HOUR" ROBERT LOWELL **(1959)** ROBERT LOWELL's homage to his friend ELIZABETH BISHOP's "The Armadillo," "Skunk Hour" is an important example of the CONFESSIONAL poetry Lowell began writing in his groundbreaking volume *Life Studies (1959).* In the irregularly rhymed and loosely metered lines for which his later work was best known, "Skunk Hour" blends aspects of Lowell's personal, psychological life with images from the modern world in order to depict the struggles of the individual self as it comes to terms with human and personal history, concluding with an unsentimentalized symbol of survival in the image of a troop of skunks raiding trash cans at midnight.

In her poem "The Armadillo," which among other things relates the poet's anxiety about nuclear holocaust, Bishop used the image of fire balloons that were loosed in Brazil as part of an annual celebration to characterize the random destruction threatened by nuclear war. The final image, of an armadillo trying to escape the flames that fell from one of these randomly falling balloons, "a mailed fist raised against the sky," stuck with Lowell, and he decided that he too wanted to write a poem that featured in its conclusion an animal surviving in spite of its surroundings. Lowell was in fact so moved by Bishop's poem that he dedicated "Skunk Hour" to her.

But rather than addressing nuclear holocaust, Lowell's poem is concerned with the disruptions of social and cultural change in the 1960s, and ultimately with the breakdown of that society. It is no coincidence that the speaker of the poem (like Lowell himself) appears constantly on the edge of a nervous breakdown, though somehow he manages to endure. Critic Charles Altieri writes that the poem "[A]rticulates a ground of values that make it possible to endure, if not overcome, the anxieties of contemporary life and the loss of traditional grounds of value" (67). If the speaker is suffering a mental breakdown but is working towards some semblance of sanity and balance, it holds that the poem reflects a parallel movement toward social balance; indeed, as James Breslin notes, Lowell learns in "Skunk Hour" "[T]o accept the imperfections of a secular world" (112).

The poem takes place in and around Castine, Maine, where Lowell, who came from a very old, upper-class American family, spent many summers. The poem opens with an evocation not only of long ancestry, but of a world where relations and history matter. An old heiress living on Nautilus Island, near Castine, has been buying "all / the eyesores facing her shore, / and lets them fall" as a way of ridding her world of the pressures of modernity and hearkening back to a safer, Victorian era. The speaker, too, feels the troubles of the present day: "The season's ill," he writes, noting the many disasters that have come to the area, including the departure (and presumed bankruptcy) of a millionaire who vacationed there in the summers. Neither money nor family history offer security against the pressures of living in the 20th century, or of living at all. Lowell himself claims "My mind's not right," and his nighttime rambles evoke the "dark night of the soul" described by the Catholic poet St. Juan de la Cruz, whom Lowell claims he was thinking of when he introduces the "dark night" he spends touring a local hill "watch[ing] for love-cars. Lights turned down, / they lay together, hull to hull / where the graveyard shelves on the town." The voyeurism of his act and the unsettling proximity of the place of *eros* (the love-cars, which provided shelter for couples seeking intimacy) and of *thanatos* (the graveyard) emphasize Lowell's own loneliness in the poem and serve to remind him of the inescapability of the end of human history—death—a fear that links Lowell's poem closely to Bishop's.

The speaker is further distressed by his isolation when he hears a folk song about seduction, murder, and suicide, and concludes, in an allusion to Satan's lines from John Milton's *Paradise Lost,* "I myself am hell; / nobody's here." But at the moment of greatest anxiety and isolation—as in Bishop's poem—the appearance of a wild animal, in this case a skunk, provides a counterforce to the devastating effects of the world at large, though by choosing a skunk and by focusing on its awkwardness and its thriving on trash, he resists the impulse to provide a full (and therefore forced) resolution to his fears of isolation and vulnerability. Rather, by introducing the skunks, he focuses on survival without beauty, perseverance without glory, an existence that is ironically supportable precisely because it does not possess or require the historical sense or the material wealth that ruined the "hermit / heiress" and the "summer millionaire" alike. Altieri connects this ugliness with Lowell's developing CONFESSIONAL style, for "[t]he skunk symbolizes what it means to search for value and self-definition when all the sustaining fictions have failed. One is left only with the garbage of one's past, which he must have the determination to explore and the courage to endure" (68).

The final image ironically reminds Lowell that survival is all life demands, and that his self-consciousness is more threatening than the loss of history, the loss of wealth, and even the loss of life portrayed in the rest of the poem. As Lowell watches on, the mother skunk licks a carton of sour cream; ugly and ungraceful, the skunk yet manages a gesture of elegance, albeit sham elegance, when she raises her ridiculous "ostrich tail." Having linked himself to Milton's Satan, and having described the skunk's "moonstruck eyes' red fire," Lowell now sees himself reflected in the skunk's marginal, trash-seeking existence, but with one difference: the mother-skunk "will not scare."

BIBLIOGRAPHY

Altieri, Charles. *Enlarging the Temple: New Directions in American Poetry in the 1960s*. Lewisburg: Bucknell University Press, 1979.

Breslin, James. *From Modern to Contemporary: American Poetry 1945–65*. Chicago: University of Chicago Press, 1984.

Hammer, Langdon. "Robert Lowell's Breakdown." *Yale Review* 79, no. 2 (1990): 172–187.

Temple Cone

"THE SMILE ON THE FACE OF A KOUROS" WILLIAM BRONK (1969) "The Smile on the Face of a Kouros" is the first poem in WILLIAM BRONK'S book *The Empty Hands,* which was named after a phrase from the poem that ends: "I tell you, death, expect no smile of pride / from me. I bring you nothing in my empty hands." This book marks the beginning of Bronk's mature work. In this poem, Bronk sees humankind as "unformed / or broken"; he is "puzzled," because he feels "we live / in a formless world." This is a postmodern understanding in which certainties are no longer creditable. Bronk's poetry insists that humans invent the terms and ways by which they attempt to understand life, but those are fictions, and the understanding is false.

In "The Smile on the Face of a Kouros," the statue of a young ancient Greek man smiles with pride at having accomplished something, an end of his own making; the word *end* in the poem means both a purpose and a termination. The statue of the boy can be seen as a metaphor for humankind that individually chooses how to live, each person making her or his own life. Most people choose an end, a purpose, and use that to shape their actions and understanding of themselves, moving toward death with the illusion of achievement, of completed lives. Yet Bronk says the other way we can go to death is "unformed / or broken, less than whole, puzzled." This is the way for a person who recognizes that the terms and forms of the world are of human construction, fictions all. The world provides no forms; the comely form, or the perfect, unbroken form, is what humans make, not knowing that these are of their own design.

Because the speaker of the poem believes we live in a formless world, he does not bring to death the self-constructed prizes of strength and virtue. There is no "smile of pride" for him, because there is no end to be "achieved." There is, however, the poetry with which Bronk's empty hands are full. If the poems are not a source of pride, it is because Bronk saw them, not as things made, but as one of the few givens in life. Bronk's belief in our ignorance of the nature of the real world is constant in all his writing, as is his belief in the nature of poetry as something substantial.

BIBLIOGRAPHY

Clippinger, David, ed. *The Body of This Life: Essays on William Bronk*. Jersey City, N.J.: Talisman House, 2001.

Foster, Edward. *Answerable To None: Berrigan, Bronk, and the American Real*. New York: Spuyten Duyvil, 1999.

Kimmelman, Burt. *The "Winter Mind": William Bronk and American Letters.* Madison, N.J.: Fairleigh Dickinson University Press, 1998.

Sherry Kearns

SMITH, DAVE (1942–) Dave Smith is one of the major southern poets of the last third of the 20th century. His poems blend ROBERT PENN WARREN's elevation of regional subjects with JAMES WRIGHT's search for beauty amid working-class life. Whether writing about the Virginia tidewater of his youth, the Midwest, or the barren Utah landscape, Smith brings a rich and dignified vernacular music to his meditations on violence, history, and the struggle for grace.

Born and raised in Portsmouth, Virginia, Smith received degrees from the University of Virginia (B.A., 1965) and Southern Illinois University (M.A., 1969) before serving in the U.S. Air Force (1969–72). After earning a Ph.D. at Ohio University (1976), Smith began a teaching career, serving most recently as the chair of the graduate writing seminars at Johns Hopkins University. His first book of poetry, *Bull Island,* was published in 1970 and has been followed by more than 20 books of poetry, a novel, and several edited collections of essays and verse. His book *Goshawk, Antelope* was a finalist for both the National Book Critics Circle Award and the Pulitzer Prize in 1979, and *Dream Flights* was a finalist for the Pulitzer in 1981. Smith has received a number of fellowships, and, as coeditor of the *Southern Review* during the 1990s and a poetry editor for Louisiana State University Press, he has significantly influenced the direction of contemporary mainstream poetry, particularly among southern authors.

Natural symbols and forceful rhythms built on enjambment create an intensity in Smith's work that Terry Hummer calls "tornadic" (76), capturing the drama and danger that sometimes disrupt daily life (see PROSODY AND FREE VERSE). Attending to "the paradoxical problem of making art out of the muck of the world around us," as Bruce Weigl observes (69), Smith often structures his poems around physical journeys that occasion psychic or spiritual ones. In "The Tire Hangs in the Yard" (1981), the poet's visit to a childhood tire swing recalls his adolescent romances and jealousies, as well as the violent, rowdy life that he escaped that others his age could not. Smith's style ranges from historical NARRATIVE to personal LYRIC POETRY, restlessly elevating ordinary speech into musical, stately utterance. As he writes in "The Roundhouse Voices" (1985), an elegy for his dead uncle, "All day I've held your hand, trying to say back a life." Smith resists the temptations of nostalgia and personal confession by emphasizing the struggle that physical existence entails. And he acknowledges that language is what makes up experience, although "Words . . . us / no damn good. Do you hear that?" Yet Smith ever strives to affirm the life in art. In "Driving Home in the Breaking Season" (1976), an almost blasphemous exclamation results in grace: "Damn death. Today I do not believe / a single sparrow will die but I will croak back his life."

BIBLIOGRAPHY

Hummer, Terry. "Dave Smith's *Homage to Edgar Allen Poe:* 'Pushed' Time and the Obsession of Memory." In *The Giver of Morning: On the Poetry of Dave Smith,* edited by Bruce Weigl, 75–87. Birmingham, Ala.: Thunder City Press, 1982.

Weigl, Bruce. "The Deep Well of Celebration: Dave Smith's *Goshawk, Antelope.*" *Poet Lore* 75, no. 1 (1980): 45–50.

Temple Cone

SMITH, WILLIAM JAY (1918–) William Jay Smith's poetry has helped to reinvigorate the language of the ordinary; it reestablishes plain speaking and nonsense as varieties of poetic dialect that continue to influence generations of poets to this day. In his light verse Smith translates the complex into simplistic verbal pictures, frequently reproducing the verbal as visual and forming his poems into rough images of his subject, such as "The Typewriter Bird" (1954). In the tradition of JOHN CIARDI, Smith's verse crosses genres into the wide realm of children's poetry, which exemplifies the ethos of light verse; for Smith, "light verse happily accepts the form that language both permits it and imposes upon it. . . . It lives on change; it thrives on variety. Rhyme is its regimen" (Smith ix). However, a large portion of Smith's poetry has focused on weightier subjects, and, like Ciardi's, his poetry can become more personal, his subjects and diction complemented by tremendous work in both translation and prose.

Smith was born in Winnfield, Louisiana, and raised, as his memoir *Army Brat* (1980) discusses, in Jefferson Barracks, near St. Louis. He was a Rhodes scholar and began writing poetry in the late 1930s. Smith was poet-in-residence at Williams College for an eight-year span starting in 1959 and spent his time in other schools, such as Columbia University and Hollins College. From 1968 until 1970, he served as poet laureate of the United States. He has been a member of the Academy of Arts and Letters since 1975, serving a brief term as vice president for literature. Smith's translations have also won him many awards and citations, most notably from the Hungarian government.

Smith's interest is in marrying the motives of light verse, its emphasis on rhyme and form, with the motives of "serious" poetry; he frequently constructs his verse in the middle of this dialectic. In "American Primitive" (1957), for example, the speaker's father becomes deconstructed and reimagined by the now-adult speaker. The familiar, childlike refrain, "Only my Daddy could look like that. / And I love my Daddy like he loves his Dollar," belies the heavier, darker reflections of his father, his gambling and desperation, the blue lips and cold hands, hanging "in the hall by his black cravat." In this poem, as in others, Smith's "light" diction and childish construction mutually reinforce and underscore the space between the child's mind and the adult's memory.

Experimenting wildly within rigid forms, Smith's verse exemplified a new movement, starting early in the 1960s, that rejected free verse and its emphasis on the deregulation of form (see NEW FORMALISM). Smith forced the idea that play could exist simultaneously with serious literary achievement and, indeed, sometimes must exist for a poem to be successful.

BIBLIOGRAPHY

Jacobsen, Josephine. "The Dark Train and the Green Place: The Poetry of William Jay Smith." *Hollins Critic* 12 (Feb. 1975): 1–14.

Smith, William Jay. *Plain Talk: Epigrams, Epitaphs, Satires, Nonsense, Occasional, Concrete and Quotidian Poems.* New York: Center for Book Arts, 1988.

———. "William Jay Smith At Eighty: An Interview," by Robert Phillips. *New Letters* 65, no. 3 (1999): 90–119.

Andy Crank

"SNAPSHOTS OF A DAUGHTER-IN-LAW" ADRIENNE RICH (1963) In its leap into radical expression and away from the fetters of tradition, this poem marks the emergence of ADRIENNE RICH as a major feminist voice in American poetry (see FEMALE VOICE, FEMALE LANGUAGE). Similar to SYLVIA PLATH's *Ariel,* written in 1962–63, "Snapshots" inflects CONFESSIONAL POETRY—which was in its infancy at the time—with the concerns of the developing second-wave feminism (which gathered momentum in the mid-1960s), abandoning more muted concerns for the unflinching embrace of issues of creativity, sexuality, and power. Before this poem, published in a book by the same name, Rich's poetry was highly wrought and praised for its exquisite style and traditional forms (see PROSODY AND FREE VERSE). The much-anthologized "Aunt Jennifer's Tigers" (1951) exemplifies this, with its formal control and careful progression of imagery. There is no *I* in the poem, which depicts its subject aloofly. Its description of tigers pacing in "sleek chivalric certainty" might equally be applied to the poetry itself. "Snapshots" is an altogether wilder animal, with its sprawling, associative imagery and multifarious allusions. The statement of poetics later articulated in "On Edges" (1969), whose speaker pledges to risk bloodshed rather than following the prescriptions and proscriptions of art—metaphorized as cutting "with blunt scissors on dotted lines"—is foreshadowed in *Snapshots of a Daughter-in-Law.*

Rich began appending dates to her poems in 1954 and cites this as the moment of the shift toward politicized poetry that *Snapshots of a Daughter-in-Law* embodies. Yet, for all its radicalism, the poem traces a theme of genealogy and inheritance, focusing on the difficult emergence of the woman poet. It centers on ideas of acceptable femininity—of "dulce ridens, dulce loquens" ("laughing and speaking sweetly"), of Thomas Campion's Corinna with her lute ("When to Her Lute Corinna Sings" [1601]), and the imperative to ladies in Shakespeare's *Much Ado about Nothing* (1600) not to sigh (instead the women should be "blithe and bonny"). It considers the punishment for the transgression of these rules, such as the labels "harpy, shrew and whore," which are applied to creative women.

The poem pivots on a tension between two sets of images—those of acceptable femininity (women doing the work of nurturing, homemaking, and sweetening others' lives) and those of the creative/transgressive woman. The two blur when the objects of domestic accommodation are employed as instruments of self-mutilation, culminating in the image of a woman burning her hand over a kettle. This suggests the oppression of the rituals of domesticity, and the subversion of this through self-laceration: The woman's agency is sublimated into the creation of her own injury, with the hand of the housekeeper (a hand described in Plath's "The Applicant" [1962] as one supposed to be "willing / to bring teacups and roll away headaches"). Allusions to this tension in the life of Emily Dickinson build to a series of sharp, hard images reflecting the determination needed to overcome a prescribed life of drudgery, imagined in the metonymy of perpetual dusting. By the last stanza images of woman as helicopter retain this tension—through flying, her fine blades cause the air to wince.

BIBLIOGRAPHY

Cooper, Jane R. *Reading Adrienne Rich: Reviews and Re-Visions, 1951–1981*. Ann Arbor: Michigan University Press, 1984.

Templeton, Alice. *The Dream and the Dialogue: Adrienne Rich's Feminist Poetics*. Knoxville: University of Tennessee Press, 1994.

Felicity Plunkett

SNODGRASS, W(ILLIAM) D(EWITT)

(1926–) Long resistant to his reputation as a founder of CONFESSIONAL POETRY, W. D. Snodgrass rejects the label for its religious, television, and tabloid connotations. From the first, his art has offered an intimacy and sharing of personal experiences and emotions that were off-limits to his predecessors, who were influenced by T. S. ELIOT and the New Critics (see FUGITIVE/AGRARIAN SCHOOL).

Born in Wilkinsburg, Pennsylvania, Snodgrass escaped a constricting home life through service in the U.S. Navy during World War II. In "Returned to Frisco, 1946" (1959), the returning serviceman senses lost freedoms in the irony offered by a flowered Alcatraz. *Heart's Needle* (1959), his acclaimed first book, won Snodgrass the 1960 Pulitzer Prize. In 1972–73 Snodgrass was accepted into the National Institute of Arts and Letters and the Academy of American Poets.

In many poems Snodgrass uses his personal history, 20th-century history, and timeless Orphic and Edenic myths to examine grief and loss. Candid and clinical, *Remains* (1970) examines his family's life and a sister's death at 25. In "The Mouse," much like poetic ancestor Robert Burns, he finds that a small creature children feared dead becomes an emblem of lost innocence after the sister's death. With cutting irony he observes, "Ridiculous children; we could bawl / Our eyes out about nothing." "After Experience Taught Me" declares training showed him that "you must call up every strength you own / And you can rip off the whole facial mask." Complacent students in "The Campus on the Hill" atop the world believe they "have nowhere to go but down." In "Heart's Needle," his child leaves, and he mourns how "Indeed our sweet / foods leave us cavities."

Snodgrass spent years on *The Fuhrer Bunker* (1977), a controversial sequence of dramatic monologues. In this multivoiced work, which Snodgrass calls "a sort of oratorio for speakers" (192), first performed theatrically in part in 1977, also adapted to the stage, various Nazi figures speak inner revelations so repulsive that some critics reject the appropriateness of such work for literary presentation. Snodgrass insists, however, that "nothing human is foreign to us" (155). This work is a crowning achievement as an examination of evil great and small.

Frequently Snodgrass has used a rhetorical strategy that moves from the general to the specific, from public to personal. While in his midcareer he tried freer forms, later, with "For me: no music, no poem" (1999), he returned to the rhymes and metrical forms of which he is a master (see PROSODY AND FREE VERSE). Gavin Ewart declared Snodgrass "one of the six best poets now writing in English" (Ewart 165). How one appraises Snodgrass depends, in large part, on larger questions about what constitutes art, as well as about accepting intimacy and trusting the artist's truthfulness. Such simplicity, ease, and directness combined with such craft makes some readers wary. Classical sincerity or a Trojan horse? Intelligence, irony, and imagery presented musically and metrically are Snodgrass's prodigious gifts. Spirited and serious with a comical name, the poet asserts "Snodgrass is walking through the universe" ("These Trees Stand" [1981]).

BIBLIOGRAPHY

Ewart, Gavin, "One Poet, Many Voices." *New York Times Book Review,* September 13, 1987.

Haven, Stephen, ed. *The Poetry of W. D. Snodgrass: Everything Human.* Ann Arbor: University of Michigan Press, 1993.

Snodgrass, W. D. *After Images.* Rochester, N.Y.: BOA Editions, 1999.

Leslie Palmer

"THE SNOW-MAN" WALLACE STEVENS (1923)

"One must have a mind of winter," announces WALLACE STEVENS at the start of "The Snow-Man," one of his most anthologized and oft-quoted poems. In this LYRIC meditation on the relation between external reality and the human self that perceives it, Stevens suggests that one might achieve a philosophically authentic experience of reality or nature without resorting to the pathetic fallacy, which projects human attributes upon the nonhuman world. By opening the poem with a winter scene that is cold and barren, and which would make anyone caught in it miserable, Stevens challenges the reader not to identify the landscape with one's own experience of it, but to perceive the world purely as it is, without judging it and thereby thinking of it in human terms. Such an attitude, Stevens suggests in the poem's closing lines, will also reveal the strangeness of the human self.

The entire poem is a single, complex sentence that begins with an important philosophical premise. The "mind of winter" that Stevens claims as a necessity is clearly linked to the world that it perceives, and one might equally read "an empty mind" or "a mind thrown open to the external world" here. Thus, one must "have been cold a long time" in order to behold "Nothing that is not there." Stevens notes a conflict between perception and judgment, where the human emotional core invariably projects its own qualities upon the nonhuman, external world, so that that world is never genuinely perceived. This failure of perception accounts in part for the haunting tone of the poem, which almost suggests that the winter landscape itself echoes with the sadness and misery of humankind's inability to experience the world for what it truly is. Helen Vendler describes the poem as one of "Stevens's great explorations into the question of the pathetic fallacy" (335), and the speaker's resistance to projection is a thematic keystone to any reading. Only if one has a mind of winter can one not perceive "any misery in the sound of the wind, / In the sound of a few leaves." Such an act of perception is essentially aesthetic, given over to the purest play of the senses and the imagination, and critics like James Longenbach praise "the act of emptying the mind [as] a highly imaginative act," noting that "Stevens returns almost obsessively to a vision of the world that is untouched by human feeling, a world in which the plain sense of things grows not only stark but also oddly compelling."

But poet and critic ROBERT PINSKY rejects the absolutism of such readings as Longenbach's, noting "That theoretical observer, oddly, has an actual representation in the snow man. . . . To reach that condition, seeing the physical world only for what it is—being 'at one' with it—and knowing it fully as nothing *to* any person, one would have to cease existing. Perfect immersion in the thing itself is a kind of stoney death" (73). To divest one's perceptions of their human, emotional qualities is to divest oneself of humanity, Pinsky suggests, reading the poem not as Stevens's advocacy of abstraction, but as an ironic warning against it. "Only an imaginary, supremely cold-minded witness could completely avoid anthropomorphizing the bitter winter scene, avoid seeing it in human terms," Pinsky cautions.

Such conflicting readings of the poem offer no easy resolution. However, whether one reads the poem as a philosophical lyric praising the wintry beauties of abstraction, or as an ironic parody of such dehumanized aesthetics, Stevens's attentions to the beauty of plain reality, of being itself, are evident, and his lyricism demonstrates the capacity of a poem to bring a reader in touch with reality. The poem's rich play of alliteration evokes the winter wind, and the carefully observed details are rendered with such precise diction ("crusted," "shagged," "the distant glitter") that the reader is made to listen, to be open to physical experience in as receptive an attitude as prayer.

BIBLIOGRAPHY

Longenbach, James. "Wallace Stevens." *American Writers: Retrospective Supplement,* 295–315. New York: Scribner's, 1998.

Pinsky, Robert. *The Situation of Poetry: Contemporary Poetry and Its Traditions.* Princeton, N.J.: Princeton University Press, 1976.

Vendler, Helen. "A. R. Ammons: Dwelling in the Flow of Shapes." In *The Music of What Happens: Poems, Poets, Critics,* 310–342. Cambridge, Mass: Harvard University Press, 1988.

Temple Cone

SNYDER, GARY (1930–) Few poets have greater "proof" than the poet Gary Snyder of what Walt Whitman called the poet's "proof . . . that his country absorbs him as affectionately as he has absorbed it" (762). Variously described (and self-described) as a SAN FRANCISCO RENAISSANCE man, BEAT poet, "wilderness-philosopher-activist" (according to ALLEN GINSBERG [203]), scholar-guru-woodsman, and, infamously, as the "number one Dharma bum of them all" (according to JACK KEROUAC [10]), Gary Snyder is perhaps one of the most important and influential American poets, as well as countercultural figures. Marked by a profound respect for the environment and a rigorous commitment to social responsibility and ethical action, Snyder weaves such notions as watershed, bioregion, reinhabitation, wild systems, mindfulness, and stewardship into his poetry, cultural theory, and public policy alike. Above all else, Snyder's writing aspires to be political and social in many radical ways: "For at least a century and a half, the socially engaged writers of the developed world have taken their role to be one of resistance and subversion," Snyder wrote in 1995. "[P]oetry can disclose the misuse of language by holders of power, it can attack dangerous archetypes employed to oppress, and it can expose the flimsiness of shabby made-up mythologies" (Snyder "What Poetry" 92).

With this in mind, it is important to point out that Snyder's poetry, poetics, and philosophy may be best approached through four main, interrelated prisms of thought: first, as mentioned, the importance of ecological and environmental concerns, manifested in his work as a kind of "ecopoetics" of bioregionalism; second, his devotion to the intricacies and complexities of American Indian and First Nations traditions, philosophies, and ways of life; third, his lifelong study of both Chinese and Japanese poetry and art, as well as his ongoing engagement with Zen Buddhism and other forms of Mahayana Buddhism; and fourth, his dialogue with the traditions and idioms of American writing, especially in the inspiration drawn from such writers as Whitman and Henry David Thoreau, and in the questioning and enlargement of modernist American poetic projects, such as those of EZRA POUND and WILLIAM CARLOS WILLIAMS (see MODERNISM).

Shortly after his birth, Snyder's family moved from San Francisco to a small farmstead on the outskirts of Seattle. It was there, in the rainy Northwest states of Washington and Oregon that Snyder grew up, reading books by Thoreau and Ernest Thompson Seton, learning a lifelong proficiency with the tools and animal life that surrounded him, and arriving at "an immediate, intuitive deep sympathy with the natural world" (Snyder *Real* 92). After graduating from high school in Portland, Snyder was awarded a scholarship to Reed College, where he studied anthropology and mythography. At Reed Snyder, along with PHILIP WHALEN and Lew Welch, began paying serious attention to writing and publishing poetry in many of the literary magazines of the West Coast. By the time Snyder moved to San Francisco in 1952, his reputation as a poet had preceded him, and he soon met KENNETH REXROTH, Ginsberg, and Kerouac. Through Ginsberg and Kerouac, Snyder came to be one of the poets who read at the Six Gallery reading in 1955, which many claim sparked the beginning of the San Francisco Renaissance.

Although trying to define any set of poetics or methodology for either the San Francisco or Beat poets is a thorny issue at best, it can be said that many of their aesthetic preoccupations overlapped, especially as seen in the extensions and revitalizations of an earlier American generation in what has come to be labeled "open form" or "organic" poetry (see PROSODY AND FREE VERSE and ARS POETICAS). Similarities can also be seen in the revival of oral poetry and the power of performance (see POETRY IN PERFORMANCE), experimentation with CONFESSIONAL modes of poetry, through the widespread use of drugs and sexual freedom as vehicles for creative expression, and, notably for Snyder, a commitment to Eastern religions. Snyder was appointed to the California Arts Council in 1974, where he served for six years as an active member. He has also been involved in local, regional, and national political and educational efforts that include the establishment of "the Art of the Wild," an annual conference focused on writing and issues concerning the environment. Snyder has taught creative writing at the University of California, Davis, since 1985. He won the Pulitzer Prize for poetry (1970), the American Book Award for poetry (1983), and the Bollingen Prize (1997). He has also received an American Academy of Arts and Letters award (1987) and the Poetry Society of America Shelley Memorial Award (1986), as well as several other awards and fellowships.

Snyder's experiences as a tanker seaman, logger, ranger, and trail-crew member in the Pacific Northwest were inspirations for his first two collections of poetry, *RIPRAP* (1959) and *Myths and Texts* (1960). Soon after the Six Gallery reading, Snyder began a long 15-year stint traveling between India, Japan, China, and the United States. During these travels he learned to speak and write Chinese and Japanese, and he became a devout Zen Buddhist in the Rinzai tradition. Prominent in *Six Selections from Mountains and Rivers without End, Plus One* (1965), a continuing cycle of poems affecting *Mountains and Rivers Without End* (1996), *Cold Mountain Poems* (1965), *The Back Country* (1967), and *Regarding Wave* (1969) is the way in which the everyday is braided with the discipline of Zen and other East Asian religious-philosophic practices. These collections also address what Snyder sees as the ethical and philosophic failures of Western culture juxtaposed against the values of Buddhism and traditions of American Indian culture. These preoccupations resonate throughout his poetry and manifest themselves in Snyder's distinct stylizations of bare simplicity, directness, and the attempts to render language as material, where "each rock a word / a creek washed stone" ("Riprap" [1965]). This rendering is expressed in terms of what Snyder often refers to as the juxtapositional logic of "riprapping" (Afterword), a mode in which words and images are placed "side by side" to "work like sharp blows on the mind" ("Statement" 421). Riprapping draws its energy from the compositional impulses of many modernist poets, seen especially in what Pound labeled the ideogrammic method (see IMAGIST SCHOOL). "Riprap" (1959), "Piute Creek" (1965), and other poems are excellent examples of Snyder's efforts to knit poetry to the physicality of the body, to work, and to the sheer immediacy of the real. As Snyder points out in "Piute Creek," "A clear, attentive mind / Has no meaning but that / Which sees is truly seen." The point is not so much to "show the world through the prism of language" but to see the world "without any prism of language, and to bring that seeing *into* language" (Snyder "What Poetry" 67).

BIBLIOGRAPHY

Dean, Tim. *Gary Snyder and the American Unconscious: Inhabiting the Ground.* Basingstoke, England: Macmillan, 1991.

Ginsberg, Allen. "My Mythic Thumbnail Biography of Gary Snyder." In *Gary Snyder: Dimensions of a Life,* edited by Jon Halper. San Francisco: Sierra Club Books, 1991.

Halper, Jon, ed. *Gary Snyder: Dimensions of a Life.* San Francisco: Sierra Club Books, 1991.

Kerouac, Jack. *The Dharma Bums.* New York: Signet, 1959.

Murphy, Patrick. *Understanding Gary Snyder.* Columbia: University of South Carolina Press, 1992.

Snyder, Gary. Afterword to *Riprap and Cold Mountain Poems.* New York: North Point Press, 1965.

———. "What Poetry Did in China." In *A Place in Space: Ethics, Aesthetics, and Watersheds.* New York: Counterpoint Press, 1995, pp. 91–93.

———. *The Real Work: Interviews and Talks 1964–1979.* New York: New Directions, 1980.

———. "Statement on Poetics." In *The New American Poetry 1945–1960,* edited by Donald Allen, 420–421. New York: Grove Press, 1960.

Whitman, Walt. "1855 Preface to Leaves of Grass." *The Complete Poems,* edited by Francis Murphy. New York: Penguin, 1975, pp. 741–762.

Jason Morelyle

SOBIN, GUSTAF (1935–2005) Gustaf Sobin is a poet of transcendence, seeking through language ways in which things of the world can be transformed and elevated into exceptional beauty and delight. Influenced by ROBERT DUNCAN, ROBERT CREELEY, and René Char, among others, his work bridges American and

French poetic traditions. He has spent his life as a writer entirely in France, which provides the setting for much of his work.

Born and reared in Boston, Sobin graduated from Brown University in 1957. He met the poet René Char, who invited him to his home in Provence in 1962. The following year Sobin made Provence his permanent home and learned "how to read the landscape [there] as one might read a text, a *textus*, a woven fabric" (Foster 27). Provence provided him with time and freedom for the intensive study of poetry and its potential transformative powers, a study that included discussions with Char and the philosopher Martin Heidegger. Sobin's first book of poems, *Wind Chrysalid's Rattle* appeared in 1980. *Voyaging Portraits* (1988) includes "Portrait of the Self as Instrument of Its Syllables," a key work in understanding Sobin's poetics. His selected poems, *By the Bias of Sound,* appeared in 1995. *Luminous Debris: Reflecting on Vestige in Provence and Languedoc* (2000) is a series of meditations on ancient objects and places in his adopted homeland. To most readers Sobin is better known for his fiction than for his poetry. His novels include *The Fly-Truffler* (2000), a best-seller that has been frequently translated. Similar to his essays and much of his poetry, the novel is set in Provence and involves transformations of the ordinary through language, inner vision, and imagination.

The specifics of landscapes and objects are necessary preconditions for Sobin's poetry. The capacity of language to suggest possibilities beyond one's immediate grasp of geography and objects, thereby going beyond the surfaces of the ordinary and everyday world, gives his poetry its fundamental dynamics. "Portrait of the Self as Instrument of Its Syllables" records this process through the final gathering of words into a poem, which is then seen as a "luminous salvage." Releasing one from the surfaces of the ordinary and everyday, language becomes an end in itself: As Sobin says in "Transparent Itineraries: 1999," collected in *In the Name of the Neither* (2002), language is "a density . . . in the service of its own evanescent releases."

BIBLIOGRAPHY

Baker, Robert. "The Manifestation of the Particular: The Thing in Sobin and Heidegger." *Talisman* 18 (fall 1998): 177–196.

———. "The Open Vocable." *American Book Review* 20, no. 2 (January/February 1999): 4, 10.

Sobin, Gustaf. "An Interview with Gustaf Sobin," by Edward Foster. *Talisman* 10 (spring 1993): 26–39. [The Gustaf Sobin Issue, edited by Foster.]

Edward Foster

"SOMEWHERE I HAVE NEVER TRAVELLED" E. E. CUMMINGS **(1931)** This poem, published in the collection *ViVa,* illustrates the influence of the modernist experimentation of such poets as EZRA POUND and T. S. ELIOT on E. E. CUMMINGS and exemplifies the poet's fusion of exuberant typographical and grammatical play, a painterly exploration of imagery, and spare lyricism. While *ViVa* demonstrates Cummings's increasingly idiosyncratic and anarchic poetics and marks his emergence as a crucial player in bringing to American poetry the questioning and experiments of European literary and visual art, "somewhere" combines formal radicalism with gentle lyricism and shows the exquisite balance of Cummings's best poetry (see EUROPEAN POETIC INFLUENCES and MODERNISM).

The world of this poem is associative in its understated metaphors and mobile in its shifting between images. A self is a flower, fingers are petals, and fragility is "intense." The poem is about the courage of a joyous trust. Eyes have voices, roses depth, and the rain is delicate handed. This imagery shows the influence of SURREALISM and evokes the sensation of the blurring of self and other that the delights of early love bring. Boundaries collapse, and the self merges with both the beloved and the world, especially the natural world. The experience of "I," the poem's speaker, is of the fear and exhilaration of loving. The poem whirls in a celebration of wonder and risk, refusing stasis and caution—a song to vitality.

Cummings called the revolutionary "i" of his poems the "non-hero" (quoted in Kennedy 175). Here "i" is paradoxical: Although far from the brash hero of classical and romantic love poetry, nevertheless "I," a vulnerably open lover, is heroic in embracing the risks of loving. The poem's economical diction reinforces this, juxtaposing fragility and power: The "most fragile gesture" can "enclose" the speaker; the "slightest look" can "unclose" him. The texture of fragility is eloquent and compelling, and it has depth as well as delicacy. From its overarching metaphor of the closed self opening and shutting, other connections ripple outward through metaphor: A self closed "as fingers" is "unclosed" one petal at a time by the lover's look and is thus also compared with the rosebud, opened by spring's persuasion.

The poem's punctuation defies standard grammar, reaching to express less rational connections. In the poem "since feeling is first," Cummings's ideas about grammar are suggested through the metaphor of putting aside "the syntax of things" to experience life more fully. Cummings, pulled from childhood toward painting as well as poetry, finds the expression of each word maximized by its placement. The silences between words invest simple term with great care. The poem "somewhere i have never travelled" avoids excess and has a simplicity in its diction and an unflinching emotional openness. In true modernist form, its hallmarks are questing and experimentation, and it shows a revitalization of form and theme.

BIBLIOGRAPHY

Kennedy, Richard S. *Dreams in the Mirror: A Biography of E. E. Cummings.* New York: W. W. Norton, 1980.

Norman Freidman. *E. E. Cummings: The Art of His Poetry.* Baltimore, Md.: Johns Hopkins University Press, 1964.

Felicity Plunkett

SONG, CATHY (1955–) Cathy Song's contribution to late 20th-century American poetry began with the publication of her first book, *Picture Bride,* which won the Yale Series of Younger Poets Award in 1982 and made Song a new figure of great promise in the Asian-American literary scene. As the recipient of one of the more prestigious literary prizes in the nation, Song not only joins a highly select and influential company of former winners, such as ADRIENNE RICH, W. S. MERWIN, JOHN ASHBERY, and ROBERT HASS, her sudden prominence also gives greater depth and dimension to what is called "emergent" or "immigrant" literature, an important body of work that has forced an expansion in the traditional canon to include texts by immigrants and people of color, such as LI-YOUNG LEE, DEREK WALCOTT, LESLIE MARMON SILKO, ALBERTO RÍOS, and LORNA DEE CERVANTES.

A Korean and Chinese American, Song was born in Honolulu, Hawaii. She graduated from Wellesley College with a B.A. in 1977 and Boston University with an M.A. in creative writing in 1981, and she returned to live in Hawaii with her husband, son, and daughter in 1987. Since her first volume of poetry, *Picture Bride,* won the 1982 Yale award and was nominated for the National Book Critics Circle Award, Song has published three other books of poems: *Frameless Windows, Squares of Light* (1988), *School Figures* (1994), and *Land of Bliss* (2001).

Song's work shows a strong talent notable for its dense, intimate, and dazzling descriptions, its penetrating exploration of those subjects closest to Song's experiences—the intricacies of Asian immigrant family relationships and histories, the places and landscapes of her childhood, especially the rural plantation culture of Hawaii, exile and reunion, and the ritual of memory—and its engagement with various modes of expression—sewing perfect seams, preparing foods (alive with all the sensory sensations of taste, smell, sound, color, and touch), or decorating the world around us with flowers, light, clothes, and sounds. In her poem "The White Porch" (1982), Song asks readers to think "of the luxury: how to use / the afternoon." Her poems offer various, original, intensely specific responses to the luxurious possibilities of how to use our time. Song shows great skill at fusing form, image, occasion, and emotion; the ability to bring concentrated life to her world; and careful explorations of the contact and occasional conflict between immigrant and nonimmigrant cultures.

BIBLIOGRAPHY

Fujita-Sato, Gayle. "'Third World' as Place and Paradigm in Cathy Song's 'Picture Bride,'" *MELUS* (spring 1988): 49–72.

Lim, Shirley. "Picture Bride." *MELUS* (fall 1983): 95–99.

Kenneth Speirs

***THE SONNETS* TED BERRIGAN (1964, 1967, 1982, 2000)** TED BERRIGAN'S *The Sonnets* was first published by Berrigan's *C* Press in 1964. The book (and Grove Press's 1967 edition) contained 65 sonnets. Reissues of *The Sonnets* by United Artists Books

(1982) and Penguin (2000) have respectively restored six and seven previously omitted sonnets. Perhaps the most "traditional" aspect of *The Sonnets* is that it can be read both as a cohesive book and as a collection of discrete poems. Thus the book belongs to the tradition of sonnet sequences stretching back to Shakespeare's sonnet sequence and Petrarch's sonnets to Laura.

Similar to Shakespeare's sonnets, Berrigan's are addressed to various characters. And yet, as ALICE NOTLEY comments, "where Shakespeare's plot is patterned chronologically [Berrigan's] is patterned simultaneously, and where Shakespeare's story is overt [Berrigan's] is buried beneath a series of names, repetitions, and fragmented experience that in this age seem more like life than a bald story does" (v–vi). Phrases, including "I like to beat people up" and "feminine, marvelous, and tough," are repeated throughout, lending a sense of consistency to the otherwise highly fragmented work.

The Sonnets also works to threaten conventional definitions of authorship and originality. Lines from other authors, without attribution, are made a part of what, in effect, is a collage—one half of "A Final Sonnet," for example, is a word-for-word selection from Prospero's final speech in Shakespeare's *The Tempest. The Sonnets* is particularly noted for its references to NEW YORK SCHOOL poets, and thus *The Sonnets* is a work in conversation with select predecessor poets. By inserting other writers' works into his own, Berrigan reestablished the practice of collage as a technique in the writing of poetry. Libbie Rifkin explains that collage can be understood as collaborative, insofar as Berrigan conceived of "collaboration as an encounter between any number of different writings, set in motion but not controlled by a single writer" (130).

Poems in *The Sonnets* are significant for their lyrical beauty and their assault on sonnet conventions. No single poem conforms to the rules of established sonnet structure. Elevated language typical of traditional sonnets—for example, "O let me burst, and I be lost at sea!"—appears throughout *The Sonnets,* yet Berrigan combines it with a street-smart and wholly contemporary rhetoric: "fucked til 7 now she's late to work" (sonnet LXIV).

Altogether *The Sonnets* radically extends the possibilities of the traditionally conservative sonnet form, as it continues to evoke 1960s ideals, including community-building and democratic redistribution of wealth—particularly the wealth of predecessor poetry.

BIBLIOGRAPHY

Berrigan, Ted. "Interview with Ted Berrigan," by Barry Alpert. In *Talking in Tranquility,* edited by Stephen Ratcliffe and Leslie Scalapino, 31–54. Bolinas, Calif.: Avenue B/O Books, 1991.

Notley, Alice. Introduction to *The Sonnets,* by Ted Berrigan. New York: Penguin, 2000, pp. v–xv.

Rifkin, Libbie. *Career Moves.* Madison: University of Wisconsin Press, 2000.

Ward, Geoff. *Statutes of Liberty.* New York: St. Martin's Press, 1993.

Daniel Kane

SOTO, GARY (1952–) Gary Soto, one of the foremost Chicano writers of the 20th century, haunted the poetry section of the library as an impoverished young man and longed for the day when his own work would reside on its shelves. At 16, Soto discovered Jules Verne, Ernest Hemingway, John Steinbeck, and ROBERT FROST. But he seemed most inspired by the work of Knut Hamsun, the Norwegian writer whose novel *Hunger* (1890) depicted a struggling and starving writer much like Soto himself.

Soto was born and raised in Fresno, California. An adolescent in the 1960s, he noted how the picture of idyllic family life presented on American television seemed an ironic contrast to his own home, where the inhabitants suffered "an ignorance that was stupefying for all of us that lived in the confines of a three-bedroom house" (Letter). Soto sold his first work at 19; a check arrived in time to purchase shoes and trousers for his graduation ceremony (Letter). A graduate of California State University, Fresno, and the University of California, Irvine, where he earned an M.F.A. in creative writing (1976), Soto is known for his poetry, short stories, and children's books. He is the author of 10 poetry collections. Among honors he has received are the Discover/*Nation* Prize (1975), two fellowships from the National Endowment for the Arts (1982 and 1991), and a fellowship from the Guggenheim Foundation (1979). He teaches at the University of California, Riverside.

Soto's work speaks to young people and those who feel out of place in the mainstream. Michael Manson suggests that Soto's writing breaks "what critics have valued as the 'continuity of American Poetry' with Puritanism" (263), confirming that even the most "American literature" is a "border product reflecting the plural origins of the United States" (264). Soto's poem "Oranges" (1985) depicts a young man of 12 attempting his first date, with a nickel and two oranges in his pocket. When the young girl chooses a candy bar that costs a dime, the speaker "took the nickel from / [his] pocket, then an orange." Their eyes meet: She knows "what it was all / About." Before this bartered exchange, the girl is referred to as "she." As the young couple exits the store, her status has changed. Soto writes that he "took my girl's hand in mine." Soto's work offers insightful reflections on childhood experiences. While it reflects the "plural origins" of American literature, it also dissolves "borders," as readers recognize elements of their own youth in his poems.

BIBLIOGRAPHY

Manson, Michael Tomasek. "Poetry and Masculinity on the Anglo/Chicano Border." In *The Calvinist Roots of the Modern Era,* edited by Aliki Barnstone. Hanover, N.H.: University Press of New England, 1997.

Soto, Gary. Letter to Pamela Highet, April 22, 2001.

Pamela Highet

SPICER, JACK (1925–1965) Jack Spicer was a part of the bohemian movement that flourished in Berkeley and San Francisco after World War II, when such writers as Henry Miller, KENNETH REXROTH, and ROBERT DUNCAN lived there. The SAN FRANCISCO RENAISSANCE lasted into the 1960s and included Duncan, Rexroth, WILLIAM EVERSON, and LAWRENCE FERLINGHETTI, among others. Spicer was also associated with writers from BLACK MOUNTAIN College, such as ROBERT CREELEY and CHARLES OLSON. While the movement featured many stylistic approaches, its poets tended to focus on language and on a poetic form shaped by the sound and rhythms of the voice; they also tried to make their poetry immediately present to the reader through everyday subject matter, words, and images. They inspired many West Coast writers who were connected with BEAT POETRY, including GARY SNYDER, MICHAEL MCCLURE, Philip Lamantia, and PHILIP WHALEN. Although Spicer was not well known during his lifetime and avoided the limelight, he did attract a dedicated following of young poets who met with him regularly at his favorite bar.

Spicer was born in southern California. He liked to say that he was born in 1946, the year he met Duncan and ROBIN BLASER at the University of California, Berkeley. He spent the rest of his life in San Francisco, except for brief stays in New York and Boston and a semester of teaching at the University of Minnesota. He worked at Berkeley as a linguistic researcher until his death.

Although Spicer was first published in the 1940s, his first well-known work, *After Lorca,* appeared in 1957, followed by *Homage to Creeley* (1959), *Billy the Kid* (1959), *The Heads of the Town up to the Aether* (1962), and *Language* (1965). Much of his work was not in print until after his death, and it now includes lectures, letters, essays, plays, and recordings. Although he was poorly understood in his own lifetime, he now attracts international favor, and his work continues to inspire gay and lesbian writers. Spicer preferred the role of cultural outcast and, similar to so many writers on the cultural margins, he found relief in alcohol, which eventually caused his death.

Spicer sees the acceptance of ambiguity and paradox as the way to what he calls the "real." As he said in his poetic "letters" to Federico García Lorca, "I would like to point to the real, disclose it," and it is the poet's task to use words to "drag the real into the poem," that is, to translate those real objects into words (*After Lorca* 1957). Poetry is a process for Spicer; rather than tapping into the subconscious, the poet receives the idea for the poem from "outside" in the form of a "dictation" (Blaser 272). Instead of controlling or manipulating that material, the poet follows it step by step through the process of composition, in what he called a "serial poem." In "Imaginary Elegies" (1959), Spicer piles words onto each other as if they were objects, questioning the power of poetry to do anything more than to provide visual images, as if it was "almost blind like a camera." He moves from there to God's "big eye" and then to all of creation, the Sun, the Moon, heaven, and hell, all unexplainable because, "Most things happen in twilight," before he offers a warning about the enormous responsibility of the poet: "Unbind the dreamers. / Poet, / Be like God." That is, the poet must lead the reader to the "real" by presenting a lasting image in an act of imaginative creation, the poem itself. In verse IV, he repeats, "Time does not finish a poem"; it cannot be finished without the reader's active participation in recreating what the poet imagined. The poem ends as the speaker transforms poetry itself into "Po-eatery," something to be consumed by the reader.

One of Spicer's most prevalent symbols is the ghost, a magical figure that brings together life and death, interior and exterior, the past and the present, and that can, as Norman M. Finkelstein says, "hint at truths the poet barely wishes to accept" (89). For example, Spicer reveals his ambivalent feeling about the past in the second of "Six Poems for Poetry Chicago" (1966): Past events are always present metaphorically, "Which evokes Eliot and then evokes suspicion. Ghosts all of them. Doers of no good." Spicer's irony is apparent in his allusion to T. S. ELIOT's famous essay "Tradition and the Individual Talent" (1919) in which Eliot stresses the importance of literary tradition to the writer (see ARS POETICAS). Because the present is formed from the past, the past is always part of the present. However, past writers are also "ghosts," never fully present, and therefore, "doers of no good." Finally, the speaker tries to envision himself as part of that procession of time: "Rest us as corpses / We poets / Vain words," but he is overwhelmed by the "impossible dimensions" of that realization. Still any communication must come from the past, because the words have already been uttered; as Spicer says in *After Lorca*, "That is how we dead men write to each other," and indeed the "Lorca" to whom Spicer writes is already a "ghost." For Spicer, things correspond rather than connect, and that allows the "real" to be communicated "across language" and "across time" (*After Lorca*), which is why his poetry speaks so powerfully today.

BIBLIOGRAPHY

Blaser, Robin, ed. *The Collected Books of Jack Spicer*. Santa Barbara, Calif.: Black Sparrow, 1980.

Ellingham, Lewis, and Kevin Killian. *Poet Be like God: Jack Spicer and the San Francisco Renaissance*. Hanover, N.H.: Wesleyan University Press, 1998.

Finkelstein, Norman M. "Jack Spicer's Ghosts and the Gnosis of History." *Boundary* IX, no. 2 (winter 1981): 81–100.

Foster, Edward. *Jack Spicer*. Boise, Idaho: Boise State University, 1991.

Gord Beveridge

SPOON RIVER ANTHOLOGY EDGAR LEE MASTERS (1915) The cemetery of Spoon River, Illinois, provides the setting and cast of characters for Edgar Lee Master's book-length collection, *Spoon River Anthology*. Comprising more than 200 short, FREE VERSE monologues by the deceased inhabitants of a small, midwestern town, Masters's book provides an often unflinching portrait of the bitterness, difficulty, and pathos of life in America in the early 20th century. The book is a historically and artistically important portrait of America's changing social and cultural landscape, one that reflects, according to the scholar John Hallwas, "an ambivalent national spirit, with contradictory thrusts toward individualism and community" (65).

In 1906, Masters first conceived of a novel dealing with the various relationships of the inhabitants of a small Illinois town, but he never wrote it. Masters later revived the plan in 1913, deciding to compose this fictional community in a modern style of free verse inspired by the demotic language of the great 19th-century poet Walt Whitman, whose biography Masters would later write, and the poised, memorable phrasings of classical Greek epigrams, which had encouraged Masters to revise the conventional style of his earlier writings. The fictional community of Spoon River is composed from details of people and places in the two river towns where Masters grew up, Lewistown, Illinois, and Petersburg, Illinois. By depicting small town life, Masters was joining a tradition distinguished by such writers as the English poet A. E. Housman, whose collection *A Shropshire Lad* (1896) was situated in Ludlow, England, and E. A. ROBINSON, many of whose characters lived in Tilbury Town, a stand-in for his hometown of Gardiner, Maine.

Organized according to the stages of Hell, Purgatory, and Heaven of Dante Alighieri's *Divine Comedy*, the book was hailed as an important work of American REALISM and was associated with Sherwood Anderson's *Winesburg, Ohio*, (1919) and Sinclair Lewis's *Main*

Street (1920), prose works from the "revolt from the village" movement from the 1910s through the 1930s. The book enjoyed great critical and commercial success, though it proved the only artistically significant work of Masters's large opus. *Spoon River Anthology* attracted readers in large part because it exposed the dark side of small-town life, including its murders, suicides, scandalous love affairs. In the opening poem of the book, "The Hill," Masters lists many of the tragedies that befell the inhabitants of Spoon River: *"One died in shameful child-birth, / One of a thwarted love, / One at the hands of a brute in a brothel. . . ."* His characters speak of guilt and loneliness, of the disappointments and thwarted ambitions caused by parenthood, insufficient talent, and bad luck, of the grief of loss and the pain of betrayal, and of the misery inflicted by small-mindedness, bigotry, and misunderstanding. More than anything, though, Masters's characters seek to tell the truth about their lives. In "Amanda Barker," for instance, the speaker reveals that, although "it is believed in the village where I lived / That Henry loved me with a husband's love," her husband got her pregnant "Knowing that I could not bring forth life / Without losing my own." Revelations such as these, which called into question the peace and harmony associated with small-town life, brought Masters equal measures of praise and notoriety among specialist and nonspecialist readers alike.

But readers also embraced the book because they found the struggles and minor achievements of their own ordinary lives reflected in the stories of Masters's characters. In "Lucinda Matlock," a poem based on Masters's mother, the speaker balances happiness and sadness equally when she says, "We were married and lived together for seventy years, / Enjoying, working, raising the twelve children, / Eight of whom we lost." And in keeping with the structural parallels with Dante's *Divine Comedy,* the monologues toward the end of *Spoon River Anthology* show an increasing sense of religious consolation. Masters professed himself a "Spinozan atheist,' by which he meant one who, like the Enlightenment philosopher Baruch de Spinoza, does not subscribe to any one religion but nevertheless finds God present in all creation. The monologue "Joseph Dixon" concludes with an affirmation of divine beneficence by a deceased piano tuner: "Surely the concord that ruled my spirit is proof / Of an Ear that tuned me, able to tune me over / And use me again if I am worthy to use." Even in an earlier poem, "Lois Spears," which is spoken by a woman blind from birth (an affliction thought by her father in "Willard Fluke" to be divine retribution for his own extramarital affairs), the goodness of life shows through. Lois Spears describes herself as "the happiest of women," who moved through the world "With an instinct as sure as sight, / As though there were eyes in my finger tips— / Glory to God in the highest."

Masters's characters reveal the twin conflicts driving America's history: the struggle for individual freedom in the face of social and cultural conformity, and the struggle of the community to negotiate and incorporate the eccentricities of its inhabitants. What Masters describes is not limited to the local level, however. Hallwas writes that the cultural divide between the individualistic and permissive but socially conservative South and the educated and socially progressive but religiously restrictive North of the Civil War era was evident in the composition of the state of Illinois itself (3–5), arguing that this had an important influence on the personalities and community divisions in *Spoon River Anthology*. Thus, like the novelist William Faulkner, Masters makes the small town a microcosm for changes and conflicts occurring within the United States as a whole during the early 20th century. His vision is at once darkly modern yet hopeful, depicting life as both "the monstrous ogre" ("Robert Fulton Tanner") and as something "we rejoice for . . . / Mirrored in us" ("Isaiah Beethoven"). The cemetery of voices in *Spoon River Anthology* becomes a garden of world-views drawn from many parts of Masters's life, no one claiming precedence but all of them linked by an all-encompassing vision that "Lucinda Matlock" acknowledges when she says, "It takes life to love Life."

BIBLIOGRAPHY

Hallwas, John E. Introduction. In *Spoon River Anthology: An Annotated Edition,* by Edgar Lee Masters, edited and with annotations by John E. Hallwas. Urbana: University of Illinois Press, 1992.

Wrenn, John H., and Margaret M. Wrenn. *Edgar Lee Masters.* Boston: Twayne Publishers, 1983.

Temple Cone

SPRING AND ALL WILLIAM CARLOS WILLIAMS (1923) First published in the periodical the *Dial* (see POETRY JOURNALS) WILLIAM CARLOS WILLIAMS's *Spring and All* is a representative modernist text (see MODERNISM). It can be read along with T. S. ELIOT's poem *The WASTE LAND* (which appeared in the *Dial* in 1922) as an example of the experimental approach to literature between the wars. But to read *Spring and All* as simply a counterpoint to *The Waste Land* is to miss the radically distinctive presence of Williams in the tradition of modernism. Eliot's formal method of allusion and quotation to and from other texts—Williams described Eliot and EZRA POUND as "men content with the connotations of their masters" (*Selected* 21)—stands in sharp contrast to Williams's embrace of the dynamic innovations of the avant-garde.

As Williams explains, *Spring and All* "was written when all the world was going crazy about typographical form and is really a travesty on the idea" (*Imaginations* 86). An improvisational sequence of 27 untitled poems and associated prose fragments, *Spring and All* is a vital example of Williams's early experiments with form. The text of *Spring and All* is distinctive for other reasons as well: It incorporates the methods of collage and juxtaposition in the visual arts of the period; it transgresses boundaries among genres, raising fundamental questions regarding the distinction between poetry and prose; it is a parody of nationalistic postwar rhetoric in the United States; and it is a modernist manifesto on the social and cultural value of art.

The text of *Spring and All* introduced the poems that would become Williams's most well known—including "Spring and All," "To Elsie," and "The Red Wheelbarrow." The poems reflect his abiding commitment to the local conditions and people of his time and place. The poem later entitled "Spring and All" registers the mind apprehending transitions in nature—"Now the grass, tomorrow / the stiff curl of wildcarrot leaf"—and the poem known as "The Right of Way" gathers the meaningful but transient particulars of our day-to-day lives—"an elderly man who / smiled and looked away."

Spring and All is not least a breathtaking commentary on the necessary and continuing activity of imaginative labor. As Williams explains, "The imagination goes from one thing to another" (*Selected* 11); therefore the reader must remain attentive to the text's movement from one thing to another. Not unlike Walt Whitman, Williams insists upon the reader's active role in the production of meaning. The experience of reading *Spring and All* is challenging for precisely this reason. As Williams insists in the prose of *Spring and All*, "There is no confusion—only difficulties." In other words, the confusion one may experience reading *Spring and All* in no way implies a confusing text; on the contrary, it is a condition naming the experience of a reader, face-to-face with the generative state in which the imagination becomes aware of itself.

BIBLIOGRAPHY

"A Symposium: Teaching (and Being Taught By) *Spring and All*." *William Carlos Williams Review* 10, no. 2 (fall 1984): 1–20.

Long, Mark C. "'no confusion—only difficulties': William Carlos Williams's Poetics of Apposition." *William Carlos Williams Review* 23, no. 2 (fall 1997): 1–26.

Palattella, John. "But If It Ends the Start Is Begun: *Spring and All*, Americanism, and Postwar Apocalypse." *William Carlos Williams Review* 21, no. 1 (spring 1995): 1–21.

Whittaker, Thomas R. *William Carlos Williams*. New York: Twayne, 1968.

Williams, William Carlos. *Imaginations*. New York: New Directions, 1970.

———. *Selected Essays*. New York: New Directions, 1969.

Mark C. Long

ST. JOHN, DAVID (1949–) David St. John holds an important place within the modern conceptualization of poetry as a mapping of consciousness (see MODERNISM). His poetry bridges the gap between linear conceptions of thought found in NARRATIVE POETRY of the mid-20th century and the elliptical patterns of the mind prominent in postmodern verse. He once remarked, as the "image of the modern mind's discovery of itself" defined "poetic activity in the early part of this century . . . I seek the movement or progression of the mind's discovery of itself" (qtd. in Jackson 78). ELIZABETH BISHOP and JOHN ASHBERY were major influences upon his early poetry. Unlike other poets of his time, St. John moves between these two poles by writing a poetry that dramatizes both Bishop's acute attention to the details of the world and Ashbery's telescopic motions of the mind.

St. John was born and raised in Fresno, California. In 1974 he earned an M.F.A. from the University of Iowa and published his first book, *Hush,* two years later. St. John is the author of six other books of poetry, including *Red Leaves of Night* (1999), a finalist for the Los Angeles Times Book Prize, and *Study for the World's Body* (1994), a finalist for the National Book Award. Along with several fellowships from the National Endowment for the Arts (1976, 1984, and 1994) and Guggenheim Foundation (1997), St. John has been awarded the Academy Award from the American Academy of Arts and Letters (2000) and the Prix de Rome (1984).

Fundamental to St. John's search for a poetic expression that enacts "the movement . . . of the mind's discovery of itself" (St. John, quoted in Jackson 78) are a sensual connection to and rendering of the physical world alongside a longing for an ideal metaphysical realm. He often plays these two elements out through characters involved in a drama of relationships, the tensions of the encounter weaving together the interior drama of the self and the public drama of interaction with others. In "A Fan Sketched with Silver Egrets" (1994), St. John uses the intensely physical to move his characters toward a metaphysical realm, beyond language, wherein two people are joined in complete comprehension of one another. The fan, a vessel for the physical touch of the lovers, unfolds as the female lover's "kiss unfolds" and reveals "This scent of animal pleasure." At the same time, the fan is also a physical emblem of the possibility of the pair communicating "With no language / Except this single pulse" of the fan, beating in the air of a crowded room.

St. John's cinematographic imagery of moments rendered in conversational tones is spiked with the flourishes of baroque elegance, accentuating the extent to which the world we perceive is the world we create with the motions and the languages of our minds.

BIBLIOGRAPHY

Jackson, Richard. "Renaming the Present." In *Acts of Mind: Conversations with Contemporary Poets.* Tuscaloosa: University of Alabama Press, 1983.

St. John, David. "David St. John," interviewed by Charles Harper Webb. Cortland Review. Available online. URL: www.cortlandreview.com/issue/11/stjohn11.htm. Downloaded March 2007.

Karla Kelsey

STAFFORD, WILLIAM (1914–1993) Rejecting the elitism, irony, and opaque techniques of the modernists (see MODERNISM), the formalism of the New Criticism (see FUGITIVE/AGRARIAN SCHOOL), in which he was educated, and the CONFESSIONAL style of his contemporaries, William Stafford wrote poetry that is personal, accessible, humane, and deceptively simple. As Judith Kitchen argues, "both his themes and his style place him as a transitional poet, between generations" (10). Influenced by ROBERT FROST, Stafford has more in common with the younger generation of poets, including JAMES WRIGHT, ROBERT BLY, and DONALD HALL, than with his near contemporary ROBERT LOWELL.

Stafford was born in Hutchinson, Kansas, into a working-class family that was liberal and nonconformist. Following a peripatetic and impoverished childhood, Stafford worked his way through the University of Kansas, where he was active in the early civil rights movement, graduating with a B.A. in 1937. During World War II, he registered as a conscientious objector and was stationed at civilian public service camps in Arkansas, California, and Illinois between 1942 and 1946, an experience that was to have a profound effect on his writing. Stafford's memoir about this experience, *Down in My Heart,* became his master's thesis at the University of Kansas and was published in 1947, the year after he graduated. He earned a Ph.D. from the University of Iowa in 1954, while on leave from a teaching position at Lewis and Clark College in Oregon, where he taught until his retirement in 1980. In 1960 when he was 46 years old, he published his first book of poetry. His second and most highly rated book by critics, *Traveling through the Dark,* was published in 1962 and won the National Book Award in 1963. He went on to receive many other prestigious awards and honors, including the Shelley Memorial Award from the Poetry Society of America (1964). In 1970 he was appointed the consultant in poetry to the Library of Congress, a position subsequently renamed poet laureate.

An incredibly prolific writer, Stafford published more than 65 volumes of poetry and prose, refusing to edit his work or limit his output. His philosophy for teaching creative writing called for equality between teacher and student. He believed that the poet and creative writing teacher had no role as critic, and he was often criticized for not setting standards. Even so, his teaching method eventually gained acceptance with the widespread influence of what is known as the "process method of teaching composition," in which the act of writing is emphasized rather than the product of that act.

Characterized by a colloquial idiom and rhythm, Stafford's poetry has often been described as conversational. His work is not conventionally formal, but Stafford adeptly uses rhythmic variations and oblique rhymes in his work for emphasis. While his diction is often simple, his syntax and usage are not; he uses language in unusual and unexpected ways. In *Writing the Australian Crawl,* he explains that "the successive distortions of language have their own kind of cumulative potential" (60).

The dominant themes in Stafford's work have been identified by Judith Kitchen as "a concern with family and home which extends to the past," "the West, which is for him equated with the wilderness and a communion with nature," and "technology and the accompanying fear that the nation will fail to put it to its proper uses" (10). These themes remained remarkably consistent throughout his career.

Stafford's work has been classified as regionalist, environmentalist, antitechnology, and pacifist—classifications that fail, however, to capture the ambivalence and complexity of his career-long explorations of both sides of every question, exemplified most clearly in his two most anthologized poems, "At the Bomb Testing Site" (1960) and "Traveling through the Dark" (1962). Both of these poems explore seeming oppositions, humans versus nature and nature versus technology. They do not favor one over the other, but instead they explore the complexity and difficulty of these issues and argue for a responsible balance between the demands of human progress and the primacy of nature.

Grounded in an ethos of personal, moral, spiritual, and civic responsibility, Stafford's work is imbued with both a childlike wonder and a sense of mortality. Many of his poems are autobiographical, although not CONFESSIONAL. The speaker in the poems is a wise, gentle, avuncular persona who perceives order and connection in the universe and offers hope for the future, while pointing out problems of the present. In the poems there can be delight in the ordinary and the possibility for transcendence through apocalypse—necessary for personal, environmental, and societal salvation to occur.

BIBLIOGRAPHY

Andrews, Tom, ed. *On William Stafford: The Worth of Local Things.* Ann Arbor: University of Michigan Press, 1993.

Carpenter, David. *William Stafford.* Boise, Idaho: Boise State University Press, 1986.

Holden, Jonathan. *The Mark to Turn: A Reading of William Stafford's Poetry.* Lawrence: University Press of Kansas, 1976.

Kitchen, Judith. *Writing the World: Understanding William Stafford.* Corvallis: Oregon State University Press, 1999.

Stafford, William. *Writing the Australian Crawl: Views on the Writer's Vocation.* Ann Arbor: University of Michigan Press, 1978.

Melissa Johnson

STEELE, TIMOTHY (1948–) Timothy Steele's formal verse implicitly critiques the subjectivism of much contemporary poetry. In books and essays Steele argues that the modernists conflated outmoded poetic diction and subject matter with meter and tradition and used free verse to destroy versification (see PROSODY AND FREE VERSE), thus severing poetry from its sources of rhythm, structure, and rational thought. Steele hopes to help restore the art of measured speech. A predominant figure in the NEW FORMALISM, Steele synthesizes the erudite elegance of RICHARD WILBUR with the counterromantic, antimodern, urbane plain style of YVOR WINTERS, J. V. CUNNINGHAM, and EDGAR BOWERS in poems that address contemporary matters against a backdrop of classical allusion and form.

Born in Burlington, Vermont, Steele attended Stanford University as an undergraduate and as a Stegner fellow, and Brandeis University, where J. V. Cunningham directed his dissertation on detective fiction. Steele has received a Guggenheim Fellowship (1984) and the Lavan Younger Poets Award from the Academy of American Poetry (1986).

While some critics praise Steele for his technical mastery, his grace, and his polish, others call his rhythms monotonous, his diction glib or crabbed, and his themes limited or unoriginal. Although Steele's subjects are occasionally banal, as in "Anecdote of the Sugar Bowl" (1994) and "The Sheets" (1986), Steele's best poems capture the motion of a scene and the mind examining it, as in *The Color Wheel's* (1994) "Dependent Nature," "Practice," and "Hortulus."

Uncertainties and Rest (1979) displays Steele's formal mastery. "Sunday Afternoon" and "Nightpiece for the Summer Solstice" treat Steele's dominant subject: domestic reality. In *Sapphics against Anger and Other Poems* (1986), Steele takes on larger philosophical themes. The free verse "Snapshots for Posterity" and the sestets of "On the Eve of a Birthday" treat the problems of maturing in a materialistic world as Stoic moral issues. "The Golden Age," a poem in syllabics (in which all lines contain a predetermined number of syllables), argues that all times are corrupt, and an era only thrives if "friends sketch / The dust with theorems and proofs." "Sapphics against Anger" meditates on anger and "the good life" and argues that though passion is "the holiest of powers," it is "sustaining / Only if mastered." *The Color Wheel* contains love lyrics, poems on academic and domestic subjects, and several poems of true wit. "Advice to a Student" counsels a delinquent student on inventing clever excuses, "On Wheeler Mountain" invites its addressee—a hiker—to contemplate nature while its speaker lags, and "Past, Present, Future" compares road rage to Greek tragedy.

As Kevin Walzer notes, Steele has been instrumental in changing the course of contemporary poetry. Unlike some New Formalists, however, Steele seems less interested in restoring form and NARRATIVE to poetry than in demonstrating that there can be no vital poetry without verse tradition.

BIBLIOGRAPHY

Sheehy, Donald G. "Measure for Measure: The Frostian Classicism of Timothy Steele." *Robert Frost Review* (fall 1995): 73–97.

Walzer, Kevin. The Ghost of Tradition: Expansive Poetry and Postmodernism. Ashland, Oreg.: Story Line Press, 1998.

Richard E. Joines

STEIN, GERTRUDE (1874–1946) Gertrude Stein's radical language experiments and central involvement in the Paris art world from the early 1900s to her death have made her work and life famous. Much of her writing remained unpublished in her lifetime, and she never received any awards, but writers, musicians, painters, filmmakers, and dancers have all found her work inspiring. Stein's favorite subject was the human experience of thinking, feeling, and doing, especially how they happen simultaneously; her favorite objects were America and family or power structures. After the 1950s, when the range of her work became better known, such poets as JOHN ASHBERY and LYN HEJINIAN quickly recognized Stein's importance. As for Stein's own influences, she read Shakespeare, and novelists from the 18th and 19th centuries: Samuel Richardson and Laurence Sterne, George Eliot and Henry James. The contemporaries who helped shape her writing were theorists in psychology and science—including William James and Alfred North Whitehead—and painters, especially Paul Cézanne and Pablo Picasso.

Shortly after her birth in Allegheny, Pennsylvania, Stein moved with her family to Vienna, then Paris; her family returned to America in 1880. English was her third language (after German and French), and she grew into adulthood on both American coasts, in Oakland, California, and Baltimore, Maryland. In 1893 Stein began study for a degree in psychology and philosophy at Radcliffe; subsequently she studied medicine at Johns Hopkins (leaving in 1901, without finishing the degree). From 1903 until her death Stein was an expatriate, an American in France. When she settled in Paris with her brother Leo, Stein's identity was firmly marked as a woman, a Jew, and a lesbian. These attributes no doubt contributed to some of the negative response her publications have received, though they rarely determined the content of her work in an overt way. There are the long poems "Lifting Belly" (1915–17), an ode to a lesbian relationship, and "Patriarchal Poetry" (1927), though neither was published in her lifetime (see LONG AND SERIAL POETRY). Stein's only "profession" was writing, but she made no money from it until the 1930s. She lived off family investments, and when necessary she sold some of the many famous paintings that she had collected. In 1910 Alice B. Toklas moved in with Gertrude and Leo, and in 1913 tensions between brother and sister resulted in Leo's move to Italy. Toklas had by 1913 become Gertrude's muse, typist, and essential partner in life.

Stein's writing can be divided into early (1903–11), middle (1910–31), and late (1932–46) periods. The early consists of the novels *Q.E.D.* (1903, published in 1950 as *Things as They Are*), *Three Lives* (1909), and *The Making of Americans* (1925). In her middle period Stein wrote poems, portraits, and plays, some of which were collected in *Geography and Plays* (1922). In the late period she wrote autobiography, opera, and lectures. Stein dispensed with the intention to represent reality in language; instead her writing embodies the reality of lived experience, something that both varies and repeats itself. Similar to the cubist painters, Stein experimented with perspective, the use of domestic materials, and writing without a "model." In *TENDER BUTTONS* (1914), a book that declared the beginning of nonlinear writing, Stein announced: "Act so that there is no use in a centre." "Why is there a difference," asks Stein, "between one window and another, why is there a difference, because the curtain is shorter." The meaning of these windows is thus determined by their context (the curtains and their different lengths); rather than being inherent to the object, meaning is established relationally.

In the 1920s and 1930s, Stein had a reputation as an extraordinary conversationalist and as a cubist writer; visiting her and Toklas at 27 Rue de Fleurus, became a rite of passage for writers, painters, and American tourists. Stein was thus already well known when *The Autobiography of Alice B. Toklas* (1933), a fanciful memoir of the Paris art world, made her a popular writer. In 1934 Stein returned to the United States for the first time in 30 years to lecture and tour. In 1929 Alice and Gertrude had begun self-publishing under their own imprint, Plain Edition. Four titles appeared, including *How to Write* (1931). The success of *Autobiography,* however, finally brought a long-term contract from Random House and interest from other American publishers so that work began to appear regularly. In this late period some of the books are *Lectures in America* (1935), *The Geographical History of America* (1936), *Everybody's Autobiography* (1937), and *Ida* (1941).

As Stein predicted in her lecture "Composition as Explanation" (1926), her work became "classic" only after she was dead (496). During her lifetime her work was "outlaw" or "irritating annoying stimulating," as she characterized it (496). It is still classified in that way, despite the number of forms she practiced: poems, portraits, plays, novels, opera, autobiography, lectures, and even a children's book. Stein's work has thus been classified as largely unclassifiable; even though her work is unmistakable, it is always unpredictable.

Stanzas in Meditation (written in 1932, unpublished until 1956) is Stein's longest poem, which she wrote at her summer home in the French countryside; much of it seems to refer to the landscape around her and the people who visit. Stein loved to discriminate between similar words—in this case, between *seeing* and *describing.* She claims that she writes what she sees without describing it. To "see" is to write about something that cannot be described but only enacted: the tension between words, as objects, in relation to other words/objects. The referents for words only play a part in meaning; language means according to how it is used. As she writes the words split: "Because I know by *weight* how *eight* are eight" (emphasis added). To know how many things there are, she assesses how much they weigh; knowledge is thus achieved indirectly. Consider these lines: "A plain is a mountain not made round," and "They say August is not April / But how say so if in the middle they can not know." When you are in the middle of something, whether August or a plain, you cannot know what it is, only what it is not (April or a mountain). "I have lost the thread of my discourse," she admits at one point; however, "it makes no difference if we find it / If we found it," since it finds her, as long as she keeps writing.

T. S. ELIOT's review of Stein in 1927 characterized her reception: "[I]t is not improving, it is not amusing, it is not interesting, it is not good for one's mind. But its rhythms have a peculiar hypnotic power not met with before. It has a kinship with the saxophone. If this is the future, then the future is [something] in which we ought not to be interested" (595). MINA LOY compared Stein in 1924 to the late 19th-century scientist Madame Marie Curie: Stein puts consciousness under a microscope "to extract / a radium of the word" (94). And in 1937 Samuel Beckett said that Stein was "a mathematician [who] is in love with his figures; a mathematician for whom the solution of the problem is of entirely secondary interest" (172–173). Treating words as a chemist or as a mathematician might, as if words were elements or numbers, strip them of reference—to other books and to history. History does not disappear; instead the past becomes something that happens in the present, much as we experience a memory as happening in the present. In this way, time present is continuous, Stein insisted; even if we never forget the past, we live in the present, whether we know it or not. MARIANNE MOORE favorably reviewed *The Making of the Americans* in 1926; in her review, she quotes a passage from the novel: "[I]t is very difficult in quarreling to be certain in either one what the other one is remembering" (129). Stein too wondered what her readers would be remembering as they read. She wanted them not to remember but rather to concentrate on the present moment of reading.

BIBLIOGRAPHY

Beckett, Samuel. *Disjecta: Miscellaneous Writings,* edited by Ruby Cohn. New York: Grove Press, 1984.

Bridgman, Richard. *Gertrude Stein in Pieces.* New York: Oxford University Press, 1970.

Curnutt, Kirk, ed. *The Critical Response to Gertrude Stein.* Westport, Conn.: Greenwood Press, 2000.

Eliot, T. S. "Charleston, Hey! Hey!" *Nation & Athenaeum* 40, no. 17 (January 29, 1927): 595.

Hoffman, Michael, ed. *Critical Essays on Gertrude Stein.* Boston: G. K. Hall, 1986.

Loy, Mina. "Gertrude Stein." In *The Lost Lunar Baedeker,* edited by Roger L. Conover, 94. New York: Noonday Press, 1996.

Moore, Marianne. "The Spare American Emotion," In *The Complete Prose of Marianne Moore,* edited by Patricia C. Willis. New York: Penguin, 1987, pp. 128–131.

Stein, Gertrude. "Composition as Explanation." In *A Stein Reader,* edited by Ulla E. Dydo. Evanston, Ill.: Northwestern University Press, 1993, pp. 495–503.

———. *Stanzas in Meditation.* Los Angeles: Sun & Moon Press, 1994.

———. *Tender Buttons. Gertrude Stein: Writings 1903–1932,* edited by Catharine R. Stimpson and Harriet Chessman. New York: Library of America, 1998, pp. 313–355.

Logan Esdale

STERN, GERALD (1925–) Gerald Stern is among the most important practitioners of voiced poetry in the later 20th century. Frequently compared with Walt Whitman, Stern often takes as his subject the natural world. Yet his poetry is more than pastoral, and he submits as his subject his own experiences as representational of the reader's. Deborah Garrison identifies the impact of this technique: "It isn't often you come across poetry that makes you want to turn to the stranger next to you on the bus, grab him by the collar, and say, 'You have to read this!'" (103). Stern's verse may be compared with that of STANLEY KUNITZ, WILLIAM STAFFORD, ROBERT BLY, and W. S. MERWIN, particularly in his use of archetypal images within the tradition of DEEP IMAGE POETRY. Stern may also be compared with JOHN ASHBERY in his use of irony. And in his use of discursive narrative, Stern's poetry is similar to that of EDWARD DORN and ROBERT PINSKY. In the Jewish-American tone of his poetry, Stern's lilt echoes that used by ALLEN GINSBERG.

Stern was born in Pittsburg, Pennsylvania, the child of Eastern European immigrant parents. Educated at the University of Pittsburgh (B.A., 1947) and Columbia University (M.A., 1949), Stern came to national attention with the publication of *Lucky Life* (1977). "I didn't start taking myself seriously as a poet / until the white began to appear in my cheek," he wrote in "The Bite" (1973). In 1998 he won the National Book Award for *This Time: New and Selected Poems.* Stern's recent work, *Last Blue* (2000) and *American Sonnets* (2002), continues to render his experiences—everyday occurrences with mythic associations conveyed in NARRATIVE—in ways that prompt identification with the speaker's voice.

In "Peaches" (2002), a characteristic poem, Stern recalls throwing a peach stone over a fence at a Metro North train station in Pennsylvania, dreaming that the stone would take root "in spite of the gravel and the newspaper, / and wasn't I like that all my life, and who isn't?" The hope of growth in a sterile urban landscape and the search for commonality are brought forward by a speaker who, as John Rodden discovered in an interview with Stern, radiates with "joy, fun, superabundance, derring-do—though never far away from the perception of good fortune is a sense of tragedy and mortality, a keen awareness of loss and sadness—

and of the fact that resurrection is impossible without death" (98). Stern's power rests in observation of the particular and a heartfelt desire to find what is universal among us.

BIBLIOGRAPHY

Garrison, Deborah. "Lyricism Unplugged." *New Yorker* 74, no. 35 (November 16, 1998): 103–104.

Somerville, Jane. "Gerald Stern among the Poets: The Speaker as Meaning." *American Poetry Review* 17, no. 6 (November/December 1988): 11–19.

Stern, Gerald. "Splendor in the Weeds: Gerald Stern," by John Rodden. In *Performing the Literary Interview: How Writers Craft Their Public Selves,* by Rodden. Lincoln: University of Nebraska Press, 2001, pp. 97–121.

Norbert Elliot

STEVENS, WALLACE (1879–1955) Along with T. S. ELIOT, WILLIAM CARLOS WILLIAMS, MARIANNE MOORE, and HART CRANE, Wallace Stevens is associated with American high MODERNISM. Similar to ROBERT FROST (with whom he sometimes fraternized on his vacations in Florida), Stevens theorized and practiced a poetry typical of writing from New England, which looked for truth and reality in nature and the seasons; however, Stevens's "mind of winter" (a favored phrase in his poetry) is often more obscure than Frost's, and though his verse is, by turns, humorous, playful, and musical, it is also stark, difficult, and deadly serious.

Stevens was born in Reading, Pennsylvania. He attended Harvard for three years (1897–1900), where he became acquainted with the philosopher George Santayana, a figure who would become a model for Stevens's own thinking and for whom he would write one of his most well-known later poems, "To an Old Philosopher in Rome" (1954). Many early Stevens poems appeared in various Harvard publications, including the *Harvard Advocate,* of which he became president in 1899. Stevens wished to make a living at writing, and his first job out of college was as a reporter for the *New York Herald Tribune,* though he quickly became unsatisfied with journalism as a profession. Stevens's father was dismissive of his son's wish to become a man of literature and encouraged him to attend law school; Stevens entered the New York Law School in 1901 and was admitted to the New York bar in 1904. He practiced law in New York City until 1916, when he moved to Hartford, Connecticut, to work for the Hartford Accident and Indemnity Company, of which he became a vice president in 1934 and for which he would work for the rest of his life. Stevens began to contribute poems to magazines in 1914, and although he did not publish his first full-length collection of poems (*Harmonium,* 1923) until he was 44 years old, Stevens managed to win nearly every major poetry prize before his death, including prizes from *Poetry* (1916) and the *Nation* (1936), the Harriet Monroe Poetry Award (1946), the Bollingen Prize (1950), two National Book Awards (1951 and 1955), and the Pulitzer Prize (1955).

"We live in the mind," Stevens writes in his 1949 essay "Imagination as Value," (140), and indeed many of Stevens's poems—including such well-known works as "NOTES TOWARD A SUPREME FICTION" (1942), "The Emperor of Ice Cream" (1923), "Thirteen Ways of Looking at a Blackbird" (1923), and "THE IDEA OF ORDER AT KEY WEST" (1936)—detail the movements and mechanisms of this most mysterious organ, exposing both its weaknesses and its strengths. The simultaneous resolution and maintenance of contradiction is what fuels Stevens's work, which often consists of unlikely and seemingly impossible fusions of ideas and emotions that become oddly reconciled, often allowing the reader to stand firmly in a new intellectual position, but one in which his or her previous position is still visible and tangible, if also in shambles. Stevens's work makes frequent use of paradox, a technique that often place the reader in a new intellectual position. In the third stanza of "Poem with Rhythms," Stevens writes of a woman who, "weeps of [her lover's] breast, though he never comes." While it may be impossible to weep on the breast of someone who is not present, the poem's previous discussion of the size of shadows relative to the things that cast them emphasizes that the mind has no trouble growing to account for the various oddities, illusions, and distortions of the physical world. For Stevens, the mind and the heart are inextricable, and in these lines the there/not-there paradox of the lover—while remaining physically unreal or impossible—is rendered emotionally and intellectually plausible. When the woman receives her lover into her heart—when her heart, like the mind, "[g]rows large against space"—it is as *if* he were there to be wept on; his absence is made present. For another example, one of his most famous poems, "The Snow Man" (1923), speaks of "Nothing that is not there and the nothing that is." The poem describes the sights and sounds of a landscape as processed by the powers and limitations of "a mind of winter." The small word *the* performs the Herculean task of separating two similar ideas ("Nothing" and "the nothing"), neither of which has an available or specific referent. By highlighting both the vagueness and the specificity that vacancy can contain, Stevens provides a clearer vision of nothingness, which is also to say a more complicated idea of what nothingness might entail. (The profundity of emptiness and the meaningfulness of small words was echoed by later such poets as ROBERT CREELEY, WILLIAM BRONK, and GEORGE OPPEN.)

Stevens's poetry is often associated with exotic places, beings, and happenings, but these transcriptions are the product of a keen and active imagination rather than a detailed record of the poet's life experiences. Although he traveled a bit on business and indulged in a few pleasure excursions to the West Coast, Florida, and Cuba, Stevens rarely left New England. He never saw Europe, yet his poems—particularly in the earlier volumes—often contain a distinctly European flair (see EUROPEAN POETIC INFLUENCE). Stevens also traveled in the mind by maintaining several long-distance correspondents, including Leonard van Geyzel (a Ceylonese plantation owner), Anatole and Paule Vidal (Parisian book and art dealers), and José Rodriguez Feo (a Cuban poet). A collector of rare and often expensive paintings and books (most of which he ordered from the Vidals), Stevens fueled his imagination not with geographic wandering, but instead by reading books, looking at paintings, and listening to music, all of which remain consistent figures in his work.

The act of reading becomes one of Stevens's most reliable tropes beginning in his second volume, *Ideas of Order* (1936), which contains "The Reader," a poem in which the speaker reads a book "as if in a book / Of sombre pages." At the end of the poem, the reading speaker—who has imagined himself to be "in a book"—looks up from the page and transfers his "bookness" to the world around him; pulled from his reverie by what is perhaps the "mumbling" of his own reading voice, the reader sees the clear winter sky as "sombre pages [which bear] no print." This "literate despair" will recur many times over the course of Stevens's poems, perhaps most noticeably in *Transport to Summer*'s "The House Was Quiet and the World Was Calm" (1947), in which he writes, "The reader became the book; and summer // night was like the conscious being of the book." In this later poem, the winter of "The Reader" gives way to summer, and the reader's becoming the book is stated rather than merely implied. While Stevens never completely deserts the playfulness and metaphor of his earlier work, his later poems tend to contain more direct statements and less fanciful sentiments. One would be hard pressed to find such a line as "One feels the life of that which gives life as it is" (from 1951's "The Course of a Particular") anywhere in his first book *Harmonium*.

DONALD JUSTICE observes that Stevens, though certainly adept at traditional meters, favored two types of free verse line throughout his published work (see PROSODY AND FREE VERSE). The first, which is evident in many of his early poems, is a short line—likely derived from the IMAGIST SCHOOL—that breaks sentences into syntactical units and varies with regard to the number of accents it may contain. This short line is perhaps best illustrated by such early poems as "Disillusionment of Ten O'Clock" and "Ploughing on Sunday" (both from *Harmonium*), yet it does reappear even in very late poems, such as "One of the Inhabitants of the West" (1954). In an attempt to describe Stevens's short-line metrics in prose, Justice relies on a loose mathematical formula—"2 accents plus or minus 1 (or more)"—while also noticing that each line "contain[s] matter of more than grammatical interest" (16–17). Stevens's longer line, which dominates the late work, is less image-oriented and likely arose, according to Justice, in order to allow for a more complex "development of ideas" that would be impossible in shorter, imagistic lines (26). Stevens's long line begins as fairly regular blank verse in early poems, such as "SUNDAY MORNING" (1923), and if, in later poems, he will stretch and torque this meter into various shapes of his own making, he never leaves his heroic iambs too far behind. "In the Element of Antagonisms" (from 1950's *The Auroras of Autumn*) is a prime example of the ways in which Stevens's long line both adheres to and deviates from the "ancient accent" of blank verse, often extending the line beyond 10 syllables and varying his feet to accommodate the rising and falling of thought: "Birds twitter pandemoniums around / The idea of the chevalier of chevaliers."

Although Stevens is occasionally branded a hedonist, a decadent, and a dandy by critics, his influence and popularity among poets is widespread and profound. Like JOHN ASHBERY, a poet whom many critics, including Harold Bloom, see as Stevens's heir, Stevens has shaped and inspired writers of all types, from formal and traditional "mainstream" poets, such as JAMES MERRILL and THEODORE ROETHKE, to more experimental writers, such as KATHLEEN FRASER and MICHAEL PALMER. Even JACK SPICER, a militant outsider, who once claimed that "everybody in English departments who hates poetry, which is just about everybody, loves Stevens," was forced to praise Stevens for his visionary—and revisionary—talents and tendencies (72).

BIBLIOGRAPHY

Bloom, Harold. *Wallace Stevens: The Poems of Our Climate.* Ithaca, N.Y.: Cornell University Press, 1977.

Justice, Donald. "The Free-Verse Line in Stevens." In Oblivion: On Writers and Writing. Ashland, Oreg.: Story Line Press, 1998, pp. 13–38.

Riddell, Joseph N. *The Clairvoyant Eye: The Poetry and Poetics of Wallace Stevens.* Baton Rouge: Louisiana State University Press, 1965.

Spicer, Jack. *The House That Jack Built: The Collected Lectures of Jack Spicer,* edited by Peter Gizzi. Hanover, N.H.: Wesleyan University Press, 1998.

Stevens, Wallace. "Imagination as Value." In *The Necessary Angel: Essays on Reality and the Imagination.* New York: Vintage Books, 1951.

Vendler, Helen. *Wallace Stevens: Words Chosen out of Desire.* Knoxville: University of Tennessee Press, 1984.

Graham Foust

STONE, RUTH (1915–) For reasons of temperament and circumstance, the development of Ruth Stone's poetry has been strikingly independent of all schools and alliances. She is, in ALICIA OSTRIKER's phrase, "a classic American maverick" (662). Stone's first book, *In An Iridescent Time* (1957), shows a marked musicality, a lightness and gaiety that echoes in the later volumes as a kind of antic irony animating the tragic and hard-won wisdom of those poems.

Ruth Perkins Stone was born in Roanoke, Virginia, into a family of writers, painters, and musicians. Stone met her husband, the poet and novelist Walter Stone, while they were students at the University of Illinois. Walter attended graduate school at Harvard, while Ruth sat in on classes and was a part of the circle of poets there that included RICHARD WILBUR, DELMORE SCHWARTZ, and RICHARD EBERHART. Some of her awards include a fellowship at the Radcliffe Institute from 1963 to 1965 (where she developed ties with other Radcliffe fellows, such as MAXINE KUMIN and Tillie Olsen), two Guggenheim fellowships (1971 and 1975), the Delmore Schwartz Award (1983), a Whiting Writers' Award (1986), and the Paterson Poetry Prize (1986). During these years Stone produced three collections. In 1990 she accepted a full-time appointment at Binghamton University (New York). Three more collections appeared over the next decade. *Ordinary Words* (1999) was honored with the National Book Critics Circle Award in 2000. Stone's eighth collection, *In the Next Galaxy,* appeared in 2002.

Her husband Walter's suicide in 1959 while the family was in England is a recurring lens through which Stone examines love, loss, and mortality. "Every day I dig you up," she tells Walter in "Habit" (1972), "you are my poem." Time does not diminish the crackling immediacy of remembered emotions: "Our bed danced on the floor / as if we had created a miracle" ("Happiness" [1987]). There is a freshness to her work, as if the poet sees the world clearly in all of its loss and sadness, as if she knows well what humanity is capable of, yet she irrepressibly holds open the hope we will choose to do better: "I am a stranger crossing the bone bridge to meet the other," she tells us in "For Eight Women" (1995), and "Our skulls shine like calligraphy in a longed-for language." Note the clarity of her unexpected images and the connective tissue of assonance. An abiding interest in the sciences and an utter lack of sentimentality also distinguish her work: "Oh world, oh galaxy," she sings in "End of Summer . . . 1969," "My error is to look for meaning in the sun / That burns for burning."

BIBLIOGRAPHY

Barker, Wendy, and Sandra M. Gilbert, eds. *The House Is Made of Poetry: The Art of Ruth Stone.* Carbondale: Southern Illinois University Press, 1996.

Bennani, Ben, ed. *The World of Ruth Stone, Paintbrush: A Journal of Poetry and Translation* XXVII (2000–2001): 6–143.

Ostriker, Alicia. Headnote to selection of poems by Ruth Stone. *Feminist Studies* 25, no. 3 (1999): 662.

Christine Gelineau

"STOPPING BY WOODS ON A SNOWY EVENING" ROBERT FROST (1923)

Although traditional in form (see PROSODY AND FREE VERSE), "Stopping by Woods on a Snowy Evening" is a modernist poem in its use of a persona with a divided sensibility (see MODERNISM). The speaker is divided between his sense of duty and a romantic aestheticism—his desire to watch the woods fill up with snow. Unlike the works of the 19th-century American transcendentalists, on which ROBERT FROST draws heavily in his poetry, "Stopping by Woods" does not reconcile these discordant selves. Like many 20th-century American poets, Frost recognizes the impossibility of a fully integrated psyche.

The speaker of the poem, who is traveling in a horse-drawn sleigh, pauses in his journey to watch someone's woods fill up with snow. From the start, the speaker admits that he knows who owns the woods by which he has stopped. His words reveal a sense of guilt, as though he were somehow trespassing. The play on legal (pragmatic) and poetic (imaginative) ownership is reminiscent of Ralph Waldo Emerson's essay "Nature" (1849) and Henry David Thoreau's *Walden* (1854). For the moment, the speaker owns the landscape, but, unlike the idealists Emerson and Thoreau, he does not believe his ownership is philosophically legitimate and permanent. Instead he makes his horse a projection of his own conscience, which judges his self-indulgence to be a moral error.

The critic Frank Lentricchia associates "Stopping by Woods" with other poems in which Frost's speakers describe landscapes filling up with snow. Lentricchia suggests that these scenes are psychologically symbolic: "[T]he speaker does not stop for long, perhaps because, in his fascination with the woods, he senses in their darkness, in their inhuman otherness, suggestions of his personal end" (96). Nevertheless he does stop, for the appeal of this aesthetic moment is aural (based on sound) as well as visual. As Richard Poirier argues, the speaker "is in danger of losing himself; and his language by the end of the third stanza begins to carry hints of seductive luxuriousness unlike anything preceding it" (183). Frost expresses this aural appeal through sensuous, liquid consonants and long vowels. This same *melopoeia* (the use of sound to charge language with emotion) continues until the final stanza, where it is countermanded by the recollection of obligations. According to Lentricchia, the "aesthetic moment is defined as a moment of stillness . . . engendered by pure contemplative appreciation. . . . But the moment of stillness and freedom is tightly circumscribed: . . . our aesthetic man must yield to quotidian man" (96). Although the dutiful side of his character overcomes his desire for aesthetic pleasure, the speaker is aware of the cost. The last two lines, identical in diction and syntax, express the speaker's weary resignation. The resonance of "miles," bespeaking the long journey, is juxtaposed with the exhaustive and liquid initial consonants of "sleep," epitomizing the struggle of two selves throughout the poem.

BIBLIOGRAPHY

Lentricchia, Frank. *Robert Frost: Modern Poetics and the Landscapes of Self.* Durham, N.C.: Duke University Press, 1975.

Poirier, Richard. *Robert Frost: The Work of Knowing.* New York: Oxford University Press, 1977.

Edwin J. Barton

STRAND, MARK (1934–)

An extensive writer of fiction, translation, and poetry, Strand's poetry has generally been associated with the surrealistic verse that reached its zenith in America during the 1960s and 1970s and has been practiced occasionally by such poets as W. S. MERWIN, ROBERT BLY, and JAMES WRIGHT. His work is characterized by minimalism and symbolic imagery, and while not all his work is of a surreal nature, Strand's poetry is generally noted for its dreamlike characteristics that investigate the limitations of the internal and external worlds of the individual. His poetry is dark, thoughtful, clear, humorous and, at times, metaphysical. Despite the fact that his poetry can be mysterious, it generally remains well grounded. Although Latin American SURREALISM greatly influenced Strand's style, the picturesque nature of his poetry is also reflective of his early training as a painter, where his spacious language is reminiscent of Albert Cuyp's serene landscapes.

Born on Canada's Prince Edward Island, Strand was educated at Antioch, Yale, and Iowa. His books of poetry include *Sleeping with One Eye Open* (1964), *Reasons for Moving* (1968), *Darker* (1970), *The Story of Our Lives* (1973), winner of the 1974 Edgar Allan Poe Award, *Selected Poems* (1980), *The Continuous Life* (1990), winner of the 1992 Rebekah Johnson Bobbitt National Prize for Poetry, *Dark Harbor* (1993), which won the 1993 Bollingen Prize, *Blizzard of One* (1998), which won the Pulitzer Prize and *Boston Book Review*'s Bingham Poetry Prize in 1999 and *Man and Camel* (2006). He has also published prose, translation, and children's books, as well as edited a number of anthologies. His latest work is also his first collection of essays, *The Weather of Words* (2000). His honors include a 1979 Academy of American Poets Fellowship, a 1987 MacArthur Fellowship, three National Endowment for the Arts grants (1968, 1978, and 1986), and an award from the Rockefeller Foundation (2000). He is a former chancellor of the Academy of American Poets and served as poet laureate of the United States in 1990.

In a post–Pulitzer Prize interview with Elizabeth Farnsworth, Strand remarked, "A poem releases itself, secretes itself slowly, sometimes almost poisonously, into the mind of the reader. . . . It does it by rearranging the world in such a way that it appears new. It does it by using language that is slightly different from the way language is used in the workday world, so that you're forced to pay attention to it" (Strand "Interview"). An example of Strand's use of this "rearranging" is the third section of *Blizzard of One,* a series of poems written from the viewpoint of five grieving dogs that are free to say the things humans cannot or will not say. These confined and domesticated dogs easily sing at night to the "great starfields," calling to the "wished-for reaches of heaven." This sense of delight and longing allows for the exposure of the truth of human disconnectedness. In a surreal world, where "The sky / Was a sheet of white" and where there "was a dog in a phone booth / Calling home," human readers find a voice for the fear of being alone in the universe. The result of this recognition of shared humanity is pure Strand, where the only recourse can be an existential release into universal oneness. In an earlier poem, "Eating Poetry" (1980), Strand again uses the image of man as dog; here the speaker becomes a dog after eating/reading poetry only to frighten a librarian, when he gets "on [his] knees and lick[s] her hand."

Strand's poetry spans the gap between what we know is real and what is ethereal. It is clear that his vision, his hope, is "that through the imaginary world that [poets] create . . . we see the real world more clearly" (Strand "Interview"). In "Eating Poetry," the speaker claims, "ink runs from the corners of my mouth. / There is no happiness like mine." While obviously imaginary, such a statement portrays the real world of the poet, and all those like him, who feast on poetry.

BIBLIOGRAPHY

Aaron, Jonathan. "About Mark Strand: A Profile." *Ploughshares* 21, no. 4 (1995–96): 202–206.

Strand, Mark. "Interview with Elizabeth Farnsworth," PBS NewsHour. Available online. URL: www.pbs.org/newshour/bb/entertainment/jan-june99/pulitzer_4-15.html. Downloaded March 2007.

Salita S. Bryant

STRICKLAND, STEPHANIE (1942–) Stephanie Strickland is one of the most celebrated poets working in hypertext, a multilinear form of writing that is specifically designed to be read on a computer, often incorporating elements of multimedia (see CYBERPOETRY). Strickland is also a print poet, but her work is only fully realized when the digital domain is also considered. She can be seen as continuing in the postmodernist tradition, as she is fascinated by the blurring of boundaries between different genres of writing as well as different modes of thought. Moreover her work incorporates the ideas of science and mathematics and is decidedly feminist in theme (see FEMALE VOICE, FEMALE LANGUAGE).

Strickland was born and raised in Detroit, Michigan. In 1978 she received an M.F.A. from Sarah Lawrence College and an M.S. in 1984 from the Pratt Institute. Her first book, *Beyond This Silence,* was published in 1988, the same year she received a grant from the National Endowment for the Arts. She won the Brittingham Prize (1993) for *The Red Virgin: A Poem of Simone Weil. True North* garnered her the Alice Fay di Castagnola Award of the Poetry Society of America (1996), the Ernest Sandeen Poetry Prize (1997), and the *Salt Hill* Hypertext Prize (1998) for the poem's hypertext version. She received the *Boston Book Review* prize and *About.com* Best of the Net Poetry Award for *Ballad of Sand and Harry Soot* in 1999, and in 2000 the Alice Fay di Castagnola Award for "V:The Wave Son.nets."

Like many writers working in hypertext, Strickland explores the larger implications of the form. In *To Be Here as Stone Is* (1999), she makes a case for the relativity and provisionality of knowledge best represented in hypertext as a guiding principle of the universe: "Objects are answers," she writes, though the natural tendency of the cosmos is toward change. Anything that appears permanent—such as "extinguished starlight"—is an illusion, though we seek these isolated bits of permanence out of our "persistent reverence for error." This is the central tension of much of Strickland's work: Human knowledge is limited and faulty, but it is all we have to make sense of experience.

Along similar lines, Strickland examines the hypertextual reading experience in *Errand upon Which We Came* (2001), written in collaboration with influential hypertext writer M. D. Coverley. On the first page, Strickland invites her readers to skip any parts of the poem he or she wants, adding, "Of course, it can be read straight through, but this is not a better reading, not a better life." Images of frogs and butterflies play heavily in the poem, as they move erratically (as the reader might) and live in more than one element during their life cycles. Here reading becomes organic and unpredictable, but Strickland's text is in constant flux as well, since each page gives way to the next after a certain amount of time. The reader may not "get anywhere" or take away any hard, stable truths, but, for Strickland, the reading is itself the point. She gives the reader a glimpse into her own restlessly inquisitive mind.

BIBLIOGRAPHY

Inez. Colette. "'Beyond This Silence'—Strickland, S." *Prairie Schooner* 62, no. 2 (1988): 134–136.

Kaufman, Ellen. Review. *Library Journal* (November 15, 1981): 86.

Muratori, Fred. "Ambiguity Isn't What It Used to Be—or Is It?" *Georgia Review* 52, no. 1 (spring 1998): 142–160.

Matthew Purdy

THE STRUCTURE OF RIME **ROBERT DUNCAN (1960)** Emerging out of the modernist tradition of the long poem (see LONG AND SERIAL POETRY), ROBERT DUNCAN's *The Structure of Rime* is a wide-ranging exploration of linguistic and material correspondences. This series of poems is influenced by romantic writers, such as William Blake and Samuel Taylor Coleridge; modernist long poems, such as Walt Whitman's *Song of Myself,* EZRA POUND's *CANTOS,* and H. D.'s *Trilogy* (see MODERNISM); and, later, by JACK SPICER's development of the serial poem. Duncan, however, distinguishes himself by his melding of tradition with the experimental, the ordinary with the mystical. As he writes early on in "Pages from a Notebook," "I don't seek a synthesis, but a melee."

The Structure of Rime first appears in *The Opening of the Field* (1960) as one of several open-ended sequences (including *PASSAGES*). Interspersed throughout later books (I to XIII appear in *Opening of the Field,* 1960; XIV to XXI appear in *Roots and Branches,* 1964; XXII to XVI appear in *Bending the Bow,* 1968; and XXVII to XVIII, as well as "structure of Rime: Of the Five Songs," appear in *Groundwork,* 1984 and 1987), these poems are connected to each other only insofar as they are generally prose pieces concerned with the larger themes of form and meaning. Otherwise they pick up on the themes and motifs of the surrounding poems while also commenting on these same themes and motifs.

The word *rime* as defined by Duncan, is either "form" and "rhythm" or "clearing" and "opening." The speaker in "The Structure of Rime I" introduces himself as both master and servant to language ("speak!

For I name myself your master, who come to serve") before going on to discover, in the course of the poem, that while language has the power to shape the way things are, the way things are also shapes the language and the writer ("In the feet that measure the dance of my pages I hear cosmic intoxications of the man I will be"). In this way, then, Duncan establishes himself as both romantic and modernist, concerned with form as much as formlessness, order as much as chaos. As he goes on to write in "The Structure of Rime II:" "'What of the Structure of Rime' I asked. / An absolute scale of resemblance and disresemblance establishes measures that are music in the actual world." It is important to note that although these first two poems are also indicative of a mystical vision of the world and a belief in the poet as seer that is evident throughout much of *The Structure of Rime,* Duncan does not endorse transcendence. Rather he invokes such figures as Mnemosyne (the goddess of memory), Jacob, and Christ to point toward his belief in the presence and power of myth in our everyday lives.

BIBLIOGRAPHY

Davidson, Michael. "Cave of Resemblances, Cave of Rimes: Tradition and Repetition in Robert Duncan." In *Conversant Essays: Contemporary Poets on Poetry*. Detroit: Wayne State University Press, 1990, pp. 282–293.

Johnson, Mark Andrew. *Robert Duncan*. Boston: Twayne, 1988.

Lori Emerson

SUN **MICHAEL PALMER (1988)** *Sun* is the title of two poems from MICHAEL PALMER's book of the same name. The *Sun* poems address political ideas and history through the medium of LANGUAGE poetry. The first poem has the same number of lines as T. S. ELIOT's *The WASTE LAND,* a poem that scholars consider central to 20th-century MODERNISM. However, *Sun* liberates modernist notions of collage and subtext from the conservative sensibilities that underscore Eliot's work.

Palmer rejects the overt way that the political often inhabits the subject matter of poetry, where poets are "more than anything else, announcing in stale poetic language, 'Look how much human feeling and fellow-feeling I have,'" in a manner that seems more self-congratulatory than a true expression of empathy or a true representation of a political event or atrocity. Instead Palmer expresses the difficulty of human crises by exploring the limitations of the language used to represent such situations. Therefore the speaker in the second poem states, "I have been writing a book, not in my native language." The language may be foreign, because it refuses to exploit personal experience as a commodity; instead it proliferates inside the multiple possibilities of experience.

These experiences result in an amplified vision of the world. In this world, dust settles on whispers, fields extend outward, and a voice invites the reader to "enter through the curtain / and swallow your words." Language collects the dust of obsolescence, whether in the form of a whisper or in the forms of words consumed by a field. To engage with the poems, readers must pass through a curtain and broaden their field of expectations of how language conveys the reality of human joy and suffering.

As a mediator conveying the experience of human suffering, language cannot be trusted; in fact, it might even be deadly. Early in the first "Sun" a voice says, "You bring death into your mouth—X / we are called—." Palmer's wariness of naming and representation subverts the traditional assumptions about meaning and the authority of the poet's voice. The poems are self-conscious, perhaps even self-critical, of their own artifice: "I now turn to my use of suffixes and punctuation, closing Mr. Circle / with a single stroke." Ultimately the poems challenge readers to define their own constructs of authority and power.

The *Sun* poems incorporate the aesthetics of Language poetry into a powerful discourse that questions popular notions of meaning. The poems address social concerns through multiple voices that are constantly aware of their presence and place in the world. Resisting the easy allure of the definitive, the poems instead revel in the complications of the abstract.

BIBLIOGRAPHY

Palmer, Michael. "'Dear Lexicon': An Interview by Benjamin Hollander and David Levi Strauss." *ACTS: A Journal of New Writing* 2, no. 1 (1986): 8–36.

Yenser, Stephen. "Open House." Review of *Sun,* by Michael Palmer. *Poetry* (Aug. 1989): 295–301.

J. Andrew Prall

"SUNDAY MORNING" WALLACE STEVENS (1915; 1923) "Sunday Morning" is not only one of WALLACE STEVENS's most brilliant successes as a poet, it also marks a pivotal moment in 20th-century American poetry whereby the philosophical and the poetic are seamlessly blended into a worldview that celebrates the world and poetry's place in that world. When the poem was first published in *Poetry* in 1915, the editor, Harriet Monroe, cut three of the stanzas and reordered the remaining ones so that the final stanza became the second. In *Harmonium* (1923), Stevens restored the poem to its original eight stanza sequence, which more clearly presents the gist of the poem as a whole: The myths that have been the mainstay of human civilization—and especially Christianity—have become hollow and empty, and we need to establish a new mode of Being that fixes its attention upon this world (the Earth), not upon the assumptions of the next (the Christian promise of eternal life and heaven). In this respect, "Sunday Morning" announces the poetics of high MODERNISM and Stevens's bold assertion that poetry, in the 20th century, should be regarded as the supreme religion.

The poem presents the tensions between this world and the images of the next through a female persona, who, in the opening stanza of the poem, is contemplating her lush domestic surroundings (instead of the interior of a church) on a Sunday morning. The explicit tension between the Epicurean setting, with its cockatoo, coffee, and oranges, is juxtaposed with the image of death—the realm of "blood and sepulchre," the cornerstones of Christianity. The central thrust of the poem is phrased as the question of whether one should give one's life over to death instead of celebrating one's life in this world. Through its various images, the poem makes an argument in favor of the pursuit of beauty and asserts that life should not be subservient to death but should follow the model of the ring of men in the poem, who announce their devotion to the splendors of the sun in an orgiastic circle.

The poem concludes, brilliantly and with great intellectual poignancy, with the image of a flock of pigeons sinking into darkness "on extended wings," which reinforces the theme of death and reframes the poem as a message to be alive in the poetic splendor of this life. In this light, "Sunday Morning" articulates the high modernist valorization of poetic artifice and the role of the artist as a lens to explore and perceive the nature of being human.

BIBLIOGRAPHY

Bloom, Harold. *Wallace Stevens: The Poems of our Climate.* Ithaca, N.Y.: Cornell University Press, 1977.

Riddel, Joseph. *The Clairvoyant Eye: The Poetry and Prose of Wallace Stevens.* Baton Rouge: Louisiana State University Press, 1965.

Vendler, Helen. *On Extended Wings: Wallace Stevens' Longer Poems.* Cambridge, Mass.: Harvard University Press, 1969.

David Clippinger

"A SUPERMARKET IN CALIFORNIA" ALLEN GINSBERG (1956) "A Supermarket in California" is ALLEN GINSBERG's paean to his closest literary forefather, the 19th-century American poet Walt Whitman. Like Ginsberg, Whitman was a radical experimenter in free verse, a celebrant of national culture, and a homosexual whose outsider status enabled him to identify with the full diversity of society. But the poem is also an investigation of the state of the American dream; when Ginsberg tells Whitman "I touch your book and dream of our odyssey in the supermarket and feel absurd," he is sounding out Whitman's hopeful vision of America in *Leaves of Grass* to see if it still pertains in the mid-20th century. The poem captures Ginsberg's exuberant voice, his spirited humor, his interest in the mundane details of the American experience, and his sense that poetry is a spiritual force appearing everywhere in human life.

The poem's setting is historically relevant and comically significant. Speaking in an apostrophe to Whitman himself, the speaker first presents himself wandering the streets of Berkeley, California, which along with San Francisco proper was a primary residence for the members of the BEAT movement in the 1950s and thus (for those allied to the Beats) the epicenter of American poetic creativity. The speaker has apparently been seeking poetic inspiration, "for I walked down the sidestreets under the trees with a headache self-conscious looking at the full moon," but is fatigued by the effort, and he tells Whitman that "shopping for images, I went into the neon fruit supermarket, dreaming of your enumerations." For Ginsberg, traditional sources of inspiration cannot help the modern poet, who must instead seek the energy of private visionary experience in mundane, public reality, no matter how unpoetic it first appears. As Laszlo Géfin notes, some of Ginsberg's finest poems from the mid-1950s "strike the difficult balance between private and public spheres, serious social awareness and absurd humor, and acceptance of human limitations along with a larger spiritual dimension." Within moments, the speaker's attitude has changed radically, the stands of produce and the store customers affording him a wild, boisterous energy that carries through the poem until the final lines.

Inside the supermarket, Ginsberg sees a man who is not identified with Whitman but appears to be Whitman himself. This encounter, which seems lunatic and visionary at once, suggests not only the profound presence of poetic energy in ordinary life but also its abnormality, the way that poetry makes people outsiders in their own surroundings. Yet for Ginsberg, such an experience intensifies connections to and the experience of this world; thus, Whitman appears utterly human, full of desires—appetitive, erotic, and imaginative—and curious about the world: "I saw you, Walt Whitman, childless, lonely old grubber, poking among the meats in the refrigerator and eyeing the grocery boys. / I heard you asking questions of each: Who killed the pork chops? What price bananas? Are you my Angel?" Ginsberg follows Whitman out of the supermarket, and the questions he overhears prompt him to ask his own questions of Whitman, first about what direction they are heading in together, then about whether they will be sharing the loneliness of America between them, but ultimately about the nature of America and the American experience. "(W)hat America did you have," Ginsberg asks his tutelary spirit, and the question is not only about whether or not Whitman found 19th-century America a place that could sustain the sort of complex lifestyle Ginsberg associates with a life of poetry, but whether such an America is present in the 20th century. Ginsberg's question is by no means rhetorical—in 1957, the San Francisco Police Department confiscated the collection *Howl* and arrested LAWRENCE FERLINGHETTI, the owner of City Lights Book Shop and the publisher of the book, on obscenity charges. The landmark obscenity trial in 1957 brought numerous prominent literary figures to Ginsberg's and Ferlinghetti's defense, and Ferlinghetti was eventually acquitted. But perhaps the final message of Ginsberg's study of the play between private and public poetry, of the links between the individual's desires and the health of the culture, is neither one of uplift nor of abject criticism, but of the good that comes of endurance, for as Ginsberg imagines Whitman carried to the underworld, his final epithet suggests that what Whitman taught America was the power to hope courageously: "Ah, dear father, graybeard, lonely old courage-teacher," Ginsberg calls to him, "what America did you have."

BIBLIOGRAPHY

Géfin, Laszlo K. "Allen Ginsberg." *Dictionary of Literary Biography, Volume 169: American Poets Since World War II, Fifth Series,* edited by Joseph Conte, 116–136. Detroit, Mich.: Gale Research Co., 1996.

Temple Cone

SURREALISM The term *surrealism* is an elision of *super and realism.* Surrealism was a movement combining painting, writing, and other arts, formally beginning as a refinement of another art movement, dada, after World War I. Surrealism cut across national boundaries, languages, and generations. Until recently surrealist art and its techniques were rarely taught in academia. Its influence on 20th-century American poetry was informal and various, but profound. Guillaume Apollinaire and Tristan Tzara founded surrealism. It was defined by André Breton's *First Surrealist Manifesto,* signed in 1925 by Louis Aragon, Antonin Artaud, Robert Desnos, Paul Élaurd, Max Ernst, and others. Breton wrote a *Second Manifesto* in 1929, but, by that time, the group had splintered.

Surrealism in poetry is characterized by dreamlike juxtaposition of images, the invitation of chance into composition, and the suspension of many types of intentional discussion of themes. Surrealist techniques are textual and psychological. Surrealist processes include automatic writing, "slippage" and "first thought

/ best thought" to turn off conscious imposition of reason. Automatic writing, in which the writer simply begins to write or draw words without intentionally controlling those words differs from spirit dictation, such as that used by William Butler Yeats, by source, although occultism shaped surrealist writing. During this type of writing, slippage and error interrupt narrative or transcription while the writer is writing: Words and images resulting from typographical mistakes during drafting, for example, are included in the work and result in a juxtaposition of symbols or words separate from linear logic. Found poetry, advertisements, and other nonpoetic sources recognized as poems and chance operations, such as rolling dice to select words from a preexisting text, remove traditional connotations or denotations of phrases or sampled poems. Surrealism was not welcomed into the academic world, in part, because surrealists used drugs, sleep deprivation, and pain to break down the boundaries of moral structures so as to enable "sight" to aid composition.

Early psychology shaped surrealism, and psychological surrealism has been welcomed into the academic world as domestic surrealism or DEEP IMAGE. Hermetic symbols and their psychological interpretation can establish a unity behind a surreal poem separate from story or form. A reading focusing on establishing relationships between the objects or persons in a surrealist poem, and therefore the relationship of a poem to mythic structures, such as journeys, can lead to an understanding of a surreal poem. Surrealism's grounding in psychological or dream reality separates it from other movements.

Surrealism is also grounded in the more extreme movement dada, which challenged the utility of language to describe reality. Dadaists, including Marcel Duchamp, sought refuge after World War I in New York, inspiring separate American surrealistic responses to dada in poetry, such as MINA LOY's. A more broadly defined, second-wave surrealism moved to New York with Salvador Dalí and Breton himself before World War II. Philip Lamantia deliberately sought out Breton in order to establish an American surrealist lineage. Lamantia, in turn, relocated to San Francisco, where he influenced the SAN FRANCISCO RENAISSANCE, BEAT, and now neosurrealist poetry. Caribbean francophone surrealist poet Aimé Césaire has influenced American poets (see CARIBBEAN POETIC INFLUENCES), as did British painter and writer Leonora Carrington, who relocated to Mexico midcareer. American poets translating surrealist writings into English include NEW YORK SCHOOL poets JOHN ASHBERY and KENNETH KOCH, RICHARD HOWARD, who also has translated Charles Baudelaire and symbolist writers, and HARRY MATHEWS, a member of OuLiPo, a largely French and Italian movement dedicated to writing that crossed surrealist textual techniques with mathematics. BERNADETTE MAYER taught surrealist and OuLiPo techniques at the St. Mark's Poetry Project in New York City (see POETRY INSTITUTIONS). Because of surrealism's longevity, it has combined with nearly every major movement of 20th-century American poetry, including the OBJECTIVIST and LANGUAGE SCHOOLS.

BIBLIOGRAPHY

Caws, Mary Ann, ed. *Surrealist Painters and Poets: An Anthology*. Cambridge, Mass.: MIT Press, 2001.

Halsall, Paul. "A Surrealist Manifesto," Internet History Sourcebook. Available online. URL: http://www.fordham.edu/halsall/mod/1925surrealism.html. Downloaded March 2007.

Catherine Daly

SWENSON, MAY (1913–1989) A native westerner who lived her entire adult life in New York and its environs, a self-proclaimed feminist who nonetheless eschewed politicized writing, and a lesbian whose love poetry, almost always sexually neutral, can often be construed as heterosexual, May Swenson wrote poems that radically challenge customary perceptions and stereotypes. Influenced by Emily Dickinson, Swenson is often compared to MARIANNE MOORE and ELIZABETH BISHOP for her ability to make us see commonplace objects in a startlingly new way. Extensively published and active as a writer-in-residence at numerous universities and artists' colonies, Swenson was one of the best-known American poets during the decades of the cold war.

Born in Logan, Utah, Swenson grew up in a Swedish immigrant, Mormon family. Upon graduation from Utah State University, she moved to New York City.

Swenson's first collection of poems, *Another Animal,* was published in 1954. Eleven volumes of poetry were published during Swenson's lifetime, including *Half Sun Half Asleep* (1967), *Iconographs* (1970), and *New and Selected Things Taking Place* (1978). She won Rockefeller (1955 and 1967), Guggenheim (1959), Ford (1964), and MacArthur (1987) Fellowships for her poetry, as well as the Bollingen Prize for poetry (1981) and a National Endowment for the Arts grant (1974). Swenson was a member of the American Academy and Institute of Arts and Letters and served as chancellor of the Academy of American Poets.

Critics have often called Swenson a nature poet, pointing to her "knowing sympathy with wild creatures" and "poems full of tents and cabins and out-of-doors" (Wilbur 2). Swenson herself remarked, however: "For me, nature includes everything: the entire universe, the city, the country, the human mind, human creatures, and animal creatures" ("Interview" 121). Indeed Swenson's poems bespeak her wide-ranging fascination with the physical world, from subway riding and space exploration to sports and modern art. Her work is marked by a vigorous playfulness, seen both in her elegant poetic riddles and her famous "shaped poems," wherein the arrangement and spacing of words on a page suggest the contour or movement of the object they describe (see VISUAL POETRY). Her understanding of the poem as a concrete, constructed unit characterized her as a formalist. At the same time, however, Swenson often acknowledged that good poetry also depends on the subconscious and a trust in randomness. In a posthumously published essay, "A Poem Happens to Me," she likened the act of writing a poem to "the opening of neuron synapses to the brain after partaking of liquor or a drug" (77). Writing, Swenson said, "is death and birth being brought to within a desperate circumferential hair's breadth of each other—as if two stars of opposite poles swept together and *almost* grazed!" (79).

Frequently Swenson wrote from an unusual viewpoint, describing a scene upside down or at extremely close range, or by forcing unexpected comparisons. She asks us to see a parallel between "The DNA Molecule" (1970) and Marcel Duchamps's *Nude Descending a Staircase:* "She is a double helix mounting and dismounting / around the swivel of her imaginary spine." In her riddle poem "Speed" (1975), Swenson depicts an insect-spattered windshield as "a tender painting / . . . a palette, thick impasto." Wedding iconoclastic vision to disciplined aesthetic structure, Swenson compels us to cast off naive ways of perceiving, to see beyond surfaces even as we glory in them.

BIBLIOGRAPHY

Swenson, May. "An Interview with May Swenson, July 14, 1978," by Karla Hammond. In *Made with Words,* edited by Gardner McFall, 121–133. Ann Arbor: University of Michigan Press, 1998.

———. "A Poem Happens to Me." In *Made With Words,* edited by Gardner McFall, 75–79. Ann Arbor: University of Michigan Press, 1998.

Wilbur, Richard. Foreword to *May Swenson: A Poet's Life in Photos,* by R. R. Knudson and Suzzanne Bigelow. Logan: Utah State University Press, 1996, pp. 1–6.

Patricia G. King

T

THE TABLETS **ARMAND SCHWERNER (1999)**
A project of an epic scale comparable to EZRA POUND'S *CANTOS* and LOUIS ZUKOFSKY'S *"A,"* ARMAND SCHWERNER'S *The Tablets* is a major poetic statement of the late 20th century (see LONG AND SERIAL POETRY). Its singular combination of deeply sincere cultural investigation and ironic self-parody, a poetic strategy Burt Kimmelman has called "at once primeval and postmodern" (70), places the work within a complex matrix of contemporary aesthetic and spiritual concerns. On the one hand, the work engages the movement known as ETHNOPOETICS, which attempted to widen the historical and cultural scope of poetic awareness to include little-known ancient and "primitive" literatures. Schwerner, a close friend of the movement's central figure, JEROME ROTHENBERG, has been associated with this movement, which proposed "to allow a *world* to come into the poem—not Europe only or a poetics bounded by an age-old partial view," but a poetics that "at its most radical" would "[carry] forward a search for poetries far outside the imperium as such" (Rothenberg 733).

At the same time, *The Tablets* should be understood in terms of the procedure-oriented compositional strategies of such contemporaries as JACKSON MAC LOW and JOHN CAGE. *The Tablets* makes use of an elaborate formal system, based on a fiction of anthropological/paleographic research, which reflects, like Mac Low's and Cage's procedures, "a typically postmodern skepticism regarding the unitary self and its expression in the poem," according to Norman Finkelstein ("Armand Schwerner"). As Schwerner himself puts it in "Tablets Journals/Divagations," a set of process notes appended to the poems themselves, "*The Tablets* live in a matrix of unbreachable, ambiguous and antique silence," but they "also exist within a context of Heisenbergian invention. Are *The Tablets* then blurrings within those two fixes, one unreachable, the other scientifically 'up-to-date'?" (133). Earlier in "Journals/Divagations," he suggests one answer to the question: "The conflict between the comedian and the mystic can make poems" (129).

The Tablets purports to be a collection of 27 texts translated from 4,000-year-old Mesopotamian clay tablets and cylinders written using a combination of Sumerian pictographs and Akkadian cuneiform. The texts are supposed to have come down to us through the labors of a figure known as the Scholar/Translator, and a large part of the humor and the pathos of the poems is derived from our sense of this figure bumbling through an immensely challenging project, always suspended between at least two poignant difficulties: either a great proportion of missing or uncertain material produces a fragmentary text whose content is highly unstable, or, at times, a fine, compressed lyric intensity shines through in what seem to be largely coherent passages—but is the Scholar/Translator projecting his own desire for coherence into a textual condition where none exists?

The sequence begins with a high degree of uncertainty: "All that's left is pattern* (shoes?)" reads the first line of Tablet I, and this is immediately followed by a nervous footnote from the Scholar/Translator: "*doubtful reconstruction" (13). The text is full of phrasings, which do not fit neatly into English: The phrase "hanging-mackerel-tail-up-smoke-death" is purported by the Scholar / Translator to be a "virtually untranslatable" evocation of a "coterminous visionary metaphysic" that refers "to both time-bound organisms . . . and the Death God, *plonz*, in his timeless brooding"; the line "they will-would-might-have-can-change the winter of NNE" contains a verb construction whose tense is "outside Indo-European categories." The multiplicity of each utterance is unsettling; at the same time we get a sense of language straining to recover the primary ground of experience. Indeed the Scholar/Translator shows himself to be obsessed with the recovery of origins: Uncertain whether to translate a particular word as "dry" or "unforgiving," he notes, "We find ourselves at or near the very point in time where the word, concrete in origin, shades off into an abstraction." Similarly, in Tablet VI, the Scholar/Translator thinks he may have located the first "particularized man" in literature, and in Tablet XI he claims to see "the first socialist voice in recorded human history." But these revelations are always undermined by our knowledge that the Scholar/Translator is inevitably distorting his originals to reflect his own desire for discovery, and his intrusions into the text increasingly betray his own doubts: "On occasion it almost seems to me as if I am inventing this sequence."

We readers know that the Scholar/Translator is a fiction as well. But as Finkelstein notes, the conceit underlying *The Tablets* should be recognized as "the deepest of deep parodies." The unstable status of authorship in the sequence ultimately reflects Schwerner's deeply held Buddhist beliefs in the unreality of the ego, and, as Willard Gingerich has written, the poems excavate the paradox "that the inescapable and necessary ground of our being is the voice of the Divine; but the Divine steadfastly refuses to speak. Therefore, we find ourselves, age after age, forced to translate an immense silence, a translation whose purpose is to obscure the forgery of its source: the inarticulate Divine" (18). If *The Tablets* can be said to have a thematic unity, it is to be found in their confrontation with the greatly mundane and greatly profound basics of existence: physical suffering, bodily functions, the natural world, sex, birth, childhood, aging, death, divinity. When in Tablet III Schwerner writes, "I am missing, my chest has no food for the maggots / there is no place for the pollen, there is only a hole in the flower," he achieves, in a timeless sense, what the Scholar/Translator has been at pains to locate historically: the point in language where the concrete and the abstract, the given and the created, intersect.

BIBLIOGRAPHY

Finkelstein, Norman. "Armand Schwerner," Jacket. Available online. URL: http://jacketmagazine.com/10/fink-r-schw.html. Downloaded December 2003.

Gingerich, Willard. "Sacred Forgeries and the Translation of Nothing in *The Tablets* of Armand Schwerner." *Talisman* 21/22 (winter/spring 2001): 18–26.

Kimmelman, Burt. "Traces of Being: Armand Schwerner's Ephemeral Episteme." *Talisman* 19 (winter 1998/1999): 70–77.

Rothenberg, Jerome. "Prologue to Origins." In *Poems for the Millenium*, Vol. One: *From Fin-de-Siècle to Negritude*, edited by Rothenberg and Pierre Joris. Berkeley: University of California Press, 1995.

Damian Judge Rollison

TAGGART, JOHN (1942–) The poetry of John Taggart gestures toward the influence of a number of important figures and movements in the landscape of 20th-century American poetry: WALLACE STEVENS and high MODERNISM; LOUIS ZUKOFSKY, GEORGE OPPEN, and the OBJECTIVIST school; and CHARLES OLSON and the BLACK MOUNTAIN SCHOOL. His poetry also draws upon a number of other artistic influences—modern and postmodern painting (especially Edward Hopper and Mark Rothko), classical music, jazz, rhythm and blues, and philosophy.

Born in Gutherie Center, Iowa, Taggart has published 13 books of poetry and two works of prose, *Remaining in Light: Ant Meditations on a Poetry by Edward Hopper* (1993) and *Songs of Degrees: Essays on Contemporary Poetry and Poetics* (1994), and he was the editor from 1966 till 1974 of *Maps*, a literary journal that featured many of the most significant but then underappreciated poets, including Oppen, WILLIAM BRONK, Olson, and Zukofsky.

Taggart's first five books of poetry—*To Construct a Clock* (1971), *Pyramid Canon* (1973), *The Pyramid Is a Pure Crystal* (1974), *Prism and the Pine Twig* (1977), and *Dodeka* (1979)—clearly invoke the sparse language and vision of objectivism and its tenet to capture reality objectively. The books of poetry that follow—*Peace on Earth* (1981) and *Dehiscence* (1983)—begin to break slightly with the earlier work and concentrate upon a poetic music indebted to jazz, especially John Coltrane (whose work is a palpable presence in *Peace on Earth*), Thelonious Monk, and other giants of the 1950s and 1960s. Beyond the clear impact of jazz upon these later books, the poems also gesture toward Olson's important 1950 essay "Projective Verse" and its proclamation that the form of the poem must embody the energy of the process of poetic discovery (see ARS POETICAS).

The most original poetry collected in the more recent works, *Loop* (1991), *Prompted* (1991), *Standing Wave* (1993), and *Crosses* (1998), seamlessly blends the visual acuity of objectivism, the musical harmonies of jazz, and the ideational and poetic dynamics of "Projective Verse" into a powerful and original poetics, as typified by the opening lines of "Rereading" from *Standing Wave*: "He has closed the door to his room and he is reading / he has closed the door and he is reading a poem." Taggart's poetry gains linguistic and semantic momentum through the repetition of words, phrases, and ideas as the poem layers and builds its argument. Similar to jazz, it establishes a theme that it asserts and repeatedly reasserts in a effort to eke out linguistic and ideational nuances. And, in keeping with "Projective Verse," the repetition builds "energy" in its pursuit of those nuances.

From these later books, "The Rothko Chapel Poem," "Marvin Gaye Suite," "Monk," and "Poem Beginning with a Line from Traherne" (all from *Loop*) and "Rereading" and "Standing Wave" (from *Standing Wave*) are noteworthy as poems of great linguistic vitality, intelligence, and poetic resonance. Taggart's poetry, in this regard, is visually, linguistically, and musically innovative, and, in an age where the value of poetry is often challenged, Taggart's philosophical investigation into the role of art as part of the living process offers a valuable statement regarding poetry's vitality.

BIBLIOGRAPHY

Daly, Lew. *Swallowing the Scroll: Late in a Prophetic Tradition with the Poetry of Susan Howe and John Taggart*. Buffalo, N.Y.: M. Press, 1994.

Howe, Susan. "Life in Darkness: John Taggart's Poetry." *Hambone* 2 (spring 1982): 37–45.

Johnson, Ronald. "On Looking up 'The Pyramid Is a Pure Crystal' in Webster." *Parnassus* 3, no. 2 (1975): 147–152.

David Clippinger

TARN, NATHANIEL (1928–) A professional translator and anthropologist who has spent time in Guatemala and Burma, Nathaniel Tarn is associated with ETHNOPOETICS. Tarn's poems revere world cultures, diverse religions, and the natural environment, while advocating political changes for their protection. His work is erudite, richly metaphorical, and rhythmically vibrant; Eliot Weinberger writes, "What holds it together is Tarn's ecstatic vision, his continuing enthusiasm for the stuff of the world" (222). Similar to CHARLES OLSON, Tarn juxtaposes various forms of poetic expression, including erotic love lyrics and political protests, with nonpoetic documents, from catalogues of Alaskan bird species to historical letters, to achieve a fullness that can "call into being everything there is" ("One" [1969]).

Tarn was born in Paris, France. After earning a Ph.D. in anthropology in 1957 from the University of Chicago, he received the Guinness Prize for poetry in 1963 (and has garnered a number of other honors over time), publishing his first book in 1964. He was founding editor of Cape-Golliard Press and a professor of comparative literature at Rutgers. Tarn has written or collaborated on more than 40 books of poetry and translations.

Motion and energy characterize Tarn's style. His sprawling, often unpunctuated lines transform the written page into a field, which depicts visually shifts in thought. His earlier poems are often spoken from the persona of the Old Savage, who critiques and pities the decay of modern culture. Many of the later poems arise from events in Tarn's own life, but he downplays his own role in the events, instead considering how individual experience opens connections to the broader world. As Tarn has said, language "is the vehicle of ever deepening attention" (222).

"Projections for an Eagle Escaped in This City, March 1965" (1967) portrays the ironic event of a bald eagle's flight from a Washington, D.C., zoo in order to critique American involvement in Vietnam during the Vietnam War. Tarn warns, "To be evil is nothing more than to be tired," and he finds an alternate symbol of freedom in the hummingbird, a hero in American Indian myths, noted for remarkable physical endurance. Tarn announces that "his lungs will flower, his heart / bear fruit. Mounting up with wings as a storm cloud, unafraid." In "Olvido Inolvidable" (1976), Tarn uses ambiguous pronouns to describe the cosmos as a pair of lovers, sometimes with Tarn, his wife, or the reader as one of the pair. The poem concludes with their union: "sun and moon wake in each other's arms surprised / and the stars make music together incessantly." Ecstatic, erudite, and energetic, Tarn's poetry embraces a world of cultural and natural riches, confident that such love can lead to radical political change.

BIBLIOGRAPHY

Tarn, Nathaniel. "Nathaniel Tarn: 'Over the fragile sails your hands would make.'" In *Talking Poetry: Conversations in the Workshop with Contemporary Poets,* edited by Lee Bartlett, 209–233. Albuquerque: University of New Mexico Press, 1987.

Weinberger, Eliot. "Nathaniel Tarn." In *Contemporary Poets.* 4th ed, edited by James Vinson and D. L. Kirkpatrick. New York: St. Martin's Press, 1985.

Temple Cone

TATE, ALLEN (1899–1979) John Orley Allen Tate was a founding member of the famed poetry magazine the *Fugitive* (see POETRY JOURNALS), a magazine that advocated a formal approach to poetry and upheld the traditional values of the agrarian South in the face of industrialism flowing down from the North (see FUGITIVE/AGRARIAN SCHOOL). Other key contributors to the movement included JOHN CROWE RANSOM and ROBERT PENN WARREN. Tate was also a leading figure in the literary movement known as New Criticism. Tate's poetry is marked by its adherence to strict poetic forms and its intellectuality.

Tate was born in Winchester, Kentucky. He attended college at Vanderbilt University in the early 1920s. After graduating from Vanderbilt, he remained in Nashville, where he helped found the *Fugitive.* He later contributed to *I'll Take My Stand* (1930), a book that became a manifesto for the Fugitive movement. As editor of the *Sewanee Review* and as an instructor at several prominent universities, Tate wrote both poetry and criticism into his seventies and continued to exert considerable force as a critic of American letters. His greatest achievement was being awarded the National Medal for literature in 1976. He won many other awards, including the Bollingen Prize in 1956. He was elected to both the American Academy of Arts and Letters (1964) and the American Academy of Arts and Sciences (1965).

Critics have argued that Tate has been relegated to the rank of minor poet, in part, because of his unwillingness to break from his self-imposed formal rigidity and overly cerebral subject matter. References to ancient philosophers and obscure concepts abound in his work. Exile is a central theme in Tate's poetry, along with a profound sense of the past as imperturbable and all-encumbering: "What shall we say of the bones, unclean, / Whose verdurous anonymity will grow?" he asks in "ODE TO THE CONFEDERATE DEAD" (1926), suggesting that our sins will outlast us. Tate's fundamental belief in our need for atonement is perhaps underscored by his conversion to Catholicism in 1950.

Tate was an important influence on several prominent members of a subsequent generation of poets, many of whom were his students, including ROBERT LOWELL, RANDALL JARRELL, and JOHN BERRYMAN. He urged adherence to traditional forms and the exploration of abstract philosophical ideas. He was unwavering in his insistence on high aesthetic standards in poetry and poetics.

BIBLIOGRAPHY

Arbery, Glenn Cannon. "Dante in Bardstown: Allen Tate's Guide to Southern Exile." *Thought: A Review of Culture and Idea* 65:256 (March 1990): 93–108.

Bishop, Ferman. *Allen Tate.* New York: Twayne, 1967.

Core, George. "Mr. Tate and the Limits of Poetry." *Virginia Quarterly Review* 62, no. 1 (winter 1986): 105–114.

Aaron Parrett

TATE, JAMES (1943–) James Tate is an unconventional poet, often described as surrealist in his aims (see SURREALISM). When he received the National Book Award in 1994, he stated that he began to write poetry at the age of 17 in order to "stay alive and make sense out of life" (26). The sense Tate has made of it, within his poems, is very much his own. Tate has a talent for making the familiar fantastic, and his work is so unusual that it is difficult to make comparisons, although elements of the work of JOHN ASHBERY might be seen in Tate's poems, and Tate's humor is similar to that of his close friend, the poet CHARLES SIMIC.

Tate was born in Kansas City, Missouri. In 1967 he received an M.F.A. in poetry from the University of Iowa, where he studied with MARVIN BELL. His first major success occurred in that year, when his book *The Lost Pilot* (1967) was selected for the Yale Series of Younger Poets. Tate was only 24 at the time. Since that initial success, he has published numerous collections of poetry, a novel, *Lucky Darryl* (1977), and a collection of short stories, *Hottentot Ossuary* (1974). He also edited the *Best American Poetry 1997*. He has been accorded nearly every poetry prize available. Tate's *Worshipful Company of Fletchers* (1994) won the National Book Award; his *Selected Poems* (1991) won both the WILLIAM CARLOS WILLIAMS Award and the Pulitzer Prize. In 1995 Tate was the winner of the prestigious Tanning Prize, the largest annual literary prize given in the United States.

The title poem from *The Lost Pilot* is perhaps Tate's most often anthologized work. It is a moving, but also unusual, elegy for his father, who was a war casualty. The poem begins, "Your face did not rot," before moving to a description of the copilot's, whose did. The horror of Tate's father's death becomes so grotesquely terrible that the effect is ultimately comic. His "Goodtime Jesus" is another good example of a poem where the worst of situations is treated with a deadpan nonchalance. In a short prose poem of unrelenting dark humor, Tate's Jesus awakens to a scene of apocalyptic nightmare, within which he decides to "take a little ride on [his] donkey," saying as he does, "I love that donkey. Hell, I love everybody."

As Tate has said elsewhere of his own work, "Truth is an elusive monster, and sometimes a poet must bend or squeeze the language to bring it into view. I'm willing to follow a poem anywhere so long as it promises some insight or revelation" (qtd. in Baker 26). His poems deliver on this objective, offering truth from his own strange perspective.

BIBLIOGRAPHY

Baker, John F. "1994 National Book Awards." *Publisher's Weekly* 241, no. 47 (November 21, 1994): 26.

Denver Quarterly 33, no. 3 (fall 1998). [James Tate: A Special Issue]

Wright, Carolyne. "On James Tate." *Iowa Review* 26, no. 1 (spring 1996): 183–188.

Anna Priddy

"TEACH US TO NUMBER OUR DAYS"

RITA DOVE (1980) "Teach Us to Number Our Days," from RITA DOVE's first full-length volume, *The Yellow House on the Corner* (1980), is significant for its ability to illustrate the ways in which individuals are shaped by both their inner and outer lives, and the poem's form—a free verse sonnet (see PROSODY AND FREE VERSE)—suggests the tensions between constriction and freedom.

In "Teach Us to Number Our Days," as in work throughout her career, Dove writes as an African American, but her work does not speak exclusively to the black experience, nor does it limit what the black experience might be. In her introduction to her *Selected Poems* (1993), Dove says that one of the questions that most interests her when she writes is: "How does where I come from determine where I've ended up?" (xxi). "Teach Us to Number Our Days" first depicts a scene that has socioeconomic and racial components to it; the poem then goes on to explore movingly the ways in which a person develops and grows up in a world of social constrictions.

The poem's complex interweaving of social realities and dreams, which can or cannot transcend external factors, recalls GWENDOLYN BROOKS's famous "kitchenette building" (1945). But Dove's poem is less hopeful and less humorous. Dove's title, which is a quotation from Moses' prayer in Psalm 90:12, places the poem within a long tradition of black spirituals, many of which take Moses as a central figure, and suggests that freedom will be found only in the next world.

The first stanza situates us, with its vernacular language and specific sensual details, in a contemporary ghetto, a world of funeral parlors and "cops." A boy tries to escape the constrictions in the world around him through his imagination and his dreams. The television antennae become for him a tic-tac-toe board. He dreams he swallows a blue bean that, like the bean in the fairy tale "Jack and the Giant Beanstalk," grows and grows. But the image of growth soon becomes ominous: Even in his dreams, the boy cannot escape constriction, the force that shapes the world around him, as the vines seem to blind him. Even the natural world now appears defined by human power, "knotting like a dark tie."

In the boy's world, "the patroller, disinterested, holds all the beans." The policeman's "blue bullets" are the beans, the source of power and what the boy dreams he has swallowed. Outside of its title, the poem offers no escape. In the poem's final image, a single-line stanza, instead of a couplet or tercet, the "mum" flowers become an image of raw emotion: a cry that will get no answer from the disinterested agents of power in this world.

BIBLIOGRAPHY

Dove, Rita. Introduction to *Selected Poems,* by Dove. New York: Pantheon, 1993.

Steffen, Therese. *Crossing Color: Transcultural Space and Place in Rita Dove's Poetry, Fiction and Drama.* New York: Oxford University Press, 2001.

Vendler, Helen. *The Given and the Made: Strategies of Poetic Redefinition.* Cambridge, Mass.: Harvard University Press, 1995.

Nadia Herman Colburn

TEASDALE, SARA (1884–1933) Sara Teasdale was an important voice of woman's poetry in the early 20th century (see FEMALE VOICE, FEMALE LANGUAGE). Her work, consistently appearing in monthly national magazines in the years before World War II, was well received by the public and critics alike. She identified with and is often compared to the 19th-century poet Elizabeth Barret Browning in theme, but her direct influence was the Victorian Christina Rossetti, about whom she had composed an unfinished biography.

Teasdale was born in St. Louis, Missouri, and lived in and out of sanitariums until her death from an overdose of sedatives. Though her work was frequently in the public eye, Teasdale herself was not; she was a quiet and private person, sheltered throughout her life by parents, friends, and husband. In her teens she and her friends founded an amateur artists society for women called the Potters and published a handwritten magazine called the *Potters Wheel,* including original photography, sketches, poems, and prose. Her first book of poetry, dedicated to a popular actress of the time, *Sonnets to Duse and Other Poems,* was published in 1907. She won the Poetry Society of America's First Prize for unpublished poetry in 1916 and, in 1918, was the first recipient of the Columbia Poetry Prize, later renamed the Pulitzer Prize for poetry.

Teasdale's poetry is classic and lyrical in nature, unaffected by the experimentation in theme, capitalization, and style of her contemporaries, such as T. S. ELIOT and E. E. CUMMINGS. She believed that traditional forms of poetry allowed the reader to understand the emotions of the poem more easily, without having to wade through MODERNISM's new challenging structures and language. Her poems deal directly with universal emotions, centering on women's experiences.

Contemporary critics often praised the musical quality of Teasdale's poetry in both its rhythm and simplicity. Teasdale remarked, "I try to say what moves me—I never care to surprise my reader. . . . For me one of the greatest joys of poetry is to know it by heart—perhaps that is why the simple songlike poems appeal to me most—they are the easiest to learn" (qtd. in Carpenter 331). The poem "The Fountain" (1915) showcases the musical quality of her writing with its strict rhythm and rhyme patterns and subtle shifting of sound, as in "The fountain sang and sang / But the satyr never stirred." In this poem the first hints of the maturity appear, which she expresses in her later writing as she contrasts cyclical characteristics of nature with those of her own experiences. In her last published collection of poems, *Strange Victory* (1933), Teasdale makes this same connection between herself and her natural surroundings: In "The Tree" she describes herself "Resting, as a tree rests / After its leaves are gone." Teasdale's poetry explores themes of love, joy, death, sorrow, and nature, rather than delving into social or political commentary.

BIBLIOGRAPHY

Carpenter, Margaret Haley. *Sara Teasdale: A Biography.* Norfolk, Va.: Pentelic, 1977.

Drake, William. *Sara Teasdale: Woman and Poet.* San Francisco: Harper and Row, 1979.

Holly Salmon

"THE TEETH MOTHER NAKED AT LAST" ROBERT BLY (1986) One of the most important poems to come out of the Vietnam protest movement, "The Teeth Mother Naked at Last" represents ROBERT BLY's seamless melding of political and contemplative poetry. Bly took inspiration from the political poems of Latin American poets, including Pablo Neruda and César Vallejo, and from American contemporaries ETHERIDGE KNIGHT, THOMAS MCGRATH, JAMES WRIGHT, and DAVID IGNATOW, as well as the earlier American poets Walt Whitman and WILLIAM CARLOS WILLIAMS, all of whom wrote about political crises. In his 1980 essay "Leaping up into Political Poetry," Bly argues for the power of contemplative poetry to engage with political questions: "The life of the nation can be imagined also not as something deep inside our psyche, but as a psyche larger than the psyche of anyone living, a larger sphere, floating above everyone. In order for the poet to write a true political poem, he has to be able to have such a grasp of his own concerns that he can leave them for awhile, and then leap up into this other psyche" (100–101).

Bly's greatest political poem was written in three versions. The first appeared in his collection of the same name (1970), the second in *Sleepers Joining Hands* (1973), and the third in *Selected Poems* (1986). In all three versions, Bly is indebted to Spanish SURREALISM, and his own DEEP IMAGE style allows him to employ powerful dreamlike images in his description of political events. In his lament over the death of spirituality and thought, he evokes the strange image of books that do not want to be with us any longer: "New Testaments . . . escaping . . . dressed as women . . . / they slip out after dark." The images are at times brutally direct. Bly describes an attack on a hut by high explosives: "The six-hour-old infant puts his fists instinctively to his eyes to keep out the light." The final image of the attack is plain and unflinching: "Blood leaps on the vegetable walls."

For Bly, the psyche of America will pay for the atrocities and lies of the Vietnam war. In a surreal passage Bly describes a speech by a lying president. Bly warns that this suggests the decline of the nation and asks, "What is there now to hold us to earth?"

Even the political arguments Bly offers take on a surreal uncanniness in their immediacy: Bly's poem is an angry lament, a prophetic warning about the psychic death that threatens America as it piles horror on horror and turns its wealth and power to the production of death.

BIBLIOGRAPHY

Bly, Robert. "Leaping up into Political Poetry: An Essay." In *Talking All Morning*. Ann Arbor: University of Michigan Press, 1980, pp. 100–101.

———. "The Magic of the Muse," Interview with Robert Bly by Roar Bjonnes, Magical Blend Magazine. Available online. URL: www.magicalblend.com/library/reading-room/interviews/bly.html. Downloaded September 2003.

Alan Bourassa

TENDER BUTTONS **GERTRUDE STEIN (1914)** Long before the popular success of her best-known work, *The Autobiography of Alice B. Toklas* (1933), the publication of *Tender Buttons* insured GERTRUDE STEIN's place among the experimental poets of the modern era. *Tender Buttons* divides into three sections of prose poems, "Objects," "Food," and "Rooms," each a unique meditation on the relationships and resemblances that structure language and thought. Stein's poetic diction is dense and complex, employing repetition, puns, and ambiguity to create a playful tone of "joyous lightness and miraculous plentitude," according to Marianne DeKoven (229). Although the skepticism of early critics seemed to affirm Stein's own claim that "the creator of the new composition in the arts is an outlaw until he is a classic" (514), Stein was conscious that her experiments partook of a historical, literary lineage. Edmund Wilson aligns her emphasis on connotation and suggestion with the methods of T. S. ELIOT, William Butler Yeats, and the symbolists, while Stein herself credits Walt Whitman as her precursor. *Tender Buttons*'s concise understatement also influenced such writers as Ernest Hemingway, and its experiments with words as objects developed alongside the avant-garde work of painters, including Pablo Picasso, who frequented her salon in Paris. In its playful linguistic innovation, Stein's poetry resembles the work of E. E. CUMMINGS, and it influenced later poets, including FRANK O'HARA of the NEW YORK SCHOOL and the contemporary experiments of CHARLES BERNSTEIN of the LANGUAGE SCHOOL.

The "carefully wrong" verbal still lifes of *Tender Buttons* present the reader with no small challenge, argues Neil Schmitz (165). Their playful, elusive logic seamlessly connects disparate words and senses, prompting some critics to suggest that the poems resemble riddles, and others to discern ambiguous connotations of lesbianism and gender polemics. But, more importantly, the poems also address the very difficulty they pose to readers, one of connection and correlation. How does "A Piece of Coffee" resemble "More of a double," or "A Cutlet" align with "blind agitation?" In what Schmidtz calls their "principled evasion of specific reference," Stein's brief lyrics address and enact the problem of relationship, a fundamental philosophical question of logic and language (165). For example, in "A Box," Stein desires "to have a green point not to red but to point again." Instead of pointing to its conventional counterpart, Stein's "green" points toward "pointing" itself, the act in which a color (or a word) directs us toward another one. Her subtle experiments pose an enormous question: Can language adequately address its own mechanisms? Stein's philosophical investigation into the nature of poetry and language underlies the entire volume; its vigor makes *Tender Buttons* a landmark of modernist experimentation (see MODERNISM), a precursor to what would later become a particularly American vein of structural and linguistic innovation.

BIBLIOGRAPHY

DeKoven, Marianne. "Breaking the Rigid Form of the Noun: Stein, Pound, Whitman and Modernist Poetry." In *Critical Essays on Modernism,* edited by Michael Hoffman, 225–234. New York: G.K. Hall, 1992.

Schmitz, Neil. *Of Huck and Alice: Humorous Writing in American Literature.* Minneapolis: University of Minnesota Press, 1983, pp. 160–199.

Stein, Gertrude. *The Selected Writings of Gertrude Stein,* edited by Carl van Vechten. New York: Random House, 1962.

Wilson, Edmund. *Axel's Castle: A Study in the Imaginative Literature of 1870–1930.* New York: Charles Scribner's Sons, 1931.

Anthony Cuda

"THEME FOR ENGLISH B" LANGSTON HUGHES (1959) One of LANGSTON HUGHES's most anthologized poems, "Theme for English B" explores issues of race, culture, and nationality, concluding with an inspiring yet subtly critical assessment of the possibility of racial harmony in America. Hughes narrates in the voice of a young African-American man writing a college theme, or English composition paper, responding to the prompt to *"let that page come out of you—/ Then, it will be true."* This young but self-assured, reflective, and cautiously hopeful narrator describes his southern past and his current life in New York, as well as his different pleasures in life, before addressing his English teacher and discussing the role of national identity in resolving racial and cultural conflict.

"I wonder if it's that simple?" the narrator asks rhetorically of the prompt. Identity for Hughes is composed of one's race, culture, locality, nationality, past, present, desires, pleasures, and dreams, among other things. But to weave these characteristics into a coherent whole presents a difficulty; "Me—who?" Hughes writes. Throughout the poem the narrator reveals many aspects of himself, sometimes directly and sometimes not, but his self-portrait remains incomplete. He states that he is "colored," 22, southern by birth, enrolled at Columbia University and living in Harlem, curious about life and knowledge, and a lover of all sorts of music, from baroque to jazz. But there are other aspects of his life that can only be inferred. He tells us he went to different schools in North Carolina before moving to New York, a pattern that traces the Great Migration of African Americans from their traditional homes in the South to urban centers in the North like New York and Chicago early in the 20th century. Such movement suggests the narrator's experience of racism and his refusal to continue enduring it. The narrator is also cautious, for while he describes his life activities in terms that seem universal or transcendent in character, writing that "I like to eat, sleep, drink, and be in love. / I like to work, read, learn, and understand life," these descriptions reveal very little in terms of particulars, suggesting his wariness about self-disclosure, especially to a white audience.

Such concealments may seem at odds with the generally affirming tone of the poem. But as formal and polite as the narrator seems to be, he admits to his teacher that "Sometimes perhaps you don't want to be a part of me. / Nor do I often want to be a part of you." Yet in spite of this dislike, he concedes "[W]e are, that's true!" By not divulging specific details about his life, Hughes simultaneously affirms a common experience with white America while also resisting the impulse to justify his life to that culture and reshape himself in its image. As Hughes once wrote, "[T]his is the mountain standing in the way of any true Negro art in America—this urge within the race toward whiteness, the desire to pour racial individuality into the mold of American standardization, and to be as little Negro and as much American as possible" (301).

Although "Theme for English B" is a FREE VERSE poem, Hughes uses occasional rhymes to make a subtle thematic argument. The instructions for the theme are in the form of rhyming couplets, suggesting the college education the young man is receiving is grounded in history and tradition. Yet for an African-American narrator, *history* signifies past racial oppression, while *tradition* evokes white, Western culture, which generally excludes distinctly African-American music or literary arts from its canon. The first lines of the "theme" portion of the poem are unrhymed, suggesting a break from the history and tradition the teacher represents. But Hughes's rhyming of *Winston-Salem* with the twice-repeated *Harlem* suggests that the young man is participating in humanism's ideal of self-knowledge by relating his past to his present, while his emphasis on Harlem, a black cultural center in the 1920s during the HARLEM RENAISSANCE, suggests the narrator's refusal to be constrained by his past. Other rhymes are scattered throughout the poem, including "love/life," "write/white," and "me/free/B," and while Hughes may not be encoding these rhymes with specific claims, they suggest the narrator intends to free himself from mainstream cultural norms and to enlighten white America about the black experience through written self-expression. Such enlightenment is not conciliatory, though. Playing on the image of written text as a field where black ink and white paper create meaning by remaining separate and distinct, the narrator claims that his paper "Being me . . . will not be white./ But it will be / a part of you, instructor." The differences between white and black America cannot and should not be erased, for they represent distinct cultural and social experiences that are nevertheless comprehensible and even meaningful to outsiders.

BIBLIOGRAPHY

Hughes, Langston. "The Negro Artist and the Racial Mountain," 301–305. In *Amistad: Writings on Black History and Culture* 1 (1970).

Temple Cone

"THIRTEEN WAYS OF LOOKING AT A BLACKBIRD" WALLACE STEVENS (1923) One of the most widely anthologized MODERNIST poems, Wallace Stevens's "Thirteen Ways of Looking at a Blackbird" uses the short IMAGIST lyric characteristic of such poets as H. D. and WILLIAM CARLOS WILLIAMS as a vehicle for exploring the nature and limits of human perception and knowledge. Poised between "[t]he beauty of inflections" and "the beauty of innuendoes," each of the poem's 13 separately numbered stanzas demonstrates the epigrammatic beauty and philosophical depth of Stevens's best work. While scholars differ as to whether the stanzas reflect individual sense impressions or philosophical epigrams about the nature of knowledge, it is clear that each explores the interrelations of human consciousness and the external natural world through the sometimes literal, sometimes metaphorical figure of the blackbird.

Although none of the poem's 13 stanzas correspond to the traditional 5-7-5 syllable pattern of the haiku, several of them echo that structure. Indeed, as Nancy Bogen has observed, several of the stanzas feature the haiku's characteristic indication of the season in which it is set (218), and the poem's utterances correspond to the formalized question and/or answer of the Japanese *katauta* (Turco, 154). Such Oriental borrowings are not surprising for Stevens, though according to Robert Buttel, Stevens was more caught up in the early 1900's popular enthusiasm for oriental art (64–65). Yet, Buttel argues, "the objectivity, indirectness, and condensation of the haiku technique seem to have had a more beneficial and lasting effect on his style" (67). Moreover, Buttel suggests a more modern source for the title, which he claims "alludes humorously to the cubists' practice of incorporating into unity and stasis a number of possible views of the subject observed over a span of time" (165).

Technique and image aside, "Thirteen Ways of Looking at a Blackbird" has proven for some a masterwork on epistemology, or the theory of knowledge, and for others an evocative but untranslatable mystery. Each stanza seems possessed of rich, philosophical claims, whether about the power of metaphor (II), the unifying effects of perception (V), the limiting effects of religiosity (VII), change (XII), or many other themes. But out of these individual points, motion and stasis prove the crucial links between stanzas, suggesting how poetry can achieve the paradox of reflecting mutability, or change through time, by means of forms created by the imagination. James Baird writes that the poem "presents thirteen phases of the imagination at play upon a winter landscape. . . . It is a matter of seeing what is around one, and of projecting the imagination upon the immediate place where one lives" (158–159).

Whether contrasting the stillness of "twenty snowy mountains" with the blackbird's shifting eye, or the shadow of a moving blackbird with an icicled window, Stevens links motion and stillness to evoke the presence of death amid life, and life inspired by the inevitability of death, a theme central to his work and apparent in such poems as "SUNDAY MORNING" and "The EMPEROR OF ICE-CREAM." Writing about section VIII, "I know noble accents," Buttel argues that Stevens's stressed lines and repetitions of "I know" "produce the total effect of confidence in the power of language to create order that includes the knowledge of death—and without any concern for the old distinctions between prose and poetry" (206). "Thirteen Ways of Looking at a Blackbird" is a beautiful meditation on life, perception, motion, nature, and death, and by the conclusion it achieves a Zen-like calmness that belies the turbulent intellectual currents running beneath its still surface, for as Stevens writes, "The river is moving. / The blackbird must be flying."

BIBLIOGRAPHY

Baird, James. *The Dome and the Rock: Structure in the Poetry of Wallace Stevens.* Baltimore, Md.: The Johns Hopkins Press, 1968.

Bogen, Nancy. "Stevens's 'Thirteen Ways of Looking at a Blackbird.'" *The Explicator* 62, no. 4 (2004): 217–221.

Buttel, Robert. *Wallace Stevens: The Making of Harmonium.* Princeton, N.J.: Princeton University Press, 1967.

Turco, Lewis. *The New Book of Forms: A Handbook of Poetics.* 2d ed. Hanover, N.H.: University Press of New England, 1986.

Vendler, Helen. *Wallace Stevens: Words Chosen Out of Desire.* Knoxville: The University of Tennessee Press, 1984.

Temple Cone

THOMAS, LORENZO (1944–) Lorenzo Thomas's poetry and criticism have helped to show the relationship of poetry to music in the 20th century. His works are infused with jazz influences and are a testament to the exploration of social, political, and economic culture in American society. As Thomas has said, "Poetry is one of the forms of music and always has been" (121). Thomas has wanted to produce poems that sound like the jazz music he has enjoyed by such artists as Lightnin' Hopkins, Eric Dolphy, John Coltrane, and Charles Mingus. He has also been influenced by poets LANGSTON HUGHES, WILLIAM CARLOS WILLIAMS, and CARL SANDBURG.

Thomas was born in Panama. His family emigrated to New York when he was a child. In the 1960s and 1970s, he was active in what became known as the BLACK ARTS MOVEMENT that, as he said, brought "full maturity and strength and African song in American English, drawing upon the syntax of traditional proverbs and the tersely sentimental tone of Rhythm and Blues" (121). Thomas has taught at the University of Houston Downtown. He has twice won the Poets Foundation Award (1966 and 1974) and the Lucille Medwick Prize (1974).

Thomas's style is nonconformist insofar as it does not follow stylized patterns of rhyme and meter (see PROSODY AND FREE VERSE). Some of his stanzas have sentences with one word, while others have up to 10 words. In his shorter sentences, he carefully chooses words whose syllables make for a short and punchy effect. He has the ability to make his words dance as each line, staggered in verse, can be read rhythmically. Reading the poems aloud allows for hearing the poems' intense beat. All of his poems contain themes of social and cultural woes in society.

In "Liquid City," (1979), a slang term for Houston, ("liquid" is slang for petroleum) Thomas treats the city as a metaphor for American greed and materialism. A repeated stanza in the poem is "No Song," meaning that Houston makes money but fails to take care of its poor and to connect, like music, with the human spirit: "Glass is a shifting liquid stunned by flame and passersby; / a shame."

BIBLIOGRAPHY

Saylor, Rita, ed. *Liquid City: Houston Writers on Houston.* Houston: Corona Publishing, 1987.

Thomas. Lorenzo. "Neo-Griots." In *Extraordinary Measures: Afrocentric Modernism and Twentieth-Century American Poetry,* edited by Charles Bernstein and Hank Lazer, 104. Tuscaloosa: University of Alabama Press, 2000.

———. "Poets on Poetry: Interview with Lorenzo Thomas," by Daniel Kane Writenet.org. Available online. URL: www.writenet.org/poetschat/poetschat_l_thomas.html. Downloaded March 2007.

Yvette R. Blair

THOMAS AND BEULAH RITA DOVE (1987)

Only the second book of poems by an African American to win the Pulitzer Prize (1987), Rita Dove's *Thomas and Beulah* is an extended love poem about the lives of Dove's maternal grandparents. Reconstructing the past "through a series of discontinuous vignettes" (Harris, 270), Dove both honors and struggles with the inscrutability of their biographies, for as Dove claims, "no matter how close two people are, there are individual moments which are entirely intimate and individual" (Cavalieri, 12). As Dove attends to central images and motifs in her grandparents' lives, her reticence about explaining their significance indicates her faith that "we will have gumption enough to stare a hole in the page until our minds leap with hers across the gaps" (Harris, 270). Though Dove wants the reader to encounter the reality of these lives, she does fictionalize their lives to facilitate the leap of the imagination, and her most significant alteration was to change her maternal grandmother's name from Georgianna to Beulah. As Dove says in an interview, "That was a decision I made—an aesthetic decision, actually—because Georgianna, though it's a wonderful name, was first of all too male based for me, and second of all didn't have the Biblical connotations that I wanted for the book. Also, it's a long name, and a very difficult name to fit on a line. So once I broke through that, I didn't have to be absolutely faithful according to biographical truth. I could go after an inner truth. That freed me" (Cavalieri, 13). The poems of *Thomas and Beulah* constitute, in part, a series of leitmotifs, recurrent images woven through the lives of her characters. These images achieve their significance through repetition, carrying an associative weight between poems; such repetition is inherently musical (*leitmotif* deriving from Wagnerian opera) so it is appropriate that the book's two sections, "Mandolin" and "Canary in Bloom," which refer to important objects in Thomas's and Beulah's lives, both have musical connotations.

"Section I: Mandolin" opens with "The Event," which Dove claims was the first poem she composed in the series. Thomas and friend Lem form a musical duo on a Mississippi riverboat: "Lem plucked / to Thomas' silver falsetto." While riding a Mississippi riverboat, Thomas dares his friend Lem to swim out and pick chestnuts from an island, and Lem drowns in the river. Back onboard, Thomas is left with only "a stinking circle of rags, / the half-shell mandolin," an archetypal legacy uniting loss with art. Almost in an act of penance, Thomas the singer will take up Lem's mandolin, the music recalling and dispelling his pain. "The Event" is the cornerstone of "Mandolin," "a master myth," as Charles Berger puts it, "for the reading of her grandfather's life" (359). With the loss of male companionship and youth's invulnerability, Thomas's life begins. He leaves the riverboat life for a settled existence in Akron, Ohio, where he meets Beulah, his love and future wife who makes him feel his own physical weakness ("Why *frail*? / Why not simply / *family man*?" he asks in "Aircraft") and whom he blames for the inevitable loss of his family name (note the bitter tallying of children in "Compendium": "Girl girl/ girl girl"). But these future events are not yet visible in the restrained language of "The Event." The absence of foreshadowing makes the art less literary and more realistic, respecting the actual lives of Dove's grandparents by not assuming an omniscient perspective.

Among the poems of the first section, there are often associative connections based on particular words or images (music, for instance, connecting "The Event," "Variation on Pain," "Jiving," and "Straw Hat," or the banana in "Refrain," which hearkens back to the banana trees on the river, and forward to the yellow scarf Thomas will wrap around Beulah). Thus, at a purely structural level, Dove represents Thomas's grief without directly stating it. But this is not to say that Thomas's life is consumed with grief. Far from it—the memories of Lem appear as unexpectedly to the reader as to Thomas. Dove portrays her grandparents through defining, though not necessarily critical, moments in their lives; as she has said, "[W]e don't actually think of our lives in very cohesive strands but we remember as beads on a necklace, moments that matter to us, come to us in flashes, and connections are submerged" (Cavalieri, 12). In Thomas's story, the submerged connections appear in the different objects and gestures repeated through the poems—the mandolin, music, the yellow scarf, the river, and the canary they keep. There is something truly masculine about this portrayal of Thomas, with its focus on objects and rituals, the sense of an early loss never quite recovered from.

If "Mandolin" captures the essence of Thomas's life through recurrent, almost symbolic, objects and figures in his life, then the poems of "Canary in Bloom," which describe Beulah's life, are linked by longings—for a cultured life, for privacy, for material elegance, for a different husband—which she must suppress, being a married black woman in the 1920s. Early on, Beulah appears as a woman of distinct imaginative powers. As a girl, she watches a Ku Klux Klan cross set burning in her front yard and transforms the threat into a self-affirming sign from beyond: "It was a sign // she would make it to Paris one day." But more often than not, disappointment plagues Beulah during her life. Patricia Wallace writes that "Beulah's poems are characterized by her sense of the distance between the material conditions of her life and the beauty of art (often represented as Paris, Versailles, or the Orient)" (13). The canary identified in the section title, which hearkens to the songbird used in coal mines to detect poison gas, small doses of which would kill the bird before the miners, is an important figure for Beulah because of its vulnerability in the world and because of its beautiful song. Many of the poems in "Canary in Bloom" feature Beulah's imagination at work, from the anxious dream that she must kill a wolf to protect her baby in "Motherhood" to the "palace" she builds during a private moment in "Daystar." This imaginative capacity is like the coal mine canary's song—absurd and beautiful, because the canary is utterly vulnerable, its song useless in its protection, and therefore, somehow priceless.

Through the submerged connections between poems, Dove lends a sense of continuity between the disparate events of the poems themselves. As the poems resist immediate narrative connections, they also resist the transcendent closure characteristic of many contemporary lyric poems. Instead of radiating outward in an epiphany that illuminates generally, Dove's endings reflect inward, shedding new light on the characters themselves. Helen Vendler writes that "Dove's discovery (as she puts it in a poem called 'Particulars') [is] that life exhibits a 'lack of conclusion,' and presents an 'eternal *denouement*'" (83). Consider, for instance, Beulah's efforts to remember a former suitor's name in "Dusting." As a young housewife, Beulah seems at best to endure her responsibilities—"Every day a wilderness—no / shade in sight. Beulah / patient among knickknacks." Left to a world, not of courts, but knicknacks, she begins thinking about her life before marriage, of a boy at a fair. The reminiscence is tinged with the disappointment she feels, in part, for her life, and when she finally hits upon his name, "Maurice," a sense of thwarted ambition and regret accrues to the name, which, spoken or thought, becomes a talismanic release for Beulah.

The submerged connections between the poems are themselves connected through the structure of the book. As Dove portrays her grandparents through scattered, oblique moments, their stories hinging on a chronology she includes at the book's end, beneath it all lies their marriage. Certainly the two are occupied with individual, intimate concerns, and the poems portraying their interaction are often tinged with ambiguities of feeling for the other ("Nothing Down" and "Daystar" in particular). But the marriage maintains continuity in spite of these differences, and what Dove has carefully withheld is the mutual devotion of two individuals. If Beulah fades from immediate attention toward the close of "Mandolin," this is because she is the anchor of Thomas's days, and is almost taken for granted. But his final thoughts in "Thomas at the Wheel" are about Beulah, and demonstrate his depth of feeling for her—"Thomas imagined / his wife as she awoke missing him, cracking a window." Likewise, Beulah, in the penultimate poem "Company," a sonnet, addresses the ghost of her husband haunting her—"*If this is code, /* she tells him, *listen: we were good, / though we never believed it.*" By means of this reticence, this withholding of the private moments of clear feeling, Dove invites the reader to return to each story and re-envision it, as she must have, with the awareness of their shared devotion.

BIBLIOGRAPHY

Berger, Charles. "The Granddaughter's Archive: Rita Dove's *Thomas and Beulah.*" *Western Humanities Review* 50–51, no. 4–1 (1997): 359–363.

Cavalieri, Grace. "Rita Dove: An Interview." *The American Poetry Review* 24, no. 2 (1995): 11–15.

Dove, Rita. "Who's Afraid of Poetry?" *Writer's Digest* (February 1995): 40–44.

Harris, Peter. "Four Salvers Salvaging: New Work by Voigt, Olds, Dove, and McHugh." *Virginia Quarterly Review* 64, no. 2 (1988): 262–276.

Vendler, Helen. *The Given and the Made: Strategies of Poetic Redefinition.* Cambridge, Mass.: Harvard University Press, 1995.

Wallace, Patricia. "Divided Loyalties: Literal and Literary in the Poetry of Lorna Dee Cervantes, Cathy Song, and Rita Dove." *MELUS* 18, no. 3 (1993): 3–20.

Temple Cone

"THOSE WINTER SUNDAYS" ROBERT HAYDEN (1962) ROBERT HAYDEN composed this 14-line elegy at a time when leading African-American artists promoted the notion that African-American poets must portray exclusively their own culture to support the struggle for freedom and equality (see the BLACK ARTS MOVEMENT). Rejecting such strictures from colleagues of any color or persuasion, Hayden created poems on various people and topics, despite sharp criticism from those who claimed that he betrayed his race.

"Those Winter Sundays" has been read autobiographically as expressing Hayden's conflicting feelings toward his foster father. It ranks high among poems on a child's emotional response to a parent (and can be profitably compared to THEODORE ROETHKE'S "MY PAPA'S WALTZ" and SYLVIA PLATH'S "DADDY"). Similar to a double exposure on film, the persona's boyhood routine merges with his perspective as an adult reevaluating his memories.

The speaker describes physical and emotional experience along with temperature changes and concomitant sounds. On Sundays his father makes a fire, cleans his son's Sunday shoes, and only wakes up his family once the rooms have warmed up. But the child gets up reluctantly for fear of "the chronic angers of that house," which represents both the creaky building and the disharmonious family. When the grown-up son remembers his father's work-worn hands, he understands that the Sunday family duties prevented them from healing. In contrast to soft-sounding alliterations on "bl" ("blueblack") and "w" ("weekday weather"), harsher sounds illustrate "the cold *s*pl*int*e*r*ing, *b*re*ak*ing" (emphasis added). The crackling of burning, disintegrating wood in an otherwise quiet home announces warmth, but, to the son, it prefigures the family's "chronic angers," which repeat the percussive *k/kr*-sounds of previous lines ("clothes," "bluebla*ck* cold," "*crack*ed," "a*ch*ed").

The adult persona illustrates his insights not only through sound patterns, but also by zeroing in on his responsibility. While the ending of the first stanza acknowledges that the family showed no appreciation for the father, the clearly personal narrative of the second stanza, in which the child awakes and rises, prepares for the third stanza, in which the speaker rebukes himself. As in the final line of the previous stanza, the speaker now uses the present continuous to stress the process, continuity, and current awareness of his ungratefulness for his father's kind deeds. The closing lines express despair at this insensitivity. Regretting his immature behavior, the grown son poetically defines his father's Sunday sacrifices as "love's austere and lonely offices." While "austere" recalls the child's impression of a seemingly stern and cold father, "lonely" conveys the man's painful understanding of his father's suffering at his son's indifference. The religious connotations of the final word, *offices,* elevate the father's devoted service to his family—as depicted throughout the poem—to the level of worship.

BIBLIOGRAPHY
Fetrow, Fred M. *Robert Hayden.* Boston: Twayne, 1984.
Hatcher, John. *From the Auroral Darkness: The Life and Poetry of Robert Hayden.* Oxon, England: George Ronald, 1984.

Nassim Winnie Balestrini

TILLINGHAST, RICHARD (1940–) Richard Tillinghast's poetry is infused with a strong regard for history and autobiography. In many of his poems, Tillinghast discovers personal history through his extensive travels. And a major theme found in his poetry is the pervasive awareness of life's impermanence: "He writes out of a sense of loss in part, but reclamation also," Wyatt Prunty has commented (968). Primarily using free verse (see PROSODY AND FREE VERSE), Tillinghast explores his personal history—childhood, relationships, and influences—but also more universally historical themes, such as the impact of the Civil War and World War II, through which he ultimately questions society's advances during postwar reconstruction. His teacher and mentor at Harvard, ROBERT LOWELL, was a major influence on his work. Lowell's CONFESSIONAL poetics and free verse poems are especially prevalent in Tillinghast's early work.

Tillinghast was born and raised in Memphis, Tennessee. *Sleep Watch,* his first book of poetry, was published in 1969. He was the recipient of an AMY LOWELL Traveling Fellowship in 1990–91. Tillinghast has been the director of the Poets' House in Ireland.

The Knife and Other Poems (1980) contains works reflecting a yearning for the past with a rather cynical view of the future. "The Knife," the title poem of this collection, is significant, because Tillinghast demonstrates a strong and positive connection with past, present, and future: His newborn son's "look" is "like the river old like rain / older than anything that dies can be." The knife, a gift from a grandfather, symbolizes a cyclical relationship between Tillinghast, his brother, and his son. With the symbol of the knife, Tillinghast embraces the past while noting the positive effect it holds for the future. Other poems in this collection express less-than-optimistic ideas about the future.

In *Our Flag Was Still There* (1984), Tillinghast continues his quest for the past through introspection. In his long poem "Sewanee in Ruins," he establishes the history of Sewanee (the University of the South) to a group of students through historical journals, letters, and local history accounts of life following the Civil War: "But why do I let these ghosts talk / and tire you with their names and histories." The purpose in this poem is to connect students with their geographical roots. "Sewanee in Ruins" displays Tillinghast's keen ability to reconstruct the past with acute detail, hoping it will remain a fixture in the present for his students. Tillinghast contrasts past and present in his poetry, often with reference to geographic location. His keen, detailed use of language and free verse convey a sense of longing for a past that can never be revisited.

BIBLIOGRAPHY
Prunty, Wyatt. "Myth, History, and Myth Again." *Southern Review* 20, no. 4 (October 1984): 958–968.
Shoaf, Diann. "Review of Stonecutter's Hand," by Richard Tillinghast. *Ploughshares* 21, no. 1 (spring 1995): 200–202.

Christopher Bloss

"THE TIRE HANGS IN THE YARD" DAVE SMITH (1981) As powerful a study of memory and place as William Wordsworth's "Tintern Abbey," Dave Smith's "The Tire Hangs in the Yard" takes as its setting not the temperate beauty of Wales but the "blackberry / thickets of darkness" of eastern Virginia, where Smith grew up. Evoking the work of JAMES DICKEY and ROBERT PENN WARREN, to whom the poem is dedicated, Smith's humid South is permeated with memories of sex, violence, and death, and the poem charts Smith's struggle to reconcile the almost mythic beauty and danger of his remembered past with the impoverished realities of the present day. This tension between past and present, between Smith's youth and what he has become as an adult, is both haunted by and becomes a figure for his inevitable confrontation with mortality itself.

The central setting and image of the poem is an old tire-swing hung from the trees in a vacant yard, a place where the young Smith "went to dream," "stared, with willing girls, into the sky," "came to fistfight," and tried to learn "what being dead was like. / Like swinging at night, they said, in the trees." As the poem's title indicates, this place continues to exist in both the physical world and in Smith's memory, though it is only over the course of the poem that Smith comes to realize the rootedness of the place in his life. When he rediscovers the tire-swing, Smith exclaims, "wouldn't you know it that the tire still hangs," but given his repeated description of the tire's black O and the rope's ticking sound throughout the poem's five FREE VERSE sections, one must question what Smith seeks to hide behind this surprise.

For Smith, the tire-swing endures because it is an important site of childhood trauma and pleasure, offering him a standard by which to judge the present state of his life and the world at large. While Smith once brought girls to this place for dreamy, romantic flings, young men and women now visit the yard for cruder purposes: "Jesus Christ," writes Smith, "look at the beer cans, the traffic, even / hung on a berry vine somebody's rubber." Once, in a fight with Jim Jenrett, Smith was "beer-brave, nearly wild . . . / pissing, taunting," but now as an older man he feels the reality of death, "his great feet jammed / halfway in the hole of your heart, / gone halfway." For better or worse, the traumas and pleasures Smith experienced in the presence of this totemic tire-swing have preserved it in his thoughts: "I imagined this place left forever behind / but it's with me as I try to see the road begin."

At the heart of the poem and of Smith's anxious memories is Jim Jenrett, whom Smith fought in jealousy over a girl. Backed by a dozen friends, Smith spat "final threats" at Jenrett, who hanged himself from the tire-swing tree the next morning. For Smith, Jenrett's suicide is a source of anxiety about his own mortality, for having loved the same girl, the two men become doubles for each other; of shame about the betrayal of love, which Smith compares to a scene of domestic abuse; and finally about the mystery of death itself, which brings Smith to ask "Where do they go who were with us on this dream road." Unconsoled by the explanations of religion or even by the authority of his elders, Smith climbs the real and the remembered tire-swing once again to experience that darkness firsthand, and finally, he has found the courage not to flinch when he learns "The whine of the rope is like a distant scream. / I think, so this is it. Really it."

BIBLIOGRAPHY

Johnson, Mark. "The Dangerous Poems of Dave Smith." *Southern Literary Journal* 38, no. 1 (2005): 91–114.

Vendler, Helen. "Southern Weather: Dave Smith." In *Soul Says: On Recent Poetry*, 43–51. Cambridge, Mass.: The Belknap Press of Harvard University Press, 1995.

Temple Cone

TOLSON, MELVIN (1898–1966) Though Melvin Tolson only published three volumes of poetry during his lifetime, he was internationally recognized as a major contributor to modernist poetics (see MODERNISM) generally and to African diasporic modernity in particular. Such recognition led to Tolson's being selected to serve as poet laureate for the Republic of Liberia (1947); he is the only American poet to have been selected as laureate of another nation. More of Tolson's works have been published posthumously, and he is increasingly seen by critics and general readers alike as among the most significant of black American poets.

Tolson was born in Moberly, Missouri. His family moved to Iowa when he was 14, and it was there that he published his first poem. He attended high school in Kansas City, then enrolled at Fisk University in 1918. The following year, he transferred to Lincoln University, which was to figure prominently in his later poetry. After graduation, Tolson assumed a teaching post at Wiley College, beginning a long and illustrious career as an educator at historically black colleges that was to take him to Langston College and back to Fisk. Later graduate work at Columbia University in New York led to his thesis, which was among the first critical examinations of the HARLEM RENAISSANCE. Though the thesis was accepted, Tolson neglected the formality of applying for his degree for some years. It was officially awarded in 1940. The thesis, *The Harlem Group of Negro Writers*, was published in book form in 2001. Nearly as much time passed between the composition of the poems for Tolson's first book and their eventual publication. In his earliest years as a poet, Tolson wrote a massive series of dramatic monologues, resembling EDGAR LEE MASTERS's *Spoon River Anthology* in conception, centered on the lives of characters in Harlem. That book, *A Gallery of Harlem Portraits* (see *HARLEM GALLERY*), appeared posthumously in 1979. The first collection of poems published in his lifetime was *Rendezvous with America* in 1944. This was followed by *Libretto for the Republic of Liberia* (1953) and *Harlem Gallery: Book I, The Curator* (1965). By the time of his last book, Tolson's poetry was beginning to achieve the sort of recognition his modern contemporaries had long enjoyed. Tolson was invited to visit the White House in the last year of his life, where he inscribed a copy of *Harlem Gallery* for President Lyndon Johnson, and he gave a reading from that book at the Library of Congress, which was recorded for the library's collection. Tolson was also awarded the American Academy of Arts and Letters Award for poetry (1966), *Poetry* magazine's Bess Hokin Award (1952), and first prize at the American Negro Exposition (1939) for his long poem "Dark Symphony" (see LONG AND SERIAL POETRY). Tolson was also a renowned drama and debate teacher, mayor of the town of Langston, Oklahoma, a frequent public speaker and a regular columnist for the *Washington Tribune* newspaper. A selection from his editorials was published in 1982 under the title *Caviar and Cabbage*, which had been the title of Tolson's column.

There has been much misunderstanding regarding the evolution of Tolson's style and aesthetics, largely because so much of his work was unavailable to most readers for so many years. With the appearance of a selected edition, it is now possible to see his movement from early free verse NARRATIVE POETRY to the highly allusive style of his later poems. What has remained constant has been his dedication to modernist experiment, his development of memorable characters, his gift for a highly lyrical narrative verse, and his ironic understanding of the racial politics of America. In *Harlem Gallery*, Tolson writes, "Black Boy often adds / the dimension of ethnic irony / to Empson's classic seven" (a reference to William Empson's widely read critical study *Seven Types of Ambiguity* [1930]). These lines typify Tolson's stance with regard to modernist poetics. He takes up a skeptical, adaptive position within a modernism that he redefines as African-derived. Throughout his career, Tolson insisted that black poets must participate in the artistic movements of their time, but he was equally insistent that their participation must be critical. The characters of his first free verse portraits, like the characters of his *Harlem Gallery*, are essentially modern people carrying with them traditions whose value is denigrated by white society, even as that society borrows heavily from them.

Like W. E. B. DUBOIS and Alain Locke, Tolson pointed often to the African and African-American roots of modern Western aesthetics. In "The Negro Scholar" (1948), Tolson observes: "The ground the Negro Scholar stands upon / Is fecund with . . . challenge and tradition." Having learned from T. S. ELIOT's *The WASTE LAND*, Tolson distances himself irreconcilably from the cultural politics that poet embodied. In contrast to Eliot's vision of Africa in his verse plays, Tolson presents Africa in *Libretto for the Republic of Liberia* as "The ladder of survival dawn men saw," and his poem, which pays tribute to more than a century of cultural contacts between Africa and America, proposes a new Africa as "A moment of the conscience of mankind!"

Throughout his career Tolson argued that African-American poets must be part of contemporary movements in poetry, such as modernism, but he was adamant that black poets could never simply be, as his colleague ROBERT HAYDEN put it, poets first who just happened to be Negro. In the end Tolson's own poems demonstrated the reliance of modernism upon black culture, even as he charted new paths for the movement.

BIBLIOGRAPHY

Bérubé, Michael. *Marginal Forces/Cultural Centers: Tolson, Pynchon, and the Politics of the Canon*. Ithaca, N.Y.: Cornell University Press, 1992.

Farnsworth, Robert M. *Melvin B. Tolson 1898–1966: Plain Talk and Prophetic Prophecy*. Columbia: University of Missouri Press, 1984.

Nielsen, Aldon Lynn. "Melvin B. Tolson and the Deterritorialization of Modernism." In *Writing between the Lines: Race and Intertextuality*. Athens: University of Georgia Press, 1994, pp. 48–70.

Aldon L. Nielsen

"TO MY TWENTIES" KENNETH KOCH (2000)

Kenneth Koch's "To My Twenties" is a characteristically humorous and exuberant paean to a period in the author's life "When everything was possible / For my legs and arms, and with hope in my heart / And so happy to see any woman." The poem comes from a collection of apostrophes, or addresses to nonpresent entities, called *New Addresses* (2000). Although many of the poems reflect on events and topics from Koch's past—as evidenced by titles such as "To My Father's Business," "To Piano Lessons," "To World War Two," "To My Old Addresses," and "To Old Age"—the book is not valetudinarian in nature (though Koch died two years after its publication). Rather, the poems manifest Koch's energetic, unpretentious, witty embrace of life's oddities and joys, and if they ever show sadness or nostalgia for the inevitable passage of life, as "To My Twenties" does at its close, they alleviate such solemnity with the intellectual slapstick and good-natured irony that characterized the mercurial Koch as a person and that makes his poems feel so delightfully alive.

Koch characterizes this decade of his life as one of companionship and garrulousness, optimism, living on the cheap, enthusiasm, lust, and hope for future accomplishments. "How lucky that I ran into you," he writes, a logically absurd observation that nevertheless rings true. The familiar tone of the opening line disarms the artifice and archaism associated with apostrophe, a device distrusted by many postmodern writers for its overtly literary quality (though Helen Vendler argues that it is the original device of lyric poetry, and thus offers a way for the lyric to return to its fundamental concerns—love and mortality). Koch's twenties are as alive and present to him as a person on the street, and he speaks to them and of them with the jocularity one reserves for a close friend. "I loved to frequent you / After my teens and before my thirties," he writes, claiming that "I always preferred you because you were midmost / Most lustrous apparently strongest."

Yet Koch resists the impulse to revise his past in retrospect. Although he can say of his twenties that "What you gave me you gave whole," he must admit that "as for telling / Me how best to use it / You weren't a genius at that." The self-mocking tone here affronts the conventional bittersweet tone of nostalgia, so that while Koch participates in the human act of remembering one's past, he resists the literary impulse to aesthetically formalize and thereby sentimentalize memory. Such an affront, managed with Koch's usual zest and wit, is one of the keystones of Koch's poetic oeuvre, so that no matter what topic Koch is addressing, he is also always addressing the art of writing poetry. Examining Koch's zany ARS POETICA "Fresh Air," David Chinitz describes the primary object of Koch's poetic criticism as "the dominant conception of poetry as a rarefied, high-aesthetic form to be valued for its artifice" (311), and he notes that Koch challenges such mainstream conceptions of poetry by means of "a barrage of comedy designed to establish how much life poetry can have if one accepts it on Koch's terms" (312). In his wise-cracking treatment of both his own past and the way that people tend to objectify their personal histories, Koch provides a delightful attack on the solemnity of modernist, image-based lyrics, while also voicing, in authentically bittersweet tones, regret for the mutability of human life: "Twenties, my soul / Is yours for the asking / You know that, if you ever come back."

BIBLIOGRAPHY

Chinitz, David. "'Arm the Paper Arm': Kenneth Koch's Postmodern Comedy." *The Scene of Myselves: New Work on New York School Poets.* Edited by Terence Diggory and Stephen Paul Miller. Orono, Maine: The National Poetry Foundation, 2001.

Vendler, Helen. *Invisible Listeners: Lyric Intimacy in Herbert, Whitman, and Ashbery.* Princeton, N.J.: Princeton University Press, 2005.

Temple Cone

TOOMER, JEAN (1894–1967) Jean Toomer is regarded as an influence on the writers of the HARLEM RENAISSANCE, yet he did not identify himself as one of them. While those writers tried to establish a new voice to communicate the black experience in America, Toomer attempted to write the literature of an American melting pot, for a new American individual representing racial unity, not a collection of component races. Though he repudiated, for the most part, the writing of explicitly African-American works, Toomer did, according to Jon Woodson, bring "the techniques of literary MODERNISM to some of the most accomplished of the young writers who gathered in Harlem in the 1920s" (30).

Toomer was born and was raised in the Washington, D.C., home of his grandfather, who had been an important Reconstruction-era politician in Louisiana.

Living in a white neighborhood and recalling no racial prejudice among his white friends, Toomer developed a sensibility different from many writers of the Harlem Renaissance. After stints at several colleges, he began to write, influenced in part by the IMAGIST poets, as well as by futurism, symbolism, and impressionism. He also met various authors, such as HART CRANE.

Toomer's reputation rests mostly upon *Cane* (1923). A vision of the rural, black South, *Cane* is a collection of poems, character sketches, and a play set in rural Georgia, Chicago, and Washington, D.C., evoking a vanishing culture. The dominant persona is a man searching for his self-identity through a connection with black heritage, though that search is unsuccessful.

A poetry selection from *Cane,* "A Portrait in Georgia," exemplifies Toomer's vision of the black experience as part of an American melting pot. An African-American woman is described as having "chestnut" hair "coiled like a lyncher's rope"—an acknowledgment of the slave past but also a representation, through her hair color, of the blending of the races into a new American one. The final lines, "her slim body, white as the ash / of black flesh after flame," reinforce Toomer's illustration of a violent slave past in America but also a new America rising out of the ashes of the past.

After *Cane* Toomer wrote short stories, articles, reviews, poetry, plays, four novels, and several works of autobiography; most were never published. Much of this work is driven by Toomer's vision of the American race, most vividly portrayed in his long poem "The Blue Meridian" (1936), a Whitmanesque discourse on this new American figure (see LONG AND SERIAL POETRY). Toomer died in 1967, feeling he had never realized his literary aims, but, ironically, he is now regarded as one of the greatest artists in the canon of African-American literature in which he did not seek inclusion.

BIBLIOGRAPHY

Fabre, Genevieve, and Michel Feith, eds. *Jean Toomer and the Harlem Renaissance.* New Brunswick, N.J.: Rutgers University Press, 2000.

Woodson, Jon. *To Make a New Race: Gurdjieff, Toomer, and the Harlem Renaissance.* Jackson: University Press of Mississippi, 1999.

Joseph Schaub

"TRAVELING THROUGH THE DARK"

WILLIAM STAFFORD (1962) In the plainspoken voice and precise imagery for which he was praised, WILLIAM STAFFORD narrates a powerful moment of moral crisis in "Traveling through the Dark," his best-known poem. A first-person LYRIC written in metrically loose ballad stanzas, the poem is spoken by a man who finds the body of a recently road-killed deer, only to discover the unborn fawn it is carrying is still alive. Confronted with the terrible choice of whether to leave the deer in the road, and risk causing an accident for some future traveler, or to push the body off a nearby cliff edge and so kill the unborn fawn, the speaker reluctantly chooses the greater good, but is saddened by the loss his choice inevitably entails: "I thought hard for us all—my only swerving." Troubled by his decision, but ultimately resolute in his commitment to doing good, Stafford offers a moving portrait of the challenge of acting morally in a relativistic world.

The dark through which the speaker is traveling at the start of the poem is more than the dark of night—it is the darkness of a morally ambiguous world, where the rules and principles that structure existence no longer seem to hold. The deer he finds has just been struck, "a recent killing," and the person who hit it has chosen, unlike Stafford, to let the body remain in the road, perhaps to cause another accident. Thus, Stafford's speaker is traveling through the moral darkness of a world where citizens fail to look after each other. Moreover, upon finding the deer, the speaker acknowledges that "It is usually best to roll them into the canyon," but in this instance, conventional behavior will not free the speaker from his moral quandary. In a world where one can no longer rely on the goodwill of others or upon ethical conventions, one is left to follow one's own path through the dark, alone. William Young notes that the poem's tone alters subtly from stanza to stanza, moving toward a point of significant moral crisis (197). George S. Lensing and Ronald Moran praise Stafford's refusal to shy away from morally troublesome issues and his resistance to cynicism or pessimism. They note that "[F]or all its romanticism, [Stafford's] poetry will not take refuge in illusions or pretensions about the state of modern society. Part of his confidence in the future is founded upon the miraculous ability of the wilderness, independent of any human agency, to renew itself" (215).

Indeed, as Young notes, the wilderness is an important presence in the poem, bearing witness to the speaker's act, and Young claims that the pulse of nature can almost be heard in the loose, five-beat lines (197). With nature bearing witness, Stafford conveys the speaker's struggle to make a difficult decision through a careful manipulation of verbal connotation and through the subtle repetition of the word *swerve* in the opening and concluding stanzas. One of the few colors that stand out in the darkness is the redness of the car's taillights, and as the speaker stands "in the glare of the warm exhaust turning red," one sees that he is himself implicated in the bloody act that is about to follow. The speaker's sense of responsibility derives in large part from Stafford's early use of the word *swerve:* the deer was struck by a driver who failed to swerve, but his failure to remove the carcass was a form of moral swerving. Now, having felt the unborn fawn, "waiting, / alive, still, never to be born," Stafford finds the poles of responsibility reversed. He cannot make the choice of disposing of the body or leaving it for someone else to hit or remove, because he now knows the fawn as an individual life.

Ultimately, however, a decision is reached, but the power of the poem is in the speaker's struggle to justify his action. Even though the speaker says he "thought hard for us all" before he "pushed her over the edge into the river," he calls his appeal to the greater good "my only swerving," because even in the midst of the general welfare, individuals suffer, and Stafford cannot reconcile himself easily with such necessity. This internal conflict is of a piece with Stafford's pacifist beliefs and his rejection of violence as a satisfactory means to political ends, but because the speaker's act is clearly for the greater good, the poem refuses any easy thematic closure. In the end, the poem reveals Stafford's fundamental belief that moral choices cannot be made by appeal to the greater collective, but only by the sanctioning force of individual conscience.

BIBLIOGRAPHY

Lensing, George S., and Ronald Moran. *Four Poets and the Emotive Imagination: Robert Bly, James Wright, Louis Simpson, and William Stafford.* Baton Rouge: Louisiana State University Press, 1976.

Young, William. "Traveling through the Dark: The Wilderness Surrealism of the Far West." *Midwest Quarterly: A Journal of Contemporary Thought* 39, no. 2 (1998): 187–201.

Temple Cone

U

UPDIKE, JOHN (1932–) John Updike has been the quintessential man of letters. In close to 50 years, he has published more than 60 books, including novels, short stories, poems, and criticism. He is most famous for his novels, which often involve American middle-class values and characters. Updike's poetry is typically metered and often rhymed (see PROSODY AND FREE VERSE); much of his early work is light verse. His poetry is related to that of RICHARD WILBUR and ANTHONY HECHT, especially in its formal elements, use of light verse, and subject matter.

Updike grew up in Shillington, Pennsylvania, in a middle-class home. He studied at Harvard and spent 1954 to 1955 at Oxford University's Ruskin School of Drawing and Fine Arts. He worked for the *New Yorker* for two years, leaving to pursue his writing career full-time. His first book was a collection of poems, *The Carpentered Hen and Other Tame Creatures* (1958). Updike has received just about every literary award that America has to offer. He has twice won the Pulitzer Prize (1982 and 1990) and has received a National Book Award (1964), American Book Award (1982), and National Book Critics Circle Award (1982 and 1990). At 32 he was the youngest invitee in the history of the American Academy of Arts and Letters.

Updike's *Collected Poems 1953–1993* (1993) has more than 400 poems, which he calls his "oeuvre's beloved waifs" (xxiv). They exhibit both a remarkable restraint and abandon. They are often carefully crafted and structured, yet their subject matter is gleaned from mundane (sometimes scandalous) sources: a newspaper article, a naked female statue, a placard on a city bus. "On the Inclusion of Miniature Dinosaurs in Breakfast Cereal Boxes" (1993), a short poem of three quatrains, concludes: "I hide within the Raisin Bran; / And thus begins the dawn of *Man*." Updike seemingly has the ability to take almost any facet of everyday American life, its blessings and burdens, and fashion it into a poem.

Updike's book of verse *Americana and Other Poems* (2002) is a continuation of familiar themes and stylistic choices. It is also, however, a slightly changed voice, showing a nostalgic appreciation for a life now in its decline: "The competition thins; so does my blood" ("On the Nearly Simultaneous Deaths of Harold Brodkey and Joseph Brodsky"). Gone is the light verse and rhyming tactics of his earlier works, although the poems remain fluent and lucid; they are what the reviewer John Taylor calls "eminently readable" (294). This collection, perhaps his last, has a preponderance of iambic pentameter and somber themes. The poem "New York," for example, shows the lyrical intensity of Updike's verse at its best: "this hell holds sacred crevices where lone / lost spirits preen and call their pit a throne."

Many of Updike's poems portray contemporary America as being gloriously flawed. A poignant fondness for and honest perception of America might very well be his most enduring legacy.

BIBLIOGRAPHY

De Bellis, Jack. *The John Updike Encyclopaedia.* Westport, Conn.: Greenwood Press, 2000.

Schiff, James A. *John Updike Revisited.* New York: Twayne, 1998.

Taylor, John. "Short Reviews." *Poetry* 179, no. 5 (February 2002): 294–302.

Updike, John. Preface to *Selected Poems 1953–1993.* London: Penguin Books, 1993, pp. xxiii–xxiv.

Michael Kuperman

V

VALENTINE, JEAN (1934–) Jean Valentine's poems do not easily yield meaning, engaging the reader in an unsettling dreamlike reality. Whether written in the first person or as a third-person close observer of others, Valentine's poems are a quiet study of the human condition. Her poems are marked by their brevity, in terms of both diction and the length of the poems themselves. "Valentine seeks refuge in a language of silence, or extreme privacy," notes Stuart Friebert (479). These deeply personal poems, offering "little exposition or context" (479), render them difficult to comprehend, but they never lack in specificity. Writing after the CONFESSIONAL poets, Valentine has the freedom to be deeply introspective without overt, blatant self-disclosure. Her poems explore the issues of womanhood and roles of lover, mother, wife, and daughter (see FEMALE VOICE, FEMALE LANGUAGE), but Valentine's poems would not properly be considered feminist. Gender issues inform her work, but the human condition guides her inquiry.

Valentine was born in Chicago and has lived most of her adult life in New York City. She won the Yale Series of Younger Poets Award for her first book, *Dream Barker and Other Poems,* in 1963. She was awarded a Guggenheim Fellowship in 1976 and won the Maurice English Prize in 1991 and the SARA TEASDALE Poetry Prize in 1992. In 2000 Valentine received the Shelley Memorial Award from the Poetry Society of America, and in 2004 she received the National Book Award for *Door in the Mountain: New and Collected Poems 1965–2003.*

Breaking from family or a beloved, whether by choice or by death, is a recurrent theme in Valentine's work. At times separation is drawn in plain language, and the emotional impact is unspoken. In "The Drinker" (2000), the speaker addresses one who is perpetually "making for the door" and trying to step out of his or her own life. The monosyllabic, flat language underscores the speaker's concession to the impossibility of being anyone but herself. The self remains, Valentine asserts: Even "death / won't take you out." Valentine also depicts separation in surrealistic terms (see SURREALISM). In "He leaves them" (2000), the effect of the schism is so extreme as to be metaphorically transformative: "He turns into a moon . . . / He turns into strips of film." For the speaker what remains of the man who leaves is ephemeral. He is transformed into the Moon, which is constant in the sky, yet ever in flux. He becomes not a fixed, photographic image of the self but "strips of film," evoking a strip of negatives or something that is torn into strips. No wholeness remains. Valentine's poems often explore a fractured world or a fractured self in the world. Silence, therefore, becomes a crucial element in her poems. That silence, which is also portrayed in the white space Valentine employs on the page, stands along with language, not in opposition to it. There is as much meaning vested in Valentine's silences as there is in her words.

BIBLIOGRAPHY

Friebert, Stuart. "Introduction to Jean Valentine." In *The Longman Anthology of Contemporary Poetry 1950–1980,*

edited by Stuart Friebert and David Young, eds. New York: Longman, 1983, pp. 478–481.
Muske, Carol. "Time into Language." *Nation* (July 21, 1987): 36–40.

Linda Levitt

VAN DUYN, MONA (1921–2004) Mona Van Duyn is an important postwar poet who, though exposed to such poetic movements as BEAT, CONFESSIONAL, feminist, and NEW FORMALISM, never sacrificed her own unique, engaging style and perspective and never succumbed to the leveling influences of various poetic schools. Van Duyn addressed a broader range of subjects than most other contemporary poets—"She is not a confessional poet fingering her emotional sores," writes Herbert Leibowitz in the *New York Times Book Review* (4)—and she experimented with a broad range of forms, both conventional and free verse (see PROSODY AND FREE VERSE), even inventing her own poetic form, the minimalist sonnet, an abbreviated version of Gerard Manley Hopkins's 19th-century curtal sonnet (Hopkins had written "sonnets" of 10 and a half lines instead of the traditional 14).

Van Duyn was raised and educated in Iowa. She moved to St. Louis in 1950, where she taught night classes for Washington University's adult education program until 1967. Her writing career began when she was 38 years old, and she eventually became one of the most highly regarded poets in the United States and received many prizes and fellowships. At age 70 she won a Pulitzer Prize (1991) for *Near Changes* (1990), and in 1992 she was named the U.S. poet laureate.

Van Duyn's first book, *Valentines to the Wide World* (1959), introduces many themes that would remain central to her poetry: the romantic concept of the child as "father to the man," the child's inevitable loss of innocence, the possibility of restoring innocence through art, the intimate relation between nature and human nature, and the stages of love. In "Falls," a longer poem from which the title of her most recent book, *Firefall,* (1994), is taken, the choice that the speaker makes as a teenager during her family's visit to Niagara Falls is emblematic of the choices she later makes as a poet. She describes driving to see the American lip from Canada's side, only to find that the whole "was beyond the grasp of [her] lens and [she] snapped instead / a family of swans, a simpler sight" (77). Never comfortable with making lofty generalizations about nature, Van Duyn carefully observed and rendered its particulars—on terms entirely her own.

BIBLIOGRAPHY

Burns, Michael, ed. *Discovery and Reminiscence: Essays on the Poetry of Mona Van Duyn.* Fayetteville: University of Arkansas Press, 1998.
Goldensohn, Lorrie. "Mona Van Duyn and the Politics of Love." *Ploughshares* 4, no. 3 (March 1978): 31–44.
Leibowitz, Herbert. Review of *Merciful Disguises* by Mona Van Duyn, *New York Times Book Review,* December 9, 1973, p. 4.
Prunty, Wyatt. *Fallen from the Symboled World: Precedents for the New Formalism.* New York: Oxford University Press, 1990.

Donna Potts

VISUAL POETRY Visual poetry has long been the poor cousin of the American poetry family, barely acknowledged by academia, but not altogether absent from the work of well-known poets, including ROBERT CREELEY, EZRA POUND, JOHN HOLLANDER, and CHARLES OLSON. Greatly overshadowed by LANGUAGE poetry as an experimental genre in the final decades of the 20th century, it has nevertheless persisted and seems likely to remain a potent alternative to conventional poetry indefinitely. There are probably nearly as many definitions of it as there are people making poems that include graphics; for simplicity's sake, however, the term will here mean simply poetry that includes visual elements that seem (to a consensus of informed judges) aesthetically necessary to the final meaning of its words.

A good example is E. E. CUMMINGS's famous poem "r-p-o-p-h-e-s-s-a-g-r" (1935). Among its many small but charming typographical tricks, this work visually shows us a grasshopper's shift from lowercase incoherence ("r-p-o-p-h-e-s-s-a-g-r") to a sudden great, energized jumble ("PPEGORHRASS") to something nearly recognizable, folded on itself (".gRrEaPsPhOs") to—at last—quiet identifiability (",grasshopper;"). Take away the typographical arrangement of the poem or use some word other than *grasshopper,* and you take away its meaning. Text and graphics are equally necessary.

A later, more sophisticated example is "Temple Bells," a minimalist haiku by Jonathan Brannen from his 1991 minibook, *Sirloin Clouds,* that consists, in its entirety, of the phrase *a petal* above the phrase *a peal.* Here six words, counting the title, make a pleasant picture of a petal and temple bells sounding in the background. The petal, being singular, is almost certainly adrift. The sounds of the words—the alliteration, assonance and consonance—and simple parallelism combine to give music to the picture. But there is not much to it—except when viewed on the page. Then it becomes evident that the visual appearance of "petal" and "peal" is crucially important, for it acts as an implicit metaphor for what those words stand for, an actual petal and actual peal of bells. A reader sensitive to visual poetry will observe at once and viscerally thrill to a wafted, exquisitely delicate but material petal's resolving itself into purely ethereal bell song, the way the word for "petal" shrinks from two syllables to one and becomes the word *peal.* The poem's words and visual appearance are equally essential for the poem's final effect.

Some scholars have traced visual poetry back to ancient Egypt. Examples can be found from just about all eras and parts of the world, notably China and pre-Columbian America. In the West, Christian-era poets occasionally printed words or phrases honoring their God in circles, in other geometric shapes, or as simple crosswords. Pre-20th-century visual poetry peaked, in the view of most observers, in the 1600s, with the "shaped" or "pattern" poems of George Herbert, whose lines, at appropriate times, are indented or cut short in such a way as to make pictures of them. Thus Herbert's most famous shaped poem, "Easter Wings" (1633), looks like a pair of wings.

The earliest widely discussed modern visual poems were published in *Calligrammes,* a book by the French poet Guillaume Apollinaire, in 1918, the year Apollinaire died in World War I. Its most famous visual poem includes words about rain printed not across the page but down it, in lines resembling streams of rain. A few years prior to this, the visual artists Pablo Picasso and Georges Braque had begun to include textual elements in their work, but the collages resulting from their experiments and those of others did not incorporate words and typography in any semantically meaningful way: They did not verbalize their pictures; they merely increased those pictures' store of visual subject matter. Around the same time, various dadaists (see SURREALISM) and Russian futurists (see EUROPEAN POETIC INFLUENCES) were doing interesting things with cut-up texts but with similarly small regard for the poetic meaning of what they were doing. Pound was actively using graphic elements then, too—in the Chinese ideogrammatic passages of his *CANTOS* (1930–70) and in "In a Station of the Metro" (1913), which when printed as Pound originally intended it to be, has two large blocks of space interrupting each of its two lines.

A major pioneer in the art was Cummings, who was exposed to Apollinaire and much else that was going on in European MODERNISM early in the century. He was writing full-blown visual poems as early as the 1920s. By 1935 he had achieved the combined visual and conceptual sophistication of such poems as "poem #70" from his collection *no thanks.* The subject of the poem is an awe-inspiringly brilliant star. In the poem Cummings (among other actions) takes the word *bright* and, by repeating it, each time with a different letter capitalized, then with question marks replacing letters, moves it from "brIght" to "????T" to convey the word's growing mysteriousness. At the same time, he carries out similar operations on the words *star* and *yes,* thus grouping "bright," "star," and the sense of affirmation—glitteringly, via the unexpected capitalizations—as interconnected essences, or the same essence. Simultaneously extremely simple and extremely subtle, his poem monitors—and "visio-metaphorically" recreates—a star's slow evolution from undifferentiated brightness into final ascendant, affirmative mystery.

Less well known and a little later than Cummings, KENNETH PATCHEN contributed (in the view of many current visual poets) equally to American visual poetry from the late 1930s through the 1940s and 1950s, experimenting with different font styles and the addition of purely graphic elements, eventually integrating his own vividly full-colored paintings with his texts, in a way that Cummings, entirely a typewriter poet (although, appropriately, also an excellent painter), did not.

Among the other lesser figures who combined graphic elements with words in poems prior to the

1950s were Harry Crosby, best known for a poem consisting of a rectangle made up of the word *black,* set in bold type to emphasize its blackness, and repeated over and over with the word *SUN* in uppercase letters, printed only once in the center of the rectangle ("Photoheliograph" [1929]); Else von Freytag-Loringhoven, who made visual poems of herself by dadaistically wearing clothes to which she had pinned—along with assorted tin cans, spoons, and shovels—painted or collaged texts; Bob Brown, whose visual poems included found writings and texts worked out in freehand drawings; Abraham Lincoln Gillespie, whose scores for vocalization and performance have sufficient extralexical devices, including dingbats and arrows, to qualify, for some, as visual poems; Walter Conrad Arensberg, an adherent of dada at one time, who specialized in the visio-poetic device of "word fracture," one of his poems beginning, with "Ing? Is it possible to mean ing?," then going on to discuss the syllable; Marsden Hartley, who included textual matter prominently in some of his paintings and who also wrote poems that deployed punctuation and different fonts in a manner that hints of later visual poetry; Wallace Berman, who wrote poetry for the page and for rock paintings that could be arranged to make different combinations of words along with Hebrew characters related to Kabbalistic mysticism and who also created collages, assemblages, and sculptures containing textual elements; and KENNETH REXROTH, whose little-known "cubist poems" are reminiscent of Cummings's most unorthodox works, as in a poem that contains four lines consisting of nothing but "vvvvvvvvvvvv," "vvvvvvvvvv," "vvvvvvvv" and "v," respectively, and a later line in which six longish words are jammed together ("Fundamental Disagreement with Two Contemporaries" [1930]).

A second generation of American visual poets rose in the late 1950s, part of a worldwide wave of interest in the field due, in large part, to the influence of Eugen Gomringer of Switzerland and the two de Campos brothers of Brazil, who drastically deemphasized the verbal content of their poems, producing work sometimes limited to a single word, as when Gomringer used the word *silence* eight times to construct a rectangle around a blank area to create another order of silence. They termed what they did "concrete poetry," a near-synonym for "visual poetry" still frequently used. Among the American concrete poets were Aram Saroyan, JONATHAN WILLIAMS, RONALD JOHNSON, Mary Ellen Solt, and Emmett Williams (these latter two were the editors responsible for the two main 20th-century anthologies of visual poetry published in the United States, *Concrete Poetry: A World View* (1968) and *An Anthology of Concrete Poetry* (1967), respectively). At about the same time, MAY SWENSON was making more traditional visual poems, Hollander was following in the footsteps of George Herbert as a maker of shaped poems, and d. a. levy was prolifically pioneering in visio-textual collage and various experiments in the aesthetically expressive damaging of texts via erasure, smearing, wholesale obliteration with layers of ink, and similar tactics.

Levy died a suicide at the age of 26; Swenson and Hollander never treated their modest ventures into visual poetry as more than secondary to their unvisual poetry, and the others mentioned went on, for the most part, to other sorts of writing after the 1960s, leaving the field to a third generation still active, which includes Karl Kempton (a pioneer in the use of op art in poetry and the editor of the longest-running American periodical devoted to visual poetry, *Kaldron*), RICHARD KOSTELANETZ (unquestionably the most prolific and best-known visual poet in the United States), Karl Young (a noted converter of Asian and pre-Columbian American materials into visual poetry and Web-master of a Web site for visual poetry, *light & dust*), K. S. Ernst (who has been a leader in the use of ceramic and other kinds of solid letters in visio-poetic sculptures), Marilyn Rosenberg (who is particularly well known for her bookworks, a major, though little-noted, form of visual poetry), Scott Helmes (a major innovator in mathematical poetry, an offshoot of visual poetry), Bill Keith (who has come closer than anyone else to capturing the flavor and beat of jazz in his visual poetry), Joel Lipman (a master of satirical but also lyrically resonant visio-poetic collages), Carol Stetser (the premier mixer of such sciences as archaeology and astronomy with words to form visual poems), Harry Polkinhorn (who was among the first to use computers to give his visual poetry a "techno-now" ambience), and Guy Beining (the content of his visio-poetic collages ranges from the crudest men's magazine images to drawings of his own that have a Matisse-like delicacy), who were fairly quickly followed by another generation that includes Crag Hill, G. Huth, Jonathan Brannen, Mike Basinski, Stephen-Paul Martin, Jake Berry, Miekal And, Liz Was, Bob Grumman, John Byrum, and John M. Bennett (some of whom are older than members of the previous generation but started later as visual poets)—with a side-generation consisting of such poets as Alan Sondheim, Ted Warnell, Jennifer Ley, and Chris Funkhouser doing intriguing things visually in CYBERPOETRY.

To suggest the value of visual poets, one can start by pointing to such efforts at epic visual poems as Berry's ongoing, multivolume *Brambu Drezi* (Vol. 1, 1994), which draws on just about every subject that can be put on paper, from alchemy to calculus, and Martin's unceasingly innovative satire on the Reagan years, *The Flood* (1992). Great strides are beginning to be made in the use of color in visual poetry, too, such as in Ernst's "weavings" (2000). A particularly charming specimen of these consists of the sentence, "I feel so nice, like thousands of tiny boats," printed 22 times right to left and 22 times sideways and perpendicular to (and on top of) the right-to-left lines. Most of the lines are in shades of blue, but five are in red. So what do we have? A silly, banal-seeming, but absolutely just-right expression of contentment: the warmth of a woven blanket, childhood delight (from the tiny boats, whether toy or real), harbored security (since you rarely see many boats except in harbors), sea-gentleness (from the colors and the rhythm of the printing), energetic cheerfulness (from the colors), and, finally, fun (due to the overprinted text's needing to be figured out).

Not much of note has yet been done with animated visual poetry (except by Kostelanetz and a few others), but the increasing use of sophisticated computer software and the ever-increasing use of the Internet for experimentation promise an explosion in that and related areas before long. In short, at the start of the 21st century, the future for American visual poetry looks to be as innovative as its past.

BIBLIOGRAPHY

Grumman, Bob. *Of Manywhere-at-Once.* Port Charlotte, Fla.: Runaway Spoon Press, 1998, pp. 112–172.

Kostelanetz, Richard. *A Dictionary of the Avant-Gardes.* New York: Schirmer Books, 2000, pp. 22, 47, 143, 648.

Young, Karl. "Notation and the Art of Reading." *Open Letter* 5, no. 7 (spring 1984): 5–32.

Bob Grumman

W

WAGONER, DAVID (1926–) David Wagoner is a regional poet of the Northwest. The influence of THEODORE ROETHKE can be felt throughout his early works. Although his poetry ranges from the LYRIC and elegiac to the satiric and the visionary, he has been most renowned for his poetic rendering of the landscape of the Northwest. A versatile writer, he has published various collections of poetry as well as novels.

Wagoner was born in Massillon, Ohio, and grew up in Whiting, Indiana. He received an A.B. from Pennsylvania State University in 1946 and an M.A. from Indiana University in 1949. His first collection of poetry, *Dry Sun, Dry Wind,* was published in 1953, followed by his first novel, *The Man in the Middle,* in 1954. *The Escape Artist* (1965) was made into a movie by Francis Ford Coppola in 1982. Wagoner's many awards and honors include an American Academy of Arts and Letters Award (1974) and the Ruth Lilly Poetry Prize (1991). A former chancellor of the Academy of American Poets, he has been the editor of *Poetry Northwest* since 1966 and has taught at the University of Washington.

Despite the versatility of his later works, Wagoner is best known for his regional and landscape poems. Critics have emphasized the importance of his "naturalist eye," pointing out the "unsentimental, animistic acceptance of and reverence for the natural world" as the prevalent life-view that informs his works, according to Sara McAulay (93). This "transmogrifying [of] landscape into language," Sanford Pinsker points out, has been seen as testifying to Roethke's influence (2). Wagoner's later works are not so much tied to a specific landscape. *New and Selected Poems* (1969) introduced magic as a recurring motif in his poetry.

"The Apotheosis of the Garbagemen," published in *Collected Poems, 1956–76* (1976) and included in *Traveling Light: Collected and New Poems* (1999), shows the mixture of the visionary and the satiric, the magic and the mundane, and the urban and the natural so characteristic of Wagoner's work. From the comical "slambang of their coming" and an elegiac invocation of the "sea of decay where our founding fathers / Rubbled their lives" to the concluding lines that conjure a celebration of nature within urban waste, the poem adroitly intermingles contrasting moods and tones. This recurrence of the magical mundane becomes most acute in his urban poems. Wagoner's poetry is grounded in the landscape of the Northwest, deriving enchantment and transcendence from the minute detailing of material objects.

BIBLIOGRAPHY

McAulay, Sara. "'Getting There' and Going Beyond: David Wagoner's Journey without Regret." *Literary Review* 28, no. 1 (1984): 93–98.

McFarland, Ron. *The World of David Wagoner.* Moscow: University of Idaho Press, 1997.

Pinsker, Sanford. *Three Pacific Norwest Poets: William Stafford, Richard Hugo, and David Wagoner.* Boston, Mass.: Twayne, 1987.

Tamara S. Wagner

"THE WAKING" THEODORE ROETHKE (1953)

The title poem of THEODORE ROETHKE's Pulitzer Prize–winning book, *The Waking, Poems: 1933–1953* (1953), is a short, haunting meditation on living and learning, and it is one of the finest villanelles in English. Other villanelles in its class are "One Art" (1979) by ELIZABETH BISHOP and "Do Not Go Gentle into That Good Night" (1952) by Dylan Thomas. The rigidity of the villanelle form makes it so difficult that the truly great ones easily stand out above the rest, and often above most other poetry. Such is the case with "The Waking," which may be a philosophical outgrowth of one of Roethke's earlier, simpler nature poems: As collected in *The Lost Son* (1948), the first poem he titled "The Waking" is a series of descriptive quatrains about how wonderful it feels to stroll "across / an open field."

In the later villanelle, Roethke seems to advocate an almost Zen approach to learning, as if education is a natural part of life: "I learn by going where I have to go." His advice is to relax and enjoy nature, not to strive too hard (like the lowly worm who pointlessly climbs the winding stair) and not to become too worried about living or learning. The truly important knowledge, he implies, will come just as easily as the trees change with the seasons. As the biographer Allan Seager quotes, Roethke once wrote, "I can sense the moods of nature almost instinctively. . . . When I get alone under an open sky . . . I'm tremendously exalted and a thousand vivid ideas and sweet visions flood my consciousness" (55).

"The Waking" seems to have been Roethke's way of putting his easygoing, nature-loving philosophy into a musical, semireligious form, a mantra that is both soothing and instructive. It shows his reverence for the earth while giving valuable advice to future generations. "The Waking" is one of his most accessible and popular poems.

BIBLIOGRAPHY

Blessing, Richard A. "The Shaking That Steadies: Theodore Roethke's 'The Waking.'" *Ball State University Forum* 12, no. 4 (1971): 17–19.

Seager, Allan. *The Glass House: The Life of Theodore Roethke.* New York: McGraw-Hill, 1968.

Jack Turner

WAKOSKI, DIANE (1937–)

Diane Wakoski's large body of work is notable for its narrative and digressionary style and its consistent use of her personal history and mythology to explore abstract themes, among them the pursuit of beauty and identity, loss, betrayal, and the world's dualities. Her influences include writers associated with the SAN FRANCISCO RENAISSANCE as well as WALLACE STEVENS.

Wakoski was born in Whittier, California, and began writing poetry at the age of seven. She published her first of more than 40 volumes, *Coins and Coffins,* in 1962. Her many honors include the Bread Loaf Writers' Conference ROBERT FROST Fellowship (1966) and the WILLIAM CARLOS WILLIAMS Prize (1989) for her selected poems, *Emerald Ice* (1988). She has taught at a number of schools, principally at Michigan State University.

Critic Mark Harris divides her career into three phases—the imagistic, the search for beauty, and the musical; however, all of Wakoski's work maintains a digressionary narrative style and uses individual experiences as a way of exploring more complex themes. Describing poetry as "a way of solving a problem" (qtd. in Erskine 5054), Wakoski is sometimes perceived as angry, because of her recurrent focus on lost love. "Justice Is Reason Enough" (1962) tells the story of a suicide, interjected with repeated questioning of "Why?" As is often the case, toward the end of the poem, Wakoski poses a resolution, "Justice is / reason enough for anything ugly. It balances the beauty in the / world."

The later work continues the exploration of loss and maintains the digressions that marked her early work; however, the problems posed in the poems tend toward more affirmative resolutions, as in "To the Thin and Elegant Woman Who Resides Inside of Alix Nelson" (1976), which critiques American consumerism and ideals of beauty by affirming the author's growing recognition of beauty in what is natural. She encourages the woman to "dump fashion" and "love your own soft peachy cheeks."

In an early interview Wakoski asserted that poetry was "control through words" (9). Though her musing, conversational style appears effortless, her exploration of conceptual dualities marks the complex refinement of her work.

BIBLIOGRAPHY

Erskine, Thomas L. "Diane Wakoski." In *Critical Survey of Poetry* 7. Vol. 7; 2d. ed., edited by Philip K. Jason. Pasadena, Calif.: Salem Press, 2003, pp. 4,052–4,060.

Harris, Mark. "Diane Wakoski." In *Dictionary of Literary Biography*. Vol. 5, *American Poets since World War II*, edited by Donald J. Greiner, 355–366. Detroit: Gale, 1980.

Wakoski, Diane. "An Interview with Diane Wakoski," by Claire Healey. *Contemporary Literature* 18, no. 1 (winter 1977): 1–19.

Sharon L. Barnes

WALCOTT, DEREK (1930–) Derek Walcott is a playwright and poet of contrasts: a Caribbean poet who weaves together the patois of his native St. Lucia and the poetic styles, themes, and diction of classical Greece and the European tradition. Walcott's work contains references to and echoes of Homer, Virgil, Shakespeare, Dante, John Donne, William Blake, Charles Baudelaire, and T. S. ELIOT. By refusing to choose between Europe and the Caribbean, Walcott creates a truly brilliant hybrid voice and identity. Although he does not explicitly identify himself as an American poet, his work echoes the American poetic tradition of Walt Whitman, the first great American poet of the democratic voice, and ROBERT LOWELL, whose historical sweep and formalism can be heard in Walcott's work. Walcott has also proclaimed an admiration for the colloquial tradition in American poetry, best represented by the African-American tradition of ETHERIDGE KNIGHT.

Walcott was born in Castries, the capital of the small Caribbean island of St. Lucia. His parents were Methodists in a largely Catholic environment, a fact that would later influence his understanding of the discipline of poetic craft. A prolific writer, Walcott published his first collection of poetry, *25 Poems,* in 1948. After a period of study in New York, he returned to the Caribbean in 1959, where he lived in Trinidad for the next two decades, until he was appointed professor of creative writing at Boston University. In Boston he became acquainted with several American poets—Lowell, JOSEPH BRODSKY, and the Irish poet Seamus Heaney. Since the publication of *In a Green Night* (1962), Walcott has made his greatest mark, producing several collections of poetry, among them *The Castaway* (1965), *Another Life* (1973), *The Arkansas Testament* (1987), *Omeros* (1990), and, most recently, *Tiopolo's Hound* (2000) and *The Prodigal* (2004). Walcott won the 1992 Nobel Prize in literature, among other awards and distinctions.

Walcott's poetry is shaped and colored by the tradition of the Old World, by the figures of Adam, Robinson Crusoe, and especially Homer. But in his book-length poem *Omeros,* readers encounter a Homer who is not simply transplanted from classical Greece, but instead is a hybrid, a Homer who can speak in the Caribbean: "I said 'Omeros,' and *O* was the conch shell's invocation, *mer* was / both mother and sea in our Antillean patois."

Walcott fears neither the poetic forms nor the EUROPEAN POETIC TRADITION. In "Ruins of a Great House" he writes, "Marble like Greece, Like Faulkner's South in stone, / deciduous beauty prospered and is gone." Later, in "The Schooner Flight" from *The Star-Apple Kingdom* (1979), using a traditional pentameter line and a complex rhyme scheme, he employs a different voice, a Caribbean voice, that of Shabine, the restless sailor: "I go draw and knot every line as tight / as ropes in this rigging; in simple speech." Walcott looks to European and biblical traditions for a set of tools to see truly and to speak of his home for the first time, like Adam, a figure that comes up in the poem "New World." Walcott speaks of Adam's post-Edenic life, of his being thrown into the world of pain and labor: "O yes, the awe of Adam / at the first bead of sweat."

For Walcott, the figure of Adam represents the poet who both names the world and who is exiled from it. This sense of exile makes Walcott a poet of traditions, because it is in the melding of European and CARIBBEAN POETIC TRADITIONS and cultures that Walcott seeks to find his place and his voice.

He is a poet of craft because it is only the craftsperson—as in Walcott's image of the disciplined carpenter in "Cul de Sac Valley"—who will be able to make a language with which to speak, a language both cosmopolitan and local, a poetry that is as material as the carpenter's wood. The poet handles words, sounds, and shapes: "the fragrant Creole / of their native grain."

Walcott is a poet of landscape because it is in the complexity and beauty of the St. Lucian tropics that he comes face to face with the irreversible blending of nature and history. In "The Sea Is History" Walcott asks where the history of monuments, of battles, of tribal memory may be found, and his answer is, "The sea. The sea / has locked them up."

Finally, Walcott is a poet of reconciliation and humanity, always working to escape the resentments and limitations of the colonial past and to construct a language that will speak history in a new voice, not a voice of the colonial master but of ethics. In his 1993 essay "The Figure of Crusoe," Walcott says, "Crusoe is no lord of magic, duke, prince. He does not possess the island he inhabits. He is alone, he is a craftsman, his beginnings are humble. He acts, not by authority, but by conscience" (37). In exile, in craft, in history, in the exploration of traditions both European and Caribbean, Walcott forges this voice of conscience.

BIBLIOGRAPHY

Bobb, June. *Beating a Restless Drum: the Poetics of Kamau Brathwaite and Derek Walcott.* Trenton, N.J.: Africa World Press, 1998.

Brown, Stewart, ed. *The Art of Derek Walcott.* Chester Spring, Pa.: Dufour Editions, 1991.

Hamner Robert D., ed. *Critical Perspectives on Derek Walcott.* Washington, D.C.: Three Continents Press, 1993.

Hamner, Robert. *Derek Walcott.* New York: Maxwell Macmillan International, 1993.

Terada, Rei. *Derek Walcott's Poetry: American Mimicry.* Boston: Northeastern University Press, 1992.

Thieme, John. *Derek Walcott.* New York: St. Martin's Press, 1999.

Walcott Derek. "The Figure of Crusoe." In *Critical Perspectives on Derek Walcott,* edited by Robert D. Hamner. Washington, D.C.: Three Continents Press, 1993, p. 37.

Alan Bourassa

WALDMAN, ANNE (1945–) Anne Waldman has been a dynamic voice in American poetry for more than three decades. While she has most commonly been associated with the BEAT writers, she also has been an active member of the post-Beat New York poetry underground. In her practice she reaches back to the archaic nature of poetry. She says of her work: "I want [my poetry] to be . . . a sustained experience, a voyage, a magnificent dream, something that would take you in myriad directions simultaneously, and you could draw on all those other voices and you could pay homage to ancestors and other languages—a poem that would include everything and yet dwell in the interstices of the imagination and action" (Ricci).

Waldman was born in Millville, New Jersey, and raised in New York City. From an early age she was influenced by the Greenwich Village arts scene of the late 1950s and early 1960s. She graduated from Bennington College in 1965, moved back to New York and, with LEWIS WARSH, started the literary magazine *Angel Hair,* and became the director at the St. Mark's Poetry Project in the Bowery (see POETRY INSTITUTIONS). In 1947 she joined with ALLEN GINSBERG to found the JACK KEROUAC School of Disembodied Poetics at Naropa Institute, an experimental Buddhist college in Boulder, Colorado. As a powerful female presence in the overwhelmingly male Beat literary movement, Waldman has served as a role model for many younger poets. She is the author of more than 40 books. Waldman has also received many awards, including the Dylan Thomas Memorial Award (1967), the Poets Foundation Award (1969), and the National Literary Anthology Award (1970).

Although she had already published several books, her reputation was firmly established with her breakthrough collection, *Fast Speaking Woman* (1975), which returned to the chant as its primary from (see POETRY IN PERFORMANCE). W. C. Bamberger has described the chants in these poems as having replaced her earlier voice with "a petroglyphic scratchiness that rose up into their space" (131). Seeing Waldman read/perform her poems is often likened to watching a shamanic ritual. Her most ambitious work is *Iovis* (1993), a long elegy, very much in the tradition of PATERSON and the CANTOS (see LONG AND SERIAL POETRY).

Iovis ambitiously incorporates many forms, including prose excerpts from letters, news reports, and narrative summaries. In the poem Waldman also explores a wide range of male personae. She aggressively pushes this poem beyond its limits not only in terms of form, taking the traditional collage nature of the elegy to extremes, but also at the level of the utterance: "work this / doesn't work it will, though / working words till they work." Just as Waldman invites her audience to participate in the energy field of her poems during an act of performance, here she invites the silent reader to watch as she struggles with the act of composition.

Early in book I of *Iovis,* Waldman gives credit to her forefathers, "those epic masters, [William Carlos] Williams, [Ezra] Pound, [Louis] Zukofsky, [Charles] Olson," while making it evident that she is also questioning the male-dominated model of the elegy itself. For more than 40 years she has been making poetry, as she remakes herself, evolving from a fast-chanting woman to a new epic master in her own right.

BIBLIOGRAPHY

Bamberger, W. C. "Emptiness inside the Compound: The Architecture of Anne Waldman's Reality." *Talisman* 13 (fall 1994–winter 1995): 130–136.

Notley, Alice. "Iovis Omnia Plena." *Chicago Review* 44, no. 1 (1998): 117–130.

Ricci, Claudia. "Anne Waldman: A Profile," Writers Online. Available online. URL: www.albany.edu/writers-inst/olv1n2.html. Downloaded March 2007.

Michael Strickland

WALDROP, KEITH (1932–) Keith Waldrop's work links metaphysical speculation to the physical textures of spoken language. His poems create momentary spaces where the spiritual and material meet. Waldrop cites the work of WILLIAM BRONK as "kin" and admires his early work "for its use of data from very disparate realms" ("Interview I" 278). Waldrop's own poems are often collages of the compositional and the conversational. He once remarked, "I'm interested in poets who start with spoken language, and then make new *written* language out of it" ("Interview II" 270). Like ROBERT CREELEY, Waldrop employs highly enjambed lines to enact the rhythm of speech and thought as they are composed into emotional reflection and echo into "the blank which follows" (Waldrop "Notes for a Preface" n.p.).

Waldrop was born in Emporia, Kansas. After military service Waldrop enrolled in the University of Michigan's Ph.D. program in comparative literature, where he completed a dissertation entitled "Aesthetic Uses of Obscenity in Literature." Since 1962 Waldrop and his wife, the poet ROSMARIE WALDROP, have been operating Burning Deck, a literary press established with the intention to join the falsely polarized camps of the BEATS and academics (see POETRY PRESSES). In 1971 Waldrop received an AMY LOWELL Fellowship to study in Europe. In Paris he met Anne-Marie Albiach and Claude Royet-Journoud, two European poets, among many others, whose work Waldrop has translated into English. Waldrop has received fellowships from the National Endowment of the Arts (1991 and 2003) and the DAAD Berlin Artists' Program (1993). *A Windmill near Calvary* (1968) received a National Book Award nomination, and *silhouette of the Bridge (Memory Stand Ins)* (1997) received the Americas Award for poetry.

Waldrop's early poems are dense lyrics that combine free and metrical verse (see PROSODY AND FREE VERSE). His recent work has become increasingly austere and draws on the book as an architectural form embodying time's passage. A book, such as *Seramis If I Remember (self portrait as mask)* (2001), becomes an extended meditation on language shifting into and emerging out of the spaces of narrative and history; a map of Babylon is that book's guiding metaphor. Always elegiac, Waldrop consistently revisits the vicissitudes of memory—subjective, physical, collective—in a variety of literary forms. For Waldrop, the body is a doomed monument—simultaneously distant and proximate—memory allows the mind to intermittently behold. In "Poem from Memory" (1983), Waldrop's pithy lines enact the process of recalling his body as he "sift[s]/ ruins for / old manuscripts." Memory and the materiality of literary history are spaces suspended between the body and the mind. The tightly enclosed lines reflect the self's precarious dependence on memory for its link to language, history, and self-consciousness. The formal clarity of Waldrop's poetry contrasts with his work's philosophical risks. Waldrop tests the edges of language with song.

BIBLIOGRAPHY

Waldrop, Keith. "Interview with Keith Waldrop 1993–1997 [I], by Peter Gizzi." *Germ* 4 (spring 2000): 275–305.

———. "Peter Gizzi Interviews Keith Waldrop 1993–1997, Part II," by Peter Gizzi *Germ*. 5 (spring 2001): 270–319.

———. "Notes for a Preface." In *The Opposite of Letting the Mind Wander: Selected Poems and a Few Songs*. Providence, R. I.: Lost Roads Publishers, 1990, p. n.p.

Kimberly Lamm

WALDROP, ROSMARIE (1935–) Rosmarie Waldrop is often aligned with the LANGUAGE movement and feminist poets, such as SUSAN HOWE, LYN HEJINIAN, BARBARA GUEST, LESLIE SCALAPINO, and MEI-MEI BERSSENBRUGGE. Her work often contains various 20th century experimental devices, including collage, concrete poetry (see VISUAL POETRY), and procedural elements, in which linguistic and formal ingredients are borrowed from other works. She is most known for her serial prose poems, which have been compared to the work of JOHN ASHBERY, ROBERT CREELEY, and RON SILLIMAN (see LONG AND SERIAL POETRY).

Waldrop was born in Kitzingen-am-Main, Germany, and emigrated to the United States in 1958 in order to attend the University of Michigan, where she received an M.A. and Ph.D. In Michigan she became associated with a group of writers who called themselves the "Walgamot Society," who consisted of KEITH WALDROP, X. J. KENNEDY, DONALD HALL, Dallas Weibe, and W. D. SNODGRASS. She has since lived in the United States as a writer, professor, and translator. She is also the copublisher of the small press, Burning Deck. Her first book of poetry, *A Dark Octave,* was published in 1967, and she has subsequently published numerous books of poetry, including *The Reproduction of Profiles* (1987), *Lawn of Excluded Middle* (1993), *A Key into the Language of America* (1994), *New and Selected Poems* (1997), and *Another Language: Selected Poems* (1997). Her list of awards are extensive and include two National Endowment for the Arts grants (1980 and 1994), a Rhode Island Governor's Art Award (1988), and a Fund for Poetry Award (1990).

Waldrop's work is rooted in a theory and practice that investigates language as both material and absence. Her experience learning English as a second language and her work as a translator have likely contributed to these artistic questions. In addition to employing various avant-garde literary techniques, her poetic discussions of language are often drawn from historical and philosophical sources. She has received most acclaim for her work in prose poems, which are usually arranged in series. In one such book, *The Reproduction of Profiles,* Waldrop writes: "Everything that can be thought at all, you said, can be thought over." When the poem's speaker asks for an explanation, an unnamed you "hastily close[s] the window," a metaphor for how language can shut out understanding. What is suggested finally, is that one might "stand outside logic"—and even be stripped of it—to reach understanding and thus return to the possibility of language. The "you" and the "I" are separated by physical and linguistic barriers. Language both shuts out expressions and also opens the door to unexplored and entirely new concepts. That which is there is often also not, and vice versa. Waldrop reveals this perplexing notion of language, which, in turn, allows poetry to reveal its own lack, beauty, limits, and bounty.

BIBLIOGRAPHY

Perloff, Marjorie. "Towards a Wittgensteinian Poetics." *Contemporary Literature* 33, no. 2 (1992): 191–213.

Retallack, Joan. "A Conversation with Rosmarie Waldrop." *Contemporary Literature* 40, no. 3 (1999): 329–377.

Waldrop, Rosmarie. "Interview with Rosmarie Waldrop," by Wendy J. Burch. *Poetry Flash* 243 (1993): 1–13.

Amy Hezel

WAR AND ANTIWAR POETRY Twentieth-century American war poetry rarely celebrates war as a great patriotic adventure; instead it often describes, in gruesome detail, the horrors of modern warfare, fought with airplanes, trenches, barbed wire, poison gas, tanks, machine guns, and, of course, the atom bomb.

The widespread destruction of World War I (1914–18) had a sobering influence on American war poetry. Although fiercely neutral during the first years, the United States entered the war in 1917. American poets, such as Alan Seeger and E. E. CUMMINGS fought in the war. Seeger, however, enlisted in the French Foreign Legion in 1914, saw much combat, and died two years later. Seeger's (and America's) most famous World War I poem is "Rendezvous" (1917), which proclaims: "I have a rendezvous with Death / When Spring brings back blue days and fair." The contrast of impending death with the idyllic imagery of spring's "blue days and fair" reflects the loss of innocence of those who fought the war and of the supposedly "civilized" Western nations who fought the first truly mechanized war that accomplished killing on such a vast and unheroic scale. The critic Paul Fussell complains that "American writing about the war tends to be spare and one-dimensional" (158). Indeed Seeger's poem lacks the connection to classical literary works that British poets, including Wilfred Owen and Siegfried Sassoon, incorporated into their war poems. While Seeger's poem seems to show an American independence from the European and classical canons, other American poets, such as T. S. ELIOT and EZRA POUND, would soon blast their American and European readers with classical references.

American poetry of the First World War was not written only by combatants. Already-famous American writers contributed their own poems on the war, and these poems often reflected the view of the American public toward the war. EDGAR LEE MASTERS, best known for the *Spoon River Anthology,* lauded France's bravery and sacrifice in "O Glorious France!" (1917). His lines, such as "O France, whose sons amid the rolling thunder / Of cannon stand in trenches where the dead / Clog the ensanguined ice," aspire to the pathos created by war in general but do not create the same irony as can be found in poems by Seeger. This difference highlights the effect of the new carnage of this war on those who experienced it intimately. Noncombatant poet Pound contrasts starkly with more patriotic poets, such as Masters, and captures the modernist view of the war and its effect on Western society in "Hugh Selwyn Mauberly (Life and Contacts)" (1920). In section IV of this poem, Pound accuses Western society of having a deceitful hand in the death of the young men who "walked eye-deep in hell / believing old men's lies." But Pound saves his most bitter condemnation of Western civilization for the slaughter of World War I for section V of "Mauberly," where he invokes the image of "an old bitch gone in the teeth, / For a botched civilization."

American poetry of the Second World War often reflects a certain ambivalence to the carnage and purpose of war. Americans were not as naïve about their place in the world nor about the evils of modern warfare as they were in 1917. "The way trench warfare dominates the imagery of World War I, the fleets of bombers and the smoking cities dominate the imagery of World War II," writes HARVEY SHAPIRO in his introduction to the 2003 *Poets of World War II* (xxlii). "The American poets of World War II wrote poems that are neither pious nor patriotic. . . . They viewed themselves as individuals caught in a machine so complex and far-flung the mind could not encompass it" (Shapiro xxli).

The most anthologized American war poem from the World War II is RANDALL JARRELL's "The DEATH OF THE BALL TURRET GUNNER" (1945), in which the speaker is described as a sort of fetus in a mother's belly. The result of the gunner's encounter with the enemy "nightmare fighters" is so gruesome that he says, "When I died they washed me out of the turret with a hose." The stark images here do not include any further statements about the destruction of war, only a graphic description of a human being who is so destroyed by the enemy that he must be washed out like an unnamed mess. James Meredith asserts that, on the whole, Jarrell's poems "are evocative of both the horror of war and the balm of hope" (13). In Jarrell's best-known war poem, however, there appears to be little hope for the slaughtered airman. Meredith, instead, focuses on Jarrell's "Eighth Air Force" (1947), a poem that suggests the ambiguity of the American response to the war and to its warriors. In this poem Jarrell takes up the problems of how soldiers keep their humanity during war and of how combatants and noncombatants respond to the death and destruction the soldiers inflict. His speaker calls the airmen *"O murderers!,"* but he also shows the soldiers between missions, playing "like puppies with their puppy." The puppy here is a symbol of the innocent who has the potential to be a murderer. Jarrell ends the poem unwilling to condemn the airmen as murderers or, conversely, to exonerate them as innocents: "Men wash their hands in blood, as best they can: / I find no fault in this just man." Despite Jarrell's ambiguous response to warriors in "Eighth Air Force," in other poems, such as "The Range in the Desert" (1947), he asserts that war trivializes its own greatest products ("Profits and death grow marginal") and laments that this destruction has failed to make a change ("And the world is—what it has been"). In "The

War in the Air" (1987), HOWARD NEMEROV portrays the curiously antiseptic and absent nature of death for those who flew. Those who died in the air "simply stayed out there / In the clean war, the war in the air."

Depictions of the ground war in World War II added in all of the carnage that Nemerov's sarcastic phrase "the clean war" left out. SAMUEL MENASHE's "Beachhead" (1961) uses the central image of a "skull / sea gulls peck." GEORGE OPPEN's "Survival: Infantry" (1962) speaks of "the smell of explosives" and of "Iron standing in mud." Where Nemerov was able to soar in a clean world, some men, including the speaker of Oppen's poem, went about on hands and knees and were "ashamed of [their] half life and [their] misery." Poems of the ground war often contain dirt, filth, and blood that reflect the soldier-poets' intimate experience of close combat.

Although many of the poems written about World War II depict battle or the results of battle, some are resolutely critical of war. In one poem pacifist WILLIAM STAFFORD feels that his brother's grave is used merely as a patriotic symbol on Independence Day and calls his brother a "reluctant hero." He asks, "Who / shall we follow next?" and "Who shall we kill / next time?" ("At the Grave of My Brother: Bomber Pilot" [1970]). Perhaps the most famous poem concerning World War II pacifism is ROBERT LOWELL's "Memories of West Street and Lepke" (1959), in which the speaker is imprisoned for a year as a "fire-breathing Catholic C.O. [conscientious objector]" along with Louis "Lepke" Buchalter, the boss of the infamous organized crime gang Murder, Inc. In this poem Lowell is aiming for the irony of a situation in which the speaker, who refuses to kill, is incarcerated in the same place as a man who has been convicted *for* killing.

World War II was also the last racially segregated war, and the segregation and inequality between Caucasian and African-American soldiers is the subject of several poems of the period. Witter Bynner's "Defeat" (1947) points out that white German prisoners on a prison train eat at the same table as that of white American soldiers, while "black soldiers sit apart"; he imagines that this separation will defeat the United States. The title character in GWENDOLYN BROOKS's poem "Negro Hero" (1945) asks, "am I good enough to die for them, is my blood bright enough to be spilled[?] . . . Am I clean enough to kill for them?" The Negro Hero, however, is not lauded like Stafford's dead brother, but is a hero who saves a people who do not wish to be saved by him.

American poetry of the Vietnam War reflected, as Jeffrey Walsh writes, a "radically new consciousness of war for Americans," which was characterized by a "moral ambivalence of advanced technology" and a "backlash of public opinion" (185). Philip Beidler observes that the early Vietnam War poems were "caught between 'diatribe' and 'documentary'" and were written by such poets as ROBERT BLY, DENISE LEVERTOV, and ALLEN GINSBERG (71–72). Bly's "The TEETH MOTHER NAKED AT LAST" (1973) chronicles the bombing of peasant huts and the burning of children by dispassionate airmen: "This is what it's like for a rich country to make war." Much poetry of the early 1970s comes from soldiers, such as D. C. Berry and Frank Cross, whose poem "Rice Will Grow Again" (1976) recounts the killing of a Vietnamese farmer and the lingering effects it has on the soldier-speaker. The world of the Vietnam poem, says Beidler, is "a world of the maimed, the blasted, the dead," which is "both literally and metaphorically too awful for meaning" (131–132). The poems of YUSEF KOMUNYAKAA reflect the observations and experience of a soldier in lyrical detail. "Starlight Scope Myopia" (1988) talks of how "the starlight scope" used to sight targets at night "brings / men into killing range," but much of the poem describes the scene of the Viet Cong moving cargo almost as a painting of "sandalwood & lotus" and of "the full moon / loaded on an ox cart." The irony of this almost pastoral approach is that the speaker is looking through the starlight scope as he aims his M16 rifle at the beautiful scene he describes.

Among poets writing since Vietnam, poet-soldier Bruce Weigl captures the lingering psychological trauma of that war on the Americans who fought it both overseas and at home in "Song of Napalm" (1985), in which he recounts the image of "the girl / running from her village, napalm / stuck to her dress like jelly." Weigl's idyllic home life with his wife (to whom the poem is dedicated) is interrupted by violent recollections of wartime atrocities represented in the famous photograph of Phan Thi Kim Phuc that appeared in *Life* magazine in June 1972. These lines are reminiscent of World War I British poet Wilfred Owen's "Dulce et Decorum Est" (1917). In "Song of Napalm," Weigl imagines that the girl "rises above the stinking jungle and her pain / eases, and your pain, and mine." Such imagining seems to be a balm for the wounded soul of the soldier, for his wife, who experiences his trauma in her own way, and for America itself, but Weigl says that this "lie swings back again," and he imagines that the girl is dead and laments that "nothing . . . can deny it." In these lines he captures the problem America faces with Vietnam: We can pretend that everything turned out all right, but the truth undeniably returns to haunt us.

Twentieth-century American war poetry thus encompasses frank descriptions of carnage and soul-searching moral dilemmas. It is not gallant and heroic. War poetry of the 20th century finds little to celebrate, except, perhaps, "man's ability, indeed his compulsion, to turn terror into art" (Shapiro xx).

BIBLIOGRAPHY

Beidler, Philip. *American Literature and the Experience of Vietnam.* Athens: University of Georgia Press, 1982.
Fussell, Paul. *The Great War and Modern Memory.* New York: Oxford University Press, 1975.
Meredith, James H. *Understanding the Literature of World War II: A Student Casebook to Issues, Sources, and Historical Documents.* Westport, Conn.: Greenwood Press, 1999.
Shapiro, Harvey, ed. *Poets of World War II.* New York: Library of America, 2003.
Walsh, Jeffrey. *American War Literature 1914 to Vietnam.* New York: St. Martin's Press, 1982.

Gregory Byrd

WARREN, ROBERT PENN (1905–1989)

Although he wrote poetry throughout his career, Robert Penn Warren was, for much of the 20th century, better known as a successful novelist and literary critic. The textbook he wrote with Cleanth Brooks, *Understanding Poetry* (1938), was extremely influential in determining the way poems have been read in the academy from the late 1930s to the late 1970s. Its insistent focus on text per se encouraged the teaching of poems without reference to anything but what the poem itself says. His works of fiction, especially *All the King's Men* (1946), were well received. It was not until late in life that Warren's poetry became his central interest, and in his sixties, seventies, and eighties he produced several books of magnificent verse.

Warren was born in Guthrie, Kentucky. He graduated from Vanderbilt University in 1925. At Vanderbilt he became involved with the FUGITIVE/AGRARIAN SCHOOL of poets, including ALLEN TATE and JOHN CROWE RANSOM. The Fugitives identified themselves with the agrarian South and argued for tradition, regionalism, and particularity of imagery in poetry. In 1929 Warren married Emma Brescia, from whom he was divorced in 1951. In 1952 he married the writer Eleanor Clark, with whom he had two children. During his long and active life, he won many awards and honors, including three Pulitzer Prizes—two for poetry (1958 and 1979) and one for fiction (1946)—the Bollingen Prize (1967), the National Medal for Literature (1970), and the Presidential Medal of Freedom (1980).

Warren's early poetry was technically accomplished and demonstrated the tenets of New Criticism, an approach to reading poetry that emphasized close reading and literary analysis. His poetry was rhymed, metered, carefully wrought, often ironic, and understated. But Warren practiced more than he preached, and, as he grew older, his poetry became freer and more discursive without completely losing its formalist underpinnings. Although many of his later poems use rhyme, many are written in long free-verse lines, sometimes with six or seven stresses (see PROSODY AND FREE VERSE).

The recurring subjects in Warren's poetry are time, memory, love, and loss. A common approach in his work is the quest for self-knowledge, though he often doubts whether such knowledge is possible. His poems frequently find metaphors in nature for states of consciousness: "Watch the great bough lashed by wind and rain. Is it / A metaphor for your soul?," he asks in "Ah, Anima" (1977). His work reveals a hunger for the glory he found in early poetry, such as Milton's *Paradise Lost* (1667), but his religious skepticism and doubt that consciousness continues after death make him ground his yearning in the experience of the present.

One of his best late collections, *Now and Then* (1978), is divided into two sections, "Nostalgic" and "Speculative." The nostalgia in the poems is complicated by an acute awareness of the elusiveness of identity, and the speculative poems are anchored in the fact of mortality each of us must confront. The division and the unity apply to most of Warren's later work. Warren's poems use language as the means for a visionary search for self-knowledge and metaphysical exploration and for the creation of the meaning to be found in beauty.

BIBLIOGRAPHY

Bloom, Harold, ed. *Robert Penn Warren: Modern Critical Views.* New York: Chelsea House, 1986.

Grimshaw, James A. *Understanding Robert Penn Warren.* Columbia: University of South Carolina Press, 2001.

Strandberg, Victor A. *The Poetic Vision of Robert Penn Warren.* Lexington: University Press of Kentucky, 1977.

Thomas Lisk

WARSH, LEWIS (1944–) Lewis Warsh is a second-generation NEW YORK SCHOOL poet most famous for his association with the poetry scene in and around St Mark's Poetry Project (see POETRY INSTITUTIONS). He can be read as a diary poet, a chronicler of his generation, and, in the New York school tradition, a collaborator with fellow poets, including *Chicago* (1969) with TOM CLARK, which Warsh has called a "sweet burst of reciprocal energy" ("Memoirs" 606). As with poets who influenced him, such as TED BERRIGAN, Warsh's unconventional forms and subject matter do not fit well within academic tastes. He once suggested that being an "American poet" means "grooving on everything that's happening in the moment" (*Part* n.p.).

Warsh was born in the Bronx, New York. He and ANNE WALDMAN met at the 1965 Berkeley Poetry Conference and married at St. Mark's Church in 1967. They cofounded *Angel Hair* magazine and books, which ran from 1966 until 1975. Upon his breakup with Waldman, Warsh moved to Bolinas, California, a location that figures prominently in *Part of My History* (1972), his travelogue written using poetry, prose, and photography. He and BERNADETTE MAYER were married from 1975 to 1985, and together they ran *United Artists,* one of the last mimeograph magazines, from their home in Lenox, Massachusetts. Warsh also writes fiction and has published several novels that have won critical praise. Among a number of honors, Warsh has received the James Shestack Award from the *American Poetry Review* (1993) and the Poets Foundation Award (1994). He has taught at a number of schools, including the State University of New York, Albany, Fairleigh Dickinson University, the New School, Queens College of the City University of New York, the Naropa Institute, and Long Island University.

Warsh's writing emphasizes the fullness of daily experience through gritty immediacy, the rush of urban details, and the wonder at travel and interpersonal exchange. Along with *Part of My History* (1972), which records his interaction with fellow poets, Warsh has also written the autobiographical *The Maharajah's Son* (1978), composed from actual letters to his parents. Warsh's poetry often reflects on its means of composition, such as by typewriter, under a particular state of consciousness, or in conversation with others. Although much of his writing is built on what Daniel Kane calls "a characteristically flat, reportage-like tone" (156), in select moments, such as "Get the News" (1970), Warsh's poetry discovers a heightened emotional urgency just beneath the quotidian: "Pay attention: / get the New York News." The verbal influx of news about friends and loved ones reveals "the great drama / of our destinies" as newsworthy poetic material in itself. In such moments his poetry offers an attentive approach to the world.

BIBLIOGRAPHY

Clay, Steven, and Rodney Phillips, eds. *A Secret Location on the Lower East Side: Adventures in Writing, 1960–1980.* New York: Granary Books, 1998.

Warsh, Lewis. "Memoirs." In *Angel hair sleeps with a boy in my head: The Angel Hair Anthology,* edited by Anne Waldman and Lewis Warsh, 573–607. New York: Granary Books, 2001.

———. *Part of My History.* Toronto: Coach House Press, 1972.

Kane, Daniel. *All Poets Welcome: The Lower East Side Poetry Scene in the 1960s.* Berkeley: University of California Press, 2003.

Kaplan Page Harris

***THE WASTE LAND* T. S. ELIOT (1922)** First published almost simultaneously in the *Dial,* then in the *Criterion* in 1922 (see POETRY JOURNALS), *The Waste Land* is often called the most influential poem of the 20th century. EZRA POUND edited the manuscript, and between his and T. S. ELIOT's excisions, the length of the poem was reduced considerably. The result is the premier poem of MODERNISM, which in many ways was a reaction to romantic and Victorian poetic and creative sensibilities. *The Waste Land* redefined poetry in the way Eliot's contemporary James Joyce redefined fiction. Many poets, such as WALLACE STEVENS, ROBERT LOWELL, MARIANNE MOORE, and WILLIAM CARLOS WILLIAMS, as well as subsequent poetic movements, such as BEAT POETRY, were forced to react to the fragmentary method and impersonal poetic aesthetic employed in *The Waste Land.*

The Waste Land is populated by both a myriad of voices and a variety of sources, including Shakespeare, Dante, St. Augustine, the Bible, the *Upanishads,* a tarot deck, Andrew Marvell, Charles Baudelaire, John Milton, Ovid, Richard Wagner, nursery rhymes, historical events, and even popular contemporary music. The poem is, however, more than a cultural and literary scavenger hunt. One need not comprehend all of Eliot's references in order to intuit the subtle historical and cultural accents each new narrative voice presents. Any reader can ascertain the chaos and hopelessness generated by the competing voices and barrage of fragments; as a speaker in part V asserts, as if in defense of Eliot's poetic method, "These fragments I have shored against my ruins." Indeed, as the word *ruins* suggests, Eliot believed that society was steadily deteriorating.

The poem manifests Eliot's critical method of aligning artistic talent with historical and artistic tradition, and it also reflects a second of Eliot's aesthetic rules: Separate the personal life of the poet from the poem, or, as he puts it in his essay "Tradition and the Individual Talent" (1919), "the more perfect the artist, the more completely separate in him will be the man who suffers and the mind which creates" (54). This separation is one reason for the poem's unpredictable narrative voice.

First-time readers may find the poem's many allusions, languages, and images challenging, yet these fragments serve multiple purposes. The fragmentation in *The Waste Land* not only evokes broken society and relationships, but also fosters a sense of disconnection between the reader and the familiar world and its history. The fragments also suggest earlier, larger wholes from which each of the fragments is derived; for this reason, Eliot's notes to the poem mention James Frazier's *Golden Bough* (1890)—famous for investigating fragments of myth in an effort to discover an ancient protomyth from which all myths derive.

Eliot's poem comprises five sections: I. "The Burial of the Dead," II. "A Game of Chess," III. "The Fire Sermon," IV. "Death by Water," and V. "What the Thunder Said." Even so, when read aloud the poem presents a series of disparate voices not coincidental with the sections. Eliot's working title was "He Do the Police in Different Voices," a reference to Charles Dickens's *Our Mutual Friend* (1865), in which a character named Sloppy is Mrs. Higden's preferred reader of the newspaper because he invents voices. Consequently the poem is appreciable not merely for its varied and esoteric allusions, but for its dramatic value.

In part I, the most prominent voice is that of Countess Marie Larisch. She speaks of her youth, a time tense with privilege and suggestive of a precocious sexual awakening. Later in part I, the speaker—who may or may not still be Larisch—recalls an event in a hyacinth garden that left her (or him) speechless and hopeless of salvation, which is evoked by a line from *Tristan and Isolde* (1865), "Oed' und leer das Meer" ("desolate and empty the sea").

Part I then undergoes a radical change in topic and voice, becoming almost playful in its rhythm and language. An anonymous speaker visits a Madame Sosostris, who speaks while providing a tarot reading. The section closes with a more somber, unidentified voice contemplating death and the flow of humanity across London Bridge, likening it to the parade of souls bound for hell in Dante's *Inferno* (ca. 1320).

Part II starts with a detailed setting that invokes the story of Philomela, from Ovid's *Metamorphoses* (A.D. 1), in which Philomela is raped by Tereus, who then cuts Philomela's tongue out so that she cannot report his cruelty. There are also new voices in this section, this time in dialogue: a beleaguered, melancholy man and a jittery, questioning woman. Critics interested in biographical readings of the poem have said that this passage might suggest Eliot's tumultuous relationship with his first wife, a woman of uncertain psychological stability. Part II then introduces a second dialogue: two women at a pub discuss the actions of a third woman, Lil, who is absent. The topic is the impending return of Lil's husband from the war and his certain expectation of sex. Lil is apparently unreceptive to his return, at least, in part, because of an abortion that left her drained and aged. The section ends as the conversation is increasingly interrupted by the English bartender's call "HURRY UP PLEASE IT'S TIME," the equivalent of "last call" for drinks.

Part III opens in the somber speaker's voice, this time invoking an older, poetic language of Alfred Lord Tennyson in the description of the river Thames flowing but strangely devoid of the former detritus—empty bottles, cigarette ends, silk handkerchiefs—because "the nymphs have departed." Critics have pointed out that the objects formerly carried by the river are the leavings of a romantic rendezvous between lovers. Indeed many amorous pairings can be found in this section—both willing and unwilling: Actaeon and Diana (hunter and goddess/huntress of Roman mythology), Sweeney and Mrs. Porter (Sweeney is a recurring character in Eliot's poetry), Tereus and Philomela, Eugenides and his companion (Eugenides is apparently unique to the poem, but the name means "born of a well," strongly suggesting his connection to cisterns later in the poem), and a young carbuncular man and his dispassionate lover, perhaps a prostitute. The voice changes a final time as the poem concludes in another description of the river and of voyages, punctuated by another couple—Queen Elizabeth I and her preferred suitor the Earl of Leicester—and by Augustine's voyage of conversion presented in his *Confessions* (ca. 397).

Part IV is an adaptation of an early Eliot poem, "Dans le Restaurant" (1918), and returns to the drowned man foretold by Madame Sosostris, continuing themes of drowning and death. A character named "Phlebas" is suggestive of *Philebus* (360 B.C.), Plato's dialogue on pleasure.

Part V is laden with biblical images, frequently of Christ's Passion; it opens with images from the Garden of Gethsemane and Christ's arrest. Later description evokes the story of the road to Emmaus. Throughout rain is sought by an unidentified beseeching voice. Another anonymous voice delivers a sermon on three commandments of the Thunder—*"Datta," "Dayadhvam," "Damyata"*—drawing from the Hindu *Upanishads.* The poem collapses in a cacophony of voices, from the Fisher King (a Celtic myth of generation) to a nursery rhyme to poets old and new, until all is quieted by a repetition of the commandments and a hushing prayer for peace. The poem ends thus, exhausted by the collective weight of its own method. In its innovative technique and representative expression of chaos felt by many during the period between world wars, *The Waste Land* deserves its critical reputation as being one of the most influential poems of the 20th century.

BIBLIOGRAPHY

Eliot, T. S. "Tradition and the Individual Talent." In *The Sacred Wood: Essays on Poetry and Criticism.* London: Methuen, 1920, pp. 47–59.

Gardner, Helen. *The Art of T. S. Eliot.* New York: Dutton, 1950.

Reeves, Gareth. *T. S. Eliot's The Waste Land.* Hertfordshire, U.K.: Harvester Wheatsheaf, 1994.

Southam, B. C. *A Guide to the Selected Poems of T. S. Eliot.* San Diego: Harcourt, 1994.

Justin L. Blessinger

WATERS, MICHAEL (1949–) Michael Waters has developed a distinctive, deeply layered, highly visual writing style. Much of his early poetry, as seen in *Not Just Any Death* (1979), follows the CONFESSIONAL practice of developing universal insights based on individual experience. During the 1980s and 1990s, however, Waters moved toward NEW FORMALISM and the IMAGIST SCHOOL, becoming more involved in the use of structure to drive meaning and in the detailed inspection of certain images that carry implicit significance, as in the work of ELIZABETH BISHOP. His poetry also shows the influences of THEODORE ROETHKE and JOHN LOGAN, the latter being the focus of *Dissolve to Island,* a 1984 collection of essays edited by Waters.

Waters was raised in Brooklyn, New York, and attended the State University of New York, Brockport, before studying in England for a year. He earned an M.F.A. at the University of Iowa and a Ph.D. from Ohio

University. Since 1978 he has taught at Salisbury University in Maryland. His first major publication was *Fish Light* (1975), and his most recent is *Parthenopi: New & Selected Poems* (2001). Waters has published seven full-length books, has won a National Endowment for the Arts fellowship (1984), two Pushcart Prizes (1984 and 1990), and numerous other honors.

The critic Floyd Collins has noted Waters's "conflation of narrative and lyric techniques," which leads to "synoptic clarity" (653). In Waters's later work, Collins says, he "couples his gift for image and metaphor with an increasingly dense musicality" (653). The content of his poetry shows a loving attention to humanity as well as a Wordsworthian appreciation for nature and its inherent ability to inspire and to heal.

One of Waters's most anthologized poems is "The Mystery of the Caves," from *Anniversary of the Air* (1985). Here one sees another familiar Waters trait—the seamless integration of literature with life. The young speaker in the poem is trying to escape his parents' quarrel by reading a story about a boy who is lost among caves that are filling with water: "I couldn't stop reading the book . . . / because my mother was leaving again. . . . / The boy wasn't able to breathe. / I think he wanted me to help." The "thin pencil of light" near the end of the poem symbolizes both the escape and the hope that literature and writing can offer. In *Bountiful* (1992), Waters shows his virtuosity in the description of nature with such poems as "Hummingbirds" and "Scorpions," the titles indicating his ability to present both the beautiful and the horrible with the same mythopoeic intensity.

Although Waters is an existentialist, the passion in his words and his obvious, voracious love for literature and nature combine to form an unusual spirituality. He exhibits a transcendence made possible by his careful attention to quotidian details.

BIBLIOGRAPHY

Collins, Floyd. "The Power of Language." *Gettysburg Review* (winter 2000): 653–663.

Hardy, Nat. "Parthenopi: *New and Selected Poems.*" *New Delta Review* 18, no. 1 (fall/winter 2000): 73–74.

Turner, Jack. "Michael Waters." In *Dictionary of Literary Biography*. Vol. 120, American Poets since World War II, edited by R. S. Gwynn. Detroit: Gale, 1992, pp. 315–324.

Jack Turner

WATTEN, BARRETT (1948–) Barrett Watten has been one of the leading proponents of the LANGUAGE SCHOOL, especially as it emerged in the San Francisco Bay area. Similar to other poets affiliated with this informal movement, he has been influenced by American avant-garde writing, such as that of LOUIS ZUKOFSKY and what has come to be called the New American poetry, named after the 1960 anthology edited by Donald Allen (see POETRY ANTHOLOGIES), and by European theorists of culture and language, especially the Russian formalist Viktor Shklovsky (see EUROPEAN POETIC INFLUENCES). From his earliest works, including the volumes *Opera-Works* (1975) and *Decay* (1977), Watten has exposed how a reader's commonsense expectations about language and art derive from institutional and historical influences that ought to be recognized as political.

Watten was born in Long Beach, California. He attended the Massachusetts Institute of Technology and received an A.B. in biochemistry from the University of California, Berkeley, in 1969. In 1972 he received an M.F.A. from the Writers' Workshop at the University of Iowa. Eight books of his poetry have been collected in the single volume, *Frame (1971–1990)* (1997). He founded two journals: *This,* with ROBERT GRENIER, in 1971, and *Poetics Journal,* with LYN HEJINIAN, in 1982. In 1979 he won a National Endowment for the Arts fellowship to complete *Plasma / Paralleles / "X"* (1979).

All of his work is characterized by an inventive treatment of poetic form. The title poem of *Complete Thought* (1982) is organized into 50 numbered two-line stanzas. Each line is a sentence and plays suggestively against its companion, though it is difficult to determine if connections between them are implied by the author or provided by the reader, as in XVI: "I am speaking in an abridged form. / Ordinary voices speak in rooms." The voices of the second line would seem to be less constrained than the speaker in the first, but a room is also a form of abridgement. No specific act of speech can be isolated from its situation. Any utterance entails a position and often a politics. To this fact Watten issues no objection. Instead his writing intercedes between displays of power and the contexts of language that make them possible.

If "Complete Thought," like many of his early works, exposes the way ordinary language can be imbued with power, from *Progress* (1985) on, he has engaged more explicitly political phenomena. For example, *Bad History* (1998), a long work in prose, questions the rhetoric of the 1991 Gulf War, taking into account how the portrayal of bombs as "smart" helped soften objections to military policy. Watten's work testifies to how such metaphors are integral to historical narratives that disguise real damage.

BIBLIOGRAPHY

Davidson, Michael. "'Skewed by Design': From Act to Speech Act in Language Writing." In *Artifice and Indeterminacy: An Anthology of New Poetics*, edited by Christopher Beach. Tuscaloosa: University of Alabama Press, 1998, pp. 70–76.

Smith, Rod, ed. *Aerial 8: Barrett Watten*. Washington, D.C.: Edge Books, 1995.

James Zeigler

"THE WEARY BLUES" LANGSTON HUGHES (1926) The title poem of his first collection, LANGSTON HUGHES's "The Weary Blues" is a landmark in African-American poetry. It features Hughes's first use of American blues in a poem, which set the precedent for the incorporation of black musical forms in poetry by such artists as ROBERT HAYDEN, STERLING BROWN, MICHAEL S. HARPER, and YUSEF KOMUNYAKAA, among others. The poem won first prize in a literary contest sponsored by *Opportunity* magazine, a publication of the Urban League, and this success helped land Hughes his first book publication, *The Weary Blues* (1926). Ostensibly narrated by Hughes himself, the poem describes an encounter with an old blues pianist and singer in Harlem. With its blues lyrics and rhythms, the poem evokes the singer's weariness, disappointment, and mournfulness, suggesting not only the difficulties, but also the stoic resilience, of African-American society.

As Arnold Rampersand notes, Hughes wrote "The Weary Blues" in 1923 after visiting a Harlem cabaret, and the sense of a musical encounter is evident throughout. Yet this encounter is anything but mere entertainment. Steven C. Tracy finds that in the weary blues singer, "Hughes presents the flip-side of the romantic vaudeville blues image of the wild and celebrated jazz player, good-timing his way through life" (220). Such a reversal counters the stereotype of the black minstrel and forces a confrontation with the social and economic realities of African-American life. The narrator finds himself drawn to the blues singer, and Hughes evokes this connection in the opening lines through a dangling modifier: "Droning a drowsy syncopated tune, / Rocking back and forth to a mellow croon, / I head a Negro play." Like many other artists in the HARLEM RENAISSANCE, Hughes promoted African-American art and culture as a way of strengthening black pride and unity, and the way the poem's narrative style adopts the blues singer's rhythms and phrasings for its own suggests how powerful Hughes believed the communal force of African-American art to be.

The narrator encountered the singer "on Lenox Avenue the other night / By the pale dull pallor of an old gas light," a somber, urban setting related to the weariness of the singer, whose plaintive blues lyrics Hughes describes as "Sweet Blues! / Coming from a black man's soul. / O Blues!" Hughes echoes the parallel patterns of blues music throughout, not only in the singer's voice, but also in the narrator's, who describes the singer by saying, "He did a lazy sway. . . . / He did a lazy sway . . . / To the tune o' those Weary Blues." Although the narrator never reveals his own circumstances, what he chooses to describe indicates much about his character. As he listens to the music, the narrator develops a sympathetic relation with the singer, who thus becomes his mirror or double, and the poem's themes of dissatisfaction, loneliness, sadness, and world-weariness come to be shared by both men.

At the end Hughes rounds out the poem by returning to an element of setting. He evokes the singer's total exhaustion after the performance by describing how "The stars went out and so did the moon." But the image does not connote a negative experience; on the contrary, Hughes suggests that singing the blues provides the singer with a catharsis, or purging of the emotions, so that although he is wearied by the failures, disappointments, and loneliness of life, his effort to express his emotions ultimately relieves him of them. That catharsis, achieved not by avoiding the difficulties of life but by fixing them in a musical form, frees him from them, so that although "the Weary

Blues echoed through his head" when the singer went home to bed, Hughes writes that "He slept like a rock or a man that's dead."

BIBLIOGRAPHY

Rampersand, Arnold. "The Poetry of the Harlem Renaissance." In *The Columbia History of American Poetry,* edited by Jay Parini and Brett C. Miller, 452–476. New York: Columbia University Press, 1993.

Tracy, Steven C. *Langston Hughes and the Blues.* Urbana: University of Illinois Press, 1988.

Temple Cone

"WEED PULLER" THEODORE ROETHKE (1948)

One of many free verse, LYRIC poems THEODORE ROETHKE wrote about his childhood experiences among the family greenhouses run by his father, "Weed Puller" features Roethke's rich vegetal language, his understated comic irony, and his use of archetypal imagery to convey the profundity of childhood experiences. As Roethke describes his boyhood chore of pulling weeds, overgrown plants, and assorted debris from the various drains in the greenhouse, his tone is conflicted. The speaker relishes the sinuous names and descriptions of plants, but the chore abases him, leaving him "Crawling on all fours." As poet Edward Hirsch notes, "The family greenhouse was for Roethke both sacred and abysmal ground, simultaneously a natural world and an artificial realm, a locale of generation and decay, order and chaos" (xix).

The poem opens from the perspective of a speaker already on hands and knees, "Hacking at black hairy roots," and we are invited to identify the speaker as the young Roethke himself, for as scholar Bernard Quetchenbach notes, "Roethke's intimate imagery locates the poem's perspective precisely and autobiographically" (45). Having brought the reader down with him "Under the concrete benches," Roethke describes the almost decadent life thriving at the ground level of the greenhouse. The language here is richly alliterative, the repeated consonant sounds suggesting the plants' dense material quality, and the sonic richness conflicts with the repulsion the speaker clearly feels toward this vegetable world. Hirsch argues that Roethke's greenhouse correlates to the poet's psychological state: "Roethke was compulsively conscious of the agony of birth, the painful effort of things to emerge out of an underworld swarming with malevolent forces" (xix). More specifically, this hidden world correlates with Roethke's own understanding of the psychological sources of poetry, for as he wrote in his notebooks, "Deep in their roots, all flowers keep the light" (*Selected,* 130). The boy, like the poet, finds himself literally and figuratively in an underworld, one that counters the romantic idealization of nature with the image of an incessant life force whose power, however repulsive, is one with the poet's own impulse to create; as Quetchenbach notes, "Roethke's greenhouse . . . derives its meaning not primarily from its appropriateness as a symbol [of Eden], or even its nearness at hand, but from its particular ties to the poet's personal life history" (44).

"Hacking," "[d]igging," "yanking," "[t]ugging," the speaker engages in an intensely physical, almost sexual manner with "Those lewd monkey-tails hanging from drainholes," and his sense of "The indignity of it!" would be almost comic if not for the desperate contrast that this vegetable underworld makes with "everything blooming above me, / Lilies, pale-pink cyclamen, roses." The nascent lyric poet, confronted with the intense floral beauty blooming above him, realizes the source of his inspiration is at ground level, "down in that fetor of weeds," in the unconscious, where vitality itself, conveyed by lush consonants and rhythms, outranks beauty as the central principle of life. The poet feels disgust at this underworld of the unconscious, but realizes it is the one force that keeps him "Alive, in a slippery grave." Caught between the flowering world above and the dark roots below, Roethke survives in poetry's intermediary place, where fecund growth never ceases, and where the flower of beauty is always close to blossoming.

BIBLIOGRAPHY

Quetchenbach, Bernard W. *Back from the Far Field: American Nature Poetry in the Late Twentieth Century.* Charlottesville: University Press of Virginia, 2000.

Roethke, Theodore. *Selected Poems,* edited by Edward Hirsch. The Library of America, 2005.

Temple Cone

WELISH, MARJORIE (1944–) Marjorie Welish is a poet, painter, and art critic. An important contemporary innovator, she is often considered alongside NEW YORK SCHOOL poets, such as BARBARA GUEST and JOHN ASHBERY, with whom her early work has been compared. But, like Guest's, Welish's recent books have turned in the direction of LANGUAGE poetics. Theoretical and disjunctive, melodic and complex, her poems can seem difficult to approach. The emphasis is on process and the multiple ways we make meaning.

Born in New York City, Welish studied art history at Columbia University and began contributing art reviews to local newspapers while still a student. Since then she has written articles and criticism for *Art in America, Art International,* and *ARTnews,* and she has provided the catalogues for various exhibitions. She has won many major awards and fellowships for her poetry and her painting, including the New York Foundation for the Arts Fellowship in 1990 and the Howard Foundation Fellowship in 1998. She has taught at the Pratt Institute in Brooklyn. Her books of poetry are *Handwritten* (1979), *Two Poems* (1981), *The Windows Flew Open* (1991), *Casting Sequences* (1993) and *The Annotated "Here"* (2000). A volume of criticism, *Signifying Art: Essays on Art after* 1960, was published in 1999.

Welish's poems do not communicate experience or an image of the world directly. They focus on our visual and linguistic means of apprehending the world. Lacking a central point of reference, the result can be disorienting. As "Respected, Feared, and Somehow Loved" (1991) explains, "In the long run we must fix our compass, / and implore our compass" in our search for direction. Instead of offering a renewed center, she opts for a poetics of *openness* (a key term for Welish) and indeterminacy, actively involving the reader in the making of poetic meaning. "The Poetry Project" (1993) simultaneously describes both reader and poem: "A wave tangled up in itself, as though antirational / . . . information making no sense."

Welish's association with Language poetry is not surprising, given that her poems are highly self-reflexive. But it is her persistent redefinition of LYRIC POETRY that places her squarely within the realm of Language poetry, next to such figures as LYN HEJINIAN and RACHEL BLAU DUPLESSIS, whose work is explicitly feminist. Standard accounts of the lyric assume a subjectivity and expressiveness that a Welish poem never asserts. As Welish has said of Guest in her online essay "The Lyric Lately" (1999), "The poet talking to herself is not at issue. . . . The impersonal, not the personal, is valid."

BIBLIOGRAPHY

Gery, John. "Ashbery's Menagerie and the Anxiety of Affluence" In *The Tribe of John: Ashbery and Contemporary Poetry,* edited by Susan M. Schultz. Tuscaloosa: University of Alabama Press, 1995.

O'Sullivan, Maggie. *Out of Everywhere: Linguistically Innovative Poetry by Women in North America & the UK.* Cambridge: Reality Street Editions, 1996.

Welish, Marjorie. "The Lyric Lately," Jacket. Available online. URL: www.jacket.zip.com.au/jacket10/welish-on-guest.html. Downloaded March 2002.

David Chirico

"WE REAL COOL" GWENDOLYN BROOKS (1960) One of the most celebrated examples of jazz poetry, "We Real Cool" evokes the tragic verve of black teenagers with sympathy and unflinching clarity. GWENDOLYN BROOKS published the lyric as part of *The Bean Eaters,* a 1960 collection noted for its explicit critique of the way in which American society denied opportunity to African Americans. "We Real Cool" does not condemn or romanticize the urban black youth it presents; instead the poem's rhythmic energy and colloquial diction bring to light an ignored milieu. The poem belongs to a tradition of politically concerned jazz poetry developed earlier by LANGSTON HUGHES and, later, by AMIRI BARAKA.

The poem tells the story of seven youths who spend their days playing pool at "the Golden Shovel" pool hall. Composed of eight sentences, the poem describes how the unnamed youths quit school, stay up late, perfect their pool shots—"We / Strike straight"—and their fighting abilities, talk tough, drink alcohol, and cavort with women. Brooks's portrait of the youths complements her portraits in other poems and in the work of African-American literature in general of black men whose lives are defined by limited and squandered opportunities.

Significantly the youths in "We Real Cool" either speak as a chorus or are spoken for by one of their unnamed members; no one has a distinct, individual identity: "The boys have no accented sense of themselves, yet they are aware of a semi-defined personal importance," Brooks explains (185). The resort to a collective identity, in part, typifies adolescence, a period in which youths do not have the full legal rights of an individual adult. The individual anonymity also represents the way in which black youths often are seen as a collective "other" rather than as fully distinguished—and deserving—individuals.

Yet Brooks presents characters who respond in a psychologically complex way to their circumstances. The opening sentence, "We real cool," allows the speakers to assert a sense of stoical pride in the face of difficulty. Although widely used in American society, *cool* originally was a black term and outlook that, like the blues, provided a way to preserve self-respect in a society that accorded little value to African Americans. The poem's opening insouciance is then detailed in the next six sentences, which describe the youth's exploits. While these claims represent bragging, they cumulatively paint a bleak portrait whose ultimate end is realized and stated bluntly at the poem's conclusion, which acknowledges imminent death.

Adding to the pathos of the poem is its jazz style. Instead of using strong rhyming couplets, Brooks improvises: She syncopates the lines by ending on "We," a move that creates a halting, variable rhythm. The use of strong rhyme and alliteration, the forceful spondaic beat of single-syllable words, and the staccato effect of three-word sentences contrast with the enjambment to evoke psychological nuance. "The ending WEs in 'We Real Cool' are tiny, wispy, weakly argumentative 'Kilroy-is-here' announcements," Brooks notes. "Say the 'We' softly" (185).

BIBLIOGRAPHY

Brooks, Gwendolyn. *Report from Part One.* Detroit: Broadside Press, 1972.

Mootry, Maria K., and Gary Smith, eds. *A Life Distilled: Gwendolyn Brooks, Her Poetry and Fiction.* Urbana: University of Illinois Press, 1987.

George W. Layng

WHALEN, PHILIP (1923–2002) Philip Whalen is a West Coast BEAT poet whose poetry records a humane responsiveness to everyday experience in a deployment of "open-field" poetics (see BLACK MOUNTAIN SCHOOL and ARS POETICAS). His poetry is also noted for its wonderfully absurdist humor and its Zen Buddhist perspective of nonjudgmental receptivity to the things, words, and thoughts of the world.

Whalen grew up outside Portland, Oregon, and attended Reed College, where his classmates included GARY SNYDER and Lew Welch. In 1955 Whalen participated in the famous Six Gallery reading in San Francisco where ALLEN GINSBERG gave the first sensational reading of *HOWL.* Much of Whalen's poetry of the 1950s and 1960s is gathered in *On Bear's Head* (1969), one of the major poetry volumes of the period. After spending most of 1966 to 1971 in Japan, Whalen became an *unsui,* or Zen monk, and for many years he was an abbot in San Francisco. His poetry of the 1970s is collected in *Heavy Breathing* (1983).

Whalen characterized his poetry as a "picture or graph of the mind moving" that aims to give a sense of gestural immediacy (50). Central to Whalen's poetic practice is notebook or journal composition: a daily and unpremeditated approach to writing, in which anything the poet happens to notice, experience, read, or think about comes into the work. The extension of Whalen's writing practice to include doodling and calligraphic script is mostly lost in his printed volumes. While tracking the leaping movements of his thoughts and perceptions, Whalen's self-reflexive writing process becomes the occasion for unanticipated tangents the poem pursues. This self-awareness also manifests itself in the humorous deflation of any tendency toward excessive self-seriousness, and in this sense Whalen stands against the prophetic earnestness of many other Beat and SAN FRANCISCO RENAISSANCE poets with whom he has been closely associated. Whalen's fine ear for the American colloquial accounts for much of the vitality and intimacy of his work, yet it is not self-tormented or typically CONFESSIONAL, despite a persistent sense of aloneness and uncertainty.

Whalen's work can be read as a sequence in process, and much of the best is found in his longer poems, carefully pieced together from the notebooks (see LONG

AND SERIAL POETRY). The early "Sourdough Mountain Lookout" (1956) records daily details and thoughts during the summer the poet spent working alone in a fire tower. Moving beyond his sense of loneliness, he ruminates on transience and history, the interconnectedness of here and elsewhere, of the private self and the larger cosmos, all of which culminates in an epiphanic acceptance that is characteristically counterbalanced by a final witty matter-of-factness: "Like they say, 'Four times up, / Three times down.' I'm still on the mountain."

BIBLIOGRAPHY

Christensen, Paul. "Philip Whalen." In *The Beats: Literary Bohemians in Postwar America.* Part 2, edited by Ann Charters, 554–572. Detroit: Gale Research, 1983.

Davidson, Michael. *The San Francisco Renaissance: Poetics and Community at Mid-century.* New York: Cambridge University Press, 1989, pp. 112–124.

Whalen, Philip. "Since You Ask Me." In *Overtime: Selected Poems,* edited by Michael Rothenberg, 50. Penguin, 1999.

Jeffrey Twitchell-Waas

"WHAT ARE YEARS?" MARIANNE MOORE **(1941)** Built upon a series of abstract, syntactically complex questions about the nature of courage, MARIANNE MOORE's "What Are Years?" is a call to moral fortitude. It examines the relation between weakness and strength, finding a paradoxical liberty in the acceptance of humankind's bondage to mortality and vulnerability. Unlike many of her earlier poems, "What Are Years?" is not a description of a material object or living being, but a deft comparative analysis of multiple abstractions. Yet the precision and attentiveness of Moore's well-known animal poems "The FISH" and "The PANGOLIN" are apparent even here, and much like the Metaphysical poetry of John Donne, Moore's "What Are Years?" extends and unfolds from its original idea, challenging the reader to join Moore in a keener vision of the relations between courage, mortality, and eternity.

Like many of Moore's poems, "What Are Years?" is written in syllabics, with each line featuring a set number of syllables. As a result of this patterning, Moore's enjambments fall in surprising places, sundering new meanings from the unit of the line itself. At the beginning, Moore asks, "What is our innocence, / what is our guilt? All are / naked, none is safe," and the placement of "All are" implies that this guilt is universal. The poem is also irregularly rhymed, and with its numerous enjambments, the recurrent sounds echo like faintly heard bells, suggesting links between words, images, and ideas without propounding them. Thus, "What Are Years?" reflects at a formal level Moore's undogmatic but nevertheless relentless philosophical inquiry of the abstractions she introduces in her initial questions. As Catherine Paul notes, the method of inquiry in "What Are Years?" is repeated throughout the collection in which it was published, *What Are Years?* (1941), and since this was the first widely available volume of her poetry which Moore herself edited (T. S. ELIOT had edited her first widely marketed collection), Paul argues, "the book seems to offer readers Moore displaying Moore" (98).

The abstractions Moore names are difficult ones to exemplify, and the relative absence of image in a poem by Moore, who was known for her rich detail, is conspicuous indeed. Moore may be suggesting the absence of such qualities from the world itself; given that the poem was finished in 1939, and that Moore scorned French collaboration with Nazi Germany, such an assertion may not be far off. John M. Slatin argues that "the inertness of the language" (79) stands metaphorically for ideological fixity, which the fluid form of the poem resists. To offer answers to her questions, whether through direct statement or through symbols, would be a capitulation to ideology; for Moore, courage is distinguished by its restless, humble inquiry, which even "in its defeat, stirs // the soul to be strong."

The paradox of liberating limitation, which was memorably portrayed by Moore's friend W. H. AUDEN in his poem "IN MEMORY OF W.B. YEATS," is captured in the poem's final image, where Moore describes a caged bird whose "mighty singing / says, satisfaction is a lowly / thing, how pure a thing is joy." Marie Baroff associates the cage and the archaic word "lowly" with Moore's unstated but ever-present Christian vision, "evident especially in poems that celebrate the voluntary meekness of a powerful being" (61). But more generally, it reflects an acceptance of mortality that can liberate humans from dread of the unknown, thereby enabling them to pursue moral, courageous acts in this world that will be remembered and judged in eternity.

BIBLIOGRAPHY

Baroff, Marie. "Marianne Moore's Promotional Prose." In *Marianne Moore,* edited by Harold Bloom, 43–72. New York: Chelsea House Publishers, 1987.

Holley, Margaret. *The Poetry of Marianne Moore: A Study in Voice and Value.* New York: Cambridge University Press, 1987.

Paul, Catherine. "Marianne Moore's Curatorial Method." *Studies in the Literary Imagination* 32, no. 1 (1999): 91–114.

Slatin, John M. "The Town's Assertiveness: Marianne Moore and New York City." In *Marianne Moore: Woman and Poet,* edited by Patricia C. Willis, 61–82. Orono, Maine: National Poetry Foundation, Inc, 1990.

Temple Cone

"THE WHEELCHAIR BUTTERFLY"

JAMES TATE (1969) Exemplary of the surrealist poetry popularized by such poets as GERALD STERN, CHARLES SIMIC, and MARK STRAND in the 1960s, JAMES TATE's free verse lyric "The Wheelchair Butterfly" defies easy explication but nevertheless demonstrates many of Tate's trademark qualities: surprising imagery, offbeat humor, and a concern with the interactions between individual humans in social communities. Here, Tate explores how the imagination unites individuals into a community through a shared sense of fragility and injury, that sense enhanced by the suggested fragility of the imagination itself. But Tate's poem does not attempt to describe the imagination systematically or to praise it in quasi-religious fashion like the romantic poets; rather, "The Wheelchair Butterfly" depicts the irrational workings of the imagination itself, coupling unlike images in startling fashion, leaping intuitively across narrative gaps, and leaving numerous ideas and narratives incomplete, but evocatively so.

The poem is an apostrophe addressed to an unidentified, modern city that Tate describes as a "sleepy city of reeling wheelchairs," "underground town / of electrical wheelchairs," and a "confident city." By associating the city with fragility and the unconscious, Tate makes it a metaphor for the imagination itself, so that the city's inhabitants represent many of the features and workings of the imagination. Yet Tate does not treat the city inhabitants simply as allegories; individual figures may resist explanation, though patterns of imagery allow for general interpretation and thus provide useful points of contrast for individual figures. For instance, throughout the poem, many individuals are in motion, a characteristic that suggests the rapid transformations the imagination undergoes. Yet Tate contrasts this general pattern of movement with a central image of stasis, "a butterfly [that] froze / in midair." The image recalls the Greek symbol of the psyche, itself associated with the imagination; it also recalls the title of the poem, though only partly, for there is no wheelchair suggested in the image. Yet when one considers how a wheelchair is both a sign of injury and a means of coping with injury, then Tate's thematic argument about the fragility and power of the imagination is made clear. When Tate writes that the butterfly is "plucked like a grape / by a child who swore he could take care // of it," he suggests that the imagination itself can be injured, and can only be protected (with no assurance that it will be) by one whose mind has not completely embraced logic at the expense of irrational play: that is, a child.

Such figurative connections operate largely at an intuitive level, though that does not make them less precise, only less easy to describe in conventional terms. Tate's surrealism promises a rebirth for the injured human soul, "the wheelchair butterfly," for although "the ordinary hornets in a human's heart / may slumber and snore . . . / we wait in our loose attics for a new season." But the world of restrictive reason still threatens to confine the imagination, as Tate suggests in a series of warnings at the conclusion of the poem. "Beware a velvet tabernacle!" Tate exclaims, "Beware the Warden of Light has married / An old piece of string!" Evoking figures for institutional religion, law, and reason, Tate warns that they threaten to confine the imagination, represented by the city, by means of ordinary, humdrum reality, represented by the old piece of string. But Tate's startling, funny, vibrant poem is its own underground resistance movement against such governance, promising the reader an anarchic utopia of the psyche.

BIBLIOGRAPHY
Gioia, Dana. "James Tate and American Surrealism." *Denver Quarterly* 33, no. 3 (1998): 70–80.
McDaniel, Craig. "James Tate's Secret Co-pilot." *New England Review* 23, no. 2 (2002): 55–72.

Temple Cone

WHEELWRIGHT, JOHN (1897–1940) John Brooks Wheelwright first established himself while an undergraduate at Harvard, with the so-called Harvard Aesthetes, which included E. E. CUMMINGS, Malcolm Cowley, and other experimental poets. In 1934, two years after joining the Socialist Party, he formed the Vanguard Verse movement with like-minded poets.

Wheelwright was born in Milton, Massachusetts, into a Unitarian Boston Brahmin family. The most significant event in Wheelwright's life was his father's suicide in 1912. From this experience came a spiritual revelation that drew the teenaged Wheelwright to the Anglican faith. He became a socialist in 1932 and edited *Arise,* the Socialist Party's cultural venue. Two years later he was recognized by the *Nation* as one of the outstanding revolutionary poets in the United States. All the same he never abandoned his Anglicanism. His poems are fusions of high church belief and left-wing rhetoric. His published volumes are: *North Atlantic Passage* (1925), *Rock and Shell* (1933), the sonnet sequence *Mirrors of Venus* (1938), *Political Self-Portrait* (1940), and the unfinished *Dusk to Dusk,* which appeared in its entirety in *Collected Poems* (1972).

In many ways Wheelwright fits the category of the "New England poet," subscribing to a theory of poetics that is, in the words of two critics, "recognizably Emersonian. . . . Like Emerson, he conceived of poetry as an unsettling force that would liberate people by rousing them from their daily habits of thought" (Rosenfeld and Damon 321, 325).

This tradition is the canvas on which his Anglicanism and his radical politics found fusion, as in his poem "Plantation Drouth" (1933), in which images of a depression-era dustbowl plantation ("It is April in the meadows / but, in the empty rice fields / it is winter") mix with thinly veiled references in the final lines to Satan ("One horned beast trots from the herd"). Alan Wald has written that "[t]he atmosphere of the poem is ominously prophetic as the poet surveys the economic wasteland of the South." Nor is the demonic symbolism lost on Wald: "Diabolical allusions constitute one source of its menacing tone—the sulfurous environment of smoldering cedar and smoking fields, the goat depicted as a 'horned beast.'"

By the time his life was ended prematurely by a drunk driver, Wheelwright was an unlikely member of a small group of Trotskyist poets working in Boston. Despite the Marxism of his comrades, he remained a devout Christian to the end.

BIBLIOGRAPHY
Rosenfeld, Alvin H., and S. Foster Damon. "John Wheelwright: New England's Colloquy with the World." *Southern Review* 8 (1972): 310–328.
Wald, Alan. "'Plantation Drouth' in Context." In *The Poetry and Politics of John Wheelwright and Sherry Mangan.* Chapel Hill: University of North Carolina Press, 1983.

Andrew E. Mathis

"WHY I AM NOT A PAINTER" FRANK O'HARA (1971) An exuberant exploration of the ways that personality and play create and shape both poetry and painting, FRANK O'HARA's "Why I Am Not a Painter" is a significant ARS POETICA of the NEW YORK SCHOOL of poetry. The poem charts the parallel creation and development of a painting called "SARDINES" by O'Hara's friend, the painter Mike Goldberg, and of a poem by O'Hara himself, called "Oranges." With characteristically comic zest and spontaneity, O'Hara expresses delight in the visual arts and in the often absurd collaboration of artists, and while "Why I Am Not a Painter" at first seems to contrast painting with poetry, O'Hara's focus on creation and revision, rather than on the artwork produced, offers a textured metaphor for the artistic process and for the play of the imagination as a whole.

"I am not a painter, I am a poet," begins O'Hara, immediately raising questions about what distinguishes the two art forms. At first, it appears that O'Hara means to contrast painting as an art of erasure with poetry as an art of amplitude; Goldberg takes out every trace of SARDINES from his painting except for the letters, saying "It was too much," while O'Hara produces page after page of a poem called ORANGES, until "My poem / is finished and I haven't mentioned / orange yet. It's twelve poems." (Ironically, O'Hara did write an earlier poem called "Oranges: 12 Pastorals," to which this poem alludes.) Yet this distinction may be a false one, made in jest. The critic Marjorie Perloff explains that O'Hara was once asked if he ever wanted to be a painter, and he said yes, but that painting required more concentration. Perloff finds O'Hara's response was characteristically tongue-in-cheek, for few of the abstract expressionists and Pop Artists O'Hara knew exhibited much concentration of their own. Perloff adds that "O'Hara is a poet not a painter for no better reason than that is what he *is*. But of course the poem is also saying that poetry and painting are part of the same spectrum" (112).

Perloff's claim that poetry and painting share the same creative spectrum is reinforced by O'Hara's use of equal-length stanzas (13 lines each) to describe first the process of Goldberg's painting, then the process of his own writing. The phrase "days go by," repeated in both stanzas, also links the two art forms, emphasizing O'Hara's view of art as daily process, not a singular event. After initially claiming to be a poet, O'Hara explains his position: "Why? I think I would rather be / a painter, but I am not." The initial enjambment is telling here. O'Hara not only might prefer to be a painter, but also simply "to be"; that is, to exist in a stable, static identity. Yet he is pushed by imagination's restless playfulness not simply to be, but to become, to maintain a constant state of creative metamorphosis. Describing the various transformations of Mike Goldberg's painting "SARDINES" and O'Hara's own poem "Oranges," O'Hara expresses a key principle in his poetic vision: art is endlessly transforming itself, driven by the desire not to be stuck in a single form but to take on as many conceivable forms as possible.

For O'Hara creativity is made possible by divesting its creations of generic labels and arbitrary divisions, and one of his primary methods for breaking down such divisions is humor. In "Why I Am Not a Painter," O'Hara parodies the semi-naïve tone of much mainstream, post-CONFESSIONAL poetry by omitting the grammatical connections between sentences, suggesting the powerful workings of the nonrational (and thus nongrammatical) unconscious. On first seeing the painting in the studio, O'Hara tells Goldberg, "'You have SARDINES in it.' / 'Yes, it needed something there.' / 'Oh.'" But false naïvete isn't the only target here. O'Hara also parodies the overly serious tones of such MODERNIST poetic manifestos as EZRA POUND's "A Few Don'ts by an Imagist" when he writes that his new poem "is even in / prose, I am a real poet." In this poem, which Perloff calls one of his greatest (112), O'Hara shows the true artistic imagination to be critical of pretense, comically self-aware, and exuberantly delighted in "how terrible orange is / and life."

BIBLIOGRAPHY

Moramarco, Fred. "John Ashbery and Frank O'Hara: The Painterly Poets." *Journal of Modern Literature* 5, no. 3 (1976): 436–462.

Perloff, Marjorie. *Frank O'Hara: Poet among Painters.* New York: George Braziller, 1977.

Temple Cone

WIENERS, JOHN (1934–2002) Considered both a BEAT writer and a practitioner of the "projective verse" of CHARLES OLSON and the BLACK MOUNTAIN poets, Wieners combined the poetic with the political and personal in his lyrical free verse (see PROSODY AND FREE VERSE); as he once said, "Lyricism is still a quality of a political career" (112). Donald Allen's groundbreaking 1960 anthology *The New American Poetry* (see POETRY ANTHOLOGIES) includes Wieners among new poets "who have evolved their own original styles and new conceptions of poetry" (xiii). Similar to HART CRANE, Wieners is considered *le poète maudit,* a poet who is cursed by the penetrating vision that allows him to see the alienation and loneliness inherent in his society.

Wieners was born in Boston, and graduated from Boston College. After hearing Olson read, he attended Black Mountain College for a year, then returned to Boston, where he published the literary magazine *Measure.* He moved to California in 1957 and connected with ROBERT DUNCAN, the painter Robert LaVigne, and other members of the SAN FRANCISCO RENAISSANCE. He was involved in antiwar and antiracism movements, and he defended the rights of women and homosexuals. Wieners was hospitalized periodically for drug and mental problems. His first book of poetry, *The Hotel*

Wentley Poems, was published in 1958; his other works include *Ace of Pentacles* (1964), *The Asylum Poems (For My Father)* (1969), and *Behind the State Capital* (1975). His *Selected Poems 1958–1984* was released in 1986.

Wieners's poetry is often CONFESSIONAL, echoing the sensibility of a person who despises the way he is, yet who celebrates his differences from conventional society. It reflects a deeply personal engagement with the world and with the reader, at times eloquently yet brutally frank. Like many of the BEATS, Wieners finds his subject in what he sees as the debased and decadent elements of life—poverty, drugs, homosexuality, insanity, despair, violence—but he also celebrates the joy of creation and of art itself. In "A Poem for Painters" (1958), he laments "Our age bereft of nobility," but he attempts to recover what is lost by turning to love and art. He crafts the poem like a painter, creating images with words, "Drawing the face / and its torture." His creative act is one of redemption that expresses the struggle of artists to work with the material they have. His later writing delves into the darkness of the human condition; in "Children of the Working Class" (1972), he describes the "poorhouses, the mad city asylums and re- / lief worklines" rather than the American that Walt Whitman wandered. The poem gives voice to the marginalized, to those who have been excluded from the rewards of modern society, and Wieners's personal despair reflects the emotional cost of bearing witness to such public suffering.

BIBLIOGRAPHY

Allen, Donald M., ed. *The New American Poetry 1945–1960.* New York: Grove Press, 1960.

Howard, Richard. "John Wieners: 'Now Watch the Windows Open by Themselves.'" *Iowa Review* 1, no. 1 (1970): 101–118.

Wieners, John. "A Talk with John Wieners," by Robert von Hallberg. *Chicago Review* 26, no. 1 (1974): 112–116.

Gord Beveridge

WILBUR, RICHARD (1921–) Richard Wilbur is arguably the most technically accomplished of the generation of poets born in the 1920s whose early work was influenced by World War II, including HOWARD NEMEROV, JAMES DICKEY, JAMES MERRILL, and LOUIS SIMPSON. Having lived nearly all his life in New England, Wilbur's LYRIC POETRY was greatly influenced by the traditional forms of ROBERT FROST and EDWIN ARLINGTON ROBINSON (see PROSODY AND FREE VERSE). Wilbur was a part of the New Critical school of poetry, which, during the 1950s and 1960s, largely through the influence of A. Richards, JOHN CROWE RANSOM, and ALLEN TATE (see FUGITIVE/AGRARIAN SCHOOL), placed emphasis on a close reading of the work itself rather than psychological or biographical interpretation. Wilbur's work exhibits self-control, wit, grace, craftsmanship, and skill.

Wilbur was born in New York City. He began writing poetry in the army (1942–45). He received a B.A. from Amherst (1942) and an M.A. from Harvard (1947). Wilbur has taught at a number of schools, most recently at Smith College (1977–86). His first book of poetry, *The Beautiful Changes and Other Poems* (1947), was published when he was only 24. Wilbur has received many honors for his poetry and translations, including the Bollingen Prize (1971). His third collection, *Things of This World* (1956), won both the Pulitzer Prize (1957) and the National Book Award (1957). In 1987 he succeeded ROBERT PENN WARREN to become the second poet laureate of the United States, and two years later he received a second Pulitzer Prize for his *New and Collected Poems.* He is a member and past president of the American Academy of Arts and Letters. In 2003 he won the Academy of American Poets' WALLACE STEVENS Award for demonstrated achievement and ability, and in 2006 he received the prestigious Ruth Lilly Poetry Prize.

As Wendy Salinger has commented, Wilbur "has always been praised for his virtuosity but too often praised and *dismissed* because of it" (20). RANDALL JARRELL, in a review of Wilbur's second book, *Ceremony and Other Poems* (1950), summed up for many readers their distrust of Wilbur's early success and what they perceived as his lack of risk-taking: "Wilbur never goes too far, but he never goes far enough" (qtd. in Salinger 48–49). As an advocate of traditional blank verse that is at odds with the free verse of his contemporaries, Wilbur's response is that, far from being restrictive, "formal verse is . . . emotionally comfortable" (27) and that the traditional techniques he employs have "freeing effects" (92).

Robert Hill has identified four qualities in Richard Wilbur's poetry: "a speculative and logical temper, sharp and true observation, technical virtuosity, and a kind of amused good humor" (19). From the beginning Wilbur was been noted for the ease and maturity of his writing. Despite his criticism Jarrell acknowledged Wilbur's skill and charm as a poet. Such poems as "Still, Citizen Sparrow" and "The Death of a Toad," both from *Ceremony,* show Wilbur's agility, but they also have a "deliberate extravagance" (Hill 80). In Peter Sacks's view, this collection leaves behind the earlier influence of Edgar Allan Poe's dream world and "dramatizes Wilbur's intended celebration of the 'things of this world'" (550). In "The Death of a Toad," for example, a common toad, even with its dying eyes, is still able "To watch . . . The haggard daylight steer." Hill sees this poem as a "gentle but high-spirited mockery" (80) that is also extravagant in its language.

"LOVE CALLS US TO THE THINGS OF THIS WORLD" (1955), a definite shift in Wilbur's poetry and the title poem from what he calls his "best book" (190), is perhaps the finest example of Wilbur's preoccupation with the imagination, which Hill identifies in Wilbur as an "active, transforming, and enriching light" (190). In the poem the soul or, alternately, the imagination "shrinks / from all that it is slow to remember," yet it must impose itself on an awakened world and clothe both "the backs of thieves" and "the heaviest nuns" so that they can live in the real world. In this third collection, Wilbur simplified his language and became more direct in his observations, as is evident in "Digging for China" (1952). The speaker realizes his goal of digging to China has come to nothing physically, but he still finds it in his altered senses: "Until I got my balance back again / All that I saw was China, China, China." In his next collection, *Advice to a Prophet* (1961), Wilbur's technical skill and grace of language find a "new outspokenness, an open commitment to personal views and feelings" (Hill 129). The imagination must be involved with the things of this world, as Wilbur himself notes: "To me, the imagination is a faculty which fuses things, takes hold of the physical and ideal world and makes them one" (185).

Many critics also see a moral design and religious quality to Wilbur's poems. Robert Sayre argues that "Wilbur is at present America's most profound moralist of man's relation with nature" (quoted in Salinger 161). Wilbur credits being raised on a farm for his "use of natural imagery" (13). He begins with the external world, the observed incident, that then takes on form shaped by the material: "Generally, what starts me off is a perception of something in the external world in which I feel the potentiality of an idea" Wilbur (23). Material objects, like a toad or wash on a line, dominate his poems and are then transformed by the imagination. In the title poem from *Walking to Sleep* (1969), the speaker says to "Open your eyes / To the general blackness not of your room alone / But of the sky you trust is over it." In "Seed Leaves" (1964), a poem written in homage to Frost, the leaves emerge, but the plant is "resigned / To being self-defined / Before it commerce with the great universe," a theme common to Wilbur and a useful summary of his view of the nature of poetry: "poetry makes order and asserts relations . . . out of a confidence in ultimate order and relatedness" (Wilbur 54).

The "ultimate order" Wilbur sees in the seed leaves underlies a lifetime devoted to poetry. His work, William Meredith maintains, "has always been about order in the universe" (quoted in Salinger 76). As a poet writing in the formalist tradition, Wilbur continues to exhibit a superb metrical ear and skill in defining poetry's ability to take the things of the world and celebrate their transformation by the mind, which is constantly attuned to nature. Thus Wilbur can be seen as a successor to the American transcendentalists, Ralph Waldo Emerson prominent among them. Wilbur agrees with the Emersonian notion that "all abstract words ultimately derive from things" (72); these things become truth "because the imagination belongs in the world" (51).

BIBLIOGRAPHY

Hill, Donald. *Richard Wilbur.* New York: Twayne, 1967.

Sacks, Peter. "Richard Wilbur." In *American Writers: A Collection of Critical Biographies,* edited by Lee Baechler and A. Walton Litz, 541–565. New York: Charles Scribner's Sons, 1991.

Salinger, Wendy, ed. *Richard Wilbur's Creation.* Ann Arbor: University of Michigan Press, 1983, pp. 153–161.

Wilbur, Richard. *Conversations with Richard Wilbur,* edited by William Butts. Jackson: University Press of Mississippi, 1990.

Gary Kerley

WILLARD, NANCY (1936–) Nancy Willard comes out of a poetic tradition that she describes in *Testimony of the Invisible Man* (1970) as "*Ding*-poetics," pioneered by Rainer Maria Rilke, WILLIAM CARLOS WILLIAMS, and Pablo Neruda, characterized by the "scrupulous examination of concrete things," and carried on in the DEEP IMAGE poetry of ROBERT BLY and JAMES WRIGHT. Willard, like RUSSELL EDSON, has taken this careful realism in the fabulist direction of magic realism, often moving ordinary objects from daily household life into the area of the fantastic or the spiritual within the space of one line. "Mercy is whiter than laundry," she writes in "Angels in Winter" (1982).

Willard was born in Michigan and educated at the University of Michigan and Stanford. Her 11 books of poetry include *Skin of Grace,* which won the Devins Award in 1967, and *A Visit to William Blake's Inn: Poems for Innocent and Experienced Travelers,* which won the Newbery Award for distinguished contribution to American literature for children in 1982.

Her first book, *In His Country,* was published in 1966. It included what was to become a staple of Willard's collections, a group of poems on a unified theme—here the sculptures of Gustav Vigeland in Frogner Park in Oslo. *Household Tales of Moon and Water* (1982) contains a sequence, "My Life on the Road with Bread and Water," which combines elements of road saga, domestic drama, and fantasy. Her "Poems from the Sports Page" sequence, in *Water Walker* (1989), moves from a literal to a spiritual/surreal reading of such headlines as "Foxes Fall to St. Francis," "Giants Meet Reviving Eagles on Monday Night," and "Stars Nip Wings" (see SURREALISM).

Other books have been entirely thematic, rather than simply collections of LYRIC POETRY. *Nineteen Masks for the Naked Poet* (1971) created the persona of a human poet (male) living in a world where one can invite the Moon for supper, enter the sleep of the bees or the eye of the snow, or, as in "The Baker's Wife Tells His Horoscope with Pretzels," have his future revealed by "hundreds of pretzels crossing their arms in prayer." *The Ballad of Biddy Early* (1987), "the wise woman of Clare," is a cycle of poems about a 19th-century Irishwoman reputed to possess magic powers. *Biddy Early* recalls the William Butler Yeats of his Crazy Jane poems in its feeling for place and character, its suggestion of a story in discrete lyrics, and even its use of refrains.

Willard's is a poetry of continuum. With grace, wit, and close observation, she bridges the distinction between children's and adult literature, between humans and angels, between the literal and the fabulous.

BIBLIOGRAPHY

Danis, Francine. "Nancy Willard's Domestic Psalms." *Modern Poetry Studies* 9 (1978): 126–134.
Tillinghast, Richard. "Poems of Innocence and Experience." *Michigan Quarterly Review* 37, no. 4 (fall 1998): 35–37.

Tad Richards

WILLIAMS, C(HARLES) K(ENNETH) (1936–) More than any other postwar poet in the United States, C. K. Williams has frankly and relentlessly challenged the anguish in our living experience. Moreover Williams has explored human suffering without the seemingly rational comfort of a formal philosophical system, such as existentialism (as in the work of W. D. SNODGRASS), without the vague consolation of faith or of a theological framework (as in the work of JOHN BERRYMAN), and certainly without the emotional-aesthetic buffer of a strong sardonic sense in the service of wary dexterity (as in the work of SYLVIA PLATH). "I realized that there was actually other people in the world who were afflicted with the same sensibilities," he has written, "the same moral confusion and uncertainty and despair I was, and realized, too, that I'd have to find a way to somehow include evidence of that in my poems, that there wasn't any point in writing unless I did" (16).

Williams was raised in Newark, New Jersey. His first book was *Lies* (1969). He has received the Morton Dauwen Zabel Prize of the American Academy and Institute of Arts and Letters (1989), the Harriet Monroe Poetry Award (1993), and in 2000, the Pulitzer Prize for his eighth collection, *Repair.* Williams is a member of the American Academy of Arts and Letters. *The Singing* (2003) won the National Book Award.

His early poems, driven by anger, were short units of clipped meter. Those poems are sonorous, yet severe, lashing out against human indifference and duplicity. *With Ignorance* (1977) marked a stylistic and thematic departure, honed by a distinct, visibly recognizable form, stretching the lines of his verse from margin to margin, exploring the psyche with a vernacular, producing a dramatic, curious quality. Critic Ray Olson argues, "His poems are ruefully, wistfully written from the perspective of someone for whom living has become a matter of watching the ongoing project of life rather than being actively immersed in it. This would all be sentimental and mawkish if it weren't for Williams' erudition and that line, that lovely, musical line" (32). His subjects are love and death, secrets kept, pain unexpressed among intimates, social disorder, despair, and everyday epiphanies.

"Grief" (1997), a four-part, 51-line poem covering four full pages of Williams's lengthy 20-plus-syllable lines, approaches his mother's death: "Gone now, after the days of desperate, unconscious gasping, the reflexive staying alive." The details of her dying are the details of his pain. He wonderingly asks himself, "Is this grief?," upon realizing that he is not making a scene, crying, or wishing to follow her in death. Slow, marching lines move in passionate spirals, like the wailing of mourners at a funeral, and build to an ecstasy in which the poet's grief is microscopic in the cosmos demonstrating adjustments made subjectively to a universal world.

BIBLIOGRAPHY

Olson, Ray, *"The Vigil: Poems." Booklist* (March 1997): 32.

Williams, C. K. *Poetry and Consciousness.* Ann Arbor: University of Michigan Press, (1998).

Gerald Schwartz

WILLIAMS, JONATHAN (1929–)

Jonathan Williams's poetry exposes the sublime in the marginalized. Believing that "'poems' are but the *deified* prosaic speech of plain men and women," Williams commonly depicts folk life and language ("Logodaedalist" [1971]). Williams spent time at Black Mountain College in the 1950s, and his work, its dynamic sense of movement and creative use of page space, can be thought of in the context of the BLACK MOUNTAIN SCHOOL; nevertheless the distinctly independent Williams displays a unique, playful exuberance, and wry, eccentric humor. Central to Williams's practice is the notion, rooted in the OBJECTIVIST SCHOOL, of the poem as object and the poet as unencumbering mediator between the mind and reality. As founder and publisher of Jargon Society Press (see POETRY PRESSES), Williams has enabled many poets to gain a wider audience and influence succeeding generations.

Born in Asheville, North Carolina, Williams has traveled extensively, eventually making Highlands, North Carolina, his primary home. In 1961 Williams, an avid hiker, walked 1,457 miles along the Appalachian Trail—from Georgia to New York State. His first book was published in 1959. Williams was one of the original poets in the groundbreaking 1960 anthology, *The New American Poetry* (see POETRY ANTHOLOGIES). In 1998 Williams was inducted into the North Carolina Literary Hall of Fame.

Williams's subject matter is bold and varied, ranging from southern Appalachian life to gay sexuality, classical music, and political satire. His highly experimental work—some of which may be characterized as concrete poetry (see VISUAL POETRY)—often incorporates found material as well as drawings and designs indicative of his talent and early training in the visual arts. Williams also invented "Meta-fours," a poetic form consisting of virtually unpunctuated, four-line poems with four words per line.

In *Mahler* (1964), a book of poems composed spontaneously to each movement of Gustav Mahler's 10 symphonies, Williams often explores the position of the imagination amidst the realities of earthly existence. The second movement of the poem, "Symphony No. 3, in D Minor," insists on nature's agency in the imaginative process, quoting the 19th-century British poet John Clare: *"I found the poems in the fields / And only wrote them down."* For Williams, nature is both subject matter and creator, inviting us to engage the world's infinite possibilities, as in the first movement of "Symphony No. 1, in D Major," in which "the sunshine sings / all things / open."

One of a series of poems documenting the words of southern Appalachian mountain people, "The Hermit

Cackleberry Brown, On Human Vanity" (1971) points out the arrogance of those who see themselves as "bettern / cowflop," when "they aint," a passage perhaps rendered ironic in its presentation of folk language as published poetry, yet revealing, through carefully enhanced line breaks, what Eric Mottram has called Williams's "uncondescending demonstration of commonality" (103). Williams's remarkable ear, sense of daring, and penchant for spontaneous inclusion produce a provocative, hardy, and moving body of work.

BIBLIOGRAPHY

Bassett, John E. "Jonathan Williams." In *Contemporary Poets, Dramatists, Essayists, and Novelists of the South,* edited by Robert Bain and Joseph M. Flora. Westport, Conn.: Greenwood Press, 1994, pp. 525–534.

Mottram, Eric. "Jonathan Williams." *Vort* 4 (1973): 54–75.

Judith Schwartz

WILLIAMS, WILLIAM CARLOS (1883–1963) Although he was deemed a "poets' poet" for most of his life, William Carlos Williams is today considered to be one of the most important modernist writers (see MODERNISM). He employed a large variety of forms and genres (novels, short stories, essays, autobiography, prose poems, long poems, and plays), but he is best known for his short free verse poems dealing with mundane objects in a language that was everyday, yet highly structured (see PROSODY AND FREE VERSE). While heavily influenced by European movements—especially cubism, SURREALISM, and dadaism—he nevertheless always insisted on the necessity of a genuinely American poetry, based on the American idiom and on contact with the immediate experience of local life and surroundings (see EUROPEAN POETIC INFLUENCES). He insisted that "[p]lace is the only universal" ("Axioms" 175) and distanced himself from the cosmopolitanism of the expatriates EZRA POUND and T. S. ELIOT. Instead he looked for role models in modernist American painters and photographers, such as Marsden Hartley, Charles Demuth, Alfred Stieglitz, and Charles Sheeler, and, similar to WALLACE STEVENS and MARIANNE MOORE, he sought to translate the findings of European modernism into an American context.

Williams was born in Rutherford, New Jersey, and, except for several short stays in Europe, spent most of his life there with his wife and his two sons—practicing (since 1910) as a small-town pediatrician, while simultaneously writing his poetry (sometimes in-between patients) and mixing with a crowd of avant-garde artists in nearby New York City on the weekends. After youthful imitations of the romantic John Keats and Walt Whitman, Williams brought out his first "official" book of poems *The Tempers* at the age of 30. The date of the small booklet is significant, since 1913 was also the year when Pound inaugurated the school of "Imagistes" in London (see IMAGIST SCHOOL) and the New York Armory Show brought modernist European painting in to a large American public for the first time. In the years to come, New York experienced the development of a genuine artistic avant-garde, which manifested itself in the opening of numerous (mostly short-lived) little galleries and magazines. Williams, while never aligning himself with any particular "school," quickly became a regular member of this sizzling scene, visiting galleries and private salons, as well as editing and contributing to various "little mags," including *Others* and *Contact* (see POETRY JOURNALS). The years between 1917 and 1923 also saw the publication of his most important early volumes: *Al Que Quiere!* (1917), *Sour Grapes* (1921), and *SPRING AND ALL* (1923), as well as the "surrealistic" prose poems of *Kora in Hell: Improvisations* (1920). These works, however, remained largely unacknowledged by critics, and Williams did not earn a literary prize until 1926, when he was given the *Dial* Award. Several smaller prizes followed in the 1930s and 1940s, but it was only in the 1950s that he received broader recognition with, among other honors, the National Book Award's Gold Medal for Poetry (1950), the Bollingen Prize (1953), and the Fellowship of the American Academy of Poets (1957). Posthumously he received the Pulitzer Prize for his last volume, *Pictures from Brueghel* (1962) in 1963.

The poems of his earlier years are often characterized as still lifes, poetry of things, or even linguistic *objets trouvés* ("found objects"), reminding many critics of Marcel Duchamp's dadaistic "antiart" of the same period (such as Duchamp's notorious "Fountain" of 1917). Descriptions such as these reflect Williams's concentration on the particular, mundane object, which he makes us see in a new light by putting it in the context of a formal piece of poetry. Famous examples of this artistic strategy are such poems as "Between Walls" (1938), "This Is Just to Say" (1934), or the famous "Red wheelbarrow," from *Spring and All,* which declares that "so much depends / upon // a red wheel / barrow." Williams famously stated, "[I]t is no longer what you paint or what you write about that counts but how you do it: how you lay on the pigment, how you place the words to make a picture or a poem" ("American Spirit" 218). The aim of such a formal transformation is the cleansing of the world and of language, the renewal of our perception of the world beyond hackneyed cliché and stereotype. "No ideas but in things" ("A Sort of a Song" [1944]) was Williams's often repeated (and often misunderstood) credo; his poetry is a permanent attempt at "seeing the thing itself without forethought or afterthought but with great intensity of perception," as he notes in the prologue to *Kora in Hell* (1957). Visual perception is what Williams, as well as the more skeptical Stevens, is particularly interested in, and many of his poems are structured along these lines. While the resulting dominance of images and the short free verse form align him with the school of imagism, Williams's concept of the poem itself as a tangible and autonomous object, "a small (or large) machine made of words"—his description in the ("Author's Introduction" to *The Wedge*) (1944) was further developed by LOUIS ZUKOFSKY and the OBJECTIVIST poets in the early 1930s.

During the political and economical crisis of the 1930s, Williams's avant-garde poetry came heavily under attack from leftist critics who demanded that the poet should devote himself to the "real" problems of "the people." Probably as a reaction to this criticism, but also as a consequence of Williams's own political stance, his next book of poems, *An Early Martyr and Other Poems* (1935), included a number of working-class portraits (reminiscent of the photographs of Walker Evans), as did his short stories and novels, which he started writing at the time. All in all, however, the 1930s were a period of artistic crisis for Williams, especially since the New York scene of artists had not fulfilled his hopes for a cultural renewal, and, with the success of Eliot's *The* WASTE LAND (1922), he saw poetry fall back into the hands of "academics."

The 1944 volume *The Wedge* in some ways marks the overcoming of that crisis; after the end of World War II, Williams entered a new phase of creative development, characterized mainly by two linked projects: the work on his long poem *PATERSON* (see LONG AND SERIAL POETRY) and the development of a new prosody—the "triadic" or "step-down line." The latter he discovered while writing a passage for book II of *Paterson* (1948, later separately republished as "The Descent"), which, fittingly, begins:

> The descent beckons
> as the ascent beckoned.

The five books of *Paterson* (1946–63), which build on the central anthropomorphic metaphors man/city and woman/flower, rank with other famous long poems of the early 20th century, including *The Waste Land* (1922), Pound's *CANTOS* (1930–70), and Hart Crane's *The BRIDGE* (1930). Moreover Williams's idea of a structured, yet flexible "variable foot" influenced CHARLES OLSON's concept of "Projective Verse" (see ARS POETICAS). Williams's volumes of poetry in the 1950s, *The Desert Music* (1954) and *Journey to Love* (1955), are written almost completely in this "new measure," which he himself considered to be his "solution of the problem of modern verse" (*Selected Letters* 334).

By the middle of the century, when he was already in his sixties and partly paralyzed by several strokes, Williams had become a tutelary figure for many younger poets, whom he supported and promoted—especially those of the just emerging BEAT generation (among them ALLEN GINSBERG, from Paterson, New Jersey) and the BLACK MOUNTAIN SCHOOL gathered around Olson, ROBERT DUNCAN, and ROBERT CREELEY, including DENISE LEVERTOV. But his influence did not remain limited to the United States; it was soon spreading to Europe as well, to such poets as Charles Tomlinson in Britain.

It was only after his death in 1963, however, that any discernible academic interest in Williams emerged. Studies initially concentrated on his double life as poet and physician, his complicated lifelong friendship with Pound, comparisons of his work with that of Stevens and MARIANNE MOORE, and the influence of painting on his poetry. In the meantime all aspects of his work have been broadly covered by studies, and Williams has become a well-established member of the literary canon. His poetry forms a substantial part of an American tradition that comes from Whitman, Pound, and Moore and leads to Ginsberg, Creeley, and Levertov.

BIBLIOGRAPHY

Axelrod, Steven Gould, and Helen Deese, eds. *Critical Essays on William Carlos Williams.* New York: G. K. Hall, 1995.

Diggory, Terence. *William Carlos Williams and the Ethics of Painting.* Princeton, N.J.: Princeton University Press, 1991.

Mariani, Paul. *William Carlos Williams: A New World Naked.* New York: McGraw-Hill, 1981.

Markos, Donald W. *Ideas in Things: The Poems of William Carlos Williams.* Rutherford, N.J.: Fairleigh Dickinson University Press, 1994.

Riddel, Joseph N. *The Inverted Bell: Modernism and the Counterpoetics of William Carlos Williams.* Baton Rouge: Louisiana State University Press, 1974.

Terrell, Caroll F., ed. *William Carlos Williams: Man and Poet.* Orono, Maine: National Poetry Foundation, 1983.

Williams, William Carlos. "The American Spirit in Art." In *A Recognizable Image: William Carlos Williams on Art and Artists,* edited by Bram Dijkstra. New York: New Directions, 1978, pp. 210–220.

———. "Axioms." In *A Recognizable Image: William Carlos Williams on Art and Artists,* edited by Bram Dijkstra, 175–176. New York: New Directions, 1978.

———. *Selected Letters,* edited by John C. Thirlwall. New York: New Directions, 1957.

Franz Meier

WINTERS, YVOR (1900–1968) Yvor Winters's development runs counter to the usual course of the career of the poet in 20th-century America. Unlike many poets of his generation who broke with traditional poetry to adopt free verse, Winters began his career by following in the footsteps of the great modernists EZRA POUND and T. S. ELIOT, but he later turned against MODERNISM in order to write very traditional verse in regular meter and rhyme (see PROSODY AND FREE VERSE). Winters justified his poetic practice in his critical writings, arguing against modernist poetic experimentation in such books as *Primitivism and Decadence* (1937) and *The Anatomy of Nonsense* (1943). His early style depended on feeling and rhythm for coherence, and it was often difficult to paraphrase, as in the following couplet from "In Winter" (1922): "No Being / I, bent. Thin nights receding." He later turned against this style in favor of a more formal and direct manner, in which ideas could be expressed explicitly. He has been an influence to many other poets, notably J. V. CUNNINGHAM, EDGAR BOWERS, and ROBERT PINSKY.

Born in Chicago, Winters was raised in Eagle Rock, California, which was then a rural area. He attended the University of Chicago but had to abandon his studies due to tuberculosis. He later attended the Universities of Colorado and Idaho, and at Stanford University he earned a Ph.D. After his studies he became a member of the Stanford faculty, teaching several generations of students, including such poets as THOM GUNN, ROBERT HASS, and JOHN MATTHIAS.

Winters's first book, *The Immobile Wind,* was published in 1921 and showed the influence of the IMAGIST SCHOOL of poetry in its sparse language and careful rendering of precise visual details. Winters's engagement with imagism and with modernism in general was strong during the early 1920s, and his correspondence with the poet HART CRANE reflects his misgivings about the modernist movement. By the time *The Proof* was published in 1930, these misgivings had led Winters to reject his early style. "Inscription for a Graveyard" (1930) and "The Empty Hills" (1930), among other poems from this period, are more traditionally formal than Winters's earlier poetry. They also reflect his new sense that the poet's work does not stop when he has rendered the world: He must also make statements about it and judge his experiences. This tendency to judgment (which is as prominent in Winters's literary criticism as it is in his poetry) has led many readers to view Winters as a moralist.

Much of the pleasure in reading Winters, however, comes not from his strong moralism, but from his powerful sense of the western places he knew so well. This is true of the early imagist poems and also of the later work, such as "A View of Pasadena from the Hills" (1947), a classic poem of the California landscape.

BIBLIOGRAPHY

Comito, Terry. *In Defense of Winters: The Poetry and Prose of Yvor Winters.* Madison: University of Wisconsin Press, 1986.

Powell, Grosvenor. *Language as Being in the Poetry of Yvor Winters.* Baton Rouge: University of Louisiana Press, 1980.

Robert Archambeau

"WOODCHUCKS" MAXINE KUMIN (1972)

MAXINE KUMIN calls "Woodchucks" her account of killing a family of woodchucks that was destroying her vegetable and flower gardens, "a terribly autobiographical poem." While this admission ties the setting to Kumin's family farm in Warner, New Hampshire, when coupled with the poem's recurrent Holocaust imagery it creates a powerful self-accusation that questions the individual's relationship to nature, to technology, and to major historical events. The poem opens in medias res with the speaker's recounting of her effort to kill the woodchucks in her garden indirectly, almost anonymously, by means of cyanide gas; when this endeavor fails, the speaker must enact the violence directly with a .22-caliber rifle. This movement from impersonal to personal violence, and the effort to justify the killings, reveals the speaker's own moral conflict with her decision, a conflict at the thematic heart of the poem. In "Woodchucks," Kumin indicts the ease with which modern technology facilitates violence, both toward nature and toward humankind, and she challenges the grand narratives of history with a reminder that history is fashioned by individual ethical decisions.

Written in rhymed sestets of iambic pentameter, "Woodchucks" demonstrates Kumin's interest in revising traditional forms with a modern, conversational voice. Here, the tension between stylized form and intimate voice parallels the tension between Kumin's desire for an indirect, almost anonymous eradication of the pests and the inevitable fact that she will have to kill them directly. Kumin represents the woodchucks as threatening her own efforts at a peaceable country life, though she herself reveals the hyperbole of her accusations that the woodchucks are taking "[t]he food from our mouths" when she calls herself "a lapsed pacifist fallen from grace / puffed with Darwinian pieties for killing." Such dramatic indignation facilitates violence, and Kumin subtly implies that the sense of injustice motivating such acts is often unwarranted; for instance, the roses into which one of the slain woodchucks falls are "everbearing," an indication that the speaker is not motivated by self-defense, but by her "overbearing" desire to possess the natural world around her.

As she details the different woodchucks she kills, Kumin notes how "the murderer inside me rose up hard, / the hawkeye killer came on stage forthwith." Wesley McNair observes that "Given the value of femaleness and nurture in *Up Country* [the volume in which "Woodchucks" first appeared], it is significant that the first animals she kills are two babies and their mother" (124). Violence and evil can be easily found in anyone, Kumin suggests, and she does not exempt herself, nor hold back self-judgment: Kumin, who is Jewish, ultimately compares her efforts to eradicate the woodchucks with the efforts by Nazi Germany to eradicate the Jews in the Holocaust. Having raised the image of cyanide gas in the first line, the poet concludes the poem by stating, regretfully, that it would all have been easier "If only they'd all consented to die unseen / gassed underground the quiet Nazi way." Kumin's reference to the Holocaust, like her earlier reference to "Darwinian pieties," challenges the grand narratives of history by emphasizing the responsibility of individual will. For Kumin, technology may invite or enable anonymity, but in the end, violence is always personal and individual. Any and every human possesses the capacity to kill, as well as to rationalize the violence (the cyanide gas she uses "was featured as merciful, quick at the bone / and the case we had against them was airtight"). Yet despite this chilling insight, Kumin also knows that every human possesses a conscience that ultimately cannot be fooled, and that will keep hunting the rational mind through all its efforts at escape and evasion. Although the speaker's material life is made better by the eradication of the woodchucks from her garden, her own thoughts are chastened and cannot let her go; she notes that the one remaining woodchuck keeps her "cocked and ready day after day after day. / All night I hunt his humped-up form. I dream / I sight along the barrel in my sleep." It is a cold consolation, but an important one given the history of violence in the 20th century, that the mind which knows its own capacities for violence cannot simply accept its having committed a violent act, but will be scourged by its memory "day after day after day."

BIBLIOGRAPHY

McNair, Wesley. "Maxine Kumin's Animal Confederates." In *Telling the Barn Swallow: Poets on the Poetry of Maxine Kumin,* edited by Emily Grosholz, 122–134. Hanover, N.H.: University Press of New England, 1997.

Raz, Hilda. "Maxine Kumin's Sense of Place in Nature." In *Telling the Barn Swallow: Poets on the Poetry of Maxine Kumin,* edited by Emily Grosholz, 98–121. Hanover, N.H.: University Press of New England, 1997.

Temple Cone

"THE WOOD-PILE" ROBERT FROST (1914)

"The Wood-Pile" offers an important example of how ROBERT FROST uses the New England pastoral landscape both as an ironic illustration of nature's indifference toward human life and as a way of considering the process of poetic creation. The poem uses a conventionally romantic subject—a nature walk—to evoke the romantic belief in nature as a source of spiritual rejuvenation and artistic inspiration, but rather than expressing harmony with nature, Frost suggests the limited connection with nature that humans can attain. The world Frost evokes in this blank verse narrative is a lonely, isolated place, where labor is performed for no apparent use but only to create some sort of human meaning in a world without meanings.

The poem begins in the middle of things with a mood of ambivalence, the speaker hesitating to enter "the frozen swamp one grey day," then changing his mind and going in. This sense of reluctance before advancing offers an important initial figure for human attitudes toward truth, particularly the truth nature reveals, as the speaker's emphasis on sight in the third line indicates. "'No, I will go on farther—and we shall see,'" Frost writes, invoking the traditional romantic idea of vision as a means of transcendence. Yet Frost simultaneously questions the possibility of such visionary experience by setting the poem in this swamp, an indistinct place without memorable scenery (in defiance of romantic ideals of the picturesque and the sublime), leaving the speaker unable "to say for certain I was here / Or somewhere else: I was just far from home." This sense of isolation and homelessness thus characterizes the human experience of nature for Frost, and it occasions the need to create meaning that the speaker will later associate with the wood pile.

Frost is not only preoccupied with romantic ideas about nature, but also with the great and lasting influence of romantic poetry, and "The Wood-Pile" is filled with puns on poetry and on fame that indicate Frost's desire to have his work remembered. The speaker regrets that "The view was all in lines / Straight up and down of tall slim trees / Too much alike to mark or name a place by." The lines of the trees correspond to the lines of a poem, and the speaker's regret that their uniformity leaves no way of marking one's territory suggests Frost's ultimate rejection of romanticism and its ideal of a transcendent experience of nature. Moreover, the speaker's observation that "The hard snow held me, save where now and then / One foot went down" evokes the metaphor of metrical feet, ironically suggesting that the only mark the speaker can leave in this romantic wilderness will be a sign of his falling (and failing).

Once in the swamp, the speaker watches a small, anonymous bird fly past him and retreat behind the eponymous wood pile, an encounter that continues Frost's dismantling of romantic tropes. If the great bird of the romantic poets was Keats's nightingale, Frost's bird fails to live up to that standard of artistic inspiration. Indeed, as Gary Roberts notes, "The twentieth-century American poet provokes the bird's defensive reaction to him, whereas the English Romantic poet would have sought his own defensive stance to the bird's elusiveness" (416). The dismantling of romantic tropes that Frost began in the opening lines, with the speaker seemingly lost in the midst of the very natural setting that was supposed to enable self-discovery, here reaches its pinnacle as Frost mocks the idea of nature as a mirror to the soul. The bird is fearful of the human intruder, but Frost indicates he has no interest in the bird, teasingly comparing it to "one who takes / Everything said as personal to himself." Yet this mockery of the romantic personification of nature also mocks the speaker's own romantic egotism, for his thoughts throughout have been self-focused.

By contrast, the unknown builder of the wood pile represents a different category of personality from the egotism of the bird and the poet. Several seasons old, the stack of split maple cords is slowly being reclaimed by nature, and as the speaker considers who might have completed and then abandoned such a project, he discovers another stance toward the work of poetry from the one the bird represented. "I thought that only / Someone who lived in turning to fresh tasks / Could so forget his handiwork," Frost writes, and Elizabeth Shepley Sergeant has noted that Frost claimed this represented the sort of person he aspired to be (118). The wood pile represents a juncture between human creation and nonhuman nature which the speaker can aspire to, and while the anonymity of the maker differs from T. S. ELIOT's ideal of artistic impersonality, Frost appears to be articulating a common MODERNIST skepticism about subjectivity. In the final lines, the speaker notes that the wood has been left "To warm the frozen swamp as best it could / With the slow smokeless burning of decay," and this subtle paradox signals Frost's approval of such a creation, which resists both pragmatic functionality and romantic sublimity in favor of the miracle of its making.

BIBLIOGRAPHY

Roberts, Gary. "The Wood-Pile." In *The Robert Frost Encyclopedia,* edited by Nancy Lewis Tuten and John Zubizarreta, 415–417. Westport, Conn: Greenwood Press, 2001.

Sergeant, Elizabeth Shepley. *Robert Frost: The Trial by Existence.* New York: Holt, Rinehart and Winston, 1960.

Temple Cone

WRIGHT, C. D. (CAROLYN WRIGHT)

(1947–) C. D. Wright maintains a maverick position in late 20th-century American poetry. With American poetry divided along aesthetic lines, she remains nonpartisan. Her work bears both the LANGUAGE poet's interest in fragment and surface as well as a NARRATIVE attention to time and place, and she cites as influences both RON SILLIMAN and such regional writers as Frank Stanford and Flannery O'Connor. She often mentions that she is the daughter of a judge and a court reporter, as if explaining her devotion to getting the story straight, and the work of many younger American women poets, such as Ange Mlinko and Stefanie Marlis, is informed by Wright's attention to strange, fragmented, and place-specific detail.

Wright was born in 1947 and raised in the Ozark Mountains of Arkansas. In 1981 she was awarded a National Endowment for the Arts Fellowship. She received Guggenheim and Bunting Fellowships in 1987, followed by a National Endowment for the Arts grant (1988), a Whiting Writer's Award (1989), and a MacArthur Fellowship (2004). She was named state poet of Rhode Island, a five-year post, in 1994 and given a Lannan Literary Award in 1999. She teaches at Brown University.

While Wright's poems can be allusive and elusive, she conveys warmth and compassion for her materials through the use of wit and a keen ear for regional dialect and detail. Her work is grounded in the lives of working- and middle-class rural Americans, relating often forgotten aspects of these stories through nonlinear and unconventional forms. Two of the most distinguishing characteristics of her poetry are the mix of high and low diction—evangelical rantings, brand names, and slang are used alongside sensual and elegant metaphor—and the shift between rapturous joy and haunted despair that feels emblematic of her southern roots.

Wright is also known for her dedication to preserving the legacy of fellow Arkansas poet Frank Stanford. In 1982 she published *Translations of the Gospel back into Tongues,* which she has called a tribute to Stanford. In it, her poems give the vernacular and the gritty details of the lives of poor southerners to bizarre magic, as Stanford did, epically, before her. In "Bent Tones," an owl watches over the people of the town getting ready for a "dance at the black school": "With her fast eye / She could see Floyd Little / Changing his shirt for the umpteenth time."

Wright's own work can also be epic. *Deepstep Come Shining* (1998) is a poetic road trip that chronicles everyday terrors and beauties in a voice both personal ("I was there. I know") and mythic ("Go to Venice; bring me back a mason jar of glass eyes. They shall multiply like shadflies"). The book has brought Wright her highest acclaim to date, and in her own words, "*Deepstep Come Shining* is my rapture" ("Interview"). Other projects, which include a photographic and poetic portrait of Louisiana prisoners with frequent collaborator Deborah Luster, supported by the Dorothea Lange-Paul Taylor Prize from the Center for Documentary Studies at Duke University in 2000, continue her unique position as a poet dedicated as much to document as to daring.

BIBLIOGRAPHY

Goodman, Jenny. "C. D. Wright." In *Dictionary of Literary Biography*. Vol. 120, *American Poets since World War II*, edited by R. S. Gwynn. Detroit: Gale, 1992, pp. 329–333.

Wright, C. D. "Looking for 'one untranslatable song': An Interview with C. D. Wright on Poetics, Collaboration, American Prisoners, and Frank Stanford," by Kent Johnson. Available online. URL: www.jacket.zip.com.au/jacket15/cdwright-iv.html. Downloaded June 2003.

Arielle Greenberg

WRIGHT, CHARLES (1935–) Charles Wright's poetry has been admired for its passion and its stunning combination of imagistic and metaphysical impulses. While the mark of EZRA POUND is unmistakable in his work, Wright transcends that influence to forge a lyrical marriage of image and prayerful praise, as in "Still Life with Stick and Word" (1995): "A slide of houselight escapes through the kitchen window. / How unlike it is. How like." With one of today's most ambitious bodies of work, Wright's poetry is deeply, though often obliquely, rooted in place and landscape and revels in the New World (even as it so often returns to the Old); it rejects a bland confessionalism in favor of, as William Butler Yeats put it, "the fascination of what's difficult" (see CONFESSIONAL SCHOOL).

Wright, born in Pickwick Dam, Tennessee, began publishing poetry in the 1960s, and his work, including his translations from the Italian, has earned him numerous important awards, among them the Pulitzer Prize for *Black Zodiac* (1997) and the National Book Award for *Country Music: Selected Early Poems* (1983). He attended Davidson College and the University of Iowa, where he studied under DONALD JUSTICE, and has taught at the University of Virginia.

Wright's work across several volumes appears as a seamless whole, a kind of contemplative quest-epic, in which three modes predominate: homage, elegy, and meditation (see LYRIC POETRY). In his elegiac mode, claims Helen Vendler, "[t]he hunger for the purity of the dead grows . . . almost to a lust" (10), as in "'Where Moth and Rust Doth Corrupt'" (1975): "I mimic the tongues of green flame in the grass. / I live in the one world, the moth and rust in my arms." In a later poem, "The Appalachian Book of the Dead" (1997), Wright binds together this "lust" for purity and his profound attachment to landscape in lines of both praise and mourning: "It always amazes me / How landscape recalibrates the stations of the dead." Such meditations liberate the poetic voice from personal history and allow it to enter a liminal world inhabited by both the living and the dead—and to face again the dilemma of the would-be visionary poet who cannot avoid seeing the image in language: "We who would see beyond seeing / see only language, that burning field" ("Looking outside the Cabin Window, I Remember a Line by Li Po" [1995]). One is reminded of WILLIAM BRONK, who, in "The Real World" (1972), articulates this quest for what cannot be known: "There is a real world which does make sense. / It is beyond our knowing or speaking but it is there." The voice of Wright's poetry longs to be both "beyond" and "there."

BIBLIOGRAPHY

Andrews, Tom, ed. *The Point Where All Things Meet: Essays on Charles Wright*. Oberlin, Ohio: Oberlin College Press, 1995.

Vendler, Helen. "The Transcendent 'I.'" In *The Point Where All Things Meet: Essays on Charles Wright*, edited by Tom Andrews. Oberlin, Ohio: Oberlin College Press, 1995, 1–12.

Rose Shapiro

WRIGHT, JAMES (1927–1980) James Wright was part of a large and diverse community of American poets born in America in the 1920s. JOHN ASHBERY, GALWAY KINNELL, W. S. MERWIN, ROBERT BLY, ROBERT CREELEY, DONALD JUSTICE, GERALD STERN, CAROLYN KIZER, MAXINE KUMIN, KENNETH KOCH, PHILLIP LEVINE, ADRIENNE RICH, and RICHARD HOWARD were all born within two years of Wright. His work as a whole speaks to the rural and industrial landscapes of the American Midwest (particularly Minnesota and his native Ohio), the sad turbulence of war and politics, the beauty and complexity of humans and animals, and the bliss and terror of addiction to both alcohol and love. Although Wright lived a shorter life than many of the major poets of his age, Wright's body of work is talked about in terms of "early" and "late" perhaps more often than that of any other poet of this generation. The early formal poems, contained in *The Green Wall* (1957) and *Saint Judas* (1959), are highly metrical, reflecting Wright's indebtedness to the work of ROBERT FROST, Thomas Hardy, and EDWARD ARLINGTON ROBINSON, while the later free verse poems, which first appeared in *The Branch Will Not Break* (1963), are heavily influenced by the many Spanish and German-language poets—including Pablo Neruda, César Vallejo, Georg Trakl, and Herman Hesse—whom Wright helped bring to readers of English.

Wright was born in the industrial town of Martins Ferry, Ohio, where he remained until he graduated from high school and joined the U.S. Army. After serving in the postwar occupation of Japan, Wright left the army to attend Kenyon College on the G.I. bill and later completed an M.S. and a Ph.D. degree at the University of Washington, where he studied under the poet THEODORE ROETHKE. (Like his mentor, Wright also suffered from alcoholism and nervous breakdowns.) His prizes included a Fulbright Scholarship, which allowed him to study in Vienna, and a Pulitzer Prize for his 1971 *Collected Poems,* which contains his first four volumes (minus a few poems from the first book) as well as his translations. He held teaching positions at the University of Minnesota, Macalaster College, and Hunter College.

In a 1979 interview, Wright stated that "an intelligent poetry is a poetry whose author has given a great deal of slow and silent attention to the problems of craft; that is, how to say something and say it in a musical way" (297). This interview was conducted near the end of his life, but the presence of an intelligent, musical attention in the younger James Wright is made evident in the seemingly effortlessly rhymed lines of "Saint Judas," the last poem from his second book (1959). After this volume's publication, Wright turned to a sparer, freer verse, which contained a slightly surreal bent likely gleaned from the authors he had been translating. Though he acknowledged SURREALISM's importance and its influence on his work and the work of his contemporaries, Wright's last book of poems, *This Journey* (1980)—published posthumously—contains a prose poem entitled "Against Surrealism." In the initial free verse poems, many of which are quite brief, Wright's attention is focused on deep, concise images (see DEEP IMAGE POETRY). A six-line poem, "Rain," for instance, consists of a definition of the poem's subject ("the sinking of things"), followed by a simple succession of imagistic events (see IMAGIST SCHOOL): flashlights in the woods, kneeling girls, the closing of an owl's eyes, the bones of the speakers hands "descending into a valley / Of strange rocks."

The state and people of Ohio are a constant presence throughout the entire body of Wright's work. In "Autumn Begins in Martins Ferry, Ohio," perhaps Wright's most well-known poem, the speaker—a spectator at a football game—addresses a population (a "ruptured nightwatchman," black blast-furnace workers, beer-drinking "Polacks," working-class wives who "cluck like starved pullets") who, though present in the poem, are absent from the stadium due to their economic or alcoholic occupations. This careful poem proves that Wright did not abandon his close attention to poetic detail, as the entire poem hinges on a single word, *therefore,* which gives the poem its powerful sense of contingency and implication. When Wright closes the poem by placing this word, followed by a comma, before the lines "Their sons grow suicidally beautiful / At the beginning of October," the effects and operations of a particular social system are suddenly and intensely displayed. Rather than simply depicting a bittersweet scene, Wright connects the facts of the world to the factors of its construction. The boys "gallop terribly against each other's bodies" in the midst of—and *because of*—the world into which they have been born.

Although the work in *Collected Poems* is far more well known than the material that followed its publication, Wright was quite prolific in the 1970s, producing three more books of poetry, numerous prose pieces, and scores of letters. (His correspondence with the poet and novelist LESLIE MARMON SILKO is collected in the 1986 volume *The Delicacy and Strength of Lace,* edited by Wright's second wife, Anne.) Critics have debated the merits of the late work relative to the first four books, although these discussions may point to Wright's turning away from tragedy and anxiety rather than to a decline in craftsmanship. The post–Pulitzer writing indicates a calmer, though certainly no less careful, poet, who eventually managed to keep his demons at a distance.

BIBLIOGRAPHY

Elkins, Andrew. *The Poetry of James Wright.* Tuscaloosa: University of Alabama Press, 1991.

Smith, David, ed. *The Pure Clear Word: Essays on the Poetry of James Wright.* Urbana: University of Illinois Press, 1982.

Stitt, Peter, and Frank Graziano. *James Wright: The Heart of the Light.* Ann Arbor: University of Michigan Press, 1990.

Wright, James. "Interview with Bruce Henricksen." In *American Poetry Observed: Poets on Their Work,* edited by Joe David Bellamy, 296–309. Urbana: University of Illinois Press, 1984.

Graham Foust

WRIGHT, JAY (1935–) Jay Wright is an African-American poet whose work combines the density and allusiveness of high MODERNISM with a fervent interest in multicultural histories and mythologies. In his poems he delves into his inheritances from African, European, and American cultures, celebrating both the hybridity and multiplicity of history. "A young man," says Wright, "hearing me read some of my poems, said that I seemed to be trying to weave together a lot of different things. My answer was that they are already woven, I'm just trying to uncover the weave" (12). Wright is also a writer of passionate lyric intensity, whose rich, musical verse echoes that of HART CRANE and Rainer Maria Rilke.

Wright was born in Albuquerque, New Mexico. He has received numerous fellowships and was named a fellow of the American Academy of Poets in 1995. He received the Lannan Literary Award for poetry in 2000, the Anisfield-Wolf Lifetime Achievement Award in 2002, and the Bollingen Prize in Poetry in 2005.

Wright's first book, *The Homecoming Singer* (1971), lays out the major themes of his career. "Chapultapec Castle," a meditation on the ill-starred Mexican emperor Maximilian, is a poem about history's continued presence and its ability to linger in places and objects. In "The Homecoming Singer," Wright celebrates the ability of art to communicate suffering, as a lonely night in Nashville fills with the voice of an anonymous woman whose song recalls "the waterboy, the railroad cutter, the jailed / the condemned, all that had been forgotten." In "Sketch for an Aesthetic Project," a mournful rumination on the slave ships that once docked in Manhattan, also becomes the occasion for a desire to delve into the past and for a statement of poetic purpose: "I have made a log for passage, / out there, where some still live."

Throughout his later work, Wright continues to explore multiple and hidden histories. His poems about Benjamin Banneker in *Soothsayers and Omens* (1976) explore the ways in which racism lurks as a tragic stain on the Enlightenment ideals that formed America. The book-length poem *The Double-Invention of Komo* (1980) combines stories from West African mythology with various Western cosmologies. This project clearly recalls the synthetic "mythical method" of T. S. ELIOT and EZRA POUND, but, as Vera Kutzinski notes, Wright wishes to "chart relationships between cultures" in such a way that "vital differences need not be negated or leveled" to any "single, absolute frame of reference" (72).

Ultimately Wright matters, because he is a poet of singular lyric force, a quality which is perhaps most on display in *Elaine's Book* (1988), a series of poems about death and desire, in which he assures us in "Veil, I" that there are harmonies promised in "the sunset's veronica'd blood."

BIBLIOGRAPHY

Kutzinski, Vera. *Against the American Grain: Myth and History in William Carlos Williams, Jay Wright, and Nicolás Guillén.* Baltimore: Johns Hopkins University Press, 1987.

Wright, Jay. "'The Unravelling of the Egg': An Interview with Jay Wright," by Charles H. Rowell. *Callaloo* 19 (autumn 1983): 3–15.

Ben Johnson

"THE WRITER" RICHARD WILBUR (1976) One of the most praised poems in RICHARD WILBUR's collection *The Mind-Reader,* "The Writer" is both typical of Wilbur's scrupulous metaphors and unusual in its relaxed form. Wilbur is known for his careful and adroit formalism, so this poem seems unusual, as it neither rhymes nor adheres to a meter. Wilbur's tercets (three-line stanzas) are in a loose or accentual meter (moving freely between iambic and anapestic feet), with three, five, and three beats per line (see PROSODY AND FREE VERSE). This is worth noting, against the comparative strictness of Wilbur's other poems, to show that one of poetry's most gifted formalists sometimes loosens the reins.

"The Writer" is more typical of Wilbur's work, however, in its strict and careful attention to metaphor. The poem opens by describing Wilbur's daughter, tentatively typing a story, as if writing meant setting out on a sea voyage: Her room is like the prow of a boat, the linden-tree outside toss like ocean-waves, the typewriter's clatter sounds like an anchor-chain dragged over the ship's edge. However, accuracy compels Wilbur to reject this first comparison in favor of another—a maneuver seen in other Wilbur pieces, such as "Mind" (1956), "The Mind-Reader" (1976), "Trolling for Blues," and "Lying" (both 1987). Hearing the intense silence between the bursts of typing—the pause while his daughter strains for the right words—Wilbur remembers a bird, a "dazed starling," that had been trapped in his daughter's room years ago. This starling, battering itself bloody against the windows until it finds the single open one, becomes the vehicle of a new metaphor: Wilbur realizes that his daughter, in her writing, is more like that wild and desperate creature than like a mercantile sailing-crew, and success in her writing means a fortunate and graceful escape. For her, as for any writer, he remembers, "It is always a matter, my darling, / Of life or death." The distant rhyme between "darling" and "dazed starling" seems to confirm this comparison. Wilbur then wishes his daughter what he wished her earlier—"a safe passage"—but, this time, as the stakes are higher, he wishes "harder." Grace Schulman has called this image "one of the best metaphors I know . . . for the creative process" (346), and it seems one of our poetry's most heartfelt benedictions for young writers.

BIBLIOGRAPHY

Edgecombe, Rodney Stenning. *A Reader's Guide to the Poetry of Richard Wilbur.* Tuscaloosa: University of Alabama Press, 1995.

Jensen, Ejner J. "Encounters with Experience: The Poems of Richard Wilbur." In *Richard Wilbur's Creation,* edited by Wendy Salinger, 243–264. Ann Arbor: University of Michigan Press, 1983.

Schulman, Grace. "'To Shake Our Gravity Up': The Poetry of Richard Wilbur." *Nation* 223 (October 9, 1976): 344–346.

Wai, Isabella. "Wilbur's 'The Writer.'" *Explicator* 53, no. 4 (summer 1995): 240–242.

Isaac Cates

Y

YAU, JOHN (1950–) John Yau's lively poetic experimentation shares the intense investigation of the sound play, texture, and multiple meanings of words with the LANGUAGE poets, CLARK COOLIDGE, and HARRY MATHEWS, as well as with the wild humor, erotic abandon, and imaginative breadth of the earlier surrealists (see SURREALISM). In demonstrating the instability of individual and collective identities and in exploring perceptions of time, his work parallels JOHN ASHBERY'S. In addition, Yau's interest in poetic sequences recalls BLACK MOUNTAIN poets, including ROBERT DUNCAN. And, like many fellow Asian-American writers, he vigorously critiques white racism.

Born in Lynn, Massachusetts, Yau grew up in the Boston area. Except for a British grandmother, his ancestors are Chinese. Along with numerous books of poetry, he has written a novel, a short story collection, and many volumes of art criticism. His first book of poems was *Crossing Canal Street* (1976). Ashbery selected *Corpse and Mirror* (1983) for the National Poetry Series contest. *Radiant Silhouette: New and Selected Work 1974–1988* appeared in 1989. Yau has gone on to receive many other awards and honors, including a Guggenheim Fellowship in 2006.

In his early work Yau's evocative descriptions stress the dignity of Chinese people in New York's Chinatown. Turning to surrealism as a way of complicating imagism (see the IMAGIST SCHOOL) and narration (see NARRATIVE POETRY) and deepening their imaginative impact, he seeks, as Priscilla Wald states, "to interrogate the rituals that foster social cohesion and position subjects within a culture" and to indicate how "the world" is "less predictable" (142). As one of the "Postcards from Trakl" (1992) declares, "You are a billiard ball / falling out of a newspaper." Part of the unpredictability conveyed in Yau's writing involves what Timothy Yu calls a "nagging" inability to "know what it means to be 'Chinese' anymore, even as we are constantly reminded of its centrality" (448). This is evident in Yau's sequence, "Genghis Chan: Private Eye" (1989, 1992, 1996), spanning three books, which exemplifies his dizzyingly parodic recycling of anti-Chinese racist tropes.

Yau's poems often trace the perplexities and delights of sexual love. Disjunctive narratives speed from comedies of miscommunication and indignation to seduction lines, apologies courtly praise, and recognition of another person's inaccessible mental inwardness to rapprochement and language's inability to achieve it. In "Conversation at Midnight" (1996), a speaker, "sorry about the lump I left in your throat," goes on to snarl, "Don't talk to me like I am some style of perishable food." A passage from "Angel Atrapado" (1992), a prose-poem sequence, views love as a crossroads that the speaker-negotiates: "I was a moniker machine working the alley between the 'you' and 'I' we constructed in the garage." Yau's poetic "moniker machine" offers fascinating wordplay, demystifying parody, and trenchant probings of identity in flux.

BIBLIOGRAPHY

Fink, Thomas. *"A Different Sense of Power": Problems of Community in Late-Twentieth-Century U.S. Poetry.* Madison, N.J.: Fairleigh Dickinson University Press, 2001, pp. 55–74.

Wald, Priscilla. "'Chaos Goes Uncourted': John Yau's Dis(-) Orienting Poetics." In *Cohesion and Dissent in American Literature,* edited by Carol Colatrella and Joseph Alkana, 133–158. Albany: State University of New York Press, 1994

Yu, Timothy. "Form and Identity in Language Poetry and Asian American Poetry." *Contemporary Literature* (fall 2000): 422–461.

Thomas Fink

"YET DO I MARVEL" COUNTEE CULLEN (1925)

In his introduction to *The Caroling Dusk* (1927), COUNTEE CULLEN rejected the presumed primacy of race as an issue in the work of Negro poets, writing that "[S]ince theirs is also the heritage of the English language, their work will not present any serious aberration from the poetic tendencies of their times" (xi). Despite this claim, however, Cullen's poetry often shows a strong concern with race, as his widely anthologized sonnet "Yet Do I Marvel" demonstrates. Lyric, formal, and full of allusions to Greek myth, the poem nevertheless uses these traditional aesthetic features to highlight the dilemma of the black poet, though to what extent this dilemma is seen as surmountable remains debated by scholars.

The poem begins with an expression of faith in the benevolence of God, but almost immediately starts naming paradoxical cases where that benevolence might be questioned. Cullen first considers what appear to be flaws in nature: the blindness of moles and the inevitable death of all humans, who were nevertheless made in the image of God eternal. In the second quatrain, Cullen reflects upon the sufferings of two mythological figures, Tantalus and Sisyphus, who were damned to an eternity of unsatisfied temptation and of unceasing labor, respectively. These reflections occupy the first eight lines, raising an interesting issue about the form of the poem. Although the rhyme scheme of Cullen's sonnet is Shakespearean, the division of its content into a problem-focused octet and a resolution-focused sestet remains the hallmark of the Petrarchan sonnet. The resolution Cullen achieves in the lines that follow, however, barely qualifies. "Inscrutable His ways are," Cullen concedes, claiming the mystery of God as an answer to the question "Why" (repeated twice in the first eight lines), the question concerning justice in the world.

The Shakespearean sonnet form again asserts itself in the concluding couplet of the poem, which stands as a proverblike response to the paradoxical conditions that Cullen has described to this point. This proverb's meaning, however, appears paradoxical as well, though it is clearly involved in some fashion with Cullen's views on race. "Yet do I marvel at this curious thing," writes Cullen, "To make a poet black, and bid him sing." The influential African-American author James Weldon Johnson called this couplet "the two most poignant lines in American literature" (268), and Allan S. Shucard argues the lines contrast darkly with the preceding "assertion of Cullen's faith, notwithstanding sundry other horrid cosmic mysteries" (26). Such readings assume Cullen's tone is heavily ironic, with the speaker ostensibly contrasting the inscrutable sufferings of the natural world and of myth with his own condition, but in fact only using them as foils in order to illustrate his own greater misery. In this light, being bid to sing is an abject fate for one whose racial identity already makes him a damned figure.

But for Fred Fetrow, the paradoxes of "Yet Do I Marvel" are paradoxical in appearance only, each of them being just within their own context. While it may be challenging or paradoxical for a black poet to sing or rejoice while his racial identity exposes him to political and social oppression, writes Fetrow, "the black poet can still articulate his blackness and express his unique racial identity while singing his humanity" (105). In terms of the poem's form, Fetrow's reading has sounder footing, for the couplet of the Shakespearean sonnet less often extends the themes of the preceding stanzas than it resolves or even contradicts them. But such transcendence is not to be had cheaply. By figuring his black identity in terms of weakness, mortality, and damnation, Cullen provides a harrowing portrait of race in America, though he ultimately invokes poetry or "song" as a force of even greater power in the service of justice.

BIBLIOGRAPHY
Cullen, Countee, ed. Introduction. In *Caroling Dusk: An Anthology of Verse by Negro Poets.* New York: Harper and Brothers, 1927.
Fetrow, Fred. "Cullen's *Yet Do I Marvel.*" *The Explicator* 56, no. 2 (1998): 103–105.
Johnson, James Weldon. *Black Manhattan.* New York: Arno Press, 1930.
Shucard, Allan S. *Countee Cullen.* Boston: Twayne Publishers, 1984.

Temple Cone

Z

ZINNES, HARRIET (1919–) Harriet Zinnes's poetry explores issues related to the fragile human condition and its chaotic environment, particularly as these issues pertain to the international political confusion of her times. Her influences include American writers, such as EZRA POUND, JOHN ASHBERY, and FRANK O'HARA, and the French poets Charles Baudelaire, Stéphane Mallarmé, and Paul Verlaine.

Zinnes was born Victoria Harriet Fich in Hyde Park, Massachusetts. She received her doctorate in 1953 and in 1964 published her first collection of poetry, *Waiting and Other Poems.* Since then Zinnes has published nine more collections. In addition to poetry, Zinnes has published two short story collections, *Lover* (1989) and *The Radiant Absurdity of Desire* (1998) and has translated poems by Jacques Prévert (*Blood and Feathers* [1998]). Zinnes has also been an influential literary and art critic, and her works on literary and visual arts are often linked, as in her book *Ezra Pound and the Visual Arts* (1980).

In Zinnes's poetry the reader notes the fusion of eclectic intellectual interests. Zinnes's husband was a professor of physics, and her bent for the humanities is complemented by an understanding and appreciation of math and science. "Wily," the first poem in *My, Haven't the Flowers Been* (1995), begins, "Time is full of wiles and mathematics. Doesn't time equal mathematics / or perhaps the other way round?" Two of her collections, *Book of Ten* (1981) and *Book of Twenty* (1992), use numeric systems as their organizing principle. Zinnes's poetic studies of chaos and order portray systems as simultaneously arbitrary, inherent, and necessary. As Zinnes states in the opening of *Entropisms* (1978), "To put it simply: the physical universe is entropic. Man's imagination is antientropic."

Art is another interest highlighted in Zinnes's poetry. Marcel Duchamp, in particular, influences both her form and content. Yet, although Zinnes's interests in art and science are pronounced, they are manifestations of a broader philosophical inquiry into the nature of life, and, finally, it is language which is her primary concern.

BIBLIOGRAPHY

Parisi, Joseph. "Harriet Zinnes." In *Contemporary Poets,* 4th ed, edited by James Vinsonand and D. L. Kirkpatrick, 960–961. New York: St. Martin's Press, 1985.

Melissa Studdard

ZUKOFSKY, LOUIS (1904–1978) Louis Zukofsky came to early public attention with his leadership of the OBJECTIVIST movement in the early 1930s, but nonetheless he spent much of his career in obscurity. Only in the 1960s, when his poetry began to be published in widely available editions, did he achieve some recognition as an important poet, and only since his death has a larger readership come to recognize Zukofsky as a major figure in 20th-century poetry, a crucial bridge between the high MODERNISM of EZRA POUND, WILLIAM CARLOS WILLIAMS, and MARIANNE MOORE and the postmodern experiments of what is called "the New American poetry," (after 1960 anthology of the same name) and the LANGUAGE school (see POETRY ANTHOLOGIES). His work is dense and highly referential and tends to twist or entirely reject conventional English syntax, yet, at the same time, his poetry attains great heights of grace and complexity.

Zukofsky was born in New York City, the child of Yiddish-speaking Eastern European Jewish immigrants. He learned English in the public schools and attended Columbia University, where he took an M.A. in 1924. He taught for a single academic year (1930–31) at the University of Wisconsin, Madison, and for most of the 1930s he worked for various Works Progress Administration (WPA) writing projects. In 1947 he joined the faculty of the Polytechnic Institute of Brooklyn, and he retired from that position at the rank of associate professor in 1966.

Zukofsky wrote and published LYRIC POETRY while in college, but his public career was sparked when he submitted his autobiographical "Poem beginning 'The,'" in part a satiric response to T. S. ELIOT's *The WASTE LAND,* to Pound's journal the *Exile* in late 1927. Pound viewed Zukofsky as a potential protégé and encouraged him to get in touch with other American poets (among them his friend Williams, with whom Zukofsky would form a lifelong friendship) and to form a literary "group" on the model of the IMAGIST SCHOOL. Zukofsky resisted the idea of such a group, but, for a while, and with some ambivalence, he advanced his own cause and that of some of his friends as "objectivists."

Zukofsky began his career writing brief lyrics and continued writing short poems throughout his life, but from 1928 on he devoted much of his energies to the 24-section-long poem *"A"* (1978). The poem begins at a performance of Bach's "St. Matthew's Passion"—"A / round of fiddles playing Bach"—and music is a constant theme in the poem. The early movements of *"A"* superficially resemble Pound's *CANTOS*, but Zukofsky's sense of poetic form is far more stringent than Pound's, and while the first six parts of *"A"* make use of the same collage elements as *The Cantos,* they are also organized in a manner analogous to the baroque fugue. *"A"*-7 is a sequence of seven sonnets, and from that point onward the movements of *"A"* become more and more formally inventive. The latter movements make use of innovative translational strategies, unconventional poetic forms, and dense and complicated collages of earlier texts. *"A"*-24, the poem's final movement, is a musical score arranged by Zukofsky's wife, Celia; it juxtaposes four different sets of Zukofsky texts to George Friedrich Handel's harpsichord pieces.

In his youth Zukofsky was deeply involved in leftist politics, and many of the early sections of *"A,"* as well as many of the short poems from the 1920s and 1930s, make use of marxist rhetoric and dialectic. That political emphasis largely disappears from Zukofsky's work after the 1930s, however, and in its place emerges a fascination with the satisfactions of familial love, reflected best in the many love poems and valentines included in his *Complete Short Poetry* (1991). Zukofsky remained enamored of systematic thinkers, however, and from first to last his writing reflects his interest in the geometrically expressed philosophy of Baruch Spinoza and the "phase theory" of history advanced by the American historian Henry Adams.

That "phase theory" led Zukofsky to his own theory of poetic language, according to which language exists in three states—solid, liquid, and gaseous, states which correspond roughly to the concrete image, the lyrically musical, and the philosophically abstract. Zukofsky clearly preferred "solid" to "gaseous" language, but his own critical prose (and sometimes his poetry) often veers from the concrete and the musical into the dauntingly abstract. Nowhere is this clearer than in *Bottom: on Shakespeare,* the massive commentary on Shakespeare's works which Zukofsky wrote between 1947 and 1960 and which attempts to explain the entire Shakespearean canon in terms of an emphasis on the "clear physical eye" over the "erring brain." Zukofsky himself described *Bottom* as a long poem of sorts, and like *"A"* it is a vast collage of quotations from previous texts that range across the entire history of Western culture. The second volume of *Bottom* consists of Celia Zukofsky's musical setting of the Shakespeare play *Pericles, Prince of Tyre,* which Zukofsky read as a narrative analogous to Homer's *Odyssey.*

Between 1958 and 1966, Zukofsky, in collaboration with his wife, translated the entire works of the Latin poet Catullus. This translation, which was published in 1969, represents a stupendous reimagination of what the act of translating a foreign poet might involve (see POETRY AND TRANSLATION). Zukofsky's aim is not to render the dictionary meaning of Catullus's words, but to "breathe the 'literal' meaning"—to follow the sounds of Catullus's Latin as closely as possible in the English translation. The result is a rich and bewildering melange of archaisms, obscure meanings, and slang, often verging upon incomprehensibility. Zukofsky, however, adopted this mode of translation—or "transliteration"—as one of his primary poetic modes in his later work, and passages of poetry directly transliterated from other languages appear in many of the later sections of *"A."*

While Zukofsky tended to devote most of his energies to large projects—*"A," Bottom: on Shakespeare,* and the Catullus translations—he also wrote a large number of short poems, many of which are arranged in thematic or imagistic sequences. Such sequences as "I's [pronounced *eyes*]" (1959–60), "Light" (1940–44), and "The Old Poet Moves to a New Apartment 14 Times" (1962) combine the slight and humorous with the philosophically profound and showcase Zukofsky's wry and sometimes recondite sense of humor.

Zukofsky was always first and foremost a formalist, a poet who was obsessed with the potentialities of the forms in which verse is written. In his early work he pursued conventional English poetic forms, such as the sonnet, and he would experiment with such Italianate forms as the sestina (in "'Mantis'" [1934]) and the canzone (in *"A"*-9), crafting these poems with a fanatical attention to requirements of these demanding shapes. In later sections of *"A,"* Zukofsky fashioned a poetics in which the length of the line is determined by word count, rather than by conventional accentual or accentual-syllabic meter: Each of the last-composed movements, *"A"*-22 and *"A"*-23, consists of 1,000 five-word lines. The poetics of these last movements—rigid word-counted lines that incorporate a breathtaking range of allusion, adaptation, and translation—is essentially identical to that of Zukofsky's last work, *80 Flowers* (1978)—81 poems (including an epigraph), each of them eight lines long, five words to the line, about various flowers. In these poems syntax has become so elastic as to disappear almost entirely, opening the poem up to a wide range of interpretations and reactions. The epigraph, for instance, begins "Heart us invisibly thyme time / round rose bud fire downland."

In the late 1950s, Zukofsky began to attract increasing attention among younger poets, including ROBERT CREELEY, THEODORE ENSLIN, ROBERT DUNCAN, RONALD JOHNSON, JONATHAN WILLIAMS, and CID CORMAN, among others. By the time of his death, he was widely recognized as an underappreciated master and had proved a crucial influence on such Language poets as MICHAEL PALMER, BOB PERELMAN, RON SILLIMAN, and CHARLES BERNSTEIN, as well as on other poets, including MICHAEL HELLER, RACHEL BLAU DUPLESSIS, and HUGH SEIDMAN.

In addition to his poetry and critical works, Zukofsky wrote a play, *Arise, arise* (1973), which deals with his mother's death; a novella, *Ferdinand* (1968), a full-length novel, *Little; for careenagers* (1970), which treats the childhood of his son Paul, the violin virtuoso; and several short stories distinguished by the precision of their language and the angularity of their wit. The scope, depth, and delicacy of his work make him one of the major 20th-century American writers.

BIBLIOGRAPHY

Ahearn, Barry. *Zukofsky's "A": An Introduction.* Berkeley: University of California Press, 1983.

Leggott, Michele J. *Reading Zukofsky's* 80 Flowers. Baltimore: Johns Hopkins University Press, 1989.

Penberthy, Jenny. *Niedecker and the Correspondence with Zukofsky, 1931–1970.* New York: Cambridge University Press, 1993.

Perelman, Bob. *The Trouble with Genius: Reading Pound, Joyce, Stein and Zukofsky.* Berkeley: University of California Press, 1994.

Quartermain, Peter. *Disjunctive Poetics: From Gertrude Stein and Louis Zukofsky to Susan Howe.* New York: Cambridge University Press, 1992.

Scroggins, Mark. *Louis Zukofsky and the Poetry of Knowledge.* Tuscaloosa: University of Alabama Press, 1998.

———., ed. *Upper Limit Music: The Writing of Louis Zukofsky.* Tuscaloosa: University of Alabama Press, 1997.

Stanley, Sandra Kumamoto. *Louis Zukofsky and the Transformation of a Modern American Poetics.* Berkeley: University of California Press, 1994.

Terrell, Carroll F., ed. *Louis Zukofsky: Man and Poet.* Orono, Maine: National Poetry Foundation, 1979.

Mark Scroggins

APPENDIX I

GLOSSARY

accent The STRESS on one or another syllable, especially when poetry is read aloud.

accentual verse A system of VERSE throughout at least a portion of a poem that depends on a certain fixed number of stresses in a line of poetry; this system, however, allows for any number of unstressed syllables.

allegory Extended metaphor or symbol with at least two levels of meaning, a literal level and an implied, figurative level; an allegorical narrative tells a story and at the same time suggests another level of meaning.

alliteration Repeating consonant sounds at the beginnings of words.

allusion Making reference to something or someone, usually in an indirect manner.

anapest A metrical foot consisting of two soft stresses followed by a hard stress. See METER.

anaphora A word or phrase that is repeated at the start of successive lines of poetry.

apostrophe A turn away from the reader to address another listener.

assonance Repetition of like vowel sounds, often in stressed syllables in close proximity to each other.

ballad A narrative in VERSE; the form derives from a narrative that was sung.

blank verse Unrhymed IAMBIC PENTAMETER.

cadence The rhythm in language, a pattern that can lend a musical order to a statement.

caesura A pause within a VERSE line, usually at approximately mid point.

canon A term originally derived from the Roman Catholic Church having to do with church law, this term also refers to a body of literature that is generally accepted as exhibiting what is best or important in terms of literary art.

collagist poetry Poetry that employs the organizing element of collage or the bringing together of disparate material to create a new statement or vision.

conceit Not unrelated to the term *concept,* an unusual supposition, analogy, metaphor, or image, often clever.

connotation Meaning that is implied rather than stated directly as in DENOTATION.

consonance Repetition of identical consonant sounds, within the context of varying vowel sounds.

couplet Two VERSE lines in succession that have the same END RHYME. When the two lines contain a complete statement in themselves, they are called a closed couplet. See also HEROIC COUPLET.

dactyl A metrical foot consisting of a hard stress followed by two soft stresses.

denotation The literal meaning of a word or statement, the opposite of CONNOTATION.

diction Word choice, the actual language that a writer employs.

dimeter A VERSE line consisting of two metrical FEET.

dramatic monologue An address to an interlocutor (another potential speaker) who is not present; a dramatic monologue has only one actual speaker.

elegy A poem mourning someone's death.

ellipsis Part of a statement left out, unspoken.

end rhyme A rhyme at the end of a VERSE line.

end-stopped A VERSE line that pauses at its end, when no ENJAMBMENT is possible.

enjambment A VERSE line whose momentum forbids a pause at its end, thus avoiding being END-STOPPED.

epic A long poem that, typically, recounts the adventures of someone in a high style and diction; classically, the adventures include a hero who is at least partially superhuman in makeup or deed, and the events have special importance in terms of the fate of a people.

epigram A brief, witty statement, often satiric or aphoristic.

epithet A word or phrase that characterizes something or someone.

eye rhyme Agreement of words according to their spelling but not their sound.

feet See FOOT.

feminine ending A VERSE line that ends with an extra soft stress.

feminine rhyme The rhyming of two words in more than a single syllable.

figurative language Language that employs figures of speech such as IRONY, HYPERBOLE, METAPHOR, SIMILE, SYMBOL, METONYMY, etc., in which the language connotes meaning.

foot A configuration of syllables to form a METER, such as an IAMB, TROCHEE, ANAPEST, DACTYL, or SPONDEE. A line of one foot is called a MONOMETER line, of two feet a DIAMETER line, of three feet TRIMETER, of four TETRAMETER, of five PENTAMETER, of six HEXAMETER, etc.

free verse Poetry lacking a metrical pattern or patterns; poetic lines without any discernible meter.

haiku A Japanese lyric form consisting of a certain number of syllables overall and in each line, most often in a five-seven-five syllabic line pattern.

half rhyme A form of CONSONANCE in which final consonant sounds in neighboring stressed syllables agree.

heroic couplet Two successive lines of END-RHYMING IAMBIC PENTAMETER.

hexameters A VERSE line consisting of six metrical FEET.

hyperbole An exaggeration meant to emphasize something.

iamb A metrical FOOT consisting of a soft stress followed by a hard stress.

iambic pentameter A five-FOOT line with a preponderance of IAMBIC FEET.

image Language meant to represent objects, actions, feelings, or thoughts in vivid terms.

internal rhyme A RHYME within a poetic line.

masculine rhyme A RHYME depending on one hard-stressed syllable only.

metaphor An implicit comparison, best when between unlike things, made without using the words *like* or *as*.

meter An arrangement of syllables in units called FEET, such as IAMB or TROCHEE, and in numbers of feet to make a pattern, such as IAMBIC PENTAMETER; the syllables can be hard- or soft-stressed according to the type of FOOT or pattern to be employed.

metonymy The substitution of a word that represents an association with, proximity to, or attribute of a thing for the thing itself; this figure of speech is not unlike SYNECHDOCHE.

monometer A VERSE line consisting of a single metrical foot.

occasional verse VERSE written to celebrate or to commemorate a particular event.

octave An eight-line stanza of poetry, also the first and larger portion of a SONNET. See OCTET.

octet An eight-line stanza of poetry. See OCTAVE.

ode A lyric poem usually in a dignified style and addressing a serious subject.

onomatopoeia A word or phrase whose sound resembles something the word or phrase is signifying.

oxymoron A phrase or statement containing a self-contradiction.

paradox A statement that seems to be self-contradictory but contains a truth that reconciles the contradiction.

pastoral A poem that evokes a rural setting or rural values; the word itself derives from the Latin *pastor,* or "shepherd."

pentameter A VERSE line consisting of five metrical FEET.

persona The speaker in a poem, most often the narrator; the term is derived from the Latin word for "mask."

personification Attributing human qualities to an inanimate entity.

prosody The study of versification; the term is at times used as a synonym for METER.

quatrain A four-line stanza of a poem, also a portion of a SONNET.

rhetorical figure An arrangement of words for one or another emphasis or effect.

rhyme Fundamentally, "agreement," the term specifically indicates the sameness or similarity of vowel sounds in an arrangement of words; there can be END RHYME, INTERNAL RHYME, EYE RHYME, HALF RHYME, FEMININE RHYME, etc.

rhyme scheme The arrangement of END RHYMES in a poem, indicated when analyzing a poem with the letters of the alphabet, such as, for a poem in successive COUPLETS, AA, BB, CC, etc.

rhythm A sense of movement created by arrangement of syllables in terms of stress and time.

sestet A six-line stanza of poetry, also the final large portion of a SONNET.

sestina A 36-line poem broken up into six SESTETS as well as a final stanza of three lines, the six words ending the first sestet's lines appearing at the conclusions of the remaining five sestets, in one or another order, and appearing in the final three lines; these repeated words usually convey key motifs of the poem.

simile A comparison using the word *like* or *as*.

slant rhyme A partial, incomplete RHYME, sometimes called a *half, imperfect, near* or *off rhyme*.

sonnet A poem of 14 lines, traditionally in IAMBIC PENTAMETER, the RHYME SCHEME and structure of which can vary. There are two predominant types of sonnets: the English or Shakespearean, which consists of three QUATRAINS and a final COUPLET, usually with a rhyme scheme of ABAB CDCD EFEF GG; and the Italian or Petrarchan sonnet, often with an initial OCTAVE rhyming ABBA ABBA and a concluding SESTET rhyming CDECDE. However, it is important to keep in mind that sonnet rhyme schemes can be very different from the above.

spondee A metrical FOOT comprised of two hard stresses.

sprung rhythm Lines or STANZAS made up of a preset number of hard syllabic stresses but any number of soft stresses; the effect is a rhythmic irregularity.

stanza A group of lines of poetry.

stress The emphasis when reading a poem accorded to a syllable.

strophe A STANZA, or VERSE paragraph in a prose poem, derived from classical Greek drama.

syllabic verse Poetry that employs a set number of syllables in a line, regardless of STRESS.

symbol A figure of speech that means what it says literally but also connotes a secondary meaning or meanings, and which usually conveys a concept, motif, or idea.

synecdoche A figure of speech in which a part of something is meant to signify the entirety of the thing, such as a hand that is meant to suggest a sailor whose hands are used in sailing a ship (as in "all hands on deck"). See METONYMY.

synesthesia The mingling or substitution of the senses, such as when talking about a sound by mentioning a color.

tanka A Japanese VERSE form consisting of five lines, with the first and third line each containing five syllables and the rest of the lines each containing seven.

tercet A three-line STANZA grouping.

terza rima Poetry comprised of TERCETS and an interlocking RHYME SCHEME: ABA, BCB, CDC, etc.

tetrameter A VERSE line of four metrical FEET.

tone A poet's manifest attitude toward the subject expressed in the poem.

trimeter A VERSE line of three metrical FEET.

trochee A metrical FOOT consisting of a hard STRESS followed by a soft stress.

trope A figurative or rhetorical mechanism, and at times a motif.

verse A line of poetry or at times a synonym for *poetry* or *poem*.

vers libre FREE VERSE.

villanelle A 19-line poem made up of six STANZAS—five TERCETS and a final QUATRAIN—with the first tercet employing an ABA RHYME SCHEME that is then replicated in the following tercets as well as in the final two lines of the quatrain. In addition, the first and third lines are repeated in lines 6, 12, and 18, and 9, 15, and 19, respectively. The poem's first and third lines, and their subsequent iterations, carry a special thematic weight, and the poem's motifs are brought together in the concluding quatrain.

voice Not unlike the poem's PERSONA, a sense of a personality or speaker's diction, point of view or attitude in a poem; voice can also simply refer to a poem's speaker.

APPENDIX II

SELECTED BIBLIOGRAPHY

Allen, Donald, and Warrent Tallman, eds. *The Poetics of the New American Poetry.* New York: Grove Press, 1973.

Altieri, Charles. *Enlarging The Temple: New Directions in American Poetry During the 1960's* Lewisburg, Pa.: Bucknell University Press, 1979.

———. *Painterly Abstraction in Modernist American Poetry: The Contemporaneity of Modernism.* University Park: Pennsylvania State University Press, 1995.

———. *Postmodernisms Now: Essays on Contemporaneity in the Arts.* University Park: Pennsylvania State University Press, 1998.

———. *Self and Sensibility in Contemporary American Poetry.* Cambridge; New York: Cambridge University Press, 1984.

Andrews, Bruce, and Charles Bernstein. *The L=A=N=G=U=A=G=E Book.* Carbondale: Southern Illinois University Press, 1984.

Armbruster, Karla, and Kathleen R. Wallace, eds. *Beyond Nature Writing: Expanding the Boundaries of Ecocriticism.* Charlottesville: The University Press of Virginia, 2001.

Baker, Jr., Houston. *Afro-American Poetics: Revisions of Harlem and the Black Aesthetic,* Madison: University of Wisconsin Press, 1988.

Baker, Peter. *Modern Poetic Practice: Structure and Genesis.* New York: Peter Lang, 1986.

Bate, Jonathan. *The Song of the Earth.* Cambridge, Mass.: Harvard University Press, 2000.

Bawer, Bruce. *The Middle Generation: The Lives and Poetry of Delmore Schwartz, Randall Jarrell, John Berryman, and Robert Lowell.* Hamden, Conn.: Archon Books, 1986.

———. *Prophets & Professors: Essays on the Lives and Works of Modern Poets.* Brownsville, Ore.: Story Line Press, 1995.

Beach, Christopher. *Artifice and Indeterminacy: An Anthology of New Poetics.* Tuscaloosa: University of Alabama Press, 1998.

———. *Cambridge Introduction to Twentieth-Century American Poetry.* Cambridge: Cambridge University Press, 2003.

———. *Poetic Culture: Contemporary American Poetry between Community and Institution.* Evanston, Ill.: Northwestern University Press, 1999.

Bernstein, Charles. *Content's Dream: Essays.* Evanston, Ill.: Northwestern University Press, 2001.

———. *A Poetics.* Cambridge, Mass.: Harvard University Press, 1992.

———. *Poetics.* Cambridge, Mass.: Harvard University Press, 1992.

Blasing, Mutlu Konuk. *Politics and Form in Postmodern Poetry: O'Hara, Bishop, Ashbery, and Merrill.* New York: Cambridge University Press, 1995.

Bloom, Clive, and Brian Docherty. *American Poetry: The Modernist Ideal.* New York: St. Martin's Press, 1995.

Bloom, Harold. *Figures of Capable Imagination.* New York: Seabury Press, 1976.

———. *American Poetry, 1915 to 1945.* New York: Chelsea House, 1987.

———, ed. *American Poetry 1946 to 1965.* New York: Chelsea House Publishers, 1987.
Bogan, Louise. *Achievement in American Poetry, 1900–1950.* Chicago: Henry Regnery, 1951.
Bolden, Tony. *Afro-Blue: Improvisations in African-American Poetry and Culture.* Urbana: University of Illinois Press, 2004.
Boyers, Robert, ed. *Contemporary Poetry in America: Essays and Interviews.* New York: Schocken Books, 1974.
Breslin, James. *From Modern to Contemporary: American Poetry, 1945–1965.* Chicago: University of Chicago Press, 1984.
Brodsky, Joseph, Seamus Heaney, and Derek Walcott. *Homage to Robert Frost.* New York: Farrar, Straus, & Giroux, 1996.
Brooks, Cleanth. *Modern Poetry and the Tradition.* Chapel Hill: The University of North Carolina Press, 1939.
Brooks, Cleanth, and Robert Penn Warren. *Understanding Poetry: An Anthology for College Students.* New York: Henry Holt, 1938.
Buell, Lawrence. *The Environmental Imagination: Thoreau, Nature Writing, and the Formation of American Culture.* Cambridge, Mass.: Belknap Press of Harvard University Press, 1995.
Castro, Michael. *Interpreting the Indian: Twentieth Century Poets and the Native American.* Norman: University of Oklahoma Press, 1983.
Comens, Bruce. *Apocalypse and After: Modern Strategy and Postmodern Tactics in Pound, Williams, and Zukofsky.* Tuscaloosa: University of Alabama Press, 1995.
Conte, Joseph. *Unending Design: The Forms of Postmodern Poetry.* Ithaca, N.Y., and London: Cornell University Press, 1991.
Costello, Bonnie. *Shifting Ground: Reinventing Landscape in Modern American Poetry.* Cambridge, Mass.: Harvard University Press, 2003.
Cronon, William. *Uncommon Ground: Rethinking the Human Place in Nature.* New York: W. W. Norton & Company, 1996.
Cucinella, Catherine, ed. *Contemporary American Women Poets: An A-to-Z Guide.* Westport, Conn.: Greenwood Press, 2002.
Cushman, Stephen. *Fictions of Form in American Poetry.* Princeton, N.J.: Princeton University Press, 1993.
Davenport, Guy. *Geography of the Imagination.* New York: Pantheon Books, 1992.
Davidson, Michael. *Ghostlier Demarcations: Modern Poetry and the Material Word.* Berkeley: University of California Press, 1997.
———. *The San Francisco Renaissance: Poetics and Community at Mid-Century.* Cambridge University Press, 1989.
Delville, Michel. *The American Prose Poem.* Gainesville: University Press of Florida, 1998.
Dickey, James. *Classes on Modern Poets and the Art of Poetry,* edited by Donald J. Greiner. Columbia: University of South Carolina Press, 2004.
Diggory, Terence, and Stephen Paul Miller, eds. *The Scene of My Selves: New Work on New York School Poets.* Orono, Maine: National Poetry Foundation; Hanover, N.H.: University Press of New England, 2001.
Donoghue, Denis. *Connoisseurs of Chaos: Ideas of Order in Modern American Poetry.* 2d ed. London, Faber, 1984.
Drake, William. *The First Wave: Women Poets in America, 1915–1945.* New York: Macmillan, 1987.
DuPlessis, Rachel Blau. *Genders, Races, and Religious Cultures in Modern American Poetry, 1908–1934.* Cambridge; New York: Cambridge University Press, 2001.
———. *Writing Beyond the Ending: Narrative Strategies of Twentieth-Century Women Writers.* Bloomington: Indiana University Press, 1985.
Dworkin, Craig. *Reading the Illegible.* Evanston, Ill.: Northwestern University Press, 2003.
Eberhart, Richard. *Of Poetry and Poets.* Urbana: University of Illinois Press, 1979.
Elder, Jonathan. *Imagining the Earth: Poetry and the Vision of Nature.* Urbana: University of Illinois Press, 1985.
Empson, William. *Seven Types of Ambiguity.* New York: New Directions, 1947.
Eysteinsson, Astradur. *The Concept of Modernism.* Ithaca, N.Y.: Cornell University Press, 1990.
Faas, Ekbert. *Towards a New American Poetics: Essays and Interviews.* Santa Barbara, Calif.: Black Sparrow, 1978.
Fink, Thomas. *"A Different Sense of Power": Problems of Community in Late Twentieth-Century U.S. Poetry.* Madison, N.J.: Fairleigh Dickinson University Press; London: Associated University Presses, 2001.
Finkelstein, Norman. *Lyrical Interference: Essays on Poetics.* New York: Spuyten Duyvil, 2003.

———. *Not One of Them in Place: Modern Poetry and Jewish American Identity.* Albany: State University of New York Press, 2001.
———. *The Utopian Moment in Contemporary American Poetry.* Rev. ed. Lewisburg, Pa.: Bucknell University Press; London: Associated University Presses, 1993.
Ford, Karen Jackson. *Gender and the Poetics of Excess: Moments of Brocade.* Jackson: University of Mississippi Press, 1997.
Foster, Edward Halsey. *Answerable to None: Berrigan, Bronk, and The American Real.* New York: Spuyten Duyvil, 1999.
———, ed. *Poetry and Poetics an a New Millenium: Interviews.* Jersey City, N.J.: Talisman House, Publishers, 2000.
———, ed. *Postmodern Poetry: The Talisman Interviews.* Hoboken, N.J.: Talisman House, 1994.
———. *Understanding the Beats.* Columbia, S.C.: University of South Carolina Press, 1992.
———. *Understanding the Black Mountain Poets.* Columbia: University of South Carolina Press, 1995.
Foster, Edward, and Joseph Donahue, eds. *The World in Time and Space: Towards a History of Innovative American Poetry in Our Time. Talisman: A Journal of Contemporary Poetry and Poetics* 23, no. 26 (2002).
Frank, Robert, and Henry Sayre. *The Line in Postmodern Poetry.* Urbana: University of Illinois Press, 1988.
Fredman, Stephen. *The Grounding of American Poetry: Charles Olson and the Emersonian Tradition.* Cambridge; New York: Cambridge University Press, 1993.
———. *Poet's Prose: The Crisis in American Verse.* 2d ed. Cambridge; New York: Cambridge University Press, 1990.
Fritzell, Peter. *Nature Writing and America: Essays upon a Cultural Type.* Ames: Iowa State University Press, 1990.
Frost, Elisabeth. *The Feminist Avant-Garde in American Poetry.* Iowa City: University of Iowa Press, 2003.
Gardner, Thomas. *Regions of Unlikeness: Explaining Contemporary Poetry.* Lincoln: University of Nebraska Press, 1999.
Gery, John. *Nuclear Annihilation and Contemporary American Poetry: Ways of Nothingness.* Gainesville: University Press of Florida, 1996.
Gilcrest, David W. *Greening the Lyre: Environmental Poetics and Ethics.* Reno: University of Nevada Press, 2002.
Gioia, Dana. *Can Poetry Matter?: Essays on Poetry and American Culture.* Saint Paul, Minn.: Graywolf Press, 2002.
Goldensohn, Lorrie. *Dismantling Glory: Twentieth-Century Soldier Poetry.* New York: Columbia University Press, 2003.
Golding, Allan. *From Outlaw to Classic: Canons in American Poetry.* Madison: University of Wisconsin Press, 1995.
Gotera, Vince. *Radical Visions: Poetry by Vietnam Veterans.* Athens: University of Georgia Press, 1994.
Gray, Richard. *American Poetry of the Twentieth Century.* London and New York: Longman, 1990.
Grumman, Bob. *Of Manywhere-at-Once.* Port Charlotte, Florida: Runaway Spoon Press, 1998.
Guillory, John. *Cultural Capital: The Problem of Literary Canon Formation.* Chicago: University of Chicago Press, 1993.
Gwynn, R. S., ed. *The Advocates of Poetry: A Reader of American Poet-Critics of the Modernist Era.* Fayetteville: University of Arkansas Press, 1996.
Harrington, Joseph. *Poetry and the Public: The Social Form of Modern U.S. Poetics.* Middletown, Conn.: Wesleyan University Press, 2002.
Hartley George. *Textual Politics and the Language Poets.* Bloomington: Indiana University Press, 1989.
Hass, Robert. *Twentieth Century Pleasures.* Hopewell, N.J.: The Ecco Press, 1984.
Hatlen, Burton, and Demetres Tryphonopoulos, eds. *William Carlos Williams and the Language of Poetry.* Orono, Maine.: National Poetry Foundation, 2002.
Heller, Michael. *Conviction's Net of Branches: Essays on the Objectivist Poets and Poetry.* Carbondale: Southern Illinois University Press, 1985.
Henderson, Stephen. *Understanding the New Black Poetry: Black Speech and Black Music as Poetic Reference.* New York: Morrow, 1973.
Hinton, Laura, and Cynthia Hogue, eds. *We Who Love to Be Astonished: Experimental Women's Writing and Performance Poetics.* Tuscaloosa, University of Alabama Press, 2001.
Holden, Jonathan. *The Rhetoric of the Contemporary Lyric.* Bloomington: Indiana University Press, 1980.
Howard, Richard. *Alone with America: Essays on the Art of Poetry in the United States since 1950.* New York: Atheneum, 1980.

Jarrell, Randall. *Poetry and the Age*. New York: Vintage, 1955.
Juhasz, Suzanne. *Naked and Fiery Forms: Modern American Poetry by Women, a New Tradition*. New York: Harper & Row, 1976.
Kalaidjian, Walter. *American Culture Between the Wars: Revisionary Modernism and PostModern Critique*. New York: Columbia University Press, 1993.
———. *Languages of Liberation: The Social Text in Contemporary American Poetry*. New York: Columbia University Press, 1989.
Kalstone, David. *Five Temperaments: Elizabeth Bishop, Robert Lowell, James Merrill, Adrienne Rich, and John Ashbery*. New York: Oxford University Press, 1977.
Kalstone, David, and Robert Hemenway, eds. *Becoming a Poet: Elizabeth Bishop with Marianne Moore and Robert Lowell*. New York: Farrar Straus & Giroux, 1989.
Keller, Lynn. *Re-making It New: Contemporary American Poetry and the Modernist Tradition*. New York: Cambridge University Press, 1987.
———. *Forms of Expansion: Recent Long Poems by Women*. Chicago: University of Chicago Press, 1997.
Keller, Lynn, and Cristanne Miller. *Feminist Measures: Soundings in Poetry and Theory*. Ann Arbor: University of Michigan Press, 1994.
Kenner, Hugh. *A Homemade World: The American Modernist Writers*. New York: Alfred A. Knopf, 1975.
———. *The Pound Era*. London, Faber, 1972.
Kimmelman, Burt. *The "Winter Mind": William Bronk and American Letters*. Madison, N.J.: Fairleigh Dickinson University Press; London: Associated University Presses, 1998.
Kostelanetz, Richard. *A Dictionary of the Avant-Gardes*. New York: Schirmer Books. 2000.
Lacey, Paul. *The Inner War: Forms and Themes in Recent American Poetry*. Philadelphia: Augsburg Fortress Publishers, 1972.
Lehman, David. *The Last Avant-Garde: The Making of the New York School of Poets*. New York: Doubleday, 1998.
———, ed. *Great American Prose Poems*. New York: Scribner. 2003.
Lensing, George S., and Ronald Moran. *Four Poets and the Emotive Imagination: Robert Bly, James Wright, Louis Simpson, and William Stafford*. Baton Rouge: Louisiana State University Press, 1976.
Lentricchia, Frank. *Modernist Quartet*. Cambridge: New York: Cambridge University Press, 1994.
Libby, Anthony. *Mythologies of Nothing: Mystical Death in American Poetry, 1940–70*. Urbana: University of Illinois Press, 1984.
Lincoln, Kenneth. *Sing with the Heart of a Bear: Fusions of Native and American Poetry, 1890–1999*. Berkeley: University of California Press, 2000.
Longenhach, James. *Modern Poetry After Modernism*. New York: Oxford University Press, 1997.
———. *Stone Cottage: Pound, Yeats, and Modernism*. New York: Oxford University Press, 1988.
Martin, Robert K. *The Homosexual Tradition in American Poetry*. Iowa City: University of Iowa Press, 1998.
Marx, Leo. *The Machine in the Garden: Technology and the Pastoral Ideal in America*. New York: Oxford University Press, 2000.
McCaffery, Steve. *North of Intention: Critical Writings 1973–1986*. 2nd ed. New York: Roof Books, 2000.
———. *Prior To Meaning: The Protosemantic and Poetics*. Evanston, Ill.: Northwestern University Press, 2001
McClatchy, J. D. *White Paper: On Contemporary American Poetry*. New York: Columbia University Press, 1989.
McDowell, Robert, ed. *Poetry after Modernism*. Brownsville, Ore.: Story Line Press, 1998.
McHale, Brian. *The Obligation toward the Difficult Whole: Postmodernist Long Poems*. Tuscaloosa: University of Alabama Press, 2003.
Middlebrook, Diane Wood, and Marilyn Yalom, eds. *Coming to Light: American Women Poets in the Twentieth Century*. Ann Arbor: University of Michigan Press, 1985.
Miller, J. Hillis. *Poets of Reality*. Cambridge, Mass.: Harvard University Press, 1965.
Molesworth, Charles. *The Fierce Embrace: A Study of Contemporary American Poetry*. Columbia: University of Missouri Press, 1979.
Montefiore, Jan. *Feminism and Poetry: Language, Experience, Identity in Women's Writing*. New York: Pandora, 1987.
Moramarco, Fred, and William Sullivan. *Containing Multitudes: Poetry in the United States Since 1950*. New York: Twayne Publishers, 1998.
Moyers, Bill. *The Language of Life: A Festival of Poets*. New York: Doubleday, 1995.
Murphy, Patrick. *Farther Afield in the Study of Nature-Oriented Literature*. Charlottesville: The University Press of Virginia, 2000.

Myers, Jack, and David Wojahn, eds. *A Profile of Twentieth-Century American Poetry.* Carbondale and Edwardsville: Southern Illinois University Press, 1991.

Naylor, Paul. *Poetic Investigations: Singing the Holes in History.* Evanston, Ill.: Northwestern University Press. 1999.

Nelson, Cary. *Our Last First Poets: Vision and History in Contemporary American Poetry.* Urbana: University of Illinois Press, 1981.

———. *Repression and Recovery: Modern American Poetry and the Politics of Cultural Memory 1910–1945.* Madison: University of Wisconsin Press, 1989.

———. *Revolutionary Memory: Recovering the Poetry of the American Left.* New York: Routledge, 2001.

Nielsen, Aldon Lynn. *Black Chant: Languages of African-American Postmodernism.* New York: Cambridge University Press, 1997.

———. *Reading Race: White American Poets and the Racial Discourse in the Twentieth Century.* Athens: University of Georgia Press. 1988.

North, Michael. *The Dialect of Modernism.* New York: Oxford University Press, 1994.

Orr, Gregory. *Poetry as Survival.* Athens: University of Georgia Press, 2002.

Osman, David. *The Sullen Art: Interviews by David Osman with Modern American Poets.* New York: Corinth, 1963.

Ostriker, Alicia Suskin. *Stealing the Language: The Emergence of Women's Poetry in America.* Boston: Beacon Press, 1986.

Palmer, Michael, ed. *Code of Signals.* Berkeley, Calif.: North Atlantic Books, 1983.

Parini, Jay. *The Columbia History of American Poetry.* New York: Columbia University Press, 1993.

Paul, Sherman. *Hewing to Experience: Essays and Reviews on Recent American Poetry and Poetics, Nature and Culture.* Ames: University of Iowa Press, 1990.

———. *In Search of the Primitive.* Baton Rouge: Louisiana State University Press, 1976.

———. *Olson's Push: Origin, Black Mountain and Recent American Poetry.* Baton Rouge: Louisiana State University Press, 1978.

Perelman, Bob. *The Marginalization of Poetry: Language Writing and Literary History.* Princeton, N.J.: Princeton University Press, 1996.

———, ed. *Writing Talks.* Carbondale: Southern Illinois University Press, 1985.

Perkins, David. *A History of Modern Poetry: From the 1890s to the High Modernist Mode.* Cambridge, Mass.: Harvard University Press, 1976.

———. *A History of Modern Poetry: Modernism and After.* Cambridge, Mass.: Harvard University Press, 1987.

Perloff, Marjorie. *The Dance of the Intellect: Studies in The Poetry of the Pound Tradition.* Evanston, Ill.: Northwestern University Press, 1996.

———. *The Futurist Moment: Avant-Garde, Avant Guerre, and the Language of Rupture.* Chicago: University of Chicago Press, 2003.

———. *Poetic License: Essays on Modernist and Postmodernist Lyric.* Evanston, Ill.: Northwestern University Press, 1990.

———. *The Poetics of Indeterminacy: Rimbaud to Cage.* Evanston, Ill.: Northwestern University Press, 1999.

———. *Poetry On & Off the Page: Essays for Emergent Occasions.* Evanston, Ill.: Northwestern University Press, 1998.

———, ed. *Postmodern Genres.* Norman: University of Oklahoma Press, 1989.

———. *Radical Artifice: Writing Poetry in the Age of Media.* Chicago: University of Chicago Press, 1991.

Pinsky, Robert. *Democracy, Culture, and the Voice of Poetry.* Princeton, N.J.: Princeton University Press, 2002.

———. *The Situation of Poetry: Contemporary Poetry and Its Traditions.* Princeton, N.J.: Princeton University Press, 1976.

Plakkoottam, J. L., and Prashant K. Sinha, eds. *Literature and Politics in Twentieth Century America.* Hyderabad, India: American Studies Research Centre. 1993.

Poirier, Richard. *Poetry and Pragmatism.* Cambridge, Mass.: Harvard University Press, 1992.

Quartermain, Peter. *Disjunctive Poetics: From Gertrude Stein and Louis Zukofsky to Susan Howe.* Cambridge; New York: Cambridge University Press, 1992.

Quartermain, Peter, and Rachel Blau DuPlessis, eds. *The Objectivist Nexus: Essays in Cultural Poetics.* Tuscaloosa: University of Alabama Press, 1999.

Quetchenbach, Bernard W. *Back From the Far Field; American Nature Poetry in the Late Twentieth Century.* Charlottesville: University Press of Virginia, 2000.

Ramazani, Jihan. *Poetry of Mourning.* Chicago: University of Chicago Press, 1994.

Rasula, Jed. *The American Poetry Wax Museum: Reality Effects, 1940–1990.* Urbana, Ill.: National Council of Teachers of English, 1996.

———. *This Compost: Ecological Imperatives in American Poetry.* Athens: University of Georgia Press, 2002.

Rexroth, Kenneth. *American Poetry of the Twentieth Century.* New York: Seabury Press, 1973.

Roberts, Neil, ed. *A Companion to Twentieth-Century Poetry.* Oxford, England: Blackwell, 2001.

Rosenthal, M. L. *Our Life in Poetry: Selected Essays and Reviews.* New York: Persea, 1991.

———. *Poetry and the Common Life.* New York: Schocken, 1983.

Rosenthal, M. L., and Sally M. Gall. *The Modern Poetic Sequence: The Genius of Modern Poetry.* New York: Oxford University Press, 1983.

Schweik, Susan. *A Gulf So Deeply Cut: American Women Poets and the Second World War.* Madison: University of Wisconsin Press, 1991.

Scigaj, Leonard. *Sustainable Poetry: Four American Ecopoets.* Lexington: The University Press of Kentucky, 1999.

Shetley, Vernon. *After the Death of Poetry: Poet and Audience in Contemporary America.* Durham: Duke University Press, 1993.

Silliman, Ron. *The New Sentence.* New York: Roof, 1989.

Simpson, Megan. *Poetic Epistemologies: Gender and Knowing in Women's Language-Oriented Writing.* Albany: SUNY Press, 2000.

Spahr, Juliana. *Everybody's Autonomy: Connective Reading and Collective Identity.* Tuscaloosa: University of Alabama Press, 2001.

Spiegelman, Willard. *How Poets See the World: The Art of Description in Contemporary Poetry.* New York: Oxford University Press, 2005.

Steele, Timothy. *Missing Measures: Modern Poetry and the Revolt Against Meter.* Fayetteville: University of Arkansas Press, 1990.

Stefans, Brian Kim. *Fashionable Noise: On Digital Poetics.* Berkeley Calif.: Atelos, 2003.

Stitt, Peter. *The World's Hieroglyphic Beauty: Five American Poets.* Athens: University of Georgia Press, 1985.

Thomas, Lorenzo. *Extraordinarv Measure: Afrocentric Modernism and 20th-Century American Poetry.* Tuscaloosa: University of Alabama Press; 2002.

Travisano, Thomas. *Midcentury Quartet.* Charlottesville: University Press of Virginia, 1999.

Vendler, Helen. *The Given and the Made: Strategies of Poetic Redefinition.* Cambridge, Mass.: Harvard University Press, 1995.

———. *Part of Nature, Part of Us: Modern American Poets.* Cambridge, Mass.: Harvard University Press, 1980.

———. *Soul Says: On Recent Poetry.* Cambridge, Mass.: Belknap Press of Harvard University Press, 1995.

———, ed. *Voices & Visions: The Poet in America.* New York: Random House, 1987.

Verdonk, Peter, Ed. *Twentieth Century Poetry: From Text to Context.* London: Routledge, 1993.

Vickery, Ann. *Leaving Lines of Gender: A Feminist Genealogy of Language Writing.* Hanover, N.H.: Wesleyan University Press, 2000.

Vincent, Stephen, and Ellen Zweig. *The Poetry Reading: A Contemporary Compendium on Language and Performance.* San Francisco: Momo's Press, 1981.

Von Hallberg, Robert. *American Poetry and Culture, 1945–1980.* Cambridge, Mass.: Harvard University Press, 1985.

Waggoner, Hyatt Howe. *The Heel of Elohim, Science and Values in Modern American Poetry.* Norman: University of Oklahoma Press, 1950.

Wagner, Jean. *Black Poets of the United States: From Paul Laurence Dunbar to Langston Hughes.* Urbana: University of Illinois Press, 1973.

Waldman, Anne, and Andrew Schelling, eds. *Disembodied Poetics: Annals of the Jack Kerouac School.* Albuquerque: University of New Mexico Press, 1994.

Wallace, Mark, and Steven Marks. *Telling it Slant: Avant Garde Poetics of the 1990s.* Tuscaloosa: University of Alabama Press, 2002.

Whitehead, Kim. *The Feminist Poetry Movement.* Jackson: University Press of Mississippi, 1996.

Williamson, Alan. *Introspection and Contemporary Poetry.* Cambridge, Mass.: Harvard University Press, 1984.

Wilson, Rob. *American Sublime: The Genealogy of a Poetic Genre.* Madison: University of Wisconsin Press, 1991.

Winters, Yvor. *Forms of Discovery: Critical & Historical Essays on the Forms of the Short Poem in English.* Chicago: The Swallow Press, 1967.

———. *In Defense of Reason: Primitivism and Decadence: A Study of American Experimental Poetry.* Chicago and New York: The Swallow Press & W. Morrow and Company, 1947.

Woznicki, John R. *Ideological Content and Political Significance of Twentieth-Century American Poetry.* Lewiston, N.Y.: Mellen, 2002.

LIST OF CONTRIBUTORS

Adams, Don – Florida Atlantic University
Alkalay-Gut, Karen – Tel Aviv University, Israel
Allegrezza, William – Indiana University Northwest
Allen, Jessica – Seattle, Washington
Archambeau, Robert – Lake Forest College
Austin, Nathan – State University of New York at Buffalo
Axelrod, Steven Gould – University of California, Riverside
Baker, Peter – Towson University
Balestrini, Nassim Winnie – Johannes Gutenberg-Universitaet Mainz, Germany
Barenblat, Rachel – Inkberry Literary Arts Center
Barker, Sue – Northwestern University
Barnes, Sharon L. – University of Toledo
Barsanti, Michael – Rosenbach Museum and Library
Barton, Edwin J. – State University of California, Bakersfield
Basinski, Michael – State University of New York at Buffalo
Bergman, David – Towson University
Bernhardt, Kimberly – Rutgers University
Bertholf, Robert – State University of New York at Buffalo
Bettridge, Joel – University of Redlands
Beveridge, Gord – University of Winnipeg, Canada
Beyer, Shaileen – Baltimore, Maryland
Blair, Yvette R. – El Centro College, Dallas, Texas
Blessinger, Justin L. – Dakota State University
Bloss, Christopher – University of South Dakota
Boggs, Rebecca Melora Corinne – Yale University
Bolt, Julie – Art Institute of Los Angeles
Bonczek, Michelle – Eastern Washington University
Bourassa, Alan – St. Thomas University, New Brunswick, Canada
Bourbeau, Lisa – Francestown, New Hampshire
Brooks, Ron – University of Oklahoma
Bryant, Salita S. – University of Mississippi
Byrd, Gregory – St. Petersburg College
Byrne, Mairéad – Rhode Island School of Design
Calihman, Matthew – Washington University, St. Louis
Camlot, Jason – Concordia University, Montreal, Canada
Cates, Isaac – Yale University
Chen, Ken – Yale University
Chinco, David – Broome Community College
Christensen, Paul – Texas A&M University
Christopher Moylan – New York Institute of Technology
Clark, J. Elizabeth – City University of New York, LaGuardia
Clippinger, David – Pittsburgh, Pennsylvania
Cocola, Jim – University of Virginia
Coffey, Dan – Iowa State University
Cohen, Alicia – Reed College
Colburn, Nadia Herman – Columbia University
Cole, Barbara – State University of New York at Buffalo
Cone, Temple – United States Naval Academy
Colligan, Colette – Queen's University, Ontario, Canada
Collins, Richard – Xavier University of Louisiana
Conte, Joseph – State University of New York at Buffalo
Cottingham, Reid – University of Chicago
Coursey, Freda Fuller – State University of New York at Binghamton
Crank, Andy – University of North Carolina, Chapel Hill
Crumpton, Margaret – Georgia Institute of Technology
Cuda, Anthony J. – Emory University
Dague, Wilma Weant – Atchison, Kansas
Daly, Catherine – Los Angeles, California
Damon, Maria – University of Minnesota
Davidson, Chad – University of West Georgia
Davis, David A. – University of North Carolina, Chapel Hill
Dobbelmann, Duncan – City University of New York, Brooklyn
Dozier, Judy Massey – Lake Forest College
Durand, Marcella – New York City
Durgin, Patrick – State University of New York at Buffalo
Durso, Patricia Keefe – Montclair State University
Dworkin, Ira – University of Miami
Earley, Bernard – State University of New York at Cortland
Elliot, Norbert – New Jersey Institute of Technology
Emerson, Lori – State University of New York at Buffalo

Encke, Jeffrey – Seattle, Washington
Esdale, Logan – Chapman University
Etter, Carrie – University of Hertforshire, Hatfield, England
Fagan, Cathy E. – Nassau Community College and Hofstra University
Ferguson, Kathryn – LaTrobe University, Victoria, Australia
Fernandez-Medina, Nicolas – Stanford University
Fifarek, Aimee – Louisiana State University
Fink, Thomas – City University of New York, LaGuardia
Fischer, Barbara – New York University
Fisher, Thomas – Portland State University
Flannagan, Rebecca – Francis Marion University
Fleischer, Doris Zames – New Jersey Institute of Technology
Foster, Edward – Stevens Institute of Technology
Foust, Graham – Drake University
Friedman, Dan – Yale University
Friedman, Robert S. – New Jersey Institute of Technology
Frye, Steven – California State University, Bakersfield
Funkhouser, Christopher – New Jersey Institute of Technology
Furlani, Andre – Concordia University, Canada
Galgan, Wendy – City University of New York, The Graduate Center
Gaughan, Frank – Hofstra University
Gelineau, Christine – State University of New York at Binghamton
Gerber, Natalie – University of California, Berkeley
Girardi, Judith S. – Notre Dame de Namur University and West Valley College
Glassmeyer, Danielle – Loyola University, Chicago
Gordon, Maggie – University of Mississippi
Gordon, Stephanie – Auburn University
Greacen, Amy Glynn – San Francisco California
Greenberg, Arielle – Columbia College, Chicago
Grotz, Jennifer – University of Houston
Grumman, Bob – Port Charlotte, Florida
Gudding, Gabriel – University of Mississippi
Gwiazda, Piotr – University of Maryland, Baltimore County
Harris, Kaplan Page – University of Notre Dame
Hart, Matthew – University of Pennsylvania
Haynes, Robert W. – Texas A&M International University
Hecker, William F. – United States Military Academy
Hernandez, Carlos – Pace University
Heuston, Sean – Vanderbilt University
Hezel, Amy – University of Iowa
Highet Hanford, Pamela – Shasta Community College
Hofer, Matthew – University of Chicago
Holbrook, Susan – University of Windsor, Ontario, Canada
Howard, W. Scott – University of Denver
Howe, Andrew – University of California, Riverside
Huehls, Mitchum – University of Wisconsin, Madison
Hulsey, Dallas – New Mexico Junior College
Humphrey, Theodore C. – California State Polytechnic University
Johnson, Ben – Rutgers University. New Brunswick
Johnson, Jeannine – Harvard University
Johnson, Melissa – Newberry College
Joines, Richard E. – Auburn University
Jones, David M. – University of Wisconsin, Eau Claire
Jones, Marie C. – University of North Texas
Kane, Daniel – University of East Anglia, Norwich, England
Kearns, Sherry – Cleverdale, New York
Kelsey, Karla – Denver, Colorado
Kelsey, Sigrid – Louisiana State University
Kerley, Gary – North Hall High School, Gainesville, Georgia
Kimmelman, Burt – New Jersey Institute of Technology
King, Patricia G. – Central American Study and Service, Guatemala City, Guatemala
Kuperman, Michael – Institute of Technology, Taiwan
Lamm, Kimberly – Pratt Institute
Lavazzi, Tom – City University of New York, Kingsborough
Layng, George W. – Westfield State College
Leising, Gary – Northern Kentucky University
Leston, Robert – University of Texas, Arlington
Levitt, Linda – University of South Florida
Lisk, Thomas – North Carolina State University, Raleigh
Lombard, Maria D. – University of South Alabama

Long, Mark C. – Keene State College
Lundblad, Michael – University of Virginia
Lundquist, Sara – University of Toledo
Marion, Carol – Guilford Technical Community College
Marsh, Nicky – University of Southampton, England
Mathis, Andrew E. – Temple University
Maynard, James L. – State University of New York at Buffalo
McBride, Sam – DeVry University, Pomona
McDaniel, Dennis D. – Saint Vincent College
McDermott, Christopher – University of Georgia
McFeely, Maureen Connolly – Hofstra University
McGrath, Barbara J. – Illinois State University
McInnis, C. Liegh – Jackson State University
McMillan, Laurie – Duquesne University
Meier, Franz – Ludwig-Maximilians-Universität, Munich, Germany
Meyer, Sabine – Rasmussen College
Meyers, G. Douglas – University of Texas, El Paso
Moore, George – University of Colorado, Boulder
Morelli-White, Nan – St. Petersburg College
Morelyle, Jason – Canmore, Alberta, Canada
Moylan, Christopher – New York Institute of Technology
Muller, Adam – University of Manitoba, Canada.
Muratori, Fred – Cornell University
Murphy, A. Mary – University of Calgary, Canada
Murphy, Kelli – University of South Dakota
Newberry, Jeff – Abraham Baldwin Agricultural College
Nielsen, Aldon L. – Pennsylvania State University
O'Connor, Jacqueline – Boise State University
O'Loughlin, Jim – University of Northern Iowa
Orange, Tom – Georgetown University
Overall, Keri – University of North Texas
Palmer, Leslie – University of North Texas
Parrett, Aaron – University of Great Falls
Payaslian, Arto – University of Massachusetts
Persoon, James – Grand Valley State University
Pettinger, Terry Lynn – University of South Carolina
Peyster, Steven J. – New Salem, Massachusetts
Phillips, Lily – John Carroll University
Plunkett, Felicity – University of New England, New South Wales, Australia
Poch, John – Texas Tech University
Potts, Donna – Kansas State University
Pozorski, Aimee L. – Central Connecticut State University
Prall, J. Andrew – University of Denver
Priddy Anna – Louisiana State University
Purdy, Matthew – University of Iowa
Pusateri, Chris – Seattle, Washington
Richards, Tad – Marist College
Robbins, Amy Moorman – University of California, Riverside
Rollison, Damian Judge – University of Virginia
Rosenow, Ce – University of Oregon
Rozendal, Michael – State University of New York at Buffalo
Russo, Linda V – State University of New York at Buffalo
Ryan, James Emmett – Auburn University
Salmon, Holly – New Haven, Connecticut
Schaub, Joseph – Newberry College
Schwartz, Gerald – Rochester, New York
Schwartz, Judith – University of Pennsylvania
Scroggins, Mark – Florida Atlantic University
Sewell, Lisa – Villanova University
Shaner, Tim – State University of New York at Buffalo
Shankar, Ravi – Central Connnecticut State University
Shapiro, David – William Paterson University
Shapiro, Rose – Fontbonne University
Sherwood, Kenneth – Indiana University of Pennsylvania
Shingavi, Snehal – University of California, Berkeley
Sievers, Stefanie – University of Wisconsin, Eau Claire
Simpson, Megan – Penn State University Altoona
Skinner, Jonathan – State University of New York at Buffalo
Smith, Joyce C. – University of Tennessee at Chattanooga
Sowder, Michael – Utah State University
Speirs, Kenneth – City University of New York, Kingsborough
Spillane, Brian A. – Shasta College
Stalling, Jonathan – State University of New York at Buffalo
Stayer, Jayme – Loyola House, Berkeley, Michigan
Stiller, Nikki – New Jersey Institute of Technology

Strickland, Michael – Elon University Studdard, Melissa Tomball College
Stumpf, Jason – Washington University in Saint Louis
Sulit, Marie-Therese C. – University of Minnesota, Twin Cities
Swihart, Megan – Duquesne University
Sylvester, Wilham – State University of New York at Buffalo
Taciuch, Dean – George Mason University
Talley, Sharon – Texas A&M University, Corpus Christi
Tanner, James T. F. – University of North Texas
Texter, Douglas W. – University of Minnesota
Tontiplaphol, Betsy Winakur – University of Virginia
Trousdale, Rachel – Agnes Scott College
Turner, Jack – Wesley College
Tursi, Mark – University of Denver
Twitchell-Waas, Jeffrey – OFS College, Singapore
Valdata, Patricia – Neumann College
Van Dyke, Michael – Michigan State University
Vickery Ann – University of Melbourne, Australia
Waddell, William – St. John Fisher College
Wagner, Tamara S. – National University of Singapore
Walpert, Bryan – Massey University, Palmerston North, New Zealand
Warner, Diane – Texas Tech University
Wattley, Ama S. – Pace University
Wellman, Don – Daniel Webster College
Whiddon, Kelly D. – Valdosta State University
Wiens, Jason – University of Calgary Alberta, Canada
Wilson, Nancy Effinger – Texas State University, San Marcos
Wilson, Steve – Texas State University, San Marcos
Wolfe, Jesse – University of Wisconsin, Madison
Woznicki, John R. – Georgian Court College
Zeigler, James – University of California, Irvine

INDEX

B

L

M

Q

R